World Guide to Abbreviations of Organizations

World Guide

to

Abbreviations of Organizations

Sixth Edition

F. A. BUTTRESS

Grand River Books

1249 Washington Boulevard
Detroit, Michigan 48226

Published by
Leonard Hill
A division of
The Blackie Publishing Group
Bishopbriggs, Glasgow G64 2NZ, and
Furnival House, 14-18 High Holborn, London WC1V 6BX

Published in the U.S.A., Canada, Central and South America by
Grand River Books
1249 Washington Boulevard, Detroit, Michigan 48226

First Edition	*1954*
Second Edition	*1960*
Third Edition	*1966*
Fourth Edition	*1971*
Fifth Edition	*1974*
This Edition	*1981*

Library of Congress Cataloging in Publication Data

Buttress, F. A.

World guide to abbreviations of organizations.

Includes bibliographical references.

1. Associations, institutions, etc. — Abbreviations
I. Title
AS8.B8 1981   060'.148   80-16633

ISBN 0-8103-2024-X

Printed in Great Britain

Introduction

Modern times have seen a bewildering proliferation of abbreviations, presenting the reader with a considerable problem of identification. This difficulty is increased, and much of the advantage of abbreviation is lost, when a reader is obliged to search a large publication for definitions inconveniently placed, or, as often happens, when editors fail to record the full meaning of an acronym at least once.

The World Guide offers a wide-ranging and up-to-date summary of the abbreviated titles of organizations and their definitions. This new edition has been expanded from 18 000 to over 27 500 entries. Apart from British, North, Central and South American and international bodies, Common Market countries account for 7 500 entries, and African states for over 1 500. Where the country of origin is not stated, it is assumed to correspond to the language of the entry, except in the case of international and continental areas. This worldwide coverage can be augmented if necessary at a more local level by reference to works dealing exclusively with British or American abbreviations, in which the addresses of many of the organizations can also be found. For a selection of these, the reader is referred to the bibliography (p. vi). An additional bibliography (p. vii) contains sources of Russian and Eastern European abbreviations not covered by the present work.

Grateful acknowledgment is made to the staff of the Library of the Department of Applied Biology, Cambridge; the Cambridge University Library; the Scientific Periodicals Library, Cambridge; the Department of Land Economy Library, Cambridge; the Cambridge Public Library, and the Food and Agricultural Organization Library, Rome. I am also especially indebted to Mr. I. G. Anderson, G. P. Henderson and S. P. A. Henderson of CBD Research Ltd., and finally to those readers who have so kindly pointed out errors and omissions.

F.A.B.

Bibliography

A. Excluding Russia and Eastern Europe

Abbreviations used by FAO for International Organizations, Congresses, Commissions, Committees etc. Terminology Bulletin no.27. 1st revision, Rome, 1976.

Abkürzungen, Abréviations, Abbreviations. Swiss Bank Corporation, London, 1964.

Acronyms, Initialisms and Abbreviations Dictionary. 5th ed. Gale Research Co., Detroit, 1976. (Mainly for USA).

ANDERSON, I.G. (Ed.) *Directory of European Associations. Part 1. National Industrial, Trade and Professional Associations.* 2nd ed. CBD Research Ltd, Beckenham, 1976.

ANDERSON, I.G. (Ed.) *Directory of European Associations. Part 2. National Learned, Scientific and Technical Societies.* CBD Research Ltd, Beckenham, 1975.

ANDERSON, I.G. (Ed.) *Marketing and Management. A World Register of Organisations.* CBD Research Publication. Beckenham, 1969.

COPE, S.T. *Glossary of Abbreviations with Particular Reference to the Telecommunications Industry.* Marconi Co., Chelmsford, 1955.

Directory of Scientific Institutes, Organizations and Services. Scientific Council for Africa South of the Sahara. Publication no.14. London, 1954.

Directory of Scientific Research Organizations in South Africa. CSIR, Pretoria, 1975.

Directory of Scientific and Technical Societies in South Africa. CSIR, Pretoria, 1975.

Encyclopedia of Associations. Vol. 1. National Organizations of the United States. 12th ed. Gale Research Co., Detroit, 1978.

Europa Year Book; a World Survey. 2 vols. London, 1977–8.

European Community Directory and Diary, 1974. Institute of Public Administration, Dublin, 1973.

FANG, J.R. and SONGE, A.H. *International Guide to Library, Archival and Information Science Associations.* Bowker, New York, 1976.

Federation of British Industries Register of British Manufacturers. London, 1965.

GALRÃO, M.J. and ARBOLEDA-SEPÚLVEDA, O. *Directorio de Siglas en Ciencias Agrícolas.* 2nd ed. IICA, Turrialba, Costa Rica, 1971.

Glossary of Symbols and Abbreviations. OEEC, Paris, 1956.

GURNETT, J.W. and KYTE, C.H.J. *Cassell's Dictionary of Abbreviations.* 2nd ed. London, 1972.

Handbook of Commonwealth Organisations. Methuen, London, 1965.

HENDERSON, G.P. and S.P.A. (Eds) *Directory of British Associations.* 5th ed. CBD Research Ltd, Beckenham, 1977–8.

Industrial Research Laboratories of the United States. 13th ed. Bowker Co., New York, 1970.

International Initialese. 2nd ed. Publication no.182. Union of International Associations, Brussels, 1963. 1st Supplement. Publication no.193. 2nd Supplement, 1973.

International Register of Organisations Undertaking Africanist Research in the Social Sciences and Humanities. International African Institute, London, 1971.

International Scientific Organisations. Library of Congress, Washington, 1962.

International Scientific Organisations. OECD, Paris, 1965.

Landbouwgids (Annual). Utrecht. (For the Netherlands).

LANDI, G. *Initials and Acronyms of Bodies, Activities and Projects concerned with Fisheries and Aquatic Sciences.* FAO Fisheries Circular no.110. 2nd revision. Rome, 1975.

MILLARD, P. *Trade Associations and Professional Bodies of the United Kingdom.* 5th ed. Letchworth, 1971.

NATO Handbook. Brussels, 1973.

OECD–ICVA Directory. Development Aid of Non-Governmental Non-Profit Organisations. Paris, 1967.

PUGH, E. *A Dictionary of Acronyms and Abbreviations.* 2nd ed. London, 1970.

PUGH, E. *Second Dictionary of Acronyms and Abbreviations.* London, 1974.

PUGH, E. *Third Dictionary of Acronyms and Abbreviations.* London, 1977.

Register of International Organisations that have Formal Relations with FAO. Rome, 1972.

ROTH, N. *Förkortnings-Lexicon.* 2nd ed. Wahlstrom & Widstrand, Stockholm, 1967.

Scientific and Learned Societies of Great Britain. Allen & Unwin, London, 1964.

Scientific, Technical and Related Societies of the United States. 9th ed. National Academy of Sciences, Washington, 1971.

Sigles Agricoles. Organisations d'Interêt Agricole à Cadre Nationale. Répertoire Alphabétique. Assemblée Permanente des Présidents des Chambres d'Agriculture, Paris, 1965.

Sociétés et Fournisseurs d'Afrique Noire et de Madagascar. 24th ed. Guide Économique NORIA. Paris, 1974.

SPILLNER, P. *Internationales Wörterbuch der Abkürzungen von Organisationen*. 2nd ed. 3 vols. Verlag Dokumentation, München–Pullach, 1970–72.

Tuinbouwgids (Annual). Den Haag. (For the Netherlands).

Whitaker's Almanack. London (Annual).

WILKES, I. *British Initials and Abbreviations*. 3rd ed. International Textbook Co., London, 1971.

WILLIAMS, M. *Directory of Trade Unions in the European Economic Community*. London, 1974.

World Airline Directory. Flight International. Special Issue, 18 May 1972.

World Directory of Social Science Institutions. UNESCO, Paris, 1977.

World Guide to Scientific Associations. 1st ed. Verlag Dokumentation, München–Pullach, 1974.

World Guide to Technical Information and Documentation Services. 2nd ed. UNESCO, Paris, 1975.

World Guide to Trade Associations. 1st ed. Part 1. Europe. Verlag Dokumentation. München–Pullach, 1973.

World Guide to Trade Associations. 1st ed. Part 2. Africa, America, Asia, Oceania. Verlag Dokumentation. München–Pullach, 1974.

World of Learning. Europa Publications, London (latest edition).

Yearbook of International Organizations. 17th ed. Union of International Associations. Brussels, 1979.

B.   Russia and Eastern Europe

BAKO, E. *Hungarian Abbreviations, A Selective List*. Library of Congress, Washington, 1961.

Dictionary of Yugoslav Abbreviations. Medunarodna Politika, Belgrade, 1971.

FURNESS, K.Z. *Bulgarian Abbreviations, A Selective List*. Library of Congress, Washington, 1961.

Glossary of Russian Abbreviations and Acronyms. Library of Congress, Washington, 1967.

HORECKY, P.L. *Czech and Slovak Abbreviations, A Selective List*. Library of Congress, Washington, 1956.

KORITSKII, B.F. (Ed.) *Dictionary of Abbreviations of the Russian Language* (Russian text). State Publishing House, Moscow, 1963.

PATRICK, G.Z. *A List Of Abbreviations Commonly Used in the U.S.S.R.* University of California, Berkeley, 1937.

PLAMENATZ, I.P. *Yugoslav Abbreviations, A Selective List*. 2nd ed. Library of Congress, Washington, 1962.

ROSENBERG, A. *Russian Abbreviations, A Selective List*. 2nd ed. Library of Congress, Washington, 1957.

WOJCICKA, J. *Polish Abbreviations, A Selective List*. 2nd ed. Library of Congress, Washington, 1957.

ZALUCKI, H. *Dictionary of Russian Technical and Scientific Abbreviations*. Elsevier, London, 1968.

A

AA	Advertising Association
AA	Akademisk Arkitektforening
AA	Alcoholics Anonymous
AA	Architectural Association
AA	Automobile Association
AA	Avisenes Arbeidsgiverforening
AAA	Agricultural Adjustment Administration (U.S.A.)
AAA	Allied Artists of America
AAA	Amateur Athletic Association
AAA	American Academy of Advertising
AAA	American Academy of Allergy
AAA	American Accounting Association
AAA	American Airship Association
AAA	American Angus Association
AAA	American Arbitration Association
AAA	American Association of Anatomists
AAA	American Anthropological Association
AAA	American Automobile Association
AAA	Anglo-American Associates (U.S.A.)
AAA	Architectural Aluminium Association
AAA	Association of Attenders and Alumni of the Hague Academy of International Law
AAAA	American Association for Advancement of Atheism
AAAA	American Association of Advertising Agencies
AAAA	American Association of Audio Analgesia
AAAA	Asian Amateur Athletic Association
AAAA	Asociación Argentina 'Amigos de la Astronomia'
AAAA	Association of Accredited Advertising Agencies of New Zealand
AAAA	Australian Association of Advertising Agencies
AAAC	Alliance Atlantique des Anciens Combattants
AAACC	Association of Asian-American Chambers of Commerce
AAACE	American Association of Agricultural College Editors
AAAE	American Association of Airport Executives
AAAEENAA	Association Amicale des Anciens Élèves de l'École National Agronomique d'Alger (*formerly* AAEIAA)
AAAEINA	Association Amicale des Anciens Élèves de l'Institut National Agronomique
AAAF	Association Aéronautique et Astronautique de France
AAAI	Advertising Agencies Association of India
AAAI	Affiliated Advertising Agencies International (U.S.A.)
AAAJ	Association Afro-Asiatique des Journalistes
AAAL	American Academy of Arts and Letters
AAALAC	American Association for Accreditation of Laboratory Animal Care
AAAM	American Association of Aircraft Manufacturers
AAAM	American Association for Automotive Medicine
AAAN	American Academy of Applied Nutrition
AAAS	American Academy of Asian Studies
AAAS	American Academy of Arts and Sciences
AAAS	American Association for the Advancement of Science
AAASA	Association for the Advancement of Agricultural Sciences in Africa
AAASS	American Association for the Advancement of Slavic Studies
AAB	Alliance Agricole Belge
AAB	American Association of Bioanalysts
AAB	Association of Applied Biologists
AABA	Associação Atletica Brasil Açucareiro
AABB	American Association of Blood Banks
AABB	Association des Archivistes et Bibliothécaires de Belgique
AABC	American Association of Bible Colleges
AABDF	Allied Association of Bleachers, Printers, Dyers and Finishers
AABE	Asian Association for Biology Education
AABEVK	Arbeitsgemeinschaft für das Archiv- und Bibliothekswesen in der Evangelischen Kirche
AABGA	American Association of Botanical Gardens and Arboretums

AABL	Associated Australasian Banks in London	**AACK**	Asociación Argentina Criadores de Karakul
AABM	American Association of Battery Manufacturers	**AACL**	Association of American Correspondents in London
AABM	Australian Association of British Manufacturers	**AACLA**	Association of American Chambers of Commerce in Latin America
AABP	Australian Association of Business Relations	**AACM**	American Academy of Compensation Medicine
AAC	Acadèmia Argentina de Cirugía	**AACMA**	All-Africa Church Music Association
AAC	Affärsarbetsgivarnas Centralförbund	**AACNP**	Asociación Argentina de Ciéncias Naturáles 'Physis'
AAC	Agrarische Adviescommissie (*of* NIBEM)		
AAC	Agricultural Advisory Council for England and Wales	**AACO**	Arab Air Carriers Organization
AAC	Anglo American Corporation	**AACOBS**	Australian Advisory Council on Bibliographical Services
AAC	Association of American Colleges	**AACP**	American Academy for Cerebral Palsy
AAC	Australian Agricultural Council	**AACP**	American Academy of Child Psychiatry
AAC	Austrian Alpine Club	**AACP**	American Association of Colleges of Pharmacy
AACB	Aeronautics and Astronautics Coordinating Board (U.S.A.)	**AACP**	American Association of Commerce Publications
AACB	Association of African Central Banks	**AACP**	American Association of Correctional Psychologists
AACC	Airport Associations Coordinating Council		
AACC	All Africa Conference of Churches	**AACP**	Anglo-American Council for Productivity
AACC	American Association of Cereal Chemists	**AACP**	Association des Agences Conseils en Publicité
AACC	American Association of Clinical Chemists	**AACPS**	American Association of Clinic Physicians and Surgeons
AACC	American Association of Commercial Colleges		
AACC	American Association for Contamination Control	**AACR**	American Association for Cancer Research
AACC	American Automatic Control Council	**AACR**	American Association of Clinical Research
AACC	Arab Air Carriers Organization	**AACR**	Association for the Advancement of Civil Rights (Gibraltar)
AACC	Asociación Argentina de Criadores de Caprinos	**AACREA**	Asociación Argentina de Consorcios Regionales de Experimentación Agrícola
AACC	Asociación Argentina de Criadores de Cebú		
AACC	Asociación Argentina de Criadores de Cerdos	**AACSL**	American Association for the Comparative Study of Law
AACC	Asociación Argentina de Criadores de Corriedale	**AACT**	American Association of Clinical Toxicology
AACCH	American Association for Child Care in Hospital	**AACTE**	American Association of Colleges for Teacher Education
AACCH	Asociación Argentina Criadores de Charolais	**AACU**	American Association of Clinical Urologists
AACE	African Association for Correspondence Education	**AAD**	American Academy of Dermatology
AACE	American Association for Cancer Education	**AADE**	American Academy of Dental Electrosurgery
AACE	American Association of Cost Engineers	**AADE**	American Association of Dental Editors
AACG	American Association for Crystal Growth	**AADFI**	Association of African Development Finance Institutions
AACI	American Association for Conservation Information	**AADM**	American Academy of Dental Medicine
		AADR	American Academy of Dental Radiology
AACIA	American Association for Clinical Immunity	**AADS**	American Academy of Dermatology and Syphilology

AE	Agrupación Astronautica Española	AÄGP	Allgemeine Ärztliche Gesellschaft für Psychotherapie
AE	American Association of Endodontists		
AE	American Association of Engineers	AAGREF	Association Amicale de Genie Rural des Eaux et des Forêts
AE	Asociación Argentina de Electrotécnicos		
		AAGS	Association of African Geological Surveys
AEA	African Adult Education Association (Nigeria)	AAGUS	American Association of Genito-Urinary Surgeons
AEA	American Agricultural Economics Association	AAHA	American Association of Handwriting Analysts
AEA	American Agricultural Editors Association	AAHD	American Academy of the History of Dentistry
AEC	Association Africaine pour l'Enseignement par Correspondence	AAHE	American Association for Higher Education
AEC	Australian Atomic Energy Commission	AAHM	American Association for the History of Medicine
AEE	American Association of Economic Entomologists	AAHO	Afro-Asian Housing Organisation (Egypt)
AEE	American Association of Electromyography and Electrodiagnosis	AAHPER	American Association for Health, Physical Education, and Recreation
AEE	Association pour l'Accueil des Étudiants Étrangers	AAHRA	Asian and Australasian Hotel and Restaurant Association (Singapore)
AEIAA	Association des Anciens Élèves de l'Institut Agricole d'Algérie et de l'École Nationale d'Agriculture d'Alger (now AAAEENAA)	AAHS	American Aviation Historical Society
		AAI	Académie des Affaires Internationales (U.S.A.)
AES	Australian Agricultural Economics Society	AAI	African-American Institute (U.S.A.)
AESU	Allgemeine Arabische Eisen und Stahl Union	AAI	Agricultural Ammonia Institute (U.S.A.)
AF	Académie d'Agriculture de France	AAI	American Association of Immunologists
AF	Agricultural Aids Foundation (U.S.A.)	AAI	Architectural Association of Ireland
AF	American Advertising Federation	AAI	Association Actuarielle Internationale
AF	American Architectural Foundation	AAI	Association of Advertisers in Ireland
AF	American Astronautical Federation	AAI	Association of Art Institutions
AF	Asociatia Artiştilor Fotografi din Republica Socialista România	AAIA	Association on American Indian Affairs
AFA	Anglo-American Families Association	AAID	American Association of Industrial Dentists
AFCO	Association of American Fertiliser Control Officials	AAIE	American Association of Industrial Editors
		AAIE	American Association of Industrial Engineers
AFE	Asociación Argentina de Fomento Equiño	AAIH	Association Amicale des Ingénieurs Horticoles et des Élèves de l'École Nationale d'Horticulture de Versailles
AFI	Association des Anciens Fonctionnaires Internationaux		
AFM	American Association of Feed Microscopists	AAIN	American Association of Industrial Nurses
AFRA	Association of African Airlines	AAIO	Afro-Asian Islamic Organization
AFS	American Academy of Forensic Sciences	AAIPS	American Association of Industrial Physicians and Surgeons
AFU	All African Farmers Union		
AG	Afdeling Agrarische Geschiedenis	AAJR	American Academy for Jewish Research
AG	Association of American Geographers	AAL	Académia Argentina de Létras
AGBA	American Angora Goat Breeders' Association	AAL	Association of Assistant Librarians
AGG	Asociación Argentina de Geofisicos y Geodestas	AALAS	American Association for Laboratory Animal Science

AALDI	Association of Agricultural Librarians and Documentalists of India
AALGCSU	American Association of Land Grant Colleges and State Universities
AALL	American Association for Labour Legislation
AALL	American Association of Law Libraries
AALS	American Association of Library Schools
AALS	Association of American Law Schools
AAM	American Academy of Microbiology
AAM	Anti-Apartheid Movement
AAM	Asociación Argentina de Marketing
AAM	Automobile Association of Malaysia
AAMA	American Academy of Medical Administration
AAMA	American Apparel Manufacturers Association
AAMA	Automotive Accessories Manufacturers of America
AAMC	Association of American Medical Colleges
AAMCH	American Association for Maternal and Child Health
AAMD	American Association on Mental Deficiency
AAMF	Association Aéromédicale de France
AAMI	Association for the Advancement of Medical Instrumentation (U.S.A.)
AAMMC	American Association of Medical Milk Commissions
AAMOA	Afro-American Music Opportunities Association
AAMOCIOS	Conseil International pour l'Organisation Scientifique Regional Committee Asia
AAMPR	American Association of Medico-Physical Research
AAMR	American Academy on Mental Retardation
AAMRL	American Association of Medical Record Librarians
AAMS	American Air Mail Society
AAMS	Associated African and Malagasy States
AAMSW	American Association of Medical Social Workers
AAMVA	American Association of Motor Vehicle Administrators
AAN	American Association of Neuropathologists
AANA	Australian Association of National Advertisers
AANO	Albanian-American National Organisation
AANP	American Association of Neuropathologists
AANS	American Academy of Neurological Surgery
AANS	American Agricultural News Service
AAO	American Academy of Osteopathy
AAO	American Association of Ophthalmology
AAO	American Association of Orthodontists
AAO	Arbeitsgemeinschaft der Altphilologen Österreichs
AAODC	American Association of Oilwell Drilling Contractors
AAOEC	Afro-Asian Organization for Economic Cooperation
AAOGAS	American Association of Obstetricians, Gynecologists and Abdominal Surgeons
AAOM	American Academy of Occupational Medicine
AAOM	American Academy of Oral Medicine
AAOMD	American Association on Mental Deficiency
AAOO	American Academy of Ophthalmology and Otolaryngology
AAOP	American Academy of Oral Pathology
AAOS	American Academy of Orthopaedic Surgery
AAOT	American Association of Orthoptic Technicians
AAP	American Academy of Pediatrics
AAP	American Academy of Periodontology
AAP	Art Association of the Philippines
AAP	Association for the Advancement of Psychoanalysis (U.S.A.)
AAP	Association for the Advancement of Psychotherapy (U.S.A.)
AAP	Association of American Physicians
AAP	Association of American Publishers
AAP	Australian Associated Press
AAPA	Advertising Agency Production Association
AAPA	American Association of Port Authorities
AAPA	Asociación Argentina de Producción Animal
AAPA	Asociación Argentina de Productores Agrícolas
AAPA	Association of Accredited Practitioners in Advertising (South Africa)
AAPA	Australian Asphalt Pavement Association
AAPB	American Association of Pathologists and Bacteriologists
AAPC	All African Peoples' Conference
AAPC	Asociación Argentina para el Progreso de las Ciencias

AAPCC	American Association of Poison Control Centres	**AARF**	Australian Accounting Research Foundation
AAPCO	Association of American Pesticide Control Officials	**AAROI**	Associazione Anestesisti Rianimatori Ospedalieri Italiani
AAPD	American Academy of Physiologic Dentistry	**AARP**	American Association of Retired Persons
AAPG	American Association of Petroleum Geologists	**AARRO**	Afro-Asian Rural Reconstruction Organisation
AAPI	Associazione Aziende Pubblicitarie Italiane	**AARS**	American Association of Railway Surgeons
AAPL	Afro-American Patrolmen's League	**AARS**	Awassa Agricultural Research Station (Ethiopia)
AAPM	American Association of Physicists in Medicine	**AART**	American Association for Rehabilitation Therapy
AAPM	Asian Association of Personnel Management	**AARU**	Association of Arab Universities (Egypt)
AAPMR	American Academy of Physical Medicine and Rehabilitation	**AAS**	American Antiquarian Society
AAPO	All African Peoples' Organisation	**AAS**	American Astronomical Society
AAPOR	American Association for Public Opinion Research	**AAS**	Archaeology Abroad Service
		AAS	Association of Architects and Surveyors
AAPPP	American Association of Planned Parenthood Physicians	**AAS**	Association des Archivistes Suisses
		AAS	Association for Asia Studies (U.S.A.)
AAPRO	Asociación Argentina de la Productividad	**AAS**	Auckland Astronomical Society (N.Z.)
AAPS	African Association of Political Science (Tanzania)	**AASA**	American Association of School Administrators
AAPS	American Association of Plastic Surgeons	**AASA**	Australian Association of Social Anthropologists
AAPS	American Association for the Promotion of Science	**AASB**	American Association of Small Businesses
		AASCW	American Association of Scientific Workers
AAPS	Asian Association of Pediatric Surgeons	**AASE**	Australian Associated Stock Exchanges
AAPS	Association of American Physicians and Surgeons	**AASG**	Association of American State Geologists
AAPSC	Afro-Asian Peoples Solidarity Council	**AASHTO**	American Association of State Highway and Transportation Officials
AAPSC	American Association of Psychiatric Services for Children	**AASL**	American Association of School Librarians
AAPSE	American Association of Professors in Sanitary Engineering	**AASL**	American Association of State Libraries
		AASM	Associated African States and Madagascar
AAPSO	Afro-Asian Peoples Solidarity Organisation (Egypt)	**AASND**	American Association for Study of Neoplastic Diseases
AAPSS	American Academy of Political and Social Sciences	**AASP**	American Association of Stratigraphic Palynologists
AAPT	American Association of Physics Teachers	**AASP**	American Association of Swine Practitioners
AAPTS & R	Australian Association for Predetermined Time Standards and Research	**AASP**	Association d'Agences Suisses de Publicité
AAR	Association of American Railroads	**AASS**	American Association for Social Security
AARC	Asociación de Agricultores del Rio Caulicán (Mexico)	**AASSREC**	Association of Asian Social Science Research Councils (India)
AARDES	Association Algérienne pour la Recherche Démographique Économique et Sociale	**AAST**	American Association for the Surgery of Trauma
		AASU	All-African Students Union (Tanzania)
AARDS	Australian Advertising Rate and Data Service	**AATA**	Anglo-American Tourist Association

5

AATCA	Austrian Air Traffic Controllers Association
AATCC	American Association of Textile Chemists and Colorists
AATM	American Academy of Tropical Medicine
AATNU	Administration de l'Assistance Technique des Nations Unies
AATP	American Academy of Tuberculosis Physicians
AATRAA	Association Argentina de Tecnicos de Refrigeración y Acondiciónamiento de Aire
AATS	American Association for Thoracic Surgery
AATS	Committee on the Application of Aerospace Technology to Society (*of* AIAA)
AATSEEL	American Association of Teachers of Slavic and East European Languages
AATT	American Association for Textile Technology
AATTA	Arab Association of Tourism and Travel Agents
AATUF	All-African Trade Union Federation
AAU	Amateur Athletic Union of Eire
AAU	Amateur Athletic Union of the United States
AAU	Association of American Universities
AAUN	American Association for the United Nations
AAUP	American Association of University Presses
AAUP	American Association of University Professors
AAUW	American Association of University Women
AAV	Nederlandse Vereniging van Algemene Aansprakelijk heids-Verzekeraars
AAVA	American Association of Veterinary Anatomists
AAVIM	American Association for Vocational Instructional Materials
AAVN	American Association of Veterinary Nutrition
AAVP	American Association of Veterinary Parasitologists
AAVSC	American Association of Volunteer Services Coordinators
AAVSO	American Association of Variable Star Observers
AAVT	Association of Audio-Visual Technicians (U.S.A.)
AAWE	Association of American Wives of Europeans
AAWSA	Addis Ababa Water and Sewerage Authority (Ethiopia)
AAYPL	Atlantic Association of Young Political Leaders

AAZPA	American Association of Zoological Parks and Aquariums
AB	Alliance Balkanique
ABA	Amateur Boxing Association
ABA	American Bankers Association
ABA	American Bakers' Association
ABA	American Booksellers' Association
ABA	Antiquarian Booksellers Association
ABA	Association Belge des Aerosols
ABA	Association of British Archaeologists
ABAA	Antiquarian Booksellers Association of America
ABAA	Association of British Adoption Agencies
ABAC	Association of British Aero Clubs
ABAC	Association of British Aviation Consultants
ABADCAM	Association des Bibliothécaires, Archivistes, Documentalistes et Muséographers du Cameroun
ABAFA	Association of British Adoption and Fostering Agencies
ABAH	Asociación de Bibliotecarios y Archiveros de Honduras
ABAM	Association of Bee Appliance Manufacturers
ABAM	Association Belge des Assureurs Maritimes
ABAN	Algemene Bond van Autorijsschoolhouders in Nederland
ABAP	Associação Brasileira de Agencias de Propaganda
ABAPE	Associaçao Brasileira de Administraçao de Pessoal
ABAPSTAS	Association of Blind and Partially Sighted Teachers
ABAS	Amateur Basketball Association of Scotland
ABB	American Board of Bioanalysis
ABB	Association Belge des Banques
ABB	Asociación Boliviana de Bibliotecarios
ABBA	Amateur Basket Ball Association
ABBF	Association of Bronze and Brass Founders
ABBL	Association des Banques et Banquiers Luxembourg
ABBMM	Association of British Brush Machinery Manufacturers
ABC	Academia Brasileira de Ciencias
ABC	Africa Bibliographic Centre (Tanzania)
ABC	American Bibliographical Centre
ABC	Asian Badminton Confederation

ABC	Asian Basketball Confederation	ABDP	Association of British Directory Publishers
ABC	Asian Benevolent Corps (U.S.A.)	ABDSA	Association of British Dental Surgery Assistants
ABC	Asian Billiards Confederation (Japan)		
ABC	Associação Brasileira de Criadores	ABE	Asociação Brasileira de Exportadores
ABC	Audit Bureau of Circulations of South Africa Ltd	ABEAS	Association Belge des Entreprises d'Alimentation à Succursales
ABC	Audit Bureau of Circulations (U.S.A.)	ABEAS	Associação Brasileira de Educação Agricola Superior
ABC	Australian Broadcasting Commission	ABEBD	Associação Brasileira de Escolas de Biblioteconomia e Documentação
ABCA	American Business Communication Association		
ABCA	Association des Banques Centrales Africaines	ABEC	Asociación Boliviana de Educación Catolica
		ABEDA	Arab Bank for Economic Development in Africa
ABCA	Association Belge des Chefs d'Approvisionnement	ABEF	Association des Bibliothèques Ecclésiastiques de France
ABCAR	Asociación Brasilena de Crédito y Asistensia Rural	ABELF	Association Belge des Éditeurs de Langue Française
ABCB	American Bottlers of Carbonated Beverages	ABEM	Association Belge pour l'Étude, l'Essai et l'Emploi des Matériaux
ABCC	Association of British Chambers of Commerce		
		ABES	Asociación de Bibliotecarios de El Salvador
ABCC	Association of British Correspondence Colleges	ABETA	Associação Brasileira de Estudos Técnicos de Agricultura
ABCD	Art, Copy and Design Association of Sweden	ABEX	Association Belge des Experts
ABCD	Association Belge de la Chaussure au Détail (France)	ABF	Aerosolindustriens Brancheforening
		ABF	American Beekeeping Federation
ABCFM	American Board of Commissioners for Foreign Missions	ABF	Arbetarnas Bildningsförbund
ABCI	Amis Belges de la Cooperation Internationale	ABF	Asian Baptist Fellowship
ABCM	Association of British Chemical Manufacturers	ABF	Association des Bibliothécaires Français
		ABF	Den Danske Antikvarboghandlerforening
ABCO	Association of British Conference Organisers	ABFACD	Association Belge des Fabricants d'Appareils de Chauffage et de Cuisine Domestiques
ABCOOP	Aliança Brasileira de Cooperativas		
ABCP	Asian Buddhist Conference for Peace (Japan)	ABFL	Association of British Foam Laminators
ABCP	Associação Técnica Brasileira de Celulose e Papel	ABFM	American Board of Foreign Missions
		ABG	Association of British Geodesists
ABCPA	Alberta Beef Cattle Performance Association (Canada)	ABG	Associazione Italiana fra gli Industriali delle Acque e Bevande
ABCT	Association Belgo-Zairoise du Textile	ABGRA	Asociación de Bibliotecarios Graduados de la República Argentina
ABD	Association Belge des Detectives		
ABD	Association Belge du Diabète	ABH	Association Belge des Hôpitaux
ABD	Association Belge de Documentation	ABH	Association of British Hairdressers
ABD	Association of British Detectives	ABHM	Association of Builders Hardware Manufacturers
ABDA	Arbeitsgemeinschaft der Berufsvertretungen Deutscher Apotheker		
		ABI	American Butter Institute
ABDI	Asoação Brasileira de Desenho Industrial	ABI	Asociación de Bienestar Infantil (Guatemala)
ABDIB	Associação Brasileira para o Desenvolvimento das Industrias de Base	ABI	Association des Bibliothèques Internationales
		ABI	Associazione Bancaria Italiana

ABIA	Associação Brasileira das Industrias da Alimentação
ABIC	Association Belge de l'Industrie du Caoutchouc
ABICIT	Association Belge d'Ingénieurs-Conseils Diplomés Ingénieurs Techniciens
ABICTIC	Association Belge des Ingénieurs, des Chimistres et des Techniciens des Industries du Cuir
ABIEAS	Asociación Boliviana de Instituciones de Educación Agrícola Superior
ABIISE	Agrupación de Bibliotecas para la Integración de la Información Socio-Económica (Peru)
ABIM	American Board of International Missions
ABIM	Association of British Insecticide Manufacturers
ABIPAR	Asociación de Bibliotecarios del Paraguay
ABIR	Associação Brasileira de Informação Rural
ABIS	Association of Burglary Insurance Surveyors
ABITA	Association Belge des Ingénieurs et Technicians de l'Aéronautique et de l'Astronautique
ABJ	Association of Brewers of Japan
ABJA	Association Belge des Journalistes Agricoles
ABJPAA	Association Belge des Journalistes Professionnels de l'Aéronautique et de l'Astronautique
ABL	Association Belge des Logopèdes
ABLC	Association of British Launderers and Cleaners
ABLGPL	Association Belgo-Luxembourgeoise des Gaz de Pétrole Liquefiés
ABLISS	Association of British Library and Information Studies Schools
ABLS	Association of British Library Schools
ABM	Associação Brasileira de Matais
ABM	Association Belge du Moulinage
ABM	Association of British Maltsters
ABM	Australian Board of Missions
ABMA	American Boiler Manufacturers Association
ABMAC	American Bureau for Medical Aid to China
ABMAC	Association of British Manufacturers of Agricultural Chemicals (*now* BAA)
ABMEX	Association of British Mining Equipment Exporters
ABMP	Association Belge des Matières Plastiques
ABMPM	Association of British Manufacturers of Printers Machinery
ABMS	American Bureau of Metal Statistics
ABMS	Associação Brasileira de Mecanica dos Solos
ABN	Algemene Nederlandse Bond van Natuursteen-bewerkende Bedrijven
ABNEI	Association Belge des Négociants Exportateurs et Importateurs
ABNT	Associaçao Brasiliera de Normas Técnicas
ABO	American Board of Ophthalmology
ABO	American Board of Otolaryngology
ABO	Associaçao Brasileira de Odontologia
ABOCF	Association of British Organic and Compound Fertilisers
ABOI	Association of British Oceanological Industries
ABOP	Algemene Bond van Onderwijzend Personeel
ABP	Association Belge des Paralysés
ABPA	Australian Book Publishers Association
ABPC	American Book Publishers Council
ABPC	Associated British Picture Corporation
ABPC	Association Belge de Photographie et de Cinématographie
ABPC	Association of British Packing Contractors
ABPE	Association Belgo-Luxembourgeoise de la Presse d'Entreprise
ABPI	Association of the British Pharmaceutical Industry
ABPM	American Board of Preventive Medicine
ABPN	American Board of Psychiatry and Neurology
ABPN	Association of British Paediatric Nurses
ABPNL	Association Belge des Pilotes et Navigateurs de Ligne
ABPVM	Association of British Plywood and Veneer Manufacturers
ABQ	Associação Brasileira de Química
ABRA	Asociação Brasileira de Reforma Agraria
ABRACE	Associação Brasileira de Computadores Electronicos
ABRAPEC	Associação Brasileira de Orientação Agro Pecuária
ABRAVA	Associação Brasileira de Refrigeração, Ar-Condicionado, Ventilação e Aquecimento
ABRFM	Association of British Roofing Felt Manufacturers

ABRO	Animal Breeding Research Organization	ABYA	Association of British Yacht Agents
ABRP	Association of British Rose Producers	ABZ	Association of British Zoologists
ABRRM	Association of British Reclaimed Rubber Manufacturers	AC	Affärsarbetsgivarnas Centralförbund
		ACA	Acoustic Corporation of America
ABRS	Association of British Riding Schools	ACA	Advertisement Contractors Association
ABS	American Bible Association	ACA	Agence Camerounaise d'Assurances
ABS	American Bureau of Shipping	ACA	Agence Congolaise d'Assurances
ABS	Association des Bibliothécaires Suisses	ACA	Agricultural Co-operative Association (now ACMS)
ABS	Association of British Spectroscopists		
ABS	Association of Broadcasting Staffs	ACA	American College of Apothecaries
ABS	Auckland Botanical Society (N.Z.)	ACA	American Composers Alliance
ABSI	Association of the Boot and Shoe Industry	ACA	Asociación Centro-americana de Anatomia
ABSM	Association of British Sterilizer Manufacturers	ACA	Asociación Colombiana de Apicultores
		ACA	Association of Canadian Advertisers
ABSTECH	American Bureau of Shipping Worldwide Technical Services	ACA	Association des Compagnies d'Assurances Agréés au Grand-Duché de Luxembourg
ABSW	Association of British Science Writers	ACA	Australian Consumers Association
ABT	Association of Building Technicians	ACA	Australian Council for Aeronautics
ABTA	Allied Brewery Trader's Association	ACAAI	Air Cargo Agents Association of India
ABTA	Association of British Travel Agents	ACABQ	Advisory Committee on Administrative and Budgetary Questions (UN)
ABTA	Australian British Trade Association		
ABTAC	Australian Book Trade Advisory Committee	ACACC	Asian Conference on Agricultural Credit and Cooperatives
ABTAPL	Association of British Theological and Philosophical Libraries	ACADEVIR	Collège Academique International de l'Environnement
ABTB	Aartsdiocesane Roomskatholieke Boeren-en Tuindersbond	ACADI	Association des Cadres Dirigeants de l'Industrie pour le Progrès Sociale et Économique
ABTCM	Association of British Textured Coating Manufacturers		
		ACAE	Ateliers et Chantiers de l'Afrique Equatoriale
ABTICS	Abstract and Book Title Index Card Service	ACAHN	Asociación Centro-Americano de Historia Natural (Guatemala)
ABTL	Association Belge des Technologues de Laboratoire		
		ACAI	Accademia Archeologica Italiana
ABTM	Association of British Transport Museums	ACAI	Associazione fra i Costruttori in Acciaio Italiani
ABTSA	Association of British Tree Surgeons and Arborists		
		ACAI	Associazione Cristiana Artigiani Italiani
ABTT	Association of British Theatre Technicians	ACAIT	Asociación Centroamericana de Industrias Textiles (Guatemala)
ABTUC	All-Burma Trade Union Congress		
ABU	Alliance Biblique Universelle	ACAM	Association des Compagnies d'Assurances Moyennes
ABU	Asian Broadcasting Union		
ABUEN	Asociación de Bibliotecas Universitarias y Especializadas de Nicaragua	ACAMAR	Asociación Centroamericana de Armadores (Guatemala)
ABV	Algemeen Belgisch Vlasverbond	ACAP	Asociación Colombiana de Agencias de Publicidad
ABWAK	Association of British Wild Animal Keepers		
ABWARC	Australian Baptist World Aid and Relief Committee	ACAPA	American Concrete Agricultural Pipe Association
ABWE	Association of Baptists for World Evangelism (U.S.A)	ACAR	Associacão de Credito e Assistencia Rural (Brazil)

ACARPESC Serviço de Extensão de Santa Catarina

ACAS Advisory Conciliation and Arbitration Service

ACAS Association Centrale des Assistants Sociaux (Belgium)

ACAST *see* ACASTD

ACASTD Advisory Committee on the Application of Science and Technology to Development (*of* UNO)

ACATS Association of Civil Aviation Technical Staffs

ACAUP Associazione Capi Aziende Pubblicitarie

ACAV American Committee on Arthropod-borne Viruses

ACB Asociación Costarricense de Bibliotecarios

ACB Association Canadienne des Bibliothèques

ACBCC Advisory Committee to the Board and to the Committee on Commodities (UNCTAD)

ACBCU Association Canadienne des Bibliothèques de Collège et d'Université

ACBD Association Canadienne des Bibliothèques de Droit

ACBI Agricultural Cooperatives Bank of Iran

ACBLF Association Canadienne des Bibliothécaires de Langue Française (*now* ASTED)

ACBM Association Canadienne des Bibliothèques Musicales

ACC Administrative Committee on Co-ordination (ECOSOC)

ACC Agricultural Credit Corporation Ltd

ACC Asian Coconut Community

ACC Associated Communications Corporation

ACCA American Clinical and Climatological Association

ACCA American Cotton Cooperative Association

ACCA Associated Chambers of Commerce of Australia

ACCA Association of Certified and Corporate Accountants

ACCAST Advisory Committee on Colonial Colleges of Arts, Science and Technology (*now* COCAST)

ACC & CE Association of Consulting Chemists and Chemical Engineers (U.S.A.)

ACCCI American Coke and Coal Chemicals Institute

ACCEC Australian Chambers of Commerce Export Council

ACCEFN Academia Colombiana de Ciencias Exactas Fisicas y Naturales

ACCET Asian Centre for Comparative Education (Iran)

ACCF Agence Centrafricaine des Communications Fluviales

ACCFA Agricultural Credit and Co-operative Financing Administration (Philippines)

ACCG American Committee for Crystal Growth

ACCHAN Allied Command Channel

ACCI Association of Chambers of Commerce of Ireland

ACCL American Council of Commercial Laboratories

ACCMLRI Association des Caisses de Crédit Mutuel Libres à Responsabilité Illimitée

ACCN Académia Chilena de Ciéncias Naturales

ACCO Algemene Classificatiecommissie voor de Overheidsadministratie

ACCO Association of Child Care Officers

ACCOR Associated Chambers of Commerce of Rhodesia

ACCP American College of Chest Physicians

ACCS Associazione del Commercio dei Cereali e Semi

ACCT Agence de Coopération Culturelle et Technique

ACCTI American Chamber of Commerce for Trade with Italy

ACCU Asian Confederation of Credit Unions

ACDA Asian Centre for Development Administration (Malaysia)

ACDA United States Arms Control and Disarmament Agency

ACDB Association du Catalogue Documentaire du Bâtiment

ACDE Asociación Cristiana de Dirigentes de Empresa (Uruguay)

ACDI Agence Canadienne de Développement International

ACDI Agricultural Cooperative Development International (U.S.A.)

ACDO Association of Civil Defence Officers

ACDRI CSIR Advisory Committee on the Development of Research for Industry (South Africa)

ACDS Anglo Continental Dental Society

ACDTPN	Association pour le Controle de la Descendance des Taureaux Pie Noirs
ACE	Acadèmia de Ciéncias Económicas (Argentina)
ACE	Advisory Centre for Education
ACE	Allied Command Europe
ACE	Americans for Childrens Relief
ACE	American Council on Education
ACE	Amitiés Chrétiennes Européennes
ACE	Association of Conference Executives
ACE	Association of Consulting Engineers
ACE	Association des Conseillers Européens
ACE	Athens Centre of Ekistiks (Greece)
ACE	Australian Christian Endeavour Union
ACEA	Asociación Costarricense de Economistas Agrícolas (Costa Rico)
ACEA	Canadian Association of African Studies
ACEAR	Atelier Central d'Études d'Aménagement Rural
ACEB	Association Canadienne des Écoles de Bibliothécaires
ACEC	Advisory Council on Energy Conservation
ACEC	Associazione Cattolica Esercenti Cinema
ACEC	Ateliers de Constructions Électriques de Charleroi
ACEHI	Association of Canadian Educators of the Hearing-Impaired
ACEI	Association for Childhood Education International (U.S.A.)
ACEIB	Association des Centrales Électriques Industrielles de Belgique
ACEID	Asian Centre of Educational Innovation for Development (Thailand)
ACEN	Assembly of Captive European Nations
ACENZ	Association of Consultant Engineers of New Zealand
ACEO	Association of Chief Education Officers
ACEP	Advisory Committee on Export Policy (U.S.A.)
ACER	Australian Council for Educational Research
ACERP	Asociación Cubana de Ejecutivos de Relaciones Públicas
ACF	Académie Canadienne Française
ACF	Agricultural Co-operative Federation
ACF	Australian Conservation Foundation
ACF	Automobile Club de France

ACFAS	Association Canadienne Française pour l'Avancement des Sciences
ACFB	Associations Culturelles Franco-Brésiliennes (Brazil)
ACFFTU	All-Ceylon Federation of Free Trade Unions
ACFHE	Association of Colleges for Further and Higher Education
ACFMO	Alliance de Constructeurs Français de Machines-Outils
ACFOA	Australian Council for Overseas Aid
ACFOD	Asian Cultural Forum on Development (Thailand)
ACFRA	Assureurs Conseils Franco-Africains
ACGB	Aircraft Corporation of Great Britain
ACGB	Arts Council of Great Britain
ACGBI	Automobile Club of Great Britain and Ireland
ACGF	Australian Citrus Growing Federation
ACGR	Associate Committee on Geotechnical Research (Canada)
ACH	Academia Colombiana de Historia
ACHA	American College of Hospital Administration
ACHA	Asociación Criadores de Holando Argentino
ACHAC	Association des Centres pour Handicapés de l'Afrique Centrale
ACHAP	Asociación Chilena de Agencias de Publicidad
ACHCN	Academia Chilena de Ciencias Naturales
ACHIF	Asociación Chilena de Ingenieros Forestales
ACHM	Asociación Chilena Microbiología
ACHTR	Advisory Committee for Humid Tropics Research (of UNESCO)
ACI	African Cultural Institute (Senegal)
ACI	Algemene Vereniging voor de Centrale Verwarmings- en Luchtbehandelingsindustrie
ACI	Alliance Coopérative Internationale
ACI	American Concrete Institute
ACI	Association Cartographique Internationale
ACI	Association of Chambers of Commerce of Ireland
ACI	Automobile Club d'Italia
ACIA	Asociación Centroamericana de Informaciones Agrícolas
ACIA	Asociación Colombiana de Ingenieros Agrónomos
ACIA	Association of the Corporation of Insurance Agents

ACIAA	Australian Commercial and Industrial Artists Association	**ACJ**	Alianz Mundial de Asociaciones Christianas de Jóvenes
ACIC	Aeronautical Charting and Information Centre (U.S.A.)	**ACL**	Académia Carioca de Létras (Brazil)
		ACL	Academia Chilena de la Lengua
ACICAFE	Association du Commerce et de l'Industrie du Café dans la CEE	**ACL**	Academia das Ciéncias de Lisboa
		ACL	Atlantic Container Line Ltd
ACID	Advisory Committee on Industrial Development (S. Rhodesia)	**ACLALS**	Association for Commonwealth Literature and Language Studies (Canada)
ACID	Association of Canadian Industrial Designers	**ACLAM**	American College of Laboratory Animal Medicine
ACIEAS	Asociación Colombiana de Instituciones de Educación Agrícola Superior	**ACLANT**	Allied Command Atlantic
ACIEL	Coordinating Action of Free Institutions of Commerce and Trade (Argentine)	**ACLS**	American Council of Learned Societies
ACIEMP	Association Catholique Internationale d'Études Médico-Psychologiques	**ACLU**	American Civil Liberties Union
		ACM	Arab Common Market
ACIESTI	Association Catholique Internationale des Enseignants et Chercheurs en Sciences et Techniques de l'Information	**ACM**	Association for Computing Machines (U.S.A.)
		ACM	Association of Crane Makers (*now* FMCEC)
ACIF	Asociación Colombiana de Ingenieros Forestales	**ACM**	Ateliers et Chantiers du Mali
ACIFA	Auxiliare Commerciale Immobilière Franco-Africaine	**ACMA**	Agricultural Co-operative Managers Association
		ACMA	Asbestos Cement Manufacturers Association
ACIL	American Council of Independent Laboratories	**ACMA**	Asphalt Coated Macadam Association
ACILECE	Association Cooperative Intersyndicale de Librairie et d'Édition du Corps Enseignant	**ACMA**	Associated Chambers of Manufacturers of Australia
		ACMC	Association of Canadian Medical Colleges
ACIM	American Committee on Italian Migration	**ACME**	Advisory Council on Medical Education (U.S.A.)
ACIMALL	Associazione Costruttori Italiani Macchine e Accessori per la Lavorazione del Legno	**ACME**	Association of Consulting Management Engineers (U.S.A.)
ACIMGA	Associazione Costruttori Italiani Macchine Grafiche e Affini	**ACMET**	Advisory Council on Middle East Trade
ACIMIT	Associazione Costruttori Italiani di Macchinario per l'Industria Tessile	**ACMF**	American Corn Millers Federation
		ACML	Anti-Common Market League
ACINDECO	Action Internationale de Développement Coopératif	**ACML**	Association of Canadian Map Libraries
ACIOPJF	Association Catholique Internationale des Oeuvres de Protection de la Jeune Fille	**ACMRR**	Advisory Committee on Marine Resources Research (FAO)
ACIS	American Committee for Irish Studies	**ACMS**	Agricultural Co-operation and Marketing Services
ACISJF	Association Catholique Internationale des Services de la Jeunesse Féminine	**ACMS**	Australasian Conference on the Mechanics of Structures and Materials
ACIT	Académie Internationale du Tourisme	**ACNA**	Aziende Colori Nazionali Affini Spa
ACIT	Association des Chimistes de l'Industrie Textile	**ACNUR**	United Nations High Commissioner for Refugees
ACIVS	Association Internationale pour la Lutte contre la Violence Associée au Sport	**ACOA**	American Committee on Africa
		ACODEX	Asociación Colombiana de Exportadores
ACIWLP	American Committee for International Wild Life Protection	**ACOEXA**	Asociación Colombiana de Expertos Agrícolas

ACOFAL	Asociación Colombiana de Fabricantes de Alimentos para Animales
ACOG	American College of Obstetricians and Gynecologists
ACOGE	Asociación Colombiana de Geógrafos
ACOH	Advisory Committee for Operational Hydrology (WMO)
ACOMEX	Asociación Colombiana de Comercio Exterior
ACOMR	Advisory Committee on Oceanic Meteorological Research (*of* WMO)
ACOOG	American College of Osteopathic Obstetricians and Gynecologists
ACOPI	Asociación Colombiana de Pequeños Industriales
ACORBAT	Association for Co-operation in Banana Research in the Caribbean and Tropical America
ACORD	Advisory Council on Research and Development
ACORD	Agency for Cooperation in Rural Development (Switzerland)
ACOSCA	Africa Cooperative Savings and Credit Association
ACOSA	Aluminium Company of South Africa
ACP	African, Caribbean and Pacific Countries associated with the European Economic Community
ACP	American College of Physicians
ACP	Association of Canadian Publishers
ACP	Associated Church Press of the Western Hemisphere (U.S.A.)
ACP	Association of Circus Proprietors of Great Britain
ACP	Association of Clinical Pathologists
ACP Group	Groupe des États d'Afrique, des Caraïbes et du Pacifique
ACPA	American Capon Producers Association
ACPA	American Concrete Paving Association
ACPA	Association des Chefs de Publicité d'Annonceurs de Belgique
ACPA	Asociación Costarricense de Productores de Algodon (Costa Rico)
ACPC	Asian Christian Peace Conference (India)
ACPCC	American Council of Polish Cultural Clubs
ACPE	Agrupación National Sindical de Constructores Promotores de Edificios Urbanos
ACPF	Asociación del Congreso Panamericano de Ferrocarrilles (Argentina)
ACPI	Associazione Consulenti Pubblicitari Italiani
ACPM	American College of Preventive Medicine
ACPM	American Congress on Physical Medicine
ACPM	Association of Corrugated Paper Makers
ACPO	Asian Committee for People's Organization (Philippines)
ACPO	Association of Chief Police Officers of England and Wales
ACPS	Arab Company for Petroleum Services (*of* OAPEC)
AC & R	American Cable and Radio Corporation
ACR	American College of Radiology
ACR	Australian Catholic Relief
ACRC	Academia de Ciencias de la República de Cuba
ACRI	American Cocoa Research Institute
ACRI	Associazione fra le Casse di Risparmio Italiano
ACRILIS	Australian Centre for Research in Library and Information Science
ACRL	Association of College and Reference Libraries (U.S.A.)
ACROA	Australian Council for Overseas Aid
ACRPP	Association pour la Conservation et la Reproduction Photographique de la Presse (France)
ACRR	American Council on Race Relations
ACRS	Advisory Committee on Reactor Safeguards (U.S.A.)
ACS	American Cancer Society
ACS	American Ceramic Society
ACS	American Chemical Society
ACS	American College of Surgeons
ACS	Association of Commonwealth Students
ACS	Australian Computer Society
ACS	Automobil Club der Schweiz
ACSA	Aerocarga SA (Mexico)
ACSA	Allied Communications Security Agency (*of* NATO)
ACSA	American Cotton Shippers Association
ACSAD	Arab Centre for the Studies of Arid Zones and Dry Lands (Syria)
ACSE	Association of Consulting Structural Engineers (Australia)

ACSEDIA	Association pour le Controle Sanitaire, l'Étude et le Développement de l'Insémination Artificielle
ACSI	Association Canadienne des Sciences de l'Information
ACSIL	Admiralty Centre for Scientific Information and Liaison
ACSP	Advisory Council on Scientific Policy
ACSP	Association Canadienne de Science Politique
ACSPA	Australian Council of Salaried and Professional Associations
ACSPFT	Asian Committee for Standardisation of Physical Fitness Tests
ACSR	Association Cinématographique Suisse Romande
ACSSM	Associate Committee on Soil and Snow Mechanics (Canada)
ACST	
see ACASTD	
ACSUS	Association for Canadian Studies in the United States (U.S.A.)
ACT	Agricultural Central Trading
ACT	Australian Capital Territory
ACTA	Association des Commissionaires de Transports Aériens (Switzerland)
ACTA	Association de Coordination Technique Agricole (of FNSEA)
ACTIS	Auckland Commercial and Technical Information Service (N.Z.)
ACTRA	Association of Canadian Television and Radio Artists
ACTT	Association of Cinematograph, Television and Allied Technicians
ACTU	Australian Council of Trade Unions
ACU	Asian Clearing Union
ACU	Association of Commonwealth Universities
ACU	Association of Cricket Umpires
ACUA	Association of Cambridge University Assistants
ACUP	Association of Canadian University Presses
ACURIL	Association of Caribbean University and Research Libraries
ACV	Algemeen Christelijk Vakverbond (Belgium)
ACV	Association Centrale des Vétérinaires
ACV	Stichting Afnemers Controle op Veevoeder
ACVAFS	American Council of Voluntary Agencies for Foreign Service

ACVPF	Association des Createurs de Variétés Potagères et Florales
ACWW	Associated Countrywomen of the World
ACYPL	Atlantic Association of Young Political Leaders
ADA	Agence Dahoméenne d'Assurances
ADA	Agricultural Development Association
ADA	Aluminium Development Association
ADA	American Dairy Association
ADA	American Dehydration Association
ADA	American Dental Association
ADA	American Diabetes Association
ADA	American Dietetic Association
ADA	Associazione Direttori Albergo
ADA	Atomic Development Authority (U.S.A.)
ADA	Australian Dental Association
ADAA	Australian Development Assistance Agency
ADACI	Associazione degli Approvvigionatori e Compratori Italiani
ADAF	Arbeitskreis Deutscher Afrika-Forschungsstellen
ADAGP	Association pour la Diffusion des Arts Graphiques et Plastiques
ADAI	Associazione degli Approvvigionatori Italiani
ADAM	Association Dauphinoise pour l'Aménagement de la Montagne
ADAPSO	Association of Data Processing Organisations (U.S.A.)
ADAS	African Demonstration Centre on Sampling Agricultural Surveys (*of* CCTA and FAO)
ADAS	Agricultural Development and Advisory Service (*formerly* NAAS)
	Army Dependants Assurance Trust
ADATIG	Anglo-Dutch African Textiles Investigation Group
ADB	African Bank for Development
ADB	Asian Development Bank (Philippines)
ADBACI	Association pour le Développement de la Documentation, des Bibliothèques et Archives de la Côte d'Ivoire
ADBP	Agricultural Development Bank of Pakistan
ADBPA	Association pour le Développement Bibliothèques Publiques en Afrique
ADBS	Association Française des Documentalistes et des Bibliothécaires Spécialisés
ADC	Agricultural Development Council (*formerly* CECA) (U.S.A.)

DC	Andean Development Corporation
DC	Arsenic Development Committee (France)
DC	Asian Development Centre (Philippines)
DC	Asociación Demografica Costarricense (Costa Rica)
DCCK	Association for the Development of Commonwealth Knowledge (Canada)
DCF	Association pour le Développement de la Culture Fourragère (Switzerland)
DCO	Andean Development Company (Ecuador)
DD	Arbeitsgemeinschaft Deutscher Detektive
DDE	Association des Dépôts Dentaires Européens
DEAC	Association d'Entrepôts en Afrique Centrale
DEARTA	Association pour le Développement de l'Équipement des Ateliers de Réparation des Tracteurs Agricoles
DEB	Association des Entrepreneurs Belges de Travaux de Génie Civil
DEC	Association pour le Développement de la Cooperation Agricole
DECO	Programa de Adiestramiento de Extensionistas en Comunicaciones, Latinoamérica
DEE	Association for Dental Education in Europe (Netherlands)
DEKRA	Arbeitsgemeinschaft Deutscher Kraftwagen-Spediteure
DELA	Atlantic Community Development Group for Latin America
DELF	Association des Écrivains de Langue Française
DEPA	Association pour le Développement de la Production Automatique
DES	Association of Directors of Education in Scotland
DESPE	Association pour le Développement de la Science Politique Européenne
DETEM	Association pour le Développement des Techniques d'Exécution et de l'Exploitation des Études de Marché
DETIM	Association pour le Développement des Techniques des Industries Mécaniques
DETOM	Association pour le Développement de l'Enseignement Technique Outre-Mer
DEVIA	Asociación de Editoras para Deficientes Visuales de Ibero-América
DEXA	Association pour le Développement des Exportations Agricoles

ADEZ	Association pour le Développement des Études Zootechniques (Belgium)
ADEZ	Association des Entrepreneurs du Zaire
ADF	Aerosolinteressenters Förening
ADF	Arbeitsgemeinschaft Deutscher Filztuchfabriken
ADF	Association Dentaire Française
ADFA	Australian Dried Fruits Association
ADGA	American Dairy Goat Association
ADGLC	Abu Dhabi Gas Liquefaction Company
ADH	Association of Dental Hospitals of Great Britain and Northern Ireland
ADI	Agrupación de Diseñadores Industriales
ADI	American Documentation Institute
ADI	Association pour le Développement International
ADI	Associazione Detectives Italiani
ADI	Associazione Dietetica Italiana
ADI	Associazione per il Disegno Industriale
ADIA	Academy of Diplomacy and International Affairs (Germany)
ADIBBEL	Association des Dirigeants des Instituts de Beauté de Belgique
ADIC	Association des Dirigeants et Cadres Chrétiens
ADICEP	Associacion des Directeurs des Centres des Matières Plastiques
ADIN	Asociación de Industrias Náuticas
ADIP	Association Nationale de Défense de Élevage et du Commerce Rural Interprofessionnel
ADIP	Associazione Italiana dei Direttori del Personale
ADIRI	Association de Droit International et de Relations Internationales (Romania)
ADK	Arbeitgeberverband der Deutschen Kautschukindustrie
ADKPZ	Arbeitskreis Deutscher Klein- und Pelztier-Züchter
ADL	Verband für Informationsverarbeitung
ADLAF	Arbeitsgemeinschaft Deutsche Lateinamerika-Forschung
ADLP	Australian Democratic Labour Party
ADLRI	Arthur D. Little Research Institute
ADM	Arbeitkreis Deutscher Marktforschungsinstitut
ADM	Asociación Dental Mexicana

ADM	Association pour le Développement du Droit Mondial
ADMA	American Drug Manufacturers' Association
ADMA	Association of Dance and Mime Artists
ADMARC	Agricultural Development and Marketing Corporation (Malawi)
ADMI	American Dry Milk Institute
ADMSt	Arbeitsgemeinschaft Deutscher Messerschmiede und Stahlwarenhändler
ADMT	Association of Dental Manufacturers and Traders of the United Kingdom
ADN	Allgemeines Deutsches Nachrichtenbüro
ADNOC	Abu Dhabi National Oil Company
ADO	Association of Dispensing Opticians
ADO	Avdelningen för Driftsorganisation
ADP	Association of Database Producers
ADP	Association for Dental Prosthesis
ADPBA	Association Internationale pour le Développement des Bibliothèques en Afrique
ADPC	Abu Dhabi Petroleum Company
ADPI	Association Internationale d'Études pour la Protection des Investissements
ADPSO	Association of Data Processing Service Organizations
ADR	Arbeitsgemeinschaft Deutscher Rinderzüchter
ADR	Association pour le Développement de la Recherche
ADRA	Animal Disease Research Association
ADRAO	Association pour le Développement du Riz en Afrique Occidentale
ADRDI	Abra Diocesan Rural Development Inc. (Philippines)
ADRI-PECHE	Armement Dakarois pour le Regroupement de l'Industrie de la Pêche
ADRIS	Association for the Development of Religious Information Systems
ADS	Arbeitsgemeinschaft Deutscher Schafzüchter
ADS	Arbeitsgemeinschaft Deutscher Schweinezüchter
ADSA	American Dairy Science Association
ADSADLT	Association de Défense des Sociétés Agricoles Dépossédées par la Loi Tunisienne du 12 Mai, 1964
ADSATIS	Australian Defence Science and Technology Information Service
ADSCAT	Associations of Distributors to the Self-Service and Coin-Operated Laundry and Allied Trades
ADSE	American Dental Society of Europe
ADSI	Agricultural Development Service, Inc. (Philippines)
ADSOC	Administrative Support Operations Centre (U.S.A.)
ADSRI	Animal and Dairy Science Research Institute (South Africa)
ADSS	Association of Direct Speech Suppliers
ADSS	Australian Defence Scientific Service
ADSSA	Association pour le Développement des Sciences Sociales Appliquées
ADTA	American Dental Trade Association
ADTC	Anglo-Dutch Trade Council
ADTCB	Association des Directeurs de Théatres Cinématographiques de Belgique
ADTM	Association pour le Diffusion des Techniques Ménagères
ADTV	Allgemeiner Deutscher Tanzlehrerverband
ADV	Addressenverleger- und Direktwerbe-Unternehmerverband
ADV	Arbeitsgemeinschaft für Datenverarbeiten
ADV	Arbeitsgemeinschaft Deutscher Verkerksflughäfen
ADVB	Associação dos Diretores de Vendas do Brasil
ADW	Verband Deutscher Werbeagenturen und Werbemittlungen
ADWA	Atlantic Deeper Waterways Association (U.S.A.)
AEA	Agence Européenne d'Approvisionnement
AEA	Agricultural Education Association
AEA	Agricultural Engineers' Association
AEA	American Economic Association
AEA	Association d'Entreprises d'Affichage (Belgium)
AEA	Association of European Airlines
AEA	Association Européenne de l'Asphalte
AEA	Atomic Energy Authority
AEAA	Asociación de Escritores y Artistas Americanos (Cuba)
AEAC	Asociación Española de Amigos de los Castillos
AEAFM	Association d'Entraide des Agriculteurs Français du Maroc

EANC	Association des Éclaireurs de l'Armée Nationale Congolaise	AEDF	Asian Economic Development Fund
EB	American Ethnology Bureau	AEDIPE	Asociación Española de Directores Jefes de Personal
EB	Asociación Ecuatoriana de Bibliotecarios	AEDP	Association Européenne pour la Direction de Personnel
EB	Atomic Energy Bureau (Japan)		
EBU	Asociación de Bancarios del Uruguay	AEDT	Association Européenne des Organisations Nationales des Commerçants Détaillants en Textiles
EC	Algemene Emigratie Centrale		
EC	American Engineering Council		
EC	Asociación Española de la Carretera	AEE	Asociacion Electrónica Española
EC	Association Européenne des Enducteurs, Calandreurs et Fabricants de Revêtements de Sols Plastiques et Synthétiques	AEE	Atomic Energy Establishment
		AEEC	Airlines Electronic Engineering Committee (International)
EC	Associação Educação Católica (Brazil)	AEED	Association Européenne des Enseignants Dentaires
EC	Association Européenne de Céramique		
EC	Association Européenne pour la Coopération	AEEF	Association Européenne des Exploitations Frigorifiques
EC	Associazione Europea per la Cooperazione		
EC	Atomic Energy Commission (U.S.A.)	AEEN	Agence Européenne pour l'Energie Nucléaire
ECA	Anglican and Eastern Churches Association	AEEP	Associação das Enfermeiras e dos Enfermeiros Portugueses
ECA	Association Européenne des Centres d'Audiophonologie	AEEP	Association of European Engineering Periodicals
ECB	Associação de Educação Católica do Brasil	AEEPA	Association d'Études Européennes de Presse Agricole
ECB	Association for the Export of Canadian Books	AEEPJ	Association Européenne des Publications pour la Jeunesse
ECC	Asociación Espanola para el Control de la Calida	AEESA	Asociación Española de Economía y Sociología Agrarias
ECC	Association des Éclaireurs Catholiques du Congo	AEET	Atomic Energy Establishment Trombay (India)
ECD	Asian Ecumenical Conference on Development	AEEW	Atomic Energy Establishment Winfrith
ECDF	Association des Exploitants de Cinéma et des Distributeurs de Films du Grand Duché de Luxembourg	AEEZ	Association des Entreprises de l'Est du Zaire
		AEF	Africa Evangelical Fellowship
ECI	African Explosives and Chemical Industries	AEF	American Economic Foundation
ECL	Atomic Energy of Canada Ltd	AEF	Asfaltentreprenørenes Forening
ECM	Association of Exhibitors and Conference Managers	AEF	Asociación Española de Financiadores
		AEF	Centre d'Action Européenne Fédéraliste
ECMA	Association Européenne de Constructeurs de Matériel Aérospatial (formerly AICMA)	AEFM	Association Européenne des Festivals de Musique
eCS	Aero Club der Schweiz	AEFS	Association des Éleveurs Française de Southdown
ECS	Australia Europe Container Services		
ED	Association of Engineering Distributors	AEFTOP	Agrupación Española de Fabricantes de Transmisiones Oleo-Hidraulicas y Pneumaticas
EDA	Asociación Española de Aerosoles		
EDA	Association Européenne pour le Droit de l'Alimentation		
		AEG	Allgemeine Elektrizitäts Gesellschaft
EDE	Association Européenne des Enseignants	AEGC	Association Européenne de Genie Civil
EDEMO	Asociación Española de Estudios de Mercado y de Opinion Comercial	AEGIS	Aid for the Elderly in Government Institutions

AEGM	Anglican Evangelical Group Movement
AEGPL	Association Européenne des Gaz de Pétrole Liquéfiés
AEI	Associated Electrical Industries
AEI	Association des Écoles Internationales
AEI	Associazione Educatrice Italiana
AEI	Associazione Ellettrotecnica ed Elletronica Italiana
AEI	Associazione Enotecnici Italiani
AEI	Auto Enthusiasts International (U.S.A.)
AEIA	Asociación Escuela Ingenieria Agronomica (Ecuador)
AEIAAF	Association Européenne de l'Industrie des Aliments pour Animaux Familiers
AEID	European Association of Development Research Institutions
AEIDC	Arctic Environmental Information and Data Centre
AEIH	Association Européenne des Industries de l'Habillement
AEIL	American Export Isbrandtsen Lines
AEIOU	Agenzia Editoriale Internazionale Organizzazioni
AEIOU	Association Européenne pour une Interaction entre les Organismes Universitaires
AEJI	Association of European Jute Industries
AEKPC	Association Européenne des Kinesitherapeutes Photographes et Cinéastes
AELE	Association Européenne de Libre-Echange
AELFA	Asociación Española de Logopedia, Foniatria y Audiologia
AELI	Asociación Europea de Libre Intercambio
AELLA	Association des Entrepreneurs Luxembourgeois des Lignes d'Autobus
AELTC	All England Lawn Tennis Club
AEM	Asociación Española de Marketing
AEMB	Association des Entrepreneurs de Montage de Belgique
AEMDA	Alliance Européenne des Associations de Myopathes
AEMIE	Association Européenne de Médecine Interne d'Ensemble
AEMP	Association of European Management Publishers
AEMT	Association of Electrical Machinery Trades
AEMTM	Association of European Machine Tool Merchants

AEN	Agence de l'UCDE pour l'Energie Nucléaire
AENA	All-England Netball Association
AENSB	Association de l'École Nationale Supérieure de Bibliothécaires
AEO	Arbeitsgemeinschaft für Elektronenoptik
AEOM	Association of European Open Air Museums
AEOZ	Association des Entreprises de l'Ouest du Zaire
AEP	Agence Européenne de Productivité (*of* OECE)
AEPB	Association pour l'Emploi des Plastiques dans le Bâtiment
AEPC	Asociación Española para el Progreso de las Ciencias
AEPCO	Association of Economic Poisons Control Officials (U.S.A.)
AEPE	Asociación Establecimientos Privados de Enseñanza (Costa Rica)
AEPE	Association pour l'Étude des Problèmes de l'Europe
AEPE	Association Européenne des Professeurs d'Espagnol
AEPIF	Association pour l'Étude et de Progrès de l'Irrigation Fertilisante
AEPT	Asociación Española de Prensa Tecnica
AEQCT	Asociación Española de Quimicos y Coloristas Textiles
AER	Association for Education by Radio (U.S.A.)
AER	Association Européenne pour l'Étude du Probleme des Réfugiés
AER	Association Européenne de Radiologie
AERA	American Educational Research Association
AERA	Association pour l'Étude et la Recherche Astronautique et Cosmique
AERAC	Association Auxiliaire pour l'Enseignement Supérieur et la Recherche Agronomique en Coopération
AERALL	Association d'Études et de Recherches sur les Aéronefs Allégés
AERD	Atomic Energy Research Department (U.S.A.)
AERE	Atomic Energy Research Establishment
AERI	Agricultural Economics Research Institute
AERO	Association of Electronic Reserve Officers (U.S.A.)
AERO-ARCTIC	International Study Society for the Exploration of Arctic Regions by Airship

AERP	Agrupación Española de Relaciones Publicas	AEU	Asia Electronics Union (Japan)
AERP	Association Européenne pour la Recherche sur le Pomme de Terre	AEV	Arbeitsgemeinschaft Erdölgewinnung und Verarbeitung (Germany)
AERTEL	Association Européenne Rubans, Tresses, Tissus Elastiques	AEVII	Federación de Veterinarios Europeos de la Industria y la Investigación
AERZAP	Association pour les Études et Recherches de Zoologie Appliquée et de Phytopathologie (Belgium)	AEWHA	All England Women's Hockey Association
		AEWLA	All England Women's Lacrosse Association
		AF	Angpanneföreningen
AES	Agricultural Economics Society	AFA	Allergy Foundation of America
AES	American Electrochemical Society	AFA	Amateur Fencing Association
AES	American Electroencephalographic Society	AFA	Amateur Football Alliance
AES	American Electroplaters' Society	AFA	American Federation of Arts
AES	American Entomological Society	AFA	American Federation of Astrologers
AES	American Epidemiological Society	AFA	American Forensic Society
AES	American Epilepsy Society	AFA	American Forestry Association
AES	American Ethnological Society	AFA	American Foundrymen's Association
AES	American Eugenics Society	AFA	Asociación Física Argentina
AES	Asian Environmental Society (Philippines)	AFA	Association Française d'Astronomie
AES	Audio Engineering Society (U.S.A.)	AFAA	Association of Faculties of Agriculture in Africa
AESA	Aerolines et Salvador SA		
AESA	Agricultural Engineering Society (Australia)	AFAA	Australian Federation of Advertising Agencies
AESA	Association pour l'Enseignement Social en Afrique (Ethiopia)	AFAB	Association Française d'Agriculture Biologique
AESC	American Engineering Standards Committee	AFABA	Association of African Basketball Federations
AESE	Association of Earth Science Editors (U.S.A.)		
AESED	Association Européenne de Sociétés d'Études pour le Développement	AFACO	Association Française des Amateurs Constructeurs l'Ordinateurs
AESF	Association des Écrivains Scientifiques de France	AFACPG	Association Française des Amateurs de Cactées et de Plantes Grasses
AESGP	Association Européenne des Spécialités Grand Public	AFAD	Association of Fatty Acid Distillers
		AFAL	Association Francophone d'Accueil et de Liaison
AESIMP	Association pour l'Étude de la Stérilité et la Médecine Périnatale	AFAP	Association Française pour l'Accroissement de la Productivité
AESN	Association of Export Subscription Newsagents	AFAQ	Association Française pour l'Expansion des Produits Agricoles de Qualité Garantie
AESOR	Association Européenne de Sous-officiers de Réserve	AFAR	Asociación Feminia de Acción Rural (Argentina)
AESU	Arabische Eisen und Stahl Union	AFAS	American Fine Arts Society
AET	Association of Auto-Electrical Technicians	AFAS	Association Française pour l'Avancement des Sciences
AET	Association Européenne de Thanatologie		
AETFAT	Association pour l'Étude Taxonomique de la Flore d'Afrique Tropicale (Belgium)	AFASE	Association for Applied Solar Energy (U.S.A.)
AEU	Amalgamated Engineering Union (*now* AUEW)	AFASIC	Association for all Speech Impaired Children
AEU	American Ethical Union	AFASTOF	Afro-Asian Federation for Tobacco Producers and Manufacturers

AFB	Arbeitsgemeinschaft Fachärztlicher Berufsverbände
AFBA	Asociación Farmacéutica y Bioquímica Argentina
AFBF	American Farm Bureau Federation
AFBS	American and Foreign Bible Society
AFC	African Football Confederation
AFC	African Forestry Commission
AFC	Asian Football Confederation
AFC	Association Française de Chimiurgie
AFC	Association Française de Cristallographie
AFC	Association France-Containers
AFC	Latin-American Forestry Commission (*of* FAO)
AFCA	Association pour la Formation des Cadres de l'Industrie et de l'Administration en Langue Française
AFCA	Association Française pour la Communauté Atlantique
AFCA	Association Professionelle des Fabricants de Compléments pour l'Alimentation Animale
AFCAC	African Civil Aviation Commission
AFCALTI	Association Française de Calcul et de Traitement de l'Information
AFCASOL	Association des Fabricants de Café Soluble des Pays de la CEE
AFCAT	Association Française de Calorimétrie et d'Analyse Thermique
AFCC	Association Française du Commerce des Cacaos
AFCET	Association Française de Cybernétique Économique et Technique
AFCIMAT	Asociación de Fabricantes de Conjuntos Importantes para la Mecanización del Agro y el Transporte (Argentina)
AFCIQ	Association Française pour le Contrôle Industriel de Qualité
AFCL	African Container Line
AFCMA	Aluminium Foil Container Manufacturers Association
AFCMA	Australian Fibreboard Containers Manufacturers Association
AFCOA	Australian Council for Overseas Aid
AFCOD	Association Française des Conseilleurs de Direction
AFCODI	Africaine Commerciale de Diffusion
AFCOFEL	Association Française Comités Économiques Agricoles de Fruits et Légumes
AFCOM	Africaine de Constructions Mécaniques (Ivory Coast)
AFCOS	Association Française des Conseils en Organisation Scientifique
AFCOT	Association Française Cotonnière
AFCR	American Federation for Clinical Research
AFCU	American and Foreign Christian Union
AFD	African Development Fund
AFDAC	Association Française de Documentation Automatique en Chimie
AfDB	African Development Bank
AFDBS	Association Française des Documentaires et des Bibliothécaires Specialisés
AFDC	Agriculture and Fishery Development Corporation (Korea)
AFDI	Association Française des Déménageurs Internationaux
AFDIN	Association Française de Documentation et d'Information
AFDOUS	Association of Food and Drug Officials of the United States
AFE	Asociación de Forestales del Ecuador
AFEA	American Farm Economic Association
AFEC	Association Française pour le Contrôle de la Qualité des Hormones Désherbantes
AFEC	Association Francophone d'Education Comparée
AFECI	Association des Fabricants Européens de Chauffebains et Chauff-eau Instantanés au Gaz
AFECOGAZ	Association de Fabricants Européens d'Appareils de Contrôle pour le Gaz et l'Huile
AFEDES	Association Française pour l'Étude et le Développement des Applications de l'Énergie Solaire
AFEE	Association Française pour l'Étude des Eaux
AFEI	Association Française pour l'Étiquetage d'Information
AFEID	Association Française pour l'Étude des Irrigations et du Drainage
AFEP	Association Française de l'École Paysanne (*now* CAEVR)
AFEQ	Association Française pour l'Étude du Quaternaire
AFERA	Association des Fabricants Européens des Rubans Auto-adhésifs

AFERO | Asia and the Far East Regional Office (FAO)
AFES | Association Française pour l'Étude du Sol
AFESA | Agrupación de Almacenistas de Ferretaria de España
AFESD | Arab Fund for Economic and Social Development
AFF | Affischeringsföretagens Forening
AFF | Association Française du Froid
AFF | Australian Farmers' Federation
AFFCO | Alaska Forest Fire Council
AFFCOD | Association Française des Firmes de Conseillers de Direction
AFFHC | Australian Freedom from Hunger Campaign
AFFI | American Frozen Food Institute
AFFW | Arab Federation of Food Workers
AFG | Association des Fabricants de Glucose de la CEE
AFG | Association Française de Gemmologie
AFGC | American Forage and Grassland Council
AFGE | American Federation of Government Employees
AFGM | American Federation of Grain Millers
AFGR | Association Française de Génie Rural
AFH | American Foundation for Homeopathy
AFI | American Film Industry
AFI | Associazione Farmacisti dell'Industria
AFI | Associazione dei Fonografici Italiani
AFI | Les Auxiliaires Féminines Internationales
AFIA | American Foreign Insurance Association
AFIA | Apparel and Fashion Industry's Association of Great Britain
AFIA | Association Française Interprofessionelle des Agrumes
AFICAU | Association de Fomento del Intercambio Comercial Anglo-Uruguayo
AFICE | Association Française des Ingenieurs et Chefs d'Entretien
AFICEP | Association Française des Ingenieurs du Caoutchouc et des Plastiques
AFICS | Association of Former International Civil Servants
AFICTIC | Association Française des Ingénieurs, Chimistes et Techniciens des Industries du Cuir
AFIEM | Association Française pour l'Information en Économie Ménagère

AFIF | Association Suisse des Fournisseurs de l'Industrie pour la Ferraille
AFII | American Federation of International Institutes
AFIMAC | Association des Fabricants et Importateurs de Matériel à Air Comprimé (Belgium)
AFIMIN | Association Française des Fabricants et Importateurs de Matériels et de Produits pour l'Industrie du Nettoyage
AFINE | Association Française pour l'Industrie Nucléaire d'Équipement
AFIP | Association Française des Indépendants du Pétrole
AFIP | Associazione Fotografi Italiani Professionisti
AFIPS | American Federation of Information Processing Societies
AFIREC | Association Financière Internationale de l'Océan Indien
AFIRO | Association Française d'Informatique et de Recherche Opérationnelle
AFIS | Amministrazione Fiduciaria Italiana della Somalia
AFISA | Aero Fletes Internationales SA (Panama)
AFISAC | Associazione Fabbricanti Italiani e Staniere di Macchinari e Apparecchiature ad Aria Compressa
AFITAE | Association Française des Ingénieurs et Techniciens de l'Aéronautique et de l'Espace
AFJA | Association Française des Journalistes Agricoles
AFJET | Association Française de Journalistes et Écrivains du Tourisme
AfK | Arbeitsgemeinschaft für Kommunikationsforschung
AFL | American Federation of Labor
AFL | Association Française Laitière
AFLA | American Foreign Law Association
AFLA | Asian Federation of the Library Association
AFL-CIO | American Federation of Labor and Congress of Industrial Organizations
AFM | Asociación Española de Fabricantes de Maquinas-Herramienta
AFM | Aussenhandelsverband für Mineralöl
AFMA | American Feed Manufacturers Association
AFMA | American Footwear Manufacturers Association
AFMA | Artificial Flower Manufacturers Association of Great Britain

AFME	American Friends of the Middle East	**AFPU**	Association Française pour la Paix Universelle
AFMH	American Foundation for Mental Hygiene		
AFMM	Association of Fish Meal Manufacturers	**AFPW**	Association Française du Poney Welsh
AFMO	Association Française de Constructeurs de Machines-Outils	**AFQ**	Association Forestière Québecoise (Canada)
		AFR	Auktoriserade Fastighetsmäklares Riksförbund
AFMR	American Foundation for Management Research	**AFRA**	American Farm Research Association
AFMR	Association pour la Formation en Milieu Rural	**AFRAA**	African Airlines Association
		AFRACA	African Regional Agricultural Credit Association
AFMS	American Federation of Mineralogical Societies	**AFRAN**	Association Française pour la Recherche de l'Alimentation Normale
AFN	Aerosolforbundet Norge		
AFN	American Forces Network	**AFRASEC**	Afro-Asian Organisation for Economic Co-operation (Egypt)
AFNIL	Agence Francophone pour la Numération Internationale du Livre	**AFRAT**	Association pour la Formation des Ruraux aux Activités du Tourisme
AFNOR	Association Française de Normalisation		
AFOB	American Foundation for Overseas Blind	**AFREC**	Association Française pour les Recherches et les Études Camerounaises
AFOCA	Association Nationale pour la Formation Professionnelle suivant les Techniques de l'Industrie du Caoutchouc	**AFREM**	Association Française de Recherches et d'Essais sur les Matériaux et les Constructions
AFOCEL	Association Forêts – Cellulose	**AFREP**	Association Française des Relations Publiques
AFOG	Asian Federation of Obstetrics and Gynaecology		
AFOMJ	Association of Fats and Oil Manufacturers of Japan	**AFRESCO**	Association Française de Recherches et Études Statistiques Commerciales
AFOSR	Air Force Office of Scientific Research (U.S.A.)	**AFRIC**	Société Africaine Française de Representations Industrielles et Commerciales
AFP	Agence France Presse	**AFRIC**	Agence Française de Representation et d'Industries au Cameroun
AFP	Asociación Forestal del Perú		
AFPA	Association de Formation et Perfectionnement Agricole (France)	**AFRICA-PLAST**	Industrie Africaine des Plastiques
AFPA	Association pour la Formation Professionnelle des Adultes	**AFRIMEX-CI**	Africaine Import-Export Côte d'Ivoire
AFPA	Australian Fire Protection Association	**AFROFED-OP**	African Regional Organization of the Public Services and Teachers
AFPE	American Foundation for Pharmaceutical Education	**AFROLIT**	Society for the Promotion of Adult Literacy in Africa
AFPE	American Foundation for Political Education	**AFRP**	American Foundation of Religion and Psychiatry
AFPEP	Association Française des Producteurs Exportateurs de Pommes		
AFPF	Association Française pour la Production Fourragère	**AFS**	American Fisheries Society
		AFS	Atlantic Ferry Service
AFPP	Association Française de Producteurs de Plantes à Protéines Legumineuses à Grosses Graines	**AFSA**	Association des Fabricants Suisses d'Accumulateurs
AFPPT	Association pour la Formation et le Perfectionnement des Planteurs de Tabac	**AFSBO**	American Federation of Small Business Organizations
AfPU	African Postal Union	**AFSBO**	Association des Fabricants Suisses de Bijouterie et d'Orfèvrerie

AFSC	American Friends Service Committee	AGA	American Goiter Association
AFSCA	Amalgamated Flying Saucer Clubs of America	AGA	Arbeitgeberverband Gross- und Aussenhandel
AFSE	Association Française de Science Économique	AGA	Architectural Granite Association
		AGA	Asociación General de Agricultores (Guatemala)
AFSEuropa	European Federation for Intercultural Learning	AGA	Association des Entreprises de Gros en Alimentation Générale (Belgium)
AFSP	Association Française des Sciences Politiques		
AFST	Association of Food Scientists and Technologists (India)	AGA	Australian Gas Association
		AGAAC	Acuerdo General sobre Aranceles Aduaneros y Comercio (GATT)
AFT	American Federation of Teachers		
AFTA	Arab Fund for Technical Assistance to Arab and African Countries (Egypt)	AGAC	American Guild of Authors and Composers
		AGADU	Asociación General de Autores del Uruguay
AFTA	Atlantic Free Trade Area	AGAF	Associazione Nazionale fra i Grossisti di Articoli Fotografici
AFTAA	Association Française des Techniciens de l'Alimentation Animale		
		AGANAPA	Asociación de Ganaderos y Agricultores de la Panamericana (Venezuela)
AFTE	American Federation of Technical Engineers		
AFTIM	Association Française des Techniciens et Ingénieurs de Sécurité et des Médecins du Travail	AGARD	Advisory Group for Aerospace Research and Development (NATO)
		AGASAL	Association des Grossistes en Appareils Sanitaires du Luxembourg
AFTM	American Foundation for Tropical Medicine		
AFTN	Aeronautical Fixed Telecommunication Network (U.K.)	AGB	Arbeitskreis Ganzheitliches Bauen
		AGC	African Groundnut Council
AFTP	Association Française des Techniciens du Pétrole	AGC	American Grassland Council
		AGC	Ashanti Goldfields Corporation (Ghana)
AFTPV	Association Française des Techniciens des Peintures, Vernis, Encres d'Imprimerie, Colles et Adhésifs	AGCC	American Guernsey Cattle Club
		AGCD	Administration Générale Belge de la Coopération au Développement
AFTRI	Association Française des Transporteurs Routiers Internationaux		
		AGCD	Association of Green Crop Driers
AFTS	Aeronautical Fixed Telecommunications Service	AGCI	Associazione Generale delle Cooperative Italiane
		AGCM	Association of Glass Container Manufacturers
AFTW	Arab Federation of Transport Workers		
AFUCA	Asian Federation of Unesco Clubs and Associations	AGDT	Advisory Group on Data Transmission (of NEDO)
		AGDW	Arbeitsgemeinschaft Deutscher Waldbesitzerverbände
AFULE	Australian Federated Union of Locomotive Enginemen		
		AGE	Asian Information Centre for Geotechnical Engineering (Thailand)
AFVP	Association Française des Volontaires du Progrès		
AfW	Arbeitskreis für Wehrforschung	AGEAM	Association pour la Gérance des Écoles d'Apprentissage Maritime
AFZ	Association Française de Zootechnie		
AG	Action Group (Nigeria)	AGEC	Arbeitsgemeinschaft Europäischer Chorverbände
AG	Actuarieël Genootschap		
AGA	Agricola Ganadera Antelana	AGECO	Agences Générales d'Exchanges Commerciaux
AGA	American Gas Association		
AGA	American Gastroenterological Association	AGECOOP	Agency for Cultural and Technical Cooperation (France)
AGA	American Genetic Association		

AGED	Association des Grandes Entreprises de Distribution de Belgique	**AGNIB**	Union of the Internal Timber Trade Associations of the EEC
AGEHR	American Guild of English Handbell Ringers	**AGNVH**	Association of Growers of the New Varieties of Hops
AGEI	Associazione Gerontologica Italiana		
AGELAF	Association des Groupes Nationaux d'Éducation Nouvelle de Langue Française	**AGO**	Arbeitsgemeinschaft der Ordenshochschulen
		AGÖ	Arbeitsgemeinschaft Österreicherischer Organisationsberater
AGEMI	Association des Groupements d'Engraisseurs de Moutons d'Importation		
		AGOD	International Association on the Genesis of Ore Deposits
AGEMOS	Associazione Nazionale Gestori di Magazzini di Vendita Generi Monopoli di Stato		
		AGOF	Arbeitsgemeinschaft Österreichischer Friedensvereine
AGET	Advisory Group on Electron Tubes (U.S.A.)		
AGF	Akademische Gesellschaft für Finanzwirtschaft	**AGOR**	Advisory Group on Ocean Research (*of* WMO)
AGF	Arbeitsgemeinschaft Getreideforschung	**AGPB**	Association Générale des Producteurs de Blé et autres Céréales (France)
AGF	Asian Games Federation		
AGFF	Arbeitsgemeinschaft zur Förderung des Futterbaues (Switzerland)	**AGP-CNO**	Assemblée Générale Permanente des Comités Nationaux Olympiques
AGFI	Assemblée Générale des Fédérations Internationales	**AGPD**	Allgemeine Gesellschaft für Philosophie in Deutschland
AGGS	Allgemeine Geschichtforschende Gesellschaft der Schweiz	**AGPH**	Association Générale des Producteurs de Houblon
AGHTM	Association Générale des Hygiénistes et Techniciens Municipaux	**AGPL**	Association Générale des Producteurs de Lin
AGI	Alliance Graphique Internationale	**AGPM**	Association Générale des Producteurs de Maïs
AGI	American Geological Institute		
AGI	Arbeitsgemeinschaft Industriebau	**AGPO**	Association Générale des Producteurs d'Oléagineux
AGI	Associazione Genetica Italiana		
AGI	Associazione Geofisica Italiana	**AGPV**	Association Générale des Producteurs de Viande
AGID	Association of Geoscientists for International Development	**Agra-Presse**	Agency Générale de Renseignements Agricoles
AGIF	Automobilgummi-Importørernes Forening	**AGREE**	Advisory Group for Reliability of Electronic Equipment (U.S.A.)
AGIFORS	Airline Group International Federation of Operational Research Societies	**AGRF**	American Geriatric Research Foundation
AGIM	Association Générale de l'Industrie du Médicament (Belgium)	**AGRI-PECHE-IVOIRE**	Société Ivoiro Sénégalaise d'Agriculture et de Pêche
AGIP	Agenzia Generale Italiana Petroli		
AGIS	Associazione Generale Italiana dello Spettacolo	**AGRIS**	International Formation System for the Agricultural Sciences and Technology (Italy)
AGK	Arbeitsgemeinschaft Korrosion	**AGROLAC**	Association des Groupements de Producteurs de Lait de Chèvre
AGLINET	Agricultural Libraries and Documentation Centres Network		
AGMA	American Gear Manufacturers' Association	**AGROMAS**	International Association for Vine-, Fruit- and Vegetable-growing Mechanization
AGMA	American Guild of Musical Artists	**AGROSEM**	Trustul pentru Asigurarea Productiei si Valorificarea Semintelor Agricole (Roumania)
AGMB	Association Générale des Meuniers Belges		
AGMÖ	Arbeitsgemeinschaft der Musikerzieher Österreichs	**AGRR**	Association Générale de Retraite par Reparition
AGMS	Arbeitsgemeinschaft Massenspektroskopie		

GRUSA Agricultores Unidos S.A.

GS American Geographical Society

GS American Geriatrics Society

GS American Goat Society

GS American Gynecological Society

GS Appalachian Geological Society (U.S.A.)

GSG Akademische Gesellschaft Schweizerischer Germanisten

GSRO Association of Government Supervisors and Radio Officers

GT Arbeitsgeververband Schweizerischer Transportunternehmungen

GT Association of Geology Teachers (U.S.A.)

GTA Agence Générale de Transit en Afrique (Congo)

GU American Geophysical Union

GU Arbeitsgemeinschaft für Umweltfragen

GV Aachener Geschichtsverein

GV Arbeitsgemeinschaft der Verbraucher

GVA American Guild of Variety Artists

GVS Autogewerbeverband der Schweiz

GW Anthropologische Gesellschaft in Wien (Austria)

GW Arbeitsgemeinschaft der Werbefachverbände

AHA American Heart Association

AHA American Hereford Association

AHA American Historical Association

AHA American Hospital Association

AHA American Humane Association

AHA American Hypnotherapy Association

AHBA Association of Hotel Booking Agents

AHC American Horticultural Council

AHD Arbeitsgemeinschaft für Hochschuldidaktik

AHDRI Animal Husbandry and Dairy Research Institute (South Africa)

AHE Association for Higher Education (U.S.A.)

AHEA American Home Economics Association

AHEM Association of Hydraulic Equipment Manufacturers

AHF Allmänna Handelslagsförbundet

AHFITB Agricultural, Horticultural and Forestry Training Board (now ATB)

AHIOI Association Historique Internationale de l'Océan Indien

AHIRS Australian Health Information and Research Service

AHITI Animal Health and Industry Training Institute (Kenya)

AHM Ateneo de Historia de la Medicina (Argentina)

AHMCA Asociación de Hombres de Mercadeo de Centro América (Guatemala)

AHPMB Alberta Hog Producers Marketing Board

AHS Agricultural History Society (U.S.A.)

AHS American Horticultural Society

AHS American Hypnodontic Society

AHSA American Hampshire Sheep Association

AHSA American Horse Shows Association

AHSA Art, Historical and Scientific Association (Canada)

AHSD Authority Health and Safety Division

AHSPM Association of Health Service Personnel Managers

AHSR Association des Horticulteurs de la Suisse Romande

AHT Animal Health Trust

AHWA Association of Hospital and Welfare Administrators

AI Asphalt Institute (U.S.A.)

AIA Abrasive Industries Association

AIA Aerospace Industries Association of America

AIA American Institute of Architects

AIA American International Association for Economic and Social Development

AIA Anglo-Indian Association

AIA Anglo-Israel Association

AIA Archeological Institute of America

AIA Artists International Association

AIA Asociación de Ingenieros Aeronáuticos

AIA Associación de Ingenieros Agronomos (Uruguay)

AIA Association for Industrial Archaeology

AIA Association of International Accountants

AIA Association Internationale des Allergistes

AIA Associazione Italiana Aerosol

AIA Associazione Italiana Allevatori

AIA Associazione Italiana delle Industrie Aerospaziali

AIA Aviation Industry Association (N.Z.)

AIAA Aircraft Industries Association of America

AIAA American Institute of Aeronautics and Astronautics

AIAA	Association Interprofessionnelle de l'Aviation Agricole	**AIBA**	Association Internationale de Boxe Amateur
AIAB	Association Internationale des Anthropobiologistes	**AIBA**	Association Interprofessionnelle des Producteurs de Betteraves et d'Alcool de Betteraves
AIAC	Air Industries Association of Canada	**AIBA**	Association of International Border Agencies (U.S.A.)
AIAC	Association des Ingénieurs en Anticorrosion		
AIAC	Association Internationale d'Archeologie Classique	**AIBA**	Associazione Italiana Brokers di Assicurazioni
AIAC	Associazione Italiana Agenti di Cambio	**AIBANIC**	Asociación de Instituciones Bancarias de Nicaragua
AIACE	Association Internationale des Anciens des Communautés Européennes	**AIBC**	Architectural Institute of British Columbia
AIAESD	American International Association for Economics and Social Development	**AIBCM**	Association of Industrialized Building Component Manufacturers
AIAF	Association de l'Industrie et de l'Agriculture Française	**AIBD**	Association of International Bond Dealers
AIAF	Associazione Italiana degli Analisti Finanziari	**AIBDA**	Asociación Interamericana de Bibliotecarios y Documentalistas Agrícolas
AIAFD	Association des Institutions Africaines de Financement du Développement	**AIBGA**	All Island Banana Growers Association (Jamaica)
AIAG	Aluminium Industrie Aktien Gesellschaft (Switzerland)	**AIBI**	International Association of the Bread Industry
AIAG	Association Internationale des Assureurs contre la Grêle	**AIBM**	Association Internationale des Bibliothèques Musicales
AIAMA	Association Internationale pour l'Art et les Moyens Audio-Visuels	**AIBS**	American Institute of Biological Sciences
AIAP	Association Internationale des Arts Plastiques	**AIC**	Académie Internationale de la Céramique
		AIC	Agricultural Improvement Council
AIAREF	Association Internationale des Anesthésistes-Réanimateurs	**AIC**	Agricultural Institute of Canada
		AIC	American Institute of Chemists
AIAS	Australian Institute of Aboriginal Studies	**AIC**	American Institute of Cooperation
AIAS	Australian Institute of Agricultural Science	**AIC**	Arab Investment Company (Saudi Arabia)
AIASR	Association des Ingenieurs Agronomes de la Suisse Romande	**AIC**	Asbestos Information Committee
		AIC	Association Internationale de la Couleur
AIAT	Association Internationale pour le Développement Économique et l'Aide Technique	**AIC**	Association Internationale Cybernétique
		AIC	Associazione Italiana di Cartografia
AIB	Academy of International Business (U.S.A.)	**AICA**	American International Charolais Association
AIB	Aerosol Industrien Brancheforening	**AICA**	Association Internationale pour Calcul Analogique
AIB	American Institute of Baking	**AICA**	Association Internationale des Critiques d'Art
AIB	American Institute of Banking	**AICA**	Associazione degli Industriali delle Conserve Animali
AIB	Associate of the Institute of Bankers		
AIB	Association des Industries de Belgique	**AICA**	Associazione Italiana per il Calcolo Automatico
AIB	Association of Insurance Brokers	**AICAR**	Association Internationale de Co-opération et d'Animation Régionales
AIB	Associazione Italiana Biblioteca		
AIBA	American Industrial Bankers Association	**AICB**	Association Internationale de Lutte contre le Bruit
AIBA	Asociación Interamericana de Bibliotecarios Agrícolas	**AICC**	All India Congress Committee

AICC	Association Internationale de Chimie Céréalière
AICC	Groupe des Chambres Syndicales et Unions Professionnelles d'Agents Independants, Courtiers et Concessionnaires du Commerce et de l'Industrie (Belgium)
AICCF	Association Internationale du Congrès de Chemins de Fer (Belgium)
AICD	Association Internationale des Compagnies de Dragage
AICD	International Association of Dredging Companies
AICDT	International Advisory Committee on Documentation and Terminology in Pure and Applied Science
AICE	American Institute of Chemical Engineers
AICE	American Institute of Consulting Engineers
AICE	American Institute of Crop Ecology
AICF	Ambassador International Cultural Foundation (U.S.A.)
AICF	American-Israel Cultural Foundation
AICFO	Asociación Internacional para las Ciencias Físicas del Océano
AICH	Asociación Internacional de Hidrología Científica
AICHE	American Institute of Chemical Engineers
AICI	Associazione Ingegneri Consultenti Italiani
AICK	Association Internationale pour la Conscience de Krishna
AICL	Association Internationale des Critiques Littéraires
AICMA	Association Internationale des Constructeurs de Matériel Aérospatial (*now* AECMA)
AICMES	Association Interprofessionelle des Constructeurs de Matériel d'Équipement Scientifiques
AICMR	Association Internationale des Constructeurs de Matériel Roulant
AICPA	American Institute of Certified Public Accountants
AICPA	Associazione Italiana Concessionari Produzione Automobilistica
AICQ	Associazione Italiana per il Controllo della Qualita
AICRIP	All India Coordinated Rice Improvement Project
AICS	Association Internationale du Cinéma Scientifique
AICT	Association Internationale des Critiques de Théâtre
AICTC	Associazione Italiana di Chimica Tessile e Coloristica
AICU	All India Cooperative Union
AICVF	Association des Ingénieurs de Chauffage et de Ventilation de France
AICVP	Association Internationale des Charités de St-Vincent
AID	Agency for International Development (*formerly* ICA)
AID	Agricultural Information Division (Philippines)
AID	Algemene Inspectiedienst
AID	Alliance Internationale de la Diffusion par Fil
AID	American Institute of Decorators
AID	Association Internationale pour le Développement
AID	Association Internationale des Documentalistes et Techniciens de l'Information
AID	Land- und Hauswirtschaftlicher Auswertungs- und Informationsdienst
AIDA	Asociación Internacional de Derecha de Aguas
AIDA	Association Internationale de la Distribution des Produits Alimentaires
AIDA	Association Internationale de Droit Africain
AIDA	Association Internationale du Droit de l'Assurance
AIDA	Associazione Industrie Dolciarie Italiane
AIDA	Associazione Italiana di Aerotecnica
AIDAA	Associazione Italiana di Aeronautica e Astronautica
AIDBA	Association Internationale pour le Développement de la Documentation, des Bibliothéques et des Archives en Afrique
AIDC	American Industrial Development Council
AIDC	Asian Industrial Development Council
AIDD	American Institute for Design and Drafting
AIDE	Asociación Interamericana de Educación
AIDE	Association Internationale de Distribution d'Eau
AIDE	Association Internationale du Droit des Eaux
AIDEC	Association for European Industrial Development and Economic Co-operation (Netherlands)

AIDEC	Association Internationale d'Expertise Chimique
AIDELA	Association Internationale d'Éditeurs pour la Linguistique Appliquée
AIDEM	Associazione Italiana degli Editori di Musica
AIDEP	Association Interentreprises pour le Développement de l'Enseignement Programmé
AIDI	Associazione Industrie Dolciarie Italiane
AIDI	Associazione Italiana per la Documentazione e Informazione
AIDI	Associazione Italiana di Illuminazione
AIDIC	Associazione Italiana di Ingegneria Chimico
AIDIS	Association Inter-Americaine de Genie Sanitaire
AIDIS	Associazione Italiana di Ingeneria Sismica
AIDL	Asociación Interamericana pro Democracia y Libertad
AIDL	Auckland Industrial Development Laboratory (N.Z.)
AIDLCM	Association Internationale pour la Defense des Langues et Cultures Menacées
AIDN	Associazione Internazionale Diritt Nucleare
AIDP	Association Internationale de Droit Pénal
AIDR	Association de Développement Rural d'Outre-mer
AIDR	Association Internationale de Développement Rural
AIDS	Australian Institute of Aboriginal Studies
AIDSEGA	Amitié Internationale des Scouts et Guides Adultes
AIDT	Association Interparlementaire du Tourisme
AIDUM	Association Internationale pour le Développement des Universités Internationales et Mondiales
AIE	Agence Internationale de l'Énergie
AIE	Associazione Italiana Editori
AIEA	L'Agence Internationale de l'Énergie Atomique
AIEA	Association Internationale des Économistes Agronomiques
AIEA	Association Internationale des Étudiants en Agriculture
AIECE	Association d'Instituts Européens de Conjoncture Économique
AIED	Association Internationale d'Entreprises de Dragage
AIED	Association Internationale des Étudiants Dentaires
AIEDP	Asian Institute for Economic Development and Planning (Thailand)
AIEE	American Institute of Electrical Engineers (*now* IEEE)
AIEE	Association des Instituts d'Études Européennes
AIEF	Association Internationale des Études Françaises
AIEGL	Association Internationale d'Epigraphie Grecque et Latine (France)
AIEI	Association of Indian Engineering Industry
AIEID	Asociación Internacional de Estudio Integral del Deporte (Argentina)
AIEJI	Association Internationale des Éducateurs de Jeunes Inadaptés
AIEL	Asociación Internacional de Estructuras Laminares
AIEL	Association Internationale d'Epigraphie Latine
AIEM	Association Internationale d'Études sur la Mécanographie et l'Informatique
AIEMA	Association Internationale pour l'Étude de la Mosaïque Antique
AIENSAN	Association des Ingénieurs de l'École Nationale Supérieure Agronomique de Nancy (France)
AIEP	Association des Importateurs d'Essence et Pétroles
AIEP	Association Internationale d'Études Patristiques
AIEP	Association Internationale des Usagers d'Embranchements Particuliers
AIEPD	African Institute for Economic Planning and Development
AIEPE	Association Internationale des Écoles Privées Européennes
AIEPM	Association Internationale des Educateurs pour la Paix Mondiale
AIER	American Institute of Economic Research
AIERI	Association Internationale d'Études et Recherches sur l'Information
AIES	Association Internationale d'Essais de Semences
AIESEC	Association Internationale des Étudiants en Sciences Économiques et Commerciales
AIESEE	Association Internationale d'Études du Sud-est Européen

AIESEP	Association Internationale des Écoles ou Instituts Supérieurs d'Éducation Physique et Sportive
AIESS	Association Internationale des Écoles du Service Social
AIEST	Association International d'Experts Scientifiques du Tourisme
AIF	Alliance Internationale des Femmes
AIF	Arbeitsgemeinschaft Industrieller Forschungsvereinigungen
AIF	Asociación Internacional de Fomento
AIF	Association des Industriels de France contre les Accidents du Travail
AIF	Association Internationale Futuribles
AIF	Associazione Italiana del Franchising
AIFA	Asociación Internacional de Fabricantes de Aceites
AIFE	Association Internationale des Femmes Ecrivains
AIFEA	All Indian Federation of Educational Association (India)
AIFL	Anglo-Israel Friendship League
AIFLD	American Institute for Free Labor Development
AIFM	Association Internationale des Femmes Médecins
AIFOB	Association Internationale des Sylviculteurs et des Utilisateurs de Produits de la Forêt et du Bois
AIFRB	American Institute of Fishery Research Biologists
AIFRO	Association Internationale Francophone de Recherche Odontologique
AIFS	African Improved Farming Scheme
AIFS	American Institute for Foreign Study
AIFS	Association Internationale des Fabricants de Superphosphate
AIFSPR	Associazione Italiana di Fisica Sanitaria e di Protezione contro le Radiazioni
AIFST	Australian Institute of Food Science and Technology
AIFT	American Institute for Foreign Trade
AIG	Association pour l'Information de Gestion
AIG	Association Internationale de Géodésie
AIGA	American Institute of Graphic Arts
AIGA	Association Internationale de Géomagnétisme et d'Aéronomie
AIGE	Asociación Interamericana de Gastroenterologia
AIGI	Association Internationale de Géologie de l'Ingénieur
AIGM	Association Internationale de Grands Magasins
AIGMF	All India Glass Manufacturers Federation
AIGREF	Association des Ingénieurs du Génie Rural, des Eaux et des Forêts
AIGSL	Alleanza Internazionale dei Giornalisti e Scrittori Latini
AIGT	Association for the Improvement of Geometrical Teaching
AIGYPFB	Asociación de Ingenieros y Geólogos de Yacimientos Petrolíferos Fiscales Bolivianos
AIH	Academie Internationale d'Heraldique
AIH	American Institute of Homeopathy
AIH	Asociación Internacional de Hispanists
AIH	Association of Independent Hospitals
AIH	Association des Ingénieurs Horticoles
AIH	Association Internationale de l'Hôtellerie
AIH	Association Internationale des Hydrogéologues
AIHA	American Industrial Hygiene Association
AIHDI	Association Internationale d'Histoire du Droit et des Institutions
AIHE	International Economic History Association (Switzerland)
AIHP	American Institute of the History of Pharmacy
AIHS	Académie Internationale d'Histoire des Sciences (France)
AIHS	American Irish Historical Society
AIHS	Association Internationale d'Hydrologie Scientifique
AII	Associazione Italiana degli Inventori
AIIA	Association of International Insurance Agents
AIIA	Atlantic Institute for International Affairs (France)
AIIA	Australian Institute of International Affairs
AIIAA	Association des Ingénieurs des Industries Agricoles et Alimentaires
AIIC	Association Internationale des Interprètes de Conférence
AIICA	Asociación Internacional para las Investigaciones sobre Contaminación de las Aguas

AIIE	American Institute of Industrial Engineers	**AILA**	Agrupación Ibero- Latinoamericana para el Estudio Cientifico de la Deficiencia Mental
AIIG	Associazione Italiana degli Insegnanti di Geografia	**AILA**	Asociación de Industriales Latino-Americanos
AIIH	Asociación Internacional de Investigaciones Hidráulicas	**AILA**	Association Internationale de Linguistique Appliquée
AIIHPH	All-India Institute of Hygiene and Public Health	**AILC**	Association Internationale de Littérature Comparée
AIIMB	Associazione Italiana di Ingegneria Medica e Biologica	**AILE**	Association Internationale des Loteries d'Etat
AIIMS	All-Indian Institute of Medical Sciences	**AIM**	American Indian Movement
AIIPA	Associazione Italiana Industriali Prodotti Alimentari	**AIM**	American Institute of Management
AIIPC	American International Institute for the Protection of Childhood	**AIM**	American Institute for Microminiaturization
AIIRM	Association Internationale des Intérêts Radio-Maritimes	**AIM**	Arbeitsgemeinschaft Information Meeresforschung und Meerestechnik
AIIS	American Institute for Imported Steel	**AIM**	Association pour les Applications de l'Informatique à la Médecine
AIIS	American Institute of Indian Studies	**AIM**	Association of Industrial Machinery Merchants
AIIS	Asian Institute of International Studies (Philippines)	**AIM**	Association Internationale de Metéorologie
AIISA	Association des Ingénieurs de l'Institut Supérieur d'Agriculture	**AIM**	Association Internationale de la Mutualité
AIISP	Associazione Italiana per l'Igiene e la Sanita Pubblica	**AIM**	Associazione Italiana di Metallurgia
		AIM	Atlantic International Marketing Committee
AIISUP	Association Internationale d'Information Scolaire, Universitaire et Professionnelle	**AIM**	Australian Institute of Management
AIIT	Association Internationale de l'Inspection du Travail	**AIMA**	All India Management Association
		AIMA	Azienda di Stato per gli Inteventi nel Mercato Agricolo
AIJA	Association Internationale des Jeunes Avocats	**AIMAS**	Académie Internationale de Médecine Aéronautique et Spatiale
AIJD	Association Internationale des Juristes Démocrates	**AIMAS**	Associazione Italiana di Medicina Aeronautica e Spaziale
AIJE	Association des Industries du Jute Européennes	**AIMAV**	Association Internationale pour la Recherche et la Diffusion des Méthodes Audio-visuelles et Structuro-globales
AIJE	Association Internationale des Juges des Enfants		
AIJE	Association Internationale des Magistrats de la Jeunesse	**AIMBE**	Association Internationale de Médecine et de Biologie de l'Environnement
AIJLF	Association Internationale des Journalistes de Langue Française	**AIMC**	American Institute of Medical Climatology
		AIMC	Associazione Italiana Maestri Cattolici
AIJP	Association Internationale des Journalistes Philateliques	**AIME**	American Institute of Mining and Metallurgical Engineers
AIJPF	Association Internationale des Journalistes de la Presse Féminine et Familiale	**AIME**	Asociación de Investigación para la Mejora de la Alfalfa
AIL	Association of International Libraries	**AIMEA**	Association Internationale des Métiers et Enseignements d'Art
AIL	Association Internationale de Limnologie Théorique et Appliquée	**AIMETA**	Associazione Italiana di Meccanica Teorica e Applicata
AILA	Agenzia Internazionale Letteraria Artistica	**AIMFA**	Asociación Internacional de Meteorología y Física Atmosférica

AIMFR	Association Internationale des Maisons Familiales Rurales
AIMH	Academy of International Military History (U.S.A.)
AIMI	Association Internationale de Meditation Transcendentale
AIMIC	Association of Insurance Managers in Industry and Commerce (*now* AIRMIC)
AIMJ	Association Internationale des Magistrats de la Jeunesse
AIMM	Association Internationale des Musées Médicaux
AIMM	Australian Institute of Mining and Metallurgy
AIMMPE	American Institute of Mining, Metallurgical and Petroleum Engineers
AIMO	Accademia Italiana di Medicina Omeopatica
AIMO	All-India Manufacturers Organisation
AIMO	Association of Industrial Medical Officers
AIMP	Associação da Indústria de Malte Portuguesa
AIMPA	Association Internationale de Météorologie et de Physique de l'Atmosphère
AIMPE	Australian Institute of Marine and Power Engineers
AIMPES	Associazione Italiana Manufatturieri Pelli Cuoio e Succedonei
AIMS	American Institute of Merchant Shipping
AIMS	American International Marchigiana Society
AIMS	Association for Improving Moral Standards
AIMS	Association for International Medical Study
AIMS	Australian Institute of Marine Science
AIN	American Institute of Nutrition
AINA	Arctic Institute of North America (Canada)
AINDT	Australian Institute for Non-Destructive Testing
AINEC	All-India Newspaper Editors Conference
AINP	Association Internationale des Numismates Professionnels
AIOA	Aviation Insurance Officers Association
AIOB	Association Internationale d'Océanografie Biologique
AIOCC	Association Internationale des Organisateurs de Courses Cyclistes
AIOP	Association Internationale d'Océanographie Physique
AIOP	Association Internationale d'Orientation Professionnelle
AIOPI	Association of Information Officers in the Pharmaceutical Industry
AIOSP	Association Internationale d'Orientation Scolaire et Professionnelle
AIP	American Institute of Physics
AIP	American Institute of Planners
AIP	Asociación Interamericana de Productividad
AIP	Associação Industrial Portuguesa
AIP	Association Internationale de Papyrologues
AIP	Association Internationale de Pédiatrie
AIP	Association Internationale de Photobiologie
AIP	Association Internationale de Psychotechnique
AIP	Associazione Italiana della Pellicceria
AIP	Associazione Italiana Prefabbricazione per l'Edilizia Industrializzata
AIPA	Association Internationale de la Psychologie Adlérienne
AIPA	Association Internationale de Psychologie Analytique
AIPA	Association Internationale de Psychologie Appliquée
AIPA	Associazione Italiana Planificazione Aziendale
AIPA	Associazione Italiana per lo Studio della Psicologia Analitica
AIPC	Association Internationale des Palais des Congrès
AIPC	Association Internationale des Ponts et Charpentes
AIPC	Association Internationale de Prophylaxie de la Cécité
AIPCEE	Association des Industries du Poisson de la CEE
AIPCN	Association Internationale Permanente des Congrès de Navigation
AIPCR	Association Internationale Permanente des Congrès de la Route
AIPE	American Institute of Plant Engineers
AIPE	Association de l'Industrie des Produits d'Entretien (Belgium)
AIPE	Association Internationale de la Presse Echiquéenne
AIPEA	Association Internationale pour l'Étude des Argiles (*formerly* CIPEA)
AIPELF	Association Internationale de Pédagogie Expérimentale de Langue Française
AIPEPO	Association Internationale de Presse pour l'Étude des Problèmes d'Outre-Mer
AIPEU	American Institute on Problems of European Unity

AIPH	Association Internationale des Producteurs de l'Horticulture	**AIRE**	Association Internationale des Ressources en Eau
AIPI	Association Internationale des Professeurs d'Italien	**AIRE**	Associazione Italiana per la Promozione degli e delle Richerche per l'Edilizia
AIPLF	Association Internationale des Parlementaires de Langue Française	**AIRG**	Agency for Intellectual Relief in Germany
AIPMA	All-India Plastics Manufacturers Association	**AIRH**	Association Internationale de Recherches Hydrauliques
AIPPI	Association Internationale pour la Protection de la Propriété Industrielle	**AIRI**	Animal Industry Research Institute (Australia)
AIPPL	Association Internationale des Professeurs de Philosophie	**AIRIT**	Association Internationale de Recherche en Informatique Toxicologique
AIPR	American Institute of Pacific Relations	**AIRMA**	All-India Radio Manufacturers Association
AIPRC	Associazione Italiana per la Promozione delle Ricerche sul Cancro	**AIRMEC**	Association Internationale pour la Recherche Médicale et les Echanges Culturels
AIPS	Association Internationale de la Presse Sportive	**AIRMIC**	Association of Insurance and Risk Managers in Industry and Commerce
AIPS	Association Internationale pour la Prévention du Suicide	**AIRO**	Associazione Italiana di Recerca Operativa
AIPS	Association Internationale pour le Progrès Social	**AIRP**	Association Internationale de Relations Professionnelles
AIPS	Australian Institute of Political Science	**AIRP**	Associazione Italiana per le Relazioni Pubbliche
AIPSA	Agro Industrias Peruanas S.A.	**AIRP**	Associazione Italiana Ricostruttori Pneumatici
AIPULF	Association Internationale des Presses Universitaires de Langue Français	**AIRPE**	Association Internationale de Recherche sur la Pollution de l'Eau
AIR	All-India Radio	**AIRXRS**	American Industrial Radium and X-Ray Society
AIR	American Institute of Refrigeration	**AIS**	Association Internationale de la Savonnerie et de la Détergence
AIR	American Institute for Research		
AIR	American Institutes for Research in the Behavioural Sciences	**AIS**	Association Internationale de Sociologie
AIR	Association des Instituteurs Réunis du Grande-Duché de Luxembourg	**AIS**	Association Internationale de la Soie
AIR	Associazione Italiana Ragioneri	**AIS**	Associazione Italiana Sociologi
AIR	Autorité Internationale de la Ruhr	**AIS**	Australian Iron and Steel Pty
AIR	Inter-American Broadcasting Association	**AISA**	Agricultural Information Society for Asia
AIRAH	Australian Institute of Refrigeration, Air Conditioning and Heating	**AISA**	Association Internationale pour la Sécurité Aérienne
AIRAPT	Association Internationale pour l'Avancement de la Recherche et de la Technologie aux Hautes Pressions	**AISAM**	Association Internationale des Sociétés d'Assurance Mutuelle
AIRBM	Associazione Italiana di Radiobiologia Medica	**AISB**	Association Internationale de Standardisation Biologique
AIRBO	Association Internationale pour les Recherches au Bas Fourneau d'Ougrée	**AISC**	American Institute of Steel Construction
AIRBR	Association Internationale du Registre des Bateaux du Rhin	**AISC**	Année Internationale du Soleil Calme
		AISC	Assistenza Internazionale Servici di Congresso
AIRCAT	Association Internationale des Régies et Commissions des Accidents du Travail	**AISC**	Association Internationale des Skal Clubs
		AISC	Associazione Italiana Santa Cecilia per la Musica Sacra

AISE	Association Internationale des Sciences de l'Éducation	**AIST**	Agenzia Italiana Spettacolo e Turismo
AISE	Association Internationale des Sciences Économiques	**AIST**	Arbeitsgemeinschaft zur Förderung und Entwicklung des Internationalen Strassenverkehrs in der Deutschen Demokratischen Republik
AISE	Association of Iron and Steel Engineers (U.S.A.)	**AISTS**	Associazione Italiana della Stampa Tecnica Scientifica e Periodica
AISF	Association Internationale de Solidarité Francophone	**AISU**	Arab Iron and Steel Union
AISFO	Associazione Italiana Sviluppo Foraggere	**AIT**	Alliance Internationale de Tourisme
AISH	Association Internationale des Sciences Hydrologiques	**AIT**	Asian Institute of Technology (Thailand)
AISI	Association Internationale des Syndicats d'Initiative et Groupements Similaires	**AIT**	Association of H.M. Inspectors of Taxes
		AITA	Association Internationale du Théâtre d'Amateurs
AISI	American Iron and Steel Institute	**AITA**	Association Internationale des Transports Aériens
AISJ	Association Internationale des Sciences Juridiques	**AITB**	Associazione Italiana dei Tecnici Birrari
AISL	Association Internationale de l'Hôpital Schweitzer de Lambaréné	**AITC**	American Institute for Timber Construction
AISL	Associazione Italiana di Studio del Lavoro	**AITC**	Association Internationale des Traducteurs de Conférence
AISLF	Association Internationale des Sociologues de Langue Française	**AITE**	Asociación de Industrias Textiles del Ecuador
AISM	Association Internationale de Signalisation Maritime	**AITEC**	Association Internationale de Technologie des Conférences
AISM	Association Internationale des Sociétés de Microbiologie	**AITEC**	Associazione Italiana Tecnico Economica del Cemento
AISM	Associazione Italiana per gli Studi di Mercato	**AITEL**	Associazione Italiana Tecnici del Latte
AISÖ	Arbeitsgemeinschaft Internationaler Strassenverkehrsunternehmer Österreichs	**AITFA**	Association des Ingénieurs et Techniciens Française des Aéroglisseurs
AISP	Académie Internationale des Sciences Politiques	**AITha**	Association Internationale de Thalassothérapie
AISP	Association Internationale de Science Politique	**AITI**	Associazione Italiana Traduttori ed Interpreti
AISP	Associazione delle Imprese Svizzere di Perforazione	**AITIM**	Asociación de Investigación Técnica de las Industrias de la Madera y Corcho
AISPA	Associazione Italiana Selezionatori Produttori Avicoli di Milano	**AITIT**	Association Internationale de la Teinture et de l'Impression Textiles (*formerly* AITT)
AISPIT	Association Internationale de Seismologie et de Physique de l'Interieur de la Terre	**AITIVA**	Associazione Italiana Tecnici Industrie Vernici e Affini
AISPO	Association Internationale des Sciences Physiques de l'Océan	**AITPCI**	Association des Ingénieurs, Techniciens et Professionels du Contrôle Industrielle
AISRU	Association Internationale pour la Statistique Regionale et Urbaine	**AITT**	Association Internationale de la Teinture Textile (*now* AITIT)
AISS	Association Internationale de la Science du Sol	**AIU**	Alliance Israelite Universelle
		AIU	Association Internationale des Universités
AISS	Association Internationale de la Sécurité Sociale	**AIU**	Association Internationale des Urbanistes
AISS	Associazione Italiana Selezionatori Sementi e Costitutori Razze	**AIUFFAS**	Association Internationale des Utilisateurs de Filés de Fibres Artificielles et Synthétiques
		AIUM	American Institute of Ultrasound in Medicine (U.S.A.)

AIV	Association Internationale de Volcanologie	**AJV**	Algemene Juweliers Vereniging
AIV	Associazione Italiana del Vuoto	**AKA**	British Amateur Karate Association
AIVCIT	Association Internationale de Volcanologie et de Chimie de l'Intérieur de la Terre	**AKAVA**	Akateemisten Järjestöjen Keskuselin
AIVM	Association Internationale pour les Voiles Minces et les Voiles Spatiaux	**AKB**	Association des Kinésithérapeutes de Belgique
AIVPA	Association Internationale Vétérinaire de Production Animale	**AKEB**	Aktiengesellschaft für Kernenergie Beteiligungen (Switzerland)
AIW	Arbeitkreis Fachagenturen und Berater für Industrie-Werbung	**AKEL**	Progressive Party of Working People (Cyprus)
AIW	Arbeitsgemeinschaft Industrieöfenbau- und Wärmeanlagen	**AKEW**	Arbeitsgemeinschaft Kernkraftwerk der Elektrizitätswirtschaft (Austria)
AIW	International Union of Allied Industrial Workers of America	**AKF**	American-Korean Foundation
AIWC	All India Women's Conference	**AKI**	Arbeitsgemeinschaft Deutsche Kunstoffindustrie
AIWFC	All India Women's Food Council	**AKI**	Arbeitsgemeinschaft Keramische Industrie
AIWM	American Institute of Weights and Measures	**AKL**	Autoalan Keskusliitto
AIWO	Agudas Israel World Organisation	**AKOR**	Gesellschaft für Operations Research in Wirtschaft und Verwaltung
AJA	Amateur Judo Association of Great Britain	**AKU**	Algemene Kunstzijde Unie NV
AJA	Australian Journalists Association	**ALA**	Afghan Library Association
AJBD	Arbeitsgemeinschaft für Juristisches Bibliotheks- und Dokumentationswesen	**ALA**	American Landrace Association
		ALA	American Library Association
AJC	Alianza Mundial de Asociaciones Cristianas de Jóvenes	**ALA**	Arbeitsgemeinschaft der Schweizerischen Aluminiumwaren-Fabrikanten
AJC	Asociación Judicial de Chile	**ALA**	Asociación de Líneas Aéreas
AJC	Association des Journalistes de la Consommation	**ALA**	Austral Lineas Aereas (Argentina)
AJC	Australian Jockey Club	**ALACF**	Asociación Latinoamericana de Ciencias Fisiológicas
AJCC	American Jersey Cattle Club	**ALAD**	Arid Lands Agricultural Development Program (Middle East)
AJCOR	Australian Joint Council for Operational Research	**ALADA**	Asociación Latinoamericana del Algodon (Venezuela)
AJDC	American Joint Distribution Committee	**ALAE**	Asociación Latinoamericana de Entomología
AJE	Association des Journalistes Européens		
AJE	Association des Juristes Européens	**ALAF**	Asociación Latino-Americana de Ferrocarriles
AJEF	Association des Jeunes Européens Fédéralistes	**ALAF**	Asociación Latinoamericana de Fitotecnia
AJEF	Association des Journalistes Économiques et Financiers	**ALAFAR**	Association Latino-Américaine des Matières Refractaires
AJEX	Association of Jewish Ex-Servicemen and Women	**ALAFO**	Asociación Latinoamericana de Facultades de Odontologia
AJH	Association des Journalistes de l'Horticulture	**ALAI**	Association Littéraire et Artistique Internationale
AJPAA	Association des Journalistes Professionnels de l'Aéronautique et de l'Astronautique		
AJPBE	Association des Journalistes Périodiques Belges et Étrangers	**ALAIH**	Asociación Latino-Americano de Ictiologos y Herpetologos
AJPF	Association Internationale des Journalistes de la Presse Féminine et Familiale	**ALALC**	Asociación Latinoamericana de Libre Comercio

ALALE	Association Latino-Américaine de Libre Echange
ALAM	Asociación Latinoamericana de Malezas
ALAM	Association of Lightweight Aggregate Manufacturers
ALAMAR	Asociación Latinoamericana de Armadores
ALAP	Agricultural Librarians Association of the Philippines
ALAP	Association Latino-Américaine d'Administration Publique
ALAR	Association of Light Alloy Refiners
ALARS	Association of Light Alloy Refiners and Smelters
ALAS	Asociación Argentina de Sociologia
ALAS	Asociación Latinoamericana del Suelo
ALASBIMN	Association Latino-Américaine des Sociétés de Biologie et Médecine Nucléaires
ALATAC	Asociación Latinoamericana del Transporte Automotor por Carreteras
ALB	Arbeitkreis Ladenbau im HDH
ALB	Arbeitsgemeinschaft Landwirtschaftliches Bauen
ALC	Agricultural Land Commission
ALC	Alberta Livestock Co-operative (Canada)
ALCA	American Leather Chemists Association
ALCA	Asociación Latinoamericana de Ciencias Agrícolas
ALCAN	Aluminium Company of Canada
ALCATEL	Société Alsacienne de Constructions Atomiques, de Telecommunications et d'Électronique
ALCL	Association of London Chief Librarians
ALCOA	Aluminium Company of America
ALDA	American Land Development Association
ALDEC	Asociación Latinoamericana de Derecho Constitucional
ALDEV	African Land Development Board (Kenya)
ALEA	Air Line Employees Association International
ALEAS	Asociación Latinoamericana de Educación Agricola
ALEASS	Association Latino-Américaine des Écoles de Service Social
ALEBCI	Asociación Latinoamericana de Biblioteconomía y Ciencias de la Información
ALEBCI	Latin American Association of Schools of Library and Information Sciences (Brazil)
ALEC	Algemeen Landbouw Emigratie-Comité (Netherlands)
ALEC	Asian Labour Education Centre (Philippines)
ALECSO	Arab League Educational, Cultural and Scientific Organization
ALEGEO	Latin American Association of Editors in the Earth Sciences (Venezuela)
ALEJ	Association Luxembourgeoise des Éditeurs de Journaux
ALENCA	Alena Enterprises of Canada
ALER	Asociación Latinoamericana de Educación Radiofónica (Argentina)
ALERB	Asociación Latinoamericana de Redactores de Revistas Biológicas (Mexico)
ALERT	All-Africa Leprosy and Rehabilitation Training Centre (Ethiopia)
ALES	American Labour Education Service
ALF	Arbeitsgemeinschaft der Lebensmittel-Filialbetriebe
ALF	Asociación Latinoamericana de Fitopatología (Colombia)
ALF	Association Laitière Française pour le Développement de la Production et des Industries du Lait
ALF	Azania Liberation Front
ALFAL	Asociación de Lingüística y Filogia de América Latina
ALFE	Association Linguistique Franco-Européenne
ALFEDIAM	Association de Langue Française pour l'Étude du Diabète et des Maladies Métaboliques
ALGES	Association of Local Government Engineers and Surveyors
ALGFO	Association of Local Government Financial Officers
ALGÖ	Arbeitsgemeinschaft Landwirtschaftlicher Geflügelzüchter Österreichs
ALGO	Association des Livres Généalogiques Ovins
ALGU	Association of Land Grant Colleges and Universities (U.S.A.)
ALI	Alfa-Laval International (Sweden)
ALI	American Library Institute
ALI	Association Luxembourgeoise des Ingénieurs
ALI	Associazione Librai Italiani
ALI	Latin American Exchange Association
ALIA	American Life Insurance Association
ALIAZO	Alianca Angolana des Originarios do Zombo

ALICA	Asociación Latinoamericana de Industrias de Conservas Alimenticias	**ALPSP**	Association of Learned and Professional Society Publishers
ALIDE	Asociación Latinoamericana de Instituciones Financieras de Desarrollo (Peru)	**ALR**	Société Luxembourgeoise de Radiologie
ALII	Association Luxembourgeoise des Ingénieurs et Industriels	**ALRA**	Abortion Law Reform Association
		ALRA	Adult Literacy Resource Agency
ALIMDA	Association of Life Insurance Medical Directors of America	**ALRC**	Anti-Locust Research Centre
		ALROS	American Laryngological, Rhinological and Otological Society
ALJE	Association Luxembourgeoise des Juristes Européens	**ALS**	Agricultural Land Service (*now* ADAS)
ALJHE	Association of Libraries of Judaica and Hebraica in Europe	**ALS**	Algemeen Landbouw Syndicaat (Indonesia)
		ALSATEX	Société Alsacienne d'Étude et d'Exploitation
ALJP	Association Luxembourgeoise des Journalistes Professionnels	**ALSPI**	Société Alsacienne de Participations Industrielles
ALKD	Association Luxembourgeoise des Kinésithérapeutes Diplomés	**ALT**	Association of Law Teachers
		ALTA	American Library Trustee Association
ALLA	Allied Long Lines Agency (*of* NATO)	**ALTU**	Association of Liberal Trade Unionists
ALM	Antillaanse Luchtvaart Maatschappij (Netherlands Antilles)	**ALUPA**	Association Luxembourgeoise pour l'Utilisation Pacifique de l'Énergie Atomique
ALM	Asociación Latinoamericana de Microbiología	**ALUS**	African Land Utilisation and Settlement Board
ALMA	Katholieke Academische Actie voor Internationale Samenwerking	**ALVAO**	Association des Langues Vivantes pour l'Afrique Occidentale
ALMER-COM	European Chambers of Commerce Group for Trade with Latin America	**ALWIC**	Anti Leprosy World Information Centre
		AMA	Accumulator Makers Association
ALMO	African Livestock Marketing Organisation	**AMA**	Adhesive Manufacturers Association (*now* BAMA)
ALN	Armée de Libération Nationale (Algeria)		
ALO	Asian Labour Organisation	**AMA**	Agricultural Marketing Administration (U.S.A.)
ALOSEV	Asamblea Latinoamerica de Organizaciones de Servicio Voluntario		
		AMA	American Machinery Association
ALP	Afdeling Arbeidsfysiologie v. h. Laboratorium v. Fysiologie d. Dieren	**AMA**	American Management Association
		AMA	American Maritime Association
ALP	Australian Labour Party	**AMA**	American Medical Association
ALPA	Asociación Latinoamericana de Producción Animal	**AMA**	American Meteor Association
		AMA	Architectural Metalwork Association
ALPAI	Air Line Pilots Association International	**AMA**	Asociación Médica Argentina
ALPAR	Association Luxembourgeoise pour l'Alimentation et l'Hygiene Rationnelles	**AMA**	Association Centrale des Moniteurs d'Auto-Écoles (Switzerland)
ALPDS	Association des Laboratories de Prothèse Dentaire de Suisse	**AMA**	Association of Manufacturers Allied to the Electrical and Electronic Industry
ALFP	Algemeen Landbouw Pensioenfonds (Indonesia)	**AMA**	Auckland Mathematical Association (N.Z.)
		AMA	Australian Medical Association
ALPL	Association Luxembourgeoise des Pilotes de Ligne	**AMA**	Australian Musical Association
		AMA	Automobile Manufacturers' Associations (U.S.A.)
ALPO	Association of Land and Property Owners		
ALPO	Association of Lunar and Planetary Observers	**AMADE**	Association Mondiale des Amis de l'Enfance
ALPRO	Alianza para el Progreso (*of* OAS)	**AMAE**	Associação Mineira de Administração Escolar (Brazil)

MAPROP Anglo American Properties Ltd

MAS Association Mondiale d'Aviculture Scientifique

MASC Association Mondiale des Anciennes Élèves du Sacré Coeur

MAT Association des Musées de l'Afrique Tropicale

MAUS Aero Medical Association of the United States

MAX American Metal Climax Inc.

MBAC Asociación Mexicana de Bibliotecarios

MBES Association of Metropolitan Borough Engineers and Surveyors

MBMO Asociación Mediterránea de Biología Marina y Oceanografía

MC Agricultural Mortgage Corporation

MC American Mining Congress

MC Association of Municipal Corporations

MCA Academia Mexicana de Ciencias Agrícolas

MCA Academia Mexicana de Ciencias Avícola

MCA Amateur Motor-Cycle Association

MCA American Mosquito Control Association

MCAN Anglo American Corporation of Canada Ltd

MCC Association Mondiale pour la Communication Chrétienne

MCCW Association of Manufacturers of Chilled Car Wheels (U.S.A.)

MCHAM American Chamber of Commerce in the Netherlands

MCL Association of Metropolitan Chief Librarians

MCOR African Metals Corporation Ltd

MD Asociación Médica Dominicana

MDB Agricultural Machinery Development Board

MDEA Association of Manufacturers of Domestic Electrical Appliances

MDEC Agricultural Marketing Development Executive Committee

MDEC Associated Manufacturers of Domestic Electric Cookers

MDEL Australian Mineral Development Laboratories

MDI Associazione Medici Dentisti Italiani

ME Accord Monetaire Européen

MEB Agrupación Mundial de Ex-Boxeadores

MECEA Association of Member Episcopal Conferences in Eastern Africa

AMECUSD Association of Manufacturers and Exporters of Concentrated and Unconcentrated Soft Drinks

AMEE Association of Managerial Electrical Executives

AMEME Association of Mining, Electrical and Mechanical Engineers

AMES Air Ministry Experimental Station

AMES Association of Marine Engineering Schools

AMEU Association of Municipal Electricity Undertakings of Southern Africa

AMEWA Associated Manufacturers of Electric Wiring Accessories

AMEX American Stock Exchange

AMFIE Association of Mutual Fire Insurance Engineers (U.S.A.)

AMFORT Association Mondiale pour la Formation Professionelle Touristique

AMGE Association Mondiale des Guides et des Éclaireuses

AMGI Associazione Medici Geriatri Italiani

AMGP Asociación Mexicana de Geólogos Petroleros

AMGRA American Milk Goat Record Association

AMGSR Association des Marchands Grainiers de la Suisse Romande

AMHS American Material Handling Society

AMI American Meat Institute

AMI Apostolat Militaire International

AMI Arbeitsgemeinschaft Mahlkorkverarbeitender Industrie

AMI Assistance Médicale Internationale (Canada)

AMI Association Maçonnique Internationale

AMI Association of Meat Inspectors

AMI Association Montessori Internationale

AMI Associazione Medica Italiana

AMIA American Metal Importers Association

AMIA Association Mondiale pour l'Union du Troisième Age (Switzerland)

AMIC Anglo American Industrial Corporation Ltd

AMIC Asian Mass Communications Research and Information Centre, Singapore (Malaysia)

AMICEE Asociación Mexicana de Ingenieros en Comunicaciónes Electricas y Electronicas

AMICI Association Mondiale des Interprètes de Conférences Internationales

AMIEV Association Médicale Internationale pour l'Étude des Conditions de Vie et de la Santé

AMIF	American Meat Institute Federation	**AMP**	Australian Mycological Panel
AMII	Association of Musical Instrument Industries	**AMPA**	Agricultural Machinery Parts Association
AMINA	Association Mondiale des Inventeurs (Belgium)	**AMPA**	American Manganese Producers' Association
AMISLA	Comité Organisateur de l'Académie Musulmane Internationale des Sciences des Lettres et des Beaux-Arts	**AMPA**	American Medical Publishers Association
		AMPA	Asociación Mexicana de Producción Animal
AMJ	Assemblée Mondiale de la Jeunesse	**AMPA**	Centro Nazionale Applicazioni Materie Plastiche Agricoltura
AMK	Arbeitsgemeinschaft Die Moderne Küche	**AMPAS**	Academy of Motion Picture Arts and Sciences (U.S.A.)
AML	American Mail Line Ltd		
AML	Applied Mathematics Laboratory (DSIR) (N.Z.)	**AMPFAC**	Asociación Mexicana de Profesionistas Forestales
AMLAR	Asociación Médico Latino-Americano de Rehabilitacion	**AMPM**	Association of Malt Products Manufacturers
AMLATFE-DOP	Latin American Federation of Employees in Public Service	**AMPrA**	Association Nationale pour les Mutations Professionnelles en Agriculture
AMLC	Australian Meat and Livestock Corporation	**AMPTC**	Arab Maritime Petroleum Transport Company
AMLF	Association des Microbiologistes de Langue Française	**AMQUA**	American Quaternary Association
		AMR	Année Mondiale de Réfugié
AMLFC	Association des Médecins de Langue Française du Canada	**AMR**	Association de Médicine Rurale
AMM	Asociación Mexicana de Microbiología	**AMRA**	American Metal Repair Association
AMM	Association of Manipulative Medicine	**AMRA**	Ancient Mediterranean Research Association
AMM	Association Médicale Mondiale	**AMRA**	Associationi Belge des Maisons de Réforme Alimentaire
AMMA	Assistant Masters and Mistresses Association	**AMRC**	Abadina Media Resource Centre (Nigeria)
AMMA	Associazione Industriali Metallurgici Meccanici Affini	**AMRC**	Australian Meat Research Committee
		AMRCB	Annales du Musée Royal du Congo Belge
AMMFI	Austrian Man-Made Fibres Institute	**AMRF**	African Medical and Research Foundation
AMMI	American Merchant Marine Institute	**AMRO**	Association of Medical Record Officers
AMMP	Association of Manufacturers of Medicinal Preparations	**AMROP**	Association Mondiale pour l'Étude de l'Opinion Publique
AMMRA	Arbeitsgemeinschaft Mittelständischer Mineralölraffinerien	**AMS**	Agricultural Marketing Service (U.S.A.)
		AMS	American Mathematical Society (U.S.A.)
AMNH	American Museum of Natural History	**AMS**	American Meteorological Society
AMÖ	Arbeitsgemeinschaft Möbeltransport Bundesverband	**AMS**	American Microchemical Society
		AMS	American Microscopical Society
AMOC	American Miscellaneous Society	**AMS**	Army Map Service (U.S.A.)
AMONO	Agricultural Machinery Operation and Management Office (China)	**AMS**	Association of Metal Sprayers
		AMS	Association des Musiciens Suisses
AMOP	Association of Mail Order Publishers	**AMSA**	American Meat Science Association
AMORC	Ordre Rosicrucien (U.S.A.)	**AMSA**	Association of Medical Schools in Africa
AMP	Associated Master Plumbers and Domestic Engineers	**AMSA**	Association Mondiale des Sciences Agricoles
		AMSA	Australian Marine Sciences Association
AMP	Association Méditerranéenne de Psychiatrie	**AMSAC**	American Society of African Culture
AMP	Australian Mutual Provident Society	**AMSAT**	Radio Amateur Satellite Corporation

AMSC	American Marine Standards Committee
AMSE	Australian Mining and Smelting Europe Ltd
AMSGA	Association of Manufacturers and Suppliers for the Graphic Arts
AMSH	Association for Moral and Social Hygiene
AMSO	Association of Market Survey Organisations
AMSS	American Milking Shorthorn Society
AMSUS	Association of Military Surgeons of the United States
AMT	Academy of Medicine Toronto (Canada)
AMT	Ateliers Metallurgiques Togolais
AMTCL	Association for Machine Translation and Computational Linguistics (U.S.A.) (*now* Association for Computational Linguistics)
AMTDA	Agricultural Machinery and Tractor Dealers' Association
AMTDA	American Machine Tool Distributors Association
AMTDS	Agricultural Machinery Training Development Society
AMTEC	Australian Meat Trades Export Group
AMTU	Agence Mondiale pour les Problèmes de Circulation en Milieu Urbain
AMTV	Allgemeiner Möbeltransportverband (Austria)
AMU	Associated Metalworkers Union
AMU	Association de Médecine Urbaine
AMUFOC	Association des Établissements Multiplicateurs de Semences Fourragères des Communautés Européennes
AMV	Association du Mérite Viticole
AMV	Association Mondiale Vétérinaire
AMVES	Asociación de Médicos Veterinarios de El Salvador
AMVMI	Association Mondiale des Vétérinaires Microbiologistes, Immunologistes et Spécialistes des Maladies Infectieuses
AMVR	Asociación Mundial de Vivienda Rural
AMVZ	Asociación de Médicos Veterinarios Zootecnistas (Colombia)
AMWG	American Movement for World Government
AMZ	Association Mondiale de Zootechnie
ANA	Agence Nigérienne d'Assurances
ANA	Accademia Nazionale di Agricoltura
ANA	All Nippon Airways (Japan)
ANA	American Nature Association

ANA	American Neurological Association
ANA	American Numismatic Association
ANA	Asociación Nacional de Agricultores
ANA	Associazione Nationale fra gli Agenti di Assicurazione
ANA	Australian National Airways
ANAAS	Australian and New Zealand Society for the Advancement of Science
ANAB	Algemene Nederlandse Agrarische Bedrijfsbond
ANABA	Asociación Nacional de Bibliotecarios, Archiveros y Arqueólogos
ANABADS	Association Nationale des Bibliothécaires, Archivistes et Documentalistes Sénégalais
ANABIC	Associazione Nazionale Allevatori Bestiame Italiano da Carne
ANAC	Associazione Nationale Autoservizi in Concessione
ANAC	Auckland Nuclear Accessory Co. (New Zealand)
ANACAFE	Asociación Nacional del Café (Guatemala)
ANACAP	Associazione Nazionale Aziende Concessionarie Affissioni e Pubblicità
ANACH	Asociación Nacional de Campesinos de Honduras
ANACNA	Associazione Nazionale Assistenti e Controllori della Navigazione Aerea
ANADISME	Associazione Nazionale Aziende Distributrici Specialità-Medicinali e Prodotti Chimico-Farmaceutici
ANAF	Association Nationale des Avocats de France
ANAGINA	Associazione Nazionale Agenti General Istituto Nazionale delle Assicurazione e le Assicurazione d'Italia
ANAGSA	Aseguradora Nacional Agrícola y Ganadera (Mexico)
ANAH	Association Nationale des Agronomes Haitiens
ANAHPS	Association Nationale Agricole et Horticole de Promotion Sociale
ANAI	Associazione Nazionale Archivistica Italiana
ANAIP	Asociación Nacional Autónoma de Industriales de Plásticos
ANALAC	Asociación Nacional de Productores e Industriales Lácteos (Colombia)
ANALJA	Asociación Nacional de la Industria del Jabón (Colombia)

ANALPES	Asociación Nacional de Productores de Pesticidas (Colombia)	**ANCAR**	Assoc. Nordestina de Credito e Assistencia Rural (Brazil)
ANALTIR	Association Nationale des Entreprises Albanaises des Transports Routiers	**ANCAR**	Australian National Committee for Antarctic Research
ANAMSO	Association Nationale des Agriculteurs Multiplicateurs de Semences Oléagineuses	**ANCB**	Association Nationale de Comptables de Belgique
ANAOA	Association Nationale des Appellations d'Origine Agricole	**ANCC**	Associazione Nazionale per il Controllo della Combustione (Italy)
ANAP	Asociación Nacional de Agricultores Pequeños (Cuba)	**ANCCR**	Association Nationale des Chanteurs et des Conteurs Ruraux
ANAP	Associazione Nazionale Agenti di Pubblicità	**ANCE**	Assemblé des Nations Captives d'Europe
ANAPO	Alianza Nacional Popular (Colombia)	**ANCE**	Associazione Nazionale del Commercio con l'Estero
ANARE	Australian National Antarctic Research Expeditions	**ANCE**	Associazione Nazionale Costruttori Edili
ANARLEP	Association Nationale des Animateurs Ruraux de Loisirs et d'Éducation Populaire	**ANCEFN**	Académia Naciónál de Ciéncias Exactas, Físicas y Naturáles (Argentina)
ANAS	Association Nationale des Assistantes Sociales et Assistants Sociaux	**ANCI**	Associazione Nazionale Calzaturifici Italiani
ANAS	Associazione Nazionale Agenzie Stampa	**ANCI**	Associazione Nazionale dei Comuni Italiani
ANASED	Associazione Nazionale Aziende Servizi Elaborazione Dati	**ANCI**	Ateliers Navals de Côte-d'Ivoire
ANATO	Asociación Colombiana de Agencias de Turismo	**ANCIA**	Association Nationale des Centres d'Insemination Artificielle
ANAV	Academia Nacional de Agronomía y Veterinaria (Argentina)	**ANCIC**	Associazione Nazionale Case di Informazioni Commerciali
ANB	Associazione Nazionale Bieticoltori Italiani	**ANCLI**	Associazione Nazionale fra le Centrali del Latte d'Italia
ANBE	Asociación Nacional de Bananeros del Ecuador	**ANCMA**	Associazione Nazionale del Ciclo, Motociclo ed Accessori
ANBEF	Association Nationale des Bibliothécaires d'Expression Française	**ANCO**	Asociación Nacional de Criadores de Ovejas (Ecuador)
ANBOS	Algemene Nederlandse Bond van Schoonheidsinstituten	**ANCO**	Associazione Nazionale dei Consorzi dell' Ortoflorofrutticoltura
ANBP	Algemene Nederlandse Bond van Postorderbedrijven	**ANCOGAS**	Associazione Nazionale Commercianti Gas Liquefatti
ANC	Academia Nacional de Ciencias (Mexico)	**ANCOL**	Associated Newsagents Co-operative Ltd (Australia)
ANC	African National Congress (Zambia)		
ANC	African National Council	**ANCOM**	Agrupación Nacional Sindical Autonoma de Constructores de Maquinaria
ANC	Australian Newspaper Council	**ANCOM**	Andean Common Market
ANCA	Allied Naval Communications Agency (of NATO)	**ANCOMAG**	Associazione Nazionale Commercianti Macchine Grafiche Cartarie e Affini
ANCA	American National Cattlemen's Association	**ANCORA**	Association Nationale pour la Coordination la Compensation des Restraites Complementaires
ANCA	Asociación Nacional Cultivadores de Algodón (Venezuela)		
ANCAD	Associazione Nazionale Commercianti Articoli Dentari	**ANCPEP**	Association Nationale de Contrôle des Performances Porcines
ANCAP	Administración Nacional de Combustiles, Alcohol y Portland (Uruguay)	**ANCPI**	Association des Négociateurs-Conseils en Propriété Industrielle (Germany)

ANCRA Associazione Nazionale Commercianti Radio, Televisione, Elettrodomestici ed Affini

ANCRIGAP Asociación Nacional de Criadores de Ganado Porcino (Venezuela)

ANCS Association Nationale des Clubs Scientifiques

ANCUN Australian National Committee for the United Nations

ANDA Administración Nacional de Acueductos y Alcantarillados (Salvador)

ANDA Associação Nacional para Difusão de Adubos (Brazil)

ANDA Associação Nordestina do Desenvolvimento Agrícola (Brazil)

ANDA Association Nationale pour le Développement Agricole

ANDB Air Navigation Development Board (U.S.A.)

ANDB Algemene Nederlandse Drogistenbond

ANDBP Association Nationale pour le Développement des Bibliothèques Publiques

ANDCP Association Nationale des Directeurs et Chefs de Personnel (France)

ANDCS Académia Nacionál de Derécho y Ciéncias Sociales (Argentina)

ANDE Asociación Nacional de Educadores (Costa Rica)

ANDE Asociación Nacional de Empresarios (Ecuador)

ANDEC Acerías Nacionales del Ecuador

ANDECE Agrupación Nacional de los Derivados del Cemento

ANDESA Asociación Nacional de Directores de la Escuelas Superiores de Agricultura (Mexico)

ANDESE Association Nationale des Docteurs ès Sciences Économiques

ANDI Asociación Nacional de Industriales (Colombia)

ANDI Associazione Nazionale degli Inventori

ANDIL Associazione Nazionale degli Industriali dei Laterizi

ANDIMA Asociación Nacional de Industriales Madereros (Venezuela)

ANDIN Associazione Nazionale di Ingegneria Nucleare

ANDIS Associazione Nazionale di Ingegneria Sanitaria

ANDSCJR Association Nationale pour le Developpement Social et Culturel de la Jeunesse Rurale

ANE Asociación Numismatica Española

ANE Associação Nacional dos Exportadores (Brazil)

ANEC Asociación Nacional de Enfermeras de Colombia

ANEC Associação Nacional dos Exportadores de Cereais (Brazil)

ANEC Association Nationale des Éleveurs de Chinchillas

ANEC Associazione Nazionale Esercenti Cinema

ANECEA Association Nationale d'Élevage du Cheval, d'Équitation et d'Agriculture

ANEDA Association Nationale d'Études pour la Documentation Automatique

ANEF Associazione Nazionale di Educazioni Fisica

ANEFPR Association Nationale d'Enseignement et de Formation Professionnelle Rurale

ANEM Association Nationale d'Études Municipales pour la Promotion de la Fonction Communale

ANENA Association Nationale pour l'Étude de la Neige et des Avalanches

ANEP Asociación Nacional de Ex-Parlamentarios (Peru)

ANESV Associazione Nazionale Esercenti Spettacoli Viaggianti

ANET Associazione Nazionale Esercenti Teatri

ANEVEI Algemene Nederlandse Vereniging van Eierhandelaren

ANF Académia Nacionál de Farmácia (Brazil)

ANFAC Agrupación Nacional de Fabricantes de Automóviles y Camiones

ANFAC Asociación Colombiana de Fabricantes de Articulos de Caucho (Colombia)

ANFACI Association Nationale des Fabricants de Colles Industrielles

ANFAMA Agrupación Nacional de Fabricantes de Maquinaria Agrícola

ANFAO Associazione Nazionale Fabbricanti Articoli di Occhialeria

ANFE Asociación Nacional de Fomento Económico (Costa Rica)

ANFIA Associazione Nazionale fra Industrie Automobilistiche

ANFIMA Associazione Nazionale fra i Fabbricanti di Imballagi Metallici ed Affini

ANFMA Associátion Nationale pour la Formation des Moniteurs Agricoles

ANFOPAR	Association Nationale pour la Formation et le Perfectionnement Professionnel des Adultes Ruraux
ANFP	Associação dos Fabricantes de Papel (Brazil)
ANFRUT	Asociación Nacional de Fruticultores (Venezuela)
ANG	Academia Nacional de Geografía (Argentina)
ANGA	Associazione Nazionale Giovani Agricoltori
ANGAISA	Associazione Nazionale Grossisti Apparecchi Igienco-Sanitari
ANGAU	Australian New Guinea Administrative Unit
ANGIP	Associazione Nazionale Grossisti Italiani Profumeria
ANGO	Association du Négoce des Graisses Oléagineuses, Huiles et Graisses Animales et Végétales et leurs Dérivés de la CEE
ANGPVCC	Association Nationale des Groupements de Producteurs (Vins de Consommation Courante)
ANGR	Association Nationale des Grossistes Répartiteurs en Spécialités Pharmaceutiques
ANGRO	Associazione Nazionale Italiana Grossisti Orologiai
ANGV	Asociación Nacional de Ganaderos de Venezuela
ANHG	Academia Nacional de Historia y Geografía (Mexico)
ANHSA	Aerovias Nacionales de Honduras SA
ANHUL	Australian National Humanities Library
ANI	Academia de Negocios Internacionales (U.S.A.)
ANIA	Asociación Nacional de Ingenieros Agronomos
ANIA	Associazione Nazionale fra le Imprese Assicuratrici
ANIAA	Association Nationale des Industries Agricoles et Alimentaires
ANIAI	Associazione Nazionale Ingegneri e Architetti Italiani
ANICA	Associazione Nazionale Instituti di Credito Agrario
ANICAF	Asociación Nacional de Industriales del Café (Venezuela)
ANICAV	Associazione Nazionale fra gli Industriali delle Conserve Alimentari Vegetali
ANICC	Association Nationale Interprofessionnelle du Champignon de Couché
ANICO-BECA	Associazione Nazionale Importatori e Commercianti di Bestiame e Carne
ANICTA	Associazione Nazionale Imprenditori Coibentazioni Termoacustiche
ANID	Associazione Nazionale Insegnanti di Disegno
ANIDECOL	Federazione Nazionale Importatori Caffè, Coloniali e Droghe
ANIE	Associazione Nazionale Industrie Elettrotecniche ed Elettroniche
ANIEM	Unione Nazionale Industrie Edili Minori
ANIERM	Asociación Nacional de Importadores y Exportadores de la República Mexicana
ANIEST	Associazione Nazionale Italiana Esperti Scientifici del Turismo
ANIFRMO	Association National Interprofessionnelle pour la Formation Rationnelle de la Main-d'Oeuvre
ANIG	Associazione Nazionale Industriali Gas
ANILEC	Association Nationale Interprofessionnelle des Légumes de Conserve (France) (*formerly* UNILEC)
ANILS	Associazione Nazionale Insegnanti di Lingue Straniere
ANIM	Asociación Nacional de Industriales Madereros (Venezuela)
ANIMA	Associazione Nazionale Industria Meccanica Varia ed Affine
ANIMeM	Associazione Nazionale Industriali Metalmeccanici Minori
ANIMPEC	Associazione Nazionale Industriali Manufatturieri delle Pelli e del Cuoio
ANIPESCA	Associazione Nazionale Importatori Produtti della Pesca Conservati
ANIPLA	Associazione Nazionale Italiana per l'Automazione
ANIR	Associazione Nazionale Industrie Refrattari
ANIT	Associazione Nazionale Imprese Teatrais e Similares
ANITA	Associazione Nazionale Imprese dei Trasporti Automobilistici
ANITPAT	Associazione Nazionale Incegnanti Tecnico-Pratici e di Applicazioni Tecniche
ANJIM	Association Nationale des Journalistes d'Information Médicale
ANKO	Algemene Nederlandse Kappersorganisatie
ANL	Argonne National Laboratory (U.S.A.)
ANL	Australian National Line

ANM	Academía Nacionál de Medicína (Brazil)
ANM	Associazione Nazionale Magistrati
ANMA	Association Nationale des Maitres Agricoles et des Maitresses Ménagères
ANMA	Associazione Nazionale Meccanizzazione Agraria
ANMB	Algemene Nederlandse Molenaarsbond
ANMC	American National Metric Council (*of* ANSI)
ANMER	L'Association Nationale de Migration et d'Établissement Ruraux
ANMF	Association Nationale de la Meunerie Française
ANMRC	Australian Numerical Meteorology Research Centre
ANNF	Association Nazionale de la Navigation Fluviale
ANOF	Algemene Nederlandse Onderwijzers Federatie
ANOFPR	Association Nationale Ouvrière pour la Formation Professionnelle Rurale
ANP	United Nations Applied Nutrition Programme
ANP	Australian Nationalist Party
ANPA	American Newspaper Publishers' Association
ANPA	Asociación Nacional de Productores de Arroz (Peru)
ANPAC	Associazione Nazionale Piloti Aviazione Commerciale
ANPAG	Associazione Nazionale Piloti Aviazione Generale
ANPAN	Associazione Nazionale Provveditori e Appaltatori Navali
ANPAT	Association Nationale pour la Prévention des Accidents du Travail (Belgium)
ANPC	Association Nationale des Promoteurs de Constructions
ANPCC	Asociación Nacional de Productores de Coco y Copra (Venezuela)
ANPE	Association Nationale des Producteurs d'Endives
ANPEA	Association Nationale pour le Développement de l'Utilisation des Engrais et Amendements
ANPEB	Association Nationale des Patrons Électriciens de Belgique
ANPES	Associação Nacional de Programação Economica e Social (Brazil)
ANPI	Association Nationale pour la Protection contre l'Incendie (Belgium)
ANPIHF	Association Nationale des Planteurs Independants de Houblons Français
ANPL	Assistencia Nestle dos Produtores de Leite (Brazil)
ANPLC	Association Nationale des Producteurs de Legumes Conservés
ANPM	Association of Name Plate Manufacturers
ANPPDOS-HR	Association Nationale Professionnelle des Personnels de Direction des Organismes Spécialisés d'Habitat Rural
ANPPSA	Association Nationale pour la Promotion Professionnelle des Salaries de l'Agriculture
ANPRDPP	Association Nationale des Propriétaires Ruraux et Défenseurs de la Propriété Privée
ANPROSE	Asociación Nacional de Productores de Semillas Certificadas (Venezuela)
ANPS	Asociación Nacional de Producción de Semillas (Chile, Colombia)
ANPSCAH	Association Nationale de Promotion Socio-Culturelle en Agriculture et en Horticulture
ANPUEP	Association Nationale des Propriétaires et Usagers d'Embranchements Particuliers
ANPUR	Associazione Nazionale Professori Universitari di Ruolo
ANPV	Algemene Nederlandse Pluimveeteelvereniging
ANQUE	Asociación Nacional de Quimicos de España
ANR	Association Nationale de Révision de la Coopération Agricole
ANR	Association Nationale de Révision (des Coopératives)
ANRC	American National Red Cross
ANRC	Animal Nutrition Research Council (U.S.A.)
ANRC	Australian National Research Council
ANRCA	Association Nationale de Revision de la Coopération Agricole
ANRFVCN-ER	Association Nationale des Ruches Familiales de Vacances de la Confédération Nationale de la Famille Rurale
ANRPC	Association of Natural Rubber Producing Countries
ANRT	Association Nationale de la Recherche Technique ,
ANS	Algemene Nederlandse Slagersbond
ANS	American Name Society
ANS	American Nuclear Society

ANS	American Nutrition Society
ANSA	Agenzia Nazionale Stampa Associazione
ANSA	Aktiebolaget Nordiske Skinnauktioner
ANSA	Association Nationale des Sociétés par Action
ANSDHA	Association Nationale pour le Développement des Sciences Humaines Appliquées
ANSEAU	Association Nationale des Services d'Eau (Belgium)
ANSI	American National Standards Institute
ANSL	Australian National Standards Laboratory
ANSMO	Association des Négociants Suisses en Machines et Outils
ANSOL	Australian National Social Sciences Library
ANSP	Australian National Socialist Party
ANSS	American Nature Study Society
ANSSMFE	Australian National Society of Soil Mechanics and Foundation Engineering
ANSTEL	Australian National Scientific and Technological Library
ANT	Administracion Nacional de Telecomunicacións (Paraguay)
ANTA	American National Theatre and Academy
ANTAI	Associazione Nazionale Tappezzieri e Arredatorie Italiani
ANTAV	Association Nationale Technique pour l'Amelioration de la Viticulture (*formerly* ATAV)
ANTeL	Associazione Nazionale Tecnici di Laboratorio
ANTI	Associazione Nazionale Tributaristi Italiani
ANTL	Association Nationale des Tisseurs de Lin (Belgium)
ANTO	Antarctic Treaty Organization
ANTOR	Association of National Tourist Office Representatives in Great Britain
ANTSAL	Association Nationale des Techniciens Supérieurs Agricoles de Laiterie
ANTSH	Association Nationale des Techniciens Supérieurs Horticoles
ANTZA	Associazione Nazionale fra i Tecnici dello Zucchero e dell' Alcole
ANU	Australian National University
ANUCAG	Asociación Nacional de Uniones de Crédito Agricola y Ganadero (Mexico)
ANUDE	Administration des Nations Unies pour le Développement Économique
ANUEG	Association des Usagers de l'Électricité et du Gaz
ANUGA	Allgemeine Nahrungs und Genussmittel-Ausstellung
ANUIES	Asociación Nacional de Universidades e Institutos de Enseñanza Superior (Mexico)
ANV	Asociación Nacional de Vitivinicultores (Mexico)
ANVAR	Agence Nationale pour la Valorization de la Recherche
ANVC	Algemene Nederlandse Vereniging van Contactlenzenspecialisten
ANVEC	Associazione Nazionale fra Aziende di Vendita per Corrispondenza
ANVR	Algemene Nederlandse Vereniging van Reisbureaus
ANVS	Algemene Nederlandse Vereniging van Speelgoedhandelaren
ANVSG	Algemene Nederlandse Vereniging voor Sociale Geneeskunde
ANVUMA	Association Nationale de Vulgarisation du Machinisme Agricole
ANVV	Algemene Nederlandse Vereniging voor Vreemdelingenverkeer
ANVW	Algemene Nederlandse Vereniging voor Wijsbegeerte
ANZ	Algemene Nederlandse Zuivelbond
ANZA	Association of New Zealand Advertisers
ANZAAS	Australian and New Zealand Association for the Advancement of Science
ANZAME	Australian and New Zealand Association for Medical Education
ANZAMRS	Australian and New Zealand Association for Medieval and Renaissance Studies
ANZASA	Australian and New Zealand American Studies Association
ANZDEC	Asian-New Zealand Development Corporation
ANZEFA	Australia and New Zealand Emigrants and Families Association
ANZHES	Australian and New Zealand History of Education Society
ANZM & S	Australian and New Zealand Merchants and Shippers Association
ANZSRLO	Australian and New Zealand Scientific Research Liaison Office

ANZUS	Australia, New Zealand, United States Pact	AOMA	American Occupational Medical Association
AO	Aide Olympique	AOO	American Oceanic Organisation
AOA	American Optometric Association	AOP	Association of Optical Practitioners
AOA	American Orthopsychiatric Association	AOPA	Aircraft Owners' and Pilots Association (International)
AOA	American Osteopathic Association		
AOA	Army Ordnance Association (U.S.A.)	AOPEC	Arab Organisation of Petroleum Exporting Countries
AOA	Asociación Odontológica Argentina	AOPI	Associazione Orticola Professionale Italiana
AOA	Association of Official Architects		
AOAC	Association of Official Analytical Chemists (U.S.A.)	AOPU	Asian-Oceanic Postal Union
AOAI	American Organist Association International	AORG	Army Operational Research Group
AOAO	American Osteopathic Academy of Orthopedics	AOS	American Ophthalmological Society
		AOS	American Otological Society
AOAS	Arab Organization for Administrative Sciences (Egypt)	AOS	Apostleship of the Sea
		AOSA	Association of Official Seed Analysts (U.S.A.)
AOAS	American Osteopathic Academy of Sclerotherapy	AOSCA	Association of Official Seed Certifying Agencies (U.S.A.)
AOAS	Arab Organization for Administrative Sciences (Egypt)	AOTA	American Occupational Therapy Association
AÖB	Arbeitsgemeinschaft Österreichischer Bausparkassen	AOU	American Ornithologists' Union
		AOUD	Alliance Universelle des Ouvriers Diamantaires
AOB	Association Ornithologique de Belgique		
AOC	American Orthoptic Council	AP	Alliance for Progress (of OAS)
AOC	Associated Overseas Countries (of EEC)	APA	All Parties Administration (Australia)
AOCI	Airport Operators Council International	APA	American Pharmaceutical Association
AOCP	Asia Oceania Congress of Perinatology (Singapore)	APA	American Philological Association
		APA	American Physicists Association
AOCS	American Oil Chemists' Society	APA	American Plywood Association
AOCTL	Association of Oriental Carpet Traders	APA	American Poultry Association
AODC	Argentine Oceanographic Data Centre	APA	American Press Association
AODRA	American Oxford Down Record Association	APA	American Protestant Association
AODT	Association Européenne des Organisations Nationales de Commerçants Détaillants en Textiles	APA	American Psychiatric Association
		APA	American Psychological Association
		APA	Asociación Peruana de Avicultura (Peru)
AÖE	Arbeitsgemeinschaft Österreichischer Entomologen	APA	Association of Preventive Medicine
		APA	Association of Public Analysts
AOEC	Airways Operations Evaluation Centre (U.S.A.)	APA	Australian Physiotherapy Association
		APA	Austria Presse Agentur
AOF	Afrique Occidentale Française	APAC	Appointment and Promotion Advisory Committee (FAO)
AOIP	Association des Ouvriers en Instruments de Précision	APAC	Asociación Peruana para el Avance de la Ciencia
ÄOL	Äidinkielen Opettajain Liitto		
AÖM	Arbeitsgemeinschaft Österreichischer Musikverleger	APACL	Asian Peoples Anti-Communist League
AOM	Overseas States, Territories and Departments associated with EEC	APADA	Asociación de Productores Agrarios del Delta Argentino

APAE	Association of Public Address Engineers
APAIS	Australian Public Affairs Information Service
APAM	Association Populaire des Amis des Musées
APAN	Administración de los Parques Nacionales (Venezuela)
APAR	Association Parlementaire Agricole et Rurale (France)
APAS	Association Paritaire d'Action Sociale du Bâtiment et des Travaux Publiques
APASP	Association pour le Perfectionnement des Approvisionnements dans les Services Publiques
APAVIT	Asociación Peruana de Agencias de Viajes y Turismo
APB	Association Pharmaceutique Belge
APBC	American Book Publishers Council
APBD	Association Professionnelle de Bibliothécaires et Documentalistes (Belgium)
APBF	Accredited Poultry Breeders Federation
APBGPL	Association Professionnelle Belge des Gaz de Pétrole Liquefiés
APBS	Accredited Poultry Breeding Stations Scheme
APC	African Groundnut (Peanut) Council
APC	All People's Congress (Sierra Leone)
APC	Atomic Power Constructions
APCA	Air Pollution Control Association (U.S.A.)
APCA	Anglo-Polish Catholic Association
APCA	Assemblée Permanente des Chambres d'Agriculture (*formerly* APPCA)
APCADEC	Associação Portuguesa dos Chefes de Aprovisionamento e de Compras (Portugal)
APCB	Associação Paulista de Criadores de Bovinos (Brazil)
APCC	Agricultural Planning and Coordinating Committee (*of* MOEA, Taiwan)
APCC	Asian and Pacific Coconut Community
APCC	Assemblée des Présidents des Chambres de Commerce
APCCI	Assemblée Permanente des Chambres de Commerce et l'Industrie
APCEI	Association pour le Perfectionnement Pratique des Cadres des Entreprises Industrielles
APCK	Association for Promoting Christian Knowledge
APCM	Assemblée Permanente des Chambres de Métiers
APCMF	Assemblée des Présidents des Chambres de Métiers de France
APCO	Asian Parasite Control Organization (Japan)
APCOL	All-Pakistan Confederation of Labour
APCS	Association de la Presse Cinématographique Suisse
APD	Associazione Aziende Italiane Pubblicità Diretta
APDC	Apple and Pear Development Council
APDCP	Associação Portuguesa dos Directores e Chefes de Pessoal
APDILA	Association des Pharmaciens Directeurs de Laboratoires d'Analyses Biologiques
APDSA	Asian Pacific Dental Student Association
APE	Assemblée Parlementaire Européenne
APEA	Asociación Peruana de Economistas Agrícolas (Peru)
APEA	Association des Producteurs Européens d'Azote
APEA	Association of Professional Engineers of Alberta (Canada)
APEA	Australian Petroleum Exploration Association
APEAI	Alliance pour l'Expansion de l'Apiculture et ses Industries
APEC	Asociación de Industriales de Puerto Rico
APEC	Asociación Paraguaya Enseñanza Católica
APEC	Atlantic Provinces Economic Council (Canada)
APECCO	Association Européenne des Promoteurs de Centres Commerciaux
APECITA	Association pour l'Emploi des Cadres, Ingénieurs et Techniciens de l'Agriculture
APECS	Association des Propriétaires et Éleveurs de Chevaux de Selle
APEDE	Asociación Panamena de Ejecutivos de Empresas (Panama)
APEE	Association for Pediatric Education in Europe (France)
APEF	Association des Pays Exportateurs de Minerai de Fer (India)
APEF	Association Professionnelle des Établissements Financiers
APEID	Asian Programme of Educational Innovation for Development
APEL	Associação Portuguesa dos Editores e Livreiros

PEL	Societé pour le Développement des Applications de l'Électricité (France)
PELUX	Association des Patrons-Électriciens du Grand-Duché de Luxembourg
PEPA	Association pour l'Encouragement de la Productivité Agricole
PEPM	Association of Professional Engineers of the Province of Manitoba (Canada)
PEPNB	Association of Professional Engineers of the Province of New Brunswick (Canada)
PEPO	Association of Professional Engineers of the Province of Ontario (Canada)
PER	Association of Publishers Educational Representatives
PERU	Asociación pro Enseñanza Rural Universitaria (Argentina)
PES	Association of Professional Engineers of Saskatchewan (Canada)
PESCA	Asociación Colombiana de Pescadores e Industriales de Pesca
PESS	Association des Professeurs de l'Enseignement Secondaire Supérieur du Grand-Duché de Luxembourg
PETI	Asociación Profesional Española de Traductores e Intérpretes
PEX	Association of Professional Executive, Clerical and Computer Staff
PF	Asian Packaging Federation Philippines
PF	Associação Portuguesa de Fundição
PF	Associazione per il Promuovimento della Foraggicoltura (Switzerland)
PF	Pontifical Association for the Propagation of the Faith
PFA	Associated Poultry Farmers of Australia
PFAV	Association des Producteurs Suisses de Films et de Production Audio-visuelle
PFC	American Plant Food Council
PFC	Asia-Pacific Forestry Commission
PFIRO	Association des Producteurs de Femelles issues de Béliers Finnois ou Romanov
PFS	African Peasant Farming Scheme
PG	Arbeitskreis Pharmazeutischer Grosshandelsverbände
PHA	American Polled Hereford Association
PHA	American Printing History Association
PHA	American Public Health Association
PHA	Australian Pneumatic and Hydraulic Association

APHB	Association Patronale Horlogère (Switzerland)
APHCA	Regional Animal Production and Health Commission for Asia, the Far East and the South-West Pacific (FAO)
APHF	American Poultry and Hatchery Federation
APHI	Association of Public Health Inspectors
APHIA	Association for the Promotion of Humour in International Affairs (France)
APHS	American Poultry Historical Society
APHV	Bundesverband des Deutschen Briefmarkenhandels
API	American Paper Institute
API	American Petroleum Institute
API	American Potash Institute
API	Association Phonétique Internationale
API	Associazione Pedagogica Italiana
API	Associazione Piscicoltori Italiani
APIA	Arkansas Poultry Improvement Association (U.S.A.)
APIA	Asociación Peruana de Ingenieros Agrónomos (Peru)
APIA	Association pour la Promotion de l'Information Agricole
APIC	Asian Packaging Information Centre (Hong Kong)
APICE	Asociación Panamericana de Instituciones de Crédito Educativo (Colombia)
APICE	Associazione fra Produttori Italiani di Calcestruzzi per l'Edilizia (Italy)
APICP	Association for the Promotion of the International Circulation of the Press
APICS	American Production and Inventory Control Society
APIDC	Andra Pradesh Industrial Development Corporation (India)
APIEAS	Asociacíon Peruana de Instituciones de Agrícola Superior
APIIPP	Association Professionnelle des Importateurs Indépendants des Produits du Pétrole
APIMO	Associazione Professionale Italiana Medici Oculisti
APIMOND-IA	Fédération Internationale des Associations d'Apiculture
APIS	Architectural and Planning Information Service (N. Ireland)
APIS	Army Photographic Intelligence Service

APJBF	Association des Producteurs de Jeunes Bovins de France	**APPA**	Association de Propagande pour les Produits Agricoles
APJT	Association Professionnelle des Journalistes du Tourisme	**APPC**	Associação Portuguesa para o Progresso das Ciéncias
APL	Association of Photographic Laboratories	**APPCA**	Assemblée Permanente des Présidents des Chambres d'Agriculture (*now* APCA)
APLA	American Patent Law Association		
APLC	Association of Patent Licensing Consultants (Germany)	**APPCB**	Association Professionnelle de la Presse Cinématographique Belge
APLE	Association of Public Lighting Engineers	**APPI**	Association Internationale d'Études pour la Promotion et la Protection des Investissements Privés en Territoires Étrangers
APLET	Association for Programmed Learning and Educational Technology		
APLIC	Association for Population/Family Planning Libraries (U.S.A.)	**APPITA**	Australian Pulp and Paper Industry Technical Association
APLICI	Association for Population, Family Planning Libraries and Information Centers International (U.S.A.)	**APPMSA**	American Pulp and Paper Mills Superintendents' Association
APLS	American Plant Life Society	**APPS**	Australian Plant Pathology Society
APLV	Association des Professeurs de Langues Vivantes de l'Enseignement Publique	**APPU**	Australian Primary Producers' Union
		APQI	Associação Portuguesa para a Qualidade Industrial
APMA	American Pharmaceutical Manufacturers' Association	**APRA**	Air Public Relations Association
APMBFP	Association de la Petite et Moyenne Brasserie Familiale de Belgique	**APRA**	American Petroleum Refiners Association
		APRA	American Public Relations Association
APMC	Allied Political and Military Commission	**APRA**	Australian Plastics Research Association
APMC	Andra Pradesh Mining Corporation (India)	**APRACA**	Asian and Pacific Regional Agricultural Credit Association
APME	Associated Press Managing Editors Association (U.S.A.)	**APRAGA**	Association des Propriétaires de Récipients à Gaz Comprimés (Belgium)
APMEP	Association des Professeurs de Mathématiques de l'Enseignement	**APREA**	American Peanut Research and Education Association
APO	African People's Organisation		
APO	Asian Productivity Organisation	**APRIA**	Association pour la Promotion Industrie-Agriculture
APO	Australian Purchasing Officers Association	**APRL**	Association for the Preservation of Rural Life
APOA	Arctic Petroleum Operators Association	**APRO**	Aerial Phenomena Research Organization (U.S.A.)
APOB	Association Professionnelle des Opticiens de Belgique		
APOS	Association Professionnelle des Opticiens Suisses de Formation Supérieure	**APROBA**	Association Professionelle pour l'Accroissement de la Productivité dans l'Industrie du Bâtiment
APPA	American Psychopathological Association	**APROSC**	Agricultural Projects Services Centre (Nepal)
APPA	American Public Power Association	**APRR**	Association for Planning and Regional Reconstruction
APPA	American Pulp and Paper Association		
APPA	Associação Brasileira de Pesquisas sobre Plantas Aromaticas e Oleos Essenciaias	**APRS**	Arab Public Relations Society (UAR)
		APRS	Association for the Preservation of Rural Scotland
APPA	Association des Pilotes et Propriétaires d'Aéronefs	**APS**	American Peace Society
APPA	Association pour la Prévention de la Pollution Atmosphérique	**APS**	American Philatelic Society
		APS	American Philosophical Society

PS	American Physical Society
PS	American Physiological Society
PS	American Phytopathological Society
PS	American Polar Society
PS	American Prosthodontic Society
PS	American Psychosomatic Society
PS	Association Patronale des Serigraphes (Switzerland)
PS	Association de la Presse Suisse
PS	Associazione Pubblicità Stampa
PS	Australian Photogrammetric Society
PS	Australian Psychological Society
PSA	Aerolineas Peruanas S.A.
PSA	American Political Science Association
PSA	Australian Political Studies Association
PSAI	Assemblée Plénière des Sociétiés d'Assurances contre l'Incendie
PSC	Asian-Pacific Society of Cardiology
PSC	Association des Producteurs de Semence du Canada
PSIB	Association Professionelle des Sociétiés Immobilières en Belgique
PSO	Afro-Asian Peoples' Solidarity Organisation
PSO	Asia-Pacific Socialist Organization
PSSEAR	Association of Pediatric Societies of the Southeast Asian Region
PSTC	Andra Pradesh State Road Transport Corporation (India)
PTA	American Physical Therapy Association
PTA	American Public Transit Association
PTA	Asian Pineapple Traders Association
PTA	Asociación de la Prensa Técnica Argentina
PTI	Association of Principals of Technical Institutions
PTI	Associazione Produttori Tabacchi Italiani
PTIC	African Pyrethrum Technical Information Centre
PTO	Association of Psychiatric Treatment of Offenders
PTU	African Postal and Telecommunications Union
PU	Arab Postal Union
PU	Asia Parliamentarians Union
PUC	Association for Promoting the Unity of Christendom

APUMAG	Asociación de Profesionales Universitarios del Ministerio de Agricultura y Ganadería de la Nación (Argentina)
APV	Arbeitsgemeinschaft für Pharmazeutische Verfahrenstechnik
APV	Association de Propagande pour le Vin
APV	Associazione Italiana Promozione Vendite e Pubblicità Punto Vendite
APWA	All Pakistan Women's Association
APWA	American Public Works Association
APWSS	Asian-Pacific Weed Science Society
AQA	Asociación Quimica Argentina
AQS	Association des Quincailliers Suisses
AQTE	Association Québécoise des Techniques de l'Eau (Canada)
ARA	Aerial Ropeways Association
ARA	Agricultural Research Administration (U.S.A.)
ARA	Aircraft Research Association
ARA	Amateur Rowing Association
ARA	American Rheumatism Association
ARA	Association of River Authorities
ARAB	Association Royale des Actuaires Belges
ARAMCO	Arabian-American Oil Company
ARAN	Association for the Reduction of Aircraft Noise
ARB	Air Registration Board
ARBA	American Rabbit Breeders Association
ARBA	American Road Builders Association
ARBE	Académie Royale des Beaux-Arts et École Supérieure d'Architecture de Bruxelles
ARBICA	Arab Regional Branch of the International Council on Archives
ARBIT	Arbeitsgemeinschaft der Bitumen-Industrie
ARBM	Association of Radio Battery Manufacturers
ARC	Action for Renewal of the Church (Trinidad)
ARC	Aeronautical Research Council
ARC	Agricultural Research Council
ARC	Anthropological Research Club
ARC	Arthritis and Rheumatism Council for Research in Great Britain and the Commonwealth
ARC	Association Romande des Conseils en Publicité (Switzerland)
ARC	Asthma Research Council
ARC	Regional Conference for Africa (FAO)

ARCCA	Agricultural Research Council of Central Africa
ARCESP	Associação Brasileira de Vendedores
ARCI	Atelier de Rectification de Côte-d'Ivoire
ARCN	Agricultural Research Council of Norway
ARCOA	Asociación Rosarina de Criadores de Ovejeros Alemanes (Argentina)
ARCOS	Anglo-Russian Co-operative Society
ARCRAN	Agricultural Research Council of Rhodesia and Nyasaland
ARCRL	Agricultural Research Council Radiobiological Laboratory
ARCUK	Architects Registration Council of the United Kingdom
ARD	Arbeitsgemeinschaft der Offentlich-Rechtlichen Rundfunkanstalten der Bundesrepublik Deutschland
ARDA	Agricultural and Rural Development Act (Canada)
ARDA	American Railway Development Association
ARDC	Agricultural Refinance and Development Corporation (India)
ARDC	Agricultural and Rural Development Corporation (Burma)
ARDC	U.S. Air Research and Development Command
ARDE	Armament Research and Development Establishment
ARDE	Associazione Romano di Entomologia
ARDECO	Aluminium Resources Development Co. (Japan)
ARDES	Association pour la Recherche Démographique, Économique et Sociale (Algeria)
ARDI	Association of Registered Driving Instructors
ARDOI	Association of Institutes for Research and Development in the Indian Ocean (Mauritius)
ARE	Association for Religious Education
AREA	Aerovias Ecuatorianas, CA
AREA	American Railway Engineering Association
AREC	Agricultural Research and Educational Centre (Lebanon)
AREC	Amitié Rurale des Étudiants Catholiques
ARELAP	Asociación Regional Latinoamericana de Puertos de Pacifico
ARELS	Association of Recognized English Language Schools

ARENA	Aliança Renovadora Nacional (Brazil)
ARER	Association Régionale d'Économie Rurale
ARERS	Association Régionale pour l'Étude et la Recherche Scientifiques
ARESA	Association pour le Recherche sur l'Énergie Solaire en Algérie
ARETO	Arab Republic of Egypt Telecommunications Organization
ARF	Advertising Research Foundation (U.S.A.)
ARF	Association of Rehabilitation Facilities (U.S.A.)
ARF	Autoriserte Reklambyåers Forening
ARFA	Allied Radio Frequency Agency (of NATO)
ARGA	American Personal and Guidance Association
ARGB	Association Royale des Gaziers Belges
ARGCA	American Rice Growers Cooperative Association
ARGCI	Agence de Representation Générale en Côte-d'Ivoire
ARGE	Arbeitsgemeinschaft der Europäischen Schloss- und Beschlag-industrie
ARGF	Automobildel- og Rekvisita-Grossistenes Forening
ARGR	Association for Research in Growth Relationships (U.S.A.)
ARHS	Australian Railway Historical Society
ARI	Agricultural Research Institute and Agricultural Board (U.S.A.)
ARI	Aluminium Research Institute (U.S.A.)
ARI	American Refractories Institute
ARI	Association of Rhodesian Industries
ARIAC	Agricultural Research Institute and Agricultural College, Glen (South Africa)
ARICN	Asian Regional Communication Network (U.S.A.)
ARIEL	Asociación Reformista Independiente de Estudiantes de Letras (Peru)
ARINC	Aeronautical Radio Incorporated (U.S.A.)
ARIP	Association pour la Recherche et l'Intervention Psychosociologiques
ARISBR	Asian Regional Institute for School Building Research
ARJA	Association Suisse Romande des Journalistes de l'Aéronautique et de l'Astronautique
ARJORA	Association des Réalisateurs de Journaux Ruraux Africains

RL	Admiralty Research Laboratory	**ARPS**	Association of Railway Preservation Societies
RL	Aeronautical Research Laboratories (Australia)	**ARPS**	Australian Royal Photographic Society
RL	Akademie für Raumsforschung und Landesplanung	**ARR**	Association for Radiation Research
RL	Autonrengasliitto	**ARRB**	Australian Road Research Board
RLIF	Académie Royale de Langue et de Littérature Françaises	**ARRL**	American Radio Relay League
		ARS	American Radium Society
RLO	Arab Literacy and Adult Education Organization	**ARS**	American Rhinologic Society
		ARS	American Rocket Society
RM	Alliance Reformée Mondiale	**ARSAP**	Agricultural Requisites Scheme for Asia and the Pacific
RMA	American Records Management Association		
RMA	American Registry of Medical Assistants	**ARSBA**	American Rambouillet Sheep Breeders Association
RMA	Australian Rubber Manufacturers Association	**ARSC**	Académie Royale des Sciences Coloniales (Belgium)
RMALIB-ERI	Associazione Armatori Liberi	**ARSO**	African Regional Organization for Standardization
RMB	Académie Royale de Médécine de Belgique	**ARSO**	Autorité pour l'Aménagement de la Région du Sud-Ouest (Ivory Coast)
RMEF	Association pour la Rationalisation et la Mécanisation de l'Exploitation Forestière	**ARSOM**	Académie Royale des Sciences d'Outremer (Belgium)
RMO	Servicio Nacional de Adiestramiento Rápido de la Mano de Obra en la Industria (Mexico)	**ARSUBA**	Société Française d'Archéologie Sub-Aquatique
RMSA	Asian Regional Medical Student Association	**ARTEMAT**	Chambre Syndicale Belge des Détaillants Specialisés en Matériel pour le Dessin, les Beaux-Arts, les Arts Appliqués
RN	Association pour la Renovation de la Noyeraie		
RnI	Association of Rhodesian Industries	**ARTFP**	Association de Recherche sur les Techniques de Forage et de Production
RO	Army Research Office (U.S.A.)		
RO	Asian Regional Organisation of ICFTU	**ARTSM**	Association of Road Traffic Sign Makers
ROMA	Groupement des Fabricants d'Essences, Huiles Essentielles, Extraits, Produits Chimiques, Aromatiques et Colorants (Belgium)	**ARU**	American Railway Union
		ARU	Asociación Rural del Uruguay
		ASA	Acoustical Society of America
ROMAR	Rumanian Marketing Association	**ASA**	Advertising Standards Authority
ROW	Association of Retailer Owned Wholesalers in Foodstuffs (Belgium)	**ASA**	African Studies Association (U.S.A.)
		ASA	Amateur Swimming Association
RP	Australian Republican Party	**ASA**	American Society of Agronomy
RPA	Advanced Research Projects Agency (U.S.A.)	**ASA**	American Sociological Association
		ASA	American Society of Anesthesiologists
RPA	Association pour les Recherches sur les Parodontopathies (Switzerland) (*ceased*)	**ASA**	American Soybean Association
RPAC	Agricultural Research Policy Advisory Committee (U.S.A.)	**ASA**	American Standards Association
		ASA	American Statistical Association
RPEL	Asociación de Asistencia Reciproca Petrolera Estatal Latino-Americano	**ASA**	American Stockyards Association
		ASA	American Surgical Association
RPF	Agricultural Research Program and Facilities Subcommittee (U.S.A.)	**ASA**	Arbeitsgemeinschaft der Schweizerischen Altstoffwirtschaft
RPLOE	Association des Rééducateurs de la Parole et du Langage Oral et Écrit	**ASA**	Army Signal Association (U.S.A.)

ASA	Asian Students Association (Hong Kong)		**ASB**	Afrikaans Studentebond
ASA	Asociación Salvadorena Agropecuaria (Salvador)		**ASB**	Arbeitsgemeinschaft für Wirtschaftliche Betriebsführung und Soziale Betriebsgestaltung
ASA	Asociación Semilleros Argentinos			
ASA	Association der Schweizerischen Aerosolindustrie		**ASB**	Association of Southeastern Biologists (U.S.A.)
ASA	Association of South-East Asia		**ASBA**	American Shorthorn Breeders Association
ASA	Association des Statisticiens Agricoles		**ASBA**	American Southdown Breeders' Association
ASA	Association Suisse des Annonceurs		**ASBAH**	Association for Spina Bifida and Hydrocephalus
ASA	Associazione per le Scienze Astronautiche		**ASBC**	American Society of Biological Chemists
ASA	Atomic Scientists Association		**ASBC**	American Society of Biophysics and Cosmology
ASA	Avicultural Society of America			
ASAB	Association for the Study of Animal Behaviour		**ASBC**	American Society of Brewing Chemists
ASAE	American Society of Agricultural Engineers		**ASBE**	American Society of Bakery Engineers
ASAE	American Society of Association Executives		**ASBI**	Advisory Service for the Building Industry
ASAE	Association Suisse pour l'Aménagement des Eaux		**ASBMT**	Annales de la Société Belge de Médecine Tropicale
ASAF	Association Suisse des Analystes Financiers		**ASBPA**	American Shore and Beach Preservation Association
ASAIHL	Association of South-East Asian Institutions of Higher Learning		**ASBS**	Association of Social and Behavioral Scientists (U.S.A.)
ASAIO	American Society for Artificial Internal Organs			
ASAJA	Asociación Sudamericana de Jueces de Atletismo		**ASBU**	Arab States Broadcasting Union
			ASC	Aardappel Studie Centrum
ASAM	American Society for Abrasive Methods		**ASC**	American Society of Cinematographers
ASAO	Association for Social Anthropology in Oceania (Hawaii)		**ASC**	American Society of Cybernetics
			ASC	American Society of Cytology
ASAP	American Society of Animal Production		**ASC**	Association Suisse des Entreprises de Transport à Câbles
ASAP	Arab Socialist Action Party			
ASAP	Australian Society of Animal Production		**ASC**	Associazione Svizzera dei Critici Cinematografica
ASAS	American Society of Abdominal Surgery			
ASAS	American Society of Agricultural Sciences		**ASC**	Conferencia Socialista Asiatica
ASAS	American Society of Animal Science		**ASCA**	Association for Science Cooperation in Asia
ASAS	Association of South-East Asian States		**ASCAN**	Asociación Canaria para Defensa de la Naturaleza (Canary Islands)
ASAS	Association Suisse des Assistants Sociaux			
ASATA	Associazione Svizzera per le Attrezzature Tecniche Agricole		**ASCAP**	American Society of Composers, Authors and Publishers
ASATOM	Association pour les Stages et l'Accueil des Techniciens d'Outre-Mer		**ASCAP**	Association Suisse pour le Commerce et l'Art Photographique
ASAUK	African Studies Association of the United Kingdom		**ASCAR**	Anglo-Soviet Co-operation on Agricultural Research
			ASCAR	Associaçao Sulina de Crédito e Assistência Rural (Brazil)
ASAVPA	Association de Salariés de l'Agriculture pour la Vulgarisation du Progrès Agricole		**ASCATEP**	Arab States Centre for Educational Planning and Administration
ASAWI	African Studies Association of the West Indies (Jamaica)		**ASCBF**	Association pour la Sélection et la Création de Betteraves Fourragères

SCC	Australian Society of Cosmetic Chemists
SCDH	Association Scientifique pour la Culture et le Développement de l'Hydroponique
SCE	American Society of Civil Engineers
SCE	Asian Society for Comparative Education (Iran)
SCEA	American Society of Civil Engineers and Architects
SCHIMICI	Associazione Nazionale dell' Industria Chimica
SCI	American Society for Clinical Investigation
SCIM	Association of Casing Importers
SCL	American Sugar Cane League of the U.S.A.
SCM	Association of Ships Compositions Manufacturers
SCM	Association of Steel Conduit Manufacturers
SCN	American Society for Clinical Nutrition
SCN	Association Suisse des Constructeurs Navals
SCO	American Society on Contemporary Ophthalmology
SCO	Association Suisse des Conseils en Organisation et Gestion
SCO	Association Suisse des Tenaciers de Cafés – Concerts
SCOBEL	Association Belge des Conseils en Organisation et Gestion
SCOFAM	Association Mondiale de Lutte Contre la Faim
SCOLBI	Asociación Colombiana de Bibliotecarios
SCOLPA	Asociación Colombiana de Cultivadores de Papa
SCOLSI	Asociación Colombiana de Sistemas
sCoMA	Associazione Nazionale Commercianti di Macchine Agricole
SCOMACE	Association des Constructeurs de Machines à Coudre de la CEE
SCP	American Society of Clinical Pathologists
SCP	American Society of Consultant Pharmacists
SCPI	Association Suisse des Conseils en Propriété Industrielle
SCREMON	Association Professionnelle des Créateurs Belge et Monopolistes de Créateurs Étrangers de Variétés de Plantes
SCTA	Association of Short-Circuit Testing Authorities
SCUN	Asociación Colombiana de Universidades

ASCV	Association Suisse des Entreprises de Chauffage et de Ventilation
AScW	Association of Scientific Workers (now ASTMS)
ASCWSA	Association of Scientific Workers of South Africa
ASD	Association Suisse de Documentation
ASD	Association Suisse des Droguistes
ASDA	Association Suisse de Droit Aérien et Spatial
ASDAN	Association Suisse de la Diététique et de l'Alimentation
ASDAR	Association pour la Selection et le Développement des Animaux de Race
ASDB	Asian Development Bank
ASDBAM	Association Sénégalaise pour le Développement de la Documentation, des Bibliothèques, des Archives et des Musées
ASDIC	Allied Submarine-Detection Investigation Committee
ASDSFB	Association of Scottish District Salmon Fishery Boards
ASDT	Association Suisse des Détaillants en Textiles
ASE	Admiralty Signal Establishment
ASE	Agence Spatiale Européenne
ASE	Amalgamated Society of Engineers
ASE	American Society of Enologists
ASE	Association for Science Education
ASE	Association Suisse des Électriciens
ASE	Association Suisse des Ergothérapeutes
ASE	Association Suisse des Experts – Comptables
ASE	Astronomical Society of Edinburgh
ASEA	Allmänna Svenska Elektriska Aktiobolaget
ASEA	American Society of Engineers and Architects
ASEA	Association Suisse des Électriciens sur Automobiles
ASEA	Associazione Svizzera di Economia delle Acque (Switzerland)
ASEA	Australian Society for Education through Art
ASEAI	Association Suisse des Experts Automobiles Indépendants
ASEAN	Association of South East Asian Nations (Thailand)
ASEAP	Association of South East Asian Publishers
ASEAS	Association Suisse pour l'Essai et l'Approvisionnement en Semenceaux des Pommes de Terre

ASECNA	Agence pour la Sécurité de la Navigation Aérienne en Afrique et Madagascar
ASECOLDA	Asociación Colombiana de Compañias de Seguros
ASEE	American Society for Engineering Education
ASEE	Association of Supervisory and Executive Engineers
ASEF	Association Suisse d'Économie Forestière
ASEF	Association Suisse des Entreprises de Forage
ASEG	Association Suisse des Entrepreneurs Généraux
ASEG	Associazione Svizzera degli Editori di Giornali
ASEIB	Asociación de Egresados de la Escuela Interamericana de Bibliotecologia (Colombia)
ASEJ	Association Suisse des Éditeurs de Journaux
ASELCA	Spanish Association Against Air Pollution
ASELF	Asociación Española de Lucha Contra et Fuego
ASELT	European Association for the Exchange of Technical Literature in the Field of Ferrous Metallurgy
ASEMOLP-RO	Asociación Nacional de Molineros de Arroz (Colombia)
ASEN	Association Suisse des Entrepreneurs en Nettoyage
ASEO	Associazion Svizra per l'Economia de las Ovas
ASEP	American Society of Electroplated Plastics
ASEP	American Society for Experimental Pathology
ASEPD	Association Suisse pour l'Étude des Problèmes Démographiques
ASEPELT	European Association for Medium and Long Term Economic Forecasting
ASERJ	Association Sénégalaise d'Études et de Recherches Juridiques (Senegal)
ASET	Association Suisse pour l'Étude des Transports
ASET	Association Suisse pour l'Étude du Travail
ASETA	Asociación de Empresas Estatales de Telecommunicaciones del Acuerdo Sub Regional Andino (Ecuador)
ASETA	Association Suisse pour l'Équipement Technique de l'Agriculture
ASF	Albatros Superfosfaat-fabrieken N.V. te Utrecht
ASF	Association des Selectionneurs Français
ASF	Association Suisse des Fonderies de Fer
ASFA	American Science Film Association
ASFAC	Regional Centre for Functional Literacy in Rural Areas in the Arab States
ASFAID	American Association for Artificial Internal Organs
ASFALEC	Association des Fabricants de Laits de Conserve des Pays de la CEE
ASFB	Australian Society for Fish Biology
ASFBT	Association Suisse des Fabricants de Briques et Juiles
ASFC	Association Suisse des Fabricants de Cigarettes
ASFD	Azienda di Stato per le Foreste Demaniali
ASFEC	Arab States Fundamental Education Centre (Egypt)
ASFFI	Association des Sociétés et Fonds Françaises d'Investissement
ASFIL-COTON	Association Belge des Filateurs de Coton et de Fibres Connexes
ASFIS	Aquatic Sciences and Fisheries Information System (FAO/IOC)
ASFPH	Association Suisse des Fabricants de Pierres d'Horlogerie et Scientifiques
ASFSE	American Swiss Foundation for Scientific Exchange
ASG	Agrarsoziale Gesellschaft
ASG	Arbeitsgemeinschaft Schweizerischer Grafiker
ASG	Association Suisse des Gravières
ASGA	Association des Services Géologiques Africains
ASGB	Adlerian Society of Great Britain
ASGB	Aeronautical Society of Great Britain
ASGB	Anthroposophical Society in Great Britain
ASGBI	Anatomical Society of Great Britain and Ireland
ASGC	Associazione Svizzera dei Grossisti di Carta
ASGE	American Society for Gastrointestinal Endoscopy
ASGP	Association Suisse des Grossistes en Papier
ASGROW	Associated Seed Growers, Inc. (U.S.A.)
ASH	Action on Smoking and Health
ASH	American Society of Haematology
ASH	Association Suisse des Horlogers

ASH	Association Suisse des Horticulteurs
ASHA	American School Health Association
ASHA	American Social Hygiene Association
ASHBA	American Saddle Horse Breeders Association
ASHG	American Society of Human Genetics
ASHRAE	American Society of Heating, Refrigerating and Air-conditioning Engineers
ASHR	Association Suisse des Ateliers d'Héliographie et de Reprographie
ASHS	American Society for Horticultural Science
ASHVE	American Society of Heating and Ventilating Engineers
ASI	Air Service Ivoirien
ASI	Asian Statistical Institute
ASI	Association Soroptimiste Internationale
ASI	Association Stomatologique Internationale
ASI	Association Suisse des Inventeurs et des Détenteurs de Brevets
ASIA	Airlines Staff International Association
ASIA	Association Scientifique Internationale d'Auriculothérapie
ASIA	Association Suisse de l'Industrie Aéronautique
ASIAG	Association Interprofessionnelle de l'Aviation Agricole
ASIAT	Association Suisse des Ingénieurs Agronomes et des Ingénieurs en Technologie Alimentaire
ASIB	Association Suisse de l'Industrie du Bois
ASIC	Association Scientifique Internationale du Café
ASIC	Association Suisse des Ingénieurs-Conseils
ASICA	Association Internationale pour le Calcul Analogique
ASICH	Confederación Cristiana de Trabajadores de Chile
ASID	American Society of Industrial Designers
ASID	Association Suisse des Infirmières et Infirmiers Diplomés
ASIDIC	Association of Scientific Information Dissemination Centers (U.S.A.)
ASIE	American Society of International Executives
ASIF	Amateur Swimming International Federation
ASIFA	Association Internationale du Film d'Animation
ASIH	American Society of Ichthyologists and Herpetologists

ASIHG	Association Suisse des Importateurs d'Huiles de Graissage
ASII	American Science Information Institute
ASIIA	Adlai Stevenson Institute of International Affairs (U.S.A.)
ASIL	American Society of International Law
ASIL	Associazione Italiana di Studio del Lavoro
ASILP	Associazione Svizzera degli Impresari di Lavori Pubblica e del Genio Civile (Switzerland)
ASILS	Association of Student International Law Societies (U.S.A.)
ASIM	American Society of Internal Medicine
ASINAPLA	Agrupación Sindical Nacional de Plaguicidas
ASIO	Australian Security and Intelligence Organisation
ASIP	Asociación Interamericana de Presupuesto Publico (Venezuela)
ASIPI	Association Interaméricaine de Propriété Industrielle
ASIPLA	Asociación de Industrias Plasticas (Chile)
ASIRA	Associazione Svizzera delle Imprese di Riscaldamento e di Aerazione
ASIRC	Aquatic Sciences Information Retrieval Center (U.S.A.)
ASIS	American Society for Information Science
ASIS	Asociación Internacional de la Sintesis
ASIS	Association for the Study of Internal Secretions (U.S.A.)
ASIT	Asociatia Stiintifica a Inginerilor si Tehnicienilor (Roumania)
ASJA	Association Suisse des Journalistes Agricoles
ASJLP	Association Suisse de Journalists Libres Professionnels
ASJS	Association Suisse des Journalistes Sportifs
ASKI	Arbeitsgemeinschaft der Schweizerischen Kunststoff-Industrie
ASL	Association Suisse des Entreprises de Linoleum et des Sols Spéciaux
ASL	Australian Society for Limnology
ASL	Avelsföreningen för Svensk Låglandsboskap
ASLA	American Society of Landscape Architects
ASLA	Australian School Library Association
ASLE	American Society of Lubrication Engineers
ASLEC	Association of Street Lighting Erection Contractors
ASLEF	Associated Society of Locomotive Engineers and Firemen

ASLEP	Asociación de Sociólogos de Lengua Española y Portuguesa
ASLIB	Association of Special Libraries and Information Bureaux
ASLIC	Indian Association of Special Libraries and Documentation Centres
ASLO	American Society of Limnology and Oceanography
ASLO	Australian Scientific Liaison Office
ASLP	Amalgamated Society of Lithographic Printers
ASLP	Association of Special Libraries of the Philippines
ASLW	Amalgamated Society of Leather Workers
ASM	Aktionsgemeinschaft Soziale Marktwirtschaft
ASM	American Society of Mammalogists
ASM	American Society for Microbiology
ASM	American Society for Metals
ASM	Arbeitgeberverband Schweizerischer Maschinen-und Metall-Industrieller
ASM	Association for Systems Management (U.S.A.)
ASMA	Arizona State Medical Association (U.S.A.)
ASMA	Association de Médecine Aéronautique et Spatiale
ASMAF	Association Scientifique des Médecins Acupuncteurs de France
ASMAP	Association of Soviet International Road Carriers
ASMAS	Association Suisse des Magasins d'Articles de Sport
ASMC	Association Suisse des Maîtres Coiffeurs
ASMC	Association Suisse des Maîtres Couvreurs
ASMCBO	Association Suisse des Maîtres-Cordonniers et Bottiers-Orthopédistes
ASME	American Society of Mechanical Engineers
ASME	Association for the Study of Medical Education
ASME	Association Suisse des Marchands d'Engrais
ASMECCA-NICA	Associazione Nazionale di Meccanica
ASMET	Arbeitsgemeinschaft Schweizerischer Metallmöbelfabrikanten
ASMEVEZ	Asociación Nacional de Médicos Veterinarios Zootecnistas (Colombia)
ASMFA	Association Suisse des Maîtres Ferblantiers et Appareilleurs
ASMFC	Atlantic States Marine Fisheries Commission
ASMFE	International Association of Soil Mechanics and Foundation Engineering
ASMG	Association Suisse des Marchands-Grainiers
ASMH	Association Suisse des Manufactures d'Horlogerie
ASMI	Associazione Stampa Medica Italiana
ASMIC	Association pour l'Organisation des Missions de Cooperation Technique
ASMM	Associazione Svizzera dei Maestri Meccanici
ASMMA	American Supply and Machinery Manufacturers Association
ASMMB	Association Suisse des Marchands de Machines à Ecrire et de Bureau
ASMMC	Association Suisse des Marchands de Matériaux de Construction
ASMO	Arab Organisation for Standardisation and Metrology
ASMP	American Society of Magazine Photographers
ASMP	Association Suisse des Marchands de Poissons
ASMPP	Association Suisse des Maîtres Plâtriers-Peintres
ASMS	American Society of Maxillofacial Surgeons
ASMS	American-Soviet Medical Society
ASMT	American Society of Medical Technologists
ASMT	Association Suisse des Maîtres Tapissiers-Décorateurs, Revêtements de Sols et des Maisons d'Ameublements
ASMT	Association Suisse de Microtechnique
ASN	American Society of Naturalists
ASNE	American Society of Naval Engineers
ASNE	American Society of Newspaper Editors
ASNEF	Agrupación Sindical Nacional de Empresas de Financiación de Ventas a Plazos
ASNEMGE	Association des Sociétés Nationales Européennes et Méditerranéennes de Gastroentérologie
ASNF	Association Suisse des Négociants en Fourrage
ASNIBI	Asociación Nicaraguense de Bibliotecarios
ASNIP	Associazione Sindacale Nazionale dell'Industria Petrolifera
ASNK	Association Suisse des Négociants de Kiosques

SNP	Association Suisse de Négociants en Timbres-Poste
SO	American Society for Oceanography
SO	Association Suisse des Opticians
SOCANA	Asociación Nacional de Cultivadores de Caña de Azúcar (Colombia)
SOCESAR	Association of Cotton Growers of Cesar (Colombia)
SODOBI	Asociación Dominicana de Bibliotecarios
SOM	Académie des Sciences d'Outre-Mer
SOMER	Association des Salaries des Organismes de Migration et d'Establissement Ruraux
SONIDA	Asociación Nacional de Industriales del Arroz (Venezuela)
SOS	Association Suisse d'Organisation Scientifique
SOSP	Association Suisse pour l'Orientation Scolaire et Professionnelle
SOVAC	Asociación Venezolana para el Avance de la Ciencia
SP	American Society of Parasitologists
SP	American Society of Pharmacognosy
SP	American Society of Photogrammetry
SP	Association Professionnelle Suisse des Commerçants en Peinture
SP	Association Scientifique de la Précontrainte
SP	Association of Self-Employed Persons
SP	Association Suisse des Pédicures
SP	Association Suisse du Pneu
SP	Association Suisse de Publicité
SP	Astronomical Society of the Pacific (U.S.A.)
SPA	American Society for Personnel Administration
SPA	American Society for Public Administration
SPA	Association Suisse des Propriétaires d'Autocamions
SPA	Australian Sugar Producers' Association
SPA	Syndicat National des Fabricants d'Agents de Surface et Produits Auxiliaires Industriels
SPAC	Asian and Pacific Council
SPACA	Asian and Pacific Cultural Association (Korea)
SPADS	Associated Sheep, Police and Army Dog Society
SPAM	Association des Producteurs d'Agrumes du Maroc
ASPAN	Association Suisse pour le Plan d'Aménagement National (Switzerland)
ASPAU	African Scholarship Program of American Universities
ASPB	Algemene Schoorsteenvegers Patroonsbond
ASPB	American Society of Professional Biologists
ASPB	Asian Student Press Bureau
ASPB	Arbeitsgemeinschaft der Spezialbibliotheken
ASPBAE	Asian-South Pacific Bureau of Adult Education (India)
ASPC	American Sheep Producers Council
ASPC	Association Suisse des Philologues Classiques
ASPCA	American Society for the Prevention of Cruelty to Animals
ASPE	Association des Firmes représentant en Suisse des Spécialités Pharmaceutiques Étrangères à Marques Déposées
ASPEA	Association Suisse pour l'Énergie Atomique
ASPEC	Association pour la Prévention et l'Étude de la Contamination
ASPEE	Association Suisse des Professionnels de l'Épuration des Eaux
ASPESCA	Asociación Colombiana de Pescadores
ASPET	American Society for Pharmacology and Experimental Therapeutics
ASPF	Australian Society of Perfumers and Flavourists
ASPFAV	Associazione Svizzera dei Produttori di Films e Audiovisivi
ASPHER	Association of Schools of Public Health in the European Region
ASPI	Arbeitsgeberverband Schweizerischer Papier-Industrieller
ASPI	Asociación Publicitaria Internacional (Honduras)
ASPLA	Agrupacion Sindical de Pilotes de Líneas Aéreas
ASPM	Association of Surgeons and Physicians of Malta
ASPO	American Society of Planning Officials
ASPO	American Society for Psychoprophylaxis in Obstetrics
ASPP	American Society of Plant Physiologists
ASPP	Association Suisse de Photographes de Presse
ASPPR	Association of Sugar Producers of Puerto Rico

ASPQ	Association Suisse pour la Promotion de la Qualité
ASPR	American Society for Psychical Research
ASPRAM	Association des Producteurs d'Agrumes du Maroc
ASPRS	American Society of Plastic and Reconstructive Surgery
ASPS	African Succulent Plant Society
ASPT	American Society of Plant Taxonomists
ASQ	Deutsche Gesellschaft für Qualität
ASQC	American Society for Quality Control
ASR	Arbeitskreis Freier Sanitär-Röhrenhändler
ASR	Association Suisse des Romanistes
ASRA	American Shropshire Registry Association
ASRC	Atmospheric Sciences Research Center (U.S.A.)
ASRCT	Applied Scientific Research Corporation of Thailand
ASRD	Astronomy, Space and Radio Division (*of* SRC)
ASRE	American Society of Refrigerating Engineers
ASRI	Academy of Sciences Research Institute (Ghana)
ASRLO	Australian Scientific Research Liaison Office
ASRM	American Association of Range Management
ASRO	Association Suisse de Recherche Opérationnelle
ASRT	Atlantic Salmon Research Trust
ASRZB	Annales de la Société Royale Zoologiques de Belgique
ASS	Asociación Salvadoreña de Sociologia
ASS	Association Suisse des Selectionneurs
ASSA	American Society for the Study of Arteriosclerosis
ASSA	Association for Sociology in Southern Africa (South Africa)
ASSA	Astronomical Association of South Africa
ASSA	Astronomical Society of South Australia
ASSALZOO	Associazione Nazionale fra i Produttori di Alimenti Zootecnici
ASSBRA	Association Belge des Brasseries
ASSBT	American Association of Sugar Beet Technologists
ASSCO	Associazione fra Società e Studi di Consulenza Organizzativa
ASSE	American Society of Safety Engineers
ASSE	American Society of Sanitary Engineering
ASSE	American Society of Swedish Engineers
ASSEDIC-COOP-AGRI	Association pour l'Emploi dans les Coopératives Agricoles
ASSELECTO	Association des Multiplicateurs de Graines Selectionées de Tomates
ASSET	Association of Supervisory Staffs, Executives and Technicians
ASSETERIE	Associazione Italiana Fabbricanti Seterie
ASSGB	Association of Ski Schools in Great Britain
ASSH	American Society for Surgery of the Hand
ASSICRED-ITO	Associazione Sindicale fra le Aziende del Credito
ASSIDER	Associazione Industrie Siderurgiche Italiana
ASSIFONTE	Association de l'Industrie de la Fonte de Fromage de la CEE
ASSILEC	Association de l'Industrie Laitière de la Communauté Européenne
ASSIN-FORM	Associazione Costruttori Macchine, Attrezzature per Ufficio e per il Trattamento delle Informazione
ASSINSEL	Association Internationale des Sélectionnels Professionels pour la Protection des Obtentions Végétales
ASSISTAL	Associazione Nazionale Installatori d'Impianti Termici e di Ventilazione, Idrici, Sanitari, Elettrici, Telefonici ed Affini
ASSITEJ	Association Internationale du Théâtre pour l'Enfance et la Jeunesse
ASSITOL	Associazione Italiana dell'Industria Olearia
ASSL	Associazione Svizzera per lo Studio del Lavoro
ASSMB	Association des Sociétés Scientifiques Médicales Belges
ASSNAS	Associazione Nazionale Assistenti Sociali
ASSOBAF	Société d'Intérêt Collectif Agricole (Guadeloupe)
ASSOBEST-IAME	Associazione Nazionale Commercianti Grossisti Esportatori Importatori di Bestiame e Carni
ASSOCAR-TA	Associazione Italiana fra gli Industriali della Carta, Cartoni e Paste per Carta
ASSOCASE-ARI	Associazione Nazionale Stagionatori e Grossisti de Prodotti Caseari
ASSOCDET-ERGENZA	Associazione Nationale dell'Industria della Saponeria, della Detergenza e dei Prodotti d'Igiene

ASSOCE-MENTO Associazione dell'Industria Italiana del Cemento, dell'Amiantocemento, della Calce e del Gesso

ASSOCHAM Associated Chambers of Commerce and Industry (India)

ASSOCO-MAPLAST Associazione Nazionale Costruttori Macchine per Materie Plastiche e Gomma

ASSOFAR-MA Associazione fra Industrie Chimico-Farmaceutiche

ASSOFER-MET Associazione Nationale dei Commercianti in Ferro e Acciai, Metalli non Ferrosi, Ferramenta e Affini, Rottami

ASSOFLUID Associazione dei Costruttori Italiani di Apparecchiature Oleodrauliche e Pneumatiche

ASSOFOND Associazione Nazionale delle Fonderie

ASSOGIO-CATTOLI Associazione Nazionale Fabbricanti Giocattoli

ASSOGOM-MA Associazione Nazionale fra le Industrie della Gomma, Cavi Elettrici ed Affini

ASSO-GRASSI Associazione Nationale Grassi Animali

ASSOITAL-PELLI Associazione Italiana fra i Commercianti di Pelli Grezze

ASSO-LAMPADE Associazione Nazionale Fabbricanti Lampade Elettriche, Valvole Termoioniche, Tubi Luminscenti, Bottiglie Isolanti, Apparecchi Termostatici

ASSO-LATTE Associazione Italiana Lattiero-Casearia

ASSOLIOS-EMI Associazione Nazionale fra gli Industriali degli Olii da Semi

ASSO-MARMI Associazione dell'Industria Marmifera Italiana e delle Industrie Affini

ASSOMET Associazione Nazionale Industrie Metalli non Ferrosi

ASSOMINE-RARIA Associazione Mineraria Italiana

ASSONAVE Associazione Nazionale fra Costruttori di Navi d'Alto Mare

ASSONIME Associazione Società Italiane per Azione

ASSONOT-AI Associazione Nazionale dei Notai

ASSO-PETROLI Associazione Nationale Commercio Petroli

ASSOPIAS-TRELLE Associazione Nationale dei Produttori di Piastrelle di Ceramica

ASSO-POMAC Association of Common Market Potato Breeders (Germany)

ASSO-POTER Associazione Nazionale Industriali Porcellane e Terraglie

ASSOSPAZ-ZOLE Associazione Nazionale Fabbricanti Spazzole, Pennelli e Preparatori Relative Materie Prime

ASSOSPORT Associazione Nazionale Produttori Articoli Sportivi

ASSOTTICA Associazione Nazionale Industriali dell' Ottica, Meccanica Fine e di Precisione

ASSOUOVA Associazione Nazionale fra Commercianti Grossisti Esportatori Importatori di Uova, Pollame e Affini

ASSP Association Suisse de Science Politique

ASSPA Association Suisse pour l'Automatisme

ASSPA Associaziun Svizra dils Specialists dalla Purificaziun d'Aqua

ASSPLV Association des Sociétés Suisses des Professeurs de Langues Vivantes

ASSS American Society for the Study of Sterility

ASSS American Suffolk Sheep Society

ASST American Society for Steel Treating

ASST Associazione Svizzera per lo Studio degli Trasporti

ASSUC Association des Organisations Professionnelles du Commerce des Sucres pour les Pays de la CEE

AST Association Suisse des Marchands de Tapis

AST Association Suisse de Thanatologie

AST Astronomical Society of Tasmania

ASTA American Seed Trade Association

ASTA American Spice Trade Association

ASTA American Society of Travel Agents

ASTA American Surgical Trade Association

ASTA Auckland Science Teachers Association

ASTC Administrative Section for Technical Cooperation (UNO)

ASTC Associazione Svizzera dei Tecnici-Catastali

ASTD American Society for Training and Development

ASTE American Society of Tool Engineers

ASTE Association pour le Développement des Sciences et Techniques de l'Environnement

ASTE Association for Study of Soviet-Type Economics (U.S.A.)

ASTEA Associazione Svizzera Tecnici Epurazione Acque

ASTED	Association pour l'Avancement des Sciences et des Techniques de la Documentation (Canada)
ASTEF	Association pour l'Organisation des Stages en France
ASTEL	Association de Spécialistes de Techniques d'Enseignement du Langage
ASTEM	Association Scientifique et Technique pour l'Exploitation des Mers
ASTEO	Association Scientifique et Technique pour l'Exploitation des Océans
ASTG	Association Suisse des Techniciens-Géomètres
ASTI	Association Suisse des Traducteurs et Interprètes
ASTIA	Armed Services Technical Information Agency (U.S.A.)
ASTIC	Agrupación Sindical del Transporte Internacional por Carretera
ASTM	American Society for Testing and Materials
ASTM	American Society of Tropical Medicine
ASTM	Association of Sanitary Towel Manufacturers
ASTME	American Society of Tool Manufacturing Engineers
ASTMH	American Society of Tropical Medicine and Hygiene
ASTMS	Association of Scientific, Technical and Managerial Staffs
ASTP	Association des Entrepreneurs Suisses de Travaux Publics
ASTRID	Association Scientifique et Technique pour la Recherche en Informatique Documentaire (Belgium)
ASTS	Association Suisse pour la Technique du Soudage
ASTUC	Anglo-Soviet Trades Union Committee
ASU	Arbeitsgemeinschaft Selbständiger Unternehmer
ASUA	Amateur Swimming Union of the Americas
ASV	Arbeitsgemeinschaft Schweizer Volkstanzkreise
ASVILMET	Associazione Italiani per lo Sviluppo degli Studi Sperimentali sulla Lavorazione dei Metalli
ASVPP	American Society of Veterinary Physiologists and Pharmacologists
ASVS	Anotera Scholi Viomichanikon Spouden
ASW	Allianz Schweizerischer Werbeberater
ASWEA	Association for Social Work Education in Africa (Ethiopia)
ASXRT	American Society of X-Ray Technicians
ASYBEL	Syndicat Belge de l'Acide Sulfurique
ASZ	American Society of Zoologists
AT	Autotuojat
ATA	Advertising Typographers Association of America
ATA	Air Transport Association of America
ATA	Air Transport Association
ATA	American Translators Association
ATA	American Transport Association
ATA	American Transit Association
ATA	American Tree Association
ATA	American Trucking Association
ATA	Animal Technicians Association
ATA	Associazione Tecnica dell'Automobile
ATA	Atlantic Treaty Association
ATAB	Association des Détaillants en Tabacs (Belgium)
ATABW	American Trade Association for British Woollens
ATAC	Air Transport Advisory Council
ATAC	Air Transport Association of Canada
ATAC	Asociación de Tecnicos Azucareros de Cuba
ATAF	Association Internationale de Transporteurs Aériens
ATAFEG	Austria Tabakeinlöse und Fermentionsgesellschaft
ATALA	Association pour l'Étude et le Développement de la Traduction Automatique et de la Linguistique Appliquée
ATAM	Asociación de Técnicos en Alimentos de México
ATAM	Association of Teaching Aids in Mathematics
ATAR	Association des Transporteurs Aériens Régionaux
ATAV	Association Technique pour l'Amelioration de la Viticulture (*now* ANTAV)
ATAVE	Asociación de Técnicos Azucareros de Venezuela
ATB	Agricultural Training Board
ATB	Arbeidertoeristenbond
ATB	Association of Tropical Biology (Costa Rica)
ATC	African Timber Company

ATC	Agence Transcongolaise des Communications
ATC	Association Européenne des Cadres Commerciaux et Technico-commerciaux
ATC	Vereniging van Automobieltechnici
ATCAS	African Training Centre for Agricultural Statistics (*of* FAO) (Nigeria)
ATCC	American Type Culture Collection
ATCDE	Association of Teachers in College and Departments of Education
ATCEU	Air Traffic Control Experimental Unit
ATCP	Asociación Mexicana de Técnicos de las Industrias de la Celulosa y del Papel
ATD	Association of Tar Distillers
ATD	Association Tunisienne des Documentalistes, Bibliothécaires et Archivistes
ATDA	Australian Telecommunications Development Association
ATDC	Asociacion Técnica de Derivados del Cemento
ATE	Automatic Telephone and Electric Company
ATEA	American Technical Education Association
ATeAC	Associazione Tecnica dell'Acciaio per Costruzioni Civili
ATEC	Agence Transequatoriale de Communications (Central Africa)
ATEC	Air Transport Electronics Council
ATECMA	Agrupación Técnica Española de Constructores de Material Aeroespacial
ATEFI	Associazione Tecnica delle Società Finanziarie
ATEFL	Association of Teachers of English and Foreign Languages (*now* IATEFL)
ATEG	Asociación Técnica Española de Galvanización
ATEGIP	Association Technique pour l'Étude de la Gestion des Institutions Publiques et des Entreprises Privées
ATEN	Association Technique pour l'Énergie Nucléaire
ATF	Association Technique de Fonderie
ATFB	Association Technique de Fonderie de Belgique
ATFS	Association of Track and Field Statisticians
ATG	Association Technique de l'industrie du Gaz en France
ATI	American Television Incorporated

ATI	Association of Technical Institutions (*now* ACFHE)
ATI	Associazione Trafiliere Italiani
ATI	Azienda Tabacchi Italiani
ATIBT	Association Technique pour l'Importation des Bois Tropicaux
ATIC	Associação Tecnica da Indústria do Cimento (Portugal)
ATIC	Association Technique pour l'Importation du Charbon en France
ATIC	Association Technique de l'Industrie du Chauffage de la Ventilation et des Branches Connexes (Belgium)
ATIC	Associazione Tecnica Italiana per la Cinematografia
ATIC	Australian Tin Information Centre
ATICELCA	Associazione Tecnica Italiana per la Cellulosa e per la Carta
ATICPA	Asociación de Tecnicos de la Industria Papelara e Celulosa Argentina
ATIFAS	Associazione Tessiture Italiana Fibre Artificiali e Sintetiche
ATIP	Association Technique de l'Industrie Papetière
ATIPCA	Asociación de Técnicos de la Industria Papelera y Celulósica Argentina
ATIPIC	Association des Technicians de l'Industrie des Peintures et des Industries Connexes
ATIRA	Ahmedabad Textile Industry's Research Association (India)
ATISEA	Associazione Tappezzori in Stoffa e Affini
ATL	American Tariff League
ATL	Autoriserte Trafikkskolers Landsforbund
ATLAS	Agrupacion de Trabajordes Latinoamericanos Sindicalistes
ATLB	Air Transport Licensing Board
ATLF	Association des Traducteurs Littéraires de France
ATLIS	Army Technical Libraries and Information Systems (U.S.A.)
ATM	Association of Teachers of Management
ATMA	Adhesive Tape Manufacturers Association
ATMA	American Textile Machinery Association
ATMA	American Textile Manufacturers Association
ATMA	Association Technique, Maritime et Aéronautique

ATME	Association International pour la Promotion des Techniques Modernes d'Enseignement
ATMI	American Textile Manufacturers Institute
ATO	African Telecommunications Union
ATO	Antarctic Treaty Organization
ATO	Arbeitskreis Topinambur
ATOA	American Tung Oil Association
ATOCI	Association de Traducteurs et Réviseurs des Organisations et Conférences Intergouvernementales
ATOI	Alliance Touristique de l'Océan Indien
ATOM	Association d'Aide aux Travailleurs d'Outre-Mer
ATONU	Assistance Technique de l'Organisation des Nations Unies
ATP	Association of Tennis Professionals
ATP	Association for Transpersonal Psychology (U.S.A.)
ATPAS	Association of Teachers of Printing and Allied Subjects
ATPI	American Textbook Publishers Institute
ATPUL	Association Technique pour la Production et l'Utilisation du Lin et Autres Fibres Liberiennes
ATR	Association Technique de la Route
ATREM	Association Technique de la Refrigération et de l'Équipement Ménager
ATRIH	Association des Transporteurs Routiers Internationaux en Hongrie (Hungary)
ATS	Agence Télégraphique Suisse
ATS	American Television Society
ATS	American Thoracic Society
ATS	American Therapeutic Society
ATS	American Thyroid Society
ATS	American Travel Service
ATS	Association Technique de la Sidérurgie Française
ATS	Atomtekniska Sällskapet i Finland
ATS	Suomen Atomiteknillinen Seura
ATSA	Aero Transportes, South America
ATSA	Association des Techniciens Supérieurs Agricoles
AT & T	American Telephone and Telegraph Company
ATTA	American Tin Trade Association
ATTI	Association of Teachers in Technical Institutions
ATU	African Telecommunication Union
ATU	Arab Tourism Union (Jordan)
ATUC	African Trade Union Confederation
ATV	Abwassertechnische Vereinigung
ATV	Agence de Transit et de Voyages (Central Africa)
ATV	Akademiet for de Tekniske Videnskaber
ATV	Associated Television Corporation
ATVF	Association Technique pour la Vulgarisation Forestière
ATWA	Association of Third World Affairs (U.S.A.)
ATYPI	Association Typographique Internationale
AUA	American Unitarian Association
AUA	American Urological Association
AUA	Associated Unions of America
AUA	Association des Universités Africaines
AUA	Austrian Airlines
AUALPA	Austrian Airline Pilots Association
AUAW	Amalgamated Union of Asphalt Workers
AUB	American University of Beirut
AUBC	Association of Universities of the British Commonwealth
AUBTW	Amalgamated Union of Building Trade Workers (*now* UCATT)
AUC	Auckland University College (N.Z.)
AUCC	Association of Universities and Colleges of Canada
AUCCTU	All-Union Central Council of Trade Unions (U.S.S.R.)
AUDAVI	Asociación Uruguaya de Agencias de Viajes Internacionales
AUDECAM	Association Universitaire pour le Développement de l'Enseignement et de la Culture en Afrique et à Madagascar
AUDI	Société Internationale d'Audiologie
AUDIVIR	Conseil International pour l'Application des Moyens Audio-Visuels à l'Environnement
AUE	Association des Universitaires d'Europe
AUEW	Amalgamated Union of Engineering and Foundry Workers
AUFM	Asociación Universal de Federalistas Mundiales
AUFS	American Universities Field Staff
AUFW	Amalgamated Union of Foundry Workers (*now* AUEW)

AUGB	Association of Ukrainians in Great Britain Ltd.	AVARD	Association of Voluntary Agencies for Rural Development (India)
AUI	Action d'Urgence Internationale	AVAS	Association of Voluntary Action Scholars (U.S.A.)
AUI	Associated Universities, Inc. (U.S.A.)		
AULA	Arab University Library Association	AVASS	Association of Voluntary Aided Secondary Schools
AULLA	Australasian Universities Language and Literature Association	AVB	Afdeling Agrarische Vertegenwoordiging Buitenland
AUMA	Ausstellungs- und Messe-Ausschuss der Deutschen Wirtschaft	AVB	Autorité pour l'Aménagement de la Vallée du Bandama (Ivory Coast)
AUMLA	Australian Universities Modern Language Association (now AULLA)	AVBB	Algemeen Verbond Bouwbedrijft
AUO	African Unity Organisation	AVC	Asociación Venezolana de Caficultores (Venezuela)
AUOD	Alliance Universelle des Ouvriers Diamantaires	AVC	Association of Vitamin Chemists (U.S.A.)
AUPELF	Association des Universités Partiellement ou Entièrement de Langue Française (Canada)	AVCFOM	Association des Villages Communautaires de France d'Outre-Mer
AURA	Association of Universities for Research in Astronomy (U.S.A.)	AFCGC	Asociación Venezolana de Criadores de Ganada Cebú (Venezuela)
AUREG	Association de Recherches Géographiques et Cartographiques	AVCZ	Algemeen Verbond der Cooperatieve Zuivelfabrieken (Belgium)
AURP	American Universities Research Program	AVDA	American Venereal Disease Association
AUSPICE	Association of University Staff to Promote Inter-University Cooperation in Europe (France)	AVDA	Asociación Venezolana de Derecho Agrario
		AVDBAD	Association Voltaique pour le Développement des Bibliothèques, des Archives et de la Documentation
AUT	Association of University Teachers	AVE	Asociación Venezolana de Ejecutivos
AUTEC	Atlantic Underwater Test Evaluation Centre	AVE	Association for Volunteer Service in Europe
AUTIG	Auto-Tilbehørs Grossist-Foreningen	AVE	Aussenhandelsvereinigung des Deutschen Einzelhandels
AUTOVIA	Autotransport-Gewerbeverband der Schweiz	AVEC	Asociación Venezolana Educación Católica
AUWE	Admiralty Underwater Weapons Establishment	AVEC	Association des Centres d'Abbatage de Volailles et du Commerce d'Importation et d'Exportation de Volailles des Pays de la EEC
AUXIMAD	Société Auxiliaire Maritime de Madagascar	AVEN-CULTA	Asociación Venezolana de Cultivadores de Tabaco
AVA	Aan en Verkoopbureau van Akkerbouwproducten	AVENEX-CAF	Asociación Venezolana de Exportadores de Café
AVA	Academy of Visual Arts	AVENSA	Aerovias Venezonalas, South America
AVA	Alberta Veterinary Association (Canada)	AVEX	Asociación Venezolana de Exportadores
AVA	Algemene Vereniging voor de Nederlandse Aardewerken Glasindustrie	AVF	Académie Vétérinaire de France
AVA	Amateur Volleyball Association (now EVA)	AVG	Asociación Venezolana de Ganaderos
AVA	American Vocational Association	AVGI	Algemene Vereniging van de Geneesmiddelenindustrie (Belgium)
AVA	Asociación Vitivinícola Argentina		
AVA	Atlantic Visitors Association (Belgium)	AVGMP	Asociación Venezolana de Geología, Minas y Petróleo
AVA	Australian Veterinary Association		
AVAB	Automatic Vending Association of Britain	AVHA	Association Vétérinaire d'Hygiène Alimentaire
AVAL	Association pour les Ventes dans Alimentation		

AVI	Arbeitsgemeinschaft der Eisen- und Metallverarbeitenden Industrie
AVI	Association Universelle d'Aviculture Scientifique
AVIANCA	Aerovías Nacionales de Colombia
AVIEAS	Asociación Venezolana de Instituciones de Educación Agrícola Superior
AVIEM	Asociación Venezolana de Ingeneiria Eléctrica y Mécanica
AVIFIA	Congrès International sur les Applications Nouvelles du Vide et du Froid dans les Industries Alimentaires
AVIJ	Algemene Vereniging voor de Ijzerhandel
AvJ	Arbeitsgemeinschaft von Jugendbuchvelegern in der Bundesrepublik Deutschland
AVK	Arbeitsgemeinschaft Verstärke Kunststoffe
AVLA	Audio Visual Language Association
AVM	Algemene Vereeniging voor Melkvoorziening
AVM	Association des Fabricants de Verres de Montres (Switzerland)
AVMA	American Veterinary Medical Association
AVMA	Automatic Vending Machine Association
AVMD	Algemene Vereniging van Leraren bij Voorbereidend Wetenschappelijk en Algemeen Voortgezet Onderwijs
AVNEG	Algemene Vereniging van Nederlandse Gieterijen
AVPA	Asociación Venezolana de Peritos Agropecuarios
AVPC	Asociación Venezolana de Productores de Cacao
AVRA	Audio-Visual Research Foundation (U.S.A.)
AVRAC	Agricultural and Veterinary Research Advisory Committee (East Africa)
AVRDC	Asian Vegetable Research and Development Centre, Taipei
AVRO	Algemene Vereniging Radio-Omroep
AVRS	American Veterinary Radiology Society
AVS	American Vacuum Society
AVS	Association of Veterinary Students of Great Britain and Ireland
AVS	Autovermieter-Verband der Schweiz
AVTRW	Association of Veterinary Teachers and Research Workers
AVV	L'Autorité d'Aménagement des Vallées des Volta (Upper Volta)
AVVE	Assemblee der Versklavten Völker Europas
AVVL	Algemeen Verbond van Leerkrachten (Belgium)
AVVN	Algemene Vereniging van Naaimachinenhandelaren
AVWV	Antilliaans Verbond van Werknemers Verenigingen
AVZ	Algemene Vereniging voor de Teelt en Handel in Zaaizaad en Pootgoed (Netherlands)
AWA	Amalgamated Wireless (Australasia)
AWAM	Association of West African Merchants
AWAS	Australian Womens Army Service
AWB	Agricultural Wages Board
AWB	Australian Wool Board
AWBA	American World's Boxing Association
AWC	American Wool Council
AWCU	Association of World Colleges and Universities (U.S.A.)
AWE	Association for World Education (U.S.A.)
AWES	Association of Western Europe Shipbuilders
AWF	American Wildlife Foundation
AWF	Asian Weightlifting Federation
AWF	Ausschuss für Wirtschaftliche Fertigung
AWGC	Australian Woolgrowers and Graziers Council
AWHA	Australian Womens Home Army
AWIS	Association for Women in Science (U.S.A.)
AWIU	Aluminium Workers International Union (U.S.A.)
AWLA	Association of Welsh Local Authorities
AWLLA	All Wales Ladies Lacrosse Association
AWMF	Arbeitsgemeinschaft Wissenschaftlich-Medizinische Fachgesellschaften
AWMM	Arbeitsgemeinschaft für Werbung, Markt- und Meinungsforschung (Switzerland)
AWMPF	Australian Wool and Meat Producers Federation
AWN	Archaeologische Werkgemeenschap voor Nederland
AWNL	Australian Womens National League
AWPA	American Wood-Preservers' Association
AWR	Arbeitsgemeinschaft der Deutschen Werksredakteure
AWR	Association for the Study of the World Refugee Problem
AWRA	American Water Resources Association

AWRA	Australian Welding Research Association	BA	British Association for the Advancement of Science
AWRA	Australian Wool Realisation Agency	BAA	Booking Agents Association of Great Britain Ltd
AWRBIAC	Arkansas-White-Red Basins Inter-Agency Committee	BAA	British Acetylene Association (*now* BCGA)
AWRC	Australian Water Resources Council	BAA	British Agrochemicals Association
AWRC	Australian Wool Realisation Commission	BAA	British Aikido Association
AWRE	Atomic Weapons Research Establishment	BAA	British Alsatian Association
AWS	Agricultural Wholesale Society	BAA	British Anodising Association
AWS	Algemene Werksgeversorganisatie Schoonmaakbedrijven	BAA	British Archaeological Association
AWS	American Welding Society	BAA	British Astronomical Association
AWST	Association of Women Science Teachers (*now* ASE)	BAA & A	British Association of Accountants and Auditors
AWT	Arbeitsgemeinschaft für Wärmebehandlung und Werkstoff-Technik	BAAB	British Amateur Athletic Board
		BAAC	Bank for Agriculture and Agricultural Co-operatives (Thailand)
AWT	Arbeitsgemeinschaft für Wirkstoffe in der Tierernährung	BAAL	British Association of Applied Linguistics
AWTA	Association for World Travel Exchange	BAALPE	British Association of Advisers in Physical Education
AWTCE	Association of World Trade Chamber Executives (U.S.A.)	BAAS	British Association for the Advancement of Science
AWU	Agricultural Workers Union (South Africa)	BAAS	British Association for American Studies
AWU	Australian Workers Union	BAAT	British Association of Art Therapists
AWV	Algemene Werkgevers-Vereniging	BAB	Berufsverband Freischaffender Architekten und Bauingenieure
AWV	Amalgamated Wireless Valve Co. (Australia)	BAB	Bond van Aannemers in de Bouwnijverheid
AWV	Ausschuss Wirtschaftliche Verwaltung	BAB	British Airways Board
AWWA	American Water-Works Association	BABEX	Bond van Aannemers met Bevoegdheid voor Explosieven
AWWM	Association of Wholesale Woollen Merchants Ltd	BABF	British Amateur Baseball Federation
AWWV	Arbeitsgemeinschaft der Wasserwirtschafsverbande	BABS	British Aluminium Building Service
AYF	Arab Youth Federation (Egypt)	BABS	British Association for Brazing and Soldering
AYH	Academia Yucateca de Historia (Mexico)	BABW	Beratender Ausschuss für Bildungs- und Wissenschaftspolitik
AYRS	Amateur Yacht Research Society	BAC	Biblioteca Agropecuaria de Colombia
AZABDO	Association Zairoise des Archivistes, Bibliothécaires et Documentalistes	BAC	Block Advisory Committee (India)
AZRC	Arid Zone Research Centre (Australia)	BAC	Bois Africaines Contreplaques (Gabon)
AZRI	Arid Zone Research in Iraq	BAC	British Aircraft Corporation
AZU	Aktionszentrum Umweltschutz	BAC	British Association of Chemists
AZV	Autofahrlehrer-Zentralverband (Switzerland)	BAC	British Atlantic Committee
		BAC	British Automatic Company
		BAC	Brouwtechnische Adviescommissie

B

BA	Booksellers Association of Great Britain and Ireland	BAC	Bureau Agricole Commun pour l'Etude de Conjoncture Economique
		BACA	British Agricultural Contractors' Association

BACAAO	Banque Centrale des Etats de l'Afrique Occidentale
BACAH	British Association of Consultants in Agriculture and Horticulture (*now* BIAC)
BACAN	British Association for the Control of Aircraft Noise
BACC	British American Chamber of Commerce (U.S.A.)
BACE	British Association of Corrosion Engineers
BACE	Bureau of Agricultural Chemistry and Engineering (U.S.A.)
BACEA	British Airport Construction and Equipment Association
BACG	British Association of Crystal Growth
BACI	British Association of Caving Instructors
BACIE	British Association for Commercial and Industrial Education
BACM	British Association of Colliery Management
BACMA	British Aromatic Compound Manufacturers Association
BACMA	British Artists' Colour Manufacturers' Association
BACR	British Association for Cancer Research
BACT	British Association of Conference Towns
BACTA	British Amusement Catering Trades Association
BACTE	British Association for Commercial and Technical Education
BAD	Associação Portuguesa de Bibliotecarios, Arquivistas e Documentalistes
BAD	Banque Africaine de Développement
BADA	British Amateur Dancers Association
BADA	British Antique Dealers' Association Ltd
BAE	Badminton Association of England
BAE	Belfast Association of Engineers
BAE	Bureau of Agricultural Economics (U.S.A.)
BAEA	British Actors Equity Association
BAEC	British Agricultural Export Council
BAECE	British Association of Early Childhood Education
BAECON	Bureau of Agricultural Economics (Philippines)
BAED	British Airways European Division
BAEF	Belgian-American Educational Foundation
BAEng	Bureau of Agricultural Engineering (U.S.A.)
BAEQ	Bureau d'Aménagement de l'Est du Québec (Canada)

BAF	British Air Ferries Ltd
BAF	Bundesarbeitsgemeinschaft der Fruchtimportmärkte
BÄF	Byggnadsämnesförbundet
BAFA	British Animated Film Association
BAFA	British Arts Festivals Association
BAfD	Banque Africaine de Développement
BAFM	British Association of Forensic Medicine
BAFM	British Association of Friends of Museums
BAFMA	British and Foreign Maritime Agencies
BAFOG	Bureau Agricole et Forestier Guyanais
BAFRA	British Aluminium Foil Rollers Association
BAFS	Banque Americano-Franco-Suisse
BAFS	British Academy of Forensic Sciences
BAFSC	British Association of Field and Sports Contractors
BAFSM	British Association of Feed Supplement Manufacturers
BAFTA	British Academy of Film and Television Arts
BAFTM	British Association of Fishing Tackle Makers
BAG	British Animation Group (*now* BAFA)
BAG	Bundesarbeitsgemeinschaft für das Schlacht- und Viehhofswesen
BAGA	British Amateur Gymnastic Association
BAGB	Baseball Association of Great Britain
BAGB	Bicycle Association of Great Britain
BAGCD	British Association of Green Crop Driers
BAGDA	British Advertising Gift Distributors Association
BAGMA	British Agricultural and Garden Machinery Association
BAH	Biologische Anstalt Helgoland
BAH	British Airways Helicopters
BAHO	British Association of Helicopter Operators
BAHOH	British Association of the Hard of Hearing
BAHPA	British Agricultural and Horticultural Plastics Association
BAHS	British Agricultural History Society
BAI	Bundesverband der Agraringenieure
BAI	Bureau des Affaires Indigènes
BAI	Bureau of Animal Industry (U.S.A.)
BAIC	Bureau of Agricultural and Industrial Chemistry (U.S.A.)
BAIE	British Association of Industrial Editors
BAIF	Bharatiya Agro-Industries Foundation (India)

AK	Bundesgemeinschaft der Architektenkammern	BAOM	Bibliothèque d'Afrique et d'Outre-Mer
AK	Bundesapothekerkammer	BAOS	British Association of Oral Surgeons
ALI	British Association of Landscape Industries	BAOT	British Association of Occupational Therapists
ALPA	British Air Line Pilots' Association	BAPA	British Air Pilots Association
AM	Brothers to All Men	BAPA	British Amateur Press Association
AM	Bundesanstalt für Materialprüfung	BAPAL	British Adult Publications Association Ltd
AMA	British Adhesive Manufacturers Association	BAPC	British Aircraft Preservation Council
AMA	British Aerosol Manufacturers Association	BAPCO	Bahrain Petroleum Company
AMA	British Amsterdam Maritime Agencies	BAPIP	British Association of Palestine-Israel Philatelists
AMA	British Army Motoring Association	BAPM & R	British Association of Physical Medicine and Rheumatology (*now* BARR)
AMB	Bureau of Administrative Management and Budget (UNDP)	BAPP	British Association of Pig Producers
AMDO	British Agricultural Marketing Development Organisation	BAPS	British Association of Paediatric Surgeons
AMES	Banque Malagasy d'Escompte et de Crédit	BAPS	British Association of Plastic Surgeons
AMEX	British Art Metal Manufacturers Export Group	BAPSA	Budget Annexe des Prestations Sociales Agricoles
AMM	British Association of Manipulative Medicine	BAPSC	Badeku Agricultural Production and Supply Company (Nigeria)
AMMATA	British Animal Medicine Makers' and Allied Traders' Association	BAPT	Incorporated British Association for Physical Training
AMRG	British Agricultural Marketing Research Group	BAQ	Bundesanstalt für Qualitätsforschung Pflanzlicher Erzeugnisse
AMS	British Air Mail Society	BAR	British Association of Removers
AMTM	British Association of Machine Tool Merchants (*now* AEMTM)	BAR	Bundesarbeitsgemeinschaft für Rehabilitation
AMW	British Association of Meat Wholesalers	BARB	British Association of Rose Breeders
AN	British Association of Neurologists	BARC	Bhabha Atomic Research Centre (India)
ANC	Biblioteca Agrícola Nacional de Colombia	BARC	British Automobile Racing Club
ANC	British Association of National Coaches	BARD	Bangladesh Academy for Rural Development
ANDECO	Banana Development Corporation of Costa Rica	BARMA	Boiler and Radiator Manufacturers Association
ANDESCO	Banco del Desarrollo Economico Espanol	BARMA	Bureau pour l'Application des Renseignements Météorologiques aux Activités Économiques et Agricoles
ANFAIC	Banco de Fomento Agricola e Industrial de Cuba		
ANS	British Association of Numismatic Societies	BARP	British Association of Retired Persons
ANSDOC	Bangladesh National Scientific and Documentation Centre	BARR	Board on Agricultural and Renewable Resources (U.S.A.)
ANZARE	British-Australian-New Zealand Antarctic Research Expedition	BARR	British Association for Rheumatology and Rehabilitation
AO	British Association of Orthodontists	BARS	British Association of Residential Settlements
AO	British Association of Otolaryngologists	BARTO	British Association of Resort Tourist Officers
AOD	British Airways Overseas Division	BAS	British Acoustical Society
AOFR	British Association of Overseas Furniture Removers	BAS	British Antarctic Survey
AOLPE	British Association of Organisers and Lecturers in Physical Education	BAS	British Association of Settlements

BASA	British Architectural Students' Association	BAUA	Business Aircraft Users' Association
BASA	British Association of Seed Analysts	BAUS	British Association of Urological Surgeons
BASA	British Automatic Sprinkler Association	BAV	Bureau Aardappelverbouw
BASAF	British and South African Forum	BAWA	British Amateur Wrestling Association
BASAM	British Association of Grain, Seed, Feed and Agricultural Merchants	BAWE	British Association of Women Executives
		BAWLA	British Amateur Weight Lifting Association
BASC	British Aerial Standards Council	BAWRA	British Australian Wool Realisation Association
BASCOL	Bauxite Alumina Study Company Ltd (Ghana)	BAYS	British Association of Young Scientists
BAsD	Banque Asiatique de Développement	BAYWA	Bayerische Warenvermittlung Landwirtschaftlicher Genossenschaften
BASE	British Association Service for the Elderly		
BASE	Bureau Africain des Sciences de l'Éducation (Zaire)	BBA	Biologische Bundesanstalt
		BBA	British Backgammon Association
BASEEFA	British Approvals Service for Electrical Equipment in Flammable Atmospheres	BBA	British Bankers' Association
		BBA	British Bee-Keepers Association
BASES	British Anti-Smoking Education Society	BBA	British Bobsleigh Association
BASF	Badische Anilin und Soda-Fabrik	BBAA	Bureau Belge des Assureurs Automobiles
BASI	British Association of Ski Instructors	BBAC	British Balloon and Airship Club
BASLC	British Association of Sports Ground and Landscape Contractors Ltd	BBB	Bedrijfslaboratorium voor Grondonderzoek
		BBBA	British Bird Breeders' Association
BASM	British Association of Sport and Medicine	BBBC	British Boxing Board of Control
BASMA	Boot and Shoe Manufacturers' Association and Leather Trades Protection Society	BBC	British Broadcasting Corporation
		BBCC	British Bottle Collectors Club
BASMM	British Association of Sewing Machine Manufacturers	BBCF	British Bacon Curers' Federation
		BBCMA	British Baby Carriage Manufacturers Association
BASO	British Association for Surgical Oncology		
BASOMED	Basutoland Socio-Medical Services	BBCS	British Beer-mat Collectors Society
BASP	British Association for Social Psychiatry	BBCS	British Butterfly Conservation Society
BASR	Bureau of Applied Social Research (U.S.A.)	BBFC	British Board of Film Censors
BASRA	British Amateur Scientific Research Association	BBFI	Baptist Bible Fellowship International (U.S.A.)
BASRM	British Association of Synthetic Rubber Manufacturers	BBG	Algemene Nederlandse Bond van Binnenlandse Groothandelaren in Groente en Fruit
BASS	Belgian Archives for the Social Sciences		
BASS	British Association of Ship Suppliers	BBGA	British Broiler Growers Association
BASSA	British Airline Stewards and Stewardesses Association	BBGOA	Boletin Bibliográfico de Geofisica y Oceanografia Americanas (Mexico)
BASW	British Association of Social Workers	BBI	British Bottlers Institute
BAT	British-American Tobacco Company	BBIRA	British Baking Industries' Research Association (now FMBRA)
BAT	Bureau de l'Assistance Technique (see TAB)		
BATA	Bakery Allied Traders Association	BBKA	British Beekeepers' Association
BATD	British Association of Teachers of Dancing	BBKC	British Bee-keeping Centre
BATMA	Bookbinding and Allied Trades Management Association	BBL	British Bridge League
		BBLO	Belgische Bond voor Lichamelijke Opvoeding
BATO	British Association of Tourist Officers	BBM	Algemene Nederlandse Bond van Bierhandelaren en Mineraalwaterfabrikanten
BATU	Brotherhood of Asian Trade Unionists (Philippines)		

BMA	British Bath Manufacturers' Association
BMA	British Brush Manufacturers Association
BMA	British Button Manufacturers' Association
BMA	Building Board Manufacturers' Association of Great Britain
BMRA	British Brush Manufacturers Research Association
BMS	British Battery Makers Society
BO	British Ballet Organisation
BO	Gesamtverband Büromaschinen, Büromöbel und Organisationsmittel
BPHA	British Poultry Breeders and Hatcheries Association
BR	Belgische Beroepsvereniging van Reisbureaus
BRS	Blair Bell Research Society
BRU	Bituminous Binder Research Unit (South Africa)
BS	Bartó Béla Szövetség
BS	British Archaeological Association
BS	British Biophysical Society
BS	British Bryological Society
BS	British Button Society
BSA	British Blind and Shutter Association
BSATRA	British Boot, Shoe and Allied Trades Research Association
BSI	British Boot and Shoe Institution
BSR	Bermuda Biological Station for Research
BTA	British Bureau of Television Advertising
BTA	Bund Baugewerblich Tätiger Architekten
CA	British Carton Association
CA	British Casino Association
CA	British Casting Association
CA	British Chicken Association
CA	British Chiropractors Association
CA	British College of Accountancy
CA	British Confectioners' Association
CAB	British Computer Association for the Blind
CAC	British Conference on Automation and Computation
CAI	British Columbia Artificial Insemination Centre
CAL	British Caledonian Airways Ltd
CAR	British Council for Aid to Refugees
CAS	British Compressed Air Society
CB	British Consultants Bureau

BCB	Bureau Congolais des Bois
BCC	Banque Commerciale Congolaise
BCC	British Caravanners Club
BCC	British Colour Council
BCC	British Communications Corporation
BCC	British Copyright Council
BCC	British Council of Churches
BCC	British Cryogenic Council
BCC	Bureau Central de Compensation
BCCCUS	British Commonwealth Chamber of Commerce in the United States
BCCF	British Cast Concrete Federation
BCCG	British Cooperative Clinical Group
BCD	Banque Camerounaise de Développement
BCD	British Crop Driers, Ltd
BCD	Bureau du Commerce et du Développement (of UNCTAD)
BCDTA	British Chemical and Dyestuffs Traders Association
BCE	Board of Customs and Excise
BCEAE	Banque Centrale des États de l'Afrique Équatoriale et du Cameroun
BCEAO	Banque Centrale des États de l'Afrique de l'Ouest
BCECA	British Chemical Engineering Contractors Association
BCECC	British and Central-European Chamber of Commerce
BCEL	British Commonwealth Ex-Services League
BCEMA	British Combustion Equipment Manufacturers Association
BCEOM	Bureau Central d'Études pour les Équipements d'Outre-Mer
BCeramRA	British Ceramic Research Association
BCF	Bacon Curers Federation
BCF	British Chess Federation
BCF	British Concrete Federation
BCF	British Cycling Federation
BCFA	British-China Friendship Association
BCFGA	British Columbia Fruit Growers' Association
BCFL	British Czechoslovak Friendship League
BCFS	British Columbia Forestry Society
BCFTE	British Commonwealth Forest Translation Exchange
BCGA	British Compressed Gases Association

BCGA	British Cotton Growing Association	**BCMN**	Bureau Central de Mesures Nucléaires (Belgium)
BCGLO	British Commonwealth Geographical Liaison Office	**BCN**	Biblioteca del Congreso de la Nación (Argentina)
BCHC	British Crane Hire Corporation	**BCOB**	Bond van Christelijke Ondernemers in het Bakkersbedrijf
BCHFA	British-Canadian Holstein Friesian Association	**BCOG**	British College of Obstetricians and Gynaecologists
BCHS	British Canadian Holstein Society	**BCORA**	British Colliery Owners' Research Association
BCI	Bedrijfsgroep Chemische Industrie	**BCPA**	British Commonwealth Pacific Airlines
BCI	Bonsai Clubs International (U.S.A.)	**BCPA**	British Concrete Pumping Association
BCI	Bureau Consultatif Interorganisations	**BCPA**	British Copyright Protection Association
BCIA	British Columbia Institute of Agrologists	**BCPC**	British Crop Protection Council
BCIA	British Cooking Industry Association	**BCPIT**	British Council for the Promotion of International Trade
BCIE	Banco Centroamericano de Integración Económica (Honduras)	**BCPMA**	British Chemical Plant Manufacturers Association (*now* PPA)
BCINA	British Commonwealth International Newsfilm Agency	**BCPMMA**	British Ceramic Plant and Machinery Manufacturers Association
BCIPPA	British Cast Iron Pressure Pipe Association	**BCPO**	British Commonwealth Producers' Organisation
BCIRA	British Cast Iron Research Association	**BCPPC**	British Christian Pen Pal Club
BCIRA	British Cotton Industries Research Association (*now* British Cotton, Silk and Man-made Fibres Association)	**BCPR**	Belgisch Centrum voor Public Relations
BCIS	Bureau Central International de Séismologie	**BCR**	Bituminous Coal Research (U.S.A.)
BCISC	British Chemical Industry Safety Council (*now* CISHEC)	**BCR**	Bureau of Commercial Research
		BCR	Bureau Communautaire de Référence
BCIT	British Columbia Institute of Technology	**BCRA**	British Carbonization Research Association
BCIU	Business Council for International Understanding (U.S.A.)	**BCRA**	British Cave Research Association
		BCRA	British Ceramic Research Association
BCK	Belgisch Centrum voor Kwaliteitszorg	**BCRA**	British Coke Research Association
BCLMA	British Columbia Lumber Manufacturers' Association	**BCRC**	British Columbia Research Council
BCM	Banque Centrale du Bali	**BCRD**	British Council for the Rehabilitation of the Disabled
BCMA	British Caramel Manufacturers Association	**BCRG**	Banque Centrale de la Republique de Guinée
BCMA	British Carpet Manufacturers Association	**BCRU**	British Committee on Radiological Units
BCMA	British Chip Board Manufacturers' Association	**BCRUM**	British Committee on Radiation Units and Measurements
BCMA	British Closure Manufacturers Association		
BCMA	British Colour Makers Association	**BCS**	Bond van Christelijke Slagerspatroons
BCMA	British Columbia Medical Association	**BCS**	British Cardiac Society
BCMA	British Council of Maintenance Associations	**BCS**	British Cartographic Society
BCMA	British Country Music Association	**BCS**	British Ceramic Society
BCMA	Bureau Commun du Machinisme Agricole (*now* BCMEA) (France)	**BCS**	British Computer Society
		BCS	British Crossbow Society
BCMEA	Bureau Commun du Machinisme et de l'Équipement Agricole	**BCSA**	British College Sports Association
BCMF	British Ceramic Manufacturers Federation	**BCSA**	British Constructional Steelwork Association

BCSH	British Committee for Standards in Haematology
BCSIR	Bangladesh Council of Scientific and Industrial Research
BCSO	British Commonwealth Scientific Office (U.S.A.)
BCTA	British Canadian Trade Association
BCTC	British Ceramic Tile Council
BCTP	British Continental Trade Press
BCU	Banco Central del Uruguay
BCU	British Canoe Union
BCU	British Commonwealth Union
BCURA	British Coal Utilization Research Association
BCVA	British Cattle Veterinary Association
BCVA	British Columbia Veterinary Association
BCWA	British Cotton Waste Association
BCWIU of A	Bakery and Confectionery Workers International Union of America
BCWLF	British Commonwealth Weightlifting Federation
BCWMA	British Clock and Watch Manufacturers Association
BCZ	Belgische Centrale Zuivelcommissie
BCZV	Bond van Cöoperatieve Zuivelverkoopverenigingen
BDA	British Deaf Association
BDA	British Dental Association
BDA	British Diabetic Association
BDA	British Dietetic Association
BDA	British Domestic Appliances, Ltd
BDA	British Dyslexia Association
BDA	Bund Deutscher Architekten
BDA	Bundesvereinigung der Deutschen Arbeitgeberverbände
BDAC	Bureau of Drug Abuse Control (U.S.A.)
BDB	Bibliotéca del Bibliotecário (Argentina)
BDB	Bund Deutscher Baumeister, Architekten und Ingenieure
BDB	Bundesverband der Deutschen Bürstenindustrie
BDB	Bund Deutscher Baumschulen
BDC	Book Development Council
BDC	Bureau International de Documentation des Chemins de Fer
BDCC	British Defence Coordinating Committee
BDD	Banque Dahoméenne de Développement

BDD	Bund Deutscher Detektive
BDDA	British Deaf and Dumb Association
BDDRG	British Deep-Drawing Research Group
BDDSA	British Deaf Amateur Sports Association
BDDV	Bund Deutscher Dolmetscherverbände
BDE	Bundesverband Deutscher Einsenbahnen
BDEAC	Banque de Développement des États de l'Afrique Centrale
BDET	Banque de Développement Économique de Tunisie
BDF	Banque de France
BDF	Bundesverband des Deutschen Güterfernverkehrs
BDFA	British Dairy Farmers' Association
BDFA	Bundesverband der Finanz- und Anlageberater
BDFG	Bundesverband des Deutschen Farbengrosshandels
BDFI	Bund Deutscher Fliesengeschäfte
BDG	Bund Deutscher Grafik-Designer
BDH	British Drug Houses, Ltd
BDHA	British Dental Hygienists Association
BDI	Bundesverband der Deutschen Industrie
BDI	Bureau of Dairy Industry (U.S.A.)
BDIA	Bund Deutscher Innerarchitekten
BDIC	Bibliothèque de Documentation Internationale Contemporaine
BDK	Bundesvervand Deutscher Kosmetikerinnen
BDL	Bund der Deutschen Landjugend im Deutschen Bauernverband
BDL	Bundesverband Deutscher Lederhändler
BDLA	Bund Deutscher Landschaftsarchitekten
BDLI	Bundesverband der Deutschen Luft- und Raumfahrtindustrie
BDM	Banque de Développement du Mali
BDMA	British Disinfectant Manufacturers Association
BDMAA	British Direct Mail Advertising Association
BDMH	Bundesverband des Deutschen Musikinstrumentenhersteller
BDN	Bundesverband des Deutschen Güternahverkehrs
BDO	Bund Deutscher Orgelbaumeister
BDP	Bundesverband des Deutschen Personenverkehrsgewerbes
BDP	Bundesverband Deutscher Pflanzenzüchter

BDPA	British Disposable Products Association	**BEA**	British European Airways
BDPA	Bureau pour le Développement de la Production Agricole	**BEAB**	British Electrical Approvals Board
		BEAC	Banque des États de l'Afrique Centrale, Paris
BDPh	Bund Deutscher Philatelisten	**BEAC**	British European Airways Corporation
BDRA	British Drag Racing Association	**BEAIRA**	British Electrical and Allied Industries Research Association
BDRN	Banque de Développement de la République du Niger	**BEAMA**	British Electrical and Allied Manufacturers Association
BDS	British Deer Society		
BDS	British Display Society	**BEAS**	British Educational Administration Society
BDS	Bund Deutscher Sekretärinnen	**BEC**	British Employers' Confederation (*now* CBI)
BDS	Bundesverband der Deutschen Schrottwirtschaft	**BEC**	British Evangelical Council
		BEC	Bureau Européen du Café
BDS	Bundesverband Deutscher Stahlhandel	**BECC**	British Empire Cancer Campaign
BDSA	British Dental Students' Association	**BECC**	Bureau d'Études Coopérative et Communautaires
BDSC	British Deaf Sports Council		
BdSW	Bundesverband der Selbstbedienungs-Warenhäuser	**BECCR**	British Empire Cancer Campaign for Research (*now* CRC)
BDT	Banque de Développement du Tchad	**BECEB**	Bedrijfs-Economisch Centrum voor de Elektrotechnische Bedrijfstak
BDTA	British Dental Trade Association		
BDTA	Bundesverband Deutscher Tabakwaren-Grosshändler und Automatenaufsteller	**BECETEL**	Centre Belge d'Études Technologiques sur Tuyauteries et Accessoires
BDU	Bund Deutscher Unternehmensberater	**BECGC**	British Empire and Commonwealth Games Council
BDÜ	Bundesverband der Dolmetscher und Übersetzer	**BECGF**	British Empire and Commonwealth Games Federation
BDV	Bundesverband Deutscher Volks- und Betriebswirte	**BECMA**	British Electro-Ceramic Manufacturers Association
BDV	Bundesverband der Versandschlachtereien	**BECOIJ**	Bureau Européen de Coordination des Organisations Internationales de Jeunesse
BDV	Bundesverband Deutscher Vorzugsmilcherzeuger		
BDVB	Bundesverband Deutscher Volks- und Betriebswirte	**BECSM**	British Electrical Conduit Systems Manufacturers (*now* BESA)
BDVI	Bund der Öffentlich Bestellten Vermessungsingenieure	**BECWLC**	British Empire and Commonwealth Weight Lifting Council
BDVT	Bund Deutscher Verkaufsforderer und Verkaufstrainer	**BEDA**	British Electrical Development Association
		BEDA	Bureau Européen des Designers Associés
BDW	Bund Deutscher Werbeberater	**BEDEK**	Israel Aircraft Industries
BDWB	Bundesverband Deutscher Wirtschaftsberater	**BEDFPU**	Brigada de Estudos da Defesa Fitossanitária dos Produtos Ultramarinos (Portugal)
BDZ	Bundesverband der Deutschen Zahnärzte	**BEDSE**	Bureau d'Étude et de Documentation sur la Santé des Étudiants (Italy)
BdZ	Bundesverband der Zigarrenindustrie		
BDZV	Bundesverband Deutscher Zeitungsverleger	**BEE**	Bureau Européen d'Environnement
BEA	British Egg Association	**BEEA**	British Educational Equipment Association
BEA	British Electrical Authority (now CEA)	**BEEP**	Bureau Européen de l'Education Populaire
BEA	British Engineers' Association	**BEF**	British Employees Federation
BEA	British Epilepsy Association	**BEF**	British Equestrian Federation
BEA	British Esperanto Association	**BEFMC**	British Educational Furniture Manufacturers Council

BEG	Brush Export Group
BEGEBI	Bureau d'Études et de Gestion des Élevages Bovines Intensifs
BEGS	British and European Geranium Society
BEHA	British Export Houses Association
BEI	Banque Européenne d'Investissement
BEIA	Bureau d'Éducation Ibéro-Américain
BEIC	Bureau Européen d'Informations Charbonnières
BEICIP	Bureau d'Études des Industrielles et de Coopération de l'Institut Français du Pétrole
BEIS	British Egg Information Service (formerly NEIS)
BEJE	Bureau Européen de la Jeunesse et de l'Enfance
BELF	Bundesministerium für Ernährung, Landwirtschaft und Forsten
BELGA	Agence Télégraphique Belge de Presse
BELRA	British Empire Leprosy Relief Association
BELVAC	Société Belge de Vacuologie et de Vacuotechnique
BEMA	British Essence Manufacturers' Association
BEMAC	British Export Marketing Advisory Committee
BEMB	British Egg Marketing Board
BEMSA	British Eastern Merchant Shippers Association
BEN	Bureau d'Études Nucléaires (Belgium)
BENA	British (Empire) Naturalists Association
BENELUX	Belgium, Netherlands, Luxembourg Union
BEO	Bureau d'Études Océanographiques
BEPA	British Egg Products Association
BEpA	British Epilepsy Association
BEPC	British Electric Power Convention
BEPI	Bureau d'Études et de Participations Industrielles (Morocco)
BEPQ	Bureau of Entomology and Plant Quarantine (U.S.A.)
BEPTOM	Bureau d'Études des Postes et Télécommunications d'Outre Mer
BERC	Basic Education Research Centre, Nairobi (Kenya)
BERCO	British Electric Resistance Company
BES	British Ecological Society
BES	British Endodontic Society
BES	Brooklyn Entomological Society (U.S.A.)

BESA	British Electrical Systems Association
BESA	British Engineering Standards Association (*now* BSI)
BESA	British Esperanto Scientific Association
BESL	British Empire Service League (Canada)
BESO	British Executive Service Overseas
BESONU	Bureau des Affaires Économiques et Sociales des Nations Unies, Beirut
BEST	Bureau d'Études de Standardisation et de Technique en Arboriculture Fruitère (*ceased*)
BET	British Electric Traction Company
BETA	Bureau for Education Technology and Administration (U.S.A.)
BETA	Business Equipment Trade Association
BETAA	British Export Trade Advertising Association
BETMA	Bureau Professionnel d'Études Techniques des Marchés Agricoles
BETRO	British Export Trade Research Organisation
BETURE	Bureau d'Études Techniques pour l'Urbanisme et l'Équipement
BEU	Benelux Economic Union
BEUC	Bureau Européen des Unions de Consommateurs
BEVA	British Equine Veterinary Association
BEVETAB	National Beroepsvereniging van Importeurs, Handelaars, Commissionairs, Makelaars en Agenten in Tabakken in Bladeren in België
BEVIA	Verband von Vieh-, Fleisch- und Fleischwarenimporteuren
BEVIFA	Vereninging der Belgische Vismeelfabrikanten
BEWAC	British West Indian Corporation
BEWEDIT	Belgische Comité voor Weverij en Diverse Textielindustrieën
BF	Banque de France
BF	Bibliotekarforeningen
BFA	British Fellmongers Association
BFA	British Film Authority
BFA	Bundestelle für Aussenhandelsinformation
BFAC	British Federation of Aesthetics and Cosmetology
BFACM	Banque Française de l'Agriculture et du Crédit Mutuel
BFAK	Bundesforschungsanstalt für Kleintierzucht
BFB	Bibliotheksforum Bayern
BFB	Bundesanstalt für Bodenforschung
BFBB	British Federation of Brass Bands

BFBN	Bond van Fabrikanten van Betonwaren in Nederland
BFBPM	British Federation of Business and Professional Women
BFBS	British Forces Broadcasting Service
BFBS	British and Foreign Bible Society
BFC	British Falconers' Club
BFC	Bureau International de Film pour les Chemins de Fer
BFCA	British Federation of Commodity Associations
BFCE	Banque Français du Commerce Extérieur
BFCS	British Friesian Cattle Society
BFE	Bedrijfsfederatie der Voortbrengers en Verdelers van Electriciteit in België
BFE	Bundesfachverband Edelmetallerzeugnisse und Verwandte Industrien
BFE	Bundesstelle für Entwicklungshilfe
BFEBS	British Far Eastern Broadcasting Service
BFEC	British Food Export Council
BFES	British Families Education Service
BFF	British Fishing Federation
BFF	Bundesverband der Deutschen Fischindustrie und des Fischgrosshandels
BFFA	British Film Fund Agency
BFFC	British Federation of Folk Clubs
BFFF	British Frozen Foods Federation
BFHMF	British Felt Hat Manufacturers Federation
BFI	British Film Institute
BFI	Verband der Schweizerischen Beutel- und Flexodruck-Industrie
BFIA	British Flower Industry Association
BFID	Brancheforeningen af Farmaceutiske Industrivirksomheder i Danmark
BFSIL	Búnadarfélag Islands
BFISS	British Federation of Iron and Steel Stockholders
BFJD	Bundesverband Freier Juristen Deutschlands
BFL	Bahamas Federation of Labour
BFM	British Furniture Manufacturers Federated Associations
BFMA	British Farm Mechanization Association
BFMA	British Floorcovering Manufacturers Association
BFMA	Building Materials Factors Association
BFMC	British Friction Materials Council
BFMF	British Federation of Music Festivals
BFMF	British Footwear Manufacturers Federation
BFMIRA	British Food Manufacturing Industries Research Association
BFMP	British Federation of Master Printers (*now* BPIF)
BFMSA	British Firework Manufacturers Safety Association
BFN	Vereniging van Beroepsfotografen in Nederland
BFPA	British Film Producers' Association
BFPC	British Farm Produce Council
BFPSA	British Fire Protection Systems Association Ltd
BFQ	Bibliotèque Fonds Quetelet (Belgium)
BFR	Banque Fédérative Rurale
BFS	British Fuchsia Society
BFSA	British Fire Services Association
BFSLYC	British Federation of Sand and Land Yacht Clubs
BFSS	British Field Sports Society
BFT	Bundesverband Freier Tankstellen und Unabhängiger Deutscher Mineralölhändler
BFTA	British Fur Trade Alliance
BFTU	Bahamas Federation of Trade Unions
BFUW	British Federation of University Women
BFW	Bread for the World (U.S.A.)
BFWA	Bundesfachverband Wasseraufbereitung
BGA	British Gaming Association
BGA	British Gliding Association
BGA	British Grit Association
BGA	Bundesverband des Deutschen Gross- und Aussenhandels
BGA	Irish Sugar Beet Growers' Association
BGB	Booksellers Association of Great Britain and Ireland
BGC	British Gas Council
BGC	British Glues and Chemicals Ltd
BGCG	British Guiana Consolidated Goldfields Ltd
BGD	Banque Gabonaise de Développement
BGD	Bureau voor Gemeenschappelijke Diensten
BGF	Banana Growers Federation (Australia)
BGF	Schweizerischer Verband der Berufs- und Geschäftsfrauen
BGGA	British Golf Greenkeepers Association

BGGRA	British Gelatine and Glue Research Association
BGH	Beroepsvereniging der Promoteurs voor Huisvesting en Ruimtelijke Ordening
BGIRA	British Glass Industry Research Association
BGL	Bundesverband Garten- und Landschaftsbau
BGMA	British Gear Manufacturers' Association
BGMA	British Glucose Manufacturers Association
BGN	Board on Geographic Names (U.S.A.)
BGR	Board of Greenkeeping Research (*now* STRI)
BGRB	British Greyhound Racing Board
BGRF	British Greyhound Racing Federation
BGRG	British Geomorphological Research Group
BGS	Bilgreinasambandid
BGS	British Gladiolus Society
BGS	British Goat Society
BGS	British Grassland Society
BGV	Bergischer Geschichtsverein
BGW	Bundesverband der Deutschen Gas- und Wasserwirtschaft
BGWF	British Granite and Whinstone Federation
BGZL	Bundesverband der Rein Gewerblichen Zahntechnischen Laboratorien
BHA	British Homoeopathic Association
BHA	British Horse Association
BHA	British Humanist Association
BHA	British Hypnotherapy Association
BHAFRA	British Hat and Allied Feltmakers Research Association
BHCF	British Hire Cruiser Federation
BHCSA	British Hospitals Contributory Schemes Association
BHE	Bureau of Home Economics (U.S.A.)
BHF	British Hardware Federation
BHG	Bundesverband Holzgrosshandel
BHGA	British Hang Gliding Association
BHI	British Horological Institute
BHI	Bureau Hydrographique International
BHKH	Bundesverband des Holz- und Kunstoffverarbeitenden
BHL	Bensinhandlernes Landsforbund
BHL	British Housewives League
BHM	Bandalag Háskólamanna
BHMA	British Hacksaw Makers Association
BHMA	British Hard Metal Association
BHMA	British Herbal Medicine Association
BHMEA	British Hard Metal Export Association
BHMRA	British Hydromechanics Research Association
BHNHE	Bureau of Human Nutrition and Home Economics (U.S.A.)
BHPC	British Hardware Promotion Council Ltd
BHRA	British Hotels and Restaurants Association (*now* BHRCA)
BHRA	British Hydromechanics Research Association
BHRCA	British Hotels, Restaurants and Caterers Association
BHS	British Herpetological Society
BHS	British Horse Society
BHSA	British Heavy Steel Association
BHTA	British Herring Trade Association
BHV	Bergshandteringens Vänner
BI	Befrienders International
BIA	Braille Institute of America
BIA	British Institute of Acupuncture
BIA	British Insurance Association
BIA	British Ironfounders Association
BIA	British Island Airways Ltd
BIAA	British Industrial Advertising Association (*now* BIMA)
BIAC	Bioinstrumentation Advisory Council (U.S.A.) (*of* AIBS)
BIAC	British Institute of Agricultural Consultants
BIAC	Business and Industry Advisory Committee to OECD
BIAD	Bureau International d'Anthropologie Différentielle
BIAE	British Institute of Adult Education
BIALL	British and Irish Association of Law Librarians
BIAO	Banque Internationale pour l'Afrique Occidentale
BIAP	Bureau International d'Audiophonologie
BIAS	Belgian International Air Services
BIAS	Brooklyn Institute of Arts and Sciences (U.S.A.)
BIATA	British Independent Air Transport Association
BIBA	British Insurance Brokers' Association
BIBF	British and Irish Basketball Federation

BIBM	Bureau International du Béton Manufacture	**BIDC**	Bureau Interafricain de Développement et du Coopération
BIBOA	Fédération Internationale des Associations de l'Industrie, de l'Artisanat et du Commerce des Diamants, Perles, Pierres Précieuses, de Bijouterie, Orfèvrerie, Joaillerie, Horlogerie	**BIDE**	Bangladesh Institute of Development Economics
BIBRA	British Industrial Biological Research Association	**BIDE**	Bureau Internationale de Documentation Éducative
BIBW	Belgisch Instituut voor Bestuurswetenschappen	**BIDI**	Banque Ivoirienne de Développement Industriel (Ivory Coast)
BIC	Baha'i International Community	**BIDIF**	Bureau International de Documentation et d'Information des Festivals (France)
BIC	Biodeterioration Information Centre	**BIDS**	Bangladesh Institute of Development Studies
BIC	British Importers Confederation	**BIE**	British Institute of Embalmers
BIC	Bureau International de la Chaussure et du Cuir	**BIE**	Bundesverband Industrieller Einkauf
		BIE	Bureau International d'Éducation
BIC	Bureau International du Cinéma	**BIE**	Bureau International des Expositions
BIC	Bureau International des Containers	**BIE**	Bureau Ivoirien d'Engineering
BICA	Bizonal International Control Administration	**BIEM**	Bureau International de l'Édition Mécanique
BICC	British Insulated Callender's Cables Ltd	**BIEM**	Bureau International des Sociétés Gérant les Droits d'Enregistrement et de Reproduction Mécanique
BICC	Bureau International des Chambres de Commerce (France)		
BICE	Banque Internationale pour la Coopération Économique	**BIES**	Bureau Interprofessionnel d'Études Statistiques Sucrières
BICE	Bureau International Catholique de l'Enfance	**BIET**	British Institute of Engineering Technology
BICEMA	British Internal Combustion Engine Manufacturers' Association	**BIF**	British Industries Fair
		BIFA	British Industrial Film Association
BICEP	British Industrial Collaborative Exponential Programme	**BIFAC**	British Isles Federation of Agricultural Co-operatives
BICERA	British Internal Combustion Engine Research Association	**BIFEDSA**	Building Industries Federation, South Africa
		BIFMA	British Industrial Floor Machine Association
BICERI	British Internal Combustion Engine Research Institute	**BIFU**	Banking Insurance and Finance Union
		BIG	Bois Industriels du Gabon
BICI	Banque Internationale pour le Commerce et l'Industrie	**BIG**	Bund der Ingenieure des Gartenbaues
BICIA-HV	Banque Internationale pour le Commerce l'Industrie et de l'Agriculture de la Haute-Volta	**BIGA**	Bundesamt für Industrie, Gewerbe und Arbeit (Switzerland)
		BIH	Bureau International de l'Heure
BICI-CONGO	Banque Internationale pour le Commerce et l'Industrie- Congo	**BIHA**	British Ice Hockey Association
		BIHFS	British Institute of Hardwood Flooring Specialists
BICO	Bureau International d'Information et de Coopération des Éditeurs de Musique	**BIICC**	Bureau International d'Information des Chambres de Commerce
BICS	Bangkok Institute for Child Study (Thailand)		
BICS	Banque Industrielle et Commerciale (France)	**BIICL**	British Institute of International and Comparative Law
BICS	British Institute of Cleaning Science	**BIID**	British Institute for Interior Design
BICTA	British Investment Casters Technical Association	**BILA**	British Insurance Law Association
		BILC	Bureau for International Language Coordination
BID	Banque Interaméricaine de Développement		

BILD	Bureau International de Liaison et de Documentation (Germany)
BIM	British Institute of Management
BIM	British Insulin Manufacturers
BIMA	British Industrial Marketing Association
BIMAS	Bimbingan Masyarakat (Indonesia)
BIMCAM	British Industrial Measuring and Control Apparatus Manufacturers' Association
BIMCO	Baltic and International Maritime Conference (Denmark)
BIML	Bureau International de Métrologie Légale (*of* OIML)
BIMR	Bureau International de Mécanique des Roches
BIMSOC	British Institute of Management Secretariat for Overseas Countries
BIN	Belgisch Instituut voor Normalisatie
BIN	Bureau of Information on Nickel
BINA	Bureau International des Normes de l'Automobile
BINAME	Biblioteca Nacional de Medicina (Uruguay)
BINC	Building Industries' National Council
BINGO	Business International Non-Governmental Organisation
BINOP	Institut National d'Étude du Travail et d'Orientation Professionnelle
BIO	Biomedical Information Processing Organisation (U.S.A.)
BIO	Bureau Interorganisations pour les Systèmes d'Information et les Activités Connexes
BIOS	British Institute of Organ Studies
BIOS	British Intelligence Objectives Sub-Committee
BIOSIS	Bio-Sciences Information Service of Biological Abstracts (U.S.A.)
BIOT	British Indian Ocean Territory
BIOTROP	Seameo Regional Center for Tropical Biology (Indonesia)
BIP	Banco Industrial del Perù
BIP	Banco Internacional de Pagos
BIP	British Industrial Plastics Ltd
BIP	Bureau Interprofessionnel du Pruneau (France) (*now* BNIP)
BIP	Union Belge des Installateurs Professionnels d'Antennes
BIPA	Bond van Importeurs van Pharmaceutische Artikelen

BIPAR	Bureau International des Producteurs d'Assurances et de Réassurances
BIPAVER	Bureau International Permanent des Associations des Vendeurs et Rechapeurs de Pneumatiques
BIPCA	Bureau International Permanent de Chimie Analytique pour les Matières Destinées à l'Alimentation de l'Homme et des Animaux
BIPE	Bureau d'Information et de Prévisions Économiques
BIPM	Bureau International des Poids et Mesures
BIPO	British Institute of Public Opinion
BIPP	British Institute of Practical Psychology
BIR	British Institute of Radiology
BIR	Bureau of Industrial Relations (U.S.A.)
BIR	Bureau International de la Récupération
BIRA	Belgisch Instituut voor Regeltechniek en Automatisatie
BIRC	British Industry Roads Campaign
BIRD	Banque Internationale pour la Reconstruction et le Développement (U.S.A.)
BIRE	British Institution of Radio Engineers
BIREME	Biblioteca Regional de Medicina (Uruguay)
BIRF	Banco Internacional de Reconstrucción y Fomento
BIRF	Brewing Industry Research Foundation (U.K.)
BIRISPT	Bureau International de Recherche sur les Implications Socials du Progrès Technique
BIRMO	British Infra-Red Manufacturers Organization
BIRPI	Bureaux Internationaux Réunis pour la Protection de la Propriété Intellectuelle
BIRS	British Institute of Recorded Sound
BIRS	Bureau International de Recherches sur la Sauvagine
BIRSH	Bureau of Information and Research on Student Health (Italy)
BIRU	Basic Ideology Research Unit (U.K.)
BIS	Bank for International Settlement (Switzerland)
BIS	British Ichthyological Society
BIS	British Information Services
BIS	British Interplanetary Society
BIS	British Iris Society
BIS	Bureau Interafricain des Sols (*now* BISER)

BIS	Bureau International du Scoutisme	**BJCEB**	British Joint Communications and Electronics Board
BISA	Banco Industrial S.A. (Bolivia)		
BISAKTA	British Iron and Steel and Kindred Trades Association	**BJCG**	British Joint Corrosion Group
		BJSM	British Joint Services Mission (U.S.A.)
BISCOFA	Schweizerischer Verband der Biscuits- und Confiseriefabrikanten	**BJTRA**	British Jute Trades Research Association
		BJU	Bundesverband Junger Unternehmer
BISEC	Board of Intermediate and Secondary Education (Pakistan)	**BKA**	British Karate Association
		BKEC	British Knitting Export Council
BISER	Bureau Interafricain des Sols et de l'Économie Rurale (Central Africa)	**BKFA**	British Kidney Fund Association
		BKFA	British Kite Flyers Association
BISF	British Iron and Steel Federation	**BKLF**	Baker-og Konditormestrenes Landsförening
BISFA	British Industrial and Scientific Film Association	**BKMV**	Belgische Kamer der Medische Voetverzorgers
BISFA	Bureau International pour la Standardisation des Fibres Artificielles (Switzerland)	**BKPA**	British Kidney Patient Association
BISI	British Iron and Steel Institute	**BKR**	British Kendo Renmei
BISITS	British Industrial and Scientific International Translation Service	**BKS**	Bildende Kunstneres Styre
		BKSK	Bundesverband Kunstoff- und Schwergewebekonfektion
BISPA	British Independent Steel Producers' Association	**BKSTS**	British Kinematograph, Sound and Television Society
BISRA	British Iron and Steel Research Association	**BKT**	Bedrijfskadertraining
BISW	Befrienders International–Samaritans Worldwide	**BKV**	Belgische Kunststoffen Vereniging
		BKVTF	Belgische Kamer van Vertalers, Tolken en Filologen
BIT	Bureau International du Travail (Switzerland)		
BITA	British Industrial Truck Association	**BL**	British Legion
BITD	Bureau International des Tarifs Douaniers	**BLA**	British Legal Association
BITEJ	Bureau International pour le Tourisme et les Échanges de la Jeunesse	**BLAC**	British Light Aviation Centre
		BLACC	British and Latin American Chamber of Commerce
BITS	Birla Institute of Technology and Science	**BLAISE**	British Library Automated Information Service
BITS	Bureau International du Tourisme Social		
BITU	Bustamente Industrial Trade Union (West Indies)	**BLASA**	Bantu Library Association of South Africa
		BLB	Brancheforeningen for Danske Leverandører af Butiksinventar
BIU	Bermuda Industrial Union		
BIU	British Import Union (Denmark)	**BLBS**	Bundesverband der Lehrer an Beruflichen Schulen
BIU	Bureau International des Universités		
BIV	Belgisch Instituut voor Verpakking	**BLC**	British Lighting Council
BIW	Bund der Ingenieure des Weinbaues	**BLE**	Budhana Ligo Esperantista (Belgium)
BIWF	British-Israel World Federation		
BIWS	Bureau of International Whaling Statistics	**BLESMA**	British Limbless Ex-Servicemen's Association
BIZ	Bank für Internationalen Zahlungsausgleich	**BLEU**	Belgisch-Luxemburgse Economische Unie
BJA	British Jewellers Association	**BLF**	Brancheforeningen for Leverandører til Frisørstanden
BJA	British Judo Association		
BJCB	British Joint Communications Board (*now* BJCEB)	**BLF**	British Leather Federation
BJCC	British Junior Chambers of Commerce	**BLF**	British Lubricants Federation

BLFAE	Bureau de Liaison France-Afrique-Europe
BLGA	Bayerische Landesgewerbeanstalt
BLH	British Legion Headquarters
BLHA	British Linen Hire Association
BLIC	Bureau de Liaison des Industries du Caoutchouc de la Communauté Économique Européenne
BLIROL	Bureau de Liaison d'Information Religieuse pour l'Océan Indien
BLL	British Library Lending Division
BLL	Bund für Lebensmittelrecht und Lebensmittelkunde
BLMA	British Lead Manufacturers Association
BLMAS	Bible Lands Missions' Aid Society
BLMC	British Leyland Motor Corporation
BLMF	British Lawnmower Manufacturers Federation
BLMRA	British Leather Manufacturers Research Association
BLO	Bureau Landelijke Opbouw (Suriname)
BLOF	British Lace Operatives Federation
BLOWS	British Library of Wildlife Sounds
BLPES	British Library of Political and Economic Science
BLPS	British Landrace Pig Society
BLR	Bundesverband der Luftfahrtzbehör- und Raketenindustrie
BLRA	British Launderers Research Association
BLRA	British Leprosy Relief Association
BLS	Bureau of Labour Statistics (U.S.A.)
BLSGMA	British Lamp Blown Scientific Glassware Manufacturers Association
BLV	Bayerischer Landwirtschaftsverlag
BLVVG	Belgisch-Luxemburgse Vakgroep Vloeibaar Gas
BLWA	British Laboratory Ware Association
BMA	Bible Memory Association International (U.S.A.)
BMA	British Manufacturers' Association
BMA	British Medical Association
BMA	Bundesverband der Möbelgrosshändler und Austlieferungslager
BMAA	British Marine Aquarists Association
BMB	Baltic Marine Biologists (Sweden)
BMBA	British Motor Boat Association

BMBW	Bundesministerium für Bildung und Wissenschaft
BMC	Banque de Madagascar et des Comores
BMC	British Match Corporation
BMC	British Metal Corporation
BMC	British Motor Corporation (now BLMC)
BMC	British Mountaineering Council
BMCC	British Metal Castings Council
BMCD	Banque Malienne de Crédit et de Dépôts
BMCRC	British Motor Cycle Racing Club
BMDC	Biomedicinska Dokumentationscentralen
BMEC	British Marine Equipment Council
BMEF	British Mechanical Engineering Federation
BMEG	Building Materials Export Group
BMELF	Bundesministerium für Ernährung, Landwirtschaft und Forsten
BMF	British Motels Federation
BMF	British Motorcyclists Federation
BMF	Bundesverband Montagebau und Fertighäuser
BMFF	British Man-Made Fibres Federation
BMFSA	British Metal Finishing Suppliers Association
BMG	British Measures Group
BMI	Battelle Memorial Institute (U.S.A.)
BML	Föreningen Bekämpningsmedels-Leverantörer
BMLA	British Maritime Law Association
BMLF	Bundesministerium für Land- und Forstwirtschaft (Austria)
BMLS	British Matchbox Label Society
BMM	Association Benelux des Conseils en Marques et Modèles
BMMA	British Mantle Manufacturers Association
BMMMA	British Mat and Matting Manufacturers Association
BMP	Bricklayers, Masons and Plasterers International Union of America
BMP	National Council of Building Material Producers
BMPA	British Medical Pilots Association
BMPA	British Metalworking Plant Makers Association
BMPMA	British Metalworking Plant Makers Association
BMR	Bundesverband der Maschinenringe (Germany)

BMRA	British Manufacturers Representatives Association (South Africa)
BMRA	British Medical Representatives Association
BMRC	British Medical Research Council
BMS	Birmingham Metallurgical Society
BMS	British Mycological Society
BMSA	British Medical Students Association
BMSA	British Metal Sinterings Association
BMSE	Baltic Mercantile and Shipping Exchange
BMSGMA	British Maize Starch and Glucose Manufacturers Association
BMSMA	British Modified Starch Manufacturers Association
BMSS	British Model Soldier Society
BMSSOA	British Motor and Sailing Ship Owners Association
BMTA	British Mining Tools Association
BMTA	British Motor Trade Association
BMTFA	British Malleable Tube Fittings Association
BMTI	Belgische Maatschappij van Technische Ingenieurs
BMV	Bundesmarktverband für Vieh und Fleisch
BMW	Bayerische Motoren Werke
BMWF	Bundesministerium für Wissenschaftliche Forschung
BMWT	Vereniging van Fabrikanten van en Handelaren in Bouwmachines, Mijn- en Wegenbouwmachines en Transportmiddelen
BMZ	Baumusterzentrale (Austria)
BNA	Bond van Nederlandsche Architecten
BNA	British Nursing Association
BNA	Maatschappij tot Bevordering der Bouwkunst Bond van Nederlandsche Architecten
BNA	Bureau de la Nutrition Animale
BNAC	British North American Committee
BNAE	Bureau de Normalisation de l'Aeronautique et de l'Espace
BNatK	Bundesnotarkammer
BNAU	Bulgarian National Agrarian Union
BNB	Bond van Nederlandse Bandfabrikanten
BNB	British National Bibliography
BNBC	British National Book Centre
BNCC	Banco Nacional de Crédito Cooperativo (Brazil)
BNCC	British National Committee for Chemistry
BNCD	Banque Nationale Centrafricaine de Dépôts
BNCI	Banque National pour le Commerce et l'Industrie (Belgium)
BNC-ICC	British National Committee of the International Chamber of Commerce
BNCM	Bibliothèque Nationale du Conservatoire de Musique
BNCM	British National Committee on Materials
BNCNDT	British National Committee for Non-Destructive Testing
BNCOE	British National Committee on Ocean Engineering
BNCOR	British National Committee for Oceanographic Research
BNCS	British National Carnation Society
BNCS	British Numerical Control Society
BNCSAA	British National Committee on Surface Active Agents
BNCSR	British National Committee for Scientific Radio
BNCWO	Belgisch Nationaal Comité voor Wetenschappelijkes
BNDA	Banque Nationale de Développement Agricole (Guinée, Ivory Coast)
BNDC	Banque Nationale de Développement Congo
BNDC	British Nuclear Design and Construction Ltd
BNDD	Bureau of Narcotics and Dangerous Drugs (U.S.A.)
BNDE	National Development Bank (Brazil)
BNDO	Bureau National des Données Océaniques
BNDS	Banque Nationale de Développement du Sénégal
BNEC	British National Export Council (*now* BOTB)
BNEC	British Nuclear Energy Council
BNES	British Nuclear Energy Society
BNETD	Bureau National d'Études Techniques de Développement (Ivory Coast)
BNF	British Nuclear Forum
BNF	British Nutrition Foundation, Ltd
BNFL	British National Fuels Ltd
BNFL	British Nuclear Fuels Ltd
BNFMF	British Non-Ferrous Metals Federation
BNFMRA	British Non-Ferrous Metals Research Association
BNFMS	British Bureau of Non-Ferrous Metal Statistics

NFSA	British Non-Ferrous Smelters' Association	BOAC	British Overseas Airways Corporation (*now* BAOD)
NG	Bayerische Numismatische Gesellschaft		
NGA	British Nursery Goods Association	BOAD	Banque Ouest-Africaine de Développement (Togo)
NHPS	Belfast Natural History and Philosophical Society	BOAG	British Overseas Aid Group
NHS	British Natural Hygiene Society	BOBA	British Overseas Banks Association
NI	Beroepsvereniging van Nederlandse Interieurarchitekten	BOBMA	British Oil-Burners Manufacturers' Association
NIA	Bureau National Interprofessionnel de l'Armagnac	BOC	British Ornithologists' Club
		BOC	British Oxygen Company
NIC	Bureau National Interprofessionnel du Cognac	BOCA	Building Officials and Code Administrators International (U.S.A.)
NICEVCP	Bureau National Interprofessionnel des Calvados et Eaux-de-Vie de Cidre et de Poire	BOCM	British Oil and Cake Mills Ltd
		BODC	Barclays Overseas Development Corporation
NIP	Bureau National Interprofessionel du Pruneau (France) (*formerly* BIP)	BODEPA	Bond van Detaillisten in de Parfumeriehandel
		BOEC	British Oil Equipment Credits, Ltd
NIRA	British Nautical Instrument Trade Association	BOF	British Orienteering Federation
NL	Banca Nationale del Lavoro	BOF	British Overseas Fairs Ltd
NL	Brookhaven National Laboratory (U.S.A.)	BÖG	Bund Österreichischer Gebrauchsgraphiker
NMA	British Non-wovens Manufacturers Association	BOGA	British Onion Growers Association
NOA	British Naturopathic and Osteopathic Association	BOGETA	Bond van Grossiers in Electrotechnische Artikelen
NOC	British National Oil Corporation	BOGFEMA	British Oil and Gas Firing Equipment Manufacturers Association
NOC	British National Opera Company	BOHS	British Occupational Hygiene Society
NOSP	Banco Nacional de Obras y Servicios Públicos (Mexico)	BÖIA	Bund Österreicherischer Innenarchitekten
NotK	Bundesnotarkammer	BOIL	British Overhead Irrigation Ltd
NRS	British National Radio School	BOLA	Betting Office Licensees Association
NS	Bond van Nederlandsche Schilderspatroons	BOLSA	Bank of London and South America
NS	Bond van Nederlandse Stedebouwkundigen	BOMA	British Overseas Mining Association
NS	British Numismatic Society	BONEFO	Bond van Nederlandse Fotodetailhandelaren
NSA	Bethlehem Natural Science Association (U.S.A.)	BÖP	Berufsverband Österreichischer Psychologen
NT	Bond van Nederlandse Tuin-en Landschapsarchitecten	BOP	Bureau of Operations and Programming (UNDP)
NTA	British Numismatic Trade Association	BOPR	Bureau d'Organisation des Programmes Ruraux (Congo)
NV	Belgische Natuurkundige Vereniging	BORAD	British Oxygen Research and Development Association
NX	British Nuclear Export Executive (*ceased*)	BORM	Bureau of Raw Materials for American Vegetable oils and Fats Industries
OA	Bank of Alexandria (Egypt)		
OA	Boliviana de Aviación	BOS	British Origami Society
OA	British Olympic Association	BOS	British Orthoptic Society
OA	British Optical Association	BOSS	Bureau of State Security (South Africa)
OA	British Orthopaedic Association	BOSTID	Board on Science and Technology for International Development (U.S.A.)
OA	British Osteopathic Association		

BOT	Board of Trade (*now* DTI)
BOTAC	British Overseas Trade Advisory Council (*now* DTI)
BOTB	British Overseas Trade Board
BOTU	Board of Trade Unit
BOU	British Ornithologists' Union
BOV	Belgische Ornithologische Vereniging
BOVA	Nederlandse Bond van Varkenshandelaren
BOVAG	Bond van Automobiel-, Garage- en Aanwerwante Bedrijven
BOVAK	Bond van Kermisbedrijfhouders
BOVAL	Bond van Agrarische Loonbedrijven in Nederland
BOVEE	Nederlandse Bond voor Veehandelaren
BOWI-SPORT	Bond van Winkeliers in Sportartikelen
BPA	Berufsverband der Praktischen Ärzte und Ärzte für Allgemeinmedizin Deutschlands
BPA	Biological Photographic Association (U.S.A.)
BPA	British Paediatric Association
BPA	British Parachute Association Ltd
BPA	British Philatelic Association
BPA	British Ploughing Association
BPA	British Pyrotechnists' Association
BPAA	British Poster Advertising Association
BPAO	Société des Pétroles BP d'Afrique Occidentale
BPAS	British Pregnancy Advisory Service
BPBF	British Paper Box Federation
BPBHA	British Poultry Breeders and Hatcheries Association
BPBIF	British Paper and Board Industry Federation
BPBIRA	British Paper and Board Industry Research Association (*now* PIRA)
BPBMA	British Paper and Board Makers' Association
BPC	Black Peoples Convention
BPC	British Productivity Council
BPCA	British Pest Control Association
BPCA	British Pro-chiropractic Association
BPCF	British Postal Chess Federation
BPCF	British Precast Concrete Federation
BPCRA	British Professional Cycle Racing Association
BPE	Bedrijfschap voor Pluimvee en Eieren

BPEAR	Bureau for the Placement and Education of African Refugees (*of* OAU)
BPEEA	British Postal Equipment Engineering Association
BPEG	British Photographic Export Group
BPF	Borst-och Penselfabrikantföreningen
BPF	British Plastics Federation
BPF	British Poultry Federation
BPF	British Polio Fellowship
BPF	British Property Federation
BPGMA	British Pressure Gauge Manufacturers Association
BPGS	British Pelargonium and Geranium Society
BPHS	British Percheron Horse Society
BPHS	British Polled Hereford Society
BPI	Belgisch Petroleum- Instituut
BPI	British Phonographic Industry
BPIA	British Photographic Importers Association
BPICA	Bureau Permanent International des Constructeurs d'Automobiles
BPICM	Bureau Permanent International des Constructeurs de Motorcyles (France)
BPICS	British Production and Inventory Control Society
BPIF	British Printing Industries Federation
BPITT	Bureau Permanent International de la Tsétsé et de la Trypanosomiase
BPL	Bedrijfspensioenfonds voor de Landbouw
BPL	British Physical Laboratories Ltd
BPL	Bundesverband Personal- Leasing
BPMA	British Photographic Manufacturers Association
BPMA	British Poultry Meat Association
BPMA	British Premium Manufacturers Association
BPMA	British Printing Machinery Association
BPMA	British Pump Manufacturers' Association
BPMF	British Postgraduate Medical Federation
BPMF	British Pottery Manufacturers Federation (*now* BCMF)
BPMMA	British Paper Machinery Makers Association
BPMTG	British Puppet and Model Theatre Guild
BPNMA	British Plain Net Manufacturers Association
BPO	Union Tarifaire Balkan Proche- Orient (Bulgaria)
BPOC	British Post Office Corporation

BPPB	Balai Penjelidikan Perkebunan Besar (Indonesia)
BPPB	Banque de Paris et Pays-Bas
BPPMA	British Power-Press Manufacturers' Association
BPPG	Balai Penjelidikan Perusahaan Gula (Indonesia)
BPRA	British Book Publishers' Representatives' Association
BPRI	British Polarographic Research Institute
BPS	British Paper Stock Merchants Association, Ltd
BPS	British Pharmacological Society
BPS	British Photobiology Society
BPS	British Phrenological Society
BPS	British Postmark Society
BPS	British Printing Society
BPS	British Psychological Society
BPSA	British Pharmaceutical Students Association
BpT	Bundesverband Praktischer Tierärzte
BPV	Buitenlandse Persvereniging in Nederland
BQSF	British Quarrying and Slag Federation
BR	Betongvaruindustrins Riksförbund
BRA	Bee Research Association
BRA	Beef Research Association (now MLC)
BRA	British Radiesthesia Association
BRA	British Records Association
BRA	British Refrigeration Association (now BRACA)
BRA	British Resorts Association
BRA	British Rheumatic Association
BRA	British Rivet Association
BRAB	Building Research Advisory Board, National Research Council (U.S.A.)
BRACA	British Refrigeration and Air Conditioning Association
BRACODI	Société des Brasseries de la Côte- d'Ivoire
BRAEC	Bureau de Recherche et d'Action Économiques
BRAK	Bundesrechtsanwaltskammer
BRALUP	Bureau of Resource Assessment and Land Use Planning (Tanzania)
BRAMA	British Rubber and Resin Adhesive Manufacturers Association
BRANIGER	Brasseries et Boissons Gazeuses du Niger
BRANZ	Building Research Association of New Zealand
BRASTACS	Bradford Scientific, Technical and Commercial Service
BRB	British Railways Board
BRC	British Rabbit Council
BRC	British Record Centre
BRCA	British Roller Canary Association
BRCMA	British Radio Cabinet Manufacturers Association
BRCS	British Railways Catering Service
BRCS	British Red Cross Society
BRDA	British Racing Drivers Association
BRDB	British Rubber Development Board
BRDC	British Racing Drivers' Club
BRDC	British Research and Development Corporation
BRDG	Bituminous Development Group
BRE	Building Research Establishment
BREDA	Bureau Régional pour l'Éducation en Afrique (of UNESCO)
BREE-DANIA	Export Board for Breeding Cattle (Denmark)
BREG	British Rivet Export Group
BREMA	British Radio Equipment Manufacturers Association
BRF	Brewing Research Foundation
BRF	British Road Federation
BRFA	British-Romanian Friendship Association
BRFFI	Biochemical Research Foundation of the Franklin Institute (U.S.A.)
BRGM	Bureau de Recherches Géologiques et Minières
BRI	Banque des Règlements Internationaux
BRIC	Bloodstock and Racehorse Industries Confederation
BRICERAM	Société Centrafricaine de Briques et Céramiques
BRIMAFEX	British Manufacturers of Malleable Tube Fittings Export Group
BRIMEC	British Mechanical Engineering Confederation
BRINCO	British Newfoundland Development Corporation
BRINEX	British Newfoundland Exploration
BritIRE	British Institution of Radio Engineers

BRL	Butterwick Research Laboratories	**BSA**	Bund Schweizer Architekten
BRMA	British Resin Manufacturers Association	**BSAA**	British School of Archaeology at Athens
BRMA	British Rubber Manufacturers Association	**BSAA**	British South American Airways Corporation (BOAC)
BRMA	Bureau de Recherches Minières de l'Algérie	**BSAC**	British Society of Antimicrobial Chemotherapy
BRMCA	British Ready Mixed Concrete Association		
BRMF	British Rainwear Manufacturers Federation	**BSAC**	British Sub-Aqua Club
BRP	Bureau de Recherches de Pétrole	**BSAF**	Berufsverband der Schweizer Augenoptiker mit Höherer Fachschulausbildung
BRPF	Bertrand Russell Peace Foundation		
BRPM	Bureau de Recherches et de Participations Minières (Morocco)	**BSAF**	British Sulphate of Ammonia Federation
		BSALS	British Society of Agricultural Labour Science
BRPRA	British Rubber Producers Research Association		
BRRA	British Rayon Research Association	**BSANZ**	Bibliographical Society of Australia and New Zealand
BRRA	British Refractories Research Association	**BSAP**	British Association of Animal Production
BRRAMA	British Rubber and Resin Adhesive Manufacturers' Association	**BSATA**	Ballast, Sand and Allied Trades Association
		BSAVA	British Small Animal Veterinary Association
BRRI	Bangladesh Rice Research Institute	**BSB**	Bangladesh Shilpa Bank
BRRI	Building and Road Research Institute (Ghana)	**BSB**	British Sugar Bureau
		BSBA	British Starter Battery Association
BRS	British Record Society	**BSBC**	British Social Biology Council
BRS	Building Research Station	**BSBI**	Botanical Society of the British Isles
BRS	Burma Research Society	**BSBSPA**	British Sugar Beet Seed Producers Association
BRSCC	British Racing and Sports Car Club		
BRTA	British Racing Toboggan Association	**BSC**	Bibliographical Society of Canada
BRTA	British Regional Television Association	**BSC**	Biological Stain Commission (U.S.A.)
BRTA	British Reinforcement Textiles Association	**BSC**	British Safety Council
BRTA	British Road Tar Association	**BSC**	British Shippers Council
BRTDC	British Recorded Tape Development Committee	**BSC**	British Shoe Corporation
		BSC	British Society of Commerce
BRTS	British Roll Turners Trade Society	**BSC**	British Steel Corporation
BRU	Bilharzia Research Unit (South Africa)	**BSC**	British Sugar Corporation
BRUFMA	British Rigid Urethane Foam Manufacturers Association	**BSC**	British Sulphur Corporation
		BSCA	British Sulphate of Copper Association (Export) Ltd
BRVMA	British Radio Valve Manufacturers Association		
		BSCA	Bureau of Security and Consular Affairs (U.S.A.)
BS	Bekloedningsindustriens Sammensluting		
BS	Biometric Society (U.S.A.)	**BSCC**	British Society for Clinical Cytology
BSA	Bibliographical Society of America	**BSCC**	British Steelmakers Creep Committee
BSA	Birmingham Small Arms Co.	**BSCC**	British Swedish Chamber of Commerce in Sweden
BSA	British Shipbreakers Association		
BSA	British Society of Aesthetics	**BSCC**	British-Swiss Chamber of Commerce in Switzerland
BSA	British Society of Audiology		
BSA	British Sociological Association	**BSCC**	British Synchronous Clock Conference
BSA	British Speleological Association	**BSCD**	British Ski Club Disabled
BSA	Building Societies Association		

BSCP	Biological Sciences Communication Project (U.S.A.)	BSIRA	British Scientific Instrument Research Association (*now* SIRA)
BSCRA	British Steel Castings Research Association (*now* SCRATA)	BSIU	British Society for International Understanding
BSCS	Biological Sciences Curriculum Study (U.S.A.)	BSJA	British Schools Judo Association
BSD	British Society of Dowsers	BSJA	British Show Jumping Association
BSDA	British Spinners and Doublers Association	BSK	Berghof Stiftung für Konfliktforschung
BSDB	British Society for Developmental Biology	BSL	Botanical Society of London
BSDE	British Society of Digestive Endoscopy	BSL	Bundesverband Spedition und Lageri
BSE	British Shipbuilding Exports	BSMA	British Secondary Metals Association
BSEA	British Steel Export Association	BSMA	British Skate Makers Association
BSEM	British Society of Electronic Music	BSMGP	British Society of Master Glass Painters
BSES	British Schools Exploring Society	BSMMA	British Sugar Machinery Manufacturers Association
BSF	British Shipping Federation (*now* GCBS)	BSMSP	Bernoulli Society for Mathematical Statistics and Probability
BSF	British Slag Federation		
BSF	British Society of Flavourists	BSNDT	British Society for Non-Destructive Testing
BSF	British Softball Federation	BSOEA	British Stationery and Office Equipment Association
BSF	British Stone Federation		
BSFA	British Sanitary Fireclay Association	BSOPF	British Stationery and Office Products Federation
BSFA	British Science Fiction Association		
BSFA	British Steel Founders Association	BSP	British Society of Phenomenology
BSFS	British Soviet Friendship Society	BSP	Bureau Sanitaire Panaméricain
BSFW	Bureau of Sport Fisheries and Wildlife (U.S.A.)	BSPA	Basic Slag Producers Association
		BSPA	British Speedway Promoters Association
BSG	British Society of Gastroenterology	BSPA	British Sports Photographers Association
BSG	Bund Schweizerischer Garten- und Landschafts-architekten	BSPG	Binnenschiffahrts-Berufsgenossenschaft
		BSPMA	British Sewage Plant Manufacturers Association
BSH	British Society of Haematology		
BSH	British Society of Hypnotherapists	BSPP	Burmese Socialist Program Party
BSHP	British Society of the History of Pharmacy	BSPS	British Show Pony Society
BSHS	British Society for the History of Science	BSPS	British Society for the Philosophy of Science
BSI	British Societies Institute	BSR	Bund Schweizerischer Reklameberater und Werbeagenturen
BSI	British Society for Immunology		
BSI	British Standards Institution	BSRA	British Ship Research Association
BSIA	British Security Industry Association Ltd	BSRA	British Society for Research on Ageing
BSIB	Boy Scouts International Bureau	BSRA	British Sound Recording Association
BSIB	British Society for International Bibliography (*now* ASLIB)	BSRA	British Sugar Refiners' Association
		BSRAE	British Society for Research in Agricultural Engineering
BSIC	British Ski Instruction Council		
BSIHE	British Society for International Health Education (*now* SHE)	BSRC	British Sporting Rifle Club
		BSRD	British Society of Restorative Dentistry
BSIP	Birbal Sahni Institute of Palaeobotany (India)	BSRI	Brewing Scientific Research Institute (Japan)
BSIR	Board for Scientific and Industrial Research (Israel)	BSRIA	Building Services Research and Information Association

BSS	Berufsverband der Sozialarbeiter
BSS	British Sailors Society
BSS	British Sheep Society
BSSM	British Society for Strain Measurement
BSSBG	British Society for Social and Behavioural Gerontology
BSSG	British Society of Scientific Glassblowers
BSSMS	British Society for the Study of Mental Subnormality
BSSO	British Society for the Study of Orthodontics
BSSPD	British Society for the Study of Prosthetic Dentistry
BSSR	Bureau of Social Science Research
BSSRS	British Society for Social Responsibility in Science
BSSS	British Society of Soil Science
BSSSA	British Surgical Support Suppliers Association
BSSSC	Baltic Sea Salmon Standing Committee
BST	Byggstandardiseringen
BSTA	British Surgical Trades Association
BStBK	Bundessteuerberaterkammer
BSTC	British Student Travel Centre
BSTF	British Student Tuberculosis Foundation
BSW	Botanical Society of Washington (U.S.A.)
BSWB	Boy Scouts World Bureau (*now* WSB)
BSWIA	British Steel Wire Industries Association
BTA	Billiards Trade Association
BTA	Blood Transfusion Association (U.S.A.)
BTA	British Tourist Authority (*formerly* British Travel Association)
BTA	British Trade Association of New Zealand
BTA	British Tugowners Association
BTAO	Bureau of Technical Assistance Operations (UNO)
BTASA	Book Trade Association of South Africa
BTBA	British Tenpin Bowling Association
BTBA	British Twinning and Bilingual Association
BTBMF	British Tin Box Manufacturers Association
BTC	British Textile Confederation
BTC	British Transport Commission
BTCC	Board of Transportation Commissioners of Canada
BTCD	Banque Tchadienne de Crédit et de Dépôts
BTCMPI	British Technical Council of the Motor and Petroleum Industries
BTCS	British Transport Catering Service
BTCV	British Trust for Conservation Volunteers
BTD	Banque Togolaise de Développement
BTDB	British Transport Docks Board
BTDR	Banque Tanzanienne de Développement Rural
BTE	Böripari Tudományos Egyesület
BTE	Bundesverband des Deutschen Textil-Einzelhandels
BTEA	British Textile Employers Association
BTEMA	British Tanning Extract Manufacturers Association
BTF	British Tarpaviors Federation Ltd
BTF	British Trampoline Federation
BTF	British Trawlers Federation (*now* BFF)
BTF	British Turkey Federation
BTF	Bundesverband Freier Tankstellen und Unabhängiger Deutscher Mineralölhändler
BTG	British Toymakers' Guild
BTG	Bundesverband des Deutschen Tankstellen und Garagengewerbes
BTGV	Belgische Technische Gieterijvereniging
BTH	British Thomson-Houston Company Ltd
BTHA	British Travel and Holidays Association (*now* BTA)
BTI	Bundesverband der Tabakwaren- Importeure
BTIA	British Tape Industry Association
BTIA	British Tar Industry Association
BTIPR	Boyce Thompson Institute for Plant Research (U.S.A.)
BTL	Bell Telephone Laboratories (U.S.A.)
BTMA	British Textile Machinery Association
BTMA	British Theatre Museum Association
BTMA	British Toy Manufacturers Association
BTMA	British Typewriter Manufacturers' Association
BTN	Bydogoskie Towarzystwo Naukowe
BTO	Boeren-en Tuinders Onderlinge
BTO	British Trust for Ornithology
BTO	Brussels Trade Organization (Belgium)
BTOF	Federation of British Trawler Officers
BTOG	British Transport Officers Guild
BTPS	Bâtiments et Travaux Publics Sénégalaise

BTR	British Telecommunications Research Ltd	BVA	British Radio Valve Manufacturers Association
BTRA	Bombay Textile Research Association (India)	BVA	British Veterinary Association
BTS	British Temperance Society	BVA	British Vigilance Association
BTS	British Transplantation Society	BVAB	Bedrijfsvereniging voor het Agrarisch Bedrijf
BTS	British Trolleybus Society	BVB	Belgische Vereniging der Banken
BTS	Burma Translation Society	BVB	Belgische Vereniging voor de Bedrijfspers
BTSA	British Tensional Strapping Association	BVB	Beroepsvereniging voor Binnenhuisarchitekten
BTTA	British Thoracic and Tuberculosis Association	BvB	Bond van Bontbedrijven
BTUC	Bahamas Trade Union Congress	BVB	Bundesverband des Bodenlegerhandwerks
BU	British Union of Great Britain and Ireland	BVB	Bundesverband der Büromaschinen-Importeure
BUA	British United Airways	BVD	Belgische Vereniging der Detectives
BUAF	British United Air Ferries	BVD	Belgische Vereniging voor Dokumentatie
BUAS	British Universities Association of Slavists	BVDB	Börsenverein des Deutscher Büchhandels
BUAV	British Union for the Abolition of Vivisection	BVDL	Bundesverband Deutscher Leibeserzieher
BUFC	British Universities Film Council	BVEM	Belgische Vereniging voor Elektronen-Mikroskopie
BUFO	British Union of Family Organisations		
BUFOFI	Bundesforschung für Fischerie	BVFA	Bundesverband Feuerlöschgeräte und Anlagen-Industrie
BUFORA	British Unidentified Flying Objects Research Association	BVG	Nederlandse Bond voor het Glasbewerkings-, Glazeniers- en Glas-in Loodbedrijf
BUIC	Bureau Universitaire d'Information sur les Carrières	BVG	Svenska Byggvarugrossistföreningen
BUIRA	British Universities Industrial Relations Association	BVI	Bundesverband Deutscher Investment-Gesellschaften
BUMICO	Bureau Minier Congolais	BVK	Bond van Kleermakerspatroons in Nederland
BUNAC	British Universities North American Club	BVK	Bundesverband Deutscher Versicherungs-kaufleute
BUOC	British Union Oil Company		
BUP	British United Press	BVL	Bergverkenes Landssammenslutning
BUPA	British United Provident Association	BVLJ	Belgische Vereniging van Landbouw-journalisten
BURISA	British Urban and Regional Information Systems Association	BVLT	Belgische Vereniging van Laboratorium-technologen
BURO	Bureau Universitaire de Recherche Operationnelle (France)	BVM	Bundesverband Deutscher Marktforscher
BUS	Bureau Universitaire de Statistique et de Documentation Scolaire et Professionnelle	BVMA	British Valve Manufacturers' Association
BUSA	British Universities Society of Arts	BVMB	Bundesvereinigung Mittelständischer Bau-unternehmunger
BUSDOM	Bureau Shell d'Outre-Mer		
BUSF	British Universities' Sports Federation	BVÖ	Berufsverband Bildender Künstler Österreichs
BUSTA	British Universities Student Travel Association	BVÖ	Bergmännischer Verband Österreichs
BUTYRA	Centrale Suisse de Ravitaillement en Beurre	BVÖ	Technisch-Wissenschaftlicher Verein 'Berg-männischer Verband Österreichs'
BUVOHA	Vereningen Bureau voor Handelsinlichtingen		
BV	Betonvereniging	BVOP	Belgisch-Luxemburgse Vereniging van de Ondernemingspers
BVA	Berufsverband der Augenärzte Deutschlands		
BVA	Bond van Adverteerders	BvP	Bond van Platenhandelaren

BVP	British Volunteer Programme
BVPA	Bundesverband der Pressebild-Agenturen, Bilderdienste und Bildarchive
BvPA	Bundesverband der Pressedienste und -agenturen
BVPG	Belgische Vakgroep voor Petroleumgassen
BVR	Belgische Vereniging van de Rubberindustrie
BVS	Bundesverband Öffenlich Bestellter und Vereidigter Sachverständiger
BVSM	Belgische Vereniging tot Studie, Beproefing en Gebruik der Materialen
BVTA	Bundesarbeitsgemeinschaft der Vereinigungen der Teer- und Asphalt-makadamherstellenden Firmen
BVUIH	Belgisch Vereniging van Uit- en Invoerhandelaars
BVV	Belgische Vereniging voor Verlamden
BVVB	Belgische Vereniging der Voedingsbedrijven met Bijhuizen
BVVK	Beroepsvereniging der Vis Groothandelaars-Verzenders van de Kust
BVVO	Beroepsvereniging Verzekerings-ondernemingen
BVZ	Belgische Vereniging der Ziekenhuizen
BWA	Baptist World Alliance
BWA	British Waterfowl Association
BWA	British Waterworks Association
BWB	British Waterways Board
BWC	Baltic World Conference (U.S.A.)
BWCC	British Weed Control Council
BWCMG	British Watch and Clock Makers Guild
BWETPA	British Water and Effluent Treatment Plant Association
BWF	Belgische Wegenfederatie
BWF	British Whiting Federation
BWF	British Wool Federation
BWG	Braunschweigische Wissenschaftliche Gesellschaft
BWIA	British West Indies Airways
BWISA	British West Indies Sugar Association
BWK	Bund der Wasser- und Kulturbauingenieure
BWMA	British Woodwork Manufacturers' Association
BWMB	British Wool Marketing Board
BWPA	British Waste Paper Association
BWPA	British Women Pilots' Association
BWPA	British Wood Preserving Association
BWPA	British Wood Pulp Association
BWPUC	British Waste Paper Utilization Council
BWRA	British Welding Research Association
BWRE	Biological Warfare Research Establishment
BWRRA	British Wire Rod Rollers' Association
BWS	British Water Colour Society
BWSF	British Water Ski Federation
BWSTMA	British Welded Steel Tube Manufacturers Association
BWTA	British Women's Temperance Association
BWTA	British Wood Turners Association
BWV	Bundesverband Werkverkehr und Verlader
BWVS	Bundeswirtschaftsvereinigung Sport-schiffahrt
BWWA	British Waterworks Association
BYBA	British Youth Band Association
BYNA	British Young Naturalists Association
BZ	Bedrijfschap voor Zuivel (Dairy Produce Corporation) (Netherlands)
BZB	Verband der Deutschen Bauzubehörindustrie

C

CA	Chambre d'Agriculture (France)
CAA	Canadian Authors' Association
CAA	Caribbean Archives Association
CAA	Catholic Art Association (U.S.A.)
CAA	Central African Airways
CAA	Centro Azucarero Argentino
CAA	Christian Adventure Association
CAA	Civil Aeronautics Administration (U.S.A.)
CAA	Civil Aviation Authority
CAA	Collectors of American Art (U.S.A.)
CAA	Commonwealth Association of Architects (U.K.)
CAA	Community Aid Abroad (Australia)
CAA	Conseil Africain de l'Arachide
CAA	Cost Accountants' Association
CAAA	Canadian Association of Advertising Agencies

CAAB	Canadian Advertising Advisory Board	**CABMA**	Canadian Association of British Manufacturers and Agencies
CAABU	Council for the Advancement of Arab-British Understanding	**CABO**	Council of American Building Officials
CAAC	Civil Aviation Administration of China	**CABRA**	Copper and Brass Research Association (U.S.A.)
CAACTD	Comité Asesor sobre la Aplicación de la Ciencia y la Tecnologia al Desarrollo (*of* UNO)	**CAC**	Canterbury Agricultural College, Lincoln (N.Z.)
CAAE	Canadian Association for Adult Education	**CAC**	Colonial Advisory Council
CAAEO	Commission des Affaires d'Aise et d'Extrême-Orient de la Chambre de Commerce Internationale	**CAC**	Comité Administratif de Coordination (ECOSOC)
		CAC	Consumers Advisory Council (U.S.A.)
CAAIM	Coopérative Agricole d'Approvisionnement des Agriculteurs de le Marche	**CAC**	Consumers Association of Canada
CAAK	Civil Aviation Administration of Korea	**CACA**	Canadian Agricultural Chemicals Association
CAANS	Canadian Association for the Advancement of Netherlandic Studies	**CACA**	Cement and Concrete Association
CAARC	Commonwealth Advisory Aeronautical Research Council	**CACAS**	Civil Aviation Council of the Arab States
		CACC	Civil Aviation Communications Centre
CAARM	Confederación de Asociaciones Algodoneras de la República Mexicana	**CACCI**	Confederation of Asian Chambers of Commerce and Industry (Philippines)
CAAS	Canadian Association of African Studies	**CACDS**	Commonwealth Advisory Committee on Defence Science
CAAS	Canadian Association for American Studies	**CACE**	Central Advisory Council for Education
CAAS	Ceylon Association for the Advancement of Science	**CACEF**	Centre d'Action Culturelle de la Communauté d'Expression Française
CAASA	Centre Africain d'Application de Statistique Agricole (of FAO) (Nigeria)	**CACEP**	Société Camerounaise de Commercialisation et d'Exportation de Produits
CAAV	Central Association of Agricultural Valuers	**CACEPA**	Centre d'Actions Concertées des Entreprises de Produits Alimentaire
CAAV	Civil Aviation Administration of Vietnam		
CAB	Canadian Association of Broadcasters	**CACEX**	Carteira de Comercio Exterior (Brazil)
CAB	Citizens Advice Bureau	**CACI**	Catholic Alumni Clubs International (U.S.A.)
CAB	Civil Aeronautics Board (U.S.A.)	**CACI**	Civil Aviation Chaplains International
CAB	Comité des Assurers Belges	**CACIA**	Compagnie d'Agriculture de Commerce et d'Industrie d'Afrique (Guinée)
CAB	Commonwealth Agricultural Bureaux (*formerly* IAB)	**CACIP**	Central American Co-operative Corn Improvement Project
CAB	Compagnie Africaine des Bois (Ivory Coast)		
CABA	Connecticut Artificial Breeding Association (U.S.A.)	**CACIP**	Confederación Argentina de Comercio de la Industria y de la Producción
CABEI	Central American Bank for Economic Integration	**CACIRA**	Chambre Syndicale des Constructeurs d'Appareils de Contrôle Industriel et de Régulation Automatique
CABEI	Intergovernmental Committee on the River Plate Basin (Uruguay)	**CACJ**	Comité de Asuntos Constitucionales y Jurídicos (FAO)
CABET	Canadian Association of Business Education Teachers	**CACL**	Canadian Association of Children's Libraries
CABIN	Campaign Against Building Industry Nationalization	**CACM**	Central American Common Market
		CACMI	Comité Africain pour la Coordination des Moyens d'Information
CABM	Commonwealth of Australia Bureau of Meteorology	**CACOM**	Central American Common Market

CACP	Chambre des Agences-Conseils en Publicité (Belgium)	**CAEES**	Centre Algérien d'Expansion Économique et Social
CACR	Council for Agricultural and Chemurgic Research (U.S.A.)	**CAEF**	Comité des Associations Européennes de Fonderie
CACRMA	Caisse Autonome Centrale de Retraites Mutuelles Agricoles	**CAEI**	Compagnie Africaine d'Équipement Industriel (Ivory Coast)
CACTAL	Conference on the Application of Science and Technology to Latin America	**CAEJ**	Communauté des Associations d'Éditeurs de Journaux de la CEE
CACTM	Central Advisory Council of Training for the Ministry	**CAEM**	Campo Agrícola Experimental de Mexicali
CACUL	Canadian Society of College and University Libraries	**CAEM**	Conseil d'Assistance Économique Mutuelle (U.S.S.R.)
CAD	Centralforeningen af Autoreparatører i Danmark	**CAEMC**	Comité d'Associations Européennes de Médecins Catholiques
CAD	Comité Agricole Départemental	**CAEND**	Centro Argentino de Ensayo no Destructivos de Materiales (Argentine)
CAD	Comité d'Aide au Développement *of* OCDE	**CAEPC**	Comisión Asesora Europea sobre Pesca Continental
CADA	Campaign Against Drug Addiction		
CADAFE	Compania Anonima de Administración y Fomento Eléctrico (Venezuela)	**CAEPE**	Centre d'Assemblage et d'Essais des Propulseurs et des Engins
CADAL	Compagnie Africaine Forestière et des Allumettes	**CAES**	Canadian Agricultural Economics Society
CADAUMA	Coopérative Agricole d'Achat et d'Utilisation de Matériel Agricole de l'Aveyron	**CAES**	Central Association of Experiment Stations (Indonesia)
CADEB	Confederación Americana de Empleados Bancarios	**CAES**	Chiba Prefecture Agricultural Experiment Station (Japan)
CADEC	Christian Action for Development in the Caribbean (Antigua)	**CAESPCI**	Central Association of Experimental Stations for Perennial Crops in Indonesia
CADEF	Centro Argentino de Estudios Forestales	**CAEU**	Council of Arab Economic Unity
CADER	Consejo Argentino de Estudios sobre la Reproducción	**CAEVR**	Comité d'Action École et Vie Rurale
CADES	Centro Argentino de Estudios Sociológicos	**CAF**	Central African Federation
CADIA	Centro Argentino de Ingenieros Agrónomos	**CAF**	Comptoir Agricole Français
CADICEC	Association des Cadres et Dirigeants Chrétiens des Entreprises au Congo et au Rwanda-Burundi	**CAF**	Confédération Africaine de Football
		CAF	Conseil de l'Agriculture Française
		CAF	Corporación Andina de Fomento (Colombia)
CADIF	Cámara Argentina de la Industria Frigorífica	**CAFA**	Chambre Agricole Franco-Allemande
CADIPPE	Comité d'Action pour le Développement de l'Interessement du Personnel à la Productivité des Entreprises	**CAFAC**	Commission Africaine de l'Aviation Civile
		CAFADE	Comisión Nacional Administración del Fondo de Apoyo al Desarrollo Económico (Argentina)
CADO	Central Air Documents Office (U.S.A.)	**CAFAL**	Compagnie Africaine Forestière et des Allumettes
CADU	Chilalo Agricultural Development Unit (Ethiopia)	**CAFC**	Compagnie Agricole et Forestière du Cameroun
CAE	Compagnie Européenne d'Automatisme Électronique	**CAFCO**	Caisse d'Allocations Familiales des Sociétés Coopératives de Consommation et de Production de la Suisse Romande
CAEA	Central American Economics Association		
CAEC	Committee of the Acta Endocrinologica Countries		
CAEC	County Agricultural Executive Committee	**CAFCO**	Compagnie Africaine de Commerce et de Commission

CAFE	Compañia Americana de Fomento Económico
CAFEA-ICC	Commission on Asian and Far Eastern Affairs of the International Chamber of Commerce
CAFESA	Compañía Costarricense del Café
CAFI	Commercial Advisory Foundation in Indonesia
CAFIC	Combined Allied Forces Information Centre
CAFMNA	Compound Animal Feedingstuffs Manufacturers National Association
CAFMS	Central American Federation of Medical Students
CAFOD	Catholic Fund for Overseas Development
CAFPTA	Comisión Aministradora del Fondo para la Promoción de la Tecnología Agropecuaria (Argentina)
CAFRAD	Centre Africain de Formation et de Recherches Administratives pour le Développement (Morocco)
CAFTA	Central American Free Trade Association
CAFTA	Comisión Administradora para el Fondo de Tecnologia Agropecuaria (Argentina)
CAFTEX	Compagnie Africaine de Textile (Ivory Coast)
CAFUM	Companhia de Fumigaçoes de Moçambique
CAG	Canadian Association of Geographers
CAG	Comparative Administrative Group of the American Society for Public Administration
CAGAC	Civil Aviation General Administration of China
CAH	Compagnie Africaine d'Hôtellerie (Congo)
CAHN	Cooperative Agricole Haute Normand
CAI	Canadian Aeronautical Institute
CAI	Club Alpino Italiano
CAI	Consumers Association of Ireland
CAIA	Céntro Argentine de Ingeniéros Agrónomos
CAIA	Congreso Argentino de la Industria Aceitera
CAIC	Caribbean Association of Industry and Commerce
CAIC	Compagnie d'Agriculture d'Industrie et de Commerce (Madagascar)
CAIFOM	Caisse de la France d'Outre-Mer
CAIM	Compagnie Agricole et Industrielle de Madagascar
CAIM	Syndicat National des Créateurs d'Architectures Intérieures et de Modèles

CAIMO	Comité Asesor de Investigaciones Meteorólogicas Oceánicas (of WMO)
CAIR	Comité d'Action Interallié de la Résistance
CAIRM	Comité Asesor sobre Investigaciones de los Recursos Marinos (of FAO)
CAIRU	Colonial Agricultural Insecticides Research Unit
CAIS	Canadian Association for Information Science
CAIS	Central American Integration Scheme
CAITA	Compagnie Agricole et Industrielle des Tabacs Africains
CAJ	Internationale Christliche Arbeiterjugend
CAJP	Clubes Agricolas Juveniles del Perú
CAL	Centro di Azione Latina
CAL	China Airlines Ltd
CAL	Cocoa Association of London
CALA	Christiana Area Land Authority (West Indies)
CALANS	Caribbean and Latin American News Service
CALB	Confédération Africano-Levantine de Billard
CALCOFI	California Cooperative Oceanic Fisheries Investigations (U.S.A.)
CALG	Compagnie des Landes de Gascogne
CALL	Canadian Association of Law Libraries
CALNU	Cooperativa Agropecuaria Limitada Norte Uruguayo
CALO	Coopérative Agricole Lainière de l'Ouest
CALPA	Canadian Air Line Pilots Association
CALQ	Centro Académico "Luiz de Queiróz" (Brazil)
CALS	Canadian Association of Library Schools
CAM	Cercle Archaeologique de Mons
CAM	Commission for Agricultural Meteorology (WMO)
CAM	Committee for Aquatic Microbiology (U.N.)
CAM	Commonwealth Association of Museums
CAMAA	Comptoir Africain de Matériel Abidjan (Ivory Coast)
CAMACOL	Cámara Colombiana de la Construcción
CAMAD	Société Camerounaise de Produits Alimentaires et Diététiques
CAMAG	Société Camerounaise de Grands Magasins
CAMARCA	Caisse Mutuelle Autonome de Retraites Complémentaires Agricoles
CAMBOIS	Société Camerounaise des Bois

CAMC	Canadian Association of Management Consultants
CAMC	Corporación Argentina de Productores Avicolas
CAMDA	Car and Motorcycle Drivers Association
CAMDEV	Cameroons Development Corporation
CAME	Conference of Allied Ministers of Education
CAME	Consejo de Ayuda Mutua Económica (Cuba)
CAMEC	Compagnie Africaine de Métaux et de Produits Chimiques (Dahomey)
CAMECO	Catholic Media Council (Germany)
CAMEP	Société Camerounaise d'Études et de Promotion pour l'Afrique
CAMES	Conseil Africaine et Malgache pour l'Enseignement Supérieur
CAMESA	Canadian Military Electronics Standards Agency
CAMGOC	Gulf Oil Company of Cameroon
CAMI	Cameroon Motors Industries
CAMIG	Companhia Agricola de Minas Gerais (Brazil)
CAMIRA	Comité d'Application des Méthodes Isotopiques aux Recherches Agronomiques (Belgium)
CAMJA	Comisión Nacional de Apoyo al Movimiento Juvenil Agrario (Uruguay)
CAML	Canadian Association of Music Libraries
CAMOA	Société Camerounaise d'Oxygène et d'Acétylène
CAMRA	Campaign for the Revitalisation of Ale
CAMROC	Cambridge Radio Observatory Committee (U.S.A.)
CAMS	Council for Asian Manpower Studies (Philippines)
CAMSI	Canadian Association of Medical Students and Interns
CAMT	Cámara Argentina Maderas Terciadas
CANA	Cooperative Agricole la Noelle, Ancenis
CANAI	Comitato Artistico Nazionale Acconciatori Italiani
CANCEE	Canadian National Committee for Earthquake Engineering
CANCIRCO	Cancer International Research Cooperative
CANEFA	Comisión Asesora Nacional de Erradicación de la Fiebre Aftosa (Argentina)
CANGO	Committee for Air Navigation and Ground Organization
CANJ	Ceramic Association of New Jersey (U.S.A.)
CANSG	Civil Aviation Navigational Services Group
CANSM	Caisse Autonome Nationale de la Sécurité dans les Mines
CANTIER-MACCHINE	Associazione Commercianti Importatori Macchine da Cantiere ed Affini
CANTV	Compania Anonima Nacional Telefonos de Venezuela
CANUSPA	Canada, Australia, New Zealand and United States Parents Association
CANWEG	Canadian National Committee of the World Energy Conference
CANYS	Ceramic Association of New York State (U.S.A.)
CAO	Canadian Association of Optometricists
CAOBISCO	Association d'Industries de Produits Sucrés de la CEE
CAOPRI	Central Arecanut and Oil Palm Research Institute (India)
CAORB	Civil Aviation Operational Research Branch
CAOSO	Coopérative Agricole Ovine du Sud-Ouest
CAOT	Canadian Association of Occupational Therapy
CAP	Canadian Association of Physicists
CAP	Central Agricultural Producers
CAP	Centres d'Alevinage Principaux (Zaire)
CAP	Committee on Agricultural Policies (of ECE)
CAP	Commonwealth Association of Planners
CAP	Compagnie Africaine d'Armement à la Pêche
CAP	Compagnie d'Agences de Publicité
CAP	Cooperative Agricole de Productie (Roumania)
CAPA	Canadian Association of Purchasing Agents
CAPA	Comisión Asesora de Politica Agraria (Venezuela)
CAPA	Compagnie Africaine de Produits Alimentaires
CAPA	Selección y Comercio de la Patata de Siembra
CAPAC	Composers' Authors' and Publishers Association of Canada
CAPAR	Centre d'Animation et de Promotion Agricole et Rurale
CAPC	Central African Power Corporation
CAPC	Comité Ampliado del Programa y de la Coordinación (UNDP)
CAPE	Centre Africain de Promotion Économique

CAPEB	Confédération de l'Artisanat et des Petites Entreprises du Bâtiment
CAPEF	Coopérative Agricole des Producteurs d'Endives de France
CAPEL	Centre pour l'Accroissement de la Productivité des Entreprises Laitières
CAPEM	Comité d'Aménagement et du Plan d'Équipement de la Moselle
CAPER	Caisse d'Accession à la Propriété et à l'Exploitation Rurales (Algeria)
CAPERAS	Comité Argentino para el Estudio de la Regiones Aridas y Semiáridas
CAPI	Comisión de Administración Pública Internacional
CAPIA	Cámara Argentina de Productores Industriales Avícolas
CAPIEL	Common Market Association for Switchgear and Control Devices
CAPIM	Consortium Africain de Produits Industriels et Ménagers (Ivory Coast)
CAPITB	Chemical and Allied Products Industry Training Board
CAPL	Canadian Association of Public Libraries
CAPL	Coastal Anti-Pollution League
CAPMA	Caisse d'Assurance et de Prévoyance Mutuelle des Agriculteurs
CAPMS	Central Agency for Public Mobilisation and Statistics (Egypt)
CAPRAL	Compagnie Africaine de Preparations Alimentaires (Ivory Coast)
CAPS	Centro de Adiestramiento para Promotores Sociales de la Universidad Rafael Landivar (Guatemala)
CAPS	Confédération Agricole des Producteurs de Plantes Saccharifères
CAPSES	Cooperativa Aragonesa de Productores de Semillas Selectas
CAPSOME	Comité d'Action des Producteurs et Stockeurs d'Oléagineux pour les Marchés Extérieurs
CAR	Canadian Association of Radiologists
CAR	Central African Republic
CAR	Centre of African Studies
CAR	Comité Agricole Régional
CAR	Corporación Autóctona Regional de la Sabana de Bogota y de los Valles de Ullate y Chinquinquirá (Colombia)
CARAC	Civil Aviation Radio Advisory Committee
CARASE	Centre Algérien de la Recherche Agronomique, Sociologique et Économique
CARAVA	Christian Association for Radio and Audio-Visual Aid (India)
CARBAP	Confederación de Asociaciones Rurales de Buenos Aires y La Lampa (Argentina)
CARC	Central Asian Research Centre (U.K.)
CARCLO	Confederación de Asociaciones Rurales del Centro y Litoral Oeste (Argentina)
CARD	Campaign Against Racial Discrimination
CARD	Center for Agricultural and Rural Development (U.S.A.)
CARDAN	Centre d'Analyse et de Recherche Documentaires pour l'Afrique Noire
CARDE	Canadian Armament Research and Development Establishment
CARE	Cooperative for American Relief for Everywhere
CAREF	Centre Algérien de Recherches et Expérimentations Forestières
CARENA	Compagnie Abidjanaise de Réparations Navales et de Travaux Industriels (Ivory Coast)
CARF	Canadian Advertising Research Foundation
CARIBANK	Caribbean Development Bank
CARIC	Compagnie Africaine de Représentations Industrielles et Commerciales (Congo, Gabon, Ivory Coast)
CARICOM	Caribbean Community
CARIFTA	Caribbean Free Trade Association
CARIPLO	Cassa di Risparmio delle Province Lombarde
CARIRI	Caribbean Industrial Research Institute (Trinidad)
CARIRI-TIS	Caribbean Industrial Research Institute. Technical Information Service
CARIS	Current Agricultural Research Information System (of FAO)
CARIS-FORM	Caribbean Institute for Social Formation
CARISOV	Caribische Institut voor Social Vorming
CARITAS INTER-NATIO-NALIS	Conférence Internationale des Charités Catholiques
CARO	Société de Fabrication de Carrelages et Revêtements au Cameroun
CARPA	Caribbean Psychiatric Association

CARPAS	Comisión Asesora Regional de Pesca para el Atlántico Sud-occidental (FAO)	**CASME**	Commonwealth Association of Science and Mathematics Educators
CARS	Canadian Arthritis and Rheumatism Society	**CASMT**	Central Association of Science and Mathematics Teachers (U.S.A.)
CARS	Central Agricultural Research Station (Somalia)	**CASRO**	Commission d'Achat de la Suisse Romande
CARTG	Canadian Amateur Radio Teletype Group	**CASRSS**	Centre of Advanced Study and Research in Social Sciences (Bangladesh)
CARVOLT	Société de Cartoucherie Voltaïque		
CAS	Caribbean Air Services	**CASSIS**	Communications and Social Science Information Service
CAS	Club Alpin Suisse		
CAS	Commission for Atmospheric Sciences (WMO)	**CAST**	Centre d'Actualisation Scientifique et Technique
CAS	Committee on Atlantic Studies (U.S.A.)	**CAST**	Confédération Africaine des Syndicats Libres
CAS	Conciliation and Arbitration Service	**CAST**	Consolidated African Selection Trust (Ghana)
CASA	Canadian Amateur Swimming Association		
CASA	Canadian Automatic Sprinkler Association	**CAST-AFRICA**	Conference of Ministers of African Member States Responsible for the Application of Science and Technology to Development
CASA	Contemporary Art Society of Australia		
CASANZ	Clean Air Society of Australia and New Zealand	**CASTALA**	Conference of Ministers of Latin American Member States Responsible for the Application of Science and Technology to Development
CASBO	Conference of American Small Business Organisations		
CASC	Caisse d'Assurances des Coopératives Suisse de Consommation	**CASTARAB**	Conference of Ministers of Arab Member States Responsible for the Application of Science and Technology to Development
CASC	Committee on African Studies in Canada		
CASCC	Canadian Agricultural Services Co-ordinating Committee	**CASTASIA**	Conference of Ministers of Asian Member States Responsible for the Application of Science and Technology to Development
CASDS	Centre for Advanced Study in the Developmental Sciences	**CASU**	Co-operative Association of Suez Canal Users
CASE	Committee on Academic Science and Engineering (U.S.A.)	**CASVAL**	Coopérative d'Approvisionnement des Syndicats Viticoles et Agricoles du Loire à Orléans
CASE	Confederation for the Advancement of State Education		
CASEC	Confederation of Associations of Specialist Engineering Contractors	**CAT**	Comité de l'Assistance Technique de l'O.N.U. (UNO)
CASHA	Centre Africain des Sciences Humaines Appliquées	**CAT**	Compagnie Africaine de Transformation (Togo)
CASI	Canadian Aeronautics and Space Institute	**CAT**	Compagnie Africaine de Transports
CASI	Commission Aéronautique Sportive Internationale	**CATA**	Compagnie Africaine de Transports Automobiles
CASLE	Commonwealth Association of Surveying and Land Engineering	**CATC**	Commonwealth Air Transport Commission
CASL-HV	Confédération Africaine des Syndicats Libres de la Haute Volta	**CATC**	Confédération Africaine des Travailleurs Croyants (Upper Volta)
CASLF	Comité d'Action pour la Sauvegarde des Libertés Forestières	**CATCA**	Canadian Air Traffic Control Association
		CATCC	Canadian Association of Textile Colourists and Chemists
CASLIS	Canadian Association of Special Libraries and Information Services	**CATECO**	Société Camerounaise d'Automobile de Technique et du Commerce

CATED   Centre d'Assistance Technique et de Documentation du Bâtiment et des Travaux Publique

CATEL   Compagnie Africaine de Télévision (Ivory Coast)

CATET   Centro Argentino de Técnicos en Estudios del Trabajo

CATEX   Société Centrafricaine des Textiles pour l'Exportation

CATG   Chinese Agricultural Technical Group (Vietnam)

CATI   Centres Administratifs et Techniques Interdépartementaux

CATIE   Centro Agrónomico Tropical de Investigación y Enseñanza (Costa Rica)

CATM   Chinese Agricultural Technical Mission to Vietnam (*now* CATG)

CATP   Compagnie Africaine de Travaux Publics (Ivory Coast)

CATPA   Comité d'Action Technique contre la Pollution Atmosphérique

CATRA   Cutlery and Allied Trades Research Association

CATRF   Central Africa Tea Research Foundation (Malawi)

CATU   Ceramic and Allied Trades Union

CAV   Cámara Agricola de Venezuela

CAV   Ceskoslovenská Akademie Ved

CAVEDINA   Cámara Venezolana de Industriales de Arroz

CAVI   Centre Audio-Visuel International

CAVIC   Corporación Agroeconómica, Viticola, Industrial y Comercial (Argentina)

CAVINEX   Société Camerounaise d'Exploitation Vinicole

CAVN   Comité d'Aménagement de la Vallée du Niari

CAVO   Centralgenossenschaft für Alkoholfreie Verwertung von Obstprodukten (Switzerland)

CAVV   Coöperatieve Aan- en Verkoop Vereniging

CAVY   Coopérative Agricole et Viticole du Départmente de l'Yonne

CAWC   Central Advisory Water Committee

CAZF   Comité des Agrumes de la Zone Franc

CAZ   Ceskoslovenská Akademie Ved Zemedelských

CAZRI   Central Arid Zone Research Institute (India)

CBA   Caribbean Atlantic Airways

CBA   Chambre Belge de l'Affichage et Média Connexes

CBA   Concrete Block Association

CBA   Council for British Archaeology

CBABG   Commonwealth Bureau of Animal Breeding and Genetics

CBAE   Commonwealth Bureau of Agricultural Economics

CBAH   Commonwealth Bureau of Animal Health

CBAMC   Chambre Belge de l'Affichage et Média Connexes

CBAN   Commonwealth Bureau of Animal Nutrition

CBAT   Central Bureau for Astronomical Telegrams (Denmark)

CBAT   Centro de Biología Aquática Tropical (Portugal)

CBB   Centrale Besturenbond v. Zuivelorganisaties in Nederland

CBB   Confédération des Betteraviers Belges

CBB   Confédération des Brasseries de Belgique

CBBA   Comissão Brasileira de Bibliotecarios Agrícolas

CBC   Canadian Broadcasting Corporation

CBC   Chad Basin Commission

CBC   Société Commerciale des Bois du Cameroun

CBCC   Canada-British Columbia Consultative Board

CBCC   Chemical-Biological Co-ordination Centre (U.S.A)

CBCISS   Centro Brasileiro de Cooperação e Intercambio de Serviços Sociais

CBCS   Commonwealth Bureau of Census and Statistics (Australia)

CBCSM   Council of British Ceramic Sanitaryware Manufacturers

CBD   Centralforeningen af Benzinforhandlere i Danmark

CBD   Comité Belge de la Distribution

CBD   Corporación Boliviana de Desarrollo

CBD   International Council of Ballroom Dancing

CBDIC   Centre Belge de Documentation et d'Information de la Construction

CBDST   Commonwealth Bureau of Dairy Science and Technology

CBE   Council of Biology Editors (U.S.A.)

CBEA   Centro Brazileiro de Estatísticas Agropecuárias

CBEFEN	Comité Belge des Expositions et des Foires et d'Expansion Nationale
CBEMA	Canadian Business Equipment Manufacturers Association
CBEN	Comisión Boliviana de Energia Nuclear
CBEVE	Central Bureau for Educational Visits and Exchanges
CBF	Corporación Boliviana de Fomento
CBG	Chambre Belge des Graphistes
CBG	Compagnie des Bauxites de Guinée
CBH	Commonwealth Bureau of Helminthology
CBHPC	Commonwealth Bureau of Horticulture and Plantation Crops
CBI	Comisión Ballenera Internacional
CBI	Confederation of British Industry
CBJO	Co-ordinating Board of Jewish Organizations for Consultation with the Economic and Social Council of the United Nations
CBK	Centraal Brouwerij Kantoor
CBL	Centraal Bureau Levensmiddelenbedrijf
CBL	Cercle Belge de la Librairie
CBL	Commission Centrale Belge du Lait
CBLIA	Centro Belgo-Luxembourgeois d'Information de l'Acier
CBLT	Commission du Bassin du Lac Tchad
CBM	Centrale Bond van Meubelfabrikanten
CBM	Centre Technique et Scientifique de la Brasserie, Malterie et des Industries Connexes (Belgium)
CBMC	Communauté de Travail des Brasseurs du Marché Commun
CBMPE	Council of British Manufacturers of Petroleum Equipment
CBN	Commission on Biochemical Nomenclature
CBNM	Central Bureau for Nuclear Measurements (of Euratom)
CBO	Conference of Baltic Oceanographers
CBOB	Christelijke Bond van Ondernemers in de Binnenwaart
CBOI	Centro Biológico del Océano Indico
CBPAE	Centro Brasileiro de Pesquisas Agrícoles em Elano
CBPAH	Council for British Plastics in Agriculture and Horticulture
CBPAV	Chambre Belge des Publicités Audio-Visuelles

CBPBG	Commonwealth Bureau of Plant Breeding and Genetics
CBPC	Canadian Book Publishers Council
CBPC	Chambre Belge de la Publicité Cinématographique
CBPDC	Canadian Book and Periodical Development Council
CBPE	Centro Brasileiro de Pesquisas Educacionais
CBPF	Centro Brasileiro de Pesquisas Fisicas
CBPFC	Commonwealth Bureau of Pastures and Field Crops
CBPM	Chambre Belge des Pédicures Médicaux
CBQ	Centre Belge pour la Gestion de la Qualité
CBR	Centraal Bureau voor de Rijwielhandel
CBR	Consejo de Bienestar Rural (Venezuela)
CBRA	Chemical Biological Radiological Agency (U.S.A.)
CBRB	Centraal Bureau voor de Rijn- en Binnenvaart
CBRI	Central Bee Research Institute (India)
CBRI	Central Building Research Institute (India)
CBRP	Centre Belge des Relations Publiques
CBRS	Coffee Board Research Station (India)
CBS	Centraal Bureau Slachtveeverzekeringen
CBS	Centraal Bureau voor Schimmelcultures
CBS	Central Bureau voor de Statistiek
CBS	Československá Botanicá Spoleenost
CBS	Columbia Broadcasting System (U.S.A.)
CBS	Commonwealth Bureau of Soils
CBSN	Centraal Bureau voor de Schapenfokkerij in Nederland
CBSN	Christelijke Bond van Schoenwinkeliers
CBT	Centre Belge de Traductions
CBT	Commission du Bassin du Tchad
CBTB	Nederlandse Christelijke Boeren- en Tuindersbond
CBTIP	Chambre Belge des Traducteurs, Interprètes et Philologues
CBV	Centraal Bureau voor de Veilingen
CBV	Central Bureau voor de Varkensfokkerij in Nederland
CBV	Coopérative Suisse pour l'Approvisionnement en Bétail de Boucherie et en Viande
CBVN	Centraal Bureau voor de Varkensfokkerij in Nederland

CC	Caribbean Commission	CCAQ	Consultative Committee on Administrative Questions (*of* UNO)
CC	Commission de Climatologie (de l'OMM)		
CCA	Canadian Chemical Association	CCASTD	Comité Consultatif sur l'Application de la Science et de la Technique au Développement (*of* UNO)
CCA	Canadian Construction Association		
CCA	Cement and Concrete Association	CCAT	Comité de Coordination de l'Assistance Technique (de l'ONU)
CCA	Chamber of Commerce of the Americas		
CCA	Chemical Corps Association Inc. (U.S.A.)	CCAVMA	Caisse Centrale d'Assurance Vieillesse Mutuelle Agricole
CCA	Commonwealth Correspondents' Association		
		CCB	Compagnie Camerounaise des Boissons
CCA	Compagnie Commerciale Africaine (Ivory Coast)	CCB	Coöperative Centrale Boerenleenbank
		CCBAT	Comité Central Belge de l'Achèvement Textile
CCA	Conférence Chrétienne d'Asie Orientale		
CCA	Consejo de Cooperación Aduanera (Belgium)	CCBB	Comité Central de la Bonneterie Belge
CCA	Copper Conductors Association	CCBDA	Canadian Copper and Brass Development Association
CCAA	Conseil de Coordination des Associations Aéroportuaires (Switzerland)		
		CCBET	Comité Central Belge de Textile l'Ennoblissement
CCAAP	Central Committee for the Architectural Advisory Panels		
		CCBM	Copper Cylinder and Boiler Manufacturers' Association
CCAAP	Comisión Consultiva en Asuntos Administrativos y de Presupuesto (UN)		
		CCBN	Central Council for British Naturism
CCAB	Canadian Circulation Audit Board	CCBSA	Central Council of Bank Staff Associations
CCAC	Compagnie Commerciale de l'Afrique Centrale	CCBV	Comité Professionnel des Coopératives des Pays du Marché Commun pour le Bétail et la Viande
CCACU	Central Co-ordinating Allocation Committee for University Project Research (South Africa)		
		CCC	Canadian Chamber of Commerce
		CCC	Caribbean Conference of Churches
CCAF	Comité Central des Armateurs de France	CCC	Caribbean Conservation Corporation
CCAF	Compagnie Agricole et Forestière	CCC	Caribbean Consumer Committee (Jamaica)
CCAFMA	Caisse Centrale d'Allocations Familiales Mutuelles Agricoles	CCC	Caribbean Council of Churches
		CCC	Central Council of Co-operatives (Czechoslovakia)
CCAHC	Central Council for Agricultural and Horticultural Co-operation		
		CCC	Centrale Cultuurtechnische Commissie
CCAI	Chambre de Commerce, d'Agriculture et l'Industrie de Bamako (Mali)	CCC	Club Cricket Conference
		CCC	Commodity Credit Corporation (U.S.A.)
CCAM	Canadian Congress of Applied Mechanics	CCC	Conseil de Coopération Culturelle (*of* CE)
CCAMAA	Caisse Centrale d'Assurances Mutuelles Agricoles contre des Accidents		
		CCC	Council for the Care of Churches
CCAMAG	Caisse Centrale d'Assurances Mutuelles Agricoles contre la Grêle	CCC	Customs Co-operation Council (Belgium)
CCAMAI	Caisse Centrale d'Assurances Mutuelles Agricoles contre l'Incendie	CCCA	Cocoa, Chocolate and Confectionery Alliance
CCAMAMB	Caisse Centrale d'Assurances Mutuelles Agricoles contre la Mortalité du Bétail	CCCA	Comité Consultivo en Cuestiones Administrativas (UNO)
CCAO	Chambre de Compensation de l'Afrique de l'Ouest (Senegal)	CCCAM	Centro de Cooperación Científica de Asia Meridional (India)
CCAP	Citizens' Crusade Against Poverty (U.S.A.)	CCCAS	Centro de Cooperación Científica de Asia Sudoriental (Thailand)
CCAP	Culture Centre of Algae and Protozoa		

CCCB	Comissáo de Comércio do Cacau da Bahia (Brazil)	**CCEB**	Conseil Canadien des Écoles de Bibliothécaires
CCCBR	Central Council of Church Bell Ringers	**CCEE**	Consilium Conferentiarum Episcopalium Europae
CCCCN	Comissão Coordenadora da Criacao do Cavalo Nacional (Brazil)	**CCEI**	Comité Consultatif Économique et Industriel auprès de l'OCDE
CCCE	Caisse Centrale de Coopération Économique	**CCEIC**	Comité de Cooperación Económica del Istmo Centroamericana
CCCET	Comité Catholique de Coordination pour l'Envoi de Techniciens (Belgium)	**CCEN**	Chilian Nuclear Energy Commission
CCCFE	Comité Consultatif de Coordination du Financement à moyen terme des Exportations	**CCEP**	Commission Consultative des Études Postales (de l'Union Postale Universelle)
CCCI	Compagnie du Congo pour le Commerce et l'Industrie	**CCEPI**	Commission Consultative Européenne pour les Pêches dans les Eaux Intérieures
CCCI	Conseil Canadien pour la Coopération Internationale	**CCERO**	Centre d'Études de Recherche Operationelle (Belgium)
CCCLP	Confederación Centroamericana y del Caribe de Levantamiento de Pesas	**CCES**	Conseil Consultatif Économique et Social de l'Union Économique (Belgium)
CCCN	Caribbean Christian Communications Network	**CCESP**	Centre County Engineers' Society of Pennsylvania (U.S.A.)
CCCR	Co-ordinating Committee for Cancer Research	**CCETI**	Commission Consultative des Employés et des Travailleurs Intellectuels (de l'OIT)
CCCS	Colonial, Commonwealth and Continental Church Society	**CCETSW**	Central Council for Education and Training in Social Work
CCCD	Centrale Contrôle Dienst	**CCEUREA**	Centre Coopératif d'Expansion et d'Utilisation Rationnelles d'Équipement Agricole
CCD	Conseil de Coopération Douanière (Belgium)		
CCDA	Commercial Chemical Development Association (U.S.A.)	**CCF**	Centrale Cultuurfondsen (Indonesia)
CCDC	Capital City Development Corporation (Malawi)	**CCF**	Co-operative Commonwealth Federation Montreal (Canada)
CCDG	Société Commerciale du Gabon	**CCF**	Crédit Commercial de France
CCDP	Comisión Centroamericana de Desarrollo Pesquero (Salvador)	**CCFA**	Cancer Cytology Foundation of America
CCDP	Compagnie Camerounaise de Dépôts Pétroliers	**CCFA**	Caribbean Cane Farmers Association
		CCFD	Comité Catholique contre la Faim et pour le Développement
CCDR	Compagnie Camerounaise de Développement Regional	**CCFOM**	Caisse Centrale de la France d'Outre-Mer
CCDS	Canadian Council on Social Development	**CCFPI**	Comité Consultatif de la Fonction Publique Internationale
CCDVT	Caisse Centrale de Dépôts et Virements de Titres	**CCGA**	Compagnie de Constructions Générales en Afrique
CCE	Comite de Cooperación Económica del Istmo Centroamericano	**CCGB**	Cycling Council of Great Britain
		CCGS	Corpus Christi Geological Society (U.S.A.)
CCE	Conseil des Communes d'Europe	**CCHA**	Compagnie Commerciale Hollando-Africaine
CCEA	Commonwealth Council for Educational Administration	**CCHE**	Central Council for Health Education
CCEAC	Comité de Coopération Économique de l'Amérique Centrale	**CCHO**	Comité Consultatif d'Hydrologie Opérationnelle (of WMO)
CCEAE	Conférence des Chefs d'État de l'Afrique Équatoriale	**CCI**	Central Campesina Independienti (Mexico)
		CCI	Chambre de Commerce Internationale

CI	Comités Consultatifs Internationaux
CI	Compagnie Camerounaise Industrielle
CI	Cotton Council International (U.S.A.)
CIA	Camera di Commercio, Industria e Agricoltura di Rieti
CIA	Commission of the Churches on International Affairs (Switzerland)
CIA	Comité Científico de Investigaciones Antárticas (ICSU)
CIA	Comptoir Commercial et Industriel Afrique
CIAESC	Coffee Commission of the Inter-American Economic and Social Council (U.S.A.)
CIC	Canadian Council for International Co-operation
CIC	Centre Catholique International pour l'Unesco
CIC	Comité Catholique International de Coordination Auprès de l'Unesco
CIC	Comité Consultatif International du Coton
CICMS	Council for the Co-ordination of International Congresses of Medicine
CIDD	Canterbury College Industrial Development Department (N.Z.)
CIEM	Catholic Committee for Intra-European Migration
CIF	Comité Consultatif International Téléphonique
CIL	Canadian Co-operative Implements Ltd
CIM	Chambre de Commerce et d'Industrie de la Martinique
CIO	Comité Cientificao de Investigaciones Oceánicas
CIP	Chambre de Compensation Internationale des Produits de Base (UNCTAD)
CIP	Commission du Commerce International des Produits de Base
CIR	Catholic Council for International Relations
CIR	Chambre de Commerce et l'Industrie de la Réunion
CIR	Comité Consultative International des Radio-communications
CIS	Compagnie Commerciale Industrielle du Sénégal
CIT	Comité Consultatif International Télégraphique
CITT	International Consultative Telegraph and Telephone Committee (of ITU)

CCITU	Coordinating Committee of Independent Trade Unions
CCIVS	Co-ordinating Committee for International Voluntary Service
CCIW	Canada Centre for Inland Waters
CCJ	Comité Européen de Coopération Juridique
CCJO	Consultative Council of Jewish Organisations
CCL	Caribbean Congress of Labour
CCL	Comité Central de la Laine
CCL	Conseil International de Continuation et de Liaison du Congrès Mondial des Forces de Paix
CCLA	Committee on Co-operation in Latin America
CCLF	Club des Congrès de Langue Française
CCLIL	Fédération Française de la Filature de Laine Cardée et Autres Fibres
CCLM	Committee on Constitutional and Legal Matters (FAO)
CCLN	Committee for Computerized Library Networks (NLISN)
CCMA	Caisse Centrale des Mutuelles Agricoles (France)
CCMA	Canadian Council of Management Association
CCMA	Cotton Canvas Manufacturers Association
CCMC	Committee of Common Market Constructors (Belgium)
CCMIE	Comité Catholique pour les Migrations Intra-européennes
CCMRG	Commonwealth Committee on Mineral Resources and Geology
CCMS	Committee on the Challenges of Modern Society (of NATO)
CCMW	Churches Committee on Migrant Workers (Switzerland)
CCNDT	Canadian Council for Non-Destructive Technology
CCNR	Central Commission for the Navigation of the Rhine
CCNR	Consultative Committee for Nuclear Research (of Council of Europe)
CCNSC	Cancer Chemotherapy National Service Center (U.S.A.)
CCNUD	Cycle de la Coopération des Nations Unies pour le Développement
CCNY	Carnegie Corporation of New York
CCOC	Comité de Coordination des Organisations des Consommateurs

CCODP	Canadian Catholic Organization for Development and Peace
CCOP/SOP-AC	Committee for the Coordination of Joint Prospecting for Mineral Resources in South Pacific Offshore Areas (*of* ECAFE)
CCOPA	Alentefo Co-ordinating Committee for Public Works (Portugal)
CCOTACAL	Conseil Coordinateur des Organisations des Travailleurs Agricoles et des Paysans d'Amérique Latine
CCP	Chinese Communist Party
CCP	Comité Cafetalero del Perú
CCP	Committee on Commodity Problems (FAO)
CCP	Confederación Científica Panamericana (Argentina)
CCP	Conférence Chrétienne pour la Paix
CCPA	Centrale Cooperative des Productions Animales
CCPE	Canadian Council of Professional Engineers
CCPES	Canadian Council of Professional Engineers and Scientists
CCPF	Comité Central de la Propriété Forestière de la CEE
CCPF	Comité de Coordination de la Production Fruitière
CCPIT	China Committee for the Promotion of International Trade
CCPMA	Caisse Centrale de Prévoyance Mutuelle Agricole
CCPMNO	Comité de Coordination des Ports Méditerranéens Nord-Occidental
CCPMO	Consultative Council of Professional Management Organisations
CCPO	Comité Central Permanent de l'Opium (Switzerland)
CCPP	Caisse Commune des Pensions du Personnel des Nations Unies
CCPR	Central Council for Physical Recreation
CCPR	Cooperativa de Cafeteros de Puerto Rico
CCPS	Commission Permanente du Pacifique Sud
CCPS	Consultative Committee for Postal Studies (*of* UPU)
CCPW	Catholic Council for Polish Welfare
CCQA	Comité Consultatif pour les Questions Administratives
CCQAB	Comité Consultative pour les Questions Administratives et Budgétaires (UN)
CCR	Center for Conflict Resolution (U.S.A.)
CCR	Commission Centrale pour la Navigation du Rhin
CCRA	Canadian Research Centre for Anthropology
CCRB	Coöperatieve Centrale Raiffeisen-Bank
CCRI	Central Coffee Research Institute (India)
CCRI	Comité Consultatif de Recherche en Informatique
CCRMO	Comité Consultatif de la Recherche Météorologique Océanique (WMO)
CCRN	Centre Commun de Recherches Nucléaires
CCRP	Corporación Centro Regional de Población (Colombia)
CCRRM	Comité Consultatif de la Recherche sur les Ressources de la Mer (FAO)
CCRS	Central Coconut Research Station (India)
CCRST	Comité Consultatif de la Recherche Scientifique et Technique
CCRTD	Committee for Coordination of Cathode Ray Tube Development
CCS	Canadian Cancer Society
CCS	Canadian Ceramic Society
CCS	Comptoir Commercial du Sénégal
CCS	Corporation of Secretaries
CCS	Council of Communication Societies (U.S.A.)
CCSA	Canadian Committee on Sugar Analysis
CCSA	Comité Chétien de Service en Algérie
CCSATU	Coordinating Council of South African Trade Unions
CCSD	Canadian Council on Social Development
CCSL	Confédération Congolaise des Syndicats Libres
CCSM	Confederation Chrétienne des Syndicats Malgaches
CCSM	Czechoslovak Committee for Scientific Management
CCSMA	Caisse Centrale de Secours Mutuels Agricoles
CCSR	Canadian Consortium for Social Research
CCSVI	Comité de Coordination du Service Volontaire International
CCT	Confederación Centroamericana de Trabajadores
CCT	Confederación Costarricense del Trabago
CCT	Consejo Centroamericana de Turismo

CTA	Centrale Chemisch-Technische Afdeling (Indonesia)	**CDDA**	Conseil Départemental de Développement Agricole
CTA	Committee for Technical Co-operation in Africa South of the Sahara	**CDDC**	Comisión de Documentación Científica (Argentina)
CTAN	Confederación de Campesinos y Trabajadores Agrícolas de Nicaragua	**CDE**	Coal Development Establishment
CTI	Conseil Central du Tourisme International	**CDF**	Capital Development Fund (UNO)
CTS	Comité de Coordination des Télécommunications par Satellites (Switzerland)	**CDFC**	Commonwealth Development Finance Corporation
		CDG	Carl Duisberg-Gesellschaft
CTU	Comité de Coordination des Télécommunications (*of* CNET)	**CDH**	Centralvereinigung Deutscher Handelsvertreter- und Handelsmakler Verbände
CUN	Collegiate Council for the United States	**CDHAR**	Comités Départementaux de l'Habitat et de l'Aménagement Rural
CURR	Canadian Council on Urban and Regional Research		
		CDHR	Comité Départemental de l'Habitat Rural
CUS	Chamber of Commerce of the United States	**CDI**	Centraal Diergeneeskunde Instituut
CVM	Centrale Commissie voor Melk Hygiene	**CDI**	Centre de Diffusion de l'Innovation (*of* ANVAR)
CWM	Congregational Council for World Mission		
CWU	Clerical and Commercial Workers Union (Guyana)	**CDI**	Centro de Documentação e Informação (Brazil)
D	Commission du Danube	**CDI**	Commission du Droit International
D	Cultuurtechnische Dienst	**CDICP**	Centrul de Documentare al Industriei Chimice si Petroliere (Romania)
DA	Canadian Dental Association		
DA	Centro de Documentação Agrária (Mozambique)	**CDIL**	Centro de Documentare Tehnica (Romania)
		CDISA	Centre de Documentation et d'Information de la Société des Africanistes
DA	Compañia Dominicana de Aviación		
DA	Copper Development Association	**CDIU**	Centrale Dienst voor de In- en Uitvoer
DAE	Centrc de Desarrollo Agrario del Ebro	**CDIUPA**	Centre de Documentation des Industries Utilisatrices de Produits Agricoles
DAF	Compagnie des Dirigeants d'Approvisionnement et Acheteurs de France	**CDJA**	Cercle Départemental des Jeunes Agriculteurs
DB	Caribbean Development Bank (Barbados)		
DB	Cyprus Development Bank	**CDL**	County and Democratic League (Australia)
DC	Cameroon's Development Corporation	**CDLDK**	Comité de Liaison des Kinésithérapeutes de la CEE
DC	Canadian Development Corporation		
DC	China Development Corporation	**CDMI**	Centre de Documentation de Musique Internationale
DC	Colonial *later* Commonwealth Development Corporation	**CDNPA**	Canadian Dairy Newspaper Publishers Association
DC	Comisión de Documentación Cientifica (Argentina)	**CDP**	Compagnie Camerounaise de Dépôts Petroliers
DC	Commonwealth Development Corporation	**CDPPP**	Centre for Development Planning, Projections and Policies (*of* UNO)
DCR	Centre for Documentation and Communication Research (U.S.A.)	**CDPT**	Centrul de Documentare şi Propagandă Tehnică (Romania)
DCTM	Centro de Documentación Científica y Tecnica de Mexico	**CDR**	Centre for Development Research (Denmark)
DCU	Centro de Documentação Científica Ultramarina (Portugal)	**CDR**	Centre de Documentation Rurale

CDRA	Committee of Directors of Research Associations	**CEA**	Compañia Ecuatoriana de Aviación
CDRB	Canadian Research Defence Board	**CEA**	Confederación de Educadores Americanos (Mexico)
CDRF	Canadian Dental Research Foundation	**CEA**	Confédération Européenne de l'Agriculture (Switzerland)
CDRI	Central Drug Research Institute (India)		
CDS	Centre de Documentation Sidérurgique	**CEAA**	Centre Européen d'Aviation Agricole
CDSH	Centre de Documentation Sciences Humaines	**CEAA**	Council of European-American Associations
		CEABH	Centre Eurafricain de Biologie Humaine
CDSO	Commonwealth Defence Science Organisation	**CEAC**	Centro de Estudos de Antropología Cultural (Portugal)
CDSP	Compagnie de Dirigeants de Services du Personnel (Belgium)	**CEAC**	Commission Européenne de l'Aviation Civile
CDSVF	Comité de Défense Scientifique du Vin Français	**CEAC**	Committee for European Airspace Coordination (*of* NATO)
CDTC	Confederation Dahoméenne des Travailleurs Croyants	**CEAC**	Confédération Européenne des Anciens Combattants
CDU	Christlich-Demokratische Union Deutschlands (East Germany)	**CEACRO**	Comisión de Energía Atómica de Costa Rica
CDU	Christlich-Demokratische Union (West Germany)	**CEACS**	Centre for East Asian Cultural Studies (Japan)
CDUCE	Christian Democratic Union of Central Europe	**CEAEN**	Centre d'Études pour les Applications de l'Énergie Nucléaire
CDUD	Christian Democratic Union of Germany	**CEAEO**	Commission Économique pour l'Asie et l'Extrême-Orient (Thailand)
CDVM	Club Dirigenti Vendite e Marketing	**CEAF**	Comité Européen des Associations de Fonderies
CDVPA	Comité Départemental de la Vulgarisation et du Progrès Agricole		
CDVTPR	Centre de Documentation du Verre Textile et des Plastiques Renforcés	**CEAI**	Cercle d'Échanges Artistiques Internationaux
CE	Conseil Économique	**CEAL**	Comité Europe-Amérique Latine (Belgium)
CE	Conseil d'État	**CEAL**	Commission Économique pour l'Amérique Latin (Chile)
CE	Council of Europe		
CEA	Canadian Electrical Association	**CEALDO**	Comité de Expertos en Ajustes por Lugar de Destino Oficial (UNO)
CEA	Central Electricity Authority (*formerly* BEA)	**CEALO**	Comisión Económica para Asia y Lejano Oriente (U.S.A.)
CEA	Centre d'Économique Alpine		
CEA	Centre des Études Andines (France)	**CEAMP**	Centrale d'Équipement Agricole et de Modernisation du Paysannat
CEA	Centre d'Étude et Arbitrage de Droit Européen	**CEANAR**	Commission on Education in Agriculture and Natural Resources (U.S.A.)
CEA	Centro de Estudos Agrícolas (Brazil)		
CEA	Cinematograph Exhibitors Association of Great Britain and Ireland	**CEAO**	Commission Économique des Nations Unies pour l'Asie Occidentale
CEA	Comité Européen des Assurances	**CEAO**	Communauté Économique de l'Afrique de l'Ouest
CEA	Commission Économique des Nations Unies pour l'Afrique		
CEA	Commission de l'Énergie Atomique (*of* U.N.)	**CEAO**	Confédération des Etudiants d'Afrique Occidentale
CEA	Commodity Exchange Authority (U.S.A.)	**CEAS**	Centro Erboristico Appenninico Sperimentale
CEA	Communauté Européenne de l'Accordéon	**CEAS**	Cooperative Educational Abstracting Service (*of* IBE)

EAT	Centre d'Études Aérodynamiques de Toulouse	**CEBV**	Communauté Économique du Bétail et de la Viande (Africa)
EB	Central Electricity Board	**CEC**	Catholic Education Council
EB	Central Electricity Board (Malaysia)	**CEC**	Centre for Economic Cooperation (UN)
EB	Comité Européen du Béton	**CEC**	Centre d'Études du Commerce
EB	Comité Européen des Constructeurs de Brûleurs	**CEC**	Centre Européen de la Culture
		CEC	Clothing Export Council of Great Britain
EB	Confédération Européenne de Billard	**CEC**	Commission of the European Communities
EBAC	Comisión Especial BrasileñoArgentina de Cooperación	**CEC**	Commonwealth Economic Committee (*formerly* IEC)
EBANOR	Comité Régional d'Expansion Économique de la Basse-Normandie	**CEC**	Commonwealth Education Cooperation
		CEC	Conference of European Churches
EBAP	Centro de Estudios de Bosques Andino-Patagónicos (Argentina)	**CEC**	Conseil Européen de l'Enseignement par Correspondance
EBEA	Centre Emile Bernheim pour l'Étude des Affaires (Belgium)	**CEC**	Consejo Economico Centroamericana (*of* CACM)
EBECO	Nationale Coöperatieve Aan- en Verkoopvereniging voor Land- en Tuinbouw	**CEC**	Co-ordinating European Council for the Development of Performance Tests for Lubricants and Engine Fuels
EBEDAIR	Centrale Belge d'Études et de Documentation de l'Air	**CEC**	Council for Education in the Commonwealth
EBEDEAU	Centre Belge d'Étude et de Documentation des Eaux	**CEC**	Council for Exceptional Children (U.S.A.)
		CECA	Carbonisation et Charbons Actifs SA
EBELA	Centro Brasiliero de Estudos Latino-Americanos	**CECA**	Communauté Européenne du Charbon et de l'Acier
EBELCOR	Centre Belge de l'Étude de la Corrosion	**CECA**	Council on Economic and Cultural Affairs, Inc (*now* ADC) (U.S.A.)
EBERENA	Centre Belge de Recherches Navales		
EBETID	Comité Belge du Tissage et des Industries Textiles Diverses	**CECA**	Cyprus Employers Consultative Organisation
EBI	Comité Européen des Bureaux d'Ingénierie	**CECAF**	FAO Fishery Committee for the Eastern Central Atlantic
EBJ	Commission of Editors of Biochemical Journals	**CECA-GADIS**	Compagnie d'Exploitations Commerciales Africaines–Société Gabonaise de Distribution
EBLS	Council of EEC Builders of Large Ships	**CECAL**	Comité Européen de Coopération avec l'Amérique Latine
EBOSINE	Centrale Bond van Scheepsbouwmeesters in Nederland	**CECAL**	Commission Episcopale de Coopération Apostolique Canada-Amérique Latine
EBRACO	Centro Brasileiro de Informação de Cobre	**CECAS**	Conference of East and Central African States
EBRAP	Centro Brasileiro de Análise et Planejamento		
EBS	Centro de Estudios del Bosque Subtropical, La Plata (Argentina)	**CECAT**	Centre for Agricultural Education and Co-operation (Italy)
EBSO	Comité d'Expansion Économique Bordeaux Sud-Ouest	**CECATI**	Centros de Capacitación para el Trabajo Industrial (Mexico)
EBSP	Centre d'Étude Belge de Publicité	**CECB**	Conseil Européen du Cuir Brut
EBTP	Centre Expérimental de Recherches et d'Études du Bâtiment et des Travaux Publics (Algeria)	**CECC**	Commonwealth Economic Consultative Council
EBUCO	Centraal Bureau voor Courantenpubliciteit van de Nederlandse Dagbladpers	**CECC**	Communaté Européenne des Coopératives de Consummateurs

CECC	Communauté Européenne de Crédit Communal
CECC	Compagnie d'Élevage et de Cultures du Cameroun
CECCB	Chambres des Experts-Comptable et des Comptables de Belgique
CECE	Centre d'Étude et Exploitation des Calculateurs Électroniques (Belgium)
CECE	Comisión Especial para la Formulación de Nuevas Medidas de Cooperación Económica Internacional
CECE	Committee for European Construction Equipment
CECEC	Communauté Européenne Culturelle des Étudiants en Chimie
CECED	Conseil Européen de la Construction Électro-Domestique
CECF	Commission Européenne des Communes Forestières et Communes de Montagne
CECG	Confédération Européenne du Commerce de la Chaussure en Gros (Belgium)
CECH	Comité Européen de la Culture du Houblon
CECI	Centre d'Étude de Cooperation Internationale (Canada)
CECI	Centre Européen du Commerce International
CECI	Centre Européen de Coopération Internationale (France)
CECIMO	Comité Européen de Cooperation des Industries de la Machine-Outil (Belgium)
CECINE	Centro de Ensino de Ciencias do Nordeste (Brazil)
CECIOS	European Council of International Committee of Scientific Management
CECIP	Comité Européen des Constructeurs d'Instruments de Pesage
CECIRNA	Centro de Coordinación de Investigaciones de Recursos Naturales y su Aplicacion (Argentina)
CECL	Comité Européen de Contrôle Laitier
CECLA	Commission Especiale de Coordinación Latinoamericana
CECLB	Comité Européen de Contrôle Laitier-Beurrier
CECLES	Conseil Européen pour la Construction de Lanceurs d'Engins Spatiaux
CECM	Commission pour l'Étude de la Construction Métallique (Belgium)
CECMA	Comité Européen des Constructeurs de Matériel Aéraulique
CECMAS	Centre d'Études des Communications de Masse
CECOAAP	Peruvian Sugar Cooperatives Association
CECOCO	Chuo Boeki Goshi Kaisha (Central Commercial Co) (Japan)
CECODE	Centre Européen du Commerce de Détail
CECODEC	Conseil Européen des Constructeurs de Cuisine
CECOM	Central European Mass Communication Research Documentation Centre (Poland)
CECOMAF	Comité Européen des Constructeurs de Matériel Frigorifique
CECORA	Central de Cooperatives de Reforma Agraria (Colombia)
CECPA	Comité Européen du Commerce des Produits Amylacés et Dérivés
CECPI	Commission Européenne Consultative pour les Pêches dans les Eaux Intérieures
CECPRA	Centre d'Études de la Commission Permanente du Risque Atomique
CECRI	Central Electrochemical Research Institute (India)
CECT	Comité Européen de la Chaudronnerie et de la Tôlerie
CECTAL	Centre for the Application of Science and Technology to the Development of Latin America
CECTK	Committee for Electro-Chemical Thermodynamics and Kinetics (Belgium)
CED	Centro de Esploro Kaj Dokumentado pri la Monda Lingvo-Problemo (U.K.)
CED	Committee for Economic Development (U.S.A.)
CEDA	Caisse d'Équipement pour le Développement de l'Algérie
CEDA	Canadian Electrical Distributors Association
CEDA	Centre for Economic Development and Administration (Nepal)
CEDA	Centre d'Édition et de Diffusion Africaines (Ivory Coast)
CEDA	Committee for the Economic Development of Australia
CEDAF	Centre for African Studies and Documentation (Belgium)
CEDAG	Centre d'Études et de Diffusion de l'Agriculture de Groupe
CEDAM	Casa Editrice Dott. Antonio Milani

CEDAMEL Centre d'Études et de Distribution des Appareils et du Matériel de l'Enseignement Linguistique

CEDAOM Centre d'Étude et de Documentation pour l'Afrique et l'Outre-Mer

CEDAP Centro de Desarrollo de Administracion Pública (Guatemala)

CEDDA Centre for Experiment Design and Data Analysis (*of* NOAA)

CEDE Centro de Estudios sobre Desarrollo Económico, Universidad de los Andes (Colombia)

CEDEAO Communauté Économique et Douanière de l'Afrique de l'Ouest

CEDEC Centre Européen de Documentation et de Compensation

CEDEFOP Centre Européen pour le Développement de la Formation Professionelle

CEDEG Centre Européen de Documentation et d'Études Gérontologiques (Belgium)

CEDEP Centre Européen d'Éducation Permanente (France)

CEDES Centre d'Étude du Développement Économique et Social (Morocco).

CEDES Corps Européen de Développement Économique et Social (Belgium)

CEDESA African Economic and Social Documentation Centre (Belgium)

CEDESE Communauté Européenne des Étudiants

CEDEV Centre d'Étude des Pays en Développement (Belgium)

CEDH Convention Européenne des Droits de l'Homme

CEDI Centre Européen de Documentation et d'Information

CEDIA Centro de Estudio, Documentación e Información de Africa (Spain)

CEDIA Centre d'Études pour l'Extension des Débouchés Industriels de l'Agriculture

CEDIAS Centre d'Études, de Documentation, d'Information et d'Action Sociales

CEDIC Comité Européen des Ingénieurs-Conseils du Marché Commun

CEDICE Centre d'Éducation et d'Information pour la Communauté Européenne

CEDIF Compagnie Européenne pour le Développement Industriel et Financier (Belgium)

CEDIGAZ Centre International d'Information sur le Gaz Naturel et tous Hydrocarbures Gazeux

CEDIM Centre d'Études de Droit International Médical

CEDIM Comité Européen des Fédérations Nationales de la Maroquinerie, Articles de Voyages et Industries Connexes

CEDIMAR Centro de Documentación e Información en Ciencias del Mar

CEDIMEX Centrafricaine de Distribution-Importation-Exportation

CEDIMON Centre Européen pour le Développement Industriel et la Mise en Valeur de l'Outre-Mer

CEDIP Centro de Estudos de Dinamica Populacional (Brazil)

CEDJ Centre d'Étude de la Délinquance Juvénile (Belgium)

CEDLA Centre d'Études et de Documentation Legislatives Africaines

CEDO Centre for Educational Development Overseas

CEDOC Centre Belge de Documentation et d'Information de la Construction

CEDOC Centro de Documentación Científica (Argentine)

CEDOCOS Centre de Documentation sur les Combustibles Solides (Belgium)

CEDOM Centre of Documentation and Teaching Materials (Peru)

CEDOPI Centre d'Études Documentaires de Propriété Industrielle

CEDORES Centre de Documentation et de Recherche Sociales (Belgium)

CEDP Centre d'Études et de Documentation Paléontologique

CEDR Comité Européen de Droit Rural

CEDRAL Comité Européen pour le Développement des Relations avec l'Amérique Latine

CEDRASE-MI Centre de Documentation et de Recherches sur l'Asie du Sud-Est et le Monde Insulindien

CEDRIC Centre d'Études de Documentation et de Recherches pour l'Industrie du Chauffage, du Conditionnement d'Air et des Branches Connexes

CEDSA Centro de Documentación del Sector Agrario (Peru)

CEDTT Committee for Economic Development of Trinidad and Tobago

CEDUS Centre d'Études et de Documentation pour l'Utilisation du Sucre

CEDVAR Centre National d'Études, de Documentation, de Vulgarisation Technique de l'Artisanat Rural

CEE Centro de Estudios Educativos (Mexico)

CEE Commission Économique pour l'Europe

CEE Commission Internationale de Réglementation en veu de l'Approbation de l'Équipement Électrique

CEE Communauté Économique Européenne

CEEA Centro de Estudos de Economia Agraria

CEEA Centro de Estudios para Empresas Agrícolas (Chile)

CEEA Communauté Européenne de l'Énergie Atomique (Euratom)

CEEBA Centre d'Études Ethnologiques de Bandundu (Zaire)

CEEC Catholic International Education Office

CEEC Commission Episcopale pour l'École Catholique (Libya)

CEEC Committee of European Economic Co-operation

CEECO Comité d'Expansion Économique du Centre-Ouest

CEED Centro de Estudios Económicos y Demográficos (Mexico)

CEEDIA Centre d'Études pour l'Extension des Débouchés Industriels de l'Agriculture

CEEGFP Centre d'Études d'Économie et de Gestion de la Forêt Privée

CEEH Centre Européen d'Écologie Humaine (Switzerland)

CEEIM Centre Européen d'Étude et d'Information sur les Sociétés Multinationales

CEEMA Centro de Ensenanza y Experimentación de la Maquinaria Agrícola (Argentina)

CEEMAT Centre d'Études et d'Expérimentation du Machinisme Agricole Tropical

CEEP Centre Européen de l'Entreprise Publique

CEEP Centre Européen d'Études de Population

CEEP Confédération Européenne d'Études de Phytopharmacie

CEEPPA Centre d'Études Économiques pour les Produits Agricoles

CEERI Central Electronics Engineering Research Institute (India)

CEESA Conference of European Engineering Students Associations

CEET Compagnie Énergie Électrique du Togo

CEF Campaign for Earth Federation (Malta)

CEF Central European Federalists

CEF Commission Européenne des Forêts (Italy)

CEF Conservation des Eaux et Forêts

CEFA Comité Europeo de Fabricantes de Azúcar (France)

CEFAC Centre de Formations des Assistants Techniques du Commerce et des Consultants Commerciaux

CEFACD Comité Européen des Fabricants d'Appareils de Chauffage et de Cuisine Domestiques

CEFB Centre d'Études des Fontes de Bâtiment

CEFCTU Central European Federation of Christian Trade Unions

CEFD Centro de Estudios de Filosofica del Derecho (Venezuela)

CEFIC Centre Européen des Fédérations de l'Industrie Chimique

CEFRACOR Centre Français de la Corrosion

CEFRES Centre Européen Féminin de Recherche sur l'Évolution de la Société (France)

CEFS Comité Européen des Fabricants de Sucre

CEFTRI Central Food Technological Research Institute (India)

CEFV Centro de Estudios del Futuro de Venezuela

CEFYM Central European Federal Youth Movement (*now* CEF)

CEG Centre d'Études de Gramat (*of* DTAT)

CEGAP European Committee of Landscape Architects

CEGAT Centro de Estudios Ganaderos de Areas Tropicales (Argentina)

CEGB Central Electricity Generating Board

CEGEP Collège d'Enseignement Générale et Professionel (Canada)

CEGET Centre d'Études de Géographie Tropicale

CEGOC Centro de Estudos de Gestão e Organizacão Cientifica (Portugal)

CEGOS Commission d'Études Générales de l'Organisation Scientifique

CEGROB Communauté Européenne des Associations du Commerce de Gros de Bière des Pays Membres de la CEE

CEH	Conférence Européenne des Horaires des Trains de Voyageurs	CELA	Committee for Exports to Latin America (*of* BNEC)
CEHILA	Comisió de Estudios de Historia de la Iglesia en America Latino	CELAC	Comité d'Études et de Liaison des Amendements Calcaires
CEHO	Compagnie Centrafricaine d'Exploitation Hôtelière	CELADE	Centro Latino-americano de Demografica
		CELADEC	Commissão Evangelica Latinoamericana de Educação Crista
CEHP	Comité Européen de l'Hospitalisation Privée		
CEI	Centre d'Études Industrielles (Switzerland)	CELAM	Conseil Episcopal Latino-Americain
CEI	Comitato Elettrotecnico Italiano	CELAME	Comité de Liaison et d'Action des Syndicats Médicaux Européens
CEI	Commission Électrotechnique Internationale		
CEI	Commission Europe de l'IOMTR	CELAP	Centro Latinoamericano de Población y Familia (Chile)
CEI	Committee for Environmental Information (UN)	CELATS	Centro Latinoamericano de Trabajo Social
CEI	Council of Engineering Institutions	CELC	Commonwealth Education Liaison Committee
CEIA	Centre d'Entr'aide Intellectuelle Africaine	CELCA	Centro Latinoamericano de Crédito Agrícola (Mexico)
CEIA	Comité Especial de Investigaciones Antárticas		
CEIA	Coopérative d'Élevage et d'Insémination Artificielle	CELE	Centre Européen pour Loisir et l'Éducation (Czechoslovakia)
CEIB	Centrul Experimental pentru Ingrasaminte Bacteriene (Roumania)	CELE	Centro Coordinamento Elettronica
		CELF	Centre d'Études Littéraires Francophones (France)
CEIB	Confédération Européenne des Industries du Bois	CELIB	Comité d'Études et de Liaison des Intérêts Bretons
CEIC	Conseil Économique International du Cuir	CELIBRIDE	Comité de Liaison des Pays Membres de la CEE pour les Industries des Broderies, Dentelles et Rideaux
CEICN	Centre Européen d'Information pour la Conservation de la Nature		
CEIE	Centre d'Études et d'Information sur l'Enseignement	CELIMAC	Comité Européen de Liaison des Industries de la Machine à Coudre
CEIF	Council of European Industrial Federations	CELME	Centro Sperimentale Lavorazione Metalli
CEIM	Centre d'Études Industrielles du Maghreb (Morocco)	CELMIC	Comité Européen de Liaison des Médecins Interprètes de Conférences
CEIP	Carnegie Endowment for International Peace (U.S.A.)	CELNUCO	Comité Européen de Liaison des Négociants et Utilisateurs de Combustibles
CEIPA	Comité d'Études et d'Informations sur les Produits Agricoles	CELOJ	Scouts' Esperanto League
		CELOS	Centrum voor Landbouwkundig Onderzoek in Suriname
CEIR	Comité Européen de l'Industrie de la Robinetterie	CELPA	Centro Espacial de Lanzamientos para la Prospección Atmosferica (Argentine)
CEIST	Centro Europeo Informazione Scientifiche e Tecniche (Italy)		
CEITJA	Centre d'Étude Internationale sur le Travail des Jeunes dans l'Agriculture	CELPUF	Comité d'Études de Liaison du Patronat de L'Union Française
CEJ	Campagne Européenne de la Jeunesse	CELTE	Constructeurs Européens de Locomotives Thermiques et Électriques
CEJH	Communauté Européenne des Jeunes de l'Horticulture	CELU	Commonwealth Education Liaison Unit
		CELU	Confederation of Ethiopian Labour Unions
CEKOM	Central European Mass Communication Research Documentation Centre	CEM	Centre d'Essais de la Méditerranée
CEL	Committee on Engineering Laws (U.S.A.)	CEM	Christian Education Movement

CEM	Conférence Européen des Horaires des Trains de Merchandises
CEM	Council of European Municipalities
CEM	Council of European Municipalities
CEM	Croisade d'Evangélisation Mondiale
CEMA	Canadian Electrical Manufacturers Association
CEMA	Catering Equipment Manufacturers Association
CEMA	Centre d'Études et de Modernisation Agricoles
CEMA	Comité pour l'Étude des Maladies et de l'Alimentation du Bétail (Belgium)
CEMA	Comité Européen des Groupements de Constructeurs de Machines Agricoles
CEMA	Council for Economic Mutual Assistance (*Soviet Bloc*)
CEMAC	Committee of European Associations of Manufacturers of Active Electronic Components (*now merged into* CEMEC)
CEMAG	Centre d'Étude de la Mécanisation en Agriculture de Gembloux (Belgium)
CEMAP	Commission Européenne des Méthodes d'Analyse des Pesticides
CEMAT	Società per la Construzione e l'Esercizio dei Mezzi Ausiliari del Transporte
CEMATEX	Comité Européen des Constructeurs de Matériel Textile (Switzerland)
CEMBS	Committee for European Marine Biological Symposia
CEMBU-REAU	European Cement Association
CEMD	Compagnie des Experts Maritimes du Dahomey
CEMDOC	Centro Multinacional de Documentación Científica sobre Geología, Geofisica de Colombia
CEME	Centro Italiano per Studio delle Relazioni Economiche e dei Mercati Esteri
CEMEC	Committee of European Associations of Manufacturers of Electronic Components
CEMI	Conseil Européen pour le Marketing Industriel
CEMLA	Centro de Estudios Monetarios Latinoamericanos (Mexico)
CEMM	Compagnie des Experts Maritimes de Madagascar

CEMO	Commission Économique pour le Moyen-Orient (UNO)
CEMP	Centre d'Étude des Matières Plastiques
CEMP	Centre d'Études et de Mesure de la Productivité
CEMS	Compagnie des Experts Maritimes du Sénégal
CEMT	Compagnie des Experts Maritimes du Togo
CEMT	Conférence Européenne des Ministres des Transports
CEMU	Centro Sperimentale per le Macchine Utensili
CEMUBAC	Centre Médical de l'Université de Bruxelles au Congo
CEN	Centre d'Études Énergie Nucléaire (Belgium)
CEN	Centro de Energia Nuclear (Brazil)
CEN	Comité Européen de Normalisation
CENA	Centre d'Études Nord-Africaines
CENA	Centre d'Experimentation de la Navigation Aérienne
CENAG	Centre des Chefs d'Entreprises Agricoles (*now* CENECA)
CENAMI	Centro Nacional de Ayuda a Mexicanos Indigenas
CENAPEC	National Centre for Promotion of Co-operative Enterprises (Ivory Coast)
CENATRA	Centre National d'Assistance Technique et de Recherche Appliquée (Belgium)
CENCER	Association of Certification (of CEN)
CENCI	Centro de Estadisticas Nacionales y Comercio International del Uruguay
CENCOS	Centro Nacional de Comunicación Social (Mexico)
CENCRA	Centro Nacional de Capacitacão em Reforma Agrária (Brazil)
CENDES	Centro de Desarrollo Industrial del Ecuador
CENDHR-RA	Centre for the Development of Human Resources in Rural Asia (Philippines)
CENDIE	Centro Nacional de Documentación e Información Educativa (Argentina)
CENDIM	Centro Nacional de Documentación e Información en Medicina y Ciencias de la Salud (Uruguay)
CENDIP	Centro Nacional de Documentación e Información Pedagógica (Colombia)
CENDOC	Centro Nacional de Documentación (Colombia)

CENECA	Centre National des Expositions et Concours Agricoles (formerly CENAG)
CENECO	Centre d'Entraînement à l'Économie
CENEL	Comité Européen de Coordination des Normes Électrotechniques
CENELCOM	Comité Européen de Coordination des Normes Électrotechniques des États Membres de la CEE
CENELEC	European Organization for Electrotechnical Standardisation
CENET	Centro Nacional de Electronica y Telecommunicaciones
CENFAM-RDP	Centro Nazionale per la Fisica della Atmosfera e la Meteorologia
CENFAR	Centre d'Études Nucléaires de Fontenay-aux-Roses
CENG	Centre d'Études Nucléaires de Grenoble
CENICIT	Centro Nacional de Información Cientifica y Técnica (Venezuela)
CENID	Centro Nacional de Información y Documentación (Chile)
CENIDE	National Centre for Educational Development and Research (Spain)
CENIM	Centro Nacional de Informação Cientifica en Microbiologia (Brazil)
CENIM	Centro Nacional de Investigaciones Metalúrgicas
CENIP	Centro Nacional de Productividad (Peru)
CENIS	Center for International Studies (U.S.A.)
CENITAL	Centro Nacional de Inseminación Artificial (Colombia)
CENPAR	Centre National de Promotion de l'Artisanat Rural
CENPHA	Centro Nacional de Pesquisas Habitacionais (Brazil)
CENPLA	Centro de Estudos, Pesquisa e Planejamento, (Brazil)
CENRA	Centro Nacional de Capacitación en Reforma Agraria (Peru)
CENS	Centre d'Étude Nucléaires de Saclay
CENSA	Committee of European and Japanese National Shipowners' Associations
CENTA	Centro Nacional de Tecnificación Agrícola (Salvador)
CENTA	Centro Nacional de Tecnologia Alimentaria (Peru)
CENTA	Combined Edible Nut Trade Association
CENTEX-BEL	Centre Scientifique et Technique de l'Industrie Textile Belge
CENTI	Centre pour le Traitement de l'Informatique
CENTO	Central Treaty Organisation (Turkey)
CENTRA-BOIS	Société Centrafricaine de Travaux du Bois
CENTRA-MINE	Compagnie Centrafricaine des Mines
CENTRI-FAN	Centre d'Institut Français d'Afrique Noire
CENTRO-COOP	Uniunea Centrala a Cooperativelor de Consum
CENTRO-MIN	Empresa Minera del Centro del Perú
CENYC	Council of European National Youth Committees
CEOA	Central European Operating Agency
CEOBOL	Centro de Documentación (Bolivia)
CEOC	Centre d'Études de l'Orient Contemporain
CEOC	Colloque Européen des Organismes de Contrôle
CEOP	Communauté Européenne des Organisations de Publicitaires
CEP	Centre d'Études des Matières Plastiques (Belgium)
CEP	European Committee for Plant Protection Research
CEPA	Centre d'Études des Problèmes Agricoles
CEPA	Cercle d'Études de la Productivité Agricole
CEPA	Comisión Económica para Africa (UNO)
CEPA	Comité d'Experts pour les Ajustements (UNO)
CEPA	Commission d'Études Pratiques d'Aviation
CEPA	Consumers Education and Protective Association International
CEPAC	Confédération Européenne de l'Industrie des Pâtes, Papiers et Cartons
CEPACC	Chemical Education Planning and Coordinating Committee (of American Chemical Society)
CEPADES	Centro Paraguayo de Estudios de Desarrollo Económico y Social
CEPAL	Comisión Económica para América Latina (UN)
CEPAL	Cooperativa Esportazione Produtti Agricoli
CEPALO	Comisión Económica para Asia y el Lejano Oriente (UNO)

CEPAO	Comisión Económica de las Naciones Unidas para el Asia Occidental	**CEPHR**	Comité d'Étude pour la Promotion de l'Habitat Rural
CEPAS	Centro di Educazione Professionale per Assistenti Sociali	**CEPIS**	Pan American Sanitary Engineering and Environmental Sciences Center (Peru)
CEPC	Central European Pipeline Committee	**CEPL**	Conférence Européenne des Pouvoirs Locaux
CEPC	Comité Élargi du Programme et de la Coordination (UNDP)	**CEPLA**	Comisión de Estudios para la Promoción de la Lana Argentina
CEPC	Comité Européen pour les Problèmes Criminels	**CEPLA**	Comité Español de Plásticos en Agricultura
CEPCEO	Comité d'Étude des Producteurs de Charbon d'Europe Occidentale	**CEPLAC**	Comissão Executiva do Plano de Recuperação Econômico-Rural da Lavoura Cacaueira (Brazil)
CEPCH	Confederación de Empleados Particulares de Chile	**CEPLAN**	Centro de Estudios de Planificación Nacional (Chile)
CEPCIECC	Comisión Ejecutiva Permanente Consejo Interamericano para la Educación, la Ciencia y la Cultura	**CEPOI**	Centre d'Études des Pays de l'Océan Indien
		CEPOM	Centre d'Études des Problèmes d'Outre Mer
CEPCIES	Comisión Ejecutiva Permanente del Consejo Interamericano Economico y Social	**CEPRIG**	Centre de Perfectionnement pour la Recherche Industrielle et sa Gestion
CEPDAC	Comité d'Études pour la Défense et l'Amélioration des Cultures	**CEPRO**	Centre d'Étude des Problèmes Humains du Travail
CEPDECC-LA	Comisión Especial de Programación y Desarrollo de la Educación, la Ciencia y la Cultura en America Latina (U.S.A.)	**CEPS**	Central Europe Pipeline System (*of* NATO)
		CEPS	Centro de Estudos e Pesquisas de Sociologia (Brazil)
CEPE	Centre d'Études Phytosociologiques et Écologiques	**CEPSA**	Compania Española de Petroleos, S.A.
CEPE	Comisión Económica para Europa	**CEPSE**	Centre d'Études Politiques et Sociales Européennes
CEPEC	Centro de Pesquisas do Cacau (Brazil)	**CEPSE**	Centre d'Execution des Programmes Sociaux et Economiques (Zaire)
CEPEC	Committee of European Associations of Manufacturers of Passive Electronic Components	**CEPSI**	Centre d'Études des Problèmes Sociaux Indigènes (Zaire)
CEPEM	Centre d'Études Européen pour les Problèmes de l'Environnement Marin	**CEPT**	Centro de Estudos de Pedologia Tropical (Portugal)
CEPEP	Centro Paraguayo de Estudios de Población	**CEPT**	Conférence Européenne des Administrations des Postes et des Télécommunications
CEPEPA	Comité Économique de la Prune d'Ente et du Pruneau d'Agen	**CEPVDVM**	Centre d'Etude des Problèmes Viticoles et de Defense des Vins Meridionaux
CEPERN	Centro Panamericano de Entrenamiento para Evaluación de Recursos Naturales (Brazil)	**CERA**	Centre d'Etudes et de Recherches sur l'Aquiculture (Belgium)
CEPES	Centro de Estudios Políticos, Económicos y Sociales (Argentina)	**CERA**	Centre d'Etudes des Religions Africaines (Zaire)
CEPES	European Centre for Higher Education (Roumania)	**CERA**	Centre d'Etudes du Risque Atomique (Switzerland)
CEPES	European Committee for Economic and Social Development	**CERA**	Civil Engineering Research Association (*now* CIRIA)
CEPFAR	Centre Européen pour la Promotion et la Formation en Milieu Agricole et Rural	**CERAC**	Centre d'Etudes pour le Ruralisme et l'Aménagement des Campagnes
CEPGL	Communauté Économique des Pays des Grand Lacs	**CERAC**	Comité d'Expansion Régionale et d'Aménagement de la Champagne

CERAFER   Centre National d'Études Techniques et de Recherches Technologiques pour l'Agriculture, les Forêts et l'Équipement Rural (*formerly* CREGR)

CERAG   Centre d'Études Regionales Antilles-Guyane

CERAME-UNIE   Common Market Liaison Bureau for the Ceramic Industries (Belgium)

CERAT   Centre d'Étude et de Recherche sur l'Administration Économique et l'Aménagement du Territoire

CERBE   Centrum voor Rationele Bedrijfsvoering Zuidhollandse Eilanden

CERBOM   Centre d'Études et de Recherches de Biologie et d'Océanographie Médicale

CERC   Centre d'Études des Revenus et des Coûts

CERC   Civil Engineering Research Council

CERC   Comité Européen des Représentants de Commerce Group CEE

CERCA   Centre d'Enseignement Rural par Correspondance d'Angers

CERCA   Centre d'Études et de Recherches Catalanes des Archives

CERCA   Commonwealth and Empire Radio for Civil Aviation

CERCA   Compagnie pour l'Étude et la Réalisation de Combustibles Atomiques

CERCHAR   Centre d'Études et Recherches des Charbonnages de France

CERCI   Compagnie d'Études et de Réalisations de Cybérnetique Industrielle

CERCLE   Centre d'Études et de Recherches sur les Collectivités Locales en Europe (France)

CERCOL   Centre de Recherches Techniques et Scientifiques des Conserves de Légumes (Belgium)

CERDAC   Centro Regional de Documentación para el Desarrollo Agrícola de América Central (Costa Rico)

CERDAS   Centre for the Co-ordination of Social Science Research and Documentation in Africa South of the Sahara (Zaire)

CERE   Centre d'Études et de Recherches de Environnement (Belgium)

CERE   Comité Européen pour les Relations Economiques

CEREA   Centre National de Recherches pour l'Étude des Animaux Nuisibles ou Utiles à l'Agriculture (Belgium)

CEREA   Comisión Especial de Representantes de Entidades Agropecuarias (Argentina)

CEREBE   Centre de Recherche sur le Bien-être

CEREC   Centre Européen de Recherches Économiques et Commerciales

CEREFA   Comision Ejecutiva de Repoblacíon Educación Forestal Agropecuaria (Cuba)

CEREGE   Centre de Recherches en Économie et Gestion des Entreprises (Belgium)

CEREN   Centre d'Études Régionales sur l'Économie de l'Énergie

CERER   Comité d'Études et de Recherches Économiques Rurales

CERES   Centre d'Assais et de Recherches d'Engins Spéciaux

CERES   Centre d'Études et de Recherches Économiques et Sociales (Tunis)

CERES   Centre de Recherches Socio-Religieuses (Burundi)

CERES   Comité d'Études Régionales Économiques et Sociales

CERES   Controlled Environment Research Laboratory (*of* CSIRO) (Australia)

CERESIS   Centro Regional de Sismologia para América del Sur (Peru)

CERF   Centre d'Études et de Recherches en Fonderies (Belgium)

CERI   Central Education Research Institute (Korea)

CERI   Centre for Educational Research and Innovation (*of* OECD)

CERI   Centre d'Étude des Relations Internationals

CERIA   Centre d'Enseignement et de Recherches des Industries Alimentaires et Chimiques (Belgium)

CERIC   Consortium d'Études et de Réalisations Industrielles et Commerciales (Dahomey)

CERIS   Centro de Estatistica Religiosa e Investigacões Socias (Brazil)

CERK   Centre d'Études et de Recherches de Kara (Togo)

CERL   Central Electricity Research Laboratories

CERLAL   Centro Regional para el Formento del Libro en la América Latina (Colombia)

CERMA   Centre d'Études et de Recherches du Machinisme Agricole

CERMAP   Centre d'Études Mathématiques pour la Planification

CERMO	Centre d'Études et de Recherches de la Machine-Outil
CERN	Organisation Européenne pour le Recherche Nucléaire (*formerly* Conseil)
CEROS	Centre Européen d'Observation par Sondages
CERP	Centre d'Études et de Recherches Psycho-techniques
CERP	Centre Européen des Relations Publiques
CERPER	Empresa Pública de Certificaciones Pesqueras del Perú
CERPHOS	Centre d'Études et de Recherches des Phosphates Minéraux
CERQUA	Centre de Développement des Certifications des Qualités Agricoles et Alimentaires
CERS	Centre d'Études et de Recherches Scientifiques
CERS	Centre Européen de Recherches Spatiales
CERSE	Centre National d'Études et de Recherches Socio-Économiques (Belgium)
CERT	Comité de Roubaix-Tourcoing d'Études et d'Actions Économiques et Sociales
CERT	Comptoir d'Etudes Radio Techniques
CERTS	Centre d'Études et Recherches en Technologie Spatiale
CERTSM	Centre d'Études et de Recherches Techniques Sous-Marines
CERUSS	Comité Permanent International des Techniques et de l'Urbanisme Souterrains et Spatials
CERVA	Consortium Européen de Réalisation et de Vente d'Avions
CERVL	Centre d'Étude et de Recherche sur la Vie Locale
CES	Centre for Environmental Studies
CES	Centre d'Études Sociologiques
CES	Comité Économique et Social (of CEE)
CES	Confédération Européenne des Syndicats
CES	Conference of European Statisticians (UN)
CES	Conseil Économique et Social
CESA	Canadian Engineering Standards Association
CESA	Central Ecuatoriana de Servicios Agraria
CESA	Centre d'Études Sociales Africaines (Zaire)
CESA	Comité Européen des Syndicats de l'Alimentation du Tabac et de l'Industrie Hôtelière dans la Communauté
CESA	Cooperative Educational Service Agency (U.S.A.)
CESAMP	Group of Experts on the Scientific Aspects of Marine Pollution
CESAP	Commission Économique et Sociale des Nations Unies pour l'Asie et le Pacifique
CESB	Centre d'Enseignement Supérieur de Brazzaville
CESC	European Confederation of Christian Trade Unions
CESCJ	Conseil Européen des Services Communautaires Juifs
CESD	Centre Européen pour la Formation de Statisticiens-Économistes pour les Pays en Voie de Développement
CESDA	Confederation of European Soft Drinks Associations
CESE	Centre d'Études de la Socio-Économie
CESE	Comisión Ecuménica de Servicio, (Brazil)
CESE	Council for Environmental Science and Engineering
CESERFO	Centro Studi e Ricerche Fondiarie.
CESH	Centre d'Études de Sciences Humaines (Zaire)
CESI	Centre for Economic and Social Information (*of* UNO)
CESIC	Catholic European Study and Information Centre (France)
CESIGU	Comité pour l'Élaboration d'un Système Informatique de Gestion Universitaire (Canada)
CESII	Centro de Sociologia Industrial e do Trabalho (Brazil)
CESIN	Centro Economico Scambi Italo-Nipponici
CESL	Camp Evans Signals Laboratory (U.S.A.)
CESL	Conseil Européen de la Jeunesse Syndicale
CESLAMD	Comité de Liaison des Secrétariats Latino-Américaines des Moyens de Diffusion
CESMAD	Association des Transporteurs Routiers Internationaux Tschécoslovaques
CESO	Canadian Executive Services Overseas
CESO	Centrum voor de Studie van het Onderwijs in Veranderende Maatschappijen
CESO	Concorde Engines Support Organisation Ltd
CESO	Council of Engineers and Scientists Organisations (U.S.A.)

CESP	European Confederation of National Unions Associations and Professional Sections of Pediatricians (Belgium)	CETIS	European Atomic Energy Community Scientific Data-processing Centre
CESPAP	Comisión Económica y Social para Asia y el Pacifico (UN)	CETISA	Compañia Española de Editoriales Tecnológicas Internacionales
CESPQ	Compañia Ecuatoriana de Sal y Productos Químicos	CETMA	Centre d'Ethno-technologie en Milieux Aquatiques
CESR	Canadian Electronic Sales Representatives	CETMA	Centre d'Études Techniques Ménagères et Agricoles
CESSE	Council of Engineering and Scientific Society Executives (U.S.A.)	CETO	Centre for Educational Television Overseas
CESSTW	Center for the Economic and Social Study of the Third World (Mexico)	CETOP	Comité Européen des Transmissions Oléohydrauliques et Pneumatiques
CESTA	Conference on Education and Scientific and Technical Training in Relation to Development in Africa	CETOPES	Centre d'Études des Techniciens de l'Organisation Professionnelle
CESTI	Centre d'Études des Sciences et Techniques de l'Information (Dakar)	CETP	Confédération Européenne pour la Thérapie Physique
CET	Centre Européen de Traduction	CETRA	Compagnie Équatoriale de Travaux (Gabon)
CET	Commission Européenne du Tourisme	CETRAMET	Compagnie Équatoriale pour la Transformation des Métaux en République Centrafricaine
CET	Council for Educational Technology for the United Kingdom	CETRAMET - CONGO	Compagnie Équatoriale pour la Transformation des Métaux au Congo
CETA	Centres d'Études Techniques Agricoles	CETS	Centre Européen de Technologie Spatiale
CETA	Centro des Estudos Technicos de Automación	CETSAS	Centre d'Études Transdisciplinaires (Sociologie, Anthropologie, Sémiologie)
CETA	Conference des Églises de toute l'Afrique	CETT	Centro de Entreamiento para Tecnicos en Telecommunicaciónes (Venezuela)
CETAM	Centre d'Etudes Techniques Agricoles Ménager	CETT	Compagnie Européenne de Télétransmissions
CETCA	Centre d'Enseignement Technique du Crédit Agricole	CEU	Constructional Engineering Union (now AUEW)
CETEHOR	Centre Technique de l'Industrie Horlogère	CEUCA	Centro de Estudios Universitarios Colombo-Americanos
CETEM	Centre d'Enseignement des Techniques d'Étude de Marché	CEUCA	Customs and Economic Union of Central Africa
CETEPA	Centre Professionnel Technique d'Études de la Pollution Atmosphérique	CEUCORS	Centre Européen de Coordination de Recherche et de Documentation en Sciences Sociales
CETEX	Committee on Extra-Terrestrial Exploration	CEUR	Centro de Estudios Urbanos y Regionales (Argentina)
CETF	Centre d'Études des Techniques Forestières	CEUSA	Committee for Exports to the United States of America (now BOTB)
CETHEDEC	Centre d'Études Théoretique de la Détection et des Communications	CEV	Coöperatieve Eierveiling van de ABTB
CETIE	Centre Technique International de l'Embouteillage	CEVECO	Centrale Organisatie van Veeafzet- en Vleesverwerkings-coöperaties
CETIEF	Centre Technique des Industries de l'Estampage	CEVOI	Comptoir d'Exportation de Vanille de l'Océan Indien (Madagascar)
CETIL	Committee of Experts for the Transfer of Information between Community Languages (EEC)	CEWC	Council for Education in World Citizenship
CETIOM	Centre Technique Interprofessionnel des Oléagineux Metropolitains	CEXIM	Carteira de Exportação e Importação (Brazil) (replaced by CACEX)

CEXO	Société des Caoutchoucs d'Extrême-Orient (Viet-Nam)	**CFAT**	Carnegie Foundation for the Advancement of Teaching (U.S.A.)
CEZ	Centre Européen pour la Formation Professionnelle dans l'Assurance (Switzerland)	**CFB**	Commonwealth Forestry Bureau
		CFB	Conselho Federal de Biblioteconomia (Brazil)
		CFBS	Canadian Federation of Biological Sciences
CEZA	Comité Européen de Zoologie Agricole	**CFC**	Compagnie Forestière du Congo
CEZMS	Church of England Zenana Missionary Society	**CFCA**	Confédération Française de la Coopération Agricole
CEZOO	Centre de Recherches Zoologiques Appliquées (Belgium)	**CFCAM**	Caisse Forestière de Crédit Agricole Mutuel et de Garantie Incendie Forestière
CF	Comité des Forêts	**CFCB**	Compagnie Française de Crédit et de Banque
CF	Commonwealth Fund (U.S.A.)	**CFCCA**	Centre de Formation des Cadres pour Coopératives Agricoles (Rwanda)
CF	Sveriges Civilingenjörsförbund		
CFA	Canadian Federation of Agriculture	**CFCE**	Conseil des Fédérations Commerciales d'Europe (*now* OIC)
CFA	Canadian Forestry Association		
CFA	Comité Français des Aérosols	**CFCO**	Chemin de Fer Congo-Océan
CFA	Committee on Food Aid Policies and Programmes (FAO/WFP)	**CFCPC**	Comité des Fruits à Cidre et des Productions Cidricoles (France)
CFA	Commission des Forêts pour l'Afrique (FAO)	**CFD**	Christlicher Friedendienst
CFA	Commonwealth Forestry Association	**CFDA**	Council of Fashion Designers of America
CFA	Communauté Financière Africaine	**CFDC**	Canadian Film Development Corporation
CFA	Compagnie Forestière Africaine	**CFDC**	Cane Farming Development Corporation (Guyana)
CFA	Comptoir Français de l'Azote		
CFA	Confédération Française de l'Artisanat	**CFDC**	Centre Français de Droit Comparé
CFA	Confédération Française de l'Aviculture	**CFDT**	Compagnie Française pour le Développement des Fibres Textiles
CFA	Conférence des Femmes Africaines		
CFA	Corporación Fruticola Argentina	**CFDT**	Confédération Française Démocratique de Travail
CFA	Council of Ironfoundry Associations		
CFA	Credit Foncier d'Afrique	**CFE**	Comision Federal de Electricidad (Mexico)
CFAE	Centre de Formation en Aérodynamique Expérimentale (Belgium)	**CFE**	Confédération de Groupements de Conseils Fiscaux des Pays de la Communauté Économique Européenne (Confédération Fiscale Européenne)
CFAE	Council for Financial Aid to Education (U.S.A.)		
CFAL	Commission des Forêts pour l'Amérique Latine	**CFEI**	Centre de Formation et d'Échanges Internationaux
CFAL	Current Food Additives Legislation (U.S.A.)	**CFEM**	Comité pour une Fédération Européenne et Mondiale
CFAN	Commission Forestière pour l'Amérique du Nord (FAO)	**CFEM**	Compagnie Française d'Entreprises Métalliques
CFAO	Chief Fire Officers Association	**CFEP**	Centre Français de Protection de l'Enfance
CFAO	Compagnie Française de l'Afrique Occidentale	**CFEU**	Conseil Français pour l'Europe Unie
		CFF	Chemins de Fer Fédéraux Suisse
CFAP	Canadian Foundation for the Advancement of Pharmacy	**CFF**	Crédit Foncier de France
		CFFA	Commonwealth Families and Friendship Association
CFAP	Commission des Forêts pour l'Asie et la Région du Pacifique	**CFG**	Compagnie Forestière du Gabon

CFGE	California Fruit Growers Exchange (U.S.A.)	CFPI	Central Family Planning Institute (India)
CFGG	Compagnie Forestière du Golfe de Guinée	CFPI	Centro de Fomento y Productividad Industrial (Guatemala)
CFH	International Information Centre of the Swiss Watchmaking Industry	CFPI	Commission de la Fonction Publique Internationale
CFHA	Colorado Forestry and Horticulture Association (U.S.A.)	CFPO	Commission des Forêts pour le Proche-Orient
CFI	Commonwealth Forestry Institute (*formerly* IFI)	CFPPT	Centre de Formation et de Perfectionnement des Planteurs de Tabac
CFI	Consejo Federal de Inversiones (Argentina)	CFRAI	Comité Français des Relations Agricoles Internationales
CFI	Corporación Financiera Internacional	CFRI	Central Fuel Research Institute (India)
CFI	Council of the Forest Industries of British Columbia	CFRT	Colorado Foundation for Research in Tuberculosis (U.S.A.)
CFIA	Comisión de Fomento e Investigaciones Agrícolas (Chile)	CFRTI	Centre Français de Renseignements Techniques Industriels
CFIE	Conseil des Fédérations Industrielles d'Europe	CFRZ	Centre Fédéral de Recherches Zootechniques (Switzerland)
CFK	Christliche Friedenskonferenz (Czechoslovakia)	CFS	Comptoir Français des Superphosphates
CFLF	Comptoir des Filasses de Lin Françaises	CFSG	Compagnie Forestière du Sud-Gabon
CFL	Confektionsfabrikanternes Landsforbund	CFSI	Comité Français de la Semoulerie Industrielle
CFLA	Comisión Forestal Latinoamericana	CFSL	Central Forensic Science Laboratory
CFM	Council of Foreign Ministers	CFSTI	Clearinghouse for Federal Scientific and Technical Information (U.S.A.) (*now* NTIS)
CFME	Compagnie Franco-Malgache d'Entreprises		
CFMU	Compagnie Française des Minerais d'Uranium	CFTC	Commonwealth Fund for Technical Cooperation
CFMVA	Centre de Formation de Moniteurs et de Vulgarisateurs Agricoles	CFTC	Confédération Française des Travailleurs Chrétiens
CFN	Corporación Financiera Nacional (Colombia)	CFTF	Centre Technique Forestier Tropical (France)
		CFTH	Compagnie Française Thomson-Houston
CFNA	Comisión Forestal Norteamericana (FAO)	CFTRI	Central Food Technological Research Institute (India)
CFNCL	Comité Fédératif National de Contrôle Laitier	CFTV	Centre de Formation de Techniciens de Vulgarisation
CFNFMPR	Centre Familial National pour la Formation Ménagère et Professionnelle Rurale	CFV	Corporación Venezolana de Fomento
CFNI	Caribbean Food and Nutrition Institute	CFWCC	Children and Families World Community Chest
CFP	Canadian Forest Products	CFZV	Centrala Farmaseutica Zoo-Veterinara (Roumania)
CFP	Compagnie Français des Pétroles		
CFP	Confédération Française de la Photographie	CGA	Canadian Gas Association
CFPC	Centre Chrétien des Patrons et Dirigeants d'Entreprise Français	CGA	Confédération Générale de l'Agriculture
		CGA	Conseil Général de l'Agriculture
CFPC	Centre Français du Patronat Chrétien	CGA	Country Gentlemen's Association
CFPD	Compagnie Française Powell Duffryn	CGA	Cyprus Geographical Association
CFPFL	Confédération Française des Producteurs de Fruits et Légumes (*formerly* CNPFL)	CGAD	Confédération Générale de l'Alimentation en Détail
CFPFLC	Confédération Française des Producteurs de Fruits, Légumes et Champignons	CGADIP	Compagnie Gazière d'Afrique et de Distribution de Primagaz

CGAF	Confédération Générale des Architectes Français
CGAF	Confédération Générale de l'Artisanat Français
CGAP	Comité Général d'Action Paysanne
CGB	Commonwealth Geographical Bureau (Sri Lanka)
CGB	Confédération Générale des Planteurs de Betteraves
CGBE	Christliche Gewerkschaft Bergbau und Energie
CGC	Commonwealth Games Council
CGC	Confédération Générale des Cadres
CGCA	Confédération Générale des Coopératives Agricoles (France) (now CFCA)
CGCI	Confédération Générale du Commerce et de l'Industrie
CGCRI	Central Glass and Ceramics Research Institute, Calcutta (India)
CGCT	Compagnie Générale de Constructions Téléphoniques
CGD	Christliche Gewerkschaftbund Deutschland
CGE	Confederación General Económica (Argentina)
CGE	Confédération Générale l'Épargne
CGEA	Confédération Générale Économique Algérienne
CGEC	Confederación General de Empleados de Comercio (Argentina)
CGECI	Compagnie Générale d'Électricité de Côte-d'Ivoire
CGER	Centre de Gestion et d'Économie Rurale
CGF	Commonwealth Games Federation
CGFPI	Consultative Group on Food Production and Investment in Developing Countries (FAO etc.)
CGFTL	Confédération Générale des Filateurs et Tisseurs de Lin
CGGP	Conference Group on German Politics
CGI	Comitato Glaciologico Italiano
CGI	Congrès Géologique International
CGIAR	Consultative Group on International Agricultural Research (FAO etc).
CGIC	Comité Général Interprofessionnel Chanvrier
CGIL	Confederazione Generale Italiana Lavora
CGLI	City and Guilds of London Institute
CGLS	Confederazione Generale dei Lavoratori della Somalia
CGLV	Breeders' Plant Licence Administration Fund
CGM	Compagnie Générale de Madagascar
CGMA	Casein Glue Manufacturers Association
CGMA	Compressed Gas Manufacturers' Association (U.S.A.)
CGMW	Commission for the Geological Map of the World
CGOT	Compagnie Générale des Oléagineux Tropicaux
CGP	Commissariat Général au Plan
CGP	Commissariat Général à la Productivité
CGPB	Confederação General dos Pescadores do Brasil
CGPB	Confédération Générale des Planteurs de Betteraves
CGPCC	Confédération Générale des Planteurs de Chicorée à Café
CGPEL	Confédération Générale des Producteurs de Fruits et Légumes
CGPLBIR	Confédération Générale des Producteurs de Lait de Brebis et des Industriels de Roquefort
CGPM	Conférence Générale des Poids et Mesures
CGPM	Conseil Général des Pêches pour la Méditerrannée (FAO)
CGPME	Confédération Générale des Petites et Moyennes Entreprises
CGPP	Confederazione Generale dei Produttori di Patate
CGPPT	Confédération Générale des Producteurs de Pommes de Terre
CGPS	Canadian Government Purchasing Service
CGPT	Confédération Générale des Paysans Travailleurs
CGRA	China and Glass Retailers Association
CGRA	Consortium Général des Recherches Aéronautiques
CGRB	Capital Gains Research Bureau
CGRB	Combinatie Groningen v. Rationele Bedrijfsvoering
CGRI	Central Glass and Ceramic Research Institute (India)
CGS	Canadian Geographical Society
CGSB	Canadian Government Specifications Board
CGSI	Confédération Générale des Syndicats Indépendants

GSLB	Centrale Générale des Syndicats Libéraux de Belgique
GT	Centro de Geografía Tropical (Ecuador)
GT	Commissariat Général au Tourisme
GT	Compagnie Générale Transatlantique
GT	Confédération Générale du Travail
GTA	General Confederation of African Workers
GTB	Canadian Government Travel Bureau
GTFB	Confederación General de Trabajadores Fabriles de Bolivia
GT-FO	Confédération Générale du Travail Force Ouvrière
GTL	Confédération Générale du Travail du Luxembourg
GTREO	Compagnie Générale de Travaux de Recherches et d'Exploitation Océaniques
GU	Confederación General Universitaria (Brazil)
GV	Confédération Générale de la Vieillesse
GV	Confédération Générale des Vignerons
GVCO	Confédération Générale des Vignerons du Centre-Ouest
GVM	Confédération Générale des Vignerons du Midi
GVSO	Confédération Générale des Vignerons du Sud-Ouest
GWB	Canadian Government Wheat Board
HA	Caribbean Hotel Association
HA	Catholic Hospital Association (U.S.A.)
HA	Chest and Heart Association
HAC	Catholic Hospital Association of Canada
HACONA	Chantier de Construction Navale
HAFREC	Chambre Syndicate Française de l'Enseignement Privé par Correspondance
HAIDIS	Chaine Africaine d'Importation, de Distribution et d'Exportation
HAIS	Consumer Hazards Analysis Information Service
HAMCOM	Chambre de Commerce d'Agriculture et de l'Industrie de la République du Tchad
HANCOM	Channel Committee (of NATO)
HAPA	Committee on the History of American Public Address
HB	Central Housing Board (Kenya)
HE	Comité Hygiène et Eau
HEA	Centre des Hautes Études Administratives
CHEAM	Centre de Hautes Études Administratives sur l'Afrique et l'Asie Modernes
CHEAR	Council on Higher Education in the American Republics
CHEC	Commonwealth Human Ecology Council
CHENOP	Companhia Hidro-Eléctrica do Norte de Portugal
CHIA	Canadian Hovercraft Industries Association
CHIDRAL	Central Hidroelectrica del Rio Anchicaya, Limitada (Colombia)
CHISS	Centre Haitien d'Investigation en Sciences Sociales (Haiti)
CHOBISCO	Chambre Syndicale des Grossiers en Confiserie Chocolaterie, Biscuits et Autres Dérivés du Sucre (Belgium)
CHOCO-SUISSE	Union des Fabricants Suisses de Chocolat
CHR	Centralforeningen af Hotelvœrter og Restauratører i Danmark
CHS	Canadian Hydrographic Service
CI	Commonwealth Institute
CIA	Central Intelligence Agency (U.S.A.)
CIA	Centre d'Insémination Artificielle
CIA	Centre International des Antiparasitaires
CIA	Centro de Inseminación Artificial (Porto Rico)
CIA	Centro de Investigaciones Agronómicas (Venezuela)
CIA	Chemical Industries Association
CIA	Cigar Institute of America
CIA	Collegium Internationale Allergologicum
CIA	Comisión Internacional del Alamo (of FAO)
CIA	Comisión Internacional del Arroz (Thailand)
CIA	Comité International d'Auschwitz
CIA	Commonwealth Industries Association
CIA	Confederación Intercooperativa Agropecuaria (Argentina)
CIA	Confédération Internationale des Accordéonistes
CIA	Confédération Nationale Belge du Commerce Indépendant de l'Alimentation
CIA	Conseil International des Archives
CIAA	Centre International d'Aviation Agricole
CIAA	Comité International d'Assistance Aéroportuaire

117

CIAA	Commission des Industries Agricoles et Alimentaires de l'Union des Industries de la CEE
CIAA	Comptoir Industriel et Agricole Abidjan (Ivory Coast)
CIAA	Confédération Internationale des Associations d'Artistes
CIAB	Centro de Investigaciones Agrícolas de El Bajio (Mexico)
CIAB	Conseil International des Agences Bénévoles
CIAC	Centrale Ivoirienne d'Achats et de Crédit
CIAC	Compagnie des Industries Africaines du Caoutchouc
CIACAM	Compagnie Industrielle d'Automobiles du Cameroun
CIACOL	Compañía de Ingenieros Agrónomos de Colombia
CIADEC	Confédération Internationale des Associations d'Anciens des Élèves de l'Enseignement Commercial Supérieur
CIADI	Centro Internacional de Arreglo de Diferencias Relativas a Inversiones
CIAECO-SOC	Consejo Interamericano Economico y Social
CIAFMA	Centre International de l'Actualité Fantastique et Magique
CIAGA	Confederación Interamericana de Ganaderos
CIAI	Comité International d'Aide aux Intellectuels
CIAI	Conférence International des Associations d'Ingénieurs
CIAL	Communauté Internationale des Associations de la Librairie
CIAL	Council International des Auteurs Littéraires
CIALA	Inter-Faculty Centre for African Anthropology and Linguistics (Zaire)
CIALS	Confédération Intérnationale des Arts, des Lettres et des Sciences
CIAM	Colegio de Ingenieros Agrónomos de México
CIAM	Congrès Internationaux d'Architecture Moderne
CIAMAC	International Conference of Associations of Amputees and Veterans
CIAME	Commission Interministerielle pour les Appareils de Mesures Électriques et Électroniques
CIANE	Centro de Investigaciones Agrícolas del Noreste (Mexico)
CIAO	Compagnie Industrielle Agricole Oubangui (Zaire)
CIAO	Conference Internationale des Africanistes de l'Ouest
CIAP	Centre d'Information Agricole des Planteurs
CIAP	Centre d'Information de l'Aviation Privée
CIAP	Centro de Investigaciones en Administracion Pública (Argentina)
CIAP	Comité Interamericano de la Alianza para el Progreso (OAS)
CIAP	Commission Internationale des Arts et Traditions Populaires
CIAP	Compagnie Ivoirienne d'Armement à la Pêche
CIAPAG	Confédération Internationale des Anciens Prisonniers de Guerre
CIAPESC	Companhia Amazónica de Pesca (Brazil)
CIAPG	Confédération Internationale des Anciens Prisonniers de Guerre
CIAPY	Centro de Investigacion Agricolas de la Peninsula de Yucatan (Mexico)
CIAQ	Centre d'Insémination Artificielle du Québec (Canada)
CIARA	Fundación para la Capacitación e Investigación Aplicada a la Reforma Agraria (Venezuela)
CIAS	Centro de Investigación y Acción Social (Colombia)
CIAS	Centro de Investigaciones Administrativas y Sociales (Venezuela)
CIAS	Centro de Investigaciones Agrícolas de Sinaloa (Mexico)
CIAS	Comité International d'Information et d'Action Sociale
CIAS	Comité Investigación Agua Subterránea (Argentina)
CIAS	Conference of Independent African States
CIAS	Consejo Inter-americano de Seguridad
CIASA	Compania Internacional Aerea S.A. (Ecuador)
CIASC	Confédération Interaméricaine d'Action Sociale Catholique
CIASE	Centro de Investigaciones Agrícolas del Sureste (Mexico)
CIAT	Centro Interamericano de Administradores Tributarios
CIAT	Centro Internacional por Agricultura Tropical (Colombia)

CIAT	Comisión Interamericana del Atún Tropical	CIC	Capital Issues Committee
CIAT	Comité des Industries de l'Achèvement Textile des Pays de la CEE	CIC	Caribbean Investment Corporation
		CIC	Centre International de Calcul (Switzerland)
CIATE	Cooperativa Industrial Agrícola Tropical Ecuatoriana	CIC	Chemical Institute of Canada
		CIC	Cinema International Corporation
CIATF	Comité International des Associations Techniques de Fonderie	CIC	Cobalt Information Centre
		CIC	Collège Internationale des Chirurgiens
CIATO	Centre Internationale d'Alcoologie/Toxicomanies	CIC	Comité International des Camps (of UIRD)
		CIC	Comité International de la Conserve
CIB	Centre Interaméricain de Biostatistique	CIC	Comité International de Coordination pour l'Initiation à la Science et le Développement des Activités Scientifiques Extra-scolaires
CIB	Centro Internacional Bibliografico		
CIB	Centro de Investigaciones Básicas (Mexico)		
CIB	Comité Interprofessionnel Bananier	CIC	Commission Internationale du Châtaignier (of FAO)
CIB	Communauté International Baha'ie		
CIB	Conseil Interfédéral du Bois	CIC	Compagnie Immobilière du Congo
CIB	Conseil International du Blé	CIC	Confédération Internationale des Cadres
CIB	International Council for Building Research Studies and Documentation	CIC	Confédération Internationale de la Coiffure
		CIC	Confédération Internationale de Défense du Cheval
CIB	International Timber Committee		
CIB	Société Congolaise Industrielle des Bois	CIC	Conférence Internationale du Crédit
CIBA	Ciba Foundation (for promotion of International Co-operation in Medical and Chemical Research)	CIC	Conseil International de la Chasse
		CIC	Conseil International des Compositeurs
		CIC	Council for International Contact
CIBAL	International Centre for Sources of Balkan History (Bulgaria)	CICA	Canadian Institute of Chartered Accountants
CIBC	Commonwealth Institute of Biological Control (West Indies)	CICA	Centro Interamericano de Ciêncas Administrativas
CIBC	Confédération Internationale de la Boucherie et de la Charcuterie	CICA	Centro de Investigaçao Cientifica Algodoeira (Portuguese W. Africa)
CIBE	Confédération Internationale des Betteraviers Européens	CICA	Comité International Catholique des Aveugles
CIBEP	Section des Six Pays du Commerce International de Bulbes à Fleurs et de Plantes Ornementales	CICA	Comité Internationale de la Crise Alimentaire
		CICA	Comité International de la Croisade des Aveugles
CIBER	Inter-African Centre for Information and Liaison in Rural Welfare	CICA	Commerciale Italiane Cooperative Agricole
CIBJO	Confédération Internationale de la Bijouterie, Joaillerie, Orfèvrerie, des Diamants, Perles et Pierres	CICA	Conférence Internationale des Contrôles d'Assurances des États Africains, Français et Malgache
CIBM	Centro de Investigación de Biología Marina (Argentina)	CICA	Confédération Internationale du Crédit Agricole
CIBRA	Comercio e Indústria de Produtos Agrícolas do Brasil	CICAA	Comisión Internacional para la Conservación del Atún del Atlántico
CIBRAZEM	Companhia Brasileira de Armazenamento (Brazil)	CICAE	Centre International des Cinémas d'Art et d'Essai
CIBS	Chartered Institution of Building Services		
CIBS	Conferencia Interamericana de Bienestar Social	CICAF	Compagnie Industrielle des Combustibles Atomiques Frittes

CICAF	International Committee for the Cinema and the Figurative Arts	**CICEIPB**	Comité Intérimaire de Coordination des Échanges Internationaux de Produits de Base
CICAJ	Centre International de Coordination de l'Assistance Juridique	**CICELPA**	Centro de Investigación de Celulosa y Papel (Argentina)
CICAM	Société Cotonnière Industrielle du Cameroun	**CICEP**	*See* CICYP
CICAP	Centre Interamericano de Capacitación en Administración Pública (Argentina)	**CICF**	Chambre des Ingénieurs-Conseils de France
CICAP	Consejo Internacional para la Colaboración en los Análisis de Plaguicidas	**CICF**	Confédération Internationale des Cadres Fonctionnaires
CICAR	Corporación Industrial Comercial Agropecuaria (Argentina)	**CICG**	Centre International du Commerce de Gros
		CICG	Centre International de Conférences Genève
CICAR	International Co-ordination Group for the Co-operative Investigations of the Caribbean and Adjacent Regions (FAO)	**CICG**	Conference Internationale Catholique du Guidisme
CICATI	Division of the Exchange and Coordination of International Technical Assistance (Brazil)	**CICH**	Centro de Información Científica y Humanística (Mexico)
		CICH	Comité Internationale de la Culture de Houblon
CICATUR	Centro Interamericano de Capacitación Turistica (Argentina)	**CICH**	Confederación Internacional Católica de Hospitales
CICB	Chambre des Ingénieurs-Conseils de Belgique	**CICHE**	Computer Information Centre for Highway Engineering (South Africa) (*now* CICTRAN)
CICB	Conférence Permanente Internationale des Centres du Bâtiment		
CICB	Société Royale Chambre des Ingénieurs Conseils de Belgique	**CICI**	Centre Industriel Centrafricaino-Israélien
		CICIAMS	Comité International Catholique des Infirmières et Assistantes Médico-Sociales
CICC	Compagnie Immobilière et Commerciale du Cameroun	**CICIG**	Commissione Italiana del Comitato Internazionale di Geofisica
CICC	Conférence Internationale de Charitiés Catholiques	**CICIH**	Confédération Internationale Catholique des Institutions Hospitalières
CICC	International Center for Comparative Criminology (Canada)	**CICILS**	Confédération Internationale du Commerce et des Industries des Légumes Secs
CICCA	Centre International de Coordination pour la Célébration des Anniversaires	**CICJ**	Comité International pour la Coopération des Journalistes
CICCH	Centre International Chrétien de la Construction d'Habilitation	**CICLA**	Comité Internacional de Coordinación para el Combate de la Langosta Centro América
CICD	Collegium Internationale Chirugiae Digestivae	**CICLA**	International Committee for Locust Control
		CICM	Centro de Investigación de Ciencias Marinas (Colombia)
CICE	Centre International de Calcul Électronique (UNO)	**CICM**	Commission Internationale Catholique pour les Migrations
CICE	Centre International de Culturisme en Europe		
CICE	Centre Ivoirien du Commerce Extérieur	**CICOLAC**	Compañia Colombiana de Alimentos Lácteos
CICE	Centro de Investigaciones en Ciencias de la Educación (Argentina)	**CICOP**	Catholic Inter-American Cooperation Program
CICE	Comité de l'Industrie Cinématographique Européenne	**CICOTE-PHAR**	Centre Technique International de Coordination Pharmaceutique
CICE	Compagnie Industrielle des Céramiques Électroniques	**CICP**	Comité Internacional para le Cooperación des los Periodistas
CICE	Information Centre of the European Railways (Italy)	**CICP**	Confédération Internationale du Crédit Populaire

CICPE	Comité d'Initiative pour le Congrès du Peuple Européen	**CID**	Centro de Investigacion Documentaria (Argentina)
CICPLA	Commission d'Information et de Coopération des Journalistes d'Amérique Latine	**CID**	Comité International du Dachau
CICPLB	Comité International pour le Contrôle de la Productivité Laitière du Bétail	**CID**	Comité International des Dérivés Tensioactifs
CICR	Comité Internationale de la Croix-Rouge	**CID**	Comité International de la Détergence
CICRA	Centre International pour la Coopération des Recherches en Agriculture (France)	**CIDA**	Canadian International Development Agency
CICRC	Commission Internationale contre le Régime Concentrationnaire	**CIDA**	Centre d'Information de Documentation et de l'Alimentation
CICRED	Comité Internationale de Coopération des Recherches Nationales en Démographie (UN)	**CIDA**	Centre International de Développement de l'Aluminium
CICRIS	Co-operative Industrial and Commercial Reference and Information Service	**CIDA**	Centre International de Documentation Arachnologique
CICS	Centre International de la Construction Scolaire	**CIDA**	Comité Interamericano de Desarrollo Agricola
CICS	Commission Internationale Catholique de la Santé	**CIDA**	Comité Intergouvernemental du Droit d'Auteur
CICS	Committee for Index Cards for Standards (*of* IOS)	**CIDA**	Confederazione Italiana dei Dirigenti di Azienda
CICSO	Centre International Culturel Social et Pedagogique de l'Université Libre de Bruxelles	**CIDA**	Inter-American Centre for Archives Development (Argentina)
CICT	Commission on International Commodity Trade (UNCTAD)	**CIDADEC**	Confédération Internationale des Associations d'Experts et de Conseils
CICT	Conseil International du Cinéma et de la Télévision	**CIDAECA**	Comité International pour le Développement des Activités Éducatives et Culturelles en Afrique
CICTA	Commission Internationale pour la Conservation des Thonidés de l'Atlantique	**CIDAL**	Centro de Información y Documentación para América Latina
CICTRAN	Computer Information Centre for Transportation (South Africa)	**CIDALC**	Comité International pour la Diffusion des Arts et des Lettres par le Cinéma
CICYP	Consejo Interamericano de Comercio y Producción	**CIDAS**	Centre d'Information et Documentation pour l'Agriculture et la Sylviculture (Roumania)
CICYT	Inter-American Committee on Science and Technology (U.S.A.)	**CIDAT**	Centre d'Informatique Appliquée au Développement et à l'Agriculture Tropicale (Belgium)
CID	Centre d'Information et de Documentation du Congo et du Ruanda-Urundi	**CIDB**	Chemie-Information und Dokumentation Berlin
CID	Centre for Information and Documentation (EURATOM)	**CIDB**	International Council for Building Documentation
CID	Centre International pour le Développement (Switzerland)	**CIDC**	Comité International de Droit Comparé
		CIDD	Conseil International de la Danse
CID	Centre International de Documentation des Producteurs de Scories Thomas (Belgium)	**CIDE**	Centre Ibéroamericain de Documentation Européenne
CID	Centro de Informacion y Documentacion	**CIDE**	Centro de Información y Documentación Económica
CID	Centro de Investigaciones para el Desarrollo (Colombia)	**CIDE**	Centro de Investigación y Desarrollo de la Educación, Santiago (Chile)

CIDE	Comisión de Inversiones y Desarrollo Económico (Uruguay)	**CIDSE**	Coopération Internationale pour le Développement Socio-économique
CIDE	Commission Intersyndicale des Deshydrateurs Européennes	**CIDSP**	Centrule de Informare şi Documentare in Ştiinţe Sociale şi Politice (Roumania)
CIDE	Conseil International pour le Droit de l'Environnement	**CIDSS**	Comité International pour la Documentation des Sciences Sociales
CIDEA	Consejo Interamericano de Educación Alimenticia (Venezuela)	**CIDST**	Committee for Scientific and Technical Information and Documentation
CIDEC	Comité Interaméricain de la Culture (U.S.A.)	**CIDU**	Centro Interdisciplinario de Desarrollo Urbana y Regional (Chile)
CIDEC	Conseil Internationale pour le Développement du Cuivre	**CIE**	Cartographie des Invertébrés Européens
CIDECT	Comité Internationale pour le Développement et l'Étude de la Construction Tubulaire	**CIE**	Centre International de l'Enfance
		CIE	Centre International de l'Environnement
CIDEM	Inter-American Music Council	**CIE**	Centro de Investigaciones Económicas (Argentina, Colombia, Mexico)
CIDEP	Centre International de Documentation et d'Études Pétrolières	**CIE**	Comité Interafricain de Statistiques
		CIE	Comité International des Échanges
CIDES	Centre de Investigación para el Desarrolo Economico Social (Argentina)	**CIE**	Comité Interaméricain d'Éducation (U.S.A.)
CIDESA	Centre International de Documentation Economique et Social Africaine (Belgium)	**CIE**	Comissão Inter-Africana de Estatistica
		CIE	Commission Internationale de l'Éclairage
CIDESCO	Comité International d'Esthetique et de Cosmetologie	**CIE**	Commonwealth Institute of Entomology
		CIE	Compagnie Ivoirienne des Étiquettes
CIDH	Comisión Interamericana de Derechos Humanos (U.S.A.)	**CIE**	Consejo Interamericano de Escultismo (Costa Rico)
CIDHEC	Centre Intergouvernemental de Documentation sur l'Habitat et l'Environnement pour les Pays de la Commission Économique pour l'Europe des Nations Unies	**CIE**	Coras Iompair Eireann (Transport Organisation of Ireland)
		CIEA	Centre International de l'Élévage pour l'Afrique
CIDI	Centre International de Documentation et d'Information	**CIEA**	Centre International d'Études Agricoles
CIDIA	Centro Interamericano de Documentacióne e Información Agrícola (Costa Rico)	**CIEA**	Ceylonese Importers and Exporters Association
CIDIA	Consejo Inter-Americano de Educación Alimenticia	**CIEC**	Centre International des Engrais Chimiques
CIDIAT	Centro Interamericano de Desarrollo Integral de Aguas y Tierras (Venezuela)	**CIEC**	Centre International d'Études Criminologiques
CIDIC	Comité Interprofessionnel de Développement de l'Industrie Chevaline	**CIEC**	Commission International de l'État Civil
CIDITVA	Centre International de Documentation de l'Inspection Techniques des Véhicles Automobiles	**CIEC**	Confédération Interaméricaine d'Éducation Catholique
CIDOC	Centro Intercultural de Documentacion (Mexico)	**CIEC**	Conference on International Economic Cooperation
CIDP	Centre International de Documentation Parlementaire (Switzerland)	**CIEC**	Conseil Internationale des Employeurs du Commerce (*now* OIC)
CIDR	Compagnie International de Développement Rural	**CIECC**	Consejo Interamericano para la Educación, la Ciencia y la Cultura
		CIECD	Council for International Economic Cooperation and Development

CIECF	Commission Internationale Européenne des Communes Forestières et Communes de Montagne
CIECMM	Comisión Internacional para la Exploración Cientifica del Mar Mediterráneo
CIEE	Consejo Internacional de Educación para la Enseñanza
CIEF	Centre Interaméricain de Formation en Statistique Économique et Financière
CIEF	Centro de Investigaciones y Estudios Familiares
CIEH	Comité Interafricain d'Études Hydrauliques
CIEH	Comité Inter États des Études Hydrauliques (Senegal)
CIEHV	Conseil International pour l'Éducation des Handicapés de la Vue
CIEIA	Centro Internazionale per degli Studi sull Irrigazione
CIEL	Centre International d'Études Latines
CIEL	Commercial Importadora Exportadora S.A. (Canary Islands)
CIEM	Conseil International pour l'Exploration de la Mer
CIEMA	Centre International des Études de la Musique Ancienne
CIEN	Comisao Interamericano de Energia Nuclear
CIENCE	Commission Internationale d'Études de Normalisation Comptable Économique
CIENES	Centro Interamericano de Ensenanza de Estadistica (Chile)
CIENTAL	Centro de Investigaciones y Estudios Internacionales para la América Latina (Ecuador)
CIEO	Catholic International Education Office
CIEP	Centre International d'Études Pédagogiques (France)
CIEP	Consorcio dos Industriais de Equipaduento Pesado
CIEPA	Comité International de l'Éducation de Plein Air
CIEPC	Commission Internationale d'Études de la Police de Circulation
CIEPI	Comité Interprofessionnel Européen des Professions Intellectuelles
CIEPRC	Confédération Internationale des Instituts Catholiques d'Éducation des Adultes Ruraux
CIEPS	Conseil International de l'Éducation Physique et Sportive
CIER	Centro Interamericano de Educación Rural
CIER	Comisión de Integración Electrica Regional (Uruguay)
CIER	Conseil International des Économies Régionales
CIERE	Centre International d'Études et de Recherches Européennes
CIERIE	Compagnie Ivoirienne d'Études et de Réalisations Informatiques et Économiques
CIERP	Centre Intersyndical d'Études et de Recherches sur la Productivité (France)
CIERSES	Centre International d'Études et de Recherches en Socio-Économie de la Santé (Fondation Royaumont)
CIES	Centre International d'Enseignement de la Statistique
CIES	Comité International des Entreprises à Succursales
CIES	Comité Inter-Unions de l'Enseignement des Sciences
CIES	Commission Internationale pour l'Exploration Scientifique de la Mer Méditerrannée
CIES	Comparative and International Education Society (U.S.A.)
CIES	Consejo Interamericano Económico y Social
CIES	Council for International Exchange of Scholars (U.S.A.)
CIESEF	Centre Interaméricaine d'Enseignement de Statistique Économique et Financière
CIESJ	Centre International d'Enseignement Supérieur de Journalisme
CIESMM	Commission Internationale pour l'Exploration Scientifique de la Mer Méditerranée
CIESPAL	Centro Internacional de Estudios Superiores de Periodismo para América Latina (Ecuador)
CIEST	Centre International d'Études Supérieures de Tourisme
CIETA	Calcutta Import and Export Trade Association (India)
CIETA	Centre International d'Étude des Textiles Anciens
CIETAP	Comité Interprofessionnel d'Études des Techniques Agricoles et Pesticides

CIETB	Centre Intercontinental d'Études de Techniques Biologiques
CIETT	Confédération Internationale des Entreprises de Travail Temporaire
CIEU	Centre Interdisciplinaire d'Études Urbaines
CIEU	Centro de Investigaciones Económicas (Chile)
CIEURP	Conférence Internationale pour l'Enseignement Universitaire des Relations Publiques
CIF	Commission Interaméricaine des Femmes
CIF	Confédération Internationale des Fonctionnaires
CIF	Conseil International des Femmes
CIF	Cork Industry Federation
CIF	Cultural Integration Fellowship (U.S.A.)
CIFA	Comité International de Recherche et d'Étude de Facteurs de l'Ambiance
CIFA	Committee for Inland Fisheries of Africa (FAO)
CIFA	Consociazione Italiani Federazioni Autotrasporti
CIFC	Council for the Investigation of Fertility Control
CIFCA	Centro Internacional de Formación de Ciencias Ambientales para Paises de Habla Española
CIFCA	Confédération Internationale des Installateurs d'Équipement de Réfrigération et de Conditionnement d'Air
CIFE	Central Institute of Fisheries Education (India)
CIFE	Centre International de Formation Européenne
CIFE	Comision Interministerial de Fomento Económico (Peru)
CIFE	Comité International du Film Ethnographique
CIFE	Conseil des Fédérations Industrielles d'Europe
CIFE	Conseil International du Film d'Enseignement
CIFEFTA	Council of the Industrial Federations of EFTA
CIFEJ	Centre International du Film pour l'Enfance et la Jeunesse
CIFES	Comité International du Film Ethnographique et Sociologique

CIFF	Centro Incremento Frutticoltura Ferraresa
CIFI	Collegio Ingegneri Ferrovieri Italiani
CIFI	Consorzio Industriali Fotomeccanici Italiani
CIFOS	Compagnie Immobilière et Foncière du Sénégal
CIFRES	Centre International de Formation, de Recherches et d'Études Séricicoles (France)
CIFRI	Central Inland Fisheries Research Institute (India)
CIFT	Central Institute of Fisheries Technology (India)
CIFT	Committee on Invisibles and Financing Related to Trade (UNSTAD)
CIFTA	Comité International des Fédérations Théâtrales d'Amateurs de Langue Française
CIG	Comité Intergouvernemental Nations Unies/FAO
CIG	Comité International de Géophysique
CIG	Conférence Internationale du Goudron pour Routes
CIG	Intergovernmental Committee on the Establishment of a Free-trade Area (*of* OEEC)
CIGA	Centro de Investigaciones de Grasas y Aceites (Argentina)
CIGA	Compagnia Italian dei Grandi Alberghi
CIGAS	Cambridge Intercollegiate Graduate Application Scheme
CIGB	Commission International des Grand Barrages de la Conférence Mondiale de l'Énergie
CIGC	Comité Interprofessionnel du Gruyère du Comte
CIGDL	Chambre Immobilière du Grand-Duché de Luxembourg
CIGE	Centre Ivoirien de Gestion des Entreprises
CIGP	Conférence Internationale sur la Guerre Politique
CIGR	Commission Internationale du Génie Rurale
CIGRE	Conférence Internationale des Grands Réseaux Électriques
CIGS	Centre International de Gérontologie Sociale
CIHA	Comité Internationale d'Histoire de l'Art
CIHAN	Centraal Instituut ter Bevordering v. d. Buitenlandse Handel
CIHEAM	Centre International des Hautes Études Agronomique Méditerranéennes

CIHM	Commission Internationale d'Histoire Maritime
CIHM	Commission Internationale d'Histoire Militaire
CII	Centro Internacional de la Infancia
CII	Chartered Insurance Institute
CII	Compagnie Internationale pour l'Information
CII	Confederation of Irish Industry
CII	Conseil International des Infirmières
CII	Council of International Investigators (U.S.A.)
CIIA	Canadian Institute of International Affairs
CIIA	Commission Internationale des Industries Agricoles et Alimentaires
CIIC	Centre d'Information de l'Industrie des Chaux et Ciments
CIIC	Centro Internacional de Investigaciones sobre el Cáncer
CIID	Centro Internacional de Investigaciones para el Desarrollo (Canada)
CIID	Commission International des Irrigations et du Drainage
CIIG	Construction Industry Information Group
CIIM	Centre International d'Information de la Mutualité
CIINTE	Centralny Instytut Informacji Naukowo-Technicznej i Ekonomicznej (Poland)
CIIR	Catholic Institute for International Relations
CIITC	Confédération Internationale des Industries Techniques du Cinéma
CIJ	Commission International de Juristes
CIJ	Cour International de Justice
CIL	Christliche Internationale von Arbeiter der Lebensmittel- und Tabakindustrie und des Gastgewerbes
CIL	Comité International de la Lumière
CIL	Comité Interprofessionel du Logement
CIL	Confédération Nationale du Secteur Immobilier et du Logement (Belgium)
CILA	Centro Interamericano de Libros Academicos (Mexico)
CILAM	Compagnie Ivoirienne de Location Automobile et de Matériel
CILAS	Compagnie Industrielle des Lasers
CILB	Comité de l'Industrie Lainière Belge
CILB	Comité Interprofessional du Lait de Brebis
CILB	Commission International de Lutte Biologique contre les Ennemis des Cultures (*now* OILB)
CILC	Confédération Internationale du Lin et du Chanvre (France)
CILECT	Centre International de Liaison des Écoles de Cinéma et de Télévision
CILF	Conseil International de la Langue Française
CILG	CIRIA Information Liaison Group
CILO	Centraal Instituut voor Landbouwkundig Onderzoek
CILOPGO	Comité International de Liaison des Gynécologues et Obstétriciens
CILPE	Conférence Internationale de Liaison entre Producteurs d'Énergie Électrique
CILSS	Comité Permanent Inter-États de Lutte contre la Sécheresse dans le Sahel
CILT	Centre for Information on Language Teaching
CIM	Canadian Institute of Mining and Metallurgy
CIM	Carte Internationale du Monde
CIM	Centro Internacional del Medio Ambiente
CIM	China Inland Mission
CIM	Comisión Interamericana de Mujeres
CIM	Commission for Industry and Manpower
CIM	Congrès International des Fabrications Mécaniques
CIM	Congrès Islamique Mondial
CIM	Conseil International de la Musique
CIM	Consejo International de Mujeres
CIM	Convention Internationale Concernant le Transport des Merchandises par Chemins de Fer
CIM	Cooperative Investigations in the Mediterranean
CIMA	Centre Interdisciplinaire d'Étude du Milieu Naturel et de l'Aménagement Rural
CIMA	Compagnie Industrielle de Miroiterie Africaine (Cameroons, Congo)
CIMA	Compagnie International des Machines Agricoles
CIMAC	Congrès International des Machines à Combustion
CIMAF	Centro de Cooperação dos Industriais de Máquinas-Ferramentas (Portugal)
CIMAFOR	Comité Interprofessionnel du Machinisme Forestier

CIMAL	Centre d'Information Mondiale Anti-lèpre	**CIMSCEE**	Comité des Industries des Mayonnaises et Sauces Condimentaires de la CEE
CIMAO	Ciments de l'Afrique de l'Ouest (Ghana, Ivory Coast, Togo)	**CIMT**	Compagnie Industrielle de Matériel de Transport (France)
CIMAP	Commission Internationale des Méthodes d'Analyse des Pesticides	**CIMTAC**	Committee for International Marine Telecommunications and Aviation Co-ordination
CIMAS	Conférence Internationale de la Mutualité et des Assurances Sociales	**CINTEL**	Cinema-Television Ltd
CIMCEE	Comité des Industries de la Moutarde de la CEE	**CIMTOGO**	Société des Ciments du Togo
CIMCLG	Construction Industry Metric Change Liaison Group	**CIMTP**	Congrès Internationaux de Médecine Tropicale et de Paludisme
CIME	Centro de Investigación de Metodos y Tecnicas para Pequenos y Medianas Empresas (Argentine)	**CIN**	Commission Internationale de Numismatique
		CINA	Centralinstitutet för Nordisk Asienforskning
CIME	Comitato Intergovernativo per le Migrazioni Europee	**CINA**	International Commission for Air Navigation
CIME	Compagnie Industrielle des Métaux Électroniques	**CINAB**	Comité des Instituts Nationaux des Agents en Brevets
CIME	Conseil International des Moyens du Film d'Enseignement	**CINAV**	Commission Internationale de la Nomenclature Anatomique Vétérinaire
CIME	Council of Industry for Management Education	**CINCC**	Coal Industry National Consultative Council
CIMEA	Comité International des Mouvements d'Enfants et d'Adolescents	**CINCHAN**	Allied Commander-in-Chief Channel
CIMEC	Comité des Industries de la Mesure Électrique et Électronique de la Communauté (*of* EEC)	**CINCWIO**	Steering Committee on Cooperative Investigations in the North and Central Western Indian Ocean
CIMENCAM	Société des Cimenteries du Cameroun	**CINDA**	Centre Inter-Universitaire pour le Développement des Andes (Chile)
CIMES	Concours International du Meilleur Enregistrement Sonore	**CINE**	Council on International Nontheatrical Events (U.S.A.)
CIMI	Centre of Industrial Microbiological Investigations (Argentina)	**CINECA**	Co-operative Investigations of the Northern Part of the Eastern Central Atlantic (FAO)
CIMM	Canadian Institute of Mining and Metallurgy	**CINFR**	Central Institute for Nutrition and Food Research (Netherlands)
CIMMYT	International Centre for Corn and Wheat Improvement (Mexico)	**CING**	Commission Internationale des Neiges et Glaces
CIMO	Club Européen des Importateurs de Fruits et Légumes d'Outre-Mer	**CINOA**	Confédération Internationale des Négociants en Oeuvres d'Art
CIMO	Commission for Instruments and Methods of Observation	**CINP**	Collegium Internationale Neuro-Psychopharmacologicum (Germany)
CIMP	Commission Internationale de la Météorologie Polaire	**CINS**	CENTO Institute of Nuclear Science
		CINS	Collegium Internationale Activitatis Nervosae Superioris (Italy)
CIMP	Conseil International de la Musique Populaire	**CINTECA**	Centro de Información Tecnica Cafetalera (Brazil)
CIMPM	Comité International de Médecine et de Pharmacie Militaires	**CINTER-FOR**	Centro Interamericano de Investigación y Documentación sobre Formación Profesional (Uruguay)
CIMPO	Central Indian Medicinal Plants Organisation		
CIMRST	Comité Interministeriel de la Recherche Scientifique et Technique	**CINU**	Centre d'Information des Nations Unies
CIMS	Centro de Investigaciones Motivacionales y Sociales (Argentina)	**CINVA**	Inter-American Housing and Planning Centre (Colombia)

CIO	Centar za Industrijsko Oblikovanje
CIO	Comité International Olympique
CIO	Commission Internationale d'Optique
CIO	Congress of Industrial Organisations (U.S.A.)
CIOA	Centro Italiano Assidatori Anodici
CIOFF	Comité International des Organisateurs de Festivals de Folklore
CIOIC	Commission Intérimaire de l'Organisation Internationale du Commerce
CIOMR	Comité Interallié des Officiers Médecins de Réserve
CIOMS	Council for International Organization of Medical Sciences
CIOPORA	Communauté Internationale des Obtenteurs de Plantes Ornementales de Reproduction Asexuée
CIOR	Confédération Interalliée des Officiers de Réserve
CIOS	Centro Italiano di Orientamento Sociale
CIOS	Comité International de l'Organisation Scientifique
CIOSL	Confederación Internacional de Organizaciones Sindicales Libres
CIOSTA	Comité International d'Organisation Scientifique du Travail en Agriculture
CIOT	Compagnie Industrielle d'Ouvrages en Textiles (Central Africa)
CIOTF	Conseil International des Organismes de Travailleuses Familiales
CIP	Cartel International de la Paix
CIP	Centre International de Paris
CIP	Centro Internacional de la Papa (Peru)
CIP	Centro de Investigaciones Pesqueras (Venezuela)
CIP	Collège International de Podologie
CIP	Comité International de Photobiologie
CIP	Commission Internationale du Peuplier
CIP	Commission Internationale de Phytopharmacie
CIP	Comptoir Ivorien des Papiers
CIP	Confédération Internationale des Parents
CIP	Council of Iron Producers
CIPA	Chartered Institute of Patent Agents
CIPA	Comité Interamericano Permanente Anti-Acridiano
CIPA	Comité Interamericano de Protección Agricola (Argentina)
CIPA	Comité International des Plastiques en Agriculture
CIPA	Council on International and Public Affairs (U.S.A.)
CIPAC	Collaborative International Pesticides Analytic Council Ltd
CIPACI	Société Commerciale et Industrielle des Produits Animaux en Côte d'Ivoire
CIPAIM	Cellule d'Intervention contre la Pollution dans les Alpes-Maritimes
CIPAM	Centro de Investigaciones de Plantas y Animales Medicinales (Mexico)
CIPAN	Commission Internationale des Pêcheries de l'Atlantique Nord-Ouest
CIPASE	Commission Internationale des Pêches pour l'Atlantique Sud-Est
CIPASH	Committee on International Programs in Atmospheric Sciences and Hydrology (U.S.A.)
CIPASO	Comisión Internacional de Pesquerías del Atlántico Sudoriental
CIPAT	Conseil International sur les Problèmes de l'Alcoolisme et des Toxicomanies
CIPBC	Centre National Interprofessionnel des Produits de Basse-Cour
CIPC	Centraal Instituut v. Physisch-Chemische Constanten
CIPC	Comité International Permanent de la Conserve
CIPCC	Comité International Permanent du Carbon Carburant
CIPCE	Information and Publicity Centre of the European Railways
CIPCI	Conseil International des Practiciens du Plan Comptable International
CIPCRO	Comité Intersecretarial sobre Programas Científicos Relacionados con la Oceanografica
CIPE	Centro Interamericana de Promoción de Exportaciones (Colombia)
CIPE	Collège International de Phonologie Expérimentale
CIPE	Comitato Inter-ministeriale per la Programmazione Economica
CIPE	Conseil International de la Préparation a l'Enseignement

CIPE	Consejo Internacional de la Película de Enseñanza		**CIPQ**	Centre International de Promotion de la Qualité
CIPEA	Centre International pour l'Élévage en Afrique		**CIPR**	Commission Internationale pour la Protection contre les Radiations
CIPEA	Comité International pour l'Étude des Argiles (*now* AIPEA)		**CIPRA**	Cast Iron Pipe Research Association (U.S.A.)
CIPEC	Conseil Intergouvernemental des Pays Exportateurs de Cuivre		**CIPRA**	Commission Internationale pour la Protection des Régions Alpines
CIPEMAT	Centre International pour l'Étude de la Marionnette Traditionnelle		**CIPROVA**	Comité Interprofessionnel pour la Promotion des Ventes des Produits Agricoles et Alimentaires
CIPEPC	Commission Internationale Permanente d'Études de la Police de la Circulation		**CIPS**	Canadian Information Processing Society
CIPEXI	Compagnie Ivoirienne de Promotion pour l'Exportation et l'Importation		**CIPS**	Comité Interprofessionnel des Productions Saccharifères
CIPF	Confédération Internationale du Commerce des Pailles, Fourrages et Dérivés		**CIPS**	Confédération Internationale de la Pêche Sportive
CIPFA	Chartered Institute of Public Finance and Accountancy		**CIPSH**	Conseil International de la Philosophie et des Sciences Humaines
CIPFE	Comité d'Initiative pour le Parti Fédéraliste Européen		**CIPSO**	Compagnie Industrielles de Plastiques Semi-Ouvres
CIPHP	Comisión Internacional de Pesquerias del Hipogloso del Pacífico		**CIPSRO**	Conseil Intersecrétariats des Programmes Scientifiques Relatifs à l'Océanographie
CIPI	Comité Interministériel de Politique Industrielle		**CIQ**	Confoederatio Internationalis ad Qualitates Plantarum Edulium Perquirendas
CIPIST	Centre International pour l'Information Scientifique et Technique		**CIQPEP**	*See* CIQ
CIPL	Comité International Permanent de Linguistes		**CIR**	Commission for Industrial Relations
			CIR	Commission International du Riz
CIPM	Comité International des Poids et Mesures		**CIRA**	Cast Iron Research Association
CIPM	Council for International Progress in Management (U.S.A.)		**CIRA**	Centre International de Recherches sur l'Anarchisme
CIPMME	Comité Intergovernemental Provisoire des Mouvements Migratories de l'Europe		**CIRA**	Centro Interamericano de Reforma Agraria (Colombia)
CIPO	Comité International pour la Protection des Oiseaux		**CIRA**	Centro Italiano Radiatori Alluminio
CIPO	Corporación Industrial de Productos Oleaginosos (Argentina)		**CIRA**	Commission Internationale pour la Réglementation des Ascenseurs et Monte-charges
CIPOL	Centre International de Publications Oecumiques des Liturgies		**CIRA**	Confederation of Industrial Research Associations
CIPP	Comisión Internacional de Problemas Pesqueros (*Apostolatus maris*)		**CIRA**	COSPAR International Reference Atmosphere
CIPP	Conseil Indo-Pacifiques des Pêches (*of* FAO)		**CIRB**	Centre International de Recherche Biologique
CIPPAS	Comité International Provisoire de Prévention Acridienne au Soudan Français		**CIRB**	Centre International de Recherches sur le Bilinguisme (Canada)
CIPPN	Commission Internationale des Pêcheries du Pacifique Nord		**CIRC**	Centre International de Recherche sur le Cancer
CIPPT	Centre International de Perfectionnement Professionnel et Technique		**CIRC**	Comité International de Réglementation du Caoutchouc

CIRCCE	Confédération Internationale de la Représentation Commerciale de la Communauté Européenne
CIRCF	Comité International de la Rayonne et des Fibres Synthétiques
CIRCOM	Centre International de Recherches sur les Communautés Coopératives Rurales
CIRDEC	Centre International de Recherche et de Documentation en Éducation Continue
CIRDI	Centre International pour le Règlement des Différends Relatifs aux Investissements
CIRDOM	Centre Interuniversitaire de Recherche et de Documentation sur les Migrations
CIRE	Confederación Internacional de Remolacheros Europeos
CIREC	Centre International de Recherches et d'Études Chréiologiques
CIRED	Centre International de Recherche sur l'Environnement et le Développement (France)
CIRES	Centre Ivoirien de Recherches Économiques et Sociales (Ivory Coast)
CIRET	Centre for International Research on Economic Tendency
CIRF	Centre International d'Information et de Recherche sur la Formation Professionnelle
CIRF	Corn Industries Research Foundation (U.S.A.)
CIRFED	Centre International de Recherche et de Formation en vue du Devéloppement Harmonisé
CIRFP	Centre International d'Information et de Recherche sur la Formation Policière
CIRFS	Comité International de la Rayonne et des Fibres Synthétiques
CIRIA	Construction Industry Research and Information Association
CIRIEC	Centre International de Recherches et d'Information sur l'Économie Collective
CIRIOL	Comitato Italiano di Rappresentanza Internazionale per l'Organizzazione del Lavoro
CIRIT	Comité Interprofessionel de Renovation de l'Industrie Textile
CIRM	Centre International Radio-Médical
CIRM	Comité International de Radio-Maritime
CIRP	Collège International pour l'Étude Scientifique des Techniques de Production Mécanique
CIRPHO	Cercle International de Recherches Philosophiques par Ordinateur
CIRR	Center on International Race Relations (U.S.A.)
CIRSA	Comité International Regional de Sanidad Agropecuaria (Latin America)
CIRSEA	Compagnia Italiana Ricerche Sviluppo Equipaggiamenti
CIRU	Colonial Insecticide Research Unit
CIRZ	Centro Italiano di Ricerche Zooeconomiche
CIS	Centre Interafricain de Sylviculture
CIS	Centre International d'Information de Sécurité et d'Hygiéne du Travail
CIS	Centre International des Stages
CIS	Centre International de Synthèse
CIS	Centro de Investigaciones Sociales (Colombia)
CIS	Centro Italiano di Sessuologia
CIS	Chartered Institute of Secretaries
CIS	Compagnie Ivoirienne de Sciages
CIS	Conference of Internationally-Minded Schools
CIS	Cranbrook Institute of Science (U.S.A.)
CIS	International Occupational Safety and Health Information Centre
CISA	Canadian Industrial Safety Association
CISA	Centro Italiano Studi Aziendali
CISA	Commission Internationale pour le Sauvetage Alpin
CISA	Confédération Internationale des Syndicats Arabes
CISA	Congresos Internacionales SA (Spain)
CISAC	Confédération Internationale des Sociétés d'Auteurs et Compositeurs
CISAE	Congrès International des Sciences Anthropologiques et Ethnologiques
CISAF	Conseil International des Services d'Aide Familiale
CISAI	Comité International de Soutien aux Antifascistes Ibériques
CISAL	Italian Confederation of Autonomous Labour Unions
CISAVIA	Civil Service Aviation Association
CISBH	Comité International de Standardisation en Biologie Humaine
CISC	Canadian Institute of Steel Construction

CISC	Confédération Internationale des Syndicats Chrétiens
CISC	Conférence Internationale du Scoutisme Catholique
CISCE	Comité International pour la Sécurité et la Coopération Européennes
CISCO	Centro Italiano Studi Containers
CISCOD	Civil Service and Cooperation Office for Developing Countries (Belgium)
CISCS	Centre International Scolaire de Correspondance Sonore Solidarité avec la Jeunesse Algérienne
CISDEN	Centro Italiano di Studi di Diritto dell'Energia Nucleare
CISE	Centro Informazioni Studi ed Esperienze
CISEPA	Centro de Investigaciones Sociales, Económicas, Politicas y Antropologicas (Peru)
CISF	Centro Internazionale Studi Famiglia
CISF	Confédération Internationale des Sages-Femmes
CISGO	Commonwealth Interchange Study Group Operations
CISH	Comité International des Sciences Historiques
CISHEC	Chemical Industry Safety and Health Council (*of* CIA)
CISIC	Centro Internazionale Sociale Istituzione Clero
CISIP	Centro Internazionale Studi Irrigazione a Pioggia
CISIR	Ceylon Institute of Scientific and Industrial Research
CISJA	Comité International de Solidarité avec la Jeunesse Algérienne
CISL	Confédération Internationale des Syndicats Libres
CISL	Confederazione Italiana Sindacati Lavoratori
CISLE	Centre International des Syndicalistes Libres en Exil
CISL-ORE	Organisation Régionale Européenne de la CISL
CISM	Centre International des Sciences Mécaniques
CISM	Conseil International du Sport Militaire
CISMEDI	Comité International de Soutien pour la Sauvegarde et la Mise en Valeur de la Mer Méditerranée
CISNAL	Confederazione Italiana dei Sindacati Nazionali dei Lavoratori
CISO	Comité International des Sciences Onomastiques
CISOR	Centro de Investigaciones Sociales y Socciorreligiosas (Venezuela)
CISP	Centro Italiano Smalti Porcellanati
CISP	Comitato Italiano per lo Studio dei Probleme della Popolazione
CISPM	Confédération Internationale des Sociétés Populaires de Musique
CISPP	Centro Italiano di Studi e Programmazioni per la Pesca
CISPR	Comité International Spécial des Perturbations Radiophoniques
CISR	Center for International Systems Research (U.S.A.)
CISR	Conférence Internationale de Sociologie Religieuse
CISRC	Computer and Information Science Research Center, Ohio (U.S.A)
CISRS	Christian Institute for the Study of Religion and Society (India)
CISS	Comité Permanente Interamericano de Seguro Social (Mexico)
CISS	Conférence Interaméricaine de Securité Sociale
CISS	Conférence Internationale de Service Social
CISS	Comité International des Sports Silencieux
CISS	Conseil International des Sciences Sociales
CISSB	Civil Service Selection Board
CISV	Children's International Summer Villages
CISWO	Coal Industry Social Welfare Organisation
CIT	Carnegie Institute of Technology (U.S.A.)
CIT	Centre International du Tabac
CIT	Chartered Institute of Transport
CIT	Comité International de Télévision
CIT	Comité International des Transports par Chemins de Fer
CIT	Comité International Tzigane
CIT	Conseil International des Tanneurs
CIT	Consejo Internacional del Trigo
CITA	Confédération Interaméricaine de Transport Aérien
CITA	Confédération Internationale des Ingénieurs et Techniciens de l'Agriculture

CITA	Conférence Internationale des Trains Spéciaux d'Agences de Voyages
CITA	Consejo Interamericano de Archiveros
CITAB	Compagnie Industrielle des Tabacs de Madagascar
CITAM	Centre International de la Tapisserie Ancienne et Moderne
CITB	Construction Industry Training Board
CITC	Canadian Institute of Timber Construction
CITC	Caribbean Interim Tourism Committee
CITC	Comisión de Investigaciones Técnicas y Científicas (*of* OUA)
CITC	Confédération Internationale des Industries Techniques du Cinéma
CITCE	Comité International de Thermodynamique et de Cinétique Électrochimiques
CITEC	Compagnie de l'Industrie Textile Cotonnière
CITEC	Compagnie pour l'Information et les Techniques Électroniques de Contrôle
CITEF	Centro de Investigaciones de Tecnologia de Frutas y Hortalizas (Argentina)
CITEFA	Instituto de Investigaciones Científicas y Técnicas de las Fuerzas Armadas (Argentina)
CITEJA	Comité International Technique d'Experts Juridiques Aériens
CITEL	Comision Interamericana de Telecomunicaciones (U.S.A)
CITEN	Comité International de Teinture et du Nettoyage
CITEPA	Centre Interprofessional Technique d'Études de la Pollution Atmosphérique
CITI	Confédération Internationale des Travailleurs Intellectuels
CITLA	Cámara Industrial Textil Lanera (Argentina)
CITLO	Centrum voor Informatieverwerking op het Gebied van Tropische Landbouw en Ontwikkeling (Belgium)
CITP	Conseil International des Télécommunications de Presse
CITPPM	Confédération des Industries de Traitement des Produits des Pêches Maritimes
CITR	Compagnie Ivoirienne de Transports Routiers
CITS	Commission Internationale Technique de Sucrerie
CITT	Commission Interaméricaine du Thon Tropical (FAO)
CITTA	Confédération Internationale des Fabricants de Tapis et de Tissus d'Ameublement
CIU	Chlorella International Union
CIUC	Consejo Internacional de Uniones Científicas
CIUFFAS	Comitato Italiano Utilizzatori Filati di Fibre Artificali e Sintetiche
CIUMR	Commission Internationale des Unités et Mesures Radiologiques
CIUPST	Commission Interunions de la Physique Solaire et Terrestre (U.S.A.)
CIUS	Conseil International des Unions Scientifiques
CIUSS	Catholic International Union for Social Service
CIUTI	Conférence Internationale Permanente de Directeurs d'Instituts Universitaires pour la Formation de Traducteurs et d'Interprètes
CIV	Centro de Investigaciones Veterinarias (Venezuela)
CIV	Christelijke Internationale van Arbeiders in Voedings-, Tabak- en Hotelbedrijven
CIV	Commission Internationale du Verre
CIV	Convention Internationale sur le Transport des Voyageurs et des Bagages
CIV	Coöperatieve Centrale Landbouw In-en Verkoopvereniging
CIVAM	Centre d'Information et de Vulgarisation Agricole et Ménager
CIVAS	Comité Interprofessionnel des Vins d'Anjou-Saumur
CIVB	Comité Interprofessionnel des Vins de Bergerac
CIVB	Comité Interprofessionnel des Vins de Bordeaux
CIVC	Comité Interprofessionnel des Vins de Champagne
CIVCP	Comité Interprofessionnel des Vins des Côtes de Provence
CIVCR	Comité Interprofessionnel des Vins des Côtes-du-Rhône
CIVDN	Comité Interprofessionnel des Vins Doux Naturels
CIVEM	Constructions Ivoiriennes Électromécaniques
CIVG	Comité Interprofessionnel des Vins de Gaillac
CIVI	Central Institute for Industrial Development (Netherlands)

CIVIJU	Association des Producteurs de Cidre, Vins, Jus de Fruits et des Embouteilleurs de Jus de Fruits (Belgium)
CIVINEX	Société Ivoirienne d'Exploitation Vinicole
CIVO	Centraal Instituut voor Voedingsonderzoek (Netherlands)
CIVPN	Comité Interprofessionnel des Vins du Pays Nantais
CIVT	Comité Interprofessionel des Vins de Touraine
CIVV	Centro Ittiologico Valli Venete
CIVV	Commission Internationale Vol à Voile
CIW	Carnegie Institute of Washington (U.S.A.)
CIWLT	Comité Permanent des Syndicats de Travailleurs de la Compagnie International des Wagon-Lits et du Tourisme
CJA	Conseil de la Jeunesse d'Afrique
CJCC	Commonwealth Joint Communications Committee
CJD	Centre des Jeunes Dirigeants d'Entreprise
CJM	Congrès Jurif Mondial
CJP	Centre des Jeunes Patrons
CKB	Christelijke Kruideniers Bond
CKH	Centrale Kamer van Handelsbevordering
CKVR	Československý Komitét pro Vedecke Rízeni
CLA	Canadian Library Association
CLA	Circolo dei Librai Antiquari
CLA	Confederación Lanera Argentina
CLA	Country Landowners' Association
CLAB	Centre Latino-Americano de Ciencias Biologicas
CLACE	Centro Latinoamericano de Coordinación de Estudios (Brazil)
CLACE	Latin American Committee of Commercial Trade
CLACSO	Consejo Latinoamericano de Ciencias Sociales (Argentina)
CLAD	Centro Latinoamericano de Administración para el Desarrollo (Venezuela)
CLADEA	Consejo Latinoamericano de Escuelas de Administración
CLADES	Centro Latino Americano de Documentación Economica y Social (Chile)
CLAF	Centro Latino-Americano de Fisica (Brazil)
CLAF	Commission Latino-Américaine des Forêts
CLAFE	Consejo Latino Americano de Física del Espacio (Mexico)
CLAH	Conference on Latin American History (U.S.A.)
CLAHCE	Comité de Liaison des Associations Hôtelières de la Communauté Européenne
CLAID	Comision Latino Americano de Irigacion y Drenaje
CLAIET	Comité de Liaison des Associations Internationales d'Entreprises Touristiques
CLAIRA	Chalk Lime and Allied Industries Research Association (*now* WHRA)
CLAM	Comité de Liaison pour l'Agrumiculture Méditeranéenne
CLAMOP	Centre Latino-Américain d'Opinion Publique
CLAO	Consejo Latinoamericano de Oceanografica
CLAPCS	Centro Latinamericano de Pesquisas en Ciencias Sociais (Brazil)
CLAPN	Comité Latinoamericano de Parques Nacionales
CLAPTUR	Corporation Latino-Americaine des Journalists Spécialisés en Tourisme
CLAQ	Centro Latinoamericano de Quimica
CLAR	Confederacion Latino Americana de Religiosos (Colombia)
CLARA	Comite Latinoamericano para las Regiones Aridas
CLARCFE	Consejo Latino Americano de Radiación Cósmica y Fisica del Espacio
CLARTE	Centre de Liaison des Activités Régionales, Touristiques et Économiques
CLAS	Center for Latin American Studies (U.S.A.)
CLASA	Confederación Latinoamericana de Sociedades de Anestesiología
CLASC	Confederación Latino-Americaine des Syndicats Chrétiens
CLASP	Consortium of Local Authorities in Wales
CLASS	Current Literature Alerting Search Service (U.S.A.)
CLAT	Central Latinoamericana de Trabajadores
CLATE	Confederación Latino-Americano de Trabajores Estatales (Argentina)
CLATEC	Comisión Latinoamericana de Trabajadores de la Educación
CLAT-RAMM	Coordinación Latinoamericana de Trabajadores Metallúrgicos y Mineros
CLAW	Consortium of Local Authorities in Wales
CLC	Caribbean Labour Congress
CLC	Commonwealth Liaison Committee

CA	Comité de Liaison de la Construction Automobile pour les Pays de la CEE
CCR	Comité de Liaison de la Construction de Carrosseries et de Remorques
EA	Centro Latinoamericano de Educación de Adultos (Chile)
EAPSE	Consortium of Local Education Authorities for the Provision of Science Equipment
EAR	Criminal Law Education and Research Center (U.S.A.)
EC	Comité de Liaison de l'Engineering Chimique Français
ECAT	Comité de Liaison Européen des Commissionnaires et Auxiliaires de Transports du Marché Commun
EIC	Comité de Liaison et d'Étude de l'Industrie de la Chaussure de la CEE
EJFL	Centre de Liaison et d'Étude pour les Jus de Fruits et de Légumes (France)
ENE	Continuing Library Education Network and Exchange (U.S.A.)
EPA	Comité de Liaison de la Construction d'Équipements et de Pièces d'Automobiles
F	Comité Linier de France
IA	Cruise Lines International Association (U.S.A.)
IF	Comité Latinoamericano de Investigaciones Forestales (Chile)
IMM	Commission de Liaison Inter-Nations Mars et Mercure
IMMAR	Centre de Liaison International des Marchands de Machines Agricoles et Réparateurs
IS	Clearinghouse for Library and Information Sciences (*of* ERIC)
ITAM	Centre de Liaison des Industries de Traitement des Algues Marines de la CEE
ITRAVI	Centre de Liaison des Industries Transformatrices de Viandes de la CEE
MR	Central Laboratory, South Manchuria Railway Company
O	Central Agricultural Organisation (Netherlands)
O	Centrum Landbouwkundig Onderzoek (Belgium)
OING	Comité de Liaison des Organisations Internationales Non-Gouvernementales
P	Club der Luftfahrtpublizisten (Austria)

CLPFF	Charles Lathrop Pack Forestry Foundation (U.S.A.)
CLRI	Central Leather Research Institute (India)
CLTC	Confederación Latinoamericana de Trabajadores de Communicaciones
CLTEA	Council for Library Training in East Africa (Uganda)
CLTRI	Central Leprosy Teaching and Research Institute (India)
CLV	Coöperatieve Landbouwvereniging
CM	Chambre des Métiers
CMA	Cable Makers' Association
CMA	Canadian Manufacturers Association
CMA	Canadian Medical Association
CMA	Catering Managers Association of Great Britain and Northern Ireland
CMA	Centre de Transport International par Véhicules Automobiles (Yugoslavia)
CMA	Chocolate Manufacturers Association of the United States
CMA	Commonwealth Magistrates Association
CMA	Confédération Mondiale de l'Accordéon
CMA	Congrès Mondial de l'Alimentation
CMA	Coopératives Marocaines Agricoles
CMA	Crédit Mutuel Agricole
CMAA	Cigar Manufacturers Association of America
CMAA	Cocoa Merchants Association of America
CMAA	Crane Manufacturers Association of America
CMAAO	Confederation of Medical Associations in Asia and Oceania
CMAB	Centro Médico Argentino-Británico
CMACP	Conseil Mondial pour l'Assemblée Constituante des Peuples
CMAE	Commission de Météorologie Aéronautique (de l'OMM)
CMAg	Commission de Météorologie Agricole (de l'OMM)
CMAO	Consejo Mundial de Artes y Oficios
CMAR	Comité Maghrebin d'Assurances et de Réassurance (Morocco)
CMAS	Confédération Mondiale des Activités Subaquatiques
CMAV	Coalition Mondiale pour l'Abolition de la Vivisection
CMBES	Canadian Medical and Biological Engineering Society

CMC	California Advisory Commission on Marine and Coastal Resources (U.S.A.)
CMC	Canadian Marconi Company
CMC	Catholic Media Council
CMC	Collective Measures Committee of the United Nations
CMC	Commission Médicale Chrétienne
CMC	Consejo Monetario Centroamericano (Guatemala)
CMC	Coöperatieve Melk Centrale
CMC	Groupement des Producteurs de Carreaux Céramiques du Marché Commun
CMCA	Constructions Métalliques du Centrafrique
CMCA	Cycle and Motor Cycle Association
CMCE	Comité Ministériel de Coordination Économique (Belgium)
CMCES	Comité Ministériel de Coordination Économique et Sociale
CMCF	Campagne Mondiale contre la Faim (*of* FAO)
CMCH	Campaña Mundial contra el Hambre (*of* FAO)
CMCPT	Comité Maghrebin de Coordination des Postes et Télécommunications
CMCR	Compagnie Maritime des Chargeurs Réunis
CMCSA	Canadian Manufacturers of Chemical Specialities Association
CMCW	Christian Mission to the Communist World
CMD	Centralföreningen af Malermestre i Danmark
CMD	Centrale Melkcontrôle Dienst
CMDC	Central Milk Distributive Committee
CME	Compagnie Mauritanienne d'Entreprises
CME	Conférence Mondiale de l'Énergie
CMEA	Council for Middle Eastern Affairs (U.S.A.)
CMEA	Council for Mutual Economic Assistance (U.S.S.R.)
CMEH	Council on Medication and Hospitals (U.S.A.)
CMERI	Central Mechanical Engineering Research Institute, Durgapur (India)
CMET	Comité Maghrebin de l'Emploi et du Travail (Morocco)
CMET	Council on Middle East Trade
CMF	Cement Makers Federation
CMF	Coal Merchants Federation of Great Britain
CMFRI	Central Marine Fisheries Research Institute (India)
CMG	Commission on Marine Geology (*of* IUGS)
CMH	Commission de Météorologie Hydrologique (de l'OMM)
CMHA	Canadian Mental Health Association
CMI	Comité Maritime International
CMI	Commission Mixte Internationale pour les Expériences Relatives à la Protection des Lignes de Télécommunication et des Canalisation Souterraines
CMI	Commonwealth Mycological Institute
CMI	Consejo Mundial de Iglesias
CMIA	Coal Mining Institute of America
CMIDOM	Centre Militaire d'Information et de Documentation sur l'Outre-Mer
CMIEB	Centre Mondiale d'Information sur l'Éducation Bilingue
CMIRNU	Centre Mondial d'Informations et de Recherches Appliquées aux Nuisances Urbaines (France)
CMITU	Centre Mondial d'Informations Techniques et d'Urbanisme (Bulgaria)
CMIU	Cigar Makers International Union (U.S.A.)
CMJP	Centre Marocain des Jeunes Patrons et des Cadres Dirigeants
CMM	Commission de Météorologie Maritime (de l'OMM)
CMMA	Crane Manufacturers Association of America
CMN	Comisia pentru Ocrotirea Monumentelor Naturii (Commission for the Protection of Natural Monuments) (Roumania)
CMN	Compagnie Malienne de Navigation
CMO	Centrale Melkhandelaren Organisatie
CMOPE	World Confederation of Organisations of the Teaching Profession
CMP	Christian Movement for Peace
CMP	Conseil Mondial de la Paix
CMPA	Chinchilla Pelt Marketing Association
CMPAA	Certified Milk Producers Association of America
CMPCO	Comité Mixta sobre Programas Científicos Relacionados con la Oceanografíca
CMPE	Comité Medical Permanent Européen
CMPO	Calcutta Metropolitan Planning Organisation (India)

CMR	Chrétiens dans le Monde Rural	**CNAB**	Confédération Nationale de Administrateurs de Biens
CMRA	Chemical Marketing Research Association (U.S.A.)	**CNAD**	Conference of National Armaments Directors
CMRC	Colonial Medical Research Committee	**CNAE**	Commisão Nacional de Actividades Especiais (Brazil)
CMREF	U.S. Committee on Marine Research, Education and Facilities	**CNAF**	Confédération Nationale de l'Aviculture Française
CMRI	Colonial Microbiological Research Unit (West Indies)	**CNAG**	Centro Nacional de Agricultura y Ganadería (Honduras)
CMRS	Central Mining Research Station (India)	**CNAG**	Commission Nationale d'Amélioration Génétique
CMRSS	Conseil Méditerranéen de Recherches en Sciences Sociales	**CNALCM**	Comité National d'Action et de Liaison des Classes Moyennes
CMS	Catholic Missionary Society	**CNAM**	Confédération Nationale de l'Artisanat et des Métiers
CMS	Church Missionary Society	**CNAN**	Compagnie Nationale Algérienne de Navigation
CMS	Commission de Météorologie Synoptique (de l'OMM)	**CNAPT**	Ceylon National Association for the Prevention of Tuberculosis
CMS	Corps Mondial de Secours	**CNAR**	Confédération Nationale pour l'Aménagement Rural
CMSCI	Council of Mechanical Speciality Contracting Industries (U.S.A.)	**CNAR**	Confédération Nationale des Artisans Ruraux
CMSER	Commission on Marine Science, Engineering and Resources	**CNASA**	Centre Nationale d'Aménagements des Structures Agricoles
CMT	Comité Maghrebin du Tourism (Tunisia)	**CNASEA**	Centre National pour l'Aménagement des Structures des Exploitations Agricoles
CMT	Confédération Mondiale du Travail	**CNAT**	Confédération Nord-Africaine des Transports (Morocco)
CMT	Construction Métallique Tropicale	**CNAV**	Christlinationaler Angestelltenverband der Schweiz
CMTC	Commission Maghrebine des Transports et Communications (Tunisia)	**CNAVMA**	Caisse Nationale d'Assurance Vieillesse Mutuelle Agricole
CMTI	Central Machine Tool Institute (India)	**CNB**	Centraal Normalisatie Bureau
CMTR	Compagnie Malienne de Transports Routiers	**CNB**	Comité National Belge
CMTT	Commission Mixte pour les Transmissions Télévisuelles	**CNB**	Confédération Nationale de la Boulangerie et Boulangerie Pâtisserie
CMV	Christlicher Metallarbeiterverband Deutschlands	**CNB**	Confédération Nord-Américaine de Billard (U.S.A.)
CNA	Central Neuropsychiatric Association (U.S.A.)	**CNBE**	Comité National Belge de l'Éclairage
CNA	Comissão Nacional de Alimentacão (Brazil)	**CNBF**	Centre National des Blés de Force
CNA	Comisión Nacional del Arroz (Ecuador)	**CNBF**	Centre National des Bureaux de Fret
CNA	Comissão Nacional de Avicultura (Brazil)	**CNBF**	Confédération Nationale de la Boucherie Française
CNA	Compagnie Nationale d'Assurance et de Réassurances (Ivory Coast)	**CNBOS**	Comité National Belge de l'Organisation Scientifique
CNA	Confédération Nationale de l'Artisanat	**CNBT**	Conseil National de la Blanchisserie et de la Teinturerie
CNA	Consejo Nacional Agrario (Peru)		
CNA	Corporación Nacional de Abastecimientos (Peru)		
CNAA	Comité National d'Action Agricole		
CNAA	Corporation Nationale de l'Agriculture et de l'Alimentation		
CNAA	Council for National Academic Awards		

CNBVSL	Confédération Nationale Belge des Industries et du Commerce des Vins, Spiritueux et Liqueurs
CNC	Comisión Nacional del Cacao (Ecuador)
CNC	Compagnie Nouvelle de Cadres
CNC	Confederación Nacional Campesina (Mexico)
CNC	Confédération Nationale de la Construction (Belgium)
CNC	Conseil National de Commerce
CNC	Conseil National du Crédit
CNC	Consejo Nacional Campesino (Costa Rica)
CNC	Conselho Nacional de Cooperativismo (Brazil)
CNC	Consorzio Nazionale Canapa
CNCA	Caisse Nacionale de Crédit Agricole
CNCA	Centre National de la Coopération Agricole
CNCA	Conselho Nacional Consultivo da Agricultura (Brazil)
CNCAF	Conseil National de la Coopération Agricole Française
CNCATA	Centre National Coopératif Agricole de Traitements Antiparasitaires
CNCC	Confédération Nationale du Commerce Charbonnier
CNCCEF	Comité National des Conseillers du Commerce Extérieur de la France
CNCCMM	Chambre Nationale des Constructeurs de Caravanes et de Maisons Mobiles
CNCD	Confederazione Nationale dei Coltivatori Diretti
CNCE	Centre National du Commerce Extérieur
CNCER	Centre National d'Économie Rurale
CNCF	Confédération Nationale de la Charcuterie de France
CNCIA	Confédération Nationale des Commerces et Industries de l'Alimentation
CNCM	Confédération Nationale du Crédit Mutuel
CNCrA	Caisse Nationale de Crédit Agricole
CNCT	Consejo Nacional de Ciencia y Tecnologia (Mexico)
CNCV	Confederación Nacional de Cooperativas de Venezuela
CNCV	Confédération Nationale des Coopératives Vinicoles
CND	Campaign for Nuclear Disarmament
CND	Comptoir National du Diamant (Central Africa)
CNDC	Comisión Nacional de Desarrollo Comunal (Peru)
CNDE	Consejo Nacional de Desarrollo Económico (Peru)
CNDEP	Conseil National des Détectives et Enquêteurs Privés
CNDES	Centre National de Documentation Économique et Sociale (Algeria)
CNDH	Centre National de Documentation Horticole
CNDP	Centre National de Documentation Pédagogique
CNDST	Centre National Belge de Documentation Scientifique et Technique
CNDV	Confédération Nationale des Distilleries Vinicoles
CNE	Centro Nacional de Economía (Nicaragua)
CNE	Confédération Nationale de l'Élévage
CNE	Consejo Nacional de Educación (Bolivia)
CNE	Consejo Nacional de la Energía (Venezuela)
CNEA	Comisión Nacional de Energía Atomica Argentina
CNEAF	Comité National des Exploitants Agricoles Forestiers
CNEAF	Confédération Nationale des Experts Agricoles et Fonciers
CNEAT	Centre National d'Études d'Agronomie Tropicale
CNECB	Collège National des Experts Compatables de Belgique
CNEEJA	Centre National d'Études Économiques et Juridiques Agricoles
CNEEMA	Centre National d'Études et d'Experimentation de Machinisme Agricole
CNEF	Cámara Nacional de Exploitación Forestal (Bolivia)
CNEF	Compagnie Nationale des Experts Forestiers
CNEIA	Comité National d'Expansion pour l'Industrie Aéronautique
CNEIL	Centre National d'Études et d'Initiatives du Logement
CNEL	Chambre Nationale Syndicale des Experts du Grand-Duché de Luxembourg
CNEN	Comision Nacional de Energia Nuclear (Mexico)
CNEN	Comitato Nazionale per l'Energia Nucleare

CNENA	Centro Nacional de Energia Nuclear na Agricultura (Brazil)		CNIA	Centro Nacional de Investigaciones Agropecuarias (Argentina, Colombia, Dominica, Salvador)
CNEP	Comptoir National d'Escompte de Paris		CNIA	Comité National Interprofessionnel de l'Amande
CNEPA	Centro Nacional de Ensino e Pesquisas Agronomicas (Brazil)		CNIA	Conseil National Interprofessionnel de l'Aviculture
CNEPDA	Comité National d'Étude des Problèmes du Développement Agricole		CNIA	Consejo Nacional de Investigaciones Agricolas (Venezuela)
CNER	Campanha Nacional de Educaçao Rural (Brazil)		CNIB	Canadian National Institute for the Blind
CNER	Centre National des Études Rurales		CNIB	Confédération Nationale des Industries du Bois
CNER	Conseil National des Économies Régionales		CNIC	Centro Nacional de Investigaciones de Café (Colombia)
CNERA	Centre National d'Études et des Recherches Aéronautiques (Belgium)		CNIC	Centro Nacional de Investigaciones Científicas (Cuba)
CNERAD	Centre National pour l'Étude, la Recherche et l'Application du Développement		CNICI	Consejo Nacional de Investigaciones Científicas y Técnicas (Argentina, Uruguay)
CNERIA	Centre National d'Études et de Recherches des Industries Agricoles		CNICT	Consejo Nacional de Investigaciones Científicas y Técnicas
CNERNA	Centre National de Coordination des Études et Recherches sur la Nutrition Animale		CNICTEI	Comité National Italien de Coopération Technique et Économique Internationale
CNES	Centre National d'Études Spatiales		CNIE	Comision Nacional de Investigaciones Especiales (Argentine)
CNET	Centre National d'Études des Télécommunications		CNIEC	China National Import and Export Corporation
CNETEA	Centre National d'Études Techniques et Économiques de l'Artisanat		CNIEL	Centre National Interprofessionnel d'Économie Laitière
CNEXO	Centre National pour l'Exploitation des Océans		CNIF	Conseil National des Ingénieurs Français
CNF	Compagnie du Niger Français		CNIH	Cámara Nacional de la Industria Hulera (Mexico)
CNFC	Centre National de Formation Coopérative (Cameroon)		CNIH	Comité National Interprofessionnel de l'Horticulture Florale et Ornementale et des Pépinières non Forestières
CNFP	Consejo Nacional de Fomento Pesquero (Venezuela)		CNIH	Comité National Interprofessionnel du Houblon
CNFR	Confédération Nationale de la Famille Rurale		CNIL	Comité National Interprofessionnel de la Laine
CNFRA	Centre National Française de la Recherche Antarctique		CNIOS	Comitato Nazionale Italiana per l'Organizzazione Scientifica del Lavoro
CNFRO	Comité National Française de Recherche Océanique		CNIP	Centre National des Indépendants et Paysans
CNG	Christlichnationaler Gewerkschaftbund der Schweiz		CNIPA	Committee of National Institutes of Patent Agents (Netherlands)
CNG	Confederación Nacional Ganadara (Mexico)		CNIPBC	Comité National Interprofessionnel des Produits de Basse-Cour
CNHR	Comité National de l'Habitat Rural			
CNHRAC	Confédération Nationale pour l'Habitat Rural et l'Aménagement des Campagnes		CNIPT	Comité National Interprofessionnel de la Pomme de Terre
CNI	Confederaçao Nacional das Industrias (Brazil)			
CNI	Consiglio Nazionale degli Ingegneri		CNIR	Centre National Interprofessionnel du Rhum

CNIT	Cámara Nacional de la Industria de Transformación (Mexico)
CNIT	Centre National des Industries et des Techniques
CNJA	Centre National des Jeunes Agriculteurs
CNJPHP	Cercle National des Jeunes Producteurs de l'Horticulture et des Pépiniéres
CNKi	Comité National du Kivu (Zaire)
CNL	Commonwealth National Library, Canberra (Australia)
CNL	Confédération Nationale Laitière
CNLA	Centre Nationale de Lutte Antiparasitaire
CNLA	Council of National Library Associations (U.S.A.)
CNLSB	Ceylon National Library Services Board
CNMA	Comitato Nazionale di Meccanica Agraria
CNMB	Central Nuclear Measurements Bureau
CNMCCA	Confédération Nationale de la Mutualité, du Crédit et de la Coopération Agricoles
CNME	Caisse Nationale des Marchés de l'État
CNMI	Camera Nazionale della Moda Italiana
CNMI	Comité National de la Meunerie Industrielle
CNO	Comisión Nacional del Olivo (Mexico)
CNO	Council of National Organisations
CNOF	Comité National de l'Organisation Française
CNOP	Conseil National de l'Orde des Pharmaciens
CNOPAR	Confédération Nationale des Organismes de Promotion Agricole et Rurale
CNOS	Comitato Nazionale per l'Organizzazione Scientifica
CNOSA	Centro Nazionale Organizzazione Scientifica in Agricoltura (Italy)
CNOV	Comité National des Producteurs d'Oeufs à Couver et des Volailles dites d'Un Jour
CNP	Comitato Nazionale per la Produttività
CNP	Comité National des Prix
CNP	Consejo Nacional de Producción
CNP	Corporation Nationale Paysanne
CNPA	Centro Nazional de Patología Animal (Peru)
CNPA	Comissão Nacional de Politica Agraria (Brazil)
CNPAR	Centre National de Progrès Agricole et Rural
CNPCC	Confédération Nationale des Planteurs de Chicorée à Café
CNPE	Consejo Nacional de Planificación Económica (Guatemala, Salvador)
CNPF	Conseil National du Patronat Français
CNPFL	Confédération Nationale des Producteurs de Fruits et Légumes (*now* CFPFL)
CNPFP	Comité National de Propagande en Faveur du Pain
CNPFV	Comité National de Propagande en Faveur du Vin
CNPI	Comisión Nacional de Productividad Industrial
CNPIO	Commisão Nacional Portuguesa para Investigacão
CNPL	Comissão Nacional da Pecuária do Leite (Brazil)
CNPPLF	Comité National de Propagande des Produits Laitiers Français
CNPRST	Centre National de Planification de la Recherche Scientifique et Technologique
CNPS	Confédération Nationale des Produits du Sol et Dérivés
CNPS	Conseil National de la Politique Scientifique (Belgium)
CNPSEPC	Confédération Nationale des Produits du Sol Engrais et Produits Connexes
CNPV	Comité National des Producteurs de Viande
CNPVE-VAOC	Confédération Nationale des Producteurs de Vins et Eaux-de-Vie de Vin à Appellations d'Origine Contrôlées
CNR	Conseil National de la Récupération (Switzerland)
CNR	Consiglio Nazionale delle Ricerche
CNRA	Centre National de Recherches Agronomiques
CNRA	Consejo Nacional de Reforma Agraria (Bolivia)
CNRC	Centro Nacional de Radiación Cosmica (Argentine)
CNRET	Centre for Natural Resources, Energy and Transport (UN)
CNRF	Centre National de Recherches Forestières
CNRM	Centre National de Recherches Métallurgiques (Belgium)
CNRN	Comitato Nazionale per le Richerche Nucleari
CNRS	Centre National de la Recherche Scientifique
CNRSH	Centre Nigérien de Recherches en Sciences Humaines (Nigeria)
CNRZ	Centre National de Recherches Zootechniques

CNS	Cyprus Numismatic Society
CNSD	Confédération Nationale des Syndicats Dentaires
CNSM	National Confederation of Trade Unions of Mali (Africa)
CNSO	Confederación Nacional de Sindicatos Obreros (Chile)
CNT	Comisión Nacional del Trigo (Ecuador)
CNT	Confederación Nacional de Trabajadores (Chile)
CNTA	Comptoir National Technique Agricole
CNTC	Confederação Nacional dos Trabalhadores no Comércio (Brazil)
CNTG	Confédération Nationale des Travailleurs Guinéens
CNTI	Confederação Nacional dos Trabalhadores na Industria (Brazil)
CNTR	Compagnie Nationale des Transports Routiers (Central Africa)
CNTS	Confédération Nationale des Travailleurs Sénégalais
CNTUC	Ceylon National Trade Union Confederation
CNUCED	Centre du Commerce International
CNUCED	Conference des Nations Unies pour le Commerce et le Développement
CNUDCI	Commission des Nations Unies pour le Droit Commercial International
CNUDMI	Comisión de las Naciones Unidas para el Derecho Mercantil Internacional
CNUIP	Commission des Nations Unies pour l'Inde et le Pakistan
CNUURC	Commission des Nations Unies pour l'Unification et le Relèvement de la Corée
CNV	Christelijk Nationaal Vakverbond in Nederlands
CNVF	Comité National des Vins de France
CNVPA	Conseil National de la Vulgarisation du Progrès Agricole
CNVS	Confédération Nationale des Industries et Commerces en Gros des Vins, Cidres, Sirops, Spiritueux et Liqueurs de France
CO	Caribbean Organisation
COA	Commissie ter Bevordering v. h. Kweken en het Onderzoek v. Nieuwe Aardappelrassen
COAER	Union Costruttori Apparecchiature ed Impianti Aeraulici (Italy) (of ANIMA)
COAG	Committee on Agriculture (FAO)

COAL	National Committee on Arid Lands (U.S.A.) (of AAAS)
COAS	Council of the Organization of American States
COB	Centre Océanologique de Bretagne (CNEXO)
COBA	Central Ohio Breeding Association (U.S.A.)
COBAE	Comissão Brasiliera de Atividades Espaciais
COBAL	Companhia Brasileira de Alimentos
COBAM	Confection-Bonneterie Africaine et Malgache
COBCCEE	Comité des Organisations de la Boucherie-Charcuterie de la CEE
COBECEP	Comité Belge des Constructeurs d'Équipement Pétrolier
COBECHAR	Comptoir Belge des Charbons
COBELDA	Compagnie Belge d'Électronique et d'Automation
COBELPA	Association des Fabricants de Pâtes, Papiers et Cartons de Belgique
COBICA	Campanhia Brasileira de Industrialização da Castanha do Caju
COBOEN	Comisión Boliviana de Energía Nuclear (Bolivia)
COBRAG	Companhia Brasileira de Agricultura
COBRASA	Companhia Brasileira de Silos e Armazens
COBRECAF	Compagnie Bretonne de Cargos Frigorifiques
COBSA	Computer Service Bureaux Association
COBSI	Committee on Biological Sciences Information (U.S.A.)
COC	Commission Officielle de Contrôle (des semences et plants)
COC	Compagnie Ouest-Cameroun
COCAAP	Comisión Centroamericana de Autoridades Portuarias
COCADA	Compagnie des Commerçants Africains du Dahomey
COCAP	Comissão Coordenadora da Alianca para o Progresso (Brazil)
COCAST	Council for Overseas Colleges of Arts, Science and Technology
COCC	Confederación de Obreros y Campesinos Cristianos (Costa Rica)
COCCEE	Comité des Organisations Commerciales des Pays de la Communauté Économique Européenne
COCDYC	Conservative and Christian Democratic Youth Community

COCEAN	Compagnie d'Études et d'Exploitation des Techniques Océans
COCEI	Compagnie Centrale d'Études Industrielles
COCEMA	Comité des Constructeurs Européen de Matériel Alimentaire
COCERAL	Comité du Commerce des Céréales et des Aliments du Bétail de la CEE
COCESNA	Corporación Centroamericana de Servicios de Navegación Aerea (Guatemala)
COCI	Consortium des Agrumes et Plantes à Parfum de Côte-d'Ivoire
COCI	Consortium on Chemical Information
COCOBRO	Coördinatie van Cultuur en Onderzoek van Broodgraan
COCODI	Compagnie de Commerce de la Côte-d'Ivoire
COCOES	Comité de Coordination des Enquêtes Statistiques
COCOM	Consultative Group Cooperation Committee
COCOM	Coordinating Committee for East-West-Trade Policy (International)
COCOR	Commission de Coordination pour la Nomenclature des Produits Sidérurgiques (*of* ECSC)
COCOS	Co-ordinating Committee for Manufacturers of Static Converters in the Common Market Countries
COCOSEER	Co-ordinating Committee on Slavic and East European Library Services
COCSA	Compañia Organizadora del Consumo, S.A.
COCTA	Committee on Conceptual and Terminological Analysis (*of* International Political Science Association)
COD	Committee of Direction of Fruit Marketing (Australia)
CODAL	Comptoir Industriel de Produits Alimentaires (Madagascar)
CODATA	Committee on Data for Science and Technology (*of* ICSU)
CODAZR	Committee on Desert and Arid Zones Research (U.S.A)
CODE-AGRO	Amazonas Agricultural Development Company (Brazil)
CODECA	Corporation for Economic Development in the Caribbean
CODEL	Coordination in Development Inc. (U.S.A.)
CODEMAC	Comité des Déménageurs du Marché Commun
CODENA	Comité de Liaison des Entreprises de Démolition Navale de la CEE
CODENA	Council for the Development of the North-East of Brazil
CODEPAR	Companhia de Desenvolvimento Econômico do Paraná (Brazil)
CODESA	Consejo de Desarrollo de Salta (Argentina)
CODESRIA	Council for the Development of Economic and Social Research in Africa (Senegal)
CODESUL	Council for the Development of the Extreme South (Brazil)
CODETAF	Compagnie d'Étancheité Africaine en Côte d'Ivoire
CODE-VINTEC	Compagnie pour le Développement Industriel et Technique
CODEXAL	Conseil Européen di 'Codex Alimentarius'
CODIA	Comité de Industrialización de Algas (Argentina)
CODIA	Comité pour l'Organisation et le Développement des Investissements Intellectuels en Afrique et à Madagascar
CODIA	Council of Defense and Space Industry Associations (U.S.A)
CODIFAC	Comité de Développement d'Industrie de la Chaussure et des Articles Chaussants
CODIMA	Société Commerciale de Diffusion de Marques (Ivory Coast)
CODIPLAM	Comissão de Divulgação do Plano Global para a Amazonia (Brazil)
CODISUCO	Compania Distribuidora de Subsistenci, Conasupo (Mexico)
CODZR	Committee on Desert and Arid Zone Research (U.S.A.)
COE	Confederation of Employee Organisations
COE	Conseil Oecuménique des Églises
COEB	Conseil d'Orientation Économique du Bas Saint-Laurent (Canada)
COEC	Comité Central d'Océanographie et d'Étude des Côtes
COESA	Committee on Extension to the Standard Atmosphere (U.S.A)
COF	Comité Olympique Française
COFA	Commonwealth and Overseas Families Association
COFA	Comptoir Français Agricole
COFACE	Comité des Organisations Familiales auprès des Communautés Européennes (Belgium)

COFACE Compagnie Française d'Assurance pour le Commerce Extérieur

COFACICO Entreprises Financières Cinématographiques et Commerciales (Congo)

COFAG Comité des Fabricants d'Acide Glutamique de la Communauté Économique Européenne

COFALEC Comité des Fabricants de Levure de Panification de la CEE

COFAMA Comptoir Franco-Africaine de Matériaux

COFAP Comité Française des Applications du Pyrèthre

COFAZ Compagnie Française de l'Azote

COFCA Coffee and Cacao Institute of the Philippines

COFEB Comité d'Études des Associations de Fabricants de Baignoires en Fonte Émaillée dans la CEE

COFI Committee of Fisheries (*of* FAO)

COFI Council of Forest Industries of British Columbia

COFIAGRO Corporación Financiera de Fomento Agropecuario y Exportaciones (Colombia)

COFIBOIS Nouvelle Compagnie Forestière et Industrielle du Bois (Congo)

COFICA Compagnie pour le Financement de l'Industrie, du Commerce et de l'Agriculture

COFIEC Companía Financiera, Ecuador

COFIFA Compagnie Financière France-Afrique

COFIMPA Compagnie Francaise Industrielle et Minière du Pacifique

COFINAN-CIERA Corporación Financiera Colombiana

COFIREP Compagnie Financière de Recherches Pétrolières

COFLA Comisión Forestal Latinoamericana (Chile)

COFNA Comisión Forestal Norteamericana (Mexico)

COFO Committee on Forestry (FAO)

COFORGA Compagnie Forestière Gabonaise

COFORIC Compagnie Forestière et Industrielle du Congo

COFRAL Comité Français Agricole de Liaison pour le Développement International

COFRAMET Compagnie Franco-Américaine des Métaux et Minérals

COFRAN-IMEX Compagnie Française pour l'Exportation et l'Importation des Animaux Reproducteurs

COFRATEL Compagnie Française des Téléphones

COFREDA Compagnie pour Favoriser la Recherche et l'Élargissement des Débouchés Agricoles

COFREND Comité Française pour l'Étude des Essais Non Destructifs

COFRUCI Coopérative Agricole de Production Bananière et Fruitière de Côte-d'Ivoire

COG Committee on Oceanography and GARP (*of* SCOR)

COGEGA Comité Général de la Coopération Agricole des Pays de la CEE

COGEI Comitato dei Geografi Italiani

COGEI Compagnie de Gestion d'Investissements Internationaux

COGENE Committee on Genetic Experimentation (Germany)

COGEO-DATA Committee on Storage, Automatic Processing and Retrieval of Geological Data (Germany)

COGEQUIN Confédération Générale de la Quincaillerie

COGERAF Compagnie Générale d'Études et Recherches pour l'Afrique

COGE-TEXIM Compagnie Générale Togolais d'Export-Import

COGIP Compagnie Générale Ivoirienne de Piles Électriques

COGRA Compãnía Colombiana de Grasas

CoGroWa Commissie Grondwaterleidingsbedrijven

COHATA Compagnie Haitienne de Transports Aériens

COHSE Confederation of Health Service Employees

COI Central Office of Information

COI Commission Internationale des Oeufs

COI Commission Océanographique Intergouvernementale Permanente

COI Conseil Oléicole International

COID Council of Industrial Design

COID Council on International Development

COIDIEA Conseil des Organisations Internationales Directement Intéressées à l'Enfance et à l'Adolescence

COIF Control of Intensive Farming

COINS Committee on Improvement of National Statistics (*of* IASI)

COIPM Comité International Permanent pour la Recherche sur la Préservation des Matériaux en Milieu Marin (*of* OECD)

COISM Conseil des Organisations Internationales des Sciences Médicales

COJEV	Comité des Organisations de Jeunesses Européennes Volontaires
COJO	Conference of Jewish Organisations
COLAC	Comité Latinoamericano de Manejo de Cuencas de Torrentes
COLAC	Confederación Latinoamericana de Cooperativas de Ahorro y Crédito
COLACOT	Confederación Latinoamericana de Cooperativos de Trabajadores
COLA-TRADE	Comisión Latinoamericana de Trabajadores de la Energía
COLBAV	Colegio de Bibliotecnomas y Archivistes de Venezuela
COLCIEN-CIAS	Fondo Colombiano para Investigaciones Cientificas
COLDI-GRASAS	Sociedad Colombiana de Industriales de Grasas Vegetales (Colombia)
COLFIN	Compañia Colombiana de Financiamiento
COLGRO	Verband Schweizerischer Grossisten der Kolonialwarenbranche
COLIME	Comité de Liaison des Industries Métalliques Européennes
COLIMO	Comité de Liaison de l'Industrie du Motorcycle des Pays de la CEE
COLIPA	Comité de Liaison des Syndicats Européens de l'Industrie de la Parfumerie et des Cosmétiques (Belgium)
COLIPED	Commission de Liaison des Pièces et Équipements de Deux Roues
COLN	Commissie Onderzoek Land-bouwwaterhuishouding Nederland
COLOMBEX	Compañia Colombiana de Comercio Exterior
COLP	Comité Latino Americano de Parques Nacionales y de Vida Silvestre
COLTA-BACO	Compañia Colombiana de Tabaco
COLUMA	Comité Français de Lutte contre les Mauvaises Herbes
COM	Centraal Orgaan voor Melkhygiene
COMACH	Confederación Maritima de Chile
COMACI	Société de Commission et d'Approvisionnement de la Côte d'Ivoire
COMAF	Comité des Constructeurs de Matériel Frigorifique de la CEE
COMAFR-IQUE	Société Ivoirienne d'Expansion Commerciale
COMAGRI-COLA	Associazione Nationale Commercianti di Prodotti per l'Agricoltura
COMAL	Compagnie Commerciale Camerounaise de l'Alumine et de l'Aliuminium
COMALFA	Comptoir Maghrebin de l'Alfa (Algeria)
COMALFI	Sociedad Colombiana de Control de Malezas y Fisiologia Vegetal
COMAMIDI	Associazione Italiana dei Commercianti e degli Utilizzatori de Amidi, Fecole e Prodotti Derivati
COMANOR	Comité Maghrebin de Normalisation (Morocco)
COMAPI	Comité d'Action pour l'Isolation et l'Insonorisation
COMARAN	Compagnie Maritime de l'Afrique Noire
COMASCI	Société Commerciale d'Applications Scientifiques (Belgium)
COMATEX	Compagnie Malienne des Textiles
COMAUBEL	Chambre Syndicale du Commerce Automobile de Belgique
COMAU-NAV	Compagnie Mauritano-Algérienne de Navigation Maritime
COMBOFLA	Comité Boliviano de Fomento Lanero
COM-CORDE	Comisión Coordinadora para el Desarrollo Económico (Uruguay)
COMDA	Canadian Office Machine Dealers Association
COMDEV	Commonwealth Development Finance Company
COME-CAFCO	Commerciale Européenne de Cafés et Cacaos
COMECON	Council for Mutual Economic Aid (U.S.S.R.)
COMEPA	Comité Européen de Liaison du Commerce de Gros des Papiers et Cartons (Belgium)
COMES	Communauté Européenne des Écrivains
COMET	Collegium Medicorum Theatri (U.S.A)
COMET	Comité d'Organisation des Manifestations Économiques et Touristiques
COMET	Council of Middle East Trade
COMETEC-GAZ	Comité d'Etudes Economiques de l'Industrie du Gaz (Belgium)
COM-EURO-CAFE	Union des Cafetiers-Limonadiers de la Communauté Economique Européenne
COMEX	Commonwealth Expedition
COMEX	Compagnie Maritime d'Expertises
COMEX	Compagnie Mauritanienne d'Explosifs
COMEXAZ	Comité de Mexico y Aztlan
COMEXO	Committee for Oceanic Exploration

OMIAO Compagnie Commerciale et Industrielle de l'Afrique de l'Ouest

OMIBOL Corporación Minera de Bolivia

OMICORD Association des Fabricants de Cordages et de Ficelles de la Communauté Économique Européenne (*now* EUROCORD)

OMIFA Commission Internationale pour l'Étude Scientifique de la Famille

OMILOG Compagnie Minière de l'Ogooué (Gabon)

OMIN-FORM Information Bureau of Communist Parties and Workers

OMINOA Comptoir des Mines et des Grands Travaux de l'Ouest Africain

OMIPHOS Compagnie Minière et Phosphatière

OMISCO Committee of International Socialist Conferences

OMI-TEXTIL Comité de Coordination des Industries Textiles de la CEE

OMLA Commonwealth Library Association (Jamaica)

OMPESCA Companhia Brasileira de Pesca

OMPLAN Comissão de Planejamento, Coordenação e Desenvolvimento Social e Econõmico e Produtividade (Brazil)

OMPLES Coopération Méditerranéenne pour l'Énergie Solaire

OMSAT Communications Satellite Corporation (U.S.A.)

OMSER Commission on Marine Science and Engineering Research (*of* UNO)

OMTELCA Comision Tecnica de la Telecomunicaciónes de Centroamericana (*of* CEMA)

OMUF Compagnie des Mines d'Uranium de Franceville (Gabon)

OMUR-HEX Société pour la Conversion de l'Uranium en Métal et en Hexafluorure

OMUVIR Institut d'Études Internationales de la Communication sur l'Environnement (France)

ONAC Comisión Nacional de Acción Comunitaria (Uruguay)

ONACAJP Comité Nacional de Clubes Agrícolas Juveniles Perú

ONACYT Consejo Nacional de Ciencia y Tecnología (Argentina)

ONADE Consejo Nacional de Desarrollo (Argentina)

ONADEP Consejo Nacional de Desarrollo y Planificacion (Haiti)

CONA-HOTU Corporación Nacional de Hoteles y Turismo (Venezuela)

CONAMAG Comité Nacional de Mercadeo Agropecuario (Venezuela)

CONAP Corporación Nacional de Abastecimientos del Perú

CONAPAC Companhia Nacional de Produtos Alimenticios Cearenses (Brazil)

CONAPLAN Consejo Nacional de Planificacion y Coordinación Economica (Salvador)

CONAREX Consortium Africain de Réalisation et Exploitation (Dahomey)

CONARG Consejo Nacional de Registros Genealógicos (Nicaragua)

CONART Consejo Nacional de Radiodifusion y Television

CONASE Consejo Nacional de Seguridad (Argentina)

CONASUPO National Service for Popular Food Supply (Mexico)

CONATRAL Congreso Nacional de Trabajadores Libres (Dominica)

CONAVI Confederación Nacional de Viñateros (Argentina)

CONAVI Consejo Nacional de la Vivienda (Bolivia)

CONCA Comité Nacional de Comercialización de Arroz (Bolivia)

CON-CACAF Confédération d'Amérique du Nord, d'Amérique Centrale et des Caraïbes de Football (Guatemala)

CONCAMIN Confederación de Cámaras Industriales de los Estados Unidos Mexicanos

CONCA-NACO Confederación de Cámaras Nacionales de Comercio (Mexico)

CONCAWE Oil Companies International Study Group for Conservation of Clean Air and Water in Europe

CONCEX Conselho Nacional de Comércio Exterior (Brazil)

CONCP Conferência das Organizações Nacionais deas Colónias Portuguesas

CONDAL Comisión Nacional del Algodón (Ecuador)

CONDECA Consejo de Defensa Centroamericana (Guatemala)

CONEP Consejo Nacional de Empresa Privada (Panama)

CONES Consejo Nacional Económico e Social (Argentina)

CONESCAL	Centro Regional de Construcciones Escolares para América Latina (Mexico)
CONESCAR	Convenio de Cooperación Tecnica, Estadistica y Cartografía (Peru)
CONET	Consejo Nacional de Educación Técnica (Argentina)
CONEX	Conservation and Extension Service (Rhodesia)
CONFAPI	Confederazione Italiana Piccola e Media Industria
CONFECA-MARAS	Confederación Colombiana de Cámaras de Comercio
CONFEDI-LIZIA	Confederazione Italiana della Proprietà Edilizia
CONFETRA	Confederazione Generale del Traffico e dei Trasporti
CONFIN	Consejo de Fomento e Investigación Agricola (Chile)
CONFI-TARMA	Confederazione Nazionale degli Armatori Liberi
CONGITA	Confédération Général Italienne de la Technique Agricole
CONGO-BOIS	Compagnie Congolaise des Bois
CONGO-MECA	Société Congolaise de Mécanographie
CONGU	Council of National Golf Unions
CONI	Comitato Olimpico Nacionale Italiano
CONIA	Consejo Nacional de Investigaciones Agrícoles (Venezuela)
CONICIT	Consejo Nacional de Investigaciones Cientificas y Tecnológicas (Venezuela)
CONIDA	Comisión Nacional de Investigación y Desarrollo Aeroespacial (Peru)
CONIE	Comisión Nacional de Investigación de Espacio
CONIN-AGRO	Confederación Intercooperativa Agropecuaria (Argentina)
CONITAL	Consorzio Italiano Allevatori
CONPROBA	Consorcio de Productores Bananeros (Ecuador)
CONSAL	Conference of South-East Asian Librarians
CONSENA	Consejo de Seguridad Nacional (Uruguay)
CONSOR-PESCA	Consorzio Nazionale fra Cooperative Pescatori ed Affini
CONSTRU-NAVES	Asociación de Constructores Navales Españoles
CONSUEL	Comité National pour la Securité des Usagers de l'Électricité
CONTAG	Confederação Nacional de Trabalhadores na Agricultura (Brazil)
CONTAC	Conference on the Atlantic Community (U.S.A.)
CONTEC	Confederação Nacional dos Trabalhadores nas Empresas de Crédito (Brazil)
CONTEL	Conselho Nacional de Telecomuniçãcoes (Brazil)
CONTU	Commission on New Technological uses of Copyrighted Works (U.S.A.)
CONVELE	Consejo Venezolano de la Leche (Venezuela)
COONA-COVEN	Confederación Nacional de Cooperativas de Venezuela
COOP	Co-opérative pour le Développement des Oléagineux
COOPEFOR	Société Coopérative Forestière d'Administration et de Gestion
COOPEN-AGRO	Cooperativa Nacional de Mercadeo Agropecuario Limitada (Colombia)
COOPLAIN-IERE	Coopérative Lainière de l'Île de France
COORD-COM	Coordinating Committee of South-East Asian Senior Officials on Transport and Communications (Malaysia)
COP	Contactgroep Opvoering Productiviteit
COPA	Comité des Organisations Professionnelles Agricoles de la CEE
COPA	Compania Panama de Aviación
COPAC	Comité Mixte pour la Promotion de l'Aide aux Coopératives (FAO)
COPAC	Committee on Pollution Abatement and Control (U.S.A.)
COPAC	Joint Committee for the Promotion of Aid to Cooperatives (FAO)
COPACA	Congresos Panamericanos de Carreteras
COPACAR	Corporación Paraguaya de Carnes
COPACE	Comité des Pêches pour l'Atlantique Centre-Est (FAO)
COPACEL	Confédération Française de l'Industrie des Papiers, Cartons et Celluloses
COPAL	Cocoa Producers Alliance (Nigeria)
COPANT	Comisión Panamericana de Normas Técnicas (Argentina)
COPARCO	Société Congolaise de Perfumerie et Cosmetiques

COPAR-MEX	Confederación Patronal de la República Mexicana
COPARROZ	Cooperativa de Productores de Arroz de Tacuarembó (Uruguay)
COPE	Committee on Political Education (U.S.A.)
COPE	Compagnie Orientale des Pétroles d'Égypte
COPEC	Conference of Politics, Economics and Christianity
COPECIAL	Comité Permanent des Congrès Internationaux pour l'Apostolat des Laïcs
COPEL	Companhia Paranaense de Energia Elétrica (Brazil)
COPERE	Cómite de Programación Económica y de Reconstrucción (Chile)
COPERS	Commission Préparatoire Européenne de Recherches Spatiales (*now* ESRO)
COPETAO	Compagnie des Pétroles Total Afrique Ouest
COPICA	Comité de Propagande pour les Industries et les Commerces Agricoles et Alimentaires
COPLAN	Development Planning Commission (Brazil)
COPLAN-ARH	Comisión del Plan Nacional de Aprovechamiento de los Recursos Hidráulicos (Venezuela)
COPMEC	Comité des Petites et Moyennes Entreprises Commerciales des Pays de la CEE
COPOL	Council of Polytechnic Librarians
COPOR-CHAD	Coopérative des Transporteurs Tchadiens
COPPSO	Conference of Professional and Public Service Organisations
COPR	Centre for Overseas Pest Research
COPRAI	Comissaõ de Productivadade da Asociação Industrial Portugesa
COPRAM	Companhia Progresso do Amapa (Brazil)
COPRAQ	Cooperative Programme of Research on Aquaculture (FAO)
COPRED	Consortium on Peace Research, Education and Development (U.S.A.)
COPRIN	Comisíon de Productividad Precios e Ingresos (Venezuela)
COPRODE	Consejo Provincial de Desarrollo (Argentina)
COPROMA	Compagnie des Produits du Mali
COPTAL	Comité Permanente Técnico para Asuntos del Asuntos del Trabajo, Latinoamerica
COPUOS	UN Committee on the Peaceful Uses of Outer Space
COR	The Club of Rome
CORA	Confederación Odontológica Regional Andina
CORA	Corporación de la Reforma Agraria (Chile)
CORAL	Corporation of Coastal Cotton Growers (Colombia)
CORC	Central Organisation for Rural Cooperatives (Iran)
CORD	Collegium Orbis Radiobiologiae Docentium (France)
CORDE	Corporación Dominicana de Expresas Estatalas
CORDI-PLAN	Central Office of Co-ordination and Planning (Africa)
CORE	Center for Operations Research and Econometrics (Belgium)
CORE	Congress of Racial Equality (U.S.A.)
CORE	CSIR Committee on Research Expenditure (South Africa)
CORECI	Compagnie de Régulation et de Contrôle Industriel
COREM	Conférences Régionales de Métiers
COREMO	Comité Revolucionario de Mocambique
CORESTA	Centre de Coopération pour les Recherches Scientifiques Relatives du Tabac
CORFO	Corporación de Fomento de la Producción (Chile)
CORGI	Confederation for the Registration of Gas Installers
CORIP	Comité de Recherches de l'Industrie Pharmaceutique (Belgium)
CORMA	Corporación Chilena de la Mandera
COROI	Comptoir de Commerce et de Représentation pour l'Océan Indien
CORPAC	Corporación Peruana de Aeropuertos y Aviación Commercial
CORPO-FRUT	Corporación de Productores de Frutas de Río Negro (Argentina)
CORPO-SANA	Corporación de Obras Sanitarias (Paraguay)
CORS	Canadian Operational Research Society
CORSAG	Corporación Santiagueña de Ganaderos (Argentina)
CORSI	Operational Research Society of India
CORSO	Council of Relief Services Overseas (New Zealand)
CORT	Council of Repertory Theatres
COSA	Cámaras Oficiales Sindicales Agrarias

CoSAMC	Commission for Special Applications of Meteorology and Climatology (WMO)
COSATA	Co-operative Supply Association of Tanzania
COSATE	Commission Syndicale Technique (*of* OEA)
COSATI	Committee on Science and Technology Information (U.S.A.)
COSBA	Computer Services and Bureaux Association
COSEBI	Corporación de Servicios Bibliotecarios (Puerto Rico)
COSEC	Coordinating Secretariat of National Unions of Students (Netherlands)
COSEM	Co-operative Seed Corn Society of Tunis
COSEMCO	Comité des Semences du Marché Commun (Belgium)
COSENA	Compagnie Sénégalaise de Navigation
COSERV	National Council for Community Services to International Visitors (U.S.A.)
COSETAM	Compagnie Sénégalaise pour tous Appareillages Mécaniques
COSIMEX	Compagnie Sénégalaise d'Importation et d'Exportation
COSIPA	Companhia Siderúgica Paulista (Brazil)
CoSIRA	Council for Small Industries in Rural Areas
COSMA	Associazione Costruttori Macchine per Cucire
COSPAR	Committee on Space Research (Netherlands)
COSPIT	Centro Orientamento Studi e Propaganda Irrigua
COSPUP	Committee on Science and Public Policy (*of* NAS) (U.S.A.)
COSRIMS	Committee on Research in the Mathematical Sciences (*of* NAS) (U.S.A.)
COSSEC	Cambridge, Oxford and Southern School Examinations Council
COST	Committee for Overseas Science and Technology
COST	Committee on Science and Technology (India)
COST	Coopération Européenne dans la Domaine de la Recherche Scientifique et Technique
COSTED	Committee on Science and Technology in Developing Countries (*of* ICSU)
COSTI	National Centre of Scientific and Technical Information (Israel)
COSTIC	Comité Scientifique et Technique de l'Industrie du Chauffage, de la Ventilation et du Conditionnement d'Air
COSUPI	Comissão Supervisora do Plano dos Institutos (Brazil)
COSVN	Central Office for South Vietnam
COSWA	Conference on Science and World Affairs
COT	Centrale Organisatie in de Tweewielerbranche
COTAL	Confederación de Organizaciones Turísticas de la América Latina
COTC	Canadian Overseas Telecommunications Corporation
COTEMA	Compagnie Technique Mauritanienne
COTIRC	Comisión Técnica Interprovincial del Río Colorado (Argentina)
COTOA	Compagnie Textile de l'Ouest Africain (Senegal)
COTOMIB	Compagnie Togolaise des Mines du Benin
COTONCO	Compagnie Cotonnière Congolaise
COTON-FRAN	Société Cotonnière Franco Tchadienne
COTON-TCHAD	Société Cotonnière du Tchad
COTRAM	Union des Constructeurs de Matériel de Travaux Publics et de Manutention
COTRAMA	Société Civile Coopérative d'Études des Transports et de Manutention
COTRIJUI	Cooperativa Regional Triticula Serra Ltda of Ijui (Brazil)
COTRINAG	Comissão de Organização de Triticultura Nacional e Armazenamento Geral (Brazil)
COTT	Central Organization for Technical Training (South Africa)
COTTI	Commission du Traitement et de la Transmission de l'Information
COVAS	Coöperatieve Vereniging voor de Afzet van Suikerbieten
COVECO	Centrale Organisatie van Veeafzet- en Vleesverwerkings-coöperaties
COVEG	Stichting Centraal Orgaan voor de Voedings- en Genotmiddelenbranche
COVENAL	Corporación Venezolana de Aluminio
COVEN-EXTA	Cooperativa Venezolana de Exportadores de Tabaco
COVENIN	Comisión Venzolana de Normas Industriales
COVENTA	Cooperativa Venezolana de Tabacaleros
COVEPRO	Cooperativa Venezolana de Productores
COVINCA	Corporación Venezolana de la Industria Naval CA

COVINEX	Société Congolaise d'Exploitation Vinicole
COVODIAM	Compagnie Voltaïque de Distribution Automobile et de Matériel
COVON	Coöperatieve Vereniging van Ondernemers in het Natuursteenbedrijf
COVOS	Groupes d'Études sur les Consequences des Vols Stratosphériques
COWA	Council for Old World Archaeology (U.S.A.)
CoWaBo	Commissie inzake Wateronttrekking aan de Bodem
COWAR	Committee on Water Research (International)
COWT	Council of World Tensions (Switzerland)
CP	Centralkommitén for Produktivitetsfragor
CP	Convention Patronale de l'Industrie Horlogère Suisse
CPA	California Pharmaceutical Association (U.S.A.)
CPA	Canadian Pacific Airlines
CPA	Canadian Pharmaceutical Association
CPA	Canadian Postmasters Association
CPA	Canadian Psychological Association
CPA	Canvas Products Association International (U.S.A.)
CPA	Centre de Perfectionnement dans d'Administration des Affaires
CPA	Centre de Préparation aux Affaires
CPA	Chick Producers Association
CPA	Cocoa Producers Alliance (West Africa)
CPA	Commonwealth Parliamentary Association
CPA	Comité Permanent Agricole (of BIT)
CPA	Contractors' Plant Association
CPA	Cour Permanente d'Arbitrage (Netherlands)
CPAC	International Collaborative Pesticides Analytical Committee
CPACO	Comité de Pesca de la FAO para el Atlántico Centro-Oriental
CPANE	Comisión de Pesquerías del Atlántico Nordeste
CPANE	Commission des Pêches de l'Atlantique Nord-Est
CPANT	Comité Panamericano de Normas Técnicas (Uruguay)
CPAS	Church Pastoral Aid Society
CPB	Centraal Planbureau

CPBP	Comisión Protectora de Bibliotecas Populares (Argentina)
CPBP	Comité Professionnel du Butane et du Propane
CPC	Christian Peace Conference
CPC	Coffee Promotion Council Ltd
CPC	Colonial Products Council
CPC	Committee for Programme and Coordination (ECOSOC)
CPC	Compagnie des Potasses du Congo
CPC	Conservative Political Centre
CPCA	Comite des Pêches Continentales pour l'Afrique (FAO)
CPCAS	Commission Permanente de Coordination des Associations Spécialisées (of FNSEA)
CPCC	Conference Permanente des Chambres de Commerce et l'Industrie de la CEE
CPCEA	Caisse de Prévoyance des Cadres d'Exploitations Agricoles
CPCERMPS	Comisión Permanente para la Conservación y Exploitación de los Recursos Maritimos del Pacifico Sur
CPCI	Centre de Perfectionnement Pratique des Cadres Commerciaux dans l'Industrie
CPCIZ	Comité Permanent du Congrès International de Zoölogie
CPCM	Comité Permanent Consultatif du Maghreb
CPDL	Canadian Patents and Development Ltd
CPDP	Comité Professionnel du Pétrole
CPE	Comité de Politique Économique (de l'OCDE)
CPE	Congrès du Peuple Européen
CPED	Commission de la Participation des Églises au Développement (Switzerland)
CPEPA	Comité de la Prune d'Ente et du Pruneau d'Agen
CPEQ	Corporation of Professional Engineers of Quebec (Canada)
CPES	Centro Paraguayo de Estudios Sociologicos
CPF	Coopération Pharmaceutique Française
CPF	Cooperative Productive Federation
CPFS	Council for the Promotion of Field Studies
CPG	Bureau of Conference Planning and General Services (UNESCO)
CPGA	Comité Professionnel des Galeries d'Art
CPGPA	Caisse Professionnelle de Garantie des Producteurs Agricoles

CPHA	Canadian Public Health Association
CPHERI	Central Public Health Engineering Research Institute (India)
CPI	Cinchona Products Institute (U.S.A.)
CPI	Commission Permanente Internationale de l'Acetylène, de la Soudure Autogène et des Industries qui s'y Rattachent
CPI	Commission Phytosanitaire Interafricaine
CPI	Communist Party of India
CPI	Conseil Phytosanitaire Interafricain
CPI	Crop Protection Institute (U.S.A.)
CPI	Stichting Coöperatief Pluimveefokkers Instituut
CPIE	Centre de l'Information Européenne
CPIP	Consejo de Pesca Indo-Pacífico
CPITUS	Comité Permanent International des Techniques et de l'Urbanisme Souterrains
CPIUS	Comité Permanent Internacional de Tecnicos y de Urbanismo Subterráneo
CPIV	Comité Permanent International du Vinaigre (Marché Commun)
CPJI	Cour Permanente de Justice Internationale
CPL	Centre Paritaire du Logement
CPL	Colonial Products Laboratory (*now* TPL)
CPM	Comisión del Pacífico Meridional
CPM	Corporación Pro-Crusada Mundial
CPME	Conseil Parlementaire du Mouvement Européen
CPN	Communistische Partij van Nederland
CPNA	Commission Paritaire Nationale pour les Entreprises Agricoles
CPNCEP	Chambre Professionnelle Nationale des Conseillers de l'Économie Privée
CPNT	Comité Panamericano de Normas Técnicas (Argentina)
CPNU	Conférence des Plénipotentiaires
CPO	Centrum voor Plantenfysiologisch Onderzoek
CPO	Commonwealth Producers Organisation
CPOI	Comisión de Pesca para el Océano Indico
CPOM	Centro de Preclasificación Océanica de México
CPP	Convention Peoples Party (Ghana)
CPPA	Canadian Pulp and Paper Association
CPPB	Comité de Problemos de Productos Básicos (FAO)
CPPC	Copper Promotion Producers Committee (*now* CIDEC)
CPPCC	Chinese People's Political Consultative Conference
CPPPD	Centre de la Planification, des Projections et des Politiques Relatives au Développement (UN)
CPPS	Comisión Permanente para la Exploitatación y Conservación de las Riquezas Marítimas del Pacífico Sur
CPRA	Chinese Public Relations Association
CPRE	Council for the Preservation of Rural England
CPREA	Canadian Peace Research and Education Association
CPRI	Canadian Peace Research Institute
CPRI	Central Potato Research Institute (India)
CPRM	Companhia de Pesquisas de Recursos Minerais (Brazil)
CPRM	Companhia Portuguesa Radio Marconi
CPRS	Canadian Public Relations Society
CPRU	Colonial Pesticides Research Unit (East Africa)
CPRW	Council for the Preservation of Rural Wales
CPS	Commission du Pacifique Sud
CPS	Committee for Penicillin Sensitivity
CPSA	Canadian Political Science Association
CPSA	Civil and Public Services Association
CPSA	Clay Pigeon Shooting Association
CPSC	Consumer Products Safety Commission (U.S.A.)
CPTB	Clay Products Technical Bureau
CPSP	Comisión Permanente para el Sur del Pacifico
CPT	Confederación Paraguaya de Trabajadores
CPT	Confederation of British Road Passenger Transport
CPTC	China Productivity and Trade Centre
CPTE	Comité Permanent des Transports Européens
CPU	Commonwealth Press Union
CPUSTAL	Congrès Permanent de l'Unité Syndicale des Travailleurs d'Amérique Latine
CPV	Centrale Proefstations Vereniging
CPWC	Central Peoples Workers Council (Burma)
CPWD	Central Public Works Department (India)
CQBF	County Quality Bacon Federation

CQCJ	Comité des Questions Constitutionnelles et Juridiques (FAO)	**CRC**	Cuba Resource Centre (U.S.A.)
CQEE	Conseil du Québec de l'Enfance Exceptionnelle	**CRCA**	Caisse Régionale de Crédit Agricole
		CRCA	Comissao Reguladora do Comércio de Arroz (Portugal)
CQPPA	Council of Quality Pig Producers Associations	**CRCAM**	Caisse Régionale de Crédit Agricole Mutuel
CQRI	Centre Québécois de Relations Internationales	**CRCC**	Canadian Red Cross Committee
		CRCP	Costa Rican Cocoa Products Co
CRA	Canadian Rheumatism Association	**CRD**	Centre de Recherches et de Documentation de l'Association Universelle pour l'Esperanto
CRA	Centres de Recherches Agronomiques		
CRA	Centres de la Recherche Appliquée (Zaire)	**CRDE**	Centre de Recherches en Développement Économique (Canada)
CRA	China Research Associates		
CRA	Confederaciones Rurales Argentinas	**CRDF**	Conseil de la Recherche et du Développement Forestiers (Canada)
CRAAM	Centro de Radio-Astronomia e Astrofisica Universidade Mackenzie (Brazil)	**CRDI**	Centre de Recherches pour le Développement International (Canada)
CRAC	Careers Research and Advisory Centre	**CRDLP**	Centre for Research and Documentation of the Language Problem
CRACCUS	Comité Régional de l'Afrique Centrale pour la Conservation et l'Utilisation des Sols		
		CRDS	Centre de Recherches et de Documentation du Sénégal
CRAE	Centre de Recherches Agronomiques de l'État (Belgium)	**CRDTO**	Regional Documentation Centre for Oral Tradition (Niger)
CRAF	Centre de Recherches Africaines		
CRAF	Comité Régional d'Arboriculture Fruitière du Bassin Parisien	**CRE**	Coal Research Establishment
		CRE	Commercial Relations Export Department
CRAM	Centre de Recherches sur les Atomes et les Molécules (Canada)	**CRE**	Standing Conference of Rectors and Vice-Chancellors of the European Universities (Switzerland)
CRAM	Collectivités Rurales Autochones Modernisées à Madagascar		
CRAPE	Centre de Recherches Anthropologiques Préhistoriques et Ethnographiques (Algeria)	**CREA**	Centre de Recherches et d'Études Agricoles
		CREA	Centro Regional de Educatión de Adultos (Venezuela)
CRAR	Committee for the Recovery of Archeological Remains (U.S.A.)	**CREA**	Committee on the Relation of Electricity to Agriculture (U.S.A.)
CRAS	Centre for Radiobiology and Radiation Protection (Netherlands)	**CREA**	Consorcio Regional de Experimentación Agrícola (Argentina)
CRATEMA	Centro di Ricerca e di Assistenza Tecnica e Mercantile alle Aziende	**CREA**	Coopérative Régionale d'Équipement Agricole
CRAV	Comisión de la Reforma Agraria y la Vivienda (Peru)	**CREACUS**	Comité Régional de l'Afrique Orientale pour la Conservation et l'Utilisation du Sol
CRB	Confederação Rural Brasileira	**CREAI**	Carteira de Credito Agricola e Industrial (Brazil)
CRBM	Centre Régional de Biologie Marine		
CRC	Cancer Research Campaign	**CREAQ**	Commission Royale d'Enquête sur l'Agriculture au Québec (Canada)
CRC	Centre de Recherches Techniques et Scientifiques Industries de la Tannerie, de la Chaussure, de la Pantoufle et des autres Industries Transformatrices du Cuir (Belgium)	**CRECIT**	Centre de Recherches Essais et Contrôles Scientifiques pour l'Industrie Textile (Belgium)
CRC	Cotton Research Corporation (*formerly* ECGC)	**CRED**	Center for Research on Economic Development (U.S.A.)

CREDE	Regional Economic Research and Documentation Centre (Togo)
CREDIFF	Centre de Recherches pour la Diffusion du Français
CREDILA	Centre de Recherches d'Études et de Documentation sur les Institutions et la Législation Africaines (Senegal)
CREDO	Centre for Curriculum Renewal and Educational Development Overseas
CREDOC	Centre de Recherches et de Documentation sur la Consommation
CREDOP	Centre de Recherche d'Étude et de Documentation en Publicité (Belgium)
CREEA	Comité Régional d'Expansion Économique de l'Auvergne
CREEGIM	Conseil Régional d'Expansion Économique de la Gaspérie et des Îles-de-la-Madeleine (Canada)
CREFAL	Centro Regional de Alfabetización Functional en las Zonas Rurale de America Latina (Mexico)
CREGR	Centre de Recherches et d'Expérimentation de Génie Rurale (France) (*now* CERAFER)
CRENO	Conférence des Régions de l'Europe du Nord-Ouest
CREO	Centre de Recherches et d'Études Océanographiques
CREPS	Centre Régional d'Éducation Physique et Sportive
CREPS	Compagnie de Recherches et d'Exploitation de Pétrole du Sahara
CRERMA	Conseillers Régionaux d'Étude de la Rentabilité du Machinisme Agricole
CRES	Centre de Recherches Économiques et Sociales
CRESA	Centre de Recherches Economiques et Sociales Appliquées
CRESHS	Centre de Recherches en Sciences Humaines et Sociales (Haiti)
CRESM	Centre de Recherches et d'Études sur les Sociétés Musulmanes
CRESR	Centre Régional d'Études Socio-Religieuses
CREST	Committee on Reactor Safety Technology (*of* ENEA)
CRET	Commission Régionale Européenne de Tourisme
CRF	Calendar Reform Foundation (U.S.A.)
CRFEA	Christian Rural Fellowship of East Africa
CRFM	Comité de Coordination de la Recherche Forestière Méditeranéenne
CRG	Cave Research Group of Great Britain
CRI	Caribbean Research Institute
CRI	Cement Research Institute (India)
CRI	Central Research Institute (India)
CRI	Croce Rossa Italiana
CRI	Children's Relief International
CRI	Coconut Research Institute (Ceylon)
CRIA	Caisse de Retraite Interenterprises Agricoles
CRIA	Centre de Recherches sur les Trypanosomiases Animales (Central Africa)
CRIC	Centre National de Recherches Scientifiques et Techniques pour l'Industrie Cimentière (Belgium)
CRIC	Centre de Recherches Industrielles sur Contrats
CRIC	Commercial Radio International Committee
CRID	Centre pour la Recherche Interdisciplinaire sur le Développement (Belgium)
CRIDAOL	Centro Regional de Investigación y Desarrollo Agraria de Galicia
CRIDE	Centre de Recherches Interdisciplinaires pour le Développement de l'Éducation (Zaire)
CRIDE	Centre de Recherches Interdisciplinaires Droit-Economie (Belgium)
CRIEL	Comité Interprofessionnel des Eaux-de-vie du Languedoc
CRIEPI	Central Research Institute of the Electrical Power Industry (Japan)
CRIF	Centre de Recherches Scientifiques et Techniques de l'Industrie des Fabrications Métalliques (Belgium)
CRIG	Cocoa Research Institute of Ghana
CRILC	Canadian Research Institute of Launderers and Cleaners
CRIN	Cacao Research Institute of Nigeria
CRIPE	Centre de Recherches et Techniques pour l'Industrie des Produits Explosifs (Belgium)
CRISP	Centre de Recherche et d'Information Sociopolitiques (Belgium)
CRIT	Co-ordinating Centre for Regional Information Training, Nairobi (Kenya)
CRL	Chemical Research Laboratory
CRLC	Coopérative Régionale Lainière du Centre
CRM	Compagnie Radio-Maritime

CRME	Committee on Research in Medical Economics (U.S.A.)
CRMS	Centro Ricerche Malattie della Selvaggina
CRO	Commissie voor Rassenonderzoek van Groenvoedergewassen
CRO	Commonwealth Relations Office
CROACUS	Comité Régional de l'Afrique Occidentale pour la Conservation et l'Utilisation du Sol
CROC	Confederación Revolucionaria de Obreros y Campesinos (Mexico)
CROSSA	Centre Régional Opérationnel de Surveillance et de Sauvetage pour l'Atlantique
CROSSMA	Centre Régional Operationnel de Surveillance et de Sauvetage pour la Manche
CRP	C. Rudolf Poensgen Stiftung zur Förderung von Führungskraften in der Wirtschaft e V.
CRPAO	Comisión Regional de Pesca para el Africa Occidental
CRPL	Central Radio Propagation Laboratory (U.S.A.)
CRPQF	Comissao Reguladora dos Productos Químicos e Farmacéuticos (Portugal)
CRR	Centre de Recherches Routières (Belgium)
CRRAG	Countryside Recreation Research Advisory Group
CRRI	Central Rice Research Institute (India)
CRRI	Central Road Research Institute (India)
CRRL	Central Reference and Research Library (Ghana)
CRRS	Central Rainlands Research Station (Sudan)
CRS	Cereals Research Station
CRSD	Co-operative Research and Service Division (U.S.A.)
CRSIM	Centre de Recherches Scientifiques, Industrielles et Maritimes
CRSV	Centre de Recherches Science et Vie
CRSVI	Conférence Régionale du Service Volontaire International
CRT	Confederación Revolucionaria de Trabajodores (Mexico)
CRU	Centre de Recherche d'Urbanisme
CRUESI	Centre de Recherches pour l'Utilisation de l'Eau Salée en Irrigation (Tunisia)
CRUTAC	Centro Rural Universitario de Treinamento e de Acao Comunitaria (Brazil)
CRWPC	Canadian Radio Wave Propagation Committee
CRWRC	Christian Reformed World Relief Committee (U.S.A.)
CRYM	Comisión Reguladora de la Produción y Comercio de la Yerba Mate (Argentina)
CSA	Canadian Standards Association
CSA	Caribbean Studies Association (U.S.A.)
CSA	Centralförbundet för Socialt Arbete
CSA	Ceskoslovenské Aerolinie
CSA	Chambre Syndicale de l'Amiante
CSA	Civil Service Assembly (Canada and U.S.A.)
CSA	Confederate States of America
CSA	Conseil Supérieur de l'Agriculture
CSA	Scientific Council for Africa South of the Sahara
CSAA	Canadian Sociology and Anthropology Association
CSAA	Child Study Association of America
CSAA	Confédération Sud-Americaine d'Athlétisme
CSAA	South American Athletic Confederation
CSAC	Alliance Cocoa Scientific Advisory Committee
CSAF	Centro di Sperimentazione Agricola e Forestale
CSAGI	Comité Spécial de l'Année Géophysique Spécial (International)
CSAI	Italian Automobile Sporting Commission
CSAP	Canadian Society of Animal Production
CSAR	Compagnie Sénégalaise d'Assurances et de Réassurances
CSATM	Confédération Sud-américaine de Tennis de Table (Uruguay)
CSB	Confédération Sud-Américaine de Billard
CSBNTP	Chambre Syndicale Belge des Négociants en Timbres Poste
CSBP	Chambre Syndicale des Banques Populaires de France
CSBVF	Chambre Syndicale de la Boulonnerie et de la Visserie Forgées
CSC	Chambre Syndicale Nationale des Industries de la Conserve
CSC	Civil Service Commission
CSC	Commercial Solvents Corporation (U.S.A.)
CSC	Commonwealth Science Council
CSC	Confédération des Syndicats Chrétiens (Belgium)

CSC	Confédération des Syndicats Chrétiens de la Suisse	**CSEU**	Confederation of Shipbuilding and Engineering Unions
CSCA	Chambre Syndicale des Constructeurs d'Automobiles	**CSF**	Coil Spring Federation
CSCA	Consejo Superior de los Colegios de Arquitectos de España	**CSF**	Comité des Salines de France
		CSF	Confederación Sudamericana de Fútbol
CSCAW	Catholic Study Circle for Animal Welfare	**CSFA**	Canadian Scientific Film Association
CSCE	Canadian Society for Chemical Engineering	**CSFA**	Confédération des Sociétés Françaises d'Architectes
CSCE	Canadian Society for Civil Engineering	**CSFE**	Canadian Society of Forest Engineers
CSCE	Conference on Security and Co-operation in Europe (*of* NATO)	**CSFIFF**	Chambre Syndicale Française des Industriels Fondeurs de Fromage
CSCF	Cast Stone and Concrete Federation	**CSFN**	Centro Siciliano di Fisica Nucleare
CSChE	Canadian Society for Chemical Engineering	**CSFRA**	Coil Spring Federation Research Organisation
CSCM	Commission Syndicale Consultative Mixte *auprès de* l'OCDE	**CSFSBA**	Chambre Syndicale des Fabricants de Supports en Béton Armé Destinés aux Canalisations Aériennes
CSCN	Chambre Syndicale des Constructeurs de Navires et de Machines Marines		
CSC-OCDE	Commission Syndicale Consultative *auprès de* l'OCDE	**CSFTI**	Committee on Southern Forest Tree Improvement (U.S.A.)
CSCR	Central Society for Clinical Research (U.S.A.)	**CSGA**	Canadian Seed Growers Association
		CSGB	Cartophilic Society of Great Britain
CSCS	Commonwealth Students Children Society	**CSGS**	Československá Gerontologická Společnost
CSD	Commonwealth Society for the Deaf	**CSH**	Chambre Suisse de l'Horlogerie
CSD	FAO's Consultative Sub-Committee on Surplus Disposal	**CSHB**	Chambre Syndicale de l'Horticulture Belge
CSDHA	Centre for Social Development and Humanitarian Affairs (UN)	**CSI**	Cartel des Syndicats Independants des Services Publics (Belgium)
CSDPP	Chambre Syndicale de la Distribution des Produits Pétroliers	**CSI**	Chartered Surveyors Institution
		CSI	Cinémathèque Scientifique Internationale
CSE	Centre de Sociologie Européenne	**CSI**	Commission Séricicole Internationale
CSE	Conférence Spatiale Européenne	**CSI**	Commission Sportive International
CSE	Conférence des Statisticiens Européens	**CSIC**	Consejo Superior de Investigaciónes Cientificas
CSEABC	Chambre Syndicale des Entreprises Artisanales du Bâtiment	**CSICC**	Canadian Steel Industries Construction Council
CSEB	Chambre Syndicale des Électriciens Belges	**CSID**	Centro de Servicios de Información y Documentación (Mexico)
CSEDB	Chambre Syndicale des Entrepreneurs de Déménagements Belgique		
CSEERI	Comité Scientifique pour l'Étude des Effets des Radiations Ionisantes (International)	**CSII**	Centre for the Study of Industrial Innovation
		CSIJ	Comité Sportif International de la Jeunesse
CSEI	Chambre Syndicale des Esthéticiens Industriels	**CSIO**	Central Scientific Instruments Organisation (India)
CSEM	Centre Séismologique Européo-Méditerranéen	**CSIR**	Council for Scientific and Industrial Research (Ghana, India etc.)
CSEMP	Chambre Syndicale des Emballages en Matières Plastiques	**CSIRO**	Commonwealth Scientific and Industrial Research Organisation (Australia)
CSESS	Cooperative State Experiment Station Service (U.S.A.)	**CSIRT**	Comité Scientifique International de Recherches sur les Trypanosomiases

CSIS	Center for Strategic and International Studies (U.S.A.)	CSNEIMB	Chambre Syndicale des Entrepreneurs d'Installations de Magasins et Bureaux et Activités Annexes
CSIS	Comisia de Stat pentru Incercarea Soiurilor (Roumania)	CSNESA	Chambre Syndicale Nationale des Électriciens et Spécialistes de l'Automobile
CSIT	Comité Sportif International du Travail	CSNFEI	Chambre Syndicale Nationale des Fabricants d'Encres d'Imprimerie
SJC	Chartered Societies Joint Committee	CSNHP	Chambre Syndicale Nationale des Entreprises et Industries de l'Hygiène Publique
SK	Comité Spécial du Katanga (Zaire)		
SL	Commonwealth Serum Laboratories (Australia)	CSNISE	Chambre Syndicale Nationale des Installateurs de Stands et d'Expositions
SL	Compagnie Sénégalaise des Lubrificants	CSNL	Chambre Syndicale Nationale de la Literie
SLATP	Canadian Society of Landscape Architects and Town Planners	CSNRD	Consortium for the Study of Nigerian Rural Development (U.S.A.)
SLO	Canadian Scientific Liaison Office	CSNRRM	Chambre Syndicale Nationale des Rectifieurs et Reconstructeurs de Moteurs
SLT	Canadian Society of Laboratory Technologists	CSO	Central Statistical Office
SM	Commission Synoptic Meteorology (Technical Commission of the World Meteorological Organisation)	CSO	Centre de Sociologie des Organisations
		CSOP	Commission to Study the Organization of Peace (U.S.A.)
SM	Compagnie Sénégalaise de Métallurgie	CSP	Chartered Society of Physio-Therapy
SM	Centrale Suikermaatschappij	CSP	Chambre Syndicale de la Phytopharmacie
SMA	Caisse de Secours Mutuels Agricoles	CSP	Council on Scientific Policy
SMA	Chemical Specialities Manufacturers Association (U.S.A.)	CSPAA	Conseil de Solidarité des Pays Afro-Asiatiques
SMCRI	Central Salt and Marine Chemicals Research Institute (India)	CSPB	Comité Spécial du Programme Biologique International
SME	Canadian Society for Mechanical Engineers	CSPBI	Comité Spécial du Programme Biologique International
SME	Confédération Syndicale Mondiale des En-seignants	CSPCA	Canadian Society for the Prevention of Cruelty to Animals
SMF	Confédération des Syndicats Médicaux Français	CSPE	Comité Scientifique pour les Problèmes de l'Environnement (of ICSU)
SMFRA	Cotton Silk and Man-Made Fibres Research Association (formerly Shirley Institute)	CSPECVM	Chambre Syndicale Patronale des Enseignants de la Conduite des Véhicules à Moteur
SMG	Československa Společnost pro Mineralogii a Geologii		
SN	Confédération des Syndicats Nationaux	CSPEFF	Chambre Syndicale des Producteurs et Exportateurs de Films Français
SN	Conseil Supérieur du Notariat	CSPFLC	Confédération Nationale des Producteurs de Fruits, Légumes et Champignons
SNA	Commonwealth Society of North America (U.S.A.)	CSPI	Citizen's Committee on Infant Nutrition (U.S.A.)
SNC	Chambre Syndicale des Constructeurs de Navires et de Machines Marines	CSPP	Centro di Studi sui Problemi Portuali
SNCRA	Chambre Syndicale Nationale du Commerce et de la Réparation de l'Automobile	CSPT	Compagnie Sénégalaise des Phosphates de Taiba
SNDP	Chambre Syndicale Nationale des Agencies Privées de Recherches et Mandataires en Obtention de Renseignements et de Preuves	CSPU	Communist Party of the Soviet Union

CSQC	Ceylon Society for Quality Control
CSR	Circolo Speleologico Romano
CSR	Conférence Suisse de Sécurité dans le Trafic Routier
CSR	Cykel– och Sporthandlarnas Riksförbund
CSRA	Comité Scientifique pour les Recherches Antarctiques (ICSU)
CSRO	Comité Scientifique pour les Recherches Océaniques (ICSU)
CSROH	Revolucniho Odborového Hnuti
CSRS	Centre Suisse de Recherches Scientifiques en Côte d'Ivoire
CSRS	Cooperative State Research Service (U.S.A.)
CSRSOM	Conseil Supérieur des Recherches Sociologiques Outre-Mer
CSS	Commodity Stabilisation Service (U.S.A.)
CSS	Compagnie Sucrière Sénégalaise
CSS	Zentralverband Schweizerischer Schneidermeister
CSSA	Cactus and Succulent Society of America
CSSA	Civil Science Systems Administration (U.S.A.)
CSSA	Conseil Supérieur pour le Sport en Afrique (Cameroons)
CSSA	Crop Science Society of America
CSSE	Compagnie Sénégalaise du Sud-Est
CSSE	Conference of State Sanitary Engineers (U.S.A.)
CSSF	Chambre Syndicale de la Sérigraphie Française
CSSF	Chambre Syndicale de la Sidérurgie Française
CSSIMS	Central States Society of Industrial Medicine and Surgery (U.S.A.)
CSSP	Committee of Scientific Society Presidents (U.S.A.)
CSSPPA	Caisse de Stabilisation et de Soutien des Prix des Productions Agricoles (Ivory Coast)
CSSR	Centro Studi Sociologia Religiosa
CSSRC	Colonial Social Sciences Research Committee (U.K.)
CSSRO	Chambre Syndicale des Soies et Rayonnes Ouvrées
CSSS	Canadian Soil Science Society
CSTA	Canadian Society of Technical Agriculturists
CSTA	Canterbury Science Teachers' Association (N.Z.)
CSTA	Consejo Sindical de Trabajadores Andinos
CSTAL	Confederación Sindical de los Trabajadores de América Latina
CSTB	Centre Scientifique et Technique du Bâtiment
CSTC	Centre Scientifique et Technique de la Construction (Belgium)
CSTC	Consejo Sindical de Trabajadores del Caribe
CSTFTAB	Confederación Sindical de Trabajadores Ferroviarios, Ramas Anexas y Transportes Aéreos de Bolivia
CSTI	Council of Science and Technology Institutes
CSTM	Calcutta School of Tropical Medicine (India)
CSTM	Centro Studi Terzo Mondo
CSTM	Compagnie Sénégalaise pour la Transformation des Métaux
CSTP	Committee for Scientific and Technical Personnel (*of* OECD)
CSTR	*see* STRC
CSU	Confédération des Syndicats Unitiés de Belgique
CSUCA	Consejo Superior Universitario Centroamericano
CSUK	Chamber of Shipping of the United Kingdom (*now merged into* GCBS)
CSURF	Colorado State University Research Foundation (U.S.A.)
CSV	Centraal Stikstof Verkoopkantoor
CSVTS	Ceskoslovenská Vědecko-Technická Společnost
CSW	Christlicher Studenten-Weltbund
CT	Conseil de Tutelle (Trusteeship Council of UNO)
CTA	Camping Trade Association of Great Britain
CTA	Canadian Tuberculosis Association
CTA	Caribbean Travel Association
CTA	Chain Testers' Association of Great Britain
CTA	Channel Tunnel Association
CTA	Collegio dei Tecnici dell'Acciaio
CTA	Commercial Travellers' Association
CTAF	Comité des Transporteurs Aériens Français
CTAL	Confederación de Trabajadores de América Latina
CTAMBJO	Syndicat National des Cadres, Techniciens, et Agents de Maîtrise de la Bijouterie, Joaillerie Orfèvrerie et des Activités qui s'y Rattachent
CTAT	Centre Technique d'Agriculture Tropicale

CTAVI	Centre Technique Audio Visuel International
CTB	Centre Technique du Bois
CTB	Commonwealth Telecommunications Board
CTBLV	Christlicher Textil-, Bekleidungs- und Lederarbeiter-Verband
CTC	Central Training Council
CTC	Centre Technique de Conserves des Produits Agricoles
CTC	Centre Technique du Cuir
CTC	Confederación de Trabajadores de Colombia
CTC	Cuban Confederation of Workers
CTCA	Commission for Technical Cooperation in Africa (*of* OAU, *now* STRC)
CTCA	Confédération des Travailleurs d'Amérique Centrale (Honduras)
CTCB	Centre Technique du Cuir Brut
CTCB	Confederación de Trabajadores de Comercio de Bolivia
CTCD	Centre Technique pour le Contrôle de la Descendance
CTCE	Comité de Thermodynamique et de Cinétique Électrochimiques (Belgium)
CTCEE	Comisão Tecnica de Cooperacae Economic Externa (Portugal)
CTCI	Classic Thunderbird Club International (U.S.A.)
CTCRA	Comité Technique de Cooperation et Réalisations Agricoles (*now* IFCT) (France)
CTCRI	Central Tuber Crops Research Institute (India)
CTCSG	Centre Technique de la Canne et du Sucre de la Guadeloupe
CTCSM	Centre Technique de la Canne du Sucre de la Martinique
CTEI	Centro Tropical de Enseñanza e Investigación (Costa Rica)
CTETOC	Council for Technical Education and Training for Overseas Countries
CTF	Catholic Teachers Federation
CTF	Coffee Trade Federation
CTF	Comité de Tourisme et des Fêtes
CTFL	Centre Technique des Fruits et Légumes
CTFM	Comité des Transports Ferroviares du Maghreb
CTFMA	Copper Tube Fittings Manufacturers Association
CTFT	Centre Technique Forestier Tropical (Ivory Coast)
CTGA	Ceylon Tea Growers Association
CTI	Centraal Technisch Instituut TNO
CTI	Confédération des Travailleurs Intellectuels
CTI	Container Transport International (U.S.A.)
CTIB	Centre Technique de l'Industrie du Bois (Belgium)
CTIC	Comisiones Técnicas Inter-Crea (Argentina)
CTIF	Centre Techniques des Industries de la Fonderie
CTIF	Comité Technique International de Prévention et Extinction du Feu
CTIFL	Centre Technique Interprofessionnel des Fruits et Légumes
CTIOM	Centre Technique Interprofessionnel des Oléagineux Métropolitains
CTIP	Compagnia Tecnica Industrie Petrole
CTM	Confederación de Trabajadores de Mexico
CTM	Conférence Technique Mondiale
CTMA	Centre Technique du Machinisme Agricole
CTMB	Canal Transport Marketing Board
CTMC	Compagnie pour la Transformation des Métaux au Cameroun
CTNE	Compania Telefonica Nacional de Espana
CTNRC	Centre for Thai National Reference Collections
CTNSS	Centre for Thai National Standard Specifications
CTO	Central Tractor Organisation (India)
CTO	Comité Technique de l'Olivier
CTP	Centre Technique de l'Industrie des Papiers, Cartons et Celluloses
CTP	Confederación de Trabajadores del Peru
CTPA	Continental Tournaments Players Association (France)
CTPL	Commission Technique et de Promotion des Laitiers
CTPS	Permanent Technical Committee for Plant Breeding (France)
CTPTA	Centro Tropical de Pesquisas e Tecnologia de Alimentos (Brazil)
CTRA	Coal Tar Research Association
CTRC	Caribbean Tourism Research Centre (Barbados)
CTRI	Catholic Tape Recorders International (U.S.A.)

CTRI	Central Tobacco Research Institute (India)		**CUMM**	Council of Underground Machinery Manufacturers
CTRI	Central Tobacco Research Institute, Rustenburg (S. Africa)		**CUNA**	Credit Union National Association (U.S.A.)
CTRL	Cotton Technological Research Laboratory (India)		**CUNY**	City University of New York (U.S.A.)
CTRM	Compagnie de Transports Routiers et de Messageries		**CUPE**	Canadian Union of Public Employees
			CUPM	Committee on Undergraduate Program in Mathematics (U.S.A.)
CTRP	Confederación de Trabajadores de la Républica de Panama		**CUPRA**	Confederazione Unitaria della Produzione Agricola
CTRU	Colonial Termite Research Unit (Nigeria)		**CURAC**	Coal Utilization Research Advisory Committee (Australia)
CTS	Committee on the Teaching of Science (*of* ICSU)		**CURB**	Campaign on the Use and Restriction of Barbiturates
CTSA	Crucible and Tool Steel Association		**CURE**	Citizens United for Racial Equality (U.S.A.)
CTSCCV	Centre Technique de la Salaison de la Charcuterie et des Conserves de Viande		**CUREI**	Centre Universitaire de Recherche Européenne et Internationale
CTT	Centrum voor Tuinbouwtechniek		**CURS**	University Scientific Research Centre (Morocco)
CTT	Irish Export Promotion Organisation			
CTU	Conservative Trade Unionists		**CUS**	Conférence Universitaire Suisse
CTUF	Ceylon Trade Union Federation		**CUSA**	Council for United States Aid (China)
CTUY	Confederation of Trade Unions of Yugoslavia		**CUSO**	Canadian University Service Overseas
CTVM	Centre for Tropical Veterinary Medicine		**CUSRPG**	Canada-United States Regional Planning Group (*of* NATO)
CTV	Confederación de Trabajadores de Venezuela		**CUSURDI**	Council of United States Universities for Rural Development in India
CUA	Department of Cultural Activities (UNESCO)		**CUSUS-WASH**	Council of U.S. Universities for Soil and Water Development in Arid and Sub-humid Areas
CUB	Confederación Universitaria Boliviana			
CUC	Canterbury University College, Christchurch (N.Z.)		**CUT**	Comité de l'Unité Togolaise
CUC	Coal Utilization Council		**CUT**	Cooperative Union of Tanganyika
CUC	Computers Users' Committee (UNDP)		**CUTAL**	Confédération Unique des Travailleurs de l'Amérique Latine
CUCES	Centre Universitaire de Coopération Économique et Sociale		**CUTCH**	Central Unica de Trabajadores de Chile
CUEA	Consejo de la Unidad Económica Arabe		**CV-AV**	International Commission CV-AV Catholic Movement for Children
CUEBS	Commission on Undergraduate Education in the Biological Sciences (*of* AIBS)		**CVB**	Centraal Veevoederbureau in Nederland
CUF	Catholicarum Universitatum Foederatio		**CVC**	Corporación Autónima Regional del Valle del Cauca (Colombia)
CUF	Companhia União Fabril (Portugal)			
CUKT	Carnegie United Kingdom Trust		**CVD**	Veterinary Department, South Cameroons
CULPAVAL	Cultivadores de Patata Valdivia		**CVF**	Corporación Venezolana de Fomento
CUMA	Canadian Urethane Manufacturers Association		**CVG**	Corporación Venezolana de Guayana
			CVI	Centraal Veevoeder Instituut
CUMA	Coopérative d'Utilisation de Matériel Agricole		**CVJM**	Weltbund der Christlichen Vereine Junger Männer
CUMATEX	Associazione Nazionale Rappresentanti Commercianti Macchine e Accessori per l'Industria Tessile, Maglierie e per Cucire		**CVJR**	Centre de Voyages de la Jeunesse Rurale
			CVLB	Christelijke Veenkoloniale Landbouwbond

CVM	Controlestation voor Melkproducten
CVM	Corporación Autónima Regional de los Valles de Magdalena y Sinú (Colombia)
CVMA	Canadian Veterinary Medical Association
CVNW	Centrale Vereniging van Nederlandse Wijnhandelaren
CVP	Christelijk Volkspartij (Belgium)
CVP	Corporación Venezolana del Petróleo
CVPCEE	Comité des Ventes Publiques de Cuirs et Peaux Verts des Pays de la CEE
CVRS	Centre Voltaique de la Recherche Scientifique (Haute-Volta)
CVSM	Central-Verband Schweizerischer Mobeltransporteurs
CVT	Centrale Vakgroep Tuinbouw van de Belgische Boerenbond
CVT	Committee on Vacuum Techniques (U.S.A.)
CVTM	Compagnie Voltaïque pour la Transformation des Métaux
CVV	Coöperatieve Veeafzetvereniging v. Noord- en Zuid-Holland
CVV	Coöperatieve Venlose Veiling Vereniging
CWA	Country Women's Association (Australia)
CWAEC	County War Agricultural Executive Committee
CWB	Canadian Wheat Board
CWB	Commonwealth Writers of Britain
CWC	Canadian Welfare Council
CWC	Catering Wages Commission
CWC	Ceylon Workers Congress
CWC	Comenius World Council (U.S.A.)
CWC	Commonwealth of World Citizens
CWCC	Childrens World Community Chest
CWDC	Canadian Wood Development Council
CWDE	Centre for World Development Education
CWDWD	Committee for World Development and World Disarmament (U.S.A.)
CWE	Co-operative Wholesale Establishment (Sri Lanka *etc.*)
CWF	Commonwealth Weightlifting Federation
CWGC	Commonwealth War Graves Commission
CWINC	Central Waterways, Irrigation and Navigation Commission (India)
CWINRS	Central Waterpower, Irrigation and Navigation Research Station (India)
CWL	Catholic Women's League

CWM	Caribbean Workers' Movement
CWM	Council for World Mission
CWME	Commission on World Mission and Evangelism of the World Council of Churches
CWOIH	Conference of World Organisations Interested in the Handicapped
CWP	Coordinating Working Party on Atlantic Fishery Statistics (FAO)
CWPC	Central Water and Power Commission (India)
CWPRS	Central Water and Power Research Station (India)
CWRA	Canadian Water Resources Association
CWRL	Citrus Wastage Research Laboratory (Australia)
CWS	Church World Service (U.S.A.)
CWS	Co-operative Wholesale Society
CWU	Chemical Workers' Union
CWU	Church Women United
CWU	Congress of World Unity (U.S.A.)
CWWA	Coloured Workers Welfare Association
CWY	Canada World Youth
CYAC	Commonwealth Youth Affairs Council
CYATCA	Cyprus Air Traffic Controllers Association
CYEC	Commonwealth Youth Exchange
CYM	Commonwealth Youth Movement
CYSA	Community Youth Service Association
CYTA	Cyprus Telecommunications Authority
CZC	Centrale Zuivelcommissie
CZL	Contrôlestation voor Zuivelproducten
CZPA	Comisia de Zonare a Produselor Agricole (Roumania)

D

DA	Dansk Agronomforening
DA	Directio Administrativa (Roumania)
DAAD	Deutscher Akademischer Austauschdienst
DAAE	Dansk Andels Aegexport
DAC	Development Assistance Committee (*of* OECD)

DACA	Institute for the Development of Agricultural Cooperation in Asia (Japan)	**DAMDA**	Dairy Appliance Manufacturers and Distributors Association
DAD	Department Administratiewe Dienste (South Africa)	**DANA**	Andelsslagteriernes Konserveseksport
DADA	Designers and Art Directors Association	**DANATOM**	Danish Association for Industrial Development of Atomic Energy
DADJ	Den Almindelige Danske Jordemoderforening	**DANBIF**	Danske Boghandleres Importørforening
DAEP	Directorate of Aircraft Equipment Production	**DANE**	Departamento Administrativo Nacional de Estadística (Colombia)
DAEP	Division of Atomic Energy Production	**DANFIP**	Dansk Føderation for Informationbehandling og Virksomhedsstyring
DAER	Departmento Autônomo de Estradas do Rodagem (Brazil)	**DANHORS**	Danish Farmers Export Union
DAF	Danmarks Automobil-Forhandler-Forening	**DANIDA**	Danish International Development Agency
DAF	Dansk Annoncør-Forening	**DANPATA-TAS**	Danske Kartoffelavleres og Kartoffeleksportørers Faellesorganisation
DAF	Dansk Arbejdsgiverforening	**DANR**	Department of Agriculture and Natural Resources (Philippines)
DAFECO	Direction des Affaires Extérieures et de la Coopération d'Électricité de France	**DANRIC**	Department of Agriculture and Natural Resources Information Council (Philippines)
DaFFO	Dansk Forening til Fremme af Opfindelser	**DAP**	Servicio de Divulgación Agrícola de Panamá
DAFS	Department of Agriculture and Fisheries for Scotland	**DAPD**	Directorate of Aircraft Production Development
DAG	Deutsche Angestellten Gewerkschaft	**DAPIS**	Danish Agricultural Products Information Service
DAG	Development Assistance Group (U.S.A. etc.)	**DAR**	Daughters of the American Revolution
DAGA	Deutsche Arbeitsgemeinschaft für Akustik	**DARA**	Deutsche Arbeitsgemeinschaft für Rechenanlagen
DAGK	Deutschen Arbeitsgemeinschaft Kybernetic	**DAS**	Dansk Akustisk Selskab
DAGV	Deutsche Arbeitsgemeinschaft Vakuum	**DAS**	Dansk Anaesthesiologisk Selskab
DAGV	Deutscher Automaten-Grosshandels-Verband	**DAS**	Den Danske Arktiske Station
DAH	Danmarks Aktive Handelsrejsende	**DASA**	Defense Atomic Support Agency (U.S.A.)
DAHOTEX	Société Dahomey-Texas du Pétrole	**DASA**	Dental Association of South Africa
DAI	Deutscher Architekten- und Ingenieur-Verband	**DASC**	Department of Agriculture, Southern Cameroons
DAIS	District Agricultural Improvement Stations (China)	**DASIAC**	Defense Atomic Support Agency Information and Analysis Centre (U.S.A.)
DAK	Deutsche Atomkommission Geschaftsfuhrung (*of* BMWF)	**DASP**	Departmento Administrativo do Servico Público (Brazil)
DAKOFO	Danske Korn-Og-Foderstof-Im-Og Eksportorers Faellesorganisation	**DASUCH**	Department of Social Action, University of Chile
DAKS	Danske Automobil Komponentfabrikkers Sammenslutning	**DATA**	Derivation and Tabulation Associates (U.S.A.)
DAL	Danske Arkitekters Landforbund	**DATA**	Draughtmen's and Allied Technicians Associations (U.K.) (*now* AUEW)
DAL	Deutscher Arbeitsring für Lärmebekämpfung		
DALA	Departmento de Asuntos Latinoamericanos (Cuba)	**DATAR**	Délégation à l'Aménagement du Territoire et à l'Action Régionale
DALIA	Distribuidora Argentina Libro Ibero-Americano	**DAtF**	Deutsches Atomforum
DALPA	Danish Air Line Pilots Association		

DATO	Discover America Travel Organisation (U.S.A.)	DCRA	Dyers and Cleaners Research Association
		DCRO	Dyers and Cleaners Research Organization
DATUM	Dokumentions und Ausbildungszentrum für Theorie und Methode der Regionalforschung	DCSM	Danish Council for Scientific Management
		DD	Data for Development International Association
DAV	Deutscher Alpenverein		
DAV	Deutscher Altphilologenverband	DDA	Dominion Department of Agriculture (Canada)
DAV	Deutscher Anwaltverein		
DAV	Deutscher Apotheker-Verein	DDB	Deutscher Dolmetscherbund
DAW	Deutsche Akademie der Wissenschaften zu Berlin	DDBF	Den Dansk Bagerstands Foellesorganisation
		DDC	Diamond Distributors Centrafrique
DAW	Deutscher Arbeitskreis Wasserforschung	DDC	U.S. Defense Documentation Centre
DB	Danmarks Biblioteksforening	DdD	Den Danske Dyrlægeforening
DB	Dansk Blomsterhandlerforening	DDF	Dental Documentary Foundation (Belgium)
DBB	Deutscher Beamtenbund	DDG	Deutsche Dendrologische Gesellschaft
DBD	Democratic Peasant's Party of Germany	DDG	Deutsche Dermatologische Gesellschaft
DBE	Development Bank of Ethiopia	DDGSR	Division of the Director-General of Scientific Research
DBF	Den Danske Boghandlerforening		
DBfk	Deutscher Berufsverband für Krankenpflege	DDR	Deutsche Demokratische Republik
DBI	Landsforening Dansk Betonvare-Industri	DDS	Dansk Dermatologisk Selskab
DBIU	Dominion Board of Insurance Underwriters (Canada)	DE	Dansk Erhvervsfrugtavl
		DEA	Department of Economic Affairs
DBIV	Deutsche Braunkohlen-Industrieverein	DEAIC	Dirección de Educación Artesanal, Industrial y Comercial (Venezuela)
DBR	Division of Building Research (Canada)		
DBS	Deutsche Berufsverband der Sozialarbeiter und Sozialpädagogen	DEBEG	Deutsche Betriebsgesellschaft für Dratlose Telegraphie
DBV	Deutscher Bäderverband	DEBRIV	Deutscher Braunkohlen-Industrie-Verein
DBV	Deutscher Bauernverband	DEC	Dollar Exports Council
DBV	Deutscher Betonverein	DECAT	Departamento de Conservación y Asistencia Técnica del Ministerio de Agricultura (Chile)
DBV	Deutscher Bibliotheksverband		
DBV	Deutsche Binnentankreedervereinigung	DECEE	Dirección de Estadística, Catastro y Estudios Económicos (Peru)
DBV	Deutscher Büchereiverband		
DCB	Decimal Currency Board	DECHEMA	Deutsche Gesellschaft für Chemisches Apparatewesen
DCCC	Domestic Coal Consumers' Council	DECP	Division de la Coordination Économique et du Plan (Morocco)
DCF	Fédération Nationale des Directeurs Commerciaux de France		
DCG	Democracia Cristiana Guatemalteca	DECSA	Departmento de Conservación de Suelos y Agua (Chile)
DChIV	Deutscher Chemie-Ingenieur-Verband	DEF	Danske Elvaerkers Forening
DCI	Directorate of Chemical Inspection	DEF	Directia Economiei Forestiere (Roumania)
DCIOO	Import Opportunities Office for Developing Countries	DEG	Danske Erhvervsgartnerforening
		DEG	Deutsche Entomologische Gesellschaft
DCIS	Delaware Country Institute of Science (U.S.A.)	DEG	Deutsche Exlibris-Gesellschaft
		DEG	Direction des Études Générales (Morocco)
DCL	Distillers Co., Ltd	DEGEBO	Deutsche Forschungsgesellschaft für Bodenmechanik
DCPE	Dominion Council of Professional Engineers (Canada)		

DEGUSSA	Deutsche Gold- und Silber Scheideanstalt
DEH	Danske Ejendomshandlerforening
DEHOGA	Deutscher Hotel- und Gaststättenverband
DEHR	Direction de l'Hydraulique et de l'Équipement Rural (Algeria)
DEIP	Division de Exploraciones e Introducción de Plantas (Argentina)
DELCO	Sierra Leone Development Company
DELIMCO	German Liberian Mining Company
DEMBA	Demarara Bauxite Company (Guyana)
DEMKO	Dansk Elektrische Materialkontrol
DEMYC	Democratic Youth Community (Germany)
DENACAL	Departamento Nacional de Acueductos y Alacantarillados (Nicaragua)
DENAGEO	Departamento Nacional de Geología (Bolivia)
DEP	Département Fédéral de l'Économie Publique (Switzerland)
DEP	Department of Employment and Productivity
DEPCA	International Study Group for the Detection and Prevention of Cancer
DEPO	Nederlandse Vereniging van Detailhandelaren in Pootaardappelen
DEPP	Société Dahoméenne d'Antreposage de Produits Pétroliers
DER	Deutscher Erfinderring
DERE	Dounreay Experimental Reactor Establishment (Scotland)
DEREL-VANS	Département d'Enseignement et de Recherche Langues Vivantes aux Non-Spécialistes
DERL	Defence Electronics Research Laboratory, Hyderabad (India)
DES	Department of Education and Science
DESAL	Centro para el Desarrollo Económico y Social de América Latina, Santiago (Chile)
DESIDOC	Defence Scientific Information and Documentation Centre (India)
DETA	Divisão de Exploração dos Transportes Aéreos (Mozambique)
DETEX	Stichting Detailhandel in Textielgoederen
DETI	Drents Economisch Technologisch Instituut
DEUA	Diesel Engine Users' Association
DEULA	Deutsche Landmaschinenschulen
DEV	Deutscher Erfinderverband
DEV	Directia Economiei Vînatului (Roumania)
DEVCO	Committee for Standardisation in the Developing Countries (of ISO)
DEZAPA	Algemene Nederlandse Bond van Detailhandelaren in Zaden en Aanverwante Artikelen
DF	Danske Fysioterapeuter
DF	Landsforeningen Dansk Frugtavl
DFBO	Deutsche Forschungsgesellschaft für Blechverarbeitung und Oberflächenbehandlung
DFCK	Development Finance Company of Kenya Ltd
DFCU	Development Finance Co. of Uganda
DFD	Democratic Women's Federation of Germany
DFD	Département Fédéral des Finances et des Douanes (Switzerland)
DFDS	Det Forenede Dampskibs-Selskab
DFF	Dansk Fotografisk Forening
DFF	Den Danske Forlaeggerforening
DFG	Deutschen Forschungsgemeinschaft
DFH	Danmarks Farmaceutiske Højskole
DFGH	Danske Fotogrossisters Handelsforening
DFIK	Dansk Forening for Industriel Kvalitetskontrol
DFK	Dansk Flaskegas Komité
DFK	Dansk Forening for Kvalitetsstyring
DFL	Deutsche Forschungsanstalt für Luftfahrt
DFOM	Départements Français d'Outre-Mer
DFR	Deutscher Fernschulrat
DFR	Diplomerade Företagsekonomers Rijksförbund
DFRA	Drop Forging Research Association
DFRC	Distillers Feed Research Council (U.S.A.)
DFV	Deutsche Feuerwehrverband
DFV	Deutscher Fischereiverband
DFVLR	Deutsche Forschungs- und Versuchsanstalt für Luft- und Raumfahrt
DFWR	Deutscher Forstwirtschaftsrat
DG	Deutsche Gesellschaft für Galvanotechnik
DGA	Deutsche Gesellschaft für Anaesthesia
DGA	Direction Générale de l'Agriculture
DGA	Durum Growers Association of the United States
DGAA	Dirección General de Asuntos Agrarios (Guatemala)

DGAB	Direction de la Gestion Administrative et du Budget (UNDP)	**DGFP**	Dirección General de Fomento Pecuario (Ecuador)
DGAE	Deutsche Gesellschaft für Angewandte Entomologie	**DGFPS**	Deutsche Gesellschaft für Psychologie
		DGfZ	Deutsche Gesellschaft für Züchtungskunde
DGAO	Deutsche Gesellschaft für Angewandt Optik	**DGG**	Deutsche Gartenbau-Gesellschaft
DGAP	Deutsche Gesellschaft für Auswärtige Politik	**DGG**	Deutsche Geologische Gesellschaft
DGAW	Deutsche Gesellschaft für Anästhesie und Wiederbelebung	**DGG**	Deutsche Glastechniche Gesellschaft
		DGG	Dirección General de Ganadería (Salvador)
DGB	Deutsche Gesellschaft für Betriebswirtschaft	**DGGM**	Dirección General de Geografica y Meteorología (Mexico)
DGB	Deutscher Gewerkschaftbund		
DGBAS	Directorate General of Budgets, Accounts and Statistics (Formosa)	**DGGR**	Direction Générale du Génie et de l'Hydraulique Agricole
DGBW	Deutsche Gesellschaft für Bewasserungswirtschaft	**DGGTOT**	Directia Generala Geo-Topografica si de Organizare a Teritoriului (Roumania)
DGD	Deutsche Gesellschaft für Dokumentation	**DGH**	Deutscher Grosshändlerverband für Heizungs-, Lüftungs- und Klimadedarf
DGE	Deutsche Gesellschaft Endokrinologie		
DGE	Deutsche Gesellschaft für Ernährung	**DGHM**	Deutsche Gesellschaft für Hygiene und Mikrobiologie
DGE	Directia Generala de Exploatare		
DGEA	Dirección General de Extensión Agropecuaria (Ecuador)	**DGIA**	Dirección General de Investigaciones Agrícolas (Salvador)
DGEC	Dirección General de Estadistica y Censos (Nicaragua)	**DGIEA**	Dirección General de Investigación y Extensión Agrícola (Guatemala)
DGEF	Direction Générale des Eaux et Forêts	**DGIFLC**	Directia Generala de Imbunatatiri Funciare si Constructii Agricole (Roumania)
DGEG	Deutsche Gesellschaft für Erd- und Grundbau		
		DGK	Deutsche Geodätische Kommission
DGemG	Deutsche Gemmologische Gesellschaft	**DGK**	Deutsche Gesellschaft für Kybernetik
DGF	Dansk Geologisk Forening	**DGLR**	Deutsche Gesellschaft f. Luft- und Raumfahrt
DGF	Deutsche Gesellschaft für Fettwissenschaft	**DGLRM**	Deutsche Gesellschaft für Luft- und Raumfahrtmedizin
DGF	Deutsche Gesellschaft für Flugwissenschaften		
		DGM	Deutsche Gesellschaft für Metallkunde
DGfA	Deutsche Gesellschaft für Amerikastudien	**DGMA**	German Society for Measuring Technique and Automation
DGfA	Deutsche Gesellschaft für Arbeitschutze		
DGFA	Dirección General de Fomento Agrícola (Argentine)	**DGMK**	Deutsche Gesellschaft für Mineralölwissenschaft und Kohlechemie
DGfB	Deutsche Gesellschaft für Betriebswirtschaft	**DGMKG**	Deutsche Gesellschaft für Mund-, Kiefer- und Gesichtschirurgie
DGfBUl	Deutsche Gesellschaft für Bluttransfusion und Immunohaematologie	**DGMS**	Deutsche Gesellschaft für Medizinische Soziologie
DGfdB	Deutsche Gesellschaft für das Badewesen	**DGMU**	Dirección General de Meteorología del Uruguay
DGfH	Deutsche Gesellschaft für Hochschulkunde		
DGFH	Deutsche Gesellschaft für Holzforschung	**DGN**	Dirección General de Normas (Mexico)
DGfH	Deutsche Gesellschaft für Hopfenforschung	**DGN**	Direccion de Geológia de la Nación (Argentina)
DGFI	Deutsches Geodätisches Forschungsinstitut		
DGFK	Deutsche Gesellschaft für Friedens- und Konfliktforschung	**DGON**	Deutsche Gesellschaft für Ortung und Navigation
DGfK	Deutsche Gesellschaft für Kartographie	**DGOR**	Deutsche Gesellschaft für Operations Research
DGFP	Deutsche Gesellschaft für Personalführung		

DGOT	Deutsche Gesellschaft für Orthopädie und Traumatologie
DGP	Deutsche Gesellschaft für Parasitologie
DGP	Deutsche Gesellschaft für Parodontologie
DGP	Deutsche Gesellschaft für Photogrammetrie
DGPA	Dirección General de Planificación y Administración (Panama)
DGPA	Directia Generala a Productiei Animale (Roumania)
DGPH	Deutsche Gesellschaft für Photographie
DGPM	Direction de la Géologie et de la Prospection Minière (Ivory Coast)
DGPN	Deutsche Gesellschaft für Psychiatrie und Nervenheilkunde
DGPPA	Dirección General de la Pequeña Propiedad Agrícola (Mexico)
DGPT	Deutsche Gesellschaft für Psychotherapie und Tiefenpsychologie
DGPV	Directia Generala a Productiei Vegetale (Roumania)
DGQ	Deutsche Gesellschaft für Qualität
DGR	Deutsche Gesellschaft für Rehabilitation
DGRA	Dirección General de Reforma Agraria (Panama)
DGRH	Dirección General de Recursos Hidráulicos (Ecuador)
DGRN	Dirección General de Recursos Naturales (Honduras)
DGRR	Deutsche Gesellschaft für Raketentechnik und Raumfahrt
DGRST	Délégation Générale à la Recherche Scientifique et Technique
DGRV	Deutscher Genossenschafts- und Raiffeisenverband
DGS	Directia Generala Silvica (Roumania)
DGS	Deutsche Gesellschaft für Sozialmedizin
DGSF	Deutsche Gesellschaft für Sexualforschung
DGSMT	Directio Generala a Statiunilor de Masini si Tractoare (Roumania)
DGSNM	Dirección General del Servicio Nacional Meteorológico (Argentina)
DGSP	Deutsche Gesellschaft für Soziale Psychiatrie in der Bundesrepublik Deutschland
DGSV	Dirección General de Sanidad Vegetal (Mexico)
DGTS	Directio Generala Tehnica Stiintifica (Roumania)
DGU	Deutsche Gesellschaft für Unternehmensforschung
DGV	Deutscher Genossenschaftsverband
DGV	Deutscher Germanistenverband
DGV	Deutscher Giessereiverband
DGV	Deutsche Gesellschaft für Völkerkunde
DGV	Deutsche Gesellschaft für Volkskunde
DGV	Deutsche Graphologische Vereinigung
DGVN	Deutsche Gesellschaft für die Vereinten Nationen
DGZMK	Deutsche Gesellschaft für Zahn-, Mund- und Kieferheilkunde
DGZFP	Deutsche Gesellschaft für Zerstörungsfreie Prüfverfahren
DH	Deutsche Heilpraktikerschaft
D & HAA	Dock and Harbour Authorities Association
DHEW	Departments of Health, Education and Welfare (U.S.A.)
DHG	Deutsche Hämophiliegesellschaft
DHG	Dungekalk- Hauptgemeinschaft
DHI	Decennie Hydrologique Internationale
DHI	Deutsches Hydrographisches Institut
DHIA	Dairy Herd Improvement Association (U.S.A.)
DHMV	Deutscher Holzmastenverband
DHR	International Commission for the Hydrology of the River Rhine Basin
DHSS	Department of Health and Social Security
DHV	Deutscher Handels- und Industrieangestelltenverband
DHV	Deutscher Hugenottenverein
DIA	Danske Interieur Arkitekter
DIA	Departmento de Investigación Agropecuaria (Colombia)
DIA	Design and Industries Association
DIAA	Direction des Industries Agricoles et Alimentaires
DIAL	Danske Indendørs Arkitekters Landsforbund
DIB	Deutsches Institut für Betriebswirtschaft
DIBEVO	Landelijke Organisatie Dibevo
DICE	Dairy and Ice Cream Equipment Association
DICORE	División de Conservación de Recursos (Chile)
DICSA	División de Investigacion de Conservación de Suelos y Aguas (Porto Rico)

DID	Drainage and Irrigation Department (Malaysia)	DIZ	Deutsches Institut für Zeitgeschichte
DID	Verband Deutscher Industrie-Designer	DJP	Département Fédéral de Justice et Police (Switzerland)
DIDA	Dirección de Inspección y Defensa Agraria (Peru)	DJT	Deutscher Juristentag
DIDEFA	División de Defensa Agropecuaria (Chile)	DJV	Deutsche Journalistenverband
DIE	Danish Institute for the International Exchange of Scientific and Literary Publications	DKB	Deutscher Konditorenbund
		DKF	Dansk Kiropraktorforening
		DKF	Danske Konsummoelkmejeriers Foellesreproesentation
DIEESE	Departamento Intersindical de Estatısticas e Estudos Sócio-Econõmicos (Brazil)	DKG	Deutsche Kautschukgesellschaft
DIELCI	Diffusion Électrique de la Côte-d'Ivoire	DKG	Deutsche Keramische Gesellschaft
DIF	Dansk Ingeniørforening	DKG	Deutsche Krankenhausgesellschaft
DIF	Deutsches Institut zur Förderung des Industriellen Führungsnachwuches	DKI	Deutsches Kunststoff Institut
		DKI	Deutsches Kupferinstitut
DIFCA	La Diffusion du Caoutchouc	DKM	Dansk Kulturhistorisk Museumsforening
DIFPOA	Divisão de Inspeção e Fiscalização de Produtos de Origem Animal (Brazil)	DK-U	Dansk Køreloerer-Union
		DKV	Deutscher Kaltetechnisher Verein
DIGAP	Direct Investigation Group Aerial Phenomena	DL	Deutscher Lehrerband
		DL	Foreningen af Danske Landskabsarkitekter
DIHT	Deutscher Industrie- und Handelstag	DLCO-EA	Desert Locust Control Organization for Eastern Africa
DIICA	Departamento Técnico Interamericano de Cooperación Agrícola (Chile)		
DILAPSA	Distribuidora Latinoamericana de Publicaciones (Chile)	DLF	Dagligvaruleverantörers Förbund
		DLF	Danmarks Loererforening
DILF	Danske Indkøbschefers Landsforening	DLF	Foreningen af Danske Lysreklame Fabrikanter
DIMES	Distribution de Matériel Électrique au Sénégal	DLF	Danske Landboforeningers Froforskning
DIMO	Danske Interne Medicineres Organisation	DLG	Deutsche Landwirtschafts-Gesellschaft
		DLH	Deutsche Lufthansa AG
DIN	Deutsche Industrie Norm	DLIS	Desert Locust Information Service (FAO)
DINFIA	Dirección Nacional de Fabricaciones e Investigaciones Aeronáuticas (Argentina)	DLV	Deutsche Lehrmittelverband
DIPAN	Directoria da Produçao Animal (Brazil)	DMB	Deutscher Museumsbund
DIPROA	División de Producción Agropecuaria (Chile)	DMDS	Deutsche Gesellschaft für Medizinische Dokumentation und Statistik
DIPUVEN	Distribuidora de Publicaciones Venezolanas	DME	Directorate of Mechanical Engineering
DIQUIVEN-JA	Distribuidora Química Venezolana	DMF	Danske Mineralbandsfabrikanters
		DMF	Dansk Møbeltransport Forening
DISCS	Domestic International Sales Corporations (U.S.A.)	DMG	Deutsche Mineralogische Gesellschaft
		DMG	Deutsche Morgenländische Gesellschaft
DISI	Dairy Industries Society International (U.S.A.)	DMG	Deutsche Mozart-Gesellschaft
		DMG	Foreningen af Danske Manufaktur-Grossiter
DISTRI-PRESS	Fédération Internationale des Distributeurs de Presse	DMI	Danske Meteorologiske Institut
DITB	Distributive Industry Training Board	DMIAA	Diamond Manufacturers and Importers Association of America
DIVENAZ	Distribuidora Venezolana de Azúcares		
DIW	Deutsches Institut für Wirtschaftforschung	DMN	Direction de la Météorologie Nationale

DMpF	Dansk Musikpoedagogisk Forening	**DNT**	Det Norske Travselskap
DMS	Danmarks Mejeritekniske Selskab	**DNTF**	De Norske Teatres Forening
DMS	Dansk Medicinsk Selskab	**DNV**	Deutscher Nautischer Verein
DMV	Deutsche Marketing Vereinigung	**DNV**	De Norske Veterinœrforening
DMV	Deutscher Markscheiderverein	**DOAT**	Direction des Opérations de l'Assistance Technique (*of* UN)
DMV	Deutscher Marmorverband		
DMV	Deutsche Mathematikervereinigung	**DOBETA**	Domestic Oil Burning Equipment Testing Association
DMV	Deutscher Musikverleger Verband		
DNA	Deutsche Normenausschuss	**DOC**	Dépôts Océan Congo
DNB	Dirección Nacional del Banano (Ecuador)	**DOCA**	Automatic Documentation Section (*of* CETIS)
DNB	Vereniging 'De Nederlandse Baksteen-industrie'	**DOCAPES-CA**	Grémio dos Armadores da Pesca de Arrasto
DNDR	Dirección Nacional de Desarrollo (Bolivia)		
DNER	National Department of Public Roads (Brazil)	**DOD**	Deutsches Ozeanographisches Datenzentrum
DNF	Den Norske Forsikringsforening	**DoE**	Department of the Environment
DNFB	De Norske Blikemballagefabrikers Forening	**DØF**	Danske Økonomers Forening
DNFF	Den Norske Fagpresses Forening	**DOF**	Dansk Ornithologisk Forening
DNGE	Dirección Nacional de Granos y Elevadores (Argentina)	**DOG**	Deutsche Ornithologen-Gesellschaft
		DOI	Department of Industry
DNH	Den Norske Husflidsforening	**DOMO**	Dispensing Opticians Manufacturing Organisation
DNH	Udgiverselskab for Danmarks Nyeste Historie		
DNIBR	Danish National Institute of Building Research	**DOP**	Direction des Opérations et de la Programmation (UNDP
		DORDEC	Domestic Refrigeration Development Committee
DNJ	Det Norske Justervesen		
DNL	Det Norske Luftartselkap	**DOREMA**	Société Européenne de Documentation, de Recherche et de Marketing
DNM	Det Norske Myrselskap		
DNO	Danske Nervelaegers Organisation	**DORS**	Danish Operations Research Society
DNOCS	Departamento Nacional de Obras contra as Sēcas (Brazil)	**DOS**	Dansk Oto-laryngologisk Selskab
		DOSCO	Dominion Steel and Coal Corporation (Canada)
DNOS	Departamento Nacional de Obras de Saneamento (Brazil)	**DOSME**	Direccion de Obra Social y Ministerio de Educacion (Argentine)
DNP	Departamento Nacional de Planeación (Colombia)		
		DOT	Department of Transport (Canada)
DNPM	Departamento Nacionál de Producaçao Mineral (Brazil)	**DOZ**	Deutsches Olympia Zentrum
		DP	Danske Psykologforening
DNPV	Departamento Nacional de Produçâo Vegetal (Brazil)	**DPA**	Deutsche Press Agentur
		DPAG	Dangerous Pathogens Advisory Group
DNPVN	Departamento Nacional de Portos e Vias Navegáveis (Brazil)	**DPC**	Defence Planning Committee (NATO)
		DPCP	Department of Prices and Consumer Protection
DNR	Deutsche Naturschutzring		
DNR	Den Norske Reisebyråforening	**DPEA**	Departamento de Pesquisa e Experimentaçao Agropecuarias (Brazil)
DNSE	Dirección Naciónal del Servicio Estadístico (Argentina)		
		DPF	Dansk Pilotforening
DNSL	De Norske Saltfisekspørters Landsforening	**DPF**	Départment Politique Fédéral (Switzerland)

DPF	Directia Plan Financiar (Roumania)	DRTE	Defence Research Telecommunications Establishment (Canada)
DPG	Deutsche Physikalische Gesellschaft	DRV	Deutscher Raiffeisenverband
DPG	Deutsche Physiologische Gesellschaft	DRV	Deutscher Reifenhändlerverband
DPhG	Deutsche Pharmakologische Gesellschaft	DRV	Deutscher Reisebüroverband
DPhV	Deutscher Philologen-Verband	DRWAW	Distillery, Rectifying, Wine and Allied Workers International Union of America
DPI	Department of Public Information (UNO)		
DPK	Deutsche Pappelkommission	DS	Danmarks Sprogloererforening
DPK	Deutsche Pudel-Klub	DS	Dansk Standardiseringsråd
DPMA	Data Processing Management Association	DSA	Direction des Services Agricoles
DPOM	Directia Planificarii si Organizarii Muncii (Roumania)	DSA	Duodecimal Society of America
		DSB	Dachverband der Schweizerischen Bekleidungsindustrie
DPP	Directia Propagandei si Presei (Roumania)	DSB	Deutscher Sauna-Bund
DPRG	Deutsche Public-Relations-Gesellschaft	DSB	Danish State Railways
DPRK	Dansk Public Relations Klub	DSB	Deutsche Schaustellerbund
DPRK	Democratic Peoples Republic of Korea	DSB	Drug Supervisory Body (Switzerland)
DPS	Dansk Pediatrisk Selskab	DSBy	Dansk Selskab for Bygningsstatik
DPS	Dansk Psykiatrisk Selskab	DSE	Deutsche Stiftung für Entwicklungsländer
DPV	Dansk Patent-og Varemaerkekonsulent-forening	DSF	Danske Salgslederes Foellesråd
		DSF	Dansk Skattevidenskabelig Forening
DPV	Deutsche Verein zur Erforschung Palästina-Verein	DSF	German-Soviet Friendship Society
		DSF	Dansk Fysiurgisk Selskab
DPWV	Deutscher Paritaetischer Wohlfahrts-verbande	DSF	Dansk Skibshandlerforening
		DSF	Dansk Socialrådgiverforening
DRB	Danske Reklamebureauers Brancheforening	DSI	Dairy Society International (U.S.A.)
DRB	Defence Research Board (Canada)	DSI	General Directorate of State Hydraulic Works (Turkey)
DRF	Dansk Rationaliserings Forening		
DRG	Deutsche Rheologische Gesellschaft	DSIM	Dansk Selskab for Intern Medicin
DRG	Deutsche Röntgengesellschaft—Gesellschaft für Medizinische Radiologie, Strahlenbiologie und Nuklearmedizin	DSIR	Department of Scientific and Industrial Research
		DSIS	Development Support Information Service (UN)
DRI	Denver Research Institute (U.S.A.)		
DRNR	Dirección de Recursos Naturales Renovables (Venezuela)	DSKV	Den Danske Sammenslutning af Konsulentev i Virksomhedsledelse
DRO	Danske Røntgendiagnostikeres Organisation	DSL	Danske Slagtermestres Landsforening
		DSO	Dansk Selskab for Optometri
DROGA	Schweizerischer Verband Angestellter Drogisten	DSOM	Dansk Selskab for Oldtids-og Middelalder-forskning
DRP	Development Resources Panel (UNDP)	DSP	Democratic Socialist Party (Japan)
DRPC	Defence Research Policy Committee	DSpÄB	Deutscher Sportärzebund
DRPLC	Département des Recherches des Plantations Lever au Congo	DSR	Dansk Sygeplejeråd
		DSRF	Dansk Salgs-og Reklameforbund
DRS	Dansk Radiologisk Selskab	DSSV	Deutschschweizerischer Sprachverein
DRTC	Documentation Research and Training Centre, Bangalore (India)	DST	Deutscher Städtetag

DStB	Deutscher Städtbund	**DVG**	Deutsche Volkswirtschaftliche Gesellschaft
DStG	Deutsche Statistische Gesellschaft	**DVGW**	Deutscher Verein van Gas- und Wasserfachmännern
DStGB	Deutscher Städte-und Gemeindebund	**DVKJ**	Deutsche Vereinigung für Kinder- und Jugendpsychiatrie
DSTO	Defence Sciences and Technology Organization (Australia)	**DVL**	Deutsche Versuchsanstalt für Luftfahrt
DSTS	Dansk Selskab for Teoretisk Statistik	**DVM**	Deutsche Verband für Materialprüfung
DSTV	Deutscher Stahlbauverband	**DVMF**	Dansk Vulkanisør- Mester-Forening
DSV	Direction des Services Vétérinaires	**DVMLG**	Deutsche Vereinigung für Mathematische Logik und Grundlagenforschung der Exakten Wissenschaften
DT	Deutsche Tierarzteschaft		
DTAT	Direction Technique des Armaments Terrestres	**DVOH**	Deutsche Verband für Oberflachenveredlung und Härtung
DTB	Danmarks Tekniske Bibliotek	**DVPW**	Deutsche Vereinigung für Politische Wissenschaft
DTC	Department of Technical Co-operation		
DTC	Départment des Transports et Communications et de l'Énergie (Switzerland)	**DVS**	Deutscher Verband für Schweisstechnik
		DVT	Deutscher Verband Technisch-Wissenschaftlicher Vereine
DTF	Domestic Textiles Federation	**DVTA**	Deutscher Verband Technischer Assistentinnen und Assistenten
DTF	Dairy Trade Federation		
DTH	Danmarks Tekniske Højskole	**DVTWV**	Deutscher Verband Technisch-Wissenschaftlicher Verbands
DTI	Dansk Textil Institut		
DTI	Department of Trade and Industry	**DVV**	Deutscher Verzinkerei Verband
DTICA	Departamento Tecnico Interamericano de Cooperación Agricola (Chile)	**DVW**	Deutscher Verein für Vermessungswesen
		DVWG	Deutsche Verkehrswissenschaftliche Gesellschaft
DTL	Dansk Teknisk Litteraturselskab		
DTL	Dansk Teknisk Loereforening	**DVWW**	Deutscher Verband für Wasserwirtschaft
DTO	Dansk Teknisk Oplysningstjeneste	**DWG**	Deutsche Weltwirt-schaftliche Gesellschaft
DTREO	Départment des Travaux, Recherches et Exploitation Océaniques	**DWG**	Deutsche Werbewissenschaftliche Gesellschaft
DTRI	Dairy Training and Research Institute (Philippines)	**DWK**	Deutsche Wissenschaftliche Kommission für Meersforschung
DTU	Dansk Textil Union		
DTV	Deutscher Transport- Versicherungs-Verband	**DWK**	Deutsches Woll-Komitee
		DWP	Verband Deutscher Werbefilmproduzenten
DUGG	Deutsche Union für Geodäsie und Geophysik	**DWT**	Deutsche Gesellschaft für Wehrtechnik
DUW	Dijksdienst voor de Uitvoering van Werken	**DWV**	Deutsche Waren-Vertriebsgesellschaft
DVA	Deutsche Versicherungs Akademie	**DWV**	Deutscher Wäscherei Verband
DVB	Deutscher Bäderverband		
DVB	Deutscher Buchereiverband	**DWV**	Deutscher Weinbauverband
DVC	Damodar Valley Corporation (India)	**DZB**	Development Bank of Zambia
DVFA	Deutsche Vereinigung für Finanzanalyse und Anlageberatung	**DZF**	Deutsche Zentrale für Fremdenverkehr
		DZG	Deutsche Zoologische Gesellschaft
DVFB	Deutscher Vieh- und Fleischhandelsbund	**DZK**	Deutsches Zentralkomitee zur Bekämpfung der Tuberkulose
DVFFA	Deutscher Verland Forstlicher Forschungsanstalten		
		DZL	Deutsche Zentralinstitut für Lehrmittel
DVfVW	Deutscher Verein für Versicherungswissenschaft	**DZT**	Deutsche Zentrale für Tourismus

DZVHA	Deutscher Zentralverein Homöopathischer Ärzte
DZW	Deutsche Dokumentations Zentrale Wasser

E

EA	Elektriska Arbetsgivareföreningen
EAA	East African Airways Corporation
EAA	Electrical Appliance Association
EAA	European Accounting Association
EAA	European Athletic Association
EAAA	European Association of Advertising Agencies
EAAC	East African Academy (Kenya)
EAAC	East African Airways Corporation
EAAC	European Agricultural Aviation Centre
EAAC	European Association of Audiophonological Centres (France)
EAACI	European Academy of Allergology and Clinical Immunology
EAAFRO	East African Agricultural and Forestry Research Organisation
EAAP	European Association of Animal Production (Italy)
EAAS	East Anglian Aviation Society
EABA	European Amateur Boxing Association
EAC	East African Community
EAC	Electro-Agricultural Centre, Kenilworth
EAC	Engineering Advisory Council
EAC	Études Agricoles par Correspondance
EAC	European Agency for Cooperation
EAC	European Banks Advisory Committee
EACA	European Association of Charter Airlines (Netherlands)
EACC	East Asia Christian Conference
EACC	European Association of Audiophonological Centres (France)
EACE	Euro-American Cultural Exchange
EACN	European Air Chemistry Network
EACR	European Association for Cancer Research
EACRP	European American Committee on Reactor Physics (of ENEA)

EACSO	East African Common Services Organisation
EADA	East African Dental Association
EADB	East African Development Bank
EADD	East African Development Division (of ODM)
EAE	Eastern Association of Electro-encephalographers (U.S.A.)
EAEC	East African Examinations Council
EAEC	East African Extract Corporation
EAEC	European Atomic Energy Community (Euratom)
EAEE	Evangelische Arbeitsgemeinschaft für Erwachsenenbildung in Europa
EAEG	European Association of Exploration Geophysicists
EAEM	Escola de Agronomica Eliseu Maciel (Brazil)
EAENF	Engineering and Allied Employers' National Federation (now EEF)
EAES	European Atomic Energy Society
EAF	Elektrokemiske Arbeidsgiverforening
EAF	Employment Agents' Federation of Great Britain
EAFFRO	East African Freshwater Fishery Research Organisation
EAFRO	East African Fisheries Research Organisation
EAG	Europäische Atomgemeinschaft (Belgium)
EAG	European-Atlantic Group
EAGGF	European Agricultural Guidance and Guarantee Fund
EAHC	East African High Commission
EAHRA	East African Railways and Harbours Administration
EAHTMA	Engineers' and Allied Hand Tool Makers' Association
EAHY	European Architectural Heritage Year
EAIMB	East Africa Industries Management Board
EAIMR	East African Institute for Medical Research (Tanzania)
EAIRB	East African Industrial Research Board
EAIRO	East African Industrial Research Organization
EAK	Cyprus Farmers Union
EALA	East African Library Association
EALB	East African Literature Bureau (Tanzania)

EALRC	East African Leprosy Research Centre (Uganda)	**EARDHE**	European Association for Research and Development in Higher Education
EALS	East African Literature Service	**EARI**	Engineer Agency for Resources Inventories (U.S.A.)
EAMA	États Africains et Malgache Associés		
EAMC	European Airlines Montparnasse Committee	**EARIC**	East African Research Information Centre
EAMD	East African Meteorological Department	**EAROPH**	Eastern Regional Organisation for Planning and Housing (India)
EAMDA	European Alliance of Muscular Dystrophy Associations	**EARS**	Eldoret Agricultural Research Station (Kenya)
EAMF	European Association of Music Festivals	**EAS**	Europese Associaties voor Samenwerking
EAMFRO	East African Marine Fisheries Research Organisation	**EASA**	Engineers Association of South Africa
EAMFS	European Association for Maxillo-Facial Surgery	**EASB**	East African Settlement Board
		EASD	European Association for the Study of Diabetes
EAMRC	East African Medical Research Council (Tanzania)	**EASE**	European Association for Special Education (Sweden)
EAMTC	European Association of Management Training Centres (*now* EFMD)	**EASHP**	European Association of Senior Hospital Physicians
EAMU	East African Malaria Unit	**EASL**	East African School of Librarianship
EAMVBD	East African Institute of Malaria and Vector-Borne Diseases (Tanzania)	**EASL**	European Association for the Study of the Liver (Germany)
EAN	Engineering Association of Nashville (U.S.A.)	**EASS**	Editura Agro-Silvica de Stat (Roumania)
EANA	European Alliance of News Agencies	**EAT**	Entreprise Africaine de Travaux
EANDC	European American Nuclear Data Committee (*of* ENEA)	**EAT**	Europäische Association für Thermographie
EANHS	East African National Health Service	**EATA**	East Asia Travel Association
EANHS	East Africa Natural History Society	**EATCS**	European Association for Theoretical Computer Science
EANRRC	East African National Resources Research Council (Kenya)	**EATEC**	East African Tanning Extract Company
EAO	Egyptian Agricultural Organization	**EATIC**	Corporation East African Tuberculosis Investigation Centre (Kenya)
EAPA	European Asphalt Pavement Association		
EAPAC	Eggs Authority Producer Advisory Committee	**EATITU**	East African Tractor and Implement Testing Unit
EAPCO	East African Pesticides Control Organization	**EATJP**	European Association for the Trade in Jute Products
EAPH	East Africa Publishing House (Kenya)		
EAPM	European Association for Personnel Management	**EATP**	European Association for Textile Polyolefins
EAPR	European Association for Potato Research (Netherlands)	**EATPHHSA**	European Association of Training Programmes in Hospital and Health Service Administration
EAPT	East African Posts and Telecommunications	**EATRO**	East African Trypanosomiasis Research Organisation
EAR	European Association of Radiology		
EARAC	East Anglian Regional Advisory Council	**EATU**	Eastern African Telecommunications Union
EARB	European Airlines Research Bureau (*now* AEA)	**EAVRI**	East African Virus Research Institute (Uganda)
EARCCUS	East African Regional Committee for the Conservation and Utilisation of the Soil	**EAVRO**	East African Veterinary Research Organisation

AWAG	Eidgenössischen Anstalt für Wasserversorgung, Abwasserreinigung und Gewässerschutz (Switzerland)
BA	English Bowling Association
BAD	École des Bibliothécaires, Archivistes et Documentalistes (Senegal)
BAE	European Bureau of Adult Education
BBA	English Basket Ball Association
BBS	European Brain and Behaviour Society
BC	European Bibliographical Centre—Clio Press
BC	European Billiards Confederation
BC	European Brewery Convention
BES	Sociétés Réunies d'Énergie du Bassin de l'Escaut (Belgium)
BF	European Baptist Federation
BIAMS	Executive Board of the International Association of Microbiological Societies
BIC	EFTA Brewing Industry Council
BIC	European Banks International Company (Belgium)
BL	European Bridge League
BM	Estación de Biologia Marina (Chile)
BM	Wirtschaftsverband Eisen, Blech und Metall-Verarbeitende
BNI	Electricity Board for Northern Ireland
B & RA	Engineer Buyers' and Representatives' Association
BSA	Estuarine and Brackish-Water Sciences Association (U.S.A.)
BU	European Boxing Union
BU	English Bridge Union
BU	European Broadcasting Union (Switzerland)
BYC	European Bureau for Youth and Childhood
CA	Economic Commission for Africa (UN)
CA	Economic Co-operation Administration (*later* MSA) (U.S.A.)
CA	Educational Centres Association
CA	Electrical Contractors Association
CA	Entreprise de Centre Afrique (Haute-Volta)
CA	Empresa de Comercio Agrícola de Chile
CA	Europe China Association
CA	European Camac Association
CA	European Confederation of Agriculture (*formerly* ICA) (Switzerland)
CA	European Congress of Accountants
ECAC	European Civil Aviation Conference
ECAFE	Economic Commission for Asia and the Far East (Thailand) (*now* ESCAP)
ECAM	Employers Consultative Association of Malawi
ECAM	Enseignement Catholique au Maroc (Morocco)
ECARBICA	East and Central African Regional Branch of the International Council on Archives
ECAS	Electrical Contractors' Association of Scotland
ECAT	École Coloniale d'Agriculture de Tunis
ECAT	Emergency Committee for American Trade
ECB	European Coordination Bureau for International Youth Organisations
ECBA	European Community Biologists Association
ECBIYO	European Coordination Bureau for International Youth Organizations
ECBO	European Cell Biology Organisation
ECC	English Ceramic Circle
ECC	European Cultural Centre (Switzerland)
ECCA	East Caribbean Currency Authority
ECCA	European Coil Coating Association
ECCASA	Empresa de Curtidos Centro Americana, S.A.
ECCC	Ecology Centre Communications Council (U.S.A.)
ECCLA	European Committee for Cooperation with Latin America
ECCM	Eastern Caribbean Common Market
ECCP	European Committee on Crime Problems
ECCS	European Union of Christian-Democratic and Conservative Students
ECCU	English Cross Country Union
ECE	Economic Commission for Europe
ECE	Export Council for Europe
ECEA	Economic Community of Eastern Africa
ECEM	Études et Construction Électro-Mécaniques et Médicales
ECEPLAN	Escritório Central de Planejamento e Contrôle (Brasil)
ECF	Eastern Counties Farmers
ECF	European Commission on Forestry and Forest Products (*of* FAO)
ECFA	European Committee for Future Activities

ECFCI	European Centre of Federations of the Chemical Industry		**ECMWF**	European Centre for Medium-Range Weather Forecasting
ECFFP	European Commission on Forestry and Forest Products		**ECNR**	European Council for Nuclear Research
ECFI	East Caribbean Farm Institute		**ECO**	European Coal Organisation (UNO)
ECFMS	Educational Council for Foreign Medical Students		**ECOCEN**	Economic Cooperation Centre for the Asian and Pacific Region (Thailand)
ECFTU	European Confederation of Free Trade Unions in the Community		**ECOLOS**	Ecological Coalition on the Law of the Sea
ECGC	Empire Cotton Growing Corporation (U.K.) (*now CRC*)		**ECOM**	Centro de Computadoras del Gobierno de Chile
ECGD	Export Credits Guarantee Department		**ECOP**	Extension Committee on Organisation and Policy (U.S.A.)
ECICW	European Centre of the International Council of Women		**ECOPEMAR**	Empresa Conservera de Pescados y Mariscos (Cuba)
ECIS	European Community Information Service		**ECO-PETROL**	Empresa Colombiana de Petróleos (Colombia)
ECITO	European Central Inland Transport Organisation.		**ECOR**	Engineering Committee on Oceanic Resources
ECITS	Ente Conzorziale Interprovinciale Toscano Sementi		**ECOROPA**	European Ecology Group
ECIWA	European Committee of Importers and Wholesaler Grocers Associations		**ECOSAL**	Equipo de Conferencias Sindicales de América Latina
ECJCS	European Council of Jewish Community Services		**ECOSEC**	European Cooperation Space Environment Committee
ECLA	Economic Commission for Latin America (U.N.)		**ECOSOC**	Economic and Social Council of the United Nations
ECLE	European Centre for Leisure and Education		**ECOSOC for OAS**	Economic and Social Council for the Organization of American States
ECLF	Centre Européen pour Loisir et l'Éducation		**ECOTAL**	Equipo de Conferencias de Trabajadores de America Latina
ECLM	Economic Community for Livestock and Meat (Africa)		**ECOWAS**	Economic Community of West African States
ECLOF	Ecumenical Church Loan Fund		**ECP**	European Confederation for Plant Protection Research
ECMA	European Carton Makers Association		**ECPA**	Expert Committee on Post Adjustments (UNO)
ECMA	European Computer Manufacturers Association		**ECPC**	Enlarged Committee for Programme and Coordination (UNDP)
ECMBR	European Committee on Milk-Butterfat Recording		**ECPD**	Engineers' Council for Professional Development, (U.S.A.)
ECMC	Electric Cable Makers Confederation		**ECPE**	European Centre for Public Enterprises
ECMC	European Container Manufacturers' Committee		**ECPR**	European Consortium for Political Research
ECME	Economic Commission for the Middle East (UNO).		**ECPS**	English Connemara Pony Society
ECMF	Electric Cable Makers' Federation		**ECRIB**	European Commissary Resale Items Board
ECMMR	European College of Marketing and Marketing Research (U.K.)		**ECRL**	Eastern Caribbean Regional Library
ECMRA	European Chemical Marketing Research Association		**ECRO**	European Chemoreception Research Organization
ECMT	European Conference of Ministers of Transport		**ECSA**	European Computing Services Association
			ECSC	European Coal and Steel Community

ECSIM	European Centre of Study and Information on Multinational Corporations
ECSWTR	European Centre for Social Welfare Training and Research (Austria)
ECTA	Eastern Caribbean Tourist Association (Antigua)
ECTA	Electrical Contractors' Trading Association
ECTCI	Entreprise Commerciale et de Transports en Côte d'Ivoire
ECU	European Chiropractors Union
ECU	European Credit Union
ECUSAT	Ecumenical Satellite Commission
ECWA	Economic Commission for Western Asia (of UN)
ECWA	Economic Community of West Africa
EDA	British Electrical Development Association (sometimes abbreviated BEDA)
EDA	Educational Development Association
EDA	English Draughts Association
EDA	Essential Oil Association of the United States
EDA	European Demolition Association
EDA	European Disposables Association
EDAC	Electronics Development Analysis Centre (Korea)
EDANA	European Disposables and Nonwovens Association
EDB	Economic Development Board (Singapore)
EDC	Economic Development Committee (of NEDC)
EDCC	Environmental Dispute Coordination Commission (Japan)
EDCCI	Economic Development Committee for the Chemical Industry
EDE	Etablissements d'Utilité Agricole d'Élevage
EDEKA	Purchasing Cooperative of German Merchants
EDF	Economic Development Foundation (Philippines)
EDF	Électricité de France. Direction Générale
EDF	European Development Fund
EDHASA	Editora y Distribuidora Hispano Americana S.A.
EDI	Economic Development Institute (Nigeria)
EDI	Entraide pour le Développement Intégral
EDICA	Egyptian Documentation and Information Centre for Agriculture

EDITEAST	Association of Editors in the South-East Asian Region (Indonesia)
EDITERRA	European Association of Earth Science Editors
EDM	Société Énergie du Mali
EDMA	European Direct Marketing Association
EDPAA	International EDP Auditors Association (U.S.A.)
EDRA	Environmental Design Research Association (U.S.A.)
EDS	Environmental Data Service (U.S.A.)
EDS	Étudiants Démocrates Européens
EDS	European Democrat Students
EDTA	European Dialysis and Transplant Association
EDUCOM	Interuniversity Communications Council (U.S.A.)
EDV	Eisendrahtvereinigung
EEA	Dirección de Economia y Estadística Agropecuaria (Venezuela)
EEA	Electronic Engineering Association
EEA	Estación Experimental de Agricultura (Bolivia)
EEA	European Evangelical Alliance
EEAT	Estación Experimental Agrícola de Tucumán (Argentina)
EEB	Eastern Electricity Board
EEB	European Environmental Bureau (Belgium)
EEBP	Estaçao Experimentál de Biologia e Piscicultura (Brazil)
EEC	English Electric Company Ltd
EEC	European Economic Community
EECA	European Electronic Component Manufacturers Association
EECE	Emergency Economic Commission for Europe
EECI	Énergie Électrique de la Côte-d'Ivoire
EED	European Enterprises Development Company
EEDC	Electronics Economic Development Committee (of NEDC)
EEF	Eisenhower Exchange Fellowships (U.S.A.)
EEF	Engineering Employers' Federation
EEG	Electroencephalographic Society
EEG	Essence Export Group
EEG	Europese Economische Gemeenschap

EEI	Edison Electric Institute (U.S.A.)
EEM	Eastern European Mission (U.S.A.)
EEMO	Exposition Européenne de la Machine Outil
EEMS	European Environmental Mutagen Society
EEOA	Compagnie des Eaux et Électricité de l'Ouest Africaine
EEOC	Equal Employment Opportunity Commission (U.S.A.)
EER	European Economic Recovery Committee (UNO)
EERI	Environmental and Ecological Research Institute (Thailand)
EETC	East Europe Trades Council
EETPU	Electrical, Electronic, Telecommunications and Plumbing Union
EETS	Early English Text Society
EEUA	Engineering Equipment Users Association
EEVC	English Electric Valve Company
EEW	Erfassung der Europäischen Wirbellosen
E & F	Eaux et Forêts (France)
EF	Engineering Foundation (U.S.A.)
EFA	École Française d'Afrique
EFA	Empire Forestry Association
EFA	European Federation of Agricultural Workers in the Community
EFA	European Finance Association
EFAA	English Field Archery Association
EFACI	Société d'Exploitations Forestières et Agricoles de la Côte-d'Ivoire
EFAPI	Euromarket Federation of Animal Protein Importers
EFBA	Entreprise Forestière des Bois Africains (Ivory Coast)
EFBACA	Entreprise Forestière de Bois Africains Centrafrique
EFBTE	Eastern Federation of Building Trades' Employers
EFC	Entreprise Forestiere Camerounaise
EFC	European Federation of Corrosion
EFC	European Forestry Commission
EFCC	European Federation of Conference Cities
EFCE	European Federation of Chemical Engineering
EFCEM	European Federation of Catering Equipment Manufacturers
EFCS	European Federation of Cytology Societies
EFCT	European Federation of Conference Towns
EFCTC	European Federation of Connective Tissue Clubs
EFDA	European Federation of Data Processing Associations
EFDSS	English Folk Dance and Song Society
EFEMA	Association des Fabricants Européens d'Emulsifiants Alimentaires
EFEO	European Flight Engineers Organization
EFF	Elektronikfabrikantforeningen
EFF	European Furniture Federation
EFGA	English Farmers Growers Association
EFI	Ekonomiska Forskningsinstitutet (Sweden)
EFI	Electronic Forum for Industry
EFIL	European Federation for Intercultural Learning
EFJC	Europäische Foderation Junger Chore
EFLA	Educational Film Library Association (U.S.A.)
EFLRY	European Federation of Liberal and Radical Youth
EFM	European Federalist Movement
EFMA	European Financial Marketing Association
EFMD	European Foundation for Management Development
EFMK	European Federation of Masseurs-Kinesitherapeutes
EFNEP	Expanded Food and Nutrition Education Program (U.S.A.)
EFNMS	European Federation of National Maintenance Societies
EFP	European Federation of Purchasing
EFPB	Employers Federation of Papermakers and Boardmakers (*of* BPBIF)
EFPMB	Employers' Federation of Papermakers and Boardmakers (*now* BPBIF)
EFPS	European Federation of Productivity Services
EFPW	European Federation for the Protection of Waters
EFS	Europäische Forschungsgemeinschaft für Stahlradiatoren (*now* EURORAD)
EFSC	European Federation of Soroptimist Clubs
EFSS	Emergency Food Supply Scheme (WFP)
EFTA	European Free Trade Association
EFTA	European Technological Forecasting Association
EFTAMALT	EFTA Malting Industry Association

EFTAPA	EFTA Plastics Association (*now* Society of Plastic Associations in Europe)
EFTA-TUC	Trade Union Committee for the European Free Trade Area
EFTC	Electrical Fair Trading Council
EFU	Europäische Frauenunion
EFVA	Education Foundation for Visual Aids
EG	Engineers' Guild
EGA	Électricité et Gaz d'Algérie
EGA	Entreprise Générale Atlantique
EGA	Europese Gemeenschap voor Atomenergie (Belgium)
EGB	Eastern Gas Board
EGCI	Export Group for the Constructional Industries
EGCM	Entreprise Gabonaise de Constructions Métalliques
EGCS	English Guernsey Cattle Society
EGGA	European General Galvanizers Association
EGGMA	European Gas Control Manufacturers' Association (*now* AFECOGAZ)
EGIG	Expédition Glaciologique Internationale au Groenland (U.K.)
EGK	Europäische Güterzugfahrplankonferenz
EGKS	Europäische Gemeinschaft für Kohle und Stahl
EGM	European Glass Container Manufacturers' Committee
EGOA	Europäische Gesellschaft für Osteo-Arthrologie
EGOS	European Group for Organization Studies
EGOTI	Egyptian General Organization for Trade and Industry
EGPA	Egyptian General Petroleum Authority
EGRSA	Edible Gelatin Research Society of America
EGS	European Geophysical Society
EGSC	Eastern Group Supply Council
EGSL	European Group for the Study of Lysosomes
EGTO	Egyptian General Trade Organisation
EGU	English Golf Union
EGZ	Europäische Gesellschaft für Zusammenarbeit
EH	International Institute of Human Economy
EHB	Europäisches Hopfenbaubüro
EHC	European Hotel Corporation
EHCC	European Hops Culture Committee

EHGC	European Hop Growers Convention
EHL	Elektriska Hushållsapparatleverantörer
EHL	Entente des Hôpitaux Luxembourgeois
EHSC	European Home Study Council
EIAC	Electronics Industries Association of Canada
EIA	Engineering Industries Association
EIAS	Institut Européen Inter-Universitaire de l'Action Sociale
EIASM	European Institute for Advanced Studies in Management (Belgium)
EIB	Economisch Instituut voor de Bouwnij-verheid
EIB	Europäische Investitionsbank
EIB	European International Business Association
EIBA	Electrical Industries Benevolent Association
EIBIS	Engineering in Britain Information Services
EIBM	Escuela Interamericana de Bibliotecología (Colombia)
EIC	Engineering Institute of Canada
EICA	East India Cotton Association
EICF	European Investment Casters Federation
EIECC	Inter-American Council for Education, Science and Culture
EIEI	General Directorate of Electrical Surveys Administration (Turkey)
EIFAC	European Inland Fisheries Advisory Commission (*of* FAO)
EIFEL	European Group for the Ardennes and the Eifel
EIFI	Electrical Industries Federation of Ireland
EIGA	Engineering Industry Group Apprenticeship
EIJC	Engineering Institutions Joint Council
EIJHE	East Indian Jute and Hessian Exchange
EIL	British Association of the Experiment in International Living
EIL	Elektroinstallatorenes Landsforbund
EIN	Escuéla Industriál de la Nación (Argentina)
EIO	Economische Voorlichtingsdienst
EIO	Elektriska Installatörganisationen
EIOI	Expedición Internacional al Océano Indico
EIP	Association Mondiale pour l'École Instrument de Paix
EIPC	European Institute of Printed Circuits
EIRC	Équipes Internationales de Renaissance Chrétienne

EIRENE	International Christian Service for Peace	**ELEP**	European Federation of Anti-Leprosy Associations (*now* ILEP)
EIRMA	European Industrial Research Management Association (France)	**ELF**	Eritrean Liberation Front
EIS	Educational Institute of Scotland	**ELF**	Esperanto-Ligo Filatelista
EIS	Elektroniikkainsinöörien Seura	**ELF**	European Landworkers' Federation
EIS	European Invertebrate Survey	**ELFA**	Electric Light Fittings Association
EISCAT	European Incoherent Scatter Organisation	**ELFO**	Elektroinstallatørernes Landsforening
EISW	Inter-University European Institute on Social Welfare	**ELGA**	European Liaison Group for Agriculture
		ELIC	Electric Lamp Industry Council
EIT	European Institute for Trans-National Studies in Group and Organisational Development	**ELIF**	Sveriges Elektroindustriförening
		ELKEPA	Ellenikon Kentron Paragogikotitos
EITB	Engineering Industry Training Board	**ELLA**	European Long Lines Agency (of NATO)
EIU	Economic Intelligence Unit	**ELMA**	Electric Lamp Manufacturers' Association
EIVT	European Institute for Vocational Training	**ELMAF**	Emballages Légers Métalliques Africains
EJC	Engineers Joint Council (U.S.A.)	**ELMIA**	European Agricultural and Industrial Fair (Sweden)
EJCS	English Jersey Cattle Society		
EJCSC	European Joint Committee of Scientific Cooperation (*of* CE)	**ELMO**	European Laundry and Dry Cleaning Machinery Manufacturers Organisation
EJMA	English Joinery Manufacturers' Association	**ELPA**	Automobile Association of Greece
		ELPA	Eléveurs Limousin Plein Air
EKESO	Europees Korps voor Ekonomische en Sociale Ontwikkeling (Belgium)	**ELRA**	European Leisure and Recreation Association
EKI	Instituto por Esperanto en Komerco kaj Industrio (Netherlands)	**ELSE**	European Life Science Editors
		ELU	English Lacrosse Union
EKRIS	Enosis Katastimatarchon Radiofonon & Illektrikon Syskevon	**ELWCHG**	European Labor and Working Class History Group (U.S.A.)
EKS	Etaireia Kypriakon Spoudon (Cyprus)	**EM**	European Movement
EKSG	Europese Kolen en Staal Gemeenschap	**EMA**	Empreza de Mecanisaçao Agricola (Brazil)
EL	Entreprenørenes Landssammenslutning	**EMA**	Entertainment Managers Association of Great Britain and Ireland
ELA	Elicottero Lavoro Aereo		
ELANE	Electronics Association for the North East	**EMA**	Evangelical Missionary Alliance
ELB	Environment Liaison Board (NGO)	**EMA**	Evaporated Milk Association (U.S.A.)
ELBS	English Language Book Society	**EMA**	European Monetary Agreement
ELC	Environment Leisure Centre (Kenya)	**EMAA**	European Mastic Asphalt Association
ELDO	European Launcher Development Organisation	**EMAB**	Enterprise Malienne du Bois
		EMAC	Educational Media Association of Canada
ELDOK	Elektronisk Dokumentationsog Patentforening	**EMACO**	Electromedicinsk Apparat Compagni
		EMAIA	Electrical Meter and Allied Industries Association (Australia)
ELEC	English Language Education Council (Japan)		
ELEC	English Language Exploratory Committee (Japan)	**EMAP**	European Marketing and Advertising Press
		EMARC	Escola Média de Agricultura da Região Cacaueira (Brazil)
ELEC	European League for Economic Co-operation	**EMA-UK**	European Marketing Association United Kingdom
ELEOUR-GIKI	Central Cooperative Union of Olive and Olive Oil Producers of Greece		
		EMB	Europäischer Metallgewerkschaftsbund

MBAL-GROS	Chambre Syndicale des Négociants en Papiers d'Emballage et Cartons en Gros (Belgium)
MBC	European Molecular Biology Conference
MBO	European Molecular Biology Organisation
MBRAER	Empresa Brasileira de Aeronautica
MBRATEL	Empresa Brasileira Telecomunicacoes
MBRATER	Empresa Brasileira de Assisténcia Técnica e Extensão Rural
MC	Enterprise Minière et Chimique
MC	European Medicum Collegium
MC	European Marketing Council
MCAPA	Empresa Capixaba de Pesquisa Agropecuaria (Brazil)
MCC	European Municipal Credit Community
MCCC	European Military Communications Coordinating Committee (of NATO)
MCF	European Monetary Cooperation Fund
MF	European Management Forum
MF	European Metalworkers Federation
MF	European Motel Federation
MGI	Ethiopian Mapping and Geography Institute
MI	Electrical and Musical Industries Ltd
MIC	Environmental Mutagen Information Centre (U.S.A.)
MP	Ethnikon Metsovion Polytechneion
MPA	Eidgenössische Materialprüfungsanstalt (Switzerland)
MPA	European Maritime Pilots Association
MPAGRI	Empresas Agricolas C.A.Ltda (Costa Rica)
MPCO	English Metal Powder Company
MRB	European Marketing Research Board
MRLS	East Midlands Regional Library Service
MS	Econometric Society (U.S.A.)
MS	Environmental Mutagen Society (U.S.A.)
MSA	Electron Microscope Society of America
MSA	Entreprenadmaskinleverantörernas Samarbetsorgan
MSS	Elisha Mitchell Scientific Society (U.S.A.)
MTA	Electro Medical Trade Association
MU	European Economic and Monetary Union
MV	Europäischer Möbel-Verband
NA	École Nationale d'Administration
NA	École Nationale d'Agriculture
NA	Émaillerie Nouvelle Afrique

ENA	European Neurosciences Association
ENAA	École Nationale d'Agriculture d'Alger
ENAF	École Nationale Agronomique Féminine
ENAF	Empresa Nacional de Fundiciones (Bolivia)
ENAG	Escuela Nacional de Agricultura y Ganadería (Nicaragua)
ENAL	Ente Nazionale Assistenza Lavoratori
ENAMI	Empresa Nacional de Minería (Chile)
ENAP	Empresa Nacional de Petróleos (Chile)
ENAP	Escuela Nacional de Administración Pública
ENAPI	Ente Nazionale Artigianato e Piccole Industrie
ENASA	Empresa Nacional de Autocamiones SA (Spain)
ENAT	Entreprise Africaine de Travaux (Ivory Coast)
ENBC	Eastern Nigeria Broadcasting Corporation
ENC	École Nationale de la Coopération (Tunisia)
ENC	Ente Nazionale Circhi
ENCA	European Naval Communications Agency (of NATO)
ENCASCO	Empresa Nacional Calvo Sotelo
ENCB	Escuela Nacional de Ciencias Biológicas
ENCC	Ente Nazionale per la Cellulose e per la Carta
ENCK	Eerste Nederlandse Coöperatieve Kunstmestfabriek
ENCOE	British National Committee on Ocean Engineering
ENCONA	Environmental Coalition for North America
ENCOTEL	Empresa Nacional de Correos y Telegrafos (Argentina)
ENDC	Eastern Nigeria Development Corporation
ENDC	Eighteen-Nation Disarmament Committee
ENDE	Empresa Nacional de Electricidad (Bolivia)
ENDESA	Hydrology Division of the National Electricity Company of Chile
ENDEV	Development Finance Co. (Eastern Nigeria)
ENDS	Empresa Nacional de Semillas (Chile)
ENEA	European Nuclear Energy Agency (OECD)
ENEF	École Nationale des Eaux et Forêts
ENEF	English New Education Fellowship
ENELCAM	Énergie Électrique du Cameroun
ENEL	Ente Nazionale per l'Energia Elettrica
ENEMA	École Nationale d'Enseignement Ménager Agricole, à Rennes

ENERCA	Énergie Centrafricaine
ENERGAS	Empresa Nacional de Gas (Spain)
ENEX	Engineering Export Association of New Zealand
ENFA	École Nationale Féminine d'Agronomie
ENFPPM	École Nationale de Formation et de Perfectionnement de Patrons de Pêche et de Mécaniciens
ENG	European Nursing Group
ENGACO	Entreprises Gabonaises de Constructions
ENGR	École Nationale du Génie Rural
ENGREF	École Nationale du Génie Rural, des Eaux et des Forêts
ENH	École Nationale des Haras
ENH	École Nationale d'Horticulture
ENHER	Empresa Nacional Hidroelectuca del Ribagorzana
ENMS	European Nuclear Medicine Society
ENI	Ente Nazionale Idrocarburi
ENIA	École Nationale des Industries Agricoles et Alimentaire
ENISA	École Nationale d'Ingénieurs Spécialisés en Agriculture
ENIT	Ente Nazionale Italiano Turismo
ENITA	École Nationale des Ingénieurs de Travaux Agricoles
ENNICO	Entreprise Nigérienne de Confiserie
ENO	Comité Hellénique de Normalisation
ENPI	Ente Nazionale Prevenzione Infortuni
ENPS	École Nationale de Promotion Sociale (Madagascar)
ENRC	European Nuclear Research Centre
ENREA	École Nationale de Radiotechnique et d'Électricité Appliquée
ENRI	Electronic Navigation Research Institute (Japan)
ENS	European Nuclear Society
ENSA	École Nationale Supérieure Agronomique
ENSAE	École Nationale de la Statistique et de l'Administration Economique
ENSAJF	École Nationale Supérieure d'Agronomie pour Jeunes Filles
ENSAN	École Nationale Supérieure Agronomique de Nancy
ENSAT	L'École Nationale Supérieure Agronomique de Toulouse
ENSEME	Entreprise Sénégalaise des Mousses et Plastiques
ENSH	École Nationale Supérieure d'Horticulture
ENSIAA	École Nationale Supérieure des Industries Agricoles et Alimentaires
ENSMIC	École Nationale Supérieure de Meunerie et des Industries Céréalières
ENSP	École Nationale de la Santé Publique
ENSPM	École Nationale Supérieure du Pétrole et des Moteurs
ENSSAA	École Nationale Supérieure des Sciences Agronomiques Appliquées
ENTEL	Empresa Nacional de Telecomunicaciónes (Bolivia, etc.)
ENUSA	Empresa Nacional del Urano SA
ENV	Écoles Nationales Vétérinaires
EOA	English Orienteering Association
EOARDC	European Office of the U.S. Air Research and Development Command
EOC	Equal Opportunities Commission
EODA	Eastern Ontario Development Association (Canada)
EOKA	National Organisation of Cypriot Combatants
EOM	Ellinikos Organismos Marketing
EONR	European Organisation for Nuclear Research
EOQC	European Organization for Quality Control
EORTC	European Organisation for Research on Treatment of Cancer
EOS	Egyptian Organization for Standardization
EOS	European Orthodontic Society
EO-WCL	European Organisation of the World Confederation of Labour
EP	European Parliament
EPA	Environmental Protection Agency (U.S.A.)
EPA	European Productivity Agency (of OECD)
EPACCI	Economic Planning and Advisory Council for the Construction Industries
EPADC	East Pakistan Agricultural Development Corporation
EPARD	East Pakistan Academy for Rural Development
EPASA	Electron Probe Analysis Society of America
EPC	Economic Policy Committee (of OECD)
EPC	Export Publicity Council

EPCA	Economic Planning and Coordination Authority (Hawaii)	**EPUL**	École Polytechnique de l'Université de Lausanne
EPCA	European Petrochemical Association	**EPWAPDA**	East Pakistan Water and Power Development Authority
EPD	Eidgenössisches Politisches Department (Switzerland)	**EQUAPAC**	International Cooperative Expedition EQUAPAC
EPDC	Electric Power Development Corporation (Japan)	**ERA**	École Régionale d'Agriculture
EPEA	Electrical Power Engineers' Association	**ERA**	Electrical Research Association
EPF	École Polytechnique Fédérale (Switzerland)	**ERA**	European Recreation Association
EPF	European Packaging Federation	**ERA**	European Rotogravure Association
EPFCL	Esso Pakistan Fertilizer Co. Ltd	**ERAP**	Entreprise de Recherches et d'Activités Pétrolières
EPFL	École Polytechnique Fédérale de Lausanne (Switzerland)	**ERB**	Educational Records Bureau (U.S.A.)
EPFTR	Expert Panel for the Facilitation of Tuna Research (FAO)	**ERC**	Economic Research Council
		ERC	Empire Rheumatism Council
EPG	European Press Group	**ERC**	Regional Conference for Europe (FAO)
EPHE	École Pratique des Hautes Études	**ERCHCW**	European Regional Clearing House for Community Work
EPIC	Electronic Properties Information Centre (U.S.A.)	**ERCO**	Electrical Reduction Company of Canada
EPIC	Export Payment Insurance Corporation (Australia)	**ERDA**	Electrical and Radio Development Association (N.S. Wales)
EPIDC	East Pakistan Industrial Development Council	**ERDA**	European Research and Development Agency
EPLA	East Pakistan Library Association	**ERDC**	Eastern Region Development Corporation (Nigeria)
EPLF	Eritrean Popular Liberation Front		
EPLMRA	European Pharmaceutical Marketing Research Foundation	**ERDC**	European Research and Development Committee
EPNS	English Place-Name Society	**ERDE**	Electronics and Radar Development Establishment, Bangalore (India)
EPOA	European Property Owners Association		
EPOC	Eastern Pacific Ocean Conference	**ERDO**	European Research and Development Organization
EPOS	Europees Pedagogisch Secretariat	**ERERCA**	Énergie Centrafricaine
EPP	European People's Party	**ERFA**	European Radio Frequency Administration (of NATO)
EPPMA	Expanded Polystyrene Product Manufacturers Association		
EPPMP	European Power Press Manufacturers Panel	**ERGOM**	European Research Group on Management
EPPO	European and Mediterranean Plant Protection Organisation (France.)	**ERIC**	Educational Resources Information Center (U.S.A.)
EPS	European Physical Society	**ERIRUP**	European Research Institute for Regional and Urban Planning
EPS	Experimental Psychology Society	**ERIW**	European Research Institute for Welding
EPSEP	Empresa Pública de Servicios Pesqueros	**ERO**	European Regional Organization (of ICFTU)
EPTA	Expanded Programme of Technical Assistance (UNO)	**EROPA**	Eastern Regional Organization for Public Administration (Philippines)
EPU	Economic Planning Unit (Malaysia)		
EPU	European Payments Union	**ERP**	European Recovery Programme (UNO)
EPU	European Picture Union	**ERPDB**	Eastern Regional Production Development Board (Nigeria)
EPU	European Press Photo Agencies Union		

ERPTUAC	European Recovery Programme Trade Unions Advisory Committee
ERRL	Eastern Regional Research Laboratory (U.S.A.)
ERS	Economic Research Service (U.S.A.)
ERU	English Rugby Union
ERVA	Erhvervaskeriernes Brancheforening
ES	Econometric Society (U.S.A.)
ESA	École Supérieure d'Agriculture et de Viticulture d'Angers (Belgium)
ESA	Ecological Society of America
ESA	Electrolysis Society of America
ESA	Employment Services Agency
ESA	Engineers and Scientists of America
ESA	Entomological Society of America
ESA	Ethnological Society of America
ESA	European Schoolmagazine Association
ESA	European Space Association
ESAA	École Supérieure d'Agriculture d'Angers
ESAA	English Schools Athletic Association
ESAAT	École Supérieure d'Application d'Agriculture Tropicale
ESAB	Elektriska Svetsningsaktiebolaget
ESABR	European Society of Animal Blood Research
ESACG	École Supérieure d'Application des Corps
ESALQ	Escola Superior de Agricultura "Luiz de Queiroz" (Brazil)
ESAN	Graduate School of Business Administration (Peru)
ESANZ	Economic Society of Australia and New Zealand
ESAP	Egyptian Society of Animal Production
ESAP	Escuela Superior de Administración Pública (Colombia)
ESAPAC	Escuela Superior de Administracion Publica America Central
ESARDA	European Safeguards Research and Development Association
ESARIPO	Industrial Property Organization of English-speaking African Countries (Cameroons)
ESAURP	Escola Superior de Agricultura da Universidade Rural de Pernambuco (Brazil)
ESAV	Escola Superior de Agricultura e Veterinaria (Brazil)
ESB	Economic Stabilisation Board (China)
ESB	European Settlement Board
ESB	Export Services Branch (*of* BOT)
ESBA	English Schools Badminton Association
ESBBA	English Schools Basket Ball Association
ESBP	European Society for Biochemical Pharmacology
ESC	Economic and Social Committee (*of* EEC)
ESC	Entomological Society of Canada
ESC	European National Shippers' Councils
ESC	European Space Conference
ESCA	East of Scotland College of Agriculture
ESCA	English Schools Cricket Association
ESCAP	Economic and Social Commission for Asia and the Pacific (UN)
ESC	European National Shippers' Councils
ESCC	Engineering Standards Co-ordinating Committee
ESCES	Experimental Satellite Communication Earth Centre (India)
ESCI	European Society for Clinical Investigation
ESCO	European Sterility and Conception Organization
ESCOFAR	Eastern Counties Farmers Ltd
ESCOM	Electricity Supply Commission (S.Africa)
ESCOP	Experiment Station Committee on Organization and Policy (U.S.A.)
ESCOR	Economic and Social Committee for Overseas Research
ESCOW	Engineering and Scientific Committee on Water (New Zealand)
ESCSP	European Society of Corporate and Strategic Planners
ESDAC	European Space Data Centre
ESDEN	Ethnikos Syndesmos Diplomatouchon Ellinidon Nosokomon
ESDP	European Social Development Programme
ESDR	European Society for Dermatological Research
ESEE	European Society for Engineering Education
ESEF	Electrotyping and Stereotyping Employers' Federation
ESEF	European Society for Engineering Education
ESF	Egyptologiska Sällskapet i Finland
ESF	European Science Foundation
ESF	European Social Fund
ESFA	English Schools Football Association
ESG	Engineers and Scientists Guild (U.S.A.)

ESGA	English Schools Gymnastics Association
ESGE	European Society of Gastrointestinal Endoscopy
ESH	European Society of Haematology
ESIC	Environmental Science Information Center (NOAA)
ESIP	Engineering Societies International Publications Committee
ESJ	Entomological Society of Japan
ESLAB	European Space Laboratory
ESLI	Esperanto Sak-Ligo Internacia
ESLO	European Satellite Launcher Organisation
ESM	European Society for Microcirculation
ESMA	Electrical Sign Manufacturers' Association
ESMOC	European Solar Meeting Organizing Committee
ESN	European Society of Nematologists
ESNA	European Society of Nuclear Methods in Agriculture
ESNE	Engineering Societies of New England (U.S.A.)
ESNZ	Entomological Society of New Zealand
ESO	European Southern Observatory
ESOC	European Space Operations Centre
ESOMAR	European Society for Opinion and Marketing Research
ESONEC	European Standard of Nuclear Electronics Committee
ESP	European Society of Pathology
ESPB	European Student Press Bureau
ESPE	European Society for Paediatric Endocrinology
ESPI	Ente Siciliano per la Promozione Industriale
ESPN	European Society for Pediatric Nephrology
ESPR	European Society for Paediatric Research
ESR	Europa Saaten Dienst
ESRA	Economische en Sociale Raad van Advies der Benelux Economische Unie
ESRANGE	European Space Launching Range
ESRC	European Science Research Council
ESRF	Economic and Scientific Research Foundation (India)
ESRI	Economic and Social Research Institute (Eire)
ESRI	European Systems Research Institute (Belgium)
ESRIN	European Space Research Institute
ESRO	European Space Research Organisation
ESRS	European Society for Rural Sociology
ESRU	English Schools Rugby Union (*now* RFSU)
ESS	Eastern Searoad Service (Australia)
ESS	Eastern Surgical Society (U.S.A.)
ESSA	Electricity Supply Association of Australia
ESSA	English Schools Swimming Association
ESSA	Environmental Science Services Administration (U.S.A.)
ESSCIRC	European Solid State Circuits Conference
ESSFA	Essens Fabrikant Foreningen
ESSRA	Economic and Social Science Research Association
ESTA	European Security Transport Association
ESTA	European String Teachers Association
ESTEC	European Space Research and Technology Centre
ESTI	European Space Technology Institute
ESTL	European Space Tribology Laboratory
ESTRA	English Speaking Tape Respondents Association
ESTRACK	European Satellite Tracking, Telemetry and Telecommand Network
ESU	English Speaking Union
ESVA	English Schools Volleyball Association
ETA	Basque Homeland and Liberty (Spain)
ETA	European Tallying Association
ETA	European Taxpayers Association
ETA	European Teacher's Association
ETA	European Thermographic Association
ETA	European Tugowners Association
ETAF	École d'Enseignement Technique Féminin
ETAP	Expanded Technical Assistance Programme (U.S.A.)
ETB	English Tourist Board
ETC	European Tea Committee
ETC	European Tourist Conference
ETC	European Translating Centre
ETC	European Travel Commission
ETDS	Electric Transport Development Society
ETE	Epitöipari Tudományos Egyesület
ETE	Experimental Tunnelling Establishment
ETFA	European Technological Forecasting Association

ETH	Eidgenössische Technische Hochschule (Switzerland)
ETIC	English-Teaching Information Centre
ETIF	Economisch-Technologisch Instituut Friesland
ETIO	Economisch-Technologisch Instituut Overijssel
ETIU	Economisch-Technologisch Instituut Utrecht
ETIYRA	El Toro International Yacht Racing Association (U.S.A.)
ETJC	Engineering Trades Joint Council
ETL	Elintarviketeollisuusliitto
ETMA	English Timber Merchants' Association
ETO	European Transportation Organisation
ETP	European Training Programme in Brain and Behaviour Research
ETPM	Société Entrepose pour les Travaux Pétroliers Maritimes
ETPO	European Trade Promotion Organisations Conference
ETRAC	Educational Television and Radio Association of Canada
ETS	Electrodepositors' Technical Society
ETTA	English Table Tennis Association
ETTU	European Table Tennis Union
ETTUC	European Teacher Trade Union Committee
ETUC	European Trade Union Confederation
ETWA	English Tiddlywink Association
EUBCA	Escuela Universitaria de Bibliotecnologia y Ciencias Afines (Uruguay)
EUBL	Europa Unuigo de Blindaj Laboruloj
EUBS	European Undersea Bio-medical Society
EUBW	European Union for Blind Workers
EUCA	Fédération Européenne des Associations de Torrefacteurs du Café
EUCARPIA	European Association for Research on Plant Breeding (Netherlands)
EUCDA	Europäische Union Christlich Demokratischer Arbeitnehmer
EUCEPA	European Liaison Committee for Pulp and Paper
EUCHEM	European Chemical Congress
EUCHEMAP	European Committee of Chemical Plant Manufacturers
EUCO	Association de l'Industrie Européenne du Coco
EUD	European Union of Dental Medicine Practitioners
EUDICE	Association Européenne pour le Développement de l'Information et la Connaissance de l'Environnement
EUF	European Union of Federalists (France)
EUFMD	European Commission for the Control of Foot and Mouth Disease
EUFODA	European Foodstuffs Distributors Association
EUFTW	European Union of Film and Television Workers
EUGROPA	Union des Distributeurs de Papiers et Cartons de la CEE
EUHOFA	Association Européenne des Directeurs d'Écoles Hôtelières
EULABANK	Banco Euro-Latinoamericano
EULAR	European League Against Rheumatism
EULEP	European Late Effects Project Group
EUM	Entr'aide Universitaire Mondiale
EUMABOIS	European Committee of Woodworking Machinery Manufacturers
EUMA-PRINT	European Committee of Associations of Printing and Paper Converting Machinery Manufacturers
EUMOTIV	European Association for Study of Economic, Commercial and Industrial Motivation
EUPA	European Union for the Protection of Animals
EUR	Europäische Union der Rechtspfleger
EURABIA	European Coordinating Committee of Friendship Societies with the Arab World
EURAFREP	Société de Recherches et Exploitation de Pétrole (Mauritania)
EURAG	European Federation for the Welfare of the Elderly
EURAS	European Anodisers Association
EURATOM	Organisation Atomique Européenne
EUREL	Association Européenne pour les Réserves Libres
EUREL	Convention of National Societies of Electrical Engineers of Western Europe
EUREMAIL	Conférence Permanente de l'Industrie Européenne de Produits Émaillés
EURES	European Group for Research on Spatial Problems

EURES	European Reticulo-Endothelial Society
EURESCO	Conseil de Coopération Culturelle Européenne
EURIM	European Conference on the Contribution of Users to Planning and Policy Making for Information Systems and Networks
EURIMA	European Insulation Manufacturers Association
EURINCAD	Fédération Européenne des Indépendants et des Cadres
EURO	Association of European Operational Research Societies
EUROAVIA	Association of European Aeronautical and Astronautical Students
EURO-BITUME	European Bitumen Association
EUROBOIS	European Group of Woodworking Journals
EUROCAE	European Organisation for Civil Aviation Electronics
EUROCEAN	European Oceanographic Association
EUROCEN-TRES	Foundation for European Language and Educational Centres
EURO-CHEMIC	European Company for the Chemical Processing of Irradiated Fuels
EUROCOM	Union Européenne des Négociants en Combustibles
EUROCOMP	European Computing Congress
EUROCON-TROL	European Organisation for the Safety of Air Navigation
EURO-COOP	Union Européenne des Centrales de Production et de Gros des Sociétés Coopératives de Consommation
EUROCOP-COST	European Cooperation and Coordination in the Field of Scientific and Technical Research
EUROCORD	Fédération des Industries de Corderie-Ficellerie de l'Europe Occidentale
EURO-COTON	EEC Committee for the Cotton and Allied Textile Industries
EURODATA	Eurodata Foundation
EURO-DIDAC	Association Européenne de Fabricants et de Revendeurs de Matériel Didactique
EURODOC	Joint Documentation Service of ESRO, EUROSPACE and the European Organisation for the Development and Construction of Space Vehicle Launchers
EURO-FEDAG	European Federation of Agricultural Workers
EURO-FEDAL	European Federation of Workers in Food and Allied Industries (of EO-WCL)
EURO-FEDOP	European Federation of Employees in Public Service
EUROFER	European Confederation of Iron and Steel Industries
EUROFEU	European Committee of the Manufacturers of Fire Engines and Apparatus
EUROFIMA	Société Européenne pour le Financement de Matériel Ferroviaire
EUROFI-NANCE	Union Internationale d'Analyse Économique et Financière
EURO-FINAS	Association of European Finance Houses
EUROFUEL	Société Européenne de Fabrication de Combustibles à Base d'Uranium pour Reacteurs à Eau Légère
EURO-GLACES	Association of the Ice Cream Industries of the EEC
EUROGRAF	Group of Federations of Graphics Industries in the EEC
EURO-GRAM	Société Européenne de Recherches et d'Études Programmées
EURO-GROPA	Union des Distributeurs de Papiers et Cartons
EURO-HKG	European High Temperature Nuclear Power Stations Society
EUROLIBRI	Association Européenne d'Éditeurs Juridiques et Économiques
EUROMAI-SIERS	Groupement des Associations des Maïsiers de la CEE
EUROMALT	Comité de Travail des Malteries de la CEE
EUROMAP	European Committee of Machinery Manufacturers for the Plastics and Rubber Industries
EURO-MECH	European Mechanics Colloquia
EURO-MICRO	European Association of Microprocessor Users
EUROMINE	European Federation of the Mining Timber Associations
EUROMOT	European Committee of Internal Combustion Engine Manufacturers' Association
EURONET	European Network for Scientific and Technical Information
EUROP	European Railway Wagon Pool
EUROPA-DRESS	European Association of Direct Mail Houses
EURO-PECHE	Association des Organisations Nationales d'Entreprises de Pêche de la CEE

EUROPHOT Association Européenne des Photographes Professionels

EUROPHYSICS European Physics Congress

EURO-PRESSE-FAMILIA Association Européenne des Éditeurs de la Presse Périodique d'Information Féminine ou Familiale

EURO-PRESS-JUNIOR Association Européenne des Éditeurs de Publications pour la Jeunesse

EUROPUMP European Committee of Pump Manufacturers

EURORAD European Association of Manufacturers of Steel-Panelled Radiators

EUROSAC Fédération Européenne des Fabricants de Sacs en Papier a grande Contenance

EUROSPACE European Industrial Space Study Group

EUROSTRUCT-PRESS European Association of Publishers in the Field of Building and Design

EUROTEST European Association of Testing Institutions

EUROTOX Comité Européen Permanent de Recherches sur la Protection des Populations contre les Risques de Toxicité à Long Terme

EUROVENT European Committee of Manufacturers of Air Handling Equipment

EUROVISION Union Européenne de Radio-Diffusion

EURP European Union of Public Relations

EUSA Evangelical Union of South America (U.K.)

EUSAFEC Eastern United States Agricultural and Food Export Council

EUSAMA European Shock Absorber Manufacturers Association

EUSEC Conférènce des Représentants de Sociétés d'Ingénieurs de l'Europe Occidentale et des États-Unis d'Amérique

EUSIDIC European Association of Scientific Information Dissemination Centres

EUSIREF European Network of Scientific Information Referral Centres

EUTO European Union of Tourism Executives

EUTOR European Association for Technical Orthopaedics and Orthopaedic Rehabilitation

EUTRA-PLAST Committee of Western European Plastics Converters Federations

EUW European Union of Women

EuWiD Europäischer Wirtschaftsdienst

EUYCD European Union of Young Christian Democrats

EV Erdöl-Vereiningung (Switzerland)

EVA Electric Vehicle Association of Great Britain

EVA English Vineyards Association

EVA English Volleyball Association

EVAF European Association for Industrial Marketing Research

EVD Eidgenössiches Volkswirtschaftsdepartement (Switzerland)

EVD Veterinary Department, Eastern Region (Nigeria)

EVEM Institute Européen de Vente et de Marketing (Belgium)

EVI Ex-Volunteers International

EVKI Europäische Vereinigung der Keramik-Industrie

EVMAC-MEX Ejecutivos de Ventas y Mercadotecnia de México

EVO Algemene Verladers-en Eigen Vervoerders Organisatie

EVP Europäische Volkspartei (Belgium)

EVS Erfinder-und Patentinhaber-Verband der Schweiz

EVSE Enosis Viomichanon Sporelaiourgon Ellados

EVT Europäische Vereinigung für Tierzucht

EWA Europäisches Währungsabkommen

EWAA European Wrought Aluminium Association

EWAC European Wheat Aneuploid Co-operative

EWF Electrical Wholesalers' Federation

EWG Europäische Wirtschaftsgemeinschaft

EWGAE European Working Group on Acoustic Emission

EWONA Educational Welfare Officers National Association

EWRC European Weed Research Council (*now* EWRS)

EWRS European Weed Research Society

EWSF European Work Study Federation (*now* EFPS)

EXBOA Export Buying Offices Association

EXIMBANK Banco de Exportación e Importacion del Gobierno de los Estados Unidos de Norte América

EXP | Exchange of Persons Service (*of* UNESCO)
EXPAINSO | Société de Développement du Sud-Ouest
EXPAN-ENTRE | Société pour l'Expansion Économique de la Région du Centre
EXTEL | Exchange Telegraph Co., Ltd
EYC | European Youth Campaign
EZS | Elektrotehniška Zveza Slovenije
EZU | Europäische Zahlungs-Union

F

FA | Forretningsbankenes Arbeidsgiverforening
FAA | Federación Agraria Argentina
FAA | U.S. Federal Aviation Agency
FAA | Foundation for American Agriculture
FAAPF | Federación Argentina de Asociaciones de Productores Forestales
FAAVCA | Federación de Asociaciones de Agencias de Viajes de Centro América
FAB | Fédération Nationale des Auto-Écoles Professionnelles de Belgique
FAB | Fédération Royale des Sociétés d'Architectes de Belgique
FABC | Federation of Asian Bishops Conferences
FABES | Vereniging van Fabrikanten van Beton-straatstenen
FABI | Fédération Royale des Associations Belges d'Ingénieurs
FABRI-METAL | Fédération des Entreprises de l'Industrie des Fabrications Métalliques (Belgium)
FAC | Confédération Africaine de Football
FAC | Fonds d'Aide et de Cooperation Technique et Économique
FACA | Federación Argentina de Cooperativas Agrarias
FACA | Fédération Algérienne de la Coopération Agricole
FACC | Federación Argentina de Cooperativas de Consumo
FACFF | Fédération des Associations de Communes Forestières Françaises
FACIM | Fondation pour l'Action Culturelle Internationale en Montagne

FACOPHAR | Syndicat National de la Fabrication et du Commerce des Produits à Usage Pharmaceutique et Parapharmaceutique
FACP | Food and Agriculture Council, Pakistan
FACREA | Federación Argentina de Consorcios Regionales de Experimentación Agrícola (*now* AACREA)
FACS | Federation of American Controlled Shipping
FACS | Fédération des Amis des Chemins de Fer Secondaires
FACSS | Federation of Analytical Chemistry and Spectroscopy (U.S.A.)
FACT | Fertilisers and Chemicals Travancore (India)
FACTS | Federation of Australian Commercial Television Stations
FACTU | Föreningen Svensk Fachpress
FAD | Fonds Africain de Développement (Ivory Coast)
FAE | Federación de Amigos de la Enseñanza
FAE | Federation of Arab Engineers
FAEAB | Federação das Associações dos Engenheiros Agrónomos do Brasil
FAECF | Fédération des Associations Européennes des Constructeurs de Fenêtres
FAEP | Federation of Association of Periodical Publishers (*of* EEC)
FAF | Finska Antikvariatforeningen
FAGAM | Groep Fabrieken van Gasmeters
FAGEC | Fédération d'Associations et Groupements pour les Études Corses
FAGS | Federation of Astronomical and Geophysical Services (ICSU)
FAGT | Federation of Agricultural Group Traders
FAH | Fédération Arabe d'Haltérophilie
FAH | Forschungsinstitut für Absatz und Handel (Switzerland)
FAI | Fédération Abolitionniste Internationale
FAI | Fédération Aéronautique Internationale
FAI | Federazione Apicoltori Italiani
FAI | Federazione Autorimesse Italiane
FAI | Federazione Autotrasportatori Italiani
FAI | Fertiliser Association of India
FAI | Football Association of Ireland
FAIAT | Federazione delle Associazioni Italiane Alberghi e Turismo
FAIB | Fédération des Associations Internationales Établies en Belgique

FAIC	Federation of Australian Investment Clubs	**FAOE**	Federation of African Organisations of Engineers
FAIMA	Federación Argentina de la Industria de la Madera y Afines	**FAPA**	Federation of Asian Pharmaceutical Associations
FAIR	Federation of Afro-Asian Insurers and Reinsurers	**FAPAL**	Groep Fabrieken van Aktieve en Passieve Elektronische Bouwelementen
FAIR	Union Professionnelle des Fabricants et Importateurs de Matériel Électronique (Belgium)	**FAPEB**	Fédération des Artisans et des Petites Entreprises du Bâtiment
FAIRT	Suomen Kansainvälisten Muuttokuljetusliikkeiden Liitto	**FAPES**	Fundacion Argentina para la Promocion del Desarrollo Económico y Social
FAITA	Federación de Asociaciones Industriales Textiles del Algodón (Mexico)	**FAPESP**	Fundaçâo de Amparo à Pesquisa do Estado de São Paulo (Brazil)
FAMA	Fachverband Messen und Ausstellungen	**FAPTA**	Fédération Suisse des Associations des Planteurs de Tabac
FAMA	Federal Agricultural Marketing Authority (Malaysia)	**FAR**	Federal Department of Agricultural Research (Nigeria)
FAMA	Foundation for Mutual Assistance in Africa South of the Sahara	**FAR**	Foreign Area Research Co-ordination Group (U.S.A.)
FAMAB	Fachverband Messe- und Ausstellungsbau	**FAR**	Föreningen Auktoriserade Revisorer
FAMED	Vereinigung Schweizerischer Fabriken der Medizinischen Technik	**FAR**	Foundation of Applied Research (U.S.A.)
FAMEM	Federation of Associations of Mine Equipment Manufacturers	**FAREC**	Unione Fabbricanti Apparecchi di Riscaldamento e Cucine
FAMEX	Foreningen af Danske Mælkekonservesfabrikker med Landbrugsministeriel Autorisation til Fremstilling af Mælkekonserves for Export	**FARGRO**	Farmers' and Growers' Industries, Ltd
		FARM	Filipino Agrarian Reform Movement
		FARM-UNIONE	Associazione Nazionale dell' Industria Farmaceutica Italiana
FAMHEM	Federation of Associations of Materials Handling Equipment Manufacturers	**FARN**	Fuerzas Armadas de la Resistencia Nacional (El Salvador)
FAMHM	Federation of Associations of Material Handling Manufacters	**FARON**	Fabrieken van Röntgen en Andere Elektromedische Apparatuur in Nederland
FAMHW	Federation of Associations of Mental Health Workers (*now* FMHW)	**FAS**	European Federation of Associations of Industrial Safety and Medical Officers
FAMID	Foreningen af Mineralvandsfabrikanter i Danmark	**FAS**	Federation of American Scientists
FAMPA	Ferro Alloys and Metals Producers Association	**FAS**	Fédération des Architectes Suisses
		FAS	Foreign Agricultural Service (U.S.A.)
FAMSA	African Medical Students Association	**FAS**	Verband Schweizerischer Fachgeschäfte für Arzt- und Spitalbedarf
FAN	Federación Agraria Nacional (Costa Rica)		
FANAL	Federación Agraria Nacional (Colombia)	**FASA**	Federación Argentina de Sindicatos Agrarios
FANCIF	Fondo Antárquico National para la Capacitación e Investigación Forestal (Argentina)	**FASA**	Federación Argentina de Sociedades Apícolas
FANOA	Fédération des Appellations et Noms d'Origine Agricole	**FASASA**	Fonds d'Action Sociale pour l'Aménagement des Structures Agricoles
FANS	Federation of Asian Nutrition Societies	**FASC**	Federation of Asian Shippers Council
FAO	Food and Agriculture Organisation (UNO)	**FASE**	Fédération des Sociétés d'Acoustique Européennes
FAOB	Federation of Asian and Oceanian Biochemists	**FASEB**	Federation of American Scientists for Experimental Biology

FASFID	Fédération des Associations et Sociétés Françaises d'Ingénieurs Diplômés
FASII	Federation of Associations of Small Industries in India
FASNUDS	Fondo Fiduciario de las Naciones Unidas para el Desarrollo Social
FASNUPPD	Fonds d'Affectation Spéciale des Nations Unies pour la Planification et des Projections en Matière de Développement
FASOMG	Fédération Avicole du Sud-Ouest et du Midi Garonnais
FASS	Federation of Associations of Specialists and Sub-contractors
FASST	Federation of Americans Supporting Science and Technology
FAST	Federazione delle Associazioni Scientifiche e Tecniche
FAT	Fonds Arabo-Africain d'Assistance Technique (Egypt)
FAT	Föreningen Auktoriserade Translatorer
FAT	Forschungsvereinigung Automobiltechnik
FATA	Fondo Assicurativo tra Agricoltori
FATIPEC	Fédération des Associations de Techniciens des Industries des Peintures et Encres d'Imprimerie de l'Europe Continentale
FATIS	Food and Agriculture Technical Information Service (of OECD)
FATME	Fabbrica Apparecchiature Telefoniche e Materiale Elettrico
FATRE	Federación Argentina de Trabajadores Rurales y Estibadores
FATS	Federation of Arab Teachers Syndicates
FATTA	Federation of Arab Travel Agents' Associations
FAVAD	Vereniging van Fabrikanten van Zwakalcoholhoudende en Alcoholvrije Dranken
FAVF	Fédération des Associations Viticoles de France
FAW	Fachverband Aussenwerbung
FAWA	Federation of Asian Women's Associations
FAWC	Federation of African Women's Clubs
FAWCO	Federation of American Women's Clubs Overseas
FB	Federation of Bakers
FBA	Farm Buildings Association
FBA	Federation of British Astrologers

FBA	Federation of British Audio
FBA	Freshwater Biological Association
FBAS	Federation of British Aquatic Societies
FBBDO	Fibre Building Board Development Organization
FBBF	Fibre Building Board Federation
FBBM	Federation of Building Block Manufacturers (now CBA)
FBCA	Federation of British Cremation Authorities
FBCAEI	Federation of Builders Contractors and Allied Employers of Ireland
FBCE	Fellowship of British Christian Esperantists
FBCM	Federation of British Carpet Manufacturers (now merged into BCMA)
FBCN	Fundação Brasileira para e Conservação da Natureza
FBEP	Fédération Belge d'Éducation Physique
FBFM	Federation of British Film Makers
FBG	Fachverband Bürobedarf für Grossverbraucher
FBG	Federation of British Growers
FBH	Fachgruppe für Brückenbau und Hochbau
FBH	Fédération Belge des Horticoles Semences
FBHTM	Federation of British Hand Tool Manufacturers
FBI	Federal Bureau of Investigation (U.S.A.)
FBI	Federation of British Industries (now CBI)
FBI	Fonds du Bien-Être Indigène (Belgium)
FBM	Fachvereinigung der Bunt- und Metallpapierfabriken
FBMA	Finnish Boat and Motor Association
FBMA	Union Suisse des Entreprises de Forge, du Bois, du Métal et de la Machine Agricole
FBMSG	Federation of British Manufacturers Sports and Games
FBMV	Federación Boliviana de Médicos Veterinarios
FBPP	Federation of Plant Pathologists
FBPS	Forest and Bird Protection Society of New Zealand
FBR	Forskningsbiblioteksrådet
FBR	Foundation for Business Responsibilities
FBRAM	Federation of British Rubber and Allied Manufacturers
FBSC	Federation of British Scooter Clubs
FBTRC	Federation of British Tape Recording Clubs

FBU	Fire Brigades Union
FBUA	Franco-British Union of Architects
FBUI	Federation of British Umbrella Industries
FBVA	Forstliche Bundesversuchsanstalt (Austria)
FBVL	Fonds ter Bevordering van de Veredeling van Landbouwgewassen
FBW	Forschungsgemeinschaft Bauen und Wohnen
FCA	Farm Credit Administration, (U.S.A.)
FCA	Foncière de la Côte d'Afrique
FCAA	Federación de Cooperativas Arroceras Argentinas
FCAATSI	Federal Council for the Advancement of Aborigines and Torres Strait Islanders (Australia)
FCACV	Federación de Cooperativas de Ahorro y Crédito de Venezuela
FCAM	Fédération Cotonnière d'Afrique Francophone et de Madagascar
FCAT	Société Franco-Centrafricaine des Tabacs
FCB	Fédération Nationale des Coopératives Agricoles de Transformation de la Betterave Industrielle
FCBA	Friesland Cattle Breeders' Association of South Africa
FCBM	Federation of Clinker Block Manufacturers
FCC	Federal Communications Commission (U.S.A.)
FCCA	Christian Federation of Craftsmen and Apprentices (Luxembourg)
FCCAM	Fédération Centrale du Crédit Agricole Mutuel
FCCC	Federación de Cámaras de Comercio del Istmo Centroamericano (Salvador)
FCCC	Federation of Commonwealth Chambers of Commerce
FCCD	Foundation for Cultural Cooperation and Development (France)
FCCST	Federal Co-ordinating Council for Science, Engineering and Technology (U.S.A.)
FCDA	Federal Civil Defense Administration (U.S.A.)
FCDC	Fertilizer and Chemical Development Council (Israel)
FCDE	Federation of Clothing Designers
FCE	Femmes Chefs d'Entreprises Mondiales
FCEC	Federation of Civil Engineering Contractors

FCECA	Fishery Committee for the Eastern Central Atlantic
FCEP	Christian Federation of Employees and Civil Servants (Luxembourg)
FCEV	Fédération des Clubs Européens de Formules IV
FCF	Footwear Components Federation
FCI	Factors Chain International (Netherlands)
FCI	Fédération Cynologique Internationale
FCI	Fertiliser Corporation of India
FCI	Fundación Científica Internacional
FCIA	Foreign Credit Insurance Association (U.S.A.)
FCJ	Fédération Internationale des Journalistes Catholiques
FCK	Central Organisation of Farmers' Co-operatives (Hungary)
FCL	Federación Campesina Latino Americana (Venezuela)
FCLA	Fisheries Council for Latin America
FCMI	Federation of Coated Macadam Industries
FCML	Christian Federation of Luxembourg Metalworkers
FCMRF	Fédération des Centres Musicaux Ruraux de France
FCO	Farmers Central Organization
FCOBC	Christian Federation of Building and Quarry Workers (Luxembourg)
FCOMF	Fédération des Coopératives Oléicoles du Midi de la France
FCOUL	Christian Federation of Luxembourg Factory Workers
FCPSP	Christian Federation of Public Service Workers (Luxembourg)
FCR	Association des Fabriques de Chaudières et Radiateurs (Switzerland)
FCRE	Foundation for Cotton Research and Education (U.S.A.)
FCRIMS	Freight Committee of the Rubber Industry of Malaysia and Singapore
FCS	Farm Cooperative Service (U.S.A.)
FCS	Federation of Concrete Specialists
FCST	Federal Council for Science and Technology (U.S.A.)
FCTA	Fédération Suisse des Travailleurs du Commerce des Transports et de l'Alimentation

FCTPAS	Christian Federation of Social Insurance Pensioners	FDJ	Free German Youth
FCTU	Federation of Associations of Catholic Trade Unionists	FDK	Fachverband Deutsche Klavierindistrie
		FDLA	Democratic Front for the Liberation of Angola
FCTV	Federación de Cooperativas de Transporte de Venezuela	FDM	Fachverband des Deutschen Maschinen- und Werkzeug-Grosshandels
FCV	Federación de Campesinos de Venezuela	FDMO	Fund for the Development of Manpower (Portugal)
FCWV	Federatie van de Katholieke en Protestants-Christelijke Werkgeversverbonden	FDO	Federatie van Nederlandse Danslerarenorganisaties
FCX	Farmers Cooperative Exchange (U.S.A.)	FDO	Fédération Départementale Ovine
FDA	Food Distribution Administration (U.S.A.)	FDO	Foreningen af Danske Osteproducenter
FDA	Food and Drug Administration (U.S.A.)	FDP	Freie Demokratische Partie (W. Germany)
FDA	Freier Deutscher Autorenverband	FDS	Fachverband der Deutschen Schulmöbelindustrie
FDAR	Federal Department of Agricultural Research (Nigeria)	FDSEA	Fédération Départementale des Syndicats d'Exploitants Agricoles
FDB	Faellesforeningen for Danmarks Brugsforeninger	FDT	Fachverband des Deutschen Tapethandels
FDBR	Fachverband Dampfkessel-, Behälter- und Rohrleitungsbau	FDVR	Federal Department of Veterinary Research (Nigeria)
FDC	Federation of Dredging Contractors	FDW	Fachverband Film- und Diapositiv-Werbung
FDC	Fiji Development Co.	FEA	Federation of European Aerosol Associations (Switzerland)
FDC	Foreningen af Dansk Civiløkonomer		
FDC	Furniture Development Council (*now* FIRA)	FEA	Fédération Internationale pour l'Éducation Artistique
FDCETA	Fédération Départementale des Centres d'Études Techniques Agricoles	FEAAF	Fédération Européenne des Associations d'Analystes Financiers
FDD	Fondation Documentaire Dentaire (Belgium)	FEACO	Fédération Européenne des Associations de Conseils en Organisation
FDD	Fundación Dominicana de Desarrollo (Dominica)	FEAICSMT	Fédération Européenne des Associations d'Ingénieurs et Chefs de Services de Sécurité et des Médecins du Travail (*now* FAS)
FDE	Fachverband Deutscher Eisenwaren- und Hausrathändler		
FDES	Fonds de Développement Économique et Social	FEAL	Fédération Nationale des Groupements de Labels Agricoles
FDF	Fachverband Deutscher Floristen	FEAM	Fédération Européenne des Associations de Mécanographes
FDF	Footwear Distributors Federation	FEANF	Fédération des Étudiants d'Afrique Noire Française
FDFR	Federal Department of Forestry Research (Nigeria)	FEANI	European Federation of National Associations of Engineers
FDFU	Federation of Documentary Film Units		
FDGB	Freier Deutscher Gewerkschaftsbund	FEAO	Federation of European American Organisations
FDGB	Confederation of Free German Trade Unions		
FDGPA	Fédération Départementale des Groupements de Productivité Agricole	FEB	Fédération des Éditeurs Belges
FDI	Fédération Dentaire Internationale	FEB	Fédération des Entreprises de Belgique
FDIC	UK Food and Drink Industries Council	FEB	Fédération des Expéditeurs de Belgique
FDIF	Fédération Democratique Internationale des Femmes	FEBAB	Federaçao Brasiliera de Associaçoes de Bibliotecários
FDIM	Federación Democrática Internacional de Mujeres		

FEBECA	Fédération Belge du Commerce Alimentaire	**FECS**	Fédération Européenne des Fabricants de Céramiques Sanitaires
FEBELBOIS	Fédération Belge des Industriels du Bois	**FED**	European Development Fund
FEBELCAR	Fédération Belge de la Carrosserie et des Métiers Connexes	**FEDAAS**	Federación Española de Asociaciones de Asitentes Sociales
FEBEL-HOUT	Belgische Federatie der Houtnijveraars	**FEDAC**	Fédération Européenne des Anciens Combattants
FEBELQUIN	Fédération Belge des Quincailliers	**FEDAR-LINEA**	Associazione Italiana dell' Armamento di Linea
FEBELTEX	Fédération de l'Industrie Textile Belge	**FEDAS**	Federación Española de Actividades Subacuáticas
FEBEVO	Federatie van de Belgische Voedingshandel	**FEDC**	Federation of Engineering Design Companies
FEBIAC	Chambre Syndicale des Constructeurs d'Automobiles et de Motocycles de Belgique et Fédération Belge des Industries de l'Automobile et du Cycle "Réunies"	**FEDEAGRO**	Federación Nacional de Asociaciones de Productores Agropecuarios (Venezuela)
		FEDE-ARROZ	Federación Nacional de Arrozeros (Colombia)
FEBIC	Fédération Belge de l'Industrie de la Chaussure	**FEDE-CACAO**	Federación Nacional de Cacaoteros (Colombia)
FEBO	Fund for Experimental Concrete Research (Netherlands)	**FEDECAM-ARAS**	Federación Venezolana de Cámeras y Asociaciones de Comercio y Producción
FEBS	Federation of European Biochemical Societies	**FEDECAME**	Fédération des Planteurs de Café Amérique
FEC	Far Eastern Commission (U.S.A.)	**FEDECHAR**	Fédération Charbonnière de Belgique
FEC	Far East Conference (U.S.A.)	**FEDECOM-LEGNO**	Federazione Nazionale dei Commercianti del Legno e del Sughero
FEC	Foundation for Environmental Conservation (Switzerland)	**FEDEGAN**	Federación Colombiana de Ganaderos (Colombia)
FEC	Fondation Européenne de la Culture	**FEDEL**	Fédération Française des Syndicats d'Éleveurs de Chevaux de Selle
FECAICA	Federación de Cámaras y Associaciones Industriales de Centroamérica (Costa Rico)	**FEDEMAR**	Fédération Belge des Exploitants Forestiers et Marchands de Bois de Mine et Papeterie
FECAMCO	Federación de Cámaras de Comercio del Istmo Centroamericano (Panama)	**FEDE-METAL**	Federación Metalúrgica Colombiana
FECAUBEL	Fédération des Concessionnaires de l'Automobile de Belgique	**FEDEMOA**	Federación Mexicana de Organizaciones Agricolas
FECB	Foreign Exchange Control Board	**FEDEMOL**	Federación Nacional de Molineros de Trigo (Colombia)
FECC	Federación Campesina Cristiana Costarricences	**FEDENAGA**	Federación Nacionale de Ganaderos (Venezuela)
FECEP	Fédération Européenne des Constructeurs d'Équipement Pétrolier	**FEDENTEL**	Fédération Nationale des Dentelles, Tulles, Broderies, Guipures et Passementeries
FECESI-TLIH	Federación Central de Sindicatos de Trabajadores Libres de Honduras	**FEDE-PALMA**	Federación Nacional de Cultivadores de Palma Africana
FECETRAG	Federación Central de Trabajadores de Guatemala	**FEDEPAS**	Federación Nacional de Fabricantes de Pastas Alimenticias (Colombia)
FECHIMIE	Fédération des Industries Chimiques de Belgique	**FEDE-POMTER**	Fédération Nationale des Syndicats de Négociants en Pommes de Terre et Légumes en Gros
FECOL-TRACOM	Federación Colombiana de Trabajadores		
FECOM	Fonds Européen de Coopération Monétaire		
FECOVE	Federación de Cooperativas de Consumo de Venezuela		
FECOVI	Fédération Nationale des Fabricants de Conserves de Viandes		

FEDERA Fédération des Sociétés Commerciales Pharmaceutiques Belges

FEDERA-BOIS Fédération Nationale des Négociants en Bois (Belgium)

FEDERA-CAFE Federación Nacional de Cafeteros (Colombia)

FEDER-AGENTI Federazione Nazionale Agenti Raccomandatori Marittimi, Agenti Aerei e Pubblici Mediatori Marittimi

FEDERAG-RONOMI Federazione Nazionale Dottori in Scienze Agrarie

FEDERAL-GODON Federación Nacional de Algodoneros (Colombia)

FEDER-CON-SORZI Federazione Italiana dei Consorzi Agrari

FEDEREC Fédération Nationale des Syndicats des Industries et Commerces de la Récupération

FEDEREL Fédération des Rélamineurs du Fer et de l'Acier de la Communauté Européenne

FEDER-FIORI Federazione Nazionale Fioristi

FEDERFISA Federazione Nazionale tra Fabbricanti ed Esportatori Italiani di Fisarmoniche ed Altri Strumenti Musicali

FEDER-GROS-SISTI Federazione Nazionale del Commercio Alimentare all'Ingrosso

FEDER-HOUT Nationale Federatie van Houthandelaars (Belgium)

FEDER-LEGNO Federazione Italiana delle Industrie del Legno, del Sughero e dell' Arredamento

FEDERMA-GAZZINI Federazione Italiana Magazzini Generali

FEDERMAR Fédération Maritime de la Côte-d'Ivoire

FEDER-MECCA-NICA Federazione Sindacale dell'Industria Metalmeccanica

FEDER-NATURA Federazione Nazionale Pro Natura

FEDER-OLIO Federazione Nazionale del Commercio Oleario

FEDER-OTTICA Federazione Nazionale dei Titolari di Esercizi di Ottica Optometrica Foto-Ottica

FEDER-PESCA Federazione Nazionale delle Imprese di Pesca

FEDERPOL Federazione Nazionale degli Istitut di Polizia Privata

FEDER-SARTI Federazione Nazionale Sarti e Sarte d'Italia

FEDER-TERME Federazione Nazionale delle Industrie Idro-Termali

FEDERVINI Federazione Italiana Industriali Produttroni Esportatori ed Importatori di Vini, Acquaviti, Liquori, Sciroppi, Aceti ed Affini

FEDES Federazione Europea dei Fabbricanti di Sachetti di Carta

FEDESPEDI Federazione Nazionale Spedizionieri

FEDETAB Fédération Belgo Luxembourgeoise du Tabac

FEDETRAM Federazione Nazionale Aziende Municipalizzate di Trasporto

FEDEX-PORT Federazione Italiana dei Consorzi Agrari

FEDHOTEL Fédération Nationale de l'Hôtellerie Belge

FEDIA Fédération des Ingénieurs Agronomes de Belgique

FEDICA Fédération des Associations de l'Industrie et du Commerce de l'Automobile (Belgium)

FEDICER Fédération des Industries Céramiques de Belgique et du Luxembourg

FEDIL Fédération des Industries Luxembourgeois

FEDIMA European Federation of Manufacturers of Bakers' and Confectioners' Ingredients and Additives

FEDIOL Fédération de l'Industrie de l'Huilerie de la CEE

FEDIPAC Fédération Nationale des Distributeurs de Produits Alimentaires et de Grande Consommation

FEDIVER Fédération de l'Industrie du Verre (Belgium)

FEDO FACT Engineering and Design Organization (India)

FEDOLIVE Fédération de l'Industrie de l'Huile d'Olive de la CEE

FEDOM Fonds Européen de Développement Outre-mer

FEDS Foreign Economic Development Service (U.S.A.)

FEE Federation of Employers of Ethiopia

FEECA Fédération Européenne pour l'Éducation Catholique des Adultes

FEFAC Fédération Européenne des Fabricants d'Aliments Composés pour Animaux (Belgium)

FEFANA Fédération Européenne des Fabricants d'Adjuvants pour la Nutrition Animale

FEFCEB Fédération Européenne des Fabricants de Caisses et Emballages en Bois

FEFCO	Fédération Européenne des Fabricants de Carton Ondulé
FEFPEB	Fédération Européenne des Fabricants de Caisses et Emballages en Bois
FEG	Föderation Europäischer Gewässerschutz
FEGAP	Fédération Européenne de la Ganterie de Peau
FEGARBEL	Fédération des Garagistes de Belgique
FEGARLUX	Fédération des Garagistes-Réparateurs du Grand-Duché de Luxembourg
FEGAZLIQ	Fédération Nationale des Centres de Liaison Régionaux de Concessionaires de Gaz Liquefiés
FEGOZI	Federatie Goud en Zilver
FEGRAB	Fédération des Industries Graphiques de Belgique
FEGRO	European Federation for the Wholesale Watch Trade
FEHA	Foreningen af Fabrikanter og Importører af Elektriske
FEHAN	Groep Fabrieken van Elektrische Huishoudelijke Apparaten in Nederland
FEHCOVIL	Federación Hondureña de Cooperativas de Vivienda (Honduras)
FEI	Federación Endodóncica Iberoamericana
FEI	Fédération Équestre Internationale
FEIA	Flight Engineers International Association (U.S.A.)
FEIC	Fédération Européenne de l'Industrie du Contreplaque
FEICA	Fédération Européenne des Industries de Colles et Adhésifs
FEICADE	Federación de Instituciones Centroamericanas de Desarrollo (Guatemala)
FEICRO	Federation of European Industrial Co-operative Research Organizations
FEIEA	Federation of European Industrial Editors' Associations
FEIM	Fédération Européenne des Importateurs de Machines de Bureau
FEIM	Fundación para las Encuentras Internacionales en las Montanas
FEITC	Fédération Européenne des Industries Techniques du Cinéma
FEJLR	Fédération Européenne des Jeunesses Libérales et Radicales
FEKO	Federatie van Kleinhandelsorganisaties

FELAC	Federación Latinoamericana de Consultores
FELACEX	Federación Latinoamericana y del Caribe de Asociaciones de Exportadores
FELA-TRABS	Federación Latinoamericana de Trabajadores Bancarios y de Seguros
FELATURS	Federación Latinoamericana de Turismo Social
FELCRA	Federal Land Consolidation and Rehabilitation Authority (Malaysia)
FELDA	Federal Land Development Authority (Malaysia)
FELEBAN	Federación Latinoamericana de Bancos (Colombia)
FEM	Fédération Européenne de la Manutention
FEM	Fédération Européenne des Metallurgistes
FEM	Fédération Européenne des Motels
FE-MA	Fédération Nationale des Unions Professionnelles de Négociants en Matériaux de Construction de Belgique
FEMAR	Fondação de Estudos do Mar
FEMAS	Far East Merchants Association (U.S.A.)
FEMC	Fédération Européenne des Médecins de Collectivités
FEMCA	Federación de Estudiantes de Medicina Centroamericanos
FEMIB	Fédération Européenne des Syndicats de Fabricants de Menuiseries Industrielles de Bâtiment
FEMIBE	Fédération Mondiale des Dirigeants des Instituts de Beauté et de l'Esthétique (Belgium)
FEMIPI	Fédération Européenne des Mandataires de l'Industrie en Propriété Industrielle
FEMK	Fédération Européenne des Masseurs-Kinésithérapeutes Praticiens en Physiothérapie
FEMO	Fédération de l'Enseignement Moyen Officiel du Degré (Belgium)
FEMOSI	Fédération Mondiale des Syndicats d'Industries
FEMPI	European Federation of Agents of Industry in Industrial Property
FEMSA	Fabrica Espanola Magnetos, S.A.
FEMUSI	Federación Mundial de Sindicatos de Industrias
FEN	Federation de l'Éducation Nationale
FENA	Fédération Européenne du Négoce de l'Ameublement

FENACEM Fédération Nationale du Commerce de l'Équipement Ménager

FENACOA Federación Nacional de Cooperativas Agropecuarias (Uruguay)

FENACOAC Federación Nacional de Cooperativas de Ahorro y Crédito de Guatemala

FENADAG Fédération Nationale des Détaillants en Alimentation Générale (Belgium)

FENAGH Federación Nacional de Agricoltores y Ganaderos de Honduras

FENAL Federazione Esercenti Latterie e Derivati del Latte

FENALCE Federación Nacional de Cultivadores de Cereales (Colombia)

FENALCO Federación Nacional de Comerciantes (Colombia)

FENARUM Fédération Nationale des Producteurs de Rhum

FENASI-BANCOL Federación Nacional de Sindicatos Bancarios Colombianos

FENA-SYCOA Fédération Nationale des Syndicats du Commerce Ouest-Africain

FENASYDA Fédération Nationale des Syndicats de la Distribution des Équipements et Outillages pour l'Automobile et Activités Annexes

FENAVIAN Fédération Nationale des Fabricants de Produits et Conserves de Viandes

FENAVINO Fédération Nationale de la Viticulture Nouvelle

FENCO Foundation of Canada Engineering Corporation

FENEC Federación Nicaraguense Educación Católica

FENECAFE Federación Nacional de Cooperativas Cafetaleras (Ecuador)

FENEDEX Federatie voor de Nederlandse Export

FENEMA Fédération des Négociants de Machines Agricoles (Luxembourg)

FENETEC Fédération des Syndicats de Négociants Techniques

FENEWOL Federatie Nederlandse Wolindustrie

FENEX Federatie van Nederlandse Expediteursorganisaties

FENFIRO Fédération Nationale des Groupements de Femelles Prolifiques issues de Béliers Finnois ou Romanov

FENIOF Federazione Nazionale Imprese Onoranze Funebri

FENIT Federazione Nazionale Imprese Trasporti

FENNO-BOARD Finnish Wallboard Industry Association

FENSIL Federación Nacional Sindical Libre (Guatemala)

FENU Fonds d'Équipement des Nations Unies

FENUDE Fondo Especial de las Naciones Unidas para el Desarrollo Económico

FEO Fishmeal Exporters Organization

FEO Flora Europea Organisation

FEODT Fédération Européenne des Organisations des Détaillants en Tabacs

FEOF Foreign Exchange Operations Fund (Laos)

FEOGA Fonds Européen d'Orientation et de Garantie Agricole

FEOTC Federal Exporters Oversea Transport Committee (UK-Continent Trade) (Australia)

FEP Federación Española de Pesca

FEPA Fédération de l'Enseignement Privé Agricole

FEPA Fédération Européenne des Fabricants de Produits Abrasifs

FEPAFAR-BIO Fédération Panaméricaine de Pharmacie et de Biochimie

FEPAFEM Pan-American Federation of Associations of Medical Schools (Colombia)

FEPE Fédération Européenne pour la Protection des Eaux

FEPE Fédération Européenne de la Publicité Extérieure

FEPEM Federation of European Petroleum Equipment Manufacturers

FEPF Fédération Européenne des Industries de Porcelaine et de Faïence de Table et d'Ornementation

FEPRABEL Fédération des Producteurs d'Assurances de Belgique

FEPRANAL Federación Nacional del Sector Privado para la Acción Comunal (Colombia)

FEPRINCO Federación de la Producción, la Industria y el Comercio (Paraguay)

FER Federation of Engine Re-manufacturers

FERA Föreningen för Elektricitetens Rationella Användning

FERC Regional Conference for Asia and the Far East (FAO)

FERE Federación Espanola de Religiosos de Enseñanza

FERE	Fondation Égyptologique Reine Elisabeth (Belgium)
FERES	Fédération Internationale des Instituts Catholiques de Recherches Socio-Religieuses
FEROPA	Fédération Européenne des Syndicats de Panneaux de Fibres
FERPI	Federazione Relazioni Pubbliche Italiana
FES	Fédération des Éditeurs Suisses
FESAC	Fondation de l'Enseignement Supérieur en Afrique Centrale
FeSAPI	Federazione Sindacati Avvocati e Procuratori Italiani
FESPF	Fédération Européenne des Syndicats de Fabricants de Parquets
FESIC	Far East Seed Improvement Conference
FESITRANH	Federación Sindical de Trabajadores Nacionales de Honduras
FESIW	Far East Seed Improvement Workshop
FESPA	Federation of European Screen Printers Associations
FESPO	Federation of European Science Policy Organizations
FESSCAP	Fédération d'Étudiants Sociaux-Chrétiens d'Amérique Centrale et Panama
FEST	Foundation for Education, Science and Technology (South Africa)
FESTAL	Fédération Syndicale du Teillage Agricole du Lin
FESYP	Fédération Européenne des Syndicats de Fabricants de Panneaux de Particules
FETA	Fire Extinguisher Trades Association
FETAB	Federación Dominicana de Cooperativas Agropecuarias y del Tabaco
FETANOR	Fédération des Industries du Blanchiment, de la Teinture et des Apprêts de la Région du Nord
FETIBALC	Federation of Workers in the Banana Industry of Latin America and the Caribbean
FETAP	Fédération Européenne des Transports Aériens Privés
FETRA	Fédération des Industries Transformatrices de Papier et de Carton (Belgium)
FETRAN-JAS	Federación Nacional de Trabajadores Agropecuarios, Recursos Naturales Renovables, Jardineros y Similares (Venezuela)
FEUCA	Fédération des Étudiants Universitaires d'Amérique Centrale
FEUGRES	Fédération Européenne des Fabricants de Tuyaux en Grès
FEUPF	Fédération Européenne des Unions Professionelles de Fleuristes
FEVC	Fédération Européenne des Villes de Congrès (Belgium)
FEVE	Fédération Européenne du Verre d'Emballage
FEVE	Ferrocarriles de Via Estrecha
FEVIR	Federation of European Veterinarians in Industry and Research
FEZ	Fédération des Entreprises du Zaire
FEZ	Fédération Européenne de Zootechnie
FF	Finlands Fysioterapeutförbund
FFA	Federation of Financial Associations (Korea)
FFA	Flygtekniska Försöksanstalten
FFA	Fédération Française d'Athlétisme
FFA	Föreningen för Arbetarskydd
FFA	Foundation for Foreign Affairs (U.S.A.)
FFA	Future Farmers of America (U.S.A.)
FFAC	Société Fiduciaire France Afrique (Cameroons, Congo)
FFAEAF	Fédération Française des Associations d'Élevages d'Animaux à Fourrure
FFAG	Fiduciare France-Afrique-Gabon
FFAS	Fiduciare France-Afrique-Sénégal
FFC	Fédération Française de Cuniculiculture
FFC	Finlands Fachföreningars Centralförbund
FFCAA	Fédération Française des Coopératives Agricoles d'Approvisionnement
FFCAC	Fédération Française des Coopératives Agricoles de Céréales
FFCAT	Fédération Française des Commissionnaires et Auxiliaires de Transport, Commissionnaires en Douane, Transitaires, Agents Maritimes et Aériens
FFCB	Federal Farm Credit Board (U.S.A.)
FFCFLH	Fédération Française de la Coopération Fruitière, Légumière et Horticole
FFCFP	Fédération Française de Cadres de la Fonction Publique
FFEA	Fédération Française d'Économie Alpestre
FFEM	Fédération Française d'Économie Montagnarde
FFEPGV	Fédération Française d'Éducation Physique et de Gymnastique

FFF	Farm Field Foundation, Washington (U.S.A.)	**FFRSA**	Fondation pour Favoriser les Recherches Scientifiques (Belgium)
FFF	Fédération des Foires-Expositions de France	**FFS**	Föreningen för Samhällsplanering
FFF	Finlands Farmaceutförbund	**FFSA**	Fédération Française des Sociétés d'Assurances
FFF	International Federations of Performers	**FFSB**	Fédération des Foires et Salons du Benelux
FFFLCAF	Fédération Française de la Filature de Laine Cardée et Autres Fibres	**FFSE**	Fédération Française des Sports Équestres
FFH-AD	Freedom from Hunger—Action for Development	**FFSL**	Fédération Française des Syndicats de Librairies
FFHC	Freedom From Hunger Campaign (of FAO)	**FFSM**	Fédération des Fondations pour la Santé Mondiale
FFI	Fachverband Faltschachtelindustrie	**FFSPBPV**	Fédération Française des Syndicats de Producteurs de Bois et Plants de Vigne
FFINTEL	Fédération Française des Importateurs Négociants-Transformateurs et Exportateurs de Laines	**FFSPIG**	Fédération Française des Syndicats Patronaux de l'Imprimerie et des Industries Graphiques
FFITP	Fédération Française des Industries Transformatrices des Plastiques	**FFSPN**	Fédération des Sociétés de Protection de la Nature
FFIVM	Fédération Française des Industries du Vêtement Masculin	**FFSU**	Fédération Française des Stations Uvales
FFJP	International Federation of Fruit-Juice Producers	**FFTB**	Fédération des Fabricants de Tuiles et de Briques de France
FFLA	Federal Farm Loan Association (U.S.A.)	**FFTC**	Food and Fertilizer Technology Centre, Taipei (China)
FFMC	Federal Farm Mortgage Corporation (U.S.A.)	**FFTL**	Fédération Française du Tissage de Laine et Autres Fibres
FFMI	Fédération Française du Matériel d'Incendie	**FFTRI**	Fruit and Food Research Institute, Stellenbosch (South Africa)
FFMIN	Fédération Française des Marches d'Intérêt National	**FFTS**	Fédération Française des Travailleurs Sociaux
FFMKR	Fédération Française des Masseurs Kinésithérapeutes Rééducateurs	**FFU**	Forskningsrådense Fellesutvag
FFMW	Federation of Fresh Meat Wholesalers	**FFZ**	Fédération Française de Zootechnie
FFNFPMAP	Fédération Familiale Nationale pour la Formation Professionnelle et Ménagère Agricole Privée	**FGA**	Fachgemeinschaft Antriebstechnik im VDMA
FFNUDS	Fondo Fiducairio de las Naciones Unidas para el Desarrollo Social	**FGA**	Fédération Générale de l'Agriculture (*of* CFTC)
FFNUPPD	Fondo Fiduciario de las Naciones Unidas para Planificación y Proyecciones del Desarrollo	**FGAT**	Fédération des Unions Professionnelles des Grossistes en Articles Tréfilés (Belgium)
FFP	Fund for Peace (U.S.A.)	**FGB**	Federation of Associations of Wholesale Dealers in Building Materials (Netherlands)
FFPE	Fédération de la Fonction Publique Européenne	**FGBI**	Federation of Soroptimist Clubs of Great Britain and Ireland
FFPLB	Fédération Française des Producteurs de Lait de Brebis	**FGBMFI**	Full Gospel Business Men's Fellowship International (U.S.A.)
FFPN	Française Frisonne Pie Noire (race bovine)	**FGCA**	Fédération Générale des Cadres de l'Agriculture
FFPRI	Forest and Forest Product Research Institute (Ghana)	**FGDS**	Fédération de la Gauche Démocrate et Socialiste
FFRC	Food Freezer Refrigeration Council		
FFRP	Fédération Française des Relations Publiques		

FGEI	Fédération des Géomètres-Experts Indépendants (Belgium)
FGF	Fachgruppe der Forstingenieure (Switzerland)
FGG	Fränkische Geographische Gesellschaft
FGGM	Federation of Gelatine and Glue Manufacturers
FGH	Forschungsgemeinschaft für Hochspannungs- und Hochstromtechnik
FGHS	Vereniging van Fabrikanten en Groothandelaren in Sportbenodigheden
FGI	Fédération Graphique Internationale
FGIL	Fédération Générale des Instituteurs Luxembourgeois
FGL	Foreningen af Grossister i Landbrugsmaskiner
FGMEE	Fédération Nationale des Syndicats de Grossistes en Matériel Électrique et Électronique
FGMOPA	Fonds de Garantie Mutuelle et d'Orientation de la Production Agricole
FGÖD	Fachwissenschaftliche Gesellschaft Österreichischen Dentisten
FGPE	Fédération Générale du Personnel Enseignant (Belgium)
FGR	Fachgemeinschaft Gusseieme Rohre
FGS	Forschungsgesellschaft für das Strassenwesen im Österreich
FGT	Fachverband der Garagen-, Tankstellen- und Service-Stations-Unternehmungen (Austria)
FGTB	Fédération General du Travail de Belgique
FGYA	Franco-German Youth Agency
FH	Fédération Horlogère Suisse
FH	Fédération Suisse des Associations de Fabricants d'Horlogerie
FHA	Farmers' Home Administration (U.S.A.)
FHA	Federal Housing Administration (U.S.A.)
FHA	Félag Husgagnarkitekta
FHA	Future Homemakers of America
FHD	Foreningen af Herreekviperingshandlere i Danmark
FHF	Federation of Hardware Factors
FhG	Fraunhofer-Gesellschaft zur Förderung der Angewandten Forschung
FHI	Fédération Haltérophile Internationale
FHI	Félag Húsgagna-og Innanhússarkitekta
FHKI	Federation of Hong Kong Industries
FHPL	Fédération Horticole Professionnelle Luxembourgeoise
FHR	Fachvereinigung Hartpapierwaren und Rundgefässe
FHRF	Finney-Howell Research Foundation (U.S.A.)
FHS	Finlands Hundstambok
FHTA	Federated Home Timber Associations
FIA	Federación Interamericana de Abogados
FIA	Fédération des Industries Agricoles et Alimentaires (Belgium)
FIA	Fédération Internationale des Aveugles
FIA	Fédération Internationale des Acteurs
FIA	Fédération Internationale de l'Artisanat
FIA	Fédération Internationale de l'Automobile
FIA	Federation of Islamic Associations in the United States and Canada
FIA	Fédération Nationale des Syndicats des Industries de l'Alimentation
FIAA	Fédération Internationale d'Athlétisme Amateur
FIAB	Federación Internacional de Asociaciones de Bibliotecarios
FIABCI	Fédération Internationale des Administrateurs de Biens Conseils Immobiliers
FIABGRAL	Federação Internacional de Associacões de Bibliotecarios-Grupo Regional América Latina
FIAC	Fédération Interaméricaine des Automobile Clubs
FIAC	Fédération Internationale des Agences Catholiques de Presse
FIAC	Fédération Internationale Amateur de Cyclisme
FIAC	Fédération Internationale de l'Artisanat de la Chaussure
FIACC	Five International Associations Co-ordinating Committee
FIAD	Fédération Internationale des Associations des Distributeurs de Films
FIADEJ	Fédération Internationale des Associations de Directeurs et d'Éditeurs de Journaux
FIAEM	Fédération Internationale des Associations des Étudiants en Médecine
FIAF	Fédération Internationale des Archives du Film

FIAI	Fédération Internationale des Associations d'Instituteurs	**FIAT**	Field Information Agency, Technical (U.S.A.)
FIAJ	Fédération Internationale des Auberges de la Jeunesse	**FIATA**	Fédération Internationale des Associations de Transitaires et Assimilés
FIAJF	Fédération Internationale des Amies de la Jeune Fille	**FIATC**	Fédération Internationale des Associations Touristiques de Cheminots
FIALEC	Federazione Italiana fra le Associazioni Laureati in Economia e Commercio	**FIATE**	Fédération Internationale des Associations de Travailleurs Évangéliques
FIAM	Fédération Internationale des Associations de Mécanographes	**FIAV**	Fédération Internationale des Agences de Voyagers
FIAMC	Fédération Internationale des Associations des Médecins Catholiques	**FIAV**	Fédération Internationale des Artistes de Variétés
FIANEI	Fédération Internationale des Associations Nationales d'Élèves Ingénieurs	**FIAV**	Fédération Internationale des Associations de Vexillologie
FIANET	Fédération Internationale des Associations Nationales d'Exploitants de Téléphériques, Funiculaires et autres Transports par Câbles pour Voyageurs	**FIAVET**	Federazione Italiana dello Associazioni degli Uffici Viaggio e Turismo
		FIB	Fédération Française de l'Industrie du Béton
FIAP	Fédération Internationale des Architectes Paysagistes	**FIB**	Fédération des Industries Belges
FIAP	Federazione Italiana Autotrasportatori Professionali	**FIB**	Federation of Insurance Brokers
		FIB	Fédération Internationale de Boules
FIAP	Fédération Internationale de l'Art Photographique	**FIBA**	Fédération Internationale de Baseball
FIAP	Fédération Internationale des Associations Pédagogiques	**FIBA**	Fédération Internationale de Basket-Ball Amateur
FIAP	Fédération Internationale des Attachés de Presse	**FIBEP**	Fédération Internationale des Bureaux d'Extraits de Presse
FIAPA	Fédération Internationale des Associations de Chefs de Publicité d'Annonceurs	**FIBEPA**	Fachverband für Imprägnierte und Beschichtete Papiere
FIAPE	Fédération des Associations de la Presse d'Église	**FIBMA**	National Federation of Ironmongers and Builders Merchants Staff Associations
FIAPF	Fédération Internationale des Associations de Producteurs de Films	**FIBP**	Federazione Italiana delle Biblioteche Popolari
FIAPS	Fédération Internationale des Associations de Professeurs des Sciences	**FIBT**	Fédération Internationale de Bobsleigh et de Tobogganing
FIAR	Vereniging van Fabrikanten, Importeurs en Agenten op Electronicagebied	**FIBTP**	Fédération Internationale du Bâtiment et des Travaux Publics
FIARBC	Federal Interagency River Basin Committee (U.S.A.)	**FIBV**	Fédération Internationale des Bourses de Valeurs
FIARO	Federazione Italiana Associazioni Regionali Ospedaliere	**FIC**	Fédération de l'Industrie Cimentière (Belgium)
FIARP	Federación Interamericana de Asociaciones de Relaciones Públicas	**FIC**	Fédération Internationale de Canoë
		FIC	Fédération Internationale des Enterprises de Couverture
FIARVEP	Federazione Italiana Agenti Rappresentanti, Viaggiatori e Piazzisti	**FIC**	Federazione Italiana Caccia
FIAT	Fabbrica Italiana Automobile Torino	**FIC**	Foundation for International Cooperation
FIAT	Fédération Internationale des Associations de Thanatopraxie	**FICA**	Fédération Internationale des Cheminots Antialcooliques
		FICAC	Fédération Internationale des Coloniaux et Anciens Coloniaux

FICAE	Federación Latinoamericana del Cariba de Asociaciones de Exportadores (Venezuela)
FICB	Federal Intermediate Credit Bank (U.S.A.)
FICC	Fédération des Industries Complémentaires de la Construction
FICC	Fédération Internationale de Chimie Clinique
FICC	Fédération Internationale de Camping et de Caravanning
FICC	Fédération Internationale de Ciné-clubs
FICCI	Federation of the Indian Chambers of Commerce and Industry
FICCIA	Fédération Internationale des Cadres de la Chimie et des Industries Annexes
FICE	Fédération Internationale des Communautés d'Enfants
FICEMA	Fédération Internationale des Centres d'Entraînement aux Méthodes d'Éducation Active
FICEP	Fédération Internationale Catholique d'Éducation Physique
FICIC	Fédération Internationale du Commerce et des Industries de Camping
FICJF	Fédération Internationale des Conseils Juridiques et Fiscaux
FICM	Fédération Internationale des Cadres des Mines
FICOB	Fédération des Industries et du Commerce des Équipements de Bureau et d'Informatique
FICP	Fédération Internationale des Clubs de Publicité
FICP	Fédération Internationale du Cyclisme Professionnel
FICPH	Fédération Internationale de Commerçants des Produits Horticoles
FICS	Fédération Internationale des Chasseurs de Sons
FICSA	Federation of International Civil Servants Associations
FICSAS	Federation of Institutions Concerned with the Study of the Adriatic Sea (Yugoslavia)
FICT	Fédération Internationale de Centres Touristiques
FICUR	Fédération Interprofessionnelle de la Congélation Ultrarapide
FID	Fédération Internationale du Diabète
FID	Fédération Internationale de Documentation
FIDA	Federación Interamericana del Algodon
FIDA	Federación Internacional de Abogadas (Chile)
FIDA	Federal Industrial Development Authority (Malaysia)
FIDA	Federation of Industrial Development Associations
FIDA	Federazione Italiana Dettaglianti dell'Alimentazione
FIDA	Nederlandse Vereniging van Fabrikanten, Importeurs en Detaillisten van Audiologische Apparatuur
FIDAC	Fédération Interalliée des Anciens Combattants
FIDAE	Federazione Istituti Dipendenti della Autorità Ecclesiastica
FIDAF	Federación Internacional de Asociaciones de Ferreteros y Almacenistas de Hierros
FIDAL	Federación Internacional del Algodón (Mexico)
FIDAP	Federazione Italiana delle Aziende di Pulimento
FIDAQ	Fédération Internationale des Associations de Quincailliers et de Fer
FIDAS	Fondation Internationale d'Art Sacré
FIDE	Fédération de l'Industrie Dentaire en Europe
FIDE	Fédération Internationale pour le Droit Européen
FIDE	Fédération Internationale des Échecs
FIDEGEP	Fédération Interalliée des Évadés de Guerre et des Passeurs
FIDEM	Fédération Internationale des Éditeurs de Médailles
FIDES	Federación Interamericana de Empresos de Seguros
FIDES	Fonds d'Investissement pour le Développement Économique et Social (of UNO)
FIDH	Fédération Internationale des Droits de l'Homme
FIDI	Fédération Internationale des Déménageurs Internationaux
FIDIA	Fédération Internationale des Intellectuels Aveugles
FIDIC	Fédération Internationale des Industries du Cinema de Film Étroit
FIDIC	Fédération Internationale des Ingénieurs-Conseils

IDIIDS Fédération Internationale des Docteurs-Ingénieurs et Ingénieurs-Docteurs-ès-Sciences

IDJC Fédération Internationale des Directeurs de Journaux Catholiques

IDO Film Industry Defence Organisation

IDOM Fonds d'Investissement et de Développement Économique des Départements d'Outre-Mer

IDOR Fibre Building Board Development Organization Ltd

IDS Falkland Islands Dependencies Survey

IDUBEL Union des Filatures Belges de Fibres Dures

IDUROP Fédération des Fabricants de Ficelles et Cordages de l'Europe Occidentale (*now* EUROCORD)

IDUROP Vereinigung der Westeuropäischen Seil- und Tauwerk-Fabrikanten

IE Fédération Internationale d'Escrime

IEA Fédération Internationale des Experts en Automobile

IEC Fédération Internationale des Associations d'Études Classiques

IEC Fédération Internationale Européenne de la Construction

IEC Fellowship of Independent Evangelical Churches

IED Fédération Internationale des Étudiants en Droit

IEDC Faculté Internationale pour l'Enseignement de Droit Comparé

IEDO Federazione Italiana Exercizi Dettaglianti Ortofrutticoli

IEEBTP Fédération Internationale des Entrepreneurs Européens de Bâtiment et de Travaux Publics

IEESA Fédération Internationale des Électriciens, Électroniciens et Spécialistes de l'Automobile

IEF Fédération Internationale pour l'Economie Familiale

IEFF Fédération Internationale de Football Féminin

IEG Federazione Italiani Editori Giornali

IEJ Fédération Internationale des Éditeurs de Journaux et Publications

IEL Foundation of Latin-American Economic Research

IELS Foreign Information Exchange for Life Scientists (U.S.A.)

FIEM Fédération Internationale de l'Enseignement Ménager

FIEM Fonds International d'Entr'aide Musicale

FIEN Forum Italiano dell' Energia Nucleare

FIEO Federation of Indian Export Organizations

FIEP Fédération Internationale des Écoles de Parents et d'Éducateurs

FIEP Fédération Internationale d'Éducation Physique

FIEP Fédération Internationale des Étudiants en Pharmacie

FIERP Federazione Italiana Esperti Relazioni Pubbliche

FIESP Fédération Internationale des Étudiants en Sciences Politiques

FIET Fédération Internationale des Employés et des Techniciens

FIEU Fonds International d'Échanges Universitaires (de la Conférence Internationale des Étudiants)

FIEV Fédération des Industries des Équipements pour Véhicles

FIF Félag Islenzkra Ferdaskrifstofa

FIF Félag Islenzkra Flugumferdarstjora

FIFA Fédération Internationale du Film d'Art

FIFA Fédération Internationale de Football Association

FIFARMA Federación Latinoamericana de la Industria Farmaceutica (Argentina)

FIFAS Fédération des Industries Françaises d'Articles de Sports

FIFCJ Fédération Internationale des Femmes des Carrières Juridiques

FIFCLC Fédération Internationale de Femmes de Carrières Libérales et Commerciales

FIFDU Fédération Internationale des Femmes Diplômées des Universités

FIFE Fédération Internationale des Associations de Fabricants de Produits d'Entretien

FIFRA Federal Insecticide, Fungicide and Rodenticide Act (U.S.A.)

FIFSP Fédération Internationale des Fonctionnaires Supérieurs de Police

FIG Fédération Internationale des Géomètres

FIG Fédération Internationale de Gymnastique

FIGA Fretted Instrument Guild of America

FIGADI Financière Gabonais de Développement Immobilier

FIGAWA	Technische Vereinigung der Firmen im Gas- und Wasserfach
FIGAZ	Fédération de l'Industrie du Gaz (Belgium)
FIGED	Fédération Internationale des Grandes Entreprises de Distribution
FIGIEFA	Fédération Internationale des Grossistes et Importateurs et Exportateurs en Fournitures Automobiles
FIGISC	Federazione Italiana Gestori Impianti Stradali Carburanti
FIGO	Fédération Internationale de Gynécologie et d'Obstetrique
FIH	Fédération Internationale de Handball
FIH	Fédération Internationale de l'Harmonica
FIH	Fédération Internationale de Hockey sur Gazon
FIH	Fédération Internationale des Hôpitaux
FIHC	Fédération Internationale Haltérophile et Culturiste
FIHC	Fédération Internationale des Hommes Catholiques
FIHU	Fédération Internationale de l'Habitation et de l'Urbanisme
FIHUAT	Fédération Internationale de l'Habitation et de l'Urbanisme et de l'Aménagement du Territoire
FII	Federation of Irish Industries, Ltd
FII	Felag Islenzkra Idnrekenda
FIIC	Fédération Interaméricaine de l'Industrie de la Construction
FIICPI	Fédération Internationale Ingénieurs-conseils en Propriété
FIIG	Fédération des Institutions Internationales Semi-officielles et Privées Etablies à Genève
FIIM	Fédération Internationale de l'Industrie du Médicament
FIIM	Fédération Internationale des Ingénieurs Municipaux
FIIP	Fédération Internationale de l'Industrie Phonographique
FIIR	Federal Institute of Industrial Research (Nigeria)
FIIRO	Federal Institute of Industrial Research Oshodi (Nigeria)
FIJ	Fédération Internationale des Journalistes
FIJ	Fédération Internationale de Judo
FIJA	Fédération Internationale des Journalistes Agricoles
FIJC	Fédération Internationale de la Jeunesse Catholique
FIJET	Fédération Internationale des Journalistes et Écrivains du Tourisme
FIJL	Fédération International des Journalistes Libres
FIJM	Fédération Internationale des Jeunesses Musicales
FIJPAA	Fédération Internationale des Journalistes Professionnels de l'Aéronautique et de l'Astronautique
FIJU	Fédération Internationale des Producteurs de Jus de Fruits
FIL	Fédération Internationale de Laiterie
FIL	Federación Internacional del Luge
FILA	Federation of Indian Library Associations
FILA	Fédération Internationale de Lutte Amateur
FILA	Föreningen Importörer av Lantbruksmaskiner
FILB	Fédération des Industries Lourdes du Bois
FILDIR	Fédération Internationale Libre des Déportés et Internes de la Résistance
FILISBEL	Syndicat Belge des Canalisations Électriques
FILLM	Fédération Internationale des Langues et Littératures Modernes
FILT	Fédération Internationale de Lawn Tennis
FIM	Fédération Internationale Motocycliste
FIM	Fédération Internationale des Musiciens
FIM	Finnish Institute of Management
FIMA	Federazione Italiana Mercanti d'Arte
FIMA	Feria Técnica Internacional de la Maquinaria Agricola
FIMAA	Federazione Italiana Mediatori e Agenti di Affari
FIMARC	Fédération Internationale des Mouvements d'Adultes Ruraux Catholiques
FIMCAP	Fédération Internationale des Mouvements de Jeunesse Catholique Paroissiales
FIMCEE	Fédération Internationale des Marbriers de la CEE
FIME	Fédération Internationale des Maisons de l'Europe
FIMEM	Fédération Internationale des Mouvements d'École Moderne
FIMF	Federación Internacional de Medicina Fisica
FIMITIC	Fédération Internationale des Mutilés et Invalides du Travail et des Invalides Civils

FIMK	Fédération Internationale des Masseurs-Kinésithérapiques Practiciens et Physiothérapie
FIMM	Fédération des Importeurs de la Métallurgie et de la Mécanique
FIMOC	Fédération Internationale des Mouvements Ouvriers Chrétiens
FIMOP	Chambre Syndicale Belge des Fabricants et Importateurs de Matériel de Transmission Oléo-Hydraulique et Pneumatique
FIMP	Fédération Internationale de Médecine Physique
FIMPR	Fédération Internationale de Médecine Physique et Réadaptation
FIMS	Fédération Internationale Médecine Sportive
FIMTM	Fédération des Industries Mécaniques et Transformatrices des Métaux
FIMU	Federación Internacional de Mujeres Universitarias
FIN	Fédération des Industries Nautiques
FIN	Futures Information Network (U.S.A.)
FINA	Fédération Internationale de Natation Amateur
FINAM	Financial Agricultural Company for the South (Italy)
FINAT	Fédération Internationale des Fabricants et Transformateurs d'Adhésifs et Thermo-Collants sur Papiers et autres Supports
FINATA	Fédération Internationale des Associations de Transporteurs et Assimilés
FINCEC	Fédération des Syndicats de Cadres et Agents de Maîtrise de l'Importation et du Négoce des Combustibles et de l'Exploitation de Chauffage
FINEFTA	Finland — European Free Trade Association
FINN-BOARD	Finnish Board Mills Association
FINNBRO-KER	Finlands Skeppsmäklareförbund
FINNCELL	Finska Cellulosaföreningen
FINNMET-AL	Suomen Metalliteollisuusyhdstys
FINNPAP	Finnish Paper Mills' Association
FINS	Fishing Industry News Service (Australia)
FINUMA	Fabrique Ivoirienne de Nuoc Mam
FIO	Food Investigation Organisation
FIO	Fédération Internationale d'Oléicultur

FIOCC	Fédération Internationale des Ouvriers de la Chaussure et du Cuir
FIOCES	Fédération Internationale des Organisations de Correspondances et d'Èchanges Scolaires
FIODS	International Federation of the Organisation of Blood Donors
FIOM	Fédération Internationale des Ouvriers Métallurgistes
FIOPI	Federaçao Interamericana de Organizaçoes des Profissionais da Imprensa
FIOPP	Federación Interamericana de Organizaciones de Periodistas Profesionales
FIORH	Fédération Internationale pour l'Organisation de Rencontres pour Handicapés
FIOST	Fédération Internationale des Organisations Syndicales du Personnel des Transports
FIOW	First International Organisation of Welcome
FIP	Federación Internacional de Periodistas
FIP	Fédération International Pharmaceutique
FIP	Fédération Internationale de Philatélie
FIP	Fédération Internationale des Phonothèques
FIP	Fédération Internationale des Piétons
FIP	Fédération Internationale de Podologie
FIP	Fédération Internationale de la Précontrainte
FIP	Federazione Italiana della Pubblicità
FIP	Félag Islenzkra Prentidnadarins
FIPA	Fédération Internationale de la Presse Agricole
FIPA	Fédération Internationale des Producteurs Agricoles
FIPA	Federazione Italiana Periti Agrari
FIPACE	Fédération Internationale des Producteurs Autoconsommateurs Industriels d'Électricité
FIPAD	Fondation Internationale pour un Autre Développement
FIPAGO	Fédération Internationale des Fabricants de Papiers Gommes
FIPAL	Fondation Internationale pour le Progrès de L'Alimentation
FIPC	Fédération Internationale des Pharmaciens Catholiques
FIPCO	Fédération Internationale pour la Philatélie Constructive
FIPDU	Fédération Internationale des Femmes Diplômées des Universités

FIPE	Federazione Italiana Pubblici Esercizi	**FIRI**	Fishing Industry Research Institute (S. Africa)
FIPESO	Fédération Internationale des Professeurs de l'Enseignement Secondaire Officiel	**FIRM**	Fédération Internationale des Rectifieurs et Reconstructeurs de Moteurs
FIPET	Federación Interamericana de Periodistas y Escritores de Turismo	**FIRMS**	Fonds d'Intervention et de Régularisation du Marché du Sucre
FIPF	Fédération Internationale des Professeurs de Français	**FIRN**	Foreningen af Importører af Raavarer til Naeringsmiddelindustrien (Denmark)
FIPG	Fédération de l'Industrie du Petit Granit	**FIRP**	Federazione Italiana Relazioni Pubbliche
FIPGV	Fédération Internationale de la Presse Gastronomique et Vinicole	**FIRP**	Fondation Internationale pour la Recherche dans le Domaine de la Publicité
FIPIF	Finnish Plastics Industry Federation	**FIRS**	Fédération Internationale de Roller-Skating
FIPJF	Fédération Internationale des Producteurs de Jus de Fruits	**FIRST**	Federal Information Research Science and Technology Network (*of* COSATI)
FIPLV	Fédération Internationale des Professeurs de Langues Vivantes	**FIS**	Fédération Internationale du Commerce des Semences
FIPM	Fédération Internationale de Psychothérapie Médicale	**FIS**	Fédération Internationale de Sauvetage
FIPMEC	Fédération Internationale des Petites et Moyennes Entreprises Commerciales	**FIS**	Fédération Internationale de Ski
FIPMI	Fédération Internationale des Petites et Moyennes Entreprises Industrielles	**FIS**	Fédération Internationale des Settlements
FIPO	Fédération Internationale de la Presse Orientale	**FIS**	Federazione Italiana Sementi
		FIS	Federazione Italiana della Strada
FIPOI	Fondation des Immeubles pour les Organisations Internationales	**FIS**	Félag Íslenzka Stórkaupmanna
FIPP	Fédération Internationale Pénale et Pénitentiare	**FIS**	Fondation Internationale pour la Science (UNESCO)
FIPP	Fédération Internationale de la Presse Périodique	**FIS**	Fondation Internationale Scientifique
FIPP	Fédération Internationale pour la Protection des Populations	**FISA**	Federation of Insurance Staffs Associations
FIPRA	Fédération Internationale de la Presse Agricole	**FISA**	Fédération Internationale des Semaines d'Art
FIPREGA	Fédération Internationale de la Presse Gastronomique, Vinicole et Touristique	**FISA**	Fédération Internationale des Sociétés Aérophilatéliques
FIPRESCI	Fédération Internationale de la Presse Cinématographique	**FISA**	Fédération Internationale des Sociétés d'Aviron
FIPTP	Fédération Internationale de la Presse Technique et Périodique	**FISAG**	Federación Interamericana de Sociedades de Autores y Compositores
FIR	Fédération Internationale des Résistants	**FISAIC**	Fédération Internationale des Sociétés Artistiques et Intellectuelles de Cheminots
FIRA	Fédération Internationale de Rugby Amateur	**FISB**	Fédération Internationale de Ski-bob
FIRA	Furniture Industry Research Association (*formerly FDC*)	**FISC**	Federation Internationale des Chasseurs du Son
		FISC	Foundation for International Scientific Co-ordination
FIRAC	Fédération Internationale des Radio Amateurs Cheminots	**FISC**	Fund for International Student Cooperation
		FISCA	Fédération Internationale des Syndicats Chrétiens de l'Agriculture
FIREC	Fédération Internationale des Rédacteurs en Chef	**FISCC**	Fruit Industry Sugar Concession Committee (Australia)

ISCETCV Fédération Internationale des Syndicats Chrétiens d'Employés Techniciens, Cadres et Voyageurs

ISCM Fédération Internationale des Syndicats Chrétiens de la Métallurgie

ISCOA Fédération Internationale des Syndicats Chrétiens d'Ouvriers Agricoles

ISCOBB Fédération Internationale des Syndicats Chrétiens d'Ouvriers du Bâtiment et du Bois

ISCTTH Fédération Internationale des Syndicats Chrétiens des Travailleurs du Textile et de l'Habillement

ISD Fédération Internationale de Sténographie et de Dactylographie

ISE Fédération Internationale des Sociétés d'Électroencéphalographie

ISE Fédération Internationale Syndicate de l'Enseignement

ISE Fonds International de Secours à l'Enfance (*of* UNO)

ISEC Fédération Internationale Sportive de l'Enseignement Catholique

ISEM Fédération Internationale des Sociétés d'Écrivains Médecins

ISGV Federazione Internazionale della Stampa Gastronomica e Vinicola

ISH Fédération Internationale des Sociétés Magiques

ISH Forskningsinstitutet vid Svensk Handelshogskolan

ISITA Fédération Internationale des Sociétés d'Ingénieurs et de Techniciens de l'Automobile

ISP Fédération Internationale des Sociétés de Philosophie

ISPIU Federazione Italiana Servizi Pubblici Igiene Urbana

ISS Fédération Internationale de Sauvetage et de Secourisme

IST Fédération de l'Industrie Suisse du Tabac

ISTAV Fédération Internationale des Syndicats des Travailleurs de l'Audio-Visuel

ISU Fédération Internationale du Sport Universitaire

IT Fédération Internationale des Traducteurs

IT Federazione Italiana Tabaccai

ITA Fédération Internationale des Techniciens Agronomes

FITA Fédération Internationale de Tir à l'Arc

FITAC Fédération Interaméricaine du Touring et des Automobile-Clubs

FITAP Fédération Internationale des Transports Aériens Privés

FITB Fédération Internationale des Techniciens de la Bonneterie

FITBB Fédération Internationale des Travailleurs du Bâtiment et du Bois

FITC Fédération Internationale du Thermalisme et du Climatisme

FITCA Fédération Internationale des Transports Commerciaux par Automobiles

FITCC-OROC Fédération Internationale de Tai Chi Chuan Orient-Occident (France)

FITCE Fédération des Ingénieurs des Télé-communications de la Communauté Européenne

FITCH Federación Industrial Ferroviaria de Chile

FITCM Federación Internacional de Trabajadores de la Construcción y la Madera

FITCRE Fédération Internationale des Travailleurs Chrétiens Refugiés et Émigrés

FITE Federación Interamericana de Trabajores del Espectáculo

FITEC Fédération Internationale du Thermalisme et du Climatisme

FITH Fédération Internationale des Travailleurs de l'Habillement

FITIM Federación Internacional de Trabajadores de las Industrias Metalurgicas

FITIM Société de Filature et de Tissage de Madagascar

FITITHC Fédération Internationale des Travailleurs des Industries du Textile de l'Habillement et du Cuir

FITITV Federación Interamericana de Trabajadores de la Industria Textil y del Vestuario (Peru)

FITP Fédération Internationale des Travailleurs du Pétrole

FITPAS Federación Internacional de los Trabajadores de las Plantaciones, Agricolas y Similares

FITPASC Fédération Internationale des Travailleurs des Plantations, de l'Agriculture et des Secteurs Connexes

FITPC Fédération Internationale des Travailleurs du Pétrole et de la Chimie

FITPQ Federación Internacional de Trabajadores Petroleros y Químicos

FITS	Fédération Internationale du Tourisme Social
FITT	Fédération Internationale de Tennis de Table
FITT	Fédération International des Travailleurs de la Terre
FIUC	Fédération Internationale des Universités Catholiques
FIV	Fédération de l'Industrie du Verre
FIVA	Fédération Internationale des Voitures Anciennes
FIVA	Federazione Italiana Venditori Ambulanti e Giornalai
FIVB	Fédération Internationale de Volleyball
FIVU	Federación Internacional de Vivienda y Urbanismo
FIVZ	Fédération Internationale Vétérinaire de Zootechnie
FIYTO	Federation of International Youth Travel Organisations
FJCEE	Fédération des Jeunes Chefs d'Entreprises d'Europe
FJF	Finlands Journalistförbund
FJK	Flyjournalisternas Klubb
FKCO	Finlands Kennel Centralorgan
FKE	Federation of Kenya Employers
FKH	Forschungskommission für Hochspannungsfragen (Switzerland)
FKI	Fachvereinigung der Deutschen Kartonagen-Industrie
FKI	Förderungs für Konsumenten-Information (Switzerland)
FKM	Forschungskuratorium Maschinenbau
FKS	Vereniging van Handelaren in Fourage-, Kunstmest-, Hooi-, Stro en Ruwvoeders
FKTG	Fernseh- und Kinotechnische Gesellschaft
FKTU	Federation of Korean Trade Unions
FKV	Fachgruppe der Kultur- und Vermessungsingenieure (Switzerland)
FLAA	Federación Latino Americana de Agrimensores (Uruguay)
FLACSO	Latin American School of Sociology (Chile)
FLAP	Federación Latinoamericana de Parasitologia
FLAPF	Federación Latinoamericana de Productores de Fonograms y Videograms
FLATE-VECU	Federación Latinoamericana de Trabajadores del Textil, Vestido, Calzado, Cuero y Conexos
FLATGRA-PA	Federación Latinoamericana de Trabajadores Gráficos, Papeleros y Afines
FLATICOM	Federación Latinoamerica de Trabajordes de la Industria de la Construcción y la Madera
FLATREP	Comité Pro-Federación Latinoamericana de Trabajadores del Espectaculo Publico
FLATT	Federación Latinoamericana de Trabajadores del Transporte
FLATVECU	Federación Latinoamericana de Trabajadores del Textil, Vestido, Calzado, Cuero y Conexos
FLB	Federal Land Bank (U.S.A)
FLDA	Federal Land Development Authority (Malaysia)
FLEC	Federatie van Land-en Tuinbouwwerktuigen Exploiterende Coöperaties
FLECE	Federación Libre de Escuelas de Ciencias de la Empresa
FLF	Finlands Läkarforbund
FLGEB	Fédération des Livres Généalogiques de l'Espèce Bovine
FLGEC	Fédération des Livres Généalogiques de l'Espèce Chevaline
FLGEP	Fédération des Livres Généalogiques de l'Espèce Porcine
FLI	Fédération Lainière Internationale
FLIDEPEC	Federation of Liberal and Democratic Parties in the European Community
FLING	Guinea National Independence Liberation Front
FLIRT	Federal Librarians Round Table of the American Library Association
FLM	Fédération Luthérienne Mondiale
FLN	Front de Libération Nationale (Algeria)
FLOAG	Front for the Liberation of the Occupied Arabian Gulf
FLOSY	Front for the Liberation of Occupied South Yemen
FLP	Forest Products Laboratory (U.S.A)
FLQ	Front de Libération du Québec (Canada)
FLRFA	Federation of Land Reform Farmers Association (Philippines)
FLS	Finska Läkaresällskapet
FLT	Fachverband Landwirtschaftlicher Trocknungswerke
FLTA	French Lawn Tennis Association

LTPR	Federación Libre de los Trabajadores de Puerto Rico
LUG	Flugfelag Islands
M	Félag Menntaskólakennara
M	Fraternité Mondiale
MA	Farm Management Association
MA	Federation of Management Associations
MA	Fertilizer Manufacturers' Association
MA	Food Machinery Association (*now* PPA)
MAC	Fédération Mondiale des Anciens Combattants
MAEM	Federazione Nazionale Aziende Elettriche Municipalizzate
MAM	Fédération Mondiale des Amis de Musées
MANU	Fédération Mondiale des Associations pour les Nations Unies
MATH	Fédération Mondiale de Travailleurs des Industries Alimentaires, du Tabac et Hôtelière
MB	Federation of Master Builders
MBRA	Flour Milling and Baking Research Association
MBSA	Farmers' and Manufacturers' Beet Sugar Association (U.S.A.)
MC	Fatstock Marketing Corporation, Ltd
MC	Federal Maritime Commission (U.S.A.)
MC	Section des Fleuristes du Marché Commun de la Fédération Européenne des Unions Professionnelles de Fleuristes
MC	Finnish Management Council
MCB	Fédération Mondiale des Organisations de Construction et du Bois
MCE	Federación Mundial Cristiana de Estudiantes
MCE	Federation of Manufacturers of Construction Equipment (*now* FMCEC)
MCEC	Federation of Manufacturers of Construction Equipment and Cranes
MCP	Federation of Manufacturers of Contractors' Plant
MCU	Federación Mundial de Ciudades Unidas (France)
MD	Foreningen af Markedsanalyse-Instittuter i Danmark
ME	Federatie Metaal- en Electrotechnische Industrie
MF	Fachverband Moderne Fremdspracen
MF	Fédération des Médecins de France
FMF	Food Manufacturers Federation
FMFR	Fédération Mondiale des Femmes Rurales
FMH	Foederatio Medicorum Helveticorum (Switzerland)
FMH	Verbindung der Schweizer Ärzte
FMHW	Federation of Mental Health Workers
FMI	Federation of Malta Industries
FMI	Fonds Monétaire Internationale
FMIG	Food Manufacturers Industrial Group
FMJC	Federation Mundial de Juventud Catolica
FMJD	Fédération Mondiale de la Jeunesse Démocratique
FMJFC	Fédération Mondiale des Jeunesses Feminines Catholiques
FMJLR	Fédération Mondiale des Jeunesses Libérales et Radicales
FMM	Fédération Mondiale de la Métallurgie (Belgium)
FMMB	Fédération des Chambres Syndicales des Métaux
FMME	Fund for Multinational Management (U.S.A.)
FMN	Fédération Mondiale de Neurologie
FMN	Fédération Motocycliste Nationale
FMO	Federation of Manufacturing Opticians
FMO	Fédération Professionnelle Agricole pour la Main-d'Oeuvre Saisonnière
FMOB	Federation of Master Organ Builders
FMOI	Fédération Mondiale des Organisations d'Ingénieurs
FMPA	Fédérations Mondiale pour la Protection des Animaux
FMPE	Federation of Master Process Engravers (*now* GRF)
FMPTE	Federation of Municipal Passenger Transport Employers
FMRA	Fertilizer Manufacturers' Research Association (New Zealand)
FMS	Fédération Mondiale des Sourds
FMSE	Federation of Medium and Small Employers
FMSI	Federazione Medicosportiva Italiano
FMSM	Fédération Mondiale pour la Santé Mentale
FMT	Federation of Merchant Tailors of Great Britain, Inc.
FMTA	Farm Machinery and Tractor Trade Association of New South Wales

FMTA	Fédération Mondiale de Travailleurs Agricoles
FMTCM	Federación Mundial de Trabajadores de la Construcción y la Madere
FMTH	Federación Mundial de Trabajadores Agricoles
FMTNM	Fédération Mondiale des Travailleurs Non Manuels
FMTS	Fédération Mondiale des Travailleurs Scientifiques
FMVI	Fachverband Metallwaren- und Verwandte Industrien
FMVJ	Fédération Mondiale des Villes Jumelées
FNAAPDAV	Fédération Nationale des Associations Agricoles pour le Développement de l'Assurance-Vie
FNAARC	Federazione Nazionale fra le Associazioni Agenti e Rappresentanti di Commercio
FNAB	Fédération Nationale des Artisans du Bâtiment et des Branches Professionnelles Annexes
FNAC	Fédération Nationale des Agents Commerciaux
FNACE	Fédération Nationale des Agents sous Contrat de l'État (Zaire)
FNAEM	Federatione Nazionale Aziende Elletriche Municipalizzate
FNAFO	Fédération Nationale de l'Agriculture Force Ouvrière
FNAH	Fonds National de l'Amélioration de l'Habitat
FNAIM	Fédération Nationale des Agents Immobiliers et Mandataires en Vente de Fonds de Commerce
FNAMAC	Fédération Nationale Artisanale des Métiers d'Art et de Création du Bijou et de l'Horlogerie
FNAMGAV	Federazione Nazionale Aziende Municipalizzate Gas, Acqua, Varie
FNAMI	Fonds National Assurance-Maladie-Invalidité
FNAMS	Fédération Nationale des Agriculteurs Multiplicateurs de Semences
FNAO	Fédération Nationale des Commerces de l'Antiquité, de l'Occasion et des Objets de Collection
FNAP	Fédération Nationale des Agences de Presse
FNARER	Fédération Nationale des Associations Régionales d'Économie Rurale
FNAS	Fédération Nationale des Chambres Syndicales des Grossistes en Équipements Sanitaires, Chauffage et Canalisation
FNASAVPA	Fédération Nationale des Associations des Salariés de l'Agriculture pour la Vulgarisation du Progrès Agricole
FNASSEM	Fédération Nationale de Sauvegarde des Sites et Ensembles Monumentaux
FNB	Fédération Nationale du Bois
FNB	Fédération Nationale des Boissons
FNB	Fédération Nationale Bovine
FNB	Food and Nutrition Board (U.S.A.)
FNBB	Fédération Nationale Belge de la Blanchisserie
FNBC	Fédération Nationale des Bibliothèques Catholiques (Belgium)
FNBTR	Fédération Nationale Belge des Transporteurs Routiers
FNC	Federación Nacional de Cafeteros (Colombia)
FNC	Federación Nacional del Campesino (Bolivia)
FNC	Fédération Nationale Chevaline
FNC	Fédération Nationale de la Coiffure
FNC	Fédération Nationale des Cressiculteurs
FNCA	Fédération Nationale de la Coopération Agricole (*now* CFNA)
FNCA	Fédération Nationale des Coopératives Apicoles
FNCA	Fédération Nationale des Coopératives Artisanales de France et d'Outre-Mer
FNCA	Fédération Nationale du Crédit Agricole
FNCAA	Fédération Nationale des Coopératives Agricoles d'Approvisionnement (*now* SYNERVA)
FNCAC	Fédération Nationale des Coopératives Agricoles de Céréales
FNCAFLPT	Fédération Nationale des Coopératives Agricoles de Fruits, Légumes et Pommes de Terre (France) (*now* FFCFLH)
FNCAM	Fédération Nationale du Crédit Agricole Mutuel
FNCASEF	Fédération Nationale des Coopératives Agricoles de Semences Fourragères
FNCAST	Fédération Nationale de la Coopération Agricole Scientifique et Technique
FNCATBI	Fédération Nationale des Coopératives Agricoles de Transformation de la Betterave Industrielle

FNCATS	Fédération Nationale de la Coopération Agricole Technique et Scientifique
FNCAUMA	Fédération Nationale des Coopératives d'Achat et d'Utilisation de Matériel Agricole
FNCAv	Fédération Nationale de la Coopération Avicole
FNCB	Fédération Nationale des Coopératives Agricoles de Transformation de la Betterave Industrielle
FNCB	Fédération Nationale des Commercants en Bestiaux de France
FNCBPV	Fédération Nationale du Commerce du Betáil, Porcs et Viande (Belgium)
FNCBV	Fédération Nationale de la Coopération Bétail et Viande
FNCC	Fédération Nationale de Conserveries Coopératives
FNCC	Fédération Nationale des Coopératives de Céréales
FNCC	Fédération Nationale des Coopératives Chrétiennes
FNCC	Fédération Nationale des Coopératives Cidricoles
FNCC	Fédération Nationale des Coopératives de Consommation
FNCC	Fondo Nacional del Café y del Cacao (Venezuela)
FNCCIB	Fédération Nationale des Chambres de Commerce et d'Industrie de Belgique
FNCCRE	Fédération Nationale des Collectivités Concédantes de Régies Électriques
FNCERO	Fédération Nationale des Comités Économiques Régionaux
FNCERVO	Fédération Nationale des Comités Économiques Régionaux de la Volaille
FNCETA	Fédération Nationale des Centres d'Études Techniques Agricoles
FNCFI	Federazione Nazionale Commercianti Filatelici Italiani
FNCFP	Fédération Nationale des Coopératives Agricoles de Fruits, Primeurs, Fleurs et Autres Produits Agricoles
FNCG	Fédération Nationale des Centres de Gestion
FNCG	Fédération Nationale du Commerce des Grains
FNCH	Fédération Nationale des Coopératives d'Huilerie
FNCHR	Fédération Nationale des Coopératives d'Habitat Rural
FNCIA	Fédération Nationale des Coopératives d'Insémination Artificielle
FNCIB	Fédération Nationale des Chambres Immobilières de Belgique
FNCIVAMA	Fédération Nationale des Centres d'Information et de Vulgarisation Agricoles et Ménagères Agricoles
FNCL	Fédération Nationale des Coopératives Lainières
FNCL	Fédération Nationale des Coopératives Laitières
FNCL	Fédération Nationale des Coopératives Linières
FNCO	Federazione Nazionale dei Collegi delle Ostetriche
FNCP	Federación Nacional de Cooperativas de Producción (Venezuela)
FNCP	Fédération Nationale des Centres de Préformation
FNCP	Fédération Nationale des Constructeurs Promoteurs
FNCPA	Fédération Nationale des Syndicats de Conserveurs de Produits Agricoles
FNCPBV	Fédération Nationale des Coopératives de Producteurs de Bétail et de Viande
FNCPSA	Fédération Nationale des Coopératives de Producteurs de Sel de l'Atlantique
FNCPV	Fédération Nationale des Cooperatives de Producteurs de Viande
FNCPVRT	Fédération Nationale des Coopératives de Production et de Vente des Raisins de Table
FNCR	Fédération Nationale des Coopératives Rizicoles
FNCRA	Fédération Nationale des Comités Régionaux de Propagande et l'Expansion de Produits Agricoles
FNCrA	Fédération Nationale du Crédit Agricole
FNCRP	Fédération Nationale des Comités Régionaux de Propagande
FNCSD	Fédération Nationale des Chambres Syndicales Dentaires (Belgium)
FNCSM	Fédération Nationale des Chambres Syndicales de Médecins
FNCSO	Fédération Nationale des Coopératives de Stockage d'Oléagineux
FNCTB	Fédération Nationale des Coopératives Agricoles de Transformation de la Betterave
FNCTSA	Fédération Nationale de la Coopération Technique Scientifique Agricole

FNCTTFEL	National Federation of Railwaymen, Transport Workers, Civil Servants and Employees of Luxembourg
FNCUMA	Fédération Nationale des Coopératives d'Achat et d'Utilisation de Matériel Agricole
FNCV	Federación Nacional de Cooperatives de Vivienda (Venezuela)
FNCV	Fédération Nationale des Coopératives Vinicoles
FNDAB	Fédération Nationale de Défense de l'Agriculture Biologique
FNDCV	Fédération Nationale des Distilleries Coopératives Vinicoles
FNDE	Fondo Nacional de Desarrollo Económico (Peru)
FNDF	Fédération Nationale des Distributeurs de Films
FNDPL	Fédération Nationale des Détaillants en Produits Laitiers
FNEAA	Fédération Nationale des Exploitants d'Autobus et Autocars
FNEAF	Fédération Nationale des Éleveurs d'Animaux à Fourrure
FNEB	Fédération Nationale des Fabricants de Caisses et Emballages en Bois de France
FNEC	Fédération Nationale des Éleveurs de Chèvres
FNECC	Fédération Nationale des Employés Commerciaux et Cadres (Zaire)
FNED	Fédération Nationale des Étudiants en Droits et en Sciences Politiques
FNEE	Fédération Nationale de l'Équipement Electrique
FNEEGA	Fédération Nationale de l'Énergie Électrique et du Gaz d'Algérie
FNEF	Fédération Nationale des Étalonniers de France
FNENF	Fédération Nationale des Entrepreneurs de Nettoyage de France
FNETA	Fédération Nationale des Entrepreneurs de Travaux Agricoles de France
FNF	Fédération Nationale de la Fourrure
FNFC	Fédération Nationale des Fabricants de Cravates
FNFC	First National Finance Corporation
FNFF	Fédération Nationale des Fleuristes de France
FNFHFTM	Federation of Needle, Fish Hook and Fishing Tackle Makers
FNFMBC	Fédération Nationale des Fabricants de Menuiseries, Charpentes et Bâtiments Industrialisés
FNFPVEI	Fédération Nationale des Fabricants de Peintures, Vernis et Encres d'Imprimerie
FNFR	Fédération Nationale de la Famille Rurale
FNFR	Fédération Nationale des Foyers Ruraux
FNFT	Fédération Nationale des Fabricants-Transformateurs de l'Industrie Cotonnière
FNG	Fédération Nationale du Genêt
FNGAA	Fédération Nationale des Groupements Agricoles d'Approvisionnement
FNGDSB	Fédération Nationale des Groupements de Défense Sanitaire du Bétail
FNGFS	Fédération Nationale des Graines Fourragères de Semence
FNGH	Fédération Nationale de l'Horlogerie en Gros
FNGPA	Fédération Nationale des Groupements de Productivité Agricole
FNGPC	Fédération Nationale des Groupements de Protection des Cultures
FNGPPTP	Fédération Nationale des Groupements et Producteurs de Pommes de Terre de Primeur
FNGRA	Fédération Nationale des Groupements Agricoles d'Approvisionnement
FNGSP	Fédération Nationale des Graines de Semences Potagères, de Fleurs, Semi-Fourragères, Betteraves Fourragères, Haricots, Pois et Fèves de Semences
FNGVPA	Fédération Nationale des Groupements de Vulgarisation et du Progrès Agricole
FNHG	Fédération Nationale de l'Horlogerie en Gros
FNHMID	Fédération Nationale des Huileries Métropolitaines et Industries Dérivées
FNHPV	Fédération Nationale des Herbagers et Producteurs de Viande
FNHR	Fédération Nationale de l'Habitat Rural
FNHRATR	Fédération Nationale de l'Habitat Rural et de l'Aménagement du Territoire Rural
FNI	Fédération Naturiste Internationale
FNIA	Fondo Nacional de Investigaciones Agropecuarias (Venezuela)
FNIB	Fédération Nationale des Infirmières Belges
FNIC	Fédération Nationale des Industries du Corset

NIC	Food and Nutrition Information and Educational Resources Center (U.S.A.)
NICG	Fédération Nationale de l'Industrie des Corps Gras
NICGV	Fédération Nationale des Industries et Commerces en Gros des Viandes
NIE	Fédération Nationale des Industries Électroniques
NIE	Fédération Nationale de l'Industrie des Engrais
NIEBI	Fédération Nationale des Installateurs-Électriciens du Bâtiment et de l'Industrie
NIEF	Federazione Nazionale Insegnanti Educazione Fisica
NIH	Fédération Nationale de l'Industrie Hôtelière de France et d'Outre-Mer
NIL	Federação Nacional dos Industriais de Lanifícios (Portugal)
NIL	Fédération Nationale des Syndicats d'Industriels Laitiers
NIM	Federação Nacional dos Industriais de Moagem (Portugal)
NIMME	Fédération Nationale des Importateurs de la Métallurgie, de la Mécanique et de l'Électronique
NINF	Fédération Nationale Interprofessionnelle de la Noix Française (of CNPFL)
NIPVEICF	Fédération Nationale des Industries des Peintures, Vernis, Encres d'Imprimerie et Couleurs Fines
NISM	Federazione Nazionale Insegnanti Scuole Medie
NITCE	Fédération Nationale des Ingénieurs, Techniciens, Cadres et Employés
NJAP	Fédération Nationale des "Jeunes Alliances Paysannes"
NLA	National Front for the Liberation of Angola
NLG	Fédération Nationale des Livres Zootechniques
NLVPT	Fédération Nationale des Loueurs de Voitures de Place à Taximètre
NMA	Fédération Nationale de la Mutualité Agricole
NMBC	Federation Nationale des Négociants en Gros en Bonneterie, Mercerie, Chaussures et Négoces Connexes de France
NMCCA	Fédération Nationale de la Mutualité du Crédit et de la Coopération Agricoles

FNMF	Fédération Nationale de la Marbrerie Funéraire
FNMIP	Fédération Nationale des Malades, Infirmes et Paralysés
FNMTTB	Fédération Nationale des Maîtres Tailleurs et Tailleuses de Belgique
FNMV	Federation Nationale des Entreprises de Miroiterie-Vitrerie
FNNBEB	Fédération Nationale des Négociants en Bières et Eaux de Boisson (Belgium)
FNNMC	Fédération Nationale des Négociants en Matériaux de Construction
FNO	Fédération Nationale Ovine
FNOA	Fédération Nationale des Organisations Agricoles
FNOCPAB	Fédération Nationale des Organismes de Contrôle des Performances des Animaux de Boucherie
FNOFPCCA	Fédération Nationale des Organismes de Formation et de Promotion des Conseillers et Cadres de l'Agriculture
FNOGA	Fédération Nationale des Organismes de Gestion Agricole
FNOM	Federazione Nazionale degli Ordini dei Medici
FNOMER	Fédération Nationale des Organismes de Migration et d'Établissement Ruraux
FNOMI	Fédération Nationale des Organismes de Migrations Intérieures
FNOOMM	Federazione Nazionale degli Ordeni dei Medici
FNOP	Federatie van Nederlandse Organisaties voor het Personenvervoer
FNOSAD	Fédération Nationale des Organisations Sanitaires Apicoles Départementales
FNOSS	Fédération Nationale des Organismes de Sécurité Sociale
FNOVI	Federazione Nazionale degli Ordini dei Veterinari Italiani
FNP	Fédération Nationale de la Pisciculture
FNP	Fédération Nationale Porcine
FNPA	Fédération Nationale de la Propriété Agricole
FNPBRF	Fédération Nationale des Producteurs de Bois et Reboiseurs Français
FNPC	Fédération Nationale des Producteurs de Chanvre
FNPECSF	Fédération Nationale des Propriétaires et Éleveurs du Cheval de Selle et de Sport Français

FNPF	Fédération Nationale de la Pisciculture Française		**FNRC**	Food and Nutrition Research Centre (Philippines)
FNPF	Fédération Nationale des Producteurs de Fraises		**FNRS**	Fonds National de la Recherche Scientifique (Belgium)
FNPF	Fédération Nationale des Producteurs de Fruits		**FNS**	Fédération Nationale des Scieries (Belgium)
FNPFB	Fédération Nationale des Entrepreneurs de Pompes Funèbres de Belgique		**FNSA**	Fédération Nationale Sanitaire Apicole (*now* FNOSAD)
FNPFC	Fédération Nationale des Producteurs de Fruits à Cidre		**FNSA**	Fédération Nationale des Sinistrés Agricoles
FNPHP	Fédération Nationale des Producteurs de l'Horticulture et des Pépinières		**FNSA**	Fédération Nationale des Syndicats Agricoles (Belgium)
FNPL	Fédération Nationale des Producteurs de Lait		**FNSACC**	Fédération Nationale des Syndicats Agricoles des Cultivateurs de Champignons
FNPL	Fédération Nationale des Producteurs de Légumes		**FNSAFER**	Fédération Nationale des Sociétés d'Aménagement Foncier et d'Établissement Rural
FNPLL	Fédération Nationale des Producteurs de Lavande et de Lavandin		**FNSAGA**	Fédération Nationale des Syndicats d'Agents Généraux
FNPP	Federation Nationale de la Photographie Professionnelle (Belgium)		**FNSBS**	Fonda Nacional de Salud y Bienestar Social (Peru)
FNPPPT	Fédération Nationale Producteurs de Plantes de Pommes de Terre		**FNSCC**	Fédération Nationale des Sociétés Coopératives de Commerçants
FNPPTC	Fédération Nationale des Producteurs de Pommes de Terre de Consommation (*now* FNPTC)		**FNSCCF**	Fédération Nationale des Syndicats de Confituriers et Conserveurs de Fruits
FNPPTI	Fédération Nationale des Producteurs de Pommes de Terre Industrielles		**FNSDPL**	Fédération Nationale des Syndicats de Détaillants en Produits Laitiers
FNPRCM	Fédération Nationale des Producteurs de Reinette Canada de Montagne		**FNSEA**	Fédération Nationale des Syndicats d'Exploitants Agricoles
FNPRT	Fédération Nationale des Producteurs de Raisins de Table		**FNSECSF**	Fédération Nationale des Syndicats d'Éleveurs de Chevaux de Selle Français
FNPSA	Fédération Nationale de Producteurs de Sel de l'Atlantique		**FNSELC**	Fédération Nationale des Syndicats d'Éleveurs de Lapins de Chair
FNPSM	Fédération Nationale des Producteurs de Semences de Maïs		**FNSFPA**	Fédération Nationale des Syndicats de Fabricants de Pâtes Alimentaires
FNPT	Federaçao Nacional dos Productores de Trigo (Portugal)		**FNSHEE**	Fédération Nationale des Syndicats d'Herbagers, Emboucheurs et Engraisseurs
FNPT	Fédération Nationale des Planteurs de Tabac		**FNSI**	Federazione Nazionale della Stampa Italiana
FNPT	Fédération Nationale des Producteurs de Topinambours		**FNSIA**	Fédération Nationale des Syndicats des Industries de l'Alimentation
FNPT	Fédération Nationale des Producteurs de Truffes		**FNSIAA**	Fédération Nationale des Syndicats des Industries de l'Alimentation Animale
FNPTC	Fédération Nationale des Groupements de Producteurs de Pommes de Terre de Consommation		**FNSIC**	Fédération Nationale des Syndicats d'Ingénieurs et de Cadres
			FNSICA	Fédération Nationale des Sociétés d'Intérêt Collectif Agricole
FNPVCC	Fédération Nationale des Producteurs de Vins de Consommation Courante		**FNSICAE**	Fédération Nationale des Sociétés d'Intérêt Collectif Agricole d'Électricité
FNPVDQS	Fédération Nationale des Producteurs de Qualité Supérieure		**FNSIL**	Fédération Nationale des Syndicats d'Industriels Laitiers

FNSIOT	Fédération Nationale des Syndicats d'Initiative et Offices de Tourisme
FNSITC-EOAA	Fédération Nationale des Syndicats d'Ingénieurs, Techniciens, Cadres Administratifs et Employés des Organisations Agricoles de l'Agriculture
FNSOAI	Fédération Nationale des Syndicats Ouvriers Agricoles Indépendants
FNSP	Fédération Nationale des Sapeurs-Pompiers Français
FNSPF	Fédération Nationale des Sociétés Photographiques de France
FNSPFS	Fédération Nationale des Syndicats de Propriétaires Forestiers Sylviculteurs
FNSPP-TCQC	Fédération Nationale des Syndicats des Producteurs de Pommes de Terre de Consommation de Qualité Contrôlée
FNSPV	Fédération Nationale des Syndicats de Pépiniéristes Viticulteurs
FNSSN	Fédération des Sociétés de Sciences Naturelles
FNSUTL	Fédération Nationale des Syndicats Utilisateurs et Transformateurs de Lait (now FNSIL)
FNT	Federación Nacional de Tabacaleros (Colombia)
FNTA	Fédération Nationale des Transporteurs Auxiliaires
FNTA	National Federation of Sugar Workers (Cuba)
FNTAF	Fédération Nationale des Travailleurs de l'Agriculture et des Forêts de France et d'Outremer
FNTAL	Fédération Nationale du Teillage Agricole du Lin
FNTCA	Fédération Nationale des Techniciens et Cadres de l'Agriculture (CGA)
FNTDP	Fédération Nationale des Transports de Denrées Périssables et Assimilés
FNTM	Federação Nacional dos Trabalhadores Marítimos (Brazil)
FNTP	Federação Nacional dos Productores de Trigo (Portugal)
FNTP	Fédération Nationale des Transformateurs de Papier
FNTR	Fédération Nationale des Transports Routiers
FNUAP	Fonds des Nations Unies pour les Activités en Matière de Population
FNUDC	Fondo de las Naciones Unidas para el Desarrollo de la Capitalización
FNUDIO	Fonds des Nations Unies pour le Développement de l'Irian Occidental
FNUMAB	Fédération Nationale Unifiée des Maîtres-Artisans du Bâtiment
FNUNF	Fédération Nationale pour l'Utilisation Naturelle des Fruits
FNUPA	Fédération Nationale des Unions Professionnelles Agricoles (Belgium)
FNUR	Fonds des Nations Unies pour les Réfugiés
FNVPA	Fonds National de la Vulgarisation et du Progrès Agricoles
FNZ	Koninklijk Nederlandse Zuivelbond
FOA	U.S. Foreign Operations Administration
FOAD	Fédération des Organisations Agricoles Diverses
FOB	Federatie van Onderlinge Brandwaarborgmaatschappij in Nederland
FOBB	Fédération Suisse des Ouvriers sur Bois et du Bâtiment
FOBFO	Federation of British Fire Organisations
FOBID	Federatie van Organisaties op het Gebied van Bibliotheek-Informatie-, en Dokumentatiewezen
FOCAP	Fédération Odontologique d'Amérique Centrale et du Panama
FOCOL	Federation of Coin-Operated Launderettes
FOCWA	Nederlandse Vereniging van Ondernemers in het Carosseriebedrijf
FOE	Friends of the Earth (U.S.A.)
FOEGIN	Vereniging voor Fabrieken op Electrotechnisch Gebied in Nederland
FOESSA	Fundación Fomento de Estudios Sociales y de Sociología Aplicada
FOEXP	Export Expansion Group (Brazil)
FOFATUSA	Federation of Free African Trade Unions of South Africa
FOFI	Federazione degli Ordini dei Farmacisti Italiani
FOFTA	Fédération Odontologique de France et des Territoires Associés
FOGA	Fonds d'Orientation de Garantie Agricole (de la C.E.E.)
FOGRA	Deutsche Gesellschaft für Forschung im Graphischen Gewerbe
FOGRA	Forschungsgesellschaft für Druck- und Reproduktiontechnik

FOLA	Federaçion Odontologica Latino-Americana (Argentina)
FOM	Federatie Organisaties in de Machinehandel
FOM	Stichting voor Fundamenteel Onderzoek der Materie
FOMH	Fédération Suisse des Ouvriers sur Métaux et Horlogers
FOMIZ	Federation des Ouvriers des Mines du Zaire
FOMO	Federatie van het Officieel Middelbaar Onderwijs van de Hogere Graad van België
FOMRE	Stichting Fundamenteel Onderzoek der Materie met Röntgen- en Electronenstralen
FONADE	Fondo Nacional para el Desarrollo (Colombia)
FONADER	Fonds National de Développement Rural (Cameroons)
FONAIAP	Fondo National de Investigaciones Agropecuarias (Venezuela)
FONASBA	Federation of National Associations of Ship Brokers and Agents
FONUBEL	Forum Nucléaire Belge
FONUR	Fondo de las Naciones Unidas para los Refugiados
FOPERDA	Père Damien Foundation
FOPRA	Federation of Private Residents Associations
FOPS	Federation of Playgoers Societies
FOPSA	Federation of Productivity Services Associations
FORALAC	Société Forestière Agricole, Industrielle et Commerciale en Afrique Équatoriale
FORATOM	Forum Atomique Européen
FOREAMI	Fonds Reine Elizabeth pour l'Assistance Médicale aux Indigènes (Belgium)
FOREX	International Association of Exchange Dealers
FORMA	Fonds d'Orientation et de Régularisation des Marchés Agricoles
FORPPA	Fondo de Ordenacion y Regulacion de Productos y Precios Agrarios
FORS	Fondation pour la Recherche Sociale
FORTRA	Federation of Radio and Television Retailers Association
FOS	Fisheries Organisation Society
FOS	Foreniging för Orientaliska Studier
FOSKOR	Phosphate Development Corporation (South Africa)
FOSS	Föreningen Ostra Sveriges Skogsarbeten

FOTIM	Fotobranchens Importørforening
FPA	Family Planning Association
FPA	Fédération de la Propriété Agricole
FPA	Film Production Association of Great Britain
FPA	Fire Protection Association
FPA	Foreign Press Association
FPA	Foyers de Progrès Agricole
FPAA	Federación Panamericana de Asociaciones de Arquitectos
FPAI	Family Planning Association of India
FPAP	Family Planning Association of Pakistan
FPBAI	Federation of Publishers' and Booksellers' Association in India
FPC	Federation of Painting Contractors Ltd. (*now* NFPDC)
FPC	Flowers Publicity Council
FPC	Fondation pour la Protection des Consommateurs (Switzerland)
FPC	United States Federal Power Commission
FPCEA	Fibreboard Packing Case Employers Association
FPCMA	Fibreboard Packing Case Manufacturers Association
FPCS	Farm Planning Computer Service
FPDA	Finnish Plywood Development Association
FPE	Fédération Professionnelle des Producteurs et Distributeurs d'Électricité de Belgique
FPF	Finska Pappersingeniörsföreningen
FPGAUS	Federated Pecan Growers Associations of the United States
FPI	Fédération Prohibitionniste Internationale
FPM	Fachverband Pulver-Metallurgie
FPPB	Family Planning and Population Board (Singapore)
FPPE	Fédération du Prêt à Porter Feminin
FPPTE	Federation of Public Passenger Transport Employers
FPRC	Flying Personnel Research Committee
FPRI	Forest Products Research Institute (Ghana, Philippines)
FPRL	Forest Products Research Laboratory
FPRS	Forest Products Research Society (U.S.A.)
FPS	Fauna Preservation Society
FPS	Federation of Personnel Services of Great Britain
FPS	Koninklijke Vereniging 'Het Friesch Paardenstamboek'

PVPC	Federation of Paint and Varnish Production Clubs (U.S.A.)
R	Fotohandlarnas Riksförbund
RA	Federación Rural Boliviana
RAME	Fund for the Replacement of Animals in Medical Experiments
RANA	Groupement des Fabricants et Représentants des Adjuvants en Nutrition Animale (Belgium)
RAP	Frente de Acción Popular (Chile)
RB	Federal Reserve Board (U.S.A.)
RB	Fédération Routière Belge
RB	Fisheries Research Board of Canada
RB	Frente de la Revolución Boliviana
RC	File Research Council
RD	Fédération Romande des Détaillants
RD	Forbrugerrådet
RE	Fédération Romande des Écoles de Conduite
REC	Forestry Research and Education Centre (Sudan)
RED	Fund for Rural Economic Development (Canada)
REJULI	Frente Justicialista do Liberacion (Argentina)
RELIMO	Mozambique Liberation Front
RG	Federal Republic of Germany
RH	Fédération pour le Respect de l'Homme et de l'Humanité
RHB	Federation of Registered House-builders
RI	Fédération Romande Immobilière (Switzerland)
RI	Food Research Institute (U.S.A.)
RI	Foreningen af Rådgivende Ingeniører
RI	Forest Research Institute (India)
RIA	Compagnie Internationale pour la Fabrication de l'Aluminium (Africa)
RICO	Friesche Coöperatieve Zuivel-Export Vereniging
RIDA	Fund for Research and Investment for the Development of Africa Ltd (U.K.)
RISA	Fuel Research Institute of South Africa
RITALUX	Union Économique France, Italie, Benelux
RL	Fisheries Research Laboratory Marine Department (N.Z.)
RM	Fédération Romande des Maîtres Marbriers
RM	Fédération Romande des Maîtres Menuisiers Ébenistes, Fabricants de Meubles, Charpentiers et Parqueteurs (Switzerland)
FRMPP	Fédération Romande des Maîtres Plâtriers-Peintres
FRO	Fire Research Organisation *see* JFRO
FROLINAT	Front de Libération Nationale Tschadienne
FROLIZI	Front for the Liberation of Zimbabwe
FRP	Fédération Romande de Publicité (Switzerland)
FRR	Foreningen af Registrerede Revisorer
FRS	Federal Reserve System (U.S.A.)
FRS	Fruit Research Station (DSIR) (N.Z.)
FRS	Schweizerischer Strassenverkehrsverband
FRSEB	Fédération Régionale des Syndicats des Éleveurs de Brebis
FRSKGD	Fauna Research Section of the Kenya Game Department
FRUBO	Nederlandse Bond van Grossiers in Zuidvruchten
FRUCOM	Fédération Européenne des Importateurs de Fruits Secs, Conserves, Épices et Miels
FRV	Fédération Romande des Vignerons (Switzerland)
FRV	Félag Rådgjafarverkfroedinga
FRW	Federation of Rural Workers
FS	Fachverband für Strahlenschutz (Switzerland)
FS	Forest Service (U.S.A.)
FSA	Farm Security Administration (U.S.A.)
FSA	Fédération Suisse des Avocats
FSA	Federazione Svizzera degli Avvocati
FSA	Föreningen Sveriges Arbetsterapeuter
FSAA	Family Service Association of America
FSAC	Folia Scientifica Africae Centralis
FSAD	Foreningen af Sygehusadministratores i Danmark
FSAI	Fédération Suisse des Architectes Indépendants
FSASR	Fédération des Sociétés d'Agriculture de la Suisse Romande
FSAV	Fédération Suisse des Agences de Voyages
FSB	Fachverband Schweizerischer Betonvorfabrikanten
FSB	Fédération Spéléologique de Belgique
FSC	Fédération Suisse des Consommateurs
FSCC	Federal Surplus Commodities Corporation (U.S.A.)

FSCRH	Fédération Suisse des Cafetiers, Restaurateurs et Hôteliers	**FSP**	Popular Socialist Front (Portugal)
FSE	Fédération des Sociétés Suisses d'Employés	**FSPD**	Fachverband Schweizerischer Privat-Detektive
FSE	Fonds Social Européen	**FSPSP**	Fédération Suisse du Personnel des Services Publics
FSF	Fédération Suisse du Franchising	**FSR**	Foreningen af Statsautoriserede Revisorer
FSF	Federazione Svissera dei Fisioterapisti Diplomati	**FSRA**	Federal Sewage Research Association (U.S.A.)
FSF	Finlands Sjuksköterskeförbund	**FSRP**	Forum Suisse des Relations Publiques
FSF	Flight Safety Foundation (U.S.A.)	**FSS**	Fédération Suisse des Sélectionneurs
FSFA	Federation of Specialised Film Associations	**FSS**	Föreningen Sveriges Skrivmaterielleverantörer
FSFF	Finlands Svenska Författareföreningen	**FSSA**	Fertilizer Society of South Africa
FSFRL	Far Seas Fisheries Research Laboratory	**FST**	Federatie Steen-, Cement-, Glas- en Keramische Industrie
FSG	Föreningen Svenska Glasstillverkare	**FSTAL**	Fédération Syndicale du Teillage Agricole du Lin
FSGD	Federation of Sports Goods Distributors		
FSI	Fachverband Schneidwarenindustrie	**FSTL**	Föreningen Svenska Tradgärds- och Landskapsarkitekter
FSI	Fédération Spirite Internationale		
FSI	Föreningen Sveriges Industrifornonodenhetsleverantörer	**FSUEO**	Fédération des Syndicats Unis des Employés et Ouvriers du Liban
FSI	International Society of Fire Service Instructors	**FSWA**	Federation of Sewage Works Associations (U.S.A.)
FSK	Fachverband Schaumkunstoffe im GKV	**FSWU**	Federation of Sudanese Workers Unions
FSK	Finlands Svenska Kommunförbund	**FTA**	Federation of Trade Associations
FSK	Finlands Svenska Köpmannaförbund	**FTA**	Fördergesellschaft Technischer Ausbus
FSK	Schweizerischer Fachverband für Sand und Kies	**FTA**	Freight Trade Associations Ltd
FSLJ	Föreningen Skogs- och Lantbruksjournalister	**FTC**	Federal Trade Commission (U.S.A.)
FSLTT	Fédération des Syndicats Libres des Travailleurs de la Terre	**FTESA**	Foundry Trades Equipment and Supplies Association
FSM	Fédération Sephardite Mondiale	**FTF**	Fibre Trade Federation
FSM	Fédération Syndicale Mondiale	**FTG**	Forschungsgemeinschaft für Technisches Glas
FSMG	Vereniging van Fabrikanten van Stempels, Matrijzen, Mallen en Andere Speciale Gereedschappen	**FTGB**	Federatie Textiel Groothandelsbonden
		FTMA	Federated Textile Managers Associations
FSMGB	Federation of Small Mines of Great Britain	**FTO**	Fruit Traffic Organisation
FSMT	Fédération Suisse des Marchands de Tabacs	**FTPR**	Federación del Trabajo de Puerto Rico
FSN	Fachverband Schweizerischer Neonfirmen	**FTPS**	Food Trades Protection Society
FSN	Federatie van Schoenwinkeliersverenigingen	**FTS**	Fédération Internationale de Sauvetage
FSNRIC	Federation Syndicate Nationale de la Répresentation Commerciale	**FTSKO**	Federation of Textile Societies and Kindred Organisations
FSNT	Federazione Svizzera dei Negozianti in Tabacchi	**FTU**	Federation of Trade Unions (Hong Kong)
		FTUN	Federación de Transportadores Unidos Nicaraguense
FSP	Fédération Suisse des Physiothérapeutes		
FSP	Foreningen Sveriges Plastfabrikanter		
FSP	Foundation for the Peoples of the South Pacific	**FUAAV**	Fédération Universelle des Associations d'Agencies de Voyages

FUACE	Fédération Universelle des Associations Chrétiennes d'Étudiants
FUCUA	Federation of University Conservative and Unionist Associations
FUDECO	Fundación para el Desarrollo de la Región Centro-Occidental de Venezuela
FUE	Federated Union of Employers (Eire)
FUEN	Federal Union of European Nationalities
FUEV	Föderalistische Union Europäischer Volksgruppen
FUGB	Federation of Ukrainians in Great Britain
FULREAC	Fondation de l'Université de Liège pour les Recherches Scientifiques en Afrique Centrale
FUMOA	Société des Fûts Métalliques de l'Ouest Africain
FUNBEG	Brazilian Foundation for the Development of Science Teaching
FUND	International Monetary Fund
FUNDA-COMUN	Fundación para el Desarrollo de la Comunidad
FUNDAR	Fundación para el Desarrollo Regional
FUNDWI	Fund of the United Nations for the Development of West Irian
FUNK	Front Uni National du Kampuchea (Cambodia)
FUNU	Force d'Urgence des Nations Unies
FUPAC	Federación de Universidades Privadas de America Central (Guatemala)
FUPADE	Fundación Panamericana de Desarrollo (U.S.A.)
FURC	Fonds pour l'Utilisation Rationelle des Combustibles
FUS	Fruit-Union Suisse
FUW	Farmers Union of Wales
FVAV	Fédération Vaudoise des Sociétés d'Agriculture et de Viticulture (Switzerland)
FVB	Fabrikanten-Verband für Beleuchtungskörper
FVCQFRA	Fruit and Vegetable Canning and Quick Freezing Research Association (U.K.) (now FVPRA)
FVG	Fachverband für das Güterbeförderungsgewerbe Österreiche
FVH	Föreningen för Vattenhygien
FVK	Landelijke Vereniging van Kaashandelaren
FVL	Fachverband Lichtwerbung

FVM	Föreningen Svenska Verktygmaskintillverkare
FVNH	Federatief Verbond Nederlandse Houtindustrie
FVPRA	Fruit and Vegetable Preservation Research Association (formerly FVCQFRA)
FVR	Federal Department of Veterinary Research (Nigeria)
FVTDV	Groep der Fabrikanten en Vertegenwoordigers van Toevoegingsmiddelen voor de Dierlijke Voeding
FWA	Farmers and World Affairs (U.S.A.)
FWCC	Friends World Committee for Consultation
FWEA	International Federation of Workers Educational Associations
FWHF	Federation of World Health Foundations
FWID	Federation of Wholesale and Industrial Distributors
FWMB	Federation of Wholesale and Multiple Bakers (*now* FB)
FWO	Federation of Wholesale Organisations (*now* FWID)
FWPCA	Federal Water Pollution Control Administration (U.S.A.)
FWQA	Federal Water Quality Administration (*later* WQO *of* EPA) (U.S.A.)
FWRMGB	Federation of Wire Rope Manufacturers of Great Britain
FYDEP	Empresa Nacional de Fomento y Desarrollo Económico del Petén (Guatemala)
FYF	Finlands Yrkeskvinnors Förbund
FZD	Finanz- und Zolldepartement (Switzerland)
FZG	Federation of Zoological Societies of Great Britain and Northern Ireland
FZLE	Federatie der Zelfstandige Landmeters-Experten (Belgium)
FZY	Federation of Zionist Youth

G

GA	General Assembly of the United Nations
GA	Gemmological Association
GA	Geographical Association

GA	Grafiska Arbetsgivareförbundet
GA	Gypsum Association (U.S.A.)
GAAM	Ghana Association for the Advancement of Management
GABA	Nederlandse Vereniging van Bedrijven in de Gemengde Branche (Glas, Aardewerk en Bijbehorende Artikelen)
GABIM	La Gabonaise Immobilière
GABOA	Société Gabonaise d'Oxygène et d'Acétylène
GABOMA	Société Gabonaise des Grands Magasins
GABONAP	Société Gabonaise de Diffusion d'Appareils Électriques
GABONEX	Société Gabonaise d'Exploitation Vinicole
GACIFAL	Groupe Consultatif de la Recherche et de l'Enseignement Forestier pour l'Amérique Latine
GAD	Groupe Africaine de Distribution
GAD	Groupe d'Aide au Développement
GADEF	Groupement des Associations Dentaires Francophones
GAE	Groupements Agricoles d'Exploitation
GAEC	Groupements Agricoles d'Exploitation en Commun
GAF	Glasmästeribranchens Arbetsgivareförbund
GAF	Gulvbeloegningsbranchens Arbejds-giverforening
GAFICA	Grupo Asesor de la FAO para la Integración Económica Centroamericana (Guatemala)
GAFTA	Grain and Feed Trade Association
GAGB	Gemmological Association of Great Britain
GAI	Guild of Architectural Ironmongers
GAIF	General Arab Insurance Federation (Egypt)
GAIF	General Assembly of International Sports Federations
GAILL	Groupement des Allergologistes et Immunologistes de Langues Latines
GAJ	Guild of Agricultural Journalists
GALA	Grupo de Acústicos Latinoamericanos
GALF	Groupement des Acousticiens de Langue Française
GALIAF	Société Gaz Liquéfiés d'Afrique
GAM	Groupement des Aciers Moulés (Belgium)
GAMA	Guitar and Accessory Manufacturers Association of America
GAMI	Groupement pour l'Avancement de la Mécanique Industrielle
GAMM	Gesellschaft f. Angewandt Mathematik und Mechanik
GAMS	Groupement pour l'Avancement des Méthodes Spectroscopiques et Physicochimiques d'Analyse
GAMTA	General Aviation Manufacturers and Traders Association
GANEFO	Federation of the Games of the New Emerging Forces (Indonesia)
GANVAM	Grupo Autonomo Nacional de Vendedores de Automobiles, Camiones y Motorcicletas del Sindicato Nacional del Metal
GAPAN	Guild of Air Pilots and Navigators
GAPAVE	Groupement des Associations de Propriétaires d'Appareils à Vapeur et Électriques
GAPINDO	Perkumpulan Koperasi Gabungan Pembelian Importir Indonesia
GAPMB	Ghana Agricultural Produce Marketing Board
GARB	Garment and Allied Industries Requirements Board
GARP	Global Atmospheric Research Programme (Switzerland)
GAS	General Aviation Services (Canada)
GAS	Group Autonomous Specialised Working Party (of CCITT)
GASC	German-American Securities Corporation
GASGA	Group for Assistance on Storage of Grains in Africa
GAT	Groupement Africain des Travaux au Cameroun
GATA	Glass and Allied Trades Association
GATCO	Guild of Air Traffic Control Officers
GATR-AMAR	Société Gabonaise de Transports Maritimes
GATT	General Agreement on Tariffs and Trade (Switzerland)
GAUFCC	General Assembly of Unitarian and Free Christian Churches
GAUK	Gamekeepers Association of the United Kingdom
GAV	Gemeinschaftsausschuss Verzinken
GAWI	Gesellschaft für Abwicklung Wirtschaftlicher Angelegenheiten
GAZ-EUROUD	Comité Européen des Fabricants d'Appareils et de Machines de Soudage aux Gaz

GBAEV	Gesellschaft für Biologische Anthropologie, Eugenik und Verhaltenforschung
GBARC	Great Britain Aeronautical Research Committee
GBDL	Gesellschaft für Bibliothekswesen und Dokumentation des Landbaues
GBDO	Guild of British Dispensing Opticians
GBF	Grafiske Bedrifters Felleskontor
GBI	Gesamtverband Besteckindustrie
GBNE	Guild of British Newspaper Editors
GBO	Groepering van de Vloer- en Muurbekledingsondernemigen (Belgium)
GBO	Groupement Belge des Omnipraticiens
GBRS	Groupe Belge de Recherche Sous-Marine
GBS	Groupement des Unions Professionnelles Belges de Médecins
GCA	Groep Fabrieken van Apparaten voor de Chemische Industrie
GCB	Greyhound Consultative Body
GCBA	Guernsey Cattle Breeders' Association
GCBS	General Council of British Shipping
GCDP	Grupo Coordinador do Desenvolvimento da Pesca (Brazil)
GCDRA	Green Crop Driers Research Association
GCE-CEE	Groupement des Caisses d'Épargne de la CEE
GCFI	Gulf and Caribbean Fisheries Institute
GCHQ	Government Communications Headquarters
GCI	Génie Climatique International
GCIAI	Grupo Consultivo sobre Investigación Agricola International (FAO etc.)
GCIC	Groupement Cinématographique International de Conciliation
GCPAI	Groupe Consultatif de la Production Alimentaire et de Investissement (FAO)
GCPAIA	Grupo Consultivo sobre Producción Alimentaria e Inversiones Agrícolas (FAO)
GCRAI	Groupe Consultatif de la Recherche Agricole Internationale (FAO etc.)
GCRI	Glasshouse Crops Research Institute
GCRO	General Council and Registrar of Osteopaths
GCS	Game Conservation Society (U.S.A.)
GCT	Groupe Consultatif Technique (UNO)
GCW	Gesellschaft der Chirurgen in Wien (Austria)
GDAPS	Grémio dos Armadores da Pesca da Sardinha (Portugal)

GdB	Gesellschaft des Bauwesens
GDBA	Genossenschaft Deutscher Bühnen-Angehörigen
GDBH	Gesellschaft Deutscher Berg- und Hüttenleute
GDCh	Gesellschaft Deutscher Chemiker
GDDA	General Desert Development Authority (Egypt)
GDE	Gemeinschaft Deutscher Einkaufskontore des Nahrungsmittelgrosshandels
GDF	Gaz de France
GDG	Gemeinschaft Deutscher Gross-Messen
GDL	Gemeinschaft Deutscher Lehrerverbände
GDL	Gesamtverband des Deutschen Leder-Gross- und -Aussenhandels
GDM	Gesamtverband Deutscher Metallgiessereien
GDM	Gesamtverband Deutscher Musikfachgeschäfte
GDMB	Gesellschaft Deutscher Metallhütten- und Bergleute
GDNÄ	Gesellschaft Deutscher Naturforscher und Arzte
GDO	Gesellschaft der Orgelfreunde
GDPF	Groupement des Directeurs Publicitaires de France
GDR	German Democratic Republic
GDS	Gesamtverband Deutscher Spielwaren-exporteure
GDSI	Global Development Studies Institute (U.S.A.)
GEA	Ghana Employers Association
GEA	Global Education Associates (U.S.A.)
GEAE	Groupement Européen des Ardennes et de l'Eifel
GEAMR	Groupement Européen des Associations des Maisons de Réforme
GEB	General Education Board (U.S.A.)
GEBCO	General Bathymetric Chart of the Oceans
GEBECOMA	Groupement Belge des Constructeurs de Matériel Aérospatial
GEBO	Golventreprenörernas Branschorganisation
GEBRAM	Gespreksgroep Fabrikanten van Brandweervoertuigen, -Apparaten en-Material
GEC	General Electric Company, Ltd
GECA	Groupe Européen de Chimiothérapie Anticancéreuse

GECA	Groupement National d'Exploitation des Conserves Agricoles (France)	**GENEMA**	Groupement d'Exportation des Navires et Engins de Mer et Acier
GECICAM	Entreprise de Génie Civil et Construction au Cameroun	**GENICIAT**	Genie Civil en Afrique Tropicale (Ivory Coast)
GECITEX	Groupement Européen de Coordination d'Industries Textiles Diverses (France)	**GEOAR**	General Egyptian Organization for Aquatic Resources
GECOMIN	General Congolese Ore Company	**GEOBOL**	Servicio Geológico de Bolivia
GECUS	Groupe d'Études et de Coordination de l'Urbanisme Souterrain	**GEP**	Groupement Intersyndical pour l'Equipement des Industries du Pétrole, du Gaz Naturel et de la Pétrochimie
GEDAG	Gesamtverband Deutscher Angestellten-Gewerkschaften	
GEDIP	Grupo Executivo do Desenvolimento da Industria de Pesca	**GEPA**	Gulf-European Freight Association (U.S.A.)
		GEPHA	Bundesverband des Genossenschaftlichen Pharmazeutischen Grosshandels in Deutschland
GEDRT	Groupe Européen d'Échange d'Experience sur la Direction de la Recherche Textile	
GEEDA	Groundnut Extractions Export Development Association (India)	**GEPLACEA**	Grupo de los Paises Latinoamericanos y del Caribe Exportadores del Azucar
GEER	Groupement d'Étude pour l'Équipement Rural	**GEPLASE**	Grupo de Estudos para o Plantio da Seringueira (Brazil)
GEERS	Groupe d'Études Européen des Recherches Spatiales	**GEPS**	Groupe d'Études des Protéines de Soja
		GER	Group of European Radiotherapists
GEFACS	Groupement des Fabricants d'Appareils Sanitaires en Céramique de la CEE	**GER**	Groupement des Entreprises de Revêtements de Sols et Murs (Belgium)
GEFAP	Groupement Européen des Associations Nationales de Fabricants de Pesticides	**GERCA**	Grupo Executivo de Racionalizaçao da Cafeicultura (Brazil)
GEFCO	Griqualand Exploration and Finance Company	**GERDAT**	Groupement d'Études et de Recherches pour le Développement de l'Agronomie Tropicale
GEFIU	Gesellschaft für Finanzwirtschaft in der Unternehmensführung	**GERDEC**	Groupe d'Études et de Recherches pour le Développement Culturel
GEIA	Executive Group for the Automotive Industry (Brazil)	**GERDES**	Groupe d'Études et de Recherches pour le Développement des Sciences Sociales
GELNA	Groupe d'Études sur la Littérature Néo-Africaine	**GEREC**	Groupement pour l'Étude et la Réalisation d'Ensembles Contrôle-Commande
GELTSPAP	Group of Experts on Long-Term Scientific Policy and Planning (UNESCO)	**GERIP**	Groupe d'Études et de Recherches des Infirmiers Psychiatriques
GEMAS	Groupement Européen des Maisons d'Alimentation et d'Approvisionnement à Succursales	**GERSPPA**	Group d'Études et de Recherches pour les Solutions aux Problèmes des Personnes Âgées
GEMEC	Grupo de Estudio para el Mejoramiento de la Ensenanza de las Ciencias en Honduras	**GES**	Gesellschaft für Electronische Systemforschung
GEMP	Groupe d'Études et de Mesures de la Productivité (*of* AFAP)	**GESAMP**	Joint Group of Experts on the Scientific Aspects of Marine Pollution
GEMS	Gilevi Exploration and Mining Syndicate (Tanzania)	**GESEM**	Groupement Européen des Sources d'Eaux Minérales Naturelles
GEN	Group of European Nutritionists (Switzerland)	**GEVES**	Groupe d'Étude et de Contrôle des Variétés et des Semences
GENCO	Société Générale de Construction au Cameroun	**GEVL**	Groupement International d'Étude pour l'Exploitation des Voitures-Lits en Europe
GENECO	Genootschap van Nederlandse Componisten	**GEW**	Gewerkschaft Erziehung und Wissenschaft

GEWINA Genootschap voor Geschiedenis der Geneeskunde, Wiskunde, Natuurwetenschappen en Techniek

GfA Gesellschaft für Arzneipflanzenforschung

GFA Groupement Foncier Africain

GFA Groupement Français d'Assurances

GFB Gemeinschaft Fachärztlicher Berufsverbände

GFB Schweizerische Gesellschaft für Bauforschung

GFC Groep Fabrikanten van Compressoren

GFCI Groupement Foncier de la Côte-d'Ivoire

GFCM General Fisheries Council for the Mediterranean (FAO)

GFDNA Grain and Feed Dealers National Association (U.S.A.)

GfdS Gesellschaft für Deutsche Sprache

GFF Gesellschaft zur Förderung der Forschung (Switzerland)

GFFC Groupement Français des Fabricants de Carton

GFI Glas Forsknings Institutet

GfK Gesellschaft für Kernforschung

GfK Gesellschaft für Konsum-, Markt- und Absatzforschung

GFM Gesellschaft f. Marktforschung

GFM Schweizerische Gesellschaft für Marktforschung

GFP Gesellschaft zur Förderung der Photographie

GFPE Gesellschaft für Praktische Energiekunde

GFPF Gesellschaft zur Förderung Pädagogischer Forschung

GFSAEPCS Groupement Fédératif des Syndicats et Associations d'Éleveurs et Propriétaires de Chevaux de Sang

GFTU General Federation of Trade Unions

GFU Gemeinschaft Freier Unternahmensberater

GfW Gesellschaft für Wehrkunde

GFWC General Federation of Womens Clubs

GFZFF Gesellschaft zur Förderung von Zukunfts- und Friedensforschung

GGB Gesellschaft für die Geschichte und Bibliographie des Brauwesens

GGC Groupe Spécialisé du Génie Chimique (Switzerland)

GGPO Gesellschaft f. d. Geschichte des Protestantismus in Österreich

GGRA Gelatine and Glue Research Association (*now merged with* BFMIRA)

GGW Groep Gereedschapswerktuigen van de Vereniging van Metaalindustrieën

GHA Gartneriets og Hagebrukets Arbeidsgiverforening

GhLM Ghaqda Letteraja Maltija

GHM Groep Houtbewerkingsmachines

GHP Groep Fabrikanten van Hydraulische et Pneumatische

GI Gesellschaft für Informatik

GI Gideons International (U.S.A.)

GIA Gemmological Institute of America

GIA Groupement Ivoirien d'Assurances

GIAC Groupement des Industries Agricoles, Alimentaires et de Grande Consommation

GIAM Conference on Global Impacts of Applied Microbiology

GIANA Groupement International des Analystes de l'Alimentation

GIAP State Institute for the Nitrogen Industry (U.S.S.R.)

GIASTA Groupement International pour l'Avancement des Sciences et Techniques Alimentaires

GIAT Groupement d'Industries Atomiques

GIBAIR Gibraltar Airways Ltd

GIC Glass Industry Club (Belgium)

GIC Guilde Internationale des Cööpératrices

GICAM Groupement Interprofessionnel pour l'Étude et le Coordination des Intérêts Économiques du Cameroun

GICRD Groupe International de Coopération et de Recherche en Documentation

GIDA Groupement Interprofessionel des Entreprises du Dahomey

GIDAVI Groupement Interprofessionnel pour la Défense et l'Amélioration des Vins de Consommation Courante

GIDNT Glówny Instytut Dokumentacji Naukowo-Technicznej

GIDOTOM Groupement Interprofessionnel pour le Développement de la Product des Oléagineux dans les Territoires d'Outre-Mer

GIF Grafiska Industriförbundet

GIFAM Groupement des Industries Françaises des Appareils d'Équipement Ménager

GIFAP Groupement International des Associations Nationales de Fabricants de Pesticides

GIFAS	Groupement des Industries Françaises Aéronautiques et Spatiales
GIFCO	Gruppo Italiano Fabbricanti Cartone Ondulato
GIFPA	Groupement Interprofessionnel des Fleurs et Plantes Aromatiques
GIIGNL	Groupe International des Importateurs de Gaz Naturel Liquéfié
GIIN	Groupe Intersyndical de l'Industrie Nucléaire
GIIP	Groupement International de l'Industrie Pharmaceutique des Pays de la Communauté Économique Européenne
GILS	Grémio dos Industriais de Lanifícios do Sul (Portugal)
GIM	Gruppe Internationale Möbelspediteure
GIMCI	Groupement des Industries de la Métallurgie en Côte-d'Ivoire
GIMEE	Groupement Syndical des Industries de Matériels d'Équipement Électrique
GIMMOM	Groupement des Industries Minières et Métallurgiques d'Outre-Mer
GIMPA	Ghana Institute of Management and Public Administration
GIMRADA	U.S. Army Geodesy, Intelligence and Mapping Research and Development Agency
GINA	Gaufretterie Industrielle Africaine
GINTEX	Groupement International des Comités Nationaux de l'Étiquetage pour l'Entretien des Textiles
GIOM	Groupement Interprofessionnel des Oléagineux Métropolitains
GIPCEL	Groupement des Industries du Polyurethane Cellulaire
GIPEC	Groupe d'Études International pour Utilizations de Profils Creux dans la Construction (Switzerland)
GIPFA	Groupement Interprofessionnel des Plantes à Parfum et Aromatiques
GIPME	Global Investigation of Pollution in the Marine Environment (FAO)
GIPP	Gremio dos Industriais de Panificação do Porto
GIQOM	Groupement Intersyndical de la Quincaillerie, de l'Outillage et du Ménage
GIRA	Groupement de l'Industrie de la Radio et de l'Électricité (Belgium)
GIRCA	Groupement Interprofessionnel pour l'Étude et de Développement de l'Économie Centrafricaine
GIRCETAPE	Groupement Interrégional des Centres d'Études Techniques Agricoles pour les Problèmes d'Entreprise
GIREP	Group International pour la Recherche sur l'Enseignement des Sciences Physiques
GIRGV	Groupe International des Ressources Génétiques Végétales
GIRP	Groupement International de la Répartition Pharmaceutique des Pays de la Communauté Européenne
GIRPIA	Groupements Interprofessionnels de Répartition des Produits Indispensables à l'Agriculture
GIRS	Groupement International pour la Recherche Scientifique en Stomatologie
GISA	Vereniging van Groothandelaren in Sanitaire Artikelen
GISECA	Groupement Ivoirien des Sociétés d'Exportation et Coopératives Agricoles
GISL	Groupement des Industries Sidérurgiques Luxembourgeoises
GISRA	Guyana Institute for Social Research and Action
GITA	Grémio dos Industriais de Transportes em Automóveis (Portugal)
GITB	Gas Industry Training Board
GITCE	Gecaga Institute of Tropical Comparative Endocrinology (Kenya)
GITO	Groupement Interprofessionnel des Entreprises du Togo
GIU	General Importers' Union (Malta)
GKC	Gesellschaft Deutscher Kosmetik-Chemiker
GKE	Geodéziai és Kartográfiai Egyesület
GKF	Beroepsvereniging van Interieurarchitecten
GKN	Gemeenschappelijke Kerneenergiecentrale in Nederland
GKSS	Gesellschaft für Kernenergieverwertung in Schiffbau und Schiffahrt
GKT	Groep Kranen en Transportinrichtingen (Netherlands)
GKV	Gesamtverband Kunststoffverarbeitende Industrie
GL	Glassmestrenes Landsforening
GLC	Greater London Council
GLECS	Groupe Linguistique d'Études Chamito-sémitiques
GLFC	Great Lakes Fishery Commission (U.S.A.)
GLINT	Gospel Literature International

GLM	Gesellschaft für Lehr- und Lernmethoden (Switzerland)	**GNET**	Gremio Nacional dos Exportadores de Têxteis
GLP-AACR	Gibraltar Labour Party and Association for the Advancement of Civil Rights	**GNF**	Grémio Nacional das Farmácias (Portugal)
GLSM	Gruppen Luftteknik inom Sveriges Mekanförbund	**GNIAA**	Groupement National des Industries de l'Alimentation Animale
GLV	Graphische Lehr- und Versuchsanstalt (Austria)	**GNIBC**	Groupement National Interprofessionnel de la Betterave, de la Canne et des Industries Productrices de Sucre et d'Alcool
GMA	Greek Management Association	**GNIC**	Grémio Nacional dos Industriais de Calçado (Portugal)
GMAA	Gold Mining Association of America		
GMBA	Gibraltar Master Bakers' Association	**GNICTMP**	Grémio Nacional dos Industriais de Composição e Transformação de Matérias Plásticas (Portugal)
GMBS	Verband Schweizerischer Grossisten der Mercerie, Bonneterie und Strickgarne		
GMC	General Medical Council	**GNIFC**	Groupement National Interprofessionnel des Fruits à Cidre
GMD	Gesellschaft für Mathematik und Datenverarbeitung	**GNIJR**	Groupement National Interprofessionnel des Jus de Raisins et Dérivés
GMEA	Groupement Médicale d'Études sur l'Alcoolisme	**GNIL**	Groupement National Interprofessionnel Linier
GMI	Grupo Mudanzas Internationales	**GNIMFVA**	Grémio Nacional dos Industriais de Montagem e Fabricação de Veículos Automóveis (Portugal)
GMITPM	Gorgas Memorial Institute of Tropical and Preventive Medicine (U.S.A.)		
GMSC	General Medical Services Council	**GNIN**	Groupement National des Importateurs et du Négoce de Laine (Belgium)
GMT	Société Générale des Moulins du Togo		
GMV	Groep Fabrieken van Machines voor de Voedings- en Genotmiddelenindustrie	**GNIPTIT**	Groupement National Interprofessionnel de la Pomme de Terre Industrielle et des Industries de Transformation
GMWU	National Union of General and Municipal Workers	**GNIS**	Groupement National Interprofessionnel de Production et d'Utilisation des Semences Graines et Plantes
GNA	Groupement National d'Achat		
GNAPO	Groupement National d'Achat des Produits Oléagineux	**GNIT**	Gremio Nacional dos Industriais de Tomate
		GNIT	Groupement National Interprofessionnel du Topinambour
GNAPRCAR	Groupement National des Associations Professionnelles Régionales des Commissionnaires Affrêteurs-Routiers	**GNITC**	Groupement National de l'Industrie de la Terre Cuite (Belgium)
GNAS	Grand National Archery Society	**GNOE**	Groupement du Nursing de l'Ouest Européen (Belgium)
GNAVT	Grémio Nacional das Agências de Viajens e Turismo		
		GNTC	Ghana National Trading Corporation
GNB	Groupement National Bulbicole	**GNV**	Gesellschaft für Nukleare Verfahrenstechnik
GNCB	Groupement National du Cuir Brut (Belgium)	**GODB**	Gal Oya Development Board (Sri Lanka)
GNEL	Grémio Nacional des Editores e Livreiros (Portugal)	**GOETO**	Grand Order of European Tour Organizers (France)
GNEPLC	Groupement National des Éleveurs Professionnels de Lapins de Chair	**GOGECA**	Comité Générale de la Coopération Agricole de la CEE
GNERFEA	Groupement National des Éleveurs "Reine de France" et Essaims d'Abeilles	**GOMAC**	Groupement des Opticiens du Marché Commun
GNESLRP	Groupement National Éleveurs Selectionneurs de Lapins de Race Pure	**GOMP**	Groupement Outre-Mer Pharmaceutique (Ivory Coast)

GOPR	Groupement pour l'Opération de Productivité Rizicole (Madagascar)	**GRAIN-UNION**	Société Commerciale de l'Union Générale des Coopératives Agricoles de Céréales
GOSPLAN	Central Planning Agency of the Union of Soviet Socialist Republics	**GRAM-ACOP**	Grain Marketing Cooperative of the Philippines
GOVPF	Groupement Obligatoire des Viticulteurs et Producteurs de Fruits (Tunisia)	**GRAO**	Group Régional de l'Afrique de l'Ouest
GPA	Groupement de Pharmaciens d'Afrique	**GRAPO**	First of October Anti-Fascist Revolutionary Group (Spain)
GPA	Groupement de Productivité Agricole	**GRB**	Gas Research Board
GPB	Groupement Professionnel des Bitumes	**GRCA**	Glassfibre Reinforcements Cement Association
GPBN	Groupement Pharmaceutique Benin-Niger	**GRCETA**	Groupement Régional de Centre d'Études Techniques Agricoles
GPC	Groupe Spécialisé des Ponts et Charpentes (Switzerland)	**GRD**	Groupe des Ressources pour le Développement (UNDP)
GPC	Groupements de Producteurs de Ciment (Belgium)	**GRDP**	Groupement National des Transporteurs Routiers de Denrées et Produits Périssables
GPDA	Gypsum Plasterboard Development Association	**GREM**	Groupement Romand pour l'Étude du Marché et du Marketing (Switzerland)
GPDA	Gypsum Products Development Association	**GREMA-DEIRAS**	Grémio dos Exportadores de Madeiras (Portugal)
GPE	Guided Projectile Establishment		
GPECC	Groupement Professionnel des Exportateurs de Café et de Cacao (Ivory Coast)	**GREPR**	Groupe de Recherches et d'Études pour la Promotion Rurale
GPEI	Gabungan Perusahaan Ekspor Indonesia	**GRF**	Graphic Reproduction Federation
GPIN	Groupement Professionnel de l'Industrie Nucléaire (Belgium)	**GRF**	Grassland Research Foundation (U.S.A.)
GPLS	Groupement Professionnel des Commercants et Industriels Libanais du Sénégal	**GRG**	Groupe Spécialisé des Ingénieurs du Génie Rural et Géomètres (Switzerland)
GPMA	Grocery Products Manufacturers Association (Canada)	**GRG**	International Committee on General Relativity and Gravitation
GPO	Association Générale des Producteurs d'Oléagineux	**GRI**	Grassland Research Institute
GPO-PIA	Government Printing Office and Printing Industry of America	**GRI**	Groupe de Recherches Ionosphériques
GPPEPA	Groupement des Producteurs de la Prune d'Ente et du Pruneau d'Agen	**GROFOR**	Deutscher Verband des Grosshandels mit Oelen, Fetten und Oelrohstoffen
GPRA	Algerian Provisional Government	**GRONTMIJ**	Grondverbetering- en Ontiginningsmaatschappij (Netherlands)
GPRA	Gesellschaft Public Relations Agenturen	**GROPACA**	Chambre Syndicale des Grossistes en Papiers et Cartons pour Écriture et Impression (Belgium)
GPRMC	Groupement des Plastiques Renforcés du Marché Commun		
GPV	Gesellschaft Pro Vindonissa (Switzerland)	**GROPO**	Nederlandse Vereniging voor de Binnenlandse Groothandel in Pootaardappelen
GPV	Groep Fabrieken van Pompen voor Vloeistoffen	**GROUP-AROMA**	Syndicat National des Fabricants et Importateurs d'Huiles Essentielles et Produits Aromatiques Naturels
GPV	Schweizerischer Glas- und Prozellanhandels-Verband	**GROUP-ISOL**	Group of Producers of Mineral Insulating Material for Electrotechnical Use (*of* EEC)
GR	Génie Rurale (Direction du)	**GRPA**	Guyana Rice Producers Association
GRA	Game Research Association	**GRTU**	General Retailers and Traders Union (Malta)
GRAE	Gouvernement Révolutionnaise de l'Angola en Exil	**GRUNK**	Cambodian National Union Government

GRUR	Deutsche Vereinigung für Gewerblichen Rechtsschutz und Urheberrecht
GS	Glassbransjens Servicekontor
GSA	Genetics Society of America
GSA	Geological Society of America
GSA	Groupe Spécialisé de l'Architecture (Switzerland)
GSC	Geographical Society of Chicago (U.S.A.)
GSF	Groupe Spécialisé des Ingénieurs Forestiers (Switzerland)
GSF	Schweizerische Genossenschaft f. Schlachtvieh u. Fleischversorgung
GSFC	Gujarat State Fertilizers Company (India)
GSG	Grosshandelszentralverband für Spielwaren und Geschenkartikel
GSIS	Group for the Standardisation of Information Services (U.S.A.)
GSK	Gesellschaft für Schweizerische Kunstgeschichte
GSL	Geological Society of London
GSL	Gesellschaft Schweizerischer Landwirte
GSL	Vereniging "De Gezamenlijke Steenkolenmijnen in Limburg"
GSM	Geological Survey of Great Britain and Museum of Practical Geology
GSMAMP	Groupement Suisse des Marchands d'Aciers Spéciaux, Métaux et Plastique
GSN	Groupement des Soufflantes Nucléaires
GSNMS	Groupement des Syndicats Nationaux de Médecins Spécialisés
GSP	Geographical Society of Philadelphia (U.S.A.)
GSRTST	German Society for Rocket Technology and Space Travel
GSSOS	Groupement des Sociétiés Scientifiques Odonto-Stomatologiques
GST	Gesellschaft Schweizerischer Tierärzte
GSZ	Gesellschaft Schweizerische Zeichenlehrer
GTA	Graduate Teachers' Association (Malta)
GTA	Groupement Togolais d'Assurance
GTC	Ghana Tobacco Company
GTCS	Groupe de Travail Intergouvernmental du Contrôle ou de la Surveillance (UNO)
GTE	Gépipari Tudományos Egyesület
GTICM	Grupo de Trabajo Intergubernamental sobre Contaminación de los Mares (IMCO)
GTIV	Grupo de Trabajo Intergubernamental sobre Vigilancia o Supervisión (UNO)
GTM	Groep Textielmachines van de Vereniging van Metaal-Industrieën
GTN	Gdańskie Towarzystwo Naukowe
GTS	Gesellschaft für Tribologie und Schmierungstechnik
GTUC	Grenada Trade Union Council
GTUC	Guyana Trades Union Council
GTW	Gesellschaft der Tierärzte in Wien (Austria)
GTZ	Deutsche Gesellschaft für Technische Zusammenarbeit
GUIMAG	Société Guinéenne de Grands Magasins
GUINELEC	Société Guinéenne d'Installations Électriques
GULP	Grenada United Labour Party
GUMR	Groupement des Utilisateurs de Matériaux Réfractaires (Belgium)
GUPCO	Gulf of Suez Petroleum Company
GUS	Great Universal Stores
GUVU	Gesellschaft für Ursachenforschung bei Verkehrsunfällen
GVA	Groupement de Vulgarisation Agricole
GVAM	Groupement de Vulgarisation Agricole et Ménagère
GVC	Gesellschaft Verfahrenstechnik und Chemieingenieurwesen
GVK	Gesellschaft f. Vergleichende Kunstforschung (Austria)
GVM	Groep Fabrieken van Verbrandingsmotoren
GVMA	Groupement de Vulgarisation Ménagère Agricole
GVN	Grafische Vormgevers Nederland
GvR	Genootschap voor Reclame
GVS	Grosshandelsverband Schreib-, Papierwaren und Bürobedarf
GVT	Forschungs-Gesellschaft Verfahrens-Technik
GWA	Gesellschaft Werbeagenturen
GWDB	Ground Water Development Bureau (Taiwan)
GWI	Gaswärme Institut
GWK	Gesellschaft zur Wiederaufarbeitung von Kernbrennstoffen
GWU	Gambia Workers Union
GWU	General Workers Union (Malta)
GYMES	Great Yarmouth Mediterranean Herring Exporters Association

H

HA	Historical Association
HA	Hydraulic Association
HAA	Helicopter Association of America
HAC	Horticultural Advisory Council for England and Wales
HAES	Hawaii Agricultural Experiment Station
HAF	Haandverkernes Arbeidsgiverforening
HAFRA	British Hat and Allied Feltmakers Research Association
HAG	Hauptarbeitsgemeinschaft des Landmaschinen-Handels und -Handwerks
HAGB	Helicopter Association of Great Britain (now incorp. in RAeS)
HAGD	Hauptvereinigung des Ambulanten Gewerbes und der Schausteller in Deutschland
HAIG	Helsinki Agreements Implementation Group (Belgium)
HAIL	Hague Academy of International Law (Netherlands)
HAKA	Verband der Deutschen Herren- und Knaben-Oberbekleidungsindustrie
HAKAF	Vereniging van Groothandelaren in Katoen- en Kunstzijdeafvallen
HAL	Holland American Line
HAO	Handelns Arbetsgivareorganisation
HAPM	Hollands-Amerikaanse Plantage Maatschappij
HAPS	Historic Aircraft Preservation Society Ltd
HAS	Hawaiian Academy of Science
HAS	Vereniging van Leveranciers van Huishoudelijke Artikelen, Speelgoederen, Houtwaren en Soortgelijke Artikelen
HASA	Editorial Hispanoamericana S.A. (Argentina)
HASI	Hubbard Association of Scientologists International
HASL	U.S. Atomic Energy Commission. Health and Safety Laboratory
HATCA	Hungarian Air Traffic Controllers Association
HATRA	Hosiery and Allied Trades Research Association
HBAA	Human Betterment Association of America
HBC	Hudson's Bay Company (Canada)
HBF	House Builders Federation
HBI	Vereniging van Handelaren in Plantenziekten-Bestrijdingsmiddelen en Landbouw-Insecticiden
HBS	Hawaiian Botanical Society
HBTI	Harcourt Butler Technological Institute (India)
HCAR	Higher Committee for Agrarian Reform (Egypt)
HCB	Huileries du Congo Belge
HCC	Hyderabad Commercial Corporation (India)
HCCC	Hyderabad Co-operative Commercial Corporation (India)
HCGB	Hover Club of Great Britain
HCITB	Hotel and Catering Industry Training Board
HCNN	Hoofdcommissie voor de Normalisatie in Nederland
HCPRU	Hot Climate Physiological Research Unit (Nigeria)
HCR	Haut-Commissaire des Nations Unies pour les Réfugiés
HCS	Harvey Cushing Society (U.S.A.)
HCSA	Hospital Consultants and Specialists Association
HDE	Hauptgemeinschaft des Deutschen Einzelhandels
HDF	Hauptverband Deutscher Filmtheater
HDGA	Hot Dip Galvanisers Association
HDH	Hauptverband der Deutschen Holzindustrie und Verwandter Industriezweige
HDP	Hauptverband für Zucht und Prüfung Deutscher Pferde
HDRA	Henry Doubleday Research Association
HDRI	Hannah Dairy Research Institute (Scotland)
HDS	Hauptverband der Deutschen Schuhindustrie
HEA	Heating Engineering Association
HEA	Horticultural Education Association
HEAA	Home Economics Association of Australia
HEC	École des Hautes Études Commerciales
HEIX	Home Economics Information Exchange of FAO
HELORS	Hellenic Operational Research Society (Greece)

HELPIS	Higher Education Learning Programmes Information Service	**HIAS**	Hebrew Immigration Aid Society (U.S.A.)
HEPCC	Heavy Electrical Plant Consultative Council	**HIB**	Herring Industry Board
HEPI	Haute École Populaire Internationale (Denmark)	**HIBIN**	Vereniging van Handelaren in Bouwmaterialen in Nederland
HERA	High Energy Reaction Analysis Group (Switzerland)	**HICS**	Holt International Children's Service Inc.
		HIDB	Highlands and Islands Development Board
HERR-AMEX	Fabricantes Exportadores de Herramientas Manuales	**HIE**	Hibernation Information Exchange
HES	Hawaiian Entomological Society	**HIID**	Harvard Institute for International Development (U.S.A.)
HETMA	Heavy Edge Tool Manufacturers' Association	**HIK**	Statens Handels-och Industrikommission
HEVAC	Heating, Ventilating and Air Conditioning Manufacturers Association	**HIOW**	Hoger Institut v. Opvoedkundige Wetenschappen (Belgium)
HEW	United States Department of Health, Education and Welfare	**HISWA**	Nederlandse Vereniging voor Handel en Industrie op het Gebied van Scheepbouw en Watersport
HFFF	Hungarian Freedom Fighters Federation		
HFI	Hemmens Forskningsinstitut	**HIVOS**	Humanistic Institute for Co-operation with Developing Countries (Netherlands)
HFI	Hjúkrunarfelag Íslands (Icelandic Nurses Association)	**HKCEC**	Hong Kong Catholic Education Council
HFIAW	International Association of Heat and Frost Insulators and Asbestos Workers	**HKI**	Fachverband Heiz- und Kochgeräte-Industrie
HFMA	Health Food Manufacturers Association	**HKMA**	Hong Kong Management Association
HFO	De Danske Handelsforeningers Foelles-Organisation	**HLA**	Hawaii Library Association
		HLCF	Holy Land Conservation Fund (U.S.A.)
HFRO	Hill Farming Research Organisation (Scotland)	**HLSRS**	High Level Sisal Research Station (E. Africa)
HFS	Hrvatski Filatelistički Savez	**HLUSA**	Honeywell Large Systems Users Association (Europe)
HFSJG	Scientific Stations of Jungfraujoch and Gornergrat (Switzerland)	**HMA**	Hellenic Marketing Association
HFWF	Hired Farm Working Force (U.S.A.)	**HMBI**	His *or* Her Majesty's Borstal Institution
HGA	Hop Growers of America	**HMC**	Horticultural Marketing Council
HGGA	Heraldische-Genealogische Gesellschaft 'Adler' (Austria)	**HMDS**	Her Majesty's Diplomatic Service
		HMNFE	Her Majesty's Norfolk Flax Establishment
HGHSC	Home Grown Herbage Seeds Committee	**HMOCS**	Her Majesty's Overseas Civil Service
HGTAC	Home Grown Timber Advisory Committee	**HMPA**	Hawaii Macadamia Producers Association
HGTMC	Home Grown Timber Marketing Corporation	**HMSO**	Her Majesty's Stationery Office
HGTPJC	Home Grown Threshed Peas Joint Committee	**HMU-CMS**	Harmonie Mondiale Universelle-Conseil Mondiale du Service (U.K.)
HGV	Hohenzollischer Geschichtsverein	**HMvL**	Hollandsche Mij. van Landbouw
HHG	Heinrich Heine-Gesellschaft	**HNGNA**	Hellenic National Graduate Nurses Association (Greece)
HHI	Harness Horse International (U.S.A.)	**HO**	Hovedorganisationen af Mesterforeninger i Byggefagene i Danmark
HI	Hotline International (U.S.A.)		
HIA	Hawaiian Irrigation Authority	**HO**	U.S. Hydrographic Office
		HOA	Huileries de l'Ouest Africain
HIA	Horological Institute of America	**HOC**	Holland Organizing Centre (Netherlands)
		HOG	Hermann-Oberth-Gesellschaft

HORECA	International Union of National Associations of Hotel, Restaurant and Café Keepers
HORECAF	Nederlandse Bond van Werkgevers in Hotel-, Restaurant-, Café- en Aanverwante Bedrijven
HORESCA	Fédération Nationale des Hôteliers, Restaurateurs et Cafetiers du Grande-Duché de Luxembourg
HORU	Home Office Research Unit
HOTAFRIC	Société de Développement Hôtelier et Touristique de l'Afrique de l'Ouest (Ivory Coast)
HPCA	Hiroshima Peace Center Associates (U.S.A.)
HPF	Horace Plunkett Foundation for Co-operative Studies
HPRS	Hellenic Public Relations Society (Greece)
HPRS	Houghton Poultry Research Station
HPV	Hauptverband der Papier, Pappe und Kun-stoffe Verarbeitenden Industrie
HRAF	Human Relations Area Files (U.S.A.)
HRB	Highway Research Board (U.S.A.)
HRCC	Humanities Research Council of Canada
HRI	Horticultural Research International
HRIS	Highway Research Information Service (*of* AAHSO)
HRN	Hotelli- ja Ravintolaneuvosto
HRS	Hop Research Station (DSIR) (N.Z.)
HRS	Hydraulics Research Station
HRTK	Hoger Rijksinstituut voor Textiel en Kunst-stoffen (Belgium)
HRU	Hydrologic Research Unit (*of* NERC)
HSAC	Hebridean Spinners Advisory Committee
HSA-UWC	Holy Spirit Association for the Unification of World Christianity
HSBA	Herdwick Sheep Breeders Association
HSFK	Hessische Stiftung für Friedens- und Konfliktsforschung
HSIU	Haile Selassie I University Library (Ethiopia)
HSMHA	Health Services and Mental Health Administration (U.S.A.)
HSNY	Horticultural Society of New York (U.S.A.)
HSPA	Hawaiian Sugar Planters' Association
HSQ	Historical Society of Queensland (Australia)
HSRC	Human Sciences Research Council (South Africa)
HSRD	National Center for Health Services Research and Development (U.S.A.)

HSS	History of Science Society (U.S.A.)
HSSA	High Speed Steel Association
HST	Hawaiian Sugar Technologists
HTA	Horticultural Trades Association
HTC	Holland-Tanganyika Compagnie
HTG	Hafenbautechnische Gesellschaft
HTG	Hemtextilgrossisterna
HTLDC	Hsinchu Tidal Land Development Planning Commission (Taiwan)
HTMA	Hawaii Territorial Medical Association
HTMAEW	Home Timber Merchants Association of England and Wales
HTRP	Humid Tropics Research Programme (*of* UNESCO)
HUK	Verband der Haftpflicht-, Unfall- und Kraftverkehrs- Versicherer
HULTIS	Hull Technical Interloan Scheme
HUMRRO	Human Resources Research Office
HVCA	Heating and Ventilating Contractors' Association
HVG	Hüttentechnische Vereinigung der Deutschen Glasindustrie
HVRA	Hawaiian Volcano Research Association
HVRA	Heating and Ventilating Research Association (*now* BSRIA)
HWMV	Schweizerischer Hartweizenmüller-Verband
HWWA	Hamburgisches Weltwirtschaftsarchiv
HYPECO	Hybrid Poultry Breeding Corporation (Belgium-Netherlands)

I

IA	Institute of Actuaries
IAA	Institut Agricole d'Algérie
IAA	Instituto do Açúcar e do Alcool (Brazil)
IAA	Institute of Automobile Assessors
IAA	Instituto Antártica Argentino
IAA	International Academy of Astronautics
IAA	International Allergy Association (U.S.A.)
IAA	International Acetylene Association
IAA	International Actuarial Association
IAA	International Advertising Association

IAA	International Aerosol Association
IAA	International Apple Association (U.S.A.)
IAA	International Association for Aerobiology
IAA	International Association of Allergology (U.S.A.)
IAA	International Association of Art-Painting, Sculpture, Graphic Art
IAA	International Association of Astacology
IAAA	Irish Association of Advertising Agencies
IAAALD	Inter-American Association of Agricultural Librarians and Documentalists (Costa Rica)
IAAAM	International Association for Aquatic Animal Medicine
IAAB	Inter-American Association of Broadcasters
IAABO	International Association of Approved Basketball Officials
IAAC	International Agricultural Aviation Centre
IAAC	International Antarctic Analysis Centre
IAAC	International Association of Art Critics
IAACC	Inter-Allied Aeronautical Commission of Control
IAACR	Instituto Agrario Argentino de Cultura Rurál
IAAE	Institution of Automotive and Aeronautical Engineers (Australia) (now SAE-Australasia)
IAAE	International Association of Agricultural Economists
IAAE	Israel Association of Agricultural Engineering
IAAEE	International Association for the Advancement of Ethnology and Eugenics
IAAER	International Association for the Advancement of Educational Research
IAAF	International Amateur Athletic Federation
IAAI	International Airports Authority of India
IAAI	International Association of Arson Investigators
IAAJ	International Association of Agricultural Journalists
IAALD	International Association of Agricultural Librarians and Documentalists
IAAM	International Association of Automotive Modelers
IAAO	International Association of Assessing Officers (U.S.A.)
IAAP	International Association for Analytical Psychology
IAAP	International Association of Applied Psychology
IAAPA	International Association of Amusement Parks and Attractions (U.S.A.)
IAAPEA	International Association Against Painful Experiments on Animals
IAARC	International Administrative Aeronautical Radio Conference
IAAS	Incorporated Association of Architects and Surveyors
IAAS	International Association of Agricultural Students
IAATM	International Association for Accident and Traffic Medicine (Sweden)
IAB	ICSU Abstracting Board
IAB	Imperial Agricultural Bureaux (UK) (now CAB)
IAB	Industrial Advisory Board
IAB	Institut Agricole de Beauvais (Oise)
IAB	International Aquatic Board
IAB	Internationale Akademie für Bäderkunde und Bädertechnik
IAB	Internationale Akademie für Bader-, Sport-, und Freizeitbau
IAB	International Council of Scientific Unions Abstracting Board
IABA	International Amateur Boxing Association
IABA	International Association of Aircraft Brokers and Agents
IABC	International Association of Business Communicators (U.S.A.)
IABE	Ibero-American Bureau of Education (Spain)
IABE	Internacia Asocio de Bankistoj Esperantistaj
IABG	International Association of Botanic Gardens
IABLA	Inter-American Bibliographical and Library Association
IABO	International Association of Biblicists and Orientalists
IABO	International Association for Biological Oceanography
IABS	International Advisory Committee for Biological Standardization
IABSE	International Association for Bridge and Structural Engineering
IABSOIW	International Association of Bridge, Structural and Ornamental Iron Workers
IAC	Indian Airlines Corporation

IAC	Industries Assistance Commission (Australia)	**IACD**	International Association of Clothing Designers
IAC	Institute of Administration and Commerce of South Africa	**IACDT**	International Advisory Committee for Documentation and Terminology
IAC	Inter Afrique Charters	**IACED**	Inter-African Advisory Committee on Control of Epizootic Diseases (*now* IACAHP)
IAC	International Advisory Committee on Research in the Natural Sciences (UNESCO)		
IAC	International Aerological Commission	**IACES**	International Air Cushion Engineering Society
IAC	Internationaal Agrarisch Centrum (Netherlands)	**IACFO**	Asociación Internacional para las Ciencias Físicas del Océano
IAC	International Artists Cooperation	**IACI**	Inter-American Children's Institute
IAC	International Athletes Club	**IACI**	Inter-American Copyright Institute
IACA	Inter-American College Association	**IACIT**	International Association of Conference Interpreters and Translators
IACA	International Air Carrier Association (U.S.A.)	**IACL**	International Academy of Comparative Law
IACA	International Air Charter Association (Switzerland)	**IACL**	International Association of Criminal Law
IACA	International Association of Consulting Actuaries	**IACM**	International Association of Circulation Managers
IACAHP	Inter-African Advisory Committee for Animal Health and Production (*formerly* IACED) (Kenya)	**IACME**	International Association of Crafts and Small and Medium-sized Enterprises
		IACO	Inter-African Coffee Organisation
IACB	Inter-Agency Consultative Board	**IACODLA**	International Advisory Committee on Documentation, Libraries and Archives (UNESCO)
IACB	International Advisory Committee on Bibliography		
IACB	International Association of Convention Bureaux (U.S.A.)	**IACOMS**	International Advisory Committee on Marine Sciences
IACBC	International Advisory Committee on Biological Control	**IACP**	International Association of Chiefs of Police
IACBDT	International Advisory Committee on Bibliography, Documentation and Terminology	**IACP**	International Association for Child Psychiatry
		IACP	International Association of Computer Programmers (U.S.A.)
IACC	Instituto Argentino de Control de la Calidad	**IACPAP**	International Association for Child Psychiatry and Allied Professions
IACC	International Agricultural Coordination Commission	**IACPP**	International Association for Cross-Cultural Psychology
IACC	International Association for Cereal Chemistry (Austria)	**IACS**	Indian Association for the Cultivation of Science
IACC	International Association of Congress Centres	**IACS**	International Academy of Christian Sociologists
IACCHE	Inter-American Confederation of Chemical Engineering	**IACS**	International Association of Classification Societies
IACCI	International Association of Credit Card Investigators	**IACS**	International Association of Counselling Services (U.S.A.)
IACCP	Inter-American Council for Commerce and Production	**IACSAC**	Inter-American Catholic Social Action Confederation
IACCP	International Association for Cross-Cultural Psychology	**IACSS**	Inter-American Conference of Social Security

IACVB	International Association of Convention and Visitors Bureaux	**IAEA**	Institute of Asian Economic Affairs (Japan) (*now* IDE)
IACVF	International Association of Cancer Victims and Friends	**IAEA**	Inter-American Educational Association
IACW	Inter-American Commission of Women	**IAEA**	International Agricultural Exchange Association (Denmark)
IAD	Instituto Agrario Dominicano	**IAEA**	International Atomic Energy Agency
IADA	Internationale Arbeitsgemeinschaft der Archiv-, Bibliotheks- und Graphik-restauratoren	**IAEC**	International Association of Environmental Coordinators
IADB	Inter-American Defense Board	**IAECO-SOC**	Inter-American Economic and Social Council
IADB	Interamerican Development Bank	**IAEE**	International Association for Earthquake Engineering
IADC	Inter-American Defense College		
IADC	International Association of Dentistry for Children	**IAEF**	Internacia Asocio de la Esperantistaj Feruo-jistoj
IADC	International Association of Dredging Companies	**IAEG**	International Association of Engineering Geology
IADC	International Association of Drilling Contractors	**IAEI**	International Association of Electrical Inspectors
IADF	Inter-American Association for Democracy and Freedom	**IAEL**	International Association of Electrical Leagues
IADIS	Irish Association for Documentation and Information Services	**IAEO**	Internationale Atoménergie Organisation
IADIWU	International Association for the Development of International and World Universities	**IAES**	Institute of Aeronautical Sciences
		IAESC	Inter-American Economic and Social Council
IADL	International Association of Democratic Lawyers	**IAESP**	Institúto Agronómico de Estado de Sao Paulo (Brazil)
IADLA	International Association for the Development of Documentation, Libraries and Archives in Africa	**IAESTE**	International Association for the Exchange of Students for Technical Experience
IADO	Instituto Argentino de Oceanografíca	**IAEVG**	International Association for Educational and Vocational Guidance
IADO	Instituto Agroindustrial de Oleaginosos (Argentina)	**IAEVI**	International Association for Educational and Vocational Information
IADO	Iran Agriculture Development Organization	**IAEWP**	International Association of Educators for World Peace
IADP	Intensive Agricultural District Programme (India)		
IADPE	Institut Asiatique pour le Développement et la Planification Économique (Thailand)	**IAF**	Inter-American Foundation
		IAF	International Abolitionist Federation
IADR	International Association for Dental Research	**IAF**	International Association Futuribles
		IAF	International Astronautical Federation
IADS	International Agricultural Development Service (U.S.A.)	**IAF**	International Automobile Federation
IADS	International Association of Dental Students	**IAFC**	Inter-American Freight Conference
IADS	International Association of Department Stores	**IAFC**	International Association of Fire Chiefs (U.S.A.)
IAE	Institut d'Administration des Entreprises	**IAFD**	International Association of Food Distribution
IAE	Institute of Automobile Engineers		
IAEA	Indian Adult Education Association	**IAFE**	International Association of Fairs and Expositions

IAFEI	International Association of Financial Executives Institutes
IAFF	International Art Film Federation
IAFF	International Association of Fire Fighters
IAFMM	International Association of Fish Meal Manufacturers
IAFP	Institúto de Anatomia y Fisiologia Patólogicas (Argentina)
IAFP	International Association of Financial Planners (U.S.A.)
IAFS	International Association of Family Sociology
IAFS	International Association of Forensic Sciences
IAFWNO	Inter-American Federation of Working Newspaperman's Organisations
IAG	IFIP Administrative Data Processing Group
IAG	Institute of American Genealogy
IAG	International Administrative Data Processing Group (of IFIP)
IAG	International Association of Geodesy
IAG	International Association of Gerontology
IAG	Internationale Arbeitsgemeinschaft f.d. Unterrichtsfilm
IAGA	Instituto Argentino de Grasas y Aceites
IAGA	International Association of Geomagnetism and Aeronomy
IAGB & I	Ileostomy Association of Great Britain and Ireland
IAGC	International Academy of Gynecological Cytology
IAGC	International Association on Geochemistry and Cosmochemistry
IAGFA	International Association of Government Fair Agencies
IAGFCC	International Association of Game, Fish and Conservation Commissioners
IAGLO	International Association of Governmental Labour Officials
IAGLP	International Association of Great Lakes Ports (Canada)
IAGLR	International Association for Great Lakes Research
IAGOD	International Association on the Genesis of Ore Deposits
IAGRE	Institution of Agricultural Engineers
IAH	International Association of Hydrogeologists
IAH	International Association of Hydrology
IAHA	Inter-American Hotel Association
IAHA	International Arabian Horse Association (U.S.A.)
IAHA	International Association of Historians of Asia
IAHB	International Association of Human Biologists
IAHCSM	International Association of Hospital Central Service Management
IAHE	International Association for Hydrogen Energy
IAHIC	International Association of Home Improvement Council
IAHM	Incorporated Association of Headmasters
IAHP	International Association of Horticultural Producers
IAHR	International Association for the History of Religions
IAHR	International Association for Hydraulic Research
IAHS	International Academy of History of Science
IAHS	International Association for Housing Science
IAHS	International Association of Hydrological Sciences
IAHU	International Association of Health Underwriters
IAI	International African Institute (U.K.)
IAI	Institute for International Collaboration in Agriculture and Forestry (Czechoslovakia)
IAI	International Anthropological Institute
IAI	International Apple Institute (U.S.A.)
IAI	International Association for Identification
IAI	Israel Aviation Industries
IAI	Istituto Affari Internazionali
IAI	International Automotive Institute (Monaco)
IAIABC	International Association of Industrial Accident Boards and Commissions
IAIAS	Inter-American Institute of Agricultural Sciences
IAIC	International Association of Insurance Counsel (U.S.A.)
IAICM	International Association of Ice Cream Manufacturers
IAIDEC	Instituto Argentino de la Industria y Exportación de Carnes

AIGC	Inter-Arab Investment Guarantee Corporation (Kuwait)
AII	Inter-American Indian Institute (*of* OAS)
AIP	International Association of Independent Producers
AIP	International Association of Individual Psychology
AIR	International Association of Industrial Radiation
AIS	Industrial Aerodynamics Information Service (*of* BHMRA)
AJC	Inter-American Juridical Committee
AJE	Internacio Asocio de Juristoj-Esperantistoj
AJRC	International Association of Jazz Record Collectors (U.S.A.)
AK	Internationales Auschwitz-Komitee
AKS	Internationalen Arbeitskreis Sportstättenbau
AL	Imperial Arts League
AL	Institut Archeologique du Luxembourg
AL	International Arbitration League
AL	International Association of Laryngectomees
AL	International Association of Theoretical and Applied Limnology
AL	Irish Academy of Letters
ALA	International African Law Association
ALA	International Association of Lighthouse Authorities
ALA	International Auxiliary Language Association
ALB	Internationalen Arbeitskreises Landwirtschaftlicher Berater
ALCRF	International Association for Liberal Christianity and Religious Freedom
ALI	International Association of Labour Inspection
ALL	International Association for Labor Legislation (U.S.A.)
ALL	International Association of Law Libraries
ALP	International Association of Logopedics and Phoniatrics (U.S.A.)
ALS	International Agency Liaison Service (*of* FAO)
ALS	International Association of Legal Science
AM	Institute of Administrative Management
AM	Institute of Advanced Motorists
AM	Institute of Aviation Medicine

IAM	International Afro-American Museum (U.S.A.)
IAM	International Association of Machinists and Aerospace Workers
IAM	International Association of Meteorology
IAM	Internationale Arbeitsgemeinschaft für Müllforschung
IAMA	Incorporated Advertising Managers Association
IAMA	International Abstaining Motorists Association
IAMA	Irish Association of Municipal Authorities
IAMAM	International Association of Museums of Arms and Military History
IAMAP	International Association of Meteorology and Atmospheric Physics
IAMAT	International Association for Medical Assistance to Travellers
IAMB	International Association of Macrobiologists
IAMB	International Association of Microbiologists
IAMB	Irish Association of Master Bakers
IAMBE	International Association for Medicine and Biology of Environment
IAMCA	International Association of Milk Control Agencies
IAMCR	International Association for Mass Communication Research
IAMD	International Association of Managing Directors (U.S.A.)
IAMFE	International Association on Mechanisation of Field Experiments
IAMFES	International Association of Milk, Food and Environmental Sanitarians (U.S.A.)
IAMG	International Association for Mathematical Geology
IAML	International Association of Music Libraries
IAMLT	International Association of Medical Laboratory Technologists
IAMM	International Association of Medical Museums
IAMO	Inter-American Municipal Organisation
IAMR	Institute of Applied Manpower Research (India)
IAMRC	International Antarctic Meteorological Research Centre
IAMS	International Association of Microbiological Societies

IAMS	International Association for Mission Studies
IAMS	International Association of Municipal Statisticians
IAMV	Internationaler Anti-Militarischer Verein
IAMWF	Inter-American Mine Workers Federation
IAN	Institúto Agrario Nacional (Venezuela etc.)
IAN	Institúto Agrónomico de Norte (Brazil)
IAN	Internationale des Amis de la Nature
IANC	Instituto de Asuntas Nucleares de Colombia
IANC	International Airline Navigators Council
IANC	International Anatomical Nomenclature Committee
IANEC	Inter-American Nuclear Energy Commission
IANSA	Industria Azucarera Nacional (Chile)
IAO	International Association of Orthodontics (U.S.A.)
IAO	Internationale Arbeitsorganisation
IAOL	International Association of Orientalist Librarians
IAOO	Irish Agricultural Officers Organisation
IAOPA	International Council of Aircraft Owner and Pilot Associations
IAOS	International Association of Oral Surgeons
IAOS	Irish Agricultural Organisation Society
IAP	Institute of Australian Photographers
IAP	Instituto Argentino del Petróleo
IAP	International Academy of Pathology
IAP	International Academy of Poets
IAP	International Academy of Proctology
IAP	International Association of Psychotechnics
IAPA	Inter-American Press Association
IAPB	International Association for the Prevention of Blindness
IAPC	International Association for Pollution Control
IAPCO	International Association of Professional Congress Organisers
IAPES	International Association of Personnel in Employment Security
IAPESGW	International Association of Physical Education and Sports for Girls and Women
IAPH	International Association of Ports and Harbours
IAPHC	International Association of Printing House Craftsmen
IAPI	Institute of Advertising Practitioners in Ireland
IAPI	Institute of American Poultry Industries
IAPI	Institúto Argentino de Promoción del Intercambio
IAPIP	International Association for the Protection of Industrial Property
IAPL	International Association for Penal Law
IAPMO	International Association of Plumbing and Mechanical Officials
IAPN	International Association of Professional Numismatists
IAPO	International Association of Physical Oceanography
IAPP	Indian Association for Plant Physiology
IAPP	International Association for Plant Physiology
IAPP	International Association of Police Professors (U.S.A.)
IAPP	International Association of Prevention Programs (U.S.A.)
IAPPLT	Inter-American Program for Linguistics and Language Teaching
IAPPW	International Association of Pupil Personnel Workers (U.S.A.)
IAPR	International Association for Pattern Recognition (U.S.A.)
IAPS	International Academy of Political Science (*Ceased*)
IAPS	International Affiliation of Planning Societies
IAPS	International Association of Pipe Smokers Clubs
IAPS	International Association on the Properties of Steam
IAPSC	Inter-African Phytosanitary Commission (U.K.)
IAPSO	International Association for the Physical Sciences of the Ocean
IAPT	International Association for Plant Taxonomy
IAPTA	International Allied Printing Trades Association
IAPW	International Association of Personnel Women
IAQ	International Academy for Quality
IAQR	Indian Association for Quality and Reliability
IAQR	International Association on Quarternary Research

IAR	International Authority for the Ruhr		**IASA**	International Association of Schools in Advertising
IARA	Inter-Allied Reparation Agency		**IASA**	International Association of Sound Archives
IARA	International Association of Rebekah Assemblies		**IASAA**	International Agricultural Students Association of the Americas
IArb	Institute of Arbitrators			
IARC	International Agency for Research on Cancer (*of* WHO)		**IASB**	International Aircraft Standard Bureau
			IASC	International Accounting Standards Committee (*of* ICCAP)
IARC	International Amateur Radio Club		**IASC**	Inter-American Safety Council (U.S.A.)
IARCB	International Asian Research Conference Board		**IASC**	International Association of Seed Crushers
IARCS	Institut Asiatique de Recherche sur les Constructions Scolaires (Sri Lanka)		**IASC**	International Association for Statistical Computing
IARF	International Association for Liberal Christianity and Religious Freedom		**IASF**	International Atlantic Salmon Foundation
			IASH	International Association of Scientific Hydrology
IARI	Indian Agricultural Research Institute		**IASI**	Inter-American Statistical Institute
IARIGAI	International Association of Research Institutes for the Graphic Arts Industry		**IASIA**	International Association of Schools and Institutes of Administration
IARIW	International Association for Research in Income and Wealth		**IASL**	Inter-American School of Librarianship (Colombia)
IARM	Instituto Argentino de Racionalización de Materiales		**IASL**	International Association of School Librarianship
IARMI	International Association of Rattan Manufacturers and Importers		**IASL**	International Association for the Study of the Liver
IARP	Indian Association for Radiation Protection		**IASLIC**	Indian Association of Special Libraries and Information Centres
IARR	International Association for Radiation Research		**IASM**	Instituto per l'Assistenzo alla Sviluppo del Mezzogiorno
IARS	Institute of Agricultural Research Statistics (India)		**IASMAL**	International Academy of Social and Moral Sciences, Arts and Letters
IARS	International Anesthesis Research Society		**IASP**	International Association of Scholarly Publishers
IARU	International Amateur Radio Union			
IARUS	International Association for Regional and Urban Statistics		**IASP**	International Association for Social Progress
			IASP	International Association of Space Philatelists
IARW	International Association of Refrigerated Warehouses		**IASP**	International Association for the Study of Pain
IAS	Association Internationale de Sémiotique			
IAS	Institute of Andean Studies (U.S.A.)		**IASP**	International Association for Suicide Prevention
IAS	Institute of the Aeronautical Sciences (U.S.A.)		**IASPEI**	International Association of Seismology and Physics of the Earth's Interior
IAS	International Association of Sedimentologists (IUGS)		**IASPM**	International Association of Scientific Paper Makers
IAS	International Association of Seismology and of Physics of the Earth's Interior		**IASRA**	International Arthur Schnitzler Research Association (U.S.A.)
IAS	International Association of Siderographers			
IAS	International Audiovisual Society		**IASPS**	International Association for Statistics in Physical Sciences
IAS	Irish Archaeological Society			
IASA	International Air Safety Association			

IASS	International Association of Security Services (U.S.A.)	**IATR**	International Association for Tamil Research (Malaysia)
IASS	International Association for Semiotic Studies	**IATR**	International Association of Teachers of Russian
IASS	International Association for Shell Structures	**IATSW**	Indian Association of Trained Social Workers
IASS	International Association of Survey Statisticians	**IATTC**	Inter-American Tropical Tuna Commission
IASSMD	International Association for the Scientific Study of Mental Deficiency	**IATU**	Inter-American Telecommunications Union
IASSW	International Association of Schools of Social Work	**IATUL**	International Association of Technical University Libraries
IASTED	International Association of Science and Technology for Development	**IAU**	International Academic Union
		IAU	International Association of Universities
IASV	Internationale Arbeitsgemeinschaft von Sortimenter Vereinigungen	**IAU**	International Astronomical Union
IAT	Institute of Animal Technicians	**IAUP**	International Association of University Presidents
IAT	International Association for Time-Keeping	**IAUPE**	International Association of University Professors of English
IATA	Instituto de Agroquimica y Tecnologia de Alimentos	**IAUPL**	International Association of University Professors and Lecturers
IATA	International Air Transport Association	**IAUR**	Instituto de Antibióticos da Universidade do Recife (Brazil)
IATA	International Amateur Theatre Association	**IAV**	International Association of Volcanology
IATAL	International Association of Theoretical and Applied Limnology	**IAVC**	International Audio-Visual Centre
IATC	International Association of Tool Craftsmen	**IAVCEI**	International Association of Volcanology and Chemistry of the Earth's Interior
IATE	International Association of Television Editors	**IAVFH**	International Association of Veterinary Food Hygiene
IATE	International Association for Temperance Education	**IAVG**	International Association for Vocational Guidance
IATEFL	International Association of Teachers of English as a Foreign Language	**IAVI**	International Association of Voice Identification
IATEM	Instituto Agrotécnico Económico de Misiones (Argentina)	**IAVRS**	International Audiovisual Resource Service
IATFIS	Inter-Agency Task Force on Information Exchange and Transfer of Technology (IOB)	**IAVTC**	International Audio-Visual Technical Centre (Belgium)
IATL	International Academy of Trial Lawyers	**IAW**	International Alliance of Women
IATL	International Association of Theological Libraries	**IAWA**	Incorporated Advertising Managers Association
IATLIS	Indian Association of Teachers of Library Science	**IAWA**	Independent American Whiskey Association
IATM	International Association for Testing Materials	**IAWA**	International Association of Wood Anatomists
IATM	International Association of Tour Managers	**IAWC**	International Association of Whaling Corporations
IATM	International Association of Transport Museums	**IAWCC**	International Association of Wall and Ceiling Contractors (U.S.A.)
IATME	International Association of Terrestrial Magnetism and Electricity	**IAWHPJ**	International Association of Women and Home Page Journalists
IATO	International Association of Theatre Public Organization	**IAWL**	International Association for Water Law

IAWM	Industrial Association of Wales and Monmouthshire	**IBAR**	Interafrican Bureau for Animal Resources
IAWMC	International Association of Workers for Maladjusted Children	**IBB**	Institute of British Bakers
		IBB	International Bowling Board
IAWP	International Association of Women Police	**IBB**	International Brotherhood of Bookbinders
IAWPR	International Association on Water Pollution Research	**IBBC**	Instituut voor Bouwmaterialen en Bouwconstructies
IAWR	Internationale Arbeitsgemeinschaft der Wasserwerke im Rheineinzugsgebiet	**IBBD**	Institúto Brasileiro de Bibliografía e Documentaçao
IAWRT	International Association of Women in Radio and Television	**IBBH**	Internationaler Bund der Bau- und Holzarbeiter
IAWS	International Academy of Wood Science	**IBBYP**	International Board on Books for Young People (Switzerland)
IAWS	Irish Agricultural Wholesale Society	**IBC**	Instituto Brasileiro do Café
IAYM	International Association of Youth Magistrates	**IBC**	Institúto Bacteriológico de Chile
		IBC	International Biographical Centre (U.K.)
IAZ	Instituto de Agricultura y Zootecnia (Peru)	**IBC**	International Biotoxicological Centre, World Life Research Institute (U.S.A.)
IB	Instituut voor Bodemvruchtbaarheid	**IBC**	International Boundary Commission (U.S.A.)
IB	Institute of Bankers		
IBA	Independent Broadcasting Authority	**IBCA**	International Braille Chess Association
IBA	Institute of British Architects	**IBCA**	International Bureau for Cultural Activities (*of* COSEC)
IBA	International Banker Association		
IBA	International Bar Association	**IBBD**	Instituto Brasileiro de Bibliografía e Documentacao
IBA	International Bauxite Association		
IBA	International Biographical Association	**IBCA**	Instituto Boliviano de Cultivos Andinos
IBA	International Bookstall Contractors Association	**IBCAM**	Institute of British Carriage and Automobile Manufacturers
IBA	International Bridge Academy	**IBCC**	International Building Classification Committee (Netherlands)
IBAA	Independent Bankers Association of America		
IBAA	Investment Bankers' Association of America	**IBCC**	International Business Communications Centers (U.S.A.)
IBAB	Institut Belge pour l'Amélioration de la Betterave	**IB-CC**	International Business Contact Club
IBAE	Institution of British Agricultural Engineers	**IBCE**	International Bureau for Cultural Exchange
IBAH	Inter-African Bureau for Animal Health (*now* IBAR)	**IBCG**	Internationaler Bund der Christlichen Gewerkschaften
IBAHP	Inter-African Bureau for Animal Health and Production (*formerly* IBED) (Kenya)	**IBCGTB**	Internationaler Bund der Christlichen Gewerkschaften im Textil- und Bekleidungswerbe
IBAM	Institute of Business Administration and Management (Japan)		
IBAM	Instituto Brasileiro de Administraçao Municipal	**IBCHBV**	Internationaler Bund Christlicher Holz- und Bauarbeiterverbände
IBAN	Institut Belge pour l'Alimentation et la Nutrition	**IBCIN**	International Biologisch Contact- en Informatie-bureau voor Nederland
IBANA	Institut de Biologie Appliquée à la Nutrition et l'Alimentation	**IBCS**	International Bureau of Commercial Statistics
IBAP	Internationales Büro für Audiophonologie	**IBD**	Incorporated Institute of British Decorators and Interior Designers
IBAP	Intervention Board for Agricultural Produce	**IBD**	International Bureau for Declarations of Death

IBDA	Instituto Brasileiro de Direito Agrário
IBDC	Institut Belge de Droit Comparé
IBDF	Instituto Brasileiro de Desenvolvimento Florestal
IBE	Institute Belge de l'Emballage
IBE	Institute of British Engineers
IBE	International Bureau of Education
IBE	International Bureau for Epilepsy
IBEAS	Instituto Boliviano de Estudio y Accion Social
IBEC	International Bank for Economic Cooperation
IBEC	International Basic Economy Corporation (U.S.A.)
IBECC	Brazilian Institute of Education, Science and Culture
IBED	Inter-African Bureau of Epizootic Diseases (*now* IBAHP)
IBEE	International Builders Exchange Executives (U.S.A.)
IBEG	International Book Export Group
IBEG	Internationaler Bund der Erziehungsgemein-schaften
IBELCO	Institut Belge de Coopération Technique
IBERSOM	Institut Belge pour l'Encouragement de la Recherche Scientifique Outre-Mer
IBERTO	Société Industrielle et Commerciale Ibéro-Togolaise
IBEW	International Brotherhood of Electrical Workers
IBF	Institute of British Foundrymen
IBF	International Badminton Federation
IBF	International Balut Federation
IBFCC	International Border Fancy Canary Club
IBFD	Instituto Brasileiro de Direito Financeiro
IBFD	International Bureau of Fiscal Docu-mentation
IBFG	Internationaler Bund Freier Gewerkschaften
IBFI	International Business Forms Industries (U.S.A.)
IBFMP	International Bureau of the Federations of Master Printers
IBFO	International Brotherhood of Fireman and Oilers
IBG	Incorporated Brewers' Guild
IBG	Institute of British Geographers

IBG	Internationales Büro für Gebirgsmechanik
IBGE	Instituto Brasileiro de Geografia e Estatistica
IBHP	Institut Belge des Hautes Pressions
IBI	Institut International des Châteaux Histori-ques
IBI	Intergovernmental Bureau for Informatics (Italy)
IBI	International Broadcast Institute
IBI	Internationales Burgen Institut
IBICC	Incorporated British Institute of Certified Carpenters
IBICT	Instituto Brasileiro de Informação en Ciencia e Tecnologia
IBIS	International Book Information Services, Inc.
IBIT	Instituto Brasileiro para Investigaçao da Tuberculose
IBK	Institute of Bookkeepers
IBK	Internationale Beleuchtungs-Kommission
IBL	Institute of British Launderers
IBL	Instytut Badawczy Lesnictwa
IBLA	Institut des Belles-Lettres Arabes (Tunis)
IBLA	Inter-American Bibliographical and Library Association
IBLC	Institut Belgo-Luxembourgeois du Change
IBM	Indian Bureau of Mines
IBM	International Brotherhood of Magicians (U.S.A.)
IBM	International Business Machines Corporation
IBMA	International Bar Managers Association
IBME	Institúto de Biológia y Medicína Experi-mental (Argentina)
IBMR	International Bureau for Mechanical Reproduction
IBN	Institut Belge de Normalisation
IBNS	International Bank Note Society
IBO	International Baccalaureate Office (Switzerland)
IBO	Instituut voor Bosbouwkundig Onderzoek
IBO	Internationale Bouworde
IBOA	Irish Bank Officials' Association
IBOB	International Brotherhood of Old Bastards
IBOPC	Instituto Brasileiro de Oftalmologia e Pre-vencao da Cegueira
IBP	Institut Belge du Pétrole
IBP	Institute of British Photographers

IBP	Institute for Business Planning	IBST	Institute of British Surgical Technicians
IBP	Instituto Boliviano del Petroleo	IBT	International Brotherhood of Teamsters, Chauffeurs, Warehousemen and Helpers of America
IBP	Instituto Brasileiro de Potasa		
IBP	International Biological Programme		
IBP	Internationaler Bund der Privatangestellten	IBTA	International Baton Twirling Association of America and Abroad
IBPA	International Bridge Press Association	IBTA	International Business Travel Association
IBPC	Institut Biologique Physico-Chimique	IBTE	Imperial Board of Telecommunications (Ethiopia)
IBPCS	International Bureau for Physico-Chemical Standards		
		IBTE	International Bureau of Technical Education
IBPGR	International Board for Plant Genetic Resources (FAO etc.)	IBTT	International Bureau for Technical Training
		IBTS	International Beer Testing Society
IBPI	International Bureau for Plant Taxonomy and Nomenclature (Netherlands)	IBTTA	International Bridge and Tunnel-Turnpike Association (U.S.A.)
IBPR	International Board for Plant Genetic Resources	IBU	International Broadcasting Union
		IBU	Internationale Bürgermeister-Union
IBPT	Instituto de Biologia e Pesquisas Tecnológicas (Portugal)	IBUPL	International Bureau for the Unification of Penal Law
IBRA	Institut Belge de Régulation et Automatisme	IBUPU	International Bureau of the Universal Postal Union
IBRA	Instituto Brasileiro de Administração		
IBRA	Instituto Brasileiro de Reforma Agraria	IBVEA	International Bureau of Veterinary Educational Aids (Australia)
IBRA	International Bee Research Association		
IBRA	International Bible Reading Association	IBVL	Instituut voor Bewaring en Verwerking van Landbouwprodukten
IBRADES	Instituto Brasileiro de Desenvolvimento	IBVT	Instituut voor Bewaring en Verwerking van Tuinbouwproducten
IBRAPE	Industria Brasileira de Produtos Electronicos e Electricos		
IBRAR	Instituto Brasileiro de Reforma Agrária Regional	IBW	Instituut voor Bestuurwetenschappen
		IBWC	International Boundary and Water Commission (USA-Mexico)
IBRC	International Bird Rescue Center (U.S.A.)		
IBRD	International Bank for Reconstruction and Development	IBWM	International Bureau of Weights and Measures
IBRE	Instituto Brasileiro de Economia	IBWS	International Bureau of Whaling Statistics
IBRI	Instituto Brasileiro de Relações Internacionais	IC	Islamic Congress
		ICA	Common Market Group of the International Confederation of Agricultural Credit
IBRO	International Brain Research Organisation		
IBS	Institut Belge de la Soudre	ICA	Fédération Internationale Chrétienne des Travailleurs de l'Alimentation, du Tabac et de l'Hôtellerie
IBS	Institute of Bankers in Scotland		
IBS	Instituut voor Biologisch en Scheikundig Onderzoek van Landbouwgewassen	ICA	Imprimerie Centrale d'Afrique
IBS	International Broadcasters Society	ICA	Industria y Comercio de Alimentación
IBSA	Institut Belge des Sciences Administratives	ICA	Information Centre for Aeronautics (India)
IBSCC	International Bureau for the Suppression of Counterfeit Coins	ICA	Institut Culturel Africain
		ICA	Institute of Company Accountants
IBSFC	International Baltic Sea Fishery Commission	ICA	Institute of Contemporary Art
IBSL	Internationaler Bund der Schum- und Lederarbeiter	ICA	Instituto Colombiano Agropêcuario
IBSL	Internationales Berufs-Sekretariat der Lehrer	ICA	Instituto Colombiano de Antropología

ICA	Institutul de Cercetari Alimentare (Roumania)	**ICAES**	International Congress of Anthropological and Ethnological Sciences
ICA	Inter-Cultural Cooperation Association	**ICAF**	International Committee on Aeronautical Fatigue
ICA	Intergovernmental Council for Automatic Data Processing	**ICAFI**	International Commission of Agriculture and Food Industries
ICA	International Caribbean Airways	**ICAI**	Instituto Católico de Artes e Industrias (Spain)
ICA	International Cartographic Association		
ICA	International Chefs Association	**ICAI**	International Commission for Agricultural Industries
ICA	International Chiropractors Association		
ICA	International Claim Association	**ICAI**	International Committee for Aid to Intellectuals
ICA	International Commission on Acoustics		
ICA	International Communications Association	**ICAITI**	Instituto Centro Americano de Investigación y Tecnologia Industrial (Guatemala)
ICA	International Control Agency		
ICA	International Co-operation Administration (U.S.A.) (*now* AID)	**ICALU**	International Confederation of Arab Labour Unions
ICA	International Co-operative Alliance	**ICAM**	Institut Culturel Africain, Malgache et Mauricien
ICA	International Council for Archives		
ICA	Jewish Colonization Association (Israel)	**ICAM**	Institute of Corn and Agricultural Merchants (U.K.) *now* BASAM
ICA	United States International Cooperation Administration	**ICAMAS**	International Centre for Advance Mediterranean Agronomic Studies
ICAA	International Civil Airport Association	**ICAME**	International Centre for the Advancement of Management Education (U.S.A.)
ICAA	International Confederation of Artists Associations	**ICAN**	International College of Applied Nutrition (U.S.A.)
ICAA	International Council on Alcohol and Addictions		
ICAAN	International Committee on Avian Anatomical Nomenclature	**ICAN**	International Commission on Air Navigation
		ICANA	Instituto Cultural Argentina Norte-Americano
ICAB	Industries Camerounaises des Annexes du Bâtiment	**ICAO**	International Civil Aviation Organisation
ICAB	International Council against Bullfighting	**ICAP**	Instituto Centroamericano de Administración Publica
ICAC	Independent Commission Against Corruption (Hong Kong)	**ICAP**	Inter-American Committee on the Alliance for Progress
ICAC	International Civil Aviation Committee		
ICAC	International Confederation for Agricultural Credit	**ICAP**	International Committee of Architectural Photogrammetry
ICAC	International Cotton Advisory Committee	**ICAPE**	International Chemical and Petroleum Engineering Exhibition
ICAD	Inter-American Committee for Agricultural Development		
		ICAPF	Instituto Centroamericano de Población y Familia (Guatemala)
ICAE	International Commission of Agricultural Engineering	**ICAR**	Indian Council of Agricultural Research
ICAE	International Commission on Atmospheric Electricity	**ICAR**	Institutul de Cercetari Agronomice al Romîniei
ICAE	International Conference of Agricultural Economists		
		ICARDA	International Centre for Agricultural Research in the Dry Areas (Middle East)
ICAE	International Council for Adult Education		
ICAES	Instituto Centroamericano de Estudios Sociales (Costa Rico)	**ICARE**	Instituto Chileno de Administración Racional de Empresas (Chile)

ICARE | International Center for the Advancement of Research and Education (Italy)

ICARES | Institut International Catholique de Recherches Sociales

ICARMO | International Council of the Architects of Historical Monuments

ICAS | Interdepartmental Committee for Atmospheric Science (U.S.A.)

ICAS | International Council of Aeronautical Sciences

ICASALS | International Centre for Arid and Semi-arid Land Studies (U.S.A.)

ICASE | Central American Institute of Educational Administration and Supervision

ICASE | International Council of Associations for Science Education

ICASSI | International Committee for Adlerian Summer Schools and Institutes

ICAT | International Committee on Autogenic Therapy

ICATO | Iranian Civil Aviation Training Organization

ICATS | International Centre of Advanced Tourism Studies (*of* IUOTO)

ICATU | International Confederation of Arab Trade Unions

ICAW | International Conference on Automation in Warehousing

ICB | Indian Coffee Board

ICB | Industrial Co-ordination Bureau

ICB | International Christian Broadcasters

ICB | International Container Bureau

ICB | International Convention Bureau (Belgium)

ICBA | International Community of Booksellers Associations

ICBB | International Commission for Bee Botany

ICBBA | International Cornish Bantam Breeders Association

ICBD | International Council of Ballroom Dancing

ICBL | International Conference on the Biology of Lipids

ICBN | International Committee on Bacteriological Nomenclature (*now* ICNB)

ICBO | International Conference of Building Officials

ICBP | International Committee for Bird Preservation

ICBY | International Council on Books for Young People

ICC | Association Internationale de Chimie Céréalière

ICC | Imprimerie Commerciale du Cameroun

ICC | International Cello Centre

ICC | International Chamber of Commerce

ICC | International Children's Centre, Paris

ICC | International Climatological Commission

ICC | International Computing Centre (Switzerland)

ICC | International Congregational Council

ICC | International Cooperation Council

ICC | International Coordinating Committee for the Presentation of Science and the Development of Scientific Out-of-School Activities (Belgium)

ICC | International Corrosion Council

ICC | International Creative Centre (Switzerland)

ICC | International Cricket Conference

ICCA | Industrie Cotonnière Centrafricaine

ICCA | Instituto Centroamericano de Ciencias Agricolas

ICCA | Intercontinental Corrugated Case Association

ICCA | International Committee on Co-ordination for Agriculture

ICCA | International Congress and Convention Association

ICCAD | International Centre for Computer-Aided Design (Italy)

ICCAIA | International Coordinating Council of Aerospace Industries Associations

ICCAM | International Committee of Children's and Adolescent's Movements

ICCAP | International Coordinating Committee for the Accountancy Profession (*now* IFA)

ICCAS | International Conference on Computer Applications in the Automation of Shipyard Operation and Ship Design

ICCAT | International Commission for the Conservation of Atlantic Tunas

ICCB | Instítuto Cultural Colombo-Británico

ICCB | International Catholic Child Bureau

ICCBC | International Committee for Colorado Beetle Control

ICCC | Indian Central Coconut Committee

ICCC | Inter-Council Co-ordination Committee (France)

ICCC	International Centre for Comparative Criminology
ICCC	International Conference of Catholic Charities
ICCC	International Conference Centers Consultants (Belgium)
ICCC	International Conference on Computer Communication
ICCC	International Conference on Co-ordination Chemistry
ICCC	International Congresses on the Communication of Culture through Architecture, Arts and Mass Media
ICCC	International Council of Christian Churches
ICCD	Institute of Chocolate and Confectionery Distributors
ICCE	Instituto Colombiano de Construcciones Escolares
ICCE	International Council of Commerce Employers
ICCE	International Council for Correspondence Education
ICCEE	International Classification Commission for Electrical Engineering
ICCF	International Committee on Canned Food
ICCF	International Correspondence Chess Federation
ICCH	International Commodity Clearing House
ICCH	International Conference on Computers and the Humanities
ICCICA	Interim Co-ordinating Committee on International Commodity Arrangements (U.S.A.)
ICCJ	International Committee for Co-operation of Journalists
ICCJ	International Council of Christians and Jews
ICCL	International Committee of Comparative Law
ICCLA	International Centre for the Co-ordination of Legal Assistance
ICCO	International Carpet Classification Organization
ICCO	International Cocoa Organization
ICCO	International Council of Containership Operators
ICCP	Institutul de Cercetari pentru Cultura Porumbului (Roumania)
ICCP	International Commission on Cloud Physics
ICCP	International Council for Children's Play
ICCR	Indian Council for Cultural Relations
ICCRA	Associazione Nazionale Importatori Carni Congelate, Refrigerate ed Affini
ICCRA	Investigaciones Cooperatives en el Mar Caribe y Regiones Adjacentes (FAO)
ICCREA	Istituto di Credito delle Casse Rurali e Artigiane
ICCS	International Catholic Conference of Scouting
ICCS	International Centre of Criminological Studies
ICCS	International Commission for Control and Supervision
ICCS	International Container and Chassis Services (Belgium)
ICCSTI	Inter-Departmental Co-ordinating Committee for Scientific and Technical Information
ICCTA	International Consultative Council of Travel Agents
ICCU	International Cross-Country Union
ICCW	Indian Council for Child Welfare
ICD	International Centre for Development (Africa)
ICD	International Committee of Dermatology
ICDA	International Catholic Deaf Association
ICDA	International Coalition for Developing Action
ICDC	Indian Cotton Development Council
ICDC	Industrial and Commercial Development Corporation
ICDCS	Interstate Permanent Committee for Drought Control in the Sahelian Zone
ICDECAA	International Committee for the Development of Educational and Cultural Activities in Africa
ICDO	International Civil Defence Organisation
ICDP	International Confederation for Disarmament and Peace
ICE	Institut Italien pour le Commerce Extérieur
ICE	Institute of Ceramic Engineers (U.S.A.)
ICE	Institution of Civil Engineers
ICE	Instituto Costarricense de Electricidad
ICE	International Centre for the Environment
ICE	International Cultural Exchange
ICE	IOMTR Committee for Europe

CE	Istituto Nazionale per il Commercio con l'Estero	**ICET**	International Council on Education for Teaching
CEA	Institut Canadien d'Éducation des Adultes	**ICETEX**	Instituto Colombiano de Especializacion Tecnica en el Exterior (Colombia)
CEA	International Childbirth Education Association (U.S.A.)	**ICETK**	International Committee of Electrochemical Thermodynamics and Kinetics
CEATCA	Icelandic Air Traffic Controllers Association	**ICETT**	Industrial Council for Educational and Training Technology
CEBY	International Conference for the Education of Blind Youth	**ICEVH**	International Council for Education of the Visually Handicapped
CECOOP	Chilean Institute for Cooperative Education	**ICF**	Ice Cream Federation
CECU	Instituto Centroamericano de Extensión y Cultura (Costa Rica)	**ICF**	Institutul de Cercetari Forestiere (Roumania)
CED	International Council for Educational Development (U.S.A.)	**ICF**	International Canoe Federation
CED	International Council on Environmental Design	**ICF**	International Casting Federation
CED	International Cryogenic Engineering Committee	**ICF**	International Cheerleading Foundation (U.S.A.)
CED	International Council for Educational Development	**ICF**	International Congress on Fracture
CEF	International Childrens Emergency Fund	**ICF**	International Consultants Foundation (U.S.A.)
CEF	International Committee for Research and Study on Environmental Factors	**ICF**	International Cultural Foundation
CEF	International Committee for Ethnographic Films	**ICF**	International Federation of Chemical and General Workers Unions
CEF	International Conference on Environmental Future	**ICF**	Société des Ingénieurs Civils de France
CEF	International Council for Educational Films	**ICFA**	International Cystic Fibrosis Association (*now* ICF(M)A)
CEI	Institute of Civil Engineers of Ireland	**ICFC**	Industrial and Commercial Finance Corporation
CEL	Instituto Colombiano de Energía Eléctrica	**ICFC**	International Centre of Films for Children
CEL	International Committee on English in the Liturgy	**ICFCYP**	International Centre of Films for Children and Young People
CEL	International Council of Environmental Law	**ICFES**	Instituto Colombiana para el Fomento de la Educación Superior
CEM	Institutul de Cercetari Metalurgice (Roumania)	**ICFG**	International Cold Forging Group
CEM	Inter-governmental Committee for European Migration	**ICF(M)A**	International Cystic Fibrosis (Mucoviscidosis) Association
CEM	International Council for Educational Media	**ICFOST**	International Committee for Food Science Technology
CEMIN	Institutul de Cercetări Miniere (Roumania)		
CER	Institute for Central European Research (U.S.A.)	**ICFPW**	International Confederation of Former Prisoners of War
CER	Information Centre of the European Railways	**ICFTA**	International Committee of Foundry Technical Associations
CES	International Council for the Exploration of the Sea	**ICFTU**	International Confederation of Free Trade Unions
CESA	International Conference on Environment Sensing and Assessment	**ICFTU-ARO**	Asian Regional Organisation of ICFTU
CET	International Centre for Economy and Technology (Belgium)	**ICFTU-ORIT**	Inter-American Regional Organisation of Workers of the ICFTU

ICFU	International Council on the Future of the University
ICFW	International Christian Federation of Food, Drink, Tobacco and Hotelworkers
ICG	International Commission on Glass
ICG	International Congress of Genetics
ICG	International Geophysical Committee
ICG	Inter-Union Commission on Geodynamics
ICGA	International Carnival Glass Association
ICGA	International Classic Guitar Association
ICGEL	International Crushing and Grinding Equipment Ltd
ICGI	International Council of Goodwill Industries
ICGS	International Catholic Girls Society
ICHC	International Committee for Horticultural Congresses
ICHCA	International Cargo Handling Co-ordination Association
ICHDA	International Cooperative Housing Development Association (U.S.A.)
ICHE	International Councils on Higher Education
I Chem E	Institution of Chemical Engineers
ICHEO	Inter-University Council for Higher Education Overseas
ICHHS	International Council of Home-Help Services
ICHMT	International Centre for Heat and Mass Transfer (Yugoslavia)
ICHPER	International Council on Health, Physical Education and Recreation
ICHR	Indian Council for Historical Research
ICHS	Interafrican Committee for Hydraulic Studies
ICHS	International Committee of Historical Sciences
ICHS	International Council of Home-Help Services
ICHT	International Committee on Haemostasis and Thrombosis
ICHV	Institutul de Cercetari Horti-Viticole (Roumania)
ICI	Imperial Chemical Industries
ICI	Inküpscentralemas Aktiebolag
ICI	Instituto de Colonización e Immigración (Colombia)
ICI	Inter-American Co-operative Institute (Panama)
ICI	Inter-American Copyright Institute (Brazil)
ICI	International Commission on Illumination
ICI	Istituto Cotoniero Italiana
ICIA	International Centre of Information on Antibiotics (Belgium)
ICIA	International Credit Insurance Association
ICIA	International Crop Improvement Association
ICIANZ	Imperial Chemical Industries of Australia and New Zealand
ICIB	Indian Commercial Information Bureau
ICIB	International Council for Building Research, Studies and Documentation
ICICI	Industrial Credit and Investment Corporation of India
ICID	International Commission on Irrigation and Drainage (India)
ICIDCA	Instituto Cubano de Investigaciones de los Derivados de la Caña de Azúcar
ICIE	International Centre for Industry and the Environment
ICIF	International Co-operative Insurance Federation
ICIFI	International Council of Infant Food Industries
ICIP	Instituto Colombiano de la Investigación Pedagógica
ICIPE	Informateur Centre International de Propagation du Jeu d'Échecs (France)
ICIPE	International Centre of Insect Physiology and Ecology (Kenya)
ICIPU	Istituto di Credito per le Imprese di Pubblica Utilità
ICIRA	Instituto de Capacitación e Investigación en Reforma Agraria (Chile)
ICIREPAT	Committee for International Cooperation in Information Retrieval among Examining Patent Offices
ICIS	International Conference on Ion Sources
ICIT	Instituto Cubano de Investigaciones Tecnológicas (Cuba)
ICITA	International Chain of Industrial and Technical Advertising Agencies
ICITA	International Co-operative Investigations of the Tropical Atlantic
ICITO	Interim Committee of the International Trade Organisation
ICIV	Instituto Cooperativo Interamericano de la Vivienda (Guatemala)
ICIW	International Confederation of Professional and Intellectual Workers

ICJ	International Commission of Jurists
ICJ	International Court of Justice
ICJA	International Criminal Justice Association (U.S.A.)
ICJW	International Council of Jewish Women
ICL	International Computers Limited
ICL	Irish Central Library for Students
ICLA	International Committee on Laboratory Animals
ICLA	International Comparative Literature Association
ICLA	Investigadores de Cafe de Latino America
ICLARM	International Center for Living Aquatic Resources Management (Philippines)
ICLG	International and Comparative Librarianship Group (of LA)
ICLM	International Christian Leprosy Mission
ICLY	International Council on Lethal Yellowing
ICM	International Confederation of Midwives
ICMA	Institute of Cost and Management Accountants
ICMA	International Center of Medieval Art
ICMA	International Christian Maritime Association
ICMA	International Circulation Managers Association (U.S.A.)
ICMA	International City Managers' Association
ICMA	International Congresses for Modern Architecture
ICMAR	Institut International de Culture Maritime
ICMC	International Catholic Migration Commission
ICMC	International Circulation Managers Commission
ICMC	International Congress on Metallic Corrosion
ICMEA	Institutul de Cercetari pentru Mecanizarea si Electrificarea Agriculturii (Roumania)
ICMF	Indian Cotton Mills Federation
ICMI	International Commission of Mathematical Instruction
ICMICA	International Catholic Movement for Intellectual and Cultural Affairs
ICMLT	International Congress of Medical Laboratory Technologists
ICMMP	International Committee of Military Medicine and Pharmacy
ICMPH	International Centre of Medical and Psychological Hypnosis (Italy)

ICMR	Indian Council of Medical Research
ICMRD	International Center for Marine Resource Development
ICMREF	Interagency Committee on Marine Science, Research, Engineering and Facilities (U.S.A.)
ICMRT	International Center for Medical Research and Training (of NIH) (U.S.A.)
ICMS	International Commission on Mushroom Science
ICMSA	Irish Creamery Milk Suppliers Association
ICMSF	International Commission on Microbiological Specifications for Foods
ICN	International Chemical and Nuclear Corporation
ICN	International Council of Nurses
ICNAF	International Commission for the Northwest Atlantic Fisheries
ICNACO	Investigaciones Cooperativas en la Parte Norte del Atlantico Centro-Oriental (FAO)
ICNATVAS	International Council of the National Academy of Television Arts and Sciences
ICNB	International Committee on Nomenclature of Bacteria
ICNDT	International Committee for Non-Destructive Testing
ICNND	Interdepartmental Committee on Nutrition for National Defense (U.S.A.)
ICNT	International Committee for Natural Therapeutics
ICNV	International Committee for the Nomenclature of Viruses
ICO	Conference of International Catholic Organizations
ICO	Intergovernmental Commission on Oceanography
ICO	International Chemistry Office
ICO	International Coffee Organisation
ICO	International Commission on Oceanography
ICO	International Commission on Optics
ICO	International Congress of Otolaryngology
ICOA	International Castor Oil Association (U.S.A.)
ICOBA	International Confederation of Book Actors
ICOC	Indian Central Oilseeds Committee
ICODA	Industrie Cotonnière du Dahomey
ICODES	Instituto Colombiano de Desarrollo Social
ICODI	Société des Impressions sur Tissus de Côte-d'Ivoire

ICOFA	International Scientific Commission on the Family
ICOFTA	Indian Council of Foreign Trade
ICOGRADA	International Council of Graphic Design Associations
ICOHM	International Committee on Occupational Mental Health
ICOHTEC	International Cooperation in History of Technology Committee
ICOLD	International Commission on Large Dams of the World Power Conference
ICOLPE	Instituto Colombiano de Pedagogía
ICOM	International Council of Museums
ICOME	International Committee on Microbial Ecology
ICOMI	Industria et Commercio de Minerios (Brazil)
ICOMIA	International Council of Marine Industry Associations
ICOMON	Conseil International des Monuments
ICOMOS	International Council of Monuments and Sites
ICON	Inter-Institutional Committee on Nutrition (U.S.A.)
ICON	Investment Company of Nigeria
ICONTEC	Instituto Colombiano de Normas Tecnicas
ICOO	Iraqi Company for Oil Operations
ICOP	Instituto Colombiano de Opinión Pública
ICOPA	International Conference of Police Associations
ICOPA	International Congress on Parasitology
ICOPRAPA	International Conference of Peace Researchers and Peace Activities
ICOR	Intergovernmental Conference on Oceanic Research
ICOS	International Committee of Onomastic Sciences
ICOSA	International Council of Seamen's Agencies (U.S.A.)
ICOSO	International Committee for Outer Space Onomastics
ICOTAF	Industrie Cotonnière Africaine
ICOU	Organisation Internationale des Unions de Consommateurs
ICP	International Committee for Learning by Participation
ICP	International Commission for Palynology
ICP	International Council of Psychologists
ICP	International Institute of Cellular and Molecular Pathology (Belgium)
ICP	Investment Corporation of Pakistan
ICPA	International Commission for the Prevention of Alcoholism
ICPA	International Co-operative Petroleum Association
ICPC	International Cable Protection Committee
ICPCE	International Great Plains Conference of Entomologists
ICPDP	International Committee for Pollution Damage to Plants
ICPFR	International Committee on Physical Fitness Research
ICPHS	International Council for Philosophy and Humanistic Studies
ICPI	Instituto Colombiano de Planeación Integral
ICPIGP	Internationale Chrétienne Professionelle pour les Industries Graphiques et Papetières
ICPM	International Commission for Plant Raw Materials
ICPM	International Committee on Polar Meteorology
ICPO	International Criminal Police Organisation
ICPP	International Conference on the Internal and External Protection of Pipes
ICPR	Indian Council of Peace Research
ICPRP	International Commission for the Protection of the Rhine Pollution
ICPS	Institute of Cost and Production Surveyors
ICPS	International Conference on the Properties of Steam
ICPS	International Congress of Photographic Science
ICPS	Trade Unions International of Chemical Oil and Allied Workers
ICPTO	International China Painting Teachers Organization (U.S.A.)
ICPU	International Catholic Press Union
ICR	Institute of Cultural Research
ICR	International Congress of Radiology
ICR	International Council for Reprography
ICRA	Instituto Costaricense de Defensa Agraria
ICRA	International Catholic Rural Association
ICRA	International Centre for Research in Accounting (U.K.)
ICRA	Irish Civil Rights Association

CRB	International Center for Research on Bilingualism (Canada)	ICSB	International Committee on Systematic Bacteriology (*of* IAMS)
CRC	Indian Cancer Research Centre	ICSC	Indian Central Sugarcane Committee
CRC	International Committee of the Red Cross	ICSC	Interim Communications Satellite Commission (*of* INTELSAT)
CRCP	International Centre for Relief to Civilian Population	ICSC	International Civil Service Commission
CRDB	International Cancer Research Data Bank (U.S.A.)	ICSC	International Council of Shopping Centers (U.S.A.)
CRE	International Centre for Remedial Education	ICSC	Inter-ocean Canal Study Commission (U.S.A.)
CRE	International Commission on Radiological Education and Information	ICSCHM	International Commission for a History of the Scientific and Cultural Development of Mankind
CREP	Instituto Chileno de Relaciones Publicas		
CRH	International Congress on Religious History	ICSDW	International Council of Social Democratic Women *now* Socialist Internationalist Women
CRICE	International Centre of Research and Information on Collective Economy (Belgium)		
CRISAT	International Crop Research Institute for the Semi-Arid Tropics (India)	ICSEAF	International Commission for the Southeast Atlantic Fisheries
CRM	Instituto Cubano de Recursos Minerales	ICSEB	International Congress of Systematic and Evolutionary Biology
CRO	International Cell Research Organisation	ICSEM	International Centre of Studies on Early Music
CRP	International Commission on Radiation Protection		
CRPMA	International Committee for Recording the Productivity of Milk Animals	ICSEMS	International Commission for the Scientific Exploration of the Mediterranean Sea
CRS	International Commission on Radium Standards	ICSHB	International Committee for Standardisation in Human Biology
CRSC	International Council for Research in the Sociology of Cooperation	ICSH	International Congress Services Holland
CRU	International Commission on Radiation Units and Measurements	ICSI	International Commission of Snow and Ice (*of* IASH)
ICS	Indian Chemical Society	ICSID	International Centre for Settlement of Investment Disputes
ICS	Institute of Caribbean Science (Puerto Rico)		
ICS	Institute of Chartered Shipbrokers	ICSID	International Council of Societies of Industrial Design
ICS	International Chamber of Shipping	ICSM	International Committee of Scientific Management
ICS	International Clarinet Society		
ICS	International Conrad Society (U.S.A.)	ICSMA	International Conference on Strength of Metals and Alloys
ICS	International Crocodilian Society (U.S.A.)		
ICS	International College of Surgeons (U.S.A.)	ICSOM	International Conference of Symphony and Opera Musicians
ICS	International Correspondence Schools (U.S.A.)		
ICSA	International Civil Service Agency	ICSP	International Council of Societies of Pathology
ICSA	International Correspondence Society of Allergists (U.S.A.)	ICSPE	International Council of Sport and Physical Education
ICSA	International Council for Scientific Agriculture	ICSPFT	International Committee for the Standardisation of Physical Fitness Tests
ICSAB	International Civil Service Advisory Board	ICSPHR	International Centre of Studies for the Protection of Human Rights (U.S.A.)
ICSB	International Centre of School-Building		

ICSPRO	Inter-Secretariat Committee on Scientific Programmes Relating to Oceanography
ICSPS	International Council for Science Policy Studies
ICSS	Instituto Colombiano de Seguros Sociales
ICSS	International Center for Strategic Studies (U.S.A.)
ICSS	International Committee for Shell Structures (*now* IASS)
ICSSD	International Committee for Social Sciences Documentation
ICSSID	International Committee for Social Science Information and Documentation
ICSSR	Indian Council of Social Science Research
ICSSW	International Committee of Schools for Social Work
ICST	Imperial College of Science and Technology, London
ICSTI	International Centre for Scientific and Technical Information (USSR)
ICSTO	International Civil Service Training Organization
ICSU	International Council of Scientific Unions
ICSUAB	International Council of Scientific Unions Abstracting Board
ICSUIA	Instituto de Ciencias Sociales de la Universidad Iberoamericana (Mexico)
ICSV	Internationale Christlich-Soziale Vereinigung (Belgium)
ICSW	International Council on Social Welfare
ICSWOA	International Centre for Scientific Work Organisation in Agriculture
ICT	Institute of Clay Technology
ICT	International Computers and Tabulators, Ltd
ICT	International Council of Tanners
ICTA	Imperial College of Tropical Agriculture (West Indies)
ICTA	Institute of Agricultural Science and Technology (Guatemala)
ICTA	International Centre for the Typographic Arts (Germany)
ICTA	International Confederation of Technical Agriculturists
ICTA	International Confederation for Thermal Analysis
ICTA	International Council for Travel Agents
ICTA	Ivory Coast Travel Agency
ICTAA	Imperial College of Tropical Agriculture Association
ICTB	International Customs Tariffs Bureau
ICTC	Indian Central Tobacco Committee
ICTC	International Cooperative Training Centre (U.S.A.)
ICTF	International Cocoa Trades Federation
ICTF	International Conference on Thin Films
ICTMM	International Congresses on Tropical Medicine and Malaria
ICTR	International Centre of Theatre Research (France)
ICTS	International Catholic Truth Society
ICTS	International Congress on Transplantation
ICTT	Internacional del Personal de los Servicios de Correos, Télegrafos y Teléfonos
ICTTC	International Consultative Telegraph and Telephone Committee
ICTU	Irish Congress of Trade Unions
ICU	Institut pour la Coopération Universitaire
ICU	International Chemistry Union
ICUAE	International Congress of University Adult Education
ICUE	International Committee on the University Emergency
ICUEPR	International Conference on University Education for Public Relations
ICUMSA	International Commission for Uniform Methods of Sugar Analysis
ICUP	International Catholic Union of the Press
ICUS	International Conference on the Unity of the Sciences
ICUSS	International Council for the United Services to Seamen
ICV	International Commission of Viticulture
ICVA	International Council of Voluntary Agencies
ICVAN	International Committee on Veterinary Anatomical Nomenclature (Austria)
ICVD	Internationale Christelijke Vredesdient
ICVG	International Council for the Study of Viruses and Virus Diseases of Grapevine
ICW	Institute of Clayworkers
ICW	Institute of Clerks of Works of Great Britain
ICW	Instituut voor Cultuurtechniek en Waterhuishouding
ICW	Inter-American Commission of Women

ICW	International Chemical Workers Union (U.S.A.)	IDAF	International Defence and Aid Fund for Southern Africa
ICW	International Council for Women	IDAMI	Istituto di Documentazione della Associazione Meccanica Italiana
ICWA	Indian Council of World Affairs	IDATEX	Industrie Dahoméenne du Textile
ICWA	Institute of Cost and Works Accountants (*now* ICMA)	IDB	Industrial Development Board (Sri Lanka)
ICWA	International Coil Winding Association	IDB	Insurance Development Bureau (Sweden)
ICWES	International Conference of Women Engineers and Scientists	IDB	Inter-American Development Bank
		IDB	International Peace Bureau (Switzerland)
ICWG	International Co-operative Womens Guild	IDBI	Industrial Development Bank of India
ICWM	International Committee of Weights and Measures	IDBP	Industrial Development Bank of Pakistan
		IDBRA	International Drivers Behaviour Research Association
ICWP	International Council of Women Psychologists	IDBT	Industrial Development Bank of Turkey
ICWS	International Co-operative Wholesale Society	IDC	Industrial Development Corporation (South Africa, Trinidad and Tobago)
ICWU	International Chemical Workers Union	IDC	International Dairy Committee
ICY	International Christian Youth	IDC	International Dance Council
ICYE	International Council for the International Christian Youth Exchange	IDC	International Documentation Centre (Sweden)
ICYF	International Catholic Youth Federation	IDC	International Dermatological Committee
ICZ	Institutul de Cercetari Zootehnice (Roumania)	IDCA	Industrial Design Council of Australia
		IDCAS	Industrial Development Centre for Arab States
ICZN	International Commission for Zoological Nomenclature	IDCHEC	Intergovernmental Documentation Centre on Housing and Environment of the Countries of the United Nations Economic Commission for Europe
IDA	Industrial Diamond Association of America		
IDA	International Defenders of Animals (U.S.A.)		
IDA	International Development Action (Australia)	IDD	Industrielle Designere Danmark
IDA	International Development Association	IDDE	Instituto para el Desarrollo de la Dirección de Empresas (Uruguay)
IDA	International Diplomatic Academy (U.S.A.)		
IDA	International Discotheque Association	IDDRG	International Deep Drawing Research Group
IDA	International Doll Association	IDDS	International Dairy Development Scheme
IDA	International Drummers Association	IDE	Institut Danois des Échanges Internationaux de Publications Scientifiques et Littéraires
IDA	Irish Dental Association		
IDA	Irish Drug Association	IDE	Institut de Développement Économique (de la Banque Mondiale)
IDAA	International Doctors in Alcoholics Anonymous (U.S.A.)		
IDAAN	Instituto de Acueductos y Alcantarillados Nacionales (Panama)	IDE	Institute of Developing Economies (Japan) (*formerly* IAEA)
IDAC	Import Duties Advisory Committee	IDEA	Instituto para el Desarrollo de Ejecutivos en la Argentina
IDACA	Institute for the Development of Agricultural Cooperation in Asia (Japan)		
		IDEA	Instituto de Estudios Africanos
IDACE	Association des Industries des Aliments Diététiques de la Communauté Économique Européenne	IDEA	International Downtown Executives Association (U.S.A.)
IDAF	Institutet f. Distribution-Ekonomisk och Administrativ Forskning	IDEAS	Institutional Development Economic Affairs Service Inc. (U.S.A.)

IDEF	Institut International de Droit des Pays d'Expression Française
IDEMA	Instituto de Mercadeo Agropecuario (Colombia)
IDEP	Institut Africain de Développement Économique et de Planification
IDER	Instituto Dominicano de Educación Rural
IDERPC	Institut de Développement Économique de la République Populaire du Congo
IDERT	Institut d'Enseignement et de Recherches Tropicales
IDES	Instituto de Desarrollo Económico y Social (Argentina)
IDET	Institut pour le Développement Économique et Technique
IDEVI	Instituto de Desarrollo del Valle Inferior del Río Negro (Argentina)
IDEX	Ivoirienne de Distribution et d'Exportation
IDF	International Dairy Federation
IDF	Institut pour le Dévelopment Forestier
IDF	International Democratic Fellowship
IDF	International Dental Federation
IDF	International Diabetes Federation
IDFA	Interessengemeinschaft Deutscher Fachmessen und Ausstellungsstädte
IDFF	Internationale Demokratische Frauenföderation
IDHA	International District Heating Association (U.S.A.)
IDHE	Institute of Domestic Heating Engineers
IDI	Institut de Droit International
IDIA	Industrial Design Institute of Australia
IDIB	Industrial Diamond Information Bureau
IDICIT	Instituto de Documentación y Información Científica y Técnica (Cuba)
IDICT	Instituto de Documentación e Información Científica y Técnica (Cuba)
IDIS	International Dairy Industries Society
IDIT	Institut du Droit International des Transports
IdK	Internationaler der Kriegsdienstgegner
IDLIS	International Desert Locust Information Service
IDLSG	International Drycleaners and Launderers Study Group
IDMA	International Diamond Manufacturers Association

IDMA	International Dancing Masters' Association (*now* IDTA)
IDMA	International Doll Makers Association
IDO	International Dental Organisation
IDOC	International Documentation and Communication Centre (Italy)
IDOC	International Documentation on the Contemporary Church (Association) (U.S.A.)
IDOE	International Decade of Ocean Exploration (U.S.A.)
IDORT	Instituto de Organizacão Racional do Trabalho (Brazil)
IDP	Institute of Data Processing
IDR	International Dental Relief
IDRA	International Desert Racing Association
IDRC	International Development Research Centre (Canada)
IDREM	Institut Européen de Documentation et de Recherche sur les Maladies
IDRF	International Disaster Relief Force
IDS	Industrieverband Deutscher Schmieden
IDS	Institute of Development Studies, University of Sussex
IDS	International Development Services
IDSA	Indian Dairy Science Association
IDSA	Industrial Designers Society of America
IDSA	International Development Service of America
IDSO	International Diamond Security Organization
IDT	Institutul de Documentare Technica (Roumania)
IDTA	International Dance Teachers' Association
IDU	International Dendrology Union
IDV	Interessengemeinschaft Deutscher Versandbier- Grosshändler
IdW	Institut der Wirtschaftsprüfer in Deutschland
IE	Institute of Engineers
I of E	Institute of Export
IE	Institution of Electronics
IEA	Institut Économique Agricole (Belgium)
IEA	Institute of Economic Affairs
IEA	Institute of Engineers, Australia
IEA	Instituto de Experimentaciones Agropecuarias (Argentina)
IEA	International Association for the Evaluation of Educational Achievement

IEA	International Economic Association
IEA	International Electrical Association
IEA	International Energy Agency
IEA	International Entomological Association
IEA	International Epidemiological Association
IEA	International Ergonomics Association
IEA	International Executives Association
IEA	Irish Exporters Association
IEAAC	Institut d'Études Agronomiques d'Afrique Centrale
IEAB	Internacia Esperanto-Asocio de Bibliotekistoj
IEAG	Instituto Ecuatoriano de Antropologiá y Geografíca
IEAJ	International Esperanto Association of Jurists
IEAV	Internationaler Eisenbahn Alkoholgegner Verband
IEAZ	Instituto Experimental de Agricultura Zootécnica
IEB	Instítúto de Estudos Brasilieros
IEB	International Education Board
IEB	International Energy Bank
IEC	Imperial Economic Committee (now CEC)
IEC	Institut d'Études Centrafricaines
IEC	International Edsal Club
IEC	International Egg Commission
IEC	International Electrotechnical Committee
IEC	International Energy Cooperative Inc. (U.S.A.)
IEC	International Extension College (U.K.)
IEC	Israel Electric Corporation
IECA	Imperial Ethiopian College of Agriculture
IECAMA	Imperial Ethiopian College of Agriculture and Mechanical Arts
IECIC	International Engineering and Construction Industries Council (U.S.A.)
IECN	Instituto Ecuatoriano de Ciencias Naturales
IED	Institut d'Études du Développement (Switzerland)
IED	Institution of Engineering Designers
IED	International Education Development
IEDA	Institut d'Études du Développement Africain
IEDD	Institution of Engineering Draughtsmen and Designers
IEDES	Institut d'Étude de Développement Économique et Social

IEDR	Institute of Economic Development and Research (Philippines)
IEE	Institute of Explosives Engineers
IEE	Institution of Electrical Engineers
IEEE	Institute of Electrical and Electronic Engineers (U.S.A.)
IEEE	Instituto Español del Envase y Embalaje
IEEFI	Institut Européen pour l'Étude des Fibres Industrielles
IEETE	Institution of Electrical and Electronics Technician Engineers
IEF	Instituto Ecuatoriano del Folklore
IEF	International Eye Foundation
IEF	International Ecumenical Fellowship
IEFC	International Emergency Food Committee (FAO)
IEG	Immunopathology Exchange Group
IEGSP	Union Intercommunale pour l'Étude et la Gestion des Services Publics à Caractère Industrial et Communal
IEHEI	Institut Européen des Hautes Études Internationales (France)
IEI	Industrial Education International
IEI	Institute of Electrical Inspectors (Australia)
IEI	Institution of Engineering Inspection
IEI	International Esperanto Institute
IEIAS	Institut Européen Interuniversitaire de l'Action Sociale (Belgium)
IEIC	Institution of Engineers-in-Charge
IEIP	Institut Européen des Industries de la Pectine (Belgium)
IEISW	Inter-University European Institute on Social Welfare
IEKA	Internacia Esperanto-Klubo Automobilista
IEKV	Internationale Eisenbahn-Kongress-Vereinigung
IEMCS	Industrial Estates Management Corporation for Scotland
IEME	Instituto Españõl de Moneda Extranjera
IEMVPT	Institut d'Élevage et de Médecine Vétérinaire des Pays Tropicaux
IEO	Instituto Español de Oceanografíca
IEP	International Economic Publishers (U.S.A.)
IEPA	International Economic Policy Association (U.S.A.)
IEPAL	Instituto de Estudios Políticos para América Latina

IEPC	NAS Committee for International Environmental Programs (U.S.A.)	**IEV**	Instítuto Experimental de Veterinária (Brazil)
		IEY	International Education Year
IER	Institute for Economic Research (Iran)	**IFA**	Industries et Forêts Africaines (Cameroons, Central Africa, Congo)
IER	Institute of Engineering Research California (U.S.A.)	**IFA**	Institut for Atomenergi
IER	Organization for International Economic Relations (U.N.)	**IFA**	Institut Français de l'Alcool
		IFA	Instituto de Fomento Algodonero (Colombia)
IERAC	Instituto Ecuatoriano de Reforma Agraria y Colonización	**IFA**	International Federation of Accountants
IERE	Institution of Electronic and Radio Engineers	**IFA**	International Federation of Actors
IERE	International Electrical Research Exchange	**IFA**	International Federation on Ageing
IEREGEM	Institut Équatorial de Recherches et d'Études Géologiques et Minières	**IFA**	International Federation of Airworthiness
		IFA	International Florists Association
IERF	Industrial Educational and Research Foundation (*now* FBR)	**IFA**	International Footprint Association
		IFA	International Franchise Association
IERH	Instituto Ecuatoriano de Recursos Hidráulicos	**IFA**	International Frisbee Association
		IFA	International Fertility Association
IERS	Institut d'Études et de Recherches Sociales (Iran)	**IFA**	International Filariasis Association
		IFA	International Fiscal Association
IERS	International Educational Reporting Service (IBE)	**IFABC**	International Federation of Audit Bureaux of Circulations
IES	Illuminating Engineering Society	**IFAC**	Institut Français d'Action Coopérative
IES	Illuminating Engineering Society (U.S.A.)	**IFAC**	Institut Français de Recherches Fruitières Outre-Mer
IES	Illuminating Engineering Societies of Australia	**IFAC**	Institut des Fruits et Agrumes Coloniaux
IES	Institute of European Studies (U.S.A.)	**IFAC**	International Federation of Advertising Clubs
IES	Institution of Engineers and Shipbuilders in Scotland	**IFAC**	International Federation of Automatic Control
IESA	Institut Français des Sciences Administratives	**IFAD**	International Fund for Agricultural Development
IESA	Instituto Español del Envase y Embalaje	**IFAE**	Interamerican Federation for Adult Education
IESA	International Society for Electrosleep and Electroanaesthesia	**IFAJ**	International Federation of Agricultural Journalists
IESC	International Executive Service Corps (U.S.A.)	**IfAL**	Institut für Ausländische Landwirtschaft, Berlin
IESNEC	Institution of Engineers and Shipbuilders of the North-East Coast	**IFALPA**	International Federation of Air Line Pilots Associations
IESRI	Institut Européen d'Études et de Relations Intercommunales (Switzerland)	**IFALS**	International Federation of Arts, Letters and Sciences
IESS	Institution of Engineers and Shipbuilders in Scotland	**IFAN**	Institut Français d'Afrique Noire
IESSA	Institute of Economic Studies and Social Action, Manila (Philippines)	**IFAN**	International Federation for the Application of Standards
IESTIS	Instituto Ecuatoriano de Sociología y Técnica, Transculturación, Integración e Investigación Social	**IFAP**	Industrie Africaine de Filets de Pêche
IESTO	Institut d'Études Supérieures des Techniques d'Organisation	**IFAP**	International Federation of Agricultural Producers

IFAPP	International Federation of the Associations of Pharmaceutical Physicians	IFCC	International Federation of Children's Communities
IFARHU	Instituto para a Formación y Aprovechamiento de Recursos Humanos (Panama)	IFCC	International Federation of Clinical Chemistry
IFAS	International Federation of Aquarium Societies	IFCCA	International Federation of Community Centre Associations
IFAT	Institut Français d'Amérique Tropicale (*of* ORSTOM)	IFCCTE	International Federation of Commercial, Clerical and Technical Employees
IFATCA	International Federation of Air Traffic Controllers Associations	IFCE	Institut Française des Combustibles et de l'Énergie
IFATCC	International Federation of Associations of Textile Chemists and Colourists	IFCE	International Federation of Consulting Engineers
IFATE	International Federation of Airworthiness Technology and Engineering (*now* IFA)	IFCI	Industrial Finance Corporation of India
IFATSEA	International Federation of Air Traffic Safety Electronic Associations	IFCJ	International Federation of Catholic Journalists
IFATU	International Federation of Arab Trade Unions	IFCM	International Federation of Christian Metalworker's Unions
IFAW	International Fund for Animal Welfare	IFCMU	International Federation of Christian Miner's Unions
IFAWPCA	International Federation of Asian and Western Pacific Contractors' Associations	IFCO	International Fan Club Organization
IFB	International Federation of the Blind	IFCO	International Fisheries Cooperative Organization
IFB	International Film Bureau	IFCO	Interreligious Foundation for Community Organization (U.S.A.)
IFBA	International Fire Buff Associations	IFCP	International Federation of Catholic Pharmacists
IFBB	International Federation of Body Builders		
IFBBF	Imported Fibre Building Board Federation	IFCT	Industrial Finance Corporation of Thailand
IFBPW	International Federation of Business and Professional Women (*now* FBBF)	IFCT	Institut Française de Coopération Technique
		IFCTU	International Federation of Christian Trade Unions
IFBSO	International Federation of Boat Show Organisers	IFCTUBWW	International Federation of Christian Trade Unions of Building and Woodworkers
IFBWW	International Federation of Building and Wood Workers	IFCTUGPI	International Federation of Christian Trade Unions of Graphical and Paper Industries
IFC	Institut Français du Caoutchouc	IFCTUSET-MSCT	International Federation of Christian Trade Unions of Salaried Employees, Technicians, Managerial Staff and Commercial Travellers
IFC	International Finance Corporation (U.S.A.)		
IFC	International Fisheries Commission		
IFCA	International Federation of Catholic Alumnae	IFCTUTCW	International Federation of Christian Trade Unions of Textile and Clothing Workers
IFCATI	International Federation of Cotton and Allied Textile Industries	IFCU	International Federation of Catholic Universities
IFCAWU	International Federation of Christian Agricultural Workers' Unions	IFCUAW	International Federation of Christian Unions of Agricultural Workers
IFCB	International Federation for Cell Biology	IFD	Institute of Food Distribution
IFCC	Institut Français du Café, du Cacao et d'Autres Plantes Stimulantes	IFD	International Federation for Documentation
IFCC	International Federation of Camping and Caravanning	IFD	Internationale Federation des Dachdeckerhandwerks

IFDA	International Federation of Data Processing Associations	**IFFF**	Internationale Frauenliga für Frieden und Freiheit	
IFDA	International Food Service Distributors Association	**IFFJ**	International Federation of Free Journalists of Central and Eastern Europe and Baltic and Balkan Countries	
IFDA	International Foundation for Development Alternatives (Switzerland)	**IFFJP**	International Federation of Fruit Juice Producers	
IFDA	International Franchised Dealers Association	**IFFPA**	International Federation of Film Producers' Associations	
IFDES	Institut Français d'Études Stratégiques			
IFDIB	International Festivals Documentation and Information Bureau (France)	**IFFS**	International Federation of Film Societies	
IFE	Asociación de Investigación Técnica de la Industria Papelera Española	**IFFS**	International Fellowship of Former Scouts and Guides	
IFE	Institut für Technische Forschung und Entwicklung (Austria)	**IFFTU**	International Federation of Free Teachers' Unions	
IFE	Institute of Fire Engineers	**IFG**	Institúto de Fisiograpia y Geológica (Argentina)	
IFEC	Institut Français de l'Emballage et du Conditionnement	**IFGA**	International Federation of Grocer's Associations	
IFEC	Institut Français des Experts Comptables	**IFGB**	Institute of Foresters of Great Britain	
IFEES	International Federation of Electro-Encephalographic Societies	**IFGO**	International Federation of Gynecology and Obstetrics	
IFEF	International Federation of Esperantist Railwaymen	**IFGVP**	International Federation of Gastronomical, Vinicultural and Touristic Press	
IFEI	Institut Français d'Esthétique Industrielle	**IFHE**	International Federation of Home Economics	
IFEIA	Instituto Franco-Ecuatoriano de Investigaciónes Agronómicas	**IFHE**	International Federation of Hospital Engineers	
IFEMS	International Federation of Electron Microscope Societies	**IFHP**	International Federation for Housing and Planning	
IFEO	International Federation of Eugenic Organizations	**IFHPSM**	International Federation for Hygiene, Preventive Medicine and Social Medicine	
IFEP	Danish Electronics Reliability Institute	**IFHTM**	International Federation for the Heat Treatment of Materials	
IFER	Fédération Internationale des Sociétés de Publicité Ferroviaire	**IFI**	Imperial Forestry Institute, Oxford (now CFI)	
IFER	Internationale Föderation des Eisenbahn-Reklame- Gesellschaften (Switzerland)	**IFI**	Information for Industry Ltd. (U.S.A.)	
IFES	International Fellowship of Evangelical Students	**IFI**	International Federation of Interior Designers	
IFEW	Inter-American Federation of Entertainment Workers	**IFI**	Internationale Föderation Innenarchitekten	
IFF	Industriens Forskningsforening	**IFI**	International Foundation for Independence (U.S.A.)	
IFF	Industrifarmaceutforeningen			
IFF	Institute for the Future (U.S.A.)	**IFI**	Israel Furniture Industry	
IFF	International Flying Farmers (U.S.A.)	**IFIA**	International Federation of Inventors' Associations	
IFFA	Institut f. Forstliche Arbeitswissenschaft			
IFFA	Institut Français de la Fièvre Aphteuse	**IFIA**	Instituto Forestal de Industrialización y Administración (Argentina)	
IFFA	International Federation of Film Archives	**IFIA**	International Federation of Ironmongers and Iron Merchants Associations	
IFFA	International Frozen Food Association			
IFFCO	Indian Farmers Fertilizer Co-operative	**IFIA**	International Fence Industry Association	

FIAS	International Federation of Institutes for Advanced Study	**IFLS**	International Federation of Law Students
		IFM	International Falcon Movement
FIDA	International Film Importers and Distributors of America	**IFM**	Institute of Fisheries Management
FIE	Instituto Forestal de Investigaciones y Experiencias	**IFMA**	International Federation of Margarine Associations
FIF	Internationale Föderation von Industriegewerkschaften und Fabrik-arbeiterverbänden	**IFMA**	International Foodservice Manufacturers Association (U.S.A.)
		IFMA	International Food Manufacturers Association (U.S.A.)
FIG	Internationales Forschungs- und Informationszentrum für Gemeinwirtschaft	**IFMA**	Irish Flour Millers Association
FIP	International Federation for Information Processing	**IFMAP**	Irish Federation of Musicians and Associated Professions
FIP	International Project in the Field of Food Irradiation	**IFMBE**	International Federation for Medical and Biological Engineering
FIPS	International Federation of Information Processing Societies	**IFMC**	International Folk Music Council
FIS	International Food Information Service	**IFME**	International Federation for Medical Electronics (*now* IFMBE)
FITU	Indian Federation of Independent Trade Unions	**IFME**	International Federation of Municipal Engineers
FIWA	International Federation of Importers and Wholesale Grocers' Associations	**IFMMS**	International Federation of Mining and Metallurgical Students
FJ	International Federation of Journalists	**IFMP**	International Federation for Medical Psychotherapy
FJU	International Federation of Fruit Juice Producers	**IFMSA**	International Federation of Medical Student Associations
FK	Industrieverband Füllhalter und Kugelschreiber	**IFM-SEI**	International Falcon Movement—Socialist Educational International
FKAB	Internationale Federatie van Katholieke Arbeiders Bewegingen	**IFMI**	Irish Federation of Marine Industries
FKM	Internationale Föderation für Kurzschrift und Maschinenschreiben	**IFMW**	International Federation of Mazdaznan Women
FKT	International Federation of Knitting Technologists	**IFNAES**	International Federation of the National Associations of Engineering Students
FL	Icelandic Federation of Labour	**IFNSA**	International Federation of the National Standardizing Association
FL	Institute of Fluorescent Lighting	**IFO**	Institut für Wirtschaftforschung
FL	Institutet för Företagsledning	**IFO**	Institute for Fermentation (Japan)
FL	International Federation of Lithographers, Process Workers and Kindred Trades	**IFO**	International Farmers Organization
FL	International Friendship League	**IFOAM**	International Federation of Organic Agriculture Movements
FLA	International Federation of Landscape Architects	**IFOCAP**	Institut de Formation pour des Cadres Paysans
FLA	International Federation of Library Associations	**IFOFSAG**	International Fellowship of Former Scouts and Guides
FLAIC	Instituto Forestal Latino-americano de Investigación y Capacitación	**IFOG**	International Federation of Olive Growers
FLFF	Internationale Frauenliga für Frieden und Freiheit	**IFOP**	Institut Français d'Opinion Publique
FLS	Institut Français de Libre Service	**IFOP**	Instituto de Fomento Pesquero, Santiago (Chile)

IFOR	International Fellowship of Reconciliation	**IFPRI**	International Food Policy Research Institute
IFORS	International Federation of Operational Research Societies	**IFPS**	International Federation of Philosophical Societies
IFORVU	International Federation of Recreational Vehicle Users	**IFPTO**	International Federation of Popular Travel Organisations
IFOS	International Federation of Oto-Rhino-Laryngological Societies	**IFPW**	International Federation of Petroleum Workers
IFOSA	International Federation of Stationers Associations	**IFPWA**	International Federation of Public Warehousing Associations
IFOTES	International Federation for Services of Emergency Telephonic Help	**IFR**	Indian Famine Relief
IFP	Institut Français du Pétrole	**IFR**	Internationaler Frauenrat
IFP	Institut Français de Polémologie	**IFRA**	INCA-FIEJ Research Association
IFP	International Federation of Purchasing	**IFRA**	International Fund-Raising Association (U.S.A.)
IFPA	Information Film Producers of America	**IFRB**	International Frequency Registration Board
IFPA	Industrial Fire Protection Association of Great Britain	**IFRC**	International Fusion Research Council
IFPA	Inter-American Federation of Personnel Administration	**IFRF**	International Flame Research Foundation
IFPA	International Fire Photographers Association	**IFRPD**	Institute of Food Research and Product Development (Thailand)
IFPAAW	International Federation of Plantation, Agricultural and Allied Workers	**IFRU**	Institut Français du Royaume-Uni
IFPCS	International Federation of Unions of Employees in Public and Civil Services	**IFRW**	International Federation of Resistance Workers
IFPCW	International Federation of Petroleum and Chemical Workers	**IFS**	International Federation of Settlements and Neighbourhood Centres
IFPE	International Federation for Parent Education	**IFS**	International Federation of Surveyors
IFPI	International Federation of the Phonographic Industry	**IFS**	International Film Seminars
IFPLAA	Internationale Föderation der Plantagen, Land- und anverwandten Arbeiter	**IFS**	International Foundation for Science (UNESCO)
IFPLVB	Internationale Föderation der Plantagen- und Landarbeiter und Verwandter Berufsgruppen	**IFSA**	Institut Français des Sciences Administratives
IFPM	International Federation of Physical Medicine	**IFSCC**	International Federation of Societies of Cosmetic Chemists
IFPMA	International Federation of Pharmaceutical Manufacturers Associations	**IFSDA**	International Federation of Stamp Dealers's Associations
IFPMM	International Federation of Purchasing and Materials Management	**IFSDP**	International Federation of the Socialist and Democratic Press
IFPNT	International Federation of Practitioners of Natural Therapeutics	**IFSEA**	International Federation of Scientific Editors' Associations
IFPRA	Inter-American Federation of Public Relations Associations	**IFSEM**	International Federation of Societies for Electron Microscopy
IFPRA	International Federation of Park and Recreation Administration	**IFSMA**	International Federation of Ship Master Associations
IFPRI	International Food Policy Research Institute (USA)	**IFSMU**	Irish Free State Medical Union
		IFSNC	International Federation of Settlements and Neighbourhood Centres
		IFSP	International Federation of Societies of Philosophy

IFSPO	International Federation of Senior Police Officers	**IFWRI**	Institute of Furniture Warehousing and Removal Industry
IFST	Institute of Food Science and Technology	**IFWTA**	International Federation of Workers Travel Associations
IFST	International Federation of Shorthand and Typewriting	**IFYC**	International Federation of Young Co-operators
IFSTA	International Fire Service Training Association	**IFYE**	International Farm Youth Exchange
IFTO	International Federation of Tour Operators	**IFYGL**	International Field Year for the Great Lakes (U.S.A.)
IFSW	International Federation of Social Workers	**IGA**	Inspection Générale de l'Agriculture
IFT	Institute of Food Technologists (U.S.A.)	**IGA**	Interessen-Gemeinschaft Aerosole
IFT	International Federation of Translators	**IGA**	International Geneva Association (U.S.A.)
IFTA	Institut Français des Transports Aériens	**IGA**	International Geographical Association
IFTA	International Federation of Teachers' Associations	**IGA**	International Gold Association
IFTA	International Federation of Thanatopraxis	**IGA**	Irish Gas Board
IFTA	International Fine Technics Association	**IGAEA**	International Graphic Arts Education Association (U.S.A.)
IFTC	International Federation of Thermalism and Climatism	**IGAM**	Internationale Gesellschaft für Allgemein-medizin
IFTC	International Film and Television Council	**IGAP**	Internationale Gesellschaft für Ärztliche Psychotherapie
IFTF	International Fur Trade Federation		
IFTOMM	International Federation for the Theory of Machines and Mechanisms	**IGAS**	International Graphic Arts Society (U.S.A.)
IFTR	International Federation for Theatre Research	**IGAS**	International Graphoanalysis Society (U.S.A.)
IFTUTW	International Federation of Trade Unions of Transport Workers	**IGB**	Internationaler Genossenschaftsbund
		IGC	International Garden Centres
IFTW	International Federation of Tobacco Workers	**IGC**	International Garden Club
		IGC	International Geological Congress
IFTWA	International Federation of Textile Workers Associations	**IGC**	International Geophysical Committee
		IGC	International Grassland Congress
IFU	Internationale Fruchtsaft-Union	**IGC**	UN/FAO Intergovernmental Committee
IFUC	Interprovincial Farm Union Council (Canada)	**IGCA**	Industrial Gas Cleaning Association
		IGCC	Intergovernmental Copyright Committee
IFUNO	Indian Federation of United Nations Associations	**IGCR**	Instituto Geográfico de Costa Rica
		IGCR	Inter-Governmental Committee on Refugees
IFUW	International Federation of University Women	**IGE**	Institution of Gas Engineers
		IGE	International Guiding Eyes (U.S.A.)
IFVA	International Federation of Variety Artistes	**IGEME**	Ihracati Geliştirme Etüd Merkezi (Export Promotion Research Centre) (Turkey)
IFVV	Internationale Federatie van Vakorganisaties van Vervoerspersoneel	**IGER**	Institut Nationale de Gestion et d'Économie Rurale
IFW	International Federation of Wargaming		
IFWA	International Federation for Weeks of Art	**IGF**	International Genetics Federation
IFWEA	International Federation of Workers Educational Associations	**IGF**	International Graphical Federation
IFWHA	International Federation of Women's Hockey Associations	**IGF**	International Gymnastic Federation
IFWL	International Federation of Women Lawyers	**IGFA**	International Game Fish Association

IGFAP	International Gesellschaft für Analytische Psychologie	**IGU**	International Geographical Union
IGFRI	Indian Grassland and Fodder Institute	**IGU**	Internationale Gewerbeunion
IGGA	International Grooving and Grinding Association	**IGV**	Internationaler Gemeindeverband
		IGWF	International Garment Workers' Federation
IGGI	Inter-Governmental Group on Indonesia	**IGY**	International Geophysical Year
IGI	Industrial Graphics International	**IHA**	International Hahnemannian Association (U.S.A.)
IGI	International Wallpaper Manufacturers Association	**IHA**	International Horse Association
IGL	Institut Gramme de Liège (Belgium)	**IHA**	International Hotel Association
IGM	Instítuto Geográfico Militar (Argentina)	**IHA**	International House Association
IGM	Internationale Gesellschaft für Moorforschung	**IHA**	Irish Hardware Association
IGMAA	International Gas Model Airplane Association (U.S.A.)	**IHAIO**	International Historical Association of the Indian Ocean
IGMB	Instituut voor Graan, Meel en Brood	**IHATIS**	International Hides and Allied Trades Improvement Society
IGMG	Internationale Gustav Mahler Gesellschaft	**IHB**	International Hydrographic Bureau
IGMW	Internationale Gesellschaft f. Musikwissenschaft	**IHB**	Internationale Hopfenbaubüro
		IHBS	International Hajji Baba Society
IGN	Institut Géographique National	**IHC**	Industrieele Handelscombinatie
IGN	Instituto Geográfica Nacional (Peru)	**IHC**	Intercontinental Hotels Association
IGN	Instituto Geológico Nacional (Colombia)	**IHC**	International Help for Children
IGNM	Internationale Gesellschaft für Neue Musik	**IHCA**	International Hebrew Christian Alliance
IGO	Inter-Governmental Organisation	**IHD**	Institute of Human Development (U.S.A.)
IGOSS	Integrated Global Ocean Station System	**IHD**	International Hydrological Decade
IGP	Grossistforeningen for Isenkram- Glas- og Porceloensbranschen	**IHE**	Institution of Highway Engineers
		IHEA	Institut des Hautes Études Agraires
IGP	Instituto Geofísico del Perú	**IHEA**	International Health Evaluation Association
IGP	International Guild of Prestidigitators	**IHEB**	International Heat Economy Bureau
IGPAI	Inspeção-Geral dos Produtes Agricolas e Industrias (Portugal)	**IHEDREA**	Institut des Hautes Études de Droit Rural et d'Économie Agricole
IGR	International Guild of Prestidigitators (U.S.A.)	**IHES**	Illinois Horticultural Experiment Station (U.S.A.)
IGROF	Internationale Rorschach-Gesellschaft	**IHEU**	International Humanist and Ethical Union
IGRS	Irish Genealogical Research Society	**IHF**	International Hockey Federation
IGS	Irish Graphical Society	**IHF**	International Hospital Federation
IGS	International Geranium Society	**IHFA**	Industrial Hygiene Foundation of America
IGSA	International Golf Sponsors Association	**IHFBC**	International High Frequency Broadcasting Conference
IGSP	Internationale Gesellschaft der Schriftpsychologie	**IHFPA**	Instituto de Higiene y Fomento de la Producción Animal (Chile)
IGSS	International Graduate Summer School in Librarianship and Information Service	**IHGB**	Instítuto Histórico e Geográfico Brazileiro
IGTYF	International Good Templar Youth Federation	**IHGC**	International Hop Growers Convention
IGU	International Gas Union	**IHGS**	Institute of Heraldic and Genealogical Studies

IHHA	International Halfway House Association (U.S.A.)	**IIAP**	Institut International d'Administration Publique
IHI	Internationales Hilfskomitee für Intellektuelle	**IIAR**	International Institute of Ammonia Refrigeration (U.S.A.)
IHK	Internationale Handelskammer	**IIAS**	Indian Institute of Asian Studies
IHL	International Hockey League	**IIAS**	Inter-American Institute of Agricultural Sciences
IHL	International Homeopathic League		
IHLADI	Instituto Hispano-Luso-Americano de Derecho Internacional	**IIAS**	International Institute of Administrative Sciences (Belgium)
IHMB	Industrie des Huiles Minérales de Belgique	**IIASA**	International Institute for Applied Systems Analysis (Austria)
IHMEE	International Hotel and Motel Educational Exposition	**IIB**	Institut International des Brevets
		IIB	International Investment Bank
IHO	International Health Organisation	**IIBD & ID**	Incorporated Institute of British Decorators and Interior Designers
IHO	International Hydrographic Organisation	**IIBEM**	Indian Institute of Biochemistry and Experimental Medicine
IHP	Intergovernmental Council of the International Hydrological Programme		
IHR	Institute of Historical Research, London	**IIC**	India International Centre
IHRB	International Hockey Rules Board	**IIC**	Institúto de Ingeneiros de Chile
IHRMA	Irish Hotel and Restaurant Managers' Association	**IIC**	International Institute of Communications (Italy)
IHS	Institute of Human Sciences (U.S.A.)	**IIC**	International Institute of Communications (U.K.)
IHS	International Haemophilia Society	**IIC**	International Institute for the Conservation of Historic and Artistic Works (U.K.)
IHS	International Hydrofoil Society		
IHSA	Inversiones Huascaran Soc. Anon (Peru)	**IIC**	International Institute for Cotton (U.S.A.)
IHVE	The Institution of Heating and Ventilating Engineers	**IICA**	Institute of Instrumentation and Control, Australia
II	Ikebana International	**IICA**	Instituto Interamericano de Ciencias Agricolas de la OEA (Costa Rica)
IIA	Institut International d'Anthropologie		
IIA	Instituto de Investigaciones Agropecuarias (Chile)	**IICA**	Instituto Internacional de las Cajas de Ahorro
IIA	International Illawarra Association	**IICA**	Instituto Internacional de Ciencias Administrativas
IIA	International Institute for Africa		
IIA	International Institute of Agriculture (*now* FAO)	**IICA**	Instituto de Investigacão Cientifica de Angola
IIAA	Institute of Inter-American Affairs	**IICAF**	Institute for International Collaboration in Agriculture and Forestry (Czechoslovakia)
IIAA	Instituto International de Asuntos Ambientales	**IICAT**	Investigación Internacional Cooperativa del Atlántico Tropical
IIAA	Instituto de Investigação Agronomica de Angola	**IICC**	International Institute for Study and Research in the Field of Commercial Competition (Belgium)
IIAG	Institut für Angewandt Geodäsie		
IIAI	Indian Institution of Art in Industry	**IICCSE**	International Information Centre for Computers in Secondary Education (U.K.)
IIAL	International Institute of Arts and Letters		
IIALM	International Institute of Adult Literacy Methods, Tehran (Iran)	**IICE**	Institut International des Caisses d'Épargne
IIAM	Institut de la Recherche Agronomique Mozambique	**IICI**	Institut International de Coopération Intellectuelle

IICM	Instituto de Investigação Científica de Moçambique		**IIEO**	International Islamic Economic Organisation
IICS	Institut International de Chimie Solvay		**IIEP**	International Institute for Educational Planning
IICT	Instítúto de Investigaciónes Científicas y Tecnologicas (Argentina)		**IIES**	Institut International d'Études Sociales (Switzerland)
IICY	International Independent Christian Youth		**IIES**	International Institute for Environmental Studies
IICY	International Investment Corporation for Yugoslavia		**IIF**	Institut International du Froid
IIDA	Institut Interaméricain de Droit d'Auteur		**IIFA**	International Institute of Films on Art
IIDARA	Instituto Iberoamericano de Derecho Agrario y Reforma Agraria (Venezuela)		**IIFCOOP**	Instituto Interamericano de Financiamienta Cooperativo (Chile)
IIDC	Instituto de Investigaciones Económicas (Mexico)		**IIFP**	Institut International des Finances Publiques (Belgium)
IIDH	Institut International de Droit Humanitaire		**IIFT**	Indian Institute of Foreign Trade
IIDP	Institut International du Droit Public		**IIGBM**	Institut International de Génie Biomédical
IIDU	Istituto Internazionale di Diritto Umanitario (Italy)		**IIGEAG**	Instituto de Investigaciones Geologicas Edafologicas y Agrobiologicas de Galicia
IIE	Institut Interaméricain de l'Enfance		**IIHA**	International Institute of the Hylean Amazon
IIE	Institut International de l'Environnement		**IIHF**	International Ice Hockey Federation
IIE	Institut International d'Embryologie		**IIHL**	International Institute of Humanitarian Law (Italy)
IIE	Institut International d'Étiopathie (France)			
IIE	Institut International de l'Épargne		**III**	Institut Isostatique International
IIE	Institution Internationale d'Esperanto		**III**	Instituto Interamericano Indigenista (Mexico)
IIE	Instituto Interamericano de Estadistica (U.S.A.)		**III**	Inter-American Indian Institute
IIE	Instituto Interamericano de Estadistica		**III**	International Institute of Interpreters (U.S.A.)
IIE	Instituto Internacional de Estadística		**III**	Internationales Institut für Industrieplanung (Austria)
IIEA	International Institute of Environmental Affairs		**III**	Istituto Italiano Imballaggio
IIEB	Institut International d'Études Bancaires		**IIIA**	Israeli Institute of International Affairs
IIEC	European Institute of Environmental Cybernetics		**IIIC**	International Institute for Intellectual Co-operation
IIEC	Istituto Internazionale di Educazione Cinematografica		**IIIC**	International Irrigation Information Centre (Israel)
IIED	International Institute for Environment and Development		**IIIHS**	International Institute of Integral Human Sciences (Canada)
IIEE	Institut International d'Études sur l'Éducation (Belgium)		**IIJP**	Instítúto de Investigaciónes Juridico-Politicas (Argentina)
IIEIC	International Institute Examinations Inquiry Committee		**IIL**	Institute of International Law (Netherlands)
IIEJ	Instituto Interamericano de Estudios Jurídicos Internacionales		**IIL**	Instituto Italo-Latinamericano
			IIL	Insurance Institute of London
IIEL	Institut International d'Études Ligures		**IILA**	Istituto Italo-Latino-Americano
IIEL	Instituto Internacional de Estudios Laborales (Switzerland)		**IILC**	Internationaal Instituut voor Landaanwinning en Cultuurtechniek
IIEM	Indian Institute of Experimental Medicine		**IILI**	Institut International de Littérature Ibéro-Américaine

IILS	International Institute for Labour Studies (*of* ILO)	IIR	Deutsches Institut für Interne Revision
IIM	Indian Institute of Management	IIR	Institute of International Relations (Trinidad and Tobago)
IIM	Indian Institute of Metals	IIR	International Institute for Refrigeration
IIM	Institute of Industrial Managers	IIRA	International Industrial Relations Association
IIM	Institúto de Investigaciónes Microquimicas (Argentina)	IIRB	Institut International de Recherches Betteravières (Belgium)
IIMC	Institut International de Musicologie Comparée	IIRE	International Institute for Resource Economics (U.S.A.)
IIMC	International Institute of Municipal Clerks (U.S.A.)	IIRG	Institut International de Recherches Graphologiques
IIMP	Institúto de Investigaciónes de Materias Primas (Chile)	IIRI	International Industrial Relations Institute
IIMT	International Institute for the Management of Technology (Italy)	IIRR	International Institute for Rice Research (Philippines)
IIMT	International Institute of Milling Technology (U.K.)	IIRR	International Institute of Rural Reconstruction (U.S.A.)
IIN	Institúto Indigenista Nacional (Guatemala)	IIRS	Institute for Industrial Research and Standards (Eire)
IIN	Instituto Interamericano del Niño	IIS	Indian Institute of Science
IIN	Istituto Italiano di Navigazione	IIS	Institut International de la Soudure
IINA	International Islamic News Agency	IIS	Institut International de Statistique
IINS	Interuniversity Institute of Nuclear Sciences (Belgium)	IIS	Institute of Industrial Supervisors (*now* ISM)
IIO	International Islamic Organization	IIS	Institute of Information Scientists
IIOE	International Indian Ocean Expedition	IIS	Institute for Intercultural Studies (U.S.A.)
IIOST	Institut International d'Organisation Scientifique du Travail (Switzerland)	IIS	Instituut voor Internationale Studien (Netherlands)
IIP	Indian Institute of Packaging	IIS	International Institute of Sociology
IIP	Indian Institute of Petroleum	IIS	Internationales Institut der Sparkassen
IIP	Institut International de la Presse	IIS	Irish Institute of Secretaries
IIP	Institute of Incorporated Photographers	IISA	Institut International des Sciences Administratives (Belgium)
IIP	International Institute of Philosophy	IISBR	International Institute of Sugar Beet Researchers (Belgium)
IIP	Israel Institute of Petroleum	IISCO	Indian Iron and Steel Company
IIP	Israel Institute of Productivity	IISE	International Institute of Social Economics (U.K.)
IIPA	Indian Institute of Public Administration	IISEE	International Institute of Seismology and Earthquake Engineering (Japan)
IIPA	Institute of Incorporated Practitioners in Advertising	IISG	International Instituut voor Sociale Geschiedenis
IIPE	Institut International de Planification de l'Éducation	IISHI	Institut International des Sciences Humaines Intégrales (Canada)
IIPE	Institution of Incorporated Plant Engineers	IISI	International Iron and Steel Institute (Belgium)
IIPER	International Institution of Production Engineering Research	IISL	International Institute of Space Law
IIPF	International Institute for Public Finance	IISL	Istituto Internazionale di Studi Liguri
IIPS	International Institute for Population Studies (India)		
IIPU	Istituto Italiano di Paleontologia Umana		

IISN	Institut Interuniversitaire des Sciences Nucléaires (Belgium)
IISO	Institution of Industrial Safety Officers
IISPS	International Institute of Social and Political Science (Switzerland)
IISR	Indian Institute of Sugar-cane Research
IISR	Institute for International Social Research (U.S.A.)
IISR	International Institution of Submarine Research
IISRP	International Institute of Synthetic Rubber Producers (U.S.A.)
IISS	International Institute for the Science of Sintering
IISS	International Institute for Strategic Studies
IISSP	Institut International des Sciences Sociales et Politiques
IIST	Institut International des Sciences Théoriques
IISWM	Institute of Iron and Steel Wire Manufacturers
IIT	Indian Institute of Technology
IIT	Institut Interafricain du Travail
IIT	Institut International du Tapis
IIT	Institut International du Théâtre
IIT	Institute of Industrial Technicians
IIT	Instituto de Investigaciones Tecnológicas (Colombia)
IIT	International Investment Trust (Africa)
IITA	International Institute of Tropical Agriculture (Nigeria)
IITS	International Institute of Theoretical Sciences
IIUPL	International Institute for the Unification of Public Law
IIVRS	International Institute for Vital Registration and Statistics
IIVW	Internationales Institut für Verwaltungswissenschaften
IIW	International Inner Wheel (U.K.)
IIW	International Institute of Welding
IJA	International Jugglers Association
IJAN	Internationale des Jeunes Amis de la Nature
IJC	International Joint Commission (Canada)
IJCIC	International Jewish Committee on Interreligious Consultations
IJF	International Judo Federation
IJG	Contactcentrum Fabrikanten Ijzerwaren en Gereedschappen

IJGD	Germany Voluntary Service
IJI	International Juridical Institute
IJIRA	Indian Jute Industry's Research Association
IJK	Internationale Juristen-Kommission
IJMA	Indian Jute Mills Association
IJMARI	Indian Jute Mills Association Research Institute
IJNPS	Instituto Joaquim Nabuco de Pesquisas Sociais (Brazil)
IJO	International Juridical Organisation for Developing Countries
IJWU	International Jewelry Workers Union
IKAPI	Ikatan Penerbit Indonesia
IKAR	Internationale Kommission für Alpines Rettungswesen
IKBK	Internationales Katholisches Bureau für das Kind
IKD	Internationale Kommission der Detektivverbände
IKEWM	Internationales Komitee zur Ermittlung der Wirtschaftlichkeit von Milchtieren
IKG	International Gift Commission
IKG	Internationale Kommission für Glas
IKI	Internationales Kali-Institut
IKJ	Internationales Kuratorium für das Jugendbuch
IKMB	Internationale Katholische Mittelstandsbewegung
IKN	Internationale Kommission für Numismatik
IKOFA	International Exhibition of Groceries and Fine Foods (Germany)
IKPE	Interministerielles Komitee für Entwicklungshilfe (Austria)
IKPO	Internationale Kriminalpolizeiliche Organisation
IKRK	Internationales Komitee von Roten Kreuz
IKS	Interkantonale Kontrolstelle für Heilmittel (Switzerland)
IKS	Internationales Kautschukbüro, Sektion Schweiz
IKSJ	Internationale Katholische Studierende Jugend
IKUE	Internacia Katolika Unuigo Esperantista
IKUP	Internationale Katholischen Union der Presse
IKV	Internationale Kartographische Vereinigung
IKV	Internationaler Krankenhausverband

IKVSA	Internationale Katholische Vereinigung für Soziale Arbeit
IKW	Industrieverband Körperpflege- und Waschmittel
IL	Institute of Linguists
IL	L'Internationale Libérale
ILA	Institute of Landscape Architects
ILA	International Laundry Association
ILA	International Law Association
ILA	International Leprosy Association
ILA	International Longshoremen's Association
ILAA	International Legal Aid Association
ILAA	International Literary and Artistic Association
ILAB	International League of Antiquarian Booksellers
ILACDE	Instituto Latinoamericano de Cooperación y Desarrollo (Venezuela)
ILACO	International Land Development Consultants (Netherlands)
ILACPS	Instituto Latinoamericano de Ciencias Políticas y Sociales
ILAFA	Instituto Latinoamericano del Fierro y el Acero (Chile)
ILAFIR	Instituto Latinoamericano de Fisiología y Reproducción
ILAI	Italian-Latin American Institute
ILAMA	International Life-Saving Appliance Manufacturers Association
ILAP	Institute Latinoamericano del Plastico
ILAPES	Instituto Latinoamericano de Planificación Económica y Social
ILAR	Institute of Laboratory Animal Resources (U.S.A.)
ILAR	International League against Rheumatism
ILARI	Instituto Latinoamericano de Relaciones Internacionales
ILAS	Institute of Latin American Studies (U.S.A.)
ILAT	Instituto Latinoamericano de Tetro
ILATES	Instituto Latinoamericano de Estudios Sociales "Humberto Valdez" (Venezuela)
ILB	Instituut voor Landbouwbedrijfsgebouwen
ILB	International Labour Board (U.S.A.)
ILB	International Liaison Bureau
ILC	Industrial Liaison Centres
ILC	International Labelling Centre

ILC	International Law Commission
ILCA	Centro Internacional de Ganadería de Africa
ILCA	International Lightning Class Association
ILCA	International Livestock Centre for Africa (Ethiopia)
ILCE	Instituto Latinoamericano de Cinematografíca Educativa (Mexico)
ILCE	Instituto Latinoamericano de la Comunicación Educativa
ILCMP	International Liaison Committee on Medical Physics
ILCOP	International Liaison Committee of Organizations for Peace
ILCORK	International Liaison Committee for Research on Korea (Korea)
ILDA	International Lutheran Deaf Association
ILDIS	Instituto Latinoamericano de Investigaciones Sociales (Chile)
ILE	Institution of Locomotive Engineers
ILEA	Inner London Education Authority
ILEC	Institut de Liaisons et d'Études des Industries de Consommation
ILEF	International League of Esperantist Amateur Photographers, Cinephotographers and Tape-Recording
ILEI	Internacia Ligo de Esperantistaj Instruistoj
ILEP	International Federation of Anti-Leprosy Associations
ILEPES	Instituto Latinoamericano de Planificación Economica y Social (Chile)
ILERA	International League of Esperantist Radio Amateurs
ILERI	Institut Libre d'Étude des Relations Internationales
ILESA	Institute of Lighting Engineers of South Africa
ILET	Instituto Latinoamericano de Estudios Transnationales (Mexico)
ILF	Industrial Leathers Federation
ILF	International Landworkers' Federation
ILF	Intreprindere de Lucrari Forestiere (Roumania)
ILFI	International Labour Film Institute
ILGO	Irish Local Government Officials Union

ILGPNWU	International Leather Goods, Plastic and Novelty Workers Union (U.S.A.)	**ILS**	International Limnological Society (ICSU)
ILGWU	International Ladies' Garment Workers Union (U.S.A.)	**ILS**	International Lunar Society
		ILS	Irish Literary Society
ILHR	International League for Human Rights	**ILSA**	Inspection des Lois Sociales en Agriculture
ILI	Inter-African Labour Institute	**ILSC**	International Learning Systems Corporation
ILIC	International Library Information Center (U.S.A.)	**ILSGB**	International Language Society of Great Britain
ILID	Institut für Landwirtschaftliche Information und Dokumentation	**ILSI**	International Life Sciences Institute
		ILSMH	International League of Societies for the Mentally Handicapped
ILLA	Irish Ladies Lacrosse Association	**ILTAM**	Institute for Literature and Mass Artistic Techniques
ILLL	International Lutheran Laymen's League		
ILM	Internationaler Landmaschinenmarkt	**ILTF**	International Lawn Tennis Federation
ILMA	Instituto Latinoamericano de Mercadeo Agricola	**ILTTA**	International Light Tackle Tournament Association
ILMAC	International Congress and Fair for Laboratory, Measuring and Automation Techniques in Chemistry	**ILU**	International Legal Union
		ILWU	International Longshoremen's and Warehousemen's Union
ILO	Instituut voor Landhouwhuishoudkundig Onderzoek	**ILZRO**	International Lead Zinc Research Organisation
ILO	International Labour Office	**ILZSG**	International Lead Zinc Research Organisation (U.S.A.)
ILO	International Labour Organisation		
ILOB	Instituut voor Landbouwkundig Onderzoek van Biochemische Producten	**IM**	Institute of Marketing
		IM	Svenska Leverantöföreningen för Instrument och Mätteknik
ILocoE	Institution of Locomotive Engineers		
ILP	Independent Labour Party	**IMA**	Industrial Marketing Association
ILPA	International Labor Press Association (U.S.A.)	**IMA**	Institute for Mediterranean Affairs (U.S.A.)
		IMA	Institutional Management Association
ILPES	Instituto Latinoamericano de Planificación Económica y Social	**IMA**	Instituto de Matemática Aplicada (Argentina)
ILPH	International League for the Protection of Horses	**IMA**	International Management Association
		IMA	International Milling Association
ILPNR	International League for the Protection of Native Races (U.S.A.)	**IMA**	International Mineralogical Association
ILR	Independent Local Radio	**IMA**	International Music Association
ILR	Instituut voor Landbouwtechniek en Rationalisatie	**IMA**	International Mycological Association
		IMA	International Mycophagist Association
ILRAD	International Laboratory for Research on Animal Diseases (Kenya)	**IMA**	Irish Medical Association
ILRCO-CSA	International Red Locust Control Organization for Central and Southern Africa	**IMA**	Stjornunarfélag (Icelandic Management Association)
ILRI	Indian Lac Research Institute	**IMA**	Schweizerisches Institut für Land-maschinenwesen und Landarbeitstechnik
ILRI	International Institute for Land Reclamation and Improvement (Netherlands)		
ILRM	International League for the Rights of Man	**IMAA**	International Maine-Anjou Association (U.S.A.)
ILS	Incorporated Law Society	**IMAB**	Comité Européen Importateurs de Machines à Bois
ILS	International Latitude Service		

MAC	International Movement of Apostolate Children	IMCS	Pax Romana, International Movement of Catholic Students
MACE	Association des Industries Margarinières des Pays de la CEE	IMCYC	Instituto Mexicano del Cemento y del Concreto
MACS	International Association for Mathematics and Computers in Simulation	IMDA	International Magic Dealers Association
		IMDA	International Mail Dealers Association
MAG	Instituut voor Mechanisatie, Arbeid en Gebouwen	IMDBI	Industrial and Mining Development Bank of Iran
MAG	Internationaler Messe und Ausstellungsdienst GmbH	IMDT	International Institute for Music, Dance and Theatre in the Audio-visual Media
MAJ	International Management Association of Japan	IME	Institut Mondial de l'Environnement
		IME	Institute of Makers of Explosives (U.S.A.)
MAPEC	Industries Mauritaniennes de Pêche	IME	Instituto de Médicos Especialistas (Brazil)
MarE	Institute of Marine Engineers	IME	International Medical Exchange
MARPE	Instituto del Mar del Perú	IMEA	Institut d'Études Métallurgiques et Électroniques Appliquées (Switzerland)
MASLA	International Muslim Academy of Sciences, Letters and Arts	IMEA	Incorporated Municipal Electrical Association
MAT	Istituto di Microbiologia Agraria e Tecnica		
MATEC	Société Internationale de Matériel Technique (Senegal)	IMechE	Institution of Mechanical Engineers
MAU	International Movement for Atlantic Union	IMEDE	Institut pour l'Étude des Méthodes de Direction de l'Entreprise (Switzerland)
MB	Internationaler Metallarbeiterbund	IMEKO	International Measurement Conference
MBEX	International Mens and Boys Exhibition	IMENUR	Institut Mondial des Cités Unies pour l'Environnement et l'Urbanisme (France)
MBM	Institute of Municipal Building Management	IMER	Institute for Marine Environmental Research
MC	Industrial Marketing Council	IMERNAR	Istituto Mexicano de Recursos Naturales Renovables (Mexico)
MC	Institute of Management Consultants		
MC	Institute of Measurement Control	IMES	Instituto Mexicano de Estudios Sociológicos
MC	Institute of Medicine of Chicago (U.S.A.)	IMESCIAL	Institut Mondial des Structures Communales et d'Information sur l'Administration Locale (France)
MC	International Mailbag Club		
MC	International Maritime Committee		
MC	International Materials Conference	IMet	Institute of Metals
MC	International Micrographic Congress	IMEXGRA	Chambre Syndicale pour le Commerce d'Importation et d'Exportation de Graines et Aliments pour le Bétail (Belgium)
MC	International Mineral and Chemical Corporation (U.S.A.)		
MC	International Missionary Council	IMF	International Marketing Federation
MC	International Music Council	IMF	International Metal Workers' Federation
MCA	International Motor Contest Association (U.S.A.)	IMF	International Metaphysical Festivals Inc. (Hawaii)
MCAR	International Movement of Catholic Agricultural and Rural Youth (Belgium)	IMF	International Monetary Fund
		IMF	International Motorcycle Federation
MCE	International Meeting of Cataloguing Experts	IMF	International Myomassethics Federation
MCO	Inter-Governmental Maritime Consultative Organisation (U.S.A.)	IMFURP	International Movement for Fraternal Union among Races and Peoples
		IMG	Industrial Marketing Group
MCOS	International Meteorological Consultant Service	IMG	International Mosel-Gesellschaft

IMH	Institute of Materials Handling
IMI	Imperial Metal Industries
IMI	Imperial Mycological Institute (U.K.) (*now* CMI)
IMI	Institute of the Motor Industry
IMI	International Maintenance Institute (U.S.A.)
IMI	International Masonry Institute (U.S.A.)
IMI	International Metaphysical Institute (U.K.)
IMI	Irish Management Institute
IMIA	Instituto Mexicano de Informacion Avícola
IMIA	International Machinery Insurers Association
IMIE	Instituto Mexicano de Investigaciones Económicas
IMIF	International Maritime Industry Forum
IMinE	Institution of Mining Engineers
IMINOCO	Iranian Marine International Oil Company
IMIQ	Instituto Mexicano de Ingenieros Químicos
IMIT	Instituto Mexicano de Investigaciones Tecnológicas
IMIT	Institute of Musical Instrument Technology
IMLO	Internationale Maatschappij v. Land-bouwkundige Ontwikkeling
IMLS	Institute of Medical Laboratory Sciences
IMM	Institute of Mining and Metallurgy
IMMK	Interkultura Monda Movado Kommunomej
IMMOA	International Mercantile Marine Officers Association
IMMRAN	International Meeting of Marine Radio Aids to Navigation
IMMS	International Material Management Society (U.S.A.)
IMO	Inter-American Municipal Organisation
IMO	International Meteorological Organisation
IMOB	Industrie van Minerale Oliën van België
IMOS	Interallied Military Organization 'Sphinx'
IMP	Ideas Marketing Pool Ltd
IMPA	Institute for Improvement of Sugar Production (Mexico)
IMPA	International Maritime Pilots Association
IMPA	International Marketing Public Relations and Advertising Consultants (U.S.A.)
IMPA	International Master Printers Association
IMPA	International Motor Press Association
IMPA	International Movement for Peace Action
IMPA	International Museum Photographers Association (U.S.A.)
IMPA	International Myopia Prevention Association (U.S.A.)
IMPA	International Personnel Management Association (U.S.A.)
IMPBA	International Model Power Boat Association (U.S.A.)
IMPGA	Institut de Météorologie et de Physique du Globe d'Algérie
IMPHOS	Institut Mondial du Phosphate (France)
IMPHQA	Institut Mondial pour la Protection de la Haute Qualité Alimentaire
IMPI	International Microwave Power Institute (U.S.A.)
IMPORT-PESCA	Associazione Nationale Importatori Grossisti Prodotti Ittici Freschi e Congelati
IMPRECO	Société des Impressions du Congo
IMPREGA	Imprimerie Gabonaise
IMPROMER	Société Ivoirienne d'Importation de Produits de la Mer
IMPS	International Plastic Modelers Society
IMRA	Industrial Marketing Research Association
IMRA	International Mission Radio Association (U.S.A.)
IMRAMN	International Meeting on Radio Aids to Marine Navigation
IMRC	International Marine Radio Committee
IMRNR	Instituto Mexicano de Recursos Naturales Renovables
IMS	Industrial Management Society (U.S.A.)
IMS	Institute of Mathematical Statistics (U.S.A.)
IMS	Institute of Manpower Studies
IMS	Institute of Mental Subnormality
IMS	International Meditation Society
IMS	International Musicological Society
IMSA	International Motor Sports Association
IMSA	International Municipal Signal Association (U.S.A.)
IMSM	Institute of Marketing and Sales Management
IMTA	Imported Meat Trade Association
IMTech	Institute of Metallurgical Technicians
IMTG	Internationale Moor und Torf-Gesellschaft
IMTI	Instituto del Minifundio y de las Tierras Indivisas (Argentina)
IMTPA	Institut de Médecine Tropicale Princesse Astrid (Belgium)

IMU	International Mailers Association (U.S.A.)
IMU	International Mathematical Union
IMU	International Molders' and Allied Workers' Union
IMun & CyE	Institute of Municipal and County Engineers
I Mun E	Institution of Municipal Engineers
IMV	Internationaler Milchwirtschaftverband
IMVS	Institute of Medical and Veterinary Science (Australia)
IMW	International Map of the World
IMWIC	International Maize and Wheat Improvement Centre (Mexico)
IMWOO	Instituut voor Maatschappij-Wetenschappelijk Onderzoek in de Ont-wikkelingslanden
IMWU	International Molders' and Allied Workers' Union
IMZ	Internationales Musikzentrum
IMZA	Association Professionnelle des Importateurs et Exportateurs Belges de Semences Fourragères
INA	Institut National Agronomique
INA	Instituto Nacional de Abastecimientos (Colombia)
INA	Instituto Nacional Agrario (Honduras)
INA	Instituto Nacional de Aprendizaje (Costa Rica)
INA	Institution of Naval Architects
INA	International Newsreel and News Film Association
INA	Ironfounders National Association
INA	Verenigung van Fabrikanten en Importeurs van Naaimachines
INAC	Istituto Nazionale per le Applicazioni del Calcolo
INACAP	Instituto Nacional de Capacitación Professional (Chile)
INACH	Instituto Antartico Chileno (Chile)
INACOL	Institut National pour l'Amélioration des Conserves de Légumes (Belgium)
INACP	Institut de Nutrition pour l'Amérique Centrale et Panama (Guatemala)
INAD	Instituto Nacional de Administracion para el Desarrollo (Guatemala)
INADES	Institut Africain pour le Développement Économique et Social
INAE	International Newspaper Advertising Executives
INAEICM	Institut Nationale Agricole d'Études et d'Initiatives Coopératives et Mutualistes
INAGRISA	Iniciativas Agrícolas, S.A.
INAH	Instituto Nacional de Anthrolopogia e Historia (Mexico)
INAIL	Instituto Nazionale per l'Assicurazione contro gli Infortuni sul Lavoro
INAIR	Internacional de Aviación SA (Panama)
INAL	Indian National Agricultural Library
INALI	Instituto Nacional de Limnología (Argentina)
INAM	Institut National d'Assurance contre la Maladie
INANDES	Instituto Andino de Estudios Sociales (Peru)
INANTIC	Instituto Nacional de Normas Tecnicas Industriales y Certificacion (Peru)
INAOV	Institut National des Appellations d'Origine des Vins et Eaux-de-Vie
INAP	Instituto Nacional de Acción Poblacional e Investigación (Chile)
INAPA	Instituto Nacional de Aquas Potables y Alcantarillados (Dominica)
INAPG	Institut National Agronomique Paris-Grignon
INARC	Institut Nord-Africain de Recherches Cotonnières
INARCH	Istituto Nazionale di Architettura
INAS	Institut Nationale d'Administration Scolaire et Universitaire
INASA	Industrias Nacionales Agrícolas (Nicaragua)
INAT	Institut National d'Assistance Technique (Belgium)
INATEIA	Istituto Nazionale di Assistenza Tecnico-Economica per Imprenditori Agricoli
INB	Institut National du Bois
INBA	Instituto Nacional de Bellas Artes (Mexico)
INBA	Instituto Nacional de Biología Animal (Bolivia & Peru)
INBH	Institut National Belge du Houblon
INBOLCA	Instituto Boliviano del Café
INC	Instituto Nacional de Colonización (Ecuador, Spain, Uruguay)
INC	Instituto Nicaraguense del Café
INC	International Nickel Company
INC	International Numismatic Commission
INC	Ironfounders National Confederation
INCA	Institut National de Crédit Agricole (Belgium)

INCA	Istituto Nazionale Confederale di Assistenza	**INDAL**	Indian Aluminium Co.
INCA	International Newspaper and Colour Association (Switzerland)	**INDC**	International Nuclear Data Committee (*of* IAEA)
INCAE	Instituto Centroamericano de Administración de Empresas	**INDE**	Instituto Nacional de Electrificación (Guatemala)
INCAP	Instituto de Nutrición de Centroamérica y Panamá	**INDEC**	Independent Nuclear Disarmament Election Committee
INCB	International Narcotics Control Board	**INDECO**	Industrial Development Corporation (Zambia)
INCE	Instituto Nacional de Cooperación Educativa (Venezuela)	**INDER**	Instituto Nacional de Deportes, Educación Fisica y Recreación (Cuba)
INCEI	Instituto Nacional de Comercio Exterior e Interior (Nicaragua)	**INDERENA**	Instituto para el Desarrollo de los Recursos Naturales (Colombia)
INCIBA	Instituto Nacional de Cultura y Bellas Artes (Venezuela)	**INDESIT**	Industria Elettrodomestici Italiana
INCIDI	International Institute of Differing Civilisations	**INDIS**	Industrial Information System (*of* UNIDO)
INCIE	Instituto Nacional de las Ciencias de Educación, Barcelona	**INDITEC-NOR**	Instituto Nacional de Investigaciones Tecnologicas y Normalización (Chile)
INCOLDA	Instituto Colombiano de Administración	**INDRHI**	Instituto Nacional de Recursos Hidráulicos (Dominica)
INCOMAS	International Conference on Marketing Systems for Developing Countries	**INDUAR-ROZ**	Federación de Industriales del Arroz (Colombia)
INCOME	Industriale Cotonicola Meridionale	**INDUN-ARES**	Servicio Comercial y Técnico de Industrias Auxiliares de la Construcción Naval
INCOMEX	Instituto Colombiano de Comercio Exterior	**INE**	Instituto Nacional de Estadística
INCOMI	Indústria e Comércio de Minerios S.A. (Brazil)	**INEA**	Istituto Nazionale de Economia Agraria
INCOOP	Instituto Nacional de Cooperativas (Peru)	**INEA**	International Electronics Association
INCOR	Indian National Committee on Oceanic Research	**INEAC**	Institut National pour l'Étude Agronomique du Congo (Belgium)
INCOR	Intergovernmental Conference on Oceanographic Research	**INEC**	Institut Européen de Cancérologie
INCOR	Israeli National Committee for Oceanographic Research	**INEC**	Institut Européen d'Écologie et de Cancérologie (Belgium)
INCORA	Instituto Colombiano de la Reforma Agraria	**INEC**	Institut Européen des Industries de la Gomme de Caroube (Belgium)
INCOSPAR	Indian National Committee for Space Research	**INEC**	Instituto Nacional para el Mejoramiento de la Enseñanza de las Ciencias (Argentina)
INCP	Instítúto Nacionál de Ciência Politica (Brazil)	**INECAFE**	Instituto Ecuatoriano del Café
INCRA	International Copper Research Association	**INED**	Institut National d'Études Démographiques
INCREF	International Children's Rescue Fund	**INEDECA**	Industria Ecuatoriana Elaboradora de Cacao
INCUBAR	Asociación Colombiana de Incubadores	**INEDES**	Instituto Ecuatoriano de Planificación para el Desarrollo
INDA	Instituto Nacional do Desenvolvimento Agrário (Brazil)	**INEMO**	Chambre Syndicale des Importateurs et Négociants en Machines-Outils et Outillages de Belgique
INDA	International Nonwovens and Disposables Association		
INDAC	Integral Nuclear Data Centre (U.S.A.)	**INEN**	Instituto National de Energia Nuclear (Guatemala)
INDACY	Industrie Dahoméenne du Cycle		
INDAG	Industrial and Agricultural Co. Ltd (Nigeria)	**INEOA**	International Narcotic Enforcement Officers Association

INEP	Institut National d'Études Politiques (Zaire)	INIA	Instituto Nacional de Investigaciones Agrícolas (Mexico)
INEP	Instituto Nacional de Estudos e Pesquisas Educacionais (Brazil)	INIA	Institúto Nacional de Investigaciones Agronómicas
INERA	Institut National pour l'Étude et la Recherche Agronomique (Zaire)	INIAP	Instituto Nacional de Investigaciones Agropecuarias (Ecuador)
INERHI	Instituto Ecuatoriano de Recursos Hidráulicos	INIBP	Instituto Nacional de Investigaciones Biológico
INERM	Institut National d'Études Rurales Montagnardes à Grenoble	INIC	Instituto Nacional de Imigraçao e Colonizaçâo (Brazil)
INETOP	Institut National de l'Enseignement Technique et d'Orientation Professionnelle	INIC	Instituto Nacional de la Investigación Científica (Mexico)
INF	Institúto Nacionál de Farmacologia (Brazil)	INIC	Instituto Nacional de Investigaciones Científicas (Paraguay)
INF	International Naturist Federation	INICHAR	Institut National de l'Industrie Charbonnière (Belgium)
INFCO	Information Committee of ISO		
INFEDOP	International Federation of Christian Trade Unions of Employees in Public Service and PTT	INIDCYA	Institute for the Intellectual Development of Children and Young Adults (Iran)
INFI	Instituto Nacional de Fomento Tabacalero (Colombia)	INIF	Industria Nacional de Insecticidas e Fertilizantes (Brazil)
INFIC	International Network of Feed Information Centres (FAO)	INII	Instituto Nacional de Investigacão Industrial (Portugal)
INFIR	Istituto Nazionale per il Finanziamento della Ricostruzione	INIP	Instituto Nacional per l'Incremento della Produttività
INFN	Istituto Nazionale de Fisico Nucleare	INIP	Instituto Nacional de Investigaciones Pecuarias (Mexico)
INFO	International Fortean Organization		
INFONAC	Instituto de Fomento Nacional (Nicaragua)	INIRO	Indonesisch Instituut voor Rubber Onderzoek
INFOP	Instituto de Fomento de la Producción (Guatemala)	INIS	International Nuclear Information System (Austria)
INFOR- EUROP	Press Information and Public Relations Service of Common Market Enterprises	INITO	Société Initiative Togolaise
INFORFILM	International Information Film Service	INL	Institut National du Logement
INFORM	International Reference Organization in Forensic Medicine and Sciences	INLA	International Nuclear Law Association
		INLD	Instituto Nacional do Livro e do Disco (Mozambique)
INFOTERM	International Information Centre for Terminology (Austria)	INLE	Instituto Nacional del Libro Espanol
ING	Instituto Nacional de Geografíca (Brazil)	INM	Institúto Nacional do Mate (Brazil)
INGC	Istituto Nazionale de Genetica per la Cerealicoltura	INMA	Institut National de Médecine Agricole
INGE	Instituto Nacional de Granos y Elevadores (Argentina)	INMARSAT	International Organization for Maritime Telecommunications by Satellites
INGO	International Non Governmental Organisation	INMAS	Institute of Nuclear Medicine and Allied Sciences (India)
INGRAF	Instituut for Grafisk Forskning	INMV	Instituto Nacional de Medicina Veterinaria (Cuba)
INGYO	International Non-Governmental Youth Organizations	INN	Instituto Nacional de la Nutrición (Argentina, Colombia, Ecuador, Venezuela)
INHADAH	Industrie d'Habillement du Dahomey	INO	Irish Nurses Association
INI	Instituto Nacional Indigenista (Mexico)	INOC	Iraq National Oil Company

INODEP	Institut Oecuménique pour le Développement des Peuples (Switzerland)
INOE	Internacia Naturista Organizo Esperantista
INORCOL	Instituto de Normas Colombiana
INOS	Instituto Nacional de Obras Sanitarias (Venezuela)
INOTEX	Industrie Nouvelle Textile (Cameroons)
INP	Institute of National Planning (Egypt)
INP	Instituto Nacional de Pinho (Brazil)
INP	Instituto Nacional de Planificación (Peru)
INP	Instituto Nacional de la Productividad (Argentina)
INPA	Institute Nacional de Pesquisas de Amazónia (Brazil)
INPA	International Newspaper Promotion Association
INPABO	Instituto Paranaense de Botanica
INPADOC	International Patent Documentation Centre, Vienna (Austria)
INPAR	Institut National de Promotion Agricole de Rennes
INPC	Irish National Productivity Committee
INPE	Instituto Nacional de Pesca del Ecuador
INPFC	International North Pacific Fisheries Commission
INPI	Institut National de la Propriété Industrielle
INPI	Instituto Nacional de Promoción Industrial (Peru)
INPPSS	Instituto Nacional para le Producción de Semillas Selectas
INPROA	Instituto de Promoción Agraria (Chile)
INPS	Institut National de la Prévoyance Sociale
INQUA	Internationale Quartärvereinigung
INR	Institut National Belge de Radio-diffusion (Belgium)
INR	Institut National de Radio-diffusion (Greece)
INRA	Institut National de la Recherche Agronomique
INRA	Instituto Nacional de Reforma Agraria (Cuba)
INRAT	Institut National de le Recherche Agronomique de Tunisie
INRDG	Institut National de Recherche et de Documentation de Guinée
INRDP	Institut National de Recherche et de Documentation Pédagogiques, Paris
INRE	Instituto Nacionale de Reforma Económica (Cuba)
INRF	Institut National de Recherches Forestières (Tunis)
INRH	Instituto Nacional de Recursos Hidráulicos (Cuba)
INRN	Instituto Nacional de Racionalización y Normalización
INRS	Institut National de Recherche Scientifique (Rwanda, Togo)
INRS	Institut National de Recherche et de Securité pour la Prévention des Accidents du Travail et de Maladies Professionelles
INRT	Instituto Nacional de Racionalización del Trabajo
INRV	Institut National de Recherche Vétérinaire (Belgium)
INS	Institut National de Sécurité
INS	International News Service
INSA	Institut National des Sciences Appliquées
INSA	International Shipowners' Association
INSAFOP	Instituto Salvadoreño de Fomento de la Producción
INSDOC	Indian National Scientific Documentation Centre
INSEA	Institut National de Statistiques et d'Économie Appliquée (Morocco)
INSEA	International Society for Education through Art (France)
INSEAD	Institut Européen d'Administration des Affaires
INSEE	Institut National de la Statistique et des Études Économiques
INSERM	Institut National de la Santé et de la Recherche Médicale
INSFOPAL	Instituto Nacional de Fomento Municipal (Colombia)
INSJ	Institute for Nuclear Study (Japan)
INSPEC	Information Service in Physics, Electrotechnology and Control (*of* IEE)
INSTAB	Information Service on Toxicity and Biodegradability (*of* WPRL)
InstBE	Institution of British Engineers
InstE	Institution of Electronics
InstMC	Institute of Measurement and Control
InstM	Institute of Metals
INSTN	Institut National des Sciences et Techniques Nucléaires

stPLA	Institute of Public Loss Assessors
NSTOP	Institut National Scientifique et Technique d'Océanographie et de Pêche (Tunisia)
stPC	Institute of Public Cleansing
stR	Institute of Refrigeration
stRA	Institute of Registered Architects
stTA	Institute of Traffic Administration
NT	Institúto Nacionál de Tecnologia (Brazil)
NT	Istituto Nazionale Trasporti
NTA	Instituto Nacional de Technologia Agropecuaria (Argentina)
NTA	Instituto Nacional de Tecnica Aerospacial
NTA	Instituto Nacional de Transformación Agrária (Guatemala)
NTA	International New Thought Alliance
NTAL	Institute for Latin American Integration
NTAMEL	International Association of Metropolitan City Libraries
NTAPUC	Association Internationale du Nettoiement
NTASAF-CON	International Tanker Safety Conference
NTD	Institut National des Techniques de la Documentation
NTE	Instituto de Investigación Técnica (Chile)
NTEC	Comité de Investigaciones Tecnológicas de Corfo (Chile)
NTECNOR	Instituto Nacional de Tecnologia y Normalizacion (Paraguay)
NTECOL	International Association for Ecology (ICSU)
NTECOM	International Council for Technical Communication
NTELCAM	Société des Télécommunications Internationales du Cameroun
NTELCI	Télécommunications Internationales de la Côte-d'Ivoire
NTELCO	Office des Télécommunications Internationales du Congo
NTELSAT	International Telecommunications Satellite Consortium
NTEM	Inter-American Institute of Music Education
NTERAN	International Conference on the Analysis of Geological Materials
NTER-ASMA	Association Internationale d'Asthmologie
NTER-BRANT	Union Intercommunale des Centrales Électriques du Brabant (Belgium)
INTER-CENTRE	International Centre for the Terminology of the Social Sciences (Switzerland)
INTERCON-TAINER	International Company for Transport by Transcontainers
INTER-COOP	International Agricultural Cooperative Society (Netherlands)
INTER-COSMOS	Council on International Cooperation in Research and Uses of Outer Space
INTER-EXPO	Committee of Organisers of National Participations in International Economic Displays
INTERFAST	International Industrial Fastener Engineering Exhibition and Conference
INTERFILM	International Inter-Church Film Centre
INTER-FINISH	International Union for Electrodeposition and Surface Finishing
INTER-FORST	International Exposition of the Technology of Forestry and Forest Industries (Germany)
INTER-FRIGO	International Railway-owned Company for Refrigerated Transport
INTER-GASTRA	International Trade Fair for the Hotel and Catering Industry
INTERGU	Société Internationale pour le Droit d'Auteur
INTER-HYBRID	Association Intercontinentale du Mais Hybride
INTER-KAMA	Internationaler Kongress mit Ausstellung f. Messtechnik und Automatik
INTER-LAINE	Comité des Industries Lainières de la CEE
INTERLAIT	Société Interprofessionnelle de Lait
INTERMAG	International Association of Television Political Magazines
INTERMET	International Association for Metropolitan Research and Development
INTER-METAL	Organization for Cooperation in the Field of Heavy Metallurgy (Hungary)
INTERPHIL	International Conference for the Study of Promotion of Philanthropy
INTER-PHOTO	Fédération Internationale des Négociants en Photo et Cinéma
INTERPOL	International Criminal Police Organisation
INTEROPS	Commission pour la Coopération Multilatérale dans l'Observation des Satellites Artificiels de la Terre
INTER-PLAN	International Group for Studies in National Planning
INTER-PROPO	Sociedade de Propaganda Internacional de Produtos Portugeses

INTERSHOE	International Federation of the Independent Shoe Trade	**INVA**	Industri Vaskerienes Forbund
INTER-STENO	International Federation of Shorthand and Typewriting	**INVE**	Instituto Nacional de Viviendas Ecónomicas (Uruguay)
INTER-SU	Bureau de Liaison des Sanatoriums Universitaires et de Protection Antituberculeuse des Étudiants	**INVEMA**	Asociación de Investigación Industrial de la Maquina-Herramienta
INTER-TANKO	International Tanker Owners' Association	**INVESTI**	Instituto Venezolano de Investigaciones Tecnológicas e Industriales
INTERTEL	International Legion of Intelligence (U.S.A.)	**INVI**	Instituto Nacional de la Vivienda (Dominica)
INTERTEL	International Television Federation	**INVSL**	Indian National Veterinary Science Library
INTERVER-SITAS	World Association of Experiments in Post-Secondary Education	**INVU**	Instituto Nacional de Vivienda y Urbanismo (Costa Rica)
INTERVICO	Inter-American Organization of Cooperative Housing Technical Service Organizations (Colombia)	**INVUFLEC**	Institut National de Vulgarisation des Fruits, Légumes et Champignons
INTER-WOO-LABS	International Association of Wool Textile Laboratories	**IO**	Institut Océanographique
		IOA	Institute of Acoustics
		IOA	International OMEGA Association (U.S.A.)
INTERZUM	International Fair of Accessories and Materials for Woodworking and Furniture	**IOA**	International Ostomy Association
INTI	Instituto Nacional de Tecnologia Industrial (Argentina)	**IOAHPR**	International Organisation for the Advancement of High Pressure Research
INTO	Irish National Teachers Organisation	**IOAP**	International Office for Audiophonology
INTOSAI	International Organisation of Supreme Audit Institutions	**IOAT**	International Organisation Against Trachoma
INTRADE	International Trade Development Organisation	**IOB**	Institute of Brewing
		IOB	Institute of Bankers
INTRANED	Internationale Transport Agenturen 'Nederland'	**IOB**	Institute of Bookkeepers
		IOB	Institute of Builders
INTRATA	International Trading and Credit Company of Tanganyika Ltd	**IOB**	Inter-Organization Board for Information Systems and Related Activities (UN)
INTROP	Information Centre of Tropical Plant Protection (Germany)	**IOBB**	International Organization of Biotechnology and Bioengineering
INTSH	Institut National Tchadien pour les Sciences Humaines (Chad)	**IOBC**	Indian Ocean Biological Centre
INTSHU	Institut Togolais des Sciences Humaines	**IOBC**	International Organisation for Biological Control of Noxious Animals and Plants
INTSOY	International Soybean Program (Puerto Rico)	**IOBI**	Institute of Bankers in Ireland
INTUC	Indian National Trade Union Congress	**IOBS**	Institute of Bankers in Scotland
INU	Institute Nazionale di Urbanistica	**IOC**	Indian Oil Corporation
INUA	Instituto Nazionale di Ultracustica	**IOC**	Institute of Chemistry
INucE	Institution of Nuclear Engineers	**IOC**	Instituto Oswaldo Cruz (Brazil)
INUTOM	Institut Universitaire des Territoires d'Outremer (Belgium)	**IOC**	Intergovernmental Oceanographic Commission
INV	Institut National du Verre (Belgium)	**IOC**	International Olympic Committee
		IOC	International Organising Committee of World Mining Congresses
INV	Instituto Nacional de Vitivinicultura (Argentina)	**IOC**	International Ornithological Congress
		IOCA	Independent Oil Compounders Association (U.S.A.)

IOCARIBE	IOC Association for the Caribbean and Adjacent Regions		IOMP	International Organisation for Medical Physics
IOCC	International Office of Cocoa and Chocolate		IOMTR	International Office for Motor Trades and Repairs
IOCHS	International Organisation for Cultivating Human Spirit (*now* OISCA-INT)		ION	Institute of Navigation (U.S.A.)
IOCU	International Organization of Consumers Unions		IOOC	International Olive Oil Council (Spain)
			IOOF	Independent Order of Oddfellows
IOCV	International Organisation of Citrus Virologists		IOOL	International Optometric and Optical League
IOD	International Institute for Organizational and Social Development (Belgium)		IOOTS	International Organisation of Old Testament Scholars
IÖD	Internationale Öffentlichen Dienste		IOP	Institute of Packaging
IODE	Imperial Order of Daughters of the Empire (Canada)		IOP	Institute of Physics
			IOP	Institute of Petroleum
IOE	Indian Ocean Expedition		IOP	Institute of Plumbing
IOE	Institute for the Officialization of Esperanto (Yugoslavia)		IOP	Institute of Printing
			IOP	International Organisation of Palaeobotany
IOE	International Office of Epizootics		IOP	Institute of Pyramidology
IOE	International Organisation of Employers		IOPAB	International Organisation for Pure and Applied Biophysics
IOED	International Office of Epizootic Diseases		IOPB	International Organization of Plant Biosystematists
IOF	Institute of Fuel			
IOF	International Oceanographic Foundation		IOPEC	International Oil Pollution Exhibition and Conference
IOF	Internationale Orientierungslauf		IOPH	International Office of Public Health
IOFC	Indian Ocean Fisheries Commission		IOQ	Institute of Quarrying
IOFI	International Organisation of the Flavor Industry		IOR	Institute for Operational Research
IOGT	International Order of Good Templars (International Supreme Lodge)		IORD	International Organisation for Rural Development
IOI	International Ocean Institute (Malta)		IORS	International Orders Research Society
IOI	International Ozone Institute (U.S.A.)		IORS	Operations Research Society of Ireland
IOIE	International Organisation of Industrial Employers		IOS	Institute of Oceanographic Sciences
			IOS	Institute of Statisticians
IOJ	Institute of Journalists		IOS	International Offshore Services (U.K.)
IOJ	International Organisation of Journalists		IOS	International Organisation for Succulent Plant Study
IOK	International Order of Kabbalists (U.K.)			
IOK	Internationales Olympisches Komitee		IOS	Iraqi Organisation for Standardization
IOKSZ	Union of Handicrafts Co-operatives (Hungary)		IOSA	International Oil Scouts Association
IOL	Institute of Librarians (India)		IOSA	Incorporated Oil Seed Association
IOL	International Old Lacers (U.S.A.)		IOSA	Irish Offshore Services Association
IOM	Institute of Metals		IOSHD	International Organization for the Study of Human Development
IOM	Institute of Office Management (*now* IAM)			
IOMA	International Oxygen Manufacturers Association		IOSOT	International Organisation for the Study of the Old Testament
IOMC	International Organisation for Medical Co-operation		IOST	International Organization of Study Tours for Teachers (Belgium)

IOSTA	Institut d'Organisation Scientifique du Travail en Agriculture	**IPAE**	Instituto Peruano de Administración de Empresas (Peru)
IOSTT	International Organization of Scenographers and Theatre Technicians	**IPAFRIC**	Inter-Pêches Afrique (Senegal)
IOT	Institute of Transport	**IPAI**	International Primary Aluminium Institute (U.K.)
IOTA	Institute of Traffic Administration	**IPAM**	Institut Pédagogique Africain et Malgache
IOTA	Institut d'Ophthalmologie Tropicale de l'Afrique Occidentale	**IPAR**	Institut de Pédagogie Appliqué à Vocation Rurale
IOV	Instituto Oceanográfico de Valparaiso (Chile)	**IPARA**	International Publishers Advertising Representatives Association
IOVST	International Organisation for Vacuum Science and Technology	**IPART**	Institute of Photographic Apparatus Repair Technicians
IOW	Institute of Welding	**IPB**	International Peace Bureau (Switzerland)
IOZV	Internationale Organisation für Zivilverteidigung	**IPBA**	India, Pakistan and Bangladesh Association (U.K.)
IPA	Industrie des Pêches Algériennes	**IPBA**	Irish Paper Box Association
IPA	Institut Pédagogique Africain	**IPBAM**	International Permanent Bureau of Automobile Manufacturers
IPA	Institut de Préparation aux Affaires	**IPBF**	International Pony Breeders Federation
IPA	Institute of Practitioners in Advertising	**IPBMM**	International Permanent Bureau of Motor Manufacturers
IPA	Institute of Public Administration (Eire)	**IPC**	Institute of Philippine Culture
IPA	Institute of Public Affairs (Australia)	**IPC**	Instituto Panameña de Café
IPA	Instituto de Pesquisas Agronómicas (Brazil)	**IPC**	Inter-African Phytosanitary Commission (U.K.)
IPA	International Paediatric Association	**IPC**	International People's College in Denmark
IPA	International Paleontological Association	**IPC**	International Photographic Council
IPA	International Peace Academy	**IPC**	International Poplar Commission
IPA	International Peach Academy	**IPC**	International Potato Centre, Lima
IPA	International Phonetic Association	**IPC**	Iraq Petroleum Company
IPA	International Pinball Association	**IPC**	International Prison Commission
IPA	International Platform Association	**IPC**	International Publishing Corporation
IPA	International Playground Association	**IPCA**	Industrial Pest Control Association (*now* BPCA)
IPA	International Police Association	**IPCA**	International Petroleum Co-operative Alliance
IPA	International Psycho-Analytical Association	**IPCA**	International Postcard Collectors Association
IPA	International Publishers Association	**IPCCIOS**	Conseil Régional Indo-Pacifique (*of* CIOS)
IPAA	Independent Petroleum Association of America	**IPCIAA**	*See* IPCRSIAA
IPAA	International Prisoners' Aid Association	**IPCL**	India Petrochemicals Ltd
IPAA	International Psycho-Analytical Association	**IPCL**	Institut du Pétrole, des Carburants et Lubrifiants
IPAC	Independent Petroleum Association of Canada	**IPCR**	Institute for Physical and Chemical Research (Japan)
IPAC	Institut Polytechnique de l'Afrique Centrale		
IPAC	International Peace Academy Committee (U.S.A.)		
IPACA	Industria Papelera Centroamericana (Honduras)		
IPACK	International Packaging Material Suppliers Association		

IPCRSIAA	Institut Professionnel de Contrôle et de Recherches Scientifiques des Industries de l'Alimentation Animale (France)
IPCS	Institution of Professional Civil Servants
IPD	Institut Panafricain pour le Développement
IPD	Institut Prumyslového Designu
IPD	Institute of Professional Designers
IPDA	International Periodical Distributors Association (U.S.A.)
IPE	Incorporated Plant Engineers
IPE	Institute of Production Engineers
IPE	Instituto Português de Embalagem
IPEAAD	Instituto de Pesquisas e Experimentação Agropecuárias da Amazõnia Ocidental (Brazil)
IPEACO	Instituto de Pesquisas e Experimentação Agropecuárias do Centro-Oeste (Brazil)
IPEACS	Instituto de Pesquisas e Experimentação Agropecuárias do Centro Sul (Brazil)
IPEAL	Instituto de Pesquisas e Experimentação Agropecuárias do Leste (Brazil)
IPEAME	Instituto do Pesquisas e Experimentação Agropecuárias do Meridional (Brazil)
IPEAN	Instituto de Pesquisas e Esperimentação Agropecuárias do Norte (Brazil)
IPEANE	Instituto de Pesquisas e Experimentação Agropecuãrias do Nordeste (Brazil)
IPEAS	Instituto de Pesquisas e Experimentação Agropecuárias do Sul (Brazil)
IPEL	International Pipeline Engineering Ltd (Canada)
IPEONGC	Institute of Petroleum Exploration Oil and Natural Gas Commission (India)
IPEP	International Permanent Exhibition of Publications (Yugoslavia)
IPEPO	Instituto para la Propaganda Exterior de los Productos del Olivar
IPEX	International Printing Machinery and Allied Trades' Exhibition
IPF	International Pen Friends (Ireland)
IPF	International Pharmaceutical Federation
IPF	Irish Printing Federation
IPFC	Indo-Pacific Fisheries Council (Thailand)
IPFE	Instituto Peruano de Fomento Educativo
IPFEO	Institut des Producteurs de Ferro-alliages d'Europe Occidentale
IPG	Independent Publishers Guild
IPG	Industrial Policy Group
IPGC	Instituto de Pesca del Golfo de Mexico y el Caribe
IPGH	Pan-American Institute of Geography and History
IPGSA	International Plant Growth Substance Association
IPH	International Association of Paper Historians
IPHC	International Pacific Halibut Commission
IPHE	Institution of Public Health Engineers
IPHF	Illinois Poultry and Hatchery Federation (U.S.A.)
IPI	Institute of Patentees and Inventors
IPI	Institute of Professional Investigators
IPI	International Press Institute
IPIA	Institutul de Patologia si Igiena Animala (Roumania)
IPIA	International Patent and Trademark Association
IPIECA	International Petroleum Industry Environmental Conservation Association
IPIRA	Indian Plywood Industries Research Association
IPIRI	Indian Plywood Industries Research Institute
IPK	Interessengemeinschaft für Pharmazeutische und Kosmetische Produkte (Switzerland)
IPKO	International Information Centre on Peace-keeping Operation (France)
IPLA	Institut Pastoral d'Amérique Latine (Chile)
IPM	Institute of Personnel Management
IPMA	International Personnel Management Association
IPMER	Institute of Post-Graduate Medical Education and Research (India)
IPMS	International Plastic Modellers Society
IPMS	International Polar Motion Service
IPNA	International Pediatric Nephrology Association
IPNCB	Institut des Parcs Nationaux du Congo Belge
IPO	Institut voor Plantenziektenkundig Onderzoek
IPO	Istituto per l'Oriente
IPO	International Progress Organization
IPOEE	Institution of Post Office Electrical Engineers
IPPA	Indo-Pacific Prehistory Association
IPPA	International Pentecostal Press Association

IPPA	International Prisoners Aid Association
IPPA	Irish Professional Photographers Association
IPPC	Industrial Promotion and Productivity Centre (Nepal)
IPPEC	Inventaire Permanent des Périodiques Étrangères en Cours. Direction des Bibliothèques
IPPF	International Penal and Penitentiary Foundation
IPPF	International Planned Parenthood Federation
IPPS	Institute of Physics and the Physical Society
IPPTA	Indian Pulp and Paper Technical Association
IPR	Institute of Pacific Relations (U.S.A.)
IPR	Institute of Population Registration
IPR	Institute of Psychophysical Research
IPR	Institute of Public Relations
IPRA	Indian Painting Research Association
IPRA	Institute of Park Recreation Administration
IPRA	International Peace Research Association
IPRA	International Public Relations Association
IPRAO	Institut de Prêvoyance et de Retraite de l'Afrique Occidentale
IPREIG	Institut Professional de Recherches et d'Études des Industries Graphiques
IPRE	Institute of Practical Radio Engineers (*now* Incorporated Practitioners in Radio and Electronics)
IPRO	International Pallet Recycling Organisation
IProd E	Institution of Production Engineers
IPRS	International Confederation for Plastic and Reconstructive Surgery
IPS	Incorporated Phonographic Society
IPS	Institute of Professional Salesmen
IPS	Instituut voor Pluimveeteelt
IPS	International Confederation for Plastic Surgery
IPS	International Peat Society
IPS	International Primatological Society
IPSA	Independent Postal System of America
IPSA	International Passenger Ship Association (U.S.A.)
IPSA	International Police and Security Association
IPSA	International Political Science Association
IPSC	International Pacific Salmon Committee
IPSCI	Industrial Promotion Services en Côte d'Ivoire
IPSF	International Pharmaceutical Students Federation
IPSFC	International Pacific Salmon Fisheries Commission (Canada)
IPSI	International Political Science Institute (U.S.A.)
IPSOA	Istituto Post-universitario per lo Studio dell'Organizzazione Aziendale
IPSRA	International Professional Ski Racers' Association
IPSSG	International Printers Supply Salesmen's Guild (U.S.A.)
IPST	Israel Programme for Scientific Translations
IPT	Inst"ituto de Pesquisas Tecnológicas (Brazil)
IPTA	International Patent and Trademark Association
IPTC	International Press Telecommunications Committee
IPTEA	Internacia Postista Kaj Telekunikista Esperanto- Asocio
IPTPA	International Professional Tennis Players' Association
IPTT	Internationale du Personnel des Postes, Télégraphes et Téléphones
IPU	International Paleontological Union
IPU	International Peasant Union
IPU	International Population Union
IPU	Inter-Parliamentary Union (Switzerland)
IPVS	International Pig Veterinary Society
IPVU	Instituto Paraguayo de Vivienda y Urbanismo
IPW	Institüt für Internationale Politik un Wirtschaft
IQ	Institute of Quarrying
IQ	International Quorum of Motion Picture Producers
IQA	Instit"uto de Químico Agricola (Brazil)
IQB	Instit"uto Químico Biológico (Brazil)
IQC	International Quality Centre (*of* EOQC)
IQCA	Irish Quality Control Association
IQPS	Institute of Qualified Private Secretaries
IQS	Institute of Quantity Surveyors
IQSY	International Year of the Quiet Sun
IRA	Institute of Registered Architects
IRA	International Racquetball Association
IRA	International Reading Association

IRA	International Recreation Association (U.S.A.) (*now* WLRA)
IRA	International Rodeo Association
IRA	International Rubber Association
IRA	Irish Republican Army
IRAA	Independent Refiners Association of America
IRABA	Institut de Recherche Appliquée du Beton Armé
IRABOIS	Institut de Recherches Appliques au Bois
IRAC	Instituto de Reforma Agraria y Colonización (Peru)
IRAC	Interdepartment Radio Advisory Committee (U.S.A.)
IRAC	International Records Administration Conference. U.S. National Archives
IRAD	Institut de Recherches Appliquées du Dahomey
IRAD	Institute for Research on Animal Diseases (*of* ARC)
IRADES	Istituto Ricerche Applicate, Documentazione e Studi
IRAG	Centre International de Recherche des Aptitudes à la Gestion
IRAM	Institut de Recherches Agronomiques de Madagascar
IRAM	Institut de Recherches et d'Application de Méthodes de Développement
IRAM	Instituto Argentino de Racionalización de Materiales
IRAM	International Reformed Agency for Migration
IRAMM	Institut de Recherche et d'Action contre la Misère Mondiale
IRANDOC	Iranian Documentation Centre
IRANORM	Instituto Nacional de Racionalización y Normalización
IRAP	Organisation Internationale pour l'Avancement de la Recherche aux Hautes Pressions
IRAS	Industriforbundets Rasjonaliseringskontor
IRASA	International Radio Air Safety Association
IRAT	Institut de Recherches Agronomiques Tropicales et des Cultures Vivrières
IRATRA	Instituto Nacional de Racionalización del Trabajo
IRB	Institute of Radiation Breeding (Japan)
IRB	Instituto de Reeseguros do Brasil
IRB	Irish Republican Brotherhood

IRC	International Rainwear Council
IRC	International Red Cross
IRC	International Rescue Committee
IRC	International Research Council
IRC	International Resources Office
IRC	International Rice Commission
IRCA	Institut de Recherches sur le Caoutchouc en Afrique
IRCA	Institution de Retraites Complémentaires Agricoles
IRCA	International Railway Congress Association
IRCAM	Institut de Recherches Scientifiques (Cameroons)
IRCAM	Institute for Research and Acoustic/Musical Co-ordination (France)
IRCC	Instrument Repair and Calibration Centre (Thailand)
IRCE	Istituto Nazionale per le Relazioni Culturali con l'Estero
IRCHA	Institut National de Recherche Chimique Appliquée
IRCI	Institut de Recherches sur le Caoutchouc en Indochine
IRCIHE	International Referral Centre for Information Handling Equipment (Yugoslavia)
IRCN	Institut de Recherches de la Construction Navale
IRCOBI	Comité International de Recherche sur la Biocinétique des Chocs
IRCT	Institut Recherche Coloniale Tropicale
IRCT	Institut de Recherches du Coton et des Textiles Exotiques
IRDA	Industrial Research and Development Authority
IRDC	International Rubber Development Committee (*now* IRRDB)
IREA	Institut de Recherches de l'Économie Alimentaire
IREC	International Rotary Engine Club (U.S.A.)
IREC	Irrigation Research and Extension Advisory Committee (Australia)
IREDA	International Radio and Electrical Distributors Association
IREE	Institute of Radio and Electronic Engineers (Australia)
IREP	Institut de Recherche Économique et de Planification

IRES	Institut de Recherches Économiques et Sociales (Zaire)
IRES	Instituto de Reinserción Social
IRESD	Institut Régional pour l'Enseignement Supérieur et le Développement (Singapore)
IRESP	Institut de Recherches Économique, Sociales et Politiques (Belgium)
IREX	International Research and Exchanges Board
IRF	International Re-education Foundation (U.S.A.)
IRF	International Reform Federation
IRF	International Road Federation
IRF	International Rowing Federation
IRFA	Imprimerie Reliure Franco-Africaine (Ivory Coast)
IRFAA	International Rescue and First Aid Association
IRFED	Institut Internationale de Recherches et de Formation en Vue du Développement Harmonisé
IRFIS	Istituto Regionale per il Finanziamento alle Industrie in Sicilia
IRFV	Internationaler Regenmantelfabrikantenverband
IRG	Internationale des Résistants à la Guerre
IRGCP	International Research Group for Carcinoembryonic Proteins
IRGOM	International Research Groups on Management
IRHA	International Rural Housing Association
IRHD	Internationaler Rat der Hauspflegedienste
IRHO	Institut de Recherches pour les Huiles de Palme et Oléagineux
IRI	Institut des Relations Internationales (Belgium)
IRI	Institution of the Rubber Industry
IRI	Inveresk Research International (Scotland)
IRI	Istituto per la Ricostruzione Industriale
IRIA	Indian Rubber Industries Association
IRIA	Institut Recherche d'Information et d'Automatique
IRIA	Instituto Regional de Investigaciones del Algodón (Salvador)
IRIA	Ivoirienne de Représentation Industrielle et Automobile
IRIEC	Institut de Recherche en Informatique et en Économie
IRIFIP	International Research Institute for Immigration and Emigration Politics
IRIJ	Institut de Recherche d'Informatique Juridique
IRIPS	Instituto di Ricerche e di Interventi Psico-Sociali
IRIS	Industrial Research and Information Services
IRL	Information Retrieval Ltd
IRL	Institute of Rural Life at Home and Overseas
IRL	Internationaler Ring für Landarbeit
IRLA	International Religious Liberty Association
IRLCO-CSA	International Red Locust Control Organisation for Central and Southern Africa
IRLCS	International Red Locust Control Service (*now* IRLCO-CSA)
IRM	Institut Suisse de Recherches Ménagères
IRMA	International Rehabilitation Medicine Association
IRMB	Institut Royal Météorologique de Belgique
IRMC	International Radio-Maritime Committee
IRMRA	Indian Rubber Manufacturers' Research Association
IRNU	Institut de Recherche des Nations Unies pour le Développement Social
IRO	International Refugees Organisation
IROPCO	Iranian Offshore Petroleum Company
IRPA	International Radiation Protection Association
IRPA	Irrigation Pump Administration (Philippines)
IRPTC	International Register of Potentially Toxic Chemicals (Switzerland)
IRQPC	International Rubber Quality and Packing Conferences
IRR	Institute of Race Relations
IRRA	Industrial Relations Research Association (U.S.A.)
IRRB	International Rubber Research Board (*now* IRRDB)
IRRDB	International Rubber Research and Development Board
IRRI	Institut Royal des Relations Internationales (Belgium)
IRRI	International Rice Research Institute
IRRT	International Relations Round Table
IRS	Institut de Recherches Sahariennes
IRS	Instituut voor Rationele Suikerproductie

S	International Referral System (Kenya)	IRYDA	Instituto Nacional de Reforma Desarrollo Agrario
S	International Rorschach Society	IRZA	Institut de Recherches sur la Zone Aride en Arabia Saoudite
S	Irrigation Research Station (N.Z.)		
SA	Istituto di Ricerca Sulle Acque	IS	Industrial Society
SAC	Institut pour la Recherche Scientifique en Afrique Centrale	ISA	Indian Society of Advertisers
		ISA	Industrie Siderurgiche Associate (Italy)
SC	Institut de Recherches Scientifiques au Congo	ISA	Instrument Society of America
SCL	International Research Society for Children's Literature	ISA	International Schools Association
		ISA	International Settlement Authority
SE	Institution of Railway Signal Engineers	ISA	International Sign Association Inc. (U.S.A.)
SEN	International Rehabilitation - Special Education Network	ISA	International Silk Association
		ISA	International Sociological Association
SF	Inland Revenue Staff Federation	ISA	International Studies Association (U.S.A.)
SFC	International Rayon and Synthetic Fibres Committee	ISAB	Institute for the Study of Animal Behaviour
SG	International Rubber Study Group	ISABR	International Society for Animal Blood Group Research
SIA	Institut pour l'Encouragement de la Recherche Scientifique dans l'Industrie et l'Agriculture (Belgium)	ISABU	Institut des Sciences Agronomiques du Burundi (Zaire)
SID	Institut de Recherches de la Sidérurgie	ISAC	International Scientific Agricultural Council
SM	Institut de Recherches Scientifiques de Madagascar	ISAC	International Security Affairs Committee (U.S.A.)
SP	Irish Republican Socialist Party	ISAC	Interuniversity South-East Asia Committee (U.S.A.)
SUR	Institut de Recherche en Sociologie Urbaine et Rurale	ISAD	Information Science and Automation Division (ALA)
T	Institute of Reprographic Technology		
T	Institut de Reboisement de Tunis	ISADA	Industries et Savonneries du Dahomey
TAC	International Round Table for the Advancement of Counselling	ISAE	Indian Society of Agricultural Economics
		ISAE	Internacia Scienca Asocio Esperantista
TC	International Road Tar Conference	ISAGA	International Simulation and Gaming Association
TE	Institute of Road Transport Engineers		
TO	Institut de Recherche Scientifique au Togo	ISAHM	International Society for Animal and Human Mycology
TO	International Radio and Television Organisation	ISAKE	Internacia Societo de Arkitektoj kaj Konstruistoj Esperantistoj
TS	International Radio and Television Society (U.S.A.)	ISAL	Iglesia y Sociedad en América Latina
		ISALPA	Incorporated Society of Auctioneers and Landed Property Agents (now ISVA)
TU	International Railway Temperance Union		
U	International Raiffeisen Union	ISAP	Instituto Superior de Administración Publica (Argentina)
U	International Relief Union		
U	International Road Transport Union	ISAP	South American Petroleum Institute
V	Internationale Rat für Vogelschutz	ISAPA	International Screen Advertising Producers' Association (U.S.A.)
VAM	Istituto per le Richerche e le Informazioni di Mercato e la Valorizzazione della Produzione Agricola	ISAR	Institut des Sciences Agronomiques du Rwanda (Zaire)
WC	International Registry of World Citizens	ISAR	International Society for Astrological Research

ISAS	Istituto di Scienze Ammistrative e Socio-Economiche
ISAS	International Screen Advertising Services
ISAW	International Society of Aviation Writers
ISB	Institute of Scientific Business
ISB	Institut für Selbstbedienung
ISB	International Society of Biometeorology
ISB	Internationaler Studentenbund
ISBA	Incorporated Society of British Advertisers
ISBB	International Society of Bioclimatology and Biometeorology
ISBC	International Society of Bible Collectors
ISBE	International Society for Business Education (U.S.A.)
ISBGA	Irish Sugar Beet Growers Association
ISBI	International Savings Banks Institute
ISBO	Instituto de Sociología Boliviana
ISBP	International Society for Biochemical Pharmacology
ISC	Interamerican Society of Cardiology
ISC	Internationale Heinrich Schütz-Gesellschaft
ISC	International Seismological Centre (U.K.)
ISC	International Sericultural Commission
ISC	International Society of Cardiology
ISC	International Society of Chemotherapy
ISC	International Society of Citriculture
ISC	International Student Conference
ISC	International Sugar Council
ISCA	International Senior Citizens Association
ISCA	International Standards Co-ordination Association
ISCAY	International Solidarity Committee with Algerian Youth
ISCB	International Society for Cell Biology
ISCD	International Society for Community Development
ISCE	International Society of Christian Endeavour
ISCEH	International Society for Clinical and Experimental Hypnosis
ISCERG	International Society for Clinical Electroretinography
ISCET	International Society of Certified Electronics Technicians
ISCFB	International Society of Cranio-Facial Biology
ISCL	US Coalition for Life (U.S.A.)
ISCLT	International Society for Clinical Laboratory Technology
ISCM	International Society for Contemporary Music
ISCM	International Society of Cybernetic Medicine
ISCMA	International Superphosphate and Compound Manufacturers Association
ISCOR	South African Iron and Steel Industrial Corporation, Ltd
ISCP	International Society for Clinical Pathology
ISCRP	International Society of City and Regional Planners
ISCS	International Scientific Co-operative Service
ISCSC	International Society for the Comparative Study of Civilizations
ISCTC	Inter-Service Components Technical Committee
ISCTP	International Study Commission for Traffic Police
ISCTR	International Scientific Committee for Trypanosomiasis Research
ISCUS	Indo-Soviet Cultural Society (India)
ISCYRA	International Star Class Yacht Racing Association (U.S.A.)
ISD	International Society for Development
ISD	International Society of Differentiation
ISDB	International Society of Developmental Biologists
ISDIBER	Instituto de Sociología y Desarrollo del Area Iberica
ISDN	Institute for the Study of Developing Nations (U.S.A.)
ISDRA	International Sled Dog Racing Association
ISDS	International Sheep Dog Society
ISE	Institution of Sales Engineers
ISE	Institution of Sanitary Engineers (*now* IPHE)
ISE	Institution of Structural Engineers
ISE	International Society of Electrochemistry
ISE	Instituto per gli Studi di Economia
ISEA	Institut de Science Économique Appliquéé
ISEA-AN	Institut de Science Économique Appliquée, Centre d'Afrique du Nord (Tunis)
ISEAS	Institute of South-East Asian Studies (Singapore)
ISEC	International Securities and Exchange Commission
ISEC	International Solvent Extraction Conference

ISEAS	Institute of Southeast Asian Studies (Singapore)	ISGA	International Study Group of Aerogrammes
ISEC	International Statistics Educational Centre	ISGC	International Society of Guatemala Collectors
ISECSI	International Society for Educational, Cultural and Scientific Interchanges	ISGE	International Society of Gastroenterology
ISEK	International Society of Electrophysiological Kinesiology	ISGI	International Service for Geomagnetic Indices (Netherlands)
ISEP	International Society for Educational Planners	ISGML	International Study Group for Mathematics Learning
ISEP	International Statistical Ecology Programme	ISGO	International Society of Geographic Ophthalmology
ISER	Institut Supérieur d'Économie Rurale	ISGRCM	International Study Group for Research in Cardiac Metabolism
ISER	Institute of Social and Economic Research (West Indies)	ISGSH	International Study Group for Steroid Hormones
ISES	Institut des Sciences Économiques et Sociales (Switzerland)	ISH	International Society of Haematology
ISES	International Schools Examination Syndicate (*now* IBO)	ISH	International Society of Hypertension
ISES	International Ship Electric Service Association	ISHAM	International Society of Human and Animal Mycology
ISES	International Society of Explosives Specialists	ISHI	International Society for the History of Ideas
ISES	International Solar Energy Society	ISHM	Institut des Sciences Humaines du Mali (Mali)
ISETU	International Secretariat of Entertainment Trade Unions (Belgium)	ISHM	International Society for Hybrid Microelectronics
ISF	International Science Foundation	ISHOBSS	International Society for the History of the Behavioral and Social Sciences
ISF	International Shipping Federation Ltd	ISHRA	Iron and Steel Holding and Realisation Agency
ISF	International Society for Fat Research	ISHS	International Society for Horticultural Science
ISF	International Softball Federation	ISI	Indian Social Institute (India)
ISF	International Spiritualist Federation	ISI	Indian Standards Institution (India)
ISF	Svenska Ingenjörssamfundet	ISI	Indian Statistical Institute
ISFA	Institute of Shipping and Forwarding Agents	ISI	International Safety Institute (U.S.A.)
ISFA	International Scientific Film Association	ISI	Institute for Scientific Information (U.S.A.)
ISFADPM	International Society for the Abolition of Data Processing Machines	ISI	International Statistical Institute
ISFC	Institut Scientifique Franco-Canadienne (Canada)	ISI	Iron and Steel Institute
ISFC	International Scholarship Fund Committee	ISIA	International Snowmobile Industry Association (U.S.A.)
ISFL	Interessengemeinschaft Schweizerischer Foto-Kino-Lieferanten	ISIB	Inter-Services Ionospheric Bureau
ISFL	International Scientific Film Library	ISIC	Instituto Salvadoreño de Investigaciónes de Café
ISFNR	International Society for Folk-Narrative Research	ISIC	International Solvay Institute of Chemistry
ISFSC	International Society of Food Service Consultants	ISICIB	Centro Internazionale Bibliografico dell' Istituto di Studi sul Lavoro
ISG	Interessengemeinschaft der Schweizerischen Gärungsessig-Industrie	ISID	Research Institute of the Iron and Steel Industry (France)
ISG	Internationale Heinrich Schütz-Gesellschaft		

ISIG	Institute of Standards and Industrial Research (Ghana)
ISIG	Instituto di Sociologia Internazionale, Gorizia
ISIL	Indian Society of International Law
ISIM	International Society of Internal Medicine
ISIO	Institute for the Study of International Organisations
ISIP	Istituto Italiano di Polemologia e di Ricerche sui Conflitti
ISIP	Internacianalna stalna izlozbo Publikacija (Yugoslavia)
ISIR	Institute of Standards and Industrial Research (Ghana)
ISIR	International Society for Invertebrate Reproduction
ISIRI	Institute of Standards and Industrial Research of Iran
ISIS	Indian School of International Studies (India)
ISIS	Integrated Scientific Information System (Switzerland)
ISIS	International Student Information Service
ISIS	Women's International Information and Communication Service
ISITB	Iron and Steel Industry Training Board
ISIUA	Institut Supérieur et International d'Urbanisme Appliqué (Belgium)
ISIYM	International Society of Industrial Yarn Manufacturers (U.S.A.)
ISJP	International Society for Japanese Philately
ISK	International Seidenbau Kommission
ISKA	Internasjonalen for Stats-og Kommunalansatte
ISKCON	International Society for Krishna Consciousness
ISL	International Soccer League (U.S.A.)
ISL	International Society of Lymphology
ISLl	Istituto di Studi sul Lavoro
ISLA	Information Services on Latin America (U.S.A.)
ISLE	Institute of Sociology of Law for Europe (Belgium)
ISLIC	Israel Society of Special Libraries and Information Centres
ISLTC	International Society of Leather Trades Chemists
ISLWF	International Shoe and Leather Workers Federation
ISLWG	International Shipping Legislation Working Group (*of* UNCTAD)
ISM	Institute of Supervisory Management
ISMA	Industrie Sénégalaise de Marbre et d'Agglomérés
ISMA	Institute for the Study of Man in Africa (South Africa)
ISMA	International Shipmasters Association of the Great Lakes (U.S.A.)
ISMA	International Superphosphate Manufacturers Association (*now* ISCMA)
ISMCM	Institut Supérieur des Matériaux et de la Construction Mécanique
ISME	Institute of Sheet Metal Engineering
ISME	International Association for Music Education
ISMEO	Istituto Italiano per il Medio e l'Estremo Oriente
ISMES	Instituto Sperimentale Modelli e Structure
ISMEX	International Shoe Machinery Exhibition
ISMFE	International Society of Soil Mechanics and Foundation Engineering
ISMG	International Scientific Management Group (*of* GARP)
ISMGF	International Stoke Mandeville Games Federation
ISMH	International Society of Medical Hydrology
ISMM	International Society of Mini- and Micro-Computers
ISMOG	Instituut voor Sociaal-Economische Studie van Minder Ontwikkelde Gebieden
ISMRC	Inter-Services Metallurgical Research Council
ISMUN	International Student Movement for the United Nations
ISN	International Society for Neurochemistry
ISN	International Society of Nephrology
ISNA	Indian Science News Association
ISNA	Instituto di Studi Nucleari per l'Agricoltura
ISNAR	International Service for Agricultural Research (Germany)
ISNP	International Society of Naturpathic Physicians
ISNVP	International Society for Non Verbal Psychotherapy

ISO	International Self-service Organisation
ISO	International Shopfitting Organisation
ISO	International Society of Organbuilders (Germany)
ISO	International Standardisation Organisation
ISO	International Sugar Organization
ISOCARP	International Society of City and Regional Planners
ISOD	International Sports Organisation for the Disabled
ISODARCO	International School on Disarmament and Research on Conflicts (Italy)
ISODOC	International Centre for Standards in Information and Documentation (of ISO)
ISONET	International Standards Information Network
ISONEVO	Instituut voor Sociaal Onderzoek van het Nederlandse Volk
ISORT	Interdisciplinary Student-Originated Research Training (U.S.A.)
ISOSC	International Society for Soilless Culture
ISP	Incorporated Society of Planters (Malaysia)
ISP	Institute of Sewage Purification
ISP	Institute for the Study of Peace (U.S.A.)
ISP	Interessengemeinschaft der Schweizerischen Parkettindustrie
ISP	International Society for Photogrammetry
ISP	Internationale des Services Publiques
ISPA	Institutul de Studii si Proiectari Agricole (Roumania)
ISPA	International Screen Publicity Association
ISPA	International Small Printers' Association
ISPA	International Society for the Protection of Animals
ISPA	International Sporting Press Association
ISPA	International Squash Players Association
ISPAS	International Society of Professional Ambulance Services (U.S.A.)
ISPCA	Ironmaking and Steelmaking Plant Contractors Association
ISPCC	Irish Society for the Prevention of Cruelty to Children
ISPE	Institute and Society of Practitioners in Electrolysis
ISPE	International Society of Planetarium Educators
ISPE	Istituto di Studi per la Programmazione Economica
ISPEMA	Industrial Safety (Protective Equipment) Manufacturers Association
ISPLS	International Society of Phonetic Sciences
ISPI	Istituto per gli Studi di Politica Internazionale (Italy)
ISPM	International Society of Plant Morphologists (India)
ISPMB	International Society for the Protection of Mustangs and Burros
ISPO	International Society for Prosthetics and Orthotics
ISPP	Indian Society for Plant Pathology
ISPP	International Society of Plant Pathology
ISPP	International Society for Portuguese Philately
ISPP	Inter-Services Plastic Panel
ISPP	International Society for Plant Pathology
ISPROM	Istituto di Studi e Programmi per il Mediterraneo
ISPS	Institutul de Studii si Proiectari Silvice (Roumania)
ISPW	International Society for the Psychology of Writing
ISQA	Israel Society for Quality Assurance
ISR	Institute of Seaweed Research, Inveresk
ISR	Institute for Social Research (South Africa)
ISR	International Society of Radiology
ISRA	International Society for Research on Aggression
ISRAIN	Institut Supérieur de Recherche Appliquée pour les Industries Nucléaires (Belgium)
ISRB	Inter-Services Research Bureau
ISRCA	Institute for Scientific Research in Central Africa
ISRCDVS	International Society for Research on Civilization Diseases and Vital Substances
ISRCSC	Inter-Service Radio Components Standardization Committee
ISRD	International Society for Rehabilitation of the Disabled
ISRF	International Squash Rackets Federation
ISRF	International Sugar Research Foundation (U.S.A.)
ISRFCTC	Inter-Services Radio-Frequency Cables Technical Committee
ISRM	International Society for Rock Mechanics

ISRO	Indian Space Research Organisation
ISRR	International Society for Rorschach Research
ISRRA	International Standard Rex Rabbit Association
ISRRT	International Society of Radiographers and Radiological Technicians
ISRS	Institute for Study of Religions and Society in Singapore and Malaysia
ISRSA	International Synthetic Rubber Safety Association
ISRU	International Scientific Radio Union
ISS	Institute for Strategic Studies
ISS	International Society for Sterology
ISS	Institute of Social Studies (Netherlands)
ISS	International Schools Services (U.S.A.)
ISS	International Seismological Summary
ISS	International Social Service
ISS	International Student Service (U.S.A.)
ISS	International Sunshine Society
ISSA	International Ship Suppliers' Association
ISSA	International Slurry Seal Association
ISSA	International Social Security Association
ISSB	Inter-Service Security Board
ISSC	International Ship Structures Conference
ISSC	International Social Science Council
ISSCB	International Society for Sandwich Construction and Bonding
ISSCL	Social Service Institution for Housing for Workers (Italy)
ISSCT	International Society of Sugar Cane Technologists
ISSER	Institute of Statistical, Social and Economic Research (Ghana)
ISSF	International Service of the Society of Friends/Quakers (U.S.A.)
ISSI	International Social Science Institute (U.S.A.)
ISSMFE	International Society of Soil Mechanics and Foundation Engineering
ISSO	International Self-Service Organisation
ISSOCO	Istituto per lo Studio della Società Contemporanea
ISSOL	International Society for the Study of the Origin of Life
ISSP	Institute for Solid State Physics (Japan)
ISSP	International Society of Sports Psychology
ISSRS	Institut de Service Social et de Recherches Sociales
ISSS	International Society for Socialist Studies
ISSS	International Society of Soil Science
ISSS	International Society for the Study of Symbols (U.S.A.)
ISST	Institut des Sciences Sociales du Travail
ISST	Instituto Scientifico Sperimental dei Tabacchi
ISST	International Society for the Study of Time
IST	Institute of Science Technology
IST	International Society on Toxinology
ISTA	Indian Scientific Translators Association
ISTA	International Seed Testing Association
ISTA	International Sight-Seeing and Tours Association
ISTA	International Society for Technology Assessment
ISTA	International Special Tooling Association
ISTA	International Statistiche Agrarinformationen
ISTAT	Istituto Nazionale di Statistica
ISTC	Institute of Scientific and Technical Communicators
ISTC	International Shade Tree Conference (U.S.A.)
ISTC	International Student Travel Conference
ISTC	International Switching and Testing Centre (U.K.)
ISTC	Iron and Steel Trades Confederation
ISTCL	International Scientific and Technical Committee on Laundering
ISTD	Imperial Society of Teachers of Dancing Incorporated
ISTD	Institute for the Study and Treatment of Delinquency
ISTD	International Society of Tropical Dermatology
ISTD	Inter-Services Topographical Department
ISTE	International Society of Tropical Ecology
ISTF	International Society of Tropical Foresters (U.S.A.)
ISTH	International Society on Thrombosis and Haemostasis
ISTPM	Institute Scientifique et Technique des Pêches Maritimes
ISTEA	Iron and Steel Trades Employers' Association

ISTESU	International Secretariat for Teaching Educational Sciences in Universities	ITA	International Taxicab Association (U.S.A.)
		ITA	International Temperance Association
ISTIC	Institute of Scientific and Technical Information of China	ITA	International Tunnelling Association
		ITA	Indian Tea Association
ISTRA	Interplanetary Space Travel Research Association	ITA	Institut Technique de l'Aviculture des Produits de Basse-cour et des Élevages de Petits Animaux (formerly ITEA)
ISTRAK	International Strassenteer Konferenz		
ISTU	International Student Theatre Union	ITA	Institut de Transport Aérien
ISTUS	Internationalen Studienkommission für Motorlosen Flug	ITA	Institute of Traffic Administration
		ITA	Institute of Travel Agents
ISTVS	International Society for Terrain-Vehicle Systems	ITA	International Thermographers Association
		ITAA	International Transactional Analysis Association
ISU	International Council of Scientific Unions		
ISU	International Salvage Union	ITAC	Interagency Textile Administrative Committee (U.S.A.)
ISU	International Skating Union		
ISU	International Society of Urology	ITAL	Institute of Food Technology (Brazil)
ISUDO	International Symposium on Ultrasonic Diagnostics in Ophthalmology (Belgium)	ITAL	Instituut voor Toepassing van Atoomenergie in de Landbouw
ISUNAM	Instituto de Investigaciones Sociales (Mexico)	ITALSIEL	Società Italiana Sistemi Informativ Elettronica
ISUSE	International Secretariat for the University Study of Education	ITAP	Institut Technique des Administrations Publiques
ISV	Interessengemeinschaft Schweizerischer Verleger	ITAU	Compania Itaú des Transportes Acéros (Brazil)
ISVA	Incorporated Society of Valuers and Auctioneers	ITAVI	Institut Technique de l'Aviculture, des Productions de Basse-Cour et des Élevages de Petits Animaux
ISVE	Istituto di Studi per lo Sviluppo Economico		
ISVET	Istituto per gli Studi sullo Sviluppo ed il Progresso Tecnico	ITAVI	Servizio Telecommunicazioni e Meteorológico dell' Aeronautica
ISVR	Institute of Sound and Vibration Research	ITB	Agricultural, Horticultural and Forestry Industry Training Board
ISVS	International Secretariat for Voluntary Service		
		ITB	Institut Français de la Betterave Industrielle
ISVSK	Internationaler Ständiger Verband für Schiffahrt-Kongresse	ITB	International Time Bureau
		ITB	Internationaler Turnerbund
ISW	Institute of Social Welfare	ITB	Irish Tourist Board
ISW	Interessengemeinschaft für den Schweizerischen Weinimport	ITBA	International Toy Buff's Association
		ITBB	Fédération Internationale des Travailleurs du Bâtiment et du Bois
ISWA	International Science Writers Association		
ISWA	International Solid Wastes and Public Cleansing Association	ITBLAV	Internationale Textil-, Bekleidungs und Lederarbeiter Vereinigung
ISWC	International Secretariat of World Citizens	ITBON	Instituut v. Toegepast Biologisch Onderzoek in de Natuur (now RIN)
ISWC	International Society for the Welfare of Cripples (now ISRD)		
		ITBTP	Institut Technique du Bâtiment et des Travaux Publiques
ISWM	Institute of Solid Wastes Management		
ITA	Independent Television Authority	ITC	Imperial Tobacco Company
ITA	Institute of Transactional Analysis	ITC	Industrial Training Council
ITA	International Tape Association	ITC	Inter-American Travel Congresses

ITC	International Institute for Aerial Survey and Earth Sciences (Netherlands)		**ITF**	Committee of Transport Workers Unions in the EEC
ITC	International Tar Conference		**ITF**	Institut Textile de France
ITC	International Tea Committee		**ITF**	Instrumenttekniska Föreningen
ITC	International Teletraffic Congress		**ITF**	International Trampolining Federation
ITC	International Textbook Company Ltd		**ITF**	International Transport Workers' Federation
ITC	International Tin Council		**ITFCA**	International Track and Field Coaches Association
ITC	International Trade Centre		**ITG**	Institut Technique du Gruyère
ITCA	Independent Television Companies Association		**ITG**	International Tabakwissenschaftliche Gesellschaft
ITCA	Inter-American Technical Council of Archives		**ITG**	International Trumpet Guild
ITCA	International Typographic Composition Association		**ITGWF**	International Textile and Garment Workers Federation
ITCAA	Institut Technique Coopératif des Aliments pour Animaux		**ITGWU**	Irish Transport and General Workers Union
ITCAS	International Training Centre for Aerial Survey		**ITI**	Indian Telephone Industries
			ITI	Institute for Technical Interchange (Hawaii)
ITCC	International Technical Cooperation Centre (Israel)		**ITI**	International Technical Institute of Flight Engineers
ITCF	Institut Technique des Céréales et des Fourrages		**ITI**	International Technology Institute (U.S.A.)
ITCPN	International Technical Conference on Protection of Nature		**ITI**	International Theatre Institute
			ITI	International Thrift Institute
ITCRA	International Textile Care and Rental Association		**ITI**	Irish Timber Industries Ltd
ITDC	International Trade Development Committee (U.S.A.)		**ITIC**	International Tsunami Information Centre (Hawaii)
ITDG	Intermediate Technology Development Group Ltd		**ITICA**	Chambre Syndicale Nationale d'Isolation Thermique, de l'Insonorisation et de la Correction Acoustique
ITE	Institute of Traffic Engineers (U.S.A.)		**ITIPAT**	Institut pour la Technologie et l'Industrialisation des Produits Agricoles Tropicaux (Ivory Coast)
ITE	Internationale Évangélique Ouvrière			
ITEA	Institut Technique de l'Élevage Avicole (France) (*now* ITA)		**ITIS**	Industrial Technical Information Service (Singapore)
ITEA	International Esperanto Tourist Association		**ITIS**	Insect Toxicologists Information Service (Netherlands)
ITEB	Institut Technique d'Élevage Bovin		**ITK**	Internationale Teerkonferenz
ITEC	International Total Energy Congress		**ITM**	Instituto di Tecnologia Meccanica
ITECA	International Educational and Cultural Association		**ITMA**	Institute of Trade Mark Agents
			ITMEB	International Tea Market Expansion Board
ITEMA	Industrie Textile du Mali		**ITMRC**	International Travel Market Research Council
ITEO	International Trade and Employment Organisation		**ITN**	Independent Television News Ltd
ITERG	Institut Technique d'Études et des Recherches des Corps Gras		**ITO**	Indian Tourist Office
			ITO	International Trade Organisation
ITESM	Instituto Tecnológico y de Estudios Superiores de Monterrey (Mexico)		**ITOCY**	Industrie Togolaise du Cycle et du Cyclometer

ITOVIC	Institut Technique de l'Élevage Ovin et Caprin
ITP	Institut Technique de la Pomme de Terre
ITP	Institut Technique du Porc
ITPA	Institut Technique de Pratique Agricole
ITPA	Irish Trade Protection Association
ITRC	Industrial Toxicology Research Centre (India)
ITRC	International Tin Research Council
ITS	Instituut voor Toegepaste Sociologie
ITS	International Technogeographical Society
ITS	International Thespian Society
ITS	International Tracing Service
ITS	International Trade Secretariats' Co-ordinating Committee
ITSC	International Telephone Service Centres
ITSG	International Tin Study Group
ITT	Instituto Torcuato di Tella, Buenos Aires (Argentina)
ITT	Industrie Textile Togolaise
ITT	Instituut voor Tuinbouwtechniek
ITTC	International Telegraph and Telephone Corporation
ITTC	International Towing Tank Conference
ITTCC	International Teachers Trade Union Cooperative Committee
ITTF	International Table Tennis Federation
ITTTA	International Technical Tropical Timber Association
ITU	International Telecommunications Union
ITU	International Temperance Union
ITU	International Typographical Union
ITV	Institut Technique du Vin
ITV	Instituto Técnico Vocacional (Guatemala)
ITVTP	Internationale Tierärztliche Vereinigung für Tierproduktion
ITVV	Internationaler Transport-Versicherungs-Verband
ITZN	International Trust for Zoological Nomenclature
IU	Interlingue Union
IU	International Environmental Protection Union
IUA	International Union of Advertising
IUA	International Union Against Alcoholism
IUA	International Union of Architects
IUA	International Union of Arts
IUAA	International Union of Advertisers Associations
IUAA	International Union of Alpine Associations
IUAC	International Union Against Cancer
IUADM	International Union of Associations of Doctor-Motorists
IUAES	International Union of Anthropological and Ethnological Sciences
IUAI	International Union of Aviation Insurers
IUAJ	International Union of Agricultural Journalists
IUAO	International Union for Applied Ornithology
IUAPPA	International Union of Air Pollution Prevention Associations
IUAS	International Union of Agricultural Sciences
IUAT	International Union against Tuberculosis
IUB	International Union of Biochemistry
IUB	International Universities' Bureau
IUBS	International Union of Biological Sciences
IUBS	International Union of Building Societies
IUC	International Union of Chemistry
IUC	Inter-University Council for Higher Education Overseas
IUC	International University Contact for Management Education
IUCAF	Inter-Union Committee for Frequency Allocations for Radio Astronomy and Space Science
IUCE	International Union of Cinematograph Exhibitors
IUCI	International Union on the Ionosphere
IUCM	Inter-Union Commission for Studies of the Moon
IUCN	International Union for Conservation of Nature and Natural Resources
IUCOG	Inter-Union Commission on Geodynamics
IUCr	International Union of Crystallography
IUCRM	Inter-Union Commission on Radio Meteorology
IUCS	Inter-Union Commission on Spectroscopy
IUCST	Inter-Union Commission on Science Teaching
IUCSTP	Inter-Union Commission on Solar-Terrestrial Physics
IUCSTR	Inter-Union Commission on Solar and Terrestrial Relationships

IUCW	International Union for Child Welfare
IUDW & C	Irish Union of Distributive Workers and Clerks
IUDZG	International Union of Directors of Zoological Gardens
IUE	International Union of Electrical Workers
IUE	International Union for Electro-heat
IUEC	International Union of Elevator Constructors
IUEC	Inter-Universitare Efficiency Commissie
IUEE	Institut Universitaire d'Études Européennes (Switzerland)
IUEF	International University Exchange Fund
IUF	International Union of Food and Allied Workers' Association
IUFDT	International Union of Food, Drink and Tobacco Workers' Associations
IUFO	International Union of Family Organisations
IUFOST	International Union of Food Science and Technology
IUFRO	International Union of Forest Research Organisations
IUFTAV	Internationale Union der Forschung, Technik und Anwendung des Vakuums
IUGB	International Union of Game Biologists
IUGG	International Union of Geodesy and Geo-physics
IUGS	International Union of Geological Sciences
IUHE	International Union for Health Education
IUHEI	Institut Universitaire de Hautes Études Internationales (Switzerland)
IUHPS	International Union of the History and Philosophy of Science
IUHR	International Union of Hotel, Restaurant and Bar Workers
IUHS	International Union of History of Sciences
IUI	Industriens Utredningsinstitut
IUI	International Union of Interpreters
IUIS	International Union of Immunological Societies
IUJCD	Internationale Union Junger Christlicher Demokraten
IUKP	Internationale Union der Katholischen Presse
IUL	International Union der Gewerkschaften der Lebens- und Genussmittelarbeiter Gewerkschaften
IULA	International Union of Local Authorities
IULCS	International Union of Leather Chemists Societies
IULCW	International Union of Liberal Christian Women
IULEC	Inter-University Labour Education Committee (U.S.A.)
IULIA	International Union of Life Insurance Agents
IUMI	International Union of Marine Insurance
IUMMSW	International Union of Mine, Mill and Smelter Workers
IUMS	International Union for Moral and Social Action
IUMSWA	Industrial Union of Marine and Shipbuilding Workers of America
IUNS	International Union of Nutritional Sciences
IUNT	Instituto Uruguayo de Normas Tecnicas
IUOE	International Union of Operating Engineers
IUOTO	International Union of Official Travel Organizations
IUP	Irish University Press
IUPA	International Union of Practitioners in Advertising
IUPAB	International Union of Pure and Applied Biophysics
IUPAC	International Union of Pure and Applied Chemistry
IUPAP	International Union of Pure and Applied Physics
IUPERJ	Instituto Universitário de Pesquisas do Rio de Janeiro (Brazil)
IUPGWA	International Union of United Plant Guard Workers of America
IUPHAR	International Union of Pharmacology
IUPIP	International Union for the Protection of Industrial Property
IUPM	International Union for Protecting Public Morality
IUPN	International Union for the Protection of Nature
IUPS	International Union of Physiological Sciences
IUPS	International Union of Psychological Science
IUPW	International Union of Petroleum Workers (U.S.A.)
IUR	International Union of Railways
IUR	International University of Radiophonics (France)
IURN	Institut Unifié de Recherches Nucléaires

IURP	Imprensa da Universidade Rural de Pernambuco (Brazil)	**IVBH**	Internationale Vereinigung für Brückenbau und Hochbau
IUS	International Union of Students	**IVBS**	Industriele Vereniging tot Bevordering van de Stralingsveiligheid
IUSA	International Underwater Spearfishing Association	**IVC**	Industrievereinigung Chemiefaser
IUSDT	International Union of Social Democratic Teachers	**IVC**	Permanent Committee for the International Veterinary Congresses
IUSF	International Union of Societies of Foresters	**IVCC**	Institut des Vins de Consommation Courante
IUSP	International Union of Scientific Psychology	**IVCLG**	Internationaler Verband Christlicher Landarbeitergewerkschaften
IUSS	International Union for Social Studies		
IUSSI	International Union for Study of Social Insects	**IVD**	Industrievereinigung Chemiefaser
		IVE	Institute of Vitreous Enamellers
IUSSP	International Union for the Scientific Study of Population	**IVE**	Instituto Veterinario Ecuatoriano
		IVE	Internationale Vereinigung des Eisenwaren- und Eisenhändlerverbände
IUSY	International Union of Socialist Youth		
IUT	International Union against Tuberculosis	**IVEL**	Instituto Veterinario Ecuatoriano del Litoral
IUTAM	International Union of Theoretical and Applied Mechanics	**IVF**	Industrieverband Friseurbedarf
		IVF	Institutet för Verkstadsteknisk Forskning
IUTCT	International Union for Thermal Medicine and Climatothalassotherapy	**IVFGR**	Internationale Vereinigung für Gewerblichen Rechtsschultz
IUVAA	Internationale Unie van Verenigingen van Artsen-Automobilisten	**IVFT**	Instituut voor Veterinaire Farmacologie en Toxicologie der Rijksuniversiteit, Utrecht
IUVDT	International Union against the Venereal Diseases and the Treponematoses	**IVFZ**	International Veterinary Federation of Zootechnics
IUVSTA	International Union for Vacuum Science, Technique and Applications	**IVG**	Internationale Vereinigung für Germanische Sprach- und Literaturwissenschaft
IUWA	International Union of Women Architects	**IVGWP**	Internationaler Verband der Gastronomie- und Weinbau-Presse
IUWDS	International Ursigrams and World Days Service		
		IVH	Industrieverband für Heimtierbedarf
IUYCD	International Union of Young Christian Democrats	**IVH**	Internationale Vereinigung des Handwerks
		IVHW	Internationaler Verband für Hauswirtschaft
IVA	Ingenjörsvetenskapsakademien	**IVIC**	Instituto Venozolano de Investigaciones Cientificas
IVA	Instítuto de Vacuna Antivariolosa (Bolivia)		
IVA	Internationale Vereinigung der Anschlussgeleisse-Benützer	**IVIO**	Instituut voor Individueel Onderwijs
		IVIP	Internationale Vereinigung f. Individualpsychologie
IVA	Swedish Academy of Engineering Sciences		
IVAAP	International Veterinary Association for Animal Production	**IVITA**	Instituto Veterinario de Investigaciones Tropicales y de Altura (Peru)
IVAC	Instituto Venezolano de Acción Comunitaria	**IVJH**	Internationale Vereinigung für Jugendhilfe
IVAKV	Internationale Vereinigung Aerztlicher Kraftfahrer-Verbände	**IVK**	Institutet för Växtforskning och Kyallagring (Sweden)
IVANK	Internationale Veterinär- Anatomische Nomenklatur- Kommission	**IVKDF**	Institut von Karman de Dynamique des Fluides (Belgium)
IVBA	International Volley-Ball Association (*now* IVBF)	**IVKM**	Internationaler Verband der Katholischen Mädchenschutzvereine
IVBF	International Volleyball Federation	**IVKMH**	International Vereinigung der Klein- und Mittelbetriebe des Handels

IVKMI	Internationale Vereinigung der Klein- und Mittelbetriebe der Industrie
IVL	Institutet för Vatten-och Luftvardsforskning
IVL	Instituut voor Veredeling van Land-bouwgewassen
IVL	Internationale Vereinigung der Lehrerver-bände
IVL	Internationale Vereinigung für Theoretische und Angewandte Limnologie
IVLD	Internationale Vereinigung der Organisationen von Lebensmittel-Detaillisten
IVMB	Internationale Vereinigung der Musikbibliotheken
IVN	Internationale Vereniging voor Nederlan-distiek
IVO	Instituut voor Veeteelkundig Onderzoek T.N.O.
IVOIRAGRI	Société Ivoirienne d'Exploitation Agricole
IVOIRAL	Compagnie Ivoirienne de l'Aluminium
IVOIRAP	Société Ivoirienne de Diffusion d'Appareils Électriques
IVOLCY	Industrie Voltaïque de Cycle et du Cyclomoteur
IVP	Industrie des Vernis et Peintures, Mastics, Encres d'Imprimerie et Couleurs d'Art
IVP	Instituto Venezolano de Petroquimica
IvP	Instituut voor Plantenveredeling
IvP	Instituut voor Pluimveeteelt
IVP	Instituut voor Visserijprodukten
IVPC	Internationaler Verband der Petroleum- und Chemie-arbeiter
IVPO	Internationale Vereniging voor Plattelandont-wikkeling
IVR	Internationale Vereinigung für Rechts- und Sozialphilosophie
IVR	Internationale Vereinigung des Rheinschiffs-registers
IVRI	Indian Veterinary Research Institute
IVRO	Instituut voor Rassenonderzoek van Land-bouwgewassen
IVS	International Voluntary Service
IVS	Internationale Verbindung für Schalen-tragwerke
IVSA	International Veterinary Students Association
IVSB	Industrieverband Schneidwaren und Bestecke
IVSP	Internationale Vereinigung für Selbstmord-prophylaxe
IVSS	Internationale Vereinigung für Soziale Sicherheit
IVSU	International Veterinary Students Union
IVT	Industrieverband Textil (Switzerland)
IVT	Instituut voor de Veredeling van Tuin-bouwgewassen
IVT	International Association of Textile Purchas-ing Societies
IVT	International Visual Theatre Research Com-munity
IVT	Internationaler Verband der Tarifeure
IVU	Instituto Veterinario Uruguay
IVU	International Vegetarian Union
IVV	Internationale Vereinigung für Vegetations-kunde
IVWO	International Vine and Wine Office
IVWSR	Internationaler Verband für Wohnungs-wesen, Städtebau und Raumordnung
IWA	Institute of World Affairs (U.S.A.)
IWA	International Wheat Agreement
IWA	International Women's Auxiliary to the Veterinary Profession
IWAHMA	Industrial Warm Air Heater Manufacturers Association
IWBP	Integration with Great Britain Party (Gibraltar)
IWC	International Commission on Whaling
IWC	International Wheat Council (U.K.)
IWCA	International World Calendar Association
IWCC	International Wrought Copper Council
IWCS	International Wood Collectors Society
IWDS	International World Days Service
IWE	Institution of Water Engineers (*now* IWES)
IWES	Institution of Water Engineers and Scientists
IWF	International Weightlifting Federation
IWF	Internationaler Währungsfonds
IWFA	International Women's Fishing Association
IWFS	International Wine and Food Society
IWG	International Writers Guild
IWG	Internationale Werbegesellschaft
IWGC	Imperial War Graves Commission
IWGIA	International Work Group for Indigenous Affairs

IWGM	Intergovernmental Working Group on Monitoring or Surveillance (UNO)
IWGMP	Intergovernmental Working Group on Marine Pollution (IMCO)
IWHS	Institute of Works and Highways Superintendents
IWIM	Institut für Wissenschaftsinformation in der Medizin
IWIS	Instituut TNO voor Wiskunde, Informatieverwerking en Statistiek
IWIU	Insurance Workers International Union
IWL	Institut für Gewerbliche Wasserwirtschaft und Luftreinhaltung
IWLA	Izaak Walton League of America (U.S.A.)
IWM	Institution of Works Managers
IWO	Institute for Works Order (U.S.A.)
IWO	International Wine Office
IWOCA	Instituut voor Wetenschappelijk Onderzoek in Centraal Africa
IWOSC	International Working-Group on Soilless Culture
IWP	Indicative World Plan for Agricultural Development (FAO)
IWPA	International Word Processing Association
IWPC	Institute of Water Pollution Control
IWRA	International Water Resources Association (U.S.A.)
IWRB	International Wildfowl Research Bureau
IWRI	International Wildfowl Research Institute
IWRMA	Irish Wholesale Ryegrass Machiners Association
IWRPF	International Waste Rubber and Plastic Federation
IWRS	International Wood Research Society
IWS	Industrial Welfare Society (*now* IS)
IWS	Institute of Water Study
IWS	Institute of Wood Science
IWS	International Wool Secretariat
IWSA	International Water-Supply Association
IWSA	International Workers Sport Association
IWSAW	Institute for Women's Studies in the Arab World (Lebanon)
IWSc	Institute of Wood Science
IWSC	International Weed Science Council
IWSG	International Wool Study Group
IWSI	Irish Work Study Institute
IWSP	Institute of Work Study Practitioners

IWTA	Inland Water Transport Authority (Pakistan)
IWTO	International Wool Textile Organisation
IWV	Internationale Warenhaus-Vereinigung
IWW	Industrial Workers of the World (U.S.A.)
IWWA	International Wild Waterfowl Conservation Association
IWY	International Women's Year (UN)
IWYF	International World Youth Friendship
IYC	International Year of the Child
IYCS	International Young Christian Students
IYF	International Youth Federation for Environmental Studies and Conservation
IYHF	International Youth Hostel Federation
IYRU	International Yacht Racing Union
IZD	Internationaler Zivildienst
IZS	Internationale Zentralstelle für Schulbau

J

JA	Jordbrukets Arbeidsgiverforening
JAALD	Japanese Association of Agricultural Librarians and Documentalists
JABC	Japan Audit Bureau of Circulation
JAC	Jeunesse Agricole Catholique
JAC	Jeunesse Agricole Chrétienne
JACA	Japan Air Cleaning Association
JACARI	Joint Action Committee Against Racial Interference
JACF	Jeunesse Agricole Catholique Féminine
JAEC	Japanese Atomic Energy Commission
JAEC	Joint Atomic Energy Committee (U.S.A.)
JAERI	Japan Atomic Energy Research Institute
JAES	Japan Atomic Energy Society
JAFC	Japan Atomic Fuel Corporation
JAIEG	Joint Atomic Information Exchange Group
JAIF	Japan Atomic Industrial Forum
JAIMS	Japan-America Institute of Management Science
JAIS	Japan Aircraft Industry Society
JAL	Japan Air Lines Company
JALMA	Japan Leprosy Mission for Asia

JAMA	Japan Automobile Manufacturers Association	**JCBMI**	Joint Committee for the British Monumental Industry
JAMC	Japan Aircraft Manufacturing Corporation	**JCBSF**	Joint Commission for Black Sea Fisheries
JAMINTEL	Jamaica International Telecommunications Ltd	**JCEA**	Junta de Control de Energía Atómica (Peru)
JAMSAT	Japan Radio Amateur Satellite Corporation	**JCEC**	Joint Communication Electronics Committee (U.S.A.)
JAMSTEC	Japan Marine Science and Technology Centre	**JCEPF**	Fédération des Jeunes Chambres Économiques des Pays Utilisant le Français dans leurs Relations Communes
JAMTS	Japan Association of Motor Trade and Service		
JAPCo	Japan Atomic Power Company	**JCET**	Joint Committee on Educational Television (U.S.A.)
JAPEX	Japan Petroleum Exploration Company	**JCFA**	Japan Chemical Fibres Association
JAPIA	Japan Auto Parts Industries Association	**JCHARS**	Joint Commission on High Altitude Research Stations (Switzerland)
JARDOR	Comité Français pour les Jardins et l'Horticulture		
JARI	Japanese Association of Railway Industries	**JCI**	Jaycees International (U.S.A.)
JARI	Jute Agricultural Research Institute (India)	**JCI**	Junior Chamber International
JARL	Japan Amateur Radio League	**JCIA**	Japan Camera Industry
JARTS	Japan Railway Technical Service	**JCLA**	Joint Council of Language Associations
JAS	Jamaica Agricultural Society	**JCM**	Junta Consultiva Mixta
JAS	Jewish Agricultural Society (U.S.A.)	**JCMF**	Jednota Ceskoslovenských Matematikua Fysiku
JAS	Jysk Arkæologisk Selskab		
JAST	Jamaican Association of Sugar Technologists	**JCP**	Japan Communist Party
JAT	Jugoslovenski Aerotransport	**JCPI**	Japan Cotton Promotion Institute
JAT	Junta de Asistencia (*see* TAB)	**JCPS**	Joint Center for Political Studies (U.S.A.)
JATCC	Joint Aviation Telecommunications Co-ordination Committee	**JCR**	Junta for Revolutionary Coordination (Argentina)
JAVIC	Japan Audio-Visual Information Centre	**JCRR**	Joint Commission (Chinese-American) on Rural Reconstruction (China)
JAWS	Japan Animal Welfare Society (U.K.)		
JBC	Jamaica Broadcasting Corporation	**JCS**	Joint Commonwealth Societies
JBC	Japanese Broadcasting Corporation	**JCSTR**	Joint Commission on Solar and Terrestrial Relationships
JBHCPIUA	Journeymen Barbers, Hairdressers, Cosmetologists and Proprietors' International Union of America		
		JCUDI	Japan Computer Usage Development Institute
JBMA	John Burroughs Memorial Association (U.S.A.)	**JCULS**	Joint Committee on the Union List of Serials (U.S.A.)
JBPA	Japan Book Publishers Association	**JDA**	Japan Defence Agency
JBCSA	Joint British Committee for Stress Analysis	**JDA**	Japan Domestic Airlines
JBTB	Jongeren Boeren-en Tuindersbond	**JDB**	Japan Development Bank
JCADR	Japan Centre for Area Development	**JDCE**	Jeunes Démocrates Chrétiens Européens
JCAE	Joint Committee on Atomic Energy (U.S.A.)	**JDREMC**	Joint Departmental Radio and Electronics Measurements Committee
JCAM	Joint Commission on Atomic Masses		
JCAPI	Junta Consultiva de Administración Publica Internacional	**JEAC**	Junta de Exportaçao do Algodao Colonial (Portugal)
		JEC	Junta de Exportaçao dos Cereais (Portugese)
JCAR	Joint Commission of Applied Radioactivity	**JECC**	Japan Electronic Industry Development Association

JECC	Joint Egyptian Cotton Committee
JECI	Jeunesse Étudiante Catholique Internationale
JECI	Jeunesse Étudiante Chrétienne Internationale
JECMA	Japan Export Clothing Makers Association
JEF	Jeunesses Européennes Fédéralistes
JEIA	Joint Export-Import Agency (U.K. & U.S.A.)
JEL	Jeunesses Européennes Libérales
JENER	Joint Establishment for Nuclear Energy Research (Netherlands & Norway)
JEOL	Japan Electron Optics Laboratory
JERC	Japan Economic Research Centre
JERI	Japan Economics Research Institute
JERS	Japan Ergonomics Research Society
JES	Japanese Electroplating Society
JESA	Japanese Engineering Standards Association
JESC	Japanese Engineering Standards Committee
JESC	Joint Electronics Standardisation Committee
JETEC	Joint Electron Tube Engineering Council (U.S.A.)
JETRO	Japanese External Trade Recovery Organisation
JF	Jordbrukets Förskningsrad
JFC	Jugend für Christus
JFCC	Japanese Federation of Culture Collections of Microorganisms
JFEA	Japan Federation of Employers Associations
JFM	Jeunesses Fédéralistes Mondiales
JFPS	Japan Fire Prevention Society
JFRCA	Japanese Fisheries Resources Conservation Association
JFRO	Joint Fire Research Organisation of DSIR and Fire Officers Committee
JFRO	Joint Fisheries Research Organisation (Zambia & Malawi)
JFTC	Joint Fur Trade Committee
JGC	Jugoslovenski Gradjevinski Centar
JHDA	Junior Hospital Doctors Association
JHEA	Junta de Historia Eclesiástica (Argentina)
JIB	Joint Intelligence Bureau
JIBA	Japanese Institute of Business
JIC	Joint Industrial Council
JIC	Joint Iron Council
JICI	Jeunesse Indépendante Chrétienne Internationale

JICNARS	Joint Industry Committee for National Readership Surveys
JICST	Japan Information Centre of Science and Technology
JICTAR	Joint Industry Committee for Television Advertising Research
JID	Junta Interamericana de Defensa
JIDA	Japan Industrial Designers Association
JIDC	Jamaica Industrial Development Corporation
JIE	Junior Institution of Engineers
JIEA	Japan Industrial Explosives Association
JIFA	Japanese Institute for Foreign Affairs
JIFE	Junta Internacional de Fiscalización de Estupefacientes
JIMA	Japan Industrial Management Association
JIMTOF	Japan International Machine Tool Fair
JINR	Joint Institute for Nuclear Research
JIOA	Joint Intelligence Objectives Agency
JIS	Jamaica Information Service
JISC	Japan Industrial Standards Committee
JITPA	Japanese International Trade Promotion Association
JIU	Junta de Investigaçao de Ultramer (Portugal)
JKA	Jugoslavenski Komitet za Aerosole
JKFC	Japan-Republic of Korea Joint Fisheries Commission
JLA	Japanese Library Association
JLA	Jordan Library Association
JLP	Jamaica Labour Party
JMA	Jamaica Manufacturer's Association
JMA	Japan Management Association
JMA	Japan Meteorological Agency
JMG	Järnmanufakturgrossisternas Förening
JMI	Japan Management Institute
JMIA	Japan Mining Industry Association
JMIF	Japan Motor Industrial Federation
JMMA	Japan Materials Management Association
JMRP	Joint Meteorological Radio Propagation Sub-Committee
JMTBA	Japan Machine Tool-Builders Association
JNA	Junta Nacional del Algodón (Argentina)
JNAU	Jawaharlal Nehru Agricultural University (India)
JNC	Junta Nacional de Carnes (Argentina)
JNG	Junta Nacional de Granos (Argentina)

JNP	Junta Nacional de Planeamiento (Bolivia)
JNPC	Junta Nacional de Planificación y Coordinación (Dominica)
JNPCE	Junta Nacional de Planificación y Coordinación Económica (Ecuador)
JNPP	Junta Nacional dos Produtos Pecuários (Portugal)
JNS	Japan Nuclear Society
JNSDA	Japan Nuclear Ship Development Agency
JNTA	Japan National Tourist Association
JNTO	Japan National Tourist Organization
JNV	Junta Nacional de la Vivienda (Peru)
JOC	Jeunesse Ouvrière Chrétienne Internationale
JOC	Joint Organizing Committee for GARP
JODC	Japanese Oceanographic Data Centre
JONSIS	Joint North Sea Information Service
JPA	Jamaica Press Association
JPC	Japan Productivity Centre
JPC	Juventud para Cristo
JPDC	Japan Petroleum Development Corporation
JPI	Japan Packaging Institute
JPIA	Japan Plastics Industry Association
JPMO	Jersey Potato Marketing Organisation
JPRG	Japan Peace Research Group
JPRS	Joint Publications Research Service (U.S.A.)
JPT	Japan Publications Trading Company
JRA	Japanese Red Army
JRB	Joint Radio Board (U.S.A.)
JRDA	Jeunesse du Rassemblement Démocratique Africain
JRDC	Japan Research and Development Corporation
JREA	Japanese Railway Engineering Association
JRIA	Japan Radioisotope Association
JRIA	Japan Rocket Industry Association
JRIA	Japan Rubber Industry Association
JRP	Jeunesse Rurale Protestante
JRR	Jeunesse Révolutionnaire Rwagasore (Burundi)
JRSMA	Japan Rolling Stock Manufacturers Association
JSA	Jesuit Seismological Association (U.S.A.)
JSAE	Japan Society of Automotive Engineering
JSAP	Japan Society of Applied Physics
JSAWC	Joint Services Amphibious Warfare Centre

JSC	Japan Science Council
JSCAACR	Joint Committee for Revision of the Anglo-American Cataloguing Rules
JSD	Jugoslovensko Statističko Društvo
JSEA	Japan Ship Exporters Association
JSEE	Japanese Society for Engineering Education
JSEM	Japan Society for Electron Microscopy
JSFC	Japanese-Soviet Fisheries Commission for the Northwest Pacific
JSIA	Japan Software Industry Association
JSLE	Japan Society of Lubrication Engineers
JSLS	Japan Society of Library Science
JSMDA	Japan Ship Machinery Development Association
JSME	Japanese Society of Mechanical Engineers
JSMEA	Japan Ship Machinery Export Association
JSP	Japanese Socialist Party
JSPB	United Nations Joint Staff Pension Board
JSPF	United Nations Joint Staff Pension Fund
JSPS	Japanese Society for the Promotion of Science
JSQC	Japan Society for Quality Control
JSSF	Japanese Society of Scientific Fisheries
JSWB	Java Suiker Werkgevers Bond
JSZS	Japanese Society of Zootechnical Science
JTAC	Joint Technical Advisory Committee (U.S.A.)
JTC	Japan Tobacco Corporation
JTES	Japan Techno-Economics Society
JTRL	Jute Technological Research Laboratory (India)
JTRU	Joint-Services Tropical Research Unit (Australia)
JTUAC	Joint Trade Union Advisory Committee
JU	Jeunesse Universelle
JUCSPA	Joint University Council for Social and Public Administration
JUDCA	Juventud Democrata Cristiana de America
JUDRAL	Democratic Revolutionary Youth of Latin America
JUF	Jordbruksare-Ungdomen Forbunds
JUKL	Jugoslovensko Udruženje Kontrolora Letenja
JUMA	Jugoslovensko Udruženje za Marketing
JUMV	Jugoslovensko Društvo za Motore i Vozila

JUN	Jordbrukets Upplysningsnamand	KAPMO	Kent Apple and Pear Marketing Organisation
JUNAL	Junta Nacional de Algodão (Brazil)	KARNA	Kweekbedrijf v. Aardappelrassen d. Nederlandse Aardappelmeelindustrie
JUNIC	Joint United Nations Information Committee		
JUS	Jugoslavenski Zavod za Standardizaciju	KAS	Kentucky Academy of Science
JUS	Jurist-och Samhällsvetareförbundet	KASEF	Katholisches Sekretariat für Europäische Fragen
JUSE	Japanese Union of Scientists and Engineers		
JUSK	Jugoslovenski Savez Organizacija za Unapredenje Kvaliteta i Pouzdanosti	KASKA	Koninklijke Academie voor Schoone Kunsten Antwerpene
JUSMAG	Joint United States Military Advisory Group	KATY	Kemikalialan Tukkukauppiasyhdistys
JUSMAP	Joint United States Military Advisory and Planning Group	KAU	Kenya African Union
		KAVB	Koninklijke Algemene Vereniging voor Bloembollencultuur
JUSTIS	Japan-United States of America Textile Information Service		
		KBBM	Koninklijke Belgische Bosbouwmaatschappij
JUTIBELIN	Association Belge du Lin, Chanvre, Jute de Fibres et Produits Apparentés Naturels et Synthétiques	KBF	Kommunale Bibliotekarers Forening
		KBKI	Indonesian Democratic Labour Organization
		KBM	Katholieke Bond Metallbewerkingsbedrijven
JUVENTO	Mouvement de la Jeunesse Togolaise	KBV	Nederlandse Katholieke Bond van Vervoers-personaal
JVA	Jordan Valley Authority (Israel)		
JWCA	Japan Watch and Clock Association	KBVE	Koninklijke Belgische Vereniging der Elektrotechnici
JWDS	Japan Work Design Society		
JWEF	Joinery and Woodwork Employers' Federation	KBVT	Koninklijke Belgische Vereniging voor Tand-heelkunde
JWPAC	Joint Waste Paper Advisory Council	KCC	Kenya Cooperative Creameries
JWS	Japan Welding Society	KCI	Key Club International (U.S.A.)
		KCNA	Korean Central News Agency
		KDB	Kenya Dairy Board
		KDF	Københavns Detailhandlerforening
		KDFC	Korea Development Finance Corporation
		KDI	Korea Development Institute
		KDI	Kwaliteitsdienst van de Industrie
		KDS	Khuzistan Development Service
		KDT	Kammer der Technik der Deutschen Demokratischen Republik

K

KÄB	Kneippärztebund		
KAC	Kuwait Airways Corporation		
KADU	Kenya African Democratic Union	KDVS	Det Kongelige Danske Videnskabernes Selskab (Royal Danish Academy of Science and Letters)
KAF	Konfeksjonsfabrikkenes Arbeids-giverforening		
KAFAB	Verband Schweizerischer Kartonfabrikanten	KEDI	Korean Education Development Institute
KAL	Suomen Kuorma-Autoliitto	KEIDAN-REN	Federation of Economic Organisation (Japan)
KAMEDO	Swedish Organizing Committee for Disaster Medicine		
		KEK	Konferenz Europäischer Kirchen
KANTAFU	Kenya African National Traders and Farmers Union	KELI	Kristina Esperantista Ligo Internacia
		KEMA	Keuring van Electrotechnische Materialen
KANU	Kenya African Nationalists Union		
KANUPP	Karachi Nuclear Power Project	KES	Kvakera Esperantista Societo
KANZEKO	Kahama Nzega Co-operative Union (Tanzania)	KES	Kwaliteitsbureau voor te Exporteren Schapen
		KESC	Karachi Electric Supply Corporation

KEST	Studiengesellschaft zur Förderung der Kernenergiewertung in Schiffbau und Schiffahrt
KF	Kooperativa Forbundet
KFA	Kammer für Aussenhandel der Deutschen Demokratischen Republik
KFA	Kenya Farmers Association
KFL	Kenya Federation of Labour
KFL	Kosmetikkfabrikkenes Landsforening
KFW	Kreditanstalt für Wiederaufbau
KGB	Komitet Gosudarstvennoi Bezopasnosti (Committee of State Security) (U.S.S.R.)
KHVS	Kunsthandelsverband der Schweiz
KIA	Kenya Institute of Administration
KIB	Arbeitskreis der beim Gesamtverband Kunststoffverarbeitende Industrie Registrierten Selbstandigen Kunstoff-Ingenieure und-Berater
KIF	Knitting Industries Federation
KIF	Konfektionsindustriföreningen
KIF	Kvarnindustriföreningen
KIFP	Korean Institute for Family Planning
KIIB	Koninklijk Instituut voor Internationale Betrekkingen (Belgium)
KIM	Kenya Institute of Management
KIO	Kenya Information Office
KIO	Kring Industriële Ontwerpers
KIRBS	Korean Institute for Research in the Behavioural Sciences
KISA	Korean International Steel Associates
KISOSZ	Kiskereskedók Országos Szervezete
KIST	Korean Institute of Science and Technology
KIT	Koninklijk Instituut voor de Tropen
KIV	Karten Industrie Verlags Verband
KIVI	Koninklijk Instituut van Ingenieurs
KIWA	Keuringsinstituut voor Waterleidingsartikelen
KJV	Kartell Juedischer Verbindungen in Great Britain
KKL	Kommunale Kinematografers Landsforbund
KLA	Kingdom of Libya Airlines
KLA	Korean Library Association
KLA	Kungl. Lantbruksakademien
KLBV	Verband der Konzertlokalbesitzer und aller Veranstalter Österreichs
KLF	Kjøttbransjens Landsforbund
KLIAU	Korea Land Improvement Association Union
KLM	Koninklijke Luchtvaart Maatschappij
KLSS	Korean Library Science Society
KLTV	Katholieke Vereniging van Land- en Tuinbouwonderwijzers
KLY	Konttorikoneliikkeiden Yhdistys
KMA	Swedish Control Institution for Dairy Products and Eggs
KMB	Katholieke Bond Metaalbewerkingsbedrijven
KMBA	Koninklijke Maatschappij voor Bouwmeesters van Antwerpen
KMC	Kenya Meat Commission
KMF	Kontormaskin- och Kontorsmöbelhandlarnas Förening
KML	Kauppamallastamojen Liitto
KMO	Koulujen Musiikinopettajat
KNAG	Koninklijk Nederlands Aardrijkskundig Genootschap
KNAK	Kongelik Norsk Automobilklubb
KNAN	Koninklijke Nederlandse Akademie voor Naturwetenschappen
KNAW	Royal Netherlands Academy of Sciences and Letters
KNBB	Katholieke Nederlandse Boerinnenbond
KNBTB	Katholieke Nederlandse Boeren- en Tuindersbond
KNBV	Koninklijke Nederlandse Brandweervereniging
KNCCI	Kenya National Chamber of Commerce and Industry
KNCU	Kilimanjaro Native Cooperation Union Ltd
KNCV	Koninklijke Nederlandse Centrale Vereniging tot Bestrijding der Tuberculose
KNCV	Koninklijke Nederlandse Chemische Vereniging
KNDP	Kamerun National Democratic Party
KNGMG	Koninklijk Nederlands Geologisch Mijnbouwkundig Genootschap
KNHM	Royal Netherlands Land Development and Reclamation Society
KNJBTB	Katholieke Nederlandse Jonge Boeren- en Tuindersbond
KNLC	Koninklijk Nederlands Landbouw Comité
KNMG	Koninklijke Nederlandsche Maatschappij tot Bevordering der Geneeskunst

KNMvD	Koninklijke Nederlandse Maatschappij voor Diergeneeskunde
KNMI	Koninklijke Nederlandse Meteorologisch Instituut
KNNP	Katholieke Nederlandse Nieuwsblad Pers
KNNV	Royal Netherlands Association of Natural History
KNPC	Kuwait National Petroleum Company
KNRV	Koninklijke Nederlandse Redersvereniging
KNSM	Koninklijke Nederlandse Stoomboot Maatschappij
KNTV	Koninklijke Nederlandse Toonkunstenaars-Vereniging
KNUB	Koninklijke Nederlandsche Uitgeversbond
KNUST	Kwame Nkrumah University of Science and Technology (Ghana)
KNVD	Koninklijk Nederlands Verbond van Drukkerijen
KNVL	Koninklijke Nederlandse Vereniging voor Luchtvaart
KNVTO	Koninklijke Nederlandse Vereniging van Transport-Ondernemingen
KNVvL	Koninklijke Nederlandse Vereniging voor Luchtvaart
KNZ	Koninklijke Nederlandse Zuivelbond
KOL	Kuvaamataidon Opettajan Liitto
KONPAPP	Kontors-och Pappersvaruleverantörernas Förening
KORDI	Korean Ocean Research and Development Institute
KORSTIC	Korean Scientific and Technological Information Centre
KOSLO	Konferenz Schweizerischer Lehrerorganisationen
KOTRA	Korea Trade Promotion Corporation
KOUDPRO-FIEL	Vereniging van Handelaren in Koudgevormde Profielen
KOV	Katholieke Onderwijzers Verbond
KOWACO	Korea Water Resources Development Corporation
KPC	Korea Productivity Centre
KPCU	Kenyan Planters' Co-operative Union
KPD	Kommunistische Partei Deutschlands
KPDR	Korean People's Democratic Republic
KPJN	Katholieke Plattelands Jongeren Nederland
KPNO	Kitt Peak National Observatory (U.S.A.)
KRAB	Kamer van Reclame-Adviesbureaus (Belgium)
KRIB	Kamer van Raadgevend Ingenieurs van België
KRIPA	Korean Research Institute of Public Administration
KRL	Vereniging Katoen, Rayon-, Linnen- en Jute-Industrie
KRO	Koustnärernas Rijksorganisation
KROM	Scandinavian Association for Penal Reform (Norway)
KRW	Vereinigung der Kessel- und Radiatoren-Werke (Switzerland)
KSA	Eidgenossisches Kommission für die Sicherheit von Atomlagen (Switzerland)
KSJ	Internationale Katholische Studierende Jugend
KSLA	Kungliga Skogs- och Lantbruksakademien
KSO	Klaedegrossisternes og Skraedderfagets Oplysningsudvalg
KSOS	Central Sultana-Raisins Co-operative Organisation (Greece)
KSS	Eidgenossisches Kommission zur Stahlenschutz (Switzerland)
KTBL	Kuratorium für Technik und Bauwesen in der Landwirtschaft
KTCCA	Kotwali Thana Central Cooperative Association (Bangladesh)
KTDA	Kenya Tea Development Authority
KTDC	Kenya Tourist Development Corporation
KTE	Kozlekedéstományi Egyesület
KTF	Kemisk-Tekniska Leverantörförbundet
KTG	Kerntechnische Gesellschaft im Deutschen Atomforum
KTGA	Kenya Tea Growers Association
KTH	Kungl. Tekniska Högskolan (Sweden)
KTIBF	Cyprus Turkish Trade Union Federation
KTL	Kuratorium f. Technik in der Landwirtschaft
KTN	Kieleckie Towarzystwo Naukowe
KTS	Kerntechnische Sektion der Schweizerischen Vereinigung für Atomenergie
KTV	Kaffee- und Teeverband (Austria)
KULSAA	Karachi University Library Science Alumni Association
KUNC	Kamerun United National Congress
KURRI	Kyoto University Research Reactor Institute (Japan)

KUVV	Katholieke Unie van Verpleegkunden en Verzorgenden
KVA	Koninklijke Vlaamse Academie voor Wetenschappen, Letteren en Schone Kunsten van België
KVARN	Sveriges Kvarnyrkesförbund
KVBG	Koninklijke Vereniging der Belgische Gasvaklieden
KvF	Svenska Kraftverksföreningen
KVHAA	Kungliga Vitterhets Historie och Antikvitets Akademien
KVIV	Koninklijke Vlaamse Ingenieursvereniging
KVL	Den Kongelige Veterinaer-og Landbohojskole
KVNT	Koninklijke Vereniging 'Het Nederlandse Trekpaard'
KVO	Katholieke Vervoeders Organisatie
KVO	Koninklijke Verbond van Ondernemers in het Kleine en Middelgrote Bedrijf
KVOB	Katholieke Vereniging van Ondernemers in het Bakkersbedijf
KVOB	Katholieke Vereniging van Ondernemers in het Bloembollenbedrijf
KVP	Katholieke Volkspartij
KVS	Kansanvalistusseura
KVWM	Katholieke Vereniging van Werkgevers in het Metaalindustrie
KWP	Korean Workers Party
KWV	Ko-operative Wijnbouwers Vereniging van Zuid-Afrika
KYDEP	Home Products Handling Administration (Greece)

L

LA	Library Association
LAA	Library Association of Australia
LAA	Libyan Arab Airlines
LAAD	Latin American Agribusiness Development Corporation
LAAS-CNRS	Laboratoire d'Automatique et de ses Applications Spatiales du CNRS
LAB	Laboratory Animals Bureau
LAB	Library Association of Barbados
LAB	Lloyd Aero Boliviano
LABAZ	Société Belge de l'Azote et des Produits Chimiques du Marly, Division Pharmaceutique
LABOR-ELEC	Laboratoire de l'Industrie Électrique (Belgium)
LABORIA	Laboratoire de Recherche en Informatique et en Automatique
LACAP	Latin-American Cooperative Acquisitions Project
LACFFP	Latin-American Commission on Forestry and Forestry Products
LACI	London Association of Conference Interpreters
LACSA	Lineas Aereas Costaricenses SA
LACSAB	Local Authorities Conditions of Service Advisory Board
LADE	Lineas Aereas del Estado (Argentine)
LANDSIR-LAC	Liverpool and District Scientific, Industrial and Research Library Advisory Council
LAE	London Association of Engineers
LAECC	Laïcat et Communauté Chrétienne (Switzerland)
LAFC	Latin American Forestry Commission
LAFTA	Latin American Free Trade Association
LAFU	Ladies Amateur Fencing Union
LAGB	Linguistic Association of Great Britain
LAGE	Lineas Aereas Guinea Ecuatorial
LaH	Landssammenslutningen af Hospitalslaboranter
LAI	Library Association of Ireland
LAI	Linee Aeree Italiane
LAIC	Les Argiles Industrielles du Cameroun
LAIICS	Latin American Institute for Information and Computer Sciences (Chile)
LAMA	Latin American Museological Association
LAMA	Locomotive and Allied Manufacturers Association
LAMCO	Liberian, American-Swedish Minerals Co.
LAMDA	London Academy of Music and Dramatic Art
LAMP	Latin American Market Planning (Centre) (U.S.A.)
LAMPA	Lampleverantörernas Förening
LAMSAC	Local Authorities Management Services and Computer Committee
LAN	Linea Aera Nacional (Chile)

LANAP	Latin American Natural Areas Program	**LAWG**	Latin American Working Group (Canada)
LANICA	Lineas Aereas de Nicaragua	**LBC**	Les Bois du Congo
LANSA	Lineas Aereas Nacionales S.A. (Peru)	**LBF**	Lantbruksförbundets Byggnadsförening
LAOSA	Librarianship and Archives Old Students Association	**LBIDI**	Liberian Bank for Industrial Development and Investment
LAP	Lineas Aereas Paraguayas	**LC**	Lärarnas Centralförbund
LAPCO	Lavan Petroleum Company (Iran)	**LC**	Lutheran Council of Great Britain
LAR	Landskapsarkitekternas Riksforbund	**LCA-GB**	Lightweight Cycle Association of Great Britain
LARC	Association for Library Automation Research Communications (U.S.A.)	**LCBC**	Lake Chad Basin Commission
LARC	Libyan-American Reconstruction Commission	**LCF**	Laboratoire Central de Fitopatologia (Argentina)
LARO	Latin American Regional Office (FAO)	**LCF**	Labour Co-operative Farms (Bulgaria)
LAS	Land Agents' Society	**LCGB**	Locomotive Club of Great Britain
LAS	Library Association of Singapore	**LCGIL**	Libera Confederazione Generale Italiana dei Lavoratori
LAS	League of Arab States		
LASA	Laboratory Animals Science Association	**LCI**	Library for Cultural Initiation (Spain)
LASA	Latin American Shipowners Association	**LCIGB**	Locomotive and Carriage Institution of Great Britain and Eire
LASA	Latin American Studies Association (U.S.A.)		
LASAS	Secretariado Latinoamericano para Asistencia Universitaria	**LCP**	League of Coloured People
		LCT	Laboratoire Central de Télécommunications
LASCA	Los Angeles State and County Arboretum (U.S.A.)	**LCWIO**	Liaison Committee of Women's International Organisation
LASCO	Latin American Unesco Science Co-operation Office	**LDA**	Lead Development Association
LASEDECO	Land Settlement and Development Corporation (Philippines)	**LDFPA**	Laboratorio da Defesa Fitossanitária dos Produtos Armazenados (Portugal)
LASIM	Los Angeles Society of Internal Medicine (U.S.A.)	**LDOS**	Lord's Day Observance Society
		LDP	Landsforeningen af Danske Plantehandlere
LASL	Los Alamos Scientific Laboratory (U.S.A.)	**LDP**	Liberal-Democratic Party (Japan)
LASMO	London and Scottish Marine Oil	**LDPD**	Liberal Democratic Party of Germany
LASPAU	Latin American Scholarship Program of American Universities	**LDRTA**	Long Distance Road Transport Association of Australia
LASRA	Leather and Shoe Research Association (N.Z.)	**LDV**	Landsforeningen Danske Vognmoend
		LEA	Ligue des États Arabes (Egypt)
LASSI	Latin American Secretariat of the Socialist International	**LEA**	Local Education Authority
LAT	Liga Argentina contra la Tuberculosis	**LEAP**	Loan and Educational Aid Programme (Nigeria)
LATICI	Latin American Technical Institute for Cooperative Integration (Puerto Rico)	**LEASEU-ROPE**	European Federation of Equipment Leasing Company Associations
LATT	Library Association of Trinidad and Tobago	**LEAT**	International Institute of Legal, Economic and Administration Terminology (France)
LAV	Landmaschinen- und Ackerschlepper-Vereinigung	**LEC**	Liberia Electricity Corporation
		LECE	Ligue Européenne de Co-opération Économique
LAV	Lineas Aeropostal Venezolana		
LAWASIA	Law Association for Asia and the Western Pacific (Australasia)	**LECT**	League for the Exchange of Commonwealth Teachers

LEDU	Local Enterprise Development Unit (N. Ireland)
LEF	Landbouw Egalisatie Fonds
LEF	Lantbruksakademiens Kommitté for Ekonomisk Forskning
LEGACOOP	Lega Nazionale delle Cooperative e Mutue
LEGPA	Laboratory of Engineering and Applied Physics
LEI	Landbouw Economisch Instituut
LEI	Landsforeningen for Elektroteknisk Industri
LEKNAS	National Institute of Economic and Social Research (Indonesia)
LEMIT	Laboratorio de Ensayo de Materiales e Investigaciones Tecnológicas (Argentina)
LEN	Ligue Européenne de Natation
LENA	Laboratorio Energia Nucleare Applicata
LEND	Linguia e Nuova Didattica
LEO	Lyons Electronic Office
LEPOR	Long-term and Expanded Programme of Oceanic Exploration and Research
LEPRA	British Leprosy Relief Association
LES	Licensing Executives Society International
LET	Laboratoire Électrotechnique de Tokyo
LETATA	Light Edge Tool and Allied Trades Association
LEY	Liberal European Youth
LFEM	Laboratoire Fédéral d'Essai des Matériaux (Switzerland)
LFF	Land- und Forstwirtschaftlicher Forschungs-rat e.v. Bonn
LFI	Laxforskningsinstitutet
LFL	Landøkonomisk Forsøgslaboratorium
LFLRASP	Lifwynn Foundation for Laboratory Research in Analytical and Social Psychiatry (U.S.A.)
LFTD	Stichting Landbouw Fysisch-Technische Dienst
LGC	Laboratory of the Government Chemist
LGEB	Local Government Examinations Board
LGTA	Ligue Générale des Travailleurs de l'Angola
LGTB	Local Government Training Board
LGU	Ladies Golf Union
LHF	Landbo- og Husmandsforeningernes
LHI	Lefthanders International
LHI	Ligue Homeopathique Internationale
LI	Liberal International (World Liberal Union)

LI	Ligue Internationale de la Représentation Commerciale (Switzerland)
LIA	Lead Industries Association (U.S.A.)
LIA	Leather Industries of America
LIA	Lebanese International Airways
LIA	Ligue Internationale d'Arbitrage
LIAT	Leeward Islands Air Transport Services
LIB	Landbrugsmaskin- Importørernes Brancheforening
LIBA	Long Island Biological Association (U.S.A.)
LIBE	Ligo Internacia de Blindaj Esperantistoj
LIBER	Ligue des Bibliothèques Européennes de Recherche
LICA	Ligue Internationale contre le Racisme et l'Antisémitisme
LICCD	Ligue Internationale contre la Concurrence Déloyale
LICOSA	Libreria Commissionaria Sansoni
LICOTRA	L'Essor Ivoirien de Construction et de Travaux Publics
LIDC	Lead Industries Development Council
LIDE	Liga de Activación de la Región del Delta (Argentina)
LIDH	Ligue Internationale des Droits de l'Homme
LIDIA	Liaison Internationale des Industries Alimentaires
LIEN	Ligue Internationale pour l'Éducation Nouvelle
LIF	Lighting Industry Federation
LIF	Läkemedelsindustriföreningen
LIFE	League for International Food Education (U.S.A.)
LIFMA	Leather Importers, Factors and Merchants Association
LIFPL	Ligue Internationale de Femmes pour la Paix et la Liberté
LIGNUM	Schweizerische Arbeitsgemeinschaft für das Holz
LIHG	Ligue Internationale de Hockey sur Glace
LIHS	Long Island Horticultural Society (U.S.A.)
LIL	Laboratoire International de la Lune
LILA	Ligue Internationale de la Librairie Ancienne
LIM	Groupement des Laboratoires Internationaux de Recherche et d'Industrie du Médicament
LIMEP	Internationale des Mères et des Éducatrices pour la Paix

IMEX	L'Ivoirienne d'Import-Export	LME	Telefonaktiebolaget L.M.Ericsson
IMPL	Liga Internacional de Mujeres pro Paz y Libertad	LMHI	Liga Medicorum Homeopathica Internationalis
INOSCO	Libraries of North Staffordshire in Co-operation	LMS	London Mathematical Society
		LMS	Riksföreningen för Lärarna i Moderna Språk
IO	Laboratorium voor Insekticidenonderzoek	LNB	Landsforbundet Norsk Brukskunst
IP	London International Press	LNBEE	Laboratoire National Belge d'Électrothermie et d'Électrochimie
IPA	Ligue Panafricaine contre le Tribalisme, le Sectarianisme, et le Racisme	LO	Landorganisasjonen i Norge
IPI	Indonesian Institute of Sciences	LO	Landorganisationen i Danmark
IRA	Lambeg Industrial Research Association	LO	Landorganisationen i Sverige
IRA	Linen Industry Research Association (Eire)	LOAS	Loyal Order of Ancient Shepherds
IRAR	Les Ingénieurs Radio Réunis	LOB	Landelijke Organisatie van Bedrijfspluimveehouders
IRI	Leather Industries Research Institute (S. Africa)	LOBB	Vereniging Landbouwkundig Overleg Bemestings Beleid
IRMA	Laboratoire International de Recherche sur les Maladies des Animaux	LOBE	Landelijke Organisatie van Bedrijfseendenhouders
IS	Light Industries Services (Singapore)	LOF	Landelijke Organisatie van Fokkers
ISC	Lions International Stamp Club	LOFA	Leisure and Outdoor Furniture Association
IST	Library Information Service for Teesside	LOG	Landbrukets Emballasjeforretning og Gartnernes Felleskjop
ITG	Lichttechnische Gesellschaft		
ITINT	Literacy International	LOK	Landelijke Organisatie van Kuikenmesters
IVI	Lämpöinsinööriyhdistys	LONRHO	London and Rhodesian Mining and Land Co.
JK	Liikeenjohdon Konsultit	LOP	Landelijke Organisatie van Piepkuikenfokkers
JUSA	Ljusarmaturleverantorerna		
K	Liiketyönantajain Keskusliitto	LORCS	League of Red Cross Societies
KD	Leverantörföreningen Kontors- och Datautrustning	LOS	Landelijke Organisatie van Pluimveeselecteurs
KP	Liberaalinen Kansanpuolue (Finland)	LOT	Polskie Linie Lotnieze
KTP	Lembaga Kemajuan Tanah Persekutuan (Malaysia)	LOV	Landelijke Organisatie van Vermeerderaars
LA	Lebanese Library Association	LPA	Leather Producers Association for England, Scotland and Wales
LEPO	Ligue Luxembourgeoise pour l'Étude et la Protection des Oiseaux	LPA	Local Planning Authority
LH	Leverantörföreningen for Lek- och Hobbyartikler	LPAB	Nederlandse Bond van Logies-, Pension- en Aanverwante Bedrijven
LLI	La Leche League International	LPAC	Launching Programmes Advisory Committee
LS	Limburgsch Landbouw Syndicaat	LPMB	Lunar and Planetary Missions Board (NASA)
LSBA	Leicester Longwool Sheep Breeders Association	LPMC	Liberian Produce Marketing Corporation
MA	Linoleum Manufacturers Association	LPO	Ligue Française pour la Protection des Oiseaux
MAGB	Locomotive Manufacturers' Association of Great Britain	LPT	Landsforeningen af Praktiserende Tandteknikere i Danmark
MC	Liga Maritima de Chile	LPV	Laboratorio de Patologia Veterinaria (Portuguese)
ME	London Metal Exchange		

LQFE	Laboratório Quimico Farmacêutico de Exército (Brazil)
LR	Lärarnas Riksförbund
LRA	Lace Research Association
LRCS	League of Red Cross Societies
LRDE	Technical Information Centre of the Electronics and Radar Development Establishment (India)
LRF	Lantbrukarnas Riksförbund
LRP	Society for Long Range Planning
LSA	Land Settlement Association
LSAA	Linen Supply Association of America
LSCR	Ligue des Sociétés de la Croix-Rouge
LSE	London School of Economics
LSHA	Louisiana State Horticultural Association (U.S.A.)
LSHTM	London School of Hygiene and Tropical Medicine
LSL	Loervare- og Sportsartikkelfabrikantenes Landsforening
LSMB	Lint and Seed Marketing Board, Tanzania
LSMI	Lake Superior Mining Institute (U.S.A.)
LSNSW	Linnean Society of New South Wales
LSNY	Linnean Society of New York (U.S.A.)
LSPN	Ligue Suisse pour la Protection de la Nature
LSRH	Laboratoire Suisse de Recherches Horlogères
LSV	Landelijke Specialisten Vereniging
LT	Lantbrukssallskapets Tidskriftsaktiebolag
LTA	Lawn Tennis Association
LTB	Katholieke Land-en Tuinbouwbond
LTC	Les Transports au Congo
LTF	Lithographic Technical Foundation (U.S.A.)
LTF	Lufttrafikkledelsens Forening
LTIB	Lead Technical Information Bureau
LTJ	Land-en Tuinbouw Jongeren
LTN	Lódzkie Towarzystwo Naukowe
LTP	Library Technology Project. American Library Association
LTRS	Low-Temperature Research Station, Cambridge (*Ceased*)
LTS	Lysteknisk Selskab
LTY	Lääketeollisuuyhistys
LU	Ligue Universelle
LUCCO	Land Utilisation Coordination Committee (Cyprus)
LUF	Ligue Universelle de Francs-Maçons
LUFORO	London Unidentified Flying Objects Research Organisation
LUFS	Land Use and Forest Resource Survey of Taiwan
LUT	Loge Unie des Théosophes
LUXAIR	Société Anonyme Luxembourgeoise de Navigation Aérienne
LUXATOM	Syndicat Luxembourgeois pour l'Industrie Nucléaire
LVCC	Landelijk Verbond der Christelijke Coöperatieven (Belgium)
LVFS	Lake Victoria Fisheries Service (Kenya)
LVM	Limburgse Vinyl Maatschappij (Belgium)
LVMEB	Landelijke Vereniging der Meesters Elektriekers van België
LWF	Lutheran World Federation
LWIU	Leather Workers International Union of America
LWMEL	Leonard Wood Memorial for the Eradication of Leprosy (U.S.A.)
LWS	Landbouw Winter Scholen
LYMEC	Liberal Youth Movement of the European Community
LZT	Beurs voor Landbouw Zuivel en Techniek

M

MA	Mathematical Association
MA	Metric Association (U.S.A.)
MAA	Maison de l'Agriculture Algérienne
MAA	Manitoba Association of Architects (Canada)
MAA	Manufacturers Agents Association of Great Britain and Ireland
MAA	Mathematical Association of America
MAA	Medical Artists Association of Great Britain
MAA	Medieval Academy of America
MAA	Motor Agents' Association
MAAC	Mastic Asphalt Advisory Council
MAAGB	Medical Artists Association of Great Britain

MAB	International Co-ordinating Council of the Programme on Man and the Biosphere
MAB	Man and the Biosphere Programme
MAB	Menswear Association of Britain Ltd
MABI	Groep Nederlandse Fabrikanten van Magazijn-, Archief- en Bibliotheekinrichtingen
MAC	Massey Agricultural College, Palmerston North (N.Z.)
MAC	Ministerio de Agricultura y Cria (Venezuela)
MACC	Manufacture d'Armes et de Cartouches Congolaises
MACI	Ministerio de Agricultura, Comercio e Industria (Panama)
MACOMA	Matériaux de Construction de Madagascar
MACS	Maharashtra Association for the Cultivation of Science (India)
MADEPA	Movimiento Apolítico de Productores Agropecuarios (Uruguay)
MAE	Magyar Agrártudományic Egyesület
MAE	Manchester Association of Engineers
MAE	Medical Association of Eire
MAER	Ministry of Agriculture, Eastern Region (Nigeria)
MAF	Motorbranschens Arbetsgivareförbund
MAFA	Maison des Agriculteurs Français d'Algérie
MAFF	Ministry of Agriculture, Fisheries and Food
MAFRIMA	Manufacture Centrafricaine de Matelasserie
MAG	Medical Association of Georgia (U.S.A.)
MAGATE	Mercados, Silos y Frigoríficos del Distrito Federal (Venezuela)
MAGB	Microfilm Association of Great Britain
MAGLI-CALZE	Associazione Italiana Produttori Maglierie e Calzetterie
MAHISSA	Maices Hibridos y Semillas, S.A.
MAILL-EUROP	Comité des Industries de la Maille des Pays de la CEE
MALAS	Midwest Association for Latin American Studies (U.S.A.)
MALIGAZ	Société Malienne des Gaz Industriels
MALRY	Malayan Leprosy Relief Association
MAMBO	Mediterranean Association for Marine Biology and Oceanology (Italy)
MAN	Mouvement pour un Alternatif Nonviolent (France)
MANA	Music Advisers National Association
MANI	Ministry of Agriculture of Northern Ireland
MANR	Ministry of Agriculture and Natural Resources (Nigeria)
MANTIS	Manchester Technical Information Service
MANU	Makedonska Akademija na Naukite i Umetnostite
MANU	Moçambique African National Union
MAOTE	Magyar Általános Orvosok Tudományos Egyesülete
MAP	Management Association of the Philippines
MAPI	Machinery and Allied Products Institute (U.S.A.)
MAPRIAL	International Association of Professors of Russian Language and Literature
MAPU	Movimiento de Acción Popular Unida (Chile)
MAPW	Medical Association for the Prevention of War
MAR	Mouvement d'Action Rurale
MARC	Monitoring and Assessment Research Centre
MARC-OGAZ	Union des Industries Gaziéres des Pays du Marché Commun (Belgium)
MARDB	Mountain Agricultural Resources Development Bureau (Taiwan)
MARDI	Malaysian Agricultural Research and Development Institute
MARINCO	Marketing International Consultants
MARKFED	Punjab State Co-operative Supply and Marketing Federation (India)
MARU	Middle American Research Unit
MAS	Military Agency for Standardization (*of* NATO)
MASA International	Mail Advertising Service Association International (U.S.A.)
MASI	Molinera Argentina Sociedad Industrial
MAT	Magyar Allerológiai Társaság
MAT	Magyar Aluminiumipari Troszt
MATA	Museums Association of Tropical Africa
MATE	Méréstechnikai és Automatizálási Tudományos Egyesület
MATFORM	Syndicat des Constructeurs Français de Matériel pour la Transformation des Matières Plastiques et du Caoutchouc
MATRA	Mauritanienne de Transit Transport Representation Assurances
MAURELEC	Société Mauritanienne d'Eau et d'Électricité
MAURINAP	Société Mauritanienne de Diffusion d'Appareils Électriques

MAVEC	Materiae Vegetabiles (Netherlands)	**MCP**	Mouvement Chrétien pour la Paix
MAVIS	Maize Virus Information Service (U.S.A.)	**MCPS**	Mechanical Copyright Protection Society
MAVOCI	Manufacture Voltaïque de Cigarettes	**MCS**	Malaysian Civil Service
MAWEV	Verband der Maschinen- und Werkzeughändler (Austria)	**MCS**	Mechanical Cultivation Services (Greece)
		MCS	Military College of Science
MAWR	Ministry of Agriculture Western Region (Nigeria)	**MCST**	Manchester College of Science and Technology
MBA	Marine Biological Association of the United Kingdom	**MCSU**	Melkcontrolestation Utrecht
MBAA	Master Brewers Association of America	**MCT**	Missão de Combate as Tripanosomiasis (Portugese)
MBAUK	Marine Biological Association of the United Kingdom	**MCTA**	Mild Coffee Trade Association (E. Africa)
MBG	Mission Biologique du Gabon	**MCWA**	Massey College Wool Association (N.Z.)
MBIA	Malting Barley Improvement Association (U.S.A.)	**MDA**	Maize Development Association
		MDA	Malt Distillers Association of Scotland
MBL	Marine Biological Laboratory (U.S.A.)	**MDAA**	Muscular Dystrophy Associations of America, Inc.
MBMA	Master Boiler Makers' Association (U.S.A.)	**MDB**	Movimento Democrático Brasileiro
MBS	Mutual Broadcasting System (U.S.A.)	**MDC**	Malawi Development Corporation
MBT	Magyar Biologiai Társaság	**MDC**	Mwanachi Development Corporation (Tanzania)
MBW	Movement for a Better World (Italy)	**MDF**	Les Meubles de France (Ivory Coast)
MC	Department of Mass Communication (France)	**MDIS**	Ministry of Industrial and Scientific Development (France)
MCA	Malaysian-Chinese Association	**MDP**	Portugese Democratic Movement
MCA	Malaysian Commercial Association (U.K.)	**MDPA**	Mines Domaniales de Potasse d'Alsace
MCA	Management Consultants Association	**MDRA**	Mouvement Démocratique du Renouveau Algérien
MCA	Manufacturing Chemists' Association of the United States	**MDS**	Minnesota Dermatologic Society (U.S.A.)
MCAA	Mechanical Contractors Association of America	**ME**	Mouvement Européen
MCAC	Marché Commun de l'Amérique Centrale	**MEA**	Marketing Executives Association of Belgium
MCB	Management Center do Brasil	**MEA**	Middle East Airlines Company
MCBSF	Mixed Commission for Black Sea Fisheries (FAO)	**MEAN**	Mission d'Étude et d'Aménagement du Niger (Nigeria)
MCC	Marylebone Cricket Club	**MEAU**	Missão de Estudos Agrónomicos do Ultramar
MCC	Mennonite Central Committee (U.S.A.)	**MEAUP**	Missão de Estudos Apícolas do Ultramar Português
MCCA	Conference of the Methodist Church in the Caribbean and the Americas	**MEBPA**	Missão de Estudos Broceanólogicas e de Pesca de Angola
MCCA	Mercado Común Centroamericano	**MEC**	Mercato Europeo Comune
MCCO	Mercado Común del Caribe Oriental	**MECAN-EMBAL**	Société Africaine d'Emballages Métalliques (Ivory Coast)
MCE	Mercado Común Europeo	**MECAS**	Middle East Centre for Arab Studies
MCF	Movement for Colonial Freedom	**MECCA**	Missionary and Ecumenical Council of the Church Assembly
MCFTU	Mauritius Confederation of Free Trade Unions		
MCIE	Midland Counties Institution of Engineers		
MCP	Malaysian Communist Party		

MECNY	Municipal Engineers of the City of New York	**MEPRA**	Misión de Estúdios de Patológia Regionál Argentina
MEDD	Middle East Development Service (*of* ODM)	**MEPW**	Ministry of Economic Planning, Western Region (Nigeria)
MEDIA-CULT	International Institute for Audio-Visual Communication and Cultural Development (Austria)	**MERALCO**	Manila Electric Company (Philippines)
MEDICA EURO-PRESS	Comité Permanent de la Presse Médicale Européenne	**MERIP**	Middle East Research and Information Project (U.S.A.)
MEDICO	A service of CARE	**MERL**	Mechanical Engineering Research Laboratory (*now* NEL)
MEDIF	Medicinalimportorforening	**MERML**	Mid-Eastern Medical Regional Library Program (U.S.A.)
MEE	Magyar Electrotechnikai Egyesület	**MERNU**	Missão de Estudo do Rendimento Nacional do Ultramar
MEEC	Middle East Economic Committee		
MEECI	Mechanical and Electrical Engineering Construction Industry	**MERRA**	Middle East Relief and Rehabilitation Administration
MEEU	Missão de Estudos Económicos do Ultramar	**MERU**	Maharishi European Research University
MEF	Maskinentreprenorenes Forbund	**MERU**	Mechanical Engineering Research Unit (S. Africa)
MEF	Mauritius Employers Federation	**MES**	Malaysian Economic Society
MEFA	Foreningen af Danske Medicinfabrikker	**MESA**	Middle East Studies Association of North America
MEFTA	Metalworking Industries in EFTA		
MEG	Max-Eyth-Gesellschaft für Agrartechnik	**MESA**	United States Mining Enforcement and Safety Administration
MEG	Münchner Entomologische Gesellschaft	**MESAN**	Mouvement d'Évolution Sociale d'Afrique Noir
MEGJR	Mitteleuropäischer Guttempler-Jugendrat		
MEIU	Medical Education and Information Unit, Spastics Society	**MESCO**	Middle East Science Co-operation Office (UNESCO)
MEKOG	N.V. Maatschappij tot Exploitatie van Kooksovengassen	**MESPF**	Malaysian Estates Staff Provident Fund
MEL	Musika Esperanta Ligo	**MESR**	Mysore Engineering Research Station (India)
MELA	Middle East Librarians Association (U.S.A.)	**MESS**	Türkiye Madenî Eşya Sanayicileri Sendikai
MEM	Mondpaca Esperantista Movada	**META**	Model Engineering Trade Association
MEMA	Marine Engine and Equipment Manufacturers' Association	**MÉTE**	Magyar Élelmezésipari Tudományos Egyesület
MEMO	Association Internationale pour l'Enseignement des Langues Vivantes par les Méthodes Modernes	**METO**	Middle East Treaty Organisation
		METRO	Metropolitan Reference and Research Library Organization, New York
MENOFER	Fédération des Unions Professionnelles des Distributeurs de Métaux Non-Ferreux et Appareils Sanitaires (Belgium)	**METU**	Middle East Technical University (Turkey)
		MEWAC	Mediterranean Europe, West Africa Conference
MENS	Middle East Neurosurgical Society		
MEOCAM	Mouvement d'Étudiants de l'Organisation Commune Africaine, Malagache et Mauricienne	**MEXE**	Military Engineering Experimental Establishment
		MEZU	Missão de Estudos Zoológicos do Ultramar
MEP	Movimento Electoral del Pueblo (Venezuela)	**MFA**	Motor Factors Association
MEPA	Missão de Estudos de Pesca de Angola	**MFAL**	Marginal Farmers and Landless Labourers Agency (India)
MEPC	Marine Environment Protection Committee (IMCO)		
MEPP	Société Mauritanienne d'Entreposage de Produits Pétroliers	**MFALDA**	Marginal Farmers and Agricultural Labourers Development Agency (India)

MFAR	Maison Familiale d'Apprentissage Rural
MFC	Movimiento Familiar Cristiano (Uruguay)
MFD	Mennonietischer Freiwilligen Dienst
MFE	Magyar Fogorvosok Egyesülete
MFE	Mouvement Fédéraliste Européen
MFECS	Mediterranean Far East Container Service
MFI	Malmö Flygindustri
MFMI	Men for Missions International (U.S.A.)
MFNO	Midland Federation of Newspaper Owners
MFP	Maremaatlou Freedom Party (Lesotho)
MFP	Ministry of Fuel and Power
MFPA	Mouth and Foot Painting Artists
MFPB	Malta Federation of Professional Bodies
MFR	Mouvement Familial Rural (France) (*now* CMR)
MFRA	Multiple Food Retailers Association
MFT	Magyar Földrajzi Társaság
MFT	Svensk Föreningen för Medicinsk Fysik och Teknik
MGA	Ministerio de Ganadería y Agricultura (Uruguay)
MGA	Missão Geográfica de Angola
MGA	Mushroom Growers Association
MGE	Magyar Geofizikusok Egyesület
MGE	Mouvement Gauche Européenne
MGF	Musikkgrossistenes Förening
MGFHU	Missão de Geografia Física e Humana do Ultramar
MGM	Missao Geografica de Moçambique
MGMI	Mining, Geological and Metallurgical Institute of India
MGMS	Manchester Geological and Mining Society
MH	Musiklärarnas Riksförening
MHA	Manila Hemp Association
MHA	Mental Health Administration (U.S.A.)
MHEA	Mechanical Handling Engineers Association
MHEDA	Material Handling Equipment Distributors Association (U.S.A.)
MHLG	Ministry of Housing and Local Government
MHN	Museo Histórico Nacionál (Argentina)
MHRA	Modern Humanities Research Association
MHS	Malta Heraldic Society
MHS	Malta Historical Society
MHS	Massachusetts Horticultural Society (U.S.A.)

MHT	Magyar Hidrológiai Társaság
MIA	Malleable Ironfounders' Association
MIA	Manitoba Institute of Agrologists (Canada)
MIA	Murrumbidgee Irrigation Area (Australia)
MIAA	Missão de Inquéritos Agrícolas de Angola
MIAM	Fédération Nationale du Matériel Industriel, Agricole et Ménager en Bois
MIAMSI	Mouvement International d'Apostolat des Milieux Sociaux Indépendants
MIAP	Mouvement International d'Action pour la Paix
MIATCO	Mid-America International Agri-Trade Council
MIB	Metal Information Bureau
MIC	Magnesium Industry Council
MIC	Malayan-Indian Congress
MICC	Malaysian International Chamber of Commerce
MICUMA	Société des Mines de Cuivre de Mauritanie
MIDADE	Mouvement International d'Apostolat des Enfants
MIDADEN	Movimiento Internacional de Apostolado de los Niños
MIDEC	Middle East Industrial Development Projects Corporation
MIDFC	Malaysian Industrial Development Finance Co.
MIDS	Madras Institute of Development Studies (India)
MIE	Mouvement pour l'Indépendance de l'Europe
MIEC	Pax Romana, Mouvement International des Étudiants Catholiques
MIF	Miners' International Federation
MIFERMA	Société des Mines de Fer de Mauritanie
MIFU	Margarine-Industriens Foelles-Udvalg
MIGB	Millinery Institute of Great Britain
MII	Muslim Intellectuals' International (Pakistan)
MIIC	Mouvement International des Intellectuels Catholiques
MIJARC	Mouvement International de la Jeunesse Agricole et Rurale Catholique
MIL	Maanmittausinsinöörien Liitto
MILC	Midwest Interlibrary Centre (U.S.A.)
MIM	Malaysian Institute of Management
MIMAF	Musicians International Mutual Aid Fund (France)

MIMC	Marconi International Marine Communication Company	**MIV**	Milchindustrie-Verband
MIME	Midland Institute of Mining Engineers	**MJA**	Movimiento de la Juventud Agraria (Uruguay)
MINESLA	Conference of Ministers of Education and those Responsible for the Promotion of Science and Technology in Relation to Development in Latin America and the Caribbean	**MJSZ**	Magyar Jogasz Svövetség
		MKA	Mezhdunarodnyj Kooperativnyj Alians
		MKE	Magyar Könyvtärosek Egyesülete
		MKFE	Magyarországi Nemzetközi Közúti Fuvarozók Egyesülete
MINETRAS	Syndicat des Constructeurs de Matériels pour Mines et Travaux Souterrains	**MKL**	Maatalouskeskusten Liitto
MINRA	Miniature International Racing Association (U.S.A.)	**MKSZ**	Magyar Képzomüvészek Szövetsége
		MLA	Malta Library Association
MIPE	Moscow Institute of Power Engineering	**MLA**	Modern Language Association (U.S.A.)
MIPI	Madjelis ilmu pengetahaun Indonesia	**MLAF**	Mainostajien Liitto Annonsörernas
MIPN	Mouvement Italien pour la Protection de la Nature	**MLAGB**	Muzzle Loaders' Association of Great Britain
MIR	Mouvement International de la Réconciliation	**MLC**	Meat and Livestock Commission
		MLEU	Mouvement Libéral pour l'Europe Unie
		MLV	Ministerie van Landbouw en Visserij
MIRA	Motor Industry Research Association	**MMA**	Meter Manufacturers Association
MIRF	Myopia International Research Foundation (U.S.A.)	**MMB**	Milk Marketing Board
MIRINZ	Meat Industry Research Institute, New Zealand	**MMFITB**	Man-made Fibres Producing Industry Training Board
MIRT	Meteorological Institute for Research and Training (Egypt)	**MMI**	Foreninger af Mobelarkitekter og Indretningsarkitekter i Danmark
MIS	Milieu Information Service (U.S.A.)	**MMM**	Mouvement Militant Mauricien
MIS	Mining Institute of Scotland	**MMM**	Mouvement Mondial des Mères
MISLIC	Mid-Staffordshire Libraries in Co-operation	**MMP**	International Organization of Masters, Mates and Pilots
MISO	Mostra Internazionale Scambi Occidente		
MISR	Macaulay Institute for Soil Research	**MMPS**	Commission Médico-Pédagogique et Psycho-Sociale (of BICE)
MISR	Makerere Institute of Social Research (Uganda)	**MMRA**	Maritime Marshland Rehabilitation Administration (Canada)
MISR	Malawi Institute of Social Research	**MMS**	Moravian Missionary Society
MIT	Massachusetts Institute of Technology (U.S.A.)	**MMSA**	Mercantile Marine Service Association
MITA	Schweizerischer Verband des Mineral- und Tafelwasserhandels	**MMSA**	Mining and Metallurgical Society of America
		MMSC	Mediterranean Marine Sorting Centre
MITEX	Federatie van Middenstandsorganisaties in de Textildetailhandel	**MMTC**	Marine Mineral Technology Center (U.S.A.)
		MMTC	Minerals and Metals Trading Corporation of India Ltd
MITI	Japanese Ministry of International Trade and Industry	**MMTC**	Mouvement Mondial des Travailleurs Chrétiens
MITI	Ministry for International Trade and Industry (Japan)	**MNA**	Mouvement National Algérien
MITRA	Management Institute for Training and Research in Asia	**MNBA**	Multinational Business Association (U.S.A.)
		MNC-L	Mouvement National Congolais-Lumumba
MIU	Microalgae International Union	**MNCP**	Mbandzeni National Convention Party (Swaziland)
MIV	Melk-Inkoop-Vereniging		

MNE	Mouvement National pour la Défense et le Développement d'Épargne
MNF	Millers' National Federation (U.S.A.)
MNHN	Museo Nacional de Historia Natural (Uruguay)
MNLF	Moro National Liberation Front (Philippines)
MNUOM	Mision de las Naciones Unidas en el Oriente Medio
MOA	Ministry of Aviation
MOAC	Ministry of Agriculture and Cooperatives (Thailand)
MOC	Melkhygiënisch Onderzoek Centrum
MOCHI	Moniteur du Commerce International
MOD	Ministry of Overseas Development
MODEF	Mouvement de Défense des Exploitations Agricoles Familiales
MODUR	Movimiento de Unidad Ruralista (Uruguay)
MOE	Ministry of Education
MOEA	Ministry of Economic Affairs (Taiwan)
MOF	Ministry of Food (*later* MAFF)
MOH	Ministry of Health
MOI	Ministry of Information (*now* COI)
MOJMRP	Meteorological Office, Joint Meteorological Radio Propagation Sub-Committee
MOK	Mezhpravitelstvennaia Okeanograficheskaia Komissiia
MOM	Musée Océanographique de Monaco
MONOTAR	Mouvement National des Travailleurs Agricoles Ruraux
MONUMO	Mission de l'Organisation des Nations Unies au Moyen-Orient
MOPC	Ministerio de Obras Publicas y Comunicaciones (Paraguay)
MORI	Market and Opinion Research International
MOS	Malta Ornithological Society
MOS	Ministry of Supply
MOSICP	Movimiento Sindical Cristiano del Perú
MOSID	Ministry of Supply Inspection Department
MOSSAD	Israeli Secret Service
MOSST	Ministry of State for Science and Technology (Canada)
MOST	Ministry of Science and Technology (Korea)
MOSZK	Central Union of Hungarian Co-operative Societies
MOT	Ministry of Transport
MOTCP	Ministry of Town and County Planning
MOTESZ	Magyar Orvostudományi Társásagok és Egyesületek Szovetsege
MOTOR-AGRIC	Agricultural Mechanisation Organization (Ivory Coast)
MPA	Magazine Publishers Association (U.S.A.)
MPA	Marketing and Promotion Association
MPA	Master Photographers Association of Great Britain
MPA	Music Publishers Association of the United States
MPAA	Motion Picture Association of America
MPAGB	Modern Pentathlon Association of Great Britain
MPAU	Mahatma Phule Agricultural University (India)
MPBP	Metal Polishers, Buffers, Platers and Helpers International Union (U.S.A.)
MPBW	Ministry of Public Building and Works
MPCA	Manpower Citizens' Association (Guyana)
MPCRI	Management Promotion Council of the Ryukyu Islands
MPF	Metallurgical Plantmakers Federation
MPG	Max-Planck-Gesellschaft zur Förderung der Wissenschaften
MPI	Meeting Planners International (U.S.A.)
MPI	Middle Path International (Buddhism)
MPIAS	Max Planck Institute for the Advancement of Science (Germany)
MPJ	Mouvement Panafricain de la Jeunesse
MPLA	Popular Movement for the Liberation of Angola
MPM	Milli Prodüktivite Merkezi (National Productivity Centre) (Turkey)
MPNI	Ministry of Pensions and National Insurance
MPPF	Malaysian Planters Provident Fund
MPRP	Mongolian Peoples Revolutionary Party
MPS	Mouvement Populaire Sénégalais
MPU	Medical Practitioners Union
MRA	Misiones Rurales Argentinas
MRA	Moral Re-Armament (International)
MRAP	Mouvement contre le Racisme, l'Antisémitisme et pour la Paix
MRC	Medical Research Council
MRCC	Mineral Resources Consultative Committee
MRCI	Medical Research Council of Ireland
MRD	Microbiological Research Department

MRE	Malaysian Rubber Exchange	MSJ	Meteorological Society of Japan
MRELB	Malaysian Rubber Exchange and Licensing Board	MSP	Association Suisse des Marchands de Papier Peints
MRf	Malaremästarnas Riksförening i Sverige	MSRA	Multiple Shoe Retailers' Association
MRF	Motorbranschens Riksförbund	MSRI	Malaysian Sociological Research Institute
MRFB	Malaysian Rubber Fund Board	MSSGB	Motion Study Society of Great Britain
MRG	Minority Rights Group	MSSL	Mullard Space Science Laboratory
MRI	Malt Research Institute (U.S.A.)	MSSP	International Association of Marble, Slate and Stone Polishers, Rubbers and Sawyers etc. (U.S.A.)
MRI	Marine Research Institute, Djakarta		
MRIS	Maritime Research Information Service (*of* NAS) (U.S.A.)	MSSRC	Mediterranean Social Sciences Research Council
MRJC	Mouvement Rural de la Jeunesse Catholique	MSSVD	Medical Society for the Study of Venereal Diseases
MRJCF	Fédération du Mouvement Rural de Jeunesse Chrétienne Féminine	MSWEG	Mild Steel Wire Export Group
MRL	Ministère de la Reconstruction et du Logement	MTA	Magyar Tudományos Akadémia
		MTA	Mica Trades Association
MRP	Mouvement Républicain Populaire	MTA	Mineral Research and Exploration Institute of Turkey
MRPP	Maoists of the Movement for the Reorganisation of the Portugese Proletariat		
MRRDB	Malaysian Rubber Research and Development Board	MTA	Mobel- og Trearbeidings- industriens Arbeidsgiverforening
MRS	Market Research Society	MTCA	Ministry of Transport and Civil Aviation
MRTA	Marketing Research Trade Association (U.S.A.)	MTCF	Multilateral Technical Cooperation Fund (*of* CENTO)
MS	Movement for Survival	MTES	Müszaki és Természettudomány Egyesületek Szövetsége
MSA	Malaysia-Singapore Airlines Ltd		
MSA	Mellan-och Sydsvenska Skogbrukets Arbets- studier	MTF	Materialteknisk Forening
		MTHL	Metalliteollisuudenharjoittajain Liitto
MSA	Motor Schools Association of Great Britain	MTI	Meinatoeknafélag Islands
MSA	Mouvement Socialiste Africian	MTI	Metal Treating Institute (U.S.A.)
MSA	Mutualité Sociale Agricole	MTIN	Ministry of Trade and Industry, Northern Region (Nigeria)
MSA	Mutual Security Agency (U.S.A.)		
MSA	Mycological Society of America	MTIRA	Machine Tool Industry Research Association
MSC	Manpower Services Commission	MTIW	Ministry of Trade and Industry, Western Region (Nigeria)
MSC	Mediterranean Sub-Commission (Silva Mediterranea) (*of* FAO)		
		MTK	Maataloustuottajain Keskusliitto
MSC	Meteorological Service of Canada	MTL	Mainostoimistojen Liitto
MSC	Mikrobiologická Spolecnost Ceskoslovenská	MTMA-UK	Methods-Time Measurement Association of the United Kingdom
MSEUE	Mouvement Socialiste pour les États-Unis d'Europe		
		MTOA	Manufacture de Tabacs de l'Ouest Africain
MSF	Multiple Shops Federation	MTP	Manufacture Togolaise des Plastiques
MSHG	Nederlandse Vereniging van Agenten in Metaalwaren, Sanitaire, Huishoudelijke en Aanverwante Artikelen en Galanterieën	MTPS	Syndicat National des Industries d'Équipement
		MTS	Marine Technology Society
MSI	Movimento Sociale Italiano	MTTA	Machine Tools Trades' Association
MSIRI	Mauritius Sugar Industry Research Institute		

MTU	Motoren- und Turbinen-Union
MTUC	Malay Trade Union Conference
MUBA	Schweizer Mustermesse in Basel
MUCIA	Midwest Universities Consortium for International Activities (U.S.A.)
MUCM	Mouvement Universel pour Confédération Mondiale
MUDRA	Training and Research Centre for the Performing Arts (Belgium)
MUF	Malta Union of Farmers
MUFM	Mouvement Universel pour une Fédération Mondiale
MUNT	Magyar Urológusok és Nephrológusok Társasága
MUP	Malta Union of Pharmacists
MURA	Midwestern Universities Research Association (U.S.A.)
MURS	Mouvement Universel de la Responsabilité Scientifique
MUT	Magyar Urbanisztikai Társaság
MUT	Malta Union of Teachers
MUZ	Institute for International Collaboration in Agriculture and Forestry (Czechoslovakia)
MVA	Missouri Valley Authority (U.S.A.)
MVDA	Motor Vehicle Dismantlers Association of Great Britain
MVL	Mekaniske Verksteders Landsforening
MVS	Mennonite Voluntary Service (Germany)
MVSofSA	Mine Ventilation Society of South Africa
MWG	Montanwissenschaftliche Gesellschaft der DDR
MWIA	Medical Women's International Association
MWTCo	Marconi's Wireless Telegraph Co. Ltd
MWV	Mineralölwirtschaftsverband
MY	Muoviyhdistys
MZS	Office Hongrois de Normalisation
MZV	Mineralöl Zentralverband

N

NA	Nordisk Amatørteaterrad
NAA	National Academy of Arbitrators (U.S.A.)

NAA	National Aeronautic Association (U.S.A.)
NAA	National Arborist Association (U.S.A.)
NAA	National Automobile Association (U.S.A.)
NAA	Nederlandse Aardappel-Associatie
NAAA	National Alliance of Athletic Associations
NAAB	National Association of Artificial Breeders (U.S.A.)
NAABC	National Association of American Business Clubs
NAABI	National Association of Alcoholic Beverage Importers (U.S.A.)
NAAC	National Association of Agricultural Contractors
NAAC	National Association of Archery Coaches
NAACIE	National Association of Agricultural, Commercial and Industrial Employees (Guyana)
NAACP	National Association for the Advancement of Coloured Peoples (U.S.A.)
NAAF	Norges Astma-og Allergiforbund
NAAF	North-African Air Force
NAAFI	Navy, Army and Air Force Institutes
NAAG	North American Advisory Group (*of* BOTB)
NAALD	Nigerian Association of Agricultural Librarians and Documentalists
NAAMSA	National Association of Automobile Manufacturers of South Africa
NAAO	North Africa Area Office (*of* UNICEF)
NAAP	National Association of Advertising Publishers (U.S.A.)
NAAR	National Association of Advertising Representatives
NAAS	National Agricultural Advisory Service (*now* ADAS)
NAAS	National Association of Art Services (U.S.A.)
NAATS	National Association of Air Traffic Specialists (U.S.A.)
NAAW	National Association of Amateur Winemakers
NAB	National Assistance Board
NAB	National Association of Broadcasters (U.S.A.)
NAB	National Association of Bookmakers, Ltd
NABAC	National Association of Bank Auditors and Comptrollers (U.S.A.)
NABB	Nationale Associatie des Compatables de Belgique
NABBA	National Amateur Body Building Association

NABC	National Association of Boys' Clubs	NACCAM	National Co-ordinating Committee for Aviation Meteorology
NABC	National Association of Building Centres		
NABE	National Association of Business Economists (U.S.A.)	NACCG	National Association of Crankshaft and Cylinder Grinders (*now* FER)
NABE	National Association for Business Education (*now amalgamated with* BACIE)	NACCU	National Association of Canadian Credit Unions
NABET	National Association of Broadcast Employees and Technicians (U.S.A.)	NACCW	National Advisory Centre of Careers for Women
NABF	Norsk Antikvarbokhandlerforening	NACD	National Association of Chemical Distributors (U.S.A.)
NABM	National Association of Biscuit Manufacturers	NACD	National Association for Community Development (U.S.A.)
NABM	National Association of British Manufacturers (*now* CBI)	NACDS	National Association of Chain Drug Stores (U.S.A.)
NABMA	National Association of British Market Authorities	NACE	National Advisory Committee on Electronics (India)
NABP	National Associations of Boards of Pharmacy (U.S.A.)	NACE	National Association of Corrosion Engineers (U.S.A.)
NABS	National Advertising Benevolent Society	NACEBO	Nationale Centrale voor Metaal-, Hout- en Bouwvakondernemingen
NABT	National Association of Biological Teachers (U.S.A.)	NACEIC	National Advisory Council on Education for Industry and Commerce
NABU	Vereniging van Nederlandse Aannemers met Belangen in het Buitland	NACF	National Agricultural Cooperative Federation (Korea)
NAC	National Agricultural Centre, Kenilworth	NACF	National Association of Church Furnishers
NAC	National Airways Corporation (South Africa)	NACFRC	North Atlantic Coastal Fisheries Research Centre
NAC	National Amusements Council	NACILA	National Council of Indian Library Associations (*now* FILA)
NAC	National Anglers Council		
NAC	National Archives Council	NACLA	North American Congress on Latin America (U.S.A.)
NAC	National Association of Choirs		
NAC	Nederlandse Akkerbouw Centrale	NACM	National Association of Charcoal Manufacturers
NAC	North American Committee of NGOs for Environment		
NACA	National Advisory Committee for Aeronautics (U.S.A.) (*now* NASA)	NACM	National Association for Cider Makers
		NACM	National Association of Colliery Managers
NACA	National Agricultural Chemicals Association (U.S.A.)	NACM	National Association of Cotton Manufacturers (U.S.A.)
NACA	National Athletic and Cycling Association	NACO	National Agricultural Company (Tanzania)
NACAA	National Association of Country Agricultural Agents (U.S.A.)	NACO	National Agricultural Credit Office (Vietnam)
NACAB	National Agricultural Centre Advisory Board	NACO	National Association of Caravan Owners
NACAE	National Advisory Council on Art Education	NACO	National Association of Cooperative Officials
NACAM	National Association of Corn and Agricultural Merchants	NACOA	National Advisory Committee on the Oceans and Atmosphere (U.S.A.)
NACAR	National Advisory Committee on Aeronautical Research (S. Africa)	NACO-BROUW	National Comité voor Brouwgerst
NACAS	National Advisory Committee on Agricultural Services (Canada)	NACODS	National Association of Colliery Overmen, Deputies and Shotfirers

NaCoVo	National Comité van Voederbouw
NACP	National Association of Creamery Proprietors and Wholesale Dairymen Inc.
NACPCC	National Advisory Committee for Pig Carcass Competitions
NACRO	National Association for the Care and Resettlement of Offenders
NACT	National Association of Careers Teachers
NACT	National Association of Cycle Traders
NACTA	National Association of Colleges and Teachers of Agriculture (U.S.A.)
NACTST	National Advisory Council on the Training and Supply of Teachers
NAD	National Association of the Deaf
NAD	National Academy of Design (U.S.A.)
NADA	National Association of Drama Advisers
NADA	National Automobile Dealers Association (U.S.A.)
NADC	Northern Region Agricultural Development Centre (Thailand)
NADECO	National Development Company (Ghana)
NADEE	National Association of Divisional Executives for Education
NADEEC	NATO Air Defence Electronic Environment Committee
NADEFCOL	Defense College (of NATO)
NADFAS	National Association of Decorative and Fine Art Societies
NADFS	National Association of Drop Forgers and Stampers
NADGE	NATO Air Defence Ground Environment System Organization
NADJ	National Association of Disc Jockeys
NADL	National Animal Disease Laboratory (Japan)
NADPAS	National Association of Discharged Prisoners' Aid Societies, Inc.
NAE	National Academy of Engineering (U.S.A.)
NAE	National Association of Exhibitors
NAEA	National Association of Estate Agents
NAEB	National Association of Educational Broadcasters (U.S.A.)
NAEC	National Aeronautical Establishment, Canada
NAEC	National Agricultural Engineering Corporation (China)
NAEC	National Association of Exhibition Contractors
NAECOE	National Academy of Engineering, Committee on Ocean Engineering (U.S.A.)
NAEDS	National Association of Engravers and Diestampers
NAEE	National Association of Environmental Education
NAEGA	North American Grain Export Association
NAET	National Association of Creamery Proprietors and Wholesale Dairymen
NAF	Nederlands Atoomforum
NAF	Norske Annonsørers Förening
NAF	Norsk Arbeitsgiverförening
NAF	Norges Apotekerförening
NAF	Norsk Arbeidgiverförening
NAFAS	National Association of Flower Arrangement Societies of Great Britain
NAFC	National Anti-fluoridation Campaign
NAFC	National Association of Food Chains (U.S.A.)
NAFC	North-American Forestry Commission (of FAO)
NAFC	North-East Atlantic Fisheries Commission (U.K.)
NAFCO	National Agricultural and Food Corporation (Tanzania)
NAFCO	National Airways and Finance Corporation (South Africa)
NAFD	National Association of Funeral Directors
NAFEKAV	Nationale Federatie der Kleinhandelaars in Algemene Voedingswaren (Belgium)
NAFEP	National Association of Frozen Egg Packers
NAFEC	National Aviation Facilities Experimental Center (U.S.A.)
NAFF	National Association for Freedom
NAFFP	National Association of Frozen Food Producers (now UKAFFP)
NAFHE	National Association of Further and Higher Education
NAFO	National Association of Fire Officers
NAFRC	National Atlantic Fisheries Research Center (of NMFS) (U.S.A.)
NAFSA	National Association of Foreign Student Advisers (USA)
NAFSA	National Fire Services Association of Great Britain
NAFTA	North Atlantic Free Trade Area
NAFTRAC	National Foreign Trade Council (U.S.A.)

AFWR	National Association of Furniture Warehousemen and Removers, Ltd	**NAII**	National Association of Ice Industries (U.S.A.)
AG	National Association of Goldsmiths of Great Britain and Ireland	**NAIL**	Neurotics Anonymous International Liaison Inc. (U.S.A.)
AG	National Association of Grooms	**NAIPRC**	Netherlands Automatic Information Processing Research Centre
AG	National Association of Groundsmen		
AG	Nederlands Akoestisch Genootschap	**NAIRO**	National Association of Intergroup Relations Officials (U.S.A.)
AG	Nederlands Architecten Genootschap		
AGARD	NATO Advisory Group for Aeronautical Research and Development	**NAISS**	National Association of Iron and Steel Stockholders
AGC	National Association of Gifted Children	**NAIWC**	National Association of Inland Waterway Carriers
AGM	National Association of Glove Manufacturers	**NAIY**	National Association of Indian Youth (U.K.)
AGS	National Allotments and Gardens Society	**NAK**	Nederlandse Algemene Keuringsdienst voor Landbouwzaden en Aardappelpootgoed
AGS	National Association of Hospital Management Committee Group Secretaries	**NAKB**	Nederlandse Algemene Keuringsdienst voor Boomkwekerijgewassen
AH	Ministry of Animal Health, Northern Region (Nigeria)	**NAKG**	Nederlandse Algemene Keuringsdienst voor Groente en Bloemzaden
AHA	National Association of Health Authorities	**NAKS**	Nederlandse Algemene Keuringsdienst voor Siergewassen
AHA	North American Highway Association		
AHA	Norwegian-American Historical Association	**NAL**	National Aeronautical Laboratory (India)
AHBO	National Association of Hospital Broadcasting Organisations	**NAL**	National Air Lines (U.S.A.)
		NAL	Norske Arkitekters Landsforbund
AHI	Nederlands Agronomisch Historisch Instituut	**NAL**	Norske Avisers Landforbund
		NAL	National Agricultural Library (U.S.A.)
AHRI	National Animal Husbandry Research Institute (Denmark)	**NALA**	National Association of Language Advisers
AHRO	National Association of Housing and Redevelopment Officials (U.S.A.)	**NALBSC**	National Association of Licensed Bingo and Social Clubs
AHS	National Association of Health Stores	**NALC**	National Association of Local Councils
AHSE	National Association of Health Services Executives (U.S.A.)	**NALCC**	National Automatic Laundry Cleaning Council
AHSO	National Association of Hospital Supplies Officers	**NALCD**	National Agricultural Library and Centre for Documentation (Hungary)
AHT	National Association of Head Teachers	**NALGO**	National and Local Government Officers Association
AI	Nordiska Afrikaninstitutet (Sweden)		
AIBD	National Association of Industries for the Blind and Disabled	**NALHM**	National Association of Licensed House Managers
AIC	National Association of Investment Clubs	**NALI**	National Association of the Laundry Industry
AIC	National Astronomy and Ionosphere Center (U.S.A.)		
		NALM	National Association of Lift Makers
AIDA	National Agricultural and Industrial Development Association (Eire)	**NALO**	National Association of Launderette Owners
AIDM	National Association of Insecticide and Disinfectant Manufacturers (U.S.A.)	**NALSAT**	National Association of Land Settlement Association Tenants
AIF	National Association for Irish Freedom	**NALSO**	National Association of Labour Student Organisations
AIG	Nippon Atomic Industry Group (Japan)		

NAM	National Association of Manufacturers (U.S.A.)
NAM	Nederlandsche Aardolie Maatschappij
NAMA	North American Mycological Association
NAMARCO	National Marketing Corporation (Philippines)
NAMB	National Agricultural Marketing Board (Canada, Zambia)
NAMB	National Association of Master Bakers, Confectioners and Caterers
NAMC	Mananga Agricultural Management Centre (*of* CDC)
NAMC	Nihon Aeroplane Manufacturing Company (Japan)
NAMCW	National Association for Maternal Child Welfare
NAME	National Association of Marine Enginebuilders
NAME	National Association of Marine Engineers of Canada
NAMG	National Association of Multiple Grocers
NAMH	National Association for Mental Health
NAMI	National Association of Malleable Ironfounders
NAMM	National Association of Margarine Manufacturers (U.S.A.)
NAMM	National Association of Master Masons
NAMMC	Natural Asphalt Mine-Owners' and Manufacturers' Council
NAMMO	NATO Multi-Role Combat Aircraft Development and Production Management Organization
NAMO	National Association of Marketing Officers (U.S.A.)
NAMPUS	National Association of Master Plumbers of the United States
NAMRU	United States Naval Medical Research Unit
NAMSO	NATO Maintenance and Supply Organisation
NANFM	National Association of Non-Ferrous Scrap Metal Merchants
NANP	National Association of Naturopathic Physicians (U.S.A.)
NANU	National Association of Non-Unionists
NANTIS	Nottingham and Nottinghamshire Technical Information Service
NAO	National Accordion Association
NAOE	National Association for Outdoor Education

NAOP	National Association of Operative Plasterers
NAP	Niger Agricultural Project (Nigeria)
NAP	Northern Agricultural Producers
NAPA	National Association of Park Administrators
NAPAEO	National Association of Principal Agricultural Education Officers
NAPB	National Agricultural Products Board (Tanzania)
NAPB	Nederlandse Aannemersbond en Patroonsbond voor de Bouwbedrijven in Nederland
NAPC	National Association of Parish Councils (*now* NALC)
NAPCA	National Air Pollution Control Administration (*of* HEW) (U.S.A.)
NAPCA	National Association of Pipe Coating Applicators (U.S.A.)
NAPD	National Association of Pharmaceutical Distributors
NAPE	National Association of Port Employers
NAPE	National Association of Power Engineers (U.S.A.)
NAPF	National Association of Pension Funds
NAPGC	National Association of Public Golf Courses
NAPIM	National Association of Printing Ink Manufacturers (U.S.A.)
NAPL	National Association of Photo-Lithographers (U.S.A.)
NAPM	National Association of Paper Merchants
NAPM	National Association of Purchasing Management (U.S.A.)
NAPO	National Association of Probation Officers
NAPO	National Association of Property Owners
NAPP	National Association of Poultry Packers
NAPR	National Association of Pram Retailers
NAPRE	National Association of Practical Refrigerating Engineers (U.S.A.)
NAPS	National Association of Personal Secretaries Ltd
NAPT	National Association for the Prevention of Tuberculosis (*now* CHA)
NAPTW	National Association of Pet Trade Wholesalers
NAPV	National Association of Prison Visitors
NAQP	National Association of Quick Printers (U.S.A.)
NAR	Nordisk Amatørteaterrad

NARACC	National Association of Refrigeration and Air Conditioning Contractors	**NASA**	National Settlement Authority (Libya)
NARAS	National Academy of Recording Arts and Sciences (U.S.A.)	**NASA**	U.S. National Aeronautics and Space Administration
NARBA	North American Regional Broadcasting Agreement	**NASA**	Nigerian Anthropological and Sociological Association
NARC	National Association for Retarded Children (U.S.A.)	**NASAB**	National Association of Shippers Advisory Boards (U.S.A.)
NARCOM	North American Research Group on Management	**NASBA**	National Automobile Safety Belt Association
NARE	National Association of Remedial Education	**NASC**	National Aeronautics and Space Council (U.S.A.)
NARF	National Association of Retail Furnishers	**NASC**	National Association of Scaffolding Contractors
NARG	Norfolk Archaeological Retrieval Group	**NASC**	National Association of Student Councils (U.S.A.)
NARGN	National Association of Retail Grocers of Norway	**NASCO**	National Academy of Sciences Committee on Oceanography (U.S.A.)
NARGUS	National Association of Retail Grocers of the United States	**NASCO**	National Agricultural Supply Company (U.S.A.)
NARI	Natal Agricultural Research Institute (S.Africa)	**NASD**	National Amalgamated Stevedores and Dockers
NARI	National Agricultural Research Institute (Japan)	**NASD**	National Association of Securities Dealers (U.S.A.)
NARI	National Association of Recycling Industries (U.S.A.)	**NASDEC**	National Assets and Services Development Export Consortium
NARIC	National Rice and Corn Corporation (Philippines)	**NASDU**	National Amalgamated Stevedores and Dockers Union
NARO	North American Regional Office (*of* FAO)	**NASEES**	National Association for Soviet and East European Studies (Scotland)
NARR	National Association of Radiator Repairers	**NASEN**	National Association of State Enrolled Nurses
NARRA	National Resettlement and Rehabilitation Administration (Philippines)	**NASH**	National Association of Specimen Hunters
NARS	National Archives and Records Service (U.S.A.)	**NASIS**	National Association for State Information Systems (U.S.A.)
NARSIS	National Association for Road Safety Instruction in Schools	**NASMAR**	National Association of Sack Merchants and Reclaimers Ltd
NARST	National Association for Research in Science Teaching (U.S.A.)	**NASPM**	National Association of Seed Potato Merchants
NARTB	National Association of Radio and Television Broadcasters (U.S.A.)	**NASRF**	National Association of Shoe Repair Factories
NARTEL	North Atlantic Radio Telephone Committee	**NASS**	National Association of Steel Stockholders
NARTM	National Association of Rope and Twine Merchants	**NASSS**	National Association for the Support of Small Schools
NAS	National Academy of Sciences (U.S.A.)	**NASU**	National Adult School Union
NAS	National Adoption Society	**NASU**	National Association of State Universities (U.S.A.)
NAS	National Association of Schoolmasters	**NASW**	National Association of Science Writers (U.S.A.)
NAS	National Association of Shopfitters		
NAS	National Audubon Society (U.S.A.)		
NAS	Noise Abatement Society		
NAS	Norges Akademikersamband		

NASW National Association of Social Workers (U.S.A.)

NASWM National Association of Scottish Woollen Manufacturers

NAT Nämnden för Avkommeundersökning av Tjurar

NATA National Association of Testing Authorities (Australia)

NATAS National Academy of Television Arts and Sciences (U.S.A.)

NATCC National Air Transport Coordinating Committee (U.S.A.)

NATD National Association of Teachers of Dancing

NATD National Association of Tobacco Distributors (U.S.A.)

NATD National Association of Tool Dealers

NATE National Association for the Teaching of English

NATEC Naval Air Technical Evaluation Centre

NATESA National Alliance of Television and Electronic Service Associations (U.S.A.)

NATEX National Textile Industries Corporation Ltd (Tanzania)

NATFHE National Association of Teachers of Further and Higher Education

NATGA National Amateur Tobacco Growers' Association

NATKE National Association of Theatrical and Kine Employees

NATMH National Association of Teachers of the Mentally Handicapped

NATN National Association of Theatre Nurses

NATO National Association of Temperance Officials

NATO National Association of Tenants Organizations (Eire)

NATO North Atlantic Treaty Organisation

NATR National Association of Tenants and Residents

NATR National Association of Toy Retailers

NATRFD National Association of Television and Radio Firm Directors (U.S.A.)

NATS National Air Traffic Services

NATS Nordisk Avisteknisk Samarbetsnämnd

NATSOPA National Society of Operative Printers, Graphical and Media Personnel

NATTKE National Association of Theatrical, Television and Kine Employees

NATTS National Association of Trade and Technical Schools (U.S.A.)

NAUA National Automobile Underwriters' Association (U.S.A.)

NAUI National Association of Underwater Instructions (U.S.A.)

NAV Nederlandse Aerosole Vereniging

NAV Nederlandse Anesthesisten

NAV Nederlandse Anthropogenetische Vereniging

NAVAC National Audio-Visual Aids Centre

NAVAS Nederlandse Aannemers Vereniging van Afbouw-en Stukadoorswerken

NaVAST Nationaal Verbond der Aannemers-Schrijnwerkers en Timmerlieden

NAVEG Nederlandse Agentenvereniging op Verlichtings- en Electrotechnisch Gebied

NAVEMHA Nationaal Verbond der Melk- en Zuivelhandelaars van België

NAVETEX Nationaal Verbond der Textieldetaillanten (Belgium)

NAVEWA Nationale Vereniging der Waterleidingbedrijven (Belgium)

NAVF Norges Almenvitenskapelige Forskningsråd

NAVH National Association of Voluntary Hostels

NAVIGA European Model Ships Federation

NAVL National Anti-Vaccination League

NAVS National Anti-Vivisection Society

NAVSA Syndicat National de Vente et Services Automatiques

NAWAFA North Atlantic Westbound Freight Association

NAWAPA North American Water and Power Alliance

NAWB National Association of Wine and Beer-makers

NAWB National Association of Workshops for the Blind Incorporated

NAWC National Association of Women's Clubs

NAWCH National Association for the Welfare of Children in Hospital

NAWDC National Association of Waste Disposal Contractors Ltd

NAWDOFF National Association of Wholesale Distributors of Frozen Foods

NAWF North American Wildlife Foundation (U.S.A.)

NAWG	National Association of Wheat Growers (U.S.A.)
NAWICS	National Anglo-West Indian Conservative Society
NAWM	National Association of Wool Manufacturers (U.S.A.)
NAWND	National Association of Wholesale Newspaper Distributors
NAWP	National Association of Women Pharmacists
NAWPM	National Association of Wholesale Paint Merchants
NAWTCH	National Association for the Welfare of Children in Hospital
NAWU	National Agricultural Workers Union (U.S.A.)
NAYC	National Association of Young Cricketers
NAYC	National Association of Youth Clubs
NAYO	National Association of Youth Orchestras
NAYSO	National Association of Youth Service Officers
NB	Norges Byforbund
NBA	National Benzole and Allied Products Association
NBA	National Brassfoundry Association
NBAA	National Business Aircraft Association
NBAHMF	National Building and Allied Hardware Manufacturers Federation
NBB	Nederlandse Boekverkopersbond
NBB	Nederlandse Bond van Bouwondernemers
NBBE	National Board for Bakery Education
NBBFP	Nationale Bond der Belgische Filmproducenten
NBBS	Nederlands Bureau voor Buitenlandse Studentenbetrekkingen
NBBZ	Nederlandse Bond van Bad- en Zweminrichtingen
NBC	National Book Council (*now* NBL)
NBC	National Broadcasting Corporation (U.S.A.)
NBC	Nordens Bondeorganisationers Centralråd
NBCK	Nederlandse Bond van Copieerders en Klein-Offsetdrukkers
NBCS	Nederlandse Bond van Christelijke Schilderpatroons
NBDC	National Broadcasting Development Committee
NBER	National Bureau of Economic Research (U.S.A.)
NBF	National Bedding Federation
NBF	Norsk Bibliotekforening
NBF	Norges Bilbransjeforbund
NBF	Norsk Botanisk Forening
NBF	Norsk Brannvern Forening
NBFBV	Nationale Belgische Federatie der Baanvervoerders
NBFU	National Bureau of Fire Underwriters (U.S.A.)
NBIRN	National Bureau of Industrial Research, Nanking (China)
NBKV	Nederlandse Bond van Konijnenfokkers-verenigingen
NBL	National Book League
NBL	Norsk Bibliotekarlag
NBL	Norsk Blomsterdyrkerlag
NBLC	Nederlands Bibliotheek en Lektuur Centrum
NBM	Nederlandse Bond van Makelaars in Onroerende Goederen
NBNI	Nasionale Bounavorsingsinstituut (South Africa)
NBO	Nordic Housing Companies Organization
NBOV	Nederlandse Banketbakkers Ondernemers Vereniging
NBPI	National Board for Prices and Incomes
NBPS	Nederlandse Bond van Patroons in het Steen-, Houtgraniet- en Kunststeenbedrijf
NBR	National Board of Roads and Water (Finland)
NBR	Norske Bedriftavisers Redaktørklubb
NBRI	National Building Research Institute (South Africa)
NBS	National Broadcasting Service (New Zealand)
NBS	National Bureau of Standards (U.S.A.)
NBS	Norsk Biokjemisk Selskap
NBS	Norske Bonde- og Småbrukarlag
NBSS	National Bible Society of Scotland
NBSS	National British Softball Society
NBTPI	National Book Trade Provident Institution
NBU	Nordiska Bankmanaunionen
NBvA	Nederlandse Bond van Assurantie-Agenten
NC	Norsk Cementforening
NCA	National Canners Association (U.S.A.)
NCA	National Coal Association (U.S.A.)

NCA	National Coffee Association of USA
NCA	National Council for Alcoholism
NCA	National Council of Aviculture
NCA	National Cranberry Association (U.S.A.)
NCA	National Cricket Association
NCAA	National Children Adoption Association
NCAB	National Citizen's Advice Bureaux
NCAB	National College der Accountants van België
NCABC	National Citizens' Advice Bureaux Committee
NCACC	National Civil Aviation Consultative Committee
NCAE	National College of Agricultural Engineering
NCAEG	National Confederation of American Ethnic Groups (U.S.A.)
NCAER	National Council of Applied Economic Research (India)
NCAFMW	National Council of Associations of Fresh Meat Wholesalers
NCAI	National Congress of American Indians
NCAI	National Council of American Importers
NCAIE	National Council of the Arts in Education (U.S.A.)
NCAPC	National Center for Air Pollution Control (*of* DHEW) (U.S.A.)
NCAR	National Centre for Atmospheric Research (New Zealand)
NCAR	National Centre for Atmospheric Research (U.S.A.)
NCARB	National Council of Architectural Registration Boards (U.S.A.)
NCASI	National Council of the Paper Industry for Air and Stream Improvement (U.S.A.)
NCAVAE	National Committee for Audio-visual Aids in Education
NCAW	National Council for Animal Welfare
NCB	National Coal Board
NCB	Nationale Confederatie van het Bouwbedrijf (Belgium)
NCB	Nederlandse Consumentenbond
NCB	Nordic Copyright Bureau
NCB	Stichting Nederlandse Centrale voor het Begrafenisbedrijf
NCBA	National Cattle Breeders' Association
NCBA	National Chinchilla Breeders of America
NCBMP	National Council of Building Material Producers
NCBRM	Nederlandse Christelijke Bond van Rijwiel- en Motorhandelaren
NCBT	Nationale Confederatie van de Belgische Textielreiniging
NCBTB	Nederlandse Christelijke Boeren- en Tuindersbond
NCC	National Caravan Council
NCC	National Climatic Center (NOAA)
NCC	National Consumer Council
NCC	National Cotton Council of America
NCC	National Council of Churches in New Zealand
NCCA	Inter-Scandinavian Committee on Consumer Matters (Norway)
NCCA	National Club Cricket Association
NCCA	National Cotton Council of America
NCCAT	National Committee for Clear Air Turbulence (U.S.A.)
NCCD	National Council on Crime and Delinquency (U.S.A.)
NCCE	Northern Counties Co-operative Enterprise (Northern Ireland)
NCCEE	Netherlands Committee for the Common Market
NCCFN	National Coordinating Committee on Food and Nutrition (Philippines)
NCCI	National Committee for Commonwealth Immigrants
NCCIA	North Carolina Crop Improvement Association Inc. (U.S.A.)
NCCK	National Christian Council of Kenya
NCCK	Nederlandse Club voor Chefkoks
NCCL	National Council of Canadian Labour
NCCL	National Council for Civil Liberties
NCCM	National Council of Catholic Men
NCCM	National Council of Concentrate Manufacturers
NCCOP	National Corporation for the Care of Old People
NCCT	National Council for Civic Theatres
NCCV	Nederlandse Cacao en Cacaoproducten Vereniging
NCCW	National Council of Catholic Women
NCD	Netherlands Centrum van Directeuren
NCDB	National Development Credit Agency (Tanzania)
NCDB	Nederlandse Christelijke Drogistenbond

NCDC	National Cooperative Development Association (India)	**NCIP**	Comision Nacional de Productividad Industrial
NCDL	National Canine Defence League	**NCIT**	National Council on Inland Transport
NCDS	National Community Development Service (U.S.A.)	**NCITD**	National Committee for International Trade Documentation (U.S.A.)
NCEA	National Catholic Education Association (U.S.A.)	**NCL**	National Carriers Limited
		NCL	National Central Library
NCEA	North Central Electric Association (U.S.A.)	**NCL**	National Chemical Laboratory (India)
NCEC	National Christian Education Council	**NCLB**	Nederlandse Christelijke Landarbeidersbond
NCERT	National Council of Educational Research and Training (India)	**NCLC**	National Council of Labour Colleges
NCES	National Center for Educational Statistics (U.S.A.)	**NCLIS**	National Commission on Libraries and Information Science (U.S.A.)
NCET	National Council for Educational Technology	**NCM**	National College of Music
		NCMA	National Contract Management Association (U.S.A.)
NCF	National Clayware Federation	**NCMB**	Nigerian Cocoa Marketing Board
NCF	Norges Colonialgrossisters Forbund	**NCMB**	Nordic Council for Marine Biology
NCFC	National Council of Farmer Cooperatives (U.S.A.)	**NCME**	National Council on Measurement in Education (U.S.A.)
NCFM	American National Commission on Food Marketing	**NCMH**	National Committee for Mental Hygiene (U.S.A.)
NCFR	National Council on Family Relations (U.S.A.)	**NCMRED**	National Council on Marine Resources and Engineering Development (U.S.A.)
NCFS	National Conference of Friendly Societies	**NCMV**	Nationaal Christelijk Middenstandsverbond (Belgium)
NCGG	National Committee for Geodesy and Geophysics (Pakistan)	**NCNA**	New China News Agency
NCGGO	National Centrum voor Grasland- en Groenvoederonderzoek	**NCNC**	National Council for Nigeria and the Cameroons
NCGT	National Council of Geography Teachers (U.S.A.)	**NCNL**	Nasionale Chemiese Navorsings-laboratorium (South Africa)
NCGV	Nationaal Centrum voor de Geestelijke Volksgezondheid	**NCOA**	National Council on the Ageing (U.S.A.)
		NCOI	National Council for the Omnibus Industry
NCHEE	National Council for Home Economics Education	**NCOR**	National Committee for Oceanographic Research (Pakistan)
NCHP	Nederlandse Centrale van Hoger Personeel	**NCOS**	Netherlands Christelijk Ondernemersverbond voor het Schildersbedrijf
NCHPTWA	National Clearing House for Periodical Abstracts Service (U.S.A.)	**NCOV**	Nederlands Christelijk Ondernemersverband
NCHS	National Center for Health Statistics (U.S.A.)	**NCPA**	National Cottonseed Products Association (U.S.A.)
NCHSO	National Committee of Hungarian Students Organization	**NCPJ**	Nederlandse Christelijke Plattelands Jongeren Bond
NCHV	Nederlandse Vereniging van Christelijke Handelsreizigers en Handelsagenten	**NCPJB**	Nederlandse Christelijke Plattelands Jongeren Bond
NCIA	National Cavity Insulation Association	**NCPL**	National Centre for Programmed Learning
NCIC	National Cancer Institute of Canada	**NCPTA**	National Confederation of Parent Teacher Associations
NCIH	National Conference on Industrial Hydraulics (U.S.A.)		

NCPUA	National Committee on Pesticide Use in Agriculture (Canada)		**NCTJ**	National Council for the Training of Journalists
NCQR	National Council for Quality and Reliability		**NCTL**	National Commercial Temperance League
NCR	Nationale Coöperatieve Raad		**NCTM**	National Council of Teachers of Mathematics (U.S.A.)
NCRAC	National Community Relations Advisory Council (U.S.A.)		**NCTYL**	National College for the Training of Youth Leaders
NCRD	National Council for Research and Development (Israel)		**NCU**	National Cyclists' Union
NCRL	National Chemical Research Laboratory (S.Africa)		**NCUA**	U.S. National Credit Union Administration
NCRP	National Committee on Radiation Protection (U.S.A.)		**NCUMC**	National Council for the Unmarried Mother and her Child
NCRR	National Center for Resource Recovery (U.S.A.)		**NCUR**	National Committee for Utilities Radio (U.S.A.)
NCRT	National College of Rubber Technology		**NCVA**	National Centre for Voluntary Action (U.S.A.)
NCRV	Nederlandsche Christelijke Radio Vereniging		**NCVCCO**	National Council of Voluntary Child Care Organisations
NCS	National Chrysanthemum Society		**NCW**	National Council of Women of Great Britain
NCSA	National Crushed Stone Association (U.S.A.)		**NCW**	Nederlands Christelijk Werkgeversbond
NCSAW	National Catholic Society for Animal Welfare (U.S.A.)		**NCWA**	National Children's Wear Association
NCSC	National Council on Schoolhouse Construction (U.S.A.)		**NCWC**	National Catholic Welfare Conference (U.S.A.)
NCSE	National Council for Special Education		**NCWCC**	North Central Weed Control Committee (U.S.A.)
NCSI	National Council for Stream Improvement (U.S.A.)		**NCWM**	National Conference on Weights and Measures (U.S.A.)
NCSPS	National Committee for Support of the Public Schools (U.S.A.)		**NCWTD**	National Centrum voor Wetenschappelijke en Technische Documentatie (Belgium)
NCSR	National Council for Social Research (S.Africa)		**NCYA**	National Catholic Youth Association
NCSS	National Cactus and Succulent Society		**NCZ**	Nationale Coöperatieve Zuivelverkoopcentrale
NCSS	National Center for Social Statistics (U.S.A.)		**NDA**	National Dairymens' Association
NCSS	National Council for the Social Studies (U.S.A.)		**NDA**	National Development Association
NCSS	National Council of Social Service, Inc.		**NDAC**	Nuclear Defence Affairs Committee (NATO)
NCSTTO	National Council for the Supply and Training of Teachers Overseas		**NDAGB**	National Darts Association of Great Britain
NCT	National Chamber of Trade		**NDALTP**	Nationale Dienst voor Afzet van Land-en Tuinbouwproduktion
NCTA	National Cable Television Association (U.S.A.)		**NDBI**	National Dairymen's Benevolent Institution
NCTA	National Council for Technological Awards		**NDC**	National Dairy Council (U.S.A.)
NCTAEP	National Committee on Technology, Automation and Economic Progress		**NDC**	National Development Corporation (Tanzania)
NCTD	National College of Teachers of the Deaf		**NDC**	NATO Defence College
NCTET	National Council for Teacher Education and Training		**NDC**	Norsk Designcentrum
			NDCS	National Deaf Children's Society
NCTF	National Check Traders' Federation		**NDEA**	National Defence Education Act (U.S.A.)
			NDEA	National Display Equipment Association

NDF	National Development Foundation (South Africa)
NDF	Norges Drosjeeier-Forbund
NDFA	National Drama Festivals Association
NDFS	National Deposit Friendly Society
NDFTA	National Dried Fruit Trade Association
NDHF	Norges Dame- og Herrefrisørmestres Forbund
NDL	National Diet Library (Japan)
NDMB	National Defense Mediation Board (U.S.A.)
NDMF	National Development and Management Foundation (South Africa)
NDOA	National Dog Owners' Association
NDP	Vereniging De Nederlandse Dagbladpers
NDPA	National Dairy Producers' Association
NDPD	National Democratic Party of Germany
NDPKC	National Domestic Poultry Keepers Council
NDPS	National Data Processing Service
NDRC	National Defence Research Committee (U.S.A.)
NDRI	National Dairy Research Institute (India)
NDS	National Dahlia Society
NDSB	Narcotic Drugs Supervisory Body (*of* UN)
NDV	Netherlands Dendrological Society
NEA	National Education Association (U.K. and U.S.A.)
NEA	Nuclear Energy Agency (OECD)
NEACT	New England Association of Chemistry Teachers (U.S.A.)
NEADEC	Near East Animal Production and Health Development Centre (Lebanon)
NEAFC	North East Atlantic Fisheries Commission
NEAHI	Near East Animal Health Institute
NEAVB	National Employers Association of Vehicle Builders
NEB	National Economic Board (Korea)
NEB	National Electricity Board of the States of Malaysia
NEB	Nederlandse Eiercontrôle Bureau
NEBA	Nederlandse Katholieke Bond van Beroeps-Assurantiebezorgers
NEBF	National Farm Bureau Federation (U.S.A.)
NEBSS	National Examinations Board in Supervisory Studies
NEBUPZA	Nederlands Bureau voor de Uitvoer van Granen, Zaden en Peulvruchten
NEBUTA	Nederlands Bureau voor Technische Hulp
NEC	National Economic Council (Pakistan or Philippines)
NECA	Nigerian Employers Consultative Association
NECC	Near East Council of Churches
NECCTA	National Educational Closed Circuit Television Association
NECIES	North-East Coast Institution of Engineers and Shipbuilders
NECOB-ETRA	Nederlandse Christelijke Ondernemersbond Electrotechniek en Radio
NECSR	North East Coast Ship Repairers
NECTA	National Electrical Contractors Trading Association
NED	Nederlandse Emigratiedienst
NEDA	National Electronics Development Association (New Zealand)
NEDACO	Vereniging Nederlandse Dakpannenfabrikanten Corporatie
NEDC	National Economic Development Council
NEDC	North-East Development Council
NedCBTB	Nederlandse Christelijke Boeren-en Tuindersbond
NEDECO	Nederlands Ingenieursbureau voor Buitenlandse Werken
NEDELSA	Nederlandse Fabrieken van Electrische Schakelapparatuur
NEDERF	Nederlandse Stichting ter Voorbereiding en Uitvoering van het Erfgewassenproject
NEDER-GRES	Nederlandse Vereniging van Gresbuizenfabrikanten
NEDO	National Economic Development Office (*of* NEDC)
NEEB	North-East Engineering Bureau
NEEB	North Eastern Electricity Board
NEEC	National Export Expansion Council (U.S.A.)
NEERI	National Electrical Engineering Research Institute (South Africa)
NEETU	National Engineering and Electrical Trades Union
NEF	Norges Eiendomsmeglerforbund
NEF	New Education Fellowship (International)
NEF	Norsk Elektroteknisk Forening
NEFA	North East Frontier Agency (India)
NEFATO	Vereniging van Nederlandse Fabrikanten van Voedertoevoegingen

NEFC	Near East Forestry Commission
NEFRS	Near East Forest Rangers' School
NEFSG	Northeastern Forest Soils Group (U.S.A. & Canada)
NEFTIC	Northeastern Forest Tree Improvement Conference (U.S.A.)
NEFYTO	Nederlandse Stichting voor Fytofarmacie
NEGB	North Eastern Gas Board
NEGI	National Federation of Engineering and General Ironfounders
NEI	Nederlandsch Economisch Instituut
NEI	Nouvelles Équipes Internationales
NEIMME	North of England Institute of Mining and Mechanical Engineers
NEIS	National Egg Information Service (*now* BEIS)
NEL	National Electronics Council (*formerly* NERC)
NEL	National Engineering Laboratory
NELSAT	National Association of Land Settlement Association Tenants
NEMA	National Electrical Manufacturers (U.S.A.)
NEMEC	Nederlandse Fabrieken van Elektrische en Elektronische Meeten Regelapparatuur
NEMI	North European Management Institute (Norway)
NEMKO	Norges Elektriske Materiellkontrol
NEMO	National Egg Marketing Organisation
NEMOG	Groep Nederlandse Fabrieken van Elektrische Motoren en Generatoren
NEN	Stichting Nederlands Normalisatie-Instituut
NEODA	National Edible Oil Distributors Association
NEOS	New England Ophthalmological Society (U.S.A.)
NEPA	Northeastern Pennsylvania Artificial Breeding Cooperative (U.S.A.)
NEPAL	National Egg Packers Association
NEPP	National Egg and Poultry Promotion
NEPPCO	Northeastern Poultry Producers Council (U.S.A.)
NEPRA	National Egg Producers Retail Association
NEPRO-PHARM	Nederlandse Vereniging van Fabrikanten van Pharmaceutische Producten
NERATU	Groep Nederlandse Fabrieken van Radio-, Televisie- en Muziekapparatuur
NERBA	New England Road Builders' Association
NERC	National Electronics Research Council (*now* NEL)
NERC	National English Rabbit Club
NERC	Natural Environment Research Council
NERC	Regional Conference for the Near East (FAO)
NERO	Near East Regional Office (*of* FAO)
NERRS	New England Röntgen Ray Society (U.S.A.)
NES	National Extension Service (India)
NESBIC	Netherlands Students Bureau for International Cooperation
NESC	Nuclear Engineering and Science Conference
NET	Vereniging Nederlandse Eigen-Textieldruckers
NETAC	Nuclear Energy Trade Associations Conference
NEV	Nederlandsche Entomologische Vereniging
NEVAC	Nederlandse Vacuumvereniging
NEVEC	Nederlandse Economische Vereniging voor de Confectie-Industrie
NEVEHAC	Nederlandse Vereniging van Handelaren in Chemicaliën
NEVEM	Nederlandse Vereniging voor Physical Distribution en Material Management
NEVEMA	Nederlandse Vereniging van Matrassenfakrikanten
NEVEPA	Vereniging van Nederlandse Papierzakken-Fabrikanten
NEVESUCO	Nederlandse Vereniging voor de Suikerwerk- en Chocoladeverwerkende Industrie
NEVEXPO	Nederlandse Vereniging van Exporteurs van Pootaardappelen
NEVI	Nederlands Vlasinstituut
NEVIE	Nederlandse Vereniging voor Inkoop-Efficiency
NEVIM	Nederlandse Vereniging voor International Meubeltransport
NEVO	Nederlandse Volksdansvereniging
NEVOK	Nederlandse Vereniging van Ondernemers in het Kappersbedrift
NEVON	Nederlandse Vereniging van Ondernemers in het Natuursteenbedrijf
NEVRA	Nederlandse Vereniging van Groothandelaren in Rioleringsartikelen
NEWO	Nederlandse Electrotechnische Winkeliers Organisatie
NEZC	New England Zoological Club (U.S.A.)

NFA	National Federation of Anglers
NFA	National Farmers Association (Eire)
NFA	National Fertilizer Association (U.S.A.)
NFA	Norsk Forening for Automatisering
NFAC	National Federation of Aerial Contractors Ltd
NFAC	National Food and Agriculture Council (Philippines)
NFAIS	National Federation of Abstracting and Indexing Services (U.S.A.)
NFB	National Federation of the Blind of the United Kingdom
NFBB	Norsk Forening for Bolig-og Byplanlegging
NFBBB	Nationale Federatie Beroepsverenigingen van Aannemers van Begrafenissen van België
NFBC	National Film Board of Canada
NFBCa	National Film Bureau of Canada
NFBF	Nationale Federatie van de Beroepsfotografie
NFBPM	National Federation of Builders and Plumbers Merchants
NFBS	Committee for Co-operation between the Nordic Research Libraries
NFBSS	National Federation of Bakery Students' Societies
NFBTE	National Federation of Building Trades Employers
NFBTO	National Federation of Building Trade Operatives
NFC	National Freight Corporation
NFCA	National Federation of Community Associations
NFCA	National Foster Care Association
NFCC	National Farm Chemurgic Council (U.S.A.)
NFCDA	National Federation of Civil Defence Associations of Great Britain and the Commonwealth
NFCG	National Federation of Consumer Groups
NFCGA	National Federation of Constructional Glass Associations
NFCI	National Federation of Clay Industries
NFCS	National Federation of Construction Supervisors
NFCSIT	National Federation of Cold Storage and Ice Trades
NFCTA	National Federation of Corn Trade Associations (*now* GAFTA)
NFCTC	National Foundry Craft Training Centre

NFCU	National Federation of Claimants Unions
NFCU	National Federation of Construction Unions
NFD	National Federation of Drapers and Allied Trades, Ltd (Eire)
NFDC	National Federation of Demolition Contractors
NFDC	National Fertilizer Development Centre (U.S.A.)
NFDSP	National Forum on Deafness and Speech Pathology (U.S.A.)
NFE	Nederlandse Vereniging van Fokkers van Edelpelsdieren
NFEA	National Federated Electrical Association
NFEC	National Foundation for Environmental Control (U.S.A.)
NFEGI	National Federation of Engineering and General Ironfounders
NFER	National Foundation for Educational Research in England and Wales
NFETM	National Federation of Engineers' Tool Manufacturers
NFF	National Federation of Fishmongers
NFF	National Froebel Foundation
NFF	Norges Farmaceutiske Förening
NFF	Norges Farvehandlerforbund
NFF	Norske Fiskeredskapfabrikanters Förening
NFF	Norges Fotografforbund
NFF	Norske Forskningsbibliotekarers Förening
NFF	Norsk Fruktgrossisters Forbund
NFF	Norske Fysioterapeuters Forbund
NFFA	National Frozen Food Association (U.S.A.)
NFFC	National Film Finance Corporation
NFFF	National Federation of Fish Friers
NFFMR	Nordisk Förening för Medicinsk Radiologi (Finland)
NFFPT	National Federation of Fruit and Potato Trades, Ltd
NFFQO	National Federation of Freestone Quarry Owners
NFFTU	National Federation of Furniture Trade Unions
NFG	Nordwestdeutsche Futtersaatbaugesellschaft
NFGC	National Federation of Grain Cooperatives (U.S.A.)
NFGS	National Federation of Gramophone Societies

NFHO	National Federation of Homophile Organisations	**NFO**	Nederlandse Federatie van Onderwijs-vakorganisaties
NFHS	National Federation of Housing Societies	**NFO**	Nederlandse Fruittelersorganisatie
NFI	National Federation of Ironmongers (*now* BHF)	**NFOAPA**	National Federation of Old Age Pensioners Associations
NFI	National Fisheries Institute (U.S.A.)	**NFOO**	National Federation of Owner Occupiers Associations
NFI	Naturfreunde-Internationale		
NFIK	Norsk Forening for Industriell Kvalitetskontroll (Norway)	**NFP**	Nederlandse Federatie voor de Handel in Pootaardappelen
NFIKB	Nationale Federatie der Immobilienkamers van België	**NFPA**	National Fire Protection Association (U.S.A.)
NFIM	Norges Forbund for Internasjonale Møbeltransporter	**NFPA**	National Foster Parents Association
NFIMA	Non-Ferrous Ingot Metal Institute (U.S.A.)	**NFPA**	National Flaxseed Processors Association (U.S.A.)
NFIP	National Foundation for Infantile Paralysis (U.S.A.)	**NFPC**	National Federation of Plastering Contractors
NFIR	National Federation of Indian Railwaymen	**NFPDC**	National Federation of Painting and Decorating Contractors
NFISM	National Federation of Iron and Steel Merchants	**NFPDHE**	National Federation of Plumbers and Domestic Heating Engineers
NFJM	National Foundation for Junior Museums (U.S.A.)	**NFPHC**	National Federation of Permanent Holiday Camps, Ltd
NFKHNB	Nationale Federatie der Kamers voor Handel en Nijverheid van België	**NFPO**	National Federation of Property Owners
NFL	Norske Fotoimportørers Landsforbund	**NFPTA**	National Federation of Parent Teacher Associations (*now* NCPTA)
NFLA	National Farm Loan Association (U.S.A.)	**NFPW**	National Federation of Professional Workers
NFLSVN	National Front for the Liberation of South Vietnam	**NFR**	Statens Naturvetenskapliga Forskningsråd
NFLV	National Federation of Licensed Victuallers	**NFRC**	National Federation of Roofing Contractors
NFMA	National Fireplace Makers Association	**NFRI**	National Food Research Institute (South Africa)
NFMP	National Federation of Master Painters and Decorators of England and Wales	**NFRN**	National Federation of Retail Newsagents, Booksellers and Stationers
NFMPS	National Federation of Master Printers in Scotland	**NFRR**	Norsk Forening af Rådgivende Rasjonaliseringsfirmaer
NFMR	National Foundation for Metabolic Research (U.S.A.)	**NFS**	Norsk Fysisk Selskap
NFMR	Norsk Forening for Medicinsk Radiologi	**NFSA**	National Federation of Sea Anglers
NFMS	National Federation of Music Societies	**NFSA**	National Fire Services Association (*now* BFSA)
NFMSLCE	National Federation of Master Steeplejacks and Lightning Conductor Engineers	**NFSAIS**	National Federation of Science Abstracting and Indexing Services (U.S.A.)
NFMTA	National Federation of Meat Traders Associations	**NFSH**	National Federation of Spiritual Healers
NFMWC	National Federation of Master Window Cleaners	**NFSO**	National Federation of Site Operators
		NFSWMM	National Federation of Scale and Weighing Machine Manufacturers
NFNL	Nationale Fisiese Navorsingslaboratorium (South Africa)	**NFT**	National Federation of Textiles (U.S.A.)
NFO	National Freight Organization (U.S.A.)	**NFTA**	National Federation of Taxicab Associations
		NFTA	National Fillings Trades Associations

NFTC	National Foreign Trade Council (U.S.A.)	**NGPR**	Nederlands Genootschap voor Public Relations
NFTF	Norges Kvalitetstekmiske Forening		
NFTMS	National Federation of Terrazzo-Mosaic Specialists	**NGRC**	National Greyhound Racing Club
		NGRH	Nationale Groepering van Ruwe Huiden
NFU	National Farmers' Union	**NGRI**	National Geophysical Research Institute (India)
NFUDCL	National Farmers Union Development Co., Ltd	**NGRS**	National Greyhound Racing Society of Great Britain (*now* NGRC)
NFUS	National Farmers Union of Scotland		
NFVB	Nederlandse Federatie van Verenigingen van Bedrijfspluimveehouders	**NGS**	National Geographic Society (U.S.A.)
		NGSDC	National Geophysical and Solar-Terrestrial Data Center (NOAA)
NFVL	National Federatie van Verenigingen van Laboratorium-assistenten (Belgium)	**NGSF**	Norges Glass-og Stentøihandleres Forbund
NFVT	National Federation of Vehicle Trades	**NGSI**	National Geographical Society of India
NFWB	Nederlandse Federatie van Werkgevers-Organisaties in het Bontbedrijf	**NGT**	National Guild of Telephonists
		NGTE	National Gas Turbine Establishment
NFWG	National Federation of Wholesale Grocers and Provision Merchants	**NGTM**	National Guild of Transport Managers
		NGU	Norges Geologiske Undersökelse
NFWIR	National Federation of Women's Institutes of Rhodesia	**NGUT**	National Group of Unit Trusts
		NGV	Nederlandse Geologische Vereniging
NFWI	National Federation of Women's Institutes	**NGV**	Nederlands Genootschap van Vertalers
NFWPM	National Federation of Wholesale Poultry Merchants	**NGZ**	Naturforschende Gesellschaft in Zürich
NFYFC	National Federation of Young Farmers' Clubs	**NH**	Norges Herredsforbund
		NHA	National Hairdressers' Association
NGA	National Graphical Association	**NHA**	National Horse Association of Great Britain
NGAA	Natural Gasoline Association of America	**NHA**	National Housewives Association
NGB	National Garden Bureau (U.S.A.)	**NHBRC**	National House-Builders Registration Council
NGB	Naturforschende Gesellschaft in Bern		
NGC	National Guild of Co-operators	**NHC**	National Health Council (U.S.A.)
NGC	Nederlands Graancentrum	**NHC**	Nederlandse Hardevezelconventie
NGCAA	National Golf Clubs Advisory Association	**NHDAA**	National Home Demonstration Agents Association (U.S.A.)
NGEA	National Gastroenterological Association (U.S.A.)	**NHF**	National Hairdressers Federation
NGF	National Grocers Federation	**NHF**	Norges Handelstands Forbund
NGF	Norges Grossistforbund	**NHG**	Neue Helvetische Gesellschaft
NGF	Norsk Gartnerforbund	**NHG**	Natuurhistorisch Genootschap im Limburg
NGI	Norsk Gerontologisk Instituut	**NHG**	Nederlands Historisch Genootschap
NGIZ	Nederlandsch Genootschap voor Internationale Zaken	**NHG**	Nederlands Huisarten Genootschap
		NHGA	National Hang Gliding Association
NGL	Nederlands Genootschap van Leraren	**NHIC**	National Home Improvement Council
NGL	Norsk Galvano-Teknisk Landsforening	**NHIF**	Norske Håndverks- og Industribedrifters Forbund
NGL	Norsk Grafisk Leverandørforening		
NGMB	Nigeria Groundnuts Marketing Board	**NHK**	Japan Broadcasting Corporation
NGO	Non-Governmental Organizations		
NGO/OPI	Executive Committee of Non-Governmental Organizations Associated with the United Nations Office of Public Information	**NHM**	Nederlandse Heidemaatschappij
		NHMRCA	National Health and Medical Research Council of Australia

NHOS	National House Owners Society
NHPLO	NATO Hawk Production and Logistics Organization
NHR	Nederlandse Huishoudraad
NHRF	Norsk Hotell- og Restaurantforbund
NHRV	Nederlandse Handelsreizigers en Handelsagent-Vereniging
NHS	National Health Service
NHS	Nordiska Handelsarbetsgivare-Föreningarnas Samarbetskommité
NHSB	National Highway Safety Bureau (U.S.A.)
NHSS	National Home Study Council (U.S.A.)
NHTPC	National Housing and Town Planning Council
NI	Numismatics International (U.S.A.)
NIA	National Irrigation Administration (Philippines)
NIAA	National Institute of Animal Agriculture (U.S.A.)
NIAB	National Institute of Agricultural Botany
NIAE	National Institute of Adult Education
NIAE	National Institute of Agricultural Engineering
NIAESS	National Institute of Agricultural Engineering Scottish Station
NIAG	NATO Industrial Advisory Group
NIAH	National Institute of Animal Health (Japan)
NIAI	National Institute of Animal Industry (Japan)
NIAID	National Institute of Allergy and Infectious Diseases (*of* NIH) (U.S.A.)
NIAM	Nederlands Instituut Agrarisch Marktonderzoek
NIAMAC	Chambre Nationale des Négociants en Gros et Agents Généraux en Machines de Fabrication, Matériel d'Émouteillage, d'Emballage et de Conditionnement pour Toutes Industries (Belgium)
NIAMD	National Institute of Arthritis and Metabolic Diseases (*of* NIH) (U.S.A.)
NIAS	National Institute of Agricultural Sciences (Japan)
NIB	Nordic Investment Bank (Finland)
NIBE	Nederlands Instituut voor het Bank- en Effectenbedrijf
NIBEM	Nationaal Instituut voor Brouwgerst, Mout en Bier
NIBID	National Investment Bank for Industrial Development (Greece)
NIBIN	Netherlands Instituut voor Beleids-Informatie
NIBS	Nippon Institute for Biological Science (Japan)
NIC	National Illumination Committee of Great Britain
NICAMAR	Compañia Nicaraguense Mercantil e Industrial de Ultramar
NICAP	National Investigations Committee on Aerial Phenomena (U.S.A.)
NICB	National Industrial Conference Board (U.S.A.)
NICD	National Institute of Cleaning and Dyeing (U.S.A.)
NICD	National Institute of Community Development (India)
NICD	National Institute of Communicable Diseases (India)
NICE	National Institute of Ceramic Engineers (U.S.A.)
NICEC	National Institute of Careers, Education and Counselling
NICEIC	National Inspection Council for Electrical Installation Contracting
NICEM	National Information Centre for Educational Media (U.S.A.)
NICHA	Northern Ireland Chest and Heart Association
NICHD	National Institute for Child Health and Human Development (*of* NIH)
NICIA	Northern Ireland Coal Importers Association
NICSO	NATA Integrated Communications System Organization
NICSS	Northern Ireland Council of Social Services
NICSSE	National Information Centre for Social Science Education (Australia)
NID	National Institute of Design (India)
NIDA	National Institute of Development Administration (Thailand)
NIDB	Nigerian Industrial Development Bank
NIDC	Nepal Industrial Development Corporation
NIDC	Northern Ireland Development Council
NIDER	Netherlands Institute for Documentation and Registration
NIDFA	National Independent Drama Festivals Association
NIDI	Nederlands Interuniversitair Demografisch Instituut

NIDIG	Netherlands Instituut van Directeuren en Ingenieurs van Gemeentewerken	**NILI**	Nederlands Instituut voor Landbouwkundige Ingenieurs
NIDO	Nationaal Instituut voor Diergeneeskundige Onderzoek (Belgium)	**NILN**	Navorsingsinstituut vir die Leernywerheid (South Africa)
NIDOC	National Information and Documentation Centre (Egypt)	**NILU**	Norsk Institutt for Luftforskning
NIECE	Nigerian International Educational and Cultural Exchange Centre	**NIM**	National Institute of Metallurgy (South Africa)
NIEF	National Ironfounding Employers Federation	**NIMA**	Nederlands Instituut voor Marketing
NIESR	National Institute of Economic and Social Research	**NIMA**	Northern Ireland Ministry of Agriculture
NIF	Nordic Institute of Folklore (Finland)	**NIMAWO**	Nederlands Instituut voor Maatschapplijk Werk Onderzoek
NIF	Nordiska Institutet for Fargforskning	**NIMD**	National Institute of Management Development (Egypt)
NIF	Norske Ingeniörforening (Norway)	**NIMH**	National Institute of Medical Health (U.S.A.)
NIFES	National Industrial Fuel Efficiency Service	**NIMH**	National Institute of Medical Herbalists
NIFOR	National Information Office, Poona (India)	**NIMH**	National Institute of Mental Health (*of* NIH) (U.S.A.)
NIFOR	Nigerian Institute for Oil Palm Research		
NIGC	National Insurance and Guarantee Corporation	**NIMO**	Nederlands Instituut voor Maatschappelijke Opbouw
NIGERCAP	Société Nigérienne de Diffusion d'Appareils Électriques	**NIMR**	National Institute for Medical Research
NIGERLEC	Société Nigérienne d'Électricité	**NIMRA**	National Industrial Materials Recovery Association
NIGER-TOUR	Société Nigérienne pour le Développement du Tourisme et de l'Hôtellerie	**NINB**	National Institute of Neurology and Blindness
NIGGECIBA	Société Nigérienne de Génie Civil et Bâtiment	**NINDB**	National Institute of Neurological Diseases and Blindness (U.S.A.)
NIGMS	National Institute of General Medical Services (*of* NIH)	**NINDS**	U.S. National Institute of Neurological Diseases and Strokes
NIGP	National Institute of Governmental Purchasing (U.S.A.)	**NIO**	National Institute of Oceanography
NIH	National Institute of Hardware	**NIOC**	National Iranian Oil Company
NIH	National Institutes of Health (*of* HEW) (U.S.A.)	**NIOM**	Nordisk Institut for Odontologisk Materialprøvning
NIHAE	National Institute of Health Administration and Education (India)	**NIOPR**	Nigerian Institute for Oil Palm Research
NIHJ	National Institutes of Health, Japan	**NIOSH**	National Institute for Occupational Safety and Health (U.S.A.)
NII	Netherlands Industrial Institute	**NIOZ**	Nederlands Instituut voor Onderzoek der Zee
NIIP	National Institute of Industrial Psychology	**NIP**	National Institute of Psychology (Iran)
NIIR	National Institute of Industrial Research (Nigeria)	**NIP**	Nederlands Instituut van Psycholegen
NIJSI	Vereniging de Nederlandse Ijzer- en Staal-producerende Industrie	**NIPA**	National Institute of Public Administration (Pakistan, Zambia)
NIL	Nederlands Instituut voor Lastechniek	**NIPDOK**	Nippon Dokumentesyon Kyokai
NIL	Norske Interiørarkitekters Landsforening	**NIPG**	Nederlands Instituut voor Praeventieve Geneeskunde
NILCO	National Instituut voor de Landbouwstudie in Congo	**NIPH**	National Institute of Poultry Husbandry
NILFO	Norsk Innkjøpslederforbund	**NIPL**	Nederlands Instituut voor Personeelsleiding
		NIPO	Nederlands Instituut voor de Publieke Opinie en het Marktonderzoek

NIPR	National Institute for Personnel Research (South Africa)	**NITR**	Nigerian Institute of Trypanosomiasis Research
NIR	Belgisch Nationaal Instituut voor Radio-Omroep	**NIV**	Nederlands Instituut voor Volksvoeding
NIRC	National Industrial Relations Court	**NIVA**	Norsk Institutt for Vannforskning
NIRD	National Institute for Research in Dairying	**NIVAG**	Nederlands Instituut van Aannemers Groot-bedrijf
NIRI	National Information Research Institute (U.S.A.)	**NIVB**	Navorsingsinstituut vir die Visserybedryf (South Africa)
NIRIA	Nederlandse Ingenieursvereniging	**NIVE**	Netherlands Institute for Efficiency
NIRNS	National Institute for Research in Nuclear Science	**NIVNO**	Nasionale Instituut vir Vuurpylnavorsing en ontwikkeling (South Africa)
NIRO	Nederlandsche Indisch Instituut voor Rub-beronderzoek	**NIVRA**	Nederlands Instituut van Registeraccoun-tants
NIRR	National Institute for Road Research (South Africa)	**NIVV**	Nederlands Instituut voor Vredesvraag-stukken
NIRRD	National Institute for Rocket Research and Development (South Africa)	**NIWO**	Stichting Nederlandsche Internationale Wegvervoer Organisatie
NIRS	National Institute of Radiological Sciences (Japan)	**NIWR**	National Institute for Water Research (South Africa)
NIRT	National Iranian Radio and Television	**NIWU**	National Industrial Workers Union (U.S.A.)
NIS	Nordiska Ingenjörssamfundet	**NIZO**	Nederlandsche Instituut voor Zuivelon-derzoek
NISCON	National Industrial Safety Conference (*of* ROSPA)	**NJ**	Norsk Journalistlag
NISC	National Industrial Space Committee	**NJ**	Norges Juristforbund
NISEE	National Information Service for Earthquake Engineering (U.S.A.)	**NJA**	National Jewellers' Association
		NJAC	National Joint Advisory Council
NISER	Nigerian Institute for Social and Economic Research	**NJBG**	Nederlandse Jeugdbond ter Bestudering van de Geschiedenis
NISI	National Institute of Sciences of India	**NJC**	National Joint Council for Local Authorities' Administrative, Professional, Technical and Clerical Services
NISRA	National Industrial Salvage and Recovery Association		
NIST	National Institute of Science and Technology (Philippines)	**NJCBI**	National Joint Council for the Building Industry Administrative Council
NISTEX	National Industrial Safety Trade Exhibition (*of* ROSPA)	**NJCC**	National Joint Consultative Committee of Architects, Quantity Surveyors and Builders
NISO	National Industrial Safety Organisation	**NJCEI**	National Joint Council for the Exhibition Industry
NISW	National Institute for Social Work		
NISWT	National Institute for Social Work Training	**NJF**	Nordic Federation of Journalists
NITA	Nicophilic Institute of Tobacco Antiquarians	**NJF**	Nordiske Jordbrugsforskeres Förening
		NJHF	Norges Jernvarehandleres Forbund
NITCs	National Information Transfer Centres	**NJIC**	National Joint Industrial Council for Gas Industry
NITEX	Société Nigérienne des Textiles		
NITHO	Nederlands Instituut voor Toegepast Huishoudkundig Onderzoek	**NJLS**	Norges Jordskiftedommer- og Landmåler-samband
NITO	Norges Ingeniorörganisasjon	**NJN**	Nederlandse Jeugdbond voor Natuurstudie
NITR	National Institute for Telecommunications Research (South Africa)	**NJPA**	New Jersey Pharmaceutical Association (U.S.A.)

NJSHS	New Jersey State Horticultural Society (U.S.A.)	NLA	National Lime Association (U.S.A.)
		NLA	Nigerian Library Association
NJSPE	New Jersey Society of Professional Engineers (U.S.A.)	NLB	National Library for the Blind
		NLC	National Liberal Club
NJU	Nordiska Järnvägsmanna-Unionen	NLC	National Liberation Council (Ghana)
NJV	Nederlandse Juristen-Vereniging	NLCA	Norwegian Lutheran Church of America
NJV	Nederlandse Vereniging van Journalisten	NLCIF	National Light Castings Ironfounders' Federation
NKA	Nordiska Kontaktorganet för Atomenergifragor	NLF	National Liberal Federation
NKB	Nederlandse Kermisbond	NLF	National Liberation Front (South Vietnam)
NKB	Nordiska Kommittén för Byggbestammelser	NLF	Norges Lastebileier-Forbund
NKE	Nordiskt Kollegium för Ekologi	NLF	Norske Litotrykkeriers Forening
NKF	Norges Kjott og Flesksentral	NLH	Norges Landbrukshogskole
NKF	Norsk Kiropraktor Forening	NLHE	National Laboratory for Higher Education (U.S.A.)
NKF	Norsk Kommunalteknisk Forening		
NKF	Norsk Korrosjonsteknisk Forening	NLL	National Lending Library for Science and Technology
NKG	Nordiska Kommissionen för Geodesi		
NKI	Norges Kjemiske Industrigruppe	NLM	National Library of Medicine (U.S.A.)
NKI	Növényvédelmi Kutató Intézet	NLM	Nederlandse Luchtvaart Maatschappij
NKI	Vereniging de Nederlandse Koeltechnische Industrie	NLMA	National Lumber Manufacturers Association (U.S.A.)
NKIM	Nederlands Kali-import Mij	NLMC	National Labour Management Council
NKJ	Nordiska Kontaktorganet för Jordbruks-forskning	NLMGB	National Liberation Movement of Guinea-Bissau
NKK	Nordiska Kulturkommisionen	NLNE	National League of Nursing Education (U.S.A.)
NKK	Nordkalottkommittén		
NKL	Norges Kooperative Landsforening	NLO	National Liberal Organisation
NKLB	Noord-Nederlandse Cooperatieve Eierhandel	NLOGF	National Lubricating Oil and Grease Federation
NKLF	Norges Kolonial- og Landhandelforbund		
NKOV	Nederlands Katholiek Ondernemers Verbond	NLPGA	National LP-Gas Association (U.S.A.)
NKP	Norges Kommunistiske Parti	NLR	National Lucht en Ruimtevaartlaboratorium
NKS	Nederlandse Kastelenstichting	NLRB	National Labour Relations Board (U.S.A.)
NKS	Norsk Keramisk Selskap	NLRY	Nordic Liberal and Radical Youth (Sweden)
NKS	Norsk Khemisk Selskap	NLS	Nordiska Läraorganisationernas Samrad
NKT	Nordiska Kommittén för Trafiksäkerhets-forskning	NLSB	National Land Survey Board (Sweden)
		NLTF	Norsk Landbruksteknisk Forening
NKTF	Nordiska Kommittén för Transport-ekonomisk Forskning	NLU	Naturvåordsverkets Limnologiska Under-sökning
NKTF	Norges Kvalitetstekniske Forening	NLVF	Norges Landbruksvitenskapelige Forskningsrad (Norway)
NKV	Nederlands Katholiek Vakverbond		
NKV	Nordiska Kommittén för Vägtrafiklagstiftung	NLYL	National League of Young Liberals
NKVT	Nederlandsche Katholieke Vereniging van Ondernemers in de Textielhandel	NM	Norsk Musikerforbund
		NMA	National Medical Association (U.S.A.)
NKWV	Nederlands Katholiek Werkgevers Verband	NMAB	Natural Materials Advisory Board of the National Academy of Sciences (U.S.A.)
NL	Norsk Lektorlag		

NMAC	National Medical Audiovisual Center (U.S.A.)	**NMSSA**	Nato Maintenance Supply Services Agency
NMBLA	North Midland Branch of the Library Association	**NMTAS**	National Milk Testing and Advisory Service
NMBS	Nationale Maatschappij e Belgische Spoorwegen	**NMTBA**	National Machine Tool Builders' Association (U.S.A.)
NM–BYGG	Scandinavian Committee on Materials Research and Testing, Subcommittee on Building	**NMTF**	National Market Traders Federation
		NMTFA	National Master Tile Fixers' Association
NMC	National Marketing Council	**NMTS**	National Milk Testing Service (U.S.A.)
NMC	National Mastitis Council (USA)	**NMV**	Nederlandse Malacologische Vereniging
NMCA	National Meat Canners Association (U.S.A.)	**NMWA**	National Mineral Wool Association (U.S.A.)
NMDC	National Mineral Development Corporation (India)	**NNA**	Nigerian National Alliance
NMERI	National Mechanical Engineering Research Institute (South Africa)	**NNA**	Norwegian Nurses Association
		NNBOB	Nieuwe Nederlandse Bond van Ondernemers in het Bouwbedrijf
NMF	Norges Markedføringsforbund	**NNC**	Noord-Nederlandse Co-operatieve
NMF	Norsk Meteorologforening	**NNDC**	New Nigeria Development Company
NMFS	National Marine Fisheries Service (*of* NOAA)(U.S.A.)	**NNDP**	Nigerian National Democratic Party
		NNF	Norsk Nopatisk Forening
NMGC	National Marriage Guidance Council	**NNF**	Northern Nurses Federation (Sweden)
NMHC	National Materials Handling Centre	**NNGA**	Northern Nut Growers Association (U.S.A.)
NMHF	Norges Musikkhandlerforbund	**NNI**	Netherlands Normalisatie-Instituut
NMHRA	National Mobile Homes Residents Association	**NNIL**	Northern Nigeria Investments Ltd
NMIA	National Meteorological Institute of Athens (Greece)	**NNLC**	Ngwane National Liberatory Congress (Swaziland)
		NNML	Norske Naturhistoriske Museers Landsforbund
NMK	Norse Marconi Kompani	**NNP**	Vereniging 'De Nederlandse Nieuwsbladpers'
NMKL	Nordisk Metodik-Komité for Levnedsmidler	**NNPA**	National Newspaper Publishers Association (U.S.A.)
NML	National Federation of Norwegian Milk Producers	**NNRC**	Neutral Nations Repatriation Commission
NML	National Metallurgical Laboratory (India)	**NNRI**	National Nutrition Research Institute (South Africa)
NML	Norske Melkeprodusenters Landsforbund	**NNRO**	Norske Nasjonalkomite for Rasjonell Organisasjon
NML	Norske Murmestres Landsforening		
NMLF	Norsk Maling- og Lakkteknisk Forening	**NNV**	Nederlandse Natuurkundige Vereniging
NMLL	Norsk Musikklaereres Landsforbund	**NNV**	Norges Naturvernforbund
NMMA	National Macaroni Manufacturers' Association (U.S.A.)	**NOAA**	National Oceanic and Atmospheric Administration (U.S.A.)
NMOC	National Marketing Organisation Committee	**NOAACP**	National Organization of African, Asian and Caribbean People
NMPA	National Marine Paint Association	**NOB**	Nationale Organisatie voor het Beroepsgoederenvervoer Wegtransport
NMPC	National Milk Publicity Council	
NMPF	National Milk Producers Federation (U.S.A.)	**NOBIN**	Stichting Nederlands Orgaan voor de Bevordering van de Informatie-verzorging
NMS	National Malaria Society (U.S.A.)	
NMS	Norske Meieriers Salgs Sentral	**NOCI**	Nederlandse Organisatie voor Chemische Informatie
NMS	Norwegian Dairies Sales Centre	
NMSS	National Multiple Sclerosis Society (U.S.A.)	**NOCIL**	National Organic Chemical Industries (India)

NOCOCA	Nouvelle Confiserie Camerounaise
NODA	National Operatic and Dramatic Association
NODC	National Oceanographic Data Centre (U.S.A.)
NOEM	Netherlands Oil and Gas Equipment Manufacturers
NOF	Nordisk Odontologisk Forening
NOFAKI	Norges Farmasoytisk-Kjemiske Industriforening
NOFI	National Oil Fuel Institute (U.S.A.)
NOFM	Nederlandse Overzeese Financierings-Maatschappij
NOFTIG	Nordic Association of Applied Geophysics (Sweden)
NÖG	Nationalökonomische Gesellschaft (Austria)
NOG	Nederlandse Oogheelkundig Gezelschap
NOGA	Nederlandse Organisatie van Glasassuradeuren
NoHaKa	Nederlandse Organisatie van Handelaren in de Kantoormachinebranche
NOIC	National Oceanographic Instrumentation Board (U.S.A.)
NOIL	Naval Ordnance Inspection Laboratory
NOISE	National Organization to Ensure a Sound-controlled Environment (U.S.A.)
NOJFU	Nordiska Järnvägars Forsknings-och Utvecklingsråd
NOK	Nordisk Okonomisk Kvaegavl
NOKIL	Norske Kinoleverandørers Landsforbund
NOKYO	Union of Agricultural Cooperatives (Japan)
NOL	Nederlandse Organisatie van Loonconfectionnairs
NOLPE	National Organisation on Legal Problems of Education (U.S.A.)
NOMA	National Office Management Association (U.S.A.)
NOMI	Norges Medisinalindustris Felleskontor
NOMOFO	Norske Motoroverhalings-verksteders Forbund
NONAS	Negros Occidental National Agricultural School (Philippines)
NOP	Nederlandse Organisatie van Pluimveehouders
NOPA	National Office Products Association (U.S.A.)
NOPHN	National Organisation for Public Health Nursing (U.S.A.)

NOPPMB	Nigeria Oil Palm Produce Marketing Board
NOPWC	National Old Peoples Welfare Council
NORAD	North American Air Defence
NORAD	Norwegian Agency for International Development
NORC	National Opinion Research Centre (U.S.A.)
NORCOFEL	Normalisation et Commercialisation des Fruits et Légumes (International)
NORDAF	Northern Federation of Advertisers Association (Sweden)
NORDEK	Organisation for Nordic Economic Cooperation
NORDEL	Organ för Nordiskt Elkraftsamarbete
NORDINFO	Nordic Council for Scientific Information and Research Libraries (Finland)
NORD-FORSK	Nordiska Forskningsdelegationen
NORD-FORSK	Nordiska Samarbets-organisationen för Teknisk-Naturvetens-kaplig Forskning
NORDGU	Nordic Council of the International Good Templar Youth Federation
NORDICOM	Nordic Documentation Centre for Mass Communication Research
NORDITA	Nordisk Institut för Teoretisk Atomfysik
NORD-PACK	International Packaging Fair
NORDPLAN	Nordic Institute for Social Planning
NORDPLAN	Nordic Institute for Urban and Regional Planning
NORDREFO	Nordiska Arbetsgruppen för Regionalpolitisk Forskning
NORG	Nederlandse Organisatie voor de Radio Groothandel
NORM	National Optimism Revival Movement
NORS	Norwegian Operational Research Society
NORSAM	Nordic Organization for the Care of the Old
NORVEN	Comisión Venezolana de Normas Industriales
NORWAID	Norwegian Aid Society for Refugees and International Development
NOS	Joint Board for the Nordic Research Councils in the National Sciences
NOSA	National Occupational Safety Association (South Africa)
NOSALF	Scandinavian Association for Research on Latin America
NOS-M	Nordiska Samarbertsnämnden för Medicinsk Forskning

NOSO	Norsk Sosionomforbund
NOSOCO	Nouvelle Société Commerciale Sénégalaise
NOSON-TRAM	Nouvelle Société Nationale des Transports Mauritaniens
NOT	Naczelna Organizacja Techniczna w Polsce
NOTBA	National Opthalmic Treatment Board Association
NOTU	Nederlandse Organisatie van Tijdschrift Uitgevers
NOU	Nederlandse Ornithologische Unie
NOV	Nederlandse Orthopaedische Vereniging
NOVA-TRANS	Société Nouvelle d'Exploitation de Transports Combinés
NOVIB	Netherlands Organization for International Development Corporation
NOVO	Nederlandse Organisatie van Oliehandelaren
NOVOK	Nederlandse Organisatie van Olie- en Kolenhandelaren
NOW	National Organization for Women (U.S.A.)
NOWEA	Nordwestdeutsche Ausstellungs-Gesellschaft
NP	Norsk Presseforbund
NPA	National Packaging Association (Australia)
NPA	National Parks Association (U.S.A.)
NPA	National Petroleum Association (U.S.A.)
NPA	National Pigeon Association
NPA	National Planning Association (U.S.A.)
NPA	National Production Authority (U.S.A.)
NPA	Newspaper Publishers Association
NPAC	National Project in Agricultural Communication (U.S.A.)
NPACI	National Production Advisory Council on Industry (U.S.A.)
NPAV	Nederlandse Patholoog Anatomen Vereniging
NPBA	National Pig Breeders' Association
NPC	National Parks Commission
NPC	National Patent Council (U.S.A.)
NPC	National Peace Council
NPC	National Peach Council (U.S.A.)
NPC	National Peanut Council (U.S.A.)
NPC	National Petroleum Council (U.S.A.)
NPC	National Pharmaceutical Council (U.S.A.)
NPC	National Potato Council (U.S.A.)
NPC	NATO Parliamentarians' Conference
NPC	Northern Peoples Congress (Nigeria)
NPCA	National Pest Control Association (U.S.A.)
NPCC	National Projects Construction Corporation (India)
NPD	Nationaldemokratische Partei Deutschlands
NPD	Nuclear Physics Division (of SRC)
NPDMC	National Property Development and Management Company (Tanzania)
NPF	Nederlandse Pluimvee Federatie
NPF	Norske Patentingeniørers Forening
NPF	Norsk Plastforening
NPF	Norsk Psykologforening
NPFA	National Playing Fields Association
NPFC	Northwest Pacific Fisheries Commission
NPFI	National Plant Food Institute
NPFSC	North Pacific Fur Seal Commission
NPG	Nuclear Planning Group (NATO)
NPI	Norsk Produktivitetsinstitut
NPIP	National Poultry Improvement Plant (U.S.A.)
NPL	National Physical Laboratory
NPL	Nederlandse Vereniging voor Produktieleiding
NPL	Norske Pelsskinneksportørers
NPL	Norske Papirhandlers Landsforbund
NPL	Norsk Planteskolelag
NPO	Nederlandse Pluimvee Organisatie
NPPF	National Poultry Producers Federation (U.S.A.)
NPPTB	National Pig Progeny Testing Board
NPRA	National Petroleum Refiners Association
NPRCG	Nuclear Public Relations Contact Group (Italy)
NPRFCA	National Petroleum Radio Frequency Co-ordinating Association (U.S.A.)
NPRL	National Physical Research Laboratory (South Africa)
NPRS	Norske Public Relations Klubb
NPS	National Philatelic Society
NPS	National Pony Society
NPTA	National Paper Trade Association (U.S.A.)
NPU	National Pharmaceutical Union
NPV	Nederlandse Planteziektenkundige Vereniging
NPVLA	National Paint, Varnish and Lacquer Association (U.S.A.)

NPWA	National Pure Water Association
NQBA	National Quality Bacon Association
NRA	National Reclamation Association (U.S.A.)
NRA	National Recreation Association (U.S.A.)
NRA	National Renderers Association (Italy)
NRA	National Rifle Association
NRA	National Rounders Association
NRAC	National Research Advisory Council (New Zealand)
NRAC	National Rural Advisory Council (Australia)
NRAO	National Radio Astronomy Observatory (U.S.A.)
NRB	Natural Resources Board (Rhodesia)
NRC	National Redemption Council (Ghana)
NRC	National Reformation Council (Sierra Leone)
NRC	National Research Council (Canada etc.)
NRC	National Research Council (U.S.A.)
NRC	Niger River Commission
NRCA	Natural Resources Council of America
NRCC	National Republican Congressional Committee (U.S.A.)
NRCD	National Reprographic Centre for Documentation
NRCP	National Research Council of the Philippines
NRCST	National Referral Center for Science and Technology (Library of Congress) (U.S.A.)
NRDB	Natural Rubber Development Association (Malaysia)
NRDC	National Research Development Corporation
NRESA	National Rural and Environmental Studies Association (*now* NAEE)
NRF	Norske Radiofabrikanters Forbund
NRF	Norges Rutebileierforbund
NRFF	National Research Foundation for Fertility (U.S.A.)
NRHA	National Roller Hockey Association
NRHC	National Rivers and Harbours Congress (U.S.A.)
NRIC	National Reserves Investigation Committee
NRIMS	National Research Institute for Mathematical Sciences (South Africa)
NRIND	National Research Institute for Nutritional Diseases (South Africa)
NRIO	National Research Institute for Oceanology (South Africa)

NRIOD	National Research Institute for Occupational Diseases (South Africa)
NRK	Norsk Rikskringkasting
NRL	Naval Research Laboratory (U.S.A.)
NRL	Nelson Research Laboratory
NRL	Norske Radio/TV-handleres Landsforbund
NRL	Norske Rørleggerbedrifters Landsforening
NRL	Nutrition Research Laboratory (India)
NRLA	Nordic Research Librarians' Association
NRLB	Northern Regional Library Bureau
NRLCC	Nordic Research Libraries' Committee of Co-operation
NRLM	National Research Laboratory of Metrology (Japan)
NRLO	National Agricultural Project Administration (U.S.A.)
NRLO	Nationale Raad voor Landbouwkundig Onderzoek
NRLSI	National Reference Library of Science and Invention
NRMA	National Roads and Motorists Association (Australia)
NRMC	National Records Management Council (U.S.A.)
NRPRA	Natural Rubber Producers Research Association
NRPTAA	National Road Passenger Transport Ambulance Association
NRRA	Northern Regional Research Laboratory (U.S.A.)
NRRD	Natural Resources Research Division (*of* UNESCO)
NRS	Nederlandsche Rundvee Stamboek
NRSA	National Rural Studies Association (*now* NRESA)
NRU	Nederlandsche Radio-Unie
NS	Natural Sciences, Department of UNESCO
NS	Newcomen Society
NSA	National Sawmilling Association
NSA	National Sheep Association
NSA	National Shellfisheries Association (U.S.A.)
NSA	National Skating Association of Great Britain
NSA	National Slag Association (U.S.A.)
NSA	Nederlands Studenten Akkoord
NSA	Norsk Svineavlslag

NSA	Norwegian Gerontological Society
NSAA	National Sulphuric Acid Association
NSAC	National Society for Autistic Children
NSACS	National Society for Abolition of Cruel Sports
NSAE	National Society for Art Education
NSAS	National Smoke Abatement Society
NSB	Norwegian State Railways
NSBA	National Sheep Breeders' Association (*now* NSA)
NSBA	National Silica Brickmakers' Association
NSC	National Safety Council (U.S.A.)
NSC	National Security Council (U.S.A.)
NSC	National Seeds Corporation (India)
NSC	National Sporting Club
NSC	Nutrition Society of Canada
NSCA	National Safety Council of Australia
NSCA	National Society for Clean Air
NSCN	National Society of Children's Nurseries
NSCR	National Society for Cancer Relief
NSDAP	Nationalsozialistische Deutsche Arbeiterpartie
NSDB	National Science Development Board (Philippines)
NSDC	National Space Development Centre (Japan)
NSDF	National Social Democratic Front (South Vietnam)
NSDO	National Seed Development Organisation
NSE	National Society of Epileptics
NSE	Nottingham Society of Engineers
NSEI	Norsk Selskap for Elektronisk Informasjonsbehandling
NSES	National Society of Electrotypers and Stereotypers
NSF	National Science Foundation (U.S.A.)
NSF	Nederlandse Sport Federatie
NSF	Nordens Skogsägareorganisationers Forbund
NSF	Norske Sivilokonomers Forening
NSF	Norsk Skuespillerforbund
NSF	Norsk Sykepleierforbund
NSFF	Norsk Selskap for Fotografi
NSFGA	Nova Scotia Fruit Growers Association (Canada)
NSFGB	National Ski Federation of Great Britain
NSFRC	National Soil and Fertiliser Research Committee (U.S.A.)
NSG	Norsk Sau- og Geitalslag
NSG	Nouvelle Société du Gabon
NSGA	National Sand and Gravel Association (U.S.A.)
NSGPMA	National Salt Glazed Pipe Manufacturers' Association
NSGT	Non-Self Governing Territories
NSH	Nouvelle Société Helvétique
NSHC	North Sea Hydrographic Commission
NSHEB	North of Scotland Hydro-Electric Board
NSI	National Sugar Institute (India)
NSI	Neytandasamtökin (Consumers Union of Iceland)
NSI	Norsk Senter for Informatik
NSIA	National Security Industrial Association (U.S.A.)
NSIC	National Small Industries Corporation (Tanzania)
NSICC	North Sea International Chart Commission
NSKO	Nationaal Secretariaat van het Katholiek Onderwijs
NSL	National Sporting League
NSL	Norske Skofabrikkers Landssammenslutning
NSLF	Norske Sporveiers og Lokalbaners Forening
NSMF	Norske Sykkel- og Mopedfabrikanters Forening
NSMHC	National Society for Mentally Handicapped Children
NSMP	National Society of Master Patternmakers
NSMR	National Society for Medical Research (U.S.A.)
NSNS	National Society of Non-Smokers
NSO	Nederlandse Sigarenwinkeliers-Organisatie
NSOA	Nouvelles Savonneries de l'Ouest Africain
NSODCC	North Sumatra Oil Development Corporation (Japan)
NSP	National Society of Painters
NSP	Nederlandse Sport Pers
NSP	Nylands Svenska Lantbruksproducentförbund
NSPA	Nova Scotia Pharmaceutical Association (Canada)
NSPB	National Society for the Prevention of Blindness (U.S.A.)

NSPCC	National Society for Prevention of Cruelty to Children	**NTC**	Nigerian Tobacco Company
NSPE	National Society of Professional Engineers (U.S.A.)	**NTDA**	National Trade Development Association
		NTDA	National Tyre Distributors Association
NSPI	National Society for Programmed Instruction (U.S.A.)	**NTDRA**	National Tire Dealers and Retreaders Association (U.S.A.)
NSPS	National Sweet Pea Society	**NTEA**	National Tax Equality Association (U.S.A.)
NSPI	National Society for Performance and Instruction (U.S.A.)	**NTEC**	National Traction Engine Club
		NTETA	National Traction Engine and Tractor Association
NSPRI	Nigerian Stored Products Research Institute	**NTF**	Nationalföreningen för Trafiksakerhetens Främjande
NSPWSND	National Society of Provincial Wholesale Sunday Newspaper Distributors		
		NTF	Norske Tannlaegeforening
NSR	Nederlandse Studenten Raad	**NTFC**	National Television Film Council (U.S.A.)
NSR	Nordiska Skogsarbets-studieernas	**NTFI**	Norsk Tekstil Forsknings Instituut
NSRA	National Smallbore Rifle Association	**NTG**	Nachrichten-Technische Gesellschaft im VDE
NSRA	Nuclear Safety Research Association (Japan)		
NSRB	National Security Resources Board (U.S.A.)	**NTG**	Nederlandse Tandheelkundig Genootschap
NSRC	National Shoe Retailers' Council	**NTH**	Norges Tekniske Hogskole
NSRDC	National Space Science Data Center (U.S.A.)	**NTHF**	Norske Turisthotellers Forening
NSRF	Norges Statsautoriserte Revisorers Forening	**NTI**	Norsk Treteknisk Institutt
NSRF	Nova Scotia Research Foundation (Canada)	**NTIAM**	National Swedish Testing Institute for Agricultural Machinery
NSRG	Northern Science Research Group (Canada)	**NTIS**	National Technical Information Service (U.S.A.) (*formerly* CFSTI)
NSRI	Nelspruit Subtropical Research Institute (South Africa)		
NSS	National Society of Stenotypists	**NTNF**	Norges Teknisk-Naturvitenskapelige Forskningsråd
NSS	National Speleological Society (U.S.A.)		
NSS	Nordisk Kommittén för Samordning av Elektriska Säkerhetsfragor	**NTO**	Nederlandse Tegelhandelaren-Organisatie
		NTOG	National Tourist Organisation of Greece
NSSA	National School Sailing Association	**NTPC**	National Technical Planning Committee (Sudan)
NSSE	National Society for the Study of Education (U.S.A.)		
		NTPS	National Turf Protection Society
NSSL	National Seed Storage Laboratory (U.S.A.)	**NTR**	Nordiska Trafiksakerhetsrådet
NSTA	National Science Teachers' Association (U.S.A.)	**NTR**	Nordiska Träskyddsrädet
		NTRL	National Telecommunications Research Laboratory (South Africa)
NSTC	National Shade Tree Conference (U.S.A.)		
NSTU	Nova Scotia Teachers Union	**NTS**	Nederlandsche Televisie Stichting
NSVV	Nederlandse Stichting voor Verlichtingskunde	**NTS**	Nordiska Tidningsutgivarnas Samarbetsnämnd
		NTS	Norske Trevarefabrikkers Servicekontor
NSWMA	National Soybean Crop Improvement Council (U.S.A.)	**NTSAC**	New Technical and Scientific Activities Committee (*of* IEEE)
NT	Nederlands Textielinstituut		
NTA	National Technical Association (U.S.A.)	**NTSB**	National Transportation Safety Board (U.S.A.)
NTA	National Trolleybus Association		
NTA	National Tuberculosis Association (U.S.A.)	**NTSC**	National Television Systems Committee (U.S.A.)
NTC	National Lending Library and the American National Translations Centre		
		NTSK	Nordiska Tele-Satelit Kommitten

NTT	Nippon Telegraph and Telephone Public Corporation (Japan)	**NUI**	National University of Ireland
NTTF	Norsk Tekstil Teknisk Forbund	**NUIW**	National Union of Insurance Workers
NTTK	Nordisk Turisttrafik-Kommitte	**NUJ**	National Union of Journalists
NTU	National Taiwan University (China)	**NULC**	National Union of Liberal Clubs
NTUC	Nigerian Trade Union Congress	**NULMW**	National Union of Lock and Metal Workers
NTUC	Nyasaland Trade Union Congress	**NULO**	National Union of Labour Organisers
NTZ	Nederlandse Vereniging voor de Teelt van en de Handel in Tuinbouwzaden	**NULV**	National Union of Licensed Victuallers
NUAAW	National Union of Agricultural and Allied Workers	**NULWAT**	National Union of Leather Workers and Allied Trades
NUAB	Italian National Union against Blasphemy	**NUM**	National Union of Manufacturers
NUAT	Nordisk Union for Alkoholfri Trafik	**NUM**	National Union of Mineworkers
NUAW	National Union of Agricultural Workers	**NUMA**	National Underwater and Marine Agency (U.S.A.)
NUBE	National Union of Bank Employees	**NUMAB**	Nederlandsche Unie van Metaalgieterijen en Aanwerwante Bedrijven
NUBSO	National Union of Boot and Shoe Operatives (*now* NUFLAT)	**NUMAS**	National Union of Manufacturers Advisory Service, Ltd
NUCLEX	International Nuclear Industrial Fair and Technical Meetings	**NuMOV**	Nah- und Mittelost-Verein
NUCO	National Union of Co-operative Officials (*now* NACO)	**NUPBPW**	National Union of Printing, Bookbinding and Paper Workers
NUCR	Nouvelle Union Corporative des Résineux	**NUPE**	National Union of Public Employees
NUCUA	National Union of Conservative and Unionist Associations	**NUR**	National Union of Railwaymen
		NURA	National Union of Ratepayers Associations
NUDBTW	National Union of Dyers, Bleachers and Textile Workers	**NURC**	National Union of Retail Confectioners (*now* RCA)
NUEA	National University Extension Association (U.S.A.)	**NURT**	National Union of Retail Tobacconists
NUF	Norges Urmakerforbund	**NUS**	National Union of Seamen
NUFAG	Northern Union of Farmers' Groups (Thailand)	**NUS**	National Union of Students of the United Kingdom
NUFCW	National Union of Funeral and Cemetery Workers	**NUSAS**	National Union of South African Students
NUFFIC	Netherlands University Foundation for International Co-operation	**NUSMW-CHDE**	National Union of Sheet Metal Workers Coppersmiths, Heating and Domestic Engineers
NUFLAT	National Union of the Footwear, Leather and Allied Trades	**NUSS**	National Union of School Students
NUFSO	National Union of Funeral Service Operators	**NUSS**	National Union of Small Shopkeepers
NUFTIC	Nuclear Fuels Technology Information Center (*of* ORNL) (U.S.A.)	**NUSUK**	National Union of Students of the United Kingdom
NUFTO	National Union of Furniture Trade Operatives	**NUT**	National Union of Teachers
NUGMW	National Union of General and Municipal Workers	**NUTA**	National Union of Tanganyika Workers
		NUTAE	Nuffield Unit of Tropical Animal Ecology (East Africa)
NUGSAT	National Union of Gold, Silver and Allied Trades	**NUTG**	National Union of Townswomen's Guilds
		NUTGW	National Union of Tailors and Garment Workers
NUHW	National Union of Hosiery Workers	**NUTI**	Nationale Unie der Technische Ingenieurs (Belgium)

NUTN	National Union of Trained Nurses	**NVG**	Nederlandse Vereniging voor Gezinscrediet
NUTS	National Union of Track Statisticians	**NVGA**	National Vocational Guidance Association (U.S.A.)
NUU	Nordic Union of Young Conservatives		
NUVB	National Union of Vehicle Builders	**NVGD**	Nederlandsche Vereniging van Gramofoonplaten-handelaren
NUVO	Nederlandse Unie van Opticiens		
NUVU	Nederlandse Unie van Ondernemers in het Uitvaartverzorgingsbedrijf	**NVGI**	Nederlandse Vereniging van Gramofoonplaten Importeurs en Fabrikanten
NUWA	National Unemployed Workers Association	**NVGZ**	Nederlandsche Vereniging van Grind- en Zandhandelaren
NUWDAT	National Union of Wallcoverings, Decorative and Allied Trades	**NVHT**	Nederlandse Vereniging voor Herpetologie en Terrariumkunde "Lacerta"
NUWWE	National Union of Water Works Employees	**NVIB**	Nederlandse Vereniging voor de Industriële Bakkerij
NVA	Nederlandsche Vereniging van Antiquaren		
NVA	Nederlandse Vereniging van Assurantie-bezorgers	**NVJ**	Nederlandse Vereniging van Journalisten
		NVK	Nederlandse Vereniging van Keuken- en Voedingdeskundigen
NVALA	National Viewers and Listeners Association		
NVB	Nederlandse Vereniging voor Biochemie	**NVKL**	Nederlandse Vereniging van Ondernemingen op het Gebied van de Koudetechniek en Luchtbehandeling
NVBA	Nederlandse Vereniging van Bedrijfs-archivarissen		
NVBB	Nationale Vereniging voor Beveiliging tegen Brand	**NVL**	Nederlandse Vereniging voor Lastechniek
		NVLG	Nederlandse Vereniging van Leveranciers van Grootkeukenapparatuur
NVBF	Nordiska Vetenskapliga Bibliotekarieför-bundet		
NVBL	Nederlandse Vereniging ter Bevordering van het Levensverzekeringswezen	**NVLP**	Nederlandse Vereniging van Lucht- en Ruimtevaart-Publicisten
		NVM	Nederlandse Vuilafvoer Maatschappij
NVBV	Nationaal Verbond van Belgische Verpleeg-sters	**NVMA**	National Veterinary Medical Association
NVC	Nederlands Verpakkingscentrum	**NVMW**	Nederlandse Vereniging van Maatschappelijk Werkers
NVC	Nederlands Vrouwen Comité	**NVNB**	Nederlandse Vereniging van Nachtveiligheids-diensten en Bewakingsbedrijven
NVD	Nederlandse Vereniging van Diëtisten		
NVE	Nederlandse Vereniging voor Ergonomie	**NVNI**	Nasionale Voedingnavorsingsinstituut (South Africa)
NVEV	Nederlandse Vrouwen Electriciteits-vereniging		
NVEW	Nederlandse Vereniging van Electrotechnische Werkgevers	**NVOB**	Nederlandse Vereniging van Ondernemers op Brandbeveil Gebied
		NVOS	Nederlandse Vereniging voor Orthodontische Studie
NVF	National Vitamin Foundation (U.S.A.)		
NVF	Nederlandse Vereniging van Fruitteelers	**NVOZ**	Nederlandse Vereniging van Ongevallen- en Ziektenverzekeraars
NVF	Norske Vaskeriers Forening		
NVF	Norske Ventilasjons-entreprenores Forening	**NVP**	Nederlandse Vereniging voor Personeelbeleid
NVFF	Nederlandse Vereniging voor Fysiologie en Farmacologie	**NVPH**	Nederlandsche Vereniging van Postzegelhan-delaren
NVFK	Nederlandse Vereniging-Federatie voor Kunststoffen	**NVR**	Nederlandse Vereniging van Rubber-fabrikanten
NVFL	Nederlandse Vereniging van Fabrikanten van Landbouwwerktuigen	**NVR**	Nederlandse Vereniging voor Ruimtevaart
		NVRD	Nederlandse Vereniging van Radio en TV Detailhandelaren
NVG	Nederlandse Vereniging voor Geodesie		
NVG	Nederlandse Vereniging voor Gerontologie	**NVRD**	Nederlandse Vereniging van Reinigings-directeuren

NVRL	Nederlandse Vereniging van Radiologisch Laboraten		**NVWFT**	Nederlandse Vereniging voor de Weten-schappelijke
NVRS	National Vegetable Research Station		**NVWH**	Nederlandse Vereniging van Werkgevers in het Heibedrijf
NVRSA	National Vegetable Research Station Association		**NWA**	North West Airlines (U.S.A.)
NVS	Nederlandse Vereniging van Schoolmeubelfabrikanten		**NWC**	New World Coalition (U.S.A.)
NVS	Nederlandse Vereniging voor Stralings-hygiene		**NWCA**	National Women Citizens Association
			NWCC	National Weed Committee of Canada
NVS	National Vegetable Society		**NWDA**	National Wholesale Druggist Association (U.S.A.)
NVSH	Nederlandse Vereniging voor Sexuele Hervorming		**NWEB**	North Western Electricity Board
NVSKPT	National Verbond der Syndikale Kamer der Praktici in de Tandheelkunde		**NWF**	National Wildlife Federation (U.S.A.)
			NWF	Norske Wallboard-fabrikkers Forening
NVT	Nederlandse Vereniging van Toneel-kunstenaars		**NWGA**	National Wholesale Grocers Alliance
			NWGA	National Wool Growers Association (U.S.A.)
NVTL	Nederlandse Vereniging Techniek in de Landbouw		**NWGA**	National Wool Growers Association (South Africa)
NVTO	Nederlandse Vereniging voor Tekenon-derwijs		**NWGB**	North Western Gas Board
			NWIC	National Wheat Improvement Committee (U.S.A.)
NVTS	Nederlandse Vereniging van Technici op Scheepvartgebied		**NWKV**	Nasionale Wolkwekersvereniging van Suid-Afrika
NVUA	Nederlands Vereniging van Universiteits Artsen		**NWMA**	National Wool Marketing Corporation (U.S.A.)
NVV	Nationaal Verbond der Vlaswevers (Belgium)		**NWPC**	Nordic Wood Preservation Council
NVV	Nederlands Verbond van Vakverenigingen		**NWPO**	Northwest Pacific Oceanographers
NVVA	Nederlandse Vereniging van Automobielassuradeuren		**NWRC**	National Weather Records Center (*of* ESSA) (U.S.A.)
NVVB	Nationale Vereniging voor Beveiliging tegen Brand (Belgium)		**NWRLS**	North Western Regional Library System
NVvGT	Nederlandse Vereniging van Gieterijtechnici		**NW&SCA**	National Water and Soil Conservation Organisation (New Zealand)
NVvIJ	Nederlandse Vereniging van Handelaren in Ijzerwaren		**NWTEC**	National Wool Textile Export Corporation
NVVK	Nederlandse Vereniging voor Koeltechniek		**NWU**	National Worker Union (Jamaica)
NVVL	Nederlandse Vereniging voor Luchttrans-port		**NYAM**	New York Academy of Medicine
			NYAS	New York Academy of Sciences
NVvL	Nederlandse Vereniging voor Luchtvaart-techniek		**NYES**	New York Entomological Society
			NYHA	National Yacht Harbour Association
NVvN	Nederlandse Vereniging van Neurochirurgen		**NYHA**	New York Heart Association
NVVT	Nederlandse Vereniging van Verftechnici		**NYL**	Norges Yrkeslaererlag
NVvV	Nederlandse Vereniging voor Vlaggenkunde		**NYLC**	National Young Life Campaign
NVVW	Nederlandse Vereniging tot Verbetering van het Welsumer		**NYSE**	New York Stock Exchange
NVvW	Nederlandse Vereniging van Wiskun-deleraren		**NYSEM**	New York Society of Electron Microscopists
NVWB	Nederlandse Vereniging van Wegenbouwers		**NYSPA**	New York State Pharmaceutical Association
NVWE	Nederlandse Vereniging van Electrotechnische Werkgevers		**NYSSIM**	New York State Society of Industrial Medicine

YT	Landsforeningen Norske Yrkestegners
NYTC	National Youth Temperance Council
NYUIMS	New York University Institute of Mathematical Sciences
NYZS	New York Zoological Society
NZAB	New Zealand Association of Bacteriologists
NZAEI	New Zealand Agricultural Engineering Institute
NZAPMB	New Zealand Apple and Pear Marketing Board
NZASc	New Zealand Association of Scientists
NZB	Netherlands Dairy Bureau
NZBC	New Zealand Broadcasting Corporation
NZBS	New Zealand Broadcasting Service
NZBTO	New Zealand Book Trade Organization
NZCER	New Zealand Council for Educational Research
NZDA	New Zealand Department of Agriculture
NZDA	New Zealand Dietetic Association
NZDCS	New Zealand Department of Census and Statistics
NZDLS	New Zealand Department of Lands and Survey
NZDSIR	New Zealand Department of Scientific and Industrial Research
NZEI	New Zealand Electronics Institute
NZES	New Zealand Ecological Society
NZFL	New Zealand Federation of Labour
NZFMRA	New Zealand Fertilizer Manufacturers Research Association
NZFP	New Zealand Forest Products Ltd
NZFRI	New Zealand Forest Research Institute
NZFS	New Zealand Forest Service
NZGA	New Zealand Grassland Association
NZGenS	New Zealand Genetical Society
NZGS	New Zealand Geographical Society
NZIA	New Zealand Institute of Architects
NZIAS	New Zealand Institute of Agricultural Science
NZIC	New Zealand Institute of Chemistry
NZIE	New Zealand Institution of Engineers
NZIER	New Zealand Institute of Economic Research
NZIF	New Zealand Institute of Foresters
NZIIA	New Zealand Institute of International Affairs

NZIM	New Zealand Institute of Management
NZIMP	New Zealand Institute of Medical Photography
NZInstW	New Zealand Institute of Welding
NZIRE	New Zealand Institute of Refrigeration Engineers
NZJCB	New Zealand Joint Communications Board
NZLA	New Zealand Library Association
NZMS	New Zealand Meteorological Service
NZNAC	New Zealand National Airways Corporation
NZNCOR	New Zealand National Committee on Oceanic Research
NZNRAC	New Zealand National Research Advisory Council
NZOI	New Zealand Oceanographic Institute
NZPOA	New Zealand Purchasing Officers Association
NZR	Vereniging Nationale Ziekenhuisraad
NZSA	New Zealand Society of Accountants
NZSA	New Zealand Statistical Association
NZSAP	New Zealand Society of Animal Production
NZSCA	New Zealand Soil Conservation Association
NZSI	New Zealand Standards Institute
NZSLO	New Zealand Scientific Liaison Office
NZSSS	New Zealand Society of Soil Science
NZVA	New Zealand Veterinary Association
NZWCC	New Zealand Weed Control Conference
NZWIRI	New Zealand Wool Industries Research Institute

O

OAA	Ontario Association of Architects (Canada)
OAA	Organisation des Nations Unies pour l'Alimentation et l'Agriculture
OAA	Orient Airlines Association (Philippines)
OAAA	Outdoor Advertising Association of Australia Inc.
ÖAAB	Österreichischer Arbeiten- und Angestelten-bund
OAAC	Outdoor Advertising Association of Canada

OAAPS	Organisation for Afro-Asian Peoples Solidarity	**OBAA**	Oil Burning Apparatus Association
OAAS	Ontario Association of Agricultural Societies (Canada)	**OBAE**	Office des Bois de l'Afrique Équatoriale (Gabon)
OAC	Oceanic Affairs Committee	**OBAP**	Office Belge pour l'Accroissement de la Productivité
OAC	Ontario Agricultural College (Canada)	**OBCE**	Office Belge du Commerce Extérieur
OAC	Outdoor Advertising Council	**OBEA**	Office Belge de l'Économie et de l'Agriculture
OACI	Organisation de l'Aviation Civile Internationale	**OBI**	Office du Baccalauréat International
OAD	Offices Agricoles Départementaux (supprimés)	**OBRA**	Overseas Broadcasting Representatives Association
ÖAeV	Österreichische Äerosol-Vereinigung	**OBSA**	Organización Boliviana de Sanidad Agropecuaria
OAF	Oljeselskapenes Arbeidgiverforening	**OCA**	Organización de Cooperativas de América
OAGB	Osteopathic Association of Great Britain	**OCAA**	Office Central des Associations Agricoles du Finistère et des Côtes-du-Nord
OAH	Organization of American Historians		
OAIA	Organisation des Agences d'Information d'Asie	**OCAM**	Organisation Commune Africaine et Mauricienne (*formerly* UAMCE)
ÖAL	Österreichischer Arbeitsring für Lärmbekämpfung	**OCAMM**	Organisation Commune Africaine, Malgache et Mauricienne
OAMA	Oil Appliance Manufacturers Association	**OCAS**	Organization of Central American States
OAMCAF	African and Malagasy Coffee Organisation	**OCAW**	Oil, Chemical and Atomic workers International Union (U.S.A.)
OAMCE	Organisation Africaine et Malgache de Coopération Économique (*now* OCAM)	**OCB**	Organisation Camerounaise de la Banane
OAMJTB	Organisation pour l'Afrique des Mouvements de Jeunesse et du Travail Bénévole	**OCBN**	Organisation Commune Benin-Niger des Chemins de Fer et des Transports
OAMPI	Office Africain et Malgache de la Propriété Industrielle	**OCCA**	Oil and Colour Chemists Association
OANA	Organisation of Asian News Agencies	**OCCGE**	Organisation de Coopération contre les Grandes Endémies
OAP	Office Algérien de Publicité	**OCCGEAC**	Organisation de Co-ordination et de Co-opération pour la Lutte Contre des Grandes Endémies en Afrique Centrale (*now* OCEAC)
OAP	Organisation Asiatique de la Productivité		
OAPEC	Organization of Arab Petroleum Exporting Countries		
OAPEP	Organisation Arabe des Pays Exportateurs de Pétrole (Kuwait)	**OCCMP**	Office Centrafricain de Commercialisation des Pierres et Métaux Précieux
OAPI	Organisation Africaine de la Propriété Intellectuelle (Cameroon)	**OCDE**	Organisation de Cooperation et de Développement Économique (*formerly* OEEC)
OAS	Organization of American States	**OCDN**	Dahomey-Niger Common Organisation
OAS	Ohio Academy of Science (U.S.A.)	**OCE**	Office de Commercialisation et d'Exportation (Morocco)
OAU	Organisation of African Unity		
ÖAV	Österreichischer Alpenverein	**OCEAC**	Organisation de Coordination pour la Lutte Contre des Endémies en Afrique Centrale
ÖAV	Österreichischer Apothekerverband		
ÖAV	Österreichische Arbeitsgemeinschaft für Volksgesundheit	**OCEC**	Oficio Central de Educación Católicos (Chile)
OAW	Österreichische Akademie der Wissenschaften	**OCFF**	Ordre des Conseils Fiscaux de France et d'Outre-Mer
		OCFT	Office du Chemin de Fer Transcamerounais
OB	Ordnance Board	**ÖCG**	Österreichische Computer Gesellschaft

OCH	Office Congolais de l'Habitat
OCI	Oficina Central de Información (Venezuela)
OCIBU	Office des Cultures Industrielles du Burundi
OCIC	Office Catholique International du Cinéma
OCIC	Office Chérifien Interprofessionel des Céréales
OCIMF	Oil Companies International Marine Forum
OCIPE	Office Catholique d'Information sur les Problèmes Européens
OCIRU	Office des Cafés Indigènes du Rwanda et Burundi
OCLA	Organisation Commune de Lutte Anti-Acridienne (*now* OCLALAV)
OCLAE	Organizacion Continental Latino-Americana de Estudiantes
OCLALAV	Organisation Commune de Lutte Antiacridienne et de Lutte Antiaviaire (Senegal)
OCLAV	Organisation Commune de Lutte Anti-Avaire (Africa) *now* OCLALAV
OCM	Ordo Constantini Magni
OCMA	Oil Companies' Material Association
OCMI	Organisation Consultative Maritime Inter-gouvernementale
OCP	Offices des Céréales Panifiables (Syria)
OCPCA	Oil and Chemical Plant Constructors Association
OCPLACS	Ontario Co-operative Program in Latin American and Caribbean Studies (Canada)
OCRA	Office Commercial du Ravitaillement et de l'Agriculture (Belgium)
OCRA	Office de Coopération Radiophonique
OCRPI	Office Central de Répartition des Produits Industriels
OCRS	Organisation Commune des Régions Sahariennes
OCRTA	Office du Chemin de Fer Transgabonais
OCS	Organ de Contrôle des Stupéfiants (UNO)
OCT	Associated Overseas Countries and Territories
OCT	Office du Commerce de la Tunisie
OCTI	Office Central des Transports Internationaux par Chemins de Fer
OCTPC	Organization for Cooperation of Socialist Countries in the domain of Tele- and Postal Communications (U.S.S.R.)

OCTRF	Ontario Cancer Treatment and Research Foundation (Canada)
OCUFA	Ontario Confederation of University Faculty Associations (Canada)
OCW	Opzoekingscentrum voor de Wegenbouw (Belgium)
OD	Office of Distribution (U.S.A.)
ODA	Official Development Assistance (*of* OECD)
ODA	Ontario Dental Association (Canada)
ODA	Overseas Development Administration
ODAMAP	Office Dahoméen des Manutentions Portuaires
ODBA	Oregon Dairy Breeders Association (U.S.A.)
ODC	Overseas Development Council (U.S.A.)
ODCA	Organización Demócrata Cristiana de América
ODCBA	Oxford and District Cattle Breeders Association
ODECA	Organización de Estados Centramericanos
ODEF	Office National de Développement et d'Exploitation des Ressources Forestières (Togo)
ODEPA	Oficina de Planificación Agrícola (Chile)
ODEPA	Organizacion Deportiva Panamericana
ÖDG	Österreichische Dermatologische Gesellschaft
ODI	Open Door International for the Economic Emancipation of the Woman Worker
ODI	Organisation Interaméricaine de Défense
ODI	Overseas Development Institute
ODM	Ministry of Overseas Development (*incorp. former* Department of Technical Co-operation)
ODSA	Overseas Development Service Association
ODSBA	Oxford Down Sheep Breeders Association
ODTA	Organisation for the Development of African Tourism
ODUCAL	Organización de Universidades Católicas de América Latina
ÖDV	Österreichische Detektiv-Verband
OEA	Organisation of European Aluminium-Smelters
OEA	Organización de los Estados Americanos
OEAS	Organisation Europäischer Aluminium Schmelzhutten
OEB	Ondervakgroep Export van Bloembollen

OEBC	Organisation Européenne de Biologie Cellulaire
OEBI	Oficina de Estadísticas Balleneras Internacionales
OEBM	Organisation Européenne de Biologie Moléculaire
OECA	Organisation des États Centro–Américains
OECD	Organisation for Economic Co-operation and Development (*formerly* OEEC)
OECE	Organisation Européenne de Coopération Économique (*now* OECD)
OECEI	Oficina de Estudio para la Colaboración Económica Internacional (Argentina)
OECL	Ordre des Experts Comptables Luxembourgeois
OECL	Organisation Européenne des Industries de la Conserve de Légumes
OE – CMT	Organisation Européenne de la Confédération Mondiale du Travail
OECQ	Organisation Européenne pour le Contrôle de la Qualité
OEEC	Organisation for European Economic Co-operation (*now* OECD)
OEEPE	Organisation Européenne d'Études Photogrammétriques Expérimentales
OEF	Organisation of Employers Federations and Employers in Developing Countries
OEFLEI	Verband Österreichischer Fleischervereinigungen
OEHI	Organisai Exportir Hasilbumi Indonesia
OEI	Oficina de Educación Ibero-americana
OEI	Organisation Européenne d'Information
OEICCF	Organisation Européenne des Industries des Confitures et Conserves de Fruits
ÖEKV	Österreichischer Energiekonsumenten-Verband
OEMOLK	Österreichischer Molkerei- und Käsereiverband
OEPP	Organisation Européenne et Méditerranéenne pour la Protection des Plantes
OER	Office Européen de Radiodiffusion
OERS	Organisation des États Riverains du Sénégal (*now* OMVS)
OERS	Organisation Européenne de Recherches Spatiales
OERTC	Organisation Européenne de Recherche sur le Traitement du Cancer
OESO	Organisatie voor Economische Samenwerking en Ontwikkeling
OETB	Offshore Energy Technology Board
OEUFSJT	Organisation Européenne des Unions de Foyers et Services pour les Jeunes Travailleurs
OEVA	Office de l'Expérimentation et de la Vulgarisation Agricoles (Tunisia)
OEWS	Oesterreichische Stickstoffwerke AG, Linz (Austria)
OFA	Office Arabe de Presse et de Documentation (Syria)
OFALAC	Office Algérien d'Action Économique et Touristique
OFAR	Office of Foreign Agricultural Relations (U.S.A.)
OFBEC	Office Franco-Britannique d'Études et de Commerce
OFC	Overseas Food Corporation
OFCA	Organisation des Fabricants de Produits Cellulosiques Alimentaires de la CEE
OFCF	Overseas Farmers Co-operative Federation Ltd
OFE	Organization de Flora Europaea
OFEROM	Office Central des Chemins de Fer d'Outre-Mer
OFESAUTO	Oficina Española de Aseguradores de Automoviles
OFFINTAC	Offshore Installations Technical Advisory Committee
OFFRO	Office of Foreign Relief and Rehabilitation Operations (U.S.A.)
ÖFG	Österreichische Forschungsgesellschaft für Philatelie und Postgeschichte
OFI	Orientation à la Fonction Internationale
OFIAMT	Office Fédéral de l'Industrie, des Arts et Métiers et du Travail (Switzerland)
OFICEMA	Oficina Central Maritima
OFIGAN	Oficina Nacional de Ganaderia (Costa Rica)
OFIPLAN	Oficina de Planificación (Costa Rica)
OFITEC	Office Tunisien de l'Expansion Commerciale et du Tourisme
OFITOMEP	Office International de Reseignements des Fabricants de Toiles Métalliques pour Papeteries
ÖFLEI	Verband Österreichischer Fleischervereinigungen
OFNACOM	Office National du Commerce (Congo)

OFR	Oliebranchens Foellesreproesentation
OFRS	Office Français de Recherches Sous-Marines
OFT	Oljeeldningstekniska Föreningen
OFTEL	Office Technique des Éleveurs
OG	Organisation Gestosis (Switzerland)
OGABI	Omnium Gabonais de Développement Immobilier
OGB	Österreicher Gewerkschaftbund
OGDB	Österreichische Gesellschaft für Dokumentation und Bibliographie
OGDI	Österreichischer Gesellschaft für Dokumentation und Information
OGE	Österreichische Gesellschaft für Ernährungsforschung
OGEA	Organisation & Gestion de l'Entreprise Agricole
OGEFA	Österreichische Gesellschaft für Arbeitstechnik und Betriebsrationalisierung
OGEW	Österreichische Gesellschaft für Erdölwissenschaften
OGF	Oslo Geofysikeres Forening
OGf M	Österreichische Gesellschaft für Musik
OGFT	Österreichische Gesellschaft für Weltraumforschung und Flugkörpertechnik
OGG	Österreichische Geographische Gesellschaft
OGH	Österreichische Gesellschaft für Holzforschung
OGHMP	Österreichische Gesellschaft für Hygiene, Mikrobiologie und Praventivmedizin
OGI	Österreichische Gesellschaft für Informatik
OGI	Österreichische Giesserei-Institut
OGP	Österreichische Gesellschaft für Politikwissenschaft
OGRR	Oesterreichische Gesellschaft f. Raumforschung und Raumplanung
OGS	Österreichische Gesellschaft für Strassenwesen
OGSI	Österreichische Gesellschaft für Statistik und Informatik
OHA	Ontario Horticultural Association (Canada)
OHE	Office of Health Economics
OHEG	Austrian Hard Cheese Export Company
OHFI	Österreichisches Holzforschungsinstitut
OHI	Organisation Hydrographique Internationale
OHKV	Österreichischer Heilbäder- und Kurorteverband

OIAC	Organisation Inter-Africaine du Café
ÖIAG	Österreichische Industrie-Verwaltungs A.G.
ÖIAV	Österreichischer Ingenieur- und Architekten-Verein
ÖIB	Österreichischer Imkerbund
OIC	International Coffee Organization
OIC	Organisation Interaméricaine du Café
OIC	Organisation Internationale Catholique
OIC	Organisation Internationale du Commerce
OICC	Office International du Cacao et du Chocolat
OICI	Oficina Internacional Católica de la Infancia
OICI	Omnium Immobilier de Côte-d'Ivoire
OICI	Organización Interamericana de Cooperación Intermunicipal
OICM	Office Intercantonal de Contrôle des Médicaments (Switzerland)
OICM	Organisation Internationale pour la Coopération Médicale
OICMA	Organisation Internationale pour le Contrôle Criquet Migrateur Africain
OICNM	Organisation Intergouvernementale Consultative de la Navigation Maritime
OICRF	Office International du Cadastre et Régime Foncier
OICS	Institute of Colonial Studies
OICS	Organe International de Contrôle des Stupéfiants
OIE	Organisation Internationale des Employeurs
OIE	Office International des Epizootics
OIEA	Office International pour l'Enseignement Agricole
OIEA	Organismo Internacional de Energia Atómica
OIEC	Office International de l'Enseignement Catholique
OIEC	Organisation Internationale d'Échanges Culturelles
OIEP	Office International d'Échange de Produits
OIETA	Office Inter-États du Tourisme Africain
ÖIF	Österreichisches Institut für Formgebung
ÖIFR	Österreichisches Institut fur Raumplanung
OIG	Organisation Intergouvernementale
OIJ	Organisation Internationale des Journalists
OILB	Organisation Internationale de Lutte Biologique contre les Animaux et les Plantes Nuisibles

OIML	Organisation Internationale de Métrologie Légale
OIN	Organisation Internationale de Normalisation
OINA	Oyster Institute of North America
OING	Organisations Internationales Non-Gouvernementales
OIP	Organisation Internationale de la Paléobotanique
OIP	Organización Internacional de Periodistas
OIP	Société Belge d'Optique et d'Instruments de Précision
OIPA	Organisation Internationale pour la Protection des Oeuvres d'Art
OIPC	Organización Internacional de Policia Criminal
OIPC	Organisation Internationale de Protection Civile
OIPEEC	Organisation Internationale pour l'Étude de l'Endurance des Câbles
OIPN	Office International pour la Protection de la Nature
OIPQA	Oficina Internacional Permanente de Química Analítica para los Alimentos Humanos y Animales
ÖIR	Österreichisches Institut für Raumplanung
OIR	Inter-American Radio Office
OIR	Organisation Internationale pour les Réfugiés
OIRP	Organisation Internationale de Régies Paléobotanique
OIRSA	Organismo Internacional Regional de Sanidad Agropecuaria (Central America)
OIRT	Organisation Internationale de Radiodiffusion et Télévision
OIS	Office of Investigatory Services (U.S.A.)
OIS	Organisation Internationale du Sucre
OISA	Office of International Scientific Affairs (U.S.A.)
OISCA – INT	Organisation for Industrial, Spiritual and Cultural Advancement International
OISE	Ontario Institute for Studies in Education (Canada)
OISS	Organización Iberoamericana de Seguridad Social
OISTT	International Organization of Scenographers and Theatre Technicians
OISTV	Organisation Internationale pour la Science et la Technique du Vide
OIT	Organisation International du Travail
OITAF	Organizzazione Internationale dei Transporti a Fune
OITRA	Organizacion Internacional de Trabajadores de Radio y Television de las Americas
OIUC	Organización Internacional de las Uniones de Consumidores
OIV	Office International du Vin
ÖIV	Österreichisches Institut für Verpackungswesen
OIVST	Organisation Internationale pour la Science et la Technique du Vide
OJIF	Ordre des Jurisconsultes Internationaux de France
OJU	Oceania Judo Union (Australia)
OK	Oljekonsumenternas Förbund
OK	Oppikoulunopettajien Keskusjärjestö
ÖKEV	Österreicherischer Klub für Englische Vorstehkunde
OKISZ	National Handicrafts Co-operative Society (Hungary)
ÖKL	Österreichisches Kuratorium für Landtechnik
OKL	Osuuspankkien Keskusliitto
ÖKV	Österreichischer Krankenflegeverband
ÖKW	Österreichisches Kuratorium für Wirtschaftlichkeit
OL	Office of Labour (U.S.A.)
OL	Ovnstøperienes Landforening
OLADE	Latin American Energy Organization
OLAP	Organizacion Latino-Americaine para Promocion de los Ciegos y Deficientes Visuales
OLAS	Organización Latinoamericana de Solidaridad (Cuba)
OLAVU	Organización Latinoamericana del Vino y de la Uva
OLC	Overseas Liaison Committee of American Council on Education
OLCP – EA	Organisation de Lutte Contre le Criquet Pèlerin dans l'Est Africain
ÖLMA	Östschweizerisch Land- und Milchwirtschaftliche Austellung
OLML	Our Lady's Missionary League
ÖLV	Österreichischer Lehrerverband
OMA	Oilskin Manufacturers Association of Great Britain Ltd

OMA	Overall Manufacturers Association of Great Britain	OMS International	Oriental Missionary Society International
OMA	Overseas Mining Association	OMVA	Office de Mise en Valeur Agricole (Morocco)
OMAAEEC	Organisation Mondiale des Anciens et Anciennes Élèves de l'Enseignement Catholique	OMVS	Organisation pour la Mise en Valeur du Fleuve Sénégal
OMAI	Organisation Mondiale Agudas Israel	OMVVM	Office de Mise en Valeur de la Vallée de la Medjerda (Tunisia)
OMASD	Office of Management Appraisal and Systems Development (U.S.A.)	OMW	Oberrheinische Mineralölwerke GmbH
OMBKE	Országos Magyar Bányászati és Kohaszati Egyesület	ÖN	Österreichisches Normungsinstitut
OMBVI	Office Malien du Bétail et de la Viande	ONA	Overseas National Airways (U.S.A.)
OMC	Organisation Mondiale du Commerce (UNO)	ONAA	Office National Anti-Acridien
OMCI	Organisation Intergouvernementale Consultative de la Navigation Maritime	ONAF	Office National des Forêts (Congo)
		ONAH	Office National des Hydrocarbures (Guinée)
OMECOMS	Organisation pour le Mécanographie la Compatibilité et la Secretariat (Ivory Coast)	ONAREST	Office National de la Recherche Scientifique et Technique (Cameroon)
OMEF	Office Machines and Equipment Federation	ÖNB	Österreichische Nationalbibliothek
OMEP	Organisation Mondiale pour l'Éducation Préscolaire	ONBG	Office National des Bois du Gabon
		ONCA	Office National de Commercialisation Agricole (Gabon)
OMF	Office of Marketing Facilities (U.S.A.)	ONCAD	Office National de Coopération et d'Assistance pour le Développement (Sénégal)
OMFP	Officine Meccan. Ferroviarie Pistoiesi		
OMG	Österreichische Mathematische Gesellschaft	ONCPA	Office Nationale de Commercialisation des Produits Agricoles (Central Africa, Congo)
OMG	Österreichische Mineralogische Gesellschaft		
OMGE	Organisation Mondiale de Gastro-Entérologie	OND	Office National des Diamants (Central Africa)
		ONDAH	Office National des Débouchés Agricoles et Horticoles (Belgium)
OMIPE	Office Mondial d'Information sur les Problèmes d'Environnement		
		ONDEPA	Organización Nacional de Profesionales Agropecuarios (Colombia)
OMIS	Organisation Mondiale de l'Image et du Son		
OMKDK	Országos Müszaki Könyvtár és Dokumentációs Központ, Budapest	ONERA	Office National d'Études et de Recherches Aéronautiques
OMM	Organisation Météorologique Mondiale	ONERN	Oficina Nacional de Evaluacion de Recursos Naturales (Peru)
OMMSA	Organisation of Museums, Monuments and Sites in Africa (Ghana)	ONF	Office National des Forêts (France, Central Africa)
ÖMOLK	Österreichischer Molkerei- und Käsereiverband		
		ONG	Organisations Non Gouvernementales
OMPA	Organizacion para el Mejoramiento de la Produccion Azucarera (Cuba)	ÖNG	Österreichische Gesellschaft für Nuclearmedizin
OMPE	Organisation Mondiale de la Profession Enseignante	ONGC	Oil and Natural Gas Commission (India)
		ONGT	Organisation Non-Gouvernementale de Portée Transnationale
OMPI	Organisation Mondiale de la Propriété Intellectuelle		
		ONHA	Office National de l'Huilerie d'Abèche (Tchad)
OMPSA	Organisation Mondiale pour la Protection Sociale des Aveugles		
		ONI	Office National d'Immigration
OMS	Office of Marketing Services (U.S.A.)	ONI	Office National des Irrigations (Morocco)
OMS	Organisation Mondiale de la Santé	ONIA	Office National Industriel de l'Azote (now EMC)

ONIB	Office National Interprofessionnel du Blé
ONIBEV	Office National Interprofessionnel du Bétail et des Viandes
ONIC	Office National Interprofessionnel des Céréales
ONISEP	Office National d'Information sur les Enseignements et les Professions
ONL	Office National du Lait et de ses Dérivés
ONM	Office National Météorologique
ONMR	Office National de la Modernisation Rurale (Morocco)
ÖNORM	Österreichischer Normenausschuss
ONR	Office of Naval Research (U.S.A.)
ONRA	National Office of Agrarian Reform (Algeria)
ONRAP	Oficina Nacional de Racionalizacion y Capacitacion de la Administracion Publica (Peru)
ONRD	Office National de la Recherche et du Développement (Zaire)
ONRI	Orde van Nederlandse Raadgevende Ingenieurs
ONS	Oriental Numismatic Society
ONSS	Office National de la Sécurité Sociale (Belgium)
ONU	Organisation des Nations Unies
ONUC	Organisation des Nations Unies au Congo
ONUDI	Organización de las Naciones Unidas para el Desarrollo Industrial
ONUDI	Organisation des Nations Unies pour le Développement Industriel
ONULP	Ontario New Universities Library Project (Canada)
ONUST	Organisme des Nations Unies Chargé de la Surveillance de la Trève (en Palestine)
OOA	Orde van Organisatiekundigen en-Adviseurs
OOMOTO	Universal Love and Brotherhood Association (Japan)
OOPS	Organismo de Obras Públicas y Socorro de las Naciones Unidas para los Refugiados de Palestina en el Cercano Oriente
OPA	Office of Price Administration (U.S.A.)
OPAC	Office des Produits Agricoles de Costermansville (Zaire)
OPAK	Office des Produits Agricoles du Kivu (Zaire)
ÖPAK	Österreichische Patentanwaltskammer
OPAM	Office des Produits Agricoles du Mali
OPANAL	Organisme pour l'Interdiction des Armes Nucléaires en Amérique Latine (Mexico)
OPAS	Office des Produits Agricoles de Stanleyville (Zaire)
OPAS	Operational Assistance
OPAT	Office des Produits Agricoles du Togo
OPC	Overseas Press Club of America
OPCD	Organisation pour la Planification de la Coopération au Développement
OPE	Omilos Pedagogikon Erevnon Kyprou
OPEC	Organization of Petroleum Exporting Countries
OPEG	OEEC Petroleum Emergency Group
OPEI	Office National de Promotion d'Entreprise Ivoirienne
OPEIU	Office and Professional Employees International Union (U.S.A.)
OPEM	Office National pour la Promotion de l'Exportation (Petites et Moyennes Entreprises)
OPEP	Organisation des Pays Exportateurs de Pétrole
OPEV	Office de Promotion de l'Entreprise Voltaïque
ÖPEV	Österreichischer Patentinhaber- und Erfinderverband
OPEX	UN Programme for the Provision of Operational Executive and Administrative Personnel
ÖPG	Österreichische Physikalische Gesellschaft
OPGC	Oil Palm Growers Council (Malaysia)
OPIC	Organización Internacional Permanente de la Carne
OPIC	Overseas Private Investment Corporation (U.S.A.)
OPICBA	Office Professionnal des Industries et Commerces du Bois et de l'Ameublement
OPMA	Overseas Press and Media Association
OPOSA	Organizacion de la Patata del Pirineo Occidental
OPPEM	Organizacion para la Protección de las Plantas en Europa y en al Mediterráneo
OPPI	Organisation of Pharmaceutical Producers of India
ÖPRG	Österreichische Public-Relations-Gesellschaft
OPRS	Oil Palm Research Station (*Now* WAIFOR)
OPS	Organisation Panaméricaine de la Santé

OPTULA	Oikeuspoliittinen Tutkimuslaitos
OPUS	Office des Publications Scientifiques de Langue Française
OPVN	Office des Produits Vivriers du Niger
ÖPWZ	Österreichisches Zentrum für Wirtschaftlichkeit
ÖPZ	Österreichisches Produktivitäts-Zentrum (Austria)
ORA	Office des Renseignements Agricoles
ORA	Organisation Régionale Asienne (of CISL)
ORAF	Organisation Régionale Africaine de la CISL
ÖRAK	Osterreichischer Rechtsanwaltkammertag
ORAMEI	Oeuvre Reine Astrid de la Mère et de l'Enfant Indigènes (Zaire)
ORANA	Organisme de Recherches sur l'Alimentation et la Nutrition Africaine
ORAP	Organisation Régionale de l'Orient pour l'Administration Publique
ORB	Observatoire Royal de Belgique
ORB	Operational Research Branch (U.S.A.)
ORCA	Ocean Resources Conservation Association
ORCA	Organisme Européen de Recherches sur la Carie
ORCD	Organisation for Regional Co-operation and Development (Iran, Pakistan, Turkey)
ORD	Organisme Régional de Développement du Nord Mossi (Upper Volta)
ORDINEX	International Organisation of Experts
ORE	Organisation Régionale Européenne de la CISL
ORE	Ornitologia Rondo Esperantlingva
ORE	Union Internationale des Chemins de Fer: Office de Recherches et d'Essais
OREALC	Oficina Regional de Educación para América Latina y el Caribe (Chile)
OREAM	Organisation d'Études d'Aires Métropolitains
ORES	European Society for Opinion Surveys and Market Research (Denmark)
ORESCO	Overseas Research Council
ORF	Ontario Research Foundation (Canada)
ÖRF	Österreichischer Rundfunk
ORGALIME	Organisme de Liaison des Industries Métalliques et Électriques Européennes
OR(I)C	Oceanographic Research (International) Committee
ORINS	Oak Ridge Institute of Nuclear Studies (U.S.A.)
ORIT	Organización Regional Interamericana de Trabajadores
ORLEIS	Office Régional Laïque d'Éducation par l'Image et par le Son
ORNAMO	Association of Finnish Designers
ORNL	Oak Ridge National Laboratory (U.S.A.)
ORRRC	Outdoor Recreation Resources Review Commission (Australia)
ORS	Operational Research Society
ORSA	Operations Research Society of America
ORSI	Operations Research Society of India
ORSI	Operations Research Society of Ireland
ORSIS	Operations Research Society of Israel
ORSJ	Operations Research Society of Japan
ORSTOM	Office de la Recherche Scientifique et Technique d'Outre-Mer
ORT	Organisation – Reconstruction – Travail, Union Mondiale
ORTF	Office de la Radiodiffusion-Télévision Française (formerly RTF)
ORTHO-BANDA	Vereniging tot het Behartigen van de Belangen van de Nederlandse Orthopedisten en Bandagisten
ORTHOMA	Nederlandse Bond van Orthopaedisch Maatschoenmakers
ORTPA	Oven-Ready Turkey Producers' Association
ORTS	Office de la Radiodiffusion et Télévision Sénégalaise
OS	Office of Supply (U.S.A.)
OSA	Optical Society of America
OSA	Organic Soil Association of Southern Africa
OSAS	Overseas Service Aid Scheme
OSCAS	Office of Statistical Coordination and Standards (Philippines)
OSCE	Office Statistique des Communautés Européennes
OSCO	Oil Service Company of Iran
OSE	Union Mondiale pour la Protection de la Santé des Populations Juives et Oeuvres de Secours aux Enfants
OSEC	Office Suisse d'Expansion Commerciale
OSFAS	Overseas Students Fee Awards Scheme (of ODA)
ÖSGK	Österreichische Studiengesellschaft für Kybernetik
OSHE	Office pour le Soutien de l'Habitat Économique (Ivory Coast)

OSHR	Organisme Spécialisé d'Habitat Rural		**OTAN**	Organisation du Traité de l'Atlantique-Nord (NATO)
OSIC	International Offshore Suppliers Information Centre		**OTAN**	Organisation of Tropical American Nematologists (Porto Rico)
OSIC	Overseas Spinning Investment Company Ltd.		**OTASE**	Organisation du Traité pour la Défense Collective de l'Asie du Sud-Est
OSIS	Office of Science Information Service (U.S.A.)		**OTC**	Organisation for Trade Co-operation
OSJD	Organisation for the Collaboration of Railways (Poland)		**OTCA**	Overseas Technical Cooperation Agency (Japan)
OSL	International Order of Saint Luke the Physician		**OTI**	Organisación de la Televisión Iberoamericana
OSLAM	Organización de Seminarios Latinoamericanos		**OTI**	Organizzazione Tecnica Internazionale
OSNZ	Ornithological Society of New Zealand		**OTIPI**	Associazione Italiana delle Agenzie di Pubblicità a Servizio Completo
OSO	Offshire Supplies Office		**OTIU**	Overseas Technical Information Unit
OSPA	Organisation Sanitaire Pan-Américaine		**OTK**	Co-operative Wholesale Association (Finland)
OSPAAL	Organisation de Solidarité des Peuples d'Afrique, d'Asie et d'Amérique Latine (Cuba)		**OTL**	Organización de la Televisión Iberoamericana (Mexico)
OSR	Organisation for Scientific Research (Indonesia)		**OTPN**	Opolskie Towarzystwo Przyjaciól Nauk
OSRB	Overseas Services Resettlement Bureau		**OTR**	Office des Transports par Route (Belgium)
OSRO	Office for the Sahelian Relief Operation (FAO)		**OTRACO**	Office d'Exploitation des Transports Coloniaux (Zaire)
OSRD	Office of Scientific Research and Development (U.S.A.)		**OTRAN**	Ocean Test Ranges and Instrumentation Conference (Honolulu)
OSSA	Office of Space Science and Applications (*of* NASA)		**OTS**	Office of Technical Services (U.S.A.)
OSShD	Organisation pour la Collaboration des Chemins de Fer		**OTS**	Organization for Tropical Studies (Costa Rica)
OST	Organisation Scientifique du Travail		**OTU**	Office of Technology Utilization (*of* NASA)
OSTAC	Ocean Science and Technology Advisory Committee (*of* NSIA)		**OTUA**	Office Technique pour l'Utilisation de l'Acier
OSTI	Office for Scientific and Technical Information (*formerly* D.S.I.R.)		**OTUS**	Office Tunisien de Standardisation
			ÖTVV	Österreichischer Transport-Versicherungs-Verband
OSTIV	Organisation Scientifique et Technique Internationale du Vol à Voile		**OUA**	Organisation de l'Unité Africaine
OSTP	Office of Scientific and Technical Personnel (OECD)		**OUAAT**	Organisation Universelle d'Associations d'Agents de Tourisme
OSTS	Official Seed Testing Station		**OV**	Optometristen Vereniging
OSUK	Ophthalmological Societies of the United Kingdom		**ÖVA**	Gesellschaft für den Volkskundeatlas in Österreich
OSWEP	Overseas Student Welfare Expansion Programme (British Council)		**OVAC**	Overseas Visual Aid Centre
			ÖVE	Österreichischer Verband für Elektrotechnik
OSZH	National Co-operative Credit Institute (Hungary)		**OVEIP**	Organisatie Verenigde Exporteurs van Indonesische Producten
OTA	World Touring and Automobile Organization		**ÖVFG**	Österreichischer Verband für Flüssiggas
OTAAI	Oficina Técnica de Asuntos Agrícolas Internacionales (Venezuela)		**ÖVG**	Österreichische Verkehrswissenschaftliche Gesellschaft
			OVM	Onderlinge Verzekeringsmaatschappij

ÖVP	Österreichische Volkspartei
OVRIJ	Organisatie van Rand-en IJsselmeervissers
ÖVS	Österreichischer Verband für Strahlenschutz
OVSL	Organisation Voltäique des Syndicats Libres
ÖVZ	Österreichisches Verpackungszentrum
OWAEC	Organization for West African Economic Co-operation
ÖWG	Österreichische Werbegesellschaft
OWRC	Ontario Water Resources Commission (Canada)
OWRT	Office of Water Research and Technology (U.S.A.)
ÖWWV	Österreicherischer Wasserwirtschaftsverband
OXEXPORT	Landbrugets Kvaeg- og Kødsalg
OXFAM	Oxford Committee for Famine Relief
ÖZEPA	Österreichische Vereinigung der Zellstoff- und Papierchemiker und Techniker
OZONE	International Bureau of Atmospheric Ozone

P

PA	Paintmakers' Association of Great Britain
PA	Direction de la Production Agricole
PA	Parapsychological Association (U.S.A.)
PA	Publishers' Association
PAA	Potato Association of America
PAA	Population Association of America
PAAA	Pan American Association of Anatomy
PAAAC	Pan-American Agricultural Aviation Centre
PAABS	Pan American Association of Biochemical Societies
PAAT	Programa Ampliado de Asistencia Técnica (see ETAP)
PAC	Packaging Association of Canada
PAC	Pan American Highway Congresses
PAC	Permanent Agricultural Committee (*of* ILO)
PACB	Pan-American Coffee Bureau
PACCIOS	Conseil Régional Panaméricain (*of* CIOS)
PACCS	Pan American Cancer Cytology Society
PACD	Presidential Arm on Community Development (Philippines)

PACDIS	Pacific Area Communicable Disease Information Service (Philippines)
PACE	Philippine Association of Civil Engineers
PACEHOPE	Fachverband der Papier-, Zellulose-, Holzstoff- und Pappenindustrie Österreichs
PACES	Political Action Committee for Engineers and Scientists (U.S.A.).
PACRA	Pottery and Ceramics Research Association (N.Z.)
PACS	Primary Agricultural Credit Societies (India)
PACT	Private Agencies Collaboration Together (U.S.A.)
PADF	Pan American Development Foundation
PADOG	Plan d'Aménagement et d'Organisation Générale de la Région Parisienne.
PAEC	Pakistan Atomic Energy Commission
PAF	Papirindustriens Arbeidsgiverforening
PAF	Petroleumbranschens Arbetsgivareförbund
PAFA	Pan-American Festival Association
PAFC	Philippine-American Financial Commission
PAFIE	Pacific Asian Federation of Industrial Engineering
PAFLU	Philippine Association of Free Labour Unions
PAFMECA	Pan African Freedom Movement of East and Central Africa
PAFMECSA	Pan-African Freedom Movement for East, Central and Southern Africa (*now* OAU)
PAG	Protein-Calorie Advisory Group of the United Nations System
PAGB	Poultry and Egg Producers Association of Great Britain Ltd
PAGB	Proprietary Association of Great Britain
PAGC	Port Area Grain Committee
PAGENACI	Participation Générale Africaine de la Côte-d'Ivoire
PAHEF	Pan American Health and Education Foundation (U.S.A.)
PARC	Pacific-Asia Resources Center (Japan)
PAHMC	Pan-American Homeopathic Medical Congress
PAHO	Pan American Health Organization
PAID	Pan-African Institute for Development
PAIGC	African Party for the Independence of Portugese Guinea and Cape Verde
PAIGH	Pan-American Institute of Geography and History

PAIMEG	Pan-American Institute of Mining Engineering and Geology	**PAPF**	Philippine Association for Permanent Forests
PAINT	Primera Asociación Internacional de Noticieros y Television	**PAPMAD**	Papeteries de Madagascar
		PARCA	Pan American Railway Congress Association
PAIS	Public Affairs Information Service (U.S.A.)	**PARD**	Pakistan Academy for Rural Development
PAJU	Pan-African Union of Journalists	**PARIBAS**	Compagnie Financière de Paris et des Pays-Bas
PAK	Panhellenic Liberation Movement (Greece)		
PAL	Philippine Air Lines	**PARL**	Prince Albert Radar Laboratory (Canada)
PAL	Pioneer Air Lines (U.S.A.)	**PAREX**	European Programme of Cooperative Research in the Social Studies of Science
PALCO	Pan-American Liaison Committee of Women's Organizations		
PALSS	Physical and Life Sciences Society (South Africa)	**PARME-HUTU**	Parti du Mouvement de l'Émancipation Hutu (Rwanda)
		PASA	Pacific American Steamship Association
PAM	Programme Alimentaire Mondial	**PASA**	Pacific Asian Studies Association
PAMA	Pan-American Medical Association	**PASA**	Powder Activated Tools Association
PAMEE	Philippine Association of Mechanical and Electrical Engineers	**PASB**	Pan-American Sanitary Bureau
		PASEGES	Panellinios Synomospondia Enoseon Georgikon Synetairismon
PAMET-RADA	Parsons and Marine Engineering Turbine Research and Developing Association		
		PASLIB	Pakistan Association of Special Libraries
PAMM	British Ceramic Plant and Machinery Manufacturers Association	**PASM**	Pan African Student Movement
		PASO	Pan-American Sanitary Organisation
PAN	Polish Academy of Sciences	**PASO**	Pan American Sports Organisation
PANA	Philippine Association of National Advertisers	**PASTIC**	Pakistan Scientific and Technological Information Centre
PANA	Pan-African Information Agency	**PATA**	Pacific Area Travel Association (U.S.A.)
PANAC	Plantations Association of Nigeria and the Cameroons	**PATA**	Proprietary Articles Trade Association
PANACH	Panafrican Chemical Industries (Ivory Coast)	**PATCO**	Professional Air Traffic Controllers Organisation (U.S.A.)
PANAFTEL	Panafrican Union of Telecommunications	**PATRA**	Printing and Allied Trades' Research Association
PANAGRA	Panorama Agrícola Nacional de los Países Latinoamericanos (Mexico)	**PAU**	Pan-American Union
PANAM	Pan American World Airways	**PAUJ**	Pan African Union of Journalists
PANASA	Productos Alimentacios Nacionales (Costa Rica)	**PAV**	Programme d'Assistance Volontaire (WMO)
		PAVE	Philippine Association for Vocational Education
PANPA	Pacific Area Newspaper Production Association	**PA of W**	Pentecostal Assemblies of the World (U.S.A.)
PANPESAS	Panamerican Confederation of Weightlifting	**PAW**	Proefstation voor Akker- en Weidebouw
PANSDOC	Pakistan National Scientific Documentation Centre	**PAWC**	Pan African Workers Congress
		PAYM	Pan African Youth Movement
PAOA	Pan-American Odontological Association	**PBCP**	Political Bureau of the Communist Party
PAP	People's Action Party (Singapore)	**PBEC**	Pacific Basin Economic Council (Australia)
PAP	Polska Agencja Prasowa	**PBF**	Papirindustrielle Bedrifters Forbund
PAPBC	Pharmaceutical Association of the Province of British Columbia (Canada)	**PBFL**	Planning for Better Family Living (FAO)
PAPC	Public Agricultural Production Corporation (Sudan)	**PBI**	Pan Britannica Industries Ltd
		PBI	Programa Biológico Internacional

PBM	Proefstation voor de Nederlandse Brouw-en Moutindustrie
PBO	Publiekrechtelijke Bedrijfsorganisatie (Netherlands)
PBU	Pali Buddhist Union
PBWG	Pakistan Bibliographical Working Group
PCA	Parochial Clergy Association
PCA	Permanent Court of Arbitration (Netherlands)
PCA	Production Credit Association (U.S.A.)
PCAC	Poultry Costings Advisory Council
PCACT	Programa de Cultivos Alimenticios del Centro de Turrialba (Costa Rica)
PCARR	Philippines Council for Agricultural Resources and Research
PCB	Nederlandse Bond van Protestants-Christelijke Beroepsgoederenvervoeders
PCBO	Protestants-Christelijke Bond voor Onder-wijzend Personeel
PCBS	Permanent Committee on Biological Standards
PCC	Palestine Conciliation Commission
PCC	Philippine Cotton Corporation
PCCC	Pakistan Central Cotton Committee
PCCEMRSP	Permanent Commission for the Conservation and Exploitation of the Maritime Resources of the South Pacific
PCCMCA	Programa Cooperativo Centroamericano para el Mejoramiento de Cultivos Alimenticios (Mexico)
PCEA	Programma Cooperativo de Experimentación Agropecuaria (*now* SIPA) (Peru)
PCEM	Parliamentary Council of the European Movement
PCF	Parti Communiste Français
PCGN	Permanent Committee on Geographical Names
PCI	Italian Communist Party
PCI	Population Council of India
PCI	Press Council of India
PCI	Prospectors Club International (U.S.A.)
PCIFC	Permanent Commission of the International Fisheries Convention
PCII	Potato Chip Institute International (U.S.A.)
PCIJ	Permanent Court of International Justice
PCIM	Programa Cooperativo de Investigaciones de Maiz (Peru)
PCIZC	Permanent Committee of International Zoological Congresses
PCJC	Pakistan Central Jute Committee
PCMA	Professional Convention Management Association (U.S.A.)
PCN	Partido Conservador de Nicaragua
PCOB	Permanent Central Opium Board (Switzerland)
PCSAS	Policy Committee for Scientific Agricultural Societies (U.S.A.)
PCSIR	Pakistan Council of Scientific and Industrial Research
PCSP	Permanent Commission of the Conference on the Use and Conservation of the Marine Resources of the South Pacific
PCVM	Research Association of British Paint, Colour and Varnish Manufacturers
PCWPC	Permanent Committee of the World Petroleum Congress
PD	Plantenziektenkundige Dienst
PDA	Democratic Party of Angola
PDA	Panhellenic Dental Association
PDAF	Taiwan Provincial Department of Agriculture and Forestry
PDC	Parti Démocratique Chrétien (Burundi)
PDC	Parti Démocratique Congolais
PDCA	Purebred Dairy Cattle Association (U.S.A.)
PDCI	Parti Démocratique de la Côte d'Ivoire
PDFLP	Popular Democratic Front for the Liberation of Palestine
PDG	Parti Démocratique de Guinée
PDIN	Indonesian National Scientific Documentation Centre
PDIUM	Partito Democratico Italiano di Unità Monarchica
PDPA	Bureau pour le Développement de la Production Agricole Outre-Mer
PDRSY	People's Democratic Republic of South Yemen
PDRY	People's Democratic Republic of Yemen
PDSA	People's Dispensary for Sick Animals
PDTS	Powell Duffryn Technical Services
PE	Parlement Européen
PEA	Physical Education Association of Great Britain and Northern Ireland
PEAB	Professional Engineers' Appointments Bureau

PEAT	Programme Élargi d'Assistance Technique des Nations Unies
PECAM	Pêcheries Camerounaises
PECI	Plastiques et Elastomères de la Côte-d'Ivoire
PEDAEP	Projet d'Expérimentation et de Démonstration en Arboriculture, Élevage et Pâturage (Tunis)
PEEAFE	Panellinios Enosis Emporikon Antiprosopon Pharmakon Exoterikou
PEF	Palestine Exploration Fund (U.K.)
PEFC	Paper Exporters Freight Committee
PEFU	Panel of Experts on Fish Utilization (FAO)
PEIA	Poultry and Egg Institute of America
PEKSI	Persatuan Exportir Indonesia
PEN	Fédération Internationale des Pen Clubs
PEN	Poets, Playwrights, Essayists and Novelists
PENB	Poultry and Egg National Board (U.S.A.)
PEO	Programme Evaluation Organization (India)
PEON	Commission pour la Production d'Électricité d'Origine Nucléaire
PEP	Political and Economic Planning
PEPSU	Patiala and East Punjab States Union
PERA	Production Engineering Research Association of Great Britain
PERI	Pakistan Economic Research Institute
PERULAC	Compañia Peruana de Alimentos Lácteos, S.A.
PES	Société Plastique et Elastomère du Sénégal
PESA	Progressive English Speaking Association (Israel)
PESGB	Petroleum Exploration Society of Great Britain
PEST	Pressure for Economic and Social Toryism
PET	Panellinois Enosis Technikon
PETROPAR	Société de Participations Pétrolières (Mauritania)
PETT	Project – Engineers and Technologists for Tomorrow
PFA	Professional Footballers' Association
PFA	Provincial Forestry Administration (Taiwan)
PFB	Provincial Food Bureau (Taiwan)
PFBCA	Pennsylvania Farm Bureau Cooperative Association (U.S.A.)
PFEL	Pacific Far East Line (U.S.A.)
PFI	Papirindustriens Forskningsinstitutt

PFIOFO	Percy FitzPatrick Institute of Ornithology (South Africa)
PFLOAG	Popular Front for the Liberation of Oman and the Arabian Gulf
PFLP	Peoples Front for the Liberation of Palestine
PFM	Political Freedom Movement
PFN	Partido Frente Nacional (Costa Rico)
PFPA	Pitch Fibre Pipe Association of Great Britain
PFPUT	Pension Fund Property Unit Trust
PFRA	Prairie Farm Rehabilitation Act (Canada)
PFU	Partie Féministe Unifié
PFW	Proefstation voor de Fruitteelt, Wilhelminadorp
PGA	Professional Golfers Association
PGAH	Pineapple Growers Association of Hawaii
PGA – NOC	Permanent General Assembly of National Olympic Committees
PGBI	Protein Grain Products International (U.S.A.)
PGL	Papirgrossistenes Landsforening
PGMTT	Professional Group on Microwave Theory and Techniques (U.S.A.)
PGRO	Pea Growers Research Organisation (*now* Process Growers Research Organisation)
PGV	Proefstation voor de Groenteteelt in de Volle Grond
PHBGB	Poll Hereford Breeders of Great Britain
PHCA	Pig Health Control Association
PHCI	Société Plantations et Huileries de Côte-d'Ivoire
PHI	Conseil Intergouvernemental du Programme Hydrologique International
PHILASAG	Philippine Association of Agriculturists
PHILCOA	Philippine Coconut Administration
PHIL-COMAN	Philippines Council of Management
PHILCUSA	Philippine Council for U.S.Aid
PHILSUGIN	Philippine Sugar Institute
PHOTO-KINA	World Fair of Photography
PHS	Personhistoriska Samfundet
PHSA	Provincial Hospital Services Association
PHYTO-PHAR	Groupement des Fabricants Belges de Produits Belges de Produits de Phytopharmacie

PI	The Plastics Institute
PIA	Pakistan International Airlines
PIA	Pharmaceutical Industries Association in EFTA
PIA	Photographic Importers Association
PIA	Pilots International Association
PIA	Plastics Institute of America
PIA	Plastics Institute of Australia
PIA	Program Implementation Agency (Philippines)
PIAC	Programa de Integración de las Naciones Unidas para la América Central
PIANC	Permanent International Association of Navigation Congresses
PIARC	Permanent International Association of Road Congresses
PIAWA	Printing Industry and Allied Workers' Union (Guyana)
PIB	Petroleum Information Bureau
PIBAC	Permanent International Bureau of Analytical Chemistry of Human and Animal Food
PIBR	Pig Industry Board of Rhodesia
PICA	Palestine Jewish Colonization Association
PICA	Private Investment Company for Asia
PICAA	Permanent International Committee of Agricultural Associations
PICAO	Provisional International Civil Aviation Organisation
PICC	Provisional International Computation Centre
PICEA	Private Information Center on Eastern Arabia (Belgium)
PICG	Programme International de Corrélation Géologique
PICGC	Permanent International Committee for Genetic Congresses
PICIC	Pakistan Industrial Credit and Investment Corporation
PICM	Permanent International Committee of Mothers
PICMME	Provisional Intergovernmental Committee for the Movement of Migrants from Europe
PICOP	Paper Industries Corporation of the Philippines
PICPA	Philippine Institute of Certified Public Accountants
PICS	Publishers Information Card Services
PICUTPC	Permanent and International Committee of Underground Town Planning and Construction
PICV	Permanent International Commission of Viticulture
PID	Partido Institucional Democrático (Guatemala)
PIDA	Pig Industry Development Authority (*now* MLC)
PIDC	Pakistan Industrial Development Corporation
PIDE	Pakistan Institute of Development Economics
PIDR	Programa Interamericano para el Desarrollo Rural (Costa Rico)
PIF	British Paper and Board Industry Federation
PIFC	Pakistan Industrial Finance Corporation
PIIF	Pakistan International Industrial Fair
PIIP	Programa Interamericano de Información Popular (Costa Rico)
PIJR	Programa Interamericano para la Juventud Rural (Costa Rico)
PIL	Pest Infestation Laboratory
PILCAM	Société Camerounaise de Fabrication de Piles Électriques
PILOT	Panel on Instrumentation for Large Optical Telescopes
PILS	Pacific Information and Library Services (Hawaii)
PIM	Plan Indicatif Mondial pour le Développement Agricole (FAO)
PIMC	Pineapple Industry Marketing Corporation (Malaysia)
PIME	Pontifical Foreign Mission Institute (Italy)
PIMEC	Programa Interamericano para Mejorar la Enseñanza de las Ciencias (*of* OEA)
PINA	Potash Institute of North America
PINA	Programa Integrado de Nutrición Aplicada (Colombia)
PINAC	Permanent International Association of Navigation Congresses
PINAPA	Panel on Interactions between the Neutral and Ionized Part of the Ionosphere
PINGW	Panstwowy Instytut Naukowy Gospodarstwa Wiejskiego w Pulawach
PINSTECH	Pakistan Institute of Nuclear Science and Technology

PINTEC	Plastics Institute National Technical Conference	**PLDT**	Philippine Long Distant Telephone Company
PINZ	Plastics Institute of New Zealand	**PLGS**	Partito Liberale dei Giovani Somali
PIOSA	Pan-Indian Ocean Science Association	**PLI**	Partido Liberal Independiente (Nicaragua)
PIPA	Pacific Industrial Property Association	**PLI**	Partito Liberale Italiano
PIRA	Research Association for the Paper and Board, Printing and Packaging Industries	**PLN**	Partido Liberacion Nacional (Costa Rico)
		PLN	Partido Liberal Nacionalista (Nicaragua)
PIRI	Paint Industries Research Institute (S. Africa)	**PLO**	Palestine Liberation Organization
PIRRCOM	Project for the Intensification of Regional Research on Cotton, Oilseeds and Millets (India)	**PLP**	Parti pour la Liberté et le Progrés (Belgium)
		PLR	Partido Liberal Radical (Paraguay)
		PLRA	Patronto de Leprosos de la Repúblic Argentina
PIRSA	Psychological Institute of the Republic of South Africa	**PLRE**	Partido Liberal Radical Ecuatoriano
PISPESCA	Asociación Colombiana de Piscicultura y Pesca	**PLRG**	Public Libraries Research Group
		PLSA	Pacific Law and Society Association (U.S.A.)
PITA	Pacific International Trapshooting Association (U.S.A.)	**PLUNA**	Primeras Lineas Uruguayas de Navegación Aerea
PITAC	Pakistan Industrial Technical Assistance Centre	**PLUVA**	Stichting voor Onderzoek van Pluimvee en Varkens
PITB	Petroleum Industry Training Board	**PMA**	Pakistan Medical Association
PIWR	Panstowy Instytut Wydawnictw Rolniczych	**PMA**	Programa Mundial de Alimentos
PJA	Pakistan Jute Association	**PMA**	Production and Marketing Administration (U.S.A.)
PJGN	Plattelands Jongeren Gemeenschap Nederland		
		PMAC	Pharmaceutical Manufacturers Association of Canada
PJMA	Pakistan Jute Mills Association		
PKL	Plast- och Kemikalieleverantörers Förening	**PMAC**	Purchasing Management Association of Canada
PKTF	Printing and Kindred Trades Federation	**PMAEA**	Port Management Association of Eastern Africa
PKV	Verband der Privaten Krankenversicherung		
PL	Parlamento Latino-Americano (Peru)	**PMATA**	Paint Manufacturers and Allied Trades Association
PLA	Pakistan Library Association		
PLA	Palestine Liberation Army	**PMBC**	Plywood Manufacturers of British Columbia
PLA	Philippine Library Association	**PME**	Petites et Moyennes Entreprises
PLA	Port of London Authority	**PMEG**	Perforated Metal Experimental Group
PLA	Private Libraries Association	**PMFC**	Pacific Marine Fisheries Commission
PLANASEM	Plano Nacional de Sementes (Brazil)	**PMH**	Pari Mutuel sur les Hippodromes
PLANATES	Plano Nacional de Assistência Técnica a Suinicultura (Brazil)	**PMIP**	Pan-Malaysian Islamic Party
		PMSD	Parti Mauricien Social Democrate
PLANAVE	Plano Nacional de Avicultura (Brazil)	**PMU**	Missionary Union of Priests, Brothers, Nuns
PLANER	Plano Nacional de Extensão Rural (Brazil)	**PMU**	Pari Mutuel Urbain
PLASCO	Latin American School of Social Sciences (Chile)	**PMV**	Pro Mundi Vita. International Research and Information Centre (Belgium)
PLAST-AFRIC	Société Africaine de Transformation de Matières Plastiques (Haute-Volta)	**PN**	Produktivitetsnämnden
		PNB	Philippine National Bank
PLATO	Programmed Learning Automatic Teaching Organisation (U.S.A.)	**PNCA**	Programa Nacional de Capacitación Agropecuaria (Colombia)

PNDC	Programa Nacional de Desarrollo de la Comunidad (Guatemala)
PNEU	Parents National Education Union
PNEUROP	European Committee of Manufacturers of Compressed Air Equipment
PNM	People's National Movement (Trinidad and Tobago)
PNOC	Philippine National Oil Company
PNP	Partido Nuevo Progresista (Puerto Rico)
PNP	People's National Party (Jamaica)
PNTA	Pakistan National Tuberculosis Association
PNUD	Programme des Nations Unies pour le Développement
PNUE	Programme des Nations Unies pour l'Environnement
PNUMA	Programa de las Naciones Unidas para el Medio Ambiente
PNYME	Papir- és Nyomdaipari Müszaki Egyesület
POAAPS	Permanent Organisation for Afro-Asian Peoples Solidarity
POC	Stichting Provinciale Onderzoekcentra
POED	Post Office Engineering Department
POEM	Palm Oil Estates Managers (Africa)
POEU	Post Office Engineering Union
POGO	Polar Orbiting Geophysical Observatory (U.S.A.)
POKE	Panellinios Organosis Kinimatografikon Epicheirision
POMAG	Société de Grands Magasins de Pointe-Noir (Congo)
POMSA	Post Office Management Staffs Association
POOL	Ad hoc Group of Experts on Pollution of the Ocean Originating on Land (IOC)
POPLAB	International Program of Laboratories for Population Statistics
PORIS	Post Office Radio Interference Station
PORLA	Palm Oil Registration and Licensing Authority (Malaysia)
POSL	Parti Ouvrier Socialiste Luxembourgeois
POSMAS	Panellinios Osmospondia Somateion Mesiton Astikon Symbaseon
POUNC	Post Office Users' National Council
POUR	President's Organization for Unemployment Relief (U.S.A.)
POWU	Post Office Workers Union
PP	Periphery Press (Norway)
PPA	Pakistan Press Association
PPA	Peat Producers Association of Great Britain and Ireland
PPA	Periodical Publishers Association
PPA	Process Plant Association
PPA	Progressive People's Alliance (Gambia)
PPAB	Programme and Policy Advisory Board (FAO)
PPBF	Pan-American Pharmaceutical and Biochemical Federation
PPCS	Primary Producers Co-operative Society (N.Z.)
PPD	Partido Popular Democrático (Puerto Rico)
PPD	Provinciale Planologische Diensten
PPDA	Produce Prepackaging Development Association, Ltd
PPE	Parti Populaire Européen (Belgium)
PPI	Pakistan Press International
PPI	Pickle Packers International (U.S.A.)
PPIP	Philippine Poultry Improvement Plan
PPM	Parti du Peuple Mauritanien
PPMA	Produce Packaging and Marketing Association
PPMC	People to People Music Committee (U.S.A.)
PPMC	Produce Prepackaging Machinery Co.
PPN	Parti Progressiste Nigérien
PPP	People's Political Party (St Vincent)
PPP	People's Progressive Party (Gambia, Guyana, Malaysia)
PPPRF	Pan Pacific Public Relations Federation
PPR	Press and Public Relations Ltd.
PPRIC	Pulp and Paper Research Institute of Canada
PPS	Parti Popular Socialista (Mexico, El Salvador)
PPS	Partido Popular Salvadoreño
PPSA	Pan-Pacific Surgical Association
PPSEAWA	Pan Pacific and Southeast Asia Women's Association
PPT	Parti Progressiste Tschadien
PPU	Peace Pledge Union
PPV	Fachverband der Papier und Pappe Verarbeitenden Industrie (Austria)
PQAA	Province of Quebec Association of Architects (Canada)
PRA	Paint Research Association

PRA	Parti du Regroupement Africaine
PRA	Partido Revolucionario Auténtico (Bolivia)
PRA	Personnel Research Association (U.S.A.)
PRA	Prairie Rail Authority (Canada)
PRAC	Pyrethrum Research Advisory Committee (Kenya)
PRAI	Planning Research and Action Institute, Lucknow (India)
PRAIS	Pesticide Residue Analysis Information Service
PRATRA	Philippines Relief and Trade Rehabilitation Administration
PRB	Partido de la Revolución Boliviana
PRC	People's Republic of China
PRD	Partido Revolucionario Dominicano
PRD	Polytechnic Research and Development Co. (U.S.A.)
PRE	Fédération Européenne des Fabricants de Produits Réfractaires
PRE	Programme de Reconstruction Européenne
PRF	Petroleumhandelns Riksförbund
PRI	Partido Republicano Italiano
PRI	Partido Revolucionario Institucional (Mexico)
PRI	Performance Registry International (U.S.A.)
PRI	Prévention Routière Internationale
PRI	Public Relations Institute of Ireland
PRIH	Pineapple Research Institute of Hawaii
PRII	Public Relations Institute of Ireland
PSIL	Philippine Society of International Law
PRIMI-FANO	Commission pour les Enfants Privés de Milieu Familial Normal (*of* BICE)
PRIN	Partido Revolucionario de Izquierda Nacionalista (Bolivia)
PRINZ	Public Relations Institute of New Zealand
PRIO	International Peace Research Institute in Oslo
PRISA	Public Relations Institute of South Africa
PRISCO	Price Stabilisation Corporation (Philippines)
PRL	Prairie Research Laboratory Canada.
PRM	Parti du Regroupement Mauritanienne
PRO	Public Record Office
PROA	Plantations Réunies de l'Ouest Africain
PROAGRO	Comisión Nacional de Promoción Agropecuario (Argentina)

PROCH-IMAD	Société des Produits Chimiques de Madagascar
PRODAC	Production Advisers' Consortium
PROD-AROM	Syndicat National des Fabricants de Produits Aromatiques
PRODEHA	Protestants-Christelijke Bond van Detaillisten in Luxe en Huishoudellijke Artikelen
PRODES	Productores de Semillas, S.A.
PRODISEGE	Syndicat Professionnel des Producteurs d'Énergie et des Services Publics Autonomes
PROHUZA	Centre d'Études et d'Information des Problèmes Humains dans les Zones Arides
PROLUMA	Produits Lubrificants de Madagascar
PROM-ARCA	Schweizerische Gesellschaft der Konsumgüterindustrie
PROMSTRA	Production Methods and Stress Research Association (Netherlands)
PRONADI	Chambre Syndicale Belge des Fabricants et Distributeurs de Produits Naturels et Diététiques
PRONASE	National Seed Production Agency (Mexico)
PRONENCA	Programa Nacional de Educación Nutricional y Complementación Alimentaria (Colombia)
PROPASI	Productores de Patata de Siembra
PROTAAL	Proyecto Cooperativo de Investigacion sobre Tecnologia Agropecuario en América Latina
PROTERRA	Programa de Redistribuição de Terras e de Estimulos a Agro-industria do Norte e do Nordeste (Brazil)
PROVO	Stichting Proefbedrijf Voedselbestraling
PRP	People's Revolutionary Party (Vietnam)
PRRM	Philippine Rural Reconstruction Movement
PRS	Groupement National des Papetiers Répartiteurs Spécialisés
PRS	Paint Research Station
PRS	Protestant Reformation Society
PRSA	Public Relations Society of America
PRSC	Partido Revolucionario Social Cristiano (Dominica)
PRSP	Public Relations Society of the Philippines
PRTA	Public Road Transport Association
PRUCIS	Philippine Rural Community Improvement Society
PS	Parapsychological Society (U.S.A.)
PS	Physical Society

PSA	Pacific Science Association (Hawaii)	PTA	Physikalisch-Technische Anstalt zu Braunschweig
PSA	Pacific Seedsmens Association (U.S.A.)	PTA	Polskie Towarzystwo Astronautyczne
PSA	Pakistan Sociological Association	PTA	Primary Tungsten Association
PSA	Parti Solidaire Africain (Zaire)	PTA	Printing Trades Alliance
PSA	Photographic Society of America	PTAiN	Polskie Towarzystwo Archeologiczne i Numizmatyczne
PSA	Poultry Stock Association (*now* BPBHA)		
PSAC	President's Science Advisory Service (U.S.A.)	PTAS	Productivity and Technical Assistance Secretariat
PSAE	Philippine Society of Agricultural Engineers	PTB	Physikalisch-Technische Bundesanstalt
PSAU	Plan de Suministros Alimentarios de Urgencia (WFP)	PTB	Polskie Towarzystwo Biometryczne
PSC	Pacific Science Council	PTBBiMF	Polskie Towarzystwo Balneologii, Bioklimatologii i Medycyny Fizykalnej
PSC	Partie Social Chrétien (Belgium)		
PSC	Peulvruchten Studie Combinatie	PTBR	Polskie Towarzystwo Badan Radiacyjnych im Marii Sktodowskiej-Curie
PSD	Parti Social Démocrate de Madagascar et des Comores		
		PTC	Polskie Towarzystwo Chemiczne
PSD	Parti Socialiste Démocratique (Morocco)	PTCh	Polskie Towarzystwo Chemiczne
PSD	Partido Social Demócrata (Bolivia)	PTCR	Patent, Trademark and Copyright Research Institute (U.S.A.)
PSDI	Partito Socialista Democratico Italiano		
PSDIS	Partito Socialista Democratico Independente Sanmarinese (San Marino)	PTD	Polskie Towarzystwo Dermatologiczne
		PTDL	Polskie Towarzystwo Diagnostyki Laboratoryjnej
PSFC	International Pacific Salmon Fisheries Commission		
		PTE	Polskie Towarzystwo Entomologiczne
PSFG	Permanent Service on the Fluctuations of Glaciers of IUGG	PTEK	Polskie Towarzystwo Ekonomiczne
		PTF	Papirindustriens Tekniske Forening
PSFN	Polskie Stowarzyszenie Filmu Naukowego	PTF	Polskie Towarzystwo Farmakologiczne
PSI	Partito Socialista Italiano	PTF	Polskie Towarzystwo Filologiczne
PSI	Pharmaceutical Society of Ireland	PTFarm	Polskie Towarzystwo Farmaceutyczne
PSI	Public Services International	PTG	Polskie Towarzystwo Geograficzne
PSIDC	Punjab State Industrial Development Corporation (India)	PTG	Polskie Towarzystwo Geologiczne
		PTGWO	Philippine Transport and General Workers Organisations
PSIP	Poultry Stock Improvement Plan		
PSIUP	Partito Socialista Italiano di Unità Proletaria	PTH	Polskie Towarzystwo Historyczne
PSMSL	Permanent Service for Mean Sea Level (*of* IAPO)	PTHiC	Polskie Towarzystwo Histochemików i Cytochemików
PSNI	Pharmaceutical Society of Northern Ireland	PTI	Press Trust of India
PSP	Pacifistich Socialistiche Partij (Netherlands)	PTIDG	Presentation of Technical Information Discussion Group
PSQC	Philippine Society for Quality Control		
PSSA	Pharmaceutical Society of South Africa	PTIO	Pesticides Technical Information Office (Canada)
PSSA	Photogrammetric Society of South Africa		
PSSC	Philippine Social Science Council	PTJ	Polskie Towarzystwo Jezykoznawcze
PSSG	International Printers Supply Salesmen's Guild (U.S.A.)	PTK	Pienteollisuuden Keskusliitto
		PTL	Polskie Towarzystwo Logopedyczne
PSU	Parti Socialiste Unifié	PTL	Polskie Towarzystwo Ludoznawcze
PSU	Partito Socialista Unitario	PTN	Polskie Towarzystwo Nautologiczne
PSWO	Picture and Sound World Organisation	PTN	Polskie Towarzystwo Neurologiczne

PTO	Polskie Towarzystwo Okulistyczne
PTO	Polskie Towarzystwo Onkologiczne
PTO	Polskie Towarzystwo Orientalistyczne
PTOiTr	Polskie Towarzystwo Ortopedyczne i Traumatologiczne
PTOM	Pays et Territoires d'Outremer (of EEC)
PTP	Polskie Towarzystwo Pediatryczne
PTP	Polskie Towarzystwo Psychologiczne
PTR	Physikalisch-Technische Reichsanstalt
PTR	Polskie Towarzystwo Religioznawcze
PTS	Polskie Towarzystwo Semiotyczne
PTT	International Federation of Christian Trade Unions of Employers in Public Service and PTT
PTT	Postes, Télégraphes, Téléphones
PTTI	Postal, Telegraph and Telephone International
PTU	Plumbing Trades Union
PTZ	Polskie Towarzystwo Zootechniczne
PTZool	Polskie Towarzystwo Zoologiczne
PUA	Pacific Union Association
PUAS	Postal Union of the Americas and Spain
PUC	Public Utilities Committee (ECE)
PUCHE	Potchefstroom University for Christian Higher Education (South Africa)
PUCR	Partido Unión Cívico Revolucionaria (Costa Rico)
PUDINE	Programa Universitario de Desenvolvimento Industrial do Nordeste (Brazil)
PUDOC	Centrum voor Landbouwpublikaties en Landbouwdocumentatie, Wageningen
PUN	Partido Unión Nacional (Costa Rico)
PUP	People's United Party (British Honduras)
PUWP	Polish United Workers Party
PV	Protection des Végétaux
PVB	Provinciale Veevoederbureau
PVC	Provinciale Voedselcommissaris
PVDA	Partij van de Arbeit (Netherlands)
PVFM	Planification pour une Vie Familiale Meilleure (FAO)
PVGA	Processed Vegetable Growers Association
PVTA	Philippine Virginia Tobacco Administration
PVV	Partij voom Vrijheid en Vooruitgang (Belgium)
PWC	Peasants' Work Co-operatives (Yugoslavia)

PWC	Peoples World Convention
PWCA	Peoples World Constituent Assembly
PWCB	Provincial Water Conservancy Bureau (Taiwan)
PWFA	Petroleum Workers Federation of Aruba
PWIF	Plantation Worker's International Federation
PWLB	Public Works Loan Board
PWPMA	Philippine Welding Products Manufacturers Association
PWU	Provision Wholesalers Union (Malta)
PZITB	Polski Zwiazek Inzynierów Techników Budownictwa
PZITS	Polskie Zrzeszenie Inzynierów i Techników Sanitarnych

Q

QANTAS	Queensland and Northern Territory Aerial Services, Ltd (Australia)
QCGA	Queensland Cane Growers' Association (Australia)
QCGC	Queensland Cane Growers' Council (Australia)
QEA	Qantas Empire Airways (Australia)
QIMA	Queensland Institute of Municipal Administration
QMFCI	Quarter-Master Food and Container Institute (U.S.A.)
QSPP	Quebec Society for the Protection of Plants (Canada)
QUANA	Authorized Newsagents Association of Queensland
QUI	Queen's University of Ireland

R

RAA	Royal Academy of Arts
RAAD	Rijks Zuivel-Agrarische Afvalwaterdienst
RAAF	Royal Australian Air Force

AAG	Research Association of Applied Geometry (Japan)
AAM	Refineria Argentina de Aceites Minerales
AAS	Racial Adjustment Action Society
AB	Rationalisatie v. d. Arbeidstechniek in de Bosbouw
ABDF	Royal Association of British Dairy Farmers
ABFM	Research Association of British Flour Millers (*now* FMBRA)
ABI	Royal Agricultural Benevolent Institution
ABPCVM	Research Association of British Paint, Colour and Varnish Manufacturers (*now* PRA)
ABRM	Research Association of British Rubber Manufacturers (*now* RAPRA)
AC	Royal Automobile Club
ACP	Royal Australian College of Physicians
ACS	Royal Australian College of Surgeons
ACSA	Radio Aeronautica de Cuba
AD	Royal Academy of Dancing
ADA	Royal Academy of Dramatic Art
ADC	Rome Air Development Centre (U.S.A.)
ADD	Royal Association in Aid of the Deaf and Dumb
AE	Radiodifusion Argentina al Exterior
AE	Royal Aircraft Establishment
AeS	Royal Aeronautical Society
AF	Redernes Arbeidsgiverforening
AF	Reklameatelierenes Forening
AF	Rörledningsfirmornas Arbetsgivareförbund
AFA	Royal Air Forces Association
AFE	Regional Office for Asia and the Far East (FAO)
AFES	Royal Air Force Educational Service
AFR	Regional Office for Africa (FAO)
AFSC	Royal Air Force Staff College
AGB	Refractories Association of Great Britain
AGB	Restaurateurs Association of Great Britain
AHS	Royal Australian Historical Society
AI	Nederlandse Vereniging de Rijwiel en Automobiel-Industrie
AI	Radiotelevisione Italiana
AI	Royal Anthropological Institute
I	Royal Archaeological Institute
AIA	Royal Australian Institute of Architects
AIC	Royal Architectural Institute of Canada

RAM	Royal Academy of Music
RAMAC	Radio Marine Associated Companies
RAMNAC	Radio Aids to Marine Navigation Application Committee
RAOB	Royal Antediluvian Order of Buffaloes
RAOU	Royal Australasian Ornithologists Unions
RAP	Rhodesian Action Party
RAPRA	Rubber and Plastics Research Association of Great Britain (*formerly* RABRM)
RARC	Ruakura Agricultural Research Centre (New Zealand)
RARDE	Royal Armament Research and Development Establishment
RAS	Royal Asiatic Society
RAS	Royal Astronomical Society
RASB	Royal Asiatic Society of Bengal
RAS of C	Royal Agricultural Society of the Commonwealth
RASC	Royal Astronomical Society of Canada
RASE	Royal Agricultural Society of England
RASK	Royal Agricultural Society of Kenya
RASU	Rangoon Arts and Science University
RATEKSA	Radiobranchens Tekniske og Kommercielle Sammenslutning
RATP	Régie Autonome des Transports Parisiens
RAU	République Arabe Unie
RAW	Rationalisierungs-Ausschusses der Deutschen Wirtschaft
RBA	Royal Society of British Artists
RBAI	Royal Belfast Academical Institution
RBS	Royal Botanical Society
RBS	Royal Society of British Sculptors
RBV	Rohrleitungsbauverband
RC	Rijksconsultentschap
RCA	Race Course Association
RCA	Radio Corporation of America
RCA	Reinforced Concrete Association
RCA	Research Council of Alberta (Canada)
RCA	Retail Confectioners Association
RCA	Royal Choral Society
RCA	Royal College of Art
RCAA	Royal Canadian Academy of Arts
RCAS	Royal Central Asia Society
RCCO	Royal Canadian College of Organists

RCD	Regional Co-operation for Development (Iran, Palestine, Turkey)	**RCSI**	Royal College of Surgeons in Ireland
RCE	Union Restaurants Collectifs Européens	**RCU**	Rural Cooperative Unions (Iran)
RCEEA	Radio Communication and Electronic Engineering Association	**RCVS**	Royal College of Veterinary Surgeons
		RDA	Rassemblement Démocratique Africain
RCGP	Royal College of General Practitioners	**RDA**	République Démocratique Allemande
RCGS	Royal Canadian Geological Society	**RDB**	Research and Development Board (U.S.A.)
RCI	Recontres Creatives Internationales	**RDB**	Ring Deutscher Bergingenieure
RCI	Research and Control Instruments, Ltd	**RDC**	Universal Esperanto Association Research and Documentation Centre
RCI	Royal Canadian Institute		
RCIA	Retail Clerks International Association (U.S.A.)	**RDCOT**	Regional Documentation Centre for Oral Tradition (Niger)
RCIVS	Regional Conference on International Voluntary Service	**RDM**	Bundesverband Ring Deutscher Makler
		RDOEI	Research and Development Organization for the Electrical Industry (India)
RCK	Research Centrum Kalkzandsteen Industrie (Netherlands)	**RDS**	Research Defence Society
RCM	République des Citoyens du Monde	**RDS**	Royal Drawing Society
RCM	Royal College of Midwives	**RDS**	Royal Dublin Society
RCM	Royal College of Mines	**RDSO**	Research Designs and Standards Organisation (India)
RCM	Royal College of Music		
RCMA	Rubber Cultuur Maatschappij 'Amsterdam'	**REA**	Rural Electrification Administration (U.S.A)
RCMP	Royal Canadian Mounted Police	**REAF**	Rutebileiernes Arbeidsgiverforening
RCN	Reactor Centrum Nederland	**REAL**	Real-Aerovias do Brasil
RCN	Royal College of Nursing	**REAP**	Reinforcing Evangelists and Pastors (Japan)
RCO	Royal College of Organists	**REBIA**	Regional Building Institute for Africa
RCOG	Royal College of Obstetricians and Gynaecologists	**REC**	Rural Electrification Corporation (India)
		RECA	Research and Education Centre (Japan)
RCP	Royal College of Physicians	**RECE**	Representación Cubana del Exilio (U.S.A.)
RCPA	Rice and Corn Production Administration (Philippines)	**RECMF**	Radio and Electronic Components Manufacturers' Association
RCPCC	Rice and Corn Production Coordinating Council (Philippines)	**RECOBAA**	Office of the Government Commissioner for Foreign Agricultural Affairs (Netherlands)
RCPI	Royal College of Physicians of Ireland	**REconS**	Royal Economic Society
RCPS	Royal College of Physicians and Surgeons	**RECSAM**	Regional Centre for Education in Science and Mathematics (Malaysia)
RCRDC	Radio Components Research and Development Committee	**REDA**	Ramo Editoriale degli Agricoltori
RCRF	Society of Roman Ceramic Archaeologists (Switzerland)	**REE**	Comité Européen de Reconstruction Économique Européenne
RCS	Royal Choral Society	**REFA**	Real Estate Fund of America
RCS	Royal Commonwealth Society	**REGABON**	Radio Électricité Gabonaise
RCS	Royal College of Science	**REHVA**	Representatives of European Heating and Ventilating Associations
RCS	Royal College of Surgeons of England		
RCSB	Royal Commonwealth Society for the Blind	**REI**	Rat der Europäischen Industrieverbände
RCSC	Radio Components Standardization Committee	**REIC**	Radiation Effects Information Centre (U.S.A)
RCSEd	Royal College of Surgeons of Edinburgh	**REKU**	Raditoren- en Ketel-Unie

REL	Riksförbundet för Electrikfieringen pa Landsbygden	**RHA**	Royal Hibernian Academy (Eire)
RELC	Regional English Language Centre (Malaysia)	**RHCSA**	Regional Hospitals Consultants and Specialists Association
REMC	Radio and Electronics Measurements Committee	**RHE**	Road Haulage Executive
		RHEL	Rutherford High Energy Laboratory, Chilton
REMP	Research Group for European Migration Problems	**RHI**	Racial Harmony International (U.K.)
RENFE	Red Nacional de los Ferrocarriles Espanoles	**RHistS**	Royal Historical Society
		RHS	Royal Horticultural Society
RENVA	Rengørings-og Vagtselskabernes Arbejds-giverforening	**RHS**	Royal Humane Society
		RHSI	Royal Horticultural Society of Ireland
REOU	Radio and Electronic Officers Union	**RHSV**	Royal Historical Society of Victoria (Canada)
REPESA	Refineria de Petroleos de Escombreras, S.A.	**RI**	Rotary International
RES	Royal Empire Society	**RI**	Royal Institute of Painters in Water Colours
RES	Royal Entomological Society of London	**RI**	Royal Institution of Great Britain
RESEDA	Réseau de Documentation en Économie Agricole	**RIA**	Railway Industry Association of Great Britain
RETMA	Radio-Electronics-Television Manufacturers Association (U.S.A.)	**RIA**	Réunions Internationales d'Architects
		RIA	Royal Irish Academy
REUR	Regional Office for Europe (FAO)	**RIAA**	Record Industry Association of America
REVIMA	Société pour la Revision et l'Entretien du Materiel Aéronautique	**RIAC**	Royal Irish Automobile Club
RF	Radiobranchens Faellesrad	**RIAI**	Royal Institute of the Architects of Ireland
RFAC	Royal Fine Art Commission	**RIAM**	Royal Irish Academy of Music
RFC	Reconstruction Finance Corporation (U.S.A.)	**RIAS**	Radio in American Sector (Germany)
		RIAS	Research Institute for Animal Science, Irene (South Africa)
RFCWA	Regional Fisheries Commission for Western Africa	**RIAS**	Royal Incorporation of Architects in Scotland
RFFSA	Rede Ferroviaria Federal, S.A. (Brazil)	**RIB**	Racing Information Bureau
RFLW	Rijksfaculteit Landbouw-wetenschappen, Gent (Belgium)	**RIB**	Research Institute of Brewing (Japan)
		RIB	Rural Industries Bureau (*now* COSIRA)
RFS	Royal Forestry Society	**RIBA**	Royal Institute of British Architects
RFSEW	Royal Forestry Society of England and Wales	**RIBI**	Rotary International in Great Britain and Ireland
RFSU	Rugby Football Schools Union		
RFU	Rugby Football Union	**RIC**	Radio Industry Council
RGA	Rubber Growers Association	**RIC**	Research and Information Commission (*of* COSEC)
RGAHS	Royal Guernsey Agricultural and Horticultural Society	**RIC**	Rice Improvement Conference (of PDAF)
RGD	Radio Gramophone Development Company	**RIC**	Royal Institute of Chemistry
RGDATA	Retail Grocery, Dairy and Allied Trades Association (Eire)	**RIC**	Union Internationale des Voitures et Fourgons
RGE	Rat der Gemeinden Europas		
RGO	Royal Greenwich Observatory	**RICA**	Research Institute for Consumer Affairs
RGS	Royal Geographical Society	**RICA**	Réseau d'Information Agricole
RGSA	Royal Geographical Society of Australasia	**RICASIP**	Research Information Center and Advisory Service on Information Processing (U.S.A.)
RGW	Rat für Gegenseitige Wirtschaftshilfe		

RICE	Rice Information Cooperative Effort (Philippines)
RICM	Registre International Citoyens du Monde
RICOB	Rice and Corn Board (Philippines)
RICOCI	Représentations Industrielles et Commerciales de l'Ouest de la Côte-d'Ivoire
RICS	Royal Institution of Chartered Surveyors
RIDA	Rural Industrial Development Authority (Malaysia)
RIEC	Research Institute for Estate Crops (Indonesia)
RIF	Radgivende Ingeniorers Forening
RIGB	Royal Institution of Great Britain
RIHED	Regional Institute of Higher Education and Development (Singapore)
RIIA	Reuniones de Intercambio de Información Agropecuaria (Argentina)
RIIA	Royal Institute of International Affairs
RIL	Suomen Rakennusinsinöörien Förbund
RILC	Racing Industry Liaison Committee
RILDD	Research Institute of Launderers, Drycleaners and Dyers (N.Z.)
RILEM	Réunion Internationale des Laboratoires d'Essais et de Recherches sur les Matériaux et les Constructions
RIM	Rhodesian Institute of Management
RIMCU	Research Institute for Mindanao Culture (Philippines)
RIN	Rijksinstituut voor Natuurbeheer
RIN	Royal Institution of Navigation
RINA	Royal Institution of Naval Architects
RINAVI	Associazione Nazionale Industriali Riparatori Navali
RINORD	Consulting Engineers in the Nordic Countries
RIOP	Royal Institute of Oil Painters
RIP	Rijksinstituut voor Pluimveeteelt
RIPA	Royal Institution of Public Administration
RIPHH	Royal Institute of Public Health and Hygiene
RIPS	United Nations Regional Institute for Population Studies (Ghana)
RISCO	Rhodesian Iron and Steel Company
RISCOM	Rhodesian Iron and Steel Commission
RISPA	Research Institute of the Sumatra Planters Association (Indonesia)
RIT	Recherches et Industries Thérapeutiques (Belgium)
RITENA	Reunión Internacional de Técnicos de la Nutrición Animal
RIV	Regolamento Internazionale Veicoli (Union Internationale des Wagons)
RIVON	Rijksinstituut voor Veldbiologisch Onderzoek ten behoeve van het Natuurbehoud (now RIN)
RIZA	Rijksinstituut voor Zuivering van Afvalwater
RJAHS	Royal Jersey Agricultural and Horticultural Society
RJAS	see RJAHS
RKJB	Rooms-Katholieke Jonge Boerenstand
RKL	Rationalisierungs-Kuratorium für Landwirtschaft
RKTL	Reichskuratorium für Technik in der Landwirtschaft
RKW	Rationalisierungs-Kuratorium der Deutschen Wirtschaft
RL	Reproducørernes Landsforening
RLA	Rhodesia Library Association
RLAT	Regional Office for Latin America (FAO)
RLBWM	Regional Library Bureau, West Midlands
RLC	Rijkslandbouwconsultentschap
RLF	Riksforbündet Landsbygdens Folk
RLH	Swedish Farmers Flax and Hemp Growers Association
RLL	Radio-Leverandorenes Landsforbund
RLL	Radioliikkeiden Liitto
RLSS	Royal Life Saving Society
RLVD	Rijkslandbouwvoorlichtingsdienst
RLWS	Rijkslandbouwwinterscholen
RMA	Royal Musical Association
RMA	Rubber Manufacturers Association (U.S.A.)
RMAI	Radio Manufacturers' Association of India
RMBC	Regional Marine Biological Centre
RMC	Regional Meteorological Centre (WMO)
RMCC	Royal Military College of Canada
RMCS	Royal Military College of Science
RMetS	Royal Meteorological Society
RMIC	Research Materials Information Center (of ORNL) (U.S.A.)
RmP	Riksföreningen mot Polio
RMPA	Royal Medico-Psychological Association
RMR	Riksförbundet mot Reumatism
RMS	Royal Medical Society

RMS	Royal Meteorological Society	RPE	Rocket Propulsion Establishment
RMS	Royal Microscopical Society	RPFLP	Revolutionary Popular Front (Lebanon)
RND	Rijksnijverheidsdienst	RPMI	Roswell Park Memorial Institute (U.S.A.)
RNEA	Regional Office for the Near East (FAO)	RPP	Republican People's Party (Turkey)
RNET	Régie Nationale des Eaux du Togo	RPPITB	Rubber and Plastics Processing Industry Training Board
RNFU	Rhodesia National Farmers' Union	RPRA	Royal Pigeon Racing Association
RNHU	Royal National Homing Union	RPRA	Rubber and Plastics Reclamation Association
RNIB	Royal National Institute for the Blind		
RNID	Royal National Institute for the Deaf	RPS	Royal Philatelic Society
RNLAF	Royal Netherlands Air Force	RPS	Royal Philharmonic Society
RNLI	Royal National Lifeboat Institution	RPS	Royal Photographic Society
RNMDSF	Royal National Mission to Deep Sea Fishermen	RPvZ	Rijksproefstation voor Zaadcontrôle
		RR	Rörledningsfirmirnas Riksorganisation
RNPL	Royal Naval Physiological Laboratory	RRCBC	Regional Research Centre of the British Caribbean (Trinidad)
RNRS	Royal National Rose Society		
RNS	Royal Numismatic Society	RRCC	Redwood Region Conservation Council (U.S.A.)
RNSAS	Royal Netherlands Society for Agricultural Science		
		RRE	Royal Radar Research Establishment
RNSS	Royal Naval Scientific Service	RRI	Rowett Research Institute (Scotland)
RNSTS	Royal Naval Supply and Transport Service	RRI	Rubber Research Institute (Malaysia)
RNTP	Régie Nationale des Transports et des Travaux Publics	RRIC	Rubber Research Institute of Ceylon
		RRII	Rubber Research Institute of India
RNZAS	Royal Astronomical Society of New Zealand	RRIN	Rubber Research Institute of Nigeria
RNZIH	Royal New Zealand Institute of Horticulture	RRIWB	River Research Institute, West Bengal
ROA	Raad van Organisatie-Adviesbureaus	RRL	Radio Research Laboratory (Japan)
ROA	Racehorse Owners Association	RRL	Regional Research Laboratory (India)
ROC	Royal Observer Corps	RRL	Road Research Laboratory
ROCAP	Regional Office for Central America and Panama	RRP	Republican Reliance Party (Turkey)
		RS	Royal Society
ROE	Royal Observatory Edinburgh (Scotland)	RSA	Rancha Santa Ana Botanic Garden (U.S.A.)
ROMANA	Société d'Archéologie Romana	RSA	Relay Services Association of Great Britain
ROMTRANS	Association Roumaine pour Transports Routiers Internationaux	RSA	Royal Scottish Academy
		RSA	Royal Society of Arts
RORC	Royal Ocean Racing Club	RSA	Royal Society of Australia
ROSCM	Research Organisation of Ships Compositions Manufacturers	RSAC	Royal Scottish Automobile Club
		RSAI	Royal Society of Antiquaries of Ireland
ROSCO	Road Operators Safety Council	RSAS	Royal Sanitary Association of Scotland
ROSPA	Royal Society for the Prevention of Accidents	RSAS	Royal Surgical Aid Society
ROSTA	Regional Office for Science and Technology for Africa (UNESCO)	RSASA	Royal South Australian Society of Arts
		RSC	Royal Society of Canada
ROSTSCA	Regional Office for Science and Technology for South and Central Asia (UNESCO)	RSCM	Royal School of Church Music
		RSD	Royal Society of Dublin
RP	Royal Society of Portrait Painters	RSE	Royal Society of Edinburgh (Scotland)
RPAA	Regional Planning Association of America		
RPC	Rijkspluimveeteeltconsulentschap		

RSF	Real Sociedad Fotográfica	**RTEB**	Radio Trades Examination Board
RSF	Riksförbundet Svensk Frukt	**RTEC**	Retail Trades Education Council
RSGB	Radio Society of Great Britain	**RTF**	Radiodiffusion et Télévision Française (*now* ORTF)
RSGS	Royal Scottish Geographical Society	**RTI**	Round Table International
RSH	Royal Society of Health		
RSI	Royal Sanitary Institute	**RTIC**	Regional Technical Information Centres (*now* ILC)
RSIC	Radiation Shielding Information Center (*of* ORNL) (U.S.A.)	**RTITB**	Road Transport Industry Training Board
RSL	Royal Society of Literature	**RTM**	Radiodiffusion Télévision Marocaine
RSM	Royal School of Mines	**RTMA**	Radio and Television Manufacturers Association (Canada or U.S.A.)
RSM	Royal Society of Medicine	**RTPB**	Radio Technical Planning Board (U.S.A.)
RSM	Royal Society of Musicians	**RTPI**	Royal Town Planning Institute
RSMA	Royal Society of Marine Artists	**RTRA**	Radio Electrical and Television Retailers Association
RSMD	Remote Sensing and Meteorological Applications Division (IAEA)	**RTRO**	Reclamation Trades Research Organisation
RSNA	Radiological Society of North America	**RTS**	Royal Television Society
RSNZ	Royal Society of New Zealand	**RTS**	Royal Toxophilite Society
RSPB	Royal Society for the Protection of Birds	**RTSA**	Retail Trading Standards Association
RSPCA	Royal Society for the Prevention of Cruelty to Animals	**RTT**	Radiodiffusion-Télévision Tunisienne
		RUA	Royal Ulster Academy
RSR	République Socialiste de Roumanie	**RUAA**	Royal Ulster Academy Association
RSS	Royal Statistical Society	**RUAS**	Royal Ulster Agricultural Society
RSSI	Royal Statistical Society of Ireland	**RUI**	Royal National University of Ireland
RSTMH	Royal Society of Tropical Medicine and Hygiene	**RUKBA**	Royal United Kingdom Beneficent Association
RSUA	Royal Society of Ulster Architects	**RUSI**	Royal United Service Institute for Defence Studies
RTA	Comité de Coordination de la Route Trans-africaine (Ethiopia)	**RVC**	Rijksveeteeltconsulentschap
RTA	Rhodesian Tobacco Association	**RVCI**	Royal Veterinary College of Ireland
RTA	Road Transport Association	**RVIA**	Royal Victoria Institute of Architects (Australia)
RTA	Rubber Trade Association of London	**RVP**	Rijksvoorlichtingsdienst voor de Pluimveeteelt
RTAC	Regional Technical Aids Center (U.S.A.)		
RTBI	National Association of Round Tables of Great Britain and Ireland	**RVS**	Reifengewerbe-Verband der Schweiz
RTC	Rijkstuinbouwconsulentschap	**RWAS**	Royal Welsh Agricultural Society
RTCEG	Rubber and Thermoplastic Cables Export Group	**RWE**	Rheinisch-Westfälisches Electrizitätswerk
		RWF	Radio Wholesalers Federation
RTCH	National Conference of Road Transport Clearing Houses	**RWS**	Royal Society of Painters in Water Colours
		RYA	Royal Yachting Association
RTCMA	Rubber and Thermoplastic Cable Manufacturers Association	**RZC**	Rijkszuivelconsulentschap
		RZSI	Royal Zoological Society of Ireland
RTE	Radio Telefis Eireann	**RZSS**	Royal Zoological Society of Scotland

S

SA   Salvation Army
SA   Skogbrukets Arbeidsgiverforening
SA   Sparebankenes Arbeidsgiverforening
SA   Svenska Agghandelsförbundet
SA   Svenska Akeriförbundet
SAA   Scottish Anglers Association
SAA   Scottish Archery Association
SAA   Schweizerische Astronautische Arbeits-
            gemeinschaft
SAA   Sociedád Argentina de Agronomia
SAA   Sociedad Argentina de Apicultores
SAA   Sociedád Argentina de Antropologia
SAA   South African Airways
SAA   Standards Association of Australia
SAA   Svenska Aerosolföreningen
SAAA   Scottish Amateur Athletic Association
SAAAS   South African Association for the Advance-
            ment of Science
SAAB   Svensk Aeroplan Aktiebolaget
SAACE   South African Association of Consulting
            Engineers
SAAD   Society for the Advancement of Anaesthesia
            in Dentistry
SAAEB   South African Atomic Energy Board
SAAEVA   Southern Association for Agricultural
            Engineering and Vocational Agriculture
            (U.S.A.)
SAAI   Specialty Advertising Association
            International (U.S.A.)
SAAMBR   South African Association for Marine
            Biological Research
SAANZ   Sociological Association of Australia and
            New Zealand
SAAO   South African Astronomical Observatory
SAARA   Sociedad de Amigos del Arbol de la
            República Argentina
SAARBS   South African Angora Ram Breeders'
            Society

SAARCI   Sindicato Autonomo Agenti Rappresentanti
            Commercio Industria
SAAT   Society of Architects and Associated
            Technicians
SAATC   Southern African Air Transport Council
SAAU   South African Agricultural Union
SAAU   Système d'Approvisionnement Alimentaire
            d'Urgence (WFP)
SAB   Schweizerische Arbeitsgemeinschaft der
            Bergbauern
SAB   Sociedád Argentina de Biologia
SAB   Sociedad Argentina de Botánica
SAB   Sociedád Arqueológica de Bolivia
SAB   Société Africaine des Bois
SAB   Société Africaine de Bonneterie (Ivory
            Coast)
SAB   Society of American Bacteriologists
SAB   Society of Applied Bacteriology
SAB   Stichting v. Aardappelbewaring
SAB   Sveriges Allmänna Biblioteksförening
SABA   Scottish Amateur Boxing Association
SABA   South African Brick Association
SABB   Société d'Arrimage des Battures de Beauport
            (Canada)
SABC   Scottish Association of Boys Clubs
SABC   Société des Brasseries du Cameroun
SABC   South African Broadcasting Corporation
SABCA   Société Anonyme Belge de Constructions
            Aéronautiques
SABCO   Society for the Areas of Biological and
            Chemical Overlap (Japan)
SABE   Société Africaine d'Exploitation des Brevets
            Eries
SABEA   Societa Alimentari Bevande e Affini
SABENA   Société Anonyme Belge d'Exploitation de la
            Navigation Aérienne
SABI   Société Africaine de Biscuiterie (Ivory
            Coast)
SABM   Société Africaine de Beton Manufacture
SABRA   Suid-Afrikaanse Bureau vir Rasse
            Aangeleenthede
SABRAO   Society for the Advancement of Breeding
            Researches in Asia and Oceania (Japan)
SABRE   Sociedad Alemã Brasileira de Refloresta-
            mento
SABS   South African Bureau of Standards

SABTS	South African Blood Transfusion Service
SAC	Schweizer Alpen Club
SAC	Scientific Advisory Committee (IAEA)
SAC	Sociedád de Agricultores de Colombia
SAC	Sociedád Agronómica de Chile
SAC	Sociedad Argentina de Criminologia
SAC	Société Africaine de Culture
SAC	Society for Analytical Chemistry
SAC	Society of Applied Cosmetology
SAC	Southern African Committee (U.S.A.)
SAC	State Advances Corporation (Australia)
SAC	Statistical Advisory Committee (FAO)
SACA	Societa per Azioni Costruzioni Aeronavali
SACA	Société Agricole de Côte d'Afrique (Ivory Coast)
SACA	Société Auxiliare de Commerce Africain (Mali)
SACA	South African Cricket Association
SACAC	South African Council for Automation and Computation
SACAF	Société Centrafricaine du Sac
SACAM	Société Auxiliaire Coopérative de Crédit Agricole Mutuel
SACANGO	Southern African Committee on Air Navigation and Ground Operation
SACAR	Société Abidjanaise de Carrelages (Ivory Coast)
SACCA	Servicio Agrónomico de los Cultivadores de Caña de Azúcar (Venezuela)
SACCB	Société Anonyme des Cultures au Congo Belge
SACDA	South African Copper Development Association
SACEM	Société des Auteurs, Compositeurs et Éditeurs de Musique
SACEM	Syndicat des Cadres et Agents de Maîtrise
SACEUR	Supreme Allied Commander Europe
SACFER	Société Africaine de Construction et de Fabrication d'Engins Roulants (Ivory Coast)
SACH	Sociedad Agronómica de Chile
SACHIA	Salone delle Tecniche Chimiche nell'Industria e nell'Agricoltura
SACHIM	Société des Amis de la Maison de la Chimie
SACI	Société Africaine de Commerce et d'Industrie (Ivory Coast)
SACIA	Société Africaine pour le Commerce l'Industrie et l'Agriculture
SACLANT	Supreme Allied Commander Atlantic
SACLANT-CEN	SACLANT Anti-Submarine Warfare Research Centre
SACLAT	Standing Advisory Committee on Local Authorities and the Theatre
SACM	Société Abidjanaise de Constructions Mécaniques (Ivory Coast)
SACM	Société Africaine de Constructions Métallurgiques
SACM	Société Alsacienne de Constructions Mécaniques
SACMA	Société Anonyme de Construction de Moteurs Aéronautiques
SACO	Société Africaine de Cacao (Ivory Coast)
SACO	Sveriges Akademikers Centralorganisation
SACOMAT	Société Africaine de Construction et Matériaux (Dahomey)
SACOS	Società Azionaria Centrali Ortofrutticole Siciliane
SACOTRA	Société Africaine de Consignation et de Transit (Dahomey)
SACPA	South African Cement Producers Association
SACRA	Société Africaine de Courtage et de Représentation d'Assurances (Ivory Coast)
SACS	Sakata Agricultural Co-operative Society (Japan)
SACS	Swedish Agro Co-operative Services
SACSEA	Supreme Allied Commander South East Asia
SACSIR	South African Council for Scientific and Industrial Research
SACSIT	Scottish Association of Cold Storage and Ice Trades
SACT	Section Administrative de la Coopération Technique (UNO)
SACT	Société Algérienne de Constructions Téléphoniques
SACTU	South African Congress of Trade Unions
SACTW	South African Council of Transport Workers
SACU	Sociedad de Avicultores y Cunicultores del Uruguay
SACU	Society for Anglo-Chinese Understanding
SACU	South African Cricket Union
SACUGS	South African Scientific Committee for the International Union of Geological Sciences
SAD	Scottish Association for the Deaf

SAD	Société Andine de Développement (Venezuela)	**SAE**	Society for the Advancement of Education (U.S.A.)
SAD	Spolecnost Antonína Dvoráka	**SAE**	Society of Automotive Engineers (U.S.A.)
SADA	Sociedad Argentina de Apicultores	**SAE**	Society of Automotive Engineers Australasia (*formerly* IAAE)
SADACI	Société Anonyme d'Applications de Chimie Industrielle (Belgium)	**SAE**	Sveriges Allmanna Exportförening
SADARET	Société Anglaise d'Études et de Réalisations d'Énergie et de Télécommunications	**SAEC**	Société Abidjanaise d'Expansion Chimique (Ivory Coast)
SADAS	Syllogos Architektonon Anotaton Scholon	**SAED**	Société Africaine d'Études et de Développement
SADC	Scottish Agricultural Development Council	**SAED**	Société d'Aménagement et d'Exploitation des Terres du Delta du Fleuve Sénégal
SADD	South African Development Division (*of* ODM)	**SAEGHT**	Société Africaine de Gestion Hôtelière et Touristique (Ivory Coast)
SADE	Società Adriatica di Ellettricità	**SAEL**	Sociedád Argentina de Estudios Lingúisticos
SADE	Société Alsacienne de Développement et d'Expansion	**SAEP**	Société Africaine d'Éditions et de Publicité
SADEL	Secretario Argentino de la Lano	**SAEPC**	Société Anonyme d'Explosifs et de Produits Chimiques
SADEP	Société Auxiliaire pour la Diffusion des Éditions de Productivité	**SAEST**	Society for the Advancement of Electrochemical Science and Technology (India)
SADER	Société Africaine de Déroulage des Déserts Rougier et Fils (Gabon)	**SAETA**	Sociedad Anonima Emisorars de Television y Anexos (Uruguay)
SADF	South African Defence Forces	**SAEWA**	South African Electrical Workers' Association
SADG	Société des Architectes Diplomés par le Gouvernment	**SAF**	Skibsfartens Arbeidsgiverforening
SADHEA	South African Dietetics and Home Economics Association	**SAF**	Skofabrikkenes Arbeidsgiverforening
SADI	Société Africaine de Développement Industriel	**SAF**	Société Africaine Forestière (Ivory Coast)
SADIA	Société Africaine de Diffusion Industrielle et Automobile (Ivory Coast)	**SAF**	Société des Agriculteurs de France
SADIA	Société Auxiliaire de l'Industrie de l'Azote	**SAF**	Société Anonyme Française
SADIAMIL	Société Africaine du Développement de l'Industrie Alimentaire du Millet et du Sorgho (Niger)	**SAF**	Société Astronomique de France
		SAF	Society of American Foresters
SADIM	Société Anonyme pour le Développement Immobilier de Monaco	**SAF**	South African Foundation
SADIO	Sociedad Argentina de Investigación Operativa	**SAF**	Sports Aid Foundation
		SAF	Svenska Aktiva Fastighetsmäklareförbundet
SADITA	Société Africaine d'Importation et de Distribution de Tabacs et Articles Divers (Ivory Coast)	**SAF**	Svenska Anestesiologisk Förening
		SAF	Svenska Antikvariatföreningen
SADMN	Sociedad Argentina de Medicina Nuclear	**SAF**	Svenska Arbetsgivareföreningen
SADOI	Sociedad Argentina de Organización Industrial	**SAF**	Syndicat Général des Affineurs de France
		SAFA	Scottish Amateur Football Association
SADP	Syndicat Agricole de Défense Paysanne	**SAFA**	Société d'Achat France-Afrique
SADRAC	South African Defence Research Advisory Committee	**SAFA**	Société Africaine Forestière et Agricole
		SAFA	Société Anon. Forestière et Agricole, Edea (French Cameroons)
		SAFA	South African Freedom Association
SADTC	SHAPE Air Defence Technical Centre	**SAFAA**	Société Française d'Appareils Automatiques

SAFAD	Swedish Agency for Administrative Development
SAFAL	Société Africaine de Fonderie d'Aluminium
SAFAMI	Société Africaine de Fabrications Métalliques Industrielles (Ivory Coast)
SAFAR	Société Africaine de Fabrication des Automobiles Renault (Ivory Coast)
SAFB	Schweizerische Arbeitsgemeinschaft für Bevölkerungsfragen
SAFBAIL	Société Africaine de Crédit Bail (Ivory Coast)
SAFCA	Société Africaine de Fabrication de Cahiers
SAFCO	Saudi Arabian Fertiliser Company
SAFCO	Société Africaine Colombani et Cie (Gabon)
SAFCO	Société Afrique Commerce (Dahomey)
SAFCO	Société Africaine de Conserveries (Ivory Coast)
SAFCO	Standing Advisory Committee on Fisheries
SAFEL	Société Agricole de Fruits et Légumes
SAFER	Sociétés d'Aménagement Foncier et Établissement Rural
SAFI	Sammenslutningen af Automobil-Fabrikanter og Importorer
SAFI	Société Africaine de Fabrication Industrielle
SAFICA	Société Africaine de Fabrication et d'Impression de Cahiers (Ivory Coast)
SAFICO	Société Abidjanaise de Fournitures pour l'Industrie et les Constructions en Côte d'Ivoire
SAFID	Sammenslutningen af Frugtpulpfabrikanter-eksportrer i Danmark
SAFIE	Société Africaine d'Installations Électriques
SAFIZ	Società Anonima Forniture Impianti Zootecnici
SAFM	Société Africaine de Fabrication Métallique (Ivory Coast)
SAFR	Schweizerische Arbeitsgemeinschaft für Raketentechnik
SAFRA	Société Africaine d'Assurances (Senegal)
SAFRIC	Société Africaine de Confection (Ivory Coast)
SAFRICA	Société Africaine d'Armement (Dahomey)
SAFRICA	Société Africaine de Management (Ivory Coast)
SAFRINEX	Société Africaine d'Exploitation Vinicole
SAFRIPA	Société Africaine de Parfumerie
SAFT	Société Africaine de Fabrication et de Transformation
SAFTEL	Société Africaine d'Électronique et de Télécommunications
SAFTO	South African Foreign Trade Organization
SAFUES	South African Federation of University Engineering Students
SAFV	Sociedad Argentina de Fisiología Vegetal
SAG	Scandinavian Society of Geneticists
SAG	Schweizerische Astronomische Gesellschaft
SAG	Secretaría de Agricultura y Ganadería (Mexico)
SAG	Shell Aviation Guinée
SAG	Société Agricole de Guinée
SAGA	Schweizerische Akademische Gesellschaft der Anglisten
SAGA	Society of American Graphic Artists
SAGB	Schizophrenia Association of Great Britain
SAGB	Spiritualist Association of Great Britain
SAGAGB	Sand and Gravel Association of Great Britain
SAGD	Suid-Afrikaanse Geneeskundige Diens
SAGE	Syndicat National des Fabricants d'Articles Galvanisés et Étamés
SAGEC	Société Africaine de Génie Rurale (Haute-Volta)
SAGECCOM	Société Africaine de Génie Civil et de Constructions Métalliques
SAGECO	Société Abidjanaise de Gerance et d'Exploitation Commercial (Ivory Coast)
SAGEM	Société d'Applications Générales d'Électricité et de Mécanique
SAGROCOL	Sociedad Agrológica Colombiana
SAGS	Schweizerische Akademische Gesellschaft der Slavisten
SAH	Sociedad Argentina de Horticultura
SAH	Sveriges Allmänna Hypoteksbank
SAHM	Société Africaine des Halles Modernes
SAHR	Society of Army Historical Research
SAHSA	Servicio Aéreo de Honduras SA
SAHT	Sallskapet for Agronomisk Hydroteknik
SAI	Scottish Agricultural Industries Ltd
SAI	Senior Advocates International (U.S.A.)
SAI	Servicio Agricola Interamericana
SAI	Società Anonima Italiana
SAI	Società Attori Italiani
SAI	Société Arabe d'Investissement (Saudi Arabia)

AI	Society of Antiquaries of Ireland
AI	Southeast Asia Institute (U.S.A.)
AIA	South Australian Institute of Architects
AIAA	South African Institute of Assayers and Analysts
AIB	Société Africaine des Industries du Bâtiment
AIC	Scottish Agricultural Improvement Council
AICA	Société Agricole et Industrielle de la Côte d'Afrique
AICCOR	South African Industrial Cellulose Corporation (Pty) Ltd
AICE	South African Institute of Civil Engineers
AIChem.E	South African Institution of Chemical Engineers
AICI	Società Agricola Industriale della Cellulosa Italiana
AICOS	Société Agricole Industrielle et Commerciale du Sénégal
AIDC	South African Inventions Development Corporation
AIE	Société Abidjanaise Import-Export (Ivory Coast)
AIEE	South African Institute of Electrical Engineers
AIET	Société Africaine d'Importation et d'Exportation Tchadienne
SAIF	Société Agricole d'Investissement Foncier
SAIF	South African Industrial Federation
SAIF	South African Institute of Foundrymen
SAIH	Société Africaine Immobilière et Hôtelière
SAII	Société Africaine d'Impressions Industrielles
SAILA	South African Indian Library Association
SAIM	Società Agraria Industriale Meridionale
SAIMech.E	South African Institution of Mechanical Engineers
SAIMM	South African Institute of Mining and Metallurgy
SAIMR	South African Institute for Medical Research
SAIO	Sociedad Argentina de Investigacion Operativa (Argentina)
SAIORG	Supreme Assembly of the International Order of Rainbow for Girls (U.S.A.)
SAIPA	South African Institute for Public Administration
SAIPA	Sociedad Argentina para la Investigación de Productos Aromaticos
SAIPE	South African Institute for Production Engineering
SAIRAC	South African Institute of Refrigeration and Air-conditioning
SAIRR	South African Institute of Race Relations
SAIS	School of Advanced International Studies, Johns Hopkins University (U.S.A.)
SAIS	Scientific Apparatus Information Service (U.S.A.)
SAIS	Sociedades Agrícoles de Interés Social (Peru)
SAIS	Società Agricola Italo Somalia
SAIS	South African Interplanetary Society
SAISSA	Scottish Amateur Ice Speed Skating Association
SAIT	Société Anonyme Internationale de Télégraphie Sans Fil (Belgium)
SAIT	South African Institute of Translators
SAIW	South African Institute of Welding
SAJ	Suomen Ammattijärjestö
SAJA	Société des Amateurs de Jardins Alpins
SAK	Kuwait Investment Company
SAK	Suomen Ammattiyhdistysten Keskusliitto
SAKF	Svenska Akustikkonsulenters Förening
SAKO	Suomen Ammattikoulunopettajien Liitto
SAL	Schweizerische Arbeitsgemeinschaft voor Logopädie
SAL	Société Astronomique de Liège
SAL	Sveriges Allmänna Lantbrukssallskap
SALA	South African Library Association
SALALM	Seminars on the Acquisition of Latin American Library Materials
SALCI	Société des Ananas de la Côte-d'Ivoire
SALF	Sveriges Agronom-och Lantbrukslärareforbund
SALINTO	Société des Salines du Togo
SALNR	South Africa Lombard Nature Reserve
SALP	Société Africaine de Librairie-Papeterie (Gabon)
SALP	South African Labour Party
SALS	South African Logopedic Society
SALT	Soviet-American Strategic Arms Limitation Talks
SAM	Sociedad Agronómica Mexicana
SAM	Société Africaine de Menuiserie (Ivory Coast)
SAM	Società Aerea Mediterrania

SAM	Society for the Advancement of Management (U.S.A.)
SAMA	Scientific Apparatus Makers of America
SAMA	Scottish Agricultural Machinery Association
SAMA	Scottish Association of Manufacturers Agents
SAMA	South African Museums Association
SAMAO	Société Auxiliare de Matériel pour l'Afrique Occidentale (Ivory Coast)
SAMB	Scottish Association of Master Bakers
SAMC	Scottish Association of Manufacturing Coppersmiths
SAMDA	Société Agricole Mutuelle d'Assurance
SAMDC	South African Medical and Dental Council
SAME	Society of American Military Engineers
SAMES	Société Anonyme de Machines Électrostatiques
SAMG	Sociedád Argentina de Mineria y Geologia
SAMH	Scottish Association for Mental Health
SAMI	Société Africaine de Matériel Industriel (Gabon Tchad)
SAMM	Société d'Applications des Machines Motrices
SAMOA	Société Agence Maritime de l'Ouest Africain (Ivory Coast)
SAMOGA	Société d'Aménagement de la Moyenne Garonne
SAMPA	Services d'Approvisionnement en Moyens de Production Agricole
SAMPE	Society of Aerospace Material and Process Engineers (U.S.A.)
SAMPM	Scottish Association of Milk Products Manufacturers
SAMRA	South African Market Research Association
SAMS	Société d'Application de Mécanisation des Semis
SAMS	South American Missionary Society
SAMSA	Silica and Moulding Sands Association
SAMTAS	Supervisory and Management Training Association of Singapore
SAN	Science Association of Nigeria
SANAA	Servicio Autonomo Nacional de Agua y Alcantarillado (Honduras)
SANAE	South African National Antarctic Expedition
SANAS	Service d'Alimentation et Nutrition Appliquée du Sénégal
SANB	South African National Bibliography
SANBRA	Sociedade Algodoeira do Nordeste Brasileiro
SANCA	South African National Council on Alcoholism and Drug Dependence
SANCAD	Scottish Association for National Certificate and Diplomas
SANCAR	South African National Committee for Antarctic Research
SANCC	South African National Consumers Council
SANCGASS	South African National Committee for Geomagnetism, Aeronomy and Space Sciences
SANCI	South African National Committee on Illumination
SANCOLD	South African National Committee on Large Dams
SANCOR	South African National Committee for Oceanographic Research
SANCOT	South African National Committee on Tunnelling
SANF	Société des Autoroutes du Nord de la France
SANLAM	Suid-Afrikaanse Nasionale Lewensassuransie-maatskappy
SANP	Sociedád de Anatomia Normal y Patológica (Argentina)
SANROC	South African Non-Racial Olympics Committee
SANTA	South African National Tuberculosis Association
SANU	Sudan African National Union
SANZ	Standards Association of New Zealand
SAO	Scottish Association of Opticians
SAONIC	Section Algérienne de l'Office National Interprofessionnel des Céréales
SAOS	Scottish Agricultural Organisation Society
SAOT	Scottish Association of Occupational Therapists
SAP	Nouvelle Société Africaine des Plastiques
SAP	Schweizerische Arztegesellschaft für Psychotherapie
SAP	Sociedad Agronómica de Panamá
SAP	Société Africaine des Peaux
SAP	Société Africaine de Pétroles
SAP	Sociedád Argentina de Pediatria
SAP	Société Africaine de Pneumatiques (Haute-Volta)
SAP	Société Agricole de Prévoyance

APA	Société d'Application de Peintures en Afrique (Congo)	**SAPS**	Servico de Alimentação da Previdencia Social (Brazil)
APA	South African Poultry Association	**SAPT**	Société Africaine de Photogrammetrie et de Topographie
APA	South African Press Association		
APA	South African Psychological Association	**SAPT**	Société d'Astronomie Populaire de Toulouse
APAC	Société Anonyme de Pêche, d'Armement et de Conservation	**SAPV**	Suid-Afrikaanse Pluimvee Vereniging
		SAQ	Schweizerische Arbeitsgemeinschaft f. Qualitätsbeforderung
APAL	Société Africaine de Produits Alimentaires		
APAR	Associazione Nazionale Sezioni Apparecchi per Pubbliche Attrazioni Ricreative	**SAR**	Secteurs d'Améliorations Rurales (Algeria)
		SAR	Société Africaine Radioélectrique
APAR	Société d'Appareillage Électrique	**SAR**	Société Africaine de Raffinage
APC	Société Africaine de Plomberie et Couverture	**SAR**	Société Africaine de Ravitaillement (Congo)
APCAM	Société Africaine de Produits Chimiques Agricoles et Ménagers	**SAR**	Société Africaine de Représentation (Haute-Volta)
APCS	Société Africaine des Produits Chimiques Shell (Ivory Coast)	**SAR**	Société Suisse d'Anesthésiologie et de Réanimation
APEB	Syndicat des Artisans et des Petites Entreprises du Bâtiment	**SAR**	Svenska Arkitekters Riksförbund
		SARA	Scottish Amateur Rowing Association
APEC	Syndicat des Fabricants d'Appareils de Production d'Eau Chaude par le Gaz	**SARA**	South African-Rhodesian Association
		SARAM	Société d'Applications Radioélectriques à l'Aéronautique et à la Marine
APECO	Société Africaine de Promotion Économique		
APEF	Société Africaine de Publicité et d'Éditions Fusionnées	**SARBICA**	South-East Asian Regional Branch of the International Council on Archives
APEGA	Société d'Approvisionnement et de Pêche du Gabon	**SARC**	South Asia Regional Council (U.S.A)
		SARCCUS	Southern African Regional Committee for the Conservation and Utilisation of the Soil
APELEC	Société Africaine des Piles Électriques (Ivory Coast)		
		SARCO	Saudi Arabian Refinery Company
APEM	Société d'Applications Pneumatiques Électriques et Méchaniques	**SAREC**	Swedish Agency for Research Cooperation with Developing Countries
APH	Société Africaine de Plantations d'Hévéas (Ivory Coast)	**SAREPA**	Société Africaine de Recherches et d'Études pour Aluminium
APHY-DATA	Systems for Acquisition, Transmission and Processing of Hydrological Data	**SARF**	South African Road Federation
		SARF	Sveriges Annons-och Reklambyraers Förbund
API	Société Africaine de Pêche Industrielle		
APM	Scottish Association of Paint Manufacturers	**SARGAS**	Station Avicole de Recherches Génétiques Appliquées à la Sélection
APM	Syndicat pour l'Amélioration de la Production Mulassière	**SARL**	Sociedade Anónima de Responsabilidade Limitada (Portugal)
APN	Société Agricole et Pastorale du Niari (Zaire)		
APPI	South African Pulp and Paper Industries Ltd	**SARL**	Société à Responsabilité Limitée
		SARL	South African Radio League
APRI	Società per Azione Produttori Riso Italiana	**SARMAG**	Société Africaine de Ravitaillement Maritime et d'Approvisionnements Généraux (Ivory Coast)
APRIM	Société Abidjanaise de Promotions Industrielles et Immobilières (Ivory Coast)		
APROC	Société d'Achats de Produits du Cameroun	**SARP**	Stowarzyszenie Architektow Polskich
APROCSY	Société Africaine de Produits Chimiques et de Synthèse (Ivory Coast)	**SARST**	Société Auxiliare de la Recherche Scientifique et Technique
APROLAIT	Société Africaine de Produits Laitiers		

SARTEX	Schweizerische Arbeitsgemeinschaft für Textil-Kennzeichnung
SARTOC	South Africa Regional Tourism Council
SARUPRI	Indonesian Plantation Workers Trade Union
SARY	Suomen Autorengasyhdistys
SAS	Scandinavian Airlines System
SAS	Schweizerischer Arbeitgeberverband für das Schneidergewerbe
SAS	Société Africaine des Silicates
SAS	Société Astronomique de Suisse
SAS	Svenska Akustikkonsulenters Förening
SASA	Scottish Amateur Swimming Association
SASA	Semilleros Argentinos S.A.
SASA	South African Sugar Association
SASAC	South African Council for Automation and Computation
SASAP	South African Society of Animal Production
SASCAR	South African Scientific Committee for Antarctic Research
SASCO	Singapore and Australia Shipping Company
SASCO	South Asia Science Cooperation Office (UNESCO)
SASI	Southern Association of Science and Industry (U.S.A.)
SASIF	Société Africaine de Soudages, Injections Forages
SASIF-CI	Société Africaine de Soudages, Forages de Côte-d'Ivoire
SASIO	Field Science Co-operation Office for South Asia
SASK	Suid-Afrikaanse Seinkorp
SASLIC	Surrey and Sussex Libraries in Co-operation
SASLO	South African Scientific Liaison Office
SASMAL	South African Sugar Millers Association Ltd
SASMI	Sindacato Autonomo Scuola Media Italiana
SASMIRA	Silk and Art Silk Mills Research Association (India)
SASO	Saudi Arabia Standards Organization
SASO	South African Students Association
SASOL	South African Coal, Oil and Gas Corporation
SASP	South African Society of Physiotherapy
SASS	Société Académique des Slavistes Suisses
SAST	Swiss Association for Space Technology
SASTA	South African Sugarcane Technologists Association
SAT	Sennacieca Asocio Tutmonda
SAT	Société Abidjanaise de Torrefaction (Ivory Coast)
SAT	Société Abidjanaise de Transport (Ivory Coast)
SAT	Société Africaine de Transit
SAT	Société Anonyme de Télécommunications
SAT	Société Archéologique de Touraine
SAT	Society of Acoustic Technology (*now* BAS)
SATA	Sociedade Acoriana de Transportes Aéreos
SATA	Société Africaine de Transit et d'Affrètement (Congo, Gabon)
SATA	Société Anonyme de Transport Aérien (Switzerland)
SATA	Student Air Travel Association
SATAM	Société Anonyme pour tous Appareillages Mécaniques
SAT-AMIKA	Association of French-Language Countries Nationless Esperantist Workers
SATC	Société Abidjanaise de Tissus et Confections (Ivory Coast)
SATC	Société d'Applications Techniques au Cameroun
SATCOM	U.S. National Academy of Sciences-National Academy of Engineering Committee on Scientific and Technical Communication
SATE	Swiss Association of Teachers of English
SATEC	Société d'Aide Technique et de Coopération (Senegal, Upper Volta)
SATEC	Société Africaine de Traitements Électrochimiques
SATEC	Société d'Assistance Technique et de Crédit
SATEL	Société Africaine des Techniques Électroniques (Dahomey)
SATENA	Servicio de Aeronavegación a Territorios Nacionales (Colombia)
SATERCO	Société Anonyme de Terrassements et de Constructions (Belgium)
SATET	Société Africaine de Travaux et d'Études Topographiques (Congo)
SATG	Schweizerische Automobiltechnische Gesellschaft
SATI	Société Anonyme de Transporte Isothermes (Belgium)
SATI-CI	Société Africaine de Transit et d'Affrètement (Ivory Coast)
SATK	Suid-Afrikaanse Toeristekorporasie
SATMACI	Société d'Assistance Technique pour la Modernisation Agricole de la Côte d'Ivoire

SATMAR	South African Torbanite Mining and Refining Company
SATNUC	Société pour les Applications de l'Énergie Nucléaire
SATO	South American Travel Organisation
SATOM	Société de Travaux d'Outre-Mer
SATPN	Société Assistance Technique pour les Produits Nestlé (Switzerland)
SATRA	Shoe and Allied Trades Research Association
SATRAM	Société Africaine de Travaux Maritimes et Fluviaux (Ivory Coast)
SATT	Société Africaine de Travaux et de Transports (Ivory Coast)
SATU	South African Typographical Union
SAUK	Suid-Afrikaanse Uitsaaikorporasie
SAUTE	Swiss Association of University Teachers of English
SAUU	South African Underwater Union
SAV	Schweizerischer Altphilogenverband
SAV	Schweizerischer Anwaltsverband
SAV	Schweizerischer Apothekerverein
SAV	Slovak Academy of Sciences
SAVA	South African Veterinary Association
SAVA	Verband Schweizerischer Annoncen-Verwaltungen und Agenturen
SAVCONGO	Savonnerie du Congo
SAVEC	Société Africaine de Vente et de Consignation (Ivory Coast)
SAVFAN	Standing Advisory Committee on Food and Nutrition (Caribbean)
SAVI	Society for the Advancement of the Vegetable Industry (Philippines)
SAVI	Suid-Afrikaanse Vertalersinstituut
SAVIA	Sociedad Agronomica Viveros Industriales Argentinos
SAVR	Special Army Volunteer Reserve
SAVS	Scottish Anti-Vivisection Society
SAWA	Scottish Amateur Wrestling Association
SAWA	Screen Advertising World Association
SAWAU	South African Women's Agricultural Union
SAWEK	Suid-Afrikaanse Akademie vir Wetenskap en Kuns
SAWGU	South African Wattle Growers Union
SAWMA	Soil and Water Management Association
SAWTRI	South African Wool Textile Research Institute
SAYC	Scottish Association of Youth Clubs
SAYFC	Scottish Association of Young Farmers' Clubs
SBA	Scottish Beekeepers' Association
SBA	Smaller Business Association
SBA	Sociedade Brasileira de Agronomia
SBAC	Société J. Bastos de l'Afrique Centrale
SBAC	Society of British Aerospace Companies
SBARMO	Scientific Ballooning and Radiations Monitoring Organization
SBAT	Service Botanique et Agronomique de Tunisie
SBAT	Sociedade Brasiliera de Autores Tetrais
SBB	Sociedade Botanica de Brasil
SBB	Société Belge de Biologie
SBBNF	Ship and Boat Builders National Federation
SBC	Sociedade Brasileira de Cartografia
SBC	Swedish Farmers Beet Growers Association
SBCBC	Société des Bitumes et Cut-backs du Cameroun
SBCCPA	Sociedade Brasileira de Criadores de Cães Pastores Alemães
SBCI	Sociedade Brasileira de Cultura Inglêsa
SBCUK	School Broadcasting Council for the United Kingdom
SBD	Société Dahoméenne de Banque
SBE	Sociedade Brasileira de Entomologia
SBE	Société Belge des Électriciens
SBE	Société Belge d'Ergologie
SBE	Society of Business Economists
SBEE	Société Belge d'Études d'Expansion
SBEF	Svenska Byggnadsentreprenörföreningen
SBET	Society of British Esperantist Teachers
SBF	Sociedade Brasileira de Floricultura
SBF	Svenska Bageriförbund
SBF	Svenska Bergsmannaföreningen
SBF	Svenska Brandförsvarsföreningen
SBF	Svenska Busstrafikförbundet
SBF	Sveriges Bildelsgrossisters Förening
SBF	Sveriges Biografägareförbund
SBFV	Schweizerischer Berufsfischerverband
SBG	Schweizerische Botanische Gesellschaft
SBG	Sociedade Brasileira de Geologia
SBG	Stichting Bevordering Galvanotechniek
SBGE	Société Belge de Gasto-Entérologie

SBGI	Society of British Gas Industries	**SBS**	Sociedad Brasileira de Silvicultura
SBGW	Städtische Büchereien der Gemeinde Wien (Austria)	**SBS**	Svenska Bibliotekariesamfundet
		SBSA	Show and Breed Secretaries Association
SBHED	Sociedade Brasileira de Herbicides e Ervas Daninhas	**SBSA**	Standard Bank of South Africa
SBHV	Schweizerischer Briefmarkenhändler-Verband	**SBSMP**	Société Bernoulli pour la Statistique Mathématique et la Probabilité
SBI	Società Botanika Italiano	**SBTC**	Sino British Trade Council
SBI	Statens Byggeforskningsinstitut (Denmark)	**SBU**	Schweizerische Butter-Union
SBI	Swedish Farmers Distillers Association	**SBU**	Scottish Badminton Union
SBIA	Société Belge des Ingénieurs de l'Automobile	**SBU**	Sociedades Bíblicas Unidas
SBIT	Société Belge des Ingénieurs Techniciens	**SBU**	Sumitomo Bayer Urethane Co., Ltd (Japan)
SBKV	Schweizerischer Bäcker-Konditorenmeister-Verband	**SBUAM**	Société Belge des Urbanistes et Architectes Modernistes
SBL	Skibsbyggerienes Landsforening	**SBV**	Schweizerischer Bank Verein
SBL	Suomen Bensiinikauppiaitten Liitto	**SBV**	Schweizerischer Baumeisterverband
SBLAM	Syndicat Belge de la Librairie Ancienne et Moderne	**SBV**	Schweizerischer Bergführerverband
		SBV	Schweizerischer Bootbauer-Verband
SBM	Sociedad Botánica de México	**SBV**	Schweizerischer Brennstoffhändler-Verband
SBM	Société Belge des Mécaniciens	**SBV**	Schweizerischer Beirbrauerverein
SBM	Société de Biologie de Montréal (Canada)	**SBV**	Schweizerischer Buchdruckerverein
SBME	Société Belge de Microscopie Électronique	**SBV**	Schweizerischer Büchsemacher-Verband
SBMV	Sociedade Brasileira de Medicina Veterinaria	**SBVV**	Schweizer Buchhändler und Verleger Verein
SBN	Schweizerischer Bund für Naturschutz	**SBWA**	Standard Bank of West Africa
SBNS	Society of British Neurological Surgeons	**SCA**	Scottish Canoe Association
SBO	Stichting Bloedgroepen Onderzoek	**SCA**	Scottish Chess Association
SBOT	Société Belge de Chirurgie Orthopédique et de Traumatologie	**SCA**	Sociedad Científica Argentina
		SCA	Société Centrale d'Apiculture
SBP	Société Belge de Photogrammétrie	**SCA**	Société Commerciale Africaine
SBP	Stowarzyszenie Bibliotekarzy Polskich	**SCA**	Society of Company and Commercial Accountants
SBPC	Sociedade Brasileira para o Progresso da Ciencia	**SCA**	Svenska Cellulose Aktiebolaget
SBPIM	Society of British Printing Ink Manufacturers	**SCAAF**	Société Centrale d'Approvisionnement des Agriculteurs de France
SBPM	Society of British Paint Manufacturers	**SCAAP**	Special Commonwealth African Assistance Plan
SBPR	Sociedad de Bibliotecarios de Puerto Rico		
SBR	Société Belge Radio-électrique	**SCAB**	Sociedad Cooperativa de Agrónomos de Bolivia
SBR	Society for Biological Rhythm (Porto Rico)	**SCAB**	Société Centrale d'Architecture de Belgique
SBR	Svenska Byggnadsingenjörers Riksförbund	**SCAD**	Société Centrafricaine de Déroulage
SBR	Sveriges Bensinhandlares Riksförbund	**SCADOA**	Service Commun d'Armements Desservant l'Ouest Africain
SBREC	Sugar Beet Research and Education Committee		
SBRF	Sveriges Bokförings-och Revisionsbyraers Förbund	**SCAEI**	Syndicat des Constructeurs d'Appareillage Électrique d'Installations
SBRS	Sheep Breeding Research Station (India)	**SCAF**	Compagnie des Scieries Africaines
SBS	Schweizerischer Berufsverband der Sozialarbeiter	**SCAF**	Société Centrale d'Aviculture de France

SCAFA | Société Centrafricaine d'Affrètement et d'Acconage
SCAFR | Société Centrale d'Aménagement Foncier Rural
SCAHUR | Société Congolaise d'Aménagement de l'Habitat Urbain et Rurale
SCALMS | Syndicat des Constructeurs d'Appareils de Levage, de Manutention et de Matériels de Stockage
SCALOM | Société Camerounaise de Location de Matériel et de Travaux Publics
SCAM | Société de Colonisation Agricole au Mayumbe (French West Africa)
SCAM | Sociétés Coopératives Agricoles Marocaines
SCAMAP | Syndicat des Cadres et Agents de Maîtrise de l'Aéroport de Paris
SCAMTRA | Société Camerounaise de Manutention, de Transport et de Transit
SCANAUS-TRAL | Scandinavian Australia Carriers Ltd (Norway)
SCANDOC | Scandinavian Documentation Centre
SCAP | Société Centrale d'Aquiculture et de Pêche
SCAPA | Society for Checking the Abuses of Public Advertising
SCAR | Scandinavian Council for Applied Research
SCAR | Scientific Committee on Antarctic Research (ICSU)
SCARA | Syndicat de Compagnies Assurant les Risques Automobiles (Belgium)
SCART | Syndicat de Constructeurs d'Appareils Radio-Récepteurs et Téléviseurs
SCASA | Servicio Cooperative Agrícola Salvadoreño Americano
SCATS | Southern Counties Agricultural Trading Society
SCAUL | Standing Conference of African University Libraries
SCAULEA | Standing Conference of African University Libraries, Eastern Area
SCAULWA | Standing Conference of African University Libraries, Western Area
SCB | Sociedad Cubana de Botánica
SCB | Schweizerische Chemische Gesellschaft
SCB | Société Camerounaise de Banque
SCB | Société Chimique de Belgique
SCB | Société d'Étude et de Développement de la Culture Bananière (Ivory Coast)
SCB | Statistiska Centralbyran

SCBE | Société Canadienne des Brevets et d'Exploitation Limitée
SCBK | Société Congolaise des Brasseries Kronenbourg
SCBM | Société Camerounaise de Beton Manufacture
SCC | Scandinavian Clothing Council
SCC | Society of Cosmetic Chemists of Great Britain
SCC | Swedish Cooperative Centre
SCCAPE | Scottish Council for Commercial, Administrative and Professional Education
SCCE | Société Camerounaise de Conditionnement et d'Entreposage
SCCF | Société Centrale Canine de France
SCCH | Sociedad Científica de Chile
SCCS | Sociedad Colombiana de la Ciencia del Suelo
SCCU | Scottish Cross Country Union
SCE | Sociedad Colombiana de Economistas
SCEAM | Symposium des Conférences Épiscopates d'Afrique et de Madagascar
SCEAR | Scientific Committee on the Effects of Radiation (U.S.A.)
SCED | Société Centrafricaine d'Exploitation Diamantifère
SCEES | Société Central des Études et des Enquêtes Statistiques
SCEF | Société Camerounaise d'Exploitation Forestière
SCEFL | Société Camerounaise Équatoriale de Fabrication de Lubrifiants
SCEL | Société Coopérative d'Édition et de Librairie
SCEL | Standing Committee on Education in Librarianship
SCEP | Société Continentale d'Éditions et Périodiques
SCEPAG | Société pour le Conditionnement et l'Exportation des Produits Agricoles (Madagascar)
SCEPS | Strategic and Corporate Europlanners Society (Belgium)
SCET-International | Société Centrale pour l'Équipement du Territoire Internationale
SCETA | Société de Contrôle et d'Exploitation des Transport Auxiliaires
SCF | Société Chimique de France
SCF | Société de Comptabilité de France
SCF | Svenska Civilekonomföreningen

SCFCEF	Syndicat des Constructeurs Française de Condensateurs Électrique Fixes
SCFMO	Syndicat des Constructeurs Français de Machines-Outils
SCG	Schweïzerische Chemische Gesellschaft
SCGAF	Société Centrale de Gestion des Agriculteurs de France
SCGB	Ski Club of Great Britain
SCGI	Société Congolaise de Gaz Industriels
SCHE	Sociedad Chilena de Entomología
SCHF	Sociedad Chilena de Física
SCHG	Sociedad Chilena de Genética
SCHHG	Sociedad Chilena de Historia y Geografía
SCHHN	Sociedad Chilena de Historia Natural
SCHI	Southern California Horticultural Institute (U.S.A.)
SCHM	International Commission for a History of the Scientific and Cultural Development of Mankind
SCHMC	Society of Catering and Hotel Management Consultants
SCHN	Société Canadienne d'Histoire Naturelle
SCHNBT	Sociedad Chilena de Nutrición, Bromatología y Toxicología
SCHP	Sociedad Chilena de Parasitología
SCHPA	Sociedad Chilena de Producción Animal
SCHQ	Sociedad Chilena de Química
SCI	Sea Containers Inc.
SCI	Service Civil Internationale
SCI	Société Camerounaise Industrielle
SCI	Society of Chemical Industry
SCI	Southern Cross International (U.K.)
SCIA	Servicio Cooperativo Interamericano de Agricultura
SCIA	Société Commerciale et Immobilière de l'Atlantique (Dahomey)
SCIBP	Special Committee for the International Biological Programme
SCIC	Société Centrale Immobilière de la Caisse des Dépôts
SCIC	Southern Corn Improvement Conference (U.S.A.)
SCICA	Société Chimique et Industrielle Camerounaise
SCIDA	Servicio Cooperativo Interamericano de Agricultura (Guatemala)

SCIDE	Servicio Cooperativo Interamericano de Educación (Bolivia)
SCIDT	Scottish Country Industries Development Trust
SCIEC	Société Civile Immobilière des Entrepôts de Coton
SCIEC	Syndicat des Commerçants Importateurs et Exportateurs du Cameroun
SCIENCE	Société des Consultants Indépendants et Neutres de la Communauté Européenne
SCIF	Servicio Cooperativo Interamericano de Irrigación, Vías de Comunicación e Industrias (Peru)
SCIFE	Servicio Cooperativo Interamericano de Fomento Económico (Panama, Peru)
SCIMA	Syndicat des Constructeurs et Constructeurs-Installateurs de Matériel Aéraulique
SCIMO	Société Commerciale et Industrielle pour la Métropole et Outre-Mer
SCIMPEX	Syndicat des Commerçants Importateurs et Exportateurs (Ivory Coast, Mali, Mauritania, Niger, Senegal, Upper Volta)
SCIMPEXNI	Syndicat des Commerçants Importateurs et Exportateurs du Niger
SCIMP-EXTO	Syndicat des Commerçants Importateurs et Exportateurs de la République Togolaise
SCIMPOS	Société Camerounaise d'Injection et de Modelage de Produits Organiques et Synthétiques
SCIPA	Servicio Cooperativo Inter-Americano de Producción de Alimentos
SCIPAG	Syndicat des Constructeurs de Machines pour les Industries du Papier, du Carton et des Arts Graphiques
SCIPLAC	Sciages et Placages Centrafricains
SCIPS	Servicio Cooperativo Interamericano Plan del Sur (Peru)
SCIR	Syndicat Central d'Initiatives Rurales (France)
SCISP	Servicio Cooperativo Interamericano de Salud Pública (Paraguay)
SCITS	Servicio de Comercio de la Industria Textil Sedara
SCIVU	Scientific Council of the International Vegetarian Union
SCLP	Scientists Committee on Loyalty Problems (U.S.A.)
SCM	Société Camerounaise Michelin

CM	Société Camerounaise de Minoterie	SCOW	Steel Company of Wales
CM	Société de Chirurgie de Montréal (Canada)	SCP	Social Credit Party (Canada)
CM	Sous-Commission de Coordination des Questions Forestières Méditerranéennes (of FAO)	SCP	Sociedad Científica de Paraguay
		SCP	Société Camerounaise des Peaux
CM	Student Christian Movement of Great Britain and Ireland	SCP	Société du Canal de Provence et d'Aménagement de la Région Provençale
CMA	Service Cinématographique du Ministère de l'Agriculture	SCP	Syndicat des Constructeurs de Pompes
		SCPA	Société Commerciale des Potasses d'Alsace
CMA	Society of Cinema Managers of Great Britain and Ireland	SCPA	Société Commerciale des Potasses et de l'Azote
CMV	Schweizerischer Coiffeurmeister-Verband	SCPI	Structural Clay Products Institute (USA)
CNEA	Sealing Commission for the Northeast Atlantic	SCPR	Scottish Council of Physical Recreation
		SCPR	Social and Community Planning Research
CNR	Scientific Committee of National Representatives (of SHAPE)	SCR	Society for Cultural Relations with the U.S.S.R.
CNVYO	Standing Conference of National Voluntary Youth Organisations	SCR	Southern Council of Research (USA)
CNWA	Sealing Commission for the Northwest Atlantic	SCRA	Secteur Côtier des Recherches Agronomiques
COA	Société Commerciale de l'Ouest Africain	SCRAL	Sociedad Cooperativa Rural Argentina Ltd.
COCLIS	Standing Conference of Co-operative Library Information Services	SCRAM	Scottish Campaign to Resist the Atomic Menace
CODI	Société des Conserves de Côte-d'Ivoire	SCRATA	Steel Castings Research and Trade Association
COFET	Syndicat des Constructeurs de Fours et d'Équipements Thermiques	SCRCC	Soil Conservation and Rivers Control Council (N.Z.)
COLLUL	Standing Conference of Librarians of Libraries of the University of London	SCRE	Scottish Council for Research in Education
COLMA	Standing Conference on Library Materials on Africa	SCRE	Syndicat des Constructeurs de Relais Électriques
COM	Société Centrale d'Organisation et Méthodes	SCREAM	Society for the Control and Registration of Estate Agents and Mortgage Brokers
COMAD	Service de Contrôle du Conditionnement de Madagascar	SCREM	Syndicat National du Commerce Radio Télévision et de l'Équipement Ménager
CONMEL	Standing Conference for Mediterranean Librarians	SCRN	Sociedad Colombiana de Recursos Naturales
CONUL	Standing Conference of National and University Libraries	SCRP	Syndicat de la Crèmerie de la Région Parisienne
COP	Société Coopératives Ouvrières de Production	SCS	Société Camerounaise de Sacherie
		SCS	Société Commerciale Sénégalaise
COPE	Scientific Committee on Problems of the Environment (of ICSU)	SCS	Society of Civil Servants
		SCS	Soil Conservation Service (U.S.A.)
COPE	Standing Committee on Professional Exchange (Denmark)	SCSA	Scottish Cold Storage Association
COR	Scientific Committee on Oceanic Research	SCSA	Société Canadienne de Sociologie et d'Anthropologie
COSTEP	Special Committee for Solar Terrestrial Physics (of ICSU)	SCSA	Soil Conservation Society of America
COTA	Scottish Offshore Training Association	SCSA	Statiunea Centrala pentru Sericicultura si Apicultura (Roumania)
COTAPLL	Standing Conference on Theological and Philosophical Libraries in London	SCSA	Supreme Council for Sports in Africa

SCSK	Shellfish Commission for the Skagerrak-Kattegat		**SDANA**	Section Dahoméenne de Nutrition et d'Alimentation Appliquée
SCSKU	Svaz Ceských Skaladatelu a Koncertních Umelcu		**SDAR**	Savez Drustava Arhivskih Radnika Jugoslavije
SCSS	Scottish Council of Social Service		**SDAT**	Sociedad Dásonómica de la América Tropical
SCT	Société Camerounaise du Tabac			
SCT	Société Cotonnière Transocéanique		**SDC**	Society of Dyers and Colourists
SCTA	Société Camerounais de Transport et d'Affrétement		**SDC**	Synthetic Diamond Company (Eire)
			SDCA	Society of Dyers and Colourists of Australia
SCTC	Société Commerciale Transocéanique des Conteneurs		**SDECE**	Service de Documentation Extérieure et de Contre-Espionnage
SCTHP	Syndicat des Constructeurs de Transmissions Hydrauliques et Pneumatiques		**SDEE**	Société Dahoméenne d'Électricité et d'Eau
SCTN	Société Agricole pour le Contrôle de la Descendance des Taureaux de Race Normande		**SDF**	Svenska Dataföreningen
			SDFM	Section Départementale des Fermiers et Métayers
SCTR	Standing Conference on Telecommunications Research		**SDG**	Schweizerische Diabetes Gesellschaft
SCTTAO	Société Commerciale de Transports Trans-atlantiques Afrique Occidentale		**SDGTE**	Société Dahoméenne des Grands Travaux de l'Est
SCTU	Security Council Truce Commission (Palestine)		**SDHBS**	South Devon Herd Book Society
SCU	Scottish Cricket Union		**SDI**	Secours Dentaire International
SCUA	Scottish Conservative and Unionist Association		**SDI**	Sociedad para el Desarrollo Internacional
SCUA	Suez Canal Users Association		**SDI**	Società Dantesca Italiana
SCUAS	Standing Conference of University Appointments Services		**SDIA**	Soap and Detergent Industry Association
			SDIC	Société de Développement Industriel du Cameroun
SCUMRA	Société Centrale de l'Uranium et des Minerais et Métaux Radioactifs		**SDIG**	Société pour le Développement de l'Industrie du Gaz
SCVANYO	Standing Conference of Voluntary Youth Organizations		**SDIT**	Service de Documentation et d'Information Techniques de l'Aéronautique
SCVM	Service Central des Ventes du Mobilier de l'État		**SDK**	Société de Kinésithérapie
			SDL	Syndicat des Distillateurs-Liquoristes de Belgique
SCVU	Svaz Ceských Výtvarných Umelcu		**SDLP**	Social and Democratic Labour Party (N. Ireland)
SCWR	Scientific Committee on Water Research (ICSU)		**SDMFAJ**	Savex Drustava Matematicara, Fizicara i Astronoma Jugoslavije
SCWS	Scottish Co-operative Wholesale Society		**SDN**	Société des Nations (replaced by UNO)
SCYA	Scottish Christian Youth Assembly		**SDP**	Swaziland Democratic Party
SCYCO-MIMPEX	Syndicat des Industries de l'Afrique Équatoriale		**SDPG**	Société Dahoméenne de Pointes Galvanisées
			SDR	Société de Développement Régional
SDA	Schweizerische Depeschenagentur		**SDRA**	Société pour le Développement de la Riviéra Africaine (Ivory Coast)
SDA	Sheep Development Association (*now* NSA)			
SDA	Société de l'Aérotrain		**SDS**	Servizio di Documentazione Spaziale
SDA	Syndicat de la Distillerie Agricole		**SDS**	Slavisticno Drustvo Slovenije
SDAI	Syndicat National de la Distribution pour l'Automobile et l'Industrie		**SDSTA**	Section Technique de l'Armée, Documentation Technique et Scientifique

SDT	Société Dahoméenne de Transports
SDT	Society of Dairy Technology
SDTIM	Society for the Development of Techniques in Industrial Marketing
SDTU	Sign and Display Trades Union
SDUK	Society for the Diffusion of Useful Knowledge
SDV	Schweizerischer Dachdeckermeister-Verband
SDV	Schweizerischer Detaillistenverband
SDV	Schweizerischer Drogisten-Verband
SDV	Stichting Doelmatig Verzinken
SE	Society of Engineers
SEA	Science and Education Administration (U.S.A.)
SEA	Shipbuilding Exports Association
SEA	Société Équatoriale d'Assurances
SEA	Société d'Électronique et d'Automatisme
SEA	Sociedad Entomológica Argentina
SEA	Société d'Études Ardennaises
SEA	Société d'Équipement pour l'Afrique (Gabon)
SEA	Stazione di Entomologia Agraria
SEAAC	South-East Asia Air Command
SEAC	Social and Economic Archives Centre
SEAC	South-East Asia Command
SEACEN	South-East Asian Central Banks
SEADAG	South-East Asia Development Advisory Group (U.S.A.)
SEADD	South-East Asia Development Division (of ODM)
SEAF	Sveriges El-och Elektronikagenters Förening
SEAFDEC	Southeast Asian Fisheries Development Centre
SEAG	Société d'Équipement pour l'Afrique-Gabon
SEAISI	South East Asia Iron and Steel Institute
SEALPA	South-East Asia Lumber Producers Association
SEAM	Servicio de Equipos Agricolas Mecanizados (Chile)
SEAMEO	Southeast Asian Ministers of Education Organisation
SEAMES	Southeast Asian Ministers of Education Secretariat
SEAN	Servicio Escolar de Alimentación y Nutrición
SEAN	Société d'Équipement pour l'Afrique-Niger
SEAP	South-East Asia Project (of IUCN)

SEAPAL	South East Asia and Pacific League against Rheumatism
SEAP-CENTRE	South East Asia Centre for the Promotion of Trade, Investments and Tourism (Japan)
SEARCA	Southeast Asian Regional Centre for Graduate Study and Research in Agriculture (Philippines)
SEARCC	South-East Asia Regional Computer Conference
SEARCF	Société d'Encouragement pour l'Amélioration des Races de Chevaux en France
SEARS	South and East Asian Regional Section (of IOBC)
SEAS	Centre for Southeast Asia Studies of Kyoto University (Japan)
SEAS	Scientific Exploration of the Atlantic Shelf
SEAS	SHARE European Association
SEAS	Société d'Équipement pour l'Afrique-Sénégal
SEASCO	Field Science Co-operation Office for South-East Asia
SEASSE	Southeast Asian Society of Soil Engineering (Thailand)
SEATAG	South East Asia Trade Advisory Group
SEATO	South-East Asia Treaty Organisation
SEAVOM	Société d'Études et d'Applications Video-Optique Mécanique
SEB	Sociedad Española de Bioquímica
SEB	Société Équatoriale des Bois (Gabon)
SEB	Société d'Exploitation des Briqueteries
SEB	Society for Economic Botany (U.S.A.)
SEB	Society for Experimental Biology
SEB	Southern Electricity Board
SEB	Syndicat des Éditeurs Belges
SEB	Syndicat des Exploitants de Bauxite
SEBA	Société Sénégalaise d'Exploitation des Bois Africains
SEBACAM	Société d'Études des Bauxites du Cameroun
SEBC	Societe d'Exploitation des Bois du Cameroun
SEBOGA	Société pour l'Expansion des Boissons Hygiéniques au Gabon
SEBT	South-Eastern Brick and Tile Federation
SEC	Société Européenne de Cardiologie
SEC	Société Européenne de Culture
SEC	State Electricity Commission of Victoria (Australia)

SECA	Société pour l'Expansion Commerciale Africaine (Togo)
SECA	Société d'Exploitation de Constructions Aéronautiques
SECA	Syndicat d'Études des Centrales Atomiques
SECAB	Secrétariat Exécutif de la Convention Andrés Bello (Peru)
SECAM	Société d'Exploitation des Cadres Maritimes
SECAM	Symposium of Episcopal Conferences of Africa and Madagascar
SECAN	Société d'Études et de Constructions Aéro-Navales
SECAP	Servicio Ecuatoria de Capacitación Profesional
SECARTYS	Servicio de Exportación de Electrónica
SECAS	Sociedad de Estudiantes de Ciencias Agronómicas Salvadoreñas
SECB	Société Européenne de Construction de l'Avion Bregeut
SECCAN	Science and Engineering Clubs of Canada
SECEA	Servicio Comercial de la Industria Textil Algodonera
SECED	Society for Earthquake and Civil Engineering Dynamics
SECF	Société des Experts Comptables Français
SECEM	Sociedad Espanola Construcciones Electro-Mecanicas
SECMA	Société d'Exploitation Cinématographique Africaine
SECO	Bureau de Contrôle pour la Sécurité de la Construction en Belgique
SECOBRAH	Société d'Encouragement de la Culture des Orges de Brasserie et des Houblons en France
SECPANE	Servicio Cooperativo Peruano-Norteamericano de Educación
SECPIA	Société d'Étude Chimiques pour l'Industrie et l'Agriculture
SECS	Sociedad Española de Ciencia del Suelo
SECT	Société des Ecrivains de Cinéma et de Télévision
SECTAB	Section Spécialisée pour le Tabac du Comité des Organisations Professionnelles Agricoles de la CEE
SEDA	Société d'Éditions Documentaires Agricoles
SEDA	Société d'Études pour le Développement de l'Automatisme
SEDAGRI	Société d'Étude et de Développement Agricole

SEDAM	Société d'Études et de Développement des Aéroglisseurs Marins, Terrestres et Amphibies
SEDAR	Sociedad Española de Anestesiología y Reanimación
SEDEC	Société d'Édition, de Documentation Économique et Commerciale
SEDECOS	Secretaríado de Comunicación Social (Chile)
SEDEIS	Société d'Études et de Documentation Économiques Industrielles et Sociales
SEDERCAL	Société d'Équipement et de Développement Rural de la Nouvelle-Calédonie
SEDES	Société pour l'Étude et le Développement Économique et Social
SEDHA	Secretariat for Dental Health in Africa
SEDIA	Société d'Étude du Développement Industriel et Agricole (Algeria)
SEDIA	Société d'Études et de Distribution Inter-Africaines (Ivory Coast)
SEDIAC	Société pour l'Étude et le Développement de l'Industrie, de l'Agriculture et du Commerce (Upper Volta)
SEDIBRA	Syndicat National d'Étude et de Défense des Intérêts de la Brasserie Française
SEDIMA	Syndicat National des Entreprises de Service et Distribution du Machinisme Agricole
SEDIVER	Société Européenne d'Isolateurs en Verre
SEDNI	Syndicat des Entrepreneurs de Dragages de Navigation Intérieure
SEDOS	Servizio di Documentazione e Studi
SEDPA	Société d'Édition et de Diffusion de la Presse Agricole
SEE	Société des Électriciens, des Électroniciens et des Radioélectriciens
SEE	Société d'Études et d'Expansion (Belgium)
SEE	Society of Electronic Engineers (India)
SEE	Society for Environmental Education
SEE	Society of Environmental Engineers
SEEA	Société Européenne d'Énergie Atomique
SEEB	South Eastern Electricity Board
SEECA	South Eastern Electricity Commercial Association
SEECF	Société d'Encouragement à l'Élévage du Cheval Français
SEEF	Service des Études Économiques et Financières
SEEF	Society of Electronics Engineers, Finland

SEEG	Société d'Énergie et d'Eau du Gabon
SEEN	Syndicat d'Études de l'Énergie Nucléaire
SEEP	Sociedad Española para el Estudio de los Pastos
SEET	Société d'Études et d'Équipements Techniques
SEF	Shipbuilding Employers' Federation
SEF	Société Entomologique de France
SEF	Société d'Ethonographie Française
SEF	Svenska Elverksföreningen
SEF	Svenska Exlibrisföreningen
SEF	Syndicat des Exportateurs Suisses de Fromage
SEFA	Genossenschaft Schweizerischer Strassenemulsions-Fabrikanten
SEFA	Scottish Educational Film Association
SEFAC	Société d'Exploitation Forestière et Agricole du Cameroun
SEFE	Suomen Ekonomiliitto
SEFEL	Secrétariat Européen des Fabricants d'Emballages Métalliques Légers (Belgium)
SEFI	Société Européenne pour la Formation des Ingénieurs
SEFI	Syndicat des Entreprises Françaises de Travaux Publics a Vocation Internationale
SEFIC	Société d'Exploitations Forestières et Industrielles du Cameroun
SEFIPA	Société Européenne de Financement et de Participation
SEFRAN	Syndicat des Embouteilleurs de France
SEFT	Society for Education in Film and Television
SEG	Saatgut-Erzeuger-Gemeinschaft Schleswig-Holstein
SEG	Schweizerische Entomologische Gesellschaft
SEG	Société d'Exploitations Gabonaises
SEG	Society of Exploration Geophysicists (U.S.A.)
SEG	Sveriges Elgrossisters Förening
SEG	Verband Schweizerischer Eier- und Geflügel-verwertungs-Genossenschaften
SEGA	Société d'Études Gabonaises
SEGA	Société d'Exploitation de Gravières en Afrique
SEGAP	Société d'Études pour l'Exploitation des Calcaires, Gypses, Argiles et Pouzzolanes de Madagascar
SEGB	South Eastern Gas Board
SEGCA	Gladstone Association of Celtic Europeans and their Friends
SEGEC	Syndicat Nationale Eau – Gas – Électricité des Cadres et Techniciens
SEGENI	Société Générale Sénégalaise pour le Négoce et l'Industrie
SEGESA	Société d'Études Géographiques, Économiques, et Sociologiques Appliquées
SEGI	Société Exploitation de Granit Ivoirien
SEGOA	Société Sénégalaise d'Oxygène et d'Acetylène
SEGRAM	Société Équatoriale de Grands Magasins
SEGRANI	Société d'Étude pour la Création d'une Usine de Graines au Niger
SEH	Société Européenne d'Hematologie
SEI	Service d'Expérimentation et d'Information (*of* I.N.R.A.)
SEI	Società Editrice Internazionale (Italy)
SEI	Societas Ergophthalmologica Internationalis
SEI	Société Générale d'Entreprises Immobilières et de Investissements (Belgium)
SEI	Société Sénégalaise d'Entreprises Industrielles
SEI	Society for Environmental Improvement
SEI	Syndicat de l'Emballage Industriel
SEICI	Société d'Exportation et d'Importation de la Côte-d'Ivoire
SEIE	Société d'Études de l'Industrie de l'Engrenage
SEIFA	Società Esportazione Importazione Fertilizanti Azotati
SEIFSA	Steel and Engineering Industries Federation of South Africa
SEIMAD	Société d'Équipement Immobilier de Madagascar
SEIN	Société d'Électronique Industrielle et Nucléaire
SEIN	Société d'Encouragement pour l'Industrie Nationale
SEINA	Société Européenne d'Instruments Numériques et Analogiques
SEIO	Sociedad Española de Investigación Operativa
SEITA	Service d'Exploitation Industrielle des Tabacs (Tunisia)
SEIU	Service Employers International Union (U.S.A.)
SEKE	Synetairistike Enosis Kapnoparagogon Ellados

SEKV	Schweizerische Einkäufer-Vereinigung
SEL	Scout's Esperanto League
SELA	Sistema Economicano Latinoamericano
SELAF	Société pour l'Étude des Langues Africains
SELEC	Société d'Étude des Électrocompresseurs
SELF	Société d'Ergonomie de Langue Française
SELF	Syndicat des Écrivains de Langue Française
SELNI	Società Elettronucleare Italiana
SELSA	Servicio de Luchas Sanitarias (Argentina)
SEM	Schweizerischer Engros-Möbelfabrikantenverband
SEM	Secretariat for European Medicine (Belgium)
SEM	Société d'Équipement de la Mauritanie
SEM	Syndesmos Epistimonon Michanikon Kyprou
SEMA	Société d'Économie et de Mathématiques Appliquées
SEMA	Société d'Équipement de Materiel Aéronautique (Congo)
SEMA	Société Équipement du Mali
SEMA	Storage Equipment Manufacturers' Association
SEMA	Spray Equipment Manufacturers Association
SEMABLE	Secteur de Modernisation d'Agriculture, Blé (Chad)
SEME	Sociedad Española de Microscopía Electrónica
SEMFA	Scottish Electrical Manufacturers' and Factors' Association
SEMI	Société des Eaux Minérales Ivoiriennes
SEMI	Société d'Ébénisterie et de Menuiserie Ivoirienne
SEMKO	Svenska Elecktriska Materielkontrollanstalten
SEMO	Société Belgo-Française d'Énergie Nucléaire Mosane
SEMRAD	Syndicat des Industries de l'Électronique Médicale et de la Radiologie (France)
SEMRY	Société d'Expansion et de Modernisation de la Riziculture de Yagoua
SEMT	Société d'Études de Machines Thermiques
SEMY	Syndesmos Ergostasiarchon Michanikis Ypodimatopoias
SEMZA	Association Professionnelle Belge des Négociants Préparateurs en Semences Agricoles
SENA	Servicio Nacional de Aprendizaje (Colombia)
SENA	Société d'Énergie Nucléaire Franco-Belge des Ardennes
SENA	Société d'Études Numismatiques et Archéologiques
SENABI	National Scientific and Technical Library and Documentation Services (South America)
SENAC	Serviço Nacional de Aprendizagem Comercial (Brazil)
SENAI	Serviço Nacional de Aprendizagem Industrial (Brazil)
SENALFA	Servicio Nacional de Lucha contra la Fiebre Aftosa (Paraguay)
SENAPET	Servicio Nacional de Programación y Evaluación Técnica (*of* INTA) (Argentina)
SENAPI	Servicio Nacional de Artesanías y Pequeñas Industrias (Panama)
SENATI	Servicio Nacional de Aprendizaje y Trabajo Industrial (Peru)
SEND	Scientists and Engineers for National Development (U.S.A.)
SENE	Servicio Nacional de Empleo (Panama)
SENEGALAP	Société Sénégalaise de Diffusion d'Appareils Électriques
SENELEC	Société Sénégalaise de Distribution d'Énergie Électrique
SENEPESCA	Société Sénégalaise pour l'Expansion de la Pêche Côtière, Surgélation et Conditionnement des Aliments
SENETRANSFIL	Société Sénégalaise de Transformation du Fil de Metal
SENFOR	Servicio Nacional de Formación Profesional (Paraguay)
SENICUA	Servizio per gli Elenchi Nominativi dei Lavoratori e per i Contributi Unificati in Agricultura
SENN	Società Elettronucleare Nazionale
SENTA	Société d'Études Nucléaires et de Techniques Nouvelles
SEOL	Suomen Elokuvateatter-inomistajain Liitto
SEOL	Suomen Erikois-Optikkojen Liitto
SEP	Sociedad Entomológica del Perú
SEP	Société Équatoriale Pharmaceutique
SEP	Société Européenne de Planification à Long Terme
SEP	Stowarzyszenie Elektryków Polskich
SEPA	Société d'Éditions et de Publications Agricoles

SEPAB	Section on Experimental Psychology and Animal Behaviour of the IUBS
SEPAM	Société d'Exploitation des Produits Animaux du Mali
SEPBA	Société d'Exploitation du Parc à Bois d'Abidjan (Ivory Coast)
SEPBC	Société d'Exploitation des Parcs à Bois du Cameroun
SEPC	Société d'Exploitation de Produits de Côte-d'Ivoire
SEPCAE	Société d'Engrais et Produits Chimiques d'Afrique Équatoriale
SEPCEM	Société d'Étude pour la Promotion de la Culture et l'Exploitation du Maïs au Cameroun
SEPCM	Société d'Engrais et de Produits Chimiques de Madagascar
SEPCO	Services Electronic Parts Co-ordinating Committee
SEPCR	Societas Europaea Physiologiae Clinicae Respiratoriae
SEPE	Secretariat pour l'Étude des Problèmes de l'Eau
SEPECAT	Société Européenne de Production de l'Avion École de Combat et d'Appui Tactique
SEPHAR	Section Internationale de Pharmacologie de l'Union Internationale de Sciences Physiologiques
SEPIA	Société d'Études et de Production Industrielle en Afrique
SEPIA	Société d'Études de Protection des Installations Atomiques
SEPM	Society of Economic Paleontologists and Mineralogists (U.S.A.)
SEPOM	Société d'Exploitation des Produits Oléagineux du Mali
SEPOR	Service des Programmes des Organismes de Recherche
SEPP	Société d'Entreposage de Produits Pétroliers (Congo)
SEPP	Société d'Étude de la Prévision et de la Planification (Switzerland)
SEPR	Société d'Étude de la Propulsion par Réaction
SEPT	Serviço de Estatistica da Previdencia e Trabalho (Brazil)
SEPT	Société d'Étude de Psychodrame Thérapeutique
SEQC	Sociedad Española de Quimicos Cosmeticos
SER	Service d'Économie Rurale (Luxemburg)
SER	Sociaal Economische Raad
SER	Svenska Elektroingenjörers Riksförening
SER	Sveriges Schaktentreprenörers Riksförbund
SERA	Socialist Environment and Resources Association
SERAI	Société d'Études de Recherches et d'Applications pour l'Industrie (Belgium)
SERAM	Service d'Études et de Recherches Antimalariennes (Zaire)
SERAS	Société d'Exploitation des Ressources Animales du Sénégal
SERC	Structural Engineering Research Centre (India)
SERC	Service d'Étude et de Recherches de la Circulation Routière (France)
SERCA	Société d'Exploitation de la République Centrafricaine
SERCE	Syndicat des Entrepreneurs de Réseaux, de Centrales et d'Équipement Industriel Électriques
SERCEL	Société d'Exploitation et de Recherches Électroniques
SERCOM	Station d'Essais et de Recherches de la Construction Métallique (Belgium)
SERCO-METAL	Servicio Técnico Comercial de Construcciones Metálicas y de Calderaria
SEREM	Sociedad Española de Radiología y Electrología Médicas y de Medicina Nuclear
SEREPCA	Société de Recherches et d'Exploitation des Pétroles du Cameroun
SERES	Société d'Études Rurales et Sociales
SERIA	Société d'Études et de Réalisations Industrielles d'Abidjan (Ivory Coast)
SERICC	Société d'Études et de Recherches pour l'Industrie et le Commerce Camerounais
SERL	Services Electronics Research Laboratory
SERLB	South Eastern Regional Library Bureau
SERM	Société d'Études et de Recherches Minières de Madagascar
SERMIS	Société d'Études et de Recherches Minières du Sénégal
SERMOTO	Servicio Técnico-Comercial de Fabricantes y Montadores de Motocicletas
SERNAUTO	Asociación Nacional de Fabricantes de Equipos y Componentes para Automoción
SERS	Société d'Étude et Recherche Sociologiques

SERT	Society of Electronic and Radio Technicians
SERTAF	Services Techniques Africains Côte d'Ivoire
SERTI	Société d'Études et de Réalisation pour le Traitement de l'Information
SERUG	Seminarie voor Toegepaste Economie bij de Rijksuniversiteit te Gent (Belgium)
SES	Scientific Exploration Society
SES	Société Européenne de Semences (Belgium)
SES	Solar Energy Society (U.S.A.)
SES	Studies and Expansion Society (Belgium)
SES	Suomen Egyptologinen Seura
SES	Swedish Engineers' Society (U.S.A.)
SES	Swiss Entomological Society
SESA	Social and Economic Statistics Administration (U.S.A.)
SESA	Société d'Études des Systèmes d'Automation
SESA	Society for Experimental Stress Analysis (U.S.A.)
SESD	Society of Experimental Station Directors (U.S.A.)
SESDA	Secretariat de Santé Dentaire de l'Afrique
SESEP	Société d'Études et de Soins pour les Enfants Poliomyélitiques
SESK	Verband Schweizerischer Schachtel-käsefabriken
SESN	Società Elvetica di Scienze Naturali (Switzerland)
SESO	Studiecentrum voor Economisch en Sociaal Onderzoek
SESPA	Scientists and Engineers for Social and Political Action (U.S.A.)
SESR	Société Européenne de Sociologie Rurale
SESSIA	Société d'Études, de Constructions de Souffleries Simulateurs et Instrumentation Aérodynamique
SESUAM	Société d'Études Sucrières en Afrique et à Madagascar
SESUHV	Société d'Études Sucrières de Haute-Volta
SET	Serviço de Expansao do Trigo (Brazil)
SET	Wirtschaftsverband Stahlbau und Energie-Technik
SETADEC	Société d'Études pour l'Amélioration, le Développement et l'Équipement des Collectivités locales
SETAO	Société d'Études et de Travaux pour l'Afrique Occidentale

SETCI	Société d'Extrusion et de Tissage de Côte-d'Ivoire
SETCO	Société d'Éditions Techniques Coloniales
SETEL	Société Européenne pour l'Étude et l'Intégration des Systèmes Spatiaux
SETFP	Syndicat de l'Extrusion et de la Transformation des Films Plastiques
SETIAC	Société des Éditions Techniques Industrielles, Agricoles et Commerciales
SETIS	Société Européenne d'Étude et d'Intégration de Systèmes Spatiaux
SETRA-CONGO	Société d'Études et des Travaux au Congo
SETRAPEM	Société Équatoriale de Travaux Pétroliers Maritimes (Gabon)
SETU	Société d'Études et de Travaux pour l'Uranium
SEV	Schweizerischer Elektrotechnischer Verein
SEV	Soviet Ekonomitcheskoi Vzaimopomochtchi
SEV	Syndesmos Ellinon Viomichanon
SEVIMA	Société d'Exploitation de la Viande à Madagascar
SEVMA-CAM	Société d'Exploitation et de Valorisation des Marbres, Cipolins et Aragonites à Madagascar
SEVPEN	Service de Vente des Publications de l'Éducation Nationale
SEYCO	Selección y Comercio de Patata
SEZEB	Société d'Ethnozoologie et d'Ethnobotanique
SF	Sagwerksförbundet
SFA	Scientific Film Association
SFA	Société Française d'Archéologie
SFA	Société Française d'Astronautique (*Incorp. in* AAAF)
SFA	Soroptimist Federation of the Americas
SFA	Syndicat Français des Adhésifs
SFAF	Société Française des Analystes Financiers
SFAJ	Société Française d'Architecture de Jardins
SFAK	Selskabet for Analytisk Kemi
SFAS	Solid Fuel Advisory Service
SFBIU	Scottish Farm Buildings Investigation Unit
SFC	Société Française de Céramique
SFC	Société Française des Chrysanthèmistes
SFC	Standing Federation Committee (West Indies)
SFCM	Société Française de Commerce à Madagascar

SFD	Société Française du Dahlia
SFDA	Small Farmers Development Agency (India)
SFDAS	Société Française de Droit Aérien et Spatial
SFE	Société Financière Européenne
SFE	Société Française d'Égyptologie
SFE	Société Française des Électriciens
SFE	Société Française d'Électrologie Médicale
SFEA	Scottish Further Education Association
SFEA	Société Française d'Études Agricoles
SFEC	San Francisco Engineering Council (USA)
SFEC	Société de Fabrication d'Éléments Catalytiques
SFEDTP	Société Française d'Entreprises de Dragages et de Travaux Publics
SFENA	Société Française d'Équipements pour la Navigation Aérienne
SFER	Société Française d'Économie Rurale (France)
SFER	Société Française des Électriciens et Radio-électriciens
SFERB	Syndicat des Fabricants d'Émulsions Routières de Bitume
SFEV	Syndicat Française des Éleveurs de Visons
SFF	Society of Filipino Foresters
SFF	Svenska Folkbibliotekarie Förbundet
SFF	Svenska Fysioterapeutiska Föreningen
SFF	Sveriges Filatelist-Förbund
SFFCCP	Syndicat Français des Fournisseurs pour Coiffeurs et Coiffeurs Parfumeurs
SFFL	Svensk Förening för Foniatri och Logopedics
SFG	Société Française de Gynécologie
SFG	Studien- und Förderungsgesellschaft (Belgium)
SFGV	Schweizerischer Frauengewerbeverband
SFH	Samfundet för Hembygdsvard
SFH	Studiengesellschaft für Hochspannungs-anlagen
SFHM	Société Française d'Histoire de la Médecine
SFHOM	Société Française d'Histoire d'Outre-Mer
SFHR	Society for Film History Research
SFHV	Schweizerischer Fischhändler-Verband
SFI	Société Financière Internationale
SFI	Société Française des Amateurs d'Iris
SFIB	Syndicat National des Fabricants d'Ensembles de Information et des Machines de Bureau
SFICE	Syndicat des Industries de Pièces Détachées et Accessoires Radio-Électriques et Électroniques
SFIE	Syndicat des Fabricants d'Isolants pour l'Électricité
SFIG	Syndicat des Fabricants Industriels de Glaces, Sorbets et Crèmes Glacées
SFIM	Société de Fabrication d'Instruments de Mesure
SFIM	Svenska Forbundet for Internationaler Möbeltransporter
SFIO	Section Française Internationale Ouvrière
SFIT	Swiss Federal Institute of Technology
SFITV	Société Française des Ingénieurs Techniciens du Vide
SFL	Statens Forskningskommitté för Lant-mannagbyggnader
SFL	Suomen Farmaseuttiliitto
SFL	Svenska Facklärarförbundet
SFL	Sveriges Fotolevantörers Förbund
SFM	Sociedad Forestal Mexicana
SFM	Société Française de Mesothérapie
SFM	Société Française de Métallurgie
SFMA	Scottish Furniture Manufacturers Association
SFME	Société Française de Médecine Esthétique
SFME	Société Française de Microscopie Électronique
SFMGV	Schweizerischer Fahrrad- und Motorrad-Gewerbe-Verband
SFMI	Société Française de Moteurs à Induction
SFMS	Société Française de Médecine du Sport
SFMT	Scottish Federation of Merchant Tailors
SFMT	Société Française de Médecine du Trafic
SFMTA	Scottish Federation of Meat Traders Associations
SFN	Société Française de Numismatique
SFNI	Suikerfabrieknavorsingsinstituut (South Africa)
SFO	Société Française d'Ophthalmologie
SFOM	Société Financière pour les Pays d'Outre-Mer
SFOM	Société Française d'Optique et de Mécanique
SFOS	Société Française d'Organo-Synthèse
SFP	Société Française de Pédagogie
SFP	Société Française de Photogrammétrie
SFP	Société Française de Photographie

SFP	Société Française de Psychologie
SFPH	Svenska Föreningen för Psykisk Hälsovard
SFPMAC	Société Française de Physiologie et de Médecine Aéronautiques et Cosmonautiques
SFR	Skogsägareföreningarnas Riksförbund
SFR	Société Française Radioélectrique
SFR	Société Française des Roses
SFR	Svenska Fargeritekniska Riksförbundet
SFR	Svenska Försäkringsbolags Riksförbund
SFR	Sveriges Färghandlares Riksförbund
SFRP	Société Française de Radioprotection
SFS	Société Française de Sociologie
SFS	Suomen Standardisoimisliitto
SFS	Svenska Fornskriftsällskapet
SFSA	Scottish Federation of Sea Anglers
SFSA	Scottish Field Studies Association
SFSA	Steel Founders' Society of America
SFSR	Socialist Federation of Soviet Republics
SFT	Société Française des Télécommunications
SFT	Société Française des Thermiciens
SFT	Société Française des Traducteurs
SFT	Society of Feed Technologists
SFTA	Society of Film and Television Arts
SFTAS	Syndicat Français des Textiles Artificiels et Synthétiques
SFTM	Société Française de Transports Maritimes
SFTSA	Scottish Forest Tree Seed Association
SFTV	Verband Gewerbsmässiger Ferntransportunternehmer der Schweiz
SFU	Société Française des Urbanistes
SFV	Schweizerischer Feuerwehrverband
SFV	Schweizerischer Floristenverband
SFV	Schweizerischer Forstverein
SFV	Schweizerische Franchising-Vereinigung
SFV	Société Française du Vide
SFZ	Sozialwissenschaftliches Forschungszentrum
SG	Société Générale
SGA	Schweizerische Gesellschaft für Automatik
SGA	Society of Graphic Artists
SGACC	Sécrétariat Général à l'Aviation Civile et Commerciale
SGAE	Schweizerische Gesellschaft für Anthropologie und Ethnologie
SGAEI	Société Gabonaise d'Aménagement et d'Équipement Immobiliers
SGAG	Schweizerische Gesellschaft für Angewandte Geographie
SGAR	Schweizerische Gesellschaft für Anästhesiologie und Reanimation
SGB	Schweizerische Gesellschaft für Betriebswissenschaft
SGB	Schweizerischer Gewerkschaftsbund
SGB	Scottish Gas Board
SGB	Sociedad Geológica Boliviana
SGB	Sociedade Geográfica Brasileira
SGB	Société des Bois du Gabon
SGBI	Santa Gertrudis Breeders International (U.S.A.)
SGBS	Société Générale de Banques au Sénégal
SGC	Service Générale de Contrôle (Belgium)
SGC	Sociedad Geográfica de Colombia
SGCE	Syndicat Général de la Construction Électrique
SGCH	Sociedad de Genética de Chile
SGCH	Sociedad Geológica de Chile
SGCI	Schweizerische Gesellschaft für Chemische Industrie
SGCTMA	Syndicat Général des Constructeurs et Machines Agricoles
SGD	Stichting Gezondheidsdienst voor Dieren
SGE	Société Gabonaise d'Entreposage
SGE	Société Gabonaise d'Entreprises
SGEP	Syndicat Général de l'Enseignement Public
SGEVE	Synomospondia Geniki Epangelmation kai Viotechnon
SGF	Scottish Growers Federation
SGF	Société Géologique de France
SGF	Studiengemeinschaft für Fertigbau
SGF	Svensk Geotekniska Föreningen
SGF	Svenska Gasföreningen
SGF	Sveriges Gjuteritekniska Förening
SGF	Sveriges Summtekniska Förening
SGFF	Schweizerische Gesellschaft für Familienforschung
SGFF	Syndicat Général des Fondeurs de France et Industries Connexes
SGFHTF	Syndicat Général des Fabricants d'Huile et de Tourteaux de France
SGFT	Schweizerische Gesellschaft für Feintechnik

SGG	Schweizerische Geisteswissenschaftliche Gesellschaft
SGG	Schweizerische Geologische Gesellschaft
SGG	Schweizerische Genossenschaft für Gemüsebau
SGG	Schweizerische Graphologische Gesellschaft
SGgG	Schweizerische Geographische Gesellschaft
SGGG	Société Générale du Golfe de Guinée
SGGMN	Schweizerische Gesellschaft für Geschichte der Medizin und der Naturwissenschaften
SGH	Schweizerische Gesellschaft für Hämatologie
SGH	Schweizerische Gesellschaft für Höhlenforschung
SGHC	Société des Grands Hôtels du Cameroun
SGI	Servicio Geodésico Interamericano
SGI	Società Geologica Italiana
SGICF	Syndicat Général de l'Industrie Cotonnière Française
SGIEO	Sistema Global Integrado de Estaciones Oceánicas
SGIJ	Syndicat Général de l'Industrie du Jute
SGIPA	Syndicat Général de l'Industrie du Plastique Armé
SGIPR	Syndicat Général de l'Industrie des Plastiques Renforcés
SGIT	Savez Gradevinskih Inzenjera i Tehnicara Jugoslavije
SGK	Stichting Verkoopkantoor voor Gras- en Klavermeel
SGKC	Schweizerische Gesellschaft für Klinische Chemie
SGKV	Studiengesellschaft für den Kombinierten Verkehr
SGM	Service Géologique de Madagascar
SGM	Société Gabonaise de Mécanique
SGM	Society of General Microbiology
SGMB	Société Géologique et Minéralogique de Bretagne
SGN	Section de Génie Nucléaire de l'Association Suisse pour l'Énergie Atomique
SGN	Servicio Geológico Nacional (Colombia, Nicaragua, Salvador)
SGO	Schweizerische Gesellschaft für Onkologie
SGOEM	Schweizerische Gesellschaft für Optik und Elektronen-mikroskopie
SGOIP	Syndicat Général de l'Optique et des Instruments de Précision
SGOP	Syndicat Générale des Ouates et Pansements
SGP	Schweizerischer Gesellschaft für Personalfragen
SGP	Schweizerische Gesellschaft für Phlebologie
SGP	Schweizerische Gesellschaft für Psychiatrie
SGP	Schweizerische Gesellschaft für Psychologie
SGP	Sociedad Geológica del Perú
SGP	Stowarzyszenie Geodetów Polskich
SGP	Syndicat des Graphologues Professionnels
SGPF	Sveriges Glas- och Porslinshandlareförbund
SGPFBM	Syndicat Générale des Producteurs Fournisseurs de Bois aux Mines
SGPMR	Schweizerische Gesellschaft für Physikalische Medizin und Rheumatologie
SGPP	Schweizerische Gesellschaft für Praktische Psychologie
SGPSM	Schweizerischer Gesellschaft für Psychosomatische Médecin
SGR	Sveriges Golvhandlares Riksförbund
SGRB	Société Générale des Représentants de Belgique
SGSH	Société Générale Suisse d'Histoire
SGSPM	Schweizerische Gesellschaft für Sozial- und Präventivmedizin
SGSR	Society for General Systems Research (U.S.A.)
SGSS	Schweizerische Gesellschaft für Skandinavische Studien
SGSS	Società Generale Svizzera di Storia
SGSV	Schweizerische Gesellschaft für Statistik und Informatik
SGT	Schweizerische Galvano-technische Gesellschaft
SGT	Société des Garde-Temps (Switzerland)
SGT	Société Guinéenne de Transport
SGT	Society of Glass Technologists
SGTE	Société Générale de Techniques et d'Études
SGTK	Schweizerische Gesellschaft für Theaterkultur
SGTS	Scottish Gaelic Texts Society
SGU	Schweizerische Gesellschaft für Umweltschutz
SGU	Scottish Golf Union
SGU	Svenska Geologiska Undersökning
SGV	Schweizerischer Geflügelzuchtverband
SGV	Schweizerische Gesellschaft für Volkskunde

SGV	Schweizerischer Gewerbeverband
SGV-NOK	Ständige Generalversammlung der Nationalen Olympischen Komitees
SHA	Sociedäd de Historia Argentina
SHA	Swiss Hotel Association
SHAC	Société Havraise Africaine de Commerce (Ivory Coast)
SHADA	Haitian-American Society for Agricultural Development
SHAL	Société d'Histoire et d'Archéologie de la Lorraine
SHALTA	Skin, Hide and Leather Trades Association
SHAPE	Supreme Headquarters of the Allied Powers in Europe
SHAS	Smallholders' Advisory Service (Malaysia and Sri Lanka)
SHAT	Sociedad Horticola para América Tropical (Costa Rico)
SHCF	Saint Hubert Club de France
SHD	Scottish Home Department
SHD	State Hydro-electric Department (New Zealand)
SHE	Society for Health Education
SHF	Société Hippique Française
SHF	Société Hydrotechnique de France
SHF	Sveriges Handelsagenters Förbund
SHFL	Sveriges Hogre Flickskolors Lararförbund
SHG	Schweizerische Heraldische Gesellschaft
SHIC	Société Hôtelière et Immobilière du Congo
SHIO	Sveriges Hantverks- och Industriorganisation
SHIV	Schweizerischer Handels- und Industrieverein
SHIV	Schweizerischer Holzindustrie-Verband
SHJPF	Société d'Horticulture et des Jardins Populaires de France
SHK	Schweizerische Hochschulkonferenz
SHL	Suomen Huonekalukauppiatten Liitto
SHN	Société des Huileries du Niger
SHNC	Société Hôtelière Nord-Cameroun
SHOM	Service Hydrographique et Océanographique de la Marine
SHRH	Servicio Hidráulico de la República Haitiana
SHR	Société Hippique Rurale
SHRI	Scottish Horticultural Research Institute
SHS	Scottish History Society
SHS	Stowarzyszenie Historyków Sztuki

SHS	Suomen Hammaslääkäriseura
SHSHV	Société des Huiles et Savons de Haute-Volta
SHSK	Schweizerische Häutschäden-Kommission
SHSN	Société Helvétique des Sciences Naturelles
SHT	Société des Hévéas de Tay-Ninh (Vietnam)
SHTF	Sveriges Handelsträdgardsmästareförbund
SHTM	Société des Hôtelleries et du Tourisme du Mali
SHU	Société Hippique Urbaine
SHU	Státni Hydrometeorologicky Ústáv
SHV	Schweizer Hotelier-Verein
SHV	Schweizerischer Hafnermeisterverband, Ofenbau- und Plattengeschäfte
SHV	Schweizerischer Hebammen-Verband
SHY	Suomen Henkilökuntalehtien Yhdistys
SHY	Suomen Hypnoosiyhdistys
SI	Smithsonian Institution (U.S.A.)
SI	Sveriges Industriförbund
SIA	Saskatchewan Institute of Agrologists (Canada)
SIA	Schweizerischer Ingenieur- und Architekten-Verein
SIA	Singapore International Airlines
SIA	Société Immobilière Agricole
SIA	Société des Ingénieurs de l'Automobile
SIA	Société Internationale d'Acupuncture
SIA	Société Interprofessionnelle de l'Aviculture et des Produits de Bassecour
SIA	Société d'Investissements Africains
SIA	Société Ivoirienne d'Assurances
SIA	Société Suisse des Ingénieurs et des Architectes
SIA	Society of Industrial Artists
SIA	Soroptimist International Association
SIA	Sprinkler Irrigation Association (U.S.A.)
SIAB	Sociedad de Ingenieros Agrónomos de Bolivia
SIAB	Stiftung für Internationalen Austauch in den Bergen (France)
SIAC	Secrétariat Inter-américain d'Action Catholique
SIAC	Secrétariat International des Artistes Catholiques
SIAC	Società Italiana Acciaierie Cornigliano
SIA-CONGO	Société Industrielle et Agricole du Congo

SIAD	Societa Italiana Autori Drammatici
SIAD	Society of Industrial Artists and Designers
SIAEN	Sociedad Iberoamericana de Estudios Numismaticos
SIAEX	Société d'Achat d'Exportation
SIAF	Société des Ingénieurs Agronomes de France
SIAF	Società Italiana di Audiologia e Foniatria
SIAG	Société Industrielle et Automobile de Guinée
SIAM	Society for Industrial and Applied Mathematics (U.S.A.)
SIAMU	Secretariado Ibero-Americano de Municipios (Spain)
SIAN	Société Industrielle et Agricole du Niari (French Equatorial Africa)
SIAP	Sociedad Interamericana de Planificación
SIAP	Société Industriel d'Articles de Papeterie (Congo)
SIAP	Société Industrielle Africaine de Plastiques
SIAPA	Società Italo-Americana Prodotti Anti-Parassitari
SIAPAP	Société Industrielle et Agricole de la Pointe-à-Pitre (Guadeloupe)
SIAPE	Société Industrielle d'Acide Phosphorique et d'Engrais
SIAR	Société de la Surveillance Industrielle
SIAR	Stiftelsen Företagsadministrativ Forskning
SIAS	Scandinavian Institute of African Studies
SIAS	Small Industries Advisory Service (Rhodesia)
SIAS	Société Industrielle et Agricole de la Somme
SIAT	Société Industrielle et Agricole du Congo
SIATSA	Servicios para la Investigación Agricola Tropical (Honduras)
SIB	Shipbuilding Industry Board
SIB	Società Italiana di Biometria
SIB	Société Internationale de Biometrie
SIB	Société Ivoirienne de Banque
SIBAF	Société Industrielle des Bois Africains
SIBAG	Société d'Industries de Bois au Gabon
SIBC	Association Mondiale des Sociétés d'Anatomie Pathologique et de Biologie Clinique
SIBEV	Société Interprofessionnelle du Bétail et des Viandes
SIBMAS	Section Internationale des Bibliothèques et Musées des Arts du Spectacle (of FIAB)
SIBRAS	Société Industrielle de Brasseries du Sénégal
SIC	Schweizerischer Verband von Comestibles-Importeuren und -Händlern
SIC	Science Information Council (of NFS) (U.S.A.)
SIC	Société Immobilière du Cameroun
SIC	Société Industrielle des Cacaos (Cameroons)
SIC	Société Intercontinentale des Containers
SIC	Société Internationale de Cardiologie
SIC	Société Internationale de Chirurgie
SICA	Société Immobilière de la Côte d'Afrique
SICA	Société Industrielle de l'Est Camerounaise
SICA	Société d'Intérêt Collectif Agricole
SICA	Société Internationale de Coopératives Agricoles
SICA	Society of Industrial and Cost Accountants of Canada
SICAB	Société Industrielle Camerounaise de Bois
SICABAG	Société d'Intérêt Collectif Agricole de Guadeloupe
SICABAM	Société d'Intérêt Collectif Agricole de la Martinique
SICAE	Société d'Intérêt Collectif Agricole d'Électricité
SICAF	Société Industrielle de Couvertures Africaines
SICAF	Société Ivoirienne de Culture d'Ananas Frais
SICAG	Société Industrielle Commerciale et Agricole de Guinée
SICAHR	Société d'Intérêt Collectif d'Habitat Rural
SICAP	Servicio Interamericano de Cooperacion Agricola en Panamá
SICAP	Société Italo-Congolaise d'Armement et de Pêche
SICAPEB	Société d'Intérêt Collectif Agricole des Planteurs et Producteurs-Exportateurs de Bananes (Guadeloupe)
SICASSO	Société d'Intérêt Collectif Agricole des Sylviculteurs du Sud-Ouest
SICC	Shell International Chemical Company Ltd
SICC	Société Suisse des Ingénieurs en Chauffage et Climatisation
SICFA	Société Industrielle et Commerciale Franco-Africaine
SICH	Sociedad Internacional de la Ciencia Hortícola
SICI	Société Immobilière et Commerciale Ivoirienne
SICIND	Società Incremento Cotonicolo Industriale nella Daunia

SICM	Secretariat International des Citoyens
SICM	Société Ivoirienne de Ciments et Matériaux
SICN	Société Industrielle de Combustible Nucléaire
SICN	Société Industrielle Commerciale Nigérienne
SICOC	Syndicat des Ingénieurs-Conseils en Organisation et Conseillers de Direction
SICOCAM	Société Industrielle et Commerciale du Cameroun
SICOD	Service Interconsulaire du Commerce et de la Distribution
SICOFEG	Société des Ingénieurs-Conseils de France en Génie Civil
SICOFEM	Société Ivoirienne de Confections Féminines et Masculines
SICOGERE	Société Ivoirienne de Copropriété et de Gérance
SICOGI	Société Ivoirienne de Construction et de Gestion Immobilière
SICOM	Società Italiana Costruzioni e Montaggi
SICOMAD	Société Industrielle de la Côte Ouest de Madagascar
SICOMED	Société Ivoirienne de Construction Médicale
SICOMI	Sociétés Immobilières pour le Commerce et l'Industrie
SICONIGER	Société Industrielle et Commerciale du Niger
SICORES	Société Internationale de Coopération pour Réalisations Économiques et Sociales
SICOT	Société Internationale de Chirurgie Orthopédique et de Traumatologie
SICOTP	Société Ivoirienne Commerciale Ouvrière de Travaux Publics et de Bâtiments
SICOTP	Société Ivoirienne de Construction et de Travaux Publics
SICOVAM	Société Interprofessionnelle pour la Compensation des Valeurs Mobilières (Organismes inter-banques)
SICOVO	Société Industrielle et Commerciale Voltaïque
SICRUS	Société Ivoirienne de Crustaces
SICS	Sociedad Internacional de las Ciencias del Suelo (Italy)
SICS	Société Internationale des Conseillers de Synthèse
SICT	Société Industrielle et Commerciale du Tchad
SID	Föreningen Svenska Industridesigner
SID	Society for International Development
SID	Society for Investigative Dermatology (U.S.A.)
SID	Verband Schweizer Industrial Designers
SIDA	Swedish International Development Authority
SIDADT	Société Industrielle pour le Développement Automobile au Dahomey et au Togo
SIDB	Société Industrielle des Bois (Congo)
SIDEA	Italian Society of Agricultural Economics
SIDEB	Société Ivoirienne de Distribution et d'Équipement de Bureaux
SIDEC	Stanford International Development Education Centre (U.S.A.)
SIDECO	Société Ivoirienne de Distribution Économique
SIDEFCOOP	Sociedad Interamericana para el Desarrollo del Financiamiento Cooperativo (Chile)
SIDELAF	Société Ivoirienne d'Électrification
SIDEPI	Seminario Internacional de Desarrollo Pesquero-Industrial (Peru)
SIDER-AFRIC	Centre d'Information et de Promotion des Produits Sidérurgiques et des Tubes d'Acier Français en Afrique
SIDERSA	Empresa Siderúrgica Boliviana
SIDES	Società Italiana di Dermatologia e Sifilografia
SIDEST	Société Indépendante de Documentation et d'Éditions Scientifiques et Techniques
SIDF	Société Ivoirienne de Développement et de Financement
SIDI	Société Ivoirienne de Développement Industriel
SIDIAMIL	International Company for the Development of Food Industries using Sorghum and Millet (Africa)
SIDITEX	Société Internationale pour le Développement de l'Industrie Textile (Cameroons)
SIDM	Società Italiana di Musicologia
SIDO	Société Interprofessionnelle de Oléagineux
SIDP	Seed Industry Development Programme (*of* FAO)
SIDS	Société Internationale de Défense Sociale
SIDS	Société Internationale de Droit Social
SIE	Servicios Industriales Especiales (UNIDO)
SIE	Società Italiana di Ergonomia
SIE	Société Internationale d'Électrochimie
SIE	Society of Industrial Engineers
SIEBEG	Société Ivoirienne d'Exploitation des Bois en Grumes

EC	Société Internationale pour l'Enseignement Commercial
ECA	Secrétariat Permanent du Traité Général d'Intégration Économique de l'Amérique Centrale
ECC	Société Internationale d'Étude des Cultures Comparées
ECUS	Sex Information and Education Council of the U.S.
ED	Société pour l'Importation et l'Exportation de Métaux Précieux au Dahomey
EDS	Società Italiana di Economia Demografia e Statistica
EF	Société Internationale d'Ethnographie et de Folklore
EHT	Société Ivoirienne d'Équipement Hôtelier et Touristique
ELOR	Société Ivoirienne d'Emballages Métalliques
EMI	Société d'Importation et d'Exportation de Matériel Industriel (Cameroons, Central Africa)
EMPA	Syndicat des Importateurs-Exportateurs de Matières Premières Aromatiques
EN	Société Internationale d'Études Néroniennes
EPM	Société Internationale pour l'Étude de la Philosophie Médiévale
ERE	Syndicat des Industries Électroniques de Reproduction et d'Enregistrement
ERI	Société Ivoirienne d'Études et de Réalisations Industrielles
ERS	Société Industrielle d'Études et Réalisations Scientifiques
ES	Société Industrielle d'Engrais au Sénégal
ES	Soils and Irrigation Extension Service (Australia)
ESC	Secrétariat International des Enseignants Secondaires Catholiques
ET	Société Internationale d'Écologie Tropicale
ETA	Société Internationale d'Études et de Travaux en Afrique (Ivory Coast)
ETHO	Société Ivoirienne d'Expansion Touristique et Hôtelière
EUSE	Secrétariat International de l'Enseignement Universitaire des Sciences de l'Éducation
EXI	Société Ivoirienne d'Exportation et d'Importation
F	Selskabets for Industriel Formgivning
F	Smøreolje Importørenes Forening
SIF	Società Italiana Fisica
SIFA	Société Industrielle pour la Fabrication des Antibiotiques
SIFB	Society of Industrial Furnace Builders
SIFCCA	Société Industrielle Forestière et Commerciale Camerounaise
SIFERCOM	Société Ivoirienne d'Entreprise et de Construction Métallique
SIFET	Società Italiana di Fotogrammetria e Topografia
SIFIDA	Société Internationale Financière pour les Investissements et le Développement en Afrique
SIFO	Società Italiana di Farmacia Ospedaliera
SIFPAF	Syndicat des Industriels Fabricants de Pâtes Alimentaires de France
SIFRA	Société Industrielle des Fruits Africains
SIFRIA	Société Immobilière de l'Aluminium (Africa)
SIG	Service d'Information Géologique
SIGA	Società Italiana di Genetica Agraria
SIGE	Società Italiana di Genetica e Eugenica
SIGE	Società Italiana Gestione Elicotteri
SIGE	Société Internationale de Gastro-Entérologie
SIGESO	Sub-committee, Intelligence German Electronics Signals Organisation
SIGEXA	Société Ivoirienne de Gestion et d'Exploitation Automobile
SIGI	Société Ivoirienne de Gestion Immobilière
SIGM	Società Italiana di Ginnastica Medica, Medicina Fisica e Riabilitazione
SIGMA	Société Industriale Générale de Mécanique Appliquée
SIGMA	Station Internationale de Géobotanique Méditerranéenne et Alpine
SIGP	Société Industrielle de la Grande Pêche
SIGRAG	Société Industrielle d'Exploitation des Granits Guinéens
SIGUE	Society for Developments in Guinea
SIH	Schweizerisches Institut für Hauswirtschaft
SIH	Société Internationale d'Hématologie
SIH	Société Ivoirienne d'Hôtellerie
SIHM	Société Internationale d'Histoire de la Médecine
SIHTCO	Société Ivoirienne Hôtelière et Touristique de la Comoé

SIIAEC	Secrétariat International des Ingénieurs, des Agronomes et des Cadres Économiques Catholiques
SIIAS	Staten Island Institute of Arts and Sciences (U.S.A.)
SIIC	Secrétariat International des Groupements Professionnels des Industries Chimiques des Pays de la CEE
SIK	Svenska Institutet för Könserveringsforsk-ning
SIL	Sähköinsinööriliitto
SIL	Secrétariat International de la Laine (IWS)
SIL	Service International des Latitudes
SIL	Societas Internationalis Limnologiae Theoretica et Applicae
SIL	Société Internationale de la Lèpre
SIL	Suomen Ilmailuliitto
SILAF	Società Italiana per Lavori Agricoli e Forestali
SILCO	Société Ivoiro-Libanaise de Commerce
SILF	Svenska Inköpsledores Förening
SILIN	Société Interprofessionnelle des Graines et Huiles de Lin
SILP	Société Internationale de Linguistique Psychologique
SILS	Société d'Investissements Libano-Sénégalaise
SIM	Singapore Institute of Management
SIM	Société Sénégalaise d'Investissements Maritimes
SIM	Société Internationale de la Moselle
SIM	Société Internationale de Musicologie
SIMA	Salon International de la Machine Agricole
SIMA	Scientific Instrument Manufacturers' Association of Great Britain
SIMA	Société d'Importation et d'Exportation Centrafricaine
SIMA	Société Industrielle de Matériel Agricole
SIMA	Société Ivoirienne de Menuiserie et d'Ameublement
SIMAC	Société Immobilière d'Afrique Centrale
SIMAC	Société Ivoirienne d'Importation de Matériaux de Construction
SIMACO	Société Ivoirienne de Matériaux de Con-struction
SIMAFRUIT	Société Interprofessionnelle Maritime et Fruitière (Ivory Coast)
SIMAQ	Syndicat des Nécogiants Importateurs Métropolitaines
SIMAR	Société Industrielle de Machines Agricoles Rotatives (Switzerland)
SIMAVIN	Société d'Importation Africaine Vinicole
SIMC	Société Internationale de Médecine Cybernétique
SIMC	Société Internationale pour la Musique Con-temporaine
SIMCA	Société Industrielle de Mécanique et Carosserie
SIMCO	Société Immobilière et de Constructions du Tchad
SIMDER	Syndicat National du Matériel de Dessin, Beaux-Arts, Reprographie
SIMEA	Società Italiana Meridionale Energia Atomica
SIMEA	Société Ivoirienne de Montage et d'Exploita-tion Automobile
SIMECO	Société Ivoirienne de Menuiserie, d'Ébénisterie et de Constructions Immobilières
SIMEI	Société Ivoirienne de Matériaux Étanches et Isolants
SIMEX	Société Ivoirienne d'Importation et d'Expor-tation
SIMG	Societas Internationalis Medicinae Generalis
SIMH	Société Internationale de Médecine Hydrologique
SIMHA	Société Internationale de Mycologie Humaine et Animale
SIMI	Società Italiana Macchine Idrauliche
SIMI	Società Italiana di Medicina Interna
SIML	Società Italiana di Medicina del Lavoro
SIMMA	Syndicat des Industries de Matériels de Manutention
SIMO	Société Ivoirienne des Matériels d'Organisation
SIMOCA	Société Industrielle du Moyen-Orient au Cameroun
SIMP	Società Italiana di Medicina Psicosomatica
SIMP	Società Italiana di Mineralogia e Petrologia
SIMP	Stowarzyszenie Inzynierów i Techników Polskich
SIMPA	Société Industrielle Moderne de Plastiques Africaines
SIMPEX	Syndicat des Commerçants Importateurs et Exportateurs (Gabon, Ivory Coast)
SIMPEXDA	Syndicat des Importateurs et Exportateurs du Dahomey

MPL	Scientific, Industrial and Medical Photographic Laboratories	SIP	Società Italiana de Pediatria
MPOL	Société Ivoirienne de Mousse Polyester	SIP	Società Italiana di Psichiatria
MRA	Scientific Instruments Manufacturers' Research Association	SIP	Société Inter-Américaine de Psychologie
MS	Scandinavian Simulation Society	SIPA	Servicio de Investigación y Promoción Agropecuaria (*formerly* SCIPA and PCEA) (Peru)
MS	Società Italiana di Medicina Sociale	SIPA	Société Industrielle de Produits Africains
MS	Student's International Meditation Society (U.S.A.)	SIPAI	Sociedad Italo Peruana Agrícola Industrial (Peru)
MT	Società Italiana di Medicina del Traffico	SIPAG	Société Industrielle de Planification de Guinée
N	Schweizerisches Institut für Nuclearforschung	SIPAG	Syndicat National des Importateurs d'Équipements pour les Industries Papetières et Graphiques
N	Società Italiana di Neurochirurgia	SIPAI	Società per l'Incremento della Produzione Avicola Italiana
N	Society for International Numismatics (U.S.A.)	SIPAK	Vereniging van Groothandelaren in Sisalpaktouw
NA	Shellfish Institute of North America	SIPARE	Syndicat des Industries de Pièces Détachées et Accessoires Radio-Électriques et Électroniques
NA	Sociedad Ibérica de Nutrición Animal		
NAGI	Sindicato Nazionale Giornalai d'Italia	SIPC	Société Interprofessionnelle pour la Production des Cocons, Graines de Vers à Soie et de Soie Grège en France
NAMOS	Sistema Nacional de Apoyo a la Movilización Social (Peru)		
NCATEX	Société Industrielle Camerounaise de Textiles	SIPCAM	Società Italiana Prodotti Chimici e per l'Agricoltura, Milano
NCO	Société Internationale de Commerce (Cameroons)	SIPE	Société Internationale de Psychologie de l'Écriture
NFAC	Syndicat Interprofessionnel des Fabricants d'Articles Manufacturés pour Chaussures	SIPE	Société Internationale de Psychopathologie de l'Expression
NFDOK	Swedish Council for Scientific Information and Documentation	SIPEC	Société Industrielle des Pêches du Cameroun
NN	Société de Imprimerie Nationale du Niger	SIPECA	Service d'Information Pastorale Européenne Catholique (Belgium)
NP	Saha Institute of Nuclear Physics (India)	SIPEGA	Société Industrielle des Pêches du Gabon
NTEF	Selskap f. Industriell og Teknisk Forskning	SIPG	Société Internationale de Pathologie Géographique
NTO	Sheffield Interchange Organisation		
NTRA	Société Industrielle des Nouvelles Techniques Radioélectriques	SIPH	Société Indochinoise de Plantation d'Hévéas (Vietnam)
O	Sisustusarkkitehdit	SIPI	Scientists Institute for Public Information (U.S.A.)
OFA	Société Interprofessionnelle des Oléagineux Fluides Alimentaires		
OG	Società Italiana di Ostetricia e Ginecologia	SIPMAD	Société Industrielle de Pêche à Madagascar
OI	Sezione Italiana per l'Organizzazione Internazionale	SIPOA	Société Industrielle Pharmaceutique de l'Ouest Africain
OP	Société Internationale d'Oncologie Pédiatrique	SIPP	Society of Irish Plant Pathologists
OT	Società Italiana di Ortopedia e Traumatologia	SIPRAG	Société Ivoirienne de Promotion Agricole
P	Sociedad Interamericana de Planificación (Porto Rico)	SIPRC	Society of Independent Public Relations Consultants
P	Sociedad Interamericana de Prensa	SIPRI	Stockholm International Peace Research Institute
P	Società Italiana di Parapsicologia		

SIPRT	Sociedad Internacional de Professionales de Radio y Televisión	**SIS**	Società Italiani di Statistica
SIPS	Società Internazionale di Psicologia della Acrittura	**SIS**	Società Italiana di Stomatologia
		SIS	Société Immobilière du Sénégal
SIPS	Società Italiana per il Progresso delle Scienze	**SIS**	Société Internationale Scotiste
SIPS	Società Italiana di Psicologia Scientifica	**SIS**	Special Industrial Services (*of* UNIDO)
SIPS	Société Industrielle de Papeterie au Sénégal	**SIS**	Sveriges Standardiseringskommission
SIR	Service International de Recherches (*of* CICR)	**SISCO**	Special Inter-Departmental Selection Committee (FAO)
SIR	Società Italiana Resine	**SISCOMA**	Société Industrielle Sénégalaise de Constructions Mécaniques et de Matériels Agricoles
SIR	Sociedad Internacional Rorschach		
SIR	Société Ivoirienne de Raffinage	**SISF**	Società Italiana di Scienze Farmaceutiche
SIR	Svenska Inredningsarkitekters Riksförbund	**SISGAC**	Scottish Industrial Safety Group Advisory Council
SIRA	Scientific Instrument Research Association		
SIRAID	Scientific Instrument Research Association Information and Data Service	**SISH**	Société Internationale de la Science Horticole
		SISIR	Singapore Institute for Standards and Industrial Research
SIRC	Socialist International Research Council		
SIRCA	Société Industrielle de République Centrafricaine	**SISMES**	Società Italiana di Statistica Medico-Sanitaria
SIRCE	Società per l'Incremento Rapporti Commerciali con l'Estero	**SISP**	Schweizerische Interessengemeinschaft f. d. Schutz von Pflanzenneuheiten
SIREP	Société Internationale pour la Recherche et l'Exploitation du Pétrole (Tchad)	**SISPA**	Società Italiana Studio e Prevenzione dell' Alcoolismo
SIRI	Société Internationale pour la Réadaptation des Invalides	**SISS**	Secrétariat International des Syndicats du Spectacle
SIRI	Sugar Industry Research Institute (Mauritius)	**SISS**	Società Italiana Serbatoi Speciali
SIRIP	Société Irano-Italienne de Pétrole	**SISS**	Société Internationale de la Science du Sol
SIRM	Società Italiana di Radiologia Medica	**SISTER**	Special Institutions for Scientific and Technological Education and Research
SIRM	Società Italiana Radio-Marittima		
SIRM	Società Italiana per le Ricerche de Mercata	**SISV**	Secrétariat International du Service Volontaire
SIRMCE	Société Internationale pour la Recherche sur les Maladies de Civilisation et l'Environnement	**SISV**	Società Italiana delle Scienze Veterinarie
		SISWO	Stichting Interuniversitair Instituut voor Sociaalwetenschappelijk Onderzoek
SIRMN	Società Italiana di Radiologia Medica e Medicina Nucleare	**SIT**	Samband Islenzkra Trygginafélaga
SIRNv	Société International de Recherches Neurovégétatives	**SIT**	Servicio de Información Técnica (Ecuador)
		SIT	Singapore Improvement Trust
SIRT	Société Internationale de la Radio et Télévision	**SIT**	Société Interafricaine de Transport
		SIT	Société Intercontinentale de Transactions
SIRT	Société Interprofessionnelle du Raison de Table	**SIT**	Society of Instrument Technology (*now* IMC
SIRTC	Société Internationale de Recherche contre la Tuberculose et le Cancer	**SITA**	Société Internationale de Télécommunications Aéronautiques
SIRTI	Società Italiana Reti Telefoniche Interurbane	**SITA**	Students International Travel Association
SIS	Samband Islenzkra Samvinnufélaga	**SITAF**	Société Industrielle des Transports Automobiles Africains (Ivory Coast)
SIS	Secret Intelligence Service	**SITAM**	Société Industrielle des Tabacs Malgaches
SIS	Senologic International Society	**SITAO**	Société Immobilière et Touristique de l'Afrique de l'Ouest

ITB	Société Industrielle de Travaux de Bureaux	SITS	Società Italiana Telecommunicazione Siemens
ITC	Swiss Insurance Training Centre	SITS	Société Internationale de Transfusion Sanguine
ITCA	Secretaria de Integración Turistica de Centroamérica (Nicaragua)	SITS	Syndicat Général des Industries pour le Traitement des Surfaces
ITEL	Société Belge des Ingénieurs des Télécommunications et d'Électronique	SITT	Syndicat des Industries Téléphoniques et Télégraphiques
ITELESC	Syndicat des Industries de Tubes Électroniques et Semiconducteurs	SITUMER	Société d'Ingénierie du Tunnel sous la Mer
ITEMSH	Société Internationale de Traumatologie de Ski et de Médecine des Sports d'Hiver	SITVAR	Syndicat National des Industries Transformateurs de Vanille et des Elements Aromatiques Naturels au Chimiques
ITH	Société Internationale de Technique Hydrothermale	SITWM	Stowarzyszenie Inzynierów i Techników Wodnych i Melioracyjnych
ITI	Sezione Imprese Traslochi Internazionali	SIU	Social Investigation Unit (of RSPCA)
ITKom	Stowarzyszenie Inzynierów i Technikow Komunikacji	SIU	Société Internationale d'Urologie
ITIM	Société Internationale des Techniques d'Imagerie Mentale	SIUNA	Seafarers International Union of North America
ITJ	Savez Inzenjera i Tehnicara Jugoslavije	SIV	Schweizerischen Inserenten-Verband
ITLiD	Stowarzyszenie Inzynierów i Techników Leśnictwa i Drzewnictwa	SIV	Société Immobilière de la Volta
ITMA	Société des Ingénieurs et Techniciens du Machinisme Agricole	SIV	Société Sénégalaise pour l'Industrie du Vêtement
ITO	Société Ivoirienne des Transports de l'Ouest	SIVA	Société Industrielle de Vêtements en Afrique
ITO	Stowarzyszenie Naukowo-Techniczne Inzynierów i Techników Ogrodnictwa	SIVAK	Société Ivoirienne Agricole et Industrielle du Kenaf
ITOFA	Société des Industries de Transformation des Oléagineux Fluides Alimentaires	SIVEL	Société Ivoirienne d'Électricité
		SIVENG	Société Ivoirienne d'Engrais
ITP	Société Ivoirienne de Transports Publics	SIVETI	Société Ivoirienne de Vêtements sur Mesures Industrielles
ITPC	Syndicat des Industries de la Transformation de la Pellicule Cellulosique	SIVIE	Société Ivoirienne d'Installations Électriques
ITPChem	Stowarzyszenie Inzynierów i Techników Przemyslu Chemicznego	SIVIT	Société des Industries de la Viande du Tchad
		SIVOA	Société Ivoirienne d'Oxygène et d'Acetylène
ITPH	Stowarzyszenie Inzynierów i Techników Przemyslu Hutniczego	SIVOM	Société Ivoirienne d'Opérations Maritimes
ITPMB	Stowarzyszenie Inzynierów i Techników Przemyslu Materialow Budowlanych	SIW	Stichting Internationale Werkkampen
		SJCM	Standing Joint Committee on Metrication
ITPP	Stowarzyszenie Inzynierów i Techników Przemyslu Papierniczego	SJF	Svenska Journalistförbundet
		SJF	Syndicat des Journalistes Français
ITPRO	U.K. Committee for the Simplification of International Trade Procedures	SJIA	Saint Joan's International Alliance
		SJK	Svenska Jordbrukskreditkassan
ITR	Stowarzyszenie Naukowo-Techniczne Inzynierów i Techników Rolnictwa	SJPA	Syndicat des Journalistes de la Presse Agricole
ITRA	South India Textile Research Association	SJU	Schweizerische Journalisten Union
ITRAC	Société Industrielle de Transformation Centrafricaine	SJUF	Scandinavisk Jodisk Ungdomsforbund
		SK	Schweizerische Käseunion
ITRAM	Société Industrielle de Transformation des Métaux (Central Africa)	SK	Svenska Kartongfabrikantföreningen
		SKAF	Sveriges Konst- och Antikhandlarförening

SKAG	Verband Schweizerischer Konzessionierter Automobilunternehmungen
SKB	Schweizerischer Konsumentenbund
SKB	Svenska Kuvertfabrikanters Branschrad
SKBT	Syndicale Kamer van de Belgische Tuinbouw
SKCV	Schweizerischer Konditor-Confiseurmeisterverband
SKF	Svenska Kylfirmors Förening
SKFB	Skandinaviska Kreatursförsäkringsbolaget
SKFB	Sveriges Köpmannaförbund
SKHS	Suomen Kirkkohistoriallinen Seura
SKK	Stichting Kernvootstuwing Koopvaardij-schepen
SKKS	Suomen Kemian Seura
SKI	Szöleszeti Kutató Intézet
SKIF	Svenska Konsulterande Ingenjörers Förening
SKIV	Schweizerischer Kioskinhaber-Verband
SKL	Suomen Kiinnteistönvälittäjäin Liitto
SKL	Sveriges Kemisk-Tekniska Leverantorförening
SKMV	Schweizerischer Kaminfegermeisterverband
SKOGA	Airline of Peoples Democratic China
SKOL	Suomen Konsulttitoimistojen Liitto
SKR	Svenska Kemiingenjörers Riksförening
SKS	Schweizerische Konferenz für Sichheit im Strassenverkehr
SKS	Stiftung für Konsumentenschutz (Switzerland)
SKS	Suomalaisten Kemistien Seura
SKS	Svenska Keramiska Sällskapet
SKT	Verband Schweizerischer Kammgarnweber, Tuch- und Decken-Fabrikanten
SKTF	Sveriges Kvalitetstekniska Förening
SKTL	Suomen Kähertäjätyönantajaliitto
SKTY	Suomen Kunnallisteknillinen Yhdistys
SKV	Schweizerischer Kaninchenzucht-Verband
SKV	Schweizerischer Kaufmännischer Verein
SKV	Schweizerischer Kochverband
SKV	Schweizerischer Reklame-Verband
SKVS	Svenska Konsulterande VVS-Ingenjörers Förening
SKY	Suomen Kuljetwstaloudellinen Yhdistys
SL	Suomen Lääkintavoimistelijaliitto
SL	Sveriges Lantbruksförbund
SL	Sveriges Lararförbund
SLA	Scottish Libraries Association
SLA	Sammenslutningen av Landbrukets Arbeidsgiverforeningen
SLA	Special Libraries Association (U.S.A.)
SLA	Svenska Lantarbetsgivareforeningen
SLAC	Stanford Linear Accelerator Centre (U.S.A.)
SLAC	Structures Lamellées d'Afrique Centrale
SLACES	Syndicat de la Librairie Ancienne et du Commerce de l'Estampe en Suisse
SLAD	Society of London Art Dealers
SLADE	Society of Lithographic Artists, Designers, Engravers and Process Workers
SLAET	Society of Licensed Aircraft Engineers and Technologists
SLAIA	Latin American Society of Agricultural Engineers
SLAMS	Syndicat des Constructeurs d'Appareils de Levage, de Manutention et de Matériels de Stockage
SLAIP	Sociedad Latinoamerica na de Investigación Pédiatrica
SLAMI	Société Agricole Minière et Industrielle (Madagascar)
SLAN	Sociedad Latinoamericana de Nutrición (Venezuela)
SLAS	Society for Latin American Studies
SLC	Scandinavian Library Centre (Denmark)
SLC	Svenska Lantbruksproducenternas Centralförbund
SLD	Savez Lekarskih Drustava
SLE	Societas Linguistica Europaea (Germany)
SLEAT	Society of Laundry Engineers and Allied Trades
SLESR	Société des Librairies de la Suisse Romande
SLF	Scottish Landowners Federation
SLF	Skandinaviska Lackteknikers Förbund
SLF	Skolledarförbundet
SLF	Svenska Laboratieassistent Föreningen
SLF	Svenska Lantbrukstjänstemannaförbundet
SLF	Sveriges Lantmätareförening
SLFP	Sri Lanka Freedom Party
SLFSP	Sri Lanka Freedom Socialist Party
SLFV	Schweizerischen Landfrauenverbandes
SLFY	Suomen Logopedis-Foniatrinen Yhdistys
SLG	Schweizerische Lichttechnische Gesellschaft

SLH	Selskabet for Levnedsmiddelteknologi og -hygiene
SLICE	St. Louis Institute of Consulting Engineers (U.S.A.)
SLiR	Société de Linguistique Romane
SLIP	Sociedad Latinoamericana de Investigadores en Papas (Venezuela)
SLITUF	Sri Lanka Independent Trade Union Federation
SLL	Skotøy- og Loervareindustriens Leverandørforening
SLL	Suomen Lääkäriliitto
SLLA	Sierra Leone Library Association
SLLA	Sri Lanka Library Association
SLLW	Société de Langue et de Littérature Wallonnes (Belgium)
SLM	Sociedad Latinoamericana de Maiz
SLMH	Schweizerischer Verband des Schmiede-, Landmaschinen-, Metall- und Holzewerbes
SLO	Stichting Landbouwhuishoudkundig Onderzoek
SLOW	Steam Launch Operations of the World (U.S.A.)
SLPMB	Sierra Leone Produce Marketing Board
SLPP	Sierra Leone Peoples Party
SLR	Svenska Lantmännens Riksförbund
SLR	Sveriges Lassmedsmästares Riksförbund
SLR	Sveriges Leksakshandlares Riksförbund
SLRP	Society for Long Range Planning
SLS	Stephenson Locomotive Society
SLS	Svenska Läkarsällskapet
SLS	Svenska Litteratursällskapet i Finland
SLSA-GB	Surf Life Saving Association of Great Britain
SLST	Sierra Leone Selection Trust
SLTA	Scottish Lawn Tennis Association
SLTC	Society of Leather Technologists and Chemists
SLV	Schweizerischen Landwirtschaftlichen Verein
SLV	Schweizerischer Lehrerverein
SLV	Schweizerischer Lichtspieltheater-Verband
SLVL	Suomen Liike-ja Virkanaisten Liitto
SLY	Suomen Lintutieteellinen Yhistys
SMA	Servico Meteorológico de Angola
SMA	Singapore Manufacturers Association
SMA	Sheffield Metallurgical Association

SMA	Société Méditerannéenne d'Acupuncture
SMA	Société des Missions Africaines (Canada)
SMA	Steel Merchants Association
SMA	Sugar Manufacturers' Association (Jamaica)
SMAE	Society of Model Aeronautical Engineers
SMAG	Société Meunière et Avicole
SMAK	Svensk Matpotatiskontroll
SMB	Sociedad Meteorológica de Bolivia
SMB	Société Mauritanienne de Banque
SMB	Société Mathématique de Belgique
SMB	Society of Missionaries of Bethlehem in Switzerland
SMBA	Scottish Marine Biological Association
SMBPA	Société Malienne de Biscuiterie et Pâtes Alimentaires
SMC	Schweizerischer Verkaufs- und Marketingleiter Club
SMC	Sealant Manufacturers Conference
SMC	Sociedad Mexicana de Cactalogía
SMC	Sveriges Möbelhandlares Centralförbund
SMCCL	Society of Municipal and County Chief Librarians
SMCS	Sociedad Mexicana de la Ciencia del Suelo
SMDN	Société Minière du Niger
SME	Sociedad Mexicana de Entomología
SMEC	Société Malienne d'Entreprises et de Constructions
SMECMA	Société Malienne d'Études et de Construction de Matériel Agricole
SMECOMA	Landbouwmechanisatiebedrijven
SMEG	Spring Makers' Export Group
SMF	Chambre Syndicale Nationale des Constructeurs et Constructeurs-Installateurs de Matériels et d'Équipements Frigorifiques
SMF	Sociedad Mexicana de Fitogenética
SMF	Sociedad Mexicana de Fitopatología
SMEI	Sales and Marketing Executives International (U.S.A.)
SMEPC	Société Suisse des Maîtres des Écoles Professionnelles Commerciales
SMER	Société Médicale Internationale d'Endoscopie et de Radio-Cinématographie
SMERT	Société Malienne de Fabrication d'Articles Métalliques
SMF	Société Météorologique de France
SMG	Schweizerische Mathematische Gesellschaft

SMG	Schweizerische Musikforschende Gesellschaft
SMGE	Sociedad Mexicana de Geografica y Estadística
SMGI	Société Mauritanienne des Gaz Industriels
SMGS	Socialist Countries Convention on Transport of Goods by Rail
SMGV	Schweizerischer Maler- und Gipsermeister-Verband
SMHI	Sveriges Meteorologiska och Hydrologiska Institut
SMHN	Sociedad Mexicana de Historia Natural
SMI	Sindacato Musicisti Italiani
SMI	Sveriges Möbelindustriförbund
SMI	Syndicat National des Constructeurs de Maisons Individuelles
SMIA	Sheet Metal Industries Association
SMIC	Syndicat des Fabricants de Meubles Métalliques Industriels et Commerciaux
SMIE	Société Mauritanienne d'Importation et d'Exportation
SMIER	Société Médicale Internationale d'Endoscopie et de Radiocinématographie
SMIF	Sveriges Motorcykel- och Mopedimportöres Förbund
SMIPCTER	Société Médicale Internationale de Photo Cinématographie et Télévision Endoscopique et Radiocinématographie (now SMIER)
SMIS	Society for Management Information Systems (U.S.A.)
SMISB	Société Mauritanienne des Industries Secondaires du Bâtiment
SMISO	Systéme Mondial Intégré de Stations Océaniques
SMIVAC	Société de Mise en Valeur de la Corse
SML	Stichting Machinale Landbouw (Suriname)
SML	Suomen Museoliitto
SML	Suomen Matkailuliitto
SMM	Sucreries Marseillaises de Madagascar
SMM	Serviço Meteorológica de Moçambique
SMMB	Scottish Milk Marketing Board
SMMCZ	Sociedad Mexicana de Medicina y Cirugía Zootécnicas
SMMT	Society of Motor Manufacturers and Traders
SMMV	Schweizerischer Mechanikermeister-Verband
SMMY	Suomen Myynti- ja Mainosyhdistys
SMN	Serviço Meterológico Nacionál (Argentina)
SMN	Société des Mélasses du Niari (Zaire)
SMOL	Suomen Musiikinopettajain Liitto
SMOM	Sovrano Militaire Ordine di Malta
SMP	Sociedad Mexicana de Parasitología
SMP	Society of Mural Painters
SMP	Suomen Maaseudun Puloue
SMPA	Scottish Master Patternmakers Association
SMPC	Scottish Milk Publicity Council
SMPC	Société Marocaine des Produits Chimiques
SMPMA	Sausage and Meat Pie Manufacturers Association
SMPMF	Scottish Metal and Plumbers' Merchants' Federation
SMPS	Socialist Countries Convention on Transport of Passengers by Rail
SMPS	Society of Master Printers of Scotland
SMPTE	Society of Motion Picture and Television Engineers (U.S.A.)
SMPV	Schweizerischer Musikpädagogischer Verband
SMR	Svenska Mejeriernas Riksförening
SMR	Svenska Mekanisters Riksförening
SMRA	Scottish Milk Records Association
SMRA	Spring Manufacturers' Research Association (now SRA)
SMRC	Scottish Motor Racing Club
SMRC	Stoneham Museum and Research Centre (Kenya)
SMRE	Safety in Mines Research Establishment
SMRI	Sugar Milling Research Institute (South Africa)
SMS	Société Mathématique Suisse
SMS	Sullivant Moss Society (U.S.A.)
SMS	Suomen Maataloustieteellinen Seura
SMS	Sveriges Malarmästareförening
SMS	Syndicat National des Fabricants de Matériels de Soudage
SMSP	Société Médicale Suisse de Psychothérapie
SMSR	Société des Meuniers de la Suisse Romande
SMSW	State Medical Society of Wisconsin (U.S.A.)
SMT	Sammenslutningen af Maskinfabrikker for Troeindustrien
SMT	Statiunea de Masini si Tractoare (Roumania)
SMTA	Scottish Motor Trade Association
SMTF	Scottish Milk Trade Federation

SMTH	Société Mauritanienne de Tourisme et d'Hôtellerie
SMTL	Suomen Muoviteollisuusliitto
SMTS	Scottish Machinery Testing Station
SMTY	Suomen Materiaalitaloudellinen Yhdistys
SMU	Schweizerische Metall-Inion
SMU	Surinaamse Mijnwerkers Unie
SMUH	Secrétariat des Missions d'Urbanisme et d'Habitat
SMUJ	Savez Muzickih Umetnika Jugoslavije
SMUSE	Socialist Movement for the United States of Europe
SMUV	Schweizerischer Metall- und Uhrenarbeiterverband
SMV	Schweizerischer Markt-Verband
SMV	Schweizerischer Musikerverband
SN	Sveriges Naturvetareförbund
SNA	Sindicato Nacional dos Arquitectos
SNA	Sociedade Nacional de Agricultura (Brazil)
SNA	Société Nationale d'Acclimatation
SNA	Société Nationale d'Assurances et de Réassurances de la République de Guinée
SNA	Syndicat National d'Apiculture
SNAA	Servicio Nacional de Acueductos y Alcantarillado (Costa Rica)
SNAA	Syndicat National des Aviculteurs Agréés
SNABM	Syndicat National des Adjuvants pour Bétons et Mortiers
SNABV	Syndicat National des Agences et Bureaux de Voyages
SNACGP	Syndicat National des Armateurs de Chalutiers de Grande Pêche
SNACH	Sociedad Nacional de Agricultura de Chile
SNAD	Sindacato Nazionale Autori Drammatici
SNADAP	Syndicat National de la Domicile et des Actions Promotionnelles
SNAF	Société Nationale des Architectes de France
SNAFOP	Société Nationale pour le Développement Forestier (Dahomey)
SNAGE	Syndicat National des Affineurs de Gruyère et d'Emmental
SNAHDA	Société Nationale des Huileries du Dahomey
SNAI	Società Nazionale Agricola Industriale (Somalia)
SNAM	Società Nazionale Metanodotii
SNAM	Syndicat National des Articles Métalliques et de leurs Dérivés
SNAME	Society of Naval Architects and Marine Engineers (U.S.A.)
SNAP	Servicia Nacional de Agua Potable (Argentina)
SNAP	Société Industrielle des Nouvelles Applications des Matières Plastiques (Cameroons)
SNAP	Syndicat National des Agences de Publicité
SNAPO	Syndicate National de la Publicité par l'Objet
SNAQ	Syndicat National Angora Qualité
SNAS	Syndicat National du Commerce de Gros des Appareils Sanitaires, de Canalisation et de Chauffage
SNASA	Sociedad Nacional de Agricultura (Mexico)
SNASA	Syndicat National des Agents de Sociétés d'Auteurs
SNASDP	Syndicat National des Annuaires et Supports Divers de Publicité
SNASE	Sindacato Nazionale Autonomo Scuola Elementare
SNATPA	Syndicat National de l'Action Technique et Professionnelle Agricole
SNAV	Société Nouvelle des Ateliers de Venissieux
SNBATI	Syndicat National du Béton Armé et des Techniques Industrialisées
SNBBR	Section Nationale des Bailleurs de Baux Ruraux
SNBC	Syndicat National des Bouilleurs de Cru Producteurs de Fruits et Professions Connexes
SNBTF	Scottish National Building Trades Federation
SNC	Cameroon National Society
SNC	Société Nationale du Cameroun
SNC	Société Nationale de Colombiculture
SNC	Société Nationale de Construction
SNC	Société Nigérienne de Cimenterie
SNC	Société en Nom Collectif
SNC	Syndicat National des Cidriers et Fabricants d'Eau-de-Vie de Cidre
SNCA	Société Nationale de Construction Aéronautique
SNCAO	Syndicat National du Commerce de l'Antiquité et de l'Occasion
SNCAR	Syndicat National des Courtiers d'Assurances et de Réassurances
SNCB	Société Nationale des Chemins de Fer Belges

SNC-BOIS	Société Nationale du Cameroun – Bois
SNCDC	Syndicat National des Commerçants Détaillants en Confiserie
SNCEA	Syndicat National des Cadres d'Exploitations Agricoles (CGA)
SNCEOOA	Syndicat National des Cadres, Employés et Ouvriers des Organisations Agricoles (CGA)
SNCF	Sindacato Nazionale Commercianti di Francobolli
SNCF	Société Nationale des Chemins de Fer Français
SNCFA	Société Nationale des Chemins de Fer Algériens
SNCGEPVO	Syndicat National du Commerce en Gros des Equipements, Pièces pour Véhicules et Outillages
SNCI	Société National de Crédit à l'Industrie
SNCIMIP	Syndicat National des Constructeurs et Installateurs de Matériels Industriels en Plastiques
SNCM	Syndicat National des Chaînes Mécaniques
SNCP	Société Nigérienne de Collecte des Cuirs et Peaux
SNCP	Syndicat National du Commerce du Porc
SNCP	Syndicat National des Conseils en Publicité
SNCRP	Syndicat National des Conseils en Relations Publiques
SNCT	Société Nationale Centrafricaine de Travaux et de Transports
SNCTN	Syndicat National des Cadres et Techniciens du Notariat
SNCTR	Syndicat National du Commerce des Tubes et Raccords
SNCV	Société Nationale des Chemins de Fer Vicinaux
SND	Syndicat National du Décolletage
SNDE	Société Nationale de Distribution d'Eau (Congo)
SNDE	Syndicat National du Découpage et de l'Emboutissage
SNDF	Syndicat National des Déshydrateurs de France
SNDM	Syndicat National des Directeurs de Mutualité
SNDOPA	Syndicat National des Directeurs d'Organismes Professionnels Agricoles
SNDSDCA	Syndicat National des Directeurs et Sous-Directeurs de Coopératives Agricoles
SNE	Société Nationale des Eaux (Haute-Volta)
SNE	Société Nationale d'Énergie (Congo)
SNE	Syndicat National des Emballeurs
SNEA	Société Nationale d'Encouragement à l'Agriculture
SNEA	Société Nationale d'Exploitation Agricole (Central Africa)
SNEALC	Syndicat National d'Elevage et d'Amélioration du Lapin de Chair
SNEC	Société Nationale des Eaux du Cameroun
SNEC	Syndicat National de l'Exploitation d'Équipements Thermiques et de Génie Climatique
SNECIPA	Sindicato Nacional dos Empregados do Comercio e da Industria da Provincia de Angola
SNECMA	Société Nationale d'Étude et de Construction et Moteurs d'Aviation
SNED	Société Nationale d'Édition et de Diffusion (Algeria)
SNED	Syndicat National des Négociants Embouteilleurs et Distributeurs en Vins et Spiritueux de France
SNEF	Syndicat National des Entreprises du Froid et du Conditionnement de l'Air
SNEF	Syndicat National de l'Estampage et de la Forge
SNEFAC	Société Nouvelle d'Entreprises Franco-Africaines de Constructions (Congo)
SNEFCA	Syndicat National des Entreprises du Froid et du Conditionnement de l'Air
SNEFP	Syndicat National des Experts Forestiers Patentes
SNEI	Société Nouvelle d'Éditions Industrielle
SNEP	Société Nationale des Entreprises de Presse
SNEP	Syndicat National des Cadres de l'Enseignement Privé
SNEPA	Syndicat National de l'Édition Phonographique et Audiovisuelle
SNEPE	Société Nigérienne d'Étude pour la Production de l'Élevage
SNEPMA	Syndicat National de l'Enseignement Professionnel et Ménager Agricole
SNEPP	Syndicat National des Extrudeurs de Profilés Plastiques
SNES	Syndicat National des Enseignements de Second Degré
SNESup	Syndicat National de l'Enseignement Supérieur

SNET	Syndicat National de l'Enseignement Technique
SNETAP	Syndicat National de l'Enseignement Technique Agricole
SNETI	Syndicat National des Entrepeneurs de Travaux Immergés
SNETP	Syndical National des Enseignements Techniques et Professionelles
SNF	Svenska Naturskyddsföreningen
SNF	Svenska Numismatiska Föreningen
SNF	Syndicat National des Industries et Commerces de la Récupération de la Ferraille
SNFBM	Syndicat National des Fabricants de Boîtes, Emballages et Bouchages Métalliques
SNFBTE	Scottish National Federation of Building Trades Employers
SNFC	Société Nationale des Chemins de Fer Français
SNFCCM	Syndicat National des Fabricants de Crèmes et Conserves de Marrons
SNFEV	Syndicat Français des Éleveurs de Visons
SNFFS	Syndicat National des Fabricants de Fruits au Sirop
SNFL	Syndicat National des Fabricants de Liqueurs
SNFM	Section Nationale des Fermiers et des Métayers
SNFPA	Syndicat National des Fabricants de Produits Abrasifs
SNFPAS	Syndicat National des Fabricants de Produits Aromatiques de Synthèse
SNFQ	Syndicat National des Fabricants de Quincaillerie
SNFP	Syndicat National des Fabricants de Ressorts
SNFS	Syndicat National des Fabricants de Sirops
SNFS	Syndicat National des Fabricants de Sucre de France
SNFTRP	Syndicat National des Fabricants de Tuyaux et Raccords en Polyoléfines
SNFU	National Farmers' Union of Scotland
SNFV	Syndicat National des Fabricants de Vinaigres
SNG	Schweizerische Naturforschende Gesellschaft
SNG	Schweizerische Neurologische Gesellschaft
SNG	Schweizerische Numismatische Gesellschaft
SNGC	Stichting Nederlands Graancentrum
SNGM	Servicio Nacional de Geología y Minería (Ecuador)
SNGP	Syndicat National des Graphistes Publicitaires
SNGP	Syndicat National des Grossistes Distributeurs en Produits de Parfumerie et Accessoires de Toilette
SNGTN	Société Nationale des Grand Travaux du Niger
SNH	Société Nationale de l'Habitat (Central Africa)
SNHBM	Société Nationale des Habitations à Bon Marché (Belgium)
SNHF	Société Nationale d'Horticulture de France
SNHMV	Syndicat National des Hybrideurs et Métisseurs Viticoles
SNHTPC	Scottish National Housing and Town Planning Council
SNI	Société Nationale d'Investissements (Madagascar, Tunisia)
SNI	Studieselskapet for Norsk Industri
SNI	Syndicat National des Instituteurs et Institutrices
SNIA	Servicio Nacional de Investigaciones Agropecuarias (Panama)
SNIA	Sindacato Nazionale Istruzione Artistica
SNIAS	Société Nationale Industrielle Aérospatiale
SNIBB	Syndicat National des Instituts de Beauté
SNIC	Singapore National Institute of Chemistry
SNICL	Syndicat National de l'Industrie et du Commerce des Lubrifiants
SNIE	Syndicat National des Industries de l'Émail
SNIECV	Syndicat National des Industries Extractives pour la Céramique et la Verrerie
SNII	Serikat Nelajan Islam Indonesia
SNIL	Suomen Neuvottelevien Insinöörien Liitto
SNIM	Société Nationale Industrielle et Minière (Mauritania)
SNIMA	Service de Normalisation Industrielle Marocaine
SNIMaBI	Syndicat National des Importateurs de Matériels de Bureau et d'Informatique
SNIP	Syndicat National de l'Industrie Pharmaceutique
SNIP	Syndicat National Interprofessionnel de Porc
SNIPOT	Société Nationale Interprofessionnelle de la Pomme de Terre
SNIPV	Syndicat National de l'Industrie Pharmaceutique Vétérinaire

SNIR	Fédération Française des Syndicats Nationaux des Industries Radioélectriques et Électroniques
SNIR	Syndicat National des Industries de la Robinetterie
SNIRA	Syndicat National des Industries de Récupérations Animales
SNIRI	Snickerifabrikernas Riksförbund
SNJ	Syndicat National des Journalistes
SNL	Serviço Nacional de Lepra (Brazil)
SNM	Sociedad Nacional de Minería (Chile)
SNMA	Servicios Nacionales de Meteorologia y Aerofotografica (Peru)
SNMG	Syndicat National de la Mécanique Générale
SNMH	Servicio Nacional de Meteorología e Hidrología (Ecuador)
SNMI	Syndicat National de la Mécanique Industrielle d'Usinage et de Constructions Spéciales
SNMM	Syndicat National des Constructeurs de Menuiserie, Murs-Rideaux et Cloisons Métalliques
SNMM	Syndicat National du Mobilier Métallique
SNMP	Syndicat National du Moulage et de la Transformation des Feuilles et Films Plastiques
SNMRMA	Syndicat National des Marchands Réparateurs de Machines Agricoles
SNN	Syndicat National des Notaires
SNO	Scottish National Orchestra Society
SNOF	Société Nationale d'Oléiculture de France
SNOP	Secrétariat National de l'Opinion Publique Secrétariat Général de l'Episcopat Français
SNP	Scottish National Party
SNPA	Serviço Nacional de Pesquisas Agrónomicas
SNPA	Scottish Newspaper Proprietors Association
SNPa	Syndicat National de la Parfumerie (Belgium)
SNPA	Syndicat National des Plastiques Alvéolaires
SNPA	Société Nationale des Pétroles d'Aquitaine
SNPA & ER	Service National de la Production Agricole et de l'Enseignement Rurale (Haiti)
SNPAMR	Syndicat National de la Presse Agricole et du Monde Rurale
SNPBR	Section Nationale des Preneurs de Baux Ruraux
SNPC	Secretaría Nacional de Planificación y Coordinación (Bolivia)
SNPCRT	Syndicat National de la Publicité Cinématographique, Radiophonique et Télévisée
SNPD	Syndicat National de la Publicité Directe
SNPE	Société Nationale des Poudres et Explosifs
SNPEN	Syndicat National des Professeurs des Écoles Normales
SNPEP	Syndicat National Professionnel des Engrais Phosphates
SNPF	Syndicat National des Pédiatres Français
SNPF	Syndicat National des Producteurs de Fraisiers
SNPI	Servicio Nacional de Productividad Industrial (Spain)
SNPIC	Syndicat National des Professionnels de l'Information et de la Communication des Entreprises et Collectivités
SNPL	Syndicat National des Pilots de Ligne
SNPLV	Syndicat National de la Promotion et de la Publicité sur le Lieu de Vente
SNPMI	Syndicat National des Producteurs de Mortiers Industriels
SNPMT	Syndicat National Professionnel des Médecins du Travail
SNPN	Société National de Protection de la Nature et d'Acclimatation de France
SNPNC	Syndicat National du Personnel Navigant Commercial
SNPNH	Syndicat National des Producteurs de Nouveautés Horticoles
SNPOQ	Syndicat National des Producteurs d'Oeufs de Qualité
SNPPA	Syndicat National du Profilage des Produits Plats en Acier
SNPPFOC	Syndicat National des Producteurs de Plantes de Fraisiers Officiellement Contrôlés
SNPPM	Syndicat National des Producteurs, Ramasseurs et Collecteurs de Plantes Médicinales, Aromatiques et Industriéles
SNPPT	Société Nationale de la Petite Propriété Terrienne (Belgium)
SNPRCI	Syndicat National des Producteurs, Ramasseurs et Collecteurs de Plantes Médicinales, Aromatiques et Industrielles
SNPT	Société Nationale de Promotion Touristique (Senegal)
SNPVAC	Sindicato Nacional de Pessoal de Vôo da Aviação Civil (Portugal)

NR	Society for Nautical Research
NRA	Servicio Nacional de Reforma Agraria (Bolivia)
NRC	Israel Atomic Energy Commission
NRTM	Sydicat National de Revêtement et du Traitement des Métaux
NRTMS	Syndicat National des Revêtements et Traitements des Métaux et Substrats
NS	Sindicato Nazionale Scrittori
NS	Société Nationale de Sidérurgie (Algeria)
NS	Studieförbundet Näringsliv och Samhälle
NSAF	Syndicat National des Spécialistes Apicoles de France
NSC	Scottish National Ski Council
NSE	Society of Nuclear Scientists and Engineers (U.S.A.)
NSM	Sindicato Nazionale Scuola Media
NSO-GATRA	Société Nouvelle Société Gabonaise de Travaux
NSRC	Swedish Natural Science Research Council
NST	Société Nationale pour la Vente des Scories Thomas
NTA	Société Nigérienne de Transport Automobile
NTA	Syndicat National des Transporteurs Aériens
NTC	Sindicato Nacional de Transportes y Comunicaciones
NTF	Syndicat National des Téléphériques et Téléskis de France
NTFM	Société Nationale des Transports Ferroviaires
NTL	Statui Nakladatelstvi Technicke Literatury (Czechoslovakia)
NTN	Société Nationale des Transports Nigériens
NTP	Société Nationale de Travaux Publics et Particuliers (Senegal)
NTPC	Scottish National Town Planning Council
NTRPCVR	Syndicat National des Fabricants de Tubes et Raccords en Polychlorure de Vinyle Rigide
NTS	Studiorum Novi Testamenti Societas (U.K.)
NTU	Société Nigérienne de Transport Urbain
NTZ	Syndicat National des Travailleurs Zairois
NUiF	Stichting Nederlandse Uienfederatie
NV	Association Suisse de Normalisation
NVF	Syndicat National des Vétérinaires Français
NVPF	Syndicat National des Vétérinaires Praticiens Français

SNVV	Stichting voor de Nederlandse Vlasteelt en Vlasbewerking
SOAE	State Organization for Administration and Employment Affairs (Iran)
SOAEM	Société Ouest-Africaine d'Entreprises Maritimes
SOAH	Syndicat de l'Outillage Agricole et Horticole
SOAM	Société d'Oxygène et d'Acetylène de Madagascar
SOAS	School of Oriental and African Studies
SOB	Sociedade de Olericultura do Brasil
SOB	Swiss Official Board of Ballroom Dancing
SOBAMAD	Société Bananière de Madagascar
SOBEMAP	Société Belge d'Économie et de Mathématique Appliquée
SOBER	Sociedade Brasileira de Economistas Rurais
SOBEVECO	Société Ophthalmologique Belge des Verres de Contact
SOBIPO	Société Bretonne Interprofessionnelle de la Pomme de Terre
SOBOA	Société des Brasseries de l'Ouest Africain
SOBOCA	Société des Bois du Sud-Ouest Cameroun
SOBOCI	Société des Boissons Hygiéniques de la Côte-d'Ivoire
SOBRAGA	Société des Brasseries du Gabon
SOBRAMIL	Sociedade Brasileira de Mineraçao Ltda
SOC	Sveriges Oljeväxtodlares Centralförening
SOCABU	Société de Caoutchouc Butyl
SOCACI	Société Commerciale et Agricole de la Côte d'Ivoire
SOCACIG	Société Centrafricaine de Cigarettes
SOCAD	Société de Commercialisation et de Crédit Agricole du Dahomey
SOCADEM	Société Camerounaise d'Emballages Métalliques
SOCADEP	Société Camerounaise d'Édition et de Publicité
SOCADI	Société Centrafricaine de Diamant Industriel
SOCADIS	Société Camerounaise de Distribution
SOCAEM	Société Ouest Africaine d'Entreprises Maritimes
SOCAFER	Société Camerounaise de Plomberie et de Ferronnerie
SOCAGI	Société Centrafricaine des Gaz Industriels
SOCAHIT	Société Camerounaise Hotélière, Immobilière et Touristique
SOCALTRA	Société Alsacienne d'Études et Travaux

SOCAM	Société Camerounaise de Menuiserie
SOCAM	Société Commerciale Africaine d'Importation (Ivory Coast)
SOCAMBO	Société Camerounaise Industrielle du Bois
SOCAMCO	Société Camerounaise de Conserveries
SOCAME	Société Camerounaise des Engrais
SOCAMETA	Société Camerounaise de Constructions Métalliques
SOCANA	Société Camerounaise de Navigation
SOCAPALM	Société Camerounaise des Palmeraies
SOCAPE	Société Camerounaise de Presse et d'Éditions
SOCAR	Société Cameroun d'Assurances et de Réassurances
SOCAREC	Société Africaine de Rectification
SOCAS	Société de Conserves Alimentaires du Sénégal
SOCASEP	Société Camerounaise de Sepultures et Transports Spéciaux
SOCATCI	Société des Caoutchoucs de Côte-d'Ivoire
SOCATEX	Société Africaine de Confection et de Bonneterie
SOCATRAL	Société Camerounaise de Transformation de l'Aluminium
SOCAVER	Société Camerounaise de Verrerie
SOCC	Super Ocean Carrier Conference (U.S.A.)
SOCCA	Société Camerounaise de Crédit Automobile
SOCEA	Société Charentaise d'Équipements Aéronautiques
SOCECO	Société Camerounaise d'Études et de Constructions
SOCEF	Société de Construction et d'Exploitation d'Installations Frigorifiques en Côte-d'Ivoire
SOCEPPAR	Sociedade Cerealista Exportadora de Produtos Paranaenses (Brazil)
SOCFI	Société d'Organisation de Congrès Français et Internationaux
SOCGPA	Seed, Oil, Cake and General Produce Association
SOCIAC	Singapore-Soviet Shipping Agency
SOCIACI	Société Commerciale et Industrielle Africaine de Côte d'Ivoire
SOCIAGRI	Société Ivoirienne d'Expansion Agricole
SOCICA	Société Cinématographique Africaine
SOCICADI	Société Dahoméenne de Promotion du Commerce et de l'Industrie
SOCICO	Société Immobilière et Commerciale du Congo
SOCIDIS	Société Ivoirienne d'Importation et de Distribution
SOCIGA	Société de Cigarettes du Gabon
SOCIM	Société Centrafricaine d'Investissements Immobiliers
SOCIM	Société de Constructions et l'Industries de la Mauritanie
SOCIMA	Société des Ciments du Mali
SOCIMEX	Société d'Importation et d'Exportation de l'Océan Indien (Madagascar)
SOCIPAR	Société Ivoirienne de Participation
SOCIPEC	Société Ivoirienne de Participations Économiques
SOCITR-ACAM	Société Camerounaise Interprofessionelle pour la Fourniture de Traverses et de Bois Débites au Transcamerounais
SOCIVER	Société Ivoirienne de Verrerie
SOCOBLE	Société Coopérative des Producteurs de Blé
SOCOBOIS	Société Congolaise des Bois
SOCOCIM	Société Ouest Africaine des Ciments
SOCOD-EBAS	Société Commerciale pour le Développement de la Basse-Sanaga
SOCODI	Société Congolaise de Disques
SOCOFFA	Société Commerciale et Financière Franco-Africaine
SOCOFIDE	Société Congolaise de Financement du Développement
SOCOFOR	Forestry Co-operative (Indo-China)
SOCOFRA	Société Commerciale Francais (Congo)
SOCOFR-ACIM	Société Commerciale Franco-Africaine des Ciments
SOCO-FROID	Société Congolaise de Conservation et de Congélation
SOCOL	Société de Construction d'Entreprises Générales (Belgium)
SOCOLOR	Sociedad Colombiana de Orquideologia
SOCOMA	Société des Conserves du Mali
SOCOMAF	Société pour le Conditionnement de Maïs Français
SOCOMID	Société de Caution Mutuelle des Industries Diverses
SOCOPA	Société Co-opérative des Produits Agricoles (Zaire)
SOCOPRE	Société Sénégalaise de Commercialisation des Produits de l'Élevage
SOCOPRISE	Société Africaine d'Entreprises Industrielles et Immobilières (Congo)

SOCORAM	Société de Constructions Radio-Électriques du Mali
SOCOTEL	Société Mixte pour le Développement de la Technique de la Communication dans le Domaine des Télécommunications
SODACA	Société Dahoméenne de Crédit Automobile
SODACOP	Société Dahoméenne de Commerce et de Pêche
SODACRUS	Société Dahoméenne de Crustaces
SODAF	Société Dahoméenne d'Ananas et de Fruits
SODAFE	Société pour le Développement de l'Afrique Équatoriale
SODAIC	Société Dahoméenne pour le Développement de l'Industrie et du Commerce
SODAK	Société Dahoméenne Agricole et Industrielle du Kénaf
SODA-METRO	Société Dahoméenne de Messageries et de Transports Routiers
SODAMI	Société Dahoméenne de Minoterie
SODAPAR	Société Dahoméenne de Parfumerie
SODAPEC	Société Dahoméenne de Peintures et Colorants
SODAPLAS-TICA	Société Dahoméenne de Plastique
SODASEL	Société Dahoméenne de Sel
SODEAM	Société pour le Développement de l'Électricité en Afrique et à Madagascar
SODECAO	Société pour le Développement de Cacao (Cameroons)
SODECI	Société de Distribution d'Eau de la Côte-d'Ivoire
SODEFEL	Société pour le Développement de la Production des Fruits et Légumes (Ivory Coast)
SODEFOR	Société pour le Développement des Plantations Forestières (Ivory Coast)
SODEL	Société pour Développement des Applications de l'Électricité
SODELAC	Société Cotonnière du Tchad
SODELEC	Société d'Études de l'Économie de Consummation
SODEMI	Société pour le Développement Minier de la Côte d'Ivoire
SODEN-ICOB	Société de Développement Regional de la Vallée du Niari et de Jacob (Congo)
SODEPALM	Société d'État pour le Développement du Palmier à Huile (Ivory Coast)
SODEPAX	Exploratory Committee on Society, Development and Peace of the Roman Catholic Church and the World Council of Churches
SODEPRA	Société pour le Développement des Productions Animales (Ivory Coast)
SODERN	Société Anonyme d'Études et Réalisations Nucléaires
SODE-SUCRE	Société pour le Développement des Plantations de Cannes a Sucre, l'Industrialisation et la Commercialisation du Sucre
SODETAM	Société pour le Développement des Voyages et du Tourisme en Afrique et à Madagascar
SODETEG	Société d'Études Techniques et d'Entreprises Générales
SODETRAM	Société d'Études pour Réalisations en Outre-Mer
SODIACAM	Société de Distribution Alimentaire du Cameroun
SODIC	Société pour la Conversion et le Développement Industriels
SODIMA	Société de Diffusion des Marques
SODIMAF	Société de Distribution des Grandes Marques pour l'Afrique (Ivory Coast)
SODIMPEX	Société Commerciale d'Import-Export (Ivory Coast)
SODIP	Société pour la Diffusion de la Presse (Belgium)
SODIPHAC	Société de Diffusion Pharmaceutique en Afrique Centrale
SODOMEI	Japan Federation of Trade Unions
SODRE	Servicio Oficial de Difusion Radio-electrica (Uruguay)
SODT	Swiss Office for the Development of Trade
SOEC	Statistical Office of the European Communities
SOEKOR	Southern Oil Exploration Corporation (South Africa)
SOF	Société Ornithologiques de France
SOF	Sveriges Ornithologische Unie
SOF	Syndicat des Osiéristes Français
SOFACO	Société Africaine de Fabrication, de Formulation et de Conditionnement (Ivory Coast)
SOFAIGUI	Society for Development of Agricultural and Industrial Products of Guinea
SOFAMI	Société de Fabrication Métallique Ivoirienne
SOFBA	Société Française des Bois Africaine
SOFCA	Société Française de Compléments Alimentaires

SOFFO Société Financière pour la France et les Pays Outre-Mer

SOFICAL Société de Financement Industriel Commercial et Agricole

SOFICO Société pour l'Exploitation des Fibres Locales (Zaire)

SOFIDAK Société pour la Foire Internationale de Dakar

SOFIDECA Société de Financement et de Développement de l'Économie Agricole

SOFIFA Société Financière et Immobilière Franco-Africaine

SOFINA Société Financière de Transports et d'Entreprises Industrielles (Belgium)

SOFIRAD Société Financière de Radiodiffusion

SOFIRAN Société Française des Pétroles d'Iran

SOFMA Société Française de Matériels d'Armement

SOFRAMER Société Française d'Achats pour l'Outre-Mer

SOFRA-TOME Société Française d'Études et de Réalisation Nucléaires

SOFRATOP Société Française de Travaux Topographiques et Photogrammétriques

SOFREAVIA Société Française d'Études et de Réalisation d'Équipements Aéronautiques

SOFRECOM Société Française d'Études et de Réalisations d'Équipements de Télécommunications

SOFREGAZ Société Française d'Études Gaz

SOFRELEC Société Française d'Études Électrique

SOFRE-MINES Société Française d'Études Minière

SOFRESID Société Française d'Études Sidérurgique

SOFREXAM Société Française d'Exportation de Matériels Naval et Militaires

SOFRAVIN Société Française des Vins (Senegal)

SOFRIGAL Société des Frigorifiques du Sénégal

SOFRINA Société Française pour l'Industrie en Afrique

SOG Schweizerische Ophthalmologische Gesellschaft

SOGABOL Société Gabonaise des Oléagineux

SOGACA Société Gabonaise de Crédit Automobile

SOGACAM Société Gabonaise de Cabotage Maritime et Fluvial

SOGACAR Société Gabonaise de Carrières

SOGACEL Société Gabonaise de Cellulose

SOGACHIM Société Gabonaise de Chimie

SOGADA Société Générale d'Approvisionnement du Dahomey

SOGAF-INEX Société Gabonaise de Financement et d'Expansion

SOGAFRIC Société Gabonaise Froid et Représentations Industrielles et Commerciales

SOGAMAR Société Gabonaise de Marbre et Matériaux

SOGAME Société Gabonaise de Matériel et d'Équipement

SOGAMIRE Société Gabonaise de Miroiterie et Ébénisterie

SOGAPECI Société Générale d'Armement et de Pêche de Côte-d'Ivoire

SOGAR-AREC Société Gabonaise de Électrification et de Mécanique Générale

SOGARES Société Gabonaise de Réalisations de Structures

SOGAS Stichting Samenwerkende Organisaties van Detaillisten in Gasapparaten

SOGAT Society of Graphical and Allied Trades

SOGATOL Société Gabonaise de Toles et Produits Sidérurgiques

SOGATRAM Société Gabonaise de Transport Maritime

SOGEC Société Gabonaise d'Électrification et de Canalisation

SOGECOR Société de Gestion et de Conseil en Organisation

SOGEDEM Société Gabonaise d'Étude et de Développement Maritimes

SOGEF Société de Gestion d'Entrepôts Frigorifiques en Côte d'Ivoire

SOGEL Société Gabonaise d'Élevage

SOGELEM Société Générale d'Électricité de Mauritanie

SOGEM Société de Gestion Moderne

SOGEP Société Générale d'Études et de Planification

SOGERCA Société pour l'Entreprise de Réacteurs et de Centrales Atomiques

SOGESCI Société Belge pour l'Application des Méthodes Scientifiques de Gestion

SOGES-ETRA Société Sénégalaise de Bâtiments et Travaux Publics

SOGETA Société Générale des Techniques Agricoles (Upper Volta)

SOGETHA Société Génerale des Techniques Hydro-Agricoles (Tunis)

SOGET-OCAM Société de Gestion pour le Tourisme au Cameroun

SOGETRA Société Générale de Travaux (Belgium)

SOGETRAF Société Générale de Travaux et de Représentations en Afrique (Ivory Coast)

SOGET-RANS	Société de Gestion pour le Tourisme au Cameroun
SOGEV	Société Générale du Vide
SOGIEXCI	Société Générale d'Importation et d'Exportation de Côte-d'Ivoire
SOGIP	Société Générale pour l'Industrialisation de la Pêche
SOGISMA	Société des Gaz Industriels de Madagascar
SOGREAH	Société Grenobloise d'Études et d'Application Hydrauliques
SOHIMA	Société Hôtelière et Immobilière de Madagascar
SOHORA	Société des Hôtels de la Riviéra Africaine (Ivory Coast)
SOHOTCI	Société Hôtelière et Touristique de Côte-d'Ivoire
SOIDAH	Société Industrielle d'Habillement du Dahomey
SOIDI	Société Ivoirienne de Distribution
SOIPAC	Società Italiana di Patologia Clinica
SOIVRE	Servicio Oficial de Inspección, Vigilancia y Regulación de la Exportaciones
SOK	Suomen Osuuskauppojen Keskuskunta
SOK	Svenska Organisations Konsulters Förening
SOKSI	Sentral Organisasi Karyawan Socialis Indonesia
SOL	Suomen Opettajain Liitto
SOLCA	Sociedad de Lucha contra el Cáncer (Ecuador)
SOLET	Società Orvietana Essiccazione e Lavorazione dei Tabacchi
SOLF	Sveriges Optikleverantöres Förening
SOLIBRA	Société de Limonaderies et Brasseries d'Afrique
SOLIDA-RIOS	Consejo de Fundaciones Americanas de Desarrollo (Guatemala)
SOLIMAC	Société Libano-Ivoirienne de Matériaux de Construction
SOM	Society of Metaphysicians
SOM	Society of Occupational Medicine
SOMA	Société Maritime de Madagascar
SOMACO	Société Nationale de Commerce (Madagascar)
SOMACOM	Société Maritime et Commerciale (Gabon)
SOMACOTP	Société Mauritanienne de Construction et de Travaux Publics

SOMACO-TRET	Société Mauritanienne de Commerce, de Transport, de Représentation et de Transit
SOMADEC	Société Mauritanienne de Développement et de Commerce
SOMAF	Société Marbrière Africaine
SOMAGA	Société Marseillaise du Gabon
SOMAIR	Société des Mines de l'Air
SOMALAC	Société Malgache Lac Alaotra-Malagasy Lake Alaotra Society (Madagascar)
SOMALIBO	Société Malienne de Boissons Gazeuses
SOMAP	Sociétés Marocaines de Prévoyance
SOMAP	Société Mauritanienne d'Armement et de Pêche
SOMAPA	Société Malienne de Parfumerie
SOMAREM	Société Nationale de Recherches et d'Exploitation des Ressources Minierès du Mali
SOMASAC	Société Malienne de Sacherie
SOMA-QUIRE	Société Mauritanienne de Quincaillerie et de Représentation
SOMAURAL	Société Mauritanienne des Allumettes
SOMDIAA	Société Multinationale de Développement pour les Industries Alimentaires et Agricoles
SOMEC	Société Mutuelle d'Études et de Coopération Industrielles
SOMECAF	Société d'Ateliers Mécaniques Africains
SOMECAF-RIQUE	Société pour la Mécanisation des Entreprises en Afrique
SOMEPI	Société Mauritanienne d'Études et de Promotion Industrielles
SOMET	Société Maroc Études
SOMETER	Société Mauritanienne d'Études Techniques et de Représentation
SOMFA	Soya Bean Meal Futures Association
SOMICOA	Société Maritime et Industrielle de la Côte Occidentale d'Afrique
SOMIEX	Société Malienne d'Importation et d'Exportation
SOMIMA	Société Minière de Mauritanie
SOMIP	Société Mauritanienne des Industries de la Pêche
SOMIREN	Società Minerali Radioattivi Energia Nucleare
SOMISA	Sociedad Mixta Siderurgia Argentina
SOMIVAC	Société pour la Mise en Valeur Agricole de la Corse

SOMMEP	Syndicat de l'Outillage à Main et des Machines Électro-Portatives
SONADER	Société Nationale pour Développement Rural (Dahomey)
SONABA	Société Nationale du Bâtiment (Tchad)
SONAC	Société Nationale de la Céramique Artisanale et Industrielle du Dahomey
SONACO	Société Nationale Agricole pour le Coton (Dahomey)
SONACO	Société Nationale de Commerce (Madagascar)
SONACO	Société Nationale de Conditionnement (Ivory Coast)
SONACOB	Société Nationale de Commercialisation des Bois et Dérivés (Algeria)
SONACOB	Société Nationale de Construction de Bâtiments (Senegal)
SONACOM	Société Nationale de Commerce (Togo)
SONACOME	Société Nationale des Construction Mécaniques
SONACOT	Société Nationale de Commercialisation du Tchad
SONADER	Société Nationale pour le Développement Rural du Dahomey
SONADIG	Société Nationale d'Investissements du Gabon
SONADIS	Société Nouvelle pour l'Approvisionnement et la Distribution au Sénégal
SONAFI	Société Nationale de Financement (Ivory Coast)
SONAFOR	Société Nationale des Forages (Senegal)
SONAFRIG	Société Nationale des Frigorifiques (Senegal)
SONAGA	Société Nationale de Garantie et d'Assistance au Commerce (Senegal)
SONAP	Sociedade Nacional de Petroleos
SONAP	Sociedad de Navigación Petrolera (Chile)
SONAP	Société Nationale des Articles de Papeterie (Central Africa)
SONAPH	Société Nationale pour le Développement de la Palmerale et des Huileries
SONARA	Société Nigérienne de Commercialisation de l'Arachide
SONAREM	Société Nationale de Recherches et d'Exploitations Minières (Algeria)
SONATAM	Société Nationale des Tabacs et Allumettes du Mali
SONATITE	Société Nationale des Travaux d'Infrastructure des Télécommunications (Algeria)
SONATRAB	Société Nationale de Transformation du Bois
SONATRAC	Société Nationale de Transit et de Consignation (Dahomey)
SONATRACH	Société Nationale de Transport de Carburant (Algeria)
SONATRAM	Société Nationale de Travaux Maritimes (Algeria)
SONEAB	Société Nationale d'Exploitation des Arachides de Bouche (Senegal)
SONEES	Société Nationale d'Exploitation des Eaux du Sénégal
SONEG	Société Nationale d'Entreprise Générale (Senegal)
SONEL	Société Nationale d'Élevage (Zaire)
SONELGAZ	Société Nationale de l'Électricité et du Gaz (Algeria)
SONEPI	Société Nationale d'Études et de Promotion Industrielle (Senegal)
SONEPRESS	Société Nationale d'Édition et de Presse (Haute-Volta)
SONERAN	Société Nigérienne d'Exploitation des Ressources Animales
SONETE	Sociedade Nacional de Estudos e Financiamento de Empreendimentos Ultramarinos (Portugal)
SONETRA	Société Nationale d'Entreprises et de Travaux Publics (Mali)
SONEXI	Société Nigérienne d'Exploitation Cinématographique
SONIBATP	Société Nigérienne de Bâtiment et de Travaux Publics
SONIC	Société Nationale des Industries de la Cellulose (Algeria)
SONICA	Société Nigérienne de Crédit Automobile
SONICAR	Société Nigérienne de Carrelage
SONIC-ERAM	Société Nigérienne de Produits Céramiques
SONIFAME	Société Nigérienne de Fabrications Métalliques
SONIMCO	Société Nationale d'Impression en Continu (Senegal)
SONIMEX	Société Nationale d'Importation et d'Exportation (Mauritania)
SONIPAL	Société Nigérienne pour la Production d'Allumettes

SONIPLA	Société Nigérienne de Plastique
SONIPRIM	Société Nigérienne de Primeurs
SONITAN	Société Nigérienne de Tannerie
SONITO	Société Nationale d'Intervention sur le Marché de la Tomate
SONITRA	Société Nationale Ivoirienne de Travaux
SONOCRAF	Société Nouvelle des Comptoirs Réunis d'Afrique
SONRA	Society of Newfoundland Radio Amateurs
SONUCI	Société Nigérienne d'Urbanisme et de Construction Immobilière
SOPAD	Société de Produits Alimentaires et Diététiques
SOPANI	Société de Parfumerie Nigérienne
SOPAO	Société de Pêche de l'Afrique Occidentale
SOPARMOD	Société des Parfums Modernes du Tchad
SOPARCO	Société Africaine de Parfumerie et de Conditionnement (Mali)
SOPECI	Société de Peinture en Côte-d'Ivoire
SOPECOBA	Société des Pêcheries Coloniales à la Baleine
SOPELEM	Société d'Optique, Précision, Électronique et Mécanique
SOPEMEA	Société pour le Perfectionnement des Matériels et Équipements Aérospatiaux
SOPESEA	Société des Pêcheries Sénégalaises de l'Atlantique
SOPEXA	Société pour la Promotion de l'Exportation des Produits Agricoles et Alimentaires
SOPIM	Société de Promotion Immobilière de la Côte-d'Ivoire
SOPIMA	Société des Piles de Madagascar
SOPIVOLTA	Société des Piles de Haute-Volta
SOPREP	Sociedade Portuguesa de Relacões Publicas
SOPRIA	Société d'Étude et de Financement pour la Promotion des Industries Agricoles et de l'Alimentation
SOPROD-AVCI	Société d'Études pour la Production de l'Avocat en Côte-d'Ivoire
SOPROGI	Société pour la Promotion et la Gestion Industrielle
SOR	Sectie Operationele Research
SOR	Society for Occupational Research (U.S.A.)
SOR	Sveriges Legitimerade Optikers Riksförbund
SORA	Svenska Operationsanalysföreningen
SORCA	Société de Recherche Operationelle et d'Économie Appliquée (Belgium)
SOREAS	Syndicat des Fabricants d'Organes et d'Équipement Aéronautiques et Spatiaux
SOREDIA	Société de Recherche et d'Exploitation Diamantiféres (French Equatorial Africa)
SOREFAME	Sociedades Reunidas Fabriacoes Metalicas (Portugal)
SOREMI	Société des Recherches et d'Exploitation Minières
SORIN	Società Richerche ed Impianti Nucleari
SORO	Special Operations Research Office, American University, Washington
SOS	International Federation of Bloodgivers Organisations
SOSAC	Société des Spécialités Agricoles et Chimiques (France)
SOSAP	Société Sénégalaise d'Armement à la Pêche
SOSATCO	Société Sénégalaise d'Assistance Technique et de Conseil de Gestion
SOSC	Smithsonian Oceanographic Sorting Centre (U.S.A.)
SOSECI	Société Sénégalaise pour le Commerce et l'Industrie
SOSECOD	Société Sénégalaise pour le Commerce et le Développement
SOSECODA	Société Sénégalaise de Courtages et d'Assurances
SOSEDECO	Société Sénégalaise pour le Développement Commercial
SOSEFIL	Société Sénégalaise de Filterie
SOSEG	Société Sénégalaise d'Amaillage et de Galvanisation
SOSETAM	Société Sénégalaise de Tannerie-Mégisserie
SOSETER	Société Sénégalaise de Terassements
SOSETRA-PROMER	Société Sénégalaise pour le Traitement des Produits de la Mer
SOSE-TRAUR	Société Sénégalaise de Travaux Urbains et Ruraux
SOSEX-CATRA	Société Sénégalaise d'Exploitation de Carrières et de Transports
SOSSI	Scouts on Stamps Society International (U.S.A.)
SOSU	Société Sucrière Voltaïque
SOSUCAM	Société Sucrière du Cameroun
SOSUMAV	Société Sucrière de la Mahavavy
SOSU-TCHAD	Société Sucrière du Tchad
SOTA	Société Coopérative pour l'Achat du Tabac (Switzerland)

SOTA	Société des Transports Africains
SOTEGA	Société Industrielles Textile du Gabon
SOTELEC	Société Mixte pour le Développement de la Technique des Télécommunications sur Cables
SOTEXCO	Société des Textiles du Congo
SOTICI	Société de Transformation Industrielle de Côte-d'Ivoire
SOTOCA	Société Industrielle et Commerciale Togolaise du Café
SOTOCAM	Société de Topographie au Cameroun
SOTO-HOMA	Société Touristique et Hôtelière de Madagascar
SOTOM	Société de Topographie de Madagascar
SOTOMA	Société des Tabacs et Oléagineux de Madagascar
SOTOMA	Société Togolaise de Marbrerie et Matériaux
SOTOMAT-ERIAUX	Société Togolaise de Matériaux
SOTOPLAN	Société Togolaise de Plantation
SOTOTRAC	Société Togolais de Transit et de Consignation
SOTRA	Société des Transports Abidjanais (Ivory Coast)
SOTRABCI	Société de Travaux Publics et de Bâtiments Côte-d'Ivoire
SOTRABO	Société de Transformation du Bois
SOTRABOI	Société de Transformation des Bois Ivoiriens
SOTREC	Société des Tréfileries et Clouteries de la Côte-d'Ivoire
SOTREF	Société Tropicale d'Exploitation Forestière (Cameroons, Ivory Coast)
SOTREP	Société Tchadienne de Réalisation et d'Entreprise de Pneumatiques
SOTROPAL	Société Tropicale des Allumettes (Ivory Coast)
SOTROPCO	Société Tropicale de Commerce
SOTUC	Société de Transports Urbains du Cameroun
SOV	Schweizerischer Obstverband
SOV	Schweizerischer Optiker-Verband
SOV	Schweizerischer Orientteppichändler-Verband
SOVEC	Société Voltaïque d'Étanchéité et de Carrelage
SOVEG	Société Voltaïque d'Engineering et de Gestion
SOVETCO	Société pour la Vente de Thons Congèles (Ivory Coast)
SOVETIV	Société de Vêtements Ivoiriens
SOVIAMAD	Société des Viandes de Madagascar
SOVICA	Société Voltaïque d'Intervention et de Coopération avec l'Agriculture
SOVIMAS	Société Voltaïque d'Importation Azar et Salam
SOVINCI	Société des Vins de la Côte d'Ivoire
SOVINCO	Société des Vins du Congo
SOVOCA	Société Voltaïque de Crédit Automobile
SOVOG	Société Voltaïque de Groupage
SOVOLCI	Société Voltaïque de Commerce et d'Industrie
SOVOLCOM	Société Voltaïque de Commercialisation
SOVOL-PLAS	Société Voltaïque de Plastique
SOVOLSEM	Société Voltaïque d'Entreprise de Surrurerie Menuiserie Métallique et Charpente
SOY	Suomen Ostopäällíköiden Yhdistys
SOXADA	Société d'Oxygène et d'Acetylène du Dahomey
SP	Commission Internationale de Phare du Cap Spartel
SPA	Föreninger Sveriges Praktiserande Arkitekter
SPA	Society of Public Analysts
SPA	Screen Printing Association International
SPA	Singapore People's Alliance
SPA	Sociedade Portuguesa de Autores
SPA	Society of St Peter Apostle for Native Clergy
SPA	Southern Pine Association (U.S.A.)
SPA	Sumatra Planters Association (Indonesia)
SPA	Syndicat de la Presse Agricole
SPA	Systems and Procedures Association (U.S.A.)
SPAB	Society for the Protection of Ancient Buildings
SPAC	Société Sénégalaise de Produits Alimentaires Congèles
SPACEM	Sociedad Puertorriquena de Autores, Compositores y Editores Musicales
SPAEF	Société des Pétroles d'Afriques Équatoriale Française
SPAG	Syndicat des Produits Alimentaires en Gros
SPAI	Service Professionnel Agricole International (*of* APPCA)
SPAM	Stowarzyszenie Polskich Artystów Muzyków
SPANA	Society for the Protection of Animals in North Africa

SPANC	Society of St Peter the Apostle for Native Clergy
SPARMO	Solar Particle Altitude Radiation Monitoring Organisation
SPAS	Chambre Syndicale des Producteurs d'Aciers Fins et Spéciaux
SPASK	Service Provincial de l'Agriculture de Sud Kivu (Zaire)
SPATC	South Pacific Air Transport Council
SPATF	South Pacific Appropriate Technology Foundation (New Guinea)
SPB	Sociedad Peruana de Botánica
SPBA	Poultry and Egg Producers Association of Great Britain
SPBS	Scottish Plant Breeding Station
SPBW	Society for the Preservation of Beers from the Wood
SPC	Seed Production Committee
SPC	Sociedade Portuguesa de Commercialização
SPC	Société Française de Ceramique
SPC	South Pacific Commission (New Caledonia)
SPC	Swiss Publishers Corporation
SPCI	Société de Promotion Commerciale Ivoirienne
SPCI	Svenska Papers- och Cellulosaingeniörs- föreningen
SPCN	Société de Produits Chimiques du Niger
SPD	Sozialdemokratische Partei Deutschlands
SPD	Svenska Privatdetektivförbundet
SPE	Society of Plastic Engineers (U.S.A.)
SPEA	Sales Promotion Executives Association (U.S.A.)
SPEA	Scottish Physical Education Association
SPEC	Society for Pollution and Environmental Control (Canada)
SPEC	South Pacific Bureau for Economic Cooperation (Fiji)
SPECI	Société de Presse et d'Édition de la Côte-d'Ivoire
SPECI-CHAMBRE	Chambre Syndicale des Fabricants et Concessionnaires de Spécialités Pharmaceutiques
SPEF	Scottish Plumbing Employers Federation
SPEF	Svenska Putsentreprenörföreningen
SPEIN	Syndicat Patronal des Entreprises et Industries du Niger
SPEL	Société Provisoire de l'Économique Laitière
SPEO	Société de Presse et d'Édition Ovine
SPEPE	Secrétariat Permanent pour l'Étude des Problèmes de l'Eau
SPER	Syndicat des Industries de Matériel Professionnel Électronique et Radioélectrique
SPF	Scottish Pharmaceutical Federation
SPF	Société Pomologique de France
SPF	Société Préhistorique Française
SPF	Svenska Pappershandlareföreningen
SPF	Svensk Pilotförening
SPF	Sveriges Papersindustriförbund
SPF	Sveriges Plastforbund
SPF	Sveriges Pomologiska Förening
SPFB	Chambre Syndicale des Producteurs de Fontes Brutes
SPFE	Society for the Preservation of the Fauna of the Empire
SPFF	Syndicat des Propriétaires Forestiers de France
SPFGBS	Syndicat des Producteurs Français des Graines de Betterave à Sucre
SPFV	Schweizerischer Pelz-Fachverband
SPG	Schweizerische Philosophische Gesellschaft
SPG	Schweizerische Physikalische Gesellschaft
SPG	Society for the Propagation of the Gospel in Foreign Parts
SPGB	Socialist Party of Great Britain
SPhV	Schweizerischer Photographenverband
SPI	Service Pédologique Inter-africain
SPI	Comité de Coordination des Secrétariats Professionnels Internationaux
SPI	Society of the Plastics Industry (USA)
SPI	Svenska Petroleum Institutet
SPIC	Society of the Plastics Industry of Canada
SPIC	Southern Petrochemical Industries Corporation (U.S.A.)
SPICA	Société Industrielle de Produits Chimiques et Aromatiques (Cameroons)
SPICRIM	Société pour la Participation Industrielle et Commerciale pour la Représentation Industrielle en Mauritanie
SPIDS	Syndicat Patronal des Industries de Dakar et du Sénégal
SPIE	Secrétariat Professionnel International de l'Enseignement
SPIEA	Syndicat Professionnel de l'Industrie des Engrais Azotés

SPIFDA	South Pacific Islands Fisheries Development Agency	**SPRL**	Society for the Promotion of Religion and Learning
SPIGED	Syndicat Professional des Industries des Goudrons et Dérivés	**SPRM**	Société des Plantations Réunies de Mimot (Vietnam)
SPIH	Syndicat des Producteurs Independants de Houblons	**SPRU**	Science Policy Research Unit
		SPS	Stichting Planbureau Suriname
SPIL	Society for the Promotion and Improvement of Libraries (India)	**SPSF**	Syndicat des Pisciculteurs-Salmoniculteurs de France
SPILS	Society for the Promotion of the Interests of Librarianship Students	**SPSL**	Society for the Protection of Science and Learning
SPIO	Spitzenorganisation der Filmwirtschaft	**SPSS**	Syndicat des Producteurs de Semences Sélectionnées
SPIRIM	Société Ivoirienne de Promotion et de Réalisations Immobilières	**SPSSI**	Society for the Psychological Study of Social Issues (U.S.A.)
SPKC	Small Pig Keepers' Council		
SPM	Société des Pétroles de Madagascar	**SPSSR**	Syndicat du Personnel Social des Services Sociaux Ruraux
SPMA	Sewage Plant Manufacturers Association	**SPT**	Brancheforeningen for Soebe- Parfumeri-, Toilet-og Kemisk-Tekniske Artikler
SPMA	Society for Post-Medieval Archaeology		
SPMF	Syndicat des Producteurs de Miel de France	**SPT**	Society of Photo-Technologists (U.S.A.)
SPML	Sociedade Portuguesa de Medicina Laboratorial	**SPT**	Sveriges Personaltidningsförening
SPN	Sociedade Portuguesa de Numismática	**SPTIY**	Suomen Puunteollisuss-insinöörien Yhdistys
SPNR	Society for the Promotion of Nature Reserves	**SPTL**	Society of Public Teachers of Law
SPO	Socialistische Partei Österreichs	**SPTL**	Suomen Pesuteollisuusliitto
SPOE	Society of Post Office Engineers	**SPTR**	Société des Plantations des Terres Rouge (Vietnam)
SPOFA	Leverantörföreningen för Sport- och Fritids-artiklar	**SPUC**	Society for the Protection of the Unborn Child
SPOOM	Syndicat des Producteurs d'Oléagineux d'Outre-mer	**SPUD**	Society for the Prevention of Unnecessary Damage (to Potatoes)
SPP	Swaziland Progressive Party	**SPUR**	Singapore Planning Urban Research Group
SPPA	Serviço de Pesquisas de Patologia Animal (Brazil)	**SPURS**	Special Program for Urban and Regional Studies of Developing Areas (U.S.A.)
SPQR	Senatus Populusque Romanus	**SPV**	Schweizerischer Pferdezuchtverband
SPR	Sociedade Portuguesa de Reumatologia	**SPV**	Schweizerische Schlachtvieh Produ-zentenverband
SPR	Société Pédagogique de la Suisse Romande		
SPR	Society for Psychical Research	**SPVEA**	Superintendência de Valorizaçao Económica da Amazonia
SPR	Studievereniging voor Psychical Research		
SPR	Sveriges Pälsdjursuppfodares Riksförbund	**SPY**	Suomen Paperi-Insinöörien Yhdistys
SPR	Sveriges Parfymhandlares Riksförbund	**SQI**	Sociedad de Quimica Industrial
SPR	Sveriges Public Relations Förening	**SQLA**	Scotch Quality Lamb Association
SPRC	Society for Prevention and Relief of Cancer	**SQM**	Sociedad Química de México
SPRDA	Solid Pipeline Research and Development Association (Canada)	**SQP**	Sociedad Química del Perú
		SR	Sagverkens Riksförbund
SPRF	Schweizer Public-Relations-Forum	**SRA**	Science Research Associates (U.S.A.)
SPRG	Schweizerische Public Relations Gesellschaft	**SRA**	Sociedad Rural Argentina
SPRI	Scott Polar Research Institute, Cambridge	**SRA**	Spring Research Association

SRA	Squash Rackets Association
SRAA	Société Royale d'Astronomie d'Anvers
SRAB	Société Royale des Beaux-Arts (Belgium)
SRAIN	Société de Représentations Automobiles et Industrielles au Niger
SRAPL	Société Romande d'Audiophonologie et de Pathologie du Langage
SRAT	Section Région d'Afrique Tropicale (*of* IOBC)
SRAT	Société de Recherches et d'Applications Techniques
SRB	Sociedad Rural Boliviana
SRB	Sociedade Rural Brasileira
SRB	Statens Rad for Byggnadsforskning
SRBB	Société Royale de Botanique de Belgique
SRBE	Société Royale Belge des Électriciens
SRBG	Société Royale Belge de Géographie
SRBII	Société Royale des Ingénieurs et des Industriels (Belgium)
SRBMD	Société Royale Belge de Médecine Dentaire
SRC	Science Research Council
SRC	Shri Ram Centre for Industrial Relations (India)
SRC	Social Research Centre (Cyprus, Hong Kong)
SRCC	Société Nationale pour la Renovation et le Développement de la Cacoyère et de Cafetière Togolaise
SRCI	Société Routière Colas de la Côte-d'Ivoire
SRCL	Service Rural de Culture et Loisirs
SRCMA	Steel Radiator and Convector Manufacturers' Association
SRCOA	Société Routière Colas de l'Ouest Africain
SRCRA	Shipowners Refrigerated Cargo Research Association
SRDA	Scottish Retail Drapers Association
SRDC	Shopfitting Research and Development Council
SRDE	Signals Research and Development Establishment (*of* MOS)
SREB	Southern Regional Educational Board (U.S.A.)
SREPB	Société Royale d'Économie Politique de Belgique
SRESA	Société de Recherche Économique et Sociologique en Agriculture
SRF	Svenska Reklambyra Forbundet
SRF	Svenska Resebyraföreningen
SRF	Sveriges Rationaliseringsförbund
SRF	Sveriges Redareförening
SRF	Syndicat des Riziculteurs de France
SRFB	Société Royale Forestière de Belgique
SRFCAM	Section de Recherches Forestières au Cameroun
SRG	Schweizerische Rundspruch Gesellschaft
SRGS	South Rhodesia Geological Survey
SRHE	Society for Research into Higher Education
SRI	Shri Ram Institute for Industrial Research (India)
SRI	Ski Retailers International (U.S.A.)
SRI	Stanford Research Institute (U.S.A.)
SRI	Sugar Research Institute (Australia)
SRIFIR	Shiram Institute for Industrial Research (India)
SRIS	Safety Research Information Service (U.S.A.)
SRIT	Section d'Études et Fabrications des Télécommunications
SRL	Science Reference Library (British Library)
SRL	Sveriges Radioleverantörer
SRL	Vereinigung der Stadt-, Regional- und Landesplaner
SRLR	Societatea Romậna de Linguistica Romanica
SRM	International Spiritual Regeneration Movement (U.K.)
SRNA	Shipbuilders and Repairers National Association
SRP	Serengeti Research Project (Tanzania)
SRP	Society for Radiological Protection
SRPO	Science Resources Planning Office (U.S.A.)
SRPTA	Scottish Road Passenger Transport Association
SRR	Società Retorumantscha
SRR	Sveriges Radiohandlares Riksförbund
SRRC	Scottish Research Reactor Centre
SRRL	Southern Regional Research Laboratory (U.S.A.)
SRS	Service de la Recherche Sociologique (Switzerland)
SRS	Soil Research Station (New Zealand)
SRS	Svenska Revisoramfundet
SRSA	Scientific Research Society of America
SRTI	Société de Recherches Techniques et In-dustrielles

SRTPA	Syndicat des Redacteurs Techniques de la Presse Agricole	**SSFA**	Stainless Steel Fabricators' Association of Great Britain
SRU	Scottish Rugby Union	**SSFC**	Société Suisse des Fabriques de Cartonnages
SRUBLUK	Society for the Reinvigoration of Unremunerative Branch Lines in the United Kingdom	**SSFF**	Skogbrukets of Skogindustrienes Forsknings-forening
SRV	Schweizerischer Reklame-Verband	**SSFF**	Solid Smokeless Fuels Federation
SRZB	Société Royale Zoologique de Belgique	**SSFODF**	Syndicat des Spécialistes Français en Orthopédie Dento-Faciale
SS	Department of Social Sciences (UNESCO)	**SSG**	Schweizerische Sprachwissenschaftliche Gesellschaft
SS	Sveriges Slakteriförbund (Sweden)		
SSA	Forskningsstiftelsen Skogsarbeten	**SSGA**	Société Suisse de Géographie Appliquée
SSA	Seismological Society of America	**SSH**	Société Suisse des Hôteliers
SSA	Social Security Administration	**SSHA**	Social Science History Association (U.S.A.)
SSA	Società Svizzera degli Albergatori	**SSHA**	Société Scientifique d'Hygiène Alimentaire
SSA	Société Suisse Amerikanisten-Gesellschaft	**SSHB**	Society for the Study of Human Biology
SSA	Society of Scottish Artists	**SSHM**	Scottish Society for the History of Medicine
SSA	Svenska Sockerfabriks Aktiebolaget	**SSHMSN**	Société Suisse d'Histoire de la Médecine et des Sciences Naturelles
SSAFA	Soldiers' Sailors' and Airmen's Families Association	**SSHRC**	Social Sciences and Humanities Research Council (Canada)
SSAE	Société Suisse d'Anthropologie et d'Ethnologie	**SSI**	Service Social International
SSAO	Société Shell de l'Afrique Occidentale	**SSI**	Smart Set International (U.S.A.)
SSC	Société Suisse de Chimie	**SSI**	Stichting Sprenger Instituut
SSC	Société Suisse des Cuisiniers	**SSIA**	Scottish Society for Industrial Archaeology
SSCC	Société Suisse de Chimie Clinique	**SSIC**	Social Science Information Center (U.S.A.)
SSE	Société Suisse des Écrivains	**SSIC**	Società Svizzera degli Impresari-Costruttori
SSE	Société Suisse des Entrepreneurs	**SSIC**	Société Suisse des Industries Chimiques
SSE	Société Suisse d'Ethnologie	**SSIDA**	Steel Sheet Information and Development Association
SSEA	Société Suisse des Exploitants d'Autotaxis et de Voitures de Remise	**SSIE**	Smithsonian Science Information Exchange Inc. (USA)
SSEC	Secondary School Examinations Council	**SSIF**	Sveriges Skogsindustriförbund
SSEC	Social Science Education Consortium (U.S.A.)	**SSIGE**	Société Suisse de l'Industrie du Gaz et des Eaux
SSEC	Société Sucrière d'Études et de Construction, Tirlemont (Belgium)	**SSIL**	Société Suisse d'Industrie Laitière
SSEF	Sveriges Städentreprenörers Förbund	**SSIMF**	Società Svizzera dei Insegnanti di Matematica e Fisica
SSEPC	Société Sénégalaise d'Engrais et de Produits Chimiques	**SSIP**	Sozialwissenschaftlicher Studienkreis f. Internationale Probleme
SSF	Società Svizzera di Farmacia	**SSISI**	Statistical and Social Inquiry Society of Ireland
SSF	Stiftelsen Svensk Skeppsforskning		
SSF	Svensk Sjuksköterskeförening	**SSIV**	Schweizerischer Spenglermeister- und In-stallateurverband
SSF	Svenska Slöjdföreningen		
SSF	Svenska Stämpelfabrikantföreningen	**SSJ**	Savez Sindikata Jugoslavije
SSF	Sveriges Stenindustri Förbund	**SSL**	Suomen Sairaanhoitajaliitto
SSF	Sveriges Stuvareförbund	**SSL**	Société Suisse de Linguistique

SSL	Société Suisse des Liquoristes	SSR	Sveriges Radiohandlares Rijksförbund
SSL	Suomen Sanomalehtimiesten Liitto	SSR	Sveriges Skogsägareföreningars Riksförbund
SSLF	Sveriges Livsmedelshandlareförbund	SSR	Sveriges Skorstensfejaremästares Riksförbund
SSM	Societatea de Stiinte Matematice din RSR		
SSMA	Scottish Steel Makers' Association	SSR	Sveriges Snickeriföretageres Riksförbund
SSMAF	Société Suisse des Mensurations et Améliorations Foncières	SSRA	Scottish Seaweed Research Association
		SSRA	Scottish Squash Rackets Association
SSMC	Société Suisse des Maîtres Charpentiers	SSRA	Secteur Soudanais des Recherches Agronomiques
SSMD	Société Suisse des Maîtres de Dessin		
SSMG	Société Suisse des Maîtres de Gymnastique	SSRB	Soil Survey Research Board (of ARC)
SSMI	Société Suisse des Maîtres Imprimeurs	SSRC	Social Science Research Council (Philippines, U.K., U.S.A. etc)
SSMLL	Society for the Study of Mediaeval Languages and Literature		
		SSRCC	Social Science Research Council of Canada
SSMUTA	Sheet and Strip Metal Users' Technical Association	SSRD	Social Science Research and Development Corporation (U.S.A.)
SSN	Sociedad Silvícola Nacional (Cuba)	SSRG	Schweizerische Studiengesellschaft f. Rationellen Guterumschlag
SSN	Société Suisse de Numismatique		
SSNTA	Scottish Seed and Nursery Trade Association	SSRI	Social Science Research Institute (Hawaii)
SSO	Société Suisse d'Odonto-Stomatologie	SSRS	Society for Social Responsibility in Science (U.S.A.)
SSO	Société Suisse d'Oncologie		
SSOL	Suomen Silmäoptikkojen Liitto	SSRT	Société Sénégalaise de Réalisation Touristique
SSOME	Société Suisse d'Optique et de Microscopie Électronique	SSS	Société Suisse de Spéléologie
		SSS	Suomen Säätöteknillinen Seura
SSOMV	Schweizerischer Schuhmacher- und Orthopädieschuhmachermeister-Verband	SSS	Svenska Spannmalsföreningarnas Samorganisation
SSP	Schweizerische Gesellschaft für Psychologie	SSSA	Soil Science Society of America
SSP	Société Suisse de Philosophie	SSSF	Sodra Sveriges Skogagares Forbund
SSP	Société Suisse de Physique	SSSH	Société Suisse des Sciences Humaines
SSP	Société Suisse de Psychiatrie	SSSI	Soil Science Society of Ireland
SSPES	Société Suisse des Professeurs de l'Enseignement Secondaire	SSSP	Society for the Study of Social Problems (U.S.A.)
SSPH	Société Suisse de Pharmacie	SSSWP	Seismological Society of the South-West Pacific (New Zealand)
SSPL	Société Suisse des Patrons Lithographes		
SSPM	Société Suisse de Pédagogie Musicale	SSTA	Secondary School Teachers Association of Malta
SSPMP	Société Suisse des Professeurs de Mathématique et de Physique	SSTEF	Svenska Sagverks-och Trävaruexport-föreningen
SSPP	Scandinavian Society for Plant Physiology (Denmark)		
		SSTL	Suomen Sähkötukkuliikkeiden Liitto
SSPP	Society for the Study of Physiological Patterns	SSTS	Scandinavian Student Travel Service
		SSV	Schweizerischer Sachversicherungsverband
SSPR	Société Suisse de Public Relations	SSV	Schweizerischer Samenhändlerverband
SSPT	Société Sénégalaise des Phosphates de Thiès	SSV	Schweizerischer Schriftstellerverband
SSPWB	Scottish Society for the Protection of Wild Birds	SSV	Schweizerischer Spiegelglasverband
SSR	Société Suisse de Radiodiffusion	SSV	Schweizerischer Städteverband

SSVC	Società Svizzera dei Viaggiatori di Commercio	**STEC**	Storage and Transport of Explosives Committee (India)
SSVC	Société Suisse des Voyageurs de Commerce	**STECI**	Société de Travaux d'Équipement de la Côte-d'Ivoire
SSWEG	Stainless Steel Wire Experiment Group	**STEE**	Société Tchadienne d'Énergie Électrique
SSZ	Société Suisse de Zoologie	**STEEP**	Société Tchadienne d'Entreposage de Produits Pétroliers
SSZ	Society of Systematic Zoologists (U.S.A.)	**STEF**	Société des Transports et Entrepôts Frigorifiques
ST	Société Théosophique (India)		
ST	Svensk Trycheriföreningen	**STEFO**	Sveriges Tecknares och Formgivares Riksförbund
STA	Science and Technology Agency (Japan)		
STA	Sociedad de Tecnicos de Automoción	**STEG**	Société Tchadienne d'Entreprises Générales
STA	Société de Travail Aérien (Algeria)	**STEL**	Société de Traitements Électrolytiques et Électrothermiques
STAA	Student Travel Association of Asia (Japan)		
STACA	Servicio Tecnico Agricola Colombian Americano	**STELO**	Stuenta Tutmonda Esperantista Ligo
		STEMI	Société de Transports et Manutentions Industriels
STACO	Society of Telecommunications Administrative and Controlling Officers		
		STEN	Société Togolaise des Engrais
STACRES	Standing Committee on Research and Statistics (FAO)	**STEPC**	Société Tropicale d'Engrais et de Produits Chimiques (Ivory Coast)
STAN	Servicio Técnico Agrícola de Nicaragua		
STANAV-FORCHAN	NATO Standing Naval Force Channel	**STET**	Società Torinese Esercizi Telefonici
		STF	Scandinavian Transport Workers Federation
STANAV-FORLANT	NATO Standing Naval Force Atlantic	**STF**	Skipsteknisk Forbund
		STF	Svenska Taxiförbundet
STAREC	Société Technique d'Application et de Recherche Électronique	**STF**	Svenska Teknologföreningen
		STF	Sveriges Takpappfabrikanters Förening
STAS	Oficiul de Stat pentru Standarde (Roumania)	**STF**	Sveriges Tandläkarförbund
STATEC	Service Central de la Statistique et des Études Économiques (Luxembourg)	**STFI**	Svenska Träforskingsinstitutet
		STG	Schiffbautechnische Gesellschaft
STAUK	Seed Trade Association of the United Kingdom	**STG**	Suomen Taidegraafikot
		STI	Société Tchadienne d'Investissement
STAV	Stiftelsen for Administrativ Vidareutbildning	**STI**	Statens Teknologiske Institutt
STB	Société Togolaise de Boissons	**StiBoka**	Stichting voor Bodemkartering
STC	Scandinavian Trade Centre	**STICA**	Servicio Técnico Inter-Americano de Cooperación Agrícola (Costa Rica)
STC	SHAPE Technical Centre		
STC	Stowarzyszenie Techników Cukrowników	**STICPA**	Société Tchadienne Industrielle et Commerciale de Produits Animale
STC	Sveriges Trä- och Byggvaruhandlares Centralförbund		
		STICUSA	Nederlandse Stichting voor Culturele Samenwerking met Suriname en de Nederlandse Antillen
STCAN	Service Technique des Constructions et Armes Navales		
STCAU	Service Technique Central d'Aménagement et d'Urbanisme	**STID**	Scientific and Technical Information Division (of NASA) (U.S.A.)
STCI	Société de Transports de la Côte-d'Ivoire	**STIL**	Service Technique Interprofessionnel du Lait
STDV	Schweizerischer Textildetaillisten-Verband	**STIMA**	Société de Techniques Industrielles et Maritimes (Ivory Coast)
STE	Société Togolaise d'Entreposage		
STEC	Société Technique d'Entreprises Chimiques	**STIP**	Science Teaching Improvement Programme (U.S.A.)

STIPEL	Società Telefonica Interregionale Piemontese e Lombarda
STISEC	Scientific and Technological Information Services Enquiry Committee (New Zealand)
STKL	Suomen Turkiseläinten Kasvattajain Liitto
STL	Standard Telecommunication Laboratories
STL	Suomen Teatteriliitto
STL	Suomen Teollisuusliitto
STL	Suomen Tukkukauppiaiden Liitto
STLV	Schweizerischer Turnlehrer-Verein
STM	International Group of Scientific, Technical and Medical Publishers
STMHV	Schweizerischer Taxi- und Mietwagenhalter-Verband
STMSA	Scottish Timber Merchants and Sawmillers Association
STOCA	Société Togolaise de Crédit Automobile
STONIC	Section Tunisienne de l'Office National Inter-professionnel des Céréales
STOP	Stowarzyszenie Techniczne Odlewników Polskich
STOPA	Stichting Overname Pootaardappelen
STP	Société Togolaise des Plastiques
STPC	Society of Technical Presentation and Communication
STPCM	Secrétariat Technique Permanent de la Conférence des Ministres de l'Éducation Nationale des États d'Expression Française d'Afrique et de Madagascar
STPTC	Standard Tar Products Testing Committee
STR	Sveriges Tandteknikers Riksförbund
STR	Sveriges Trafikbilägares Rijksorganisation
STR	Sveriges Trähusfabrikers Riksförbund
STRA	Scottish Textile Research Association
STRC	Scientific, Technical and Research Commission (of OAU)
STRI	Smithsonian Tropical Research Institute (Panama)
STRI	Sports Turf Research Institute
STRIM	Société Technique de Recherches Industrielles et Mécanique
STS	Société Textile Sénégalaise
STS	Suomen Teknillinen Seura
STSA	Science Technology and Society Association
STSN	Società Toscana di Scienze Naturali
STTA	Service Technique des Télécommunications de l'Air
STTIF	Sveriges Tval-och Tvättmedelsindustriförening
STU	Swedish Board for Technical Development
STUC	Scottish Trade Union Congress
STULM	Stichting tot Uitvoering van Landbouw-Maatregelen
STUMOKA	Studiekring voor Moderne Kantoortechniek
STUVA	Studiengesellschaft für Interidische Verkehrarlagen
STV	Schweizerischer Technischer Verband
STV	Schweizerischer Tonkünstlerverein
STV	Schweizerischer Transport-Versicherungs-Verein
SUACI	Service d'Utilité Agricole a Compétence Interdépartementale (of CA)
SUAD	Services d'Utilité Agricole de Développement
SUBAW	Scottish Union of Bakers and Allied Workers
SUCEE	Socialist Union of Central-Eastern Europe
SUCESU	Sociedade de Usarios de Computadores Electronicos e Equipmentos Subsidiaros (Brazil)
SUCO	Service Universitaire Canadian Outre-Mer
SUCOMA	Sugar Corporation of Malawi
SUCRP	Société des Usines Chimiques Rhône-Poulenc
SUCSE	Scottish Universities Council on Studies in Education
SUDAM	Superintendência do Desenvolvimento da Amazônia (Brazil)
SUDAP	Superintendência da Agricultura e Produção (Brazil)
SUDENE	Superintendency for the Development of the North-East (Brazil)
SUDEPE	Superintendency for Fisheries Development (Brazil)
SÜDV	Schweizerischer Übersetzer- und Dolmetscherverband
SUE	Sociedad Uruguaya de Entomología
SUERF	Société Universitaire Européenne de Recherches Financières
SUF	Svenska Uppfinnareföreningen
SUFJ	Savez Udruzenja Folklorista Jugoslavije
SUHAF	Sveriges Universitets- och Högskoleamanuensers Förbund
SUKOL	Suomen Kieltenopettajien Liitto
SUM	Servicio Universitario Mundial
SUMOC	Superintendência da Moeda e Crédito (Brazil)

SUN	Spiritual Unity of Nations
SUN	Symbols, Units and Nomenclature Commission (*of* IUPAP)
SUNAB	National Superintendency of Supplies (Brazil)
SUNFED	Special United Nations Fund for Economic Development
SUNKLO	Suomen Näytelmäkirjailijaliitto
SUPARCO	Space and Upper Atmosphere Research Committee (Pakistan)
SUPLAN	Sub-secretaria de planejamento e orçamento Ministério da Agricultura Brazil
SURDD	Southern Utilisation Research and Development Division (U.S.A.)
SUS	Schweizerischer Verband des Seilbahnunternehmungen
SUS	Suomalais-Ugrilainen Seura
SUSTA	Scottish Union of Students Travel Association
SUT	Society for Underwater Technology
SUVA	Schweizerische Unfallversicherungs-Anstalt
SV	Stifterverband für die Deutsche Wissenschaft
SVA	Schweizerische Vereinigung für Altertumswissenschaft
SVA	Schweizerische Vereinigung für Atomenergie
SVAE	Schweizerischer Verband der Auto-Elektriker
SVAJ	Schweizerische Vereinigung der Agrarjournalisten
SVAM	Società per lo Sviluppo Agricolo del Mezzogiorno
SVB	Schweizerischer Verband für Berufsberatung
SVB	Speleologisch Verband van België
SVB	Stichting voor Bodemkartering
SVBF	Schweizerischer Verband für das Arbeitsstudium
SVBF	Schweizerischer Verband von Betriebsfachleuten
SVBL	Schweizerische Vereinigung zur Förderung der Betriebsberatung in der Landwirtschaft
SVC	Svejsecentralen
SVC	Svenska Västkustfiskarnas Centralförbund
SVCC	Schweizerischer Verein der Chemiker-Coloristen
SVCF	Schweizerischer Verband der Cementwarenfabrikanten
SVCN	Sociedad Venezolana de Ciencias Naturales
SVCP	Société Voltaïque des Cuirs et Peaux
SVCS	Sociedad Venezolana de la Ciencia del Suelo
SVD	Schweizerischer Drogisten-Verband
SVD	Schweizerische Vereinigung f. Dokumentation
SVDK	Schweizerischer Verband Diplomierter Krankenschwestern und Krankenpfleger
SVDP	Schweizerischer Verband Diplomierter Psychiatrieschwestern und -pfleger
SVE	Sociedad Venezolana de Entomología
SVE	Society for Visual Education (U.S.A.)
SVEABUND	Svenska Väg-och Vattenbyggarnas Arbetsgivareförbund
SVEB	Schweizerische Vereinigung für Erwachsenenbildung
SVEFF	Sveriges Färgfabrikanters Förening
SVERTEX	Sveriges Textilindustriförbund
SVF	Schweizerischer Vereinigung von Färbereifachleuten
SVF	Stiftelsen för Värmeteknisk Forskning
SVF	Svenska Vägföreningen
SVF	Sveriges Varvsindustriförening
SVF	Sveriges Veterinärförbund
SVFJ	Schweizerische Vereinigung Freier Berufsjournalisten
SVG	Schweizerischer Fachverband für Gemeinschaftsverpflegung
SVG	Sociedad Venezolana de Geólogos
SVGP	Schweizerischer Verband der Gartenbauproduzenten
SVGU	Schweizerischer Verband der Glas- und Gebäudereinigungs-Unternehmer
SVGW	Schweizerischer Verein von Gas- und Wasserfachmännern
SVHA	Société Vaudoise d'Histoire et d'Archéologie
SVI	Vereinigung Schweizerisches Verpackungsinstitut
SVIA	Schweizerischer Verband der Ingenieur-Agronomen
SVIA	Sociedad Venezolana de Ingenieros Agrónomos
SVIAL	Schweizerischer Verband der Ingenieur-Agronomen und der Lebensmittel-ingenieure
SVIF	Sociedad Venezolana de Ingenieros Forestales
SVIH	Sociedad Venezolana de Ingeniería Hidráulica
SVIL	Schweizerische Vereinigung für Innerkolonisation und Industrielle Landwirtschaft

SVIM	Sociedad Venezolana de Minas y Metalurgicos
SVIMU	Associazione Italiana per lo Sviluppo della Ricerca nelle Macchine Utensili
SVIQ	Sociedad Venezolana de Ingenieros Químicos
SVIS	Schweizerischer Verband der Innen-dekorateure und Sattler
SVIT	Schweizerischer Verband der Immobilien-Treuhänder
SVK	Schweizerische Vereinigung für Kleintiermedizin
SVKAZ	Schweizerischer Verband Kantonal Approbrierter Zahnärzte
SVKS	Schweizerischer Verband der Klavierbauer und- Stimmer
SVKW	Schweizerischer Verband der Konfektions- und Wäsche-Industrie
SVL	Suomen Vähittäiskauppiasliitto
SVL	Suomen Valokuvaajain Liitto
SVLFC	Schweizerische Vereinigung der Lack- und Farbenchemiker
SVLP	St Vincent Labour Party
SVLR	Schweizerische Vereinigung für Luft- und Raumrecht
SVLT	Schweizerischer Verband für Landtechnik
SVM	Service Volontaire Mennonite (Germany)
SVM	Stichting voor Melkhygiëne
SVMF	Sveriges Vertygsmaskinaffärers Förening
SVMIU	Associazione Italiana per lo Svipuppo della Ricerca nelle Macchine Utensili
SVMT	Schweizerischer Verband für die Materialprüfungen der Technik
SVMY	Suomen Vene- ja Mootoriyhdistys
SVNLF	South Vietnamese National Liberation Front
SVO	Stiching voor Oliehoudende Zaden
SVO	Stichting voor Veevoedings Onderzoek
SVOB	Schweizerischer Verband der Orthopädisten und Bandagisten
SVOI	Staatsveeartsenijkundig Onderzoekings In-stituut
SVOR	Schweizerische Vereinigung f. Operations Research
SVOT	Schweizer Verband der Orthopädie-Techniker
SVP	Schweizerischer Pedicure-Verband
SVP	Schweizerischer Verband Staatlich Anerkannter Physiotherapeuten
SVP	Sociedad Venezolana de Planificación
SVP	Stichting v. Plantenveredeling
SVP	Studiekring voor Plantenveredeling
SVPC	Société Voltaïque de Peintures
SVPC	Syndicat des Entreprises de Vente par Correspondance
SVPG	Schweizerisches Verband für Photo-Handel und -Gewerbe
SVPP	Schweizerisches Vereinigung für Para-psychologie
SVQ	Sociedad Venezolana de Química
SVR	Svenska Väg- och Vattenbyggares Riksför-bund
SVS	Schweizerische Verein für Schweisstechnik
SVS	Société des Vétérinaires Suisses
SVS	Society of Visiting Scientists
SVSF	Sveriges Vetenskapliga Specialbiblioteks Förening
SVSN	Société Vaudoise des Sciences Naturelles (Switzerland)
SVST	Slovenská Vysoká Skola Technická
SVT	Schweizerische Vereinigung für Tierzucht
SVTM	Schweizerischer Verband der Tapezierermeister-Dekorateure und des Möbel-Detailhandels
SVVIA	Schweizerischer Verband der Versicherungs-Inspektoren und- Agenten
SVVK	Schweizerischer Verein für Vermessungs-wesen und Kulturtechnik
SVW	Schweizerischer Verband für Waldwirtschaft
SVWG	Schweizerische Verkehrswissenschaftliche Gesellschaft
SVWS	Schweizerischer Verband der Wirkerei- und Strickerei-Industrie
SVWT	Schweizerische Vereinigung für Weltraum-technik
SVY	Suomen Voimalaitosyhdistys
SVZ	Sociedád Veterinaria de Zootecnia de Espãna
SW	Samaritans Worldwide
SW	Seaboard World Airlines (U.S.A.)
SWA	Sozialwissenschaftliche Arbeitsgemeinschaft (Austria)
SWAFAC	South West Atlantic Fisheries Advisory Commission
SWANU	South West Africa National Union
SWANUF	South West Africa National United Front

SWAPO	South West Africa People's Organisation
SWB	Schweizerischer Werkbund
SWCRD	Soil and Water Conservation Research Division (U.S.A.)
SWDA	Scottish Wholesaler Druggists Association
SWEB	South Western Electricity Board
SWF	Svenska Wallboardföreningen
SWG	Society of Woman Geographers (U.S.A)
SWGA	Société des Exportateurs de Vins Suisse
SWGB	South Western Gas Board
SWHV	Schweizerischer Weinhändlerverband
SWIE	South Wales Institute of Engineers
SWIF	Svenska Wellpappindustriföreningen
SWIFT	Society for Worldwide Interbank Financial Telecommunications (Belgium)
SWIG	South-Western Irrigated Cotton Growers Association (U.S.A.)
SWIRECO	Southwestern Institute of Radio Engineers Conference and Electronics Show (U.S.A.)
SWKI	Schweizerischer Verein von Wärme- und Klimaingenieuren
SWLA	South Western Library Association (U.S.A.)
SWMA	Steel Wool Manufacturers' Association
SWO	Surinaamse Werknemers -Organisatie
SWOA	Scottish Woodland Owners Association
SWOV	Stichting Wetenschappelijk Onderzoek Veerkeersveiligheid
SWP	Stowarzyszenie Wtokienników Polskich
SWRLS	South Western Regional Library System
SWS	Sozialwissenschaftliche Studiengesellschaft
SWSF	Society for a World Service Federation (U.S.A.)
SWT	Scottish Wild Life Trust
SWTE	Society for Water Treatment and Examination (*now* IWES)
SWTEA	Scottish Woollen Trade Employers Association
SWTMA	Scottish Woollen Trade Mark Association
SWV	Schweizerischer Wasserwirtschaftsverband
SWV	Schweizerischer Webeblatt-Fabrikanten-Verband
SWV	Schweizerischer Wirtverein
SWWJ	Society of Women Writers and Journalists
SYBAZ	Syndicat du Bâtiment du Zaire
SYBELIC	Syndicat Belge d'Études et de Recherches Électroniques
SYBESCO	Syndicat Belge des Scories Thomas
SYBESI	Syndicat Belge pour le Séparation Isotopique
SYBETRA	Syndicat Belge d'Entreprises à l'Étranger
SYCEF	Syndicat des Constructeurs Français de Condensateurs
SYCOMEL	Syndicat National des Constructeurs Français de Matériel et Équipement Laitier Industriel
SYCOM-IMPEX	Syndicat des Commerçants Importateurs et Exportateurs (Central African Republique, Congo)
SYCOMOM	Syndicat des Constructeurs Belge de Machines-outils pour le Travail des Métaux
SYCOSER	Syndicat des Constructeurs et Constructeurs-Installateurs
SYFAC	Syndicat des Fabricants d'Aliments Composés pour l'Alimentation Animale
SYFACAR	Chambre des Fabricants des Négociants en Papiers d'Emballage et Cartons en Gros (Belgium)
SYFAMER	Syndicat National des Fabricants de Moteurs, Matériel Naval, Équipements de Bords et Remorques pour la Navigation
SYFODIA	Syndicat des Fabricants d'Outillage et de Produits à Base de Diamant
SYGECAM	Syndicat Général des Constructeurs d'Équipements pour la Chimie, les Matières Plastiques et le Caoutchouc, l'Alimentation et pour Industries Diverses
SYLAITEX	Syndicat du Commerce d'Exportation de Produits Laitiers et Avicoles
SYMA	Syndicat des Constructeurs de Machines pour l'Alimentation
SYMACAP	Syndicat des Constructeurs Français de Matériel pour le Caoutchouc et les Matières Plastiques
SYMACO	Syndicat des Constructeurs de Matériels de Conditionnement
SYMCA	Syndicat des Constructeurs de Machines et Appareils pour les Industries Chimiques et Industries de l'Alimentation
SYMCAP	Syndicat des Constructeurs Français de Matériel pour le Caoutchouc et les Matières Plastiques
SYMCO	Syndicat des Constructeurs de Matériels de Conditionnment
SYMAFO	Chambre Syndicale des Fabricants et Négociants en Machines et Fournitures pour Chaussures (Belgium)

SYMATEX Syndicat des Constructeurs Belges de Machines Textiles

SYNABATI Syndicat National des Fabricants et Constructeurs de Bâtiments Industrialisés

SYNACID Syndicat National des Commerçants et Industriels Africains du Dahomey

SYNACO-BOIS Syndicat National des Constructeurs Français de Machines à Bois et Outillages Annexes

SYNAC-OMEX Syndicat National du Commerce Extérieur des Céréales

SYNAD Syndicat National des Producteurs de Béton Prêt à l'Emploi

SYNAFA Syndicat National des Fabricants d'Aliments pour les Animaux

SYNAGRA Syndicat National du Commerce des Céréales et Légumes Secs (Belgium)

SYNAME Syndicat National de la Mesure Électrique et Électronique

SYNAP Syndicat National des Attachés de Presse Professionnels

SYNAQ Syndicat National d'Amélioration de la Qualité pour les Coopératives Agricoles

SYNCOBEL Syndicale Kamer der Fabrikanten van Confectie van België

SYNCOPAC Syndicat National des Coopératives Préparant des Aliments Composés

SYNCOPEX Syndicat National des Coopératives Agricoles Exportatrices

SYNCOT Syndicat National du Commerce des Tourteaux sons et Issues

SYNDI-CALU Syndicat National des Fabricants d'Articles de Ménage en Aluminium

SYNDICH-AMPAGNE Chambre Syndicale des Agents Accrédités par les Maisons de Champagne de Marque

SYNDICUIR Syndicat Général des Cuirs et Dérivés (Belgium)

SYNDI-SCOTCH Chambre Syndicale des Agents Accrédités de Scotch Whisky (Belgium)

SYNDUS-TREF Syndicat des Industries de l'Afrique Équatoriale

SYNDUST-RICAM Syndicat des Industriels du Cameroun

SYNECOT Syndicat National des Fabricants d'Engrenages et Constructeurs d'Organes de Transmission

SYNERCAU Syndicat National d'Études de la Recherche pour les Coopératives Agricoles et Leurs Unions

SYNERVA Syndicat National d'Études de Revision et de Vulgarisation des Coopératives Agricoles

SYNPA Syndicat National des Producteurs d'Additifs Alimentaires

SYNTEC Chambre Syndicale des Sociétés d'Études et de Conseils

SYNTECAM Société Camerounaise pour la Fabrication des Tissus Synthétiques

SYPAL Syndicat National des Fabrikants et Fabricants Distributeurs de Palettes en Bois

SYR Sveriges Yrkesfruktodlares Riksförbund

SYSNA Société des Systemes d'Aides à la Navigation

SZBV Schweizer und Zürcher Buchhändlervereine

SZF Schweizerische Vereinigung für Zukunftforschung

SZG Schweizerische Zoologische Gesellschaft

SZH Schweizerische Zentrale für Handelsförderung

SZN Stazione Zoologica di Napoli

SZOT Magyar Szakszervezetek Országos Tanácsa

SZS Schweizerische Zentralstelle für Stahlbau

SZU Sociedad Zoológica del Uruguay

SZV Schweizerischer Saatzuchtverband

SZV Schweizerischer Zahntechnikerverband

SZV Schweizerischer Zeitungsverlegerverband

SZV Schweizerischer Zimmermeisterverband

SZVT Szervezési és Vezetési Tudományos Társaság

SZZV Schweizerischer Ziegenzuchtverband

T

TAA Technical Assistance Administration (UNDP)

TAA Trans-Australia Airlines

TAAF Terres Australes et Antarctiques Françaises

TAALS The American Association of Language Specialists

TAAS Telegraphic Agency of the Union of Socialist Soviet Republics

TAB Technical Assistance Board (UNDP)

TABA Timber Agents and Brokers Association of the United Kingdom

TABA	Société Agricole Tchadienne de Collecte et de Traitement des Tabacs	**TAT**	Transportes Aéreos de Timor
TABA	Transportes Aeras de Buenos Aires (Argentina)	**TAUN**	Technical Assistance of the United Nations
TAC	Tanganyika Agricultural Corporation (*now* NDC)	**TAVR**	Territorial Army Voluntary Reserve
TAC	Technical Assistance Committee (UNO)	**TAZARA**	Tanzania-Zambia Railway Authority
TAC	Technische Advies Commissie van het NaCaBrouw	**TBD**	Türk Belediyecilik Dernegi
TAC	Tobacco Advisory Committee	**TBE**	European Federation of Tile and Brick Manufacturers
TAC	Trades Advisory Council	**TBMA**	Timber Building Manufacturers Association
TACAC	Trans Atlantic Committee on Agricultural Change	**TBPA**	Tenpin Bowling Proprieters Association
TAM	Technical Association of Malaysia	**TBTAK**	Scientific and Technical Research Council of Turkey
TAMCO	Société de Transports, d'Automobile et de Mécanique au Congo	**TC**	Taraxacum Club (Netherlands)
TAMDA	Timber and Allied Materials Development Association (South Africa)	**TC**	Trusteeship Council (UNO)
		TCA	Tanners' Council of America
TAMTU	Tanganyika Machinery Testing Unit	**TCA**	Technical Co-operation Administration (U.S.A.)
TAN	Transportes Aeros Nacionales (Honduras)	**TCA**	Trans-Canada Air Lines
TANCA	Technical Assistance to Non-Commonwealth Countries	**TCC**	Transport and Communications Commission (UNO)
TANU	Tanganyika African National Union	**TCCA**	Textile Colour Card Association of the United States
TAO	Technical Assistance Operations (UNDP)	**TCCA**	Textile and Clothing Contractors Association
TAP	Technical Advisory Panel (UNO)	**TCCB**	Test and County Cricket Board
TAP	Technical Assistance Program (U.S.A.)	**TCD**	Trinity College, Dublin
TAP	Svenska Tapetfabrikanternas Förening	**TCEA**	Training Centre for Experimental Aerodynamics (Belgium)
TAP	Transportes Aéroes Portugueses	**TCGA**	Tanzania Coffee Growers Association
TAPA	Tanzania African Parents Association	**TChP**	Towarzystwo Chirurgów Polskich
TAPI	Tropical Agricultural Products Institute (Thailand)	**TCI**	Tall Clubs International (U.S.A.)
TAROM	Transporturi Aeriene Rômine (Roumania)	**TCI**	Traffic Clubs International (U.S.A.)
TAPPI	Technical Association of the Pulp and Paper Association (U.S.A.)	**TCJCC**	Trades Councils' Joint Consultative Committee
		TCL	Tanganyika Creameries Ltd
TARC	Tropical Agriculture Research Center (Japan)	**TCM**	Trustul Centrolelor Mecanice (Roumania)
TARI	Taiwan Agricultural Research Institute (China)	**TCMA**	Textile Commission Manufacturers Association
		TCMA	Telephone Cable Makers' Association
TAROM	Transporturi Aeriene Române	**TCMA**	Tufted Carpet Manufactures Association
TARS	Technical Assistance Recruitment Service (of UN)	**TCN**	Tekniska Nomenklaturcentralens
		TCO	Tjänstemannens Centralorganisation
TARS	Tropical African Regional Section (*of* IOBS)	**TCOT**	Transit Congo-Oubanqui-Tchad
TAS	Tennessee Academy of Science (U.S.A.)	**TCPA**	Town and Country Planning Association
TASMA	Tanganyika Sisal Marketing Board	**TCRC**	Tobacco Chemists Research Conference (U.S.A.)
TASPO	Thalacker Allgemeine Samen- u. Pflanzen Offerte	**TCS**	Technology Club of Syracuse (U.S.A.)

CZB	Turkiye Cumhuriyeti Ziraat Bankasi (Turkey)	TELIMALI	Télécommunications Internationales du Mali
DA	Textile Distributors' Association	TEMA	Telecommunication Engineering and Manufacturing Association
DA	Timber Development Association (U.S.A.)	TEPCO	Tokyo Electric Power Company (Japan)
DB	Trade and Development Board (UNCTAD)	TEPCORN	Tobacco Export Promotion Council of Rhodesia and Nyasaland
DC	Tanganyika Development Corporation (now NDC)	TERG	Technical Education Resources Group
DC	Trade Development Council (Hong Kong)	TESCO	Hungary's International Scientific Co-operation Bureau
DFL	Tanzania Development Finance Company Ltd	TESOL	Teachers of English to Speakers of other Languages (U.S.A.)
DK	Türk Dil Kurumu	TESSILABIT	Associazione Italiana degli Industriali dell' Abbigliamento
EA	Trans-European Airways (Belgium)		
EAM	The European-Atlantic Movement (U.K.)	TESSIL-VARI	Associazione Nazionale Produttori Tessili Vari e del Cappello
EAR	The Evangelical Alliance Relief Fund		
EBROC	Tehran Book Processing Centre (Iran)	TETOC	Technical Education and Training Organisation for Overseas Countries (of ODM)
ECA	Trans-Europa Compañia de Aviación SA		
ECHNI-CHAR	Association pour le Perfectionnement Technique des Appareils Domestiques d'Utilisation du Charbon (Belgium)	TEVA	Tutmonda Esperanta Vegetara Asocio
		TEXTEL	Trinidad and Tobago Telecommunications Company
ECHNI-COL	Association pour le Perfectionnement Technique des Appareils Domestiques d'Utilisation des Combustibles Liquides (Belgium)	TF	Textile Foundation (U.S.A.)
		TFA	Taiwan Forest Administration (China)
ECHNO-CEAN	Société Technique pour l'Océanologie	TFA	Tanganyika Farmers Association
		TFA	Texas Forestry Association (U.S.A.)
ECHNO-NET	Asia Network for Industrial Technology Information and Extension (Singapore)	TFCRI	Tropical Fish Culture Research Institute (Malaysia)
ECNI-BERIA	Asociación Española Empresas de Estudios y Proyectos	TFDL	Technisch Fysische Dienst voor de Landbouw
ECO	Tanzania Extract Company	TFF	Association of Technical Physicists (Sweden)
ECO	Technical Cooperation Committee (of OECD)		
		TFF	Tekniska Fysikers Förening
ECTRO	Société de Techniques Tropicales	TFIF	Tekniska Foreningen i Finland
ED	International Association for Training, Education and Development	TFK	Transportforskningskommissionen
		TFRI	Taiwan Fisheries Research Institute
EDCO	Thames Estuary Development Company	TFRI	Transnational Family Research Institute (U.S.A.)
EEM	Trans-Europ Express Marchandises		
EFO	Svenska Textilforskningsinstitutet	TFTDWU	Taiwan Federation of Textile and Dyeing Workers Union
EGEWA	Verband der Textilhilfsmittel-, Lederhilfsmittel-, Gerbstoff- und Waschrohstoff-Industrie		
		TG	Theosophische Gesellschaft (India)
		TGF	Tekstilgrossistenes Forbund
EGMA	Terminal Elevator Grain Merchants Association (U.S.A.)	TGS	Texas Geographic Society (U.S.A.)
		TGSA	Tropical Grassland Society of Australia
EJA	Tutmonda Esperantista Jurnalistica Asocio	TGV	Schweizerischer Transportgewerbeverband
EJO	Tutmonda Esperantista Junulara Organizo	TGWU	Transport and General Workers' Union
EK	Turkiya Elektrik Kurumu (Turkey)	THD	Türk Hemsireler Dernegi
ELI	Technisch-Literarische-Gesellschaft	THE	Technical Help for Exporters

THL	Teollisuudenharjoittajain Liitto	**TISK**	Türkiye Isveren Sendikalari Konfederasyonu
THRA	Tasmanian Historial Research Association	**TIT**	Tutományos Ismeretter-jesztö Társulat
THY	Turun Historiallinen Yhdistys	**TITUS**	Textile Information Treatment Users Service
THYT	Teollisuudenharjoittajain Yleinen Ryhmä	**TKD**	Türk Kütüphaneciler Dernegi
TI	Textile Institute	**TKI**	Tejgazdasági Kiserleti Intézet
TIA	Trans-International Airlines (U.S.A.)	**TKP**	Türkiye Komünist Partisi
TIAC	Travel Industry Association of Canada	**TL**	Trehusindustriens Landsforbund
TIB	Tanzania Investment Bank	**TL**	Trelasthandlernes Landsforbund
TIB	Transivoirienne des Bois	**TL**	Turistvognmoendenes Landsorganisation
TIBE	Société Travaux Isolation, Bâtiment Étanchéité	**TLA**	Thai Library Association
		TLP	Tasmania Labour Party
TIBEA	Société Travaux Isolation-Bâtiment Étanchéité-Afrique (Congo)	**TLDPC**	Tidal Land Development Planning Commission of the Executive Yuan (Taiwan)
TIBO	Träindustrins Branschorganisation	**TLIF**	Traktor- og Landbruksmaskin-Importörenes Forening
TIC	Tantalum Producers International Study Centre (Belgium)	**TLJW**	Stichting Technisch Landbouw Jongerenwerk
TIC	Timber Industries Confederation	**TLS**	Tekniska Litteratursällskapet
TICCI	Technical Information Centre for Chemical Industry, Bombay (India)	**TM**	Tiedotusmiehet
TICER	Temporary International Council for Educational Reconstruction	**TMA**	Trans-Mediterranean Airways (Lebanon)
		TMA	Trinidad Manufacturers Association
TIDA	Travel and Industrial Development Association	**TMA**	Turkish Management Association
TIDU	Technical Information and Documents Unit of D.S.I.R.	**TMAC**	Transmeridian Air Cargo Ltd
		TMAMA	Textile Machinery and Accessory Manufacturers Association
TIE	The Institute of Ecology (U.S.A.)	**TMB**	Tobacco Marketing Board (Rhodesia)
TiFC	Towarzystwo im Fryderyka Chopina	**TMHiZK**	Towarzystwo Milosyników Historii i Zabytków Krakowa
TIFR	Tata Institute of Fundamental Research, Bombay (India)		
TIG	Télécommunications Internationales Gabonaises	**TMIS**	Technical Meetings Information Service (U.S.A.)
TIIAL	The International Institute of Applied Linguistics	**TMJP**	Towarzystwo Milosyników Jezyka Polskiego
		TMMB	Türkiye Muhendisler ve Mimarlar Birligi
TIMCON	Timber Packaging and Pallet Confederation	**TMMOB**	Turk Mühendis ve Mimar Odalari Birligi
TIMS	Institute of Management Sciences (U.S.A.)	**TMO**	Toprak Mahsulleri Offisi
TINFO	Tieteellisen Informoinnin Neuvosto	**TMSA**	Telephone Manufacturers of South Africa
TINTUC	Trinidad and Tobago National Trade Union Congress	**TMSE**	Tobacco Manufacturers Standing Committee
		TMTE	Textilpari Müszaki és Tudományos Egyesület
TIP	Towarzystwo Internistów Polskich	**TNDC**	Thai National Documentation Centre
TIP	Turkish Labour Party	**TNI**	Transnational Institute (Netherlands)
TIPER	Tanzanian and Italian Petroleum Refining Co.	**TNIMA**	Tubman National Institute of Medical Arts (Liberia)
TIRC	Tobacco Industry Research Committee	**TNIP**	Transkei National Independence Party (South Africa)
TIRU	Traitement Industriel des Résidus Urbains		
TIS	Technical Information Service (Canada)	**TNO**	Organisatie v. Toegepast Natuurwetenschappelijk Onderzoek
TISCO	Tata Iron and Steel Company (India)		

TNOIK	Towarzystwo Naukowe Organizacji i Kierownictwa
TNT	Towarzystwo Naukowe w Toruniu
TOAG	Research Division on Agriculture and Forestry (Turkey)
TOBETON	Société Togolaise de Béton
TØF	Transportøkomisk Forening
TOFINSO	Société Toulousaine Financière et Industrielle du Sud-Ouest
TOGO-FRUIT	Société Nationale de Développement de la Culture Fruitière (Togo)
TOGOGAZ	Société Togolaise des Gaz Industriels
TOK	Türk Otomatik Kontrol Kurumu
TOPRAKSU	General Directorate of Spil Conservation and Irrigation (Turkey)
TOT	Telephone Organization of Thailand
TOURAC	Association Internationale Auxiliaire des Touring Clubs de l'Afrique Centrale
TOURIS-MAD	Société Hôtelière et Touristique de Madagascar
TPC	Taiwan Pineapple Association
TPDC	Tanzania Petroleum Development Corporation
TpF	Talepoedagogisk Forening
TPG	Trésorier Payeur Général
TPI	Tropical Products Institute (*formerly* CPL)
TPI	Royal Town Planning Institute
TPIS	Tropical Pesticides Information Service
TPL	Tanganyika Packers Ltd
TPLA	Turkish People's Liberation Army
TPRC	Thermophysical Properties Research Center (U.S.A.)
TPRC	Tropical Pesticides Research Unit, Porton Down
TPRI	Tropical Pesticides Research Institute
TPTPA	Table Poultry and Turkey Producers Association
TR	Teatrarnas Riksförbund
TR	Textilgrossisternas Riksförbund
TRA	Thoroughbred Racing Association (U.S.A.)
TRACO-GRAS	Association Belge des Transformateurs de Corps Gras Industriels
TRADA	Timber Research and Development Association
TRAFO	Transportmateriel-Foreningen
TRAMA-GRAS	Transformateurs de Matières Grasses
TRAMET	Groupement du Négoce International et du Traitement Industriel des Déchets Métalliques
TRANSCAP	Société Eurafricaine de Voyages, de Transit et de Camionnage Portuaire
TRANS-COFER	*see* INTERCONTAINER
TRANS-EQUAT	Société de Transit Equatorial (Cameroons)
TRANS-FRIA	Société de Transport et d'Approvisionnement de l'Aluminium (Africa)
TRBR	Tobacco Research Board of Rhodesia
TRC	Technical Reports Centre, Ministry of Technology
TRC	Trade Relations Council of the United States (U.S.A.)
TRDB	Tanzanian Rural Development Bank
TRANSUD	Société des Transports du Sud de Madagascar
TRC	Textile Research Council
TRDC	Tana River Development Company (Kenya)
TRE	Telecommunications Research Establishment
TRI	Tape Respondents International
TRI	Tea Research Institute (Sri Lanka)
TRI	Textile Research Institute (U.S.A.)
TRI	Tin Research Institute
TRI	Tribal Research Institute and Training Centre (India)
TRICOMAD	Société Industrielle des Tricotages de Madagascar
TRIDO	Table Ronde Internationale pour le Développement de l'Orientation
TRIEA	Tea Research Institute of East Africa
TRITURAF	Société Ivoirienne pour la Trituration de Graines Oléagineuses et le Raffinage d'Huiles Végétales
TRI-UN	Department of Trusteeship and Information from Non-Self-Governing Territories
TRRB	Trade Relations Research Bureau
TRRL	Transport and Road Research Laboratory
TRS	Tobacco Research Station (New Zealand)
TRS	Tree-Ring Society (U.S.A.)
TRT	Télécommunications Radioélectriques et Téléphoniques

TRT	Turkish Radio
TRTA	Traders Road Transport Association (*now* FTA)
TS	Theosophical Society (India)
TSBA	Trustee Savings Banks Association
TSC	Taiwan Sugar Corporation
TSE	Turk Standardlari Enstitusu
TSF	Compagnie Générale de Télégraphie Sans Fil
TSGA	Tanzania Sisal Growers Association
TSIA	Trading Stamp Institute of America
TSK	Tradgardsnäringens Standardiseringskommitté
TSKB	Turkiye Sinai Kalinma Bankasi, A.S.
TSPC	Tropical Stored Products Centre (*of* MOD)
TSSA	Transport Salaried Staffs' Association
TTA	Tanzania Tea Authority
TTA	Teknillisten Tieteiden Akademia
TTC	Tanzania Tourist Corporation
TTC	Transit Transports Camerounais
TTDC	Thana Training and Development Centre (Pakistan)
TTEC	Thai Technical and Economic Cooperation Office
TTF	Timber Trade Federation
TTFTU	Trinidad and Tobago Federation of Trade Unions
TTGA	Tanganyika Tea Growers' Association
TTIC	Taiwan Tea Improvement Committee
TTIS	Translation and Technical Information Services
TTK	Türk Tarih Kurumu
T & TPC	Trinidad and Tobago Management Development and Productivity Centre
TTWMB	Taiwan Tobacco and Wine Monopoly Bureau
TU	Svenska Tidningsutgivareföreningen
TUA	Tractor Users Association
TUAC	Trade Union Advisory Committee (*of* OECD)
TUBE	Union of Bookmakers Employees
TUBITAK	Turkish Science and Technology Research Council
TUC	Trades' Union Congress
TUCSA	Trades Union Council of South Africa
TUF	Tokyo University of Fisheries
TUFEC	Thailand-Unesco Fundamental Education Centre
TUFMAC	Uganda Fish Marketing Corporation
TUIAFPW	Trade Unions International of Agricultural, Forestry and Plantation Workers (Italy) (*formerly* TUIAFW)
TUIWC	Trade Union International of Workers in Commerce
TUP	Towarzystwo Urbanistów Polskich
TUPLAN	Textil Uruguaya de Productos de Lana
TÜRDOK	Turkish Scientific and Technical Documentation Centre
TURKIS	Turkish Trade Union Confederation
TURSAB	Türkiye Seyahat Acentalari Birligi
TUSM	World Federation of Ukrainian Student Organizations of Michnowsky
TÜV	Vereinigung der Technischen Uberwachungs-Vereine (Austria)
TVA	Tennessee Valley Authority (U.S.A.)
TVS	Technical Valuation Society (U.S.A.)
TVA	Teglverkenes Arbeidsgiver-forening
TVK	Toimihenkilö- ja Virkamiesjärjestöjen
TVVL	Nederlandse Technische Vereniging voor Verwarming en Luchtbehandeling
TWA	Trans-World Airlines (U.S.A.)
TWARO	Textile Workers Asian Regional Organisation
TWAU	Transvaal Women's Agricultural Union (South Africa)
TWICO	Tanzania Wood Industries Corporation
TWIF	Tug of War International Federation
TWIU	Tobacco Workers International Union (U.S.A.)
TWK	Polskie Towarzystwo Walki z Kalectwem
TWL	Nederlandse Technische Vereniging voor Verwarming en Luchtbehandeling
TWOZ	Commissie voor Toegepast Wetenschappelijk Onderzoek in de Zeevisserij (Belgium)
TWP	Committee for the Provision of Technical Assistance for the Welfare of the People (Thailand)
TWU	Tobacco Workers Union
TWUA	Transport Workers' Union of America
TZF	Technische Zentralstelle der Deutschen Forstwirtschaft

U

UA	Ulkomaankaupan Agenttiliitto
UA	Underwater Association
UAA	United Arab Airlines (Egypt)
UAA	Union des Avocats Arabes
UAAEE	United Arab Atomic Energy Establishment
UAB	Universities Appointments Board
UABS	Union of American Biological Societies
UAC	Unified Agricultural Co-operatives (Czechoslovakia)
UAC	United Africa Company
UACB	Union des Agglomérés di Ciment de Belgique
UACEE	Union de l'Artisanat de la CEE
UACO	United Africa Company
UACP	Union des Agences et Conseils en Publicité
UACS	Union des Associations Cinématographiques Suisses
UADI	Union Argentina de Asociaciones de Ingenieros
UADW	Universal Alliance of Diamond Workers
UAE	United Arab Emirates
UAEE	Union des Associations Européennes d'Etudiants
UAFA	Union Arabe du Fer et de l'Acier
UAG	Österreichische Arbeitsgemeinschaft für Ur- und Frühgeschichte
UAI	Union Académique Internationale
UAI	Union des Associations Internationales
UAI	Union Astronomique Internationale
UAIA	Union des Agences d'Information Africaines
UAJ	Udruzenje Anesteziologa Jugoslavije
UAL	United Air Lines, Inc. (U.S.A.)
UAM	Union Africaine et Malgache (*now* OCAM)
UAMBD	Union Africaine et Malgache des Banques pour le Développement
UAMCE	Union Africaine et Malgache de Coopération Économique (*now* OCAM)
UAMD	Union Africaine et Malgache de Défense

UAMPT	Union Africaine et Malgache des Postes et Télécommunications
UANA	Union of African News Agencies
UANA	Union de Natation Amateur des Amériques
UANC	United African National Council
UAOS	Ulster Agricultural Organisation Society (N. Ireland)
UAP	Union des Assurances de Paris
UAP	United Australia Party
UAP	Uniunea Artistilor Plastici din Republica Socialista România
UAPA	Union des Agences de Presse Africaines
UAPF	Union des Amateurs à la Pêche de France
UAPT	United Association for the Protection of Trade
UAR	Union Asiatique de Radiodiffusion (Japan)
UAR	United Arab Republic
UARAEE	United Arab Republic Atomic Energy Establishment
UARN	Union des Chambres Artisanales du Bâtiment
UAS	Union of African States
UAS	University of Agricultural Sciences (India)
UASIF	Union des Associations Scientifiques et Industrielles Françaises
UASTM	Universidad Agraria de la Selva de Tingo María (Peru)
UAT	Union Aéromaritime de Transport
UATI	Union des Associations Techniques Internationales
UAU	Universities Athletic Union
UAW	International Union of United Automobile, Aerospace and Agricultural Workers of America
UBA	Union Belge des Annonceurs
UBA	Union Belge de l'Automatique
UBA	Union of Burma Airways Board
UBAC	Union Bancaire en Afrique Centrale
UBAF	Union des Banques Arabes et Françaises
UBAH	Union des Branches Annexes de l'Horlogerie (Switzerland)
UBBS	University of Basutoland, Bechuanaland Protectorate and Swaziland
UBESA	Unión de Bananeros Ecuatorianos
UBF	Universal Buddhist Fellowship (U.S.A.)
UBFTG	Union Belge des Fabricants de Tôles Galvanisées

UBG	Union Belge des Géomètres-Experts Immobiliers
UBIC	Union Belge des Installateurs en Chauffage Central, Ventilation et Tuyauteries
UBM	Union Balkanique Mathématique
UBOS	Union de la Bijouterie et de l'Orfèverie Suisse
UBS	Union Belge des Sérigraphes
UBS	United Bible Societies
UBT	Union Togolaise de Banque
UBZI	Unie der Belgische Zuivelindustrie
UCAAF	Union des Coopératives Agricoles et Alimentaires Françaises
UCADIA	Unión Centroamericana de Asociaciones de Ingenieros y Arquitectos (Costa Rico)
UCAE	Universities Council for Adult Education
UCAEYL	L'Union des Coopératives d'Élevage de l'Yonne-Loiret
UCAL	Union des Cinémathèques d'Amérique Latine (Mexico)
UCAM	Universidad Nacional Autonoma de México
UCAP	United Coconut Association of the Philippines
UCAR	University Corporation for Atmospheric Research (U.S.A.)
UCASEF	Union Nationale des Coopératives Agricoles de Semences Fourragères
UCAT	Universidad Católica de Chile
UCATT	Union of Construction, Allied Trades and Technicians
UCB	Uitvoer-Contrôle-Bureau
UCB	Union Camerounaise des Brasseries
UCB	Union Chimique Belge
UCB	Union Nationale des Coopératives Agricoles de Transformation de Betterave
UCC	Union Corporative de la Couleur
UCC	Union de la Critique du Cinéma (Belgium)
UCC	University College, Cork
UCCA	Union Cotonnière Centrafricaine
UCCA	Universities Central Council on Admissions
UCCAO	Union des Coopératives de Café Arabica de l'Ouest (Cameroons)
UCCD	Union des Producteurs Belges de Chaux, Calcaires, Dolomies et Produits Connexes
UCCE	Union des Capitales de la Communauté Européenne
UCCEGA	Union des Chambres de Commerce et Établissements Gestionnaires d'Aéroports
UCCI	Union Carbide Côte d'Ivoire
UCCMA	Union des Caisses Centrales de la Mutualité Agricole
UCD	University College, Dublin
UCDEC	Union Chrétienne Démocrate d'Europe Centrale
UCECOM	Uniunea Centrala a Cooperativelor Mestesugaresti (Roumania)
UCEI	Union des Centres d'Échanges Internationaux
UCEPA	Unidad de Comercio Exterior de Productos Agricolas (Venezuela)
UCERC	Union des Centres d'Études Rurales par Correspondance
UCF	Union des Chausseurs Français
UCF	Union Culturelle Française
UCF	Unions Chrétiennes Féminines
UCF	United Cooperative Farmers, Inc. (U.S.A.)
UCF	United Counties Farmers Ltd
UCFAF	Union Centrale des Syndicats Agricoles de France
UCG	University College, Galway
UCH	Union Nationale des Chambres Syndicates d'Entreprises en Génie Climatique
UCI	Ufficio Centrale Italiano
UCI	Union Canine Internationale
UCI	Union Cycliste Internationale
UCIC	Unione Costruttori Impianti di Combustione
UCICIS	Union Costruttori Italiani Carrelli Industriali Semoventi ed Affini
UCID	Union Cristiana Imprenditori Dirigenti
UCIDT	União Cátolica de Industriais e Dirigentes de Trabalho
UCIFA	Union Centralschweizerischer Cigarrenfabrikanten
UCIIM	Unione Cattolica Italiana Insegnanti Medi
UCIL	Uranium Corporation of India
UCIMU	Unione Costruttori Italiani Macchine Utensili
UCINA	Unione Nazionale Cantieri e Industrie Nautiche ed Affini
UCIP	Union Catholique Internationale de la Presse
UCIP	Union del Comercio la Industria y la Produccion (Argentina)
UCIS	University Center for International Studies (U.S.A.)
UCISP	Unione Costruttori Italiani Strumenti per Pesare

UCISS	Union Catholique Internationale de Service Social	**UCTA**	United Commercial Travellers' Association of Great Britain and Ireland
UCJG	Alliance Universelle des Unions Chrétiennes de Jeunes Gens	**UCTAT**	Union des Co-opératives de Travaux Agricoles de Tunisie
UCL	Uganda Creameries Ltd	**UCTF**	Union Culturelle et Technique de Langue Française
UCLA	University of California at Los Angeles (U.S.A.)	**UCW**	University College of Wales
UCLAP	Union Catholique Latino-Américaine de la Presse (Uruguay)	**UCWI**	University College of the West Indies
UCLG	United Cement, Lime and Gypsum Workers International Union (U.S.A.)	**UCWRE**	Under-Water Counter-Measures and Weapons Research Establishment
UCMA	Unione Costruttori Macchine Alimentari	**UDA**	Union des Annonceurs
UCML	University of California Microwave Laboratory	**UDACI**	Unione Donne di Azione Cattolica Italiana
UCMTF	Union des Constructeurs de Matériel Textile de France	**UDAO**	Union Douanière de l'Afrique de l'Ouest (*now* CEAO)
UCNW	University College of North Wales, Bangor	**UDC**	Uganda Development Corporation
UCOA	Union Chimique de l'Ouest-Africain (Guinée)	**UDCEC**	Unión Democrática Cristiana de Europa Central
UCODIMA	Union Commerciale de Diffusion de Marques	**UDD**	Association pour l'Utilisation et la Diffusion de la Documentation
UCODIS	Union pour le Commerce et la Distribution des Grandes Marques	**UDDIA**	Union Démocratique de Défense des Intérêts Africains
UCOMA	Union des Commerçants Maliens	**UDE**	Union Douanière Équatoriale (*formerly* UDEAC)
UCOMAF	Union Commerciale Africaine		
UCOMESA	Unione Costruttori Macchine Edili, Stradali, Minerarie ed Affini	**UDEAC**	Union Douanière et Économique de l'Afrique Centrale (*now* UDE)
UCONAL	Unión de Cooperativas Nacionales (Colombia)	**UDEAO**	Union Douanière des États de l'Afrique de l'Ouest
UCOPS	Universal Coterie of Pipe Smokers (U.S.A.)	**UDEC**	Union d'Entreprises de Constructions (Ivory Coast)
UCOWR	Universities Council on Water Resources Research (U.S.A.)	**UDECEVER**	Union Européenne des Détaillants en Céramique et Verrerie
UCPL	Union Centrale des Producteurs de Lait (Switzerland)	**UDEL**	Union des Éditeurs de Littérature
UCPTE	Union pour la Coordination de la Production et du Transport de l'Électricité (Austria)	**UDELAV**	Union pour la Défense de la Lavande et du Lavandin
UCR	Union Corporative des Résineux (France) (*now* UIR)	**UDEMAG**	Union de Empleados Profesionales del Ministerio de Agricultura y Ganaderia (Costa Rica)
UCRIFER	Unione Costruttori e Riparatori Ferrotramviari		
UCRL	University of California Radiation Laboratory	**UDENAMO**	Uniao Democratica Nacional de Moçambique
UCRM	University College of Rhodesia and Malawi	**UDEPAC**	Union Professionnelle des Détaillants en Porcelain et Cristaux (Belgium)
UCS	Union des Centrales Suisses d'Électricité	**UDI**	Unione Donne Italiane
UCS	Union des Coopératives de Semences	**UDIAS**	Union des Constructeurs et Importateurs d'Appareils Scientifiques, Médicaux et de Contrôle (Belgium)
UCSMB	Union des Carrières et Scieries de Marbres de Belgique		
UCSWM	University College of South Wales and Monmouthshire	**UDP**	Institut International pour l'Unification du Droit Privé

UDPO	Union pour la Défense des Peuples Opprimés (L'Internationale de la Liberté)
UDPT	Democratic Union of Togolese Peoples
UDS	Union des Dentistes et Stomatologistes de Belgique
UDSSD	Union des Sociétés Suisses de Développement
UDT	United Dominions Trust
UDUAL	Unión de Universidades de América Latina
UEA	Union Européenne de l'Ameublement
UEA	Universala Esperanto-Asocio (Netherlands)
UEAC	Union des États de l'Afrique Centrale (Chad)
UEBL	Union Économique Belgo-Luxembourgeoise
UEC	Union Européenne de la Carrosserie
UEC	Union Européenne des Experts Comptables Économiques et Financiers
UECB	Union Européenne des Commerces du Bétail
UECBV	Union Européenne du Commerce et de la Viande
UECGPT	Union Européenne du Commerce de Gros des Pommes de Terre
UECL	Union Européenne des Constructeurs de Logements
UECP	Union Européenne des Coupeurs de Poil pour Chapellerie et Filature
UECR	Union des Ententes et Communautés Rurales
UEDC	Union Européenne Démocrate Chrétienne
UEDE	Union Économique et Douanière Européenne
UEEB	Union des Exploitations Electriques de Belgique
UEF	Union Européenne des Fédéralistes
UEF	Union Européenne Feminine
UEFA	Union of European Football Associations
UEIC	United East India Company
UEIG	Union des Expéditeurs Internationaux de Grèce
UEJ	Union Européenne de Judo
UEJDC	Union Européenne des Jeunes Démocrates-Chrétiens
UEM	Union Évangélique Mondiale
UEMO	Union Européenne des Médecins Omnipracticiens
UEMOA	Union des Exposants de Machines et d'Outillage Agricoles
UEMS	Union Européenne de Médecine Sociale
UEMS	Union Européenne des Médecins Spécialistes
UENCPB	Union Européenne des Négociants en Cuirs et Peaux Bruts
UENDC	Union Européenne des Négociants Détaillants en Combustibles
UEO	Union de l'Europe Occidentale
UEPMD	Union Européenne des Practiciens en Médecine Dentaire
UEP	Union Européenne de Paiements
UEP	Union Européenne de Pédopsychiatres
UEPGH	Union Européenne des Portiers des Grandes Hôtels
UEPMD	Union Européenne de Practiciens de Médecine Dentaire
UER	Union Européenne de Radiodiffusion
UERP	Union Européenne de Relations Publiques
UESC	Union Européenne du Spectacle Cinématographique
UESEM	Union Européenne des Sources d'Eaux Minérales Naturelles du Marché Commun
UET	United Engineering Trustees (U.S.A.)
UETA	Union Européenne des Travailleurs Aveugles
UETDC	Union Européenne des Travailleurs Démocrates Chrétiens
UETU	Union Européenne des Théâtres Universitaires
UEVH	Union Européenne des Vélodromes d'Hiver
UEVP	Union Européenne des Vétérinaires Practiciens
UFAC	Union des Fabricants d'Aliments Composés
UFACD	Union des Fabricants d'Appareils de Cuisine et de Chauffage Domestique
UFALEX	Union des Exportateurs Français de Demi-produits en Aluminium
UFARAL	Union des Fournisseurs des Artisans de l'Alimentation (Belgium)
UFAW	Universities Federation for Animal Welfare
UFC	Université Fédérale du Cameroun
UFC	Union Fédérale de la Consommation
UFCAC	Union Féderale des Coopératives Agricoles de Céréales (France)
UFCE	Union Fédéraliste des Communautés Ethniques Européennes
UFDC	Union des Femmes Démocrates Chrétiennes (Switzerland)
UFE	Union des Groupements Professionnels de l'Industrie de la Féculerie de Pommes de Terre (*of* CEE)

UFEA	Union Française pour l'Équipement Agricole	**UGAASA**	Union General de Autores y Artistas de El Salvador
UFEMAT	Union des Fédérations Nationales des Négociants en Matériaux de Construction de la CEE	**UGAF**	Union des Groupements Apicoles Français
		UGAL	Union des Groupements d'Achat de l'Alimentation (Belgium)
UFER	Mouvement International pour l'Union Fraternelle entre les Races et les Peuples	**UGAT**	Union Générale de l'Agriculture Tunisienne
UFESAS	Universal Fair and Exhibition Service Ltd	**UGB**	Union Gabonaise de Banque
UFI	Union des Foires Internationales	**UGBF**	Union Générale de la Brasserie Française
UFIDEC	Union pour l'Information et la Défense des Consommateurs (Belgium)	**UGC**	University Grants Committee
UFIE	Union Française des Industries Exportatrices de Biens de Consommation	**UGCAA**	Union Générale des Coopératives Agricoles d'Approvisionnement
UFIPTE	Union Franco-Ibérique pour la Production et le Transport de l'Électricité	**UGCAC**	Union Générale des Coopératives Agricoles de Céréales
UFINAL	Union Financière pour le Développement des Industries Alimentaires	**UGCAF**	Union Générale des Coopératives Agricoles Françaises
UFK	Universala Framasona Ligo (Belgium)	**UGEA**	Union des Groupements pour l'Exploitation Agricole
UFL	Underraettelser fraan Flygledningen	**UGEAN**	Union Générale des Étudiants d'Afrique Noire
UFLC	Union Internationale des Femmes Libérales Chrétiennes	**UGEAO**	Union Générale des Étudiants d'Afrique Occidentale
UFMAT	Union des Fédérations Nationales des Négociants en Matériaux de Construction de la CEE	**UGECO-BAM**	Union Générale des Coopératives Bananières du Mungo (Cameroons)
UFNE	Unión Federalista de Nacionalidades Europeas	**UGEL**	Union der Genosschaftlichen Einkaufsorganisationen für Lebensmittel
UFOD	Union Française des Organismes de Documentation	**UGET**	General Union of Tunisian Students
UFORA	Unidentified Flying Objects Research Association	**UGEXPO**	Union Générale des Exposants de Matériels et de Produits Destinés à Agriculture (Belgium)
UFP	United Federal Party (N. Rhodesia)	**UGGI**	Union Géodésique et Géophysique Internationale
UFRGS	Federal University of Rio Grande do Sul (Brazil)	**UGI**	Union Géographique Internationale
UFRO	International Union of Forest Research Organisations	**UGIMA**	Unione Generale degli Industriali Apuani del Marmo ed Affini
UFSAM	Union Féminine Suisse des Arts et Métiers	**UGLE**	United Grand Lodge of England
UPSEB	Uttar Pradesh State Electricity Board (India)	**UGOCM**	Unión General de Obreros y Campesinos de México
UFSS	Union Française des Syndicats Séricicoles	**UGOPJ**	Union Générale des Oeuvres Pastorales pour la Jeunesse (Italy)
UFT	Union des Fédérations de Transports		
UFTA	United Farmers Trading Agency	**UGSA**	Union Générale Sidérurgie Arabe
UFTAA	Universal Federation of Travel Agents Associations	**UGSBF**	Union Générale des Syndicats de la Brasserie Française
UFTF	Union des Fabricants de Tapis de France	**UGSD**	Union Générale des Syndicats du Dahomey
UFU	Ulster Farmers' Union	**UGSR**	Uniunea Generala a Sindicatelor din România
UFUCH	Unión de Federaciones Universitarias de Chile	**UGT**	Unión General de Trabajadores de España
UFWOG	United Farm Workers' Organising Committee (U.S.A.)	**UGTAN**	General Union of Workers of Black Africa

UGTD	Union Générale des Travailleurs du Dahomey	**UICB**	Union Internationale des Centres du Bâtiment
UGTM	Union Générale des Travailleurs du Maroc	**UICC**	Union Internationale Contre le Cancer
UGTT	Union Générale Tunisienne du Travail	**UICCIA**	Unione Italiana della Camere di Commercio, Industria, Artigianto, Agricoltura
UHA	Union der Hörgeräte-Akustiker		
UI	Utrikespolitiska Institutet	**UICF**	Unión Internacional de Ciencias Fisiológicas
UIA	Union Immobilière Africaine (Congo)	**UICG**	Unión Internacional de Ciencias Geológicas
UIA	Unión Industrial Argentina	**UICGF**	Union Internationale du Commerce en Gros de la Fleur
UIA	Union of International Associations		
UIA	Union Internationale contre l'Alcoolisme	**UICM**	Union Internationale Catholique des Classes Moyennes
UIA	Union Internationale Antiraciste		
UIA	Union Internationale des Architectes	**UICN**	Union Internationale pour la Conservation de la Nature et de ses Ressources
UIA	Union Internationale des Avocats		
UIA	Union International des Travailleurs des Industries Alimentaires et Connexes	**UICPA**	Union Internationale de Chimie Pure et Appliquée
UIAA	Union Internationale des Associations d'Alpinisme	**UICR**	Union Internationale des Chauffeurs Routières
UIAA	Union Internationale des Associations d'Annonceurs	**UICT**	Union Internationale Contre la Tuberculose
		UID	Union Internationale Dendrologie
UIACM	Union Internationale des Automobile-Clubs Médicaux	**UIDA**	Union Internationale des Arts
UIAE	Union Industrielle pour l'Afrique	**UIDA**	Union Internationale des Organisations de Détaillants de la Branche Alimentaire
UIAF	Union Interprofessionnelle de l'Angora Français	**UIDIS**	Union International de Interlinguistic Service
UIAMS	Union Internationale d'Action Morale et Sociale	**UIDJZ**	Union Internationale des Directeurs de Jardins Zoologiques
UIAOM	Union Internationale des Agriculteurs de l'Outre-Mer	**UIE**	Union Internationale des Éditeurs
UIAP	Union Intérféderale des Armateurs à la Pêche	**UIE**	Union Internationale d'Électrothermie
		UIE	Union Internationale des Étudiants
UIAPME	Union Internationale de l'Artisanat et des Petites et Moyennes Entreprises	**UIEA**	Union Internationale de Étudiants en Architecture
UIAT	Union Internationale des Syndicats des Industries de l'Alimentation et du Tabac	**UIEC**	Union Industrielle et d'Entreprise pour le Congo
UIB	Union Internationale de la Boulangerie	**UIEC**	Union Internationale de l'Exploitation Cinématographique
UIB	Syndikale Unie der Immobiliënberoepen van België	**UIEIS**	Union Internationale pour l'Étude des Insectes Sociaux
UIBPA	Union Internationale de Biophysique Pure et Appliquée	**UIEO**	Union of International Engineering Organisations
UIBWM	Trade Unions International of Workers of Building, Wood and Building Materials Industries	**UIEOA**	Union Internationale des Études Orientales et Asiatiques
		UIEP	Union Internationale des Entrepreneurs de Peinture
UIC	Union of Independent Companies		
UIC	Union Industrielle pour le Cameroun	**UIES**	Union Internationale pour l'Éducation Sanitaire
UIC	Union des Industries Chimiques		
UIC	Union Internationale des Chemins de Fer	**UIES**	Union Internationale d'Études Sociales
UICB	Unión Internacional de Ciencias Biológicas	**UIESP**	Union International pour l'Étude Scientifique de la Population

UIFA	Union Internationale des Femmes Architectes
UIFI	Union Internationale des Fabricants d'Imperméables
UIFL	Union Internationale des Fédérations de Détaillants en Produits Laitiers
UIFPA	Union Internacional de Física Pura y Aplicada
UIG	Union Industrielle de Gruyère
UIGA	Unione Italiana Giornalisti dell' Automobile
UIGDC	Unione Internazionale del Giovani Democratici Cristiani
UIGG	Unión Internacional de Geodesia y Geofisica
UIH	Union Internationale Hôtelière
UIHE	Union Internationale de l'Humanisme et de l'Éthique
UIHL	Union Internationale de l'Humanisme Laïque
UIHMSU	Union Internationale d'Hygiéne et de Médecine Scolaries et Universitaries
UIHP	Union Internationale de l'Hospitalisation
UIHPS	Union Internationale d'Histoire et de Philosophie des Sciences
UIHS	Union Internationale d'Histoire des Sciences
UIIG	Union Internationale de l'Industrie du Gaz
UIIRF	Union Internationale des Instituts de Recherches Forestières
UIJA	Union Internationale des Journalistes Agricoles
UIJDC	Union Internationale de Jeunesse Démocrate Chrétienne
UIJPLF	Union Internationales des Journalistes et de la Presse de Langue Française
UIJS	Union Internationale de la Jeunesse Socialiste
UIL	Unione Italiana del Lavoro
UILB	Union de l'Industrie Laitière Belge
UILC	Unione Italiana Lavoratori Chimici
UILE	Union Internationale pour la Liberté d'Enseignement
UILI	Union Internationale des Laboratoires Indépendants
UILJ	Union International pour les Livres de Jeunesse
UILM	Unione Italiana Lavoratori Metallurgici
UIM	Union Internationale des Métis
UIM	Union Internationale Motonautique
UIM	Union of International Motorboating
UIMC	Union Internationale des Services Médicaux des Chemins de Fer
UIMJ	Union Internationale des Maisons de Jeunesse (*of* FIJC)
UIMM	Union des Industries Métallurgiques et Minières
UIMP	Union Internationale pour la Protection de la Moralité Publique
UIMTCT	Union Internationale de Médecine Thermale et de Climatothalassothérapie
UIMV	Union Internationale des Miroitiers-Vitriers
UINF	Union Internationale de la Navigation Fluviale
UINL	Union Internationale du Notariat Latin
UIO	Union Internationale des Orientalistes
UIOA	International Union for Applied Ornithology
UIOF	Union Internationale des Organismes Familiaux
UIOIF	Unión Internacional de Organizaciones de Investigación Forestal
UION	Uniunea Internationala pentru Ocrotirea Naturii (Roumania)
UIOOPT	Union Internationale des Organisations Officielles de Propagande Touristique
UIOOT	Union Internationale des Organismes Officiels de Tourisme
UIORF	Union Internationale des Organisations de Recherches Forestières
UIP	Union Internationale d'Associations de Propriétaires de Wagons de Particuliers
UIP	Union Internationale de Patinage
UIP	Union Internationale Paysanne
UIP	Union Internationale des Professeurs et Maîtres de Conférences des Universités Techniques et Scientifiques et des Instituts Post-Universitaires de Perfectionnement Technique et Scientifique
UIP	Union Internationale de la Publicitaires
UIP	Union Interparlementaire
UIPC	Union Internationale de la Presse Catholique
UIPC	Unione Italiana per il Progresso della Cultura
UIPCA	Union Internationale de Chimie Pure et Appliquée
UIPCG	Union Internationale de la Pâtisserie, Confiserie, Glacerie
UIPDE	Union Internationale des Producteurs et Distributeurs d'Énergie Électrique

UIPE	Union Internationale de Protection de l'Enfance
UIPFB	Union Internationale de la Propriété Foncière Bâtie
UIPGH	Union Internationale des Portiers des Grands Hôtels
UIPI	Unión Internacional de Protecciòn a la Infancia
UIPM	Union Internationale de Pentathlon Moderne
UIPM	Union Internationale de la Press Médicale
UIPMB	Union Internationale de Pentathlon Moderne et Biathlon
UIPN	Union Internationale pour la Protection de la Nature
UIPPA	Union Internationale de Physique Pure et Appliquée
UIPPI	Union Internationale pour la Protection de la Propriété Industrielle
UIPVT	Union Internationale contre le Péril Vénérien et les Tréponematoses
UIQPA	Unión Internacional de Química Pura y Aplicada
UIR	Union Internationale de Radio-diffusion
UIR	Union Interprofessionnelle des Résineux
UIRD	Union Internationale de la Résistance et de la Déportation
UIS	Union Internationale de Secours
UISA	Union Internationale des Sciences Agronomiques
UISAE	Union Internationale des Sciences Anthropologiques et Ethnologiques
UISB	Union Internationale des Sciences Biologiques
UISE	Union Internationale de Secours aux Enfants
UISG	Union Internationale des Sciences Géologiques
UISG	Union Internationale des Supérieurs Générales
UISLAF	Unione Internationale dei Sindicati dei Lavoratori Agricoli e Forestali
UISM	Union Internationale des Syndicats des Mineurs
UISMM	Union Internationale des Syndicats des Industries Métallurgiques et Mécaniques
UISN	Union Internationale des Sciences de la Nutrition
UISP	Union Internationale des Sciences Physiologiques
UISP	Union Internationale des Sociétés de la Paix
UISPP	Union Internationale des Sciences Préhistoriques et Protohistoriques
UISPTT	Union Internationale Sportive des Postes, des Téléphones et des Télécommunications
UISTABP	Union Internacional de Sindicatos de Trabajadores de la Agricultura, de los Bosques y de las Plantaciones
UISTAFP	Union Internationale des Syndicats des Travailleurs de l'Agriculture, des Forêts et des Plantations
UISTAV	Union Internationale pour la Science, la Technique et les Applications du Vide
UISTC	Union Internationale des Syndicats des Travailleurs du Commerce
UISTICPS	Union Internationale des Syndicats des Travailleurs des Industries Chimiques, du Pétrole et Similaires
UIT	Union Internationale Contre la Tuberculose
UIT	Union Internationale des Télécommunications
UITA	Unión Internacional de Associaciones de Trabajadores de Alimentos y Ramos Afines
UITAM	Union Internationale de Mécanique Théorique et Appliquée
UITBB	Union Internationale des Syndicats des Travailleurs du Bâtiment, du Bois et des Matériaux de Construction
UITP	Union Internationale des Transports Publics
UITU	Union Internationale des Théâtres Universitaires
UIUSD	Union Internationale Universitaire Socialiste et Démocratique
UIV	Union Internationale des Villes et Pouvoirs Locaux
UIVB	Union Interprofessionnelle des Vins du Beaujolais
UJAF	Union de la Jeunesse Agricole de France
UJEF	Union des Journaux d'Entreprise de France
UJNR	United States-Japan Cooperative Program in Natural Resources
UKA	United Kingdom Alliance
UKAC	United Kingdom Automation Council
UKAEA	United Kingdom Atomic Energy Authority
UKAFFP	United Kingdom Association of Frozen Food Producers
UKAMBY	United Kingdom Association of Manufacturers of Bakers Yeast

UKAPE	United Kingdom Association of Professional Engineers	UKSA	United Kingdom Sponsoring Authority for the Exchange of Young Agriculturists
UKASA	United Kingdom Agricultural Students Association	UKSATA	United Kingdom South African Trade Association
UKASTA	United Kingdom Agricultural Suppliers and Trade Association	UKSM	United Kingdom Scientific Mission
UKCA	United Kingdom Coffee Association	UKSMA	United Kingdom Sugar Merchants' Association
UKCBDA	United Kingdom Carbon Block Distributors' Association	UKWAL	United Kingdom West African Line
UKCCFSR	U.K. Co-ordinating Committee for Food Science and Technology	UL	Universal League
		ULA	Uganda Library Association
UKCIS	United Kingdom Chemical Information Service	ULABEL	Union Professionelle des Loueurs de Voiteurs sans Chauffeur de Belgique
UKCOSA	United Kingdom Council for Overseas Student Affairs	ULADE	Unión Latino American del Embalaje
		ULAJE	Unión Latinoamericana de Juventudes Evangélicas
UKCSBS	United Kingdom Civil Service Benefit Society	ULAPC	Union Latino-Américaine de la Presse Catholique
UKCSMA	United Kingdom Cutlery and Silverware Manufacturers Association	ULAST	Unión Latino Americana de Sociedades de Tisiologia
UKCTA	United Commercial Travellers Association of Great Britain and Ireland	ULC	Union Luxembourgeoise des Consommateurs
UKDA	United Kingdom Dairy Association	ULC	United Labour Congress (Nigeria)
UKF	Unie van Kunstmestfabrieken	ULF	Universitetslärarförbundet
UKFA	United Kingdom Fellmongers Association	ULI	Union pour la Langue Internationale Ido
UKFFCA	United Kingdom Freight Forwarders Container Association	ULICS	University of London Institute of Computer Science
UKGPA	United Kingdom Glycerine Producers Association	ULT	United Lodge of Theosophists
		ULTAB	Brazilian Agricultural Workers Union
UKHS	United Kingdom Hovercraft Society	ULU	Union of Latin American Universities
UKI	Uniono Katolik Idista	UMA	Ultrasonic Manufacturers Association (U.S.A.)
UKIAS	United Kingdom Immigrant Advisory Service		
UKISC	United Kingdom Industrial Space Committee	UMA	Union Marocaine de l'Agriculture
UKISES	United Kingdom Section of the International Solar Energy Society	UMA	Unión de Mujeres Americana
		UMA	Universal Medical Assistance International Centre
UKJGA	United Kingdom Jute Goods Association		
UKMAN-ZRA	United Kingdom Manufacturers and New Zealand Representatives Association	UMA	Utenti Motori Agricoli
		UMAA	Union Mondiale des Anciennes Élèves de l'Assomption
UKMMA	United Kingdom Metal Mining Association		
UKOBA	United Kingdom Outboard Boating Association	UMAEC	Union Monétaire de l'Afrique Équatoriale et du Cameroun
UKOOA	United Kingdom Offshore Operators Association	UMAH	Union Mondiale d'Avancée Humaine
UKOP	United Kingdom Oil Pipelines	UMAI	Unión Mexicana de Asociaciones de Ingenieros
UKPA	United Kingdom Pilot's Association		
UKPTF	United Kingdom Provision Trade Federation	UMARCO	Union Maritime et Commerciale
UKRA	United Kingdom Reading Association	UMARCO	Union Maritime et Commerciale Cameroun
UKRAS	United Kingdom Railway Advisory Service	UMB	Union Médicale Balkanique

UMB	Union Mondiale de Billard
UMBC	United Malayan Banking Corporation
UMC	Upper Mantle Committee
UMCA	Unión Monetaria Centroamericana (Salvador)
UMCA	Universities Mission to Central Africa
UMCA	Uraba, Medellin and Central Airways Inc. (Columbia)
UMCC	United Maritime Consultative Council
UMDC	Union Mondiale Démocrate Chrétienne
UME	Unitas Malacologica Europaea
UMEA	Universala Medicina Esperanto Asocio
UMEC	Union Mondiale des Enseignants Catholiques
UMEJ	Union Mondiale des Étudiants Juifs
UMEMPS	Union of Middle East Mediterranean Paediatric Societies
UMFIA	Union Médicale Latine
UMHE	United Ministries in Higher Education (U.S.A.)
UMHP	Union Mondiale des Sociétés d'Histoire Pharmaceutique
UMI	Union Mundial pro Interlingua
UMI	Unione Matematica Italiana
UMIMA	Union Malienne d'Industries Maritimes
UMIMA	Union Mauritanienne d'Industries Maritimes
UMIST	University of Manchester Institute of Science and Technology
UMJL	Union Mondiale pour un Judaïsme Libéral
UMML	Union Médicale de la Méditerranée Latine
UMNO	United Malays' National Organisation
UMNS	Union Mondiale des Nationaux Socialistes
UMOA	Union Monétaire Ouest Africaine
UMOFC	Union Mondiale des Organisations Féminines Catholiques
UMOSBESL	Union Mondiale des Organisations Syndicales sur Base Économique et Sociale Libérale
UMOSEA	Union Mondiale des Organismes pour la Sauvegarde de l'Enfance et de l'Adolescence
UMP	Uganda Meat Packers Ltd
UMP	Upper Mantle Project
UMPB	Union Professionnelle des Maîtres Photograveurs Belges
UMPC	Uganda Milk Processing Company Ltd
UMPF	Union Mondiale de la Presse Féminine
UMPH	Union Mondiale des Sociétés d'Histoire Pharmaceutique
UMS	Union Maraîchère Suisse
UMS	Union des Meuniers Suisses
UMS	Union Suisse des Marchands Forains
UMS	University Mailing Service
UMSN	Union Mondiale de Ski Nautique
UMSR	Universal Movement for Scientific Responsibility
UMT	Union Marocaine du Travail
UMVF	Union Mondiale des Voix Françaises
UMWA	United Mine Workers of America
UN	*See* UNO
UNA	Union Nationale de l'Aviculture et des Productions Rattachées
UNA	Unione Nazionale dell'Avicoltura
UNA	United Nations Association
UNAA	United Nations Association of Australia
UNAAFR	Union Nationale des Associations d'Aides Familiales Rurales
UNACA	Unión Nacional de Astronomia y Ciencias Afines
UNACAFE	Unión Nacional Agrícola de Cafeteros (Mexico)
UNACAP	Union Nationale des Coopératives Apicoles
UNACAST	United Nations Advisory Committee on the Application of Science and Technology to Development
UNACC	United Nations Administrative Committee and Co-ordination
UNACI	Union Africaine pour le Commerce et l'Industrie en Côte-d'Ivoire
UNACIL	United Africa Commercial and Industrial Ltd
UNACOMA	Unione Nazionale Costruttori Macchine Agricole
UNACO-OPRL	Unión Nacional de Cooperatives (Costa Rica)
UNADA	United Nations Atomic Development Authority
UNADI	United Nations Asian Development Institute
UNAEC	United Nations Atomic Energy Commission
UNAF	Union Nationale de l'Apiculture Française
UNAF	Union Nationale des Associations Familiales
UNAFIMA	Union Nationale des Associations de Formation et d'Information Mutualistes Agricoles
UNAFR	Union Nationale des Aides Familiales Rurales

UNAG	Verband Schweizerischer Zeitungsagenturen und Büchergrossisten	**UNCAC**	Union Nationale de Coopératives Agricoles Chanvrières
UNAGA	Unión Nacional de Asociaciones Ganaderas (Colombia)	**UNCAFL**	Union Nationale des Coopératives Agricoles de Fruits et Légumes
UNAIS	United Nations Association International Service	**UNCAMB**	Union Nationale des Coopératives Agricoles de Meunerie et de Meunerie-Boulangerie
UNALOR	Union Allumettière Équatoriale (Cameroons)	**UNCAMTC**	Union Nationale des Coopératives Agricoles de Meunerie et de Transformation des Céréales
UNAM	Union Nationale des Analystes Médicales (Belgium)		
UNAM	Universidad Nacional Autónoma de México	**UNCAP**	National Union of the Agricultural Production Cooperatives of Roumania
UNAP	Union Nationale des Artistes Professionnels des Arts Plastiques et Graphiques (Belgium)	**UNCARR**	Union Nationale des Comités d'Action Renovation Rurale
UNAP	Union Nationale des Attachés de Presse	**UNCASTD**	United Nations Advisory Committee on the Application of Science and Technology to Development
UNAPACE	Unione Nazionale Aziende Produttrici Auto-Consumatrici di Energia Elettrica		
UNAPHAL	Union Nationale des Pharmaciens Luxembourgeois	**UNCATA**	Union Nationale des Coopératives Agricoles des Traitements Antiparasitaires
UNASAD	Union Nationale des Associations Sanitaires Apicoles Départementales (France) (*now* FNOSAD)	**UNCC**	Union Nacional de Colegios Católicos (Dominican Republic)
		UNCC	Union Nigérienne de Crédit et de Coopération
UNASCA	Unione Nazionale Autoscuole e Studi di Consulenza Automobilistica	**UNCCP**	United Nations Conciliation Commission for Palestine
UNASCO	Uniao Nacional das Associacoes de Cooperativas (Argentina)	**UNCDC**	Union Nationale des Caves et Distilleries Coopératives
UNAT	Union Nationale des Associations de Tourisme	**UNCDCV**	Union Nationale des Caves et Distilleries Coopératives Vinicoles
UNAT	Unione Nazionale Artisti Teatrali	**UNCDF**	United Nations Capital Development Fund
UNATCA	Union Nationale des Associations de Techniciens du Conseil Agricole	**UNCEA**	Union Commerciale pour l'Europe et l'Afrique
UNAU	Unione Nazionale Assistenti Universitari	**UNCEF**	Union Nationale des Caisses d'Épargne de France
UNAULA	Universidad Autonoma Latinoamericana (Colombia)	**UNCEIA**	Union Nationale des Coopératives d'Élevage et d'Insémination Artificielle
UNA-USA	United Nations Association of the USA		
UNAVCA	Union Nationale des Associations de Vulgarisation et de Conseillers Agricoles	**UNCEM**	Unione Nazionale Comuni ed Enti Montani
UNBSA	United Nations Bureau of Social Affairs	**UNCFI**	United Nations Commission for Indonesia
UNBTAO	United Nations Bureau of Technical Assistance Operations	**UNCGABV**	Union Nationale des Coopératives et Groupements Agricoles de Bétail et de Viande
UNC	Union Nazionale Chinesiologi	**UNCHBP**	Centre for Housing, Building and Planning (UNO)
UNC	Union Suisse des Négociants en Combustibles	**UNCI**	Unione Nazionale Chimici Italiani
UNC	Unione Nazionale Consumatori	**UNCI**	United Nations Commission for Indonesia
UNC	Universidad Nacional de Colombia	**UNCIET**	Unione Nazionale Costruttori Impianti Elettrici e Telefonici
UNCAA	Union Nationale des Coopératives Agricoles d'Approvisionnement		
UNCAC	Union National des Coopératives Agricoles de Céréales	**UNCIO**	United Nations Conference on International Organisation

UNCIP	United Nations Commission for India-Pakistan
UNCITRAL	United Nations Commission on International Trade Law
UNCL	Union Nationale des Cafetiers-Limonadiers
UNCL	Union Nationale des Coopératives Laitières
UNCLOTS	United Nations Conference on the Law of the Sea
UNCLS	United Nations Conference on the Law of the Sea
UNCO	United Nations Civilian Operations Mission (Zaire)
UNCOK	United Nations Commission on Korea (*formerly* UNTCOK)
UNCP	United Nations Conference of Plenipotentiaries
UNCSAI	Unione Nazionale Costruttori Serramenti in Alluminio e Leghe Pregiate
UNCSAT	United Nations and Conference on the Application of Science and Technology for the Benefit of Less Developed Areas
UNCSCMP	Union Nationale des Chambres Syndicales de Charpente, Menuiserie et Parquets
UNCSTD	United Nations Conference on Science and Technology for Development
UNCTAD	United Nations Conference on Trade and Development
UNCULTA	Unión Nacional de Cultivadores de Tabaco (Venezuela)
UNCURK	United Nations Commission for the Unification and Rehabilitation of Korea
UNCVDC	Union Nationale des Coopératives Viticoles et Distilleries Coopératives
UNDA	International Catholic Association for Radio and Television
UNDAT	United Nations Multinational Interdisciplinary Advisory Teams
UNDCC	United Nations Development Cooperation Cycle
UNDD	United Nations Development Decade
UNDOF	United Nations Disengagement Observer Force
UNDP	United Nations Development Programme
UNDRO	United Nations Disaster Relief Co-ordinator's Office
UNEAP	Union Nationale de l'Enseignement Agricole Privé
UNEB	Union Nationale des Industries Françaises de l'Emballage Utilisant le Bois
UNEBECE	Association d'Utilisateurs et Négociants Belges de Combustibles
UNEC	Unión Nacional Educación Católica (Uruguay)
UNEC	Union Nationale des Établissements Catholiques (Upper Volta)
UNEC	United Nations Education Conference
UNECA	Union Européenne des Fondeurs et Fabricants de Corps Gras Animaux
UNECA	United Nations Economic Commission for Africa
UNECO-LAIT	Union Européenne du Commerce Laitier
UNEDA	United Nations Economic Development Administration
UNEEPF	Union Nationale des Éditeurs-Exportateurs de Publications Périodiques Françaises
UNEESA	Union Nationale des Étudiants de l'Enseignement Supérieur Agricole
UNEF	Union Nationale des Étudiants de France
UNEF	United Nations Emergency Force
UNEGA	Union Européenne des Fondeurs et Fabricants de Corps Gras Animaux
UNELAM	Movement for Evangelical Unity in Latin America (Uruguay)
UNEMAF	Union des Employers Agricoles et Forestiers (Ivory Coast)
UNEMI	Union Editori di Musica Italiani
UNEMO	National Union of Mozambican Students
UNEO	United Nations Emergency Operation
UNEP	Union Nationale des Éleveurs de Porcs
UNEP	United Nations Environmental Programme
UNEPA	Unión Económica Patagónica (Argentina)
UNESCO	United Nations Educational, Scientific and Cultural Organisation
UNESDA	Union des Associations de Boissons Gazeuses des Pays Membres de la CEE
UNESEM	Union Européenne des Sources d'Eaux Minérales du Marché Commun
UNESID	Union de Empresas y Entidades Siderurgicas
UNESOB	United Nations Economic and Social Office in Beirut
UNETAS	United Nations Emergency Technical Aid Service
UNEUROP	Association Économique Européenne

UNEXSO	International Underwater Explorers Society
UNFAO	United Nations Food and Agriculture Organisation
UNFB	United Nations Film Board
UNFDAC	United Nations Fund for Drug Abuse Control
UNFC	United Nations Food Conference
UNFICYP	United Nations Peacekeeping Force in Cyprus
UNFP	Union Nationale des Forces Populaires (Morocco)
UNFPA	United Nations Fund for Population Activities
UNFRFJ	Union Nationale des Foyers Ruraux de la Famille et des Jeunes
UNGA	United Nations General Assembly
UNGP	Union Nationale des Grandes Pharmacies
UNHCR	Office of the High Commissioner for Refugees (of UNO)
UNHHSF	United Nations Habitat and Human Settlements Foundation
UNHQ	United Nations Headquarters
UNI	Ente Nazionale Italiano di Unificazione
UNI	Union Nationale des Intellectuels
UNIA	Union Nationale des Industries Agricoles
UNIA	Union Nationale des Ingénieurs Agricoles
UNIADUS-EC	Union Internationale des Associations de Diplômés Universitaires en Sciences Économiques et Commerciales
UNIAPAC	Union Internationale des Associations Patronales Catholiques
UNIARTE	Unión Nacional de Industriales y Artesanos (Venezuela)
UNIATEC	Union Internationale des Associations Techniques Cinématographiques
UNIBA	Unione Nazionale Industrie Bigiotterie ed Affini
UNIBEV	Union Nationale Interprofessionnelle du Bétail et des Viandes
UNIBEX	Union des Brasseries Belges d'Exportation
UNIC	Union Nationale Interprofessionnelle du Cheval
UNIC	Unione Nazionale Industria Conciaria
UNIC	United Nations Information Centre
UNICA	Association of Universities and Research Institutes from the Caribbean
UNICA	Union Internationale du Cinéma d'Amateurs

UNICA	Universidad Nacional, Instituto Colombiano Agropecuario
UNICAF	Union d'Importationes Industrielles et Commerciales Africains
UNICAP	Unione Nazionale Italiana Collegi Associazioni Periti
UNICE	Union des Industries de la Communauté Européenne
UNICEF	United Nations International Children's Emergency Fund
UNICELPE	Association Européenne des Producteurs de Protéines Unicellulaires
UNICEM	Union Nationale Interprofessionnelle des Carrières et Matériaux de Construction
UNICEMA	Union Nationale des Industriels, Commerçants et Entrepreneurs de Mauritanie
UNICERE-ALES	Union Nationale Interprofessionnelle des Céréales
UNICETA	Union Nationale des Ingénieurs des Centres d'Études Techniques Agricoles
UNICHAD	Union Interprofessionelle du Tchad
UNICHAL	Union Internationale des Distributeurs de Chaleur
UNICHOCO	Union des Chambres Syndicales des Chocolatiers Confiseurs Fabricants Détaillants
UNICID	Union Nationale Interprofessionnelle Cidricole
UNICLIMA	Union Intersyndicale des Constructeurs de Matériel Aéraulique
UNICOCYM	Union Internationale du Commerce et de la Réparation du Cycle et du Motorcycle
UNICOLHV	Union Industrielle et Commerciale des Oléagineux de Haute-Volta
UNICOMA	Union des Coopératives du Morbihan et le Loire-Atlantique
UNICOMAT	Union Intersyndicale des Constructeurs de Matériel Aéraulique, Thermique et Frigorifique
UNICOMER	Union des Comptoirs d'Outre-Mer
UNICONGO	Union Patronale et Interprofessionnelle du Congo
UNICON-SERVE	Union Nationale Interprofessionnelle de la Conserve
UNICOOP	Union Coopérative de Viticulteurs Charentais
UNICUIR	Union Internationale des Négociants en Cuir

UNIDO	United Nations Industrial Development Organisation
UNIDROIT	International Institute for the Unification of Private Law
UNIEG	Unione Nazionale Industrie Editoriali e Grafiche
UNIEM	Union Nationale des Entrepreneurs-Menuisiers et Charpentiers (Belgium)
UNIEMA	Union des Industries et Entreprises de Mauritanie
UNIENSA	Union des Ingénieurs Diplomés des Écoles Nationales
UNIEP	Union Internationale des Entrepreneurs de Peinture
UNIFA	Union Nationale des Industries Français de l'Ameublement
UNIFE	Union des Industries Ferroviaires Européennes
UNIFICYP	Force de Maintien de la Paix des Nations-Unies à Chypre
UNIFIL	United Nations Interim Force in Lebanon
UNIFL	Union Nationale Interprofessionnelle des Fruits et Légumes
UNIFO-DENT	Union Professionnelle des Négociants en Fournitures Dentaires de Belgique
UNIFRUITS	Union Nationale Interprofessionnnelle des Fruits, Légumes et Pommes de Terre
UNIGABON	Union Interprofessionnelle Économique et Sociale du Gabon
UNIGRA	Union des Industries Graphiques et du Livre (Belgium)
UNIGRAINS	Union Financière pour le Développement de l'Économie Céréalière
UNIL	United Nordic Importers Ltd (Denmark)
UNILEC	Union Nationale Interprofessionnelle des Légumes de Conserve (France) (*now* ANILEC)
UNIM	Union Nationale des Industries de la Manutention dans les Ports Français
UNIMA	Union Internationale de Grands Magasins
UNIMA	Union Internationale de la Marionnette
UNIMA	Union Nazionale Imprese di Meccanizzazione Agricola
UNIMA	Union Internationale des Marionettes
UNIMES	Union des Importateurs-Exportateurs Sénégalaise
UNIMETAL	Union Nationale des Petites et Moyennes Entreprises du Métal (Belgium)

UNINAT	Union des Industries de Matériaux Naturels
UNIO	United Nations Information Organisation
UNIOM	Union Nationale Interprofessionnelle des Oléagineux Métropolitains
UNION	Union des Conseils Européens en Brevets
UNIONCHI-MICA	Unione Nazionale Piccole e Medie Industrie Chimiche ed Affini
UNION FLEURS	International Association of Flowers Wholesalers
UNION-LEGNO	Unione Nazionale Piccole e Medie Industrie del Legno
UNION-PLAST	Unione Nazionale Industrie Materie Plastiche
UNIONRISO	Unione Italiana dell'Industria Risiera
UNIP	Unión Interamericana de Padres de Familia
UNIP	United National Independent Party (Zambia)
UNIPAC	Union Industrielle des Fabricants de Papiers et Cartons
UNIPAR	Union de Participations de France et d'Outre-Mer
UNIPEDE	Union Internationale des Producteurs et Distributeurs d'Énergie Électrique
UNIPI	Unione Industriali Pastai Italiani
UNIPLPL	Union Nationale Interprofessionnelle de Propagande pour le Lait et les Produits Laitiers (France)
UNIPOL	Union des Industries de Produits Oléagineux
UNIPRO	Unione Nazionale delle Industrie di Profumeria Cosmesi, Saponi da Toilette e Affini
UNIPRO-LAIT	Union Nationale Interprofessionnelle des Produits Laitiers
UNIRIZ	Union Nationale Interprofessionnelle du Riz
UNIS	United Nations Information Service
UNIS	United Nations International School (U.S.A.)
UNISA	Union Nazionale Italiana Stampatori Acciaio
UNISCAN	British-Scandinavian Economic Committee
UNISCAT	United Nations Expert Committee on the Application of Science and Technology
UNISIST	World Science Information System (*of* ICSU-UNESCO)
UNISTOCK	Union Professionnelle des Stockeurs de Céréales dans la CEE
UNISYNDI	Union Intersyndicale d'Entreprises et d'Industries de l'Ouest Africain
UNIT	Union Nationale des Ingénieurs Techniciens (Belgium)

UNITA	Union for the Total Independence of Angola
UNITAB	Internationalen Union der Tabakspflanzer
UNITAN	Union de la Tannerie et de la Mégisserie Belge
UNITAP	United Nations Intermunicipal Technical Assistance Programme
UNITAR	United Nations Institute for Training and Research
UNITEC	Union Togolaise de Commerce
UNITEC	University Information Technology Corporation (U.S.A.)
UNITESA	Union Nazionale dell'Istruzione Tecnica e Professionale
UNITRA	Union pour l'Industrie et les Travaux Publics (Senegal)
UNIVCC	Union Nationale Intercoopérative des Vins de Consommation Courante
UNIVENCA	Unión Venezolana Criadores de Aves
UNIVIAN-DES	Union Nationale Interprofessionnelle des Viandes
UNIVIGNE	Union Nationale Interprofessionnelle de la Vigne
UNIVOL-AILLE	Union Nationale Interprofessionnelle de la Volaille
UNIVSERV	United Nations International Voluntary Service Fund
UNJSPB	United Nations Joint Staff Pension Board
UNKRA	United Nations Korean Reconstruction Agency
UNLC	United Nations Liaison Committee
UNLF	Uganda National Liberation Front
UNLG	Union Nationale des Livres Généalogiques
UNMC	United Nations Mediterranean Commission
UNME	Union Nationale des Maisons de l'Élevage
UNMEM	United Nations Middle East Mission
UNMFAR	Union Nationale des Maisons Familiales d'Apprentissage Rural
UNMOGIP	United Nations Military Observer Group in India and Pakistan
UNO	United Nations Organisation
UNOAI	Union Nationale des Ouvriers Agricoles Indépendants
UNOB	Union Nationale des Opticiens de Belgique
UNOC	United Nations Congo Operation
UNO-CARA-PEN	Union Internationale pour la Coopération Culturelle
UNOCCER	Union Nationale des Offices de Compatibilité et des Centres d'Économie Rurale
UNOE	Union Nationale des Oenologues
UNOH	Union Nationale des Ouvriers d'Haiti
UNOLE-ARIA	Associazione Nazionale dell' Industria Olearia
UNOOB	Union Nationale des Optométristes et Opticiens de Belgique
UNPA	United Nations Postal Administration
UNPADI	Unión Panamericana de Asociaciónes de Ingeneiros
UNPAL	Unión Nacional de Productores de Aceite de Limón (Mexico)
UNPASA	Unión Nacional de Productores de Azúcar de Caña (Mexico)
UNPBF	Union Nationale des Producteurs Belges de Films
UNPC	United Nations Palestine Commission
UNPCC	United Nations Conciliation Commission for Palestine
UNPEG	Unión Nacional de Produtores y Exportadores de Garbanzo (Mexico)
UNPF	National Union of Popular Forces (Morocco)
UNPFA	United Nations Fund for Population Activities
UNPJF	Union Nationale des Producteurs et Distributeurs de Jus de Fruits et de Légumes (France)
UNPL	Union Nationale des Professions Libérales
UNPOC	United Nations Peace Observation Commission
UNPVF	Union Nationale des Peintres-Vitriers de France
UNRAE	Unione Nazionale Rappresentanti Autoveicoli Esteri
UNREF	United Nations Refugee Fund
UNREP	Union Nationale Rurale d'Éducation et de Promotion
UNRISD	United Nations Research Institute for Social Development
UNROD	United Nations Relief Operation, Dacca
UNRPR	United Nations Relief for Palestine Refugees
UNRRA	United Nations Relief and Rehabilitation Administration
UNRST	Union Nationale des Revêtements de Sol et du Tapis
UNRTD	United Nations Resources and Transport Division

UNRWA	United Nations Relief and Works Agency
UNRWA-PRNE	United Nations Relief and Works Agency for Palestine Refugees in the Near East
UNRWI	United Nations Representative for West Irian
UNSC	United Nations Security Council
UNSC	United Nations Social Commission
UNSCC	United Nations Standards Co-ordinating Committee
UNSCCUR	United Nations Scientific Conference on the Conservation and Utilisation of Resources
UNSCEAR	United Nations Scientific Committee on the Effects of Atomic Radiation
UNSCOB	United Nations Special Commission to the Balkans
UNSCOP	United Nations Special Commission on Palestine
UNSDD	United Nations Social Development Division
UNSDRI	United Nations Social Defence Research Institute (Italy)
UNSE	Union Nationale des Syndicats de l'Étang
UNSEPF	Union Nationale des Syndicats d'Entrepreneurs Paysagistes de France
UNSF	United Nations Special Fund
UNSFL	Union Nationale des Syndicats de Fabricants de Lunetterie
UNSOF	Union Nationale des Syndicats d'Opticiens de France
UNSTHV	Union Nationale des Syndicats des Travailleurs de la Haute Volta
UNSU	United Nations Study Unit
UNTAA	United Nations Technical Assistance Administration
UNTAB	United Nations Technical Assistance Board
UNTAM	United Nations Technical Assistance Mission
UNTC	Union Nationale des Travailleurs Congolais
UNTC	United Nations Trusteeship Council
UNTCOK	United Nations Temporary Commission on Korea (*now* UNCOK)
UNTEA	United Nations Temporary Executive Authority, West New Guinea
UNTEL	Union Nationale des Syndicats des Tissus Élastiques
UNTFDPP	United Nations Trust Fund for Development Planning and Projections
UNTFSD	United Nations Trust Fund for Social Development
UNTRA	Union of National Radio and Television Organisations of Africa
UNTS	Union Nationale des Travailleurs du Sénégal
UNTSO	United Nations Truce Supervision Organisation
UNTT	Union Nationale des Travailleurs Togolais
UNTT	United Nations Trust Territory
UNU	Uganda National Union
UNU	United Nations University
UNUCI	Unione Nazionale Ufficiali in Congedo d'Italia
UNV	United Nations Volunteers
UNWCC	United Nations War Crimes Commission
UNWG	United Nations Women's Guild
UNY	United Nations of Yoga
UNYOM	United Nations Yemen Observation Mission
UNZALPI	Universities of Nottingham and Zambia, Agricultural Labour Productivity Investigation
UOASE	Union des Organisations Agricoles du Sud-Est
UOF	Union Ovine de France
UOTAA	Universal Organisation of Travel Agents' Associations
UOVS	Universiteit van die Oranje Vrystaat (South Africa)
UP	Unione Petrolifera
UP	Union Pétrolière (Switzerland)
UP	Union des Propriétaires du Grand-Duché de Luxembourg
UPA	Unions Professionnelles Agricoles (Belgium)
UPA	Union of Angolan Peoples
UPA	Union Postale Arabe
UPA	United Printers Association
UPA	Utenti Pubblicità Associati
UPAB	Fédération des Unions Professionnelles Agricoles de Belgique
UPACCIM	Union des Ports Autonomes et des Chambres de Commerce et d'Industrie Maritimes
UPADI	Union Panamericana de Asociaciones de Ingenieros (Mexico)
UPAE	Union Postale des Amériques et de l'Espagne
UPAF	Union Postale Africaine
UPAFI	Union Professionnelle d'Agents, Fabricants et Importateurs Exclusifs d'Objets d'Art et de Cadeaux (Belgium

UPAJ	Union Panafricaine des Journalistes
UPAM	United Planters' Association of Malaya
UPAO	Union Postale de l'Asie et de l'Océanie
UPASI	United Planters' Association of Southern India
UPAU	Uttar Pradesh Agricultural University (India)
UPAV	Union Professionnelle Belge des Agences des Voyages
UPAVE	Unión de Productores de Azúcar de Venezuela
UPBAN	Union Professionnelle Belge des Approvisionneurs de Navires
UPBIF	Union Professionnelle Belge des Industriels du Froid
UPBMC	Union Professionnelle Belge des Médecins Ophtalmologistes
UPBOB	Union Professionnelle des Bandagistes et Orthopédistes de Belgique
UPBPP	Union Professionnelle Belge de la Police Privée
UPC	Union des Pelleteries et Confectionneurs en Fourrure
UPC	Union du Peuple Corse (Corsica)
UPCA	Union Professionnelle des Coopératives Agricoles (Belgium)
UPCA	University of the Philippines College of Agriculture
UPCIL	Union Interfédérale des Producteurs, des Coopératives et des Industriels Laitiers
UPCL	Union Professionnelle des Promoteurs de Logements et d'Aménagement du Territoire (Belgium)
UPDAL	Union Professionelle de Commerce de Gros des Produits Laitiers Indigènes et d'Importation autre que Beurre et Fromage (Belgium)
UPDBF	Union Professionnelle des Distributeurs Belges de Films
UPE	Union Parlementaire Européenne
UPE	Union de la Presse Étrangère en Belgique
UPDEA	Union of Producers, Conveyors and Distributors of Electric Power in African Countries, Madagascar and Mauritius (Ivory Coast)
UPEA	Union Professionnelle des Entreprises d'Assurances (Belgium)
UPEB	Unión de Países Exportadores de Banano (Philippines)
UPEFE	Union de la Presse Économique et Financière Européenne

UPET	Ufficio per la Esportazione Tabacco
UPETITA	Union Professionnelle des Entreprises de Travaux d'Isolation Thermique et Acoustique (Belgium)
UPETTC	Union Professionnelle des Exploitants de Taxis et de Taxis-Camionnettes
UPGA	United Progressive Grand Alliance (Nigeria)
UPGWA	International Union United Plant Guard Workers of America
UPHA	Utah Public Health Association
UPI	Union Syndicale des Professions Immobilières de Belgiques
UPI	United Press International
UPIA	Union Pharmaceutique Inter-Africaine
UPICV	Revolutionary Committee of the Cape Verde Islands People's Union
UPIGO	Union Professionnelle Internationale des Gynécologues et Obstétriciens
UPIL	Union des Pharmaciens d'Industrie Luxembourgeoise
UPIP	Union des Pharmaciens de l'Industrie Pharmaceutique (Belgium)
UPIR	Uttar Pradesh Irrigation Research Institute (India)
UPIU	United Paperworkers International Union
UPL	International Institute for the Unification of Private Law
UPLAC	Union des Producteurs de Levure-aliment de la CEE
UPLB	University of the Philippines Los Banos
UPN	Urad Pro Normalisaci (Czechoslovakia) (Standards Office)
UPNI	Unionist Party of Northern Ireland
UPOV	Union Internationale pour la Protection des Obtentions Végétales
UPOW	Union of Post Office Workers
UPP	United Peoples Party (Nigeria)
UPPB	Union de la Presse Périodique Belge
UPPIC	Union Syndicale Interprofessionnelle pour la Promotion de la Conserve
UPPN	Union Postale des Pays du Nord (Finland)
UPR	Union Professionnelle des Représentants de Commerce de Belgique
UPRF	Union Professionnelle Belge du Commerce des Fromages
UPROCA	Union Professionelle des Producteurs du Caoutchouc (Belgium)

UPRONA	Party for Unity and Progress (Burundi)	**URO**	Union des Remorquers de l'Océan
UPROTAB	Union Professionnelle Nationale des Importateurs Négociants, Commissionnaires, Courtiers et Agents en Tabacs en Feuilles en Belgique	**URPE**	Union for Radical Political Economics (U.S.A.)
		URPE	Union des Resistants pour une Europe Unie
UPS	Union Producteurs Suisses	**URSI**	Union Radio-Scientifique Internationale
UPS	Union Progressive Sénégalaise	**URSSAF**	Union pour le Recouvrement des Cortisations de la Sécurité Sociale et les Allocations Familiales
UPSA	Union Professionnelle Suisse de l'Automobile		
UPSTC	Uttar Pradesh State Textile Corporation (India)	**URTI**	Université Radiophonique et Télévisuelle Internationale
UPTC	Union Panafricaine des Travailleurs Croyants	**URTNA**	Union des Radiodiffusions et Télévisions Nationales d'Afrique
UPTD	Union Professionnelle des Teinuriers-Dégraisseurs (Belgium)	**URTU**	United Road Transport Union
UPTRI	Union Professionnelle Belge des Transporteurs Routiers Internationaux	**URW**	United Rubber, Cork, Linoleum and Plastic Workers of America
UPU	Universal Postal Union	**USAAPEB**	Union Syndicale Ardennaise des Artisans et Petites Entreprises du Bâtiment
UPW	Union of Post Office Workers		
UQP	Universities and the Quest for Peace	**USACASP**	Union des Sociétés d'Assurances et de Capitalisation par Actions du Secteur Privé
URANEX	Groupement d'Intérêt Économique pour la Commercialisation de l'Uranie		
		USAEC	United States Atomic Energy Commission
URBAN-ICOM	Association Internationale Urbanisme et Commerce	**USAFCRL**	U.S. Air Force Cambridge Research Laboratories
URCAM	Union Régionale des Coopératives du Midi	**USAI**	Union Sud-Americana de Asociaciones de Ingeniores
URCC	Union Régionale des Coopératives Cidricoles	**USAID**	United States Agency for International Development
URCCE	Union des Régions des Capitales de la Communauté Européenne		
		USAIRE	United States of America Aerospace Industries Representatives in Europe
URD	Union Republicana Democrata (Venezuela)		
UREGER	Union pour la Recherche et l'Expansion de la Gestion et de l'Économie Rurale	**USAL**	Union Suisse des Acheteurs de Lait
		USAM	Union Suisse des Arts et Métiers
UREMG	Universidade Rural do Estado de Minas Gerais (Brazil)	**USAM**	Union des Syndicats Autonomes de Madagascar
URF	Union des Services Routiers des Chemins de Fer Européens	**USAR**	Union des Syndicats Agricoles Romands (Switzerland)
URGA	Unión Recibidores de Granos y Anexos (Argentina)	**USARP**	United Nations Antarctic Research Programme
URGCI	Union Romande des Gérants et Courtiers en Immeubles	**USASI**	United States of America Standards Institute (*now* ANSI)
URI	Université Radiophonique et Télévisuelle Internationale	**USB**	Union Schweizerischer Briefumschlagfabriken
URISA	Urban and Regional Information Systems Association (U.S.A.)	**USB**	Union Sénégalaise de Banque
		USBGN	United States Board on Geographic Names
URJ	Union Romande de Journaux (Switzerland)	**USBM**	United States Bureau of Mines
URLAC	Union Régionale Laitière Agricole Coopératives	**USBR**	United States Bureau of Reclamation
URMA	Union Romande de Moulins Agricoles (Switzerland)	**USC**	Union Suisse des Coopératives de Consumation
		USC	Unione Svizzera dei Cartolai

USC	Universidad de San Carlos (Guatemala)
USCA	Union Syndicale des Courtiers en Assurances
USCAP	Union Syndicate des Cadres du Pétrole
USCAR	United States Civil Administration, Ryukyu Islands
USCAS	South American Union of Societies of Cardiology (Venezuela)
USCI	Union Suisse du Commerce et de l'Industrie
USCIGW	Union of Salt, Chemical and Industrial General Workers
USCL	United Society for Christian Literature
USCO	Union Steel Corporation (South Africa)
USCOLD	United States Committee on Large Dams
USCSC	United States Civil Service Commission
USCSC	United States Cuban Sugar Council
USCV	Union Scientifique Continentale du Verre
USDA	Union Suisse des Acheteurs
USDA	United States Department of Agriculture
USDAM	Union Suisse des Artistes Musiciens
USDAW	Union of Shop, Distributive and Allied Workers
USDC	Union Svizzera dei Compratori
USDC	United States Department of Commerce
USDI	United States Department of the Interior
USDIS	Union Suisse des Métiers de la Décoration d'Intérieure et de la Sellerie
USDL	United States Department of Labor
USELPA	Usinas Eletricas do Paranapanema (Brazil)
USEM	Confederación de Unions Sociales de Enpresarios Mexicanos
USF	Unione Svizzera dei Fotografi
USFB	Union Suisse des Fabricants de Boîtes de Montres
USFDA	United States Food and Drug Administration
USFGC	U.S. Feed Grains Council
USFHTF	L'Union Syndicate des Fabricants d'Huile et de Tourteaux de France
USFJ	Union Suisse des Fabricants de Jouets
USFLF	Union Syndicale des Fabricants de Limes de France
USFMC	Union Syndicale des Fabricants de Matières Colorantes et d'Hydrosulfites
USFO	Union Syndicale Française du Carton Ondulé
USFWS	United States Fish and Wildlife Service
USG	Union Suisse de la Glace Polie
USG	Union of Superiors-General (Italy)
USGA	United States Travel Service
USGOS	Union des Stockeurs de Graines Oléagineuses de Semences
USGPO	United States Government Printing Office
USGS	United States Geological Survey
USHF	L'Union Syndicale de l'Huilerie Française
USI	Union of Students in Ireland
USI	United Schools International
USIA	U.S. Information Agency
USIAS	Union Syndicale des Industries Aéronautiques et Spatiales (*now* GIFAS)
USIC	Union Sportive Internationale des Cheminots
USIC	Union Suisse des Industriels en Carrosserie
USIEM	Union des Syndicats d'Intérêt Économique de Madagascar
USIMA	Union Sénégalaise d'Industries Maritimes
USINEN	Société Ivoirienne d'Usinage
USINOR	Union Sidérurgique du Nord et de l'Est de la France
USIO	Union Syndicale Interprofessionnelle Oléicole
USIPA	Union des Syndicats des Industries des Produits Amylacés et de leurs Dérivés
USIRF	Union Syndicale des Industries Routières Françaises
USIS	United States Information Service
USITA	United States Independent Telephone Association
USITT	U.S. Institute for Theatre Technology
USJ	Union Suisse des Journalistes
USL	Union Suisse pour la Lumière
USL	United States Lines
USLSA	United States Livestock Sanitary Association
USLTA	United States Lawn Tennis Association
USLV	Union des Schweizerischen Lichtspieltheater-Verbände
USM	Union des Semouliers de Maïs
USMAP	Union Syndicale de la Maîtrise du Pétrole
USMB	Union Suisse des Marchands de Beurre
USMC	Union Suisse des Marchands de Chaussures
USMC	Union Suisse des Marchands de Cuir
USMC	United States Maritime Commission
USMCM	Union Suisse des Mécaniciens en Cycles et Motos
USMMASA	Union Scientifique Mondiale des Médecins Acupuncteurs et des Sociétés d'Acupuncture

USNCFID	United States National Committee for FID		**USSR**	Union of Soviet Socialist Republics
USNEF	Union Syndicale National des Exploitations Frigorifiques		**UST**	Union des Entreprises Suisses de Transports Publics
USNM	United States National Museum		**UST**	Union of Speech Therapists
USNSA	United States National Student Association		**USTA**	United States Trademark Association
USNTCE-OOPA	Union des Syndicats Nationaux de Techniciens, Cadres, Employés et Ouvriers des Organisations Professionnelles Agricoles		**USTC**	United States Tariff Commission
			USTD	University Science and Technology Division (of SRC)
USNTIS	United States National Technical Information Service		**USTEL**	Union Syndicale du Tréfilage, Étirage et Laminage à Froid de l'Acier
USOE	United States Office of Education		**USTIL**	Syndicat National des Fabricants d'Utensiles Industriels de Laiterie
USOI	U.S. Office of Information			
USOM	United States Overseas Mission (now AID)		**USTS**	United States Travel Service
USOO	United States Oceanographic Office		**USTTA**	United States Table Tennis Association
USP	Union Suisse des Papetiers		**USUARIOS**	Association of Maritime Transport Users in the Central American Isthmus (Guatemala)
USP	Union Suisse des Photographes			
USPA	Union Syndicale Panafricaine		**USUCA**	United Steelworkers Union of Central Africa
USPC	United States Pharmacopoeial Convention		**USUN**	United States Mission to the United Nations
USPE	Utah Society of Professional Engineers		**USVB**	Union Syndicale Vétérinaire Belge
USPG	United Society for the Propagation of the Gospel		**USVBA**	United States Volleyball Association
			USVC	Union Suisse des Fabricants de Vernis et de Couleurs
USPHS	United States Public Health Service			
USPI	Unione della Stampa Periodica Italiana		**USWA**	United Steelworkers of America
USPM	Union des Syndicats Patronaux de Madagascar		**USWB**	United States Weather Bureau
			USWD	Undersurface Warfare Division
USPMOM	Union des Sociétés de Pédiatre du Moyen-Orient et de la Méditerranée		**UT**	Conférence Internationale pour l'Unité Technique des Chemins de Fer
USPO	United States Post Office		**UTA**	Ulster Transport Authority
USR	Union Suisse des Industries Graphiques de Reproduction		**UTA**	Union des Transports Aériens
			UTAC	Union Technique de l'Automobile et du Cycle
USRM	Union Suisse des Reconstructeurs de Moteurs		**UTAFRIQ**	Union Trading Afrique tout pour l'Auto (Ivory Coast)
USRT	Union Suisse des Installateurs Concessionnaires en Radio et Télévision		**UTAL**	Universidad de los Trabajadores de América Latina (Venezuela)
USS	Union Syndicale Suisse			
USSASA	University Science Students Association of South Africa		**UTC**	Union de Trabajadores de Colombia
USSCC	University Social Sciences Council Conference (East Africa)		**UTCGA**	Union Tunisienne de la Confédération Générale de l'Agriculture
USSEA	United States Scientific Export Association		**UTCPT**	Union Internationale des Organismes Touristiques et Culturels des Postes et des Télécommunications
USSI	Union des Sociétés Suisses d'Ingénieurs-Conseils			
USSI	Unione Stampa Sportiva Italiana		**UTDA**	Ulster Tourist Development Association
USSM	Uniunea Societatilor de Stiinte Medicale din RSR		**UTE**	Union Technique de l'Électricité
			UTE	Usinas Electricas los Telefonos del Estado (Uruguay)
US-SPE	Union Syndicale- Service Public Européen (Belgium)		**UTE**	Universidad Técnica del Estado (Chile)

UTEHA	Unión Tipográfica Editorial Hispano Americana (Mexico)
UTEXI	Union Textile de Côte d'Ivoire
UTGC	Uganda Tea Growers Corporation
UTH	Union Touristique et Hôtelière
UTHI	Ukrainian Technical Husbandry Institute, New York (U.S.A.)
UTI	Unione Tabacchicoltori Italiani
UTI	Union Technique Interprofessionnelle des Fédérations
UTICA	Union Tunisienne de l'Industrie, du Commerce et de l'Artisant
UTIFAR	Unione Tecnica Italiana Farmacisti
UTIP	Union Technique Intersyndicale Pharmaceutique
UTM	Union Trading Monaco
UTMM	Union Technique des Constructeurs de Menuiserie Métallique (Belgium)
UTO	United Towns Organization (France)
UTO	Universal Tourism Organisation
UTOP	United Technological Organisations of the Philippines
UTPP	United Thai People's Party
UTPUR	Union des Transports Publics Urbains et Régionaux
UTRAMM-ICOL	Union de Trabajadores Metalurgicos y Mineros de Colombia
UTRAT-EXCO	Unión de Trabajadores Textiles de Colombia
UTS	Union Technique Suisse
UTU	Universidad del Trabajo del Uruguay
UTWA	United Textile Workers of America
UTZ	Union Nationale des Travailleurs Zairoises
UUUC	United Ulster Unionist Council
UVAT	Unie van Assurantietussenpersonen
UVCB	Union des Villes et Communes Belges
UVS	Union des Villes Suisses
UVT	Union Voltaïque de Transport
UVTP	Union des Usagers de Véhicules de Transport Privé
UWH/WCS	Universal World Harmony World Council of Service
UWI	University of the West Indies
UWIST	University of Wales Institute of Science and Technology
UWM	United World Mission (U.S.A.)
UWPC	United World Press Cooperative (U.S.A.)
UWT	Union of Women Teachers
UY	Universal Youth
UZD	Umetnostnozgodovinsko Drustvo Slovenije
UZRA	United Zionist Revisionists of America

V

VAA	Verband angestellter Akademiker der Chemischen Industrie
VAB	Voluntary Agencies Bureau
VABB	Vereniging van Archivarissen en Bibliothecarissen van België
VAC	Verbond van Nederlandse Fabrikanten van Asbestcementwaren
VAD	Directia Aprovizionarii si Desfacerii (Roumania)
VAD	Vereinigung von Afrikanisten in Deutschland
VAHA	Vereniging Fabrieken van Aluminium Huishoudelijke Artikelen
VAHVA	Vahinkovakuutusyhdistys
VAK	Verband der Aufbau- und Geräte-Industrie für Kommunalzwecke
VALA	National Viewers' and Listeners' Association
VALCO	Volta Aluminium Co. (Ghana)
VAM	Vereniging voor Algemene Machinehandel
VAN	Vereniging van Archivarissen in Nederland
VANDPF	Vietnam Alliance of National, Democratic and Popular Forces
VAÖ	Verband der Agrarjournalisten in Österreich
VAÖ	Verband der Antiquare Österreichs
VAP	Verband Schweizerischer Anschussgeleise- und Privatgüterwagenbesitzer
VAP	Voluntary Assistance Programme (WMO)
VAPI	Vereniging der Apotekers van de Pharmaceutische Industrie (Belgium)
VAR	Vereniging voor Agrarisch Recht
VARA	Vereniging v. Arbeiders Radio-Amateurs
VARIM	Vattenreningsgruppen inom Sveriges Mekanförbund
VASCA	Electronic Valve and Semi-conductor Manufacturers Association

VASF	Verband der Angestelten des Schweizer Fernsehens	**VBNA**	Vereniging ter Behartiging van den Nederlandschen Aardappelhandel
VASGB	Vasectomy Advancement Society of Great Britain	**VBNN**	Society for Nature Conservation in the Netherlands
VASP	Viacao Aérea Sao Paulo (Brazil)	**VBÖ**	Verband der Baustoffhändler Österreichs
VATE	Victorian Association for the Teaching of English (Australia)	**VBO**	Vereinigung für Bankbetriebsorganisation
		VBO	Vereniging Belge des Omnipraticiens
VATEVA	Vaatetuseollisuuden Keskuslitto	**VBP**	Vlaamse Bond van Postzegelverzamelaars
VAV	Svenska Vatten- och Avloppsverksföreningen	**VBRA**	Vehicle Builders and Repairers Association
VAVI	Vereninging voor de Aardappelverwerkende Industrie	**VBS**	Verbond der Belgische Beroepsverenigingen van Geneesheren-Specialisten
VBA	Vereniging der Belgische Aannemers van Werken van Burgerlijke Bouwkunde (Belgium)	**VBSG**	Vereniging van Belgische Steden en Gemeenten
VBAM	Vereniging der Belgische Aannemers van Montagewerk	**VbU**	Verband Bergbaulicher Unternehmen und Bergbauverwandter Organisationen
VBB	Veenkoloniale Boerenbond	**VBV**	Vereniging Band-, Vlecht- en Kantindustrie
VBB	Verein der Bibliothekare an Öffentlichen Büchereien	**VBV**	Vereniging voor Bedrijfsvoorlichting
		VBV	Vereinigung Beratender Betriebs- und Volkswirte
VbBV	Verband Beratender Betriebs- und Volkswirte, Wirtschaftsjuristen und Sachverstandiger	**VBVB**	Vereniging ter Bevordering van het Vlaamse Boekwezen
VBC	Vereningen Bedrijfsleven Curacao	**VBW**	Vereniging voor Bitumineuze Werken
VBE	Verband Bildung und Erziehung	**VBZ**	Verband der Lieferanten für Brandschutz, Zivilschutz und Erste Hilfe
VBI	Verband der Beleuchtungs-Industrie (Switzerland)	**VCC**	Veteran Car Club of Great Britain
VBI	Verein Beratender Ingenieure	**VCG**	Vereniging tot Behartiging v. d. Belangen v. Coöperatieve Grasdrogerijen
VBI	Vereniging van Blikverwerkende Industrieën	**VCI**	Variety Clubs International (U.S.A.)
VBK	Verband der Deutschen Bodenbelags-, Kunststoff- Folien- und Beschichtungs-Industrie	**VCI**	Verband der Chemischen Industrie
		VCL	Vereinigung Christlicher Lehrer an den Höheren Schulen Österreichs
VBKD	Verband Bildender Künstler Deutschlands, Sektion Gebrauchsgraphik	**VCN**	Vereniging van Classici in Nederland
VBKDDR	Verband Bildender Künstler Deutsche Demokratische Republik	**VCOAD**	Voluntary Committee on Overseas Aid and Development
VBLJ	Vereniging van Belgische Landbouwjournalisten	**VCOD**	Vereniging van Christelijke Ondernemers in de DHZ Detailhandel
VBMWG	Vereniging van de Belgische Medische Wetenschappelijke	**VCP**	Vêtements et Chemiserie de Paris (Ivory Coast)
VBN	Vereniging van Bedrijfsredacteuren in Nederland	**VCRS**	Verband Chemischer Reingungsanstalten der Schweiz
VBN	Vereniging voor Bedrijfsrestaurateurs in Nederland	**VCTA**	Victorian Commercial Teachers Association (Australia)
VBN	Vereniging van Betonmortelfabrikanten in Nederland	**VCTV**	Verbond der Coöperatieve Tuinbouwveilingen
VBN	Vereniging van Boeren en Pluimveefokbedrijven in Nederland	**VCU**	Vereniging van Christelijke Uitgevers
		VCU	Vereinigung Christlicher Unternehmer der Schweiz

VCUÖ	Verband Christlicher Unternehmer Österreichs
VCV	Vlaamse Chemische Vereniging (Belgium)
VCW	Vereniging van Werkgevers in de Chemische Wasserijen en Ververijen
VD	Veeartsenijkundige Dienst
VDA	Schweizerischer Verband Diplomieter Arztegehilfinnen
VDA	Verband der Automobilindustrie
VDA	Verband Deutscher Agrarjournalisten
VDA	Verband Deutscher Antiquare
VdA	Verein Deutscher Archivare
VDAI	Verband der Deutschen Automatenindustrie
VdB	Verband der Bautenschutzmittel-Industrie
VDB	Verein Deutscher Bibliothekare
VDB	Verband Deutscher Badebetriebe
VDB	Verband Deutscher Biologen
VDB	Verein Deutscher Buchbindereien für Verlag und Industrie
VDBF	Verband der Briefumschlag- und Papierausstattungs-Fabriken
VDC	Verband Deutscher Fachschulchemiker
VDD	Industrieverband Bituminöse Dach- und Dichtungsbahnen
VDD	Verein Deutscher Dokumentare
VDD	Verband Deutscher Drogisten
VdD	Verband der Druchfarbenindustrie
VDD	Vereinigung der Drahtflechtereien
VdDB	Verein der Diplom-Bibliothekare an Wissenschaftlichen Bibliotheken
VDDI	Verband Deutscher Diplom-Ingenieure
VDDS	Vereinigung Diplomieter Kaufleute des Detailhandels der Schweiz
VDDW	Verband der Deutschen Wasserzählerindustrie
VDE	Verband Deutscher Elektrotechniker
VDEfa	Verein Deutscher Emailfachleute
VDEh	Verein Deutscher Eisenhüttenleute
VDEN	Vereniging van Directeuren van Electriciteitsbedrijven in Nederland
VDEW	Vereinigung Deutscher Elektrizitätswerke
VDF	Verband der Deutschen Faserplattenindustrie und verwandter Betriebe
VDF	Verband Deutscher Feuerverzinkereien
VDF	Verband der Deutschen Fruchtsaft-Industrie
VDF	Verband Deutscher Flugleiter
VDG	Verein Deutscher Giessereifachleute
VDG	Vereinigung Deutsch Gewässerschutz
VDH	Verband Deutscher Häutehändler
VDH	Verband Deutscher Heilbrunnen
VDH	Verein Deutscher Holzeinfuhrhäuser
VDI	Verband der Importeure van Kraftfahrzeugen
VDI	Verein Deutscher Ingenieure
VDID	Verband Deutscher Industrie-Designer
VDJ	Deutscher Journalisten-Verband
VDK	Verband Deutscher Dokumentar- und Kurzfilmproduzenten
VDKF	Verband Deutscher Kälte-Klima-Fachleute
VDKF	Verband Deutscher Kur- und Fremdenverkehrsfachleute
VDL	Verband Deutscher Akademiker für Landwirtschaft, Ernährung und Landespflege
VDL	Verband Deutscher Diplomandwirte
VDL	Verband Deutscher Luftfahrttechniker
VDL	Vereinigung Deutscher Landesschafzuchtverbände
VdL	Verband der Lackindustrie
VDLU	Verband Deutscher Luftfahrt-Unternehmen
VDLUFA	Verband Deutscher Landwirtschaftlicher Untersuchungs- u. Forschungsanstalten
VDM	Verband Deutscher Makler für Grundbesitz und Finanzierungen
VDM	Verband der Deutschen Milchwirtschaft
VDM	Verband Deutscher Mineralbrunnen
VDM	Verband der Deutschen Möbelindustrie
VdM	Verband der Mineralfarbenindustrie
VDMA	Verein Deutscher Maschinenbauanstalten
VDMG	Verband Deutscher Meteorologischer Gesellschaften
VDMK	Verband Deutscher Musikerzieher und Konzertierender Künstler
VDN	Verband Deutscher Nähmaschinenhändler
VDN	Verband des Deutschen Nahrungsmittelgrosshandels
VDP	Verband Deutscher Papierfabriken
VDP	Verband Deutscher Pradikätsweingüter
VDP	Verband der Deutschen Parkett-Industrie
VDPh	Verband Deutscher Physiotherapeuten
VDPI	Verband der Deutschen Photographischen Industrie
VDPI	Verband Deutscher Post-Ingenieure

VdPÖ	Verband der Professoren Österreichs
VDPW	Verband der Patentwirtschaftler (Germany)
VDR	Verband Deutscher Realschullehrer
VDR	Verband Deutscher Reeder
VDRG	Verband Deutscher Rundfunk- und Fernseh-Fachgrosshändler
VDRI	Verein Deutscher Revisions-Ingenieure
VDRJ	Vereinigung Deutscher Reisejournalisten
VDRZ	Verband Deutscher Rechenzentren
VDS	Verband Deutscher Schiffswerften
VDS	Verband Deutscher Schulmuskerzieher
VDS	Verband Deutscher Studienschaften
VDS	Vereinigung Deutscher Sägewerksverbände
VDS	Verband Deutscher Schirmfachgeschäfte
VDSB	Verein Deutschschweizerischer Bienenfreunde
VDSI	Verein Deutscher Sicherheits-Ingenieure
VDSt	Verband Deutscher Stahlwarenhändler
VDT	Verband Deutscher Tapetenfabrikanten
VDT	Verband Deutscher Techniker
VDT	Verband des Deutschen Tischlerhandwerks
VdTUV	Vereinigung der Technischen Überwachungs-Vereine
VDU	Verband der Deutschen Uhrenindustrie
VDÜ	Verband Deutschsprachiger Übersetzer Literarischer und Wissenschaftlicher Werke
VDV	Verband Deutscher Vermessungsingenieure
VDV	Verband der Versandgeschäfte
VDVM	Verein Deutscher Versicherungsmakler
VdW	Verband der Deutschen Fruchtwein- und Fruchtschaumwein-Industrie
VDW	Verband Deutscher Weinexporteure
VdW	Verband der Waggonindustrie
VDW	Verband der Wellpappen-Industrie
VDW	Verein Deutscher Werkzeug-maschinenfabriken
VDWW	Vereinigung Deutscher Werks- und Wirtschaftsarchivare
VDZ	Verband Deutscher Zeitschriftenverleger
VDZ	Verein Deutscher Zementwerke
VDZ	Verband des Deutscher Zweiradhandels
VdZ	Vereinigung von Verbänden der Deutschen Zentralheizungswirtschaft
VDZI	Verband Deutscher Zahntechniker-Innungen
VEA	Nederlandse Vereniging voor Erkende Adverteniebureaux
VEA	Verband der Energie-Abnehmer
VEA	Vereinigung von Fabriken Elektrothermischer Apparate (Switzerland)
VEB	Vereniging Effectenbescherming
VEB	Vereniging der Electriciteitsbedrijven in België
VEB	Vereinigung Evangelischer Buchhändler
VEBIDAK	Vereniging van Bitumineuze Dakbedekkingsbedrijven
VEBO	Vereniging voor Brouwerij Onderzoek en Onderwijs
VEBUKU	Vereinigung der Buchantiquare und Kupferstichhändler der Schweiz
VECE	Coöperatieve Verkoopcentrale voor Eieren
VECO	Vereniging van op Coöperatieve Grondslag werkende Afzetorganisaties voor Zaaizaad en Pootgoed
VECOL	Empresa Colombiana de Productos Veterinarios
VECOR	Vanderbijl Engineering Corporation (South Africa)
VECTA	Vereniging van Ondernemers van Concertbureaux
VED	Verband der Exhibition-Designer
VED	Verkerks- und Energiewirtschaftsdepartement (Switzerland)
VEDAG	Verband Deutschschweizerischer Ärztegesellschaften
VEDC	Vitreous Enamel Development Council
VEDEWA	Vereinigung der Wasserversorgungsverbände und Gemeinden mit Wasserwerken
VEEN	Vereniging v. Exploitanten v. Electriciteitsbedrijven in Nederland
VEF	Vereniging van Emaillefakrieken
VEG	Bundesverband des Elektro-Grosshandels
VEG	Verband Österreichischer Elektro-Grosshändler
VEG	Vereniging van Exploitanten van Gasbedrijven
VEGA	Vegetable Growing Association of America
VEGAT	Verband Schweizerischer Garn- und Tricotveredler
VEGIN	Vereniging van Exploitanten van Gasbedrijven in Nederland
VEGROCOS	Nederlandse Vereniging van Groothandelaren in Cosmetica en Parfumerieën

VEHAVLAS	Vereniging der Handelaars in Vlasvezels
VEICB	Vereniging der Electrische Industriële Centrales van België
VEIMMAVO	Vereniging van Importeurs van en Handelaren in Machines voor de Zuivel-Dranken-Voedings- en Genotmiddelenindustrie
VEK	Veterana Esperentista Klubo (Germany)
VELEBI	Vereniging van Leraren in de Biologie
VELEDES	Schweizerischer Verband der Lebensmittel-Detaillisten
VELF	Verwaltung für Ernährung, Landwirtschaft und Forsten
VELINES	Vereniging van Leraren in Natuur- en Scheikunde
VEMI	Vereniging van Importeurs en Fabrikanten van en Groothandelaren in Melkwinning- en Bewaarapparatuur
VEMI	Vereniging van Muziekinstrumenten-handelaren
VENEAGRO	Venezolana de Exportaciones Agricolas
VENEDAK	Vereniging van Nederlandse Dakrolfabrikanten
VENEFAB	Vereniging van Nederlandse Fabrikanten van Bestrijdingsmiddelen
VENEPAL	Venezolana de Pulpa y Papel
VENEXA	Vereniging van Nederlandse Exporteurs van Aardappelen
VENISS	Visual Education National Information Service for Schools
VENO	Verbond Algemene Exporthandel
VEÖ	Verband der Elektrizitätswerke Österreichisches
VEPAVE	Vereniging van Papierverwerkers
VERAS	Vereinigung Schweizerischer Asphalt-unternehmungen
VERBISKO	Vereniging van Fabrikanten van Banket, Beschuit, Biscuit, Koek en Aanverwante Produkten
VEREM-ABEL	Groupement Belge des Vendeurs-Réparateurs de Tracteurs et Machines Agricoles
VERNOF	Vereniging van Nederlandse Fabrikanten van Eetbare Oliën en Vetten
VERTGLAS	Genossenschaft der Schweizerischen Glasgrosshändler
VERTRIKO	Vereniging van Tricot- en Kousenfabrikanten
VERVOER	Vereniging van Oesterkwekers en Exporteurs
VES	Voluntary Emergency Service
VESEIGA	Verband Schweizerischer Seidengarnfarbereien
VESKA	Verband Schweizerischer Krankenanstalten
VESKOF	Vereinigung Schweizerischer Kontrollfirmen f. Sämereien
VESTRA	Verband Schweizerischer Unternehmungen für Strassenbeläge
VETSALL	Veterinarians Alliance
VEV	Vereniging ter Bevordering van de Export van Vleeswaren en Vleesconserven
VEV	Vlaams Economische Verbond
VEWIN	Vereniging van Exploitanten van Waterleidingsbedrijven in Nederland
VF	Sveriges Verkstadsförening
VF	Vestlandske Fartybyggjarlag
VFB	Vereniging van Fabrikanten van Bakkerij-Installaties
VFDB	Vereinigung z. Förderung d. Deutschen Brandschutzes
VFFS	Verband der Freiberuflichen Fahrzeug-sachverständigen
VFG	Verband für Flüssiggas
VFG	Verein zur Förderung der Giesserei-Industrie
VFG	Versuchanstalt f. Getreideverwertung
VFI	Verkfroedingafélag Íslands
VFK	Vereniging v. Fourage-en Kunstmest-handelaren
VFK	Vereniging van Nederlandse Fabrieken van Ketels, Drukhouders en Tanks
VFM	Verband der Fahrrad- und Motorradindustrie
VFMA	Verband der Führungskräfte der Metall- und Electroindustrie
VFMG	Vereinigung der Freunde der Mineralogie und Geologie
VFN	Vereniging van Financieringsondernemingen in Nederland
VFP	Verband der Fellgrossisten und Pelzkonfektionäre
VFR	Verband der Radio Fernsch- und Elektro-Fachhandels Österreichs
VFW	Vereinigte Flugtechnische Werke
VGAA	Vegetable Growers' Association of America
VGAS	Verband Galvanischer Anstalten der Schweiz
VGB	Vereniging van Groothandelaren in Brandstoffen
VGB	Vereinigung der Grosskraftwerksbetreiber
VGCT	Verein für Gerberei-Chemie und -Technik

VGD	Vereniging van de Grote Distributie-ondernemingen van België
VGG	Verband der Hersteller von gewerblichen Geschirrspülmaschinen
VGHM	Vereniging voor de Groothandel in Huishoudelijke Artikelen en Metaalwaren
VGIG	Vereniging voor de Groothandel in Gasverwarmings- en Verbruikstoestellen en Andere Verwarmingstoestellen
VGL	Schweizerische Vereinigung für Gewasser-schutz und Lufthygiene
VGM	Verband Gross-Städtischer Milchver-sorgungsbetriebe
VGN	Verein für Geschichte der Stadt Nürnberg
VGN	Vereniging van Gasfabrikanten in Nederland
VGN	Vereniging Gereedschapsfabrieken in Nederland
VGN	Vereniging van Geschiedenisleraren in Nederland
VGP	Vereinigung von Grossiten für den Photohandel
VGRO	Vereniging van Grafische Reproductie On-dernemingen
VGS	Vereniging van Gespecialiseerde Schoolleveranciers
VGSW	Verein für Geschichte der Stadt Wien (Austria)
VGT	Nederlandse Vereniging van Groothan-delaren in Tandheelkundige Benodigdheden
VGT	Verband des Garagen- und Tankstellengewerbes
VGV	Vereniging van Gespecialiseerde Vloeren-bedrijven
VGW	Verband der Deutschen Gas- und Wasserwerke
VH	Versuchsanstalt der Hefeindustrie
VHF	Veterinaerhygienisk Forening
VHI	Verband der Deutschen Holzwerkstoff-Industrie
VHK	Verband der Hersteller von Konditoreihilf-stoffen
VHN	Vereniging van Houtimpregneerinrichtingen in Nederland
VHOK	Vereniging van Handelaren in Oude Kunst in Nederland
VHP	Nederlandse Vereninging voor de Handel in Pluimvee en Wild
VHPI	Verband der Schweizerischen Holzverpackungs- und Palettenindustrie
VHR	Vereniging voor de Handel in Rubber-artikelen
VHS	Vereniging Fabrieken van Hang- en Sluitwerk
VHTL	Verband der Handels-, Transport- und Lebensmittelarbeiter der Schweiz
VHV	Vereinigung der Holzhandelsverbände
VHVH	Nederlandse Vereniging van Handelaren in Verwarmings- en Huishoudelijke Apparaten
VHZ	Vereniging voor de Handel in Land-bouwzaaizaden
VHZMK	Vereinigung der Hochschullehre für Zahn-, Mund- und Kieferheilkunde
VIAR	Volcani Institute of Agricultural Research (Israel)
VIASA	Venezolana Internacional de Aviación, S.A.
VIB	Nederlandse Vereniging in het Isolatiebedrijf
VIB	Vereniging van Importeurs van Bouwmaterialen
VIB	Voedselvoorzienings in-en Verkoopbureau
VIBÖ	Vereinigung Industrieller Bauunter-nehmungen Österreichs
VICA	Vocational Industrial Clubs of America
VICORP	Virgin Islands Corporation
VID	Volunteers for International Development (U.S.A.)
VIE	Victorian Institute of Engineers (Australia)
VIF	Svenska Värmeisolermaterialfakrikanterna
VIF	Verband von Importeuren der Fisch- und Fischproduktenbranche
VIFKA	Vereniging van Importeurs en Fabrikanten van Kantoormachines
VIGE	Royal Institute of Agricultural Research (Greece)
VIGPA	Nederlandse Vereniging van Importeurs van en Groothandelaren in Glas, Porcelan en Aardewerk
VILF	Verband der Ingenieure des Lack- und Far-benfaches
VILLA	Ventes Immobilières de Logement et de Lotissements en Afrique (Congo)
VILS	Verband Schweizerischer Industrielieferan-ten für Shrott
VIMAG	Vereniging van Importeurs van Machinegereedschappen voor de Metaalbewerking
VIMETAAL	Vereniging van Importeurs van Gereedschapswerktuigen

VIMHOUT	Vereniging van Importeurs van en Handelaren
VIMKO	Vereniging van Importeurs van Koelmachines en Koelkasten
VIMPOL	Vereniging v. Importeurs v. Landbouwwerktuigen
VIMPOLTU	Vereniging van Importeurs van en Groothandelaren in Land- en Tuinbouwmachines
VIMPOS-TAAL	Vereniging van Handelaren in Speciaalstaal
VIMTU	Vereniging v. Importeurs v. Tuinbouwwerktuigen
VIP	Verein der Industriefilmproduzenten
VIP	Vereniging Importeurs Pneumatische Werktuigen
VIP Teams	Visiting International Psychiatric Teams Inc. (U.S.A.)
VIPS	Vereinigung der Importeure Pharmazeutischer Spezialtäten (Switzerland)
VIR	Vereniging Informatie en Recherche-Bureauhouders
VIRO	Netherlands United Nations Association
VIS	Veterinary Investigation Service
VISACAM	Société des Viandes et Salaisons du Cameroun
VISTA	Volunteers in the Service of America
VITA	Volunteers for International Technical Assistance (U.S.A.)
VITAR	Veterinary Institute for Tropical and High Altitude Research (Peru)
VIV	Food Import Bureau (Holland)
VIV	Verband Schweizer Vieh-Importeure
VIV	Vereniging van Importeurs van Verbrandingsmotoren
VKD	Verband der Köche Deutschlands
VKE	Verband Kunststofferzeugende Industrie und Verwandt Gebiete
VKF	Vereniging van Kartonnagefabrikanten in Nederland
VKF	Vereinigung Schweizerischer Kabel-Fabriken
VKFA	Vereinigung Kantonaler Feuerversicherungsanstalten
VKG	Verband der Kraftfahrzeugteile
VKI	Groep Verwarmings- en Kookapparatenindustrie
VKI	Verband Kunststoff Verarbeitender Industriebetriebe der Schweiz
VKI	Vereniging Klei Industrie
VKIFD	Von Karman Institute for Fluid Dynamics (Belgium)
VKL	Vereniging van Kleuterschool Leveranciers
VKL	Vereniging van Katholieke Leraren "Sint-Bonaventura"
VKÖ	Verband der Köche Österreichs
VKS	Verband Kommunaler Städtereinigungsbetriebe
VLA	Vereniging Fabrieken van Luchttechnische Apparaten
VLB	Versuchs- und Lehranstalt für Brauerei in Berlin
VLET	Vereniging van Leveranciers van Electrotechnische
VLG	Vereniging van Leveranciers voor de Galvano-Techniek
VLGN	Verband Landwirtschaftlicher Genossenschaften der Nordwestschweiz
VLGZ	Verband Landwirtschaftlicher Genossenschaften der Zentralschweiz
VLHT	Vereniging van Laboratoriumhoudende Tandtechnici in Nederland
VLK	Verband der Landwirtschaftskammern
VLKB	Schweizerischer Verband der Lehrer an Kaufmännischen Berufsschulen
VLL	Nederlandse Vereniging van Leraren in Landbouw-Mechanica
VLM	Vereniging van Leveranciers van Merkspeelgoed
VLN	Vereniging tot Bevordering v. d. Landbouwtuigpaardfokkerij in Nederland
VLP	Schweizerische Vereinigung für Landesplanung
VLRP	Vitamin Laboratories of Roche Products (Australia)
VLSF	Verband der Lastwagen-Spediteure und Ferntransportunternehmer (Switzerland)
VKV	Vlaams Kinesitherapeutem Verbond
VLT	Vereniging van Loonveredilingsbedrijven voor de Textielindustrie
VLVB	Verband von Lieferanten Versilbenter Bestecke (Switzerland)
VLW	Bundesverband der Lehrer an Wirtschaftsschulen
VMAI	Veterinary Medical Association of Ireland
VMB	Vereniging van Metaalbeschermingsbedrijven
VMCC	Vintage Motor Cycle Club

VMD	Vereniging Milieudefensie
VMF	Vieilles Maisons Françaises
VMI	Vereniging van Metaal-Industrieën
VMM	Volunteer Missionary Movement
VMNICM	Vaikunth Mehta National Institute of Cooperative Management (India)
VMÖ	Verband der Marktforscher Österreichs
VMPA	Verband der Materialprüfungsämter
VMR	Vereniging van Metalen-Ramenfabrikanten
VMS	Verband der Museen der Schweiz
VMVM	Verbond der Middelgrote Verzekerings-maatschappijen
VNA	Vereniging van de Nederlandse Aardolie-Industrie
VNA	Vietnamese News Agency
VNCI	Vereniging van de Nederlandse Chemische Industrie
VNG	Verbond van de Nederlandse Groothandel
VNG	Vereniging van Nederlandse Gemeenten
VNG	Vereniging van Nederlandse Grasdrogerijen
VNGF	Vereniging van Kleuterschool Leveranciers
VNK	Vereniging voor Japanse Kunst
VNK	Vereniging Nederlandse Kerftabakindustrie
VNKI	Vereniging van Nederlandse Kolenimporteurs
VNM	Vereniging Nederlandse Fabrieken van Melktransportkannen
VNM	Vereniging Nederlandse Motorenrevisiebedrijven
VNMF	Vereniging van Nederlandse Mengvoederfabrikanten
VNO	Verbond van Nederlandse Ondernemingen
VNP	Vereninging van Nederlandsche Papierfabrikanten
VNR	Vereniging van Nederlandse Reformhuizen
VNRC	Vegetarian Nutritional Research Centre
VNS	Verenigde Nederlandse Slijters
VNU	Volontaires des Nations Unies
VNV	Vereniging van Nederlandse Verkeersvliegers
VNV	Vereniging van Nederlandse Vleeswaren- en Vleesconservenfabrikanten
VNZ	Vereniging van Nederlandse Fabrikanten van Zuivelwerktuigen
VÖA	Verband Österreichischer Archivare
VOA	Vereniging Ontwikkeling Arbeidstechniek
VOA	Vereniging voor Organisatieen Arbeidskunde

VÖÄ	Vereinigung Österreichischer Ärzte
VÖAG	Verband des Österreichischen Automatengewerbes
VÖB	Verband Öffentlicher Banken
VÖB	Vereinigung Österreichischer Bibliothekare
VÖCh	Verein Österreichischer Chemiker
VOCOSS	Voluntary Organisations Co-operating in Overseas Social Service
VOEST	Vereinigte Österreichische Eisen – und Stahlwerke AG
VOF	Verband der Fabrikanten von Technischen Ölen, Fetten und Verwandten Produkten
VÖFVL	Verband Österreichischer Flugsverkehrsleiter
VOFyTOZ	Vereniging voor Studie en Onderzoek over Fytopatologie en Toegepaste Zoologie
VÖG	Verein Österreichischer Giessereifachleute
VÖI	Verband Österreichische Ingenieure
VÖI	Vereinigung Österreichischer Industrieller
VÖK	Vereinigung Österreichischer Kunst-stoffverarbeiter
VOLBRIC-ERAM	Société Voltaïque de Briqueterie et de Céramique
VOLG	Verband Ostschweizerischer Landwirtschaft-icher Genossenschaften
VOLINFLO	Voluntary Action Information Flow
VOLTAICA	Société Voltaïque pour l'Avancement de l'Industrie, du Commerce et de l'Agriculture
VOLTAP	Société Voltaïque de Diffusion d'Appareils Électriques
VOLTAVIN	Société des Vins de la Haute-Volta
VOLTELEC	Société Voltaïque d'Électricité
VOLTEX	Société Voltaïque des Textiles
VOLTOA	Société Voltaïque d'Oxygène et d'Acetylène
VOM	Vereniging voor Oppervlaktetechnieken van Metalen
VÖN	Verband der Österreichischen Neuphilologen
VOO	Vereniging voor Openbaar Onderwijs
VOP	Stichting tot Bevordering van de Vakopleiding voor de Handel in Pluimvee, Wild en Tamme Konijnen
VÖR	Vereinigung des Österreichischen Rüben-bauerorganisationen
VORI	Viticultural and Oenological Research Institute (South Africa)
VOSA	Voluntary Overseas Service Association
VÖTC	Verein Österreichischer Textilchemiker Coloristen

VÖV	Verband Öffentlicher Verkehrsbetriebe
VOW	Vereniging van Ondernemers in Wand-bekleding
VÖWA	Verband Österreichischer Wirtschafts-akademiker
VÖZ	Verband Österreichischer Ziegelwerke
VÖZ	Verband Österreichischer Zeitungs-herausgeber
VÖZ	Verein Österreichischen Zementfabrikanten
VPA	Virginia Pharmaceutical Association
VPBS	Verband Papier, Bürobedarf und Schreibwaren in der Hauptgemeinschaft des Deutschen Einzelhandels
VPCA	Vereniging der Publiciteitschefs der Adver-teerders van België
VPCM	Vereniging van Protestants-Christelijke Metaalindustriëlen in Nederland
VPI	Nederlandse Vereniging van Producenten en Importeurs van Wegen- en Water-bouwmaterialen
VPI	Virginia Polytechnic Institute (U.S.A.)
VPLC	Vereniging v. Pluimveeselecteurs in Dienst v. Landbouwcoöperaties
VPM	Nederlandse Vereniging van Fabrikanten van Verbandstoffen, Pleisters en Maandverband
VPN	Verein für Psychiatric and Neurologie (Austria)
VPOD	Schweizerischer Verband des Personals Offentlicher Dienste
VPRI	Victorian Plant Research Institute (Australia)
VPRO	Vrijzinnig Protestantse Radio-Omroep
VPRP	Vietnam People's Revolutionary Party
VPS	Verband Privater Städtereinigungsbetriebe
VPSG	Verband Schweizerischer Papier- und Papierstoff- Fabrikanten
VRB	Vereniging van Religieus-Wetenschappelijke Bibliothecarissen
VRF	Verband der Radio, Fernseh- und Elektro-Fachhandels Österreichs
VRH	Verband der Reformwaren-Hersteller
VRKD	Verband Reisender Kaufleute Deutschlands
VRKÖ	Verband Reisender Kaufleute Österreichs
VRKS	Verband Reisender Kaufleute der Schweiz
VRM	Vereinigung der Regierungsbaumeister des Maschinenwesens "Motor"
VS	Verband Deutscher Schriftsteller
VSA	Föreningen Värmlands Skogarbetsstudier
VSA	Verband Schweizerischer Annoncen-Expeditionen
VSA	Vereinigung Schweizerischer Akkumulatorenfabrikanten
VSA	Vereinigung Schweizerischer Angestelltenverbände
VSA	Vereinigung Schweizerischer Archivare
VSAK	Verband Schweizer Antiquare und Kunsthändler
VSB	Schweizerischer Bierbrauerverein
VSB	Verband Schweizer Badekurorte
VSB	Verband Schweizerischer Baumschulbesitzer
VSB	Verband Schweizerischer Bücherexperten
VSB	Vereniging voor Strategische Beleidsvorming
VSB	Vereinigung Schweizerischer Bibliothekare
VSB	Vereinigung Schweizerischer Bohrfirmen
VSBF	Verband Schweizerischer Blechemballagen-Fabrikanten
VSBH	Verband Schweizerischer Baumaterial-Händler
VSBH	Verband Schweizerischer Baumwollabgang-Händler
VSBH	Vereinigung Schweizerischer Buchdruck-Hilfsarbeiter
VSBM	Verband Schweizerischer Baumaschinen – Fabrikanten und -Händler
VSBPF	Verband Schweizerischer Bürsten- und Pinselfabrikanten
VSBS	Verband Schweizerischer Bildhauer- und Steinmetzmeister
VSC	Verband Schweizerischer Carbesitzer
VSCC	Vintage Sports Car Club
VSCF	Verein Schweizerischer Cartonnage-Fabriken
VSchM	Verband Schweizerischer Müller
VSCI	Verband der Schweizerischer Carosserie-Industrie
VSCTU	Vereinigung Schweizerischer Chemischreinigungs- und Textilpflege-Unternehmen
VSD	Verband des Schweizerischen Darmhandels
VSD	Verband Schweizerischer Düngerhändler
VSE	Verband der Schweizerischen Edelstein-branche
VSE	Verband Schweizerischer Eisengiessereien
VSE	Verband Schweizerischer Eisenwarenhändler
VSE	Verband Schweizerischer Elektrizitätswerke

VSEF	Verband Schweizersicher Edelmetallwaren-Fabrikanten		**VSH**	Verband Schweizerischer Hadernsortierwerke
VSEI	Verband Schweizerische Elektro-Installationsfirmen		**VSH**	Verband Schweizerischer Hartschotterwerke
VSEMK	Verband Schweizerischer Edelstahl-, Metall- und Kunststoffhändler		**VSH**	Verband Schweizerischer Heuhandelsfirmen
VSF	Värme- och Sanitetstekniska Föreningen i Finland		**VSH**	Vereinigung Schweizerischer Hafermühlen
VSF	Verband Schweizerischer Seidenstoff-Fabrikanten		**VSHF**	Verband Schweizerischer Holzbearbeitungsmaschinen- und Werkzeug-Fabrikanten
VSF	Vereinigung des Schweizerischen Farbenfachhandels		**VSHL**	Verband Schweizerischer Heizungs- und Lüftungsfirmen
VSF	Vereinigung Schweizerischer Futtermittelfabrikanten		**VSI**	Bundesverband des Sanitär-Fachhandels
VSFAV	Verband Schweizerischer Film und AV-Produzenten		**VSI**	Verband Schmierfett-Industrie
VSFBR	Verband Schweizerischer Fabrikanten van Besen aus Reisig		**VSI**	Verband Schweizerischer Immobilienbureaux
VSFE	Verband Schweizerischer Fabrikanten von Einbauküchen		**VSI**	Verband Schweizerischer Isolierfirmen
VSFF	Verband Schweizerischer Fleischwaren-Fabrikanten		**VSI**	Verband Selbständiger Ingenieure
VSFK	Verein Schweizerischer Fabrikanten von Kunststoffpackungen		**VSI**	Vereinigung Schweizer Innenarchitekten
VSG	Verband Schweizerischer Gärtnermeister		**VSI**	Vinnuveitandasamband Islands
VSG	Verband Schweizerischer Gaswerke		**VSIA**	Verband Schweizerischer Industrie-Lieferanten für Altpapier
VSG	Verband Schweizerischer Gerbereien		**VSIEA**	Vereinigung Schweizerischer Importeure Elektrischer Apparate
VSG	Verband Schweizerischer Goldschmiede		**VSIG**	Vereinigung des Schweizerischen Import- und Grosshandels
VSG	Verband Schweizerischer Graphiker		**VSJE**	Vereinigung Schweizerischer Juwelen- und Edelmetallbranchen
VSG	Verband Schweizerischer Grastrocknungsbetriebe		**VSK**	Verband Schweizerischer Konsumvereine
VSG	Verband des Schweizerischen Spirituosengewerbes		**VSKB**	Vereniging voor het Theologisch Bibliothecariaat
VSG	Verein Schweizerischer Gymnasiallehrer		**VSKE**	Verband Schweizerischer Käseesporteure
VSGF	Vereinigung Schweizerischer Gasherd-Fabrikanten		**VSKF**	Verband Schweizerischer Kachelofenfabrikanten
VSGH	Verband Schweizerischer Geflügelhalter		**VSKF**	Verein Schweizerischer Kondensatoren-Fabrikanten
VSGI	Verband Schweizerischer Geflügel- und Wild-Importeure		**VSKI**	Verband der Schweizerischen Keramischen Industrie
VSGN	Vereinigung Schweizerischer Grosshandelsfirmen in Abfällen von Nichteisenmetallen		**VSKM**	Verband Schweizerischer Kundenmüller
VSGP	Verband Schweizerischer Gemüseproduzenten		**VSL**	Verband Schweizerischer Firmen für Linoleum und Spezialbodenbeläge
VSGT	Verband Schweizerischer Gummi- und Thermoplast-Industrieller		**VSL**	Verband Schweizerischer Lagerhäuser
VSGU	Verband Schweizerischer General-unternehmer		**VSL**	Verband Schweizerischer Leinen-Industrieller
			VSLB	Verein Schweizerischer Lithographiebesitzer
			VSLF	Verband Schweizerischer Lack- und Farbenfabrikanten
			VSLF	Vereinigung Schweizerischer Leichtbauplattenfabrikanten

VSLG	Verband Schweizerischer Grossisten für Linoleum und Spezialbodenbeläge
VSLR	Verband Schweizerischer Lichtpaus- und Reprografie-Betriebe
VSM	Verband Schweizerischer Marmor- und Granitwerke
VSM	Verein Schweizerischer Maschinen-Industrieller
VSM	Verband Schweizerischer Mineralquellen
VSM	Verein Schweizerischer Maschinen-Industrieller
VSM	Vereinigung Schweizerischer Modehäuser
VSM	Vereniging Fabrikanten van Stalen Kantooren Bedrijfsmeubelen
VSMB	Verband Schweizerischer Modellbaubetriebe
VSMBD	Verband Schweizerischer Mercerie- und Bonnerie-Detaillisten
VSMF	Vereinigung Schweizerischer Metallschutz-Firmen
VSMG	Verband Schweizerischer Metallgiessereien
VSMP	Verein Schweizerischer Mathematik- und Physiklehrer
VSMR	Verband Schweizerischer Motor-Revisionsbetriebe
VSMWH	Verband des Schweizerischen Maschinen- und Werkzeughandels
VSN	Vereinigung Schweizerischer Naturwissenschaftslehrer
VSN	Vereniging Smeerolieondernemingen Nederland
VSO	Voluntary Service Overseas
VSP	Verband Schweizerischer Papeteristen
VSP	Verband Schweizerischer Patentanwälte
VSP	Verband Schweizerischer Pferdemetzgereien
VSP	Verband Schweizerischer Pflasterermeister
VSP	Verein der Schweizer Presse
VSP	Vereinigung Schweizer Petroleum-Geologen und Ingenieure
VSPG	Verband Schweizerischer Papier-Grossisten
VSPPF	Verband Schweizerischer Papier- und Papierstoff-Fabrikanten
VSR	Verband Schweizerischer Rolladen-und Storenfabriken
VSR	Vereinigung Schweizerischer Reproduktionsbetriebe
VSR	Vereniging Fabrieken van Staalplaat Radiatoren
VSRD	Verband Schweizer Reform- und Diätfachgeschäfte
VSRT	Verband Schweizerischer Radio- und Televisionsfachgeschäfte
VSS	Verband Schweizerischer Schirmfabrikanten
VSS	Verband Schweizerischer Schmierölimporteurs
VSS	Verband Schweizerische Schuhindustrieller
VSS	Vereinigung Schweizerischer Strassenfachmänner
VSS	Verband Schweizerischer Studentenschaften
VSS	Vereinigung Schweizerischer Siebdruckereien
VSSB	Verband Schweizerischer Schloss- und Beschlägefabrikanten
VSSB	Verband Schweizerischer Schreib- und Büromaschinenhändler
VSSD	Verband Schweizerischer Spielwaren-Detaillisten
VSSF	Verband Schweizerischer Schallplatten-Fachgeschäfte
VSSF	Verband Schweizerischer Spielwarenfabrikanten
VSSJ	Verband Schweizer Sportjournalisten
VSSL	Verband Schweizerischer Schallplatten-Lieferanten
VSSM	Verband Schweizerischer Schreinermeister und Möbelfabrikanten
VSSÖ	Verband der Sportausrüster und Sportartikelerzeuger Österreichs
VSSTF	Verband Schweizerischer Sperrholz- und Tischlerplatten-Fabrikanten
VSSZ	Verein Schweizerischer Seidenzwirner
VST	Verband Schweizerischer Teigwarenfabrikanten
VST	Verband Schweizerischer Transportanstalten
VST	Verband Schweizerischer Transportunternehmungen des Öffentlichen Verkehrs
VST	Vereinigung Schweizerischer Teppichhändler
VST	Vereinigung Schweizerischer Tiefbauunternehmer
VSTF	Verein Schweizerischer Teppichfabrikanten
VSTG	Verband Schweizerischer Teppich-Grossisten
VSTG	Verband Schweizerischer Topfpflanzen- und Schnittblumengärtnereien
VSTH	Verband Schweizerischer Tabakhändler
VSTH	Verband Schweizerischer Technischer Händler

VSTH	Verband Schweizerischer Traubensaft-hersteller
VSTI	Verein Schweizerischer Textilindustrieller
VSTV	Verband der Schweizerischen Textil-Veredlungs-Industrie
VSU	Verband Schweizerischer Uhrenfachgeschäfte
VSU	Verband Selbständiger Unternehmen der Nährmittelindustrie
VSV	Verband Schweizerischer Verkehrsvereine
VSVF	Verband der Schweizer Versandmetzgereien und des Fleischhandels
VSVM	Verband der Schweizer Versandmetzgereien
VSVM	Vereinigung Schweizerischer Versicherungs-mathematiker
VSVT	Verband Schweizerischer Vermessungs-techniker
VSVVS	Vereinigung Schweiz Versuchs-und Ver-mittlungsstellen für Saatkartoffeln
VSW	Verband Schweizerischer Werbe-gesellschaften
VSWF	Vereinigung Schweizerischer Weisskalkfabrikanten
VSWK	Verband der Schweizerischen Waren- und Kaufhäuser
VSWM	Vereniging Fabrikanten van Stalen Woning-meubelen
VSWS	Verband Schweizerischer Woll- und Seidenstoff-Fabrikanten
VSZ	Verband Schweizerischer Zigarrenfabrikanten
VSZKGF	Verein Schweizerischer Zement-, Kalk- und Gips-Fabrikanter
VSZS	Verband Schweizerischer Ziegel- und Steinfabrikanten
VTCC	Verein der Textil-Chemiker und Coloristen
VTCVG	Vereniging Technische Commissie Vloeibaar Gas
VTFF	Verband Technischer Betriebe für Film- und Fernsehen
VTG	Verband Schweizer Tierarzneimittel-grossisten
VTO	Vereniging van Textielondernemingen in Nederland
VTO	Vsemirnaja Turisticheskaja Organizatsija
VTR	Verband Schweizerischer Unternehmungen für Tankreinigungen

VUBI	Verband Unabhängig Beratender Ingenieurfirmen
VUC	Victoria University College, Wellington (New Zealand)
VUNB	Vereniging van Uitgevers van Nederlands-talige Boeken
VUPC	Výskúmny Ústav Papiera a Celulózy
VUPP	Výskúmny Ústav Prumysly Papírenského
VUV	Výzkumný ústav Vodohosppodárský
VVA	Vee an Vlees Aankoopbureau
VVBADP	Vlaamse Vereniging van Bibliotheek-, Archief- en Documentatiepersoneel
VVBAP	Vlaamse Vereniging van Bibliotheek- en Archiefpersoneel
VVD	Volkspartij voor Vrijheid en Democratie (Netherlands)
VVDF	Vereniging van Drukinktfabrikanten
VVK	Verband Vollpappe- Kartonagen
VVK	Verein für Volkskunde (Austria)
VvL	Vereniging van Letterkundigen
VVMA	Vereniging van Medische Analysten
VVS	Kungliga Vetenskaps- och Vitterhets-Samhället i Göteborg
VVS	Svenska Rörgrossistförening
VVS	Vereniging voor Statistiek
VvU	Vereinigung von Unternehmerinnen
VVV	Vliegtuigeienaars- en Vlieëniersvereniging
VVVF	Vereniging van Vernis- en Verffakrikanten in Nederland
VVVH	Vereiniging van Verfhandelaren in Nederland
VVZM	Vereniging voor Zuivelindustrie en Melkhygiene
VWA	Bundesverband Deutscher Verwaltungs- und Wirtschafts-Akademien
VWA	Vereinigung der Werbeleiter und Werbe-assistenten
VWF	Verband der Wissenschaftler an Forschungs-instituten
VWFA	Verband Unabhängiger Wirtschafts-, Finanz- und Anlageberater
VWI	Vereniging van Weegwerktuig-Industrieën
VWO	Verbond van Wetenschappelijke Onder-zoekers
VWP	Vietnam Workers' Party
VZB	Vereniging van Zelfbedienings-Bedrijven
VZH	Nederlandse Bond van Verzenhandelaren in Groenten en Fruit

VZI	Verband der Zigarettenpapier verarbeitenden Industrie
VZLS	Verband Zahntechnischer Laboratorien der Schweiz

W

WAA	Western Association of Africanists (U.S.A.)
WAAA	Women's Amateur Athletic Association
WAACCS	Western Australian Automobile Chamber of Commerce
WAAE	World Association for Adult Education
WAAER	World Association for the Advancement of Educational Research
WAALD	West African Association of Agricultural Librarians and Documentalists
WAAP	World Association for Animal Production
WAAS	World Academy of Art and Science
WAASP	World-Wide Association for Anomalous Scientific Phenomena
WAAVP	World Association for the Advancement of Veterinary Parasitology
WAC	Water Allocation Council (New Zealand)
WAC	West African Committee (U.K.)
WAC	Women's Advisory Committee of the British Standards Institution
WACA	Western Agricultural Chemicals Association (U.S.A.)
WACA	World Airlines Clubs Association
WACB	World Association for Christian Broadcasting
WACC	World Association for Christian Communication
WACH	West African Clearing House (Senegal)
WACL	World Anti-Communist League
WACMR	West African Council for Medical Research
WACO	World Air Cargo Organisation
WACP	West African College of Physicians (Ghana)
WACRAL	World Association of Christian Radio Amateurs and Listeners
WACRI	West African Cacao Research Institute, (Ghana)
WACU	West African Customs Union

WACY 2000	World Association for Celebrating Year 2000
WAD	World Association of Detectives (U.S.A.)
WADA	Wum Area Development Agency (Cameroons)
WADB	West African Development Bank (Togo)
WADC	Wright Air Development Centre (U.S.A.)
WADE	World Association of Document Examiners
WADVBS	World Association of Daily Vacation Bible Schools (U.S.A.)
WAE	World Association of Estonians (U.S.A.)
WAEC	War Agricultural Executive Committee
WAEC	West African Economic Community (Upper Volta)
WAEC	West African Examinations Council
WAEPA	Worldwide Assurance for Employees of Public Agencies (U.S.A.)
WAERSA	World Agricultural Economics and Rural Sociology Abstracts
WAFC	West African Fisheries Commissioner (FAO)
WAFRI	West-African Fisheries Research Institute
WAFRU	West African Fungicide Research Unit
WAGBI	Wildfowlers Association of Great Britain and Ireland
WAGGGS	World Association of Girl Guides and Girl Scouts
WAHO	World Arab Horse Organization
WAHS	West African Health Secretariat
WAIFOR	West African Institute for Oilpalm Research (*formerly* OPRS) (Nigeria)
WAIFTR	World Alliance for International Friendship through the Churches
WAIIC	Western State Agricultural and Industrial Investment Company (Nigeria)
WAISER	West African Institute of Social and Economic Research
WAITR	West African Institute for Trypanosomiasis Research
WAITRO	World Association of Industrial and Technological Research Organisations
WAJ	World Association of Judges
WAJAL	West African Joint Agency Ltd
WAL	Western Air Lines (U.S.A.)
WAL	World Association of Lawyers
WALA	West African Library Association
WAMRAC	World Association of Methodist Radio Amateurs and Clubs

WAMRU	West African Maize Research Unit
WAMS	World Association of Military Surgeons
WAMU	West African Monetary Union
WAOS	Welsh Agricultural Organisation Society
WAPDA	Water and Power Development Authority of West Pakistan
WAPET	West Australian Petroleum (Pty) Ltd.
WAPOR	World Association for Public Opinion Research
WAPMC	West African Postgraduate Medical College (Nigeria)
WAPT	Wild Animal Propagation Trust
WAPTT	World Association for Professional Training in Tourism
WARC	Women's Amateur Rowing Council
WARC	World Alliance of Reformed Churches
WARDA	West African Rice Development Association
WARI	Waite Agricultural Research Institute (Australia)
WARPATH	World Association to Remove Prejudice Against the Handicapped (U.S.A.)
WARRS	West African Rice Research Station
WAS	Washington Academy of Sciences (U.S.A.)
WAS	Witwatersrand Agricultural Society (South Africa)
WASA	West African Science Association
WASAL	Wisconsin Academy of Sciences, Arts and Letters
WASCO	National Water and Soil Conservation Organisation (New Zealand)
WASCU	World Association for the Senior Citizens Union (Switzerland)
WASID	Water and Soil Investigation Department (Pakistan)
WASP	World Association of Societies of Anatomic and Clinical Pathology
WASPRU	West African Stored Products Research Unit
WASU	West African Students Union
WAT	World Airport Technology (France)
WATA	World Association of Travel Agencies
WATBRU	West African Timber Borer Research Unit
WATTE	West African Tropical Testing Establishment
WAVA	World Association of Veterinary Anatomists
WAVE	World Association of Video-Makers and Editions
WAVFH	World Association of Veterinary Food Hygienists
WAVMI	World Association of Veterinary Microbiologists, Immunologists and Specialists in Infectious Diseases
WAVP	World Association of Veterinary Pathologists
WAWE	World Association of Women Executives
WAWF	World Association of World Federalists
WAY	World Alliance of Y.M.C.A's
WAY	World Assembly of Youth
WB	World Brotherhood
WBA	World Boxing Association
WBC	World Boxing Council
WBBG	Weltbund der Bibelgesellschaften
WBCA	Weltbewegung der Christlichen Arbeiter
WBC	World Business Council (U.S.A.)
WBDJ	Weltbund der Demokratischen Jugend
WBF	World Bridge Federation
WBG	Wiener Beethoven Gesellschaft
WBG	Wiener Bibliophilen-Gesellschaft
WBL	Nederlandse Vereniging tegen Water-, Bodem- en Luchtverontreiniging
WBMS	World Bureau of Metal Statistics (U.K.)
WBS	Wassmann Biological Society (U.S.A.)
WBS	Wellington Botanical Society (N.Z.)
WBSI	Western Behavioral Sciences Institute
WBV	Schweizerischer Weinbauverein
WCA	Women's Cricket Association
WCA	World Calendar Association
WCBA	Weltbewegung der Christlichen Arbeiter
WCC	World Cheerleader Council (U.S.A.)
WCC	World Council of Clergymen (U.S.A.)
WCC	World Council of Churches
WCC	World Crafts Council
WCCB	World Committee for Christian Broadcasting
WCCE	World Council of Christian Education
WCCESSA	World Council of Christian Education and Sunday School Associations
WCCI	World Council for Curriculum and Instruction (U.S.A.)
WCCS	World Chamber of Commerce Service (U.S.A.)
WCEMA	West Coast Electronic Manufacturers Association (U.S.A.)
WCEU	World's Christian Endeavour Union
WCF	World Congress of Faiths

WCFBA	World Catholic Federation for the Biblical Apostolate		**WEDA**	Wholesale Engineering Distributors Association
WCL	World Confederation of Labour		**WEF**	World Education Fellowship
WCMMF	World Congress of Man-Made Fibres		**WEF**	World Evangelical Fellowship (Switzerland)
WCOTP	World Confederation of Organisations of the Teaching Profession (U.S.A.)		**WEFC**	West European Fisheries Conference
WCP	World Council of Peace		**WEG**	Wirtschaftsverband Erdölgewinnung
WCPA	World Constitution and Parliament Association (U.S.A.)		**WEK**	Weltweiter Evangelisations-Kreuzzug
			WELG	Women's Ecumenical Liaison Group
WCPS	World Confederation of Productivity Science		**WEM**	Western European Metal Trades Employers Organizations
WCPT	World Confederation of Physical Therapy		**WEMA**	Wirtschaftsverband Eisen-, Maschinen- und Apparatebau
WCPWC	World Council for the Peoples World Convention		**WEPARM**	Werkgroep Export Propaganda Agrarisch Reproductiemateriaal
WCRA	Weather Control Research Association (U.S.A.)		**WERC**	World Environment and Resources Council
WCRA	Women's Cycle Racing Association		**WES**	Women's Engineering Society
WCRP	World Conference of Religion for Peace		**WETUC**	Workers Educational Trade Union Committee
WCSC	World Correctional Service Center for Community and Social Concerns Inc. (U.S.A.)		**WEU**	Western European Union
WCWB	World Council for the Welfare of the Blind		**WEXAS**	World Expeditionary Association
WCYMSC	World Council of Young Men's Service Clubs		**WF**	Wallboardfabrikkenes Felleskontor
WDC	World Data Centre		**WFA**	War Food Administration (U.S.A.)
WDK	Wirtschaftsverband der Deutschen Kautschukindustrie		**WFA**	White Fish Authority
			WFA	Women's Football Association
WDM	World Development Movement (U.K.)		**WFA**	World Friendship Association (U.S.A.)
WDRC	World Data Referral Centre (France)		**WFAA**	Weltföderation Agrarischer Arbeiter
WdW	Weltbund der Weltföderalisten		**WFAC**	World Federal Authority Committee
WE	World Evangelism (U.S.A.)		**WFALW**	Weltbund Freiheitlicher Arbeitnehmerverbände auf Liberaler Wirtschaftsgrundlage
WEA	Royal West of England Academy			
WEA	Workers' Education Association		**WFAW**	World Federation of Agricultural Workers
WEAA	Western European Airports Association		**WFB**	Weltrat für Bildung
WEAAC	Western European Airports Association Conference		**WFB**	World Federation of Buddists
WEAAP	Western European Association for Aviation Psychology (Belgium)		**WFBMA**	Woven Fabric Belting Manufacturers Association
			WFBW	World Federation of Building and Woodworkers Unions
WEBA	World Educational Broadcasting Assembly			
WEC	World Energy Conference		**WFC**	World Food Congress (FAO)
WEC	World Engineering Conference		**WFC**	World Food Council (UN)
WEC	Worldwide Evangelisation Crusade		**WFCC**	World Federation for Culture Collections
WECAFC	Western Central Atlantic Fishery Commission		**WFCLC**	World Federation of Christian Life Communities
WECo	Western Company (U.S.A.)		**WFCS**	World's Fair Collectors Society (U.S.A.)
WECON	Western Electronics Show and Convention (U.S.A.)		**WFCY**	World Federation of Catholic Youth
WEDA	Wholesale Egg Distributors Association		**WFCYWG**	World Federation of Catholic Young Women and Girls

WFD	World Federation of the Deaf		**WFS**	World Fertility Survey
WFDA	Wholesalers Floorcovering Distributors Association		**WFS**	World Food Security
WFDA	Wholesale Footwear Distributors Association		**WFS**	World Future Society (U.S.A.)
			WFSA	World Federation of Societies of Anaesthesiologists
WFDY	World Federation of Democratic Youth		**WFSF**	World Future Studies Federation
WFEA	World Federation of Education Associations		**WFSW**	World Federation of Scientific Workers
WFEO	World Federation of Engineering Organisations		**WFTU**	World Federation of Teachers Unions
WFF	World Friendship Federation		**WFTU**	World Federation of Trade Unions
WFFL	World Federation of Free Latvians		**WFUNA**	World Federation of United Nations Associations
WFFM	World Federation of Friends of Museums (Belgium)		**WFV**	Werkfeuerwehrverband
WFFTH	World Federation of Workers in Food, Tobacco and Hotel Industries		**WFVTH**	Wereldfederatie van Arbeiders in Voedings-, Tabaks- en Hotelbedrijven
WFGA	Women's Farm and Garden Association		**WFW**	Weltföderation der Wissenschaftler
WFH	Worldwide Federation of Healing (U.K.)		**WFY**	World Federalist Youth
WFI	Wirtschaftsförderungsinstitut (Austria)		**WGA**	Writers Guild of America
WFIJI	World Federation of International Juridical Institutions		**WGB**	Weltgewerkschaftsbund
			WGC	Womens Global Congress for International Friendship, Education and Culture
WFIM	World Federation of Islamic Missions (Pakistan)		**WGC**	World Gospel Crusades (U.S.A.)
WFIS	Wagner Free Institute of Science (U.S.A.)		**WGE**	Wissenschaftliche Gesellschaft für Europarecht
WFL	Women's Freedom League		**WGfF**	Westdeutsche Gesellschaft für Familienkunde
WFLRY	World Federation of Liberal and Radical Youth		**WGFSK**	Wiener Gesellschaftzur Förderung der Schönen Künste (Austria)
WFLTH	Weltföderation von Arbeiter in Lebensmittel, Tabak und Hotelindustrien		**WGGB**	Writers Guild of Great Britain
WFM	World Federation for the Metallurgic Industry		**WGM**	World Gospel Mission (U.S.A.)
			WGRA	Western Governmental Research Association
WFMH	World Federation for Mental Health		**WHA**	Wholesale Horticultural Association
WFMW	World Federation of Methodist Women		**WHGS**	Wyoming Historical and Geological Society (U.S.A.)
WFN	World Federation of Neurology			
WFNMB	World Federation of Nuclear Medicine and Biology (U.S.A.)		**WHO**	World Health Organisation
WFNS	World Federation of Neurosurgical Societies		**WHOI**	Woods Hole Oceanographic Institution (U.S.A.)
WFOT	World Federation of Occupational Therapists		**WHRA**	Welwyn Hall Research Association (*formerly* CLAIRA and WIPRC)
WFP	World Federation of Parasitologists			
WFP	World Food Programme (Italy)		**WHRC**	World Health Research Centre
WFPA	World Federation for the Protection of Animals		**WIA**	Willow Importers' Association
			WIA	Wool Importers Association
WFPFFC	Worldwide Fairplay for Frogs Committee (U.S.A.)		**WIAB**	Wistar Institute of Anatomy and Biology (U.S.A.)
WFPMM	World Federation of Proprietary Medicine Manufacturers		**WIAC**	Women's International Art Club
WFR	Weltfriedensrat			

WIACO	World Insulation Acoustics Congress Organization
WIBC	Women's International Bowling Congress (U.S.A.)
WIC	Water Information Centre (U.S.A.)
WIC	West Indian Committee (U.K.)
WICA	Witches International Craft Association (U.S.A.)
WICBC	West Indies Cricket Board of Control
WIDF	Women's International Democratic Federation
WIG	Verband Schweizerischer Wein-Importgrossisten
WIG	Weltverband der Industriegewerkschaften
WIIU	Workers International Industrial Union
WILCIC	Women's International Liaison Committee for International Cooperation Ye
WILPF	Women's International League for Peace and Freedom
WIM	Wirtschaftsvereinigung Industrielle Meerestechnik
WIM	Women in Management
WINBAN	Windward Islands Banana Association
WIO	Women's International ORT (Organisation-Reconstruction-Travail)
WIPO	World Intellectual Property Organisation
WIPOG	Wirtschaftspolitische Gesellschaft
WIPRC	Whiting and Industrial Powders Research Council (now WHRA)
WIRA	Wax Importers and Refiners Association (U.S.A.)
WIRA	Wool Industries Research Association
WIRF	Women's International Religious Fellowship (U.S.A.)
WIRFMD	Wellcome Institute for Research into Foot and Mouth Disease (E. Africa)
WIS	Wheat Information Service (Japan)
WISA	West Indies Sugar Association
WISC	West Indian Standing Conference
WISC	Women's Information and Study Centre
WISCO	West Indies Sugar Company
WISDA	Wirtschaftsgruppe Schweizerischer Dachpappenfabriken
WISI	World Information System on Informatics
WISICA	West Indies Sea Island Cotton Association
WIT	Winnebago International Travelers (U.S.A.)
WITB	Wool Industry Training Board
WIZ	Wissenschaftliches Informationzentrum
WIZO	Women's International Zionist Organisation
WJA	World Jazz Association (U.S.A.)
WJC	World Jewish Congress
WJCB	World Jersey Cattle Bureau
WJEC	Welsh Joint Education Committee
WJG	Wiener Juristische Gesellschaft (Austria)
WKFO	Weltunion der Katholischen Frauen-Organisationen
WKJ	Weltbund der Katholischen Jugend
WLA	Womens Land Army
WLDA	Wholesale Leather Distributors Association
WLF	Women's Liberal Federation
WLG	Witwatersrand Landbougenootskap (South Africa)
WLHB	Women's League of Health and Beauty
WLPSA	Wild Life Preservation Society of Australia
WLRA	World Leisure and Recreation Association (U.S.A.)
WLSA	Welsh Land Settlement Association
WLTBU	Watermen, Lightermen, Tugmen and Bargemen's Union
WLU	World Lebanese Union
WLUS	World Land Use Survey
WMA	Wellington Mathematical Association (N.Z.)
WMA	World Medical Association
WMC	World Methodist Council
WMCW	World Movement of Christian Workers
WMGB	West Midlands Gas Board
WMI	Wildlife Management Institute (U.S.A.)
WMM	World Movement of Mothers
WMMA	Woodworking Machinery Manufacturers Association
WMO	World Meteorological Organisation
WMOAS	Women's Migration and Oversea Appointments Society
WMPCE	World Meeting Planners Congress and Exposition
WMPL	World Mission Prayer League (U.S.A.)
WMR	World Medical Relief (U.S.A.)
WMS	World Magnetic Survey
WMWFG	World Movement for World Federal Government
WN	World Neighbours (U.S.A.)

WNNR	Wetenskaplike en Nywerheids-Navorsingsraad (South Africa)	**WPA**	World Parliament Association
		WPA	World Pheasant Association
WNR	World New Religion (U.S.A.)	**WPA**	Works Projects Administration (U.S.A.)
WOBA	Werkgroep Onderzoek Bestrijding Aardappelcystenaaltjes	**WPA**	World Presbyterian Alliance
		WPADC	West Pakistan Agricultural Development Corporation
WOBT	Welt-Organisation Bild und Ton		
WOCCU	World Council of Credit Unions	**WPBS**	Welsh Plant Breeding Station
WODA	World Dredging Association	**WPC**	World Peace Council
WODCON	World Dredging Conference	**WPC**	World Petroleum Congress
WOE	Women Overseas for Equality (Belgium)	**WPC**	World Power Conference
WOECE	World Organisation for Early Childhood Education	**WPCC**	Water Pollution Control Council (New Zealand)
WOFIWU	World Federation of Industrial Workers' Unions	**WPCF**	Water Pollution Control Federation (U.S.A.)
		WPF	World Prohibition Federation
WOGSC	World Cybernetics and Systems Organisation	**WPFC**	Commission for Fisheries Research in the West Pacific
WOHP	World Organization for Human Potential (U.S.A.)	**WPFL**	West Pakistan Federation of Labour
		WPI	World Press Institute (U.S.A.)
WOIEP	World Office of Information on Environmental Problems	**WPIDC**	West Pakistan Industrial Development Corporation
WOIH	Council of World Organizations Interested in the Handicapped (U.S.A.)	**WPK**	Wirtschaftsprüferkammer
		WPLO	West Pakistan Library Association
WOM	Weltorganisation für Meteorologie	**WPMA**	Wall Paper Merchants' Association of Great Britain
WOMAN	World Organization of Mothers of all Nations		
WOMPI	Women of the Motion Picture Industry International (U.S.A.)	**WPNA**	World Proof Numismatic Association (U.S.A.)
WONCA	World Organisation of National Colleges, Academies and Academic Associations of General Practitioners and Family Physicians	**WPO**	Water Programs Office (of EPA) (U.S.A.)
		WPO	World Packaging Organization
		WPO	World Ploughing Organization
WONG	Netherlands Foundation for the Advancement of Research in New Guinea (now WOTRO)	**WPOA**	Western Pacific Orthopaedic Association
		WPRA	Wallpaper, Paint and Wallcovering Retailers Association
WONPA	World Organisation of Negro Plastic Arts		
WORMS	World Organisation for the Retention of Male Supremacy	**WPRA**	Waste Paper Recovery Association
		WPRL	Water Pollution Research Laboratory
WOSIC	Watchmakers of Switzerland Information Bureau	**WPRS**	West Palaearctic Regional Section (of IOBC)
		WPS	World Population Society (U.S.A.)
WOSUNA	Stichting Wetenschappelijk Onderzoek Suriname-Nederlandse Antillen (now WOTRO)	**WPSA**	World's Poultry Science Association
		WPSMA	Welsh Plate and Steel Makers Association
WOTP	World Organisation of the Teaching Profession	**WPTLC**	World Peace Through Law Center (U.S.A.)
		WPU	Women's Protestant Union
WOTRO	Stichting voor Wetenschappelijk Onderzoek van de Tropen (formerly WONG and WOSUNA)	**WPV**	Weltpostverein
		WPY	World Population Year
WOWI	Women on Words and Images (U.S.A.)	**WQO**	Water Quality Office (now WPO of EPA) (U.S.A.)
WPA	Wisconsin Pharmaceutical Association (U.S.A.)		
		WRA	Water Research Association

WRAC	Women's Royal Army Corps
WRADAC	Water Research Association Distribution Analogue Centre
WRAF	Women's Auxiliary Air Force
WRB	Water Resources Board
WRC	Water Research Centre
WRC	World Relief Commission (U.S.A.)
WRCC	Wildlife Research Co-ordinating Committee (E. Africa)
WRI	War Resister's International
WRK	Westdeutsche Rektorenkonferenze
WRMA	Woollen Mills Research Association (N.Z.)
WRNS	Women's Royal Naval Service
WRO	Weed Research Organization
WRONZ	Wool Research Organization of New Zealand
WRPC	Water Resources Planning Commission (Taiwan)
WRPDB	Western Regional Production Development Board (Nigeria)
WRRL	Western Regional Research Laboratory (U.S.A.)
WRRU	Water Resources Research Unit (Ghana)
WRSA	World Rabbit Science Association
WRSIC	Water Resources Scientific Information Center (U.S.A.)
WRU	Western Reserve University (U.S.A.)
WRVS	Women's Royal Voluntary Service
WRY	World Refugee Year
WSA	World Service Authority
WSAC	Water Space Amenity Committee
WSAVA	World Small Animal Veterinary Association
WSB	World Scout Bureau
WSC	World Spiritual Council
WSCF	World's Student Christian Federation
WSCS	Western Society of Crop Science (U.S.A.)
WSE	Western Society of Engineers (U.S.A.)
WSE	World Society of Ekistics (Greece)
WSET	Writers and Scholars Educational Trust
WSF	World Sephardic Federation
WSFS	World Science Fiction Society (U.K.)
WSGF	Welsh Seed Growers Federation
WSISI	West of Scotland Iron and Steel Institute
WSL	Warren Spring Laboratory
WSL	Weldbund zum Schultze des Lebens
WSLF	Western Somalia Liberation Front
WSO	World Simulation Organisation
WSRA	Women's Squash Rackets Association
WSS	World Ship Society
WSSI	Weed Science Society of Indonesia
WSSS	Western Society of Soil Science (U.S.A.)
WSTEC	Western Samoa Trust Estates Corporation
WTA	World Transport Agency
WTAA	World Trade Alliance Association
WTB	Welttierschutzbund
WTBA	Water-Tube Boilermakers' Association
WTCA	World Trade Centres Association
WTD	Wool Textile Delegation
WTG	Welt-Tierärztegesellschaft
WTGS	West Texas Geological Society (U.S.A.)
WTI	Wirtschaftlich-Technischer Informations-dienst (Austria)
WTIS	World Trade Information Service (U.S.A.)
WTLMF	Warszawskie Towarzystwo Lekarzy Medycyny Fizykalnej
WTMA	Welded Tool Manufacturers Association
WTN	Wroclawskie Towarzystwo Naukowe
WTO	World Tourism Organization
WTP	World Tape Pals
WTRD	Water Treatment Research Division (South Africa)
WTTA	Wholesale Tobacco Trade Association of Great Britain and Northern Ireland
WTUC	World Trade Union Conference
WU	Women's Union
WUA	Workers' Unions' Association (Sudan)
WUCT	World Union of Catholic Teachers
WUCWO	World Union of Catholic Women's Organisations
WUF	World Underwater Federation
WUF	World Union of Free Thinkers
WUJS	World Union of Jewish Students
WULTUO	World Union of Liberal Trade Union Organisations
WUM	Women's Universal Movement (U.S.A.)
WUM	World Union Movement
WUOSY	World Union of Organisations for the Safeguard of Youth
WUPJ	World Union for Progressive Judaïsm
WUPO	World Union of Pythagorean Organisations

WUR	World University Roundtable
WURDD	Western Utilisation Research and Development Division (U.S.A.)
WUS	World University Service
WUSA	World University Service in Australia
WUSL	Women's United Service League
WVA	Wereld Verbond van de Arbeid
WVA	Wirtschaftsverband Asbest
WUNS	World Union of National Socialists
WUUN	Women United for United Nations
WVA	World Veterinary Association
WVAO	Wissenschaftliche Vereinigung für Augenoptik und Optometrie
WVBH	Weltband der Bau- und Holzarbeiterorganisationen
WVD	Wereldverbond van Diamantbewerkers
WVF	World Veterans Federation
WVGM	Wirtschaftliche Vereinigung Grosshandel Metallhalbfabrikate
WVHS	West Virginia Horticultural Society (U.S.A.)
WVL	Weltverband der Lehrer
WVLI	Wirtschaftsvereinigung der Lebensmittelindustrie
WVM	Wereldfederatie voor de Metaalindustrie
WVOP	Wereld Vakverbond van Onderwijzend Personeel
WVPA	World Veterinary Poultry Association
WVRSC	Wholesale Vegetable and Root Seeds Committee
WVSMA	West Virginia State Medical Association (U.S.A.)
WVSPA	West Virginia State Pharmaceutical Association (U.S.A.)
WVT	Weltvereinigung für Tierzucht
WVV	Wissenschaftlicher Verein für Verkehrswesen e.V.
WVZ	Wirtschaftliche Vereinigung Zucker
WWABCC	World Wide Avon Bottle Collectors Club (U.S.A.)
WWC	World's Wristwrestling Championship (U.S.A.)
WWCC	Western Weed Control Conference (U.S.A.)
WWCTU	World's Woman's Christian Temperance Union
WWF	World Wildlife Fund (*Adviser* IUCN)
WWI	Werkgroep van Winkelinrichtingsbedrijven

WWML	Wood, Wire and Metal Lathers' International Union
WWSU	World Water Ski Union
WWTA	Woollen and Worsted Trades Association
WWTF	Woollen and Worsted Trades Federation
WWTT	Worldwide Tapetalk (U.K.)
WWW	World Weather Watch (WMO)
WWWC	World Without War Council
WYF	World Youth Forum (U.S.A.)
WYWCA	World Young Women's Christian Association
WZO	World Zionist Organisation (Israel)

X

XR	External Relations Service (UNESCO)

Y

YARS	Yugoslav Astronautical and Rocket Society
YASGB	Youth Association of Synagogues in Great Britain
YBDSA	Yacht Brokers, Designers and Surveyors Association
YCF	Yacimientos Carboniferos Fiscales (Argentine)
YCS	International Young Catholic Students
YCW	International Young Christian Workers
YEA	Yanhee Electricity Authority (Thailand)
YEPWA	Youth Environmental Programme for West Africa
YFC	Young Farmers' Clubs
YFC	Youth for Christ, International (U.S.A.)
YFCI	Youth for Christ International
YFCU	Young Farmers' Clubs of Ulster (N. Ireland)
YGS	Yorkshire Grassland Society
YHA	Youth Hostels Association

YHANI	Youth Hostel Association of Northern Ireland
YMCA	The World Alliance of Young Men's Christian Associations
YMHA	World Federation of Young Men's Hebrew Associations and Jewish Community Centres
YMISIG	Young Mensa International Special Interest Group
YOL	Yleinen Ossuskauppojen Liitto
YPEM	Service of Productive Works of Macedonia
YPF	Yacimentos Petroliferos Fiscales (Argentina)
YPFB	Yacimientos Petroliferos Fiscales Bolivianos
YPSCE	Young People's Society for Christian Endeavour
YSKOR	Suid-Afrikaanse Yster en Staal Industriële Korporasie Beperk
YSSYEM	Service for the Completion and Maintenance of Works of Macedonia
YTP	Yeni Türkiye Partisi
YVFF	Young Volunteer Force Foundation
YWCA	Young Women's Christian Association
YWF	Young World Federalists
YWFD	Young World Food and Development (FAO)
YWPG	Young World Promotion Group (FAO)

Z

ZADCA	Zinc Alloy Die Casters' Association
ZAED	Zentralstelle f. Atomkernenergie Dokumentation
ZAMEFA	Metal Fabricators of Zambia
ZANLA	Zimbabwe African National Liberation Army
ZANU	Zimbabwe African National Union
ZAP	Zaaizaadvereniging Anna-Paulowna
ZAP	Zwiazek Polskich Artystów Plastyków
ZAPU	Zimbabwe African People's Union
ZASP	Union of Polish State Artists Abroad
ZAV	Zentralarbeitsgemeinschaft des Strassenverkehrsgewerbes
ZAW	Zentralausschuss der Werbewirtschaft
ZBHD	Zambia Broken Hill Development Co.

ZBI	Zentralverband Berufsständischer Ingenieurvereine
ZBZ	Zentrum Berlin für Zukunftsforschung
ZCCI	Zippy Collectors Club International (U.S.A.)
ZCI	Zambian Copper Investment Ltd
ZDA	Zinc Development Association
ZDB	Zentralverband des Deutschen Baugewerbes
ZDG	Zentralverband der Deutschen Geflügelwirtschaft
ZDH	Zentralverband des Deutschen Handwerks
ZDK	Zentralverband des Kraftfahrzeughandels
ZDV	Zentralverband des Deutschen Vulkaniseur-Handwerks
ZELLCHE-MING	Verein der Zellstoff- und Papier-Chemiker und Ingenieure
ZENKO	All-Japan Federation of Metal Miners Union
ZENRO	All-Japan Trade Union Congress
ZENSEN DOMEI	National Federation of Textile Industry Workers Unions (Japan)
ZENTEI	Japanese Postal Workers Union
ZEV	Zuivel-Export-Vereniging
ZFD	Zentralverband der Fusspfleger Deutschlands
ZFGBI	Zionist Federation of Great Britain and Ireland
ZFMA	Zip Fasteners Manufacturers Association (India)
ZFV	Deutsche Zentrale fur Fremdenverkehr
ZGA	Zambia Geographical Association
ZHI	Stichting v. d. Nederlandse Zelfstandige Handel en Industrie
ZHZ	Zuid-Hollandse Zuivelbond
ZI	Zonta International (U.S.A.)
ZIDA	Zentrum für Information und Dokumentation der Aussenwirtschaft
ZIID	Zentralinstitut für Information und Dokumentation
ZIMCO	Zambia Industrial and Mining Corporation
ZINCOM	Zambian Industrial and Commercial Association
ZINS	Zionist Information Service (U.S.A.)
ZIPRA	Zimbabwe People's Revolutionary Army
ZITS	Zveza Inzenirjev in Tehnikov SR Slovenije
ZIV	Zentrale Informationsstelle für Verkehr in der Deutschen Verkehrswissenschaftlichen
ZKB	Zuivel Kwaliteitscontrôle Bureau

ZKF	Zentralverband Karosserie- und Fahrzeug-technik	**ZSKBIP**	Zväz Slovenských Knihovnikov Bibliografov Informacných Pracovnikov
ZKP	Zwiazek Kompozytorów Polskich	**ZSN**	Zoological Stations of Naples
ZLA	Zambia Library Association	**ZTG**	Zentralverband des Tankstellen- und Garagengewerbes
ZLDI	Zentralstelle f. Luftfahrdokumentation und Information	**ZUPO**	Zimbabwe United Peoples Organization
ZMB	Zentrale f. Maikäfer- Bekampfungsaktionen	**ZUU**	Zemedelsky ústav Ucetnicko-sprayoredný (Czechoslovakia)
ZMP	Zentrale Markt- u. Presberichtstelle der Deut-schen Landwirtschaft	**ZVA**	Zentralverband der Augenoptiker
ZMPD	Zrzesenie Miedzynarodowych Przewózników Drogowych w Polsce	**ZVEI**	Zentralverband der Elektrotechnischen In-dustrie
ZNP	Zanzibar Nationalist Party	**ZVFIFU**	Zentralverband Forstindustrie und Forst-unternehem
ZNTB	Zambia National Tourist Bureau	**ZVK**	Zentralverband des Kraftfahrzeughandwerks
ZNZ	Zuid-Nederlandse Zuivelbond	**ZVK**	Zentralverband Krankengymnastik
ZOA	Zentralverband der Organisationen des Automaten-Aufstell-Gewerbes	**ZVM**	Zentralverband Deutscher Mechaniker-Handwerke
ZOA	Zionist Organisation of America	**ZVR**	Zentralverband des Raumausstatter-handwerks
ZPC	Zaaizaad en Pootgoed Cooperatieve	**ZVSH**	Zentralverband Sanitär- und Heizungs-Technik
ZPDA	Zinc Pigment Development Association		
ZPHT	Zrzeszenie Polskich Hoteli Turystycznych	**ZVSHK**	Zentralverband Sanitär-, Heizungs- und Klimatechnik
ZPP	Zjednoczenie Przemyslu Piwowarskiego	**ZVSM**	Zentralverband Schweizerischer Milchprodu-zenten
ZPPP	Zanzibar and Pemba Peoples Party		
ZPTL	Zrzeszenie Polskich Towarzystw Lekarskich	**ZVSU**	Zentralverband Schweizerischer Uhrmacher
ZSA	Zululand Swaziland Association (U.K.)	**ZWO**	Nederlandse Organisatie voor Zuiverweten-schappelijk Onderzoek
ZSIG	Zürcherische Seidenindustrie-Gesellschaft		